MW01196856

American Casebook Series
Hornbook Series and Basic Legal Texts
Nutshell Series

of

WEST PUBLISHING COMPANY
P.O. Box 64526
St. Paul, Minnesota 55164–0526

ACCOUNTING

Faris' Accounting and Law in a Nutshell, 377 pages, 1984 (Text)

Fiflis, Kripke and Foster's Teaching Materials on Accounting for Business Lawyers, 3rd Ed., 838 pages, 1984 (Casebook)

Siegel and Siegel's Accounting and Financial Disclosure: A Guide to Basic Concepts, 259 pages, 1983 (Text)

ADMINISTRATIVE LAW

Davis' Cases, Text and Problems on Administrative Law, 6th Ed., 683 pages, 1977 (Casebook)

Davis' Basic Text on Administrative Law, 3rd Ed., 617 pages, 1972 (Text)

Gellhorn and Boyer's Administrative Law and Process in a Nutshell, 2nd Ed., 445 pages, 1981 (Text)

Mashaw and Merrill's Cases and Materials on Administrative Law–The American Public Law System, 2nd Ed., 976 pages, 1985 (Casebook)

Robinson, Gellhorn and Bruff's The Administrative Process, 3rd Ed., 978 pages, 1986 (Casebook)

ADMIRALTY

Healy and Sharpe's Cases and Materials on Admiralty, 2nd Ed., 876 pages, 1986 (Casebook)

Maraist's Admiralty in a Nutshell, 390 pages, 1983 (Text)

Sohn and Gustafson's Law of the Sea in a Nutshell, 264 pages, 1984 (Text)

AGENCY—PARTNERSHIP

Fessler's Alternatives to Incorporation for Persons in Quest of Profit, 2nd Ed., 326 pages, 1986 (Casebook)

AGENCY—PARTNERSHIP—Cont'd

Henn's Cases and Materials on Agency, Partnership and Other Unincorporated Business Enterprises, 2nd Ed., 733 pages, 1985 (Casebook)

Reuschlein and Gregory's Hornbook on the Law of Agency and Partnership, 625 pages, 1979, with 1981 pocket part (Text)

Seavey, Reuschlein and Hall's Cases on Agency and Partnership, 599 pages, 1962 (Casebook)

Selected Corporation and Partnership Statutes and Forms, 555 pages, 1985

Steffen and Kerr's Cases and Materials on Agency-Partnership, 4th Ed., 859 pages, 1980 (Casebook)

Steffen's Agency-Partnership in a Nutshell, 364 pages, 1977 (Text)

AGRICULTURAL LAW

Meyer, Pedersen, Thorson and Davidson's Agricultural Law: Cases and Materials, 931 pages, 1985 (Casebook)

ALTERNATIVE DISPUTE RESOLUTION

Kanowitz' Cases and Materials on Alternative Dispute Resolution, 1024 pages, 1986 (Casebook)

AMERICAN INDIAN LAW

Canby's American Indian Law in a Nutshell, 288 pages, 1981 (Text)

Getches and Wilkinson's Cases on Federal Indian Law, 2nd Ed., approximately 870 pages, 1986 (Casebook)

ANTITRUST LAW

Gellhorn's Antitrust Law and Economics in a Nutshell, 3rd Ed., about 425 pages, 1987 (Text)

List current as of July, 1986

ANTITRUST LAW—Cont'd

Gifford and Raskind's Cases and Materials on Antitrust, 694 pages, 1983 with 1985 Supplement (Casebook)

Hovenkamp's Hornbook on Economics and Federal Antitrust Law, Student Ed., 414 pages, 1985 (Text)

Oppenheim, Weston and McCarthy's Cases and Comments on Federal Antitrust Laws, 4th Ed., 1168 pages, 1981 with 1985 Supplement (Casebook)

Posner and Easterbrook's Cases and Economic Notes on Antitrust, 2nd Ed., 1077 pages, 1981, with 1984–85 Supplement (Casebook)

Sullivan's Hornbook of the Law of Antitrust, 886 pages, 1977 (Text)

See also Regulated Industries, Trade Regulation

ART LAW

DuBoff's Art Law in a Nutshell, 335 pages, 1984 (Text)

BANKING LAW

Lovett's Banking and Financial Institutions in a Nutshell, 409 pages, 1984 (Text)

Symons and White's Teaching Materials on Banking Law, 2nd Ed., 993 pages, 1984 (Casebook)

BUSINESS PLANNING

Painter's Problems and Materials in Business Planning, 2nd Ed., 1008 pages, 1984 (Casebook)

Selected Securities and Business Planning Statutes, Rules and Forms, 470 pages, 1985

CIVIL PROCEDURE

Casad's Res Judicata in a Nutshell, 310 pages, 1976 (text)

Cound, Friedenthal, Miller and Sexton's Cases and Materials on Civil Procedure, 4th Ed., 1202 pages, 1985 with 1985 Supplement (Casebook)

Ehrenzweig, Louisell and Hazard's Jurisdiction in a Nutshell, 4th Ed., 232 pages, 1980 (Text)

Federal Rules of Civil-Appellate Procedure—West Law School Edition, about 550 pages, 1986

Friedenthal, Kane and Miller's Hornbook on Civil Procedure, 876 pages, 1985 (Text)

Kane's Civil Procedure in a Nutshell, 2nd Ed., 306 pages, 1986 (Text)

Koffler and Reppy's Hornbook on Common Law Pleading, 663 pages, 1969 (Text)

Marcus and Sherman's Complex Litigation–Cases and Materials on Advanced Civil Procedure, 846 pages, 1985 (Casebook)

Park's Computer-Aided Exercises on Civil Procedure, 2nd Ed., 167 pages, 1983 (Coursebook)

CIVIL PROCEDURE—Cont'd

Siegel's Hornbook on New York Practice, 1011 pages, 1978 with 1985 Pocket Part (Text)

See also Federal Jurisdiction and Procedure

CIVIL RIGHTS

Abernathy's Cases and Materials on Civil Rights, 660 pages, 1980 (Casebook)

Cohen's Cases on the Law of Deprivation of Liberty: A Study in Social Control, 755 pages, 1980 (Casebook)

Lockhart, Kamisar, Choper and Shiffrin's Cases on Constitutional Rights and Liberties, 6th Ed., about 1300 pages, 1986 with 1986 Supplement (Casebook)—reprint from Lockhart, et al. Cases on Constitutional Law, 6th Ed., 1986

Vieira's Civil Rights in a Nutshell, 279 pages, 1978 (Text)

COMMERCIAL LAW

Bailey's Secured Transactions in a Nutshell, 2nd Ed., 391 pages, 1981 (Text)

Epstein and Martin's Basic Uniform Commercial Code Teaching Materials, 2nd Ed., 667 pages, 1983 (Casebook)

Henson's Hornbook on Secured Transactions Under the U.C.C., 2nd Ed., 504 pages, 1979 with 1979 P.P. (Text)

Murray's Commercial Law, Problems and Materials, 366 pages, 1975 (Coursebook)

Nordstrom and Clovis' Problems and Materials on Commercial Paper, 458 pages, 1972 (Casebook)

Nordstrom, Murray and Clovis' Problems and Materials on Sales, 515 pages, 1982 (Casebook)

Nordstrom, Murray and Clovis' Problems and Materials on Secured Transactions, about 500 pages, 1987 (Casebook)

Selected Commercial Statutes, 1389 pages, 1985

Speidel, Summers and White's Teaching Materials on Commercial and Consumer Law, 3rd Ed., 1490 pages, 1981 (Casebook)

Stockton's Sales in a Nutshell, 2nd Ed., 370 pages, 1981 (Text)

Stone's Uniform Commercial Code in a Nutshell, 2nd Ed., 516 pages, 1984 (Text)

Uniform Commercial Code, Official Text with Comments, 994 pages, 1978

UCC Article 9, Reprint from 1962 Code, 128 pages, 1976

UCC Article 9, 1972 Amendments, 304 pages, 1978

Weber and Speidel's Commercial Paper in a Nutshell, 3rd Ed., 404 pages, 1982 (Text)

White and Summers' Hornbook on the Uniform Commercial Code, 2nd Ed., 1250 pages, 1980 (Text)

LAW SCHOOL PUBLICATIONS—Continued

COMMUNITY PROPERTY

Mennell's Community Property in a Nutshell, 447 pages, 1982 (Text)
Verrall and Bird's Cases and Materials on California Community Property, 4th Ed., 549 pages, 1983 (Casebook)

COMPARATIVE LAW

Barton, Gibbs, Li and Merryman's Law in Radically Different Cultures, 960 pages, 1983 (Casebook)
Glendon, Gordon and Osakive's Comparative Legal Traditions: Text, Materials and Cases on the Civil Law, Common Law, and Socialist Law Traditions, 1091 pages, 1985 (Casebook)
Glendon, Gordon, and Osakwe's Comparative Legal Traditions in a Nutshell, 402 pages, 1982 (Text)
Langbein's Comparative Criminal Procedure: Germany, 172 pages, 1977 (Casebook)

COMPUTERS AND LAW

Maggs and Sprowl's Computer Applications in the Law, about 300 pages, 1986 (Text)
Mason's An Introduction to the Use of Computers in Law, 223 pages, 1984 (Text)

CONFLICT OF LAWS

Cramton, Currie and Kay's Cases-Comments-Questions on Conflict of Laws, 3rd Ed., 1026 pages, 1981 (Casebook)
Scoles and Hay's Hornbook on Conflict of Laws, Student Ed., 1085 pages, 1982 with 1986 P.P. (Text)
Scoles and Weintraub's Cases and Materials on Conflict of Laws, 2nd Ed., 966 pages, 1972, with 1978 Supplement (Casebook)
Siegel's Conflicts in a Nutshell, 469 pages, 1982 (Text)

CONSTITUTIONAL LAW

Barron and Dienes' Constitutional Law in a Nutshell, about 400 pages, 1986 (Text)
Engdahl's Constitutional Power in a Nutshell: Federal and State, 411 pages, 1974 (Text)
Lockhart, Kamisar, Choper and Shiffrin's Cases-Comments-Questions on Constitutional Law, 6th Ed., 1601 pages, 1986 with 1986 Supplement (Casebook)
Lockhart, Kamisar, Choper and Shiffrin's Cases-Comments-Questions on the American Constitution, 6th Ed., about 1200 pages, 1986 with 1986 Supplement (Casebook)—abridgment of Lockhart, et al. Cases on Constitutional Law, 6th Ed., 1986
Manning's The Law of Church-State Relations in a Nutshell, 305 pages, 1981 (Text)
Miller's Presidential Power in a Nutshell, 328 pages, 1977 (Text)

CONSTITUTIONAL LAW—Cont'd

Nowak, Rotunda and Young's Hornbook on Constitutional Law, 3rd Ed., Student Ed., approximately 1100 pages, 1986 (Text)
Rotunda's Modern Constitutional Law: Cases and Notes, 2nd Ed., 1004 pages, 1985, with 1986 Supplement (Casebook)
Williams' Constitutional Analysis in a Nutshell, 388 pages, 1979 (Text)
See also Civil Rights

CONSUMER LAW

Epstein and Nickles' Consumer Law in a Nutshell, 2nd Ed., 418 pages, 1981 (Text)
McCall's Consumer Protection, Cases, Notes and Materials, 594 pages, 1977, with 1977 Statutory Supplement (Casebook)
Selected Commercial Statutes, 1389 pages, 1985
Spanogle and Rohner's Cases and Materials on Consumer Law, 693 pages, 1979, with 1982 Supplement (Casebook)
See also Commercial Law

CONTRACTS

Calamari & Perillo's Cases and Problems on Contracts, 1061 pages, 1978 (Casebook)
Calamari and Perillo's Hornbook on Contracts, 2nd Ed., 878 pages, 1977 (Text)
Corbin's Text on Contracts, One Volume Student Edition, 1224 pages, 1952 (Text)
Fessler and Loiseaux's Cases and Materials on Contracts, 837 pages, 1982 (Casebook)
Friedman's Contract Remedies in a Nutshell, 323 pages, 1981 (Text)
Fuller and Eisenberg's Cases on Basic Contract Law, 4th Ed., 1203 pages, 1981 (Casebook)
Hamilton, Rau and Weintraub's Cases and Materials on Contracts, 830 pages, 1984 (Casebook)
Jackson and Bollinger's Cases on Contract Law in Modern Society, 2nd Ed., 1329 pages, 1980 (Casebook)
Keyes' Government Contracts in a Nutshell, 423 pages, 1979 (Text)
Schaber and Rohwer's Contracts in a Nutshell, 2nd Ed., 425 pages, 1984 (Text)

COPYRIGHT

See Patent and Copyright Law

CORPORATIONS

Hamilton's Cases on Corporations—Including Partnerships and Limited Partnerships, 3rd Ed., 1213 pages, 1986 with 1986 Statutory Supplement (Casebook)
Hamilton's Law of Corporations in a Nutshell, 379 pages, 1980 (Text)
Henn's Teaching Materials on Corporations, 2nd Ed., about 1200 pages, 1986 (Casebook)

CORPORATIONS—Cont'd

Henn and Alexander's Hornbook on Corporations, 3rd Ed., Student Ed., 1371 pages, 1983 with 1986 P.P. (Text)

Jennings and Buxbaum's Cases and Materials on Corporations, 5th Ed., 1180 pages, 1979 (Casebook)

Selected Corporation and Partnership Statutes, Regulations and Forms, 555 pages, 1985

Solomon, Stevenson and Schwartz' Materials and Problems on Corporations: Law and Policy, 1172 pages, 1982 with 1986 Supplement (Casebook)

CORPORATE FINANCE

Hamilton's Cases and Materials on Corporate Finance, 895 pages, 1984 with 1986 Supplement (Casebook)

CORRECTIONS

Krantz's Cases and Materials on the Law of Corrections and Prisoners' Rights, 3rd Ed., 855 pages, 1986 (Casebook)

Krantz's Law of Corrections and Prisoners' Rights in a Nutshell, 2nd Ed., 386 pages, 1983 (Text)

Popper's Post-Conviction Remedies in a Nutshell, 360 pages, 1978 (Text)

Robbins' Cases and Materials on Post Conviction Remedies, 506 pages, 1982 (Casebook)

CREDITOR'S RIGHTS

Bankruptcy Code, Rules and Forms, Law School and C.L.E. Ed., about 800 pages, 1986

Epstein's Debtor-Creditor Law in a Nutshell, 3rd Ed., 383 pages, 1986 (Text)

Epstein and Landers' Debtors and Creditors: Cases and Materials, 2nd Ed., 689 pages, 1982 (Casebook)

LoPucki's Player's Manual for the Debtor-Creditor Game, 123 pages, 1985 (Coursebook)

Riesenfeld's Cases and Materials on Creditors' Remedies and Debtors' Protection, 4th Ed., about 800 pages, 1987 (Casebook)

White's Bankruptcy and Creditor's Rights: Cases and Materials, 812 pages, 1985 (Casebook)

CRIMINAL LAW AND CRIMINAL PROCEDURE

Abrams', Federal Criminal Law and its Enforcement, 882 pages, 1986 (Casebook)

Carlson's Adjudication of Criminal Justice, Problems and References, about 124 pages, 1986 (Casebook)

Dix and Sharlot's Cases and Materials on Criminal Law, 2nd Ed., 771 pages, 1979 (Casebook)

CRIMINAL LAW AND CRIMINAL PROCEDURE—Cont'd

Federal Rules of Criminal Procedure—West Law School Edition, about 465 pages, 1986

Grano's Problems in Criminal Procedure, 2nd Ed., 176 pages, 1981 (Problem book)

Israel and LaFave's Criminal Procedure in a Nutshell, 3rd Ed., 438 pages, 1980 (Text)

Johnson's Cases, Materials and Text on Criminal Law, 3rd Ed., 783 pages, 1985 (Casebook)

Kamisar, LaFave and Israel's Cases, Comments and Questions on Modern Criminal Procedure, 6th Ed., about 1600 pages, 1986 with 1986 Supplement (Casebook)

Kamisar, LaFave and Israel's Cases, Comments and Questions on Basic Criminal Procedure, 6th Ed., about 800 pages, 1986 with 1986 Supplement (Casebook)—reprint from Kamisar, et al. Modern Criminal Procedure, 6th ed., 1986

LaFave's Modern Criminal Law: Cases, Comments and Questions, 789 pages, 1978 (Casebook)

LaFave and Israel's Hornbook on Criminal Procedure, Student Ed., 1142 pages, 1985 with 1985 P.P. (Text)

LaFave and Scott's Hornbook on Criminal Law, 2nd Ed., Student Ed., about 800 pages, 1986 (Text)

Langbein's Comparative Criminal Procedure: Germany, 172 pages, 1977 (Casebook)

Loewy's Criminal Law in a Nutshell, 302 pages, 1975 (Text)

Saltzburg's American Criminal Procedure, Cases and Commentary, 2nd Ed., 1193 pages, 1985 with 1986 Supplement (Casebook)

Uviller's The Processes of Criminal Justice: Investigation and Adjudication, 2nd Ed., 1384 pages, 1979 with 1979 Statutory Supplement and 1986 Update (Casebook)

Uviller's The Processes of Criminal Justice: Adjudication, 2nd Ed., 730 pages, 1979. Soft-cover reprint from Uviller's The Processes of Criminal Justice: Investigation and Adjudication, 2nd Ed. (Casebook)

Uviller's The Processes of Criminal Justice: Investigation, 2nd Ed., 655 pages, 1979. Soft-cover reprint from Uviller's The Processes of Criminal Justice: Investigation and Adjudication, 2nd Ed. (Casebook)

Vorenberg's Cases on Criminal Law and Procedure, 2nd Ed., 1088 pages, 1981 with 1985 Supplement (Casebook)

See also Corrections, Juvenile Justice

DECEDENTS ESTATES

See Trusts and Estates

DOMESTIC RELATIONS

Clark's Cases and Problems on Domestic Relations, 3rd Ed., 1153 pages, 1980 (Casebook)
Clark's Hornbook on Domestic Relations, 754 pages, 1968 (Text)
Krause's Cases and Materials on Family Law, 2nd Ed., 1221 pages, 1983 with 1986 Supplement (Casebook)
Krause's Family Law in a Nutshell, 2nd Ed., 444 pages, 1986 (Text)
Krauskopf's Cases on Property Division at Marriage Dissolution, 250 pages, 1984 (Casebook)

ECONOMICS, LAW AND

Goetz' Cases and Materials on Law and Economics, 547 pages, 1984 (Casebook)
See also Antitrust, Regulated Industries

EDUCATION LAW

Alexander and Alexander's The Law of Schools, Students and Teachers in a Nutshell, 409 pages, 1984 (Text)
Morris' The Constitution and American Education, 2nd Ed., 992 pages, 1980 (Casebook)

EMPLOYMENT DISCRIMINATION

Jones, Murphy and Belton's Cases on Discrimination in Employment, about 930 pages, 1986 (Casebook)
Player's Cases and Materials on Employment Discrimination Law, 2nd Ed., 782 pages, 1984 (Casebook)
Player's Federal Law of Employment Discrimination in a Nutshell, 2nd Ed., 402 pages, 1981 (Text)
See also Women and the Law

ENERGY AND NATURAL RESOURCES LAW

Laitos' Cases and Materials on Natural Resources Law, 938 pages, 1985 (Casebook)
Rodgers' Cases and Materials on Energy and Natural Resources Law, 2nd Ed., 877 pages, 1983 (Casebook)
Selected Environmental Law Statutes, about 850 pages, 1986
Tomain's Energy Law in a Nutshell, 338 pages, 1981 (Text)
See also Environmental Law, Oil and Gas, Water Law

ENVIRONMENTAL LAW

Bonine and McGarity's Cases and Materials on the Law of Environment and Pollution, 1076 pages, 1984 (Casebook)
Findley and Farber's Cases and Materials on Environmental Law, 2nd Ed., 813 pages, 1985 (Casebook)
Findley and Farber's Environmental Law in a Nutshell, 343 pages, 1983 (Text)

ENVIRONMENTAL LAW—Cont'd

Rodgers' Hornbook on Environmental Law, 956 pages, 1977 with 1984 pocket part (Text)
Selected Environmental Law Statutes, about 950 pages, 1986
See also Energy Law, Natural Resources Law, Water Law

EQUITY

See Remedies

ESTATES

See Trusts and Estates

ESTATE PLANNING

Kurtz' Cases, Materials and Problems on Family Estate Planning, 853 pages, 1983 (Casebook)
Lynn's Introduction to Estate Planning, in a Nutshell, 3rd Ed., 370 pages, 1983 (Text)
See also Taxation

EVIDENCE

Broun and Meisenholder's Problems in Evidence, 2nd Ed., 304 pages, 1981 (Problem book)
Cleary and Strong's Cases, Materials and Problems on Evidence, 3rd Ed., 1143 pages, 1981 (Casebook)
Federal Rules of Evidence for United States Courts and Magistrates, 337 pages, 1984
Graham's Federal Rules of Evidence in a Nutshell, 429 pages, 1981 (Text)
Kimball's Programmed Materials on Problems in Evidence, 380 pages, 1978 (Problem book)
Lempert and Saltzburg's A Modern Approach to Evidence: Text, Problems, Transcripts and Cases, 2nd Ed., 1232 pages, 1983 (Casebook)
Lilly's Introduction to the Law of Evidence, 490 pages, 1978 (Text)
McCormick, Elliott and Sutton's Cases and Materials on Evidence, 5th Ed., 1212 pages, 1981 (Casebook)
McCormick's Hornbook on Evidence, 3rd Ed., Student Ed., 1156 pages, 1984 (Text)
Rothstein's Evidence, State and Federal Rules in a Nutshell, 2nd Ed., 514 pages, 1981 (Text)
Saltzburg's Evidence Supplement: Rules, Statutes, Commentary, 245 pages, 1980 (Casebook Supplement)

FEDERAL JURISDICTION AND PROCEDURE

Currie's Cases and Materials on Federal Courts, 3rd Ed., 1042 pages, 1982 with 1985 Supplement (Casebook)
Currie's Federal Jurisdiction in a Nutshell, 2nd Ed., 258 pages, 1981 (Text)

FEDERAL JURISDICTION AND PROCEDURE—Cont'd

Federal Rules of Civil-Appellate Procedure—West Law School Edition, about 550 pages, 1986

Forrester and Moye's Cases and Materials on Federal Jurisdiction and Procedure, 3rd Ed., 917 pages, 1977 with 1985 Supplement (Casebook)

Redish's Cases, Comments and Questions on Federal Courts, 878 pages, 1983 with 1986 Supplement (Casebook)

Vetri and Merrill's Federal Courts, Problems and Materials, 2nd Ed., 232 pages, 1984 (Problem Book)

Wright's Hornbook on Federal Courts, 4th Ed., Student Ed., 870 pages, 1983 (Text)

FUTURE INTERESTS

See Trusts and Estates

IMMIGRATION LAW

Aleinikoff and Martin's Immigration Process and Policy, 1042 pages, 1985 (Casebook)

Weissbrodt's Immigration Law and Procedure in a Nutshell, 345 pages, 1984 (Text)

INDIAN LAW

See American Indian Law

INSURANCE

Dobbyn's Insurance Law in a Nutshell, 281 pages, 1981 (Text)

Keeton's Cases on Basic Insurance Law, 2nd Ed., 1086 pages, 1977

Keeton's Basic Text on Insurance Law, 712 pages, 1971 (Text)

Keeton's Case Supplement to Keeton's Basic Text on Insurance Law, 334 pages, 1978 (Casebook)

York and Whelan's Cases, Materials and Problems on Insurance Law, 715 pages, 1982, with 1985 Supplement (Casebook)

INTERNATIONAL LAW

Buergenthal and Maier's Public International Law in a Nutshell, 262 pages, 1985 (Text)

Folsom, Gordon and Spanogle's International Business Transactions – a Problem-Oriented Coursebook, 1160 pages, 1986 (Casebook)

Henkin, Pugh, Schachter and Smit's Cases and Materials on International Law, 2nd Ed., about 1200 pages, 1987 with Documents Supplement (Casebook)

Jackson and Davey's Legal Problems of International Economic Relations, 2nd Ed., about 1250 pages, 1986, with Documents Supplement (Casebook)

Kirgis' International Organizations in Their Legal Setting, 1016 pages, 1977, with 1981 Supplement (Casebook)

INTERNATIONAL LAW—Cont'd

Weston, Falk and D'Amato's International Law and World Order—A Problem Oriented Coursebook, 1195 pages, 1980, with Documents Supplement (Casebook)

Wilson's International Business Transactions in a Nutshell, 2nd Ed., 476 pages, 1984 (Text)

INTERVIEWING AND COUNSELING

Binder and Price's Interviewing and Counseling, 232 pages, 1977 (Text)

Shaffer's Interviewing and Counseling in a Nutshell, 353 pages, 1976 (Text)

INTRODUCTION TO LAW STUDY

Dobbyn's So You Want to go to Law School, Revised First Edition, 206 pages, 1976 (Text)

Hegland's Introduction to the Study and Practice of Law in a Nutshell, 418 pages, 1983 (Text)

Kinyon's Introduction to Law Study and Law Examinations in a Nutshell, 389 pages, 1971 (Text)

See also Legal Method and Legal System

JUDICIAL ADMINISTRATION

Nelson's Cases and Materials on Judicial Administration and the Administration of Justice, 1032 pages, 1974 (Casebook)

JURISPRUDENCE

Christie's Text and Readings on Jurisprudence—The Philosophy of Law, 1056 pages, 1973 (Casebook)

JUVENILE JUSTICE

Fox's Cases and Materials on Modern Juvenile Justice, 2nd Ed., 960 pages, 1981 (Casebook)

Fox's Juvenile Courts in a Nutshell, 3rd Ed., 291 pages, 1984 (Text)

LABOR LAW

Gorman's Basic Text on Labor Law—Unionization and Collective Bargaining, 914 pages, 1976 (Text)

Leslie's Labor Law in a Nutshell, 2nd Ed., 397 pages, 1986 (Text)

Nolan's Labor Arbitration Law and Practice in a Nutshell, 358 pages, 1979 (Text)

Oberer, Hanslowe, Andersen and Heinsz' Cases and Materials on Labor Law—Collective Bargaining in a Free Society, 3rd Ed., about 1200 pages, 1986 with Statutory Supplement (Casebook)

See also Employment Discrimination, Social Legislation

LAND FINANCE

See Real Estate Transactions

LAW SCHOOL PUBLICATIONS—Continued

LAND USE

Callies and Freilich's Cases and Materials on Land Use, 1233 pages, 1986 (Casebook)

Hagman's Cases on Public Planning and Control of Urban and Land Development, 2nd Ed., 1301 pages, 1980 (Casebook)

Hagman and Juergensmeyer's Hornbook on Urban Planning and Land Development Control Law, 2nd Ed., Student Edition, approximately 580 pages, 1986 (Text)

Wright and Gitelman's Cases and Materials on Land Use, 3rd Ed., 1300 pages, 1982 (Casebook)

Wright and Wright's Land Use in a Nutshell, 2nd Ed., 356 pages, 1985 (Text)

LEGAL HISTORY

Presser and Zainaldin's Cases on Law and American History, 855 pages, 1980 (Casebook)

See also Legal Method and Legal System

LEGAL METHOD AND LEGAL SYSTEM

Aldisert's Readings, Materials and Cases in the Judicial Process, 948 pages, 1976 (Casebook)

Berch and Berch's Introduction to Legal Method and Process, 550 pages, 1985 (Casebook)

Bodenheimer, Oakley and Love's Readings and Cases on an Introduction to the Anglo-American Legal System, 161 pages, 1980 (Casebook)

Davies and Lawry's Institutions and Methods of the Law—Introductory Teaching Materials, 547 pages, 1982 (Casebook)

Dvorkin, Himmelstein and Lesnick's Becoming a Lawyer: A Humanistic Perspective on Legal Education and Professionalism, 211 pages, 1981 (Text)

Greenberg's Judicial Process and Social Change, 666 pages, 1977 (Casebook)

Kelso and Kelso's Studying Law: An Introduction, 587 pages, 1984 (Coursebook)

Kempin's Historical Introduction to Anglo-American Law in a Nutshell, 2nd Ed., 280 pages, 1973 (Text)

Kimball's Historical Introduction to the Legal System, 610 pages, 1966 (Casebook)

Murphy's Cases and Materials on Introduction to Law—Legal Process and Procedure, 772 pages, 1977 (Casebook)

Reynolds' Judicial Process in a Nutshell, 292 pages, 1980 (Text)

See also Legal Research and Writing

LEGAL PROFESSION

Aronson, Devine and Fisch's Problems, Cases and Materials on Professional Responsibility, 745 pages, 1985 (Casebook)

Aronson and Weckstein's Professional Responsibility in a Nutshell, 399 pages, 1980 (Text)

LEGAL PROFESSION—Cont'd

Mellinkoff's The Conscience of a Lawyer, 304 pages, 1973 (Text)

Mellinkoff's Lawyers and the System of Justice, 983 pages, 1976 (Casebook)

Pirsig and Kirwin's Cases and Materials on Professional Responsibility, 4th Ed., 603 pages, 1984 (Casebook)

Schwartz and Wydick's Problems in Legal Ethics, 285 pages, 1983 (Casebook)

Selected Statutes, Rules and Standards on the Legal Profession, 276 pages, Revised 1984

Smith's Preventing Legal Malpractice, 142 pages, 1981 (Text)

Wolfram's Hornbook on Modern Legal Ethics, Student Edition, 1120 pages, 1986 (Text)

LEGAL RESEARCH AND WRITING

Cohen's Legal Research in a Nutshell, 4th Ed., 450 pages, 1985 (Text)

Cohen and Berring's How to Find the Law, 8th Ed., 790 pages, 1983. Problem book by Foster, Johnson and Kelly available (Casebook)

Cohen and Berring's Finding the Law, 8th Ed., Abridged Ed., 556 pages, 1984 (Casebook)

Dickerson's Materials on Legal Drafting, 425 pages, 1981 (Casebook)

Felsenfeld and Siegel's Writing Contracts in Plain English, 290 pages, 1981 (Text)

Gopen's Writing From a Legal Perspective, 225 pages, 1981 (Text)

Mellinkoff's Legal Writing—Sense and Nonsense, 242 pages, 1982 (Text)

Rombauer's Legal Problem Solving—Analysis, Research and Writing, 4th Ed., 424 pages, 1983 (Coursebook)

Squires and Rombauer's Legal Writing in a Nutshell, 294 pages, 1982 (Text)

Statsky's Legal Research, Writing and Analysis, 2nd Ed., 167 pages, 1982 (Coursebook)

Statsky and Wernet's Case Analysis and Fundamentals of Legal Writing, 2nd Ed., 441 pages, 1984 (Text)

Teply's Programmed Materials on Legal Research and Citation, 2nd Ed., 358 pages, 1986. Student Library Exercises available (Coursebook)

Weihofen's Legal Writing Style, 2nd Ed., 332 pages, 1980 (Text)

LEGISLATION

Davies' Legislative Law and Process in a Nutshell, 2nd Ed., 346 pages, 1986 (Text)

Nutting and Dickerson's Cases and Materials on Legislation, 5th Ed., 744 pages, 1978 (Casebook)

LEGISLATION—Cont'd

Statsky's Legislative Analysis: How to Use Statutes and Regulations, 2nd Ed., 217 pages, 1984 (Text)

LOCAL GOVERNMENT

McCarthy's Local Government Law in a Nutshell, 2nd Ed., 404 pages, 1983 (Text)
Reynolds' Hornbook on Local Government Law, 860 pages, 1982 (Text)
Valente's Cases and Materials on Local Government Law, 2nd Ed., 980 pages, 1980 with 1982 Supplement (Casebook)

MASS COMMUNICATION LAW

Gillmor and Barron's Cases and Comment on Mass Communication Law, 4th Ed., 1076 pages, 1984 (Casebook)
Ginsburg's Regulation of Broadcasting: Law and Policy Towards Radio, Television and Cable Communications, 741 pages, 1979, with 1983 Supplement (Casebook)
Zuckman and Gayne's Mass Communications Law in a Nutshell, 2nd Ed., 473 pages, 1983 (Text)

MEDICINE, LAW AND

King's The Law of Medical Malpractice in a Nutshell, 2nd Ed., 342 pages, 1986 (Text)
Shapiro and Spece's Problems, Cases and Materials on Bioethics and Law, 892 pages, 1981 (Casebook)
Sharpe, Fiscina and Head's Cases on Law and Medicine, 882 pages, 1978 (Casebook)

MILITARY LAW

Shanor and Terrell's Military Law in a Nutshell, 378 pages, 1980 (Text)

MORTGAGES

See Real Estate Transactions

NATURAL RESOURCES LAW

See Energy and Natural Resources Law

NEGOTIATION

Edwards and White's Problems, Readings and Materials on the Lawyer as a Negotiator, 484 pages, 1977 (Casebook)
Williams' Legal Negotiation and Settlement, 207 pages, 1983 (Coursebook)

OFFICE PRACTICE

Hegland's Trial and Practice Skills in a Nutshell, 346 pages, 1978 (Text)
Strong and Clark's Law Office Management, 424 pages, 1974 (Casebook)
See also Computers and Law, Interviewing and Counseling, Negotiation

OIL AND GAS

Hemingway's Hornbook on Oil and Gas, 2nd Ed., Student Ed., 543 pages, 1983 with 1986 P.P. (Text)

OIL AND GAS—Cont'd

Kuntz, Lowe, Anderson and Smith's Cases and Materials on Oil and Gas Law, 857 pages, 1986 (Casebook)
Lowe's Oil and Gas Law in a Nutshell, 443 pages, 1983 (Text)
See also Energy and Natural Resources Law

PARTNERSHIP

See Agency—Partnership

PATENT AND COPYRIGHT LAW

Choate and Francis' Cases and Materials on Patent Law, 2nd Ed., 1110 pages, 1981 (Casebook)
Miller and Davis' Intellectual Property—Patents, Trademarks and Copyright in a Nutshell, 428 pages, 1983 (Text)
Nimmer's Cases on Copyright and Other Aspects of Entertainment Litigation, 3rd Ed., 1025 pages, 1985 (Casebook)

PRODUCTS LIABILITY

Noel and Phillips' Cases on Products Liability, 2nd Ed., 821 pages, 1982 (Casebook)
Noel and Phillips' Products Liability in a Nutshell, 2nd Ed., 341 pages, 1981 (Text)

PROPERTY

Bernhardt's Real Property in a Nutshell, 2nd Ed., 448 pages, 1981 (Text)
Boyer's Survey of the Law of Property, 766 pages, 1981 (Text)
Browder, Cunningham and Smith's Cases on Basic Property Law, 4th Ed., 1431 pages, 1984 (Casebook)
Bruce, Ely and Bostick's Cases and Materials on Modern Property Law, 1004 pages, 1984 (Casebook)
Burke's Personal Property in a Nutshell, 322 pages, 1983 (Text)
Cunningham, Stoebuck and Whitman's Hornbook on the Law of Property, Student Ed., 916 pages, 1984 (Text)
Donahue, Kauper and Martin's Cases on Property, 2nd Ed., 1362 pages, 1983 (Casebook)
Hill's Landlord and Tenant Law in a Nutshell, 2nd Ed., 311 pages, 1986 (Text)
Moynihan's Introduction to Real Property, 254 pages, 1962 (Text)
Uniform Land Transactions Act, Uniform Simplification of Land Transfers Act, Uniform Condominium Act, 1977 Official Text with Comments, 462 pages, 1978
See also Real Estate Transactions, Land Use

PSYCHIATRY, LAW AND

Reisner's Law and the Mental Health System, Civil and Criminal Aspects, 696 pages, 1985 (Casebooks)

LAW SCHOOL PUBLICATIONS—Continued

REAL ESTATE TRANSACTIONS

Bruce's Real Estate Finance in a Nutshell, 2nd Ed., 262 pages, 1985 (Text)

Maxwell, Riesenfeld, Hetland and Warren's Cases on California Security Transactions in Land, 3rd Ed., 728 pages, 1984 (Casebook)

Nelson and Whitman's Cases on Real Estate Transfer, Finance and Development, 2nd Ed., 1114 pages, 1981, with 1986 Supplement (Casebook)

Nelson and Whitman's Hornbook on Real Estate Finance Law, 2nd Ed., Student Ed., 941 pages, 1985 (Text)

Osborne's Cases and Materials on Secured Transactions, 559 pages, 1967 (Casebook)

REGULATED INDUSTRIES

Gellhorn and Pierce's Regulated Industries in a Nutshell, 394 pages, 1982 (Text)

Morgan, Harrison and Verkuil's Cases and Materials on Economic Regulation of Business, 2nd Ed., 666 pages, 1985 (Casebook)

See also Mass Communication Law, Banking Law

REMEDIES

Dobbs' Hornbook on Remedies, 1067 pages, 1973 (Text)

Dobbs' Problems in Remedies, 137 pages, 1974 (Problem book)

Dobbyn's Injunctions in a Nutshell, 264 pages, 1974 (Text)

Friedman's Contract Remedies in a Nutshell, 323 pages, 1981 (Text)

Leavell, Love and Nelson's Cases and Materials on Equitable Remedies and Restitution, 4th Ed., 1111 pages, 1986 (Casebook)

McCormick's Hornbook on Damages, 811 pages, 1935 (Text)

O'Connell's Remedies in a Nutshell, 2nd Ed., 320 pages, 1985 (Text)

York, Bauman and Rendleman's Cases and Materials on Remedies, 4th Ed., 1029 pages, 1985 (Casebook)

REVIEW MATERIALS

Ballantine's Problems

Black Letter Series

Smith's Review Series

West's Review Covering Multistate Subjects

SECURITIES REGULATION

Hazen's Hornbook on The Law of Securities Regulation, Student Ed., 739 pages, 1985 (Text)

Ratner's Securities Regulation: Materials for a Basic Course, 3rd Ed., 1000 pages, 1986 (Casebook)

Ratner's Securities Regulation in a Nutshell, 2nd Ed., 322 pages, 1982 (Text)

SECURITIES REGULATION—Cont'd

Selected Securities and Business Planning Statutes, Rules and Forms, 470 pages, 1985

SOCIAL LEGISLATION

Hood and Hardy's Workers' Compensation and Employee Protection Laws in a Nutshell, 274 pages, 1984 (Text)

LaFrance's Welfare Law: Structure and Entitlement in a Nutshell, 455 pages, 1979 (Text)

Malone, Plant and Little's Cases on Workers' Compensation and Employment Rights, 2nd Ed., 951 pages, 1980 (Casebook)

SPORTS LAW

Schubert, Smith and Trentadue's Sports Law, 395 pages, 1986 (Text)

TAXATION

Dodge's Cases and Materials on Federal Income Taxation, 820 pages, 1985 (Casebook)

Dodge's Federal Taxation of Estates, Trusts and Gifts: Principles and Planning, 771 pages, 1981 with 1982 Supplement (Casebook)

Garbis and Struntz' Cases and Materials on Tax Procedure and Tax Fraud, 829 pages, 1982 with 1984 Supplement (Casebook)

Gelfand and Salsich's State and Local Taxation and Finance in a Nutshell, 309 pages, 1986 (Text)

Gunn's Cases and Materials on Federal Income Taxation of Individuals, 785 pages, 1981 with 1985 Supplement (Casebook)

Hellerstein and Hellerstein's Cases on State and Local Taxation, 4th Ed., 1041 pages, 1978 with 1982 Supplement (Casebook)

Kahn and Gann's Corporate Taxation and Taxation of Partnerships and Partners, 2nd Ed., 1204 pages, 1985 (Casebook)

Kragen and McNulty's Cases and Materials on Federal Income Taxation: Individuals, Corporations, Partnerships, 4th Ed., 1287 pages, 1985 (Casebook)

McNulty's Federal Estate and Gift Taxation in a Nutshell, 3rd Ed., 509 pages, 1983 (Text)

McNulty's Federal Income Taxation of Individuals in a Nutshell, 3rd Ed., 487 pages, 1983 (Text)

Posin's Hornbook on Federal Income Taxation of Individuals, Student Ed., 491 pages, 1983 with 1985 pocket part (Text)

Selected Federal Taxation Statutes and Regulations, about 1400 pages, 1986

Solomon and Hesch's Cases on Federal Income Taxation of Individuals, about 800 pages, 1987 (Casebook)

TAXATION—Cont'd

Sobeloff and Weidenbruch's Federal Income Taxation of Corporations and Stockholders in a Nutshell, 362 pages, 1981 (Text)

TORTS

Christie's Cases and Materials on the Law of Torts, 1264 pages, 1983 (Casebook)
Dobbs' Torts and Compensation—Personal Accountability and Social Responsibility for Injury, 955 pages, 1985 (Casebook)
Green, Pedrick, Rahl, Thode, Hawkins, Smith and Treece's Cases and Materials on Torts, 2nd Ed., 1360 pages, 1977 (Casebook)
Green, Pedrick, Rahl, Thode, Hawkins, Smith, and Treece's Advanced Torts: Injuries to Business, Political and Family Interests, 2nd Ed., 544 pages, 1977 (Casebook)—reprint from Green, et al. Cases and Materials on Torts, 2nd Ed., 1977
Keeton, Keeton, Sargentich and Steiner's Cases and Materials on Torts, and Accident Law, 1360 pages, 1983 (Casebook)
Kionka's Torts in a Nutshell: Injuries to Persons and Property, 434 pages, 1977 (Text)
Malone's Torts in a Nutshell: Injuries to Family, Social and Trade Relations, 358 pages, 1979 (Text)
Prosser and Keeton's Hornbook on Torts, 5th Ed., Student Ed., 1286 pages, 1984 (Text)
Shapo's Cases on Tort and Compensation Law, 1244 pages, 1976 (Casebook)
See also Products Liability

TRADE REGULATION

McManis' Unfair Trade Practices in a Nutshell, 444 pages, 1982 (Text)
Oppenheim, Weston, Maggs and Schechter's Cases and Materials on Unfair Trade Practices and Consumer Protection, 4th Ed., 1038 pages, 1983 with 1986 Supplement (Casebook)
See also Antitrust, Regulated Industries

TRIAL AND APPELLATE ADVOCACY

Appellate Advocacy, Handbook of, 2nd Ed., 182 pages, 1986 (Text)
Bergman's Trial Advocacy in a Nutshell, 402 pages, 1979 (Text)
Binder and Bergman's Fact Investigation: From Hypothesis to Proof, 354 pages, 1984 (Coursebook)
Goldberg's The First Trial (Where Do I Sit?, What Do I Say?) in a Nutshell, 396 pages, 1982 (Text)
Haydock, Herr and Stempel's, Fundamentals of Pre-Trial Litigation, 768 pages, 1985 (Casebook)
Hegland's Trial and Practice Skills in a Nutshell, 346 pages, 1978 (Text)
Hornstein's Appellate Advocacy in a Nutshell, 325 pages, 1984 (Text)

TRIAL AND APPELLATE ADVOCACY—Cont'd

Jeans' Handbook on Trial Advocacy, Student Ed., 473 pages, 1975 (Text)
Martineau's Cases and Materials on Appellate Practice and Procedure, about 550 pages, 1987 (Casebook)
McElhaney's Effective Litigation, 457 pages, 1974 (Casebook)
Nolan's Cases and Materials on Trial Practice, 518 pages, 1981 (Casebook)
Parnell and Shellhaas' Cases, Exercises and Problems for Trial Advocacy, 171 pages, 1982 (Coursebook)
Sonsteng, Haydock and Boyd's The Trialbook: A Total System for Preparation and Presentation of a Case, Student Ed., 404 pages, 1984 (Coursebook)

TRUSTS AND ESTATES

Atkinson's Hornbook on Wills, 2nd Ed., 975 pages, 1953 (Text)
Averill's Uniform Probate Code in a Nutshell, 425 pages, 1978 (Text)
Bogert's Hornbook on Trusts, 5th Ed., 726 pages, 1973 (Text)
Clark, Lusky and Murphy's Cases and Materials on Gratuitous Transfers, 3rd Ed., 970 pages, 1985 (Casebook)
Gulliver's Cases and Materials on Future Interests, 624 pages, 1959 (Casebook)
Gulliver's Introduction to the Law of Future Interests, 87 pages, 1959 (Casebook)—reprint from Gulliver's Cases and Materials on Future Interests, 1959
McGovern's Cases and Materials on Wills, Trusts and Future Interests: An Introduction to Estate Planning, 750 pages, 1983 (Casebook)
Mennell's Cases and Materials on California Decedent's Estates, 566 pages, 1973 (Casebook)
Mennell's Wills and Trusts in a Nutshell, 392 pages, 1979 (Text)
Powell's The Law of Future Interests in California, 91 pages, 1980 (Text)
Simes' Hornbook on Future Interests, 2nd Ed., 355 pages, 1966 (Text)
Turano and Radigan's Hornbook on New York Estate Administration, approximately 575 pages, 1986 (Text)
Uniform Probate Code, 5th Ed., Official Text With Comments, 384 pages, 1977
Waggoner's Future Interests in a Nutshell, 361 pages, 1981 (Text)
Waterbury's Materials on Trusts and Estates, 1039 pages, 1986 (Casebook)

WATER LAW

Getches' Water Law in a Nutshell, 439 pages, 1984 (Text)

WATER LAW—Cont'd

Sax and Abram's Cases and Materials on Legal Control of Water Resources in the United States, 941 pages, 1986 (Casebook)

Trelease and Gould's Cases and Materials on Water Law, 4th Ed., 816 pages, 1986 (Casebook)

See also Energy and Natural Resources Law, Environmental Law

WILLS

See Trusts and Estates

WOMEN AND THE LAW

Kay's Text, Cases and Materials on Sex-Based Discrimination, 2nd Ed., 1045 pages, 1981, with 1986 Supplement (Casebook)

Thomas' Sex Discrimination in a Nutshell, 399 pages, 1982 (Text)

See also Employment Discrimination

WORKERS' COMPENSATION

See Social Legislation

NEW YORK ESTATE ADMINISTRATION

By

Margaret Valentine Turano

Associate Professor of Law
St. John's University School of Law

Honorable C. Raymond Radigan

Judge
Nassau County Surrogate's Court

HORNBOOK SERIES

WEST PUBLISHING CO.
ST. PAUL, MINN., 1986

50 West Kellogg Boulevard
P.O. Box 64526
St. Paul, Minnesota 55164–0526

Printed in the United States of America

Library of Congress Cataloging-in-Publication Data

Turano, Margaret Valentine, 1948–
New York estate administration.

(Hornbook series)
Includes index.
1. Executors and administrators—New York (State)
2. Probate law and practice—New York (State)
I. Radigan, Raymond. II. Title. III. Series.
KFN5210.T87 1986 346.747'056 86–11067
347.470656

ISBN 0–314–98675–8

Turano & Radigan, N.Y.Est.Admin. HB

To John

M.V.T.

To my wife, Aileen, and family and to my mentor, John D. Bennett, former Surrogate of Nassau County and chairman of the Temporary State Commission on the Modernization, Revision, and Simplification of the Law of Estates.

C.R.R.

*

Preface and Acknowledgement

In writing this book on estate administration, I relied on the assistance of several persons to whom I must express my gratitude.

Special thanks to Patricia McLernon and Pat Castelluccio for reading and editing the manuscript. Their experience and perceptions added a texture to the book for which I am most grateful. Similarly, Vincent McNamara gave valuable assistance in editing the chapter on wrongful death proceedings, and Patricia Gallagher read several chapters, adding thoughtful comments throughout. To these four, thank you.

Sincere thanks to the students (some of them now attorneys) who shepardized and checked citations and gave general editorial assistance, especially Patrick Hackett, David Gallo, Patricia Hill, Elizabeth Hess, Judi LaMountain, Richard Balletta, Mary Beth Walsh, James Lamb, Frances Gruber, Susan Cember and Eileen White.

I must also state my gratitude to Professor Paul S. Graziano and the late Dean John J. Murphy, who guided me into the academic community and nurtured me when I got there. I think of them often with a thankful sense of their place in my professional development and the writing of this book.

My thanks and love to my patient sons, Dan, Pat and Chris, and to my loving parents, Alice and Ben Valentine.

Finally, I must try to find the words to thank my husband John, for his support, his good humor, his patience, his flexibility and his help during the entire period of writing this book. He has, as always, been a handful of dream-dust, and I could not have done it without him.

MARGARET VALENTINE TURANO

We have endeavored to provide a practical guidebook to aid the student in learning the statutory procedure of Surrogate's practice with an insight on the reasons for the provisions, a guide to the general practitioner who ventures into the estate practice from time to time to a source that will expedite his research as to what is required in order to handle a particular facet of estate practice and for those who regularly practice in the field a bird's eye view of the statutory provisions, case interpretation, and the ongoing development of the practice. As a member of the Nassau County Surrogate's staff for almost all of my legal career and having served Surrogate Bennett while he was chairman of the Commission on Estates, and then being elected Surrogate, I was privileged to witness the experts at work in this field. I have studied the cases that developed as a result of the Commission's work and experienced the day-to-day implementation of the practice and played a role in the drafting of statutory changes to further the overall goals of the Bennett Commission in order to make estate practice modern, expeditious, and simplified. I am also indebted to the many estate practitioners for aiding me in acquiring the knowledge on a day-to-day practical basis in my working with them at the court.

I do hope that this book will be a valuable tool for those interested in estate practice to gain insight to the meaning of the procedural practice and to use those provisions that will aid in the efficient administration of estates.

I wish to thank Surrogate Bennett for his confidence in me in all the years that I have been associated with him and for his offering me so many opportunities to learn in the field of trusts and estates. To the staff, interns, and countless number of people who have aided us in planning the overall view of our assignment, I thank them for their contribution in planning a true Hornbook for the estate practitioner; and last but not least, I thank my family for their support.

C. RAYMOND RADIGAN

WESTLAW Introduction

Turano and Radigan's, *New York Estate Administration* offers a detailed and comprehensive treatment of the basic rules and principles of estate administration. However, legal researchers frequently need to find additional authority. In an effort to assist with comprehensive research, a WESTLAW Appendix is included with this hornbook. The WESTLAW Appendix gives concise, step-by-step instruction on how to coordinate WESTLAW computer-assisted research with this hornbook.

THE PUBLISHER

*

Summary of Contents

*

Table of Contents

NEW YORK ESTATE ADMINISTRATION

*

Chapter One

JURISDICTION

SECTION A. INTRODUCTION

Any discussion of the Surrogate's jurisdiction must be separated into two components: subject matter jurisdiction and jurisdictional predicate (personal or in rem) for exercising the subject matter jurisdiction. The Surrogate's Court Procedure Act ("SCPA") specifically covers both these points.

SECTION B. SUBJECT MATTER JURISDICTION

1. CONSTITUTIONAL AND STATUTORY BASIS

The subject matter jurisdiction of the Surrogate's Court is broad; the general rule is that the court can exercise jurisdiction over matters that relate to the affairs of a decedent. This broad jurisdiction is grounded in the New York Constitution, which specifically confers jurisdiction over "all actions and proceedings relating to the affairs of decedents, probate of wills, administration of estates and actions and proceedings arising thereunder or pertaining thereto, guardianship of the property of minors, and such other actions or proceedings, not within the exclusive jurisdiction of the Supreme Court, as may be provided by law." [1] The constitution also grants the Surrogate "such equity jurisdiction as provided by law." [2]

Before September 1, 1962, the powers of the Surrogate to exercise jurisdiction over estates were derived mostly from statute, not from the state constitution. Historically, the Surrogate's jurisdiction was very limited, and through the years, as studies were made to determine whether to consolidate the Surrogate's Court with a common law forum, the legislators instead expanded the jurisdiction of the Surrogate's Court. As more extensive jurisdiction was given to the Surrogate's Court, fragmentation of cases between the Surrogate's Court and other civil courts lessened.

The state constitutional amendment giving the Surrogate jurisdiction over all actions and proceedings relating to the affairs of a decedent was effective September 1, 1962. Hence if a matter has to do

Sec. B

1. McKinney's Const. Art. 6, section 12(d).

2. McKinney's Const. Art. 6, section 12(e).

with the affairs of a decedent or the administration of his estate, it is now the state constitution and not the SCPA that gives the court its powers, except for its equity powers. Article 2 of the SCPA does, however, specifically codify the jurisdiction conferred by the constitution [3] and, pursuant to the constitutional authority, grants full equity jurisdiction.[4] Article 2 empowers the court to try, upon the return of process, all legal or equitable issues arising between persons over whom the court has personal jurisdiction. Article 2 is helpful in that it recites (and alerts the practitioner to) the constitutional authority of the Surrogate's Court. The constitution authorizes the legislature to assign additional powers to the Surrogate, and Article 2 of the SCPA gives the court jurisdiction over those additional matters, which need not relate to the settlement of a decedent's estate. For example, the legislature has given the Surrogate jurisdiction over inter vivos trusts [5] (concurrent with the Supreme Court), guardianships of the person of infants [6] (concurrent with the Supreme Court and the Family Court) (as opposed to guardianships of the property of infants provided for in the constitution), guardianship of mentally retarded persons, [7] adoption proceedings [8] (concurrent with the Family Court), ownership disputes between living persons in discovery proceedings [9] (concurrent with the Supreme Court), and conservatorships when a person requiring a conservator has an interest in an estate [10] (concurrent with the Supreme Court).

The rest of the SCPA sets forth the powers of the court in great detail,[11] but this attention to detail does not delimit the court's subject matter jurisdiction, since Article 2 specifies that the court can exercise any of its jurisdiction in any proceeding, whether the proceeding is enumerated in the SCPA or not, and whether the jurisdiction could be exercised in another proceeding or not.[12] In addition, case law has construed the Surrogate's constitutional and statutory subject matter jurisdiction broadly.[13]

2. JURISDICTION OVER DOMICILIARIES' ESTATES

The Surrogate's Court has jurisdiction over the estates of decedents.[14] That jurisdiction is concurrent with the Supreme Court's

3. McKinney's SCPA 201(1).

4. McKinney's SCPA 201(2), (3).

5. McKinney's SCPA 207.

6. McKinney's SCPA 1701.

7. McKinney's SCPA 1750.

8. McKinney's Family Court Act 641 (1983); McKinney's Domestic Relations Law Article VII (1977).

9. McKinney's SCPA 2104(5).

10. McKinney's Mental Hygiene Law 77.01 (Supp.1984–85).

11. The hundreds of enumerated powers are discussed seriatim in the respective chapters that cover them.

12. McKinney's SCPA 202. See "McKinney's SCPA Section 201: The Jurisdiction Facilitator," infra at 23–24.

13. See, e.g., Matter of Piccione, 57 N.Y.2d 278, 456 N.Y.S.2d 669, 442 N.E.2d 1180 (1982), discussed this chapter infra at 14–17, and cases cited in notes 92 through 99, this section infra.

14. McKinney's Const. Art. 6, Section 12(d).

jurisdiction,[15] but in practice the Supreme Court never exercises it. The Surrogate's jurisdiction persists until all issues relating to the estate have been settled.[16] Every Surrogate in New York has jurisdiction over the estate of any New York domiciliary, and the county of domicile is the only proper venue.[17] Improper venue is not a jurisdictional defect; the court of improper venue can transfer the proceeding to the proper venue either on its own motion or on the motion of a party. The practical value of this is that the parties do not have to start all the preliminary proceedings, such as an examination of attesting witnesses in a probate proceeding,[18] anew.

Under the predecessor to SCPA 205, the Surrogate's Court of each county had exclusive jurisdiction over the estate of any domiciliary of the county at the time of his death, disappearance or internment.[19] If a probate proceeding was brought in a county other than the decedent's domicile, the court lacked subject matter jurisdiction entirely. It therefore could not transfer the proceeding; the petitioning party had to start a new proceeding (and presumably incur a new filing fee) or move in the Supreme Court for a transfer.[20] This was the law until June 21, 1984.

The current SCPA 205 is somewhat more consistent with Supreme Court practice, where an action or proceeding begun in the wrong county can be transferred to the proper venue.[21] However, in Surrogate's practice proper venue will be strictly enforced.[22] The amendment to the statute was not intended to change the practice of commencing an action in the county of the decedent's domicile. Transfer for the purpose of fair trial, convenience of witnesses and forum-shopping, so frequent in other civil practice,[23] in general will not be allowed in Surrogate's Court practice.

The 1984 legislation is a result of much deliberation on the subject-matter-jurisdiction/venue issue.[24] The current legislation loosens the

15. Matter of Tabler, 55 A.D.2d 207, 389 N.Y.S.2d 899 (3d Dep't 1976).

16. That jurisdiction, however, should not be tortured. See Matter of Braker, N.Y.L.J., April 3, 1985, at 12, col. 1 (New York County) where the Surrogate declined to exercise jurisdiction over a proceeding relating to dissolution of a charitable corporation created by a decedent's will in 1908. The Surrogate reasoned that the Supreme Court had jurisdiction over not-for-profit corporations and their incidental creation by a decedent's will was not a reason for bringing the proceeding in the Surrogate's Court.

17. McKinney's SCPA 205.

18. McKinney's SCPA 1404, discussed in chapter on "Probate," infra at 90–93.

19. L.1966, c. 953.

20. McKinney's CPLR 325(a).

21. McKinney's CPLR 510.

22. See Leg.Doc. [1984] No. 65(E); Matter of Dickinson, 129 Misc.2d 184, 492 N.Y.S.2d 923 (Nassau 1985); Matter of Gray, N.Y.L.J., June 17, 1985, at 15, col. 3 (Bronx) (court would not grant order to examine safe deposit box when petitioner did not prove that decedent was domiciled in that county).

23. See McKinney's CPLR 510. See also McKinney's SCPA 206, Prac.Comm. at 31–32 (Supp. 1984–85), where Prof. Siegel takes an opposing view.

24. See, e.g., Matter of Coletti, 91 Misc. 2d 7, 397 N.Y.S.2d 330 (Nassau 1977), Surrogate Bennett suggested that every Surrogate's Court in the state should have subject matter jurisdiction over the estates of every New York domiciliary, and that the proper venue should then be determined by the convenience of the court, the dece-

rigidity of the old law while still recognizing that the county of domicile is the proper one to entertain the proceeding and administer the estate.

Thus we must look at the concept of domicile, predicated on the idea that every person has formed ties with one place sufficient to make that place "home." Domicile is the permanent home to which a person, during an absence, intends to return. Everyone has a domicile,[25] and once a person has acquired a domicile, it remains his domicile until he takes up residence in a new location with the intent of making that his domicile.[26] The existing domicile continues until the new one begins,[27] and some cases hold that where the facts on domicile conflict, there is a presumption in favor of the original domicile over the newly acquired one.[28]

A person may have several residences but cannot have more than one domicile.[29] When an issue arises as to which of multiple homes is a person's domicile, it is a question of fact to be decided on the unique circumstances of each case, such as where he voted, where his car was registered, where his business activities took place, where the church and clubs of which he was a member were located, and where he filed his income taxes.[30] The amount of time a person spends in a place, what he does while there, what possessions he has there, who lives with him, and his feelings toward other places where he also resides, are factors in the determination of domicile.[31] The decedent's own assertion in the will that a place is his domicile is not dispositive; the court still looks into the underlying facts.[32]

A few examples of domicile cases will suffice to give a flavor. In one, a woman lived with her married sister in the Bronx until eighteen months before her death, when she took an apartment in Brooklyn to be nearer her job. She voted in the Bronx, left clothes there, went there on holidays and listed her Bronx address on tax returns, and the court found her to be a Bronx domiciliary.[33] In another case, a

dent's main residence and the location of the assets, a position he later reconsidered as not being in the best interests of administering estates. See Legislative Proposal Files of Surrogate Bennett.

25. United States Trust Co. v. Hart, 150 App.Div. 413, 135 N.Y.S. 81 (1st Dep't 1912), modified on other grounds 208 N.Y. 617, 102 N.E. 1115 (1913).

26. Matter of Chrisman, 43 A.D.2d 771, 350 N.Y.S.2d 468 (3d Dep't 1973).

27. Bodfish v. Gallman, 50 A.D.2d 457, 378 N.Y.S.2d 138 (3d Dep't 1976).

28. Ratkowsky v. Browne, 267 App.Div. 643, 47 N.Y.S.2d 905 (3d Dep't 1944), appeal denied 268 A.D. 835, 50 N.Y.S.2d 464 (1944); Matter of Sumpter, N.Y.L.J., April 23, 1985, at 14, col. 3 (Nassau).

29. Matter of Newcomb, 192 N.Y. 238, 84 N.E. 950 (1908).

30. These factors are taken from a New York estate tax return, TT–141A, the "Estate Tax Domicile Affidavit," required in estates where the fiduciary claims that the decedent was not a New York domiciliary.

31. See Texas v. Florida, 306 U.S. 398, 59 S.Ct. 563, 83 L.Ed. 817 (1939); Pignatelli v. Pignatelli, 169 Misc. 534, 8 N.Y.S.2d 10 (New York County 1938).

32. Matter of Sumpter, N.Y.L.J., April 23, 1985, at 14, col. 3, (Nassau); Matter of Riley, 148 Misc. 588, 266 N.Y.S. 209 (Niagara 1933).

33. Matter of Rutto, N.Y.L.J., Jan. 11, 1979, at 14, col. 2 (Bronx). See also Matter of Stern, where a woman was found not to have changed her domicile when she moved in with her nephew after becoming unable to care for herself, but maintained her former apartment.

decedent had a wife and children in two separate locations. The court reasoned that his Nassau County address was used for his more "important" papers, such as car registration and tax returns, and held him to be domiciled there.[34]

A child is domiciled with his custodial parent.[35]

Intent to change domiciles is not sufficient; the decedent's acts must establish that he actually changed his domicile.[36] For example, if a person moves to a new residence, but nonetheless maintains his prior residence, votes and banks and attends church at the former location, that prior residence is his domicile.

If a person is incompetent, there must be some proof that he has the ability to formulate the necessary intent to change his domicile.[37] Thus, a comatose person who is moved out of his domicile to another state retains the original domicile,[38] unless a court of competent jurisdiction or a person with authority to make such a change does so.[39] Similarly, a change of residence for the purpose of procuring medical care does not change domicile unless the decedent intended a change.[40]

If a party claims that the decedent changed his domicile, the burden is on that party to prove the change.[41] Domicile, however, is at the very heart of subject matter jurisdiction and the parties cannot by agreement confer jurisdiction over a non-New York domiciliary.[42]

Domicile also has enormous importance in the area of state death taxes, since states normally tax all intangible personal property, wherever situated, of their domiciliaries.[43]

If a dispute arises as to which county was the decedent's domicile, a hearing ("domicile" hearing) has to be held to determine the issue.[44]

34. Matter of Bellitti, N.Y.L.J., Jan. 23, 1979, at 14, col. 6 (Nassau).

35. Matter of Polier, N.Y.L.J., Sept. 22, 1978, at 18, col. 1 (Suffolk).

36. Matter of Shindell, 60 A.D.2d 393, 400 N.Y.S.2d 67 (1st Dep't 1977), affirmed 55 N.Y.2d 655, 446 N.Y.S.2d 942, 431 N.E.2d 303 (1981).

37. Matter of Liebell, N.Y.L.J., June 5, 1985, at 14, col. 4 (Queens); Matter of Webber, 187 Misc. 674, 64 N.Y.S.2d 281 (Kings 1946).

38. Matter of Cantor, N.Y.L.J., May 22, 1985, at 14, col. 2 (Nassau).

39. Gibbs v. Berger, 59 A.D.2d 282, 399 N.Y.S.2d 304 (3d Dep't 1977).

40. Ratowsky v. Browne, 267 A.D.2d 643, 47 N.Y.S.2d 905 (3d Dep't 1944), appeal denied 268 A.D. 835, 50 N.Y.S.2d 464 (1944); Matter of Sumpter, N.Y.L.J., April 23, 1985, at 14, col. 3 (Nassau).

41. Matter of Shindell, 60 A.D.2d 393, 400 N.Y.S.2d 67 (1st Dep't 1977), affirmed 55 N.Y.2d 655, 446 N.Y.S.2d 942, 431 N.E.2d 303 (1981); Matter of Selzer, 237 N.Y.S.2d 484 (Nassau 1963); Matter of Sumpter, N.Y.L.J., April 23, 1985, at 14, col. 3 (Nassau).

42. But see discussion of McKinney's SCPA 509 in chapter on "Trials," infra at 507.

43. See Matter of Dorrance, 115 N.J.Eq. 268, 170 A. 601 (1934), affirmed per curiam sub nom. Dorrance v. Thayer—Martin, 13 N.J.Misc. 168, 176 A. 602 (1935), affirmed per curiam 116 N.J.L. 362, 184 A. 743 (1936), certiorari denied, 298 U.S. 678, 56 S.Ct. 949, 80 L.Ed. 1399 (1936), rehearing denied, 298 U.S. 692, 56 S.Ct. 957, 80 L.Ed. 1410 (1936). See chapter on "Estate Taxes," infra at 556 et seq.

44. Jurisdiction to hold this hearing is not specifically conferred by the SCPA. However, courts have the jurisdiction to determine their own jurisdiction over a matter. Stoll v. Gottlieb, 305 U.S. 165, 59 S.Ct. 134, 83 L.Ed. 104 (1938), rehearing denied 305 U.S. 675, 59 S.Ct. 250, 83 L.Ed. 437 (1938).

The practice has generally been, and will probably continue to be, that the court where the instrument latest in date has been offered for probate will hold the hearing to determine domicile. If there is no later instrument, normally the court that first obtained jurisdiction by the commencement of a proceeding will hold the domicile hearing.[45] Often the parties bring the matter to the attention of the respective courts, which then resolve where the status hearing should take place. The courts will take appropriate steps to stay proceedings until the status hearing is complete.[46]

In the next section of this chapter we discuss cases where two courts are permissible venues, and the first to act becomes the proper venue for the proceeding. This is inapplicable here, because only one court (that of the decedent's domicile) is the proper venue, and the purpose of the hearing is to determine which one.

Once a will is admitted to probate in one court, that court retains jurisdiction and a Surrogate's Court of another county cannot entertain an application regarding that estate.[47]

3. JURISDICTION OVER NONDOMICILIARIES' ESTATES

The Surrogate's Courts of every county have subject matter jurisdiction of the estates of nondomiciliaries who have left property in New York.[48]

Two points, one practical and one constitutional, fit in well at this point before discussion of the technical aspects of section 206. First, the Surrogate's Court can exercise its subject matter jurisdiction over a non-domiciliary's estate either by granting ancillary letters, where New York's role is to supplement the primary administration occurring in the decedent's domicile, or less frequently, by granting original probate. Those matters are discussed in detail elsewhere,[49] and the discussion in this chapter is limited to whether the court has the subject matter jurisdiction to grant any kind of letters.

Secondly, the jurisdictional predicate for exercising subject matter jurisdiction over the estate of a non-domiciliary is usually in rem: the non-domiciliary's property is physically located in New York, and its presence here gives the court the basis to exercise jurisdiction over its disposition. The estate is usually seeking not a money judgment, but a determination as to who is entitled to an asset within the jurisdiction of the Surrogate's Court. Because the rem is in New York, the court can give notice by personal or substituted service to interested persons, make them parties to a proceeding, and determine who is entitled to the assets. This type of jurisdiction is truly in rem. It is not an

45. E.g., Matter of Margolin, 493 N.Y.S.2d 972 (New York County 1985).

46. McKinney's SCPA 209, 102; McKinney's CPLR 2201.

47. See Matter of Kaufman, 145 Misc. 450, 261 N.Y.S. 212 (Richmond 1932).

48. McKinney's SCPA 206.

49. These matters are covered by McKinney's SCPA article 16 and discussed in chapter on "Ancillary Proceedings," infra at 509 et seq.

attachment of the respondent's property to gain jurisdiction over him for the purpose of obtaining a money judgment, which the Supreme Court has found constitutionally defective.[50]

The law provides that "[t]he Surrogate's Court of any county has jurisdiction over the estate of any non-domiciliary decedent who leaves property in the state, or a cause of action for wrongful death against a domiciliary of the state." [51] If the decedent left property in only one county, that county is the proper venue for proceedings relating to the estate. The same is true if he left personal property which since his death, disappearance or interment has come into one county and remains unadministered, or if he had at death a cause of action against a domiciliary of that county for personal injuries or for wrongful death and left no property in any other county. The place of his death is irrelevant. If the decedent left property in more than one county, each of the two counties is potentially the proper venue and the first to exercise jurisdiction becomes the proper venue. Other Surrogates must transfer matters relating to the estate to that court.

If someone brings the decedent's property into New York for the purpose of creating jurisdiction here, he may succeed. The Surrogate's exercise of jurisdiction over the estates of non-domiciliaries is discretionary,[52] and the court will weigh the New York contacts in deciding whether to exercise its discretion.[53] If some reasonable New York contacts exist, such as the presence of the beneficiaries or fiduciaries or most of the assets here, then the court will exercise jurisdiction based on assets brought into New York after the decedent's death. On the other hand, if someone brought the assets here for fraudulent or collusive reasons, such as to avoid stricter right of election statutes, the courts in New York will decline jurisdiction.[54] The courts also tend to disregard property that is here only temporarily, even if not brought here for collusive purposes.[55]

Subject matter jurisdiction is exercised through the commencement of a proceeding. In the Surrogate's Court the proceeding commences at the filing of the petition,[56] and commencement of any proceeding, such as a proceeding to open a safe deposit box, to probate a will, to

50. Shaffer v. Heitner, 433 U.S. 186, 97 S.Ct. 2569, 53 L.Ed.2d 683 (1977).

51. McKinney's SCPA 206.

52. Matter of Heller-Baghero, 26 N.Y.2d 337, 310 N.Y.S.2d 313, 258 N.E.2d 717 (1970).

53. The factors are discussed in this chapter infra at 30.

54. Matter of De Camillis, 66 Misc.2d 882, 322 N.Y.S.2d 551 (New York County 1971), affirmed 38 A.D.2d 687, 327 N.Y.S.2d 554 (1st Dep't 1971); Matter of Guadagno, N.Y.L.J., Aug. 21, 1985, at 12, col. 5 (Richmond), where the court revoked ancillary letters of administration from a decedent's husband who stated in his petition that the decedent had a bank account in New York "not exceeding $1,000" when in fact the only New York asset was thirty dollars placed in a Totten Trust for the decedent's benefit when she was comatose.

55. See Hoes v. New York, New Haven and Harlem Railroad Co., 173 N.Y. 435, 66 N.E. 119 (1903); Matter of Boda, 124 Misc. 2d 464, 476 N.Y.S.2d 476 (Tompkins 1984) (jewelry left by decedent at sister's house while on visit).

56. McKinney's SCPA 301, discussed in chapter on "Procedure," infra at 53.

administer an estate or even to administer a small estate, permits one county to retain jurisdiction and require all others to relinquish it to the first.

The current statute was enacted in 1984.[57] Its predecessor conferred exclusive subject matter jurisdiction on the county where the property was situated or where the defendant in the wrongful death action was domiciled,[58] or when more than one county had concurrent jurisdiction, in the first county to exercise it. To commence a proceeding in another county was a jurisdictional defect; the court of the wrong county totally lacked subject matter jurisdiction and did not even have the power to transfer the proceeding to a proper court. Now, a court of improper venue can (and must) transfer the proceeding to the proper venue.[59]

a. Situs of Assets

Since jurisdiction of and venue in a non-domiciliary's estate depends on where property is located, the statute assigns a situs to intangible property whose location is not immediately clear.[60]

For example, a wrongful death lawsuit against a New York domiciliary is personal property in the county of the domiciliary, and if there is more than one defendant-domiciliary, in the county of either domiciliary. The same rule applies to a debt owed by a New York domiciliary. If the debtor is not a natural person, its domicile will be in the county of its principal office. Where, however, the debt is evidenced by a negotiable instrument, jurisdiction will lie in the county where the instrument is located, not in the county of the debtor's domicile.

If an insurance policy on a nondomiciliary's life, or stock owned by a nondomiciliary, is physically situated within a county in New York, its situs for jurisdictional purposes will be the county where it is located. If the policy or stock is not physically present in New York, its situs will be at the principal office in New York of the issuing insurance company or corporation.

A discussion of the presence of assets in New York sufficient to confer subject matter jurisdiction on the New York courts would be incomplete without a mention of negligence actions, although as we discuss in some detail in another chapter,[61] the Surrogate's role in a

57. L.1984, c. 128.

58. L.1966, c. 953, repealed L.1984, c. 128. Matter of Wyche, 84 A.D.2d 223, 446 N.Y.S.2d 504 (3d Dep't 1982), affirmed 56 N.Y.2d 748, 452 N.Y.S.2d 20, 473 N.E.2d 279 (1982), is a good example of the pre-1984 law. There the decedent's sole New York property was a cause of action against a resident of New York County who had killed her. The court held that New York County was the only Surrogate's Court with jurisdiction of her estate.

59. As we discussed in the preceding section, supra at 3, the parties cannot get a change in venue for the convenience of the witnesses or for the purpose of obtaining a fair trial.

60. McKinney's SCPA 208.

61. See chapter on "Wrongful Death Proceedings," infra at 527 et seq.

negligence action is not usually to try the case, but to appoint the fiduciary to commence the action, supervise the distribution of the proceeds and review the accounting after the case has been tried in another civil court.

In the context of negligence actions, the United States Supreme Court in Rush v. Savchuk [62] has resolved the issue of the jurisdiction of a state court conferred by the presence of a defendant's insurance carrier within the state. Before that case, a court could obtain jurisdiction over a non-resident defendant by finding that his insurance carrier with an office in this state was a domiciliary for jurisdictional purposes even though the carrier's principal office was outside the state. The theory was that the insurance carrier owed a debt to the non-domiciliary.[63] The obligation of the carrier doing business in New York to defend and indemnify a non-domiciliary constituted a "res" and hence provided a basis for in rem jurisdiction. In Rush v. Savchuk the Court held that a domiciliary of one state could not obtain jurisdiction over a non-domiciliary through in rem jurisdiction by garnishing the contractual obligation of an insurance carrier to defend and indemnify the non-domiciliary. The Court held that the defendant did not have minimum contacts with the forum necessary to satisfy due process. The fictional presence of an insurance policy, along with the obligation to defend and indemnify, was not a sufficient relationship with the state to permit the court to acquire jurisdiction over the defendant, and therefore the SCPA provision giving the Surrogate jurisdiction in cases where there is property in New York cannot be used to confer jurisdiction in that situation.

4. JURISDICTION IN CONSERVATORSHIP CASES

The Surrogate has acquired the power to appoint conservators in cases relating to the administration of estates.[64] A person entitled to estate property, including proceeds of a negligence action, or the proceeds of a wrongful death recovery, must be under legal disability, must reside in the county where the Surrogate's Court proceeding is pending, and must be a person for whom a conservator could be appointed in the Supreme Court. In addition, the Surrogate must be satisfied by clear and convincing proof of the need for a conservator. If the conservatee was not a New York domiciliary, the Surrogate's Court of the county where the conservatee's property is located is the proper venue.[65]

62. 444 U.S. 320, 100 S.Ct. 571, 62 L.Ed. 2d 516 (1980), on remand 290 N.W.2d 633 (Minn.1980).

63. Seider v. Roth, 17 N.Y.2d 111, 269 N.Y.S.2d 99, 216 N.E.2d 312 (1966); Matter of Riggle, 11 N.Y.2d 73, 226 N.Y.S.2d 416, 181 N.E.2d 436 (1962).

64. McKinney's SCPA 2220(4); McKinney's Mental Hygiene Law § 77.01(3) (Supp.1984–85).

65. See Matter of Fabell, 121 Misc.2d 176, 467 N.Y.S.2d 792 (Bronx 1983).

5. JURISDICTION OVER TRUSTS

a. Inter Vivos Trusts

Historically the Surrogate did not take jurisdiction of inter vivos trusts, and the original SCPA that superseded the Surrogate's Court Act in 1967 granted the Surrogate subject matter jurisdiction which excluded lifetime trusts.[66] The Surrogates nevertheless felt that such jurisdiction was within their constitutional boundaries and when the trust was closely related to the affairs of a decedent, they frequently exercised jurisdiction over it.[67] The controversy has become obsolete since a 1980 amendment to the SCPA which explicitly confers jurisdiction, concurrent with that of the Supreme Court, over inter vivos trusts[68] if the trust assets are located in New York, or if the grantor was a New York domiciliary when the proceeding began, or if the trustee resides or (in the case of a corporate trustee) has a principal office in New York.[69]

The proper venue for proceedings relating to inter vivos trusts is the county where the assets are, or where the grantor was domiciled, or where the trustee is.[70] If venue could be in more than one county (because the assets, the creator and the trustee are in different counties), the first court to exercise its jurisdiction by entertaining a proceeding retains jurisdiction, and the Surrogate's Courts of other counties must transfer to that court any proceedings relating to the trust. Like its counterparts governing domiciliaries'[71] and non-domiciliaries'[72] estates, the law governing jurisdiction in inter vivos trusts was amended in 1984 for the purpose of expanding subject matter jurisdiction of the Surrogate's Courts over trusts not within their county so that a matter erroneously started in the wrong county could be transferred to the court of proper venue.[73]

It remains to be seen whether the Supreme Court will continue to exercise its jurisdiction over inter vivos trusts, or will permit the Surrogate's Court to take over administration of most of these trusts. It is likely that at least trusts for which intermediate accountings have already been filed in the Supreme Court will continue to be reviewed there for purposes of continuity, because of that court's familiarity with the trust administration and the presence there of previous court records are found there.

66. McKinney's SCPA 209(4), enacted in L.1966, c. 953.

67. E.g., Matter of Fornason, 88 Misc.2d 736, 389 N.Y.S.2d 1003 (Nassau 1976); Matter of Bleier, N.Y.L.J., Nov. 17, 1978, at 12, col. 2 (New York County). See Midonick, Do Surrogates Have Jurisdiction in Cases Involving Living Trusts?, N.Y.L.J., June 16, 1975, at 19, col. 1.

68. L.1980, c. 503.

69. McKinney's SCPA 207.

70. McKinney's SCPA 207.

71. McKinney's SCPA 205.

72. McKinney's SCPA 206.

73. L.1984, c. 128, § 2.

b. Testamentary Trusts

Article 15 [74] and Article 2 overlap substantially in the area of the court's jurisdiction over testamentary trusts. Under Article 15, the Surrogate has jurisdiction over testamentary trusts in three instances:

(i) if the testator was a New York domiciliary.[75]

(ii) if the will of a non-New Yorker was probated here.[76]

(iii) if the will of a non-New Yorker was probated in the decedent's domicile, but the trust situs is here.[77]

The situs of a trust of real property is where the real property is located. Both Article 2 [78] and Article 15 [79] contain provisions on the situs of a trust of personal property. The situs is in New York if the personalty was in New York when the trust was established (that is, at the testator's death or at the creation of the inter vivos trust), and is held and administered here, or if it was brought into New York for administration here and such move was not forbidden by the terms of the trust or the law of the creator's domicile. For example, a District of Columbia domiciliary could direct payment of the entire net estate to a New York trustee for administration here.[80] Some "forum-shopping" is thus possible.

There will be occasions where the New York Court, though it concededly has jurisdiction, will (rightly) decline to exercise it. If the New York contacts are very slim (for example, a New York testator creates an out-of-state trust to benefit out-of-state beneficiaries, or the trust situs is in New York but all the personae are elsewhere), the court may allow a more convenient forum of competent jurisdiction to take jurisdiction on a forum non conveniens reasoning,[81] so long as that does not thwart the testator's intent.[82]

If the court has subject matter jurisdiction, a question may arise as to which Surrogate should exercise that jurisdiction. Article 2 and Article 15 both state rules on venue, not always consistent. We discuss that topic in the chapter on "Trusts and Trustees." [83]

Sometimes a Surrogate in New York has jurisdiction over a testamentary trust, and a beneficiary with a power of appointment over the corpus exercises it in favor of the trustee of an out-of-state trust over which the Surrogate does not have jurisdiction. The EPTL offers some

74. Article 15 is discussed in chapter on "Trusts and Trustees," infra at 455 et seq.

75. McKinney's SCPA 1501(1)(a).

76. McKinney's SCPA 1501(1)(a); Matter of Vanneck, 158 Misc. 704, 286 N.Y.S. 489 (1936) (jurisdiction over testamentary trust created by a Canadian where will was admitted to probate in New York).

77. McKinney's SCPA 1501(1)(b). See Matter of Walker, 117 Misc. 805, 191 N.Y.S. 676 (New York County 1921) (jurisdiction over trust created by will of Englishman and admitted to probate in England when trust corpus was real property in New York).

78. McKinney's SCPA 208.

79. McKinney's SCPA 1501(2).

80. Matter of Ryan, 11 Misc.2d 205, 169 N.Y.S.2d 804 (N.Y.County 1957).

81. McKinney's CPLR 327.

82. Matter of Smart, 15 Misc.2d 906, 181 N.Y.S.2d 647 (Sup.Ct. New York County 1958) (court permitted transfer of trust assets to Maryland).

83. Infra at 455 et seq.

guidance; it states that once the power is exercised in favor of a trust other than the one that created the power, the court with jurisdiction of the appointee trust acquires jurisdiction of the property transferred.[84] The funds are thus delivered to the appointee trust by the original trustee. Although the New York court loses jurisdiction over the continuing trust,[85] there is clearly a good deal of residual jurisdiction left in the New York court. Obviously, the New York court has to approve and judicially settle the final accounting of the original testamentary trust, and it has the power to settle issues relating to the trust at that time.[86] After the accounting, however, the New York court would no longer have jurisdiction and the other state's court would take over jurisdiction.[87]

Of course, even if the court has jurisdiction, the court would not necessarily apply New York law. Rather, where other laws than that of New York are involved, the court would apply choice of law principles to determine whether to apply New York law or the law of another jurisdiction.

6. JURISDICTION OVER MATTERS RELATING TO THE AFFAIRS OF DECEDENTS

In 1982 the New York Court of Appeals decided Matter of Piccione,[88] settling many (though not all) of the troubling issues of the breadth of Surrogate's Court jurisdiction over matters that related, sometimes centrally, sometimes only peripherally, to a decedent's estate. Because decedents were often partners, shareholders, spouses, exspouses, trust and insurance beneficiaries, tortfeasors and parties to contracts, questions constantly arose as to whether these matters were within the Surrogate's jurisdiction to decide.

Although the grant of jurisdiction given to Surrogates by the constitution in 1962 (and by statute before) was broad, the Surrogate's Court did not immediately assume all of its jurisdiction. For instance, in discovery proceedings under SCPA 2103, the statute envisioned a replevy action, and for a long time the courts held that they did not have jurisdiction over a fiduciary's attempts to discover real property, insurance proceeds, contract actions, or other "choses in action."[89] Similarly, the courts did not take jurisdiction of inter vivos trusts; in fact, when the Bennett Commission proposed the SCPA, it clearly

84. McKinney's EPTL 10–6.9.

85. Matter of Rose, 256 N.Y. 557, 177 N.E. 139 (1931); Matter of Shea, 191 N.Y.S.2d 1014 (Westchester 1959).

86. See Matter of Security Trust Co., 71 A.D.2d 786, 419 N.Y.S.2d 26 (4th Dep't 1979), appeal denied 48 N.Y.2d 603, 421 N.Y.S.2d 1028, 396 N.E.2d 207 (1979) (the New York contacts made it equitable for the New York court to decide, at the accounting, the issue of how estate taxes should be apportioned against the testamentary trust).

87. McKinney's EPTL 10–6.9.

88. 57 N.Y.2d 278, 456 N.Y.S.2d 669, 442 N.E.2d 1180 (1982).

89. See, e.g., Matter of Trevor, 309 N.Y. 389, 131 N.E.2d 561 (1956); Matter of Chapin, 167 Misc. 351, 3 N.Y.S.2d 936 (Monroe 1938); Matter of Sichel, 162 Misc. 2, 293 N.Y.S. 559 (Kings 1937).

excluded jurisdiction of inter vivos trusts.[90] At about the time that the Surrogate's Court Act was replaced by the SCPA in 1967, with article 2 of the SCPA restating the constitutional grant of jurisdiction, the Surrogates began increasingly to exercise their jurisdiction over the affairs of decedents and the overall administration of estates under their supervision.[91] For example, they exercised jurisdiction over such matters as rescission of a contract,[92] shareholders' derivative actions,[93] actions to determine the validity of divorce before granting letters of administration to someone other than the decedent's former spouse,[94] inter vivos trusts,[95] discovery of royalties under a publishing agreement [96] discovery of funds under a stockholders' agreement,[97] discovery of rents and profits from real property,[98] interpretation of an agreement,[99] and entitlement to life insurance proceeds on decedent's life.[1]

No serious challenge to the Surrogate's jurisdiction succeeded at the Appellate Division level, and the Surrogates continued to entertain more and more proceedings which they felt would expedite the administration of estates.

In addition, the Surrogates would occasionally take jurisdiction derivatively of actions commenced in the Supreme Court. This creative device would occur when an action was started in the Supreme Court because the Surrogate feared that the Surrogate's Court lacked jurisdiction. Then, because the New York State Constitution [2] and the stat-

90. McKinney's SCPA 209(4), enacted in L.1966, c. 953. See section on "Inter vivos Trusts," supra at 10.

91. It would be misleading to say that the Surrogates had not exercised these powers before. See, e.g., Pierce v. Pierce, 71 N.Y. 154 (1877) (validity of ante-nuptial agreement); Matter of Jones, 19 Misc.2d 234, 189 N.Y.S.2d 389 (Nassau 1959), modified and affirmed 9 A.D.2d 778, 193 N.Y.S.2d 604 (2d Dep't 1959), reversed on other grounds 8 N.Y.2d 24, 200 N.Y.S.2d 638, 167 N.E.2d 336 (1960) (validity of contract and availability of specific performance as remedy); Matter of Farley, 91 Misc. 185, 155 N.Y.S. 63 (Clinton County 1915) (validity of common law marriage and validity of assignment of common law wife's interests in estate). However, armed with the new constitutional provisions, the courts obviously felt more comfortable to expand their jurisdiction.

92. Matter of Rothko, 69 Misc.2d 752, 330 N.Y.S.2d 915 (New York County 1972), affirmed 40 A.D.2d 1083, 338 N.Y.S.2d 855 (1st Dep't 1972).

93. Maki v. Estate of Ziehm, 55 A.D.2d 454, 391 N.Y.S.2d 705 (3d Dep't 1977).

94. Matter of Carter, 69 Misc.2d 630, 331 N.Y.S.2d 257 (New York County 1972), affirmed 42 A.D.2d 925, 347 N.Y.S.2d 1007 (1st Dep't 1973).

95. Matter of Frohlich, 87 Misc.2d 518, 385 N.Y.S.2d 922 (N.Y.1976).

96. Matter of Young, 80 Misc.2d 937, 365 N.Y.S.2d 695 (N.Y.1975).

97. Matter of Goldstein, 79 Misc.2d 4, 358 N.Y.S.2d 923 (Nassau 1974); Matter of Hall, 54 Misc.2d 923, 283 N.Y.S.2d 540 (New York County 1967).

98. Matter of Rungo, 74 Misc.2d 239, 342 N.Y.S.2d 929 (Nassau 1973).

99. Matter of Ryan, 63 Misc.2d 415, 311 N.Y.S.2d 719 (Erie 1970).

1. See Matter of Pedersen, N.Y.L.J., July 25, 1978, at 14, col. 4 (Suffolk), where the dispute over the life insurance proceeds was between the decedent's wife and his children by an earlier marriage. Though the estate did not even claim to be a beneficiary, the court took jurisdiction because the issue could have had estate tax ramifications.

2. McKinney's Const. Art. 6, section 19(a).

utes[3] authorized the Supreme Court to transfer proceedings to the Surrogate's Court, voila! the Surrogate would obtain jurisdiction.[4]

Another means for avoiding fragmentation of estate administration was to designate the Surrogate as an acting Supreme Court justice with special terms of the Supreme Court held at the Surrogate's Court. A Surrogate doubting jurisdiction could transfer a matter to himself as acting Supreme Court justice.[5]

Obviously, a definitive statement of the jurisdiction of the Surrogate's Court was needed. The statement came from the New York Court of Appeals in Matter of Piccione.[6]

In Piccione, the executors of the estate had to marshal assets to pay taxes and administration expenses, and had to sell real property in order to avoid foreclosure. The real property was burdened by a lease terminating on June 30, 1980, and the contract of sale was conditioned on the premises' being vacant. On May 1, 1980, the tenants were informed of the contract by letter and told to vacate the premises by July 1, 1980. Eventually the tenant refused to vacate. The executors forwarded a letter to the tenant attempting to give him thirty days notice to surrender, and began summary proceedings in the district court, which were dismissed on the basis of the inadequacy of the thirty-day notice.

At that point the situation had become desperate, for the contract vendee had a right to cancel if the premises were not conveyed. The mortgage on the premises had matured and was due, although extensions had been obtained in contemplation of the sale. Failure to sell the property could have resulted in a foreclosure and serious loss to the estate. The executors commenced a proceeding in the Surrogate's Court to evict the unauthorized hold-over tenant in order to close title. The tenant contended that the Surrogate did not have jurisdiction because the Surrogate's Court is not one of the courts entitled to hear summary proceedings under the Real Property Actions and Proceedings Law.[7]

The Surrogate held (and the Court of Appeals affirmed)[8] that the legislature could not take away from the Surrogate's Court what the New York Constitution[9] and the statute[10] grant: jurisdiction over all actions and proceedings relating to the affairs of a decedent. Therefore, the Real Property Actions and Proceedings Law's failure to list the

3. McKinney's SCPA 209, 501; McKinney's CPLR 325(e).

4. See Matter of Suchoff, 55 Misc.2d 284, 285 N.Y.S.2d 134 (Nassau 1967); Schoelles v. Zausmer, 2 A.D.2d 979, 157 N.Y.S.2d 190 (2d Dep't 1956) (dissenting opinion); 5A Warren's Heaton 473.

5. This procedure is authorized by the McKinney's Const. Art. 6, section 26.

6. 57 N.Y.2d 278, 456 N.Y.S.2d 669, 442 N.E.2d 1180 (1982).

7. McKinney's Real Prop. Actions & Proc.L. § 701(1) (1979).

8. 106 Misc.2d 898, 432 N.Y.S.2d 840 (Nassau 1980), reversed 85 A.D.2d 604, 444 N.Y.S.2d 689 (2d Dep't 1981), reversed 57 N.Y.2d 278, 456 N.Y.S.2d 669, 442 N.E.2d 1180 (1982).

9. McKinney's Const. Art. 6, section 12(d).

10. McKinney's SCPA 201(3).

Surrogate's Court did not matter; the court could still exercise its jurisdiction in a proceeding to recover possession of a decedent's real property if it related to the administration of his estate. SCPA 202, a section we discuss shortly, permits the court to exercise its general jurisdiction even though the procedure may not be specifically enumerated under the SCPA.[11]

The executors in Piccione also commenced a discovery proceeding against the tenant, and again the tenant moved to dismiss on the ground that the Surrogate's Court lacked subject matter jurisdiction. In the discovery proceeding the executor sought damages caused by the tenant's refusal to vacate the premises timely, which prevented an expeditious sale and caused the fiduciaries to secure an extension on the mortgage at a higher rate of interest. In addition, the executors claimed that the tenant physically damaged the property, which had to be repaired before the closing. The executors also sought to recover real estate taxes that the estate had to pay on behalf of the tenant. The Surrogate upheld his jurisdiction.[12] The Court of Appeals in dicta approved the Surrogate's exercise of jurisdiction, conceding that discovery proceedings had historically dealt with replevy and had been unavailable for choses in action, but approving the trend to permit discovery proceedings under the broadly-worded jurisdiction section, SCPA 202.[13] When the matter was reviewed again in the Appellate Division, after the Court of Appeals decision, the court decided that the Surrogate's Court did have jurisdiction.[14] Thus, the Surrogate emphatically can exercise all of the jurisdiction afforded under the constitution.

Finally, in Piccione the tenant commenced a malicious prosecution tort action in the Supreme Court against the fiduciaries, who moved to transfer that proceeding from the Supreme Court to the Surrogate's Court. The New York Court of Appeals held that the Surrogate did not have jurisdiction over the tort action, because it was a dispute between living persons, even though the fiduciaries were named in their fiduciary capacity only.[15]

11. See section on "McKinney's SCPA 202: The Jurisdiction Facilitator," infra at 23.

12. 106 Misc.2d at 900, 432 N.Y.S.2d at 843.

13. 57 N.Y.2d at 290, 456 N.Y.S.2d at 674, 442 N.E.2d at 1185.

14. N.Y.L.J., July 27, 1983, at 14, col. 3 (2d Dep't).

15. 57 N.Y.2d at 291, 456 N.Y.S.2d at 674, 442 N.E.2d at 1185. The Surrogate had recommended to the Supreme Court that the transfer of the action to the Surrogate's Court would be in the best interests of the estate, following Matter of Suchoff, 55 Misc.2d 284, 285 N.Y.S.2d 134 (Nassau 1967). This is hardly an extreme position, since the Supreme Court can always transfer a matter within the Surrogate's subject matter jurisdiction to the Surrogate's Court, with or without the Surrogate's recommendation or consent. See discussion of transfer of proceedings in chapter on "Trials," infra at 495–96. See also Matter of Keith, N.Y.L.J., Oct. 11, 1979, at 10, col. 5 (New York County) (Surrogate must accept transfer of accounting from Supreme Court); Matter of Wichfeld, N.Y.L.J., May 2, 1979, at 10, col. 1 (New York County) (Surrogate gave consent to transfer by Supreme Court). The Court of Appeals' holding is impliedly that the Surrogate's recommendation was inappropriate because the threshold subject matter jurisdiction requirement had not been met.

The legislature has considered a bill to expand SCPA Article 2 to grant jurisdiction to the Surrogate's Court over issues between living persons tangentially affecting an estate if such grant would expedite the administration of an estate, but it was not enacted.[16]

The Court of Appeals decision in Piccione made the need for legislation much less imperative, but it has not completely unclouded the issue. The question remains whether a blanket rule denying jurisdiction over matters between living persons will unnecessarily fragment estate administration in cases where the matter relates closely to the estate administration and the estate in fact may be liable for the expenses or damages that are the subject of the litigation. For example, in Matter of Zalaznick,[17] the decedent had been serving as executrix of an estate at the time of her death, and had retained attorneys to represent her as executrix and prepare the accounting. After her death, the estate of which she had been fiduciary sought to surcharge her estate for losses, and her estate filed a cross-petition for indemnification against the attorneys who had represented her. The respondents moved to dismiss, claiming that the Surrogate lacked subject matter jurisdiction over third party malpractice actions. The Surrogate exercised jurisdiction over the cross-petition, holding that under the statute,[18] the Surrogate's Court could determine all questions, legal and equitable, between all parties and any persons having any claim or interest in the matter litigated before the court. Since the CPLR provides for third party practice, the Surrogate could exercise his jurisdiction over the matter raised by the joinder of the third party.[19]

In such cases, where the estate of a deceased fiduciary stands to be surcharged for her wrongful acts in the administration of an estate, and both estates are being administered in the same Surrogate's Court, it makes sense to allow the fiduciary's estate to implead the attorneys who prepared the accounting. If the fiduciary's estate suffers a surcharge for wrongdoing attributable to the wrong advice of her attorneys, the Surrogate would be the logical jurist to resolve the question of liability. The same is true of the Piccione facts: if the plaintiff sues the fiduciaries in their representative capacity for malicious prosecution, and the fiduciaries are entitled (or may be) to

16. S. 8560 and A. 9964 of 1982. This legislation was drafted after the Appellate Division opinion in Matter of Piccione, 85 A.D.2d 604, 444 N.Y.S.2d 689 (2d Dep't 1981), reversing 106 Misc.2d 898, 432 N.Y.S.2d 840 (Nassau County 1980). The legislation passed the assembly and the senate but was not approved by the governor.

17. Matter of Zalaznick, 84 Misc.2d 715, 375 N.Y.S.2d 522 (Bronx 1975).

18. McKinney's SCPA 201(3).

19. McKinney's SCPA 102 states that unless the SCPA has contrary provisions, the provisions of the CPLR applies to Surrogate's Court practice. See also Matter of Chusid, 60 Misc.2d 462, 301 N.Y.S.2d 766 (Kings 1969), where the Surrogate ordered the testamentary trustees to pay sums due to a beneficiary to his wife instead, under a Family court support order. The court cited its general statutory grant of jurisdiction, McKinney's SCPA 201(3).

reimbursement from the estate for any funds they expend, it may be sensible to leave the matter with the Surrogate.[20]

The upholding of the Surrogate's jurisdiction in matters between living persons which closely affect an estate administration is bolstered by McKinney's EPTL 11–4.7, enacted in 1980 to clarify the extent of a fiduciary's liability arising out of the administration of an estate. Under the statute it is presumed that a fiduciary is working within his fiduciary powers unless proven otherwise. The indirect effect of a denial of jurisdiction in the Surrogate's Court may be a prejudging that the fiduciary was not acting within his fiduciary powers. Perhaps the Surrogate, who is presiding over the very litigation in issue, is better able to determine whether abuse of process or malicious or vexatious litigation has taken place. The issue invites legislative action.

a. Status of the Law After **Piccione**

As a result of Piccione, the law is now clear that if a matter relates to the affairs of a decedent or the administration of an estate, the Surrogate's Court has jurisdiction.

Piccione furthers the trend of concentrating matters dealing with decedents' estates in the Surrogate's Court unless the issues could be better resolved in a forum with more expertise or better facilities to handle them (such as medical malpractice, multiple eviction of an entire apartment complex, small claims matters).

On the other hand, the Surrogate will not and need not entertain every matter that can be commenced in the Surrogate's Court. Some matters, such as probate and final accounts, can be brought as a matter of right in the Surrogate's Court. However, most of the miscellaneous proceedings require entertainment by the court, and the court can refuse to take a proceeding.[21]

The Surrogate's calendars are up to date, and in order to insure expeditious administration of estates, the court may refrain from entertaining proceedings, although that is the exception, not the rule.

7. THIRD PARTY PRACTICE

In some cases, the Surrogate has specifically been given jurisdiction over third party practice. For example, in discovery proceedings the Surrogate can determine a dispute as to ownership between respondents if he finds that the estate does not have an interest in an asset.[22]

20. Judge Cardozo's words in Raymond v. Davis, 248 N.Y. 67, 72, 161 N.E. 421 (1928) would be appropriate here: "To remit the claimant to another forum after all the advances and retreats, these reconnaissances and skirmishes, would be a postponement of justice equivalent to a denial."

21. See Matter of Gifford, 279 N.Y. 470, 18 N.E.2d 663 (1939) (no exercise of jurisdiction over will of domiciliary disposing only of personal property located in another jurisdiction); Matter of Wolf, 144 Misc. 256, 258 N.Y.S. 444 (New York County 1932) (no exercise of jurisdiction over will of non-domiciliary whose New York assets were minimal). See also SCPA 2101(1)(b), where the court may decline to entertain a discovery proceeding.

22. McKinney's SCPA 2104(5).

Where the SCPA is silent, the provisions of the CPLR are applicable in the Surrogate's Court,[23] and the CPLR liberally allows the impleading of third parties to resolve disputes before the court.[24] Accordingly, the Surrogates have in the past permitted third party practice.

However, the New York Court of Appeals' recent restatement of the traditional rule that unless the statute specifically confers such jurisdiction (as, for example, in discovery proceedings),[25] the Surrogate does not have jurisdiction over disputes between living persons [26] casts doubt on the cases permitting the Surrogate to decide issues between third parties, even if the issues relate closely to the affairs of a decedent. The court in Matter of Piccione held that the Surrogate's Court did not have jurisdiction over a malicious prosecution action commenced against the fiduciary by a respondent in proceedings brought by the fiduciary in the Surrogate's Court.[27] The same reasoning has resulted in the denial of the Surrogate's jurisdiction of a dispute between a legatee of an estate and her creditor; the court held that it could not direct the legatee to assign her interest to the creditor.[28]

As we discussed above, that aspect of the Piccione holding invites legislative action.

SECTION C. FULL FAITH AND CREDIT

If the court of another state has subject matter jurisdiction and personal jurisdiction over the parties,[1] New York will enforce a decree from that court under the full faith and credit clause of the Constitution. A counterpart to the full faith and credit clause is the due process clause, and the two can conflict in a case such as the following: A New York decedent made a will and in it gave a power to another person (say, his spouse) to appoint the property by will. The spouse

23. McKinney's SCPA 102.

24. McKinney's CPLR 1007.

25. McKinney's SCPA 2104(5).

26. Matter of Piccione, 57 N.Y.2d 278, 456 N.Y.S.2d 669, 442 N.E.2d 1180 (1982), discussed supra in preceding section.

27. Its theory was that it was a dispute between living people and did not relate to the administration of an estate. See "Piccione" Ruling Makes Clear Surrogate's Court Jurisdiction, N.Y.L.J., Feb. 7, 1983, at 1, col. 2. The court cited Matter of Lainez, 79 A.D.2d 78, 435 N.Y.S.2d 798 (2d Dep't 1981), affirmed 55 N.Y.2d 657, 446 N.Y.S.2d 942, 431 N.E.2d 303 (1981) (no jurisdiction to adjudicate claim between estate beneficiary and the Department of Social Services); Matter of Goelet, 28 A.D.2d 149, 283 N.Y.S.2d 545 (1st Dep't 1967) (no jurisdiction to order specific performance of separation agreement); Matter of Ullman, 56 Misc.2d 495, 289 N.Y.S.2d 833 (N.Y.1968) (no jurisdiction to direct legatee to make payment of his interest to his creditor, unless the legatee had assigned his interest, in which case the court could direct payment to the assignee).

28. Matter of Goelet, 28 A.D.2d 149, 283 N.Y.S.2d 545 (1st Dep't 1967); Matter of Ullman, 56 Misc.2d 495, 289 N.Y.S.2d 833 (N.Y.1968). Once the assignment is made, however, the court can direct the fiduciary to make payment to the creditor. See also Matter of Naughton, 87 Misc.2d 530, 386 N.Y.S.2d 321 (Orange 1976) (no jurisdiction over dispute between executor and decedent's business partner).

Sec. C

1. See section on "Personal Jurisdiction," infra at 25 et seq.

moves away from New York and executes a will. The spouse's state does not require that takers in default of exercise be made parties to probate proceedings, and the will is probated without their having any notice of it. The trustees of the trust commence a proceeding for judicial settlement of their account in a Surrogate's Court in New York, where the trust is located. The takers in default of exercise are necessary parties, and they object to the spouse's exercise of the power on the ground that her will was procured by undue influence. In such a case, New York law determines the validity of the will as it relates to property that came from the New York decedent,[2] and New York's failure to recognize the foreign decree does not violate the full faith and credit clause because New York's own due process requirements were not met.[3]

Naturally, the New York court need not recognize the decree of another court unless that court had subject matter jurisdiction, and sometimes the question of whether the foreign court has subject matter jurisdiction is a close one. For example, in Matter of Acheson [4] the decedent's grandmother created a trust in New York and named Morgan Guaranty trustee. Income was to be paid to her son, and at his death income was to be paid to the decedent for life, remainder as he appointed by will, or in default to his issue. The decedent died in California in 1965. His will purported to exercise the power in favor of a daughter in a manner which violated both New York's and California's rules against perpetuities.

In 1966, Morgan Guaranty commenced a proceeding in New York for a final accounting and construction of the California will to determine whether there had been a valid exercise of the power. Before it was resolved, the decedent's executor obtained in California a cy pres reformation of the will, which validated the exercise of the power. The California court had obtained jurisdiction over the takers in default (the decedent's five other children) but not over Morgan Guaranty. The daughter, in the New York proceeding, sought recognition of the California construction based on the full faith and credit clause. She prevailed, the New York Court of Appeals holding that the California judgment was entitled to full faith and credit and that therefore parties over whom the California court had jurisdiction were bound. Morgan Guaranty was not bound but its absence was irrelevant since the court was not ruling on the validity of the trust or the validity of the exercise of the power, but rather the construction of the will.

2. Matter of New York Life Insurance and Trust Co., 209 N.Y. 585, 103 N.E. 315 (1913).

3. Matter of Brown, 120 Misc.2d 799, 466 N.Y.S.2d 988 (Westchester 1983). See also Blount v. Walker, 134 U.S. 607, 10 S.Ct. 606, 33 L.Ed. 1036 (1890), where a South Carolina court refused to recognize a North Carolina decree validating the will of the donee of a power conferred by a South Carolina decedent because it was not duly executed under South Carolina law.

4. Matter of Acheson, 28 N.Y.2d 155, 320 N.Y.S.2d 905, 269 N.E.2d 571 (1971), certiorari denied sub nom. Dowell v. Acheson, 404 U.S. 826, 92 S.Ct. 58, 30 L.Ed.2d 55 (1971).

A strong dissent in Acheson cogently argued that the California court did not have subject matter jurisdiction because the California probate court is not a court of general jurisdiction and because this was not a California will being construed, but a New York trust.

SECTION D. INCIDENTAL POWERS

SCPA 209 sets forth the incidental powers of the Surrogate's Court. Many of the powers were already provided for by the constitution and parts of 209 merely repeat that jurisdiction. The Bennett Commission, in drafting section 209, purposefully set forth powers repetitive of constitutional provisions. Because of the historical limitations that had been placed on the Surrogate's Court in the past, the Commission wanted to make clear that the Surrogate's Court had the necessary incidental powers to administer estates.

Other paragraphs of SCPA 209 implement the constitutional provisions authorizing the legislature to delegate additional powers to the Surrogate's Court, so long as they do not lie exclusively in the Supreme Court.

The statute specifically lists the following powers:

> The Surrogate can sign decisions, decrees and orders, which are then binding,[1] and change decrees and orders directing distribution made before probate and without knowledge of the existence of a will, and order the refund of wrongly distributed property.[2]
>
> The Surrogate can also determine what assets are subject to estate administration and what assets are available for distribution under a will or by intestacy.[3] The Surrogate can decide the validity of claims, and even resolve a controversy between the parties or between the estate and the parties as to ownership of estate assets.[4] The court can further construe any instruments executed by the decedent which may affect devolution of the property of an estate.
>
> The Surrogate can entertain a proceeding relating to a charitable trust[5] created by a will,[6] and he can dismiss a proceeding for lack of diligent prosecution.[7]
>
> The Surrogate can settle the account of a fiduciary of a common trust fund as provided under the banking law[8] and entertain proceedings relating to inter vivos trusts.[9] The Surro-

Sec. D

1. McKinney's SCPA 209(2).

2. McKinney's SCPA 209(2).

3. McKinney's SCPA 209(4).

4. McKinney's SCPA 209(4); see also SCPA 2104(5).

5. The charitable trust is defined by McKinney's EPTL 8–1.1.

6. McKinney's SCPA 209(7).

7. McKinney's SCPA 209(8).

8. McKinney's SCPA 209(5).

9. McKinney's SCPA 209(6). Both McKinney's SCPA 209(5) and McKinney's SCPA 209(6) are additional powers delegated to the Surrogate's Court by the legislature.

gate can complete the work of his predecessor,[10] and that includes the power to review the record on a hearing and render a decision without conducting a new hearing,[11] and can exercise the same powers the Supreme Court has.[12]

Despite the specificity of the statute, the enumeration of powers is not exclusive,[13] for the statute cannot take away from the Surrogate's Court the powers granted by the constitution.

The Surrogate's Court can transfer a case from a court other than the Supreme Court to itself if the case relates to the administration of an estate,[14] and can receive an action or proceeding from the Supreme Court if the Supreme Court orders it transferred to the Surrogate's Court.[15] In two respects this section varies from the constitutional provisions permitting transfers from one court to another, but in fact there is no real conflict. The statute requires a prior order from the Surrogate's Court to have an action transferred to it from the Supreme Court. Constitutionally, this is not necessary,[16] but it is helpful for the Surrogate to advise the Supreme Court whether or not the transfer would be beneficial to the overall expeditious administration of an estate.[17]

Secondly, the Surrogate can order a matter transferred from a lower court to itself.[18] The constitution contemplates a transfer out of the court rather than a transfer into the court.[19] The power given to the Surrogate to transfer up is not in conflict with the constitution, but is rather an additional power given by the legislature, which is authorized by the constitution.[20] The Surrogate can also transfer cases to another court of competent jurisdiction if for some valid reason it does not belong in the Surrogate's Court.[21]

10. McKinney's SCPA 209(9).

11. Matter of Newhoff, 107 A.D.2d 417, 486 N.Y.S.2d 956 (2d Dep't 1985).

12. McKinney's SCPA 209(10). While McKinney's SCPA 209(10) gives the Surrogate the powers of a Supreme Court justice in the exercise of its jurisdiction, when a statute confers jurisdiction specifically on a Supreme Court justice and not to the Surrogate, the Surrogate does not get such power under 209(10). For example, in a proceeding to fix New York estate taxes, the petitioner has sixty days to appeal a Surrogate's order (McKinney's SCPA 2008), and has two years to apply to the Supreme Court to reassess the taxes if the Surrogate's order was, among other things, erroneous. McKinney's Tax Law § 249–x. To confer that Supreme Court power, to reassess the taxes after sixty days, on the Surrogate would fly in the face of logic, and Matter of Bradley, 84 Misc.2d 1007, 376 N.Y.S.2d 874 (Albany 1975), so held.

13. McKinney's SCPA 209(11).

14. McKinney's SCPA 209(3).

15. See, e.g., Matter of Keith, N.Y.L.J., Oct. 11, 1979, at 10, col. 5.

16. McKinney's Const. Art. 6, section 19(h).

17. See Matter of Suchoff, 55 Misc.2d 284, 285 N.Y.S.2d 134 (Nassau 1967) (McKinney's SCPA 209 merely requires advisory information from Surrogate to Supreme Court).

18. McKinney's SCPA 209(3).

19. McKinney's Const. Art. 6, section 19(h).

20. McKinney's Const., Art. 6, section 12(d). See chapter on "Trials," infra at 495–96, for a discussion of transfers into and out of the Surrogate's Court.

21. McKinney's Const. Art. 6, section 19(d); Matter of Anonymous, N.Y.L.J., June 24, 1976, at 13, col. 3 (Queens) (transfer of adoption proceeding to Family Court).

SECTION E. SUPREME COURT'S JURISDICTION OVER SURROGATE'S MATTERS

Since the Supreme Court is a court of general jurisdiction, it has concurrent jurisdiction over Surrogate's matters with the Surrogate's Court, but has been admonished not to accept jurisdiction.[1] If the Surrogate is the first to exercise jurisdiction, the Supreme Court, like other Surrogate's Courts, must defer to that court.[2]

SECTION F. PRESUMPTION OF JURISDICTION

If a Surrogate signs a decree or order, a person aggrieved by it can move (in the court that issued it) to vacate or modify the decree or order,[1] or can appeal from it.[2] If the court lacked subject matter jurisdiction, that issue can be raised in the motion or appeal. If it is raised on a motion to vacate, the Surrogate's Court can decide the issue of its own jurisdiction.[3]

The SCPA creates a special rule for cases where the attack on the Surrogate's subject matter jurisdiction comes not directly, but collaterally, for example a challenge by a defendant in another forum who questions the authority of the Surrogate to appoint the fiduciary who commenced the action.[4]

All petitions starting proceedings in the Surrogate's Court must state the facts on which the court's jurisdiction is based,[5] and the rule is that unless these facts are contested, the Surrogate is presumed to have had jurisdiction of the subject matter and the parties. If the person contesting the court's jurisdiction cannot prove fraud or collusion, the presumption of subject matter jurisdiction is conclusive.[6] However, this does not enable the parties, by misstating the jurisdictional basis, to confer jurisdiction on the Surrogate's Court, because the type of fraud that precludes the conclusive establishment of jurisdiction in-

Sec. E

1. Raymond v. Davis, 248 N.Y. 67, 161 N.E. 421 (1928); Shearn v. Lord, 16 Misc.2d 224, 156 N.Y.S.2d 32 (Sup.Ct. New York County 1956), affirmed 3 A.D.2d 823, 161 N.Y.S.2d 822 (1st Dep't 1957).

2. Matter of Tabler, 55 A.D.2d 207, 389 N.Y.S.2d 899 (3d Dep't 1976), and authorities cited therein.

Sec. F

1. McKinney's SCPA 209(1).

2. Appeals in the Surrogate's Court are governed by McKinney's CPLR Art. 55 and 57. McKinney's SCPA 2701.

3. Matter of Gilman, 109 Misc.2d 749, 440 N.Y.S.2d 819 (1981).

4. See Windbourne v. Eastern Airlines, Inc., 479 F.Supp. 1130 (E.D.N.Y.1979), reversed on other grounds 632 F.2d 219 (2d Cir.1980); Matter of Guadagno, N.Y.L.J., Aug. 21, 1985, at 12, col. 5 (Richmond).

5. McKinney's SCPA 304(2), discussed in chapter on "Procedure," infra at 55. See Schwal v. Meyer, 93 Misc.2d 1051, 403 N.Y.S.2d 629 (Rockland 1978).

6. McKinney's SCPA 204. No such conclusive presumption arises concerning the court's personal jurisdiction over necessary parties. If the court issues an order or decree in a proceeding where it lacked personal jurisdiction over a necessary party, that party is not bound by it. See McKinney's SCPA 204, Prac.Comm. at 156 (1967); see discussion of personal jurisdiction this chapter infra at 25–28.

cludes constructive or unintentional fraud, where one mistakenly sets forth false facts in a verified pleading.[7]

Only a person with an interest in the proceeding can launch the attack on jurisdiction. For example, a legatee under the will who was not a necessary or proper party to the probate proceeding (because not a distributee or other adversely affected person), and who has no standing to object to probate,[8] cannot attack the jurisdiction of the court.[9] While a party could challenge directly, the non-party's attack on jurisdiction is collateral, and in the absence of fraud or collusion, jurisdiction is conclusively established by the allegation of the jurisdictional fact of domicile in the probate petition.

Moreover, a decree in the Surrogate's Court is res judicata as to all parties to the proceeding.[10] Thus, if a petitioner in a probate petition named the decedent's spouse as distributee and the court granted probate, the petitioner could not in a later right of election proceeding challenge the validity of the marriage.[11]

SECTION G. McKINNEY'S SCPA 202: THE JURISDICTION FACILITATOR

SCPA 202 creates, in two ways, a valuable flexibility in the exercise of the court's jurisdiction.

Over sixty different proceedings can be commenced in the Surrogate's Court. The SCPA gives the procedures for many of them, such as probate,[1] administration,[2] discovery,[3] and accounting,[4] but under SCPA 202, the proceedings enumerated in the SCPA are not exclusive. The Surrogate can, in any proceeding, exercise all the jurisdiction granted by law. Therefore, a proceeding not specifically provided for in the SCPA can be commenced under SCPA 202. For instance, an attorney who wishes to discover property which is the subject of a contract may not do so under SCPA 2103 because that section does not permit discovery of choses in action such as contracts. However, the Surrogate does have subject matter jurisdiction granted by the state constitution if the contract relates to a decedent's affairs,[5] so the

7. Lapiedra v. American Surety Co., 247 N.Y. 25, 159 N.E. 710 (1928); Stolz v. New York Central Railroad Co., 7 N.Y.2d 269, 196 N.Y.S.2d 969, 164 N.E.2d 849 (1959). See McKinney's SCPA 204, Prac. Comm. at 156 (1967).

8. Probate proceedings and necessary parties to probate proceedings, and parties entitled to object, are discussed in chapter on "Probate," infra at 71 et seq.

9. Matter of Deitch, N.Y.L.J. February 3, 1978 at 12, col. 4.

10. See Matter of LeRoy, 118 Misc.2d 382, 461 N.Y.S.2d 161 (Onondaga 1983).

11. Surviving spouses' right of election is discussed in chapter on "Surviving Spouses," infra at 302 et seq.

Sec. G

1. McKinney's SCPA Article 14, discussed infra at 71 et seq.

2. McKinney's SCPA Article 10, discussed infra at 125 et seq.

3. McKinney's SCPA Article 21, discussed infra at 326 et seq.

4. McKinney's SCPA Article 22, discussed infra at 179 et seq.

5. McKinney's Const. Art. 6, section 12(d).

attorney can commence the action under SCPA 202.[6] Similarly, if a fiduciary hoping to discover real property starts his proceeding under SCPA 2103, which does not permit discovery of realty, the court can entertain it anyway under 202, because it has subject matter jurisdiction.

Secondly, under SCPA 202 the court can exercise all of the jurisdiction granted to it by law (that is, the state constitution and statute) in any proceeding regardless of whether jurisdiction could have been exercised in a different proceeding. Thus if an attorney starts a proceeding under the wrong section of the SCPA, the court can retain the proceeding and make a determination, as long as it has subject matter jurisdiction and personal jurisdiction over the parties. A court could, for example, remove an executor from office in the course of an accounting proceeding.[7]

Similarly, if someone started a miscellaneous proceeding under Article 21 where he should have started an accounting proceeding under Article 22, the court need not dismiss the miscellaneous proceeding, but can treat it as an accounting proceeding.[8]

This is not to say, however, that the Surrogate will never decline to exercise one of its powers in a proceeding. For example, in one case [9] the court refused to hear evidence, during an accounting proceeding, on the validity of a testamentary provision, saying that the issue should be raised in a proceeding to vacate the probate decree.

SECTION H. EXERCISE OF THE COURT'S SUBJECT MATTER JURISDICTION

If the court has subject matter jurisdiction, it can make a decree or other determination. The jurisdiction of the court is exercised when the proceeding commences[1], at the filing of the petition, not at service of process as in the Supreme Court. There is no getting around this rule. When there is some reason to rush a proceeding, the court can obtain personal jurisdiction over the parties by order to show cause instead of citation,[2] but until a petition is filed, the court does not have jurisdiction to order service of the order.

6. See Matter of Rungo, 74 Misc.2d 239, 342 N.Y.S.2d 929 (Nassau 1973).

7. See Matter of Israel, 64 Misc.2d 1035, 315 N.Y.S.2d 453 (Nassau 1970), where the executor was removed from office during an accounting proceeding. The guardian ad litem raised the issue, and the court tried the question as part of the objections to the account.

8. See Matter of Perry, 123 Misc.2d 273, 473 N.Y.S.2d 335 (Nassau 1984), where a creditor commenced a proceeding to determine the validity of a claim under McKinney's SCPA 1808 and the court, fearing that the estate might be insolvent, used its authority under McKinney's SCPA 202 to convert it into a proceeding under McKinney's SCPA 1809, which requires citations of other creditors.

9. Matter of Brush, 46 Misc.2d 277, 259 N.Y.S.2d 390 (New York County 1965).

Sec. H

1. McKinney's SCPA 203.

2. See chapter on "Procedure," infra at 39.

The state constitution gives the Surrogate's Court jurisdiction over actions and proceedings,[3] but in fact under the statute all proceedings in the Surrogate's Court are special proceedings. Each proceeding, such as probate, tax, or accounting, is commenced separately unless there is a reason to consolidate several proceedings in one (such as a construction proceeding with a probate or an accounting). The subject matter and parties are different in each proceeding, so the jurisdiction obtained in a probate proceeding does not carry over to an accounting proceeding in the same estate. The petitioner must start a new special proceeding and the court must acquire (or reacquire, as the case may be) personal jurisdiction over the parties.[4]

An action commenced in another forum can be transferred to the Surrogate's Court if it relates to the administration of an estate.[5]

SECTION I. JURISDICTIONAL PREDICATE: PERSONAL OR IN REM JURISDICTION

Even if the court has subject matter jurisdiction, it cannot exercise that jurisdiction unless it has personal jurisdiction over the parties or "in rem" jurisdiction over the property, and unless it has given the parties to be bound procedural due process (notice and opportunity to be heard). A person who has not received process or has not appeared will not be bound by the order or decree.[1]

1. JURISDICTION TO DETERMINE JURISDICTION

As a preliminary matter, the court has jurisdiction to determine at a hearing whether or not it has jurisdiction of the subject matter or the parties.[2] The parties are not entitled to a jury trial on that preliminary question.[3]

2. PERSONAL JURISDICTION

a. Traditional Bases and Long-Arm Jurisdiction

The Surrogate's Court is expressly authorized to exercise jurisdiction over persons "as heretofore or hereafter permitted by law." [4] Thus, a person submits himself personally to the jurisdiction of the

3. McKinney's Const. Art. 6, section 12(d).

4. See, e.g., Matter of O'Brien, N.Y.L.J., Nov. 20, 1978, at 14, col. 6 (Bronx).

5. The transfer and consolidation of proceedings are discussed in this chapter supra at 21 and in chapter on "Trials," infra at 495–96.

Sec. I

1. See Matter of Zalaznick, 84 Misc.2d 715, 375 N.Y.S.2d 522 (Bronx 1975).

2. Matter of O'Brien, 54 A.D.2d 880, 389 N.Y.S.2d 2 (1st Dep't 1976). See Stoll v. Gottlieb, 305 U.S. 165, 59 S.Ct. 134, 83 L.Ed. 104 (1938), rehearing denied 305 U.S. 675, 59 S.Ct. 250, 83 L.Ed. 437 (1938). See also Matter of O'Meara, N.Y.L.J., Dec. 12, 1978, at 14, col. 3 (Queens).

3. Matter of Fay, 70 Misc.2d 51, 332 N.Y.S.2d 322 (New York County 1972), affirmed 41 A.D.2d 703, 340 N.Y.S.2d 861 (1st Dep't 1973).

4. McKinney's SCPA 210(1). See McKinney's CPLR 301, the Supreme Court counterpart to this retention of all bases of jurisdiction previously possessed.

Surrogate's Court by physical presence in the state and by domicile in the state.

Moreover, the presence of property (a "res") in the state gives the court jurisdiction to adjudicate interests in that property, whether or not the persons claiming an interest in the property are personally subject to the court's jurisdiction. While the court has jurisdiction over the res and need not obtain jurisdiction over the person, adequate notice must be given, and can be done by any means the court directs.[5]

In addition, the SCPA has a long-arm statute to secure jurisdiction over persons otherwise inaccessible under the traditional personal and rem theories. This long-arm provision is found in 210(2) and has two parts, a very broad one in subparagraph (2)(a) and a narrower one in subparagraph (2)(b).

Under SCPA 210(2)(a), a non-domiciliary who is not present in the state subjects himself (or his fiduciary) to the Surrogate's jurisdiction by any act or omission within the state committed either personally or by an agent, so long as the act or omission relates to the matter before the court. To determine whether a person is subject to jurisdiction under the long-arm statute, one must first ask, as Professor David Siegel so aptly states it, "Is the claim being asserted against the respondent, or the matter as to which his interest is sought to be affected, one which arises out of something he did in New York, or should have done but did not do in New York?"[6] For example, if a decedent's out-of-state relative, while in New York, transferred the decedent's ring to a jewelry repairman, and the repairman took it to his New Jersey shop to do the repairs, both the relative and the repairman have done something in New York which prompts the executrix's attempt to get the jewelry back. The next question is whether the exercise of jurisdiction is constitutional under the due process standards, which require that the party have at least minimum contacts with the state "such that the maintenance of the suit does not offend traditional notions of fair play and substantial justice."[7] In the jewelry hypothetical, the actual transfer of the property within the state is an act creating sufficient contacts to satisfy due process. A closer case arises where a person refuses to hand over property allegedly belonging to a New York estate. Cases have held that if the refusal takes place in New York, the New York contacts are sufficient to confer long-arm jurisdiction on the court,[8] and conversely, if a person's sole New York "act or omission"

5. McKinney's SCPA 307(2), discussed in chapter on "Procedure," infra at 40 et seq.

6. McKinney's SCPA 210, Prac.Comm. at 292 (1967).

7. International Shoe Co. v. Washington, 326 U.S. 310, 66 S.Ct. 154, 90 L.Ed. 95 (1945).

8. See Matter of Cooke, 112 Misc.2d 167, 446 N.Y.S.2d 189 (Nassau 1982), where the respondent, while in New York, refused to hand over to fiduciary securities, also allegedly in New York, under respondent's control, and the court found its exercise of jurisdiction was constitutionally supportable. In Gasarch v. Ormand Industries, Inc., 346 F.Supp. 550 (S.D.N.Y.1972), the respondent had presented stock certificates to a New York transfer agent of a Delaware corporation for exchange pursuant to a no-action letter of the Securities

was the failure to deliver property when the delivery should have taken place in New York, that omission is insufficient, without more, to confer jurisdiction.[9]

Since, in our hypothetical, the repairman's contacts with New York were sufficient to satisfy due process, the statute confers personal jurisdiction over him. This, in effect, enables the court to get the property back within its jurisdiction. If the repairman refused to follow the court's decree, a decree rendered against him would be binding against him everywhere under the full faith and credit clause,[10] and a New Jersey court would enforce the New York judgment. Without the long-arm grant of personal jurisdiction in McKinney's SCPA 210, there would have been no person and no res subject to the court's powers.

SCPA 210(2)(b) adds another basis for long-arm jurisdiction: the receipt of estate property constitutes a submission to the court's jurisdiction on matters relating to that payment.[11]

Needless to say, the court must have subject matter jurisdiction before it can enlist the aid of section 210, which deals solely with personal jurisdiction and does not expand subject matter jurisdiction. It simply assists the court that has subject matter jurisdiction in securing personal jurisdiction over those who, prior to enactment of the statute, would not have been available as parties to a proceeding because they were not domiciled or otherwise present in the state.

b. Additional Bases for Personal Jurisdiction

If the Surrogate's Court has subject matter jurisdiction, it may exercise personal jurisdiction over a person to the same extent the Supreme Court could do so.[12] In most cases, because of the long-arm statute of SCPA 210, this section need not be invoked. It will be useful, however, in obtaining jurisdiction in situations covered by CPLR 301,[13] such as the presence of a foreign corporation doing business in New York, or the submission to personal jurisdiction by a party who appears specially to contest the court's jurisdiction but then participates (even informally) in the merits in a proceeding.[14]

and Exchange Commission, and the agent refused to transfer. The court held that was a tort sufficient to give the court jurisdiction over the Delaware corporation.

9. Schenin v. Micro Copper Corp., 272 F.Supp. 523 (S.D.N.Y.1967).

10. U.S. Const. art. IV, § 1.

11. See McKinney's SCPA 210, D. Siegel, Practice Commentary at 297–98 (1967), for a discussion of when application of this basis of long-arm jurisdiction would be constitutional.

12. McKinney's SCPA 211.

13. McKinney's CPLR 301 provides: "A court may exercise such jurisdiction over persons, property, or status as might have been exercised heretofore."

14. Special appearances are discussed in chapter on "Appearances," infra at 237.

3. NOTICE AND OPPORTUNITY TO BE HEARD

Article 2 determines whether the court has a basis for personal jurisdiction; once that threshold has been met, the attorney must then address the question of whether the procedural requirements of due process (notice and an opportunity to be heard)[15] can be met. The court's exercise of personal jurisdiction over a party is discussed in detail in chapter 2 on "Procedure." Briefly put, personal jurisdiction can be obtained by service of process (a citation or an order to show cause), by waiver of process, by appearance of an adult competent party in person or by attorney, by a pleading, by service on a representative of a legally disabled person and on the disabled person if he is fourteen or older, and even by no service at all when a person is virtually represented by someone over whom the court has obtained personal jurisdiction.[16]

When the court has obtained personal jurisdiction over a party and has rendered a decree, that decree is binding on the party and can be converted to a judgment and enforced in other states under the full faith and credit clause of the United States Constitution.[17] The converse is also true: a party not served in a proceeding is not bound by the decree and can relitigate the issue in a court with personal jurisdiction over the parties. For example, in a case where a Delaware court was asked to give full faith and credit to a Georgia decree to which one of the parties in the Delaware proceeding had not been a party, the court held that the decree was not binding on the party who had not been cited in the Georgia proceeding.[18] Similarly, in another case the residuary legatees, who were not distributees and were therefore not parties in the probate proceeding, were not bound on the issue of the validity of a testamentary provision although it had been decided in the probate proceeding.[19]

Once a party is cited in the Surrogate's proceeding to probate a will and appears by an attorney, he is subject to the jurisdiction of that court and cannot offer another instrument for probate in a different forum until the Surrogate's Court determines the validity of the instrument propounded in that court.[20]

4. SERVICE OF PROCESS AS IT RELATES TO JURISDICTION

If the court has a basis for personal jurisdiction, service of process can be made in any part of the state and outside the state.[21] Under the

15. These requirements are set forth in McKinney's SCPA 203 and various sections of McKinney's SCPA Article 3, discussed in chapter on "Procedure," infra at 39–53.

16. McKinney's SCPA 307 and 315, discussed infra in chapter 2 on "Procedure."

17. U.S. Const. art. IV, § 1.

18. See Matter of Riley, 315 U.S. 343, 62 S.Ct. 608, 86 L.Ed. 885 (1942), rehearing denied 315 U.S. 829, 62 S.Ct. 903, 86 L.Ed. 1223 (1942).

19. Matter of Brush, 46 Misc.2d 277, 259 N.Y.S.2d 390 (New York County 1965).

20. Matter of Marshall, 57 Misc.2d 419, 292 N.Y.S.2d 973 (Nassau 1968).

21. McKinney's SCPA 212. Service of process is discussed in chapter on "Procedure," infra at 39–53.

state constitution,[22] the Surrogate's Court may direct process in the state, and the SCPA 212 broadens the provision to include service outside the state.[23]

SECTION J. CHOICE OF JURISDICTION AND CHOICE OF LAW

Occasionally a non-New Yorker writes a will to include a direction that it be probated in New York and that New York law apply to its construction and administration. The next two sections of this chapter discuss the SCPA sections that permit the Surrogate to probate such a will [1] and to resolve the conflict of laws in favor of New York law,[2] and the case law that fills the gaps left by the statute.

1. JURISDICTION TO PROBATE

SCPA Article 16 covers the administration of estates of non-domiciliaries who leave property in New York. Such administration can be ancillary, that is, a secondary administration where a New York fiduciary delivers the New York assets to the primary administrator elsewhere after satisfying the interests of New York creditors.[3] Article 16 also allows original probate of the will of a non-New Yorker.[4] Whether original probate will be allowed depends on what has taken place in the other jurisdiction. The basic rules are set forth in SCPA 1605 and several cases add gloss to the statute.

a. Wills Proved or Established in Another Jurisdiction

When a will has been admitted to probate or "established" in the testator's domicile,[5] the general rule is not to permit original probate in New York.[6] The rationale of this section is that the New York property is more appropriately administered by ancillary probate. There are, however, exceptions to this general prohibition against original probate.[7] First, a will probated or established elsewhere can be admitted to original probate here if the court finds that ancillary probate would be impossible or unduly expensive or inconvenient. The kinds of inconvenience or impossibility contemplated are a "state of war, massive destruction of records by bombing, or organized persecution of or discrimination against minorities * * *." [8] The will may

22. McKinney's Const. Article 6, section 1(c).

23. McKinney's SCPA 212. The legislature is authorized to confer more powers on the Surrogate than the Constitution does by McKinney's Const. Article 6, section 12(d).

Sec. J

1. McKinney's SCPA 1605.

2. McKinney's EPTL 3–5.1(h).

3. See chapter on "Ancillary Administration," infra at 509 et seq.

4. Original probate of a foreign will is discussed in chapter on "Ancillary Administration," infra at 522–24.

5. McKinney's SCPA 1605(2). The phrase "established in the testator's domicile" is intended to cover situations in foreign countries where the will is "proved" by a method other than probate.

6. McKinney's SCPA 1605(2).

7. McKinney's SCPA 1605(2)(a), (b), (c).

8. McKinney's SCPA 1605, P. Powers, Practice Commentary at 632 (1967).

also be originally probated here despite its probate elsewhere if the testator directed that it be probated here,[9] or if the laws of the testator's domicile discriminate against New York domiciliaries.[10]

Thus, if a will has been probated (or "established") in the decedent's domicile, one of the exceptions must apply or original probate in New York will not be allowed. Further, even if one of the exceptions does apply, the Surrogate's Court will not automatically exercise its jurisdiction to probate the will. The exercise of jurisdiction is discretionary. The principles of comity require deference to the domicile, and original jurisdiction in New York will be allowed only if certain factors justify it.

The factors were set forth in Matter of Heller-Baghero,[11] and they are:

(i) how substantial the New York assets are;

(ii) whether the executors and beneficiaries reside in New York;

(iii) whether it appears that proof of the will in the other jurisdiction would require extensive and costly litigation; and

(iv) whether the New York proceeding was brought in good faith with no intention of thwarting the law of the domicile.

As a practical matter, the presence of a bulk of the assets in New York ranks high among the factors listed.[12]

In Matter of Renard,[13] the Surrogate added another interesting factor in deciding to grant original probate. The testatrix had requested New York jurisdiction and had also directed application of New

9. This is useful in cases where a "testator may explicitly direct probate in this jurisdiction but the law of his own domicile may make it necessary first to prove the will there." McKinney's SCPA 1605, P. Powers, Practice Commentary at 632 (1967).

10. See, e.g., Matter of Goldstein, 34 A.D.2d 764, 310 N.Y.S.2d 602 (1st Dep't 1970), discussed below in text accompanying footnote 18; Matter of Siegel, 83 Misc. 2d 1062, 373 N.Y.S.2d 812 (Erie County 1975) (original probate in New York granted because New York corporate fiduciary not permitted to qualify in Florida).

11. 26 N.Y.2d 337, 345, 310 N.Y.S.2d 313, 320, 258 N.E.2d 717, 722 (1970).

12. For example, jurisdiction to probate was exercised in Matter of Heller-Baghero, 26 N.Y.2d 337, 310 N.Y.S.2d 313, 258 N.E.2d 717 (1970) (90% of assets in New York); Matter of Goldstein, 34 A.D.2d 764, 310 N.Y.S.2d 602 (1st Dep't 1970) (100% of assets in New York); Matter of Renard, 108 Misc.2d 31, 437 N.Y.S.2d 860 (New York County 1981), affirmed without op. 85 A.D.2d 501, 447 N.Y.S.2d 573 (1st Dep't 1981), affirmed 56 N.Y.2d 973, 453 N.Y.S.2d 625, 439 N.E.2d 341 (1982) (80% of assets in New York); Matter of Vischer, 53 Misc.2d 912, 280 N.Y.S.2d 49 (N.Y.1967) (90% of assets in New York). Jurisdiction to probate was declined in Matter of Brunner, 72 Misc.2d 826, 339 N.Y.S.2d 506 (New York County 1973), affirmed on other grounds 51 A.D.2d 995, 380 N.Y.S.2d 744 (1st Dep't 1977), affirmed 41 N.Y.2d 917, 394 N.Y.S.2d 621, 363 N.E.2d 346 (1977) ($1,000 in New York out of an estate of over one million dollars); Matter of Oakley, N.Y.L.J. March 29, 1978, p. 17, col. 6 (Westch. County) (most of estate assets in Pennsylvania; only safe deposit box in New York); Matter of Wolf, 144 Misc. 256, 258 N.Y.S. 444 (N.Y.1932) (almost all property in Pennsylvania; only small personal effects in New York).

13. 100 Misc.2d 347, 417 N.Y.S.2d 155 (N.Y.1979), affirmed 71 A.D.2d 554, 418 N.Y.S.2d 553 (1st Dep't 1979), motion for leave to appeal denied 48 N.Y.2d 609, 424 N.Y.S.2d 1027, 400 N.E.2d 1351 (1979).

York law in an attempt to bar her son from taking a "forced share" under French law. In deciding to exercise jurisdiction, the Surrogate preliminarily analyzed the choice of law question and concluded that New York law might ultimately be found to apply (and since the conflicts question was later decided by the same Surrogate, it is not surprising that New York law was indeed found to apply).[14] Thus, the court reasoned, it would be advantageous to have the issue decided by a New York court. "This conclusion makes it at least possible that the decedent's evident intent to bar her son and to have the courts of this state pass upon the efficacy of her attempt to do so will be served to the maximum degree possible." [15] Theoretically, it should not matter where a choice of law issue is argued. This statement by the Surrogate impliedly recognizes that in practice, however, the outcome of the choice of law question may be affected by the choice of forum.

b. Wills Not Proved or Established in Another Jurisdiction

Where a will of a non-domiciliary has not been probated (or "established") in another state or country, the Surrogate in his discretion can grant original probate to the will if it was validly executed.[16] The Surrogate must decide whether original probate in New York is appropriate, and he will make that decision by weighing the same "Heller-Baghero" factors, set forth in the preceding section, that he weighed in deciding whether to probate a will proved in another jurisdiction. The difference is that when the will has not been probated or established elsewhere, the Surrogate considers only those factors, whereas he must also find one of the enumerated statutory exceptions [17] if the will has been proven elsewhere.

Thus, even though the testator did not direct probate in New York in Matter of Goldstein,[18] the will, which had not been probated elsewhere, was entitled to probate in New York because all the assets were here, all the distributees and most of the legatees lived here, and the domiciliary state (Florida) would not permit the named New York executors to qualify. The party objecting to New York probate was a residuary legatee with a relatively minor interest in the estate.

These cases usually arise when the court of the decedent's domicile, although it has not probated the will, has exercised jurisdiction over some other aspect of the estate. For example, in Matter of Renard,[19]

14. 108 Misc.2d 31, 437 N.Y.S.2d 860 (N.Y. County 1981), affirmed without op., 85 A.D.2d 501 (1st Dep't 1981), affirmed 56 N.Y.2d 973, 453 N.Y.S.2d 625, 439 N.E.2d 341 (1982).

15. 100 Misc.2d 347, 363, 417 N.Y.S.2d 155, 164 (N.Y. County 1979), affirmed 71 A.D.2d 554, 418 N.Y.S.2d 553 (1st Dep't 1979), motion for leave to appeal denied 48 N.Y.2d 609, 424 N.Y.S.2d 1027, 400 N.E.2d 1351 (1979).

16. McKinney's SCPA 1605(1). A will is validly executed under New York law if at the time of execution it was valid under the law of New York, or the testator's domicile, or the place where it was executed. McKinney's EPTL 3-5.1.

17. McKinney's SCPA 1605(2).

18. 34 A.D.2d 764, 310 N.Y.S.2d 602 (1st Dep't 1970).

19. 108 Misc.2d 31, 437 N.Y.S.2d 860 (New York County 1981), affirmed without

the testatrix had executed a "New York will" and a "French will," and the French will had been established in France; and in Matter of Brunner,[20] a later document said to supersede the New York will had been offered in a French court. Both courts weighed the New York connections against those of the domicile in deciding whether to probate the will in New York.

2. CHOICE OF LAW

Closely related to the choice of forum is the choice of law. Occasionally a testator directs in his will that New York law apply to the administration of his estate and disposition of his assets. Most often he does this to avoid a law of his own jurisdiction which he finds burdensome, such as a substantial right of election for the surviving spouse. EPTL 3–5.1 explicitly permits a testator to direct that New York law apply to the disposition of his property, and the New York Court of Appeals in Matter of Renard has interpreted this to extend both to dispositions under his will and to dispositions by operation of law, such as forced shares for heirs.[21]

The question whether a testator can opt for application of New York's right of election instead of his domicile's more substantial one was not directly answered by the Court of Appeals in Matter of Renard, so the practitioner is well advised to know the history behind Renard before assuming that a testator can safely move his assets to New York and opt for application of New York's right of election.

In Matter of Clark,[22] a domiciliary of Virginia died with a will directing that the will be construed pursuant to New York law. There was bi-state administration of the estate, but the bulk of his assets was administered in New York. The decedent's widow, still a Virginia resident, filed a right of election in New York against the New York property, and the question was whether New York law (less favorable to spouse) or Virginia law (more favorable to spouse) applied. The Court of Appeals held that Virginia law controlled; although a testator had a statutory right to have New York law determine issues relating to testamentary dispositions,[23] that statute did not apply to the right of election, which is not a testamentary disposition but a statutory grant. Under choice of law principles, Virginia had the predominant, if not the sole, interest in the protection of its residents.

op. 85 A.D.2d 501, 447 N.Y.S.2d 573 (1st Dep't 1981), affirmed 56 N.Y.2d 973, 453 N.Y.S.2d 625, 439 N.E.2d 341 (1982).

20. 72 Misc.2d 826, 339 N.Y.S.2d 506 (New York County 1973), affirmed on other grounds 51 A.D.2d 995, 380 N.Y.S.2d 744 (1st Dep't 1977), affirmed 41 N.Y.2d 917, 394 N.Y.S.2d 621, 363 N.E.2d 346 (1977).

21. 56 N.Y.2d 973, 453 N.Y.S.2d 625, 439 N.E.2d 341 (1982).

22. 21 N.Y.2d 478, 288 N.Y.S.2d 993, 236 N.E.2d 152 (1968).

23. The law in effect at the time of testator's death, and thus the law applicable to his estate, was D.E.L. 47. L. 1909, c. 18.

In Matter of Renard,[24] the decedent was born in France, worked in New York and lived in New York for thirty years. She then returned to France where she died, leaving major assets in New York.

Her son, a citizen of both France and the United States, was an adult domiciled in California. The will, admitted to probate in New York, directed that New York law apply. The decedent's son received less under the will than under the forced heirship laws of France, and he objected, contending that he was entitled to one-half the estate. The Surrogate held that New York law controlled because EPTL 3–5.1(h) was intended to permit a non-resident testator to invoke New York law with respect to assets physically located here and thereby avoid forced heirship.[25] The Appellate Division affirmed,[26] and the Court of Appeals also affirmed,[27] basing its decision on that part of the Surrogate's opinion which spoke of the legislative changes to the statute.

The Surrogate had noted that in Clark, the statute permitted application of New York law only to testamentary dispositions, and the right of election had nothing to do with testamentary dispositions. The current law, EPTL 3–5.1(h), has broader language than its predecessor. It permits New York law to govern the disposition of one's property located within the state, not just the disposition of that property by will.

Future case law (or legislation) will determine whether Clark has been overruled by Renard or not.[28] Distinctions could be made on the facts. In Clark, the decedent's wife was a Virginia domiciliary, so she had greater interest in application of Virginia law than the heir in Renard, a California domiciliary who was attempting to impose French law. In fact, in the Surrogate's opinion in Renard, an apparently critical determinant was that the son was domiciled in California.[29] The Surrogate held that both France and New York had adequate points of contact to apply their own law within reasonable standards of due process and fundamental fairness. In addition, in Renard the decedent always kept her United States citizenship and retained contacts here. Her son had very little contact with France other than French citizenship. Thus, even if EPTL 3–5.1(h) did not control, the choice of New York law would be warranted under a "paramount

24. 108 Misc.2d 31, 437 N.Y.S.2d 860 (N.Y. County 1981), affirmed without op. 85 A.D.2d 501 (1st Dep't 1981), affirmed 56 N.Y.2d 973, 453 N.Y.S.2d 625, 439 N.E.2d 341 (1982).

25. 108 Misc.2d 31, 437 N.Y.S.2d 860 (N.Y. County 1981), affirmed without op. 85 A.D.2d 501 (1st Dep't 1981), affirmed 56 N.Y.2d 973, 453 N.Y.S.2d 625, 439 N.E.2d 341 (1982).

26. 85 A.D.2d 501, 447 N.Y.S.2d 573 (1st Dep't 1981).

27. 56 N.Y.2d 973, 453 N.Y.S.2d 625, 439 N.E.2d 341 (1982).

28. For a discussion of Renard, see Turano, "In re Renard", Trusts and Estates, Jan. 1984 at 35; Midonick and Ordover, "Spousal Claims after Renard," 123 Trust & Estates, No. 6, 14–36 (June, 1984); Hendrickson, "Choice of Law Direction for Disposing of Assets Situated Elsewhere Than the Domicile of Their Owner, The Refractions of Renard", A.B.A., Real Property, Probate and Trust Journal, vol. 18, p. 407 (1983).

29. 108 Misc.2d at 39, 437 N.Y.S.2d at 865–66.

interest" test. Moreover, and perhaps more importantly, New York has a strong public policy interest in protecting surviving spouses and no policy at all in favor of forcing a decedent to give a share of his estate to his children. In fact, testators from every state but Louisiana are free to disinherit their children completely.

However, the Court of Appeals did not use the "paramount interest" theory and did not discuss New York's public policy in favor of spouses, but affirmed on the Surrogate's opinion stating that the linguistic changes in the statute mandated a different result in Renard from that in Clark.[30] The dissent in Renard felt that Renard overruled Clark and, by implication, that a testator can now place assets in New York and insulate them from the spousal right of election of his domicile. However uncertain the issue may be, Matter of Renard indicates at a minimum that there is a trend to permit jurisdiction in New York and application of New York law if there is sufficient contact and if public policy is not violated.

SECTION K. JURISDICTION OF THE FEDERAL COURTS

It is rare that estates issues are litigated in the federal courts because probate and administration are so peculiarly "state-law" phenomena. Occasionally, however, the parties bring, on a diversity basis, a lawsuit in the federal court to adjudicate a claim against the estate. The federal courts have the jurisdiction to do so.[1] They cannot, however, assume jurisdiction in the probate proceeding,[2] or in any other proceeding where the Surrogate would have been, in fact, the only New York court to assume jurisdiction. For example, the Surrogate's Court is the appropriate forum to decide the probate itself, attorneys' fees and commissions for the estate administrator.[3] If, on the other hand, the matter was such that a court of general jurisdiction would likely have decided it, the federal court can hear it.[4]

30. 108 Misc.2d at 38, 437 N.Y.S.2d at 865.

Sec. K

1. Markham v. Allen, 326 U.S. 490, 66 S.Ct. 296, 90 L.Ed. 256 (1946); 13B C. Wright, A. Miller and E. Cooper, Federal Practice and Procedure, section 3610 (1984).

2. Waterman v. Canal-Louisiana Bank & Trust Co., 215 U.S. 33, 30 S.Ct. 10, 54 L.Ed. 80 (1909).

3. See Giardina v. Fontana, 733 F.2d 1047 (2d Cir.1984) (court refused to order accounting and to impose constructive trust in an estate still subject to probate proceedings).

4. Lamberg v. Callahan, 455 F.2d 1213 (2d Cir.1972). See Dannhardt v. Donnelly, 604 F.Supp. 796 (E.D.N.Y.1985) (federal court assumed jurisdiction of case where legatee under earlier joint will claimed to be entitled to entire estate despite decedent's execution of a later will giving him only a nominal gift.

Chapter Two

PROCEDURE

SECTION A. INTRODUCTION

Article 3 of the SCPA, the general article on procedure (with emphasis on process), applies to Surrogate's Court practice unless other sections of the SCPA contain contrary rules for particular proceedings. Where the SCPA is silent on a procedural matter, the CPLR governs.[1] Therefore, the lawyer researching a question of procedure in the Surrogate's Court should start with the SCPA articles dealing with specific proceedings, and if the question is unanswered there, proceed to SCPA article 3, and finally to the CPLR.

There are no actions in the Surrogate's Court, but only special proceedings.[2] A petition commences the special proceeding and the court issues process to be served on necessary parties. If someone later commences another proceeding relating to the same estate, the court's jurisdiction over the parties to the first proceeding does not continue automatically; process must be served again on all necessary parties to the second proceeding.

A general caveat is worthwhile here: when a paper must be filed with the Surrogate's Court, that filing will be accomplished when the court receives the paper, not when the attorney mails it. It is therefore advisable to deliver the papers to the Surrogate's Court by hand, especially whenever time is of the essence (for example, if a statute of limitations is about to run.)[3]

SECTION B. THE CITATION

The citation is the usual form of process in the Surrogate's Court. It is functionally equivalent to the summons used in most courts of civil jurisdiction, and it fulfills the same constitutional requirement of notice. If the court lacks personal jurisdiction over a necessary party, an order or decree it issues does not bind that party, who can, when he finds out about it, attack its validity. If the court does have personal

Sec. A

1. McKinney's SCPA 102 states that the "CPLR and other laws applicable to practice and procedure apply to the surrogate's court except where other procedure is provided by this act."

2. McKinney's SCPA 203.

3. Matter of Ziems, 120 Misc.2d 502, 466 N.Y.S.2d 159 (Oswego 1983) (court's failure to receive timely notice of election defeated the claim, though notice had been mailed timely).

jurisdiction over a party who defaults, that party is bound by the decree unless he succeeds in a motion to vacate the default.

Despite the similarities between the summons used in other civil courts and the citation used in the Surrogate's Court, in practice an important difference exists. The citation is issued by the court, not by the attorney.[1] In practice the attorney prepares the petition and the citation and takes them to the clerk, who then issues the citation in the name of the judge and places the seal of the court on them. The clerk files the original (the one submitted by the attorney) in the court, and the petitioner's attorney makes copies for service. The citation is returnable before the court that issued it. The citation has to be substantially like the official form appended to the SCPA,[2] and in most cases attorneys get the official form from the court and modify it, if necessary, for the proceeding at bar.

The attorney should be aware of two points of timing. First, the return date may not be more than four months after the date of issuance.[3] Secondly, the statute of limitations is tolled by the filing of the petition, and not by service of process, as long as process is issued and service made within sixty days after the filing of the petition.[4] If it is not, the statute of limitations continues to run as though the petition had not been filed. This is a significant difference in Surrogate's practice from other civil courts, where service of process tolls the statute of limitations.[5] If the running of the statute of limitations does not loom near, there is no time limit on when, after filing the petition, the attorney must serve the citation, except that once the citation is issued, the four-month limitation begins to run.

The citation must include the names of parties entitled to process (those interested in the proceeding[6] who have not signed waivers or otherwise consented to the relief requested), the name and domicile of the petitioner, the type of proceeding, the return date, the relief sought, and the name, address and telephone number of the petitioner's attorney, so that the person cited can communicate with the attorney and seek information to determine whether to appear or not. The citation alerts the person served that he need not appear, but that if he does not, he is assumed to have consented to the relief sought by the petitioner. This amounts to a default.

On the back of the official form of citation is an affidavit for proof of service. In it the person who made service describes the person served and swears that service was made properly. The petitioner

Sec. B

1. Under McKinney's SCPA 2609(1)(a), (3), either the chief clerk, the deputy chief clerk or the Surrogate can issue process.

2. Official Form Number 1.

3. The return date is discussed this chapter infra at 49–51.

4. McKinney's SCPA 301.

5. McKinney's CPLR 203(b)(1).

6. The parties necessary to each proceeding are discussed in the respective chapters on the proceedings.

must submit the completed affidavit to the court before the return date.[7]

SECTION C. PERSONS TO BE CITED (AND EXCEPTIONS)

The importance of proper service of process on all necessary parties cannot be gainsaid. The court which does not have personal jurisdiction over a necessary party cannot make a decree binding on that party.

Ordinarily every person with an interest in the proceeding must be cited, and we discuss necessary parties in the chapters on the respective proceedings, but a few exceptions exist and those we can dispose of here. First, no citation need be served on those persons who have waived service,[1] and it is customary for an attorney to send waivers to adult competent persons entitled to service.[2] If they sign the waivers, the petitioner avoids the expense and trouble of personal (or alternative) service. The waiver is a simple notarized statement that the person signing waives service of process and consents to the relief requested by the petitioner. Samples are included in some of the official forms in the SCPA, and a form for waivers is available from the court. A person who reads the waiver and signs it is chargeable with knowledge of what it says and what its effect is,[3] but it is still advisable for the attorney to explain in the cover letter the contents and effect of the waiver. The court will not lightly reopen a decree,[4] but it will do so if it finds that someone convinced the person to sign the waiver by fraud,[5] overreaching,[6] misrepresentation or other misconduct.[7]

Secondly, if a necessary party is not served, the court nevertheless acquires jurisdiction if the party is a competent adult and appears in person or by an attorney's written notice of appearance.[8] This is not true for persons under legal disability; while a committee, conservator

7. See "Proof of Service and Admission of Service," this chapter infra at 51–52.

Sec. C

1. McKinney's SCPA 203.

2. In large estates some attorneys make it a practice not to use waivers, but to serve process on all necessary parties despite the added expense, just to ensure finality of the decree. A validly executed waiver confers jurisdiction, but the fear of these attorneys is that the waiving party may not, or may claim not to, understand the effect of the waiver.

3. Matter of Boyle, 107 A.D.2d 807, 484 N.Y.S.2d 642 (2d Dep't 1985).

4. Matter of Leeper, 53 A.D.2d 1054, 385 N.Y.S.2d 887 (4th Dep't 1976) (bereavement and fear of being served with process not sufficient grounds to set aside probate decree).

5. Matter of Frutiger, 62 Misc.2d 163, 308 N.Y.S.2d 692 (Broome 1970), reversed on other grounds 35 A.D.2d 755, 314 N.Y.S.2d 949 (3d Dep't 1970), reversed 29 N.Y.2d 143, 324 N.Y.S.2d 36, 272 N.E.2d 543 (1971).

6. Matter of Frutiger, 62 Misc.2d 163, 308 N.Y.S.2d 692 (Broome 1970), reversed on other grounds 35 A.D.2d 755, 314 N.Y.S.2d 949 (3d Dep't 1970), reversed 29 N.Y.2d 143, 324 N.Y.S.2d 36, 272 N.E.2d 543 (1971).

7. Matter of Westberg, 254 App.Div. 320, 5 N.Y.S.2d 31 (1st Dep't 1938).

8. McKinney's SCPA 203.

or guardian is allowed to appear for a person under a disability,[9] if that representative is not served with process, the court will not obtain jurisdiction of the legally disabled person.[10]

Thirdly, if a necessary party files a pleading (petition, objections, answer or accounting) [11], the court gets personal jurisdiction over him.[12]

Lastly, when the number of persons in a class to be served exceeds fifty, the petitioner does not have to list their names but can direct the citation to the class by some title which the court considers adequate.[13] As a practical matter, the Surrogate almost never allows this; the members of the class are listed and cited, because the court has to safeguard the due process rights of the class.[14]

Another class of interested persons who, though not listed as statutory exceptions,[15] need not be named in the citation or served are those who are "virtually represented" by another party to the proceeding, a topic we discuss at length below.[16]

SECTION D. RELIEF REQUESTED

The citation must set forth with a fair amount of specificity the relief the petitioner seeks. If it does not, the court will not have jurisdiction to grant such relief because the respondent did not have notice.[1]

The attorney should be very explicit in his request for relief and should always add a general request for any other relief necessary to effectuate justice, taking a lesson from one case where a defaulting party in a construction proceeding was held bound by a decree destroying his interest in the estate although the prayer for relief in the citation was set out in dichotomous form, neither of which would have affected him.[2] The court noted that a petitioner may commence a construction proceeding only with the court's permission and that therefore the court, and not the petitioner's attorney, was responsible for fashioning the citation. Probably more significant was the inclusion in the citation of the general prayer for relief as well.

9. For a discussion of appearances generally, and appearances by persons under a disability, see chapter on "Appearances," infra at 232 et seq.

10. McKinney's SCPA 203; 307(3), (4). As we discuss infra at 45–46, the person under disability (except for infants under fourteen) must also receive process.

11. McKinney's SCPA 302(1)(a), discussed this chapter infra at 54–56.

12. McKinney's SCPA 203.

13. McKinney's SCPA 306(1)(b).

14. See Mullane v. Central Hanover Bank & Trust Co., 339 U.S. 306, 70 S.Ct. 652, 94 L.Ed. 865 (1950).

15. That is, not listed in McKinney's SCPA 306.

16. Virtual representation is governed by McKinney's SCPA 315 and discussed this chapter infra at 60–70.

Sec. D

1. Matter of Kilborn, 232 App.Div. 580, 251 N.Y.S. 113 (1st Dep't 1931); Matter of Franciscus, 17 Misc.2d 355, 173 N.Y.S.2d 144 (Queens 1958).

2. Matter of Axe, 89 Misc.2d 86, 390 N.Y.S.2d 378 (Westchester 1976).

SECTION E. ORDER TO SHOW CAUSE

In an emergency, an order to show cause can sometimes be used instead of a citation to expedite a proceeding.[1] The normal time limitations for return of process, which we discuss below,[2] would not then apply.

SECTION F. SERVICE OF PROCESS

The SCPA provides rules for the service of process in Surrogate's practice.[1] If the SCPA does not cover a situation, the CPLR applies.[2]

The following discussion of service of process assumes that the court has a basis for jurisdiction over the party (the party's domicile or presence within the state, or long-arm jurisdiction).[3] It also assumes that the attorney was unable to get waivers of process, which would have eliminated the need for service.

1. PERSONAL SERVICE

The ideal method of serving process, the one most calculated to satisfy the constitutional requirement of notice, is personal service, and when the respondent is a domiciliary natural person, personal service should be made whenever possible.[4] The Surrogate will not sign an order for an alternative means of service unless it is shown that, with due diligence,[5] the petitioner could not deliver the process to the domiciliary within the state [6] (for example, if the domiciliary is outside the state and remains there, and if it would represent an undue hardship to deliver process personally). In that case, the court has discretion to order alternative means of service on the domiciliary. On the other hand, a court order for alternative means of service can automatically be obtained for non-domiciliaries outside the state.[7]

With a few exceptions, which follow, personal service is the only kind the attorney can make without a court order.[8] Once the attorney has received the citation issued by the clerk of the court, he can

Sec. E

1. See McKinney's CPLR 2211, 2214(d).

2. See section on "Return Date," this chapter infra at 49–51.

Sec. F

1. McKinney's SCPA 307.

2. McKinney's SCPA 102.

3. Personal jurisdiction is discussed in chapter on "Jurisdiction," supra at 25–28.

4. Mullane v. Central Hanover Bank and Trust Co., 339 U.S. 306, 70 S.Ct. 652, 94 L.Ed. 865 (1950).

5. See section on "The Petition," this chapter infra at 54–55, for a discussion of due diligence.

6. McKinney's SCPA 307(2).

7. See McKinney's SCPA 307, Prac. Comm. at 341 (1967).

8. Service can be made without court order on representatives of an infant, see text accompanying note 45 this section, and on the secretary of state for a corporation, see text accompanying note 54 this section. It can also be made by simple mailing without court order on a group of more than twenty-five creditors. See text accompanying note 61 this section.

arrange for service on any natural person by personal delivery of a copy of the citation either within or without the state.[9]

If the party to be served is in New York, the attorney usually hires a process server, who serves the citation and gives the attorney a signed, notarized proof of service. The attorney should warn the process server to hand the citation directly to the party he is serving, not drop it near the party unless he has told the party what is being dropped and the party has clearly refused to accept service.[10]

The person serving the citation does not have to be a professional process server. Even a party to the proceeding may serve process,[11] which is not true in other civil practice. If the server serves the process on a Sunday, it is void.[12]

If the party in New York is avoiding service or if service for some other reason cannot be made with due diligence, the court can order an alternative means of service even within the state.[13]

If the party to be served is not in New York, the petitioner can arrange for personal service outside the state (without any necessity for a court order), either by a New York resident eighteen years or older (even a party) or by a person authorized in his own state to serve process,[14] often a process server, who then furnishes the necessary proof of service to be filed with the court. As a practical matter, the attorney usually applies to the court for an alternative means of service instead of hiring a process server out-of-state. The courts routinely order service by mail on out-of-state persons.

2. ALTERNATIVE MEANS OF SERVICE

If the petitioner cannot make service by personal delivery or if personal service would be inconvenient, he must apply to the court for permission to use an alternative means of service.[15] He can make this application either in the petition itself or in an affidavit.[16]

The application for alternative means of service is made ex parte by the petitioner. To obtain a court order, the attorney submits an application for an order of service by alternative means, explaining the reason such service is necessary, and an order for the judge's signature. If the facts are not true, the service will be invalid.[17] The court can order any of the following methods, each of which is discussed below:

9. McKinney's SCPA 307(1).

10. See Matter of Davidson, N.Y.L.J. Sept. 15, 1983 at 15, col. 6 (Nassau) (process server's act of attaching citation to front fence was inadequate notice; service invalid).

11. McKinney's SCPA 310(1).

12. Matter of Mortimer, 84 Misc.2d 1086, 380 N.Y.S.2d 216 (Orange 1976).

13. McKinney's SCPA 307(2). The court does not do so lightly, however. See Matter of Cohen, N.Y.L.J., March 27, 1985, at 12, col. 2 (Bronx), where the court refused to order alternative service because the petitioner showed only one unsuccessful attempt to serve process. See discussion of "Alternative Means of Service," this chapter infra at 40–49.

14. McKinney's CPLR 313; McKinney's SCPA 310.

15. McKinney's SCPA 307(2).

16. McKinney's SCPA 307(2).

17. See Clarkson v. Butler, 173 App. Div. 143, 159 N.Y.S. 343 (1st Dep't 1917)

(i) Service by mail;

(ii) Service by delivery and mail;

(iii) Service by nail and mail;

(iv) Service on a designee or a person likely to give notice to party;

(v) Service by publication;

(vi) Service on a designee for a person under legal disability;

(vii) Service on entities;

(viii) Service by other means within the Surrogate's discretion;

(ix) Service under some additional miscellaneous rules.

There is no order of preference among these alternative means of service except that service by publication is the least favored. The court will always choose the one most likely to give actual notice to the respondent. It is within the Surrogate's discretion to mold or devise any method sufficient to satisfy due process.[18]

a. Service by Mail

The court very often orders service by mail, which includes air-mail or registered or certified mail, with or without return receipt requested.[19] If the court does not require a return receipt, the attorney will normally be required to inform the court if the envelope is returned. In case of an extraordinary number of respondents where the cost would be prohibitive, or in other cases in the Surrogate's discretion, the Surrogate can order ordinary mailing.[20]

After mailing the citation in the manner directed by the court, the attorney submits an affirmation, or another adult (often the petitioner's attorney's secretary) submits an affidavit, in which he swears to having dropped the citation, with the correct address and postage, in an official United States post box.[21]

b. Service by Delivery and Mail

The court can order the petitioner to arrange personal delivery of a copy of the citation inside or outside the state to a person of suitable age and discretion at the home or actual place of business of the person to be served, and to mail a copy of the process to the person to be served at his last known residence.[22]

c. Service by Nail and Mail

The court can order the petitioner to affix the citation to the door of either the home or actual place of business of a person to be served,

(order for substituted service vacated because facts supporting it were untrue).

18. See "Service by Another Method in the Surrogate's Discretion," infra at 48.

19. McKinney's SCPA 307(2)(c).

20. McKinney's SCPA 307(2)(b), (c).

21. McKinney's SCPA 314.

22. McKinney's CPLR 308(2). See discussion of this type of service in D. Siegel, New York Practice 77 (1978).

inside or outside the state, and then to mail a copy of the citation to the person at his last known residence.[23]

d. Service on Designee or Person Likely to Give Notice to Party

The court can order personal delivery to a person duly designated by respondent to receive process on his behalf, or to a person whose relationship to the respondent (by blood or otherwise) makes it probable, under the circumstances, that actual notice will reach the party.[24]

This section is sometimes used in situations such as service on a person of suitable age and discretion in the person's home or service on a person's agent,[25] but its primary use is ensuring that service can always be made on a fiduciary of a New York estate or trust by service on the clerk of the court. Before a fiduciary is qualified to serve, he must designate the clerk to receive service of process issuing from that Surrogate's Court.[26] If someone wishes to start a proceeding in the Surrogate's Court against the fiduciary, but he cannot find the fiduciary to serve within the state, service on the clerk is equivalent to service on the fiduciary.[27] This designation does not authorize service of a summons or other process from other courts, but only process issued from the Surrogate's Court where the clerk presides. The clerk, when served, must mail a copy of the process to the fiduciary at his last known address.[28] The function of the designation is to ensure that the Surrogate retains personal jurisdiction over a fiduciary in an estate under the Surrogate's control.[29]

e. Service by Publication

Before discussion of the technical and formal details of publication as a means of service, we must mention its disfavored status. Of all forms of service, publication is the least likely to give notice of the proceeding to the person served. It is a necessary alternative because interested persons are constitutionally entitled to notice of lawsuits which concern them, and when their identities or whereabouts are unknown, service by publication in a newspaper is the only way to give them that "notice," however unlikely that they actually receive it. Where the citation, besides being served only by publication, is also directed to a fictitious name ("John Doe"), the Alice-in-Wonderland quality of the notice increases. Nevertheless, publication is sometimes the only way to safeguard the constitutional rights of the person served by it, and when no other type of service is possible, service by publica-

23. McKinney's CPLR 308(4). See discussion of this type of service in D. Siegel, New York Practice 79 (1978).

24. McKinney's SCPA 307(2)(e).

25. E.g., Totero v. World Telegram, 41 Misc.2d 594, 245 N.Y.S.2d 870 (Sup.Ct. New York County 1963) (service on defendant's literary agent).

26. McKinney's SCPA 708(2).

27. McKinney's SCPA 307(2)(e).

28. McKinney's SCPA 2609(4).

29. Michigan Trust Co. v. Ferry, 228 U.S. 346, 33 S.Ct. 550, 57 L.Ed. 867 (1913).

tion permits the parties to move forward with the proceeding and to obtain a judgment or decree binding on the party thus served. The court will order it only when there is no more effective means available and will use it only as a last resort.

Service by publication is governed partly by the SCPA [30] and partly by the CPLR.[31] The person seeking it includes the request either in the petition or in an affidavit accompanying the petition, and the validity of the court's order of service by publication will depend on whether the facts in the petition or affidavit were true.[32]

When the Surrogate determines that as a last resort service must be made by publication, his order directs the publication of the information contained in the official form of citation.[33] The order ordinarily directs publication in two newspapers (at least one in the English language) most likely to give notice to the persons to be served. It also mandates the number of publications; the minimum is one per week for four consecutive weeks. The publications need not run concurrently but both must otherwise be timely. The first publication of the citation must appear within thirty days after the order is granted,[34] and service is complete on the 28th day after the first publication.[35]

Sometimes necessary parties include a class of persons, such as a decedent's distributees in a probate proceeding.[36] If the petitioner does not know the names of some of the persons in the class he must list the names he does know and a general description of all other persons belonging to the class and their interests. The court orders service on the unknown members of the class by publication. For example:

> TO: MARY DOE and any and all unknown persons whose names or parts of whose names and whose place or places of residence are unknown and cannot after diligent inquiry be ascertained, distributees, heirs-at-law and next-of-kin of said JOHN DOE, deceased, and if any of the said above distributees named specifically or as a class be dead, their legal representatives, their husbands or wives, if any, distributees and successors in interest whose names and/or places of residence and post office addresses are unknown and cannot after diligent inquiry be ascertained.

The court also appoints a guardian ad litem to represent their interests in the proceeding.

If the petitioner does not know the names of any of the class members, he should give a general description of them, and state their interest in the proceeding. In that case the court will order the

30. McKinney's SCPA 307(2)(a).

31. McKinney's CPLR 316.

32. Matter of Roberts, 19 A.D.2d 391, 243 N.Y.S.2d 780 (4th Dep't 1963) (court vacated its order because person to be cited in fact lived within several miles of petitioner's office and could have been found with due diligence).

33. McKinney's CPLR 316.

34. McKinney's CPLR 316(c).

35. McKinney's SCPA 309(2)(d). See discussion of completion of service, infra at 49–51.

36. Probate proceedings are discussed in chapter on "Probate," infra at 71.

petitioner to cite the unknown persons (by publication), as well as the state attorney general and the county public administrator, by means that we will discuss shortly.[37] For example:

> MARY SMITH, PUBLIC ADMINISTRATOR OF THE COUNTY OF NASSAU, and any and all of the persons cited upon this proceeding as heirs-at-law and next-of-kin of said JOHN DOE, deceased, are unknown, and cannot, after diligent inquiry, be ascertained; and, that if said persons or any of them be dead, that the names or parts of the names, and place or places of residence, of any and all unknown persons, who are the respective executors, administrators, heirs-at-law, next-of-kin, distributees, legatees, devisees, husbands or wives, or successors in interest of said deceased persons are unknown, and cannot after diligent inquiry be ascertained and that personal service of the citation cannot, with due diligence, be made upon them within the state.

In cases where the petitioner does not know the name of the person to be served, he may use a fictitious name or as much of the name as he does know. Since these citations are most frequently served by publication, the court prescribes the form best calculated to give notice to the interested party. The court also appoints a guardian ad litem to represent them.

Publication in one newspaper is enough in adoption proceedings and in proceedings relating to the surrender of parental rights.[38] One newspaper also suffices when all persons to be served by publication have an aggregate interest of less than $50,000 in the proceeding.[39] The determination of the value of the estate must be bona fide; the court will invalidate single-newspaper service upon a finding that the executors did not diligently seek out estate assets in arriving at the threshold figure.[40] On the other hand, the court does not require definite proof that the estate is below the threshold; it will order publication in a single newspaper when to do otherwise would seem futile and wasteful. For example, if the decedent's only asset is a lawsuit for personal injuries which may have been worth more or less than the threshold amount, and the decedent has no known relatives, the court may decide to order publication in a single newspaper.[41]

Where a petitioner is trying to serve an absentee or one alleged to be deceased,[42] the court may (and typically does) direct that process also be published in a newspaper near the place where that person was last known to be.[43]

37. See McKinney's SCPA 311.

38. McKinney's SCPA 307(2)(a)(iv).

39. McKinney's SCPA 307(2)(a)(i).

40. Matter of Manley, 33 Misc.2d 367, 226 N.Y.S.2d 21 (New York County 1962).

41. See Matter of Davis, 54 Misc.2d 539, 282 N.Y.S.2d 1005 (New York County 1967).

42. See McKinney's EPTL 2–1.7, McKinney's SCPA Article 9, and chapter on "Temporary Administration," infra at 289 et seq.

43. McKinney's SCPA 307(2)(a)(iii).

f. Service on Person Under Legal Disability

Service on disabled persons is governed partly by the SCPA [44] and partly by the CPLR.[45]

i. Infants

Service of process may be made on an infant by serving his father, his mother, his guardian, or any adult person having care and control of him or with whom he resides, whether within or without the state.[46] Where the court finds it necessary to intervene, it can instead order service on another person interested in the child's welfare, by personal or substituted service. The SCPA provides no level of priority as to the individuals who can be served on the infant's behalf. The attorney can, without court order, choose one of the persons listed, and the court is free to designate a different person to receive the process. It then also directs the manner of service and the time service is complete.

In addition, if the infant is over fourteen years, he too must be served.[47] If a child has a guardian, under the statute that guardian does not necessarily have to receive process for the child, so long as an adult living with the child receives it. It is good practice, however, to serve the guardian every time the child is served with process.

Appointment of a guardian ad litem to represent the child's interests in the proceeding does not obviate the need for service of process.[48]

ii. Incompetents and Conservatees

If a person to be served has been judicially declared incompetent to manage his affairs or has had a committee or conservator appointed, SCPA 307(4) dictates that service must be made personally on the committee or conservator.[49] The incompetent or conservatee should also be served, but the court may dispense with that service.

Unlike the CPLR, which requires service on the committee within the state, the SCPA also permits personal service outside the state and the alternative court-ordered types of service.[50] In effect, SCPA 307(4) actually does no more than name the persons who can receive service of process for an incompetent or conservatee. The method of service on these persons and entities is still governed by the general service-of-process provisions of the SCPA. Thus if the committee or conservator is a domiciliary natural person, the petitioner has to show due diligence in trying to serve him within the state, and if such service cannot be made, the petitioner can submit application for a court order to serve

44. McKinney's SCPA 311.

45. McKinney's CPLR 309.

46. McKinney's SCPA 307(3).

47. McKinney's SCPA 307(3).

48. Davis v. Crandall, 101 N.Y. 311, 4 N.E. 721 (1886) (appearance by guardian ad litem did not constitute appearance of infant who had not been served).

49. McKinney's CPLR 309(b), incorporated into the Surrogate's Court by McKinney's SCPA 307(4).

50. McKinney's SCPA 307(1), (2).

the committee or conservator by mail, by publication, by substituted service, or by other alternate means of service in the court's discretion.

iii. Incapacitated Persons, Unknown Persons and Prisoners

Infants, conservatees and incompetents have special SCPA provisions governing service of process on them. All other persons under a legal disability, including incapacitated persons,[51] unknown persons or persons whose whereabouts are unknown, and prisoners, are treated together for service-of-process purposes. The court may, sua sponte, or in response to an affidavit by the petitioner or his attorney, order the citation to be delivered to a person designated by the court, and may specify the manner and time of service as well.[52] The designee is treated for all purposes as a guardian ad litem. He is not a party to the proceeding. The designee need not be an attorney, but the court generally does appoint an attorney, because in most cases this designee is also named as guardian ad litem on the return date.[53] In short, where a person seems immature though an adult, feeble-minded, senile, or terribly unsophisticated, to the point of being legally disabled, the court is likely to appoint a guardian ad litem not only for the receipt of process, but also to protect the ward's interests during the proceeding.

Appointment of this designee can also be a time-saving device. Very often when a proceeding is pending, if the court foresees that a guardian ad litem will have to be appointed, it permits the proposed guardian ad litem (that is, the designee for receipt of process) to start reviewing the account or other court proceedings without having to wait for the return date. Appointment of a designee is also useful in cases where the court is not ready to make a person a party to a proceeding. For instance, in an adoption proceeding where an adoptee wishes to review the adoption records, the court can preliminarily designate an attorney who can commence a review of the proceedings and possibly communicate with the natural parent to determine whether or not the adoption record should be unsealed.

g. Service on Entities

Since the SCPA is silent on service on persons other than natural persons, the CPLR governs. Where the person to be served on behalf of the entity is a domiciliary natural person, he should be served personally. If he is not a domiciliary, counsel can apply to the court for

51. An incapacitated person is a person "incapable adequately to protect his rights, although not judicially declared an incompetent," McKinney's SCPA 103(25).

52. McKinney's SCPA 311. For instructions on service of process on incompetent and allegedly incompetent patients in state and private institutions, see section 22.1 of the Official Codes, Rules and Regulations of the Office of Mental Health, found as a historical note, McKinney's Mental Hygiene Law § 4.21 (McKinney 1978).

53. Guardians ad litem are governed by McKinney's SCPA Article 4 discussed in chapter on "Appearances," infra at 238–44.

alternate service.[54] The diagram below gives the salient points of the CPLR sections on service to entities:

PERSON TO BE SERVED	METHOD OF SERVICE	CPLR
Persons conducting business as partners	Personal service within state on any of partners	310
Partnership	Service on any of partners	1025
Unincorporated association	Service on president or treasurer	1025
Corporation	Personal service on officer, director, managing agent, general agent, or other agent authorized by appointment or law to receive service of process [55]	311
New York State	Service on assistant attorney general at an office of the attorney general or on the attorney general	307
New York City	Service on the corporation counsel or any person designated by him in a written instrument filed in the New York County Clerk's office	307
City other than New York City	Service on the mayor, comptroller, treasurer, counsel or clerk (or office performing corresponding functions)	307
County	Service on the chairman or clerk of the board of supervisors, county clerk, attorney or treasurer	307
Town	Service on the supervisor or clerk	307
Village	Service on the mayor, clerk or any trustee	307
School district	Service on school officer (defined by Education Law)	307

54. See D. Siegel, New York Practice 69 (1978) for an excellent discussion on service on non-natural persons.

55. Since section 304 of the Business Corporation Law designates the Secretary of State as agent to receive process on behalf of New York corporations, the Secretary of State should receive personal service unless the court orders an alternative means of service under McKinney's SCPA 307(2). It would appear that personal service can be made on the secretary without court order; such service falls under McKinney's SCPA 307(1) and not 307(2). See McKinney's SCPA 307, Siegel, 1972 Practice Commentary at 52 (Supp. 1984–85).

PERSON TO BE SERVED	METHOD OF SERVICE	CPLR
Sewer or water district	Service on clerk or trustee or board member	307
Court	Service on the judge, or to one of them if there are three or more	307
Board or Commission	Service on the chairman, any member or officer	307
New York State Tax Commission re New York estate tax proceedings	Service on tax commission or local attorney for the New York State tax commission	Tax Law 249w

h. Service by Another Method in the Surrogate's Discretion

If the SCPA does not cover the manner of service on a person or entity, SCPA 313 gives the court authority to dictate the means and time requirements of service. The court's directions may be set forth on the citation or on the application for alternative service, and it will have the same force as if it were an order for alternative service.

Because special proceedings often have their own methods of notice specified in the statute, SCPA 313 is to some degree superfluous. It remains helpful as a reminder to the practitioner that when SCPA 307 gives no rule, the court can direct service.

In addition, the Surrogate arguably can order substituted service in proceedings which have their own form of service prescribed. For example, the order commencing a discovery proceeding [56] must be served by delivery of a certified copy of the order and the subpoena fee to the respondent. If the respondent is a New York resident evading service, the court can order an alternative means of service on him, on the theory that under SCPA 103(40), the order itself is process, so the court can apply SCPA 307(2) to it and order service by another means.[57]

As long as due process requirements are satisfied, the court can be quite creative in its orders for alternative service. For example, in one case the court allowed the petitioner to serve a necessary party by sending the citation to a governmental agency which refused to disclose the party's address (under the Privacy Act) but which agreed to forward the papers to him.[58] In another, the court directed service on the attorney of a non-domiciliary who transacted business in New York; the attorney had refused to reveal the non-domiciliary's address to the petitioner.[59]

56. Discovery proceedings are governed by McKinney's SCPA 2103 and discussed in chapter on "Miscellaneous Proceedings," infra at 337–44.

57. Matter of Marko, 56 Misc.2d 138, 287 N.Y.S.2d 776 (New York County 1968).

58. Matter of Banks, N.Y.L.J., Apr. 3, 1979, at 13, col. 6. [Queens]

59. Matter of Leichter, N.Y.L.J., Jan. 6, 1982, at 15, col. 6.

i. Service Under Miscellaneous Rules

The legislature has incorporated several rules of convenience into the statute. If the interest of a non-domiciliary alien in the estate is less than $500, or his address is unknown, or the estate is less than $5,000, the court can direct delivery of a copy of the process to the consular official of the alien's nation.[60] Service on a non-domiciliary alien whose interest is greater than $500 must be by personal delivery or by an alternative method ordered by the court.

If a person is located in a country at war with the United States, or if the country does not maintain postal communication, the court can direct that a copy of process be mailed on behalf of a person residing in such country to the officer appointed to take possession of the property of alien enemies.[61]

When there are more than twenty-five creditors, the petitioner may serve process on them, without court order, by mailing a copy of the process to each one of them whether they are New York domiciliaries and natural persons or not. Of course where there are fewer than twenty-five creditors, they may be served by mailing also, but in that case a court order is required.[62]

SECTION G. RETURN DATE

1. GENERAL RULES

As a preliminary caveat, compliance with the time requirements for the return date is essential. If a petitioner fails to comply, the court does not get jurisdiction over the party, and its decree is void as to that person.

The return date of the citation may not be more than four months after the date of issuance of the citation, and must be at least ten days after service of the citation if the person was served within the state, at least twenty days if the person was served outside the state but in the United States or its territories, and at least thirty days in all other cases.[1] These time periods depend on the place of service; the domicile of the person served is irrelevant. When service is made in a bifurcated manner, for example by nailing to the door of respondent's New York business and mailing to his last known address, which is out of state, the longer return date for the more distant location should be used.[2]

The time period for the return date starts running from the time service is complete,[3] and that depends on how the service was made.

60. McKinney's SCPA 307(2)(f).

61. McKinney's SCPA 307(2)(a)(ii).

62. McKinney's SCPA 307(5).

Sec. G

1. McKinney's SCPA 308.

2. See McKinney's SCPA 308, Practice Commentary at 358 (1967).

3. McKinney's SCPA 309.

When service is made by personal delivery, it is complete as soon as the server hands the citation to the respondent, and the ten-, twenty- or thirty-day time period then begins to run.[4]

When service is made by mail, it is complete upon the mailing, whether regular, registered or certified, unless otherwise directed by the court.[5] Even if the court directs that the return receipt be filed, the service is still complete upon the mailing, unless the court orders otherwise, or unless the person to be served refuses to accept it, in which case the court will not mark service complete.[6]

When "nail and mail" service is ordered, it is complete on the later of the nailing or the mailing.[7] If the court orders a variation in "nail and mail" service from that prescribed in the CPLR, service is complete when the last step directed by the court has been accomplished. The court could also follow CPLR practice and direct that service will not be complete until ten days after proof of service is filed,[8] but this is not an ordinary practice in the Surrogate's Court.

Service is complete on a designee of the respondent, or a person or consular official designated by the court, when it is made to that designee.[9] When a fiduciary has designated the clerk of the court for service of process, for example, service is complete when made on the clerk, not when the clerk later mails the copy to the fiduciary.

When service is made by publication, it is complete on the 28th day after the first publication.[10] Very often weekly newspapers are actually published prior to their announced publication date. If, for example, a weekly paper's front page says Friday and the paper is actually published and distributed on Wednesday, an affidavit from the publisher will satisfy the court that the twenty-eight day period should be measured from Wednesday, curing the problem of short service.

SCPA 309 does not specify when service is complete on an infant, and 309(2)(c), making service complete upon delivery to the designee, is not always applicable because it refers to persons designated by the court to receive process, and a father, mother, or other adult can receive process for the infant without a court order. If 309(c) does not apply, the court has to direct under 309(2)(e) when service is complete, and not surprisingly, the court usually orders that it is complete when delivered to the father, mother, or other adult. If the infant is over fourteen, service is not complete until both the person receiving process for the infant and the infant himself have received delivery.

If any alternative form of service is used, the court can always determine when service is complete regardless of the statutory provisions.[11] In any event service must be complete the ten, twenty or thirty

4. McKinney's SCPA 309(1).

5. McKinney's SCPA 309(2)(a).

6. Matter of Mackey, 91 Misc.2d 736, 398 N.Y.S.2d 605 (Dutchess 1977).

7. McKinney's SCPA 309(2)(b).

8. McKinney's CPLR 308(1)(a)(i).

9. McKinney's SCPA 309(2)(c).

10. McKinney's SCPA 309(2)(d).

11. McKinney's SCPA 309(2)(e).

days before the return of process, and the return date may not be more than four months after the issuance of process.

2. SETTING THE RETURN DATE

In practice the clerk of the court usually fills in the return date of the citation, because each of the Surrogate's Courts has different days set aside for various proceedings.[12] The attorney may select the return date in standard proceedings like probate, administration, final accountings and guardianships if he knows the calendar practice of the court, and the clerk will accept it if it is proper. In many cases, however, the Surrogate can decide whether or not to entertain the proceeding,[13] and it is better in those cases to wait for the clerk to select a return date.

3. RETURN DATE FOR PROCESS OTHER THAN THE CITATION

The SCPA's rules on return date and completion of process [14] both refer to service of citation and not other kinds of process. When process other than a citation is ordered, the order will direct the method of service and will set the time requirements. For example, the court can permit a proceeding to be commenced by an order to show cause,[15] and set the return date in the order itself. The minimum ten-, twenty- and thirty-day time periods for return of process would then not apply.[16]

SECTION H. PROOF OF SERVICE AND ADMISSION OF SERVICE

The Surrogate's jurisdiction over the parties is not complete until the court has received proof of service. That proof is due two days before the return date.[1] In computing the two-day period, Saturdays, Sundays and holidays are ignored. If the proofs are not filed two days before the return date, the matter may be marked off the calendar. An attorney who has failed to comply with the two-day rule should get to the courtroom early, before the calendar call, to submit the proofs of service to the clerk.

Proof of service in the Surrogate's Court is normally made in one of two ways: either proof submitted by the person serving the process, or

12. For example, in the city of New York and Westchester County, the return days are Tuesday and Friday; in Nassau, Wednesday; in Suffolk, Tuesday.

13. The attorney usually does not have to submit an order for entertainment; rather, the clerk will stamp an entertainment order on the petition for the judge's signature. See chapter on "Miscellaneous Proceedings," infra at 327–28.

14. McKinney's SCPA 308, 309.

15. McKinney's CPLR 403(d).

16. See McKinney's SCPA 308, Practice and Commentary at 362 (1967).

Sec. H

1. Uniform Statewide Rules of the Surrogate's Courts section 207.7.

admission by the person receiving the service.[2] The person serving the process (or subpoena) can sign a writing describing the papers served, the person served (by height, weight, gender, color of hair and skin) and the date, place and manner of service. The writing must swear that service was made by an authorized person in an authorized manner. This writing will be a certificate if the server was an authorized public officer such as a sheriff, or an affidavit if the server was another person.[3] If an attorney makes service, an affirmation of service is sufficient, and no affidavit is required.

In the case of service by publication, proof of service will be by affidavit from the publisher.[4] The printer, publisher, foreman or principal clerk of the newspaper must sign this affidavit of proof. When the affidavit is annexed to the copy of the published notice, it is prima facie evidence of publication.

The person receiving process can also sign a writing admitting the service. The admission states that the person signing is over the age of sixteen and competent [5] and admits personal service of the citation on a stated date. It is then dated, signed and acknowledged. An adult can add a waiver of time periods for return of process provided by statute.

In Matter of Orenstein,[6] the court ruled that the admission of service, to be valid, had to be made within the times prescribed by SCPA 308 (ten, twenty or thirty days). Though the language in Orenstein is general, the person admitting service in that case was an infant, and probably the holding should be limited to those facts. In view of Orenstein, however, the attorney should certainly arrange to have the service admitted within the SCPA 308 time frame, and also to state the compliance with SCPA 308 in the admission. As an alternative, the person admitting service, if adult, could waive the time period requirement, and could so state in the admission. Impliedly, under Orenstein, the admission of service has no more effect than an affidavit of service, so the person served retains the right to object on grounds of method and timeliness.

SECTION I. WHO MAY SERVE PROCESS

Anyone over eighteen, even a party to the proceeding, can serve process within the state.[1] As a general practice it is better to have a disinterested person, rather than a party, serve process to avoid placing the party in the position of fighting a respondent's allegation that he was not served, or was served untimely or improperly.

2. McKinney's SCPA 314, incorporating McKinney's CPLR 306.

3. McKinney's CPLR 306(d).

4. McKinney's CPLR 4532, incorporated into McKinney's SCPA 314.

5. This differs from ordinary civil practice, where anyone can admit service. McKinney's CPLR 306.

6. 61 Misc.2d 306, 305 N.Y.S.2d 443 (Nassau 1969).

Sec. I

1. McKinney's SCPA 310(1).

The SCPA allows personal service without court order outside the state as well as within,[2] but the CPLR contains some limitations on who can serve outside the state.[3] It states that those persons qualified to serve process in New York, or in the state where service is being made, can make service out of state. Thus, if the state where service is made permits minors to serve, service by a minor would be valid despite its invalidity in New York. However, the manner of service made out-of-state must be valid in New York. If, for instance, another state permitted service on Sunday, service made there on Sunday would be invalid because it is invalid here.[4]

SECTION J. SUPPLEMENTAL PROCESS

The court can, on its own or at the request of another, direct service of supplemental process.[1] The court will typically issue supplemental process in two instances: first, if a party was not properly or timely served, and second, when the court determines that additional parties are necessary to the proceeding. It is common to see the court directing supplemental citations in cases initially allowing virtual representation.[2] In those cases, if the court finds that the virtual representation is inadequate to protect the representees' interests, it will order supplemental process served on them.

Supplemental process is also appropriate in cases where an issue arises that was not set forth in the initial citation. Since the court does not have jurisdiction to grant relief not requested in the citation, the supplemental process is necessary where a new issue is unearthed.[3]

The court can direct the means of service, and if it does not, supplemental process will be by citation and all of the SCPA provisions on methods of service[4] and on the return date of service[5] will apply.

SECTION K. STATUTE OF LIMITATIONS

The statute of limitations provisions in the CPLR governing civil practice are applicable to Surrogate's practice[1] with a significant exception: a proceeding in the Surrogate's Court commences when the petition is filed if service of process occurs within sixty days thereafter.[2] Subject to that, the CPLR rules regarding interposition of defenses and

2. McKinney's SCPA 307(1).

3. McKinney's CPLR 313.

4. Eisenberg v. Citation-Langley Corp., 99 A.D.2d 700, 471 N.Y.S.2d 595 (1st Dep't 1984) (service in California on Sunday, though valid in California, invalid because New York law does not permit it).

Sec. J

1. McKinney's SCPA 312.

2. Virtual representation is governed by McKinney's SCPA 315 and discussed this chapter infra at 60–70.

3. See discussion of "Relief Requested," this chapter supra at 38.

4. McKinney's SCPA 307.

5. McKinney's SCPA 308.

Sec. K

1. McKinney's SCPA 102.

2. McKinney's SCPA 301.

counterclaims, tolling of the statute of limitations, amended pleadings, etc., govern practice in the Surrogate's Court.[3]

We discuss the statutes of limitations in particular proceedings, such as right of election and claims, in the sections on those proceedings.

SECTION L. PLEADINGS

The pleadings in a Surrogate's Court proceeding play a vital procedural role, because they commence the proceeding, establish the starting point of the proceeding for the statute of limitations, and set forth the predicate for the court's subject matter jurisdiction. This section of the text covers the general requirements of pleadings in all proceedings. We discuss the special requirements of particular proceedings in the respective chapters on those proceedings.

The pleadings in the Surrogate's Court are the petition, the answer or objections, and the account.[1] There may be other pleadings in two instances: (a) if the SCPA provides for them [2] and (b) if the court directs them.[3] The court may, for example, want a reply from the petitioner to an affirmative defense or new issue raised in the answer, or may direct the filing of a cross-petition.

All pleadings must be verified,[4] and all other instruments submitted to the court, such as waivers, should be acknowledged.[5]

1. THE PETITION

The SCPA contains forms of petitions acceptable in every Surrogate's Court in the state.[6] As a practical matter, the clerk of the Surrogate's Court will provide sample forms for petitions in proceedings for probate, administration, and other standard matters. In some cases, these forms can be submitted with the appropriate information inserted. Whether the attorney uses a form petition or drafts it, it must contain all the information required by Article 3 [7] and all the information required for petitions in other proceedings.[8] Under the "bare minimum" Article 3 requirements, the petition must give the proceeding a title, such as "Matter of Adoption of Catherine by John and Mary Smith," "Matter of Construction of the Will of Sarah Jones." It must give the petitioner's name and domicile, and the name and

3. See D. Siegel, New York Practice 34–58 (1978) for an excellent discussion of the statute of limitations.

Sec. L

1. McKinney's SCPA 302.

2. McKinney's SCPA 302(1)(a).

3. McKinney's SCPA 302(1)(b).

4. McKinney's SCPA 303.

5. See Matter of Frutiger, 62 Misc.2d 163, 308 N.Y.S.2d 692 (Broome 1970), reversed on other grounds 35 A.D.2d 755, 314 N.Y.S.2d 949 (3d Dep't 1970), reversed 29 N.Y.2d 143, 324 N.Y.S.2d 36, 272 N.E.2d 543 (1971).

6. Official Form Number 2 (Petition for Letters of Administration); Official Form Number 4 (Probate Petition); Official Form Number 5 (Petition for Guardianship).

7. McKinney's SCPA 304.

8. McKinney's SCPA 304. These will be discussed infra in the sections dealing with those proceedings.

domicile of the decedent or person to whom the proceeding relates (the child in a guardianship proceeding, the fiduciary in an accounting). The petition must state the basis of the court's subject matter jurisdiction,[9] such as domicile, presence of property of a non-domiciliary in the county, or the domicile of the adoptive parents in the county.

The petitioner must list the names and addresses of all persons interested in the proceeding upon whom service of process is required,[10] so far as they can be ascertained with due diligence. "Due diligence" requires a thorough search and includes inquiries at such places as offices of vital statistics, armed services, voting polls, motor vehicle departments, banks, utilities, schools, churches, the census bureau, police missing persons bureaus and telephone directories.[11] The list of interested persons is divided into two sections: those who are not under a disability (competent persons eighteen years or older) and those who are legally disabled: infants, incompetents, incapacitated persons, conservatees, unknown persons, persons whose whereabouts are unknown, and prisoners. For each category, the petition must give facts designed to inform the court how best to protect the interests of these persons under a disability (typically, the names and addresses of parents, committees, conservators, guardians, and a statement of the efforts made to ascertain and locate unknown persons). Though these facts are usually right in the petition, they can be instead in an accompanying affidavit.[12]

The petition must also state that no other persons are interested in the proceeding, and must include a "wherefore" clause requesting relief.

2. ANSWER OR OBJECTIONS

The words "answers" and "objections" are often used interchangeably in Surrogate's practice to denote a response to a pleading. However, objections are the usual response to a probate or accounting petition; in the objections the contestant of the will or the objectant to the account sets forth precisely why the relief sought should be denied. For example, the objections may state that the propounded instrument should be denied probate because the decedent was not of sound mind and memory at the time of the execution, or that a claim in an accounting proceeding should have been denied rather than allowed because the statute of limitations had expired.

An answer, on the other hand, is usually the response to all the other miscellaneous petitions, setting forth reasons why the relief should be denied and possible counter-claims and defenses. For exam-

9. McKinney's SCPA 203, 304(2).

10. The parties necessary to each proceeding will be discussed in the sections on the respective proceedings.

11. See Matter of Layh, 55 Misc.2d 92, 284 N.Y.S.2d 511 (Nassau 1967).

12. Matter of Langell, 3 Misc.2d 532, 155 N.Y.S.2d 892 (Suffolk 1956) (affidavit detailing diligent search was sufficient when attached to the petition).

ple, in a compulsory accounting proceeding against the fiduciary, the fiduciary's answer to the petition may be that the petitioner lacks standing in that he does not have any interest in the estate or he has executed a waiver which precludes him from compelling an accounting.

When objections are used, the allegations set forth in the petition need not be specifically denied. The objections can be in general terms.[13] When an answer is interposed, it very often contains specific denials.

The petition and answer or objections define the issues and limit the relief.[14]

3. ACCOUNT

The account is the fiduciary's recording and reporting of the administration of the estate. We discuss it at length in its own chapter.[15]

4. EFFECT OF NOT RESPONDING TO PLEADINGS

In most proceedings the petitioner submits just one pleading, the petition, unless he is a fiduciary seeking a voluntary accounting, where he submits two, the petition and the account. These initial pleadings invite response (answer or objections). If the respondent does not serve an answer or objections, the facts alleged in the petition (or account) are proof of the facts stated.[16] Responsive pleadings (the answer and objections) do not require responses, so their allegations are deemed denied.[17]

An account may be an initial pleading (voluntary account),[18] or it may be a responsive pleading.[19] In the former case, its facts will be deemed proven unless denied by an answer or objections. A compulsory account filed as a responsive pleading should be deemed denied since no response is necessary, but because of the literal language of SCPA 509, the petitioner for the compulsory account should object to the account if he wishes to controvert the facts alleged in it. Otherwise the court is likely to accept the account.

The impact of this statute may not be as great as one might expect on a first reading. The allegations are proof of the facts stated, but this

13. See section on "Sufficiency of Pleadings," this chapter infra at 58–59. See Matter of Schneider, 64 Misc.2d 299, 314 N.Y.S.2d 587 (Westchester 1970); McKinney's SCPA 302, Prac.Comm. at 47 (1984–85).

14. See Matter of Schaich, 55 A.D.2d 914, 391 N.Y.S.2d 135 (2d Dep't 1977), appeal denied 42 N.Y.2d 802, 397 N.Y.S.2d 1026, 366 N.E.2d 293 (1977) (surcharge cannot be predicated on a ground neither alleged nor proved).

15. See chapter on "Accounting," infra at 179 et seq.

16. McKinney's SCPA 509.

17. McKinney's CPLR 3018(a); McKinney's SCPA 302, Practice Commentary at 309 (1967); McKinney's SCPA 509, Practice Commentary at 465–66 (1967).

18. See McKinney's SCPA 509 and 2203.

19. See McKinney's SCPA 2206.

does not mean that the allegations are accepted as true.[20] The Surrogate is not bound to accept them.[21] In fact the judge must be satisfied that they are true before accepting them. Moreover, the pleading may be controverted by "answer, objection or other proof," and the "other proof" is a broad term, including evidence obtained by the Surrogate in the course of a hearing [22] as well as denial of the allegations by affidavit.[23]

Needless to say, failure to deny facts on which subject matter jurisdiction rests will not confer jurisdiction on the court. Lack of subject matter jurisdiction can be contested at any stage of the proceeding, including appeal. However, although the court cannot get subject matter jurisdiction by agreement of the parties, if a jurisdictional fact is set forth in a petition or a pleading and is not denied, the court has a right to assume its truth and any party over whom the court has jurisdiction will be bound if he fails to refute that fact.[24]

5. THE CROSS CLAIM

An additional category of pleadings, imported into the Surrogate's Court through the CPLR's third-party practice, is the cross-claim. Only very recently seen in the Surrogate's Court,[25] it may well become more common there as the Surrogate's subject matter jurisdiction expands.[26] In Matter of Zalaznick,[27] the court held that the term "petition" in Article 3 [28] impliedly included "cross-petition" and permitted the executors of a deceased fiduciary to join the deceased fiduciary's attorneys as parties. The executors had filed an accounting to which objections were made. In response to the objections, the executors filed a "cross-petition" on the attorneys, whom they accused of malpractice in the handling of the estate. Having found that it had subject matter jurisdiction of the malpractice claim, the court permitted cross-petitions to bring in both a party and a non-party, a practice authorized by the CPLR.[29] In Zalaznick the court noted that personal jurisdiction could be obtained over the non-party by service of a supplemental citation.[30]

20. See Matter of Hyde, 218 N.Y. 55, 112 N.E. 581 (1931); Matter of Clemens, 174 Misc. 1052, 22 N.Y.S.2d 168 (Ontario County 1940).

21. See Matter of Falvey, 7 A.D.2d 476, 184 N.Y.S.2d 496 (4th Dep't 1959); Matter of Israelite, 155 Misc. 259, 279 N.Y.S. 699 (Bronx 1935).

22. Matter of Falvey, 7 A.D.2d 476, 184 N.Y.S.2d 496 (4th Dep't 1959).

23. McKinney's SCPA 509, Practice Commentary at 466 (1967).

24. See McKinney's SCPA 509, Practice Commentary at 466 (1967).

25. In his 1972 Practice Commentary to McKinney's SCPA 201, Professor David Siegel urged acceptance of the use of McKinney's SCPA 201 and 209 to secure the benefits of third party impleader for the Surrogate's Court.

26. See discussion of the Surrogate's expanding jurisdiction in chapter on "Jurisdiction," supra at 12–18.

27. 84 Misc.2d 715, 375 N.Y.S.2d 522 (Bronx County 1975).

28. McKinney's SCPA 302.

29. McKinney's CPLR 3019(d). The Surrogate's finding of subject matter jurisdiction in Zalaznick may no longer be valid since the New York Court of Appeals decision in Matter of Piccione, discussed supra at 14–17.

30. For further discussion of third party practice, see chapter on "Jurisdiction," supra at 17–18.

6. SERVICE OF RESPONSIVE PLEADINGS

The answer or objections must be served upon the return of process. One copy should be served on the petitioner and another filed in the court. A respondent can apply for an extension of time to answer a petition,[31] and the Surrogate usually grants the extension. For example, in probate proceedings, on the return date the respondent may request examinations of attesting witnesses under SCPA 1404,[32] and the court will often direct that objections be filed ten days after the filing of the transcripts of the examinations with the court, or at some other time.[33]

7. PARTIES ENTITLED TO COPIES OF PLEADINGS

Copies of the pleadings (except the account) must be served on parties who, having appeared in the proceeding, have demanded copies, and those on whom the court directs that service be made. Thus, the attorney in a proceeding should, upon appearing, notify all other parties of his appearance and demand copies of all pleadings. If a party then fails or refuses to serve the papers demanded, he may be treated as a defaulting party.[34]

If a new party receives supplemental process and appears after the proceeding has started, the court can order all the other parties to serve copies of pleadings on the newcomer and the court can direct the amendment of all prior pleadings to reflect the presence of the new party.

Subject to varying rules in some counties, the parties are not automatically entitled to a copy of the accounting; this different rule for accountings was enacted because accountings are usually far longer than other pleadings and automatic distribution would be potentially very costly. A party can review the copy filed with the court or ask the court to direct the petitioner to give him a copy. If it is voluminous, the court may direct the party requesting it to pay the reproduction cost. An accounting party should always be prepared to give a copy of the account to a guardian ad litem.

8. SUFFICIENCY OF PLEADINGS

A pleading must contain sufficient particularity to give notice of the claim, objection or defense to the court and to the parties.[35] Fraud and undue influence are often grounds for a will contest, and in Surrogate's practice the pleading simply has to give notice that fraud and undue influence will be litigated. While the CPLR requires more specificity in a pleading alleging fraud,[36] the legislature did not impose those requirements on pleadings in the Surrogate's Court, where the

31. McKinney's CPLR 2004.

32. McKinney's SCPA 1404(1).

33. See chapter on "Probate," infra at 101–09.

34. McKinney's SCPA 302(3).

35. McKinney's SCPA 302(2).

36. McKinney's CPLR 3016(b).

terms "fraud" and "undue influence" have a universal meaning.[37] The predecessor to SCPA 302(2) required "a plain and concise statement of the facts constituting the claim, objection or defense," [38] and the courts construed that to allow a general pleading.[39] The current version is even more liberal; it requires that the court and the parties have "notice" of the claim, objection or defense.[40] Hence, the liberal pleading rules of the CPLR apply in the Surrogate's Court, even to fraud claims, and the pleadings should contain plain concise statements in consecutively numbered paragraphs, each containing a single allegation.[41]

9. AMENDMENT OF PLEADINGS

The parties to a proceeding may move in the Surrogate's Court to amend the pleadings. The SCPA is silent on amendment, and consequently Surrogate's practice conforms with civil practice in this area. The courts liberally allow amendment if no prejudice results from the delay,[42] and the decision is within the court's discretion.[43]

If a party needs more information, he can demand a bill of particulars or obtain other disclosure. He can also move for an expanded pleading, which in practice is rare.

10. VERIFICATION OF PLEADINGS

In the Surrogate's Court, all pleadings must be verified.[44] Ordinarily the client verifies the pleadings, and should do so,[45] but the attorney can do so if the client cannot.[46] If the attorney verifies the pleading, he must set forth the grounds for his belief on all matters that he does not know himself.[47]

37. Fraud and undue influence are discussed in chapter on "Probate," infra at 105–09.

38. L.1962, c. 308.

39. See, e.g., Matter of Dixon, 7 Misc.2d 812, 160 N.Y.S.2d 177 (Westchester 1956), affirmed 2 A.D.2d 987, 158 N.Y.S.2d 770 (2d Dep't 1956); Matter of Hone, 226 App. Div. 715, 233 N.Y.S. 400 (4th Dep't 1929).

40. McKinney's CPLR 3013, 3014; Matter of Schneider, 64 Misc.2d 299, 314 N.Y.S.2d 587 (Westchester 1970).

41. But see Matter of Grotzinger, 81 A.D.2d 268, 440 N.Y.S.2d 189 (1st Dep't 1981), where the court upheld the petition even though it was not plain and concise because it did give notice of the litigated issues.

42. McKinney's CPLR 3025(b); Fahey v. County of Ontario, 44 N.Y.2d 934, 408 N.Y.S.2d 314, 380 N.E.2d 146 (1978); Sindle v. New York City Trans. Auth., 33 N.Y.2d 293, 352 N.Y.S.2d 183, 307 N.E.2d 245 (1973).

43. See Bilhorn v. Farlow, 60 A.D.2d 755, 401 N.Y.S.2d 115 (4th Dep't 1977); Martin v. PPS Capital Corp., N.Y.L.J., May 14, 1985, at 13, col. 4 (Westchester).

44. McKinney's SCPA 303.

45. Matter of Ray, 150 Misc. 728, 270 N.Y.S. 333 (Orange 1934) (allowing attorney's verification but discouraging the practice).

46. See McKinney's CPLR 3020 for the situations in which an attorney may verify the pleading for the client, including the absence of the parties from the county. See Matter of Reed, 214 N.Y. 383, 108 N.E. 565 (1915).

47. McKinney's CPLR 3021; See Matter of Ganfuss, N.Y.L.J., April 19, 1985, at 13, col. 1 (New York County) (court required verifying attorney to give names of persons providing information in bill of particulars, rather than statement that his knowledge was based on conversations with a named person, members of that person's family and unnamed others).

SECTION M. VIRTUAL REPRESENTATION

Because of the nature of Surrogate's practice, often many persons are interested in a proceeding as direct or contingent beneficiaries. Article 3 requires service of process on all interested persons, except those who are "virtually represented" under SCPA 315.

Section 315 is very useful in reducing the number of persons who would have to be cited, or for whom a guardian ad litem would have to be appointed, in its absence (at expense to the estate).[1] It also aids the court in gaining jurisdiction over parties who, though indispensible, are unborn or unascertained.

1. CONCEPT OF VIRTUAL REPRESENTATION

The theory of virtual representation is that those who are already parties to a proceeding and have the same financial interests as others who are not parties will, in protecting their own self-interest, protect the others. Under the statute, it is not necessary to serve process on the persons whose interests are adequately represented by a party to the proceeding.

An example of virtual representation is where a decedent creates a trust by will to provide income to his wife and remainder to his son, or if his son predeceases his wife, then remainder to the son's issue. In an accounting proceeding the wife and son would have to be cited, but the son's children (the representees) would not because they have the same financial interest as their father (the representor), who can virtually represent them.[2]

Similarly, where a trust provides for income to the decedent's wife for her life, at her death income to her son for his life, and at his death remainder to the son's issue, the wife could virtually represent the son. SCPA 315 applies to interests in income as well as principal.[3]

Virtual representation applies in proceedings in the Surrogate's Court unless a statute governing a specific proceeding states that it does not.[4]

Sec. M

1. In drafting McKinney's SCPA 315, the Bennett Commission sought to insure expeditious administration of estates in New York at the least expense possible by adopting and expanding the concept of virtual representation which had been used since the early 1940's in Supreme Court inter vivos trust proceedings. L.1962 c. 308, formerly McKinney's CPA 1311, currently McKinney's CPLR 7703.

2. This is often referred to as vertical virtual representation. A discussion of lateral or horizontal representation follows, infra at 68–69.

3. McKinney's SCPA 315(1).

4. See, e.g., McKinney's SCPA 2106(2), governing compromise proceedings, which states that persons not in being and persons under disability must be represented by a guardian ad litem. See Matter of Wegner, August 14, 1985, at 14, col. 2 (Nassau), refusing to allow virtual representation in a compromise proceeding.

2. USE OF VIRTUAL REPRESENTATION

An attorney hoping to dispense with service on an interested person under SCPA 315 must satisfy two tests. First, the person or class to be represented must fit within the statute. Second, that person's (or class's) interests must actually be represented by the party to the action.

a. Persons or Classes in the Statute

i. Class of Contingent Beneficiaries

When a testator or grantor makes a disposition of property to a class, conditioned on some contingency, the members of the class, alive or unborn, are all contingent beneficiaries. SCPA 315 allows virtual representation of the unborn or infant or otherwise disabled members by the class members who would be entitled to take if the contingency mentioned in the instrument had occurred just before the proceeding.[5]

For example, if a trust provides income to the grantor's widower, remainder to her descendants alive at the widower's death, and at the time the intermediate trust accounting is brought, the grantor's descendants are three children and two grandchildren (from a deceased daughter), only the three children and the two grandchildren need be served.[6] If the contingency (the widower's death) had occurred just before the accounting proceeding had started, the living descendants would have been the only class members; it is therefore sufficient to serve them only.[7]

ii. Class of Relatives

When a future interest will go to a class of persons described in terms of their relationship to the party with the same interest as theirs, only the party and not the class must be cited. For instance, if a trust provides income to the decedent's widower, remainder to her son or, if the son predeceases, to his issue, only the son need be cited, because the future interests belong to a class described as relatives of his.[8]

5. McKinney's SCPA 315(2)(a)(i).

6. See Matter of Winn, 58 Misc.2d 965, 297 N.Y.S.2d 207 (Suffolk 1968), a probate proceeding in which the will created a residuary trust, income to wife for life, remainder to issue, and a subsequent codicil, by making an outright gift of money, had the effect of reducing the residuary trust. The court allowed the persons who would have constituted the class of "issue" if the widow had died just before the proceeding (the decedent's three children) to represent their own minor children, who were potentially, but not currently, in the class.

7. McKinney's SCPA 315(2)(a)(i). It is possible to have more than one level of virtual representation occurring within a single case. If two classes of persons are contingent beneficiaries (e.g., remainder to decedent's issue, or if there are none, to decedent's parents' issue), and members of each class are alive at the time of the proceeding, they can represent their respective classes. See Matter of Krech, N.Y.L.J., Jan. 17, 1983, at 19, col. 1.

8. McKinney's SCPA 315(2)(a)(ii). See Matter of Ulsh, N.Y.L.J., June 10, 1985, at 15, col. 4 (Nassau) (decedent's grandson, contingent income beneficiary, permitted to represent decedent's great-grandson, contingent income beneficiary and remainderman, in executor's accounting); Matter of Wenzel, N.Y.L.J., March 26, 1980, at 15, col. 2 (Nassau) (daughter, income beneficiary under decedent's testamentary trust,

iii. Class of Unborn or Unascertained Persons

When unborn or unascertained persons may be the beneficiaries of an interest in a trust or estate, they have to be cited only when there is no living person who can protect their interests, in which case the court will appoint a guardian ad litem to represent them.[9]

For instance, if a trust provides income to the widower, remainder to grandchildren, or if there are none, to grandnieces, and no grandchildren or grandnieces are alive at the time of the proceeding, the class of contingent remaindermen has no representative to protect its interests. The court will have to appoint a guardian ad litem to represent the unborn grandchildren and grandnieces. If grandchildren existed, they could represent the unborn grandchildren and grandnieces.[10] If grandnieces existed but no grandchildren, they could represent the unborn grandchildren,[11] since the representor's interest may follow the representee's interest,[12] so long as it is not too remote to insure valid representation of the unborns.[13]

iv. Individual Contingent Beneficiaries

If a party to a proceeding has the same interest in an estate or trust as a person whose possession of that interest is subject to a future contingency, the party can represent the other person.[14] For example, if income is payable to the widower, remainder to the son, or if he predeceases the widower, to the daughter, it is sufficient to serve the son at the time of the proceeding. His protection of his interests will protect the daughter's.

b. Actual Protection of the Representee's Interests

Even if a representee fits within the technical language of SCPA 315, if his interests are not actually protected by the representor (or if they may not be), the court has the authority under SCPA 315(7) to disallow the use of virtual representation, and to require that he be served with process.

The party can usually be counted on to look after the non-party's interests because he is representing his own self-interest. The court will not assume adequate protection of the non-party's interests, however. It must satisfy itself that the representor is actually protecting the common interest.

permitted to represent her children and unborn issue).

9. McKinney's SCPA 315(2)(a)(iii).

10. McKinney's SCPA 315(2)(a)(i).

11. McKinney's SCPA 315(2)(a)(i), (iii).

12. McKinney's SCPA 315(2)(a)(iii); Matter of Forgan, N.Y.L.J., April 26, 1985, at 13, col. 1 (New York County); Matter of Lawrence, 106 Misc.2d 19, 430 N.Y.S.2d 533 (New York County 1980).

13. See Matter of Lawrence, 106 Misc. 2d 19, 430 N.Y.S.2d 533 (New York County 1980), where a contingent remainderman with a very remote interest was not permitted to represent an infant contingent remainderman who would take before her because she was not likely to protect such a remote contingency aggressively.

14. McKinney's SCPA 315(3).

Under the statute, the interests of the representor and the representee must be the same, and some courts have required that they be identical. For instance, in a trust which gives income to the widower for life, then income to the son until he turns thirty, then remainder to him or if he is dead, to his issue, the son has the same interest as his issue (remainder of the trust), but he also has an income interest, so his interests are not identical to those of his issue, and some courts have refused to allow him to represent the issue.[15] Other courts have not required identity of interests; they have construed the definition of "same interest" to mean an interest the protection of which will necessarily protect the interests of the representees, and have permitted representation of contingent remaindermen by one who has an interest in the income and the remainder.[16] As one court phrased it, the representor can represent the non-party's interest because "the requisite identity of interest was identity of economic interests in the particular proceeding rather than the literal congruence of the property interests." [17] This is the preferable view.

To answer the question, "Would the interest of these issue in fact be protected by the representor's protection of his own interest?", one must know the nature of the proceeding. In the hypothetical of the last paragraph, for example, if the proceeding is an executor's accounting, in most cases both the son and his issue will want the maximum funding of the trust created by the will. In that case the son can represent his issue. His protecting his interests will, necessarily, protect theirs.[18]

Similarly, if the proceeding is a surviving spouse's election against a decedent's will, a remainderman of the trust created in the will can represent his issue, subsequent contingent remaindermen, despite the fact that he also has a right to income, since both he and his issue have the same interest in defeating the spouse's right of election.[19]

15. See Matter of Lawrence, 106 Misc. 2d 19, 430 N.Y.S.2d 533 (New York County 1980); Matter of Trigger, 66 Misc.2d 110, 319 N.Y.S.2d 792 (New York County 1971). This holding, that the representor's interest must be neither more nor less than the representee's, was seen frequently under the law relating to inter vivos trusts, McKinney's CPLR 1311. Matter of Childs, 129 N.Y.S.2d 830 (Sup.Ct. Suffolk County 1952); Matter of Blake, 208 Misc. 22, 141 N.Y.S.2d 194 (Sup.Ct. New York County 1955).

16. See, e.g., Matter of Pinkerson, N.Y. L.J., Dec. 18, 1978, at 14, col. 6; Matter of Sunderhauf, N.Y.L.J., Aug. 2, 1978, at 11, col. 2; Matter of Adler, 77 Misc.2d 651, 354 N.Y.S.2d 353 (New York County 1974); Matter of Leyshon, 67 Misc.2d 492, 324 N.Y.S.2d 472 (New York County 1971); Matter of Fuller, 57 Misc.2d 174, 291 N.Y.S.2d 455 (New York County 1968).

17. Matter of Connable, 102 Misc.2d 406, 423 N.Y.S.2d 421 (New York County 1979).

18. See Matter of Fountain, N.Y.L.J., April 3, 1985, at 16, col. 1 (Suffolk); Matter of Loening, N.Y.L.J., Aug. 23, 1978, at 13, col. 2 (Suffolk). But see Matter of Sanders, 123 Misc.2d 424, 474 N.Y.S.2d 215 (Nassau 1984), which refused to allow virtual representation because of a potential conflict between the income-beneficiary/remainderman, who might desire high yield, and the mere remainderman, who would prefer greater growth potential. Accord, Matter of Holland, 84 Misc.2d 922, 377 N.Y.S.2d 854 (Bronx 1974), (dictum).

19. Matter of Adler, 77 Misc.2d 651, 354 N.Y.S.2d 353 (New York County 1974).

If, on the other hand, the proceeding is a trustee's accounting, the son has an interest in the income account which could conflict with his issue's interest in the remainder, and he cannot represent them; they must be cited. The son may attempt to justify income payments made to him, and that is likely to conflict with the contingent remainder interests of his issue.

If the proceeding is an accounting and the potential representor is the accounting fiduciary, or one of them, the court might find a conflict and require service or appointment of a guardian for the remote beneficiaries who otherwise could have been virtually represented.[20]

The lawyer must also look at the facts as they exist at the time of the proceeding to determine whether the interests of the successive parties are the same. For example, if a person is a permissible income beneficiary[21] and is also a remainderman, his ability to represent contingent remaindermen under section 315 will depend on whether or not he has received any income payments. If he has, he may then be in a position of conflict with the remaindermen.[22] In Matter of Schwartz,[23] a will created a trust with income payable to the decedent's widow, a daughter, and the daughter's issue until the widow's death, then income to the daughter and her issue until the daughter reached age thirty, the remainder then payable outright to the daughter or if she did not survive the widow and reach the age of thirty, to her surviving issue. The income payments were entirely within the trustee's discretion. In the final estate accounting, the court allowed the daughter to represent her issue because she had not received any income payments. Because she had not received any income, her interest (like those of the other remaindermen) would be in funding the trust to the greatest extent possible. If she had received income, her interest would have been in justifying those payments as well as in funding the trust maximally, different interests from those of her issue.

If the representation is (or may be) inadequate, the court will require service of process.[24] The phrase "adequacy of representation"

20. Matter of Bingham, 97 Misc.2d 370, 411 N.Y.S.2d 516 (New York County 1978). No such conflict necessarily exists, however, where the fiduciary is not accounting. See Matter of O'Connor, 72 Misc.2d 490, 339 N.Y.S.2d 726 (New York County 1973), where, in a will construction proceeding, the court found no conflict of interest between a father and daughter who were both contingent remaindermen, though father was also fiduciary of the estate. See also Matter of Forgan, N.Y.L.J., April 26, 1985, at 13, col. 1 (New York County), where the Surrogate refused to allow the fiduciaries to represent unborns in a proceeding to terminate the trust.

21. The creator of a trust may give a trustee discretion to "spray" or "sprinkle" income among several beneficiaries.

22. See Matter of Putignano, 82 Misc.2d 389, 368 N.Y.S.2d 420 (Kings 1975) (virtual representation allowed because representor had not received any income payments); Matter of Borax, 60 Misc.2d 645, 303 N.Y.S.2d 739 (New York County 1969) (virtual representation not allowed because representor had received discretionary income and principal payments).

23. 71 Misc.2d 80, 335 N.Y.S.2d 243 (Nassau 1972).

24. McKinney's SCPA 315(7). See Matter of Alexander, N.Y.L.J., Jan. 2, 1979, at 12, col. 2 (New York County) (representor's interests were too remote to allow virtual representation).

has two possible constructions. If the words are construed objectively, the representor must merely have the same interests; that is, he must strictly comply with the statute. The cases sustaining attacks on virtual representation have illustrated this type of inadequacy.[25] If the phrase is construed subjectively, the representation will be inadequate if the representor has not actually taken the proper steps to protect his own (and hence the representee's) rights. For instance, he may not have actively participated in a decision to appear, default, acquiesce or contest. This type of attack on adequacy of the actual representation has not yet been made, although it would certainly be authorized by the statutory language.

Virtual representation results in a decree binding on the representees, but only if it is properly used. The court should therefore require service [26] in all cases where the representor for any reason may not give full and true protection of the representee's interests. In such cases, virtual representation does not assure the same finality as when a guardian ad litem is appointed to represent persons under a disability or when the competent adult interested persons are cited.[27] If the court does order service, the order must contain the reason for it.[28]

Occasionally a court will consent to virtual representation but will attach some condition to it to insure the adequacy of the representation, such as the requirement that the parties obtain court approval before settling the case.

The use of SCPA 315 in a prior proceeding is subject to review in a subsequent proceeding.[29] The appropriateness of virtual representation must be evaluated separately in every proceeding relating to an estate.[30] If the decree results in an advantage to the representor vis a vis the representee, this is prima facie proof of either inadequacy of representation or conflict of interest.[31]

In an attack on virtual representation, the representor is a party to the litigation for his failure adequately to protect the representee's interests, but he is not liable to the representee for failure to act. The litigation, if successful, will open up a proceeding that the representor thought was final. However, he is not a fiduciary, and such a role

25. E.g., Matter of Silver, 72 Misc.2d 963, 340 N.Y.S.2d 335 (Kings County 1973); Matter of Schwartz, 71 Misc.2d 80, 335 N.Y.S.2d 243 (Nassau 1972). See also Matter of Willis, 6 Misc.2d 218, 162 N.Y.S.2d 989 (Suffolk 1957), decided before the enactment of SCPA 315, where an attack on virtual representation was sustained when an after-born grandchild challenged her representation by existing grandchildren in a proceeding to construe a testamentary trust to limit the remainder to the class of existing grandchildren.

26. McKinney's SCPA 315(7).

27. See Matter of Silver, 72 Misc.2d 963, 340 N.Y.S.2d 335 (Kings 1973).

28. McKinney's SCPA 315(7).

29. Matter of Holland, 84 Misc.2d 922, 377 N.Y.S.2d 854 (Bronx 1974).

30. In Matter of Holland, 84 Misc.2d 922, 377 N.Y.S.2d 854 (Bronx 1974), the court found that the virtual representation of a son, the contingent remainderman of a testamentary trust, by his mother, the income beneficiary and remainderman, had been proper in the executor's accounting proceeding but was inadequate in the trustee's accounting, because their interests were no longer the same.

31. Matter of Willis, 6 Misc.2d 218, 162 N.Y.S.2d 989 (Suffolk 1957).

cannot be forced on him. The legislature did not intend to make an individual do anything more than he wished to do on his own or to subject him to liability for his failure to act prudently. It is the responsibility of the one undertaking to use virtual representation to see to it that the representees are being adequately protected.[32]

3. VIRTUAL REPRESENTATION IN PROBATE PROCEEDINGS

Probate proceedings differ somewhat from other proceedings because the parties generally share the desire either to get the will admitted to probate or to disprove it; they may have the "same interest" though one is entitled to principal and the other to income. Hence, the statute contains a special rule allowing virtual representation in probate proceedings if there is a common interest in proving or disproving the will.[33]

For example, a decedent's will might leave the entire residuary estate in trust, income to her daughter for life, remainder to her issue per stirpes. If the decedent dies in 1986 survived by her daughter and a granddaughter (child of decedent's predeceased son), the daughter can represent the granddaughter in the probate proceeding because they have the same interest in proving the will, even though the daughter's interest is in income and the granddaughter's interest is in principal.

Even if the persons both have an interest in proving the will (because both are named in it), if the representor would do better if the will were denied probate, virtual representation will not apply. The converse is also true: even if the persons both have an interest in disproving the will (for example, both are intestate distributees), if the representor would benefit more under the will than the representee, virtual representation will not be allowed.[34]

For example, if the testator left a gift in trust, income to his wife, remainder to his children, or if they predeceased him, remainder to his grandchildren, and then executed a codicil leaving specific bequests to the children, they cannot virtually represent the grandchildren because they would gain, and the grandchildren would lose, if the codicil were admitted to probate.[35]

32. Uniform Rules of the Surrogate's Court 207.18.

33. McKinney's SCPA 315(4); Matter of Fuller, 57 Misc.2d 174, 291 N.Y.S.3d 455 (New York County 1968).

34. This special rule for probate proceedings was amended in 1981 to allow representation in cases where the parties had a common interest in disproving the will. Before the amendment, the courts stretched to permit such virtual representation. See Matter of Sandefur, 95 Misc.2d 24, 406 N.Y.S.2d 245 (N.Y. County 1978) (service not required in probate proceeding on persons who would take as contingent remaindermen of a trust in default of exercise of power of appointment because the income beneficiary who would take in default was a party to the action and had the same interest in disproving the will, which exercised the power of appointment, as the representee).

35. Matter of Young, 68 Misc.2d 943, 328 N.Y.S.2d 325 (Nassau 1972).

4. VIRTUAL REPRESENTATION AND POWERS OF APPOINTMENT

If a person has a special power of appointment,[36] he can virtually represent the potential appointees.[37] For example, if a trust provides for income to the creator's daughter for life, remainder as the daughter appoints among her children, the daughter can represent her children in a proceeding relating to the trust.

Where a person has a general power of appointment, he can virtually represent not only the potential appointees but also those who would take in default of his exercise of the general power of appointment.[38]

5. VIRTUAL REPRESENTATION IN ACCOUNTING PROCEEDINGS

Virtual representation applies in formal judicial accounting proceedings. Moreover, it can also be used in informal accounting proceedings.

a. Informal Accountings on Receipts and Releases

One way for a fiduciary to settle an account is to obtain receipts and releases from the beneficiaries of the trust or estate.[39] Virtual representation is allowed in informal accounting proceedings settled by receipts and releases, unless the governing instrument prohibits it.[40]

The statute provides that the receipts and releases in an informal accounting proceeding are binding on all the virtual representees to the same extent they are binding on the parties who executed them. That section contemplates that a receipt and release is only as good as the underlying accounting given to the party who executed the release. The adequacy of the virtual representation is questionable if receipts and releases are executed by a representor who did not review the account, and the representee, upon reaching majority or upon the disappearance of the disability, may be able to attack the release on the ground of inadequate representation.

Moreover, the receipts and releases will discharge a fiduciary only as to the matters embraced in the account. Where the underlying disclosure is incomplete or the account is inaccurate, the release does not relieve the fiduciary of liability, and where the signer of the release

36. A special power of appointment is any power of appointment which is not general. McKinney's EPTL 10–3.2(c). A general power is one which can be exercised in favor of the holder of the power, or his estate, or his creditors, or the creditors of his estate. EPTL 10–3.2(b). A power of appointment is defined as "an authority to do any act in relation to property * * * which the donor of the power might himself do. * * *" EPTL 10–2.1.

37. McKinney's SCPA 315(2)(b).

38. McKinney's SCPA 315(2)(b). In a probate proceeding, where the decedent held the power of appointment, the default takers are necessary parties. See chapter on "Probate," infra at 80.

39. McKinney's SCPA 2202, discussed in chapter on "Accounting," infra at 180–82.

40. McKinney's SCPA 315(8), codifying what had been the general practice.

virtually represented others, arguably not only the representor but also the representee (where the representor refuses to act or is not acting in the representee's best interests) can challenge the release, force the filing of an amended account, or petition for a judicial settlement of the account.

In order to avoid the possibility of an attack on the manner in which one was virtually represented, the court will carefully review the steps taken to insure adequate representation. It may decide to require citations or appoint a guardian ad litem for persons under disability if it finds that the interests to be protected may not be adequately represented.[41]

b. Decree on Informal Accounting

A fiduciary can also obtain a judicial decree based on receipts and releases,[42] and virtual representation is available in the proceeding.[43]

Everything said in the preceding section on the validity of virtual representation in informal accountings based on receipts and releases applies also to a decree based on those receipts and releases. The representor must review the account, which must be thorough and accurate. If the representation was inadequate, the party being represented can move to set aside the decree.

6. LATERAL OR HORIZONTAL VIRTUAL REPRESENTATION

The whole discussion thus far has been of vertical representation, where a person represents another whose interest is one step more remote or contingent than his own. The statute also allows lateral or horizontal representation, where a party can represent a person under a disability on his own level.[44] Horizontal representation is allowed only if the instrument expressly permits it.[45] For example, if a trust provided income to the widower, remainder to his two children, an adult and a minor, the adult could virtually represent the minor only if the will allowed it. Similarly, if both the representor and the representee are "sprinklees" of the income of a trust in the trustee's discretion, their interests are concurrent rather than successive and the court will order virtual representation only if the will permits it.[46] As a practical matter, an attorney should consider adding a clause to wills providing that where a person under disability has an interest in the estate or the proceedings, and another party to the proceeding has the same interest, the disabled person need not be cited.

41. McKinney's SCPA 315(7).

42. McKinney's SCPA 2203(3). See discussion of informal accountings in chapter on "Accounting," infra at 180–82.

43. McKinney's SCPA 315(8).

44. McKinney's SCPA 315(5).

45. Prior to this amendment, L.1981, c. 178, the permissibility of lateral representation was not clear. In Matter of Murnane, N.Y.L.J., March 27, 1975, at 17, col. 3 (Nassau), for example, the court in dicta said it would not allow lateral representation. Accord, Matter of Peck, N.Y.L.J., June 13, 1979, at 12, col. 2, (New York County); Matter of Raimo, N.Y.L.J., Nov. 14, 1977, at 12, col. 2.

46. Matter of Sanders, 123 Misc.2d 424, 474 N.Y.S.2d 215 (Nassau 1984).

In cases where the petitioner proposes to use horizontal virtual representation, he (or his attorney) must submit an affidavit to assure the court that the representation will be adequate. It must give the statutory basis for the use of virtual representation and must state the steps the representor has taken to make a decision whether to appear, default, acquiesce or contest. It must also state whether the representor has any conflict of interest with the representee.[47]

Because a will must contain authorization for the use of horizontal virtual representation, a most interesting question arises during a probate proceeding when someone requests the use of lateral virtual representation. A will during a probate proceeding is in a sense not a valid instrument. It becomes effective only when the court accepts it and issues a probate decree. Hence that will should not be effective to authorize lateral virtual representation.[48] It would nevertheless be wise to state specifically in a will that the will does not have to be probated in order to supply the authorization for horizontal representation. Though this provision may not have any legal effect, since the law is not settled, the drafter should include it in cases where there are multiple beneficiaries of an interest in property.

7. REQUEST FOR USE OF VIRTUAL REPRESENTATION

In any proceeding where the petitioner wants to use virtual representation for some parties, the petition must give information justifying it. It must first list them as necessary parties, give their addresses and legal disabilities,[49] and set forth the nature of their interests and the basis of dispensing with service. It must describe any discretion on the part of the fiduciary or any other person to affect the present or future beneficiaries' interests and describe the manner in which it has been exercised, if it has.[50]

In addition, in accounting proceedings where horizontal virtual representation is used or in any case where the court questions the adequacy of the representation, the petitioner and the virtual representor must submit affidavits to justify virtual representation.[51] The affidavit must demonstrate among other things that the representees are in fact being adequately represented. For example, in an accounting proceeding, the virtual representor can swear that he has fully reviewed the account and executed the receipt and release, or, in a judicial proceeding, that he has evaluated the merits and decided

47. Uniform Rules of the Surrogate's Courts, 207.18.

48. The only case to decide that point held that an unprobated will could not authorize the use of horizontal virtual representation. Matter of Ginsburg, 115 Misc.2d 122, 453 N.Y.S.2d 587 (Nassau 1982) held that it did not.

49. McKinney's SCPA 315(7); McKinney's SCPA 304(3).

50. This information is required whenever a petitioner requests that service of process be dispensed with, both under 315 and under 2210, which dispenses with service on trust beneficiaries in a proceeding in which a fiduciary is accounting to himself as trustee if an independent co-trustee is also serving.

51. Uniform Rules of the Surrogate's Court, 207.18.

not to interpose any objections because he is satisfied that there is no basis for any. He should also vouch that he found no basis for objections, and that there is no conflict in his representing those not cited. It is also wise to require the petitioner formally to advise the virtual representor of the fact that he is protecting not only his own interests but the interests of others. This procedure is intended not to dilute the aims of SCPA 315, but to insure that it is used properly, and that decrees will be final and not later subject to attack on the ground that the court lacked jurisdiction over a necessary party because that party was not truly represented.

Chapter Three

PROBATE PROCEEDINGS

SECTION A. INTRODUCTION

Probate is the process of proving that a will the decedent supposedly wrote and executed is in fact his will and reflects his wishes. Its purpose is to prove the validity of the will, get the fiduciary appointed, and let the administration begin.

A will is a written instrument [1] taking effect at death. It may state how property shall not be disposed of [2] ("before anything else is done [I direct that] fifty cents be paid to my son-in-law to enable him to buy for himself a good stout rope with which to hang himself, and thus rid mankind of one of the most infamous scoundrels that ever roamed this broad land or dwelt outside of a penitentiary") [3], or simply appoint a fiduciary, make funeral arrangements,[4] dispose of body parts,[5] or exercise a power of appointment,[6] but most often it disposes of the decedent's property. It is revocable (ambulatory) during the decedent's lifetime and becomes irrevocable at the moment of death.[7]

Sec. A

1. A will can also be oral in limited situations discussed this chapter infra at 98.

2. Matter of Guarcello, 236 N.Y.S.2d 931 (Westchester 1963) ("I have no intention of bequeathing or devising any property of any kind to [one of decedent's five children]"). Wills of persons who died before Sept. 1, 1967 which did nothing more than disinherit someone were not valid. Matter of Morgenstern, N.Y.L.J., May 14, 1985, at 12, col. 6 (Suffolk); Matter of Bachmann, 45 Misc.2d 297, 256 N.Y.S.2d 665 (Erie 1965).

3. Gest, Some Jolly Testators, 8 Temp. L.Q. 297 (1934).

4. But see Public Health Law 4200 et seq. (decedent cannot direct burial in an unauthorized place).

5. Disposition of bodily organs can be done in the will itself and should certainly also be done on a card carried in the donor's wallet. This card, like a will, is signed by two witnesses.

6. McKinney's EPTL 10–6.2(a)(3) states that "[w]here the donor has made the power exercisable only by deed, it is also exercisable by a written will unless exercise by will is expressly excluded." See Matter of Beckwith, 87 Misc.2d 649, 386 N.Y.S.2d 615 (Broome 1976), modified on other grounds 57 A.D.2d 415, 395 N.Y.S.2d 499 (3d Dep't 1977), where a power of appointment exercisable only by deed was held also exercisable by written will because it was not expressly excluded.

7. See, e.g., Rubenstein v. Mueller, 19 N.Y.2d 228, 278 N.Y.S.2d 845, 225 N.E.2d 540 (1967). The instrument should evidence that the decedent anticipated that it would take effect on his death. See Matter of Berecz, N.Y.L.J., April 23, 1985, at 11, col. 4 (Bronx), where the instrument did not show decedent's understanding that it would take effect at death, but the Surrogate nevertheless admitted it because all parties were competent and consented and no one was prejudiced.

The definition of a will includes all codicils,[8] which are defined as supplements to the will whose function is to add or subtract from the will, change it, or republish a revoked will.[9]

A strong theme running through New York law is freedom of testation. Except for a few prohibitions, such as disinheriting a spouse,[10] violating the Rule against Perpetuities,[11] violating public policy,[12] or attempting to dispose of property which passes by operation of law,[13] a testator is given enormous freedom to dispose of his property as he likes.[14]

When executing a will, a testator must comply with strict formalities of execution,[15] and probate is the post-death process of proving that he did. During the process of probate, because the decedent cannot explain his own version of the estate plan, the court will strictly construe the formality requirements, but it is aided by a presumption that a will executed under the supervision of an attorney was executed with the necessary statutory formalities.[16]

A will enjoys no presumption in favor if its validity; [17] it becomes a valid and operative instrument only after its admission to probate.[18]

8. McKinney's EPTL 1–2.18(b).

9. McKinney's EPTL 1–2.1.

10. See McKinney's EPTL 5–1.1 and discussion of "Surviving Spouse's Right of Election," infra at 302 et seq.

11. See McKinney's EPTL 9–1.1; Kalish v. Kalish, 166 N.Y. 368, 59 N.E. 917 (1901).

12. See Matter of Walker, 64 N.Y.2d 354, 486 N.Y.S.2d 899, 476 N.E.2d 298 (1985), where the court found that though the decedent's residuary clause which left all personal property to his children was broad enough to cover their adoption decrees, it is New York's policy to keep such records sealed so the clause would not be given effect; Matter of Liberman, 279 N.Y. 458, 18 N.E.2d 658 (1939) (legacy attempting to restrict legatee's right to marry held invalid); Matter of Haight, 51 App.Div. 310, 64 N.Y.S. 1029 (2d Dep't 1900) (legacy encouraging divorce held invalid).

13. See Levenson v. Levenson, 229 App. Div. 402, 242 N.Y.S. 165 (2d Dep't 1930) (jointly owned property); Matter of McHugh, 226 App.Div. 153, 234 N.Y.S. 541 (4th Dep't 1929) (wrongful death proceeds).

14. McKinney's EPTL 3–1.1, 3–1.2. See, e.g., Matter of Guarcello, 236 N.Y.S.2d 931 (Westchester 1963) (testator gave all his property to three of his children and disinherited the two others).

15. McKinney's EPTL 3–2.1, discussed this chapter infra at 84–86.

16. See Matter of Cottrell, 95 N.Y. 329 (1884), where the will was admitted to probate against the testimony of both attesting witnesses that they were not present when it was executed because their signatures were proven by other evidence and because the supervision by attorneys created a presumption of compliance with the requirements of the statute. See also Matter of Kiefer, 78 Misc.2d 262, 356 N.Y.S.2d 520 (Yates 1974), where a will was admitted to probate though it was actually signed by only one of two attesting witnesses. Because this was a clear violation of statute, the will in Kiefer should not have been admitted to probate despite the other ample proof of its validity.

17. Matter of Cameron, 47 App.Div. 120, 62 N.Y.S. 187 (3d Dep't 1901), affirmed 166 N.Y. 610, 59 N.E. 1120 (1901) ("existence of a valid will cannot be presumed, but it must be shown to have been executed and published as prescribed by our statutes, by a person having testamentary capacity * * *.")

18. Matter of Cameron, 47 App.Div. 120, 62 N.Y.S. 187 (3d Dep't 1901), affirmed 166 N.Y. 610, 59 N.E. 1120 (1901); Matter of Ginsburg, 115 Misc.2d 122, 453 N.Y.S.2d 587 (Nassau 1982) (a will not yet probated could not permit horizontal virtual representation as provided by SCPA 315).

This chapter discusses the usual proceeding to probate a will or codicil: the proponent presents to the Surrogate the original of the will, a petition for a decree of probate and appointment of an executor, a death certificate, and depositions or affidavits of attesting witnesses. The proponent must arrange to serve process on all necessary parties and to give notice to all other persons interested as beneficiaries under the will.[19] They are given an opportunity to object, and the court decides whether the will is a valid instrument properly executed by a person with the mental capacity to do so. If it is, the court grants probate and issues letters testamentary, authorizing the executor to administer the estate.

A decedent's will must be probated if the estate contains assets that cannot be administered without letters, such as bank accounts and securities in the decedent's individual name. Under other circumstances, probate is unnecessary. For example, if the decedent owned all his property jointly, probate may be superfluous.[20] If the person named as sole beneficiary and executor in the will has predeceased the decedent, the court can issue letters of administration.[21] Moreover, if the personal property owned individually by the decedent was worth $10,000 or less, the estate can be settled expeditiously without probate under the simplified procedures applicable to small estates contained in SCPA Article 13.[22]

SECTION B. PRELIMINARY STEPS IF THE CLIENT DOES NOT HAVE THE WILL

If the client does not have the will, the attorney may have to take some preliminary steps to obtain it. The drafter may have kept the original in a will vault. In that case, the decedent usually has a "conformed copy," which gives the lawyer's name and office address. The attorney will deliver the will to the family or offer it for probate upon request.

The will may have been filed for safekeeping in the Surrogate's Court before the testator's death, so if a will cannot be found, the court files are a good place to search.[1] In fact, a petitioner for probate or administration must search for a will filed for safekeeping to ensure that no other wills of the testator supersede the one offered for probate. In the petition, the petitioner must state that he has made the search. As a safeguard, when the petitioner files for probate, most Surrogates

19. Service and notice are discussed in sections on "Persons to Be Cited" infra at 78–82, and "Notice of Probate," infra at 82–84.

20. The attorney should be aware of possible tax ramifications, however, even when probate is unnecessary. See chapter on "Estate Taxes," infra at 556 et seq.

21. Matter of Santiago, N.Y.L.J., March 28, 1979, at 11, col. 2 (Bronx). See Matter of Von Ripper, 95 Misc.2d 952, 408 N.Y.S.2d 686 (New York County 1978) (no need to probate a will when its provisions are a nullity).

22. See chapter on "Small Estates," infra at 246 et seq.

Sec. B

1. McKinney's SCPA 2508.

have their staff check to see if there is a will of the testator on file, and if so, they will produce it in the course of the probate proceeding.

The testator may, against his attorney's advice, have put the will in a safe deposit box, and the petitioner must then seek an order directing the bank to open the box.[2] The court may order the opening of the box ex parte upon a petition alleging that a will (or deed to a burial plot or insurance policy) is or may be in the safe deposit box. A bank officer and a member of the state tax commission must be present to inventory the contents of the box, which (except for the will, the cemetery deed and any insurance policies with a value of $50,000 or less naming designated beneficiaries) will not be released until the court appoints a fiduciary.

If a person takes the property out of the safe deposit box owned by the decedent individually or in joint names with another person and it results in tax evasion, he is guilty of a misdemeanor.[3]

A similar procedure is available for examining a home or apartment. If a person dies at home and has no close relatives,[4] the police will come and seal the home, and a family member or interested person will have to petition for an order to search through the apartment for a will, insurance policies, funeral instructions or the deed to a burial plot. If the court grants the order, a police officer and a representative of the state tax commission will accompany the petitioner to the house. If they find insurance policies, they give the policies to the beneficiaries named in the policies, and the petitioner may take the deed and funeral instructions. If the petitioner does not find a will in the apartment, he can inventory the contents of the apartment so the court will know what amount of a bond to set.

Later in this chapter we discuss cases where the will is truly unavailable for presentation to the court (such as a lost will, a destroyed will, an oral will, and a will in the possession of someone other than the fiduciary who does not make it available) and the methods that can be used to probate such a will.[5]

SECTION C. WHO MAY OFFER A WILL FOR PROBATE

The statute is specific on who is allowed to offer a will for probate, and that is the subject of this section, but as a preliminary statement, most often the nominated executor is the one to do so. If more than

2. McKinney's SCPA 2003. This proceeding should be brought in the county of decedent's domicile, which is the only proper venue. McKinney's SCPA 205. See Matter of Gray, N.Y.L.J., June 17, 1985, at 15, col. 3 (Bronx).

3. McKinney's Tax Law § 249–cc. The fine is up to $5,000 and the prison term up to one year.

4. In practice the degree of relationship is different from county to county.

5. These unavailable wills are discussed in section on "Ways of Proceeding When There is No Document," this chapter infra at 98–101.

one executor is nominated, they should all petition, but if that is impractical, one of them can petition and the others can submit oaths and designations.[1]

Any one of the following interested persons may petition for the probate of a will: [2]

(a) a person named in the instrument as legatee, devisee, fiduciary or guardian;

(b) the guardian of an infant legatee or devisee;

(c) the committee of an incompetent legatee or devisee;

(d) the conservator of a legatee or devisee;

(e) a creditor of the estate. Although a creditor is a person interested in having a fiduciary appointed in order to present a claim, and can therefore theoretically commence probate proceedings, in practice a creditor usually commences administration proceedings [3] rather than offering a will for probate. His claim has priority over all will beneficiaries [4] and intestate distributees, and thus he has no reason to offer the will to probate.

(f) any person having an interest in the estate, including a person with a pecuniary interest [5] an assignee of such a person,[6] or the beneficiary of a post-deceased beneficiary under a decedent's will.[7]

(g) anyone who would be entitled to letters of administration with the will annexed under SCPA 1418; [8]

(h) any party to an action brought or about to be brought in which the decedent if living would be a party;

(i) The public administrator or the county treasurer on order of the court where the will has been filed in the court and proceedings for its probate have not been instituted or diligently prosecuted.

For example, if a decedent dies survived by his mother, his three adult children, one child of each of his children, his brother and his brother's two daughters,

Sec. C

1. Oaths and designations are discussed in chapter on "Fiduciaries," infra at 391–92.

2. McKinney's SCPA 1402(1).

3. McKinney's SCPA 1002, discussed in chapter on "Administration," infra at 126–27.

4. For priorities among claimants and beneficiaries, see chapter on "Claims," infra at 164–72.

5. McKinney's SCPA 103(36).

6. Matter of Jordan, 202 App.Div. 710, 195 N.Y.S. 193 (2d Dep't 1922) (assignee may petition for probate of a will but he has no right to be appointed administrator c.t.a.).

7. Matter of Brew, 11 Misc.2d 802, 172 N.Y.S.2d 1007 (New York County 1958); Matter of Bell, 4 Misc.2d 286, 157 N.Y.S.2d 99 (Broome 1956).

8. See discussion of letters of administration with the will annexed this chapter infra at 115–18.

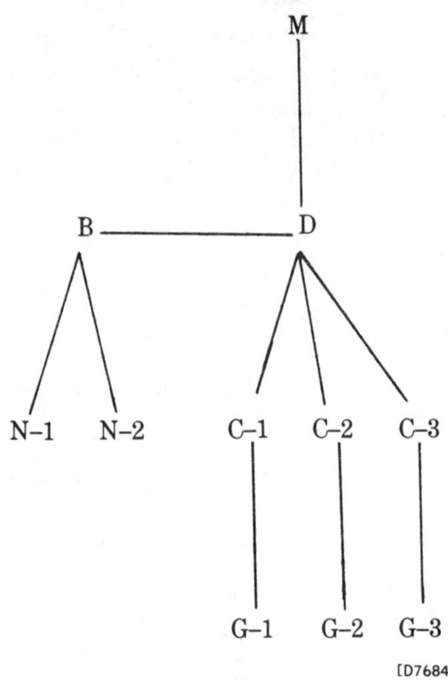

and in his will leaves $40,000 to G2, $10,000 to his brother and the residue to his descendants per stirpes, and names C1 as executor, the following persons alone can offer the will for probate:

Brother (as legatee)

C1 (as legatee and fiduciary)

C2 (as legatee)

C3 (as legatee)

G2 (as legatee, but only if adult; otherwise, his guardian).

If the appropriate person has filed a probate petition but has not diligently pursued it, the court may direct the Public Administrator or County Treasurer or any party to take steps to bring the matter to a decree.[9] For example, in one case where a proponent attempted to withdraw a petition for probate, the court noted that infants' rights might be adversely affected by withdrawal and it directed the Public Administrator to take over the probate proceeding.[10]

SECTION D. THE PETITION

Like all petitions, the one used for probate must contain all the basics required in Surrogate's Court practice generally.[1] The probate petition has additional special requirements.[2] The petition must state

9. McKinney's SCPA 1402(3)(a).

10. Matter of Wool, 57 Misc.2d 757, 293 N.Y.S.2d 678 (Nassau 1968).

Sec. D

1. These requirements are found in SCPA 304 and discussed in chapter on "Procedure," supra at 54–55.

2. McKinney's SCPA 1402(2).

that the testator is dead [3] (or is an alleged decedent [4]) and give the citizenship of the petitioner and the testator. It must describe the will (and codicils, if there are any), which in practice means to give the dates of the instrument and the names of the attesting witnesses. It must state whether any other wills of the same testator are on file in the court. It must state the names and addresses of all the distributees and any other persons entitled to be cited,[5] divided into categories of legally disabled and adult competent persons, to the extent ascertainable with due diligence.[6] It must also identify all the legatees, devisees and fiduciaries named in the will or any other will filed in the court, because they are entitled to notice of the proceeding.[7] The petition must be verified, and the nominated executor must qualify in advance, that is, must designate the clerk of the Surrogate's Court for process, sign an oath that he will faithfully discharge his duties,[8] and post a bond if the will so directs.[9]

The petition must state the size of the estate, for the purpose of setting a filing fee,[10] and that figure should include all "probate" assets, in New York. Probate assets are those that pass under the will; they do not include joint property, Totten Trusts, pensions or insurance payable to a named beneficiary, or other assets that pass outside the will. The petitioner need not include real property outside New York, but must list personal property wherever located. If the petitioner overestimates the estate, he can get a refund of the excess filing fee.[11]

If the petition seeks any extraordinary relief, such as a will construction, abandonment, status, or rights of after-born children, the petitioner should clearly state it.

Most lawyers use the statutory official probate forms issued by the court where the will is to be probated,[12] amended if necessary to accommodate out-of-the-ordinary situations such as a will of an alleged decedent, a lost or destroyed will, or a nuncupative or holographic will. If the attorney-drafter or a member of his family is receiving a benefit under the will, the proponent must submit a "Putnam" affidavit [13] explaining the circumstances surrounding the bequest. Some courts require a family tree with the petition. The attorney should also check the Uniform Surrogate's Court Rules and should ask the probate clerk if there are any local court rules requiring additional information. For

3. The proof of death is by death certificate.

4. For a discussion of the proceeding in which the court can declare a testator dead under EPR 2–1.7 and then proceed to probate his will, see chapter on "Temporary Administration, infra at 291–92.

5. McKinney's SCPA 1403 and discussion infra at 78–82.

6. See discussion of due diligence in chapter on "Procedure," infra at 55.

7. Notice of probate is governed by 1409 and discussed infra at 82–84.

8. McKinney's SCPA 708. The verification, oath and designation are part of the official form.

9. Bonds are discussed in chapter on "Fiduciaries," infra at 391–92.

10. McKinney's SCPA 2402.

11. McKinney's SCPA 2402.

12. See Official Form No. 7.

13. Matter of Putnam, 257 N.Y. 140, 177 N.E. 399 (1931). See chapter on "Attorney's Fees," infra at 359 et seq.

example, some courts file the wills separately, and the probate file contains a copy, not the original, of the will. In that case the proponent must submit an affidavit that the copy is exactly like the original. Similarly, if the staples have been (or appear to have been) removed from the will, the "stapling affidavit" may vary a little from court to court. Some courts require an affidavit if the surviving distributees were distant relatives (aunts and uncles and their issue or more distant relations) or if only one distributee survived, and some require an affidavit of decedent's domicile. The requirements of additional information vary from county to county and in some cases they are unpublished and depend on the factual situation at the time of probate.

If the petition states that necessary parties [14] are unknown or their addresses as unknown, the attorney must attach to the petition an affidavit of due diligence as to attempts made to locate and identify those parties.[15] Due diligence requires a thorough search of all sources likely to have information of the existence or whereabouts of distributees.[16] As a practical matter much of the "due diligence" headache can be avoided if the drafter, either in the will or in a family tree kept in the file, includes a description and the full names and addresses of the distributees, beneficiaries and anyone else who would be necessary to the probate proceeding.

SECTION E. PERSONS TO BE CITED

As in other proceedings, the attorney can obtain waivers of process from necessary parties who do not object to probate. In practice, most wills are admitted to probate on waivers.[1] The clerks review the waivers, the petition, the will, the death certificate and other documents submitted, and if everything is in order, they submit a decree to the Surrogate for signature.

Service of process in probate proceedings is crucial, even more so than in administration proceedings. The stakes in a probate proceeding are high: a share of the decedent's estate. In an administration proceeding, they are lower; the court merely determines who will administer the estate, and if there is any dispute about who shares in the estate, the court usually resolves it later in an accounting proceeding.

The following persons must be served with process unless they are petitioners, or have waived or appeared voluntarily.[2] Their common

14. See discussion of McKinney's SCPA 1403 immediately following.

15. See Matter of Clark, 144 Misc. 705, 259 N.Y.S. 377 (Orange 1932).

16. The specifics of a due diligence search are discussed in the chapter on "Procedure," supra at 55.

Sec. E

1. In large estates some attorneys make it a practice to cite all necessary parties and not to rely on waivers.

2. McKinney's SCPA 1403 states that process must issue to all the parties listed, but the logical implication is that a person who has waived or appeared voluntarily need not be served.

bond is that they could be adversely affected if the will were granted probate: [3]

(a) The decedent's distributees. If, for example, the decedent was survived by two children, C1 and C2, and two grandchildren, G1, son of his predeceased child, C3, and G2, daughter of C1, citations would go to C1, C2 and G1 (the distributees).[4]

(b) The person designated in the will as primary executor. Substitute or successor executors need not be served unless the designated executor has died or cannot serve.

(c) Any beneficiary, executor, trustee or guardian under the will whose rights or interests are adversely affected by a later instrument or an instrument modifying the one offered for probate. For example, if a testator made a specific bequest in a codicil, the residuary beneficiaries under the will would have to be cited because their residuary share would be reduced by the gift.

(d) Any person named in another will of the same testator on file in the same Surrogate's Court where probate is sought whose rights are adversely affected by the instrument offered for probate.[5] This provision contemplates a will filed by the decedent's attorney or executor after his death but in practice the courts construe it to include a will filed for safekeeping by the decedent before his death. The reason for making these persons necessary parties is to allow them to protect their rights under the second will by objecting to the first if necessary. Persons named in another of decedent's wills not on file are not necessary parties because the filing gives the will some aura of importance, however easily dissipated. A curious judicial gloss has been added to this section. The Court of Appeals has held in Matter of Brinkman [6] that a joint will executed by a husband and his wife and probated on the wife's earlier death is not a "will on file" at the husband's death, and hence the beneficiaries under it are not necessary parties to the probate of the husband's will. A joint will can be construed to be the will of both parties (if they agreed not to revoke it) or the will only of the first party to die, and the Brinkman rule apparently applies in both cases. In Brinkman, the will was construed not to bind the second decedent, because the parties had not agreed to keep the will in effect after the first spouse's death. Under those

3. McKinney's SCPA 1403(1).

4. See Matter of Frey, 40 A.D.2d 1013, 338 N.Y.S.2d 769 (1972) (because decedent and his wife were not divorced (though separated), his mother was not a distributee and therefore not a necessary party to probate proceeding); Matter of O'Daniels, 67 Misc.2d 571, 323 N.Y.S.2d 345 (1971) (legatee, because not necessary party, could not object to probate on ground that decedent was not domiciled in county alleged in petition).

5. L.1984, c. 223 (eff. June 19, 1984). Before the amendment everyone named in the will on file had to be cited, whether they were adversely affected or not. The amendment conforms 1403(1)(d) with 1403(1)(c) and comports with the policy of section 1403 to require service on those who have an interest in seeing the will denied probate.

6. Matter of Brinkman, 21 N.Y.2d 804, 288 N.Y.S.2d 634, 235 N.E.2d 773 (1968).

circumstances, it makes sense not to cite the persons named in that will, since it is not another will of the same decedent on file. However, the Court of Appeals went further than that; it expressly disagreed with Matter of Elwyn,[7] where the court in the second probate proceeding required service of process on the persons named in the joint will which had been probated on the death of the first decedent. In Elwyn the court found implicit in the language of the will a contract not to revoke, and hence found that the will was also the will of the second spouse. On this ground the Brinkman court could have distinguished Elwyn, but instead chose to disagree, so the rule appears to be that it is unnecessary in the probate proceeding of the second decedent's will to cite the persons named in the joint will, even though the earlier construction proceeding found the joint will binding on the survivor. The result seems illogical and inequitable.[8]

(e) The alleged decedent if it is such a case.[9] That person is, perforce, served by publication.[10]

(f) The state tax commission if the decedent was not a New York domiciliary.[11] This is to permit the state to protect its revenues should any New York estate taxes be due.

(g) The Attorney General if there are no distributees, or if the proponent does not know whether any exist.[12]

(h) Persons who would take in default of the exercise of a power of appointment possessed by the testator.[13] For example, if the will of testator's father created a trust, income to the testator for life, remainder as the testator appointed by will, or if the testator failed to exercise the power of appointment, remainder to X, X would be a necessary party in the probate of the testator's will.

Shortly we discuss the class of persons entitled to object to probate: those whose interests are adversely affected by the will offered for probate. It could happen that a person would have a right to contest the will if he knew of it, but falls between the cracks of those entitled to service in a probate proceeding. Thus some cases, albeit rare, a person with a right to object would never find out about the proceeding. If the

7. 285 App.Div. 91, 135 N.Y.S.2d 431 (3d Dep't 1954).

8. See McKinney's SCPA 1403, Practice Commentary at 48 (Supp.1986), where Professor Powers discussed the Brinkman decision.

9. Alleged decedents and the probate and administration of their estates are discussed in chapter on "Temporary Administration," infra at 289 et seq.

10. See discussion of service by publication in chapter on "Procedure," supra at 42–44.

11. A non-New Yorker's will may be probated in New York either originally or ancillarily, under circumstances described in chapter on "Ancillary Probate," infra at 509 et seq.

12. The attorney general is listed as a necessary party not under McKinney's SCPA 1403, but under McKinney's SCPA 316.

13. Matter of Wells, 36 Misc.2d 829, 233 N.Y.S.2d 940 (New York County 1962); Statewide Uniform Rules for the Surrogate's Court section 207.19(f).

petitioner is aware of any such person, he should serve a citation to ensure finality of the probate decree. Such a conclusion is dictated by the tenets of due process.[14]

A creditor, though entitled to petition for probate, is not a necessary party to a probate proceeding brought by someone else.[15] The reason is that his claim, if valid, has priority over the beneficiaries under the will, so the probate does not jeopardize his position.

If a necessary party survives the decedent but dies before being served in the probate proceeding, the citation must be served on his fiduciary. If there is none, process must be served on all his distributees, nominated fiduciaries, legatees and devisees.[16]

Necessary parties are determined at the time of probate of the decedent's will even if he disposes of some property by exercising a power of appointment granted under a former decedent's will.[17]

If the petitioner believes that an otherwise necessary party is disqualified because of abandonment, failure to support or other statutory wrongdoing,[18] the petitioner should cite that person and the court can determine his status in the probate proceeding.

The citation in a probate proceeding must include the name of the proponent so the person knows who is trying to commence the estate administration. If the will is oral, the citation must also note that it is.[19]

If a necessary party is under disability, the court must appoint a guardian ad litem to represent his interests.[20] However, the virtual representation provisions of SCPA 315 [21] apply to probate proceedings.[22] This can be valuable to a proponent, for if one of the necessary parties is under a legal disability and shares an interest in upholding or defeating the will with another party not under a legal disability, the proponent can dispense with process on the disabled party.

Although virtual representation has been discussed at length already,[23] its special probate aspects bear repetition here. Virtual representation in other proceedings requires analysis of whether the inter-

14. See Matter of Brachfeld, 118 Misc. 2d 200, 459 N.Y.S.2d 999 (Bronx 1983) (where the court ordered the petitioner to serve process on beneficiary of Totten Trust account revoked by the will).

15. McKinney's SCPA 1403; Matter of Hoffman, N.Y.L.J., March 11, 1985, at 15, col. 6 (Nassau).

16. McKinney's SCPA 1403(1)(g).

17. Matter of Thibault, N.Y.L.J., Oct. 16, 1978, at 16, col. 4 (New York County) (necessary parties determined at date of life beneficiary's death, not at death of the life beneficiary's father, creator of the power).

18. See McKinney's EPTL 5–1.2 and McKinney's EPTL 4–1.4 and discussion of abandonment and other grounds for disqualification in chapter on "Administration," infra at 129.

19. McKinney's SCPA 1403(2).

20. Matter of Arneson, 84 Misc.2d 128, 374 N.Y.S.2d 973 (Westchester 1975) (probate decree reopened because decedent's son, a necessary party to probate, was under disability (epileptic) and had not been cited).

21. Virtual representation is discussed in chapter on "Procedure," supra at 60–70.

22. McKinney's SCPA 1403(1)(h).

23. See chapter on "Procedure," supra at 60–70.

ests of the representor and representee are identical, or at least very similar. Not so in probate proceedings. The representor and representee in the estate do not have to have identical interests, so long as they both share an interest in having the will admitted to probate or denied probate. For example, if a mother is income beneficiary of a residuary trust and her son is remainderman, the mother can represent the son despite the eventual obvious conflict in their interests. At the moment of probate their interests are the same: to probate the will and get the trust established.[24]

Virtual representation in its most common form permits one interest to represent another interest one step more remote. In fact the additional contingency is often that the representee survive the representor (e.g., "remainder to my daughter or if she is dead, to her issue"). This is aptly called "vertical" representation. "Horizontal" representation, where a competent adult beneficiary can represent a disabled person on his own level ("remainder to my daughter and son in equal shares"), is permitted only if the will specifically allows it.[25] A question arises whether the will can be held specifically to allow it when the will has not been probated. The only case on this issue to date soundly concludes that it cannot, and refuses to allow horizontal virtual representation in probate proceedings.[26]

SECTION F. NOTICE OF PROBATE

The persons named in the will or codicil who do not have to be served with a citation are entitled to notice of probate.[1] This usually means legatees who are not distributees, such as friends, non-distributee relatives, and charities. It gives those named in the will who would not otherwise have an interest in the estate an opportunity to know that probate proceedings are under way and to protect their interests under the will. They need not be cited because the proponent and the named executor can adequately protect their interests. The proponent simply sends to them, usually by mail,[2] a copy of the notice of probate.

The notice is not jurisdictional, but merely informational. It is not process and therefore while the court will supervise the service of notice of probate, failure to give the notice does not jeopardize the probate decree.[3]

24. But see Matter of Sanders, 123 Misc.2d 424, 474 N.Y.S.2d 215 (Nassau 1984), discussed supra page 63 n. 18.

25. McKinney's SCPA 315(5).

26. Matter of Ginsburg, 115 Misc.2d 122, 453 N.Y.S.2d 587 (Nassau 1982).

Sec. F

1. McKinney's SCPA 1409.

2. McKinney's SCPA 1409(2).

3. See Matter of Dillon, 28 N.Y.2d 597, 319 N.Y.S.2d 850, 268 N.E.2d 646 (1971) (notice of probate to non-necessary party was sufficient and party had no right to move for vacatur of probate decree). See also Matter of Brush, 46 Misc.2d 277, 259 N.Y.S.2d 390 (New York County 1965), where the court held that a residuary legatee not cited in probate proceeding was not bound by the decree; the validity of a testamentary disposition was not res judicata, and the residuary beneficiary was entitled to move to vacate the probate decree. The questionable disposition was one made in a convoluted fashion to the attor-

The notice must state the name of the testator, the name and address of the proponent and the fact that the will has been offered for probate. It must give the name and address and status (legatee, devisee or fiduciary) of each person named in the petition who has not received or waived service or appeared. When the proponent is not the nominated executor, the name and address of the latter must be set forth in the notice.[4]

The original notice must be filed in court with proof by affidavit of mailing signed by the person who mailed it.[5] If the persons to be served are infants or incompetents, the notice is mailed to those who would receive process on their behalf.[6] Notice is unnecessary if those who should receive it are unknown or their addresses are unknown.[7]

While the statute authorizes the service of the notice before or after the decree, in practice the court usually requires proof of service before it issues the probate decree. This gives the persons named in the will an opportunity to come forward if they think there is some reason the court should not issue letters to the nominated fiduciary.

There is a miniature virtual representation provision within SCPA 1409.[8] This is technically necessary because the virtual representation statute, SCPA 315, applies to service of process, and notice is not process. Where a class of persons has a contingent interest in a trust or property, notice need be served only on the persons alive at the decedent's death who would constitute the class if the event had happened immediately before the issuance of the notice.[9] Naturally, if any of the persons in being has been served or has appeared or waived service of process, he need not receive notice. Similarly, where a primary beneficiary has an interest in the trust or property, and a class of his relatives has a contingent interest in it, it is sufficient to serve the primary beneficiary with the notice; it is not necessary to serve notice on the class.[10] If the primary beneficiary has waived service or appeared, that will also satisfy the notice requirement for the class.

If more than one will or codicil is offered for probate, the practice is for the court to try the validity of the last instrument before allowing litigation over a prior instrument.[11] If a petitioner seeks probate of a

ney-drafter-executor, and the residuary beneficiary contended that it had been procured by undue influence.

4. McKinney's SCPA 1409, Practice Commentary at 314 (1967).

5. McKinney's SCPA 1409(1) and (2).

6. Service on persons under legal disability is governed by McKinney's SCPA 307(3) and (4) and discussed in chapter on "Procedure," supra at 45–46.

7. McKinney's SCPA 1409(2).

8. See discussion of virtual representation in chapter on "Procedure," supra at 60–70.

9. McKinney's SCPA 1409(1)(a).

10. McKinney's SCPA 1409(1)(b).

11. Matter of Stacer, 10 A.D.2d 810, 198 N.Y.S.2d 63 (4th Dep't 1960); Matter of McCabe, 116 Misc. 637, 190 N.Y.S. 490 (New York County 1921). But compare Matter of Manville, N.Y.L.J., Feb. 6, 1969, at 19, col. 1 (Westchester), where the court held a hearing on the validity of an earlier will because of doubts as to the validity of signatures, and Matter of Vieillard, 15 Misc.2d 836, 186 N.Y.S.2d 506 (Nassau 1959), where the court granted a preliminary hearing to determine the status of contestants named as beneficiaries in a

will and a later will is on file, the petitioner should also petition for denial of probate of the later will.[12]

SECTION G. PROPONENT'S BURDENS: PROVING DUE EXECUTION AND TESTAMENTARY CAPACITY

1. DUE EXECUTION

The proponent has the burden of proving due execution by a fair preponderance of the evidence,[1] and he can rely on a presumption of regularity if an attorney supervised the execution.[2]

The elements of proper execution are

(a) The testator must have signed at the end of the will or another person must have signed his name at the end at his direction.

(b) The testator must have signed in the presence of the attesting witnesses (formerly called subscribing witnesses before the enactment of the EPTL) or acknowledged to them that the signature was his.

(c) The testator must have declared to the attesting witnesses that the instrument was his will (or they must have at least had a "meeting of the minds" on that issue). In other words there must be publication by the testator to the witnesses that they are attesting witnesses to his will.

(d) The attesting witnesses must have both signed within a thirty-day period.[3]

a. *Signature Must Be at the End*

The testator's signature should be at the very end of the will, just before the attestation clause signed by the attesting witnesses. Any material after the signature is invalid[4] but the will can still be probated without that material unless the deleted material is necessary to understand the will or to carry out the testator's general plan, in which case the whole will will be denied probate.[5]

Any material added later in time than the testator's signature is invalid whether it precedes or follows (in space) the signature.[6] The burden of establishing when the additions or alterations were made

prior will which had a red line drawn through the decedent's signature.

12. Matter of Buratovich, N.Y.L.J., April 29, 1975, at 18, col. 5 (New York County); Matter of Rose, N.Y.L.J., June 3, 1971, at 17, col. 5 (Kings).

Sec. G

1. Matter of Martin, 98 N.Y. 193 (1885).

2. E.g., Matter of Hedges, 100 A.D.2d 586, 473 N.Y.S.2d 529 (2d Dep't 1984) (Surrogate erred in refusing to charge jury on presumption of regularity).

3. McKinney's EPTL 3–2.1.

4. McKinney's EPTL 3–2.1(a)(1)(A).

5. McKinney's EPTL 3–2.1(a)(1)(B).

6. McKinney's EPTL 3–2.1(a)(1)(B).

should be on the person who benefits from them.[7] If no proof exists, therefore, the court will ignore the alterations and grant probate to the will as originally written.[8] Moreover, because a codicil can incorporate by reference only materials which were themselves executed with the formalities required for a will, a codicil does not validate materials added to a will after the will's execution.[9] An occasional case has said that if the alteration is fair on its face, a presumption arises that it was made prior to execution.[10]

If the testator cannot sign his own name because of physical infirmity, another person can sign for him, but that other person cannot be counted as an attesting witness (so two others are needed), and must sign his own name or the will will be invalid.[11] The courts are strict about this requirement.[12] The testator may also sign with a mark, such as an "X," so long as he made the mark to signify his signature on the will.[13]

The attesting witnesses should sign at the end,[14] but unlike the strict compliance required for the placement of the testator's signature at the end, the courts are not so strict about the placement of the attesting witnesses' signatures,[15] which can be to the right or left, under or over the testator's signature.

b. Attesting Witnesses Must Know the Signature Is Testator's

The most common and soundest practice is for the testator to sign in the attesting witnesses' presence, but if he does not, he can acknowledge his signature to them. He can acknowledge the signature before or after the attesting witnesses sign,[16] although presumably if he acknowledges it after, it should be soon after.

7. Matter of Fodera, 96 A.D.2d 559, 465 N.Y.S.2d 65 (2d Dep't 1983) (proponents, who stood to gain from alteration, had burden of proving that alterations preceded execution of will).

8. Matter of Rose, 22 Misc.2d 993, 199 N.Y.S.2d 305 (Columbia 1960).

9. Matter of Rose, 22 Misc.2d 993, 199 N.Y.S.2d 305 (Columbia 1960).

10. See Crossman v. Crossman, 95 N.Y. 145 (1884); and Matter of Beattie, 154 N.Y.S.2d 696 (Kings 1956).

11. McKinney's EPTL 3–2.1(a)(1)(C).

12. Matter of Andrews, 162 N.Y. 1, 56 N.E. 529 (1900).

13. See, e.g., Matter of Irving, 153 App. Div. 728, 138 N.Y.S. 784 (1912), affirmed 207 N.Y. 775, 101 N.E. 1106 (1st Dep't 1912); Matter of Galvin, 78 Misc.2d 22, 355 N.Y.S.2d 751 (Erie 1974).

14. McKinney's EPTL 3–2.1(a)(4).

15. See Matter of Macchiarola, N.Y. L.J., Jan. 9, 1979, at 15, col. 1 (Bronx), where the attesting witnesses had signed their names at the top of the last page because there was no room at the bottom, and the court admitted the will to probate, holding that statutory technicalities should be construed liberally; Matter of Kobrinsky, 51 Misc.2d 222, 273 N.Y.S.2d 156 (Kings 1966) (witnesses signed around the margins, the only space available in a small holographic will).

16. Matter of Baldwin, 67 Misc. 329, 124 N.Y.S. 612 (Kings 1910), affirmed 142 A.D. 904, 126 N.Y.S. 1121 (2d Dep't 1910), affirmed 202 N.Y. 548, 95 N.E. 1222 (1911).

c. *Attesting Witnesses Must Know It Is Testator's Will*

Although the testator does not have to tell the attesting witnesses directly that the document they are witnessing is a will,[17] there must be some act on his part which gets that fact across to them; if they do not know it, the attestation (and hence, the will) is invalid.[18] The attesting witnesses need not (and usually do not) know the dispositive provisions of the will.

d. *Attesting Witnesses Must Sign Within a Thirty-Day Period*

The statute does not set a thirty-day limit on the whole execution process; rather, it requires that the attesting witnesses sign within thirty days of each other.[19] For example, if the testator signs the will on April 1 and the first attesting witness signs on April 5, the second witness must sign by May 4, not necessarily by April 30. In fact the statute specifically states that the procedure need not be followed in the exact order noted (that is, testator signing first, followed by the attesting witnesses), so long as all the requirements are met.[20]

2. TESTAMENTARY CAPACITY

It is the proponent's burden to prove testamentary capacity.[21] A testator need not have a superior or even an average intellect. A person has testamentary capacity if he understands in a general way three things: (i) what property he owns, (ii) which persons society would consider the natural objects of his bounty, and (iii) what his will provides. He need not understand these things with perfect specificity,[22] but he must know them in a general way and understand how they relate to each other and be able to make decisions in light of his knowledge.[23]

The focus in determining whether a testator had testamentary capacity is always the time of execution. If a person was usually of sound mind and memory but was not so at the time of execution,

17. Matter of Hunt, 110 N.Y. 278, 18 N.E. 106 (1888).

18. See Matter of Hedges, 100 A.D.2d 586, 473 N.Y.S.2d 529 (2d Dep't 1984), where the court said that "the requirement of express declaration need not be followed literally as long as sufficient information is conveyed to the subscribing witnesses during the execution ceremony" that the testator knows the instrument is his will.

19. McKinney's EPTL 3–2.1(4).

20. McKinney's EPTL 3–2.1(b).

21. Matter of Kaplan, 50 A.D.2d 429, 387 N.Y.S.2d 105 (3d Dep't 1976), affirmed 41 N.Y.2d 870, 393 N.Y.S.2d 993, 362 N.E.2d 623 (1976).

22. See, e.g., Matter of Bush, 85 A.D.2d 887, 446 N.Y.S.2d 759 (4th Dep't 1981), where there was some question whether the decedent knew the precise size of his estate, but he clearly knew it consisted of bank accounts and Veterans Administration funds. The court admitted the will to probate.

23. See Matter of Slade, 106 A.D.2d 914, 483 N.Y.S.2d 513 (4th Dep't 1984), where the following factors precluded the probate of the will: testatrix thought she had $10,000 when in fact she had $650,000; she could not transact business with her stockbroker because she did not know what stocks and bonds she owned; she had not paid taxes; her house was littered with $30,000 cash; and her medical diagnosis was degenerative dementia, which only gets worse.

because of, say, drunkenness, that will is invalid. On the other hand, if a person's mind and memory are usually unsound, for example because of senility or drug addiction, but the will is executed in a lucid interval during which the testator understands what he is doing, that will is valid.[24] It is, of course, relevant that the testator executed the will on his deathbed.[25] While testimony on the testator's mental condition before and after execution is relevant, it is relevant only because it may reflect on the testator's mental condition at the time of execution.[26] Two presumptions work here: if the testator was incompetent before the execution, the presumption is that he remains incompetent.[27] Similarly, a person whose mind was sound before the execution is presumed still to be competent at the execution.[28]

The mental capacity required for wills is less than that required for any other legal instrument,[29] because no arm's length negotiations are necessary for a will as they are for other legal documents. In fact, the level of intelligence and memory needed is quite low,[30] and oddness and eccentricity do not necessarily mean a lack of testamentary capacity.[31]

The attesting witnesses may give their opinion on whether the testator had testamentary capacity at execution.[32] Psychiatrists and

24. Children's Aid Society v. Loveridge, 70 N.Y. 387 (1877); Matter of Hedges, 100 A.D.2d 586, 473 N.Y.S.2d 529 (2d Dep't 1984) (102 year old woman).

25. Matter of Robinson, 102 A.D.2d 995, 477 N.Y.S.2d 877 (3d Dep't 1984) (will executed 32 minutes before decedent was pronounced dead denied probate on evidence that testator had no palpable pulse, blood pressure of 50 over 20, and a temperature of 105.4 degrees, and was unable to respond to verbal stimuli).

26. Matter of Hedges, 100 A.D.2d 586, 473 N.Y.S.2d 529 (2d Dep't 1984); Matter of Stern, 28 A.D.2d 207, 284 N.Y.S.2d 286 (3d Dep't 1967) (Surrogate allowed discovery of decedent's hospital records for four years before and three years after date of will).

27. Matter of McCarthy, 269 App.Div. 145, 54 N.Y.S.2d 591 (1st Dep't 1945), affirmed 296 N.Y. 987, 73 N.E.2d 566 (1947) (eighty-three year old man incompetent before execution); Matter of Widmayer, 74 App.Div. 336, 77 N.Y.S. 663 (1st Dep't 1902) (eighty-year old testator adjudged incompetent one week before will execution presumed to remain incompetent in absence of evidence to contrary).

28. Rintelen v. Schaefer, 158 App.Div. 477, 143 N.Y.S. 631 (2d Dep't 1913) (testator judicially declared incompetent in 1904, and judicially declared competent in 1905, presumed competent at execution of will in 1908). A division exists in the case law on the issue of whether the presumption remains in the case along with the evidence to rebut it, Brotherton v. People, 75 N.Y. 159 (1878), or whether the presumption disappears when evidence rebutting it is introduced. People v. Egnor, 175 N.Y. 419, 67 N.E. 906 (1903). See N.Y. Pattern Jury Instructions, Will Contests, 1183, 7:48.

29. Matter of Coddington, 281 App.Div. 143, 118 N.Y.S.2d 525 (3d Dep't 1952), affirmed 307 N.Y. 181, 120 N.E.2d 777 (1954) (will admitted to probate, despite testimony by doctor and psychiatrist that decedent was incompetent, because decedent was managing his own affairs and "less capacity is required to make a will than to make other contract").

30. See Matter of Strong, 179 App.Div. 539, 166 N.Y.S. 862 (3d Dep't 1917), where the court refused to decide the issue of capacity as a matter of law despite 74-year old testatrix's history of convulsions and her illness just before execution so serious as to require the presence of two doctors.

31. Matter of Bush, 85 A.D.2d 887, 446 N.Y.S.2d 759 (4th Dep't 1981).

32. Clapp v. Fullerton, 34 N.Y. 190 (1866) (attesting witnesses are present at the act of execution and their statements regarding testamentary capacity are admissible).

other experts can also give their opinions on testamentary capacity,[33] although it will be only minimally helpful if the expert did not treat the decedent personally.[34] The proponent may interpose the doctor-patient privilege [35] but if he does not, or if he opens the door to medical testimony by his own offer of privileged testimony,[36] the typical will contest presents enough special circumstances [37] to warrant this expert testimony.[38] Where the expert testimony contradicts the facts, the facts prevail.[39] Other persons may testify about the testator's actions and may state that his actions struck them as being irrational, but may not offer an opinion on his testamentary capacity.[40]

If the proponent makes a prima facie case and the objectant fails to raise any issues of fact, the Surrogate has the authority to grant summary judgment, but in fact that happens very rarely.[41] The Surrogate can also, in a jury trial, direct a verdict or set aside a jury verdict if it is unsupported by the record.[42]

Because the Surrogate presides and hears the testimony of all the witnesses, his findings are entitled to great weight.[43] The appellate court can overturn the Surrogate's finding if it is unsupported by the record.[44]

SECTION H. ATTESTING WITNESSES

The next few sections discuss the role of the attesting witnesses' testimony in the probate proceedings. By far the most usual practice is simply to submit written affidavits by two attesting witnesses. There are cases, however, where the witnesses come to the court to testify, where the court dispenses with one witness's testimony, where the

33. Matter of Horton, 26 Misc.2d 843, 203 N.Y.S.2d 978 (Suffolk 1960), affirmed 13 A.D.2d 506, 214 N.Y.S.2d 653 (2d Dep't 1961).

34. Matter of Vukich, 53 A.D.2d 1029, 385 N.Y.S.2d 905 (4th Dep't 1976), affirmed 43 N.Y.2d 668, 400 N.Y.S.2d 817, 371 N.E.2d 535 (1977); Matter of Slade, 106 A.D.2d 914, 483 N.Y.S.2d 513 (4th Dep't 1984).

35. McKinney's CPLR 4504.

36. E.g., Steinberg v. New York Life Insurance Co., 263 N.Y. 45, 188 N.E. 152 (1933); Strader v. Collins, 280 App.Div. 582, 116 N.Y.S.2d 318 (1st Dep't 1952).

37. McKinney's CPLR 3101(a)(4).

38. See Matter of Corey, 275 App.Div. 53, 87 N.Y.S.2d 208 (4th Dep't 1949); Matter of Danilow, 118 N.Y.S.2d 522 (New York County 1948); Matter of Postley, 125 Misc.2d 416, 479 N.Y.S.2d 464 (Nassau 1984).

39. Matter of Horton, 272 App.Div. 646, 75 N.Y.S.2d 45 (3d Dep't 1947), affirmed 297 N.Y. 891, 79 N.E.2d 736 (1948); Matter of Slade, 106 A.D.2d 914, 483 N.Y.S.2d 513 (4th Dep't 1984). But see Matter of Sylvestri, 44 N.Y.2d 260, 405 N.Y.S.2d 424, 376 N.E.2d 897 (1978) (handwriting expert).

40. Holcomb v. Holcomb, 95 N.Y. 317 (1884); Matter of Ross, 87 N.Y. 514 (1882).

41. See Matter of Pollock, 64 N.Y.2d 1156, 490 N.Y.S.2d 732, 480 N.E.2d 346 (1985); Matter of Pascal, 309 N.Y. 108, 127 N.E.2d 835 (1955); Matter of Witkowski, 85 A.D.2d 807, 445 N.Y.S.2d 639 (3d Dep't 1981), appeal denied 56 N.Y.2d 505, 451 N.Y.S.2d 1027, 437 N.E.2d 286 (1982); Matter of Betz, 63 A.D.2d 769, 404 N.Y.S.2d 737 (3d Dep't 1978); Matter of Kaplan, 50 A.D.2d 429, 378 N.Y.S.2d 105 (3d Dep't 1976), affirmed 41 N.Y.2d 840, 393 N.Y.S.2d 993, 362 N.E.2d 623 (1976).

42. Matter of Hedges, 100 A.D.2d 586, 473 N.Y.S.2d 529 (2d Dep't 1984).

43. Matter of Thorne, 108 A.D.2d 865, 485 N.Y.S.2d 383 (2d Dep't 1985).

44. Matter of Hedges, 100 A.D.2d 586, 473 N.Y.S.2d 529 (2d Dep't 1984).

testimony of an out-of-state witness is submitted in the form of a commission, where the witness forgets the details of the execution or testifies against it, and where no attesting witnesses are available, and this chapter discusses these situations as well.

1. TESTIMONY BY AFFIDAVIT

To expedite probate proceedings and to curtail expenses, the law permits proof of wills by out-of-court affidavits of attesting witnesses.[1] Before 1963, the attesting witnesses would have to appear at the courthouse and be examined whether there were objections to the will or not. In practice today, unless there is a contest or some difficulty in proving the propounded instrument, the proof taken from attesting witnesses is submitted in the form of written testimony obtained out of court. Because of this practice, competent practitioners today attach the "1406 affidavit" [2] to the will and the attesting witnesses sign it (and have it notarized) at the time the will is executed.

The proponent cannot always use the SCPA 1406 affidavits. In the following instances, the affidavits alone are not sufficient to prove a will: [3]

1. Where the will contains changes, writing between the lines, deletions or mutilations in its dispositive portions, or where

Sec. H

1. McKinney's SCPA 1406, enacted by L.1963, c. 405. For a discussion of the use of affidavits, see Bay, "Affidavits of Attesting Witnesses," 55 N.Y. State B.J. 13 (Dec. 1983).

2. A sample of the McKinney's SCPA 1406 affidavit follows:

STATE OF NEW YORK }
ERIE COUNTY } ss:

We, the undersigned, being duly sworn, say:

1. We witnessed the execution of the foregoing Last Will and Testament, dated ———, of the Testator, JOHN JONES. Said testator subscribed said will at the end thereof at the offices of JANE DOE, Esq., on [date] in our presence. At the time of making such subscription said Testator declared the said instrument so subscribed by him to be his will, and we thereupon signed our names as witnesses at the end of such instrument, at the request of said Testator, and in his presence and sight, and in the presence of each other.

2. In the opinion of the undersigned:

A. The said Testator at the time of so executing said instrument, was over the age of 18 years, and of sound mind, memory and understanding, and not under any restraint or in any respect incompetent to make a will.

B. The said Testator could read, write and converse in the English language and was suffering from no defect or impairment which would affect his capacity to make a valid will. The will was executed as a single instrument and was not executed in counterparts.

3. Each of the undersigned was acquainted with said Testator and we make this affidavit at the request of said Testator.

4. The said instrument was executed by said Testator and each of the undersigned, as witnesses, under the supervision of JANE DOE, who is an attorney-at-law licensed to practice in the State of New York.

____

____

Sworn to before me this
day of ______, 19__.

____
Notary Public

3. See Surrogates' Press Release, N.Y. L.J., November 15, 1973, at 1, col. 5.

something about the appearance of the will requires an explanation and the affidavits do not explain it.

2. Where the testator was illiterate or unable to read English.

3. Where more than one will was executed and not all counterparts are produced, or where a carbon or reproduced copy is produced and the ribbon copy is not.

4. Where the will was executed within ninety days of the decedent's death.

5. Where the attorney-draftsman or a member of his family is a beneficiary under the will, or where the decedent and an unrelated beneficiary had a confidential relationship, such as doctor-patient or attorney-client. This is often referred to as a "Putnam" matter.[4]

6. Where the testator is blind or otherwise unable to execute a will in the usual manner.

7. Where the execution was not supervised by an attorney.

8. Where the testator signed with a mark instead of a signature.

If the attesting witnesses did not sign an affidavit at the will execution, they can sign them after the decedent's death,[5] and if they do, they must review either the original will or, if that is already filed with the court, a court-certified photographic reproduction of the will, and then sign a written deposition to be filed along with the affidavits. The deposition (available from the court) essentially restates the allegations of the attesting witnesses' affidavits.

If no one contests the affidavit, and the court on its own does not require the presence of the witness (or witnesses) to testify, the court will accept the sworn affidavit as testimony of the genuineness of the will, the validity of its execution, the competence of the testator and his freedom from restraint.

2. EXAMINATION OF ATTESTING WITNESSES

In a case other than the typical uncontested probate proceeding where the attesting witnesses' testimony is submitted in writing,[6] the attesting witnesses may have to appear to testify. Any party to the probate proceeding has a right to examine any attesting witness, whether or not that party has filed objections to probate.[7]

The attesting witnesses' responsibility is to testify that the will is genuine and validly executed, and that the testator was competent and free from restraint. These points are the bases for objections in

4. Matter of Putnam, 257 N.Y. 140, 177 N.E. 399 (1931).

5. They can do so at the request of the named executor, the proponent, the attorney or a person interested. McKinney's SCPA 1406(1).

6. See McKinney's SCPA 1406 and discussion immediately preceding this section.

7. McKinney's SCPA 1404(4).

probate proceedings,[8] and the scope of the examination of the attesting witnesses covers "all relevant matters which may be the basis for objections to the probate of the propounded instrument."[9] The broad examination now allowed differs from prior practice which allowed questions only on what happened when the will was executed; an attesting witness could later be subjected to a full examination under the predecessor to CPLR Article 31.[10] The current statute combines the two examinations, and the examining party is entitled to one full examination of the attesting witnesses and cannot examine them again unless the court allows it.[11] The court allows it rarely, usually in cases of newly discovered evidence, and even then it may restrict the examining party to questions about new matters only and prohibit him from questioning the attesting witnesses on any matter covered in the original examination.[12] Thus, the SCPA 1404 examination may cover due execution, testamentary capacity, fraud and undue influence and any other matter relating to the probate of a decedent's will. The courts are very liberal in the depth of the inquiry as long as it relates to probate and complies with the "3–2" timing rule, which states that questions asked of attesting witnesses must relate to the period three years before the date of execution of the propounded instrument and two years after it (or through the date of decedent's death if that is sooner).[13] The five-year period can be expanded in special circumstances;[14] the procedure is for the examining party, after finishing the examination relating to the five-year period, to ask the court to allow questions covering an expanded period.

The attorneys for the proponent and the objectant conduct the examination of the attesting witnesses at the courthouse before the official court reporter[15] whether the examination is before or after objections have been filed. If the attesting witness is sick or frail, the court can order examination at the witness's house,[16] or on written

8. See McKinney's SCPA 1408.

9. McKinney's SCPA 1404(4). See discussion of "Objections to Probate," this chapter infra at 101–09.

10. L.1962, c. 308.

11. Matter of Roberg, N.Y.L.J., Dec. 28, 1979, at 6, col. 3 (New York County) (contestant was allowed reexamination of attesting witnesses on the strength of new hospital records, but court refused to reopen probate because reexamination showed nothing on which objections could be based).

12. See Matter of Poon, N.Y.L.J., July 20, 1979, at 7, col. 2 (New York County) (scope of second examination limited to those matters not covered in first).

13. See Uniform Rules of the Surrogate's Court, section 207.24; Matter of Dillon, N.Y.L.J., June 26, 1978, at 12, col. 2 (Bronx) (examination of charity to determine whether attorney-drafter was a beneficiary of the charity's services or an active fundraiser for three years before and two years after the examination).

14. See, e.g., Matter of Ford, N.Y.L.J., Feb. 15, 1980, at 7, col. 3 (New York County), where decedent's chronic alcoholism was considered sufficient to bring the case within the exception to the three-year rule. A close personal relationship between the decedent and another person sometimes qualifies as a "special circumstance," Matter of Kaufmann, 11 A.D.2d 759, 202 N.Y.S.2d 423 (1st Dep't 1960), and sometimes does not, Matter of Heller, N.Y.L.J., July 15, 1985, at 15, col. 3 (New York County).

15. Uniform Rules of the Surrogate's Court, section 207.28.

16. Matter of Howard, N.Y.L.J., April 23, 1984, at 15, col. 2 (Westchester); Mat-

questions,[17] or it can make other appropriate accommodations. If the examination would cause undue hardship on the witness, the court can order testimony to be taken by commission.[18] Usually the proponent examines first to obtain his prima facie proof and then the objectant's attorney examines. In the larger counties ordinarily the surrogates do not preside over the SCPA 1404 examination, but law assistants (acting as referees) [19] are available to make rulings during the examination.

On the return date of process, the court usually asks the parties whether they wish to examine the attesting witnesses under SCPA 1404 and if they say yes, the court usually directs that objections, if any, be filed ten days after the filing of the SCPA 1404 transcript with the court.

In practice, it is the proponent's task to produce the attesting witnesses. In most cases the witnesses are not hostile to the proponent's attorney since they often are either members or employees of his firm or employees or friends of the testator, and a simple telephone call is all it takes to produce the witnesses. If, however, a witness refuses to cooperate, the proponent's attorney should serve a subpoena on the witness if he is in New York or ask the court to direct a commission to obtain his testimony outside New York. The estate pays for the court's copy of the examination, subject to the court's discretion to award costs to the proponent when a decree is signed.[20]

A few cases have placed the burden on the contestant to produce the attesting witnesses for examination and pay their fees.[21] These cases are the exception and not the rule. Since the proponent wants the will admitted to probate, he should do everything possible to produce the witnesses so the SCPA 1404 examination can be completed.

The statements obtained during the examination of attesting witnesses are available to all parties on a motion for discovery and inspection. The probate proceeding is an in rem proceeding in which all parties have a right to any information on whether the decedent had a will or died intestate.[22]

The usual chronology is that the contestant examines the attesting witnesses and then, if the contestant has alleged fraud or undue influence and all requested disclosure is complete, the proponent serves

ter of Vedder, N.Y.L.J., March 20, 1978, at 16, col. 4 (Suffolk).

17. Matter of Shapiro, 14 Misc.2d 942, 178 N.Y.S.2d 840 (Westchester 1958); Matter of Grote, N.Y.L.J., Nov. 26, 1984, at 14, col. 3 (New York County). See McKinney's CPLR 3108.

18. See SCPA 1405(2).

19. See McKinney's SCPA 2609(5).

20. Matter of Mentes, N.Y.L.J., July 1, 1976, at 10, col. 3 (New York County).

21. See Matter of Elias, 128 Misc. 122, 217 N.Y.S. 847 (New York County 1926), appeal denied 222 App.Div. 728, 225 N.Y.S. 294 (1st Dep't 1927). The parties may also stipulate that the objectant shall bear that burden if he wants the examination. See Matter of Sedita, N.Y.L.J., June 20, 1985, at 12, col. 6 (Bronx).

22. McKinney's CPLR 3101(d). See Matter of Roe, 65 Misc.2d 143, 316 N.Y.S.2d 785 (Suffolk 1970).

the contestant with a request for a bill of particulars on those issues.[23] Even if the contestant is dilatory about examining the attesting witnesses, the courts are generally liberal in allowing the examination.[24]

3. COURT'S DISPENSING WITH TESTIMONY OF ATTESTING WITNESSES

EPTL 3–2.1 requires the signatures of two attesting witnesses on a will. Many attorneys follow the sound practice of using three attesting witnesses in the hope that at least two will be available at the time of probate. If one or more of the attesting witnesses are unavailable, however, the court can dispense with their testimony and admit the will to probate on the testimony of one or even none of them under the rules set forth in SCPA 1405.

The court by order or decree can dispense with the testimony of (1) an attesting witness who is dead, absent from the state or incompetent, (2) an attesting witness who after due diligence cannot be found within the state, or (3) an attesting witness who suffers a physical or mental condition that would preclude him from testifying.[25] When the court dispenses with the testimony of an attesting witness, the court may admit the will to probate on the testimony of one other attesting witness. If an attesting witness is dead, the proponent should submit the proof of the death, usually by a death certificate.

If one of the attesting witnesses cannot remember the circumstances of the execution or testifies against the validity or due execution of the will, the court can dispense with his testimony.[26] In this case, besides the testimony of the other attesting witness, the proponent must produce "such other facts as would be sufficient to prove the will," and in practice, these "other facts" are often satisfied by the attestation clause. They could also include the testimony of the attorney-drafter, proof of handwriting, testimony concerning the physical appearance of the will,[27] and testimony concerning declarations made by the testator after the will's execution.[28]

If both of the attesting witnesses forget the circumstances surrounding the execution, the court can admit the will to probate on

23. See Matter of Reynolds, 38 A.D.2d 788, 328 N.Y.S.2d 155 (4th Dep't 1972); Matter of Tribble, 34 Misc.2d 130, 230 N.Y.S.2d 74 (Suffolk 1962).

24. See, e.g., Matter of Gallo, N.Y.L.J., May 8, 1985, at 16, col. 5 (Nassau) (allowing contestant to examine attesting witnesses after proponents had moved for an order of preclusion for failure to file a bill of particulars).

25. McKinney's SCPA 1405(1).

26. McKinney's 1405(3). See Matter of Bright, 20 Misc.2d 789, 189 N.Y.S.2d 234 (New York County 1959), affirmed 12 A.D.2d 745, 210 N.Y.S.2d 754 (1st Dep't 1961) (jury disbelieved testimony of subscribing witness, the sister of the contestant, who testified against the will, and the Appellate Division affirmed); Matter of Zipkin, 3 Misc.2d 396, 153 N.Y.S.2d 783 (Westchester 1956) (will admitted to probate despite conflicting testimony of attesting witness).

27. Matter of Wolf, 11 Misc.2d 936, 176 N.Y.S.2d 671 (New York County 1958).

28. Matter of Price, 254 App.Div. 477, 5 N.Y.S.2d 457 (1st Dep't 1938), affirmed 279 N.Y. 700, 18 N.E.2d 320 (1938).

other proof of the will's validity.[29] This Court of Appeals interpretation seems at first to contradict the statute, which states that "[w]hen an attesting witness has forgotten the occurrence * * * and at least 1 other attesting witness has been examined the will may be admitted to probate upon the testimony of the other witness or witnesses and such other facts as would be sufficient to prove the will." [30] The result is a sound one, however, well-rooted in pre-SCPA law.[31] It is consistent with the spirit of the statute, which permits the court to grant probate without any attesting witnesses' testimony if the attesting witnesses are dead or outside New York. It interprets the statute to mean simply that the court, in a case where one attesting witness forgets the will execution, cannot dispense with the other attesting witness's testimony, but then, if the other witness also forgets the will execution, the court can admit the will to probate if the other proof satisfies the court that the will was validly executed.

Sometimes an attesting witness whose testimony could be obtained with reasonable diligence is not in New York. If a party demands it, the court must order the testimony to be taken by commission, and it may do so on its own whether a party demands it or not.[32]

If all the attesting witnesses are unavailable (dead, incompetent, mentally or physically unable to testify, or outside New York), the proponent must first satisfy the court that they are dead (with death certificates, affidavits of friends or relatives concerning their deaths, or other proof) or missing (by proof of a due diligence search) [33] or unable to testify and then the court may admit the will to probate on the proof of the handwriting of the testator and at least one of the attesting witnesses and other facts sufficient to prove the will (often the attestation clause).[34]

4. NO-CONTEST CLAUSES AND EXAMINATION OF ATTESTING WITNESSES

A testator with a cantankerous relative has a weapon available in the form of a no-contest ("in terrorem") clause which states, essentially, that if any beneficiary contests the will he loses any bequests or devises under it.[35] The beneficiary can, however, examine the attesting witnesses without violating the no-contest clause.[36] In fact he can examine not only the attesting witnesses, but the proponent's other witnesses in the rare instances the proponent has others.[37]

29. Matter of Collins, 60 N.Y.2d 466, 470 N.Y.S.2d 338, 458 N.E.2d 797 (1983), on remand 101 A.D.2d 694, 476 N.Y.S.2d 30 (1984).

30. McKinney's SCPA 1405(3).

31. See McKinney's SCPA 1405, Prac. Comm. at 55–56 (Supp.1984–85).

32. McKinney's SCPA 1405(2). Commissions are discussed in chapter on "Trials," infra 506–07.

33. The due diligence search is discussed in chapter on "Procedure," supra at 55.

34. McKinney's SCPA 1405(4); see Matter of Capezza, N.Y.L.J., December 20, 1979, at 14, col. 3 (Bronx).

35. McKinney's EPTL 3–3.5.

36. McKinney's EPTL 3–3.5.

37. The statute, McKinney's EPTL 3–3.5(b)(3)(D) is not crystal clear on this

5. WITNESS-BENEFICIARIES

Since the court has the power to dispense with the testimony of an attesting witness who is absent or dead, when three witnesses subscribed the will, and one is dead, one available and disinterested, and one a beneficiary under the will, the court will not necessarily require the interested attesting witness to testify. It can dispense with the witness-beneficiary's testimony unless someone objects.[38]

SECTION I. THE PROBATE DECREE—COURT SATISFACTION

A decree of probate is the end result of the probate proceedings. A will enjoys no presumption of validity;[1] it must be probated to be validated.[2] The court may not grant the decree admitting the will to probate unless it is satisfied that the will deserves probate.[3] The grounds for the court's denying a will probate are the same as the grounds for objections to probate: lack of testamentary capacity, failure of due execution, fraud and undue influence.[4]

If the court finds that the will was duly executed and that the decedent at the time of execution was competent to make a will and not under restraint, the court must admit the will to probate and the will and decree must be recorded.[5]

Many wills are admitted to probate on waivers,[6] without contest, but even there, if something is out of the ordinary, the Surrogate will personally review the documents to be satisfied that the will should be probated. If the will has any function left to perform, such as the naming of a fiduciary or the revoking of prior wills, the court should

point, phrased as it is "preliminary examination, under McKinney's SCPA 1404, of a proponent's witnesses in a probate proceeding." McKinney's SCPA 1404 refers only to attesting witnesses. In addition, McKinney's EPTL 3–3.5's predecessor, SCA 141, specifically permitted examination of all the proponent's witnesses, while the current law specifies section 1404. However, the law was clearly meant to include other witnesses. See McKinney's SCPA 1404, Practice Commentary at 160 (1967); Matter of Lachman, 100 Misc.2d 21, 418 N.Y.S.2d 512 (New York County 1979).

38. Matter of Chieriko, N.Y.L.J., March 27, 1968, at 21, col. 6 (Kings). Compare Matter of Williams, N.Y.L.J., Feb. 7, 1969, at 19, col. 1 (Westchester) where the court required proof of handwriting of all three attesting witnesses and refused to grant probate on proof of handwriting of two.

Sec. I

1. Matter of Cameron, 47 App.Div. 120, 62 N.Y.S. 187 (3d Dep't 1900), affirmed 166 N.Y. 610, 59 N.E. 1120 (1901); Matter of Kiefer, 78 Misc.2d 262, 356 N.Y.S.2d 520 (Yates 1974).

2. Matter of Ginsburg, 115 Misc.2d 122, 453 N.Y.S.2d 587 (Nassau 1982).

3. McKinney's SCPA 1408.

4. McKinney's SCPA 1408(2).

5. McKinney's SCPA 1408(2). An interesting problem arises if the court is satisfied of the validity of the will, but there is also an earlier joint will containing a contract not to revoke it, and the propounded will does revoke it. In Matter of Chesnin, N.Y.L.J., July 2, 1985, at 12, col. 2 (Bronx), the court properly admitted the propounded will to probate, leaving the beneficiaries under the joint will the right to enforce their claim under a contract theory, citing Matter of Coffed, 46 N.Y.2d 514, 414 N.Y.S.2d 893, 387 N.E.2d 1209 (1979).

6. Waivers are discussed in section on "Persons to Be Cited," this chapter supra at 78.

not refuse probate on the ground that the pre-decease of the beneficiaries makes the dispositive provisions inoperative.[7] If the will's net effect would be the same as though the decedent had died intestate, the court can dispense with probate.[8]

Sometimes the will cannot be admitted to probate exactly the way it was at the decedent's death. This would be true, for example, when the court had to construe a will, or the will was modified by a stipulation of settlement, or parts of a will were deleted, or pages were interchanged, or provisions were added after the attestation clause. In these cases, the court can determine the text or tenor of the will as admitted to probate and may incorporate the will or any part of it into the decree.[9]

In probate and administration proceedings, the Surrogates require a death certificate proving that the decedent is in fact dead.[10] Where the fact of death is not certain and the petition alleges that a missing person is deceased, the court holds a hearing and the proponent submits evidence to justify such an allegation.[11] If the proponent makes adequate proof, the court in its decree reclassifies the missing person as a decedent, and the parties then proceed as in an ordinary probate proceeding.

The court has authority to grant a motion for summary judgment that the instrument offered for probate is not the decedent's will, but in practice the court will grant summary judgment only if the document is egregiously wrong-looking.[12] One rare example was where a non-relative offered hand-written papers of uneven size with glued additions obviously cut from larger pages. Decedent's distributees petitioned for letters of administration and sought, in a motion for summary judgment, a ruling that the instrument was not a will. The court ordered a hearing for production of the missing portions of the instrument [13] and stated that if those missing portions could not be explained, the motion for summary judgment would be granted.[14]

When all parties consent that a portion of a will be admitted to probate and that the balance be litigated, the court, if it is also

7. Matter of Davis, 182 N.Y. 468, 75 N.E. 530 (1905) (will admitted to probate though sole beneficiary and executor had died; court ruled that it at least had the effect of revoking all prior wills); Matter of Sanicola, N.Y.L.J., January 22, 1968, at 18, col. 1 (Kings) (will admitted to probate though sole legatee had predeceased testator).

8. Matter of Santiago, N.Y.L.J., March 28, 1979, at 11, col. 2. (Bronx); Matter of Von Ripper, 95 Misc.2d 952, 408 N.Y.S.2d 686 (New York County 1978).

9. McKinney's SCPA 1402(3)(b).

10. See Uniform Rules of the Surrogate's Court section 207.15.

11. Alleged decedents and the procedure for administering their estates, both temporarily and permanently, are discussed in chapter on "Temporary Administration," infra at 289 et seq.

12. Matter of Pascal, 309 N.Y. 108, 127 N.E.2d 835 (1955) (summary judgment denied though will was handwritten and there was an issue whether will was conditional).

13. This proceeding to discover a lost will is governed by McKinney's SCPA 1401, discussed this chapter infra at 99–100.

14. See Matter of Healy, 60 Misc.2d 447, 304 N.Y.S.2d 63 (Nassau 1969).

satisfied, will admit the uncontested portion to probate.[15] If a will is uncontested but a party challenges the codicil, the sound practice would be to admit the will to probate and impose restrictions on the executor prohibiting him from effectuating any will provisions that would be revoked if the codicil were admitted to probate.[16]

The validity and genuineness of a will cannot be submitted to arbitration; the Surrogate has the responsibility to judge those issues. To delegate it would violate public policy.[17]

The Surrogate can vacate a probate decree if someone presents evidence that raises the issue of that instrument's invalidity. When a subsequent will is offered, for example, along with some creditable evidence of its validity, the court will vacate the earlier decree and set a trial date to determine the validity of the later will.[18]

SECTION J. ANCIENT DOCUMENTS

If a will is very old, the courts will occasionally relax the rules of SCPA 1405 under the ancient document rule of evidence, which permits the court to look to factors like the unsuspicious appearance of the document and the naturalness of the place it was kept over the years. If these conditions exist, the court can admit the will to probate with something less than strict compliance with the formality requirements.[1] The age that makes a document ancient varies somewhat;[2] the attorney should consider involving the ancient document rule in cases where the will is twenty or more years old.[3]

15. Matter of Atlas, 101 Misc.2d 677, 421 N.Y.S.2d 815 (Nassau 1979) (court granted partial probate of that portion of the will directing creation of a trust for decedent's mother).

16. See McKinney's SCPA 1408, Prac. Comm. at 69 (Supp.1986); but see Matter of Okin, 100 Misc.2d 1020, 420 N.Y.S.2d 464 (Westchester 1979), denying both instruments probate on the theory that they were an indivisible whole, and appointing a preliminary executor.

17. Matter of Jacobovitz, 58 Misc.2d 330, 295 N.Y.S.2d 527 (Nassau 1968).

18. See Matter of Lium, N.Y.L.J., June 18, 1985, at 15, col. 2 (Westchester).

Sec. J

1. In Matter of Samelson, 40 Misc.2d 623, 243 N.Y.S.2d 345 (Kings 1963), the court admitted a thirty-eight year old will to probate on proof of the handwriting of the decedent and one attesting witness; it dispensed with proof of the handwriting of the other attesting witness. The decedent had known the missing attesting witness for two years before the execution, and that witness had later returned permanently to his homeland. The court relied heavily on the fact that the witnesses signed the attestation clause stating that the testator was of sound mind and that the will was properly executed. See also Matter of Hehn, 6 Misc.2d 801, 160 N.Y.S.2d 417 (Nassau 1957) (document over thirty years old considered ancient).

2. See Fed.R.Ev. 901(b)(8); 803(17); See Matter of Hehn, 6 Misc.2d 801, 160 N.Y.S. 2d 417 (Nassau 1957) (document over thirty years old); Matter of Samelson, 40 Misc.2d 623, 243 N.Y.S.2d 345 (Kings 1963) (thirty-eight year old document).

3. See also Matter of Hehn, 6 Misc.2d 801, 160 N.Y.S.2d 417 (Nassau 1957); Matter of Barney, 185 App.Div. 782, 174 N.Y.S. 242 (1st Dep't 1919); C. McCormack, Evidence at 401 et seq. (1954).

SECTION K. WAYS OF PROCEEDING WHEN THERE IS NO DOCUMENT

1. ORAL WILLS

A proponent may wish to offer an oral (nuncupative) will for probate. A nuncupative will is valid in New York [1] if it is made in the presence of two witnesses in wartime aboard ship by a member of the armed services, a mariner at sea, or a person accompanying or serving someone in the armed forces, and if the death occurs within one year of making it. If the testator is not a serviceman in a wartime setting, the New York courts will not accept an oral will even if it was valid where made or valid at the testator's domicile, since, besides the oral will in the wartime setting just described, only written and signed wills can be probated in New York.[2] To probate the nuncupative will, the proponent must produce two witnesses who attested the will and can verify its contents.[3] They need not have been present at the same time but they both must testify to all the provisions of the nuncupative will.[4] As with lost or destroyed wills that are admitted to probate, the practice is to have the decree contain the full text of the will.

Occasionally a will is on file in a court of another jurisdiction which will not allow it to be removed to New York, or will allow it to be removed but require it to be returned. Such a will can be probated in New York if the Surrogate in the New York court issues a commission to an authorized person (usually an attorney in the other jurisdiction) to take testimony on its provisions, its existence at the time of the testator's death, and its due execution. The New York probate decree must contain the full text of the will.[5]

2. PROCEEDING TO COMPEL PRODUCTION OF A WILL

An interested person may suspect that a will has been lost or destroyed, and he can use two sections of the SCPA, 1407 and 1401, to locate the will and get it admitted to probate. Section 1407 gives the requirements for probating a will that actually is lost or destroyed, and is discussed presently; section 1401 sets forth a proceeding to compel production of a missing will.

Under SCPA 1401, if an interested person believes that someone is concealing a will or codicil [6] or has destroyed it, that person can summon the "suspect" (or any person likely to have knowledge of the will) and require him to explain. The person to be examined must be

Sec. K

1. McKinney's EPTL 3–2.2.
2. McKinney's EPTL 3–5.1(c).
3. McKinney's SCPA 1404(3).
4. Matter of Thompson, 191 Misc. 109, 76 N.Y.S.2d 742 (Steuben 1948).
5. McKinney's SCPA 1404(2).
6. Although codicils are not specifically mentioned under McKinney's SCPA 1401, they are included in the definition of wills in McKinney's SCPA 103(52), and hence are discoverable under McKinney's SCPA 1401. See McKinney's SCPA 1401, Practice Commentary at 129 (1967).

served with a certified copy of the order and paid a witness fee. The Surrogate can order the production of any will under the respondent's control.

The sole purpose of the proceeding is to compel the production of the will. All other collateral matters, including revocation, due execution, and validity of the instrument, are resolved in subsequent proceedings, usually the probate proceeding, once the instrument's existence has been established.

Anyone authorized to petition for probate of a will can also petition for its production under SCPA 1401. This is accomplished by the incorporation into SCPA 1401 of the permissible probate petitioners listed in SCPA 1402: the court will entertain "the petition of a person authorized under the succeeding section of this act to present a petition for the probate of the will * * *." Because of that incorporation, a "person interested" can use this search tool of section 1401, and the category of "person interested" is quite a broad one. If, for example, a person suspects he was named in a will, he may submit a petition including a verified allegation of his interest, and that suffices to give him the standing of an "interested person." [7]

Even if another will of the decedent has already been admitted to probate, a proceeding can be begun under SCPA 1401 for the production of a will,[8] whether that will was executed subsequently or previously to the one that has been probated.

There is no express time limitation for the commencement of a proceeding under SCPA 1401, but the Surrogate can use his discretion to refuse to order production of wills too remote from the probated instrument.[9]

If the SCPA 1401 examination leads to the production of the will, it is then offered for probate and the parties follow the usual probate procedure.

3. A LOST OR DESTROYED WILL

If a will is in fact lost or destroyed, the proponent has three burdens to meet. He must prove that it was duly executed, and the required proof is identical to that which is required in the ordinary probate proceeding; [10] it is irrelevant whether the proponent is offering an existing will or a lost one. He must also prove all provisions of the will clearly and distinctly by each of at least two credible witnesses or by a copy or draft of the will proved to be true and complete.[11] Usually

7. McKinney's SCPA 103(39).

8. Matter of Work, 151 App.Div. 707, 136 N.Y.S. 218 (1st Dep't 1912).

9. See Matter of Hutton, 35 Misc.2d 992, 232 N.Y.S.2d 608 (Nassau 1962), where the attorney-drafter produced four wills earlier than the one offered for probate, dating back nine years from that instrument, and the court refused to order him to produce even earlier instruments.

10. McKinney's SCPA 1407(2).

11. McKinney's SCPA 1407. Thus, if there are not two witnesses who can testify, but there is proof of the authenticity of a copy or draft of a will, the will may be admitted to probate. This overrules Mat-

the attesting witnesses do not know the contents of a will, but a lost will may nonetheless be admitted to probate where, for example, an attorney drafter's secretary who typed the will can identify a copy or draft of it and state that it is true and complete. Other likely persons able to prove the contents of a lost will include the attorney-drafter or a trust officer nominated as a fiduciary under the instrument. They are not required to remember the exact language of the instrument but must know its substance.[12]

The proponent's third burden is to prove that the will was not revoked.[13] A person can revoke an entire will by executing with the same formalities required for a will another instrument which revokes the former, or by ripping up, burning or otherwise destroying the will with an intention to revoke it.[14] He can revoke part of a will only by an instrument, not by an act of destruction or mutilation.[15] As a practical matter, if part of a will is completely excised or obliterated and the missing part cannot be proved by a copy or witness, the court will admit the will to probate without that clause.[16]

A presumption arises that a lost or destroyed will in the testator's control was revoked by a testator during his lifetime.[17] For example, in one case the decedent's attorney could not find the original of decedent's will and could not remember whether he had kept the original or given it to the decedent. The only copy was in the hands of the non-related sole beneficiary, who was disqualified from testifying about what had happened to the original because of the Dead Man's Statute.[18] The court held that the proponent had not overcome the presumption of revocation and refused to grant probate.[19] It is not, however, impossible to rebut the presumption. For example, in one case the attorney and both disinterested attesting witnesses testified that the attorney had retained the original will, meaning to file it in the Surrogate's Court, and that the attorney had then moved his offices amid abundant chaos. The will, executed only a year before the decedent's death, left the decedent's whole estate to his distributees. The attorney and his wife remembered the entire contents of the will, and the court ruled the presumption of revocation overcome.[20] Similarly, when at the decedent's death the proponent found a copy of the will

ter of Kleefeld, 55 N.Y.2d 253, 448 N.Y.S. 2d 456, 433 N.E.2d 521 (1982).

12. Matter of Musacchio, 146 Misc. 626, 262 N.Y.S. 616 (Madison 1933).

13. See Matter of Young, 82 Misc.2d 871, 371 N.Y.S.2d 114 (Suffolk 1975).

14. McKinney's EPTL 3–4.1(a)(1), (2).

15. McKinney's EPTL 3–4.1(a)(1).

16. See Matter of Steffenhagen, 77 Misc.2d 624, 353 N.Y.S.2d 361 (Cattaraugus 1974), for a comprehensive discussion of revocation.

17. Matter of Fox, 9 N.Y.2d 400, 214 N.Y.S.2d 405, 174 N.E.2d 499 (1961); Matter of Kramer, N.Y.L.J., July 22, 1985, at 14, col. 3 (Westchester); Matter of Danziger, 57 Misc.2d 1014, 293 N.Y.S.2d 979 (Nassau 1968).

18. McKinney's CPLR 4519.

19. Matter of Di Nisio, 54 Misc.2d 10, 280 N.Y.S.2d 999 (Dutchess 1967). See also Matter of Engelken, 103 Misc.2d 772, 426 N.Y.S.2d 894 (Nassau 1980).

20. Matter of Graeber, 53 Misc.2d 640, 279 N.Y.S.2d 429 (Erie 1967); see also Matter of Stolzenberg, N.Y.L.J., March 8, 1979, at 11, col. 4 (Bronx); Matter of Donovan, N.Y.L.J., March 7, 1979, at 11, col. 4 (Bronx).

and the original codicil together among the personal effects of the decedent, the court held that the decedent evidently intended not to revoke the original will and granted probate to the will and codicil. The court held that the decedent would not have retained the original codicil if he desired to revoke the original will.[21]

SCPA 1407 is the statutory formulation of what a proponent has to do when a will was not revoked but was destroyed by someone other than the decedent, or lost. He must rebut the presumption of revocation, prove due execution, and prove the contents of the missing will. If a duplicate of the will exists, the court can admit the duplicate to probate if the proponent has met his burdens.[22]

SECTION L. OBJECTIONS TO PROBATE

1. STANDING TO OBJECT

A person with an interest in the estate which would be jeopardized by admission of the will to probate can object to the petition for probate.[1] With the exception of a fiduciary nominated in an earlier will, who can object under certain circumstances discussed shortly, the objectant's interest must be pecuniary.[2] For example, a distributee who receives nothing (or less than his intestate share) under the will can object, even if the will contains a no-contest clause that causes the beneficiary to lose his bequest if he objects,[3] and a person who would get less in intestacy than under the will cannot object because he has no pecuniary interest.[4] A person who is not a distributee cannot object

21. Matter of Herbert, 89 Misc.2d 340, 391 N.Y.S.2d 351 (Nassau 1977); Matter of Dawson, N.Y.L.J., Nov. 28, 1983, at 15, col. 6 (Kings) (court admitted conformed copy and original of codicil to probate). See also Matter of Kessler, N.Y.L.J., October 5, 1979, at 6, col. 1 (Bronx) (photostat admitted to probate when disinterested witness testified that decedent withdrew the will from her bank vault and stated that it was her will, and presumably gave it to someone for safekeeping).

22. Matter of Leitner, N.Y.L.J., Jan. 9, 1984, at 14, col. 1 (Bronx) (executed duplicate); Matter of DeBeaumont, N.Y.L.J., Feb. 26, 1985, at 11, col. 1 (New York County) (court admitted duplicate will to probate when original had been in attorney's office; attorney had died and proponent proved due execution, testamentary capacity, absence of undue influence and absence of revocation).

Sec. L

1. McKinney's SCPA 1410.

2. See, e.g., Matter of Eisenfeld, 52 Misc.2d 209, 275 N.Y.S.2d 434 (1966) (court on its own motion struck objections of person whose financial interests were same under will as in intestacy); Matter of Haddock, 22 Misc.2d 694, 200 N.Y.S.2d 800 (Nassau 1960) (though children had possible right to letters of administration if will was denied probate, they had no standing to object because they would receive more under the will than in intestacy).

3. See Matter of Lippner, 104 Misc.2d 819, 429 N.Y.S.2d 839 (1980), where the court held that a "forfeiture" clause does not deny standing to contest the will. If the proponent wins and the objections are dismissed, the objectant loses his bequest, but so long as the objectant stands to sustain a pecuniary loss if the will is probated, the testator cannot, by using a no-contest clause, deprive that person of his standing to object.

4. Matter of Stapper, N.Y.L.J., September 22, 1978, at 18, col. 6 (Westchester) (daughter who would receive less in intestacy than under the will had no standing to object to probate); Matter of Haddock, 22 Misc.2d 694, 200 N.Y.S.2d 800 (Nassau 1960) (distributees who would receive 25% in intestacy and 33⅓% under will have no standing to object).

unless he was a beneficiary under an earlier will and is ousted (or given less) by the later one offered for probate.[5] However, a beneficiary who establishes a pecuniary interest has standing to object even if that interest is not directly threatened; that is, he can object to the appointment of a named fiduciary if he believes that fiduciary obtained his nomination by fraud or undue influence.[6] His interest in having the estate administered by an executor freely chosen by the testator is the equivalent of a pecuniary interest.

If the estate is insufficient to satisfy the objectant's legacy though he theoretically has one, he does not risk pecuniary injury and the court will dismiss his objections.[7] If his interest under the will is larger than in intestacy, but there is a chance that the intestate share will increase, he has standing to object.[8]

While the objectant is frequently a distributee or a legatee under an earlier instrument and hopes to see the whole will denied probate, that does not always have to be the case. The objectant has standing even if he is damaged by the admission of only a part of the will to probate. For example, in one case the objectant was beneficiary of one-half the residuary estate, and claimed that the clause leaving the other half to the attorney-draftsman's wife was induced by fraud and undue influence. The court held that he had standing, interpreting the statute to read that any person "whose interest in property or in the estate of the testator would be adversely affected by the admission of the will [or any portion thereof] to probate may file objections to the probate of the will or any portion thereof * * *."[9] The court can admit part of the will to probate while deciding the contested issues.[10]

5. Matter of Chadwell, 55 Misc.2d 1033, 286 N.Y.S.2d 725 (Dutchess 1968). See Matter of Turner, 86 Misc.2d 132, 382 N.Y.S.2d 235 (Albany 1976). In Turner, the objectant received the entire estate in each of decedent's two successive wills. On the same day the testator executed the second will, however, he also executed a deed transferring realty to a third party. The probate of the second will would have injured the objectant because it would constitute a finding that the testator had testamentary capacity, thus validating the deed. The court ruled that she had no standing to object.

6. See Matter of Brumer, 69 A.D.2d 438, 419 N.Y.S.2d 155 (2d Dep't 1979), appeal dismissed 48 N.Y.2d 667, 421 N.Y.S.2d 879, 397 N.E.2d 390 (1979). Compare the approach in Brumer, where the court affirmed the Surrogate's decision to admit the will to probate without the fiduciary clause, with that in Matter of Weinstock, 40 N.Y.2d 1, 386 N.Y.S.2d 1, 351 N.E.2d 647 (1976), where the court expressed the view that the entire will could be admitted to probate and the executor subsequently removed under McKinney's SCPA 709. The former is the more accepted practice. See McKinney's SCPA 1410, Practice Commentary at 78 (Supp.1984–85).

7. Matter of Vance, 263 App.Div. 840, 31 N.Y.S.2d 694 (2d Dep't 1941).

8. Matter of Basile, 63 Misc.2d 845, 313 N.Y.S.2d 513 (Suffolk 1970).

9. See McKinney's SCPA 1410, Prac. Comm. at 82 (Supp.1986); Matter of Wharton, 114 Misc.2d 1017, 453 N.Y.S.2d 308 (Westchester 1982).

10. Matter of Atlas, 101 Misc.2d 677, 421 N.Y.S.2d 815 (Nassau 1979) (where objections related to residuary clause, court allowed probate of part of will that provided for trust for decedent's elderly mother). But see Matter of Okin, 100 Misc.2d 1020, 420 N.Y.S.2d 464 (Westchester 1979), where the court refused to admit the will to probate when objections had been leveled against the codicil.

The parties may enter into an agreement that limits the time during which the objectant can file his objections.[11]

There can be a preliminary hearing on the contestant's status, but more often the objectant is not put to such a test; [12] if it appears that the objectant has standing to make objections, he can do so.[13]

An executor nominated in an earlier will whose nomination is superseded by the will offered for probate cannot object to probate unless he has some better reason to do so than the loss of the commissions he would have earned.[14] The legislature passed this provision in 1971 to ensure that such deposed fiduciaries could not thwart settlement of a probate contest.[15] The superseded fiduciary can, however, object for "good cause," which is determined by the court. It can include allegations of fraud, undue influence or lack of testamentary capacity.[16] This good cause standard seeks to strike a balance. The legislature did not want to cut out completely a person who may very well have pertinent facts regarding the testator's estate plan and the voluntariness and validity of the will, but it also wanted to eliminate the possibility that a nominated fiduciary would try to thwart probate of the will or a family settlement of a will contest.[17] Toward this end, the Surrogate can impose some conditions on the fiduciary; in one case the court permitted the fiduciary nominated in the earlier will to object to probate on condition that he agree not to object to a compromise among family members and not to appeal (unless someone else also appealed) from the order of probate.[18] The "good cause" standard also

11. Matter of Greenspan, 43 A.D.2d 998, 352 N.Y.S.2d 263 (3d Dep't 1974), affirmed 36 N.Y.2d 737, 368 N.Y.S.2d 162, 328 N.E.2d 791 (1974).

12. See Matter of Chadwell, 55 Misc.2d 1033, 286 N.Y.S.2d 725 (Dutchess 1968).

13. See Matter of Rikert, 25 Misc.2d 492, 205 N.Y.S.2d 498 (Dutchess 1960) (contestant did not have to refute the revocation of a prior instrument); Matter of Cohen, 151 Misc. 98, 270 N.Y.S. 907 (Kings 1934) (contestant did not have to prove validity of a prior instrument). See also Matter of Lefante, N.Y.L.J., Oct. 30, 1978, at 14, col. 5 (Kings), where the court found that a distributee may, after proving his relationship with the (male) decedent, rely on the presumption of legitimacy and establish his standing to file objections if no one rebuts that presumption. Under current law a person's status as distributee (and hence, his right to object) would be determined by the rules governing proof of paternity, McKinney's EPTL 4-1.2, discussed in chapter on "Administration," infra at 130-32.

14. McKinney's SCPA 1410; Matter of Hatzistefanou, 77 Misc.2d 594, 354 N.Y.S.2d 553 (New York County 1974).

15. L.1971, c. 362; Legislative Note to 1971 Senate 3510, Assembly 5379.

16. See, e.g., Matter of Melcher, 54 A.D.2d 830, 388 N.Y.S.2d 97 (1st Dep't 1976) (executor nominated in earlier will objected to testator's competence when later will was executed); Matter of Fields, N.Y.L.J., Feb. 23, 1978, at 11, col. 1 (New York County) (fact that decedent had been admitted to a hospital for a terminal disease was sufficient to constitute good cause); Matter of Silverman, 91 Misc.2d 125, 397 N.Y.S.2d 319 (New York County 1977) (executor nominated in earlier will objected because testator was very weak when second will was executed).

17. See Matter of Molnar, 76 Misc.2d 126, 350 N.Y.S.2d 855 (New York County 1973).

18. Matter of Molnar, 76 Misc.2d 126, 350 N.Y.S.2d 855 (New York County 1973).

helps the court to meet its obligation not to admit a will to probate unless satisfied with its validity and genuineness.[19]

2. PROCEDURE

The objectant should file the objections in court and send copies of the objections to all persons who have appeared in the probate proceeding and demanded copies of all pleadings.[20] He should do so by the return date of process or, if an SCPA 1404 examination of attesting witnesses occurs,[21] within ten days after the return of process. At the time of filing, the objectant should pay the filing fee.[22] The court has discretion to extend the time for filing objections [23] and does so liberally if no prejudice occurs to the proponent.[24] The parties can also agree to a different return date for objections.[25]

SECTION M. NOTICE OF OBJECTIONS

When the contestant has filed the objections, the proponent must then give notice of the objections to all persons named in the will who have not appeared in the probate proceedings by attorney,[1] even persons who have received process or waived process, if they did not appear in the proceeding by attorney. They have to get notice of the objections so they can appear and argue for the will's validity.[2] The court directs the time and manner of giving notice.[3]

Although the proponent serves notice and not process, this notice is jurisdictional in nature. A party who does not get notice of objections is not bound by the decree that issues after the proceeding,[4] and conversely, if he does get notice, he is bound by the decree whether he appears or not.[5] Thus, although it is the proponent's job to serve the notice, in reality the objectant has the stake in making sure that all

19. McKinney's SCPA 1408, discussed this chapter supra at 95–97.

20. McKinney's SCPA 302, discussed in chapter on "Procedure," supra at 58.

21. McKinney's SCPA 1404, discussed this chapter supra at 90–93.

22. McKinney's SCPA 2402. If several objectants file the same set of objections, only one filing fee is due. Calabrese v. Tomlinson, 106 A.D.2d 843, 484 N.Y.S.2d 242 (3d Dep't 1984).

23. McKinney's SCPA 1410.

24. See, e.g., Matter of Mills, N.Y.L.J., November 9, 1978, at 14, col. 3 (Bronx).

25. McKinney's SCPA 1410 permits the parties to extend the time for filing objections in cases where the objectant intends to examine the attesting witnesses, McKinney's SCPA 1410, and where the parties stipulate to a different date whether or not the examination will take place, and the court can set the return date.

Sec. M

1. McKinney's SCPA 1411(1)(b)(ii).

2. See, by analogy, Matter of Clark, 24 Misc.2d 1001, 205 N.Y.S.2d 445 (Nassau 1960), where a special guardian concluded that the will was not duly executed and the proponent ultimately conceded that it was not. The court ordered the proponent to submit a petition for denial of probate and to serve all interested parties with process.

3. McKinney's SCPA 1411(3).

4. McKinney's SCPA 1411(5).

5. See Matter of Gehlert, 179 Misc. 193, 38 N.Y.S.2d 151 (Westchester 1942). See also Matter of Vail, 120 Misc. 430, 198 N.Y.S. 661 (Orange 1923), where the court said that a person served with notice is a party to the action and therefore subject to examination.

necessary parties have received it. If the proponent fails to give notice of objections, the court can authorize another party to do so, so if the objectant discovers that a necessary party has not received notice, he should bring that to the court's attention and the court will allow him to arrange for service of the notice. Whatever the theory for contesting the will, a legatee named in it is a necessary party and the court should stay all other pre-trial proceedings until the legatee is given notice and an opportunity to be heard.[6]

The notice of objections must give the testator's name and the names and addresses of the proponent and all those named in the will who have not appeared by attorney. It must state that the will was offered for probate and that objections were filed, and must state the date on which the court will hear the objections.[7]

A person with objections to the probate of only part of a will may find himself in the interesting position of objecting to probate on his own behalf and being a person with a right to notice of objections by another person. This dual role is logically permissible; the right to appear in the proceeding relating to another person's objections does not take away a person's right to lodge his own objections to probate of the will.[8]

SECTION N. THE CONTESTANT'S PROOF—UNDUE INFLUENCE AND FRAUD

If a person coerced the testator into writing and executing a will, it is not the testator's will at all, for it does not express his wishes. The same is true if a person exercised undue influence on the testator; the will cannot be admitted to probate.

Undue influence is a question of fact. To be undue, the influence must have been true moral coercion that destroyed the testator's ability to act independently. When undue influence is exerted, the testator does what is against his own wishes because he cannot refuse or is too weak to resist.[1] Undue influence is a systematic working away at the testator's mind. It can be in the form of force, flattery, threats, appeals to the testator's prejudices, or play on his emotions.

Exercising some control over the testator's activities, giving advice and trying to persuade the testator may be influence, but is not undue influence unless the testator's free will was overcome.[2] Unless the

6. Uniform Rules of the Surrogate's Court section 207.26(c); Matter of Holden, 75 Misc.2d 905, 349 N.Y.S.2d 261 (Dutchess 1973) (court stayed proceedings for 30 days from filing proof of service).

7. McKinney's SCPA 1411(1).

8. Matter of Wharton, 114 Misc.2d 1017, 453 N.Y.S.2d 308 (Westchester 1982) (co-residuary legatee entitled to file objections to part of will; irrelevant that she would receive a notice of objections filed and could appear in the proceeding).

Sec. N

1. Matter of Walther, 6 N.Y.2d 49, 188 N.Y.S.2d 168, 159 N.E.2d 665 (1959); Matter of Beneway, 272 A.D. 463, 71 N.Y.S.2d 361 (1947).

2. See, e.g., Matter of Klitgaard, 83 A.D.2d 651, 442 N.Y.S.2d 590 (3d Dep't 1981), where, although the testatrix's son

contestant can produce substantial evidence inconsistent with a finding that the testator's will reflected his real wishes, the court should not permit the issue to go to the jury.[3]

Objectants have made out a prima facie case of undue influence by showing that the "influencer" was a beneficiary under the will, that he participated somehow in the preparation or execution of the will, and that he exercised influence on the testator.[4] It is not sufficient to show that the influencer had an opportunity to exert undue influence and the motive to do so without some other evidence of the influence.[5]

Because undue influence is a question of fact, the court will consider all the circumstances: the relationship between the testator and the influencer, the opportunity for exerting the influence, the relationship of the testator with the (other) natural objects of his bounty, the physical, mental and emotional condition of the testator,[6] the role of independent counsel in the drafting and execution of the will, the will provisions, the existence and provisions of former wills, the testator's contact with his family or other loved ones, his knowledge of what was in the will, the naturalness of the will provisions, the size of the bequest for the influencer, the whereabouts of the influencer during the will execution, and the testator's dependence on the influencer,[7] and prior judgments against the influencer finding undue influence against other testators.[8]

A very common issue arising in undue influence cases is the validity of a bequest to someone in a confidential relationship with the testator, such as an attorney, guardian, clergyman, doctor, or (probably) nursing home director.[9] If the contestant can show the confidential relationship and some other circumstance that could point to undue influence, the jury (or judge as trier of the facts) can infer that undue influence was exercised. The burden of proof is the same as in the ordinary undue influence case, namely that the contestant must prove

lived with her and exercised control over her activities, the contestant could not prove that the son influenced her to make a will against her wishes.

3. Matter of Fiumara, 47 N.Y.2d 845, 418 N.Y.S.2d 579, 392 N.E.2d 565 (1979).

4. Matter of Walther, 6 N.Y.2d 49, 188 N.Y.S.2d 168, 159 N.E.2d 665 (1959); Matter of Hedges, 100 A.D.2d 586, 473 N.Y.S.2d 529 (2d Dep't 1984).

5. Matter of Burke, 82 A.D.2d 260, 441 N.Y.S.2d 542 (2d Dep't 1981).

6. Matter of Stacer, 13 A.D.2d 164, 214 N.Y.S.2d 746 (4th Dep't 1961).

7. See, e.g., Matter of Mahnken, 92 A.D.2d 949, 460 N.Y.S.2d 671 (3d Dep't 1983), where the court especially weighed two factors: first that decedent had contact with his friends and community, and second that a prior will had, like the contested will, left nothing to his children, in dismissing the objection of undue influence.

8. See Matter of Brandon, 79 A.D.2d 246, 436 N.Y.S.2d 329 (2d Dep't 1981), affirmed 55 N.Y.2d 206, 448 N.Y.S.2d 436, 433 N.E.2d 501 (1981) (court allowed two prior judgments against proponent decreeing that he had exercised undue influence against nursing home residents, as evidence of a common scheme).

9. See Matter of Arnold, 125 Misc.2d 265, 479 N.Y.S.2d 924 (Bronx 1983), where the court subjected the relationship between a decedent and the person with responsibility for his day-to-day care in a nursing home to the Putnam scrutiny, but found that under the circumstances, no inference of undue influence could be drawn. See also Matter of Harris, N.Y. L.J., March 14, 1984, at 12, col. 6.

undue influence by a preponderance of the evidence, but once the contestant shows the confidential relationship and other circumstances, such as a change in the dispositive provisions of the will, or a motive and opportunity for exercising undue influence, the influencer has to come forward with some evidence to rebut or the judge or jury can infer that he did unduly influence the testator,[10] even without direct proof of undue influence.[11]

If an issue of undue influence arises out of a confidential relationship, the court must inquire into it even if no one objects.[12] Very commonly the testator makes a bequest to the attorney-drafter or a close relative of the attorney-drafter, and the attorney is then obliged to explain the circumstances and to show that his relationship with the testator does not give rise to a finding of any improper influence.[13] In practice the attorney does this by an affidavit, sometimes supported by an affidavit of the attesting witnesses. The court will consider the long relationship of the attorney with the testator,[14] the lack of objections, the other provisions of the will,[15] the biological relationship, if any, between the testator and the attorney, the size of the bequest,[16] and the provisions in prior wills.

Because of the added expense and delay in these cases, the attorney whose client wishes to leave him a bequest should suggest that the client retain another (independent) attorney to draft the will.

The objectants have a right to examine the proponent on all relevant non-privileged evidence.[17] The court can decide the issue of

10. Matter of Putnam, 257 N.Y. 140, 177 N.E. 399 (1931).

11. See Matter of Doe, N.Y.L.J., June 3, 1985, at 15, col. 5 (Queens) (court rejected attorney-beneficiary-son's testimony on testator's capacity and found undue influence); Matter of Thompson, N.Y.L.J., May 7, 1985, at 15, col. 6 (Nassau).

12. Matter of Arnold, 125 Misc.2d 265, 479 N.Y.S.2d 924 (Bronx 1983); Matter of Zurkow, 74 Misc.2d 736, 345 N.Y.S.2d 436 (New York County 1973).

13. Matter of Putnam, 257 N.Y. 140, 177 N.E. 402 (1931). If the attorney-drafter is given a bequest either to keep for himself or to distribute among the decedent's relatives and charities, he will not have to submit a Putnam affidavit if he distributes the property among the designated beneficiaries and has no pecuniary benefit. Matter of Kelly, N.Y.L.J., June 12, 1985, at 14, col. 5 (Bronx).

14. See Matter of Schmitz, 104 A.D.2d 1093, 481 N.Y.S.2d 14 (2d Dep't 1984), where the testator left property to the attorney-drafter's wife, and the testator's cousins objected on the ground of undue influence. The court granted probate on the theory that the attorney-drafter's wife was a lifetime friend and the most natural object of the decedent's bounty.

15. See, e.g., Matter of Arnold, 125 Misc.2d 265, 479 N.Y.S.2d 924 (Bronx 1983), where the bequest to the attorney-drafter's wife, a friend of testator's, was one of several to friends. See also Matter of Thompson, N.Y.L.J., May 7, 1985, at 15, col. 6, where the court refused to set aside the jury's finding of undue influence despite the testator's long-standing relationship with his attorney-drafter-neighbor, because, inter alia, the testator left no bequests to other neighbors with whom he was even more friendly.

16. See, e.g., Matter of Klinko. N.Y.L.J., April 10, 1985, at 12, col. 2 (Bronx), where the court admitted to probate a will leaving $30,000 to the attorney and his brother out of an estate of $500,000. The court considered the relative modesty of the bequest along with the long-standing relationship between the attorney and the testator in rejecting any inference of undue influence.

17. McKinney's CPLR 3101; Allen v. Cromwell-Collier Publishing Co., 21 N.Y.2d 403, 288 N.Y.S.2d 449, 235 N.E.2d 430 (1968); Matter of Fox, 473 N.Y.S.2d 631

undue influence at the probate proceeding or at a later discovery proceeding.[18]

Fraud is a related ground for objections to probate, usually pleaded together with undue influence but conceptually different from it. The fraud must induce the will in order to invalidate it. For example, if the decedent had a falling-out with his child and ordered the child out of the house, and later someone told a malicious lie about that child, the lie could not be said to have necessarily caused the disinheritance, and therefore does not invalidate the will.[19] Similarly, if a decedent leaves money to the woman he thought he was married to for fifty years, while in reality she had defrauded him into marrying her, knowing that she had not dissolved her former marriage, the fraud may have induced the marriage but the years of faithful "marriage" probably induced the bequest, so the fraud should not invalidate the bequest. On the other hand, if the spouse defrauded the testator into marriage in order to get the bequest, it would affect the validity of the will.[20]

There is authority that the issue of fraud can be raised at the accounting proceeding even if not raised at probate.[21] There is also authority that if the person committing the fraud was in a fiduciary relationship with the person on whom it was committed, such as attorney-client or trustee-beneficiary, the burden shifts to the one accused of fraud because of his superior knowledge of the facts.[22]

The court will usually frame the issues for the jury.[23] A typical order framing the issues would read as follows:

> A trial may be had with respect to the following issues of fact:
>
> 1. Did testatrix subscribe the paper offered for probate at the end thereof in the presence of the attesting witnesses or acknowl-

(4th Dep't 1984) (discovery of proponent's knowledge of decedent's assets and her dispositions of assets within three years of her death).

18. See Matter of Brandon, 78 A.D.2d 246, 436 N.Y.S.2d 329 (2d Dep't 1981), affirmed 55 N.Y.2d 206, 448 N.Y.S.2d 436, 433 N.E.2d 501 (1981).

19. Matter of Sullivan, 229 N.Y. 440, 128 N.E. 594 (1920).

20. Matter of Rockwell, 2 N.Y.S. 378 (Sup.Ct.1888).

21. Matter of Laflin, N.Y.L.J., June 14, 1984, at 16, Col. 2 (Nassau), affirmed 111 A.D.2d 924 (2nd Dep't 1985); Matter of Harris, 123 Misc.2d 247, 473 N.Y.S.2d 125 (Nassau 1984). In *Harris* the attorney-drafter and his partner had been nominated as executors. At the final accounting, the co-executors sought two full commissions, which was allowable under McKinney's SCPA 2307, and the objectant argued that the attorneys had procured their nomination by fraudulently misleading the testator about the double commissions. Attorneys are of course not allowed to procure their own appointment as fiduciaries without proper disclosure, Matter of Weinstock, 40 N.Y.2d 1, 386 N.Y.S.2d 1, 351 N.E.2d 647 (1976), and the Surrogate allowed the objectants to raise the issue for the first time on the accounting, on the theory that the Weinstock scrutiny should not cease after probate. The court's other ground for allowing the issue at the accounting stage was that it went to the qualification of the fiduciary under McKinney's SCPA 711(1), which is not limited to the probate petition proceeding.

22. Cowee v. Cornell, 75 N.Y. 91 (1878); Matter of Paul, 105 A.D.2d 928, 482 N.Y.S.2d 121 (3d Dep't 1984); Matter of Levy, 19 A.D.2d 413, 244 N.Y.S.2d 22 (1st Dep't 1963).

23. Orders framing issues are discussed in chapter on "Trials," infra at 501–02.

edge to each of them that such subscription appearing on said paper had been made by her?

2. At the time of making such subscription or acknowledgment did testatrix declare to the attesting witnesses that the paper offered for probate was her last will and testament?

3. Were there at least two attesting witnesses, each of whom signed his or her name at the end of said paper at the request of testatrix?

4. At the time of execution of the paper offered for probate was testatrix of sound mind and disposing memory?

5. At the time of execution of said paper was testatrix free from restraint?

6. Was the execution of said paper by testatrix caused or procured by fraud of the legatees, or by any other person or persons? [24]

An order in an undue influence case should be specific and should not charge unnamed "other persons" with undue influence.[25]

The appellate division can overturn the Surrogate's Court judgment if it is unsupported by the record.[26]

The order framing the issues is not conclusive on either side. The court can during the proceeding or during jury deliberations alter or simplify the questions, submit additional questions, or remove the question from the jury if the evidence raises only questions of law.[27]

SECTION O. CONSTRUCTION OF THE WILL

In the course of the probate proceeding an interested person may petition the court for an interpretation of the will or part of it that seems to be unclear, or for a ruling that a will provision is invalid under the law, or for some other matter of construction.[1] Since the court cannot construe a will that has not been admitted to probate, it will decide the probate issue first and then look to the matter of construction.[2]

Probate is not the only appropriate time for this proceeding; it can also be commenced in an independent construction proceeding or as part of a fiduciary's accounting. The issue itself must be ripe for decision, however.[3]

24. Matter of Glover, N.Y.L.J., Sept. 18, 1959, at 14 (Queens).

25. Matter of Basile, 63 Misc.2d 845, 313 N.Y.S.2d 513 (Suffolk 1970).

26. Matter of Hedges, 100 A.D.2d 586, 473 N.Y.S.2d 529 (2d Dep't 1984).

27. Matter of Greenman, N.Y.L.J., September 28, 1966, at 11 (New York County).

Sec. O

1. McKinney's SCPA 1420.

2. Matter of Zurkow, 74 Misc.2d 736, 345 N.Y.S.2d 436 (New York County 1973); Matter of Rothwachs, 57 Misc.2d 152, 290 N.Y.S.2d 781 (Kings 1968).

3. See Matter of Swett, 52 A.D.2d 330, 383 N.Y.S.2d 770 (4th Dep't 1976), where the will provided for distribution after the

The "interested person" entitled to bring this petition may be the fiduciary who wants to avoid a surcharge if his construction is wrong, a legatee hoping that his legacy is specific so it will not abate so quickly, or a residuary legatee who stands to gain if a specific or general bequest is invalidated. Courts have held that the decedent's relatives cannot seek a construction when any possible reading of the will excludes them as beneficiaries,[4] and that a creditor of a life beneficiary under a trust created by will may not seek a construction.[5] The court can entertain the proceeding or can decide to defer a decision until a later time, such as the accounting.[6] The petitioner must show that it is necessary. If the court entertains the construction proceeding, it issues process and the petitioner arranges to serve it on all persons whose interests could be affected by the construction, usually beneficiaries under the will who have not appeared in the probate proceeding.[7] If someone seeks a construction during another proceeding, the court also orders notice of the request for construction on all the parties who have appeared,[8] since their appearance alone would not assure that they knew of the construction proceeding.

On the return date of process the court may order a hearing and make a decision which it incorporates into a decree. Its decision is based on a systematic reading of the entire instrument to ascertain the testator's intent,[9] and extrinsic evidence is not admissible,[10] unless the will is ambiguous.[11] The burden of proving the testator's intent is on

life beneficiary's death, and the fiduciary sought construction during the life beneficiary's lifetime. The court dismissed the proceeding. But see Matter of Halleran, 28 A.D.2d 1008, 284 N.Y.S.2d 111 (1967) (court decided issue rather than postponing it when it appeared that the postponement might in effect unconstitutionally deprive a person of his property).

4. Matter of Stoffel, 117 Misc.2d 1036, 459 N.Y.S.2d 707 (1983).

5. Matter of Penn Yan Manor Nursing Home, 96 Misc.2d 463, 409 N.Y.S.2d 201 (1978).

6. See Matter of Halleran, 28 A.D.2d 1008, 284 N.Y.S.2d 111 (1967), where the Appellate Division held that the Surrogate should entertain the proceeding if the deferral might amount to an unconstitutional taking. Here the Surrogate had deferred until the widow's death a construction proceeding that might have resulted in payment to her of her intestate share.

7. McKinney's SCPA 1420(1). Because the court has discretion to entertain a proceeding or not and to direct the manner of service and the contents of process, arguably a citation that fails to give notice of the real relief sought is the court's fault, not that of the attorney of the party serving it. In Matter of Axe, 89 Misc.2d 86, 390 N.Y.S.2d 378 (1976), on this reasoning, a person served with process which did not give him notice that his own interest might be affected in the construction proceeding was nevertheless bound by it.

8. McKinney's SCPA 1420(3).

9. See, e.g., Matter of Jones, 38 N.Y.2d 189, 379 N.Y.S.2d 55, 341 N.E.2d 565 (1975); Matter of Bellows, 103 A.D.2d 594, 480 N.Y.S.2d 925 (2d Dep't 1984); Matter of Falvey, 15 A.D.2d 415, 224 N.Y.S.2d 899 (4th Dep't 1969), affirmed 12 N.Y.2d 759, 234 N.Y.S.2d 713, 186 N.E.2d 563 (1962); Matter of Symonds, 79 A.D.2d 24, 434 N.Y.S.2d 838 (4th Dep't 1981); Matter of Outerbridge, 91 Misc.2d 986, 398 N.Y.S.2d 517 (New York County 1977).

10. Matter of Cord, 58 N.Y.2d 539, 462 N.Y.S.2d 622, 449 N.E.2d 402 (1983); Matter of Wierzbieniec, 93 A.D.2d 978, 461 N.Y.S.2d 653 (2d Dep't 1983).

11. E.g., Matter of Ragone, 116 Misc.2d 993, 459 N.Y.S.2d 649 (New York County 1981), modified on other grounds 87 A.D.2d 457, 452 N.Y.S.2d 410 (1st Dep't 1982), appeal dismissed 57 N.Y.2d 1046, 457 N.Y.S.2d 788, 444 N.E.2d 38 (1982); Matter of Taitt, 87 Misc.2d 586, 386 N.Y.S.2d 308 (Bronx 1976).

the one who seeks a construction that that is in fact the testator's intent.[12] The parties adversely affected have a right to appeal, but if they do not, the decree is binding on all parties and their successors in interest.[13]

SECTION P. DECREE OF PROBATE AND ISSUANCE OF LETTERS TESTAMENTARY

When the court is satisfied that the will is valid, it issues a decree admitting the will to probate. At that point, the Surrogate [1] must grant letters testamentary to any person who (i) appears in the proceeding and is entitled to letters under the will and (ii) is eligible [2] (that is, not an infant, incompetent, non-domiciliary alien, felon or person incapable of performing fiduciary duties because of drunkenness, dishonesty, improvidence or want of understanding), and (iii) qualifies [3] (that is, signs an oath, submits a designation of the clerk for service of process, and files a bond if necessary).[4] Mere nomination as executor in a will confers no authority on the nominated person, except to pay a reasonable funeral bill and to preserve assets. He must appear and qualify and obtain letters.[5]

Some testators provide for appointment of a fiduciary on a contingency, such as being of age or being married to a named person. If the contingency happens, the nominated fiduciary can then appear and request letters.[6] Whether he serves with the fiduciaries already serving or ousts them depends on the directions in the will, and if the will is silent the court makes that decision. Notice of this person's application for letters is in the court's discretion,[7] and most courts order service of citations on all interested parties.[8] Since the beneficiaries have the right to seek removal of the fiduciary from office after his appointment,[9] it is logical to give them a chance to voice their objections before his appointment.

12. See, e.g., Matter of Revson, 86 A.D.2d 872, 447 N.Y.S.2d 297 (2d Dep't 1982).

13. McKinney's SCPA 1420(4).

Sec. P

1. Under the New York Constitution, the Supreme Court has concurrent jurisdiction with the Surrogate's Court over the estates of decedents. In the extremely rare case where the Supreme Court entertains a probate proceeding and renders a judgment, the Surrogate must record the will and issue the letters directed by the judgment. McKinney's SCPA 1414(2). For an old case in which such an event occurred, see Noll v. Ruprecht, 256 App. Div. 926, 9 N.Y.S.2d 651 (2d Dep't 1939), affirmed 282 N.Y. 598, 25 N.E.2d 386 (1940).

2. McKinney's SCPA 707, discussed in chapter on "Fiduciaries," infra at 388–91.

3. McKinney's SCPA 708, discussed in chapter on "Fiduciaries," infra at 391–92.

4. McKinney's SCPA 1414(1).

5. Matter of Coleman, 150 Misc. 76, 269 N.Y.S. 617 (Richmond 1934).

6. McKinney's SCPA 1414(3).

7. Matter of Griffin, 193 Misc. 419, 83 N.Y.S.2d 579 (Erie 1948) (court did not require notice of application).

8. See McKinney's SCPA 1414, Practice Commentary at 357 (1967).

9. McKinney's SCPA 711, discussed in chapter on "Fiduciaries," infra at 393–400.

Some testators give to another person the right to designate an executor. For example, a testator may provide, "I nominate X as my executor, but if X should fail or cease to serve, I direct that my eldest child shall choose a successor executor." If in that case the testator's oldest child chooses Y as successor executor, Y must, upon appearance, file a paper, acknowledged by the eldest child, stating that Y has been chosen.[10]

If the nominated executor obtained his nomination by fraud or constructive fraud, the court can admit the will to probate but refuse to appoint the nominated executor on the ground that no one should profit from his own wrong. The court has sanctioned two different ways of achieving this end: It can admit the will to probate without the clause appointing the fiduciary,[11] or it can admit the entire will to probate but then refuse [12] to issue letters to the nominated executor because of his wrongdoing.[13]

Rarely a proponent files a probate petition and then fails to follow it through. In that case the court can direct the proponent or another interested party to pursue the probate decree and if he does not, appoint the public administrator to do so.[14]

SECTION Q. SUPPLEMENTARY LETTERS

Occasionally a nominated executor cannot qualify at the time of probate because he is a minor or a non-domiciliary alien.[1] If during the course of estate administration he reaches the age of majority or establishes a United States domicile or becomes a citizen, he can petition for supplementary letters testamentary and serve as executor for the duration of the estate administration.[2] In practice, the nominated executor makes the application ex parte and in the petition names the persons interested in the proceeding. The court then has

10. McKinney's SCPA 1414(4).

11. Matter of Brumer, 69 A.D.2d 438, 419 N.Y.S.2d 155 (2d Dep't 1979), appeal dismissed 48 N.Y.2d 667, 421 N.Y.S.2d 879, 397 N.E.2d 390 (1979) (court admitted will to probate without clause naming proponent as sole executrix because he had obtained that nomination against the testatrix's intention).

12. Such refusal would be grounded in McKinney's SCPA 709.

13. Matter of Weinstock, 40 N.Y.2d 1, 386 N.Y.S.2d 1, 351 N.E.2d 647 (1976) (removal of father and son as executors because of their overreaching in obtaining their appointment); Matter of Vermilye, 101 A.D.2d 865, 475 N.Y.S.2d 888 (2d Dep't 1984) (appellate division held removal of preliminary executor on unsubstantiated charge of undue influence was abuse of Surrogate's discretion and ordered resolution of the problem at a probate contest). See discussion of the possible unconstitutional breadth of the court's powers to remove a fiduciary under McKinney's SCPA 719(19) in SCPA 719, Prac.Comm. at 599 (1967).

14. See, e.g., Matter of Hammons, N.Y. L.J., Feb. 27, 1985, at 13, col. 3 (Bronx). See McKinney's SCPA 1402(3)(a); 1418(2); 1116; 1123(j); Matter of Leitner, N.Y.L.J., Aug. 13, 1985, at 11, col. 5 (Bronx).

Sec. Q

1. See McKinney's SCPA 708(2), which states that to qualify one must be eligible, and McKinney's SCPA 707, which states that minors and non-domiciliary aliens are ineligible.

2. McKinney's SCPA 1415.

discretion to require notice to those with an interest in the estate, and usually does so.[3]

When a testator names two executors and one cannot serve because he is an infant or a non-domiciliary alien, the court will issue letters only to the qualified nominee. The statute states that when the infant becomes of age or the alien becomes a domiciliary and there are assets still to administer, this recently qualified executor serves along with the person already serving. If the fiduciary serving was not nominated under the will (an administrator c.t.a.) there is some confusion whether he continues to serve as co-fiduciary.[4]

SECTION R. RENUNCIATION OF LETTERS AND FAILURE TO QUALIFY OR RENOUNCE

If a nominated executor does not want to serve, he may renounce his right to letters by filing an acknowledged renunciation with the court.[1] The nominated executor does not have to explain his decision to renounce, but the renunciation must be clear and unequivocal and cannot be conditioned on subsequent events.[2] The renunciation is not necessarily irrevocable. If no letters testamentary, letters c.t.a. or letters of administration have issued to anyone else, the nominated executor can retract his renunciation merely by giving the court an acknowledged retraction.[3] The court then has discretion as to whether to issue letters to that person or not.[4] If the court has granted letters to someone else, the nominated executor can retract his renunciation only if the fiduciary has ceased to serve (because of death, incompetence or revocation of letters) and no other fiduciary is serving.[5] If a nominated executor tries to retract his renunciation, the court decides who, if anyone, should get notice of the retraction.[6] In practice the court usually orders notice to all persons with an interest in the estate so they will have an opportunity to object to the appointment.[7] It is

3. McKinney's SCPA 1415, Practice Commentary at 364 (1967).

4. See McKinney's SCPA 1415, Practice Commentary at 364 (1967).

Sec. R

1. McKinney's SCPA 1417(1). The appropriate court for filing is the Surrogate's Court with jurisdiction over the estate. McKinney's SCPA 1417(4). See chapter on "Jurisdiction," supra at 1 et seq.

2. See Matter of Kruesi, 25 Misc.2d 73, 206 N.Y.S.2d 3 (New York County 1960) (where husband renounced his appointment as executor on condition that letters be issued to a certain trust company, court held that the alternate executor named in the will would be entitled to letters unless the husband retracted his renunciation within five days).

3. McKinney's SCPA 1417(2). Note that this group does not include letters of temporary administration, and presumably their issuance should not bar the discretionary retraction of a renunciation. See Matter of Mitchell, N.Y.L.J., March 29, 1979, at 16, col. 3 (Suffolk), so holding.

4. McKinney's SCPA 1417(3) says that "letters testamentary may be issued * * *."

5. McKinney's SCPA 1417(2).

6. McKinney's SCPA 1417(3).

7. The basis for their objections would have to be grounds set forth in McKinney's SCPA 709 or 711, such as dishonesty or

then within the court's discretion whether to grant letters to the retracting, renouncing executor or not.[8]

Until a nominated executor files a renunciation, the court cannot take away his right to letters without giving him notice and an opportunity to be heard. In most cases the nominated fiduciary qualifies promptly, as the statute contemplates.[9] However, if the nominated executor neither renounces nor qualifies, the court can order him to qualify within a specified period (set by the court). If he fails to do so, he has, by his neglect, renounced the appointment.[10] The application for this order can be made by a fiduciary, a person interested in the estate, or a creditor.[11] The application can be made fifteen days after probate, or fifteen days after the nominated executor's designation by someone other than the testator if the will gives someone that power, or five days after resolution in the nominated executor's favor of objections to his appointment.[12]

The court's direction to qualify should be served on the nominated executor personally within the state.[13] If the court is satisfied that such service cannot be made, it will order appropriate alternative service.[14] If the executor does not then qualify within the time the court allows, the court signs an order that the nominated executor has renounced his appointment.

The court can even dispense entirely with service on the nominated executor if his whereabouts are unknown. In one case, for example, the decedent left a modest estate and was survived by his son as sole distributee and sole beneficiary under the will. He nominated two fiduciaries who could not be found at the time of probate. The court found that publication for the missing fiduciaries would waste estate assets and appointed the son as sole administrator, subject to the nominated executors' right to be heard on the issue if they returned before the estate was finally settled.[15]

If the nominated executor who defaults under this provision later wants to serve, he is under the same restrictions as the executor who has deliberately renounced; namely, if no fiduciary has yet been appointed, he can file an acknowledged writing and the court may revoke its order, or if the court has appointed a fiduciary, he can ask the court to appoint him only if the fiduciary has died, has become

drunkenness, discussed in chapter on "Fiduciaries," infra at 393–400.

8. McKinney's SCPA 1417(3).

9. See Matter of Stavin, 56 A.D.2d 68, 391 N.Y.S.2d 412 (1st Dep't 1977), affirmed 43 N.Y.2d 669, 400 N.Y.S.2d 817, 371 N.E.2d 535 (1977) (section 711 contemplates quick qualification).

10. McKinney's SCPA 1416(1).

11. McKinney's SCPA 1416.

12. McKinney's SCPA 1416(1).

13. McKinney's SCPA 1416(2).

14. McKinney's SCPA 1416(2).

15. Matter of Dinten, N.Y.L.J., June 29, 1983, at 12, col. 2 (Bronx). It was also significant that the missing fiduciary's sole interest in the estate would have been in commissions, and the courts do not like to slow down the estate administration process when that is the only interest at stake.

incompetent, or has had his letters revoked (and no other fiduciary is serving).[16]

SECTION S. LETTERS OF ADMINISTRATION WITH THE WILL ANNEXED (C.T.A.)

Sometimes a will admitted to probate has failed to name an executor or to provide for selection of one. Sometimes the nominated executor has predeceased the testator or is, at the time of the testator's death, incompetent or unwilling to serve. Sometimes the executor receives letters and subsequently dies or ceases to serve. If for any of these reasons no fiduciary is qualified to act in the estate of a decedent who had a will, the proper procedure is to seek letters of administration "with the will annexed" (c.t.a.).[1] The administrator c.t.a. is actually more akin to an executor than to an administrator; he administers the estate under the terms of the will, not under the rules of intestate administration.[2]

Any person who may petition for probate of the will [3] may apply for letters of administration c.t.a.[4] (that is, persons named in the will or their legal representatives, creditors, parties to lawsuits in which the decedent would have been a party, and other persons interested in the estate).

The following are entitled, in order of priority, to letters of administration c.t.a.[5] The court has no discretion to alter the priorities.

1. The sole beneficiary (or if he is dead, his fiduciary).

2. One or more of the residuary beneficiaries (or if any is dead, his fiduciary).

3. If there is no one from the first two categories available, or if they are not eligible,[6] the court may issue letters to one or more persons interested in the estate (or if any are dead, to their fiduciaries). This would include specific or general legatees or devisees.

As to persons within a class, there is no priority; the court uses its discretion in appointing the administrator c.t.a.[7]

16. McKinney's SCPA 1416(3).

Sec. S

1. McKinney's SCPA 1418.

2. Intestate administration is governed by McKinney's SCPA Article 10 and discussed in chapter on "Administration," infra at 125 et seq.

3. See McKinney's SCPA 1402, discussed this chapter supra at 74–76.

4. McKinney's SCPA 1418(1).

5. McKinney's SCPA 1418(1)(a), (b), (c).

6. Eligibility to receive letters is defined in McKinney's SCPA 707, discussed in chapter on "Fiduciaries," infra at 388–91.

7. See Matter of Fleet, N.Y.L.J., October 12, 1978, at 19, col. 4 (Westchester) (daughter and grandson were residuary legatees; court appointed grandson though daughter claimed a larger share); Matter of Hoard, 78 Misc.2d 1083, 358 N.Y.S.2d 625 (Westchester 1974) (both mother and father of nonmarital child were entitled to letters, and court had discretion to grant them to either). Note that an assignee, who does have a right under McKinney's SCPA 1402 to petition for probate, has no right to serve as administrator c.t.a. See

If a person otherwise entitled to letters is an infant, incompetent or conservatee, the court may instead issue letters of administration c.t.a. to the guardian of the property of the infant, the committee of the property of the incompetent or the conservator of the property of the conservatee.[8] That fiduciary has the same priority as the infant, incompetent or conservatee would have had if not for the disability.[9] If the disabled person has a fiduciary of his person only, and not of his property, that fiduciary is not entitled to letters c.t.a.[10]

Since the fiduciary of a sole beneficiary who survived the decedent and subsequently died has first priority to receive letters of administration c.t.a.[11] a question arises whether that fiduciary can serve if it is a non-New York trust company. For example, assume a decedent left his entire estate to his daughter and named her as executor, and upon her death after the decedent's, a foreign trust company qualified as her executor. That trust company's eligibility depends on the existence of a reciprocity statute enabling New York fiduciaries to qualify in the foreign state.[12] If the other state does not have a reciprocity statute, the foreign fiduciary will be ineligible to serve as administrator c.t.a.,[13] and would also be precluded from consenting to the appointment of a New York administrator c.t.a. That should be true even if the foreign bank is the only one whose consent is required and even if the alternative is appointment of the public administrator. The bank cannot consent because only eligible beneficiaries can consent, and the bank is neither a beneficiary nor eligible.[14]

The beneficiaries can get together and agree to the appointment of a person not otherwise entitled to serve.[15] To do this, all the beneficiaries must themselves be eligible, except that a guardian of the property, committee of the property, or conservator of the property may consent on behalf of a child, incompetent or conservatee,[16] unless the guardian, committee or conservator is foreign.[17] If the chosen fiduciary

Matter of Jordan, 202 App.Div. 710, 195 N.Y.S. 193 (2d Dep't 1922).

8. McKinney's SCPA 1418(5).

9. Matter of Neeley, 64 Misc.2d 419, 314 N.Y.S.2d 683 (Nassau 1970).

10. McKinney's SCPA 1418(5).

11. McKinney's SCPA 1418(1)(a).

12. McKinney's Banking Law 131(3) (1971).

13. See Matter of Edwards, 56 Misc.2d 902, 290 N.Y.S.2d 314 (New York County 1968).

14. In Matter of Edwards, 56 Misc.2d 902, 290 N.Y.S.2d 314 (New York County 1968), the court allowed the bank to consent under a predecessor statute to McKinney's SCPA 1418 which conditioned that consent not on eligibility but on absence of legal disability. The court found that the foreign bank was not under disability and could therefore consent to appointment of a New York attorney as administrator c.t.a.

15. McKinney's SCPA 1418(6).

16. McKinney's SCPA 1418(6).

17. See Matter of Robertson, N.Y.L.J., June 13, 1983, at 14, col. 4 (Queens). The rules governing consent to appointment of an administrator in McKinney's SCPA 1001(7) specifically require that the guardian, committee or conservator consenting for a ward be appointed in New York, while the rules governing consent to appointment of an administrator c.t.a. in McKinney's SCPA 1418(6) do not so limit the guardian, committee or conservator. The definition of a guardian in McKinney's SCPA 103(24), however, includes only those appointed in New York. The late Professor Paul Powers, in his 1983 Practice Commentary to McKinney's SCPA 1418, at

is a trust company or other corporate fiduciary, the rule is further relaxed: even non-domiciliary aliens can consent despite their own ineligibility,[18] and the personal representatives of minors, conservatees and incompetents can consent on their behalf.[19]

If neither a beneficiary nor a person chosen by the beneficiaries is available and eligible, the court will issue letters c.t.a. to the public administrator (or if there is none, to the county treasurer).[20]

If the public administrator refuses to accept letters (because he may have a conflict with another estate), the court may issue them to the petitioner,[21] and if the petitioner refuses to accept them, the court may designate a person to receive letters.[22] In these rare cases the court attempts to have a trust company accept the appointment.

If a corporation is entitled to letters (because it is, for example, a sole or residuary beneficiary), it can serve despite the absence in its charter or in any statute of authorization to act as fiduciary.[23] Because of this, a charitable institution can administer an estate in which it has an interest although it is otherwise not authorized to act as an executor or administrator of an estate. Though the statute does not specify, it is interpreted to apply only to domestic corporations.[24]

When a fiduciary dies and not much remains to be done to wind up the estate, the fiduciary of the deceased fiduciary can, with a court order, finish the estate administration.[25] In those circumstances, an administrator c.t.a. will not be necessary; the fiduciary of the deceased fiduciary can distribute the estate.[26]

When someone petitions for letters c.t.a., the court must issue process and the petitioner must arrange for its service on all persons with an equal or prior right to the petitioner's to serve as administrator c.t.a., including minors, incompetents and conservatees. Even if no fiduciary has yet been appointed for the person under legal disability,

106–107 (Supp.1986) impliedly agreed that only New York guardians can consent.

18. McKinney's SCPA 1418(7). Prior to a 1985 amendment to McKinney's SCPA 1418(7), L.1985, c. 536, sec. 1, a literal reading of McKinney's SCPA 1418(7) would appear to have precluded a trust company from acting if there were infant, incompetent or conservatee beneficiaries, but arguably McKinney's SCPA 1418(6) would have allowed those parties to consent, through a legal representative, to a trust company's (or anyone else's) appointment.

19. See McKinney's SCPA 1418(7), Prac. Comm at 373 (1967).

20. McKinney's SCPA 1418(2); Matter of Hungerford, 117 Misc.2d 272, 458 N.Y.S.2d 177 (Nassau 1983) (since no application was made either by residuary beneficiary or trustee, court issued letters to public administrator).

21. The petitioner might be a creditor who, though he has a right to petition for appointment of an administrator c.t.a., does not have a right to serve, unless the court grants letters under this section.

22. McKinney's SCPA 1418(3).

23. McKinney's SCPA 1418(4).

24. See Matter of Bolton, 65 Misc.2d 846, 319 N.Y.S.2d 113 (Erie 1971) (court granted letters after ascertaining that corporation had no debts and was domestic); Matter of Duelund, 177 Misc. 569, 31 N.Y.S.2d 4 (Bronx 1941), citing White v. Howard, 46 N.Y. 144 (1871).

25. McKinney's SCPA 2207. That section is discussed in detail in chapter on "Accounting," infra at 210–12.

26. McKinney's SCPA 1418(8).

that person should be cited.[27] Then, if an interested person wants to petition for appointment of a guardian, committee or conservator to seek appointment as administrator c.t.a., they can do so. If they do not, that should end the disabled person's interest in the proceeding, and the court should not appoint a guardian ad litem.[28]

If a party has waived service or renounced appointment, he need not be served. If an otherwise necessary party is not a New York domiciliary, the court can in its discretion dispense with service on him.[29] After service of process, the proceedings are the same as those for appointment of an administrator in the estate of an intestate; that is, if there are no objections, the court reviews the papers submitted and determines whether letters should issue, and if there are objections, the court holds a hearing.[30]

SECTION T. PRELIMINARY LETTERS TESTAMENTARY

Frequently delays occur in probate. For example, if someone objects to probate, the court will not grant the decree of probate until examinations, negotiations and perhaps a hearing or trial have taken place. If the proponent does not know the identities or whereabouts of the decedent's distributees, he will have to conduct a time-consuming search. Since the executor nominated in the will receives letters only when probate is granted, a delay in probate means a delay in the appointment of a fiduciary. If that delay could be detrimental to the estate (for example because there is a depreciating asset that needs to be sold or property, such as securities, that needs active management), the executor named in the will can ask the court for preliminary letters testamentary.[1] If the court grants them, the estate administration can proceed during the resolution of the problem that delayed probate. This very flexible procedure gives the court broad (but, as we will discuss, not unlimited) discretion in supervising the administration.

Before the creation of preliminary letters in 1963,[2] the only device available in cases of delayed appointment of a fiduciary was temporary letters of administration,[3] which was unsatisfactory for several reasons. The powers of a temporary administrator are severely limited.[4] The temporary administrator must file a bond, an expense to the estate

27. For the ways to cite a person under disability, see McKinney's SCPA 307 and the chapter on "Procedure," supra at 45–46.

28. McKinney's SCPA 1419, Practice Commentary at 110 (Supp.1986).

29. McKinney's SCPA 1419.

30. See chapter on "Administration," infra at 125 et seq.

Sec. T

1. McKinney's SCPA 1412.

2. L.1963, c. 405, SCA 153–a.

3. See McKinney's SCPA Article 9 and discussion of temporary letters of administration infra at 289 et seq.

4. McKinney's SCPA 903, discussed in chapter on "Temporary Administration," infra at 297–301.

frequently not imposed on a preliminary executor.[5] In addition, under prior law the probate proceeding had built-in potential for the following extortionist plan: a person feeling aggrieved by his poor treatment in the will could object to its probate, whether or not the objections were supportable by fact or law, knowing that in a contest the court would have to appoint a temporary administrator and hoping to receive an offer for settlement. That hope was frequently realized because the named executor was willing to pay the nuisance value of the claim just to be able to proceed with administration. Because of the current availability of preliminary letters to the named executor, an office that permits rather broad powers and allows administration to proceed almost normally, that ploy is now much less useful.[6] Now, after the nominated executor applies for preliminary letters, if the court believes that probate will follow in due course and has no reason to doubt the eligibility or qualification of the executor, it will grant preliminary letters.

1. PROCEDURE

Because preliminary letters are meant to be used in interim or emergency situations, the statute governing them provides considerable flexibility and leaves much to the court's discretion. There are, however, some minimum non-discretionary requirements.

The named executor can file the request for preliminary letters testamentary only after filing the probate petition.[7] If the court sees that a fiduciary is needed immediately, it can entertain the request and grant the letters even before issuing process in the underlying probate proceeding.[8] This usually occurs when the decedent's distributees are unknown or their whereabouts are unknown, and the proponent must conduct a diligent search. To obtain a grant of preliminary letters before process issues, the petitioner must produce whatever proof the court considers necessary,[9] usually a statement as to why process cannot be served, what steps have been taken to locate distributees, what steps remain to be taken, and how long a delay is anticipated.[10] The proof required is clearly less than an affidavit of due diligence, because the statute and its legislative history contemplated a pre-citation issuance of letters in cases where the due diligence search is the very cause of the delay.[11] If the due diligence search had been

5. McKinney's SCPA 806.

6. The creation of preliminary letters was one step in an attempt by the Bennett Commission to simplify probate without going quite as far as probate in common form. The other steps toward simplification were the use of attesting witnesses' affidavits under McKinney's SCPA 1406 and administration of small estates under McKinney's SCPA Article 13.

7. McKinney's SCPA 1412(1).

8. McKinney's SCPA 1412(1).

9. McKinney's SCPA 1412(1).

10. McKinney's SCPA 1412, 1971 Practice Commentary at 96 (Supp.1986).

11. McKinney's SCPA 1412(1) was amended by L.1971, c. 883, to permit the issuance of preliminary letters before process issues. The legislature acted for the specific purpose of extending preliminary letters to those cases where a diligent search was needed. See McKinney's SCPA 1412, Prac.Comm. at 96 (Supp.1986). See

conducted, process could issue and this part of the statute would have no utility. The broad flexibility incorporated into the language "upon such proof as the court shall deem necessary" allows the issuance of preliminary letters before the diligent search.[12]

The court must order notice of the request for preliminary letters to be served on any other named executors in the will not joining in the application,[13] because they have a right to letters equal to the petitioner's. Successor executors are not entitled to notice unless their predecessor has died or ceased serving.[14] If a later will of the same testator is on file in the court, notice must also be given to the named executors in that will,[15] because they have a prior right to preliminary letters unless good cause is shown.[16] The named executor in the later will must offer the later will for probate before he can get preliminary letters.[17] If preliminary letters were already issued to someone named in an earlier will, the named executor in the later will can seek revocation of the prior letters in addition to his own appointment as preliminary executor. The court then has the discretion to appoint the executor named in the later will, or appoint both, or confirm the appointment it already made and deny letters to the executor named in the later will if good cause is shown.[18] The manner and time of serving the notice are within the court's discretion, and the court can even order notice after it issues the preliminary letters if the estate needs a fiduciary immediately.[19]

Any person with a right to serve as executor equal or prior to the applicant's can join in the application for preliminary letters [20] or can request that preliminary letters also be issued to him if the court has already granted preliminary letters.[21]

A preliminary executor must qualify by signing an oath, filing a designation of the clerk of the court for service of process and filing a

the description of a diligent search in chapter on "Procedure," supra at 55.

12. McKinney's SCPA 1412, Practice Commentary at 96 (1986).

13. McKinney's SCPA 1412(2)(a).

14. McKinney's SCPA 1412(2)(a).

15. McKinney's SCPA 1412(2)(a).

16. McKinney's SCPA 1412(2)(a). See Matter of Auerbach, N.Y.L.J., Aug. 4, 1968, at 10, col. 1 (New York County), where the court appointed executors named in both earlier and later wills because it found that good cause was shown in two ways: first, when the decedent executed the second will, incompetency proceedings were pending, and she was in fact declared incompetent, and second, one of the executors in the earlier will had no interest in the estate except in the commissions he would earn.

17. McKinney's SCPA 1412(2)(b).

18. See Matter of Ellenberg, N.Y.L.J., June 12, 1978, p. 13, col. 6 (New York County), where the court granted preliminary letters to the executor named in the will rather than to the one named in the codicil because the executor named in the codicil had drafted it, and his son and wife were the other executors named in it. The draftsman had died before the decedent and his estate had claims against the decedent's estate. The court, noting that the two estates would be in litigation over the claim and that the other named executors in the codicil were distributees of the draftsman, found those facts to be sufficient good cause to deny preliminary letters to the wife and son.

19. McKinney's SCPA 1412(2)(a).

20. McKinney's SCPA 1412(2)(a).

21. McKinney's SCPA 1412(2)(b).

bond if necessary. It is necessary if the will specifically requires it, and even if the will is silent or dispenses with it,[22] the court has discretion to order the preliminary executor to file a bond and sometimes does so in cases where an interested person objects to the appointment.[23] The statute provides, "Upon due qualification * * * and upon the issuance of process, preliminary letters testamentary must thereupon be issued to the person or persons who appear to the court to be entitled thereto * * *."[24] However, a careful analysis of the statute reveals that the court still has discretion to refuse to grant a nominated executor preliminary letters if it believes that the named executor is not an appropriate interim fiduciary. If, for example, some evidence points to the conclusion that the nominated executor exercised undue influence on the testator or procured the will by fraud, the court can refuse to grant him preliminary letters on the ground that in order to qualify he must be able to state in his oath that he is eligible to serve, and a dishonest person is not eligible.[25] Moreover, since the court can always revoke preliminary letters where it believes that to be in the best interests of the estate,[26] the court can base its refusal to grant the letters in the first place on the theory that it is pointless to issue the letters and then immediately revoke them.[27] If the testator named an alternate executor, the court will grant him preliminary letters; if not, it will appoint a temporary administrator. However, the showing of good cause for not appointing the nominated executor must be substantial, or the court will appoint that nominated executor.[28]

22. McKinney's SCPA 1412(5); McKinney's SCPA 708. Even if the will dispenses with the necessity of a bond, the court can nevertheless order one if it believes it necessary. McKinney's SCPA 1412(5).

23. McKinney's SCPA 1412(5); Matter of Sager, N.Y.L.J., May 15, 1985, at 13, col. 6 (Nassau).

24. McKinney's SCPA 1412(3).

25. The analysis is that McKinney's SCPA 1412(5) requires a preliminary executor to qualify under McKinney's SCPA 708, and 708 states that a fiduciary must sign an oath swearing that he is not ineligible, and McKinney's SCPA 707 includes in the definition of ineligibility incompetence to execute fiduciary duties because of drunkenness, dishonesty, improvidence or want of understanding. See Matter of Mann, N.Y.L.J., April 10, 1978, at 12, col. 1 (New York County) (bona fide issue of undue influence is good cause for not appointing nominated executor); Matter of Smith, 71 Misc.2d 248, 336 N.Y.S.2d 68 (Erie 1972) (where Surrogate named the public administrator instead of named executor (unrelated female friend) or widow (a legatee of her elective share in trust), because of the allegations of undue influence and because of the mental and physical infirmities of the decedent). Bald allegations of undue influence or fraud will not suffice. Matter of Vermilye, 101 A.D.2d 865, 475 N.Y.S.2d 888 (1984).

26. McKinney's SCPA 1412(6). Revocation of preliminary letters is discussed infra at 123–24.

27. Matter of Bayley, 72 Misc.2d 312, 339 N.Y.S.2d 129 (Suffolk 1972), affirmed 40 A.D.2d 843, 337 N.Y.S.2d 500 (1972), appeal denied 31 N.Y.2d 1025, 341 N.Y.S. 2d 898, 294 N.E.2d 658 (1973).

28. See Matter of Bayerdorfer, N.Y.L.J., April 3, 1985, at 14, col. 4 (Richmond), where the court appointed the nominated executor despite some hazy allegations of removal of estate property from the decedent's home. The court distinguished the very serious allegations of undue influence in Matter of Smith, discussed in note 25 supra. See also Matter of Sager, N.Y.L.J., May 15, 1985, at 13, col. 6 (Nassau), where the court granted preliminary letters to the named executor despite the objectant's claim that the named executor lacked responsibility and was improvident, when the objectant did not support those claims with substantial evidence.

All persons with an interest in the estate have the right to object to issuance of preliminary letters, not just the persons with a prior or equal right to serve as preliminary executor.[29]

2. POWERS OF A PRELIMINARY EXECUTOR

The starting point for determining the preliminary executor's powers, like any other fiduciary's, is the will. If the testator has not restricted the fiduciary in any way, the preliminary executor's powers are those of an administrator,[30] except that he cannot distribute legacies or intestate shares and he cannot sell property specifically disposed of without the consent of the specific legatee or devisee.[31] In this latter restriction he is no different from other fiduciaries,[32] and this provision merely serves as a reminder that the preliminary executor can marshal the assets generally but can liquidate specifically bequeathed or devised property only on consent. The Surrogate cannot permit the preliminary executor to make a partial distribution of the estate even though all the parties consent, because the statute specifically prohibits it. To get around this problem part of the will can be admitted to probate and letters testamentary issued for the sole purpose of making a distribution.[33]

The preliminary executor, unlike the temporary administrator, can take possession of real property, manage it, collect the rents, pay taxes and utility bills and make essential repairs, all without court order.[34] Preliminary executors can sell real property not specifically disposed of.[35]

Preliminary executors may pay claims and may apply for a judicial determination of the validity of a claim.[36] The sixty-day statute of limitations to sue in a civil court other than the Surrogate's Court

29. See Matter of Ragone, 116 Misc.2d 993, 459 N.Y.S.2d 649 (New York County 1981), modified on other grounds 87 A.D.2d 457, 452 N.Y.S.2d 410 (1st Dep't 1982), reversed and Surrogate's opinion reinstated 58 N.Y.S.2d 864, 460 N.Y.S.2d 528, 447 N.E.2d 76 (1983), where the widow whose status was proven in the course of a probate proceeding had standing to object to issuance of preliminary letters to decedent's sisters.

30. See McKinney's EPTL 11–1.1, discussed in chapter on "Fiduciaries," infra at 402–05.

31. McKinney's SCPA 1412(3).

32. McKinney's EPTL 11–1.1(b)(5).

33. See Matter of Atlas, 101 Misc.2d 677, 421 N.Y.S.2d 815 (Nassau 1979) (partial distribution allowed where only part of will was objected to).

34. McKinney's EPTL 11–1.1(b)(5)(a). See Matter of Griffith, 44 Misc.2d 94, 252 N.Y.S.2d 984 (Kings 1964) (court granted petition to remove from decree of preliminary letters the language empowering the preliminary executor the "power to collect rents and if necessary to pay fuel bills" on the ground that it was superfluous, since the fiduciary already had that power). A temporary administrator must obtain a court order to exercise these powers. McKinney's SCPA 903(2)(c).

35. A 1968 amendment to McKinney's SCPA 1412 eliminated the prohibition against selling real property. L.1968, c. 259, section 25, eff. May 14, 1968. See Matter of Way, 56 Misc.2d 552, 289 N.Y.S. 2d 272 (Jefferson 1967), which, before the amendment, permitted the preliminary executor to sell realty on the authority of McKinney's EPTL 11–1.1.

36. Matter of Thoens, 88 Misc.2d 1006, 392 N.Y.S.2d 774 (New York County 1975); Matter of Cooper, 55 Misc.2d 159, 284 N.Y.S.2d 464 (Kings 1967), affirmed 30 A.D.2d 642, 292 N.Y.S.2d 820 (2d Dep't 1968).

begins to run when the preliminary executor rejects the claim; the creditor cannot wait until the appointment of a permanent fiduciary.[37]

The court can also place limitations on a preliminary executor, such as a limitation on which of the decedent's assets the preliminary executor can collect, a prohibition against selling real property or a limitation on paying claims. It may direct the collection and preservation of the decedent's papers and order the preliminary executor to make them available for inspection by other parties.[38]

The court may place a time limit on the preliminary executor's term of office, and the Surrogates of certain counties routinely do so.[39]

3. COMMISSIONS

The preliminary executor's commissions are the statutory commissions for an executor if he eventually is appointed and administers the estate.[40] If the will is denied probate or the preliminary letters are revoked for another reason, the court can award the preliminary executor reasonable compensation not more than the statutory commissions.[41] The court will base its award on the value of the fiduciary's services to the estate.[42]

Preliminary letters are not available for administration c.t.a., or for lost or destroyed wills. The rationale is that the preliminary letters run to the executor named in the will, and if there is none named, or if the contents of the will are uncertain because the will is lost or destroyed, preliminary letters are inappropriate. Temporary administration would have to be used in those cases.

4. REVOCATION OF PRELIMINARY LETTERS

When a will is probated, the court issues letters testamentary to the executor and revokes the preliminary letters.[43] In practice this usually happens because the decree admitting the will to probate and granting letters testamentary specifically revokes the preliminary letters, but even where the decree does not, the preliminary letters should be revoked automatically.[44] If the will is ultimately denied probate, the decree revokes preliminary letters unless the court specifically directs

37. McKinney's SCPA 1810; Matter of Cooper, 55 Misc.2d 159, 284 N.Y.S.2d 464 (Kings 1967), affirmed 30 A.D.2d 642, 292 N.Y.S.2d 820 (2d Dep't 1968) (claimant cannot wait until permanent fiduciary is appointed to start the sixty-day period running).

38. McKinney's SCPA 1412(4).

39. For instance, in New York County and the other counties in the New York City metropolitan area, the Surrogates usually limit preliminary letters to six months.

40. Executors' commissions are governed by McKinney's SCPA 2307 and discussed in chapter on "Commissions," infra at 426–29.

41. See McKinney's SCPA 2307, discussed in chapter on "Commissions," infra at 426–29.

42. Matter of Bernstein, 94 Misc.2d 898, 405 N.Y.S.2d 958 (New York County 1978).

43. McKinney's SCPA 1413.

44. See also Matter of Durban, 175 App.Div. 688, 160 N.Y.S. 945 (2d Dep't 1916), affirmed 220 N.Y. 589, 115 N.E. 1038 (1917) (where probate decree was reversed on appeal, the original appointment as temporary administrator is not automatically revived).

continuation of the letters until the termination of the appeals process.[45] Before the grant or denial of probate, the court can revoke preliminary letters if the preliminary executor does not move reasonably quickly in obtaining probate,[46] or if the court finds that such revocation would be in the best interests of the estate.[47] The court can also revoke if the preliminary executor does something which would cause revocation of letters of administration or letters testamentary, for example if he fails to account, fails to obey a court order, commits a felony, fails to remain amenable to service of process, commingles funds, wastes estate assets or removes property from the state.[48] When a preliminary executor's letters are revoked, the subsequent fiduciary and all persons with an interest in the estate are entitled to an accounting. Of course, if the reason for revocation is that the preliminary executor becomes the "real" executor, he need not account at that time. The successor fiduciary must request the accounting or he risks surcharge for his predecessor's mismanagement.[49] If the preliminary executor refuses to account voluntarily, the successor can petition for a compulsory accounting.[50]

45. McKinney's SCPA 1412(6).

46. McKinney's SCPA 1412(6)(a). See, e.g., Matter of Caporuscio, N.Y.L.J., Jan 2, 1979, at 12, col. 5 (Bronx) (two years delay).

47. McKinney's SCPA 1412(6)(c).

48. McKinney's SCPA 719 and 711, enumerating the grounds for revocation of letters, are incorporated into McKinney's SCPA 1412(6) and are therefore specifically applicable to preliminary executors.

49. McKinney's SCPA 1413, Practice Commentary at 353 (1967).

50. See McKinney's SCPA 2205(1)(g) and discussion of compulsory accountings in chapter on "Accounting," infra at 183–86.

Chapter Four

ADMINISTRATION OF INTESTATE ESTATES

SECTION A. INTRODUCTION

When a person dies without a will, the disposition of his property is governed by the intestate scheme set forth in Article 4 of the EPTL. Similarly, if a person has a will but does not successfully dispose of all his property under it, that undisposed-of property passes under the laws of intestacy.[1] Under the laws of intestacy, if the decedent left a spouse and children, no one else shares in the estate.[2] If there is no spouse but there are children (or issue of pre-deceased children), they take the entire estate.[3] If there are no children, the spouse shares with the decedent's parents.[4] If there are no children or parents the spouse takes the whole estate.[5] If there is neither a spouse nor children, the decedent's parents take the estate.[6] If there are no spouse, children or parents, the decedent's brothers and sisters take the estate, and the distribution is per stirpes, so predeceased brothers' and sisters' issue take their parents' shares.[7] If there are no brothers, sisters or their issue, the estate goes to grandparents or their issue, but the distribution at this level is not per stirpes; it is per capita to the decedent's nearest relative (or relatives of equal degree).[8] If there are no grandparents or their issue, the property escheats to the estate unless the decedent was a minor or an adjudicated incompetent,[9] the rationale being that a minor cannot make a will, and an incompetent is likely to lack the testamentary capacity to do so.

Sec. A

1. There is, however, a presumption that a person who took the trouble to write a will did not wish to die intestate. Matter of Hayes, 263 N.Y. 219, 188 N.E. 716 (1934); Matter of Pennsylvania Bank, 107 A.D.2d 1084, 486 N.Y.S.2d 502 (4th Dep't 1985).

2. McKinney's EPTL 4–1.1(a)(1), (2). If the decedent left only one child or issue of one child, the spouse takes $4,000 plus half of the remainder and the child or issue takes the rest. If the decedent left more than one child or issue of more than one child, the spouse takes $4,000 plus one-third of the remainder, and the children or issue share the rest.

3. McKinney's EPTL 4–1.1(a)(6). They share the estate per stirpes, except that if they are all equally related to the decedent, they take per capita.

4. McKinney's EPTL 4–1.1(a)(3), (4). The spouse takes the first $25,000 and one-half of the remainder, and the parents share the rest.

5. McKinney's EPTL 4–1.1(a)(5).

6. McKinney's EPTL 4–1.1(a)(3), (4).

7. McKinney's EPTL 4–1.1(a)(7).

8. McKinney's EPTL 4–1.1(a)(8).

9. McKinney's EPTL 4–1.1(a)(9).

This chapter discusses the procedural rules governing intestate decedents, found in SCPA Article 10. The proceeding is similar in many ways to probate: the court reviews a petition and issues process to interested persons, the petitioner arranges for its service on them, and after the return of process they have an opportunity to object to the issuance of letters to the nominated administrator. The court can hear all the parties and appoint an administrator, whose powers and duties are somewhat like those of an executor. The administrator collects the estate assets, pays debts, claims and taxes, accounts for his actions and distributes the property to the beneficiaries entitled to it under the intestate scheme.

A significant difference between probate and administration proceedings is that the former determines those entitled to share in the estate, while administration proceedings decide only who is entitled to administer the estate. The persons entitled to share in the estate are usually established in the accounting proceeding.

SCPA Article 10 is also used in cases where a decedent is alleged to be deceased and his family seeks administration and distribution of his estate,[10] and it can also be used even when the decedent died with a will, if that will is not being probated promptly.[11]

SECTION B. PERSONS ENTITLED TO PETITION

There are two reasons to petition for appointment of an administrator: first, an intestate decedent owned property that needs administering (stocks to be transferred, debts to be paid, deeds to be executed), or second, a person has a claim or lawsuit against the estate and wants someone at the helm against whom to proceed.

Not surprisingly, the class of persons who can petition for letters of administration is broad: anyone with an interest in an intestate estate,[1] the public administrator (or chief fiscal officer of the county), a creditor or a person interested in a lawsuit in which the decedent would have been a party.[2]

If all the distributees consent to the appointment of a non-distributee as administrator, that person can petition, so long as the consenting distributees themselves are eligible, except that the representative of a minor, incompetent or conservatee can consent for his ward, and non-

10. Alleged decedents are discussed this chapter infra at 142, and in chapter on "Temporary Administration," infra at 289 et seq.

11. McKinney's SCPA 1001(9), discussed this chapter infra at 137–39.

Sec. B

1. Everything said in this chapter about an estate of a decedent applies equally to the estate of a person alleged to be deceased. That class refers to persons who are inexplicably missing for a period of five years (or less, if they were exposed to a specific period) and who have not been located despite a diligent search. McKinney's EPTL 2–1.7. Those unfortunates can be judicially declared dead and when they are, their wills are probated or their estates administered in intestacy.

2. McKinney's SCPA 1002.

domiciliary alien distributees otherwise eligible may consent to appointment of a corporate fiduciary.[3]

If the estate is insolvent, or so small that it is clear that the shares will not be paid, one who may otherwise have been a distributee loses his status as such, along with his right to petition for letters.[4] In that case the proceeding may be commenced by another distributee (such as the surviving spouse, who is entitled to the first $4,000 even if the decedent had issue), a creditor or the public administrator.

Unlike the priority that exists among persons entitled to serve as administrator, which we discuss shortly, there is no order of priority as to who may petition. Petitioning does not confer any status that the petitioner would not otherwise have had in being appointed administrator. Usually the petitioner is the one seeking letters, but the petition may request that letters issue to another person.[5] For example, when a creditor or a potential plaintiff is the petitioner, the court will appoint an appropriate distributee or other person, or the public administrator, since the creditor has no interest in administering the estate; he merely wants someone in place so he can press his claim.

The petitioner should file the petition in the county where the decedent was domiciled,[6] or if the decedent was not a New Yorker, in one of the counties where the decedent's property is located or where the defendant in a negligence or personal injury action resides.[7]

SECTION C. CONTENTS OF PETITION

In addition to the fundamentals required of all petitions in the Surrogate's Court,[1] the petition must allege the citizenship of the petitioner[2] and of the decedent.[3] The statute requires the petition to state that the decedent left no will[4] but this should be read "that decedent left no valid will,"[5] or alternatively that even though a will has been filed, it is not being probated promptly.[6] In practice if the

3. McKinney's SCPA 1002(1).

4. Matter of Payne, 75 Misc.2d 425, 346 N.Y.S.2d 131 (Nassau 1973).

5. SCPA 1002(1); see e.g., Matter of Kassam, 144 Misc. 366, 252 N.Y.S. 706 (1931), affirmed 235 App.Div. 609, 255 N.Y.S. 835 (1932).

6. McKinney's SCPA 205.

7. McKinney's SCPA 206. Once one of the Surrogates has entertained a proceeding, all other proceedings should be brought in that court. See chapter on "Jurisdiction," supra at 1 et seq.

Sec. C

1. McKinney's SCPA 304, discussed in chapter on "Procedure," supra at 54–55.

2. The purpose of this statement is to determine his eligibility under McKinney's SCPA 707, discussed in chapter on "Fiduciaries," infra at 388–91.

3. McKinney's SCPA 1002(2).

4. McKinney's SCPA 1002(2). See Matter of Cameron, 47 App.Div. 120, 62 N.Y.S. 187 (3d Dep't 1900), affirmed 166 N.Y. 610, 59 N.E. 1120 (1900).

5. McKinney's SCPA 1002, Revisers Notes.

6. See McKinney's SCPA 1001(9) and discussion this chapter infra at 137–38, for a discussion of the granting of letters of administration in cases where probate of a will has not been diligently prosecuted.

decedent's will has been probated but failed to dispose of some of his property, the executor of the will ordinarily administers that property even though it passes to the decedent's intestate distributees.

The petitioner should demonstrate that he searched for a will in the decedent's safe deposit box, among the decedent's personal papers and in the files of the Surrogate's Court.[7] The burden of proving that there is a will, however, is on the person opposing the issuance of letters of administration.[8]

The decedent must be dead in order for the court to grant letters of administration. The petitioner usually submits a death certificate which suffices as proof of death. In case of an alleged decedent, the court holds a hearing and makes a determination of death within the administration proceeding.[9]

The petition must state whether the decedent had any non-marital children,[10] and must set forth the value of any personal property, a description and the value of any real property and the estimated gross rents from real property for eighteen months.[11] The petitioner need not list assets that pass by operation of law, such as life insurance and pensions payable to named beneficiaries other than the estate, jointly held property, Totten Trusts, and tenancies by the entirety. If the estate has no assets requiring administration, the court cannot appoint an administrator.[12]

Official forms for the petition containing all the necessary allegations are available from the Surrogate's Court.[13]

If only one distributee survived the decedent, or if the distributees were more remote relatives than the decedent's brothers and sisters, the petitioner must offer proof (1) to establish the relationship of the decedent to those named in the petition; and (2) to establish that no other persons of the same or a nearer degree of relationship survived the decedent. That proof must be by affidavit or a disinterested person's testimony and must include a chart of the family tree.[14]

7. Wills may be filed in the Surrogate's Court under the authority of McKinney's SCPA 2507.

8. Matter of Cameron, 47 A.D. 120, 62 N.Y.S. 187 (3d Dep't 1900), affirmed 166 N.Y. 610, 59 N.E. 1120 (1901).

9. Alleged decedents are discussed this chapter infra at 142.

10. Uniform Rules of the Surrogate's Court section 207.16.

11. McKinney's SCPA 1002(2).

12. In Matter of Perno, 30 A.D.2d 1037, 294 N.Y.S.2d 853 (4th Dep't 1968), although a temporary administrator had fully administered the estate, the Surrogate nevertheless entertained a petition for letters by the decedent's second wife and denied letters after finding that the foreign divorce from the first wife was invalid. The appellate division held that the Surrogate had no authority to make such a determination because administration was unnecessary.

13. See Official Form No. 2.

14. Uniform Rules of the Surrogate's Court section 207.17.

SECTION D. PERSONS ENTITLED TO SERVE

1. GENERAL RULES

When a decedent dies intestate, the court must grant letters to one of his distributees who is eligible [1] and can qualify [2] in the following order of priority: surviving spouse,[3] children, grandchildren, father and mother, brothers and sisters.[4] Parents of a decedent may be disqualified from serving if they abandoned or failed to support the child,[5] and spouses may be disqualified from serving if they divorced, abandoned or failed to support the decedent.[6] Relatives of the half-blood have rights equal to those of relatives of the whole blood.[7] If none of the distributees mentioned survives and is eligible and qualifies, then the court may appoint any other distributee (such as grandparents, aunts, uncles or cousins), with preference given to the one with the largest share in the estate. Arguably, if the estate is insufficient to pay a distributee's share, that distributee loses his right to serve.[8]

If more than one member of a class qualifies, the court has discretion to choose among them and may grant letters of administration to one or more of them.[9] The court has broad discretion to choose among class members; its decision can be upset only on a showing that

Sec. D

1. Under McKinney's SCPA 707 a person is eligible unless he is an infant, incompetent, non-domiciliary alien, felon or person unable to serve because of dishonesty, drunkenness or improvidence. See e.g., Matter of Avery, 111 Misc.2d 818, 445 N.Y.S.2d 672 (Wayne 1981) (husband disqualified as administrator because he was felon). See discussion of eligibility in chapter on "Fiduciaries," infra at 388–91.

2. Under McKinney's SCPA 708, a person qualifies by filing an oath and a designation of the clerk to receive service of process, and filing a bond. See discussion of qualification in chapter on "Fiduciaries," infra at 391–92.

3. The spouse has the burden of proving his status, but certain presumptions, discussed in chapter on "Surviving Spouses," infra at 315–17, aid him in meeting his burden, and in addition, if the spouse alleges in the petition that he is the decedent's spouse and produces documentary evidence, and if no one contests it, the allegations in the petition are proof of the facts. McKinney's SCPA 509, discussed in chapter on "Trials," infra at 507. See Matter of Tulloch, N.Y.L.J., July 8, 1985, at 12, col. 4 (Bronx).

4. McKinney's SCPA 1001(1).

5. McKinney's EPTL 4–1.4; Matter of O'Dell, N.Y.L.J., Jan. 15, 1979, at 18, col. 3 (Suffolk). The statute disqualifies parents who abandoned or failed to support the child before age twenty-one, or until the child's death if sooner. If the parent resumed a relationship with the child or resumed support before the child's death, the disqualification is purged.

6. McKinney's EPTL 5–1.2. The statute disqualifies a spouse who was divorced in a valid New York divorce, or whose marriage was annulled or dissolved because of absence ("Enoch Arden" decree), McKinney's EPTL 5–1.2(a)(1), or whose marriage was incestuous, bigamous or a prohibited remarriage, McKinney's EPTL 5–1.2(a)(2). A spouse who obtained an out-of-state divorce against the decedent is disqualified even if the divorce is invalid, McKinney's EPTL 5–1.2(a)(3), as is a spouse against whom the decedent obtained a final decree of separation. McKinney's EPTL 5–1.2(a)(4). Finally, the spouse who abandoned or, having a duty to support, failed to do so, is disqualified. See Matter of Helfinstein, N.Y.L.J., Aug. 8, 1983, at 13, col. 4 (Bronx); and Matter of Ferguson, N.Y.L.J., April 26, 1985, at 17, col. 4 (Suffolk), for a discussion of abandonment by a spouse.

7. McKinney's EPTL 4–1.1(d).

8. See Matter of Payne, 75 Misc.2d 425, 346 N.Y.S.2d 131 (Nassau 1973).

9. McKinney's SCPA 1001(1).

the court abused its discretion.[10] The court need not necessarily appoint the person who asserts the greatest familiarity with the decedent's affairs, but that familiarity will be a factor, as will the decedent's probable preference.[11] The court will choose whoever seems the most competent member of the class.[12] If the parties can agree on a candidate, the court will ordinarily appoint that one. Though it has the power to appoint two or more of the candidates, many of the Surrogates prefer to avoid the appointment of multiple fiduciaries because it can cause delay (in getting them to agree on actions) and extra expense (in extra commissions) in the administration of an estate.[13]

To illustrate the priorities, if a decedent is survived only by his mother, his sister and an adult child, his child will be the first in priority for letters.[14] If he is survived by his mother, brother and sister, his mother is entitled to letters, but if he is survived only by his brother and his sister, the court may grant letters to one or both of them.[15] If he is survived only by his uncle and two cousins, his uncle will get letters; the cousins are not distributees at all, since per capita and not per stirpes distributions are made at this level.[16]

If the person seeking letters claims to be the surviving spouse, the court has jurisdiction to determine whether that is true; it can decide whether a foreign divorce decree is valid.[17] In a case where a person's status as distributee is questioned, or where his suitability as fiduciary is uncertain, the court can grant temporary letters to another party, so that administration can proceed while the court decides the issue.[18]

A child born out of wedlock is a child of his mother entitled to priority in receiving letters of administration, and is entitled to letters in his father's estate if one of the following standards is met: (1) paternity was established by an order of filiation, or (2) a signed and acknowledged acknowledgment of paternity was filed with the Putative Father's Registry, or (3) the father openly and notoriously acknowl-

10. Matter of Edelson, 88 A.D.2d 640, 450 N.Y.S.2d 223 (2d Dep't 1982).

11. Matter of Scher, N.Y.L.J., Oct. 28, 1976, at 15, col. 4 (Bronx); Matter of Adelman, N.Y.L.J., Feb. 8, 1972, at 19, col. 1 (Nassau).

12. See Matter of Edelson, 88 A.D.2d 640, 450 N.Y.S.2d 223 (2d Dep't 1982) (distributee's assertion that she was more familiar with decedent's estate than her brother whom the court in its discretion appointed was insufficient to show abuse of the court's discretion); Matter of Ryan, 81 Misc.2d 1079, 367 N.Y.S.2d 452 (Albany 1975).

13. See Matter of Nolan, N.Y.L.J., June 6, 1985, at 14, col. 5 (Nassau) (court appointed decedent's mother only though father had equal right to serve); Matter of Casey, N.Y.L.J., Dec. 4, 1979, at 15, col. 1 (Westchester) (to avoid hampering administration, court appointed decedent's mother alone, though father had equal right to serve).

14. McKinney's SCPA 1001(1)(c).

15. McKinney's SCPA 1001(1) (last paragraph).

16. McKinney's EPTL 4–1.1(b).

17. Matter of Carter, 69 Misc.2d 630, 331 N.Y.S.2d 257 (New York County 1972), affirmed 42 A.D.2d 925, 347 N.Y.S.2d 1007 (1973).

18. See Matter of Shifrel, 57 Misc.2d 860, 293 N.Y.S.2d 818 (Nassau 1968), where the court granted temporary letters to decedent's son because decedent's widow had pleaded not guilty by reason of insanity to her husband's murder.

edged the child as his own and there is also clear and convincing proof of paternity.[19] The same rules apply on the death of an intestate person born out of wedlock; if he is not survived by a spouse, children or issue, his mother is entitled to letters of administration, as is his father if any of the three proofs of paternity described above was established.[20]

A father's open acknowledgment of paternity is a question of fact. The legislature added that test (coupled with clear and convincing evidence) to the statute in 1981 [21] to reflect the modern reality of the de facto nonmarital family. Case law is still sparse on the issue, but some of the factors to be considered are whether the father's name was on the birth certificate, whether he supported the child, lived with or visited the child, sent cards or gifts on birthdays, claimed the child as a dependent on income tax returns,[22] participated in school activities, and told people that he was the child's father.

It is significant, and worth mentioning here though only peripherally related to administration proceedings, that out-of-wedlock children are treated differently in wrongful death proceedings. A nonmarital child need not meet the proofs just described to share in the wrongful death proceeds payable as a result of his father's death; [23] he must merely show paternity by clear and convincing evidence. Thus, in a wrongful death action in which the decedent's children born out of wedlock can prove paternity by clear and convincing evidence, they are entitled to notice and their representative is entitled to limited letters to commence the wrongful death action.[24] If the proceeding is for administration of the entire estate, and not just for prosecution of the

19. McKinney's EPTL 4–1.2(a). See Matter of Davis, N.Y.L.J., March 18, 1985, at 15, col. 1 (New York County) (notorious acknowledgment and clear and convincing evidence standard met); Matter of Campbell, N.Y.L.J., March 7, 1984, at 11, col. 2 (New York County) (notorious acknowledgment and clear and convincing evidence standard not met); Matter of Diaz, 102 Misc.2d 817, 424 N.Y.S.2d 590 (New York County 1979) (letters granted to decedent's mother, not decedent's out of wedlock child, because statutory proof of paternity not satisfied).

20. McKinney's EPTL 4–1.2(b).

21. L.1981, c. 75, § 2.

22. These factors were lacking in Matter of Campbell, N.Y.L.J., March 7, 1984, at 11, col. 2 (New York County), and the court rejected the father's claim of paternity.

23. McKinney's EPTL 5–4.5. This rule, and the reason for the "double standard" for intestacy versus wrongful death, are discussed in chapter on "Wrongful Death," infra at 530–31.

24. See Matter of Cesario, 103 Misc.2d 1, 425 N.Y.S.2d 238 (Bronx 1980) (decedent's nonmarital children had priority over decedent's parents if they could make satisfactory proof of paternity). But see Matter of Diaz, 102 Misc.2d 817, 424 N.Y.S.2d 590 (New York County 1979), where the court issued letters to the decedent's mother in a wrongful death action because the necessary statutory proof of paternity, which at that time required a court order of filiation or an acknowledgment filed with the Putative Father's Registry, was not made and the children were therefore not distributees. This proof should not be required for the nonmarital children if the only function they will perform as administrators is to start the wrongful death action, for which clear and convincing proof is sufficient under McKinney's EPTL 5–4.5.

wrongful death action, the higher statutory level of proof should be required.[25]

An anomalous situation can arise in a case where the decedent's out-of-wedlock child can meet the clear and convincing proof burden and is therefore entitled to the entire wrongful death recovery, but cannot meet the stricter proof of paternity that would permit him to inherit in intestacy, and therefore is not entitled to letters of administration. In one such case,[26] the decedent's mother, who was entitled to be appointed administrator to bring the action as representative of the decedent's distributees,[27] but who was not entitled to share in the recovery because she was not a distributee, petitioned for letters, as did the out-of-wedlock child, who was entitled to share in the recovery but not to serve as administrator. The court's solution in protecting all parties was creative; it granted letters to both, requesting that they mutually consent, although in fact only distributees can consent.[28]

The "open-acknowledgment plus clear and convincing proof" standard, which was added to the other two more formal proofs in 1981,[29] should blur the line between wrongful death actions and intestacy proceedings somewhat. In the example in the preceding paragraph, for example, under current law the out-of-wedlock child would have been entitled to serve as administratrix if her father had openly acknowledged her and there was clear and convincing proof of paternity.[30] However, the possibility still exists for the uneven treatment of nonmarital children. Where the child can meet the clear and convincing test but not the open acknowledgment test, he will be able to share in wrongful death proceeds but not in his father's estate, and as we discuss in the chapter on wrongful death, any personal injury recovery is part of the estate. Hence, that child will be able to share in the wrongful death recovery but not in the recovery for the decedent's pain and suffering.[31]

The order of priority established in SCPA 1001 for letters of administration is mandatory: "letters of administration must be granted * * *."[32] If, however, a distributee with a prior right has been disqualified from sharing in the estate by one of the wrongful acts that

25. See Matter of Thomas, 81 Misc.2d 891, 367 N.Y.S.2d 182 (1975).

26. Matter of Ross, 67 Misc.2d 320, 323 N.Y.S.2d 770 (Kings 1971), decided before the 1981 amendment to McKinney's EPTL 4–1.2(a) allowing nonmarital children to inherit from their fathers on clear and convincing proof and notorious acknowledgment of paternity.

27. McKinney's EPTL 5–4.1(1).

28. McKinney's SCPA 1001(5).

29. L.1981, c. 75, § 2.

30. The Surrogates have split on the issue of whether this amendment is retroactive. Compare Matter of Youngblood, N.Y.L.J., March 25, 1985, at 13, col. 4 (New York County) (no retroactive application), and Matter of Smith, 114 Misc.2d 346, 451 N.Y.S.2d 546 (Queens 1982) (no retroactive application to father who died in 1980), and Matter of Smith, 118 Misc.2d 165, 460 N.Y.S.2d 441 (Bronx 1985) (accord), with Matter of Kenny, 114 Misc.2d 203, 450 N.Y.S.2d 1003 (Kings 1982) (retroactive application allowed), Matter of Crist, 116 Misc.2d 1078, 457 N.Y.S.2d 182 (Orange 1982) (accord), and Matter of Schweiker, 569 F.Supp. 1341 (E.D.N.Y.1983) (accord).

31. See chapter on "Wrongful Death," infra at 530–31.

32. McKinney's SCPA 1001(1).

disqualify parents [33] or surviving spouses,[34] he has lost his status as distributee and cannot serve.[35] The person with the next priority will serve, or a member (in the court's discretion) of the class with next priority will serve, and the disqualified person will be treated as though he had predeceased.[36]

A trust company can serve, as can another corporation authorized to act as fiduciary by law or by its charter, if all the distributees are eligible and they consent to the appointment.[37]

The beneficiaries, if they are competent adults, can agree on an administrator even if that person is not a distributee.[38] All interested persons have a right to be heard and can object to the appointment of the fiduciary.

If the court appoints an administrator, following the mandated priorities, and someone (perhaps a defendant sued by that administrator) challenges the appointment collaterally, the administrator can invoke SCPA 204, which states that the court's jurisdiction to appoint an administrator, when attacked collaterally, is presumptively established, and in the absence of fraud or collusion, conclusively established by the statement of jurisdictional facts in the petition. That collateral attacker thus must show fraud, either intentional fraud or constructive, unintentional fraud.[39]

2. PRIORITY WHEN DISTRIBUTEES WITH PRIOR RIGHT DO NOT OR CANNOT SERVE

If a person would have had priority to serve but is dead [40] or under another legal disability or refuses to serve, the court has several statutory guidelines to follow.

33. McKinney's EPTL 4–1.4, discussed supra at 129.

34. McKinney's EPTL 5–1.2, discussed supra at 129.

35. For a discussion of the status of a spouse who obtains an "Enoch Arden" divorce decree against his spouse and then petitions for letters of administration in the spouse's estate, see Matter of Hahn, 57 Misc.2d 231, 291 N.Y.S.2d 491 (Kings 1968). There the court distinguishes between the ineligibility of such spouse to serve when the decedent is known to be dead (see McKinney's 5–1.4) and his possible eligibility to serve when the spouse is alleged to be dead.

36. McKinney's EPTL 4–1.4(b).

37. McKinney's SCPA 1001(7); see Matter of Nichols, 124 Misc.2d 204, 475 N.Y.S.2d 787 (Clinton 1984) (church not permitted to serve because neither the law nor its charter authorized it). Compare McKinney's SCPA 1418(4) which permits a corporation to serve even without authorization in its charter if the corporation is the sole or residuary legatee.

38. McKinney's SCPA 1001(6); Matter of Aikman, N.Y.L.J., March 28, 1979, at 11, col. 2 (Bronx).

39. McKinney's SCPA 204, Practice Commentary at 156 (1967), and discussion of this section in chapter on "Jurisdiction," supra at 22–23. See Windbourne v. Eastern Airlines, 479 F.Supp. 1130, 1153 (E.D. N.Y.1979), reversed on other grounds 632 F.2d 219 (2d Cir.1980).

40. To clarify a point that may be obvious, a person who had a right to letters of administration is one who survived the decedent, so we refer in this discussion to a person who survived the decedent and then died.

a. *Sole Distributee*

If the sole distributee is deceased or is an infant, incompetent or conservatee, the court must grant letters of administration to his representative (guardian, committee or conservator),[41] if eligible and qualified.[42] Thus, if a decedent is survived by his mother, his sister and his minor child, the guardian of the child's property is entitled to serve, since the child is the sole distributee.

Frequently the guardian or committee represent both the person and the property of the ward. If he is representative of the person only, however, the court may deny him letters of administration [43] on the theory that he has no real interest in the ward's property. Moreover, a "natural guardian" such as a parent is not automatically entitled to letters as representative of the minor.[44]

If a person relinquishes in a separation agreement the right to serve as administrator of his spouse's estate, he can nevertheless serve as administrator if he is the guardian of the property of the decedent's child who is sole distributee.[45] The theory is that the relinquishment in the separation agreement binds the spouse in his individual capacity, not in his representative capacity as guardian of the child. This is consistent with the general rule in New York that separation agreements are strictly construed and should not be extended beyond the four corners of the agreement.[46]

b. *Two or More Distributees*

When a distributee with a prior right to serve as administrator has died or is an infant, incompetent or conservatee, the court may grant letters to his representative if he is eligible and qualified.[47] It is discretionary, not mandatory, and the court can instead appoint anoth-

41. McKinney's SCPA 1001(2) and 1001(3)(a) now codify the conservator's right to serve as administrator in place of his ward, L.1981, c. 115, § 118, a position supported by case law before this codification. See Matter of Cantor, 80 Misc.2d 555, 363 N.Y.S.2d 79 (Kings 1975). Included under these provisions is the guardian of a mentally retarded person appointed under McKinney's SCPA Article 17A, who is entitled to letters as representative of his ward. See Matter of Resnick, 76 Misc. 2d 541, 351 N.Y.S.2d 269 (Kings 1973). Guardianships generally and guardianships of mentally retarded persons are discussed in chapter on "Guardians," infra at 257 et seq.

42. McKinney's SCPA 1001(2); 1001(3)(a).

43. McKinney's SCPA 1001(2).

44. See Matter of Winkhous, 157 Misc. 560, 284 N.Y.S. 52 (Kings 1935), where a minor child born out of wedlock was the sole distributee in his father's estate. His mother, though natural guardian, was not his legal representative and was not entitled to letters. See chapter on "Guardianship," infra at 257 et seq., for a discussion of the procedure for appointing a guardian to serve as administrator.

45. Matter of Porrata, 89 Misc.2d 663, 392 N.Y.S.2d 221 (Bronx 1977).

46. See Matter of Maruccia, 54 N.Y.2d 196, 445 N.Y.S.2d 73, 429 N.E.2d 751 (1981) (relinquishment in separation agreement of statutory marital property rights did not extend to bequests under the will); Matter of Laney, 274 App.Div. 250, 80 N.Y.S.2d 421 (4th Dep't 1948), affirmed 298 N.Y. 834, 84 N.E.2d 145 (1949); Matter of Colaci, 288 N.Y. 158, 42 N.E.2d 466 (1942).

47. McKinney's SCPA 1001(4)(a).

er eligible distributee, even one with an inferior right to serve.[48] For example, where the decedent is survived by a spouse and a child but the spouse dies a month after the decedent, the court can grant letters of administration to the spouse's fiduciary, or in its discretion can appoint the child (or, as we see in the next paragraph, his guardian).

Where all the distributees are deceased or are infants, incompetents or conservatees, the court may grant letters to the eligible and qualified representative of one such distributee, giving preference to the representative of the distributee entitled to the largest share in the estate.[49] Thus, if the decedent is survived only by his brother, an adjudicated incompetent, and the minor children of a predeceased sister, the court will grant letters to the brother's committee, because the brother had the right to the largest share of the estate.[50]

If a person with a prior right to serve declines to do so, and all the other distributees are under legal disability, the court may grant letters to one of their fiduciaries, giving preference to the fiduciary of the distributee with the right to the largest share.[51] Thus, if a decedent is survived by a spouse, a minor child, and two minor grandchildren of a predeceased child, and the spouse refuses to serve, the court will appoint the child's guardian. If the other distributees are equally entitled to share, the court can issue letters to one or more of their representatives.[52] Thus, if the decedent is survived by his spouse, who declines to serve, and by two minor grandchildren, the court can appoint either or both of the grandchildren's representatives.

If it is unclear whether there are any distributees closer than the class described in the petition, the court may decline to appoint a person from that class, and appoint the public administrator instead.[53] It usually will not do so unless there is some reasonable evidence that there are some closer-related distributees. For example, if the petitioners are the decedent's maternal cousins, and a question arises whether the decedent's paternal aunt survived, the court can appoint the public administrator.

48. Matter of Kleefeld, 93 A.D.2d 713, 467 N.Y.S.2d 200 (1st Dep't 1983), leave for appeal denied 59 N.Y.2d 606, 466 N.Y.S.2d 1026, 453 N.E.2d 55) (1983) (appellate division upheld Surrogate's appointment of distributee instead of fiduciary of deceased distributee with prior right); Matter of Papadogiannis, N.Y.L.J., April 23, 1985, at 13, col. 3 (Kings) (court appointed decedent's sons rather than fiduciary of decedent's mother, who had been serving until her death). See McKinney's SCPA 1001, Revisers' Notes, which says that McKinney's SCPA 1001(4)(a) was meant to preserve the priorities of McKinney's SCPA 1001(1) if the court decides to exercise its discretion and appoint the fiduciary of the person specified in 1001(1).

49. McKinney's SCPA 1001(3)(a).

50. Under McKinney's EPTL 4–1.1(a)(7), the brother takes one-half the estate and the sister's children take one-quarter each.

51. McKinney's SCPA 1001(4)(b); See Matter of Alaburta, N.Y.L.J., March 12, 1985, at 12, col. 5 (Bronx) (surviving spouse stated she had no present intention to apply for letters and court granted letters to decedent's mother).

52. McKinney's SCPA 1001(4)(c).

53. McKinney's SCPA 1001(8).

As an alternative to appointing the public administrator, the court may restrict the administrator's powers, require a bond, or prohibit distribution of the proceeds without further court order.

c. *Co–Administration*

If the distributee with priority does not wish to serve, the attorney may advise him to consider co-administration: he may petition to serve jointly with an eligible distributee or non-distributee (or more than one), including a corporate fiduciary.[54] The petitioning fiduciary need not obtain the consents of those with inferior rights.[55] The co-fiduciary, like the fiduciary, is entitled to commissions for his fiduciary services.[56]

d. *Selection by Consent*

If the distributees with priority do not want to serve, with a co-administrator or alone, they can consent to the selection of an administrator, either a distributee with lower priority or a non-distributee. If they do, and their choice of administrator is eligible,[57] the court may grant letters of administration to that person.[58] The distributees' choice of an administrator has priority over the public administrator or chief county fiscal officer.[59]

The general rule is that the distributees cannot consent unless they are all themselves eligible.[60] Two exceptions exist. First, if a distributee is ineligible because of legal disability, consents may be given by his guardian, committee, or conservator, but only if appointed in New York;[61] out-of-state representatives may not consent for their wards. Secondly, letters of administration may be granted to a corporate fiduciary on the acknowledged and filed consents of all distributees, including non-domiciliary aliens, and disabled distributees can consent through their guardians, committees or conservators, as long as they are otherwise eligible.[62]

54. McKinney's SCPA 1001(5).

55. McKinney's SCPA 1001(5); Matter of Fichter, 155 Misc. 399, 279 N.Y.S. 597 (Westchester 1935).

56. McKinney's SCPA 1001(5). Administrators' commissions are governed by McKinney's SCPA 2307 and discussed in chapter on "Commissions," infra at 426–29.

57. Under McKinney's SCPA 707 a person is eligible unless he is an infant, incompetent, non-domiciliary alien, felon or person unable to serve because of dishonesty, drunkenness or improvidence.

58. McKinney's SCPA 1001(6).

59. See McKinney's SCPA 1001(6), 1001(8), and Matter of Bernich, 98 Misc.2d 1036, 415 N.Y.S.2d 201 (Dutchess 1979), where the sole distributee had been appointed and had requested revocation of his letters because of a conflict of interest, and the chief fiscal officer had been appointed. The sole distributee's father, who was not a distributee of the decedent's estate, petitioned with the consent of the sole distributee to remove the chief fiscal officer and have himself appointed. The court granted his petition.

60. McKinney's SCPA 1001(6).

61. McKinney's SCPA 1001(6).

62. McKinney's SCPA 1001(7).

e. Public Administration

When no distributees can serve, either because there are none, or because none are eligible, or because none take the necessary steps to qualify,[63] or because the one serving is removed for wrongdoing and there are no others,[64] the court will issue letters to the public administrator or the chief fiscal officer of the county.[65] If an eligible distributee is willing to accept the appointment, the public administrator has no right to serve. On the other hand, if the public administrator is in line to serve under this section, he cannot renounce letters without court order.[66] The court will always consider whether there are other eligible persons willing to serve before allowing the public administrator or county officer to renounce letters.[67]

If the public administrator does not qualify (because of a possible conflict with another estate of which he is administrator), the court in its discretion may appoint the petitioner or another person. This category of "another person" includes such persons as the consul of a foreign country,[68] a creditor of the estate,[69] or a friend of the disabled sole legatee.[70]

SECTION E. APPOINTMENT OF ADMINISTRATOR WHEN THE DECEDENT HAD A WILL

The usual proceeding for letters of administration requires that the decedent die intestate. In addition, the court can grant letters of administration in cases where a decedent's will has been filed with the court, either for safekeeping[1] or in a probate proceeding, but no one has either begun probate proceedings within a reasonable time or has diligently prosecuted them.[2]

63. See Matter of Wyche, 96 Misc.2d 324, 408 N.Y.S.2d 1018 (Albany 1978), where the decedent was survived only by an infant son. The child's father, the divorced spouse of the decedent, refused to petition for letters of guardianship on his son's behalf.

64. See Matter of Bodin, N.Y.L.J., Nov. 26, 1979, at 11, col. 5 (Bronx) (administrator failed to account). Removal of fiduciaries is governed by McKinney's SCPA 711 and McKinney's SCPA 719 and discussed in chapter on "Fiduciaries," infra at 393–400.

65. McKinney's SCPA 1001(8). See, e.g., Matter of Marks, 101 Misc.2d 115, 420 N.Y.S.2d 696 (1979).

66. Matter of Warren, 121 Misc.2d 660, 468 N.Y.S.2d 836 (Kings 1983).

67. Matter of Page, 107 N.Y. 266, 14 N.E. 193 (1887).

68. Matter of Conde, 144 Misc. 357, 259 N.Y.S. 129 (Columbia 1932) (public administrator has prior right to serve over consul of non-resident alien).

69. Matter of Morel, 103 Misc. 555 (Bronx 1918) (public administrator has prior right to serve over a creditor).

70. Matter of Baltimore, N.Y.L.J., April 3, 1979, at 12, col. 5 (Bronx) (public administrator had prior right over friend of legatee).

Sec. E

1. McKinney's SCPA 2507 (living testator), McKinney's SCPA 2508 (decedent).

2. McKinney's SCPA 1001(9). Historically, letters of administration were also issued in cases where the decedent had executed a will, but had done so invalidly or had revoked it, e.g., Matter of Cameron, 47 App.Div. 120, 62 N.Y.S. 187 (3d Dep't 1900), affirmed 166 N.Y. 610, 59 N.E. 1120

While the courts are reluctant to disregard the testamentary intentions of a decedent and ordinarily direct probate proceedings if the decedent had a will, in some cases a court will permit a family (with no legally disabled members) to join together and agree not to probate an instrument, for example in an estate in which the distribution of the estate would be the same under the will as in intestacy and the petitioner prefers administration to probate,[3] perhaps because the attesting witnesses are unavailable.[4]

Occasionally a court allows administration in a case where the petitioner-sole distributee would receive less in intestacy than under the will.[5] In one, the sole beneficiary under the will of an insolvent decedent was a non-distributee who agreed to appointment of an administrator on condition that he be cited and permitted to object in the judicial accounting. The court granted letters of administration.[6]

If a petitioner for letters of administration thinks that the instrument on file is invalid, he should state the reason briefly in the petition and expand on it in an affidavit filed with the petition.

If those cited as beneficiaries under the instrument default and the court, after reading the petition and affidavit, is satisfied that the will should be denied probate, it will issue letters. If the court feels that the will should be offered for probate and no one will petition to do so, the court can direct the public administrator or county treasurer to

(1901); Matter of Billet, 187 App.Div. 309, 175 N.Y.S. 482 (2d Dep't 1919), and in cases where the will was valid but all the legacies in it had lapsed because of the death of all legatees, Matter of Hammel, 33 Misc.2d 335, 223 N.Y.S.2d 647 (Suffolk 1962); Matter of Millar, 156 N.Y.S.2d 944 (Nassau 1956). (This assumes that the legatees under the will either were not the decedent's issue, brothers or sisters, or that they died without issue, because otherwise the anti-lapse statute, McKinney's EPTL 3–3.3, would cause the pre-deceased beneficiary's share to pass to his issue.)

Several courts expanded the scope of administration proceedings under McKinney's SCPA 1001(9)'s predecessor, SCA 119(1), to permit administration not only in cases of invalid wills, but also in all cases where the will had not been admitted to probate, Matter of Friedman, 164 Misc. 440, 299 N.Y.S. 103 (Bronx 1935); Matter of Sielcken, 162 Misc. 54, 293 N.Y.S. 721 (New York County 1937), and the current law, permitting administration in cases where probate is delayed, codifies that precedent. See Matter of Von Ripper, 95 Misc.2d 952, 408 N.Y.S.2d 686 (New York County 1978).

3. See Matter of Von Ripper, 95 Misc. 2d 952, 408 N.Y.S.2d 686 (New York County 1978); Matter of Caravano, 95 Misc.2d 952, 408 N.Y.S.2d 686 (New York County 1978).

4. Matter of Riley, 95 Misc.2d 952, 408 N.Y.S.2d 686 (New York County 1978). The mere fact that the attesting witnesses to a will cannot be located or are deceased does not mean that a will must be denied probate. The will can still be proved by proof of the handwriting of the testator and the witnesses. See chapter on "Probate," supra at 93–94.

5. Matter of Young, N.Y.L.J., July 25, 1978, at 14, col 5. (Suffolk); Matter of Von Ripper, 95 Misc.2d 952, 408 N.Y.S.2d 686 (New York County 1978).

6. See Matter of Brugaletta, 95 Misc.2d 952, 408 N.Y.S.2d 686 (New York County 1978), where the sole surviving beneficiary under the will was the decedent's uncle, a non-distributee for whom a conservator had been appointed. The estate (approximately $10,000) was insolvent and the guardian ad litem for the uncle did not object to the public administrator's petition for letters of administration on stipulation that the uncle would be cited and could object in the public administrator's judicial accounting proceeding.

probate the filed instrument.[7] In the alternative, it will appoint an administrator.

SECTION F. APPOINTMENT OF FOREIGN CORPORATE FIDUCIARIES

The New York Banking Law [1] states when foreign corporate fiduciaries may serve. Briefly stated, the rule is that the court can appoint foreign trust companies with a right under SCPA article 10 to serve as administrator, if they can act as fiduciaries in their state of incorporation, and if similar New York corporations are granted reciprocal rights to act as a fiduciary in that jurisdiction. Thus, if a decedent's sole distributee died and a foreign trust company received letters as the distributee's fiduciary, the trust company could serve as administrator of the decedent's estate if it could serve as fiduciary in its own jurisdiction and if a New York trust company could qualify in the other state.

SECTION G. PERSONS ENTITLED TO PROCESS

The necessary parties in administration proceedings are all eligible persons with prior or equal right to letters of administration to that of the petitioner.[1] As in probate or other proceedings, the petitioner's attorney should attempt to obtain waivers of process from all adult competent persons entitled to service.[2] The waiver is available from the clerk of the court, and it should be signed, acknowledged and filed in the court. In it the signing party waives the right to process and the right to serve as administrator.

If not all necessary parties sign waivers, the petitioner submits a citation, the court issues it and the petitioner arranges to serve it on the eligible persons with a prior or equal right to letters who have not renounced. The attorney for the petitioner should not unilaterally make the decision as to who is eligible unless the ineligibility is unmistakable (such as infancy or adjudicated incompetency). It is safer to serve all those who have prior or equal rights unless the court has already decided that a distributee is ineligible. For example, a prisoner is a person under disability and should be cited, and a guardian ad litem should be appointed to represent him.[3] The citation gives the necessary parties an opportunity to be heard on the appointment of a fiduciary.

7. These parties can do so under McKinney's SCPA 1402. See Matter of Brugaletta, 95 Misc.2d 952, 408 N.Y.S.2d 686 (New York County 1978), discussed supra in note 6.

Sec. F

1. McKinney's Banking L. 131(3) (1971).

Sec. G

1. McKinney's SCPA 1003(2).

2. See discussion of waivers in chapter on "Procedure," supra at 37.

3. Matter of Shifrel, 57 Misc.2d 860, 293 N.Y.S.2d 818 (Nassau 1968).

If a person is alleged to be deceased, the petitioner must arrange for service of process on him (by publication) and on his presumptive distributees.[4]

If the petitioner is the public administrator or county treasurer, he must serve all incompetent or conservatee domiciliary distributees whose names and addresses he knows. If the petitioner is a creditor or potential plaintiff against the estate, he has to serve all appointed representatives of domiciliary distributees who are incompetents, conservatees and infants. The court may dispense with the issuance and service of process on non-domiciliaries.[5]

If a party is seeking letters of administration because of an unreasonable delay in probate of a will on file with the court,[6] he must serve process on all those who would have been entitled to it if the instrument had been offered for probate,[7] that is, all legatees, devisees, distributees, executors named in the instrument, persons adversely affected by later instruments offered for probate, persons named in another instrument on file in the court adversely affected by the will offered for probate, and the testator if he is alleged to be dead.[8] If those persons default by failing to appear, the court can extinguish their rights in the estate.

If the decedent had no distributees, process must be served on the public administrator [9] and the state attorney general.[10]

Those with inferior rights to letters are not entitled to service, or even notice that an administration proceeding is under way. For example, if the decedent's spouse, while serving as administratrix, learns of an out-of-wedlock child of the decedent, the court can permit a "nunc pro tunc" amendment of the petition for letters to reflect the existence of the child; his omission from the proceeding is not a jurisdictional defect, since the decedent's spouse had a prior right to letters and he consequently is not a party entitled to service.[11] The court may and usually does direct that a non-jurisdictional notice be given to those with an inferior right to letters.[12]

Unlike in probate proceedings, where the court determines who is entitled to share in the testamentary estate, in administration proceedings the court usually determines only the person who will serve as fiduciary. Those entitled to share in the estate are usually determined by subsequent informal or judicial accountings or kinship hearings. Consequently, in administration proceedings, while personal jurisdiction over interested parties is important, it is not as critical as in

4. McKinney's SCPA 1003(1).

5. McKinney's SCPA 1003(2).

6. McKinney's SCPA 1001(9), discussed this chapter supra at 137–139.

7. McKinney's SCPA 1003(5).

8. See McKinney's SCPA 1403 and chapter on "Probate," supra at 78–82.

9. See Matter of Morel, 103 Misc. 555, 171 N.Y.S. 759 (Bronx 1918); Matter of Anderton, 112 Misc. 686, 184 N.Y.S. 277 (Suffolk 1920).

10. McKinney's SCPA 311.

11. See Matter of Johnson, 114 Misc.2d 100, 450 N.Y.S.2d 740 (Nassau 1982).

12. McKinney's SCPA 1005.

probate proceedings. The court will, in those subsequent proceedings, get personal jurisdiction over the parties entitled to share in the estate.

An exception to this general rule is service on a person whose status as distributee is challenged. The court holds a hearing to decide whether the person is a distributee, and if he is a distributee whether he has forfeited his rights because of abandonment, failure to support, or other grounds. The result of the status hearing may be to preclude him from receiving letters and from sharing in the estate under the laws of intestacy. Failure to serve that person is a jurisdictional defect. Of course, if a party whose status as distributee is challenged receives process and fails to appear and contest, he loses his rights to share in the estate.

SECTION H. DISPENSING WITH SERVICE

The court may dispense with the service of process on those persons having a prior or equal right to letters to the petitioner's if their names or whereabouts are unknown and cannot be discovered with due diligence.[1] In that case, however, the decree granting letters must direct that process issue to such persons in the judicial accounting proceeding, so that then they will have the opportunity to establish their status to share in the estate.[2]

The court's discretion in dispensing with service reflects once again the fact that the "stakes" in administration proceedings are merely who shall serve as fiduciary, not who shall share in the estate.

SECTION I. PROCEEDINGS UPON RETURN OF PROCESS

On the return date, two different proceedings may occur, one for a decedent, the other for an "alleged decedent."[1] In the vast majority of administration cases, the decedent is known to be dead, and the petitioner proves it by submitting a death certificate. In relatively few cases, the petitioner seeks letters for an alleged decedent who disappeared under circumstances that afford reasonable ground to believe he is dead. We discuss the alleged decedent elsewhere,[2] and we mention here only the salient points that relate to administration.

1. DECEDENTS

In proceedings where the decedent is known to be dead, the court requires the death certificate as proof of death. Once the court ac-

Sec. H

1. McKinney's SCPA 1003(4). See, e.g., Matter of Ramm, 22 N.Y.2d 926, 295 N.Y.S.2d 523, 242 N.E.2d 88 (1968), dispensing with service on one son after petitioner, decedent's other son, conducted a fruitless diligent search for him.

2. McKinney's SCPA 1003(4).

Sec. I

1. McKinney's SCPA 1004.

2. See chapter on "Temporary Administration," infra at 289 et seq.

quires jurisdiction on the return date over those with a prior or equal right to letters, or, in a delayed-probate case,[3] over those who would have been entitled to process if the instrument on file had been offered for probate, if no one objects, the court can grant letters without a hearing to the petitioner or another person.[4]

If a party does object to the petition, the court holds a hearing to determine whether the petitioner has the right to serve.

Once the court issues letters, the administrator can obtain from the court clerk a certificate of letters to present when he performs his fiduciary functions.

2. ALLEGED DECEDENTS

Where the petitioner alleges that the decedent is dead, on the return date the court holds a hearing to take proof, look at the facts, and determine whether the person is in fact dead and whether appointment of an administrator is necessary.[5]

The alleged decedent must be served with process,[6] and a guardian ad litem will be appointed to represent him. Obviously a great deal is at risk for the alleged decedent, and the court cannot issue letters based on waivers, default or agreement of the parties.[7]

If the court determines after the hearing that the decedent is indeed dead, it may state so in a decree and issue letters of administration to the petitioner or another person.[8] The Surrogate's decree determining death is, for practical purposes, the equivalent of a death certificate.

Once the court issues letters, the administrator, like the administrator for a "true" decedent, can obtain a certificate of letters indicating his authority to act.

SECTION J. NOTICE OF APPLICATION FOR LETTERS

The court has discretion to require the petitioner to mail written notice of the administration proceedings to the decedent's distributees who did not receive process, that is, those with an inferior right to letters of administration.[1] Like the notice of probate given to legatees,[2] the notice of administration is not jurisdictional;[3] it is to notify the

3. McKinney's SCPA 1001(9), discussed this chapter supra at 137–38.

4. McKinney's SCPA 1004(2).

5. McKinney's SCPA 1004(1).

6. McKinney's SCPA 1003(1).

7. McKinney's SCPA 1003(1).

8. McKinney's SCPA 1004(1).

Sec. J

1. McKinney's SCPA 1005(1). Such notice need not be served, of course, on any party who has appeared in the proceeding or waived service of process.

2. McKinney's SCPA 1409, discussed in chapter on "Probate," supra at 82–84.

3. Matter of Smith, 175 Misc. 688, 24 N.Y.S.2d 704 (Kings 1940).

interested persons that someone has petitioned for letters, so they can appear in the proceeding to protect their interests if they wish.

The courts typically order this notice to be served and are fairly strict about compliance with the statute. The original notice must be filed in the Surrogate's Court with proof of mailing by affidavit (or by affirmation if made by an attorney).[4] The court can delay the issuance of letters or the granting of the decree until the petitioner complies with the notice requirement.

The notice states the caption of the proceedings, all the names by which the intestate was known, the fact that the petitioner has applied for a decree granting letters of administration and the date the letters will issue, the name of the person to whom letters will issue, the name and address of the petitioner and all the distributees listed in the petition, and a statement that the person serving the notice knows of no other distributees.[5]

SECTION K. FAILURE TO QUALIFY

Once a person asserts his right to letters of administration in a decedent's estate, he must qualify as administrator by signing an oath, designating the court clerk to receive process, and filing a bond.[1] The bond is fixed by the value of personal property in the intestate estate, including money, securities and bank accounts, plus estimated gross rents for eighteen months from real property, and the probable recovery the estate will receive in a cause of action the fiduciary intends to commence.[2] The value of the bond does not have to include non-testamentary assets such as Totten Trusts, joint property, insurance or pensions unless the estate is the beneficiary. The petitioner usually signs the oath and designation and obtains a bond before filing the petition, and files them along with (or as part of) the petition.[3]

Sometimes a person eligible to serve as administrator anticipates a lawsuit against the estate and tries to prevent its commencement by failing to qualify as administrator. In that case the court can force the fiduciary to qualify.[4] A person interested in the estate, a creditor or the public administrator can invoke this power by submitting an application, and the court will then require (by citation or order to show cause) the administrator to qualify within a specified time, usual-

4. McKinney's SCPA 1005(3).

5. McKinney's SCPA 1005(2).

Sec. K

1. McKinney's SCPA 708, discussed in chapter on "Fiduciaries," infra at 391–92.

2. McKinney's SCPA 801(1). As we discuss in chapter on "Fiduciaries," infra at 386–87, and in chapter on "Wrongful Death," infra at 529, the court often severely restricts an administrator's powers vis a vis a wrongful death or personal injury recovery and does not require a bond to cover that fund.

3. If the court appoints a successor fiduciary, qualification usually occurs after the filing of the petition.

4. McKinney's SCPA 1006.

ly fifteen days. If he does not, the court treats him as though he renounced his appointment and appoints someone else to serve.[5]

SECTION L. ADMINISTRATION DE BONIS NON

An administrator de bonis non is a successor administrator who continues the administration of an estate after the original administrator has died or left the position for some other reason.[1] When the office becomes vacant, the court may appoint letters of administration to other persons in the same order of priority in which it could originally have appointed them.[2]

If the sole fiduciary dies and a fiduciary is appointed in his estate, that fiduciary can wind up the estate if it has been substantially administered and merely awaits distribution [3] or the court can appoint an administrator d.b.n. if more substantial administration is required.[4]

There is some interplay here between the various provisions of Article 10. If a sole distributee dies, his fiduciary is entitled to letters of administration.[5] Thus the court can either let him wind up an almost-administered estate in his capacity as fiduciary of the deceased fiduciary,[6] or can appoint him administrator of the original decedent's estate if some work remains to be done.[7] The court has similar discretion in granting letters to the fiduciary of the distributee entitled to the largest share of the estate when that distributee dies.[8]

Where co-administrators are serving, one vacancy does not trigger the necessity for an administrator d.b.n.; the remaining fiduciary can wind up the estate.[9] Only when none of the appointed administrators is able to continue his duties will the court appoint an administrator d.b.n., who must be eligible and must qualify.

5. See Matter of Boehm, 207 N.Y.S.2d 43 (Suffolk 1960); Matter of Bemis, 116 Misc. 516, 190 N.Y.S. 269 (Westchester 1921).

Sec. L

1. McKinney's SCPA 1007.

2. See Matter of Mraz, 111 Misc.2d 804, 445 N.Y.S.2d 405 (Nassau 1981), where a son of the decedent died and the court appointed another of decedent's sons as administrator d.b.n. The wife of the deceased son had applied for letters d.b.n., and the court refused to grant them. Though she did not state whether she was the deceased son's executor, the court found that the other son had priority because the fiduciary of a deceased fiduciary can serve only when administration is substantially completed, and here it was not.

3. McKinney's SCPA 2207.

4. See Matter of Marks, 101 Misc.2d 115, 420 N.Y.S.2d 696 (Rensselaer 1979), in which the court held that the deceased fiduciary's fiduciaries could not continue administration of the estate either under McKinney's SCPA 2207 (because the estate was not substantially administered) or McKinney's SCPA 1007 (because the deceased fiduciary was not a distributee), and appointed the public administrator, who does have a right to serve under McKinney's SCPA 1001(8).

5. McKinney's SCPA 1001(2).

6. McKinney's SCPA 1007; 2207.

7. McKinney's SCPA 1001(2); 1007(1); Matter of Briasco, 69 Misc. 278, 126 N.Y.S. 1001 (Suffolk 1910).

8. McKinney's SCPA 1001(4)(a); Matter of Gallagher, 194 Misc. 180, 86 N.Y.S.2d 589 (Kings 1949). See McKinney's SCPA 1007, Prac.Comm. at 62–63 (1967).

9. McKinney's SCPA 706(1), discussed in chapter on "Fiduciaries," infra at 388.

The petition and proceedings are the same as those used for original letters of administration, except that the petition and the citations should also state that the office of administrator has become vacant.

Where the estate was already partially administered, the court may fix the bond in a sum not less than the value of the assets remaining unadministered. The court has discretion to determine the amount of bond to be filed.[10]

10. McKinney's SCPA 801(1)(a).

Chapter Five

CLAIMS

SECTION A. INTRODUCTION

One of the responsibilities of a fiduciary is to pay all legitimate debts of the decedent before distributing the assets, and to resist unjustified claims by asserting all appropriate defenses.[1] If he distributes the estate assets prematurely, he will be personally liable to the creditors. SCPA Article 18 governs the fiduciary's payment of the decedent's debts, and this chapter discusses Article 18: the fiduciary's liability for claims, the ways of giving notice to creditors, the allowance and rejection of claims, contingent or unliquidated claims, priorities among claims and compromises with claimants.

Creditors are also bound to follow the rules of Article 18; they need to be especially careful about timing. Besides the obvious statute of limitations that attaches to the claim itself under the CPLR or other statutes,[2] which stops running when the claimant files a claim with the fiduciary,[3] the claimant must be aware of three statute of limitations expressly set forth in Article 18: a seven-month statute of limitations,[4] a three-month statute of limitations,[5] and a sixty-day statute of limitations.[6]

SECTION B. PRESENTATION OF CLAIMS

Claimants must present a notice of their claims in writing to the fiduciary.[1] The fiduciary need not search for creditors; it is assumed that creditors will, with ordinary diligence, send bills within a reasonable time to persons who owe them money, causing the fiduciary to get

Sec. A

1. Matter of Taylor, 251 N.Y. 257, 167 N.E. 434 (1929) (lack of consideration); Butler v. Johnson, 111 N.Y. 204, 18 N.E. 643 (1888) (defense of statute of limitations); Matter of Sage, 54 Misc.2d 779, 283 N.Y.S.2d 442 (New York County 1967) (fiduciary of a deceased income beneficiary had fiduciary obligation to resist claim that decedent's estate repay for benefit of principal remaindermen excess amounts of income received); Matter of Meyering, 184 Misc. 233, 55 N.Y.S.2d 553 (Monroe 1945) (claim served on Surrogate, but not on fiduciary, within statute of limitations).

2. For example, see McKinney's CPLR 214 (three-year statute), McKinney's CPLR 213 (six-year statute).

3. McKinney's SCPA 1808(6).

4. McKinney's SCPA 1802, discussed this chapter infra at 148–50.

5. McKinney's SCPA 1801, discussed this chapter infra at 150–51.

6. McKinney's SCPA 1810, discussed this chapter infra at 162.

Sec. B

1. McKinney's SCPA 1803.

notice of the claim. If the claimant has not been paid and learns of the decedent's death, he should present his claims to the fiduciary in writing, either personally or by mail, using either the address listed in the designation the fiduciary filed with the clerk of the court,[2] or, if the notice to the claimant was made by publication,[3] the address listed in the published notice.

In the claim, the claimant must state the amount due and the facts underlying the claim. The fiduciary may also ask the claimant for an affidavit swearing that the claim is justly due, that he has credited the decedent with any payments the decedent made, that he owes the estate nothing, and that he holds no collateral for the debt except that listed in the affidavit. If the claim is for repayment of a loan to the decedent, the claimant must support the claim with substantial documentary evidence.[4]

Certain claims need not be in writing: claims for administration expenses[5] (on the theory that the fiduciary, who is after all the one incurring them, knows of these expenses); claims of the United States or New York State[6] (on the theory that the state cannot prevent the federal or state government from attempting to collect its taxes);[7] and claims reduced to judgment by a court of competent jurisdiction[8] (on the theory that the fiduciary is charged with knowledge of those claims); in that case the claimant may ask the court for an order of execution against the property even if he has not filed a claim with the fiduciary.[9] As a practical matter, claims mailed to the decedent before his death also do not meet the formality requirements, but the fiduciary knows of them (or should) and can pay them without their formal presentation if he deems them proper.

The claimant has a right to file a claim at any time,[10] but he needs to be mindful of two alternative statutes of limitations, a seven-month statute and a three-month statute, one of which will apply to him and may drastically alter his rights to payment.

2. See McKinney's SCPA 708 and discussion of the designation in chapters on "Fiduciaries," infra at 391–92, "Probate," supra at 111, and "Administration," supra at 129.

3. McKinney's SCPA 1801, discussed this chapter infra at 150–51.

4. McKinney's SCPA 1803(1).

5. McKinney's SCPA 1803(1).

6. McKinney's SCPA 1803(1).

7. See McKinney's SCPA 1803, Prac. Comm. at 89 (1967). For a discussion of the sometimes uncomfortable position this places the fiduciary in vis a vis unpaid taxes, see Ferguson, The Fiduciary's Personal Liability for Federal Taxes of the Decedent and His Estate: the Problems of Distribution and Partial Distribution, 25 N.Y.U.Inst. on Fed.Tax. 1185 (1967).

8. McKinney's SCPA 1803(3). See Matter of Geraerdt, 211 N.Y.S.2d 915 (Westchester 1961) (fiduciary relationship between executor and judgment creditor prevents running of statute of limitations).

9. See Matter of Chester National Bank, 72 Misc.2d 310, 339 N.Y.S.2d 174 (Orange 1972).

10. McKinney's SCPA 1803; Matter of Goldberg, 14 A.D.2d 294, 220 N.Y.S.2d 559 (1st Dep't 1961), affirmed in part, reversed in part 12 N.Y.2d 911, 237 N.Y.S.2d 1008, 188 N.E.2d 271 (1963).

SECTION C. FIDUCIARY'S LIABILITY FOR CLAIMS

1. SEVEN MONTH STATUTE OF LIMITATIONS

A fiduciary unaware of a claim is not personally liable to a claimant who does not present his claim within seven months of the issuance of letters if the fiduciary satisfies other lawful claims or distributes estate assets after seven months in good faith.[1]

This narrow statute of limitations does not define or limit the liability of the estate or the beneficiaries who have received the property. Its purpose is to eliminate the fiduciary's personal liability if he distributes the estate after seven months in good faith.[2] In cases where a claimant fails to present his claim within the seven months, if the fiduciary has not distributed the assets and finally accounted, the claimant can still recover on a valid claim not barred by the underlying CPLR statute of limitations [3] by asserting it or compelling an accounting.[4] If, however, the fiduciary has paid the assets to beneficiaries in good faith, or used the assets to pay other claims, the claimant cannot compel an accounting. He can follow the estate assets to the beneficiaries under the will or intestate distributees who received them,[5] and we discuss that issue presently,[6] but the fiduciary's liability has, at that point, ended.

If the executor is also the sole beneficiary of the estate, the claimant can file his claim before or after the seven months, because this statute of limitations is meant to protect an executor only after the estate property is out of his hands.[7]

The seven-month rule protects only fiduciaries acting in good faith. The fiduciary's good faith is a question of fact and the court can hold a hearing to decide it.[8] If the fiduciary knows (or should have known) of a claim, even if the claimant did not present it formally, he fails the

Sec. C

1. McKinney's SCPA 1802. The fiduciary does not have to pay any claims before the end of the seven months unless the will or court order directs early payment. McKinney's EPTL 11–1.5(a). If a claimant wants early payment, he can petition for a court order under McKinney's SCPA 2102(4), discussed in chapter on "Miscellaneous Proceedings," infra at 332–33.

2. Matter of Disalvo, N.Y.L.J., March 29, 1985, at 14, col. 2 (Bronx); Matter of Lee, 107 Misc.2d 928, 436 N.Y.S.2d 180 (City Court Buffalo 1981).

3. Matter of Lent, 82 N.Y.S.2d 904 (New York County 1948).

4. Matter of Mullon, 145 N.Y. 98, 39 N.E. 821 (1895) (creditor can compel accounting); Matter of Goldberg, 14 A.D.2d 294, 220 N.Y.S.2d 559 (1st Dep't 1961), affirmed 12 N.Y.2d 911, 237 N.Y.S.2d 1008, 188 N.E.2d 271 (1962) (accord). Compulsory accountings are governed by McKinney's SCPA 2205 and discussed in chapter on "Accounting," infra at 183–86.

5. McKinney's EPTL 12–1.1(a).

6. See "Claimants' Remedies After Distribution of Estate Assets," infra at 151.

7. See Rubin v. Kurzman, 436 F.Supp. 1044 (S.D.N.Y.1977) (the executor in effect "trades hats" and can be pursued as a beneficiary under McKinney's EPTL 12–1.1(a)).

8. Matter of Lukin, 26 Misc.2d 176, 207 N.Y.S.2d 318 (Nassau 1960) (issue of whether fiduciary had knowledge of claim against estate before he made distribution would be determined at hearing).

good faith test if he distributes the assets without paying the claim.[9] In that case the claimant can recover from the fiduciary personally if the estate does not contain enough property to satisfy the claim.[10] In addition, a fiduciary is charged with knowledge of some claims, such as funeral expenses,[11] hospital and doctor bills,[12] and judgments against the decedent.[13]

For statute of limitations purposes, the presentation of the claim commences a special proceeding which tolls the statute.[14] Naturally, if a claimant is time-barred in another court, he cannot enforce his claim in the Surrogate's Court.[15]

a. How to Compute the Seven Months in Cases of Successor Fiduciaries

Occasionally the fiduciary nominated to administer the estate does not immediately assume office, but a temporary administrator or preliminary executor serves first until some conflict or delay can be resolved and the ultimate fiduciary appointed. In that case a claimant has seven months to present his claim and the statute states that the seven-month period starts from the issuance of the first letters, even if they are temporary or preliminary letters.[16] The sound rationale for this rule is that temporary administrators and preliminary executors have the power to pay claims, preliminary executors on their own and temporary administrators with a court order,[17] so a creditor should not

9. Matter of Segall, 287 N.Y. 52, 38 N.E.2d 126 (1941) (law does not protect executor who distributes estate with knowledge of outstanding claim); Matter of Lee, 107 Misc.2d 928, 436 N.Y.S.2d 180 (Yates 1981) (accord); Matter of Simon, 48 Misc.2d 851, 265 N.Y.S.2d 818 (Nassau 1966).

10. See Matter of Schaeffner, 96 Misc. 2d 846, 410 N.Y.S.2d 44 (Nassau 1978).

11. Matter of Reinhardt, 202 Misc. 424, 114 N.Y.S.2d 208 (Kings 1952).

12. Matter of Swaab, 40 Misc.2d 767, 244 N.Y.S.2d 83 (New York County 1963); Matter of Schoenberger, N.Y.L.J. May 16, 1978, at 12, col. 2 (Queens). If reimbursement or assistance is available from Medicare or some such source, the fiduciary should establish the decedent's eligibility for those funds when the hospital or doctor bills are presented. See Matter of Lazarides, N.Y.L.J., April 5, 1978, at 13, col. 3, where the court struck the fiduciary's affirmative defense against the hospital that the hospital should have collected the payment from Medicare, holding that the fiduciary had the burden of establishing eligibility for Medicare benefits, and that it had failed to do so. Without answering the question of whether the hospital owed the decedent the duty of attempting to collect from Medicare, the court ruled that the estate had not proved enough even to assert that claim.

13. See Matter of Chester National Bank, 72 Misc.2d 310, 339 N.Y.S.2d 174 (Orange 1972).

14. McKinney's SCPA 1808(6); Matter of Feinberg, 18 N.Y.2d 499, 277 N.Y.S.2d 249, 223 N.E.2d 780 (1966).

15. Matter of Thom, 76 Misc.2d 132, 350 N.Y.S.2d 568 (Monroe 1973).

16. McKinney's SCPA 1802, amended by L.1970, c. 15. Contrast this with the six-month period a surviving spouse has to exercise the right of election, which starts to run only at the issuance of letters of administration or letters testamentary. The surviving spouse can exercise the right before the fiduciary is appointed or at any time until six months after the appointment.

17. See McKinney's SCPA 1412, discussed in chapter on "Probate," supra at 118–24, and McKinney's SCPA 903, discussed in chapter on "Temporary Administration," infra at 297–300.

be given a second chance to present his claim after having missed the first one.

There is no conflict between this rule and the rule set forth in SCPA 705 that, in estates where successive fiduciaries serve, the statute of limitations starts to run from the issuing of the first letters except where the first letters were preliminary or temporary letters or letters of administration later revoked when a will was admitted to probate.[18] SCPA 705 makes an exception where the law specifically provides otherwise, and SCPA 1802 does.[19]

The issuance of letters to a permanent fiduciary does not interrupt the seven-month period, but a gap between the temporary or preliminary fiduciary and the permanent fiduciary during which no fiduciary is serving will not count in measuring the seven months.[20]

2. THREE MONTH STATUTE OF LIMITATIONS

A fiduciary who wants to distribute the assets before the end of the seven month period may do so by giving creditors notice of the decedent's death by publication.[21] Publication is used for unknown creditors, because if a fiduciary knows of a creditor, he may not pay out estate assets without first paying the claim.

The notice must appear once a week for three consecutive months in a newspaper printed in the county of decedent's domicile. The notice informs all creditors to present their claims to the fiduciary at a place and by a date set forth in the notice. The date must be at least three months from the date of the first publication. If the publications are not completed, because, for example, the fiduciary dies or resigns or the newspaper stops publishing, the court can direct the publication of a new notice for a time sufficient to complete the three-month period. It need not be in the same newspaper and all publications need not be within a three-month period, so long as they cover three months in total.

In major cities [22] the notice can be published in alternate weeks for a fourteen-week consecutive period. The rationale for the shorter publication period is twofold: the notice in these larger-circulation

18. Under McKinney's SCPA 1413, the decree admitting the will to probate must revoke the former letters.

19. McKinney's SCPA 705 originally contemplated procedures that could be begun only after probate. The legislature considered revising 705 to conform with McKinney's SCPA 1802, L.1970, c. 15, but declined to do so because of these post-probate procedures. The two such procedures mentioned were objections to excess charitable gifts under McKinney's EPTL 5–3.3, which was repealed in 1980, L.1980, c. 461, and the right of election under McKinney's EPTL 5–1.1, which was revised in 1971 to permit a pre-probate exercise of the right. L.1971, c. 796. McKinney's SCPA 705 therefore has very little continuing validity. See Tate v. McQuade, 83 Misc.2d 951, 373 N.Y.S.2d 263 (Westchester 1975).

20. McKinney's SCPA 1802.

21. McKinney's SCPA 1801.

22. That is, the boroughs of New York City or counties containing a "city of the first or second class." A city of the first class has a minimum population of 175,000, and a city of the second class has a minimum population of 50,000. McKinney's Veh. & Traffic L. § 107 (1970).

urban newspapers is likely to reach more creditors, and since the cost of advertising in the larger newspapers is higher than in rural or suburban areas, the costs to the estate are kept within moderation.

Most fiduciaries do not use publication as a means of notifying creditors. It can accelerate the distributions by no more than four months,[23] so its costs are often not warranted. Usually fiduciaries take more than three months to complete administration, so such urgency to distribute assets is rare.

If a fiduciary does publish for creditors and a creditor does not present his claim, the fiduciary acting in good faith can distribute the estate assets without liability to the claimant. If the fiduciary still has estate assets, the claimant can assert his claim. If the claimant eventually presents his claim after the fiduciary has distributed the estate assets, the claimant can bring an action against the beneficiaries.[24]

SECTION D. CLAIMANT'S REMEDIES AFTER DISTRIBUTION OF ESTATE ASSETS

If a claimant fails to present his claim within the seven-month (or three-month) period just described, and his claim is still valid (that is, not time-barred by the underlying CPLR statute of limitations), his first step is to try to recover from the fiduciary.[1] If he cannot, because the fiduciary has distributed the assets or paid other claims and does not have sufficient assets to pay the claim, the claimant may bring an action in the Supreme Court or another civil court of competent jurisdiction against the distributees and beneficiaries who received the estate assets,[2] following the statutory order of priority among them.[3]

Intestate distributees are the first class to lose their distributions if the estate is insufficient to cover all claims and expenses. If the decedent had a will but part of his property passed in intestacy (for example, if the residuary estate was left to the decedent's sister and she predeceased the decedent without issue), the distributees' intestate shares would abate entirely before the shares of any other beneficiaries would be touched.[4] If the intestate shares were used up and a balance remained to be paid on the claim, the residuary beneficiaries' shares [5] would next abate ratably, and when they were gone the general beneficiaries' shares would abate ratably.[6] When the general disposi-

23. See McKinney's SCPA 1802, discussed in preceding section, for the usual seven-month rule.

24. See discussion of a creditor's right to proceed against beneficiaries in the next section of this chapter.

Sec. D

1. McKinney's EPTL 12–1.1(b)(2).

2. McKinney's EPTL 12–2.1. The interest of a distributee or beneficiary is subject to enforcement of a money judgment. McKinney's CPLR 5201(b).

3. McKinney's EPTL 12–1.2.

4. McKinney's EPTL 12–1.2.

5. A residuary disposition is the disposition of property remaining after all the pre-residuary, that is, general, demonstrative and specific, dispositions.

6. A general disposition is a "testamentary disposition of property not amounting

tions were gone the demonstrative [7] and specific [8] beneficiaries' shares would abate ratably together, unless the fund out of which the demonstrative beneficiaries' share was to be taken is no longer in existence, in which case the demonstrative beneficiaries' shares would abate along with the general beneficiaries'.[9] Finally, the share given to a surviving spouse which qualifies for the estate tax marital deduction would abate last.[10]

The claimant has to foreclose on a mortgage or enforce a lien he has on specifically devised or bequeathed estate property before going against the beneficiaries generally, and he must also attempt to recover his claim from the proceeds of life insurance payable to a named beneficiary before going against other estate property in beneficiaries' hands.[11]

If one of the beneficiaries within this hierarchy is not in New York or otherwise subject to the court's personal jurisdiction, or is insolvent, the claimant can proceed against a beneficiary from a subsequent class.[12] For example, if the residuary beneficiary is a non-New Yorker who has not given the court any ground for exercising personal jurisdiction, the claimant can sue a specific beneficiary who is within the court's jurisdiction.

To illustrate this rule, if a person had extended a loan to a decedent and taken back a mortgage, that person would have first to foreclose on the mortgage, second to go against the fiduciary for any deficiency, and finally bring an action against the beneficiaries for any ultimate deficiency,[13] following the statutory order of abatement.

The distributee or beneficiary can interpose as a defense the existence of another claim entitled to preference over the creditor at bar.[14]

The claimant may recover the whole amount the beneficiary received if it does not exceed the claim, but the beneficiary is ultimately responsible only for his ratable proportion of the claim and can recover the excess from the other beneficiaries.[15] If the beneficiary owes more than one claim, the claims are subject to the SCPA priorities, which we

to a demonstrative, residuary or specific disposition." McKinney's EPTL 1–2.8.

7. A demonstrative disposition is "a testamentary disposition of property to be taken out of specified or identified property." McKinney's EPTL 1–2.3.

8. A specific disposition is "a disposition of a specific or identified item of testator's property." McKinney's EPTL 1–2.16.

9. McKinney's EPTL 12–1.2(a)(4).

10. McKinney's EPTL 12–1.2(a)(5).

11. McKinney's EPTL 12–1.1(b)(3); see Matter of Figliola's, 81 Misc.2d 979, 367 N.Y.S.2d 384 (1975).

12. McKinney's EPTL 12–1.1(b)(2).

13. Jemzura v. Jemzura, 36 N.Y.2d 496, 369 N.Y.S.2d 400, 330 N.E.2d 414 (1975). McKinney's EPTL 12–1.1(b)(3). The foreclosure would be authorized by McKinney's EPTL 3–3.6, which says that a beneficiary who receives property encumbered by a lien or mortgage must pay it unless the will directs otherwise.

14. McKinney's EPTL 12–1.2(d)(2).

15. McKinney's EPTL 12–1.3(a); 12–1.1, Prac.Comm. at 319 (1967).

discuss shortly.[16] The distributee can also vary the preferences and the order of abatement by will.[17]

In short, the Article 18 statutes of limitations protect the fiduciary against personal liability, but do not completely bar the claimant from all relief.

SECTION E. CONTINGENT CLAIMS

Sometimes a fiduciary cannot distribute the estate to the beneficiaries because someone has either a contingent claim or a claim of an uncertain amount against the state. If that happens, a claimant can give the fiduciary an affidavit showing the facts relating to the claim and estimating the amount of the claim.[1] The fiduciary then has to reserve an amount the court considers sufficient to cover the contingent or unliquidated claim. The court determines the amount by looking at all the facts and circumstances of the claim, including any security to which the claimant can resort for satisfaction of the claim. It usually orders reservation of more than enough to meet the obligation, for example twice the actuarial worth of the claim [2] and in some cases, the entire net estate.[3]

For example, if the decedent was obligated under a separation agreement or divorce decree to make payments to his spouse until death or remarriage, the spouse could request the reservation of funds.[4] The court where possible computes the amount by using actuarial tables. Similarly, if the decedent had rented real property and his estate was liable for the rent unless certain contingencies occurred, the court could order a reserve fund to cover the contingent claim.[5] The court can also order the reservation of funds when the decedent was principal on an outstanding bond, recognizance or undertaking.[6]

This rule is mandatory.[7] Unless the will provides otherwise, the executor must hold and administer the reserve fund, and the courts rather strictly construe it. Where the claim is for periodic payments for life, for example, the courts frown on allowing a lump sum payment

16. McKinney's SCPA 1811, discussed this chapter infra at 164–72.

17. McKinney's EPTL 12–1.2(c).

Sec. E

1. McKinney's SCPA 1804(1).

2. See Matter of Reid, 165 Misc. 207, 300 N.Y.S. 1083 (New York County 1937), affirmed 254 App.Div. 850, 6 N.Y.S.2d 360 (1st Dep't 1937), where a husband set up an inter-vivos trust to pay his former wife $30,000 per year. When he died, she challenged its sufficiency. The court ruled that she had not bound herself by accepting the payments during her former husband's lifetime.

3. Matter of Biel, N.Y.L.J., April 3, 1985, at 15, col. 4 (Suffolk); Matter of Grimley, 200 Misc. 901, 107 N.Y.S.2d 129 (New York County 1951).

4. See Cohen v. Cronin, 39 N.Y.2d 42, 382 N.Y.S.2d 724, 346 N.E.2d 524 (1976) (reserve fund established to continue terms of separation agreement granting wife $400 per month until she died or remarried); Matter of Runals, 68 Misc.2d 967, 328 N.Y.S.2d 966 (Cattaraugus 1972) (accord).

5. Matter of DeMartino, N.Y.L.J., Dec. 3, 1964, at 17, col. 5 (New York County).

6. See Matter of Burrows, 283 N.Y. 540, 29 N.E.2d 77 (1940) (past due bond and mortgage).

7. McKinney's SCPA 1804(1).

based on the actuarial value of those payments.[8] While a will can authorize an executor to purchase an annuity to discharge the decedent's obligation, the court will not interfere with the executor's decision not to do so,[9] and even if the will gives the fiduciary the authority to make "a different settlement or adjustment of said obligation," the court will evaluate the fiduciary's decision and may require him to set aside the fund despite his own contrary plan.[10]

If the amount of the claim becomes certain before the fiduciary files his final account, the claimant can simply file a formal claim with the fiduciary.[11] If, on the other hand, the fiduciary is ready to finalize his account and the claim is still contingent or unliquidated, the court can, in the final accounting, direct that the fiduciary retain an amount sufficient to cover the probable claim, and distribute the rest.[12]

Sometimes the unliquidated claim is for New York estate taxes; [13] this may occur if the fiduciary has filed a state estate tax return but the state has not finished the audit by the time the fiduciary is ready to account. In these cases the court orders some amount reserved and permits the rest to be paid to the beneficiaries. The State Tax Commission is a necessary party to the accounting proceeding.[14] The court is often very conservative and directs a reserve fund large enough to cover the worst (for the taxpayer) possible outcome of the tax audit, while still permitting, where possible, some distributions to beneficiaries. The same reservation of funds can be made for payment of federal estate taxes,[15] or fiduciary income taxes.[16]

The fiduciary should make the contingent claimant a party to the accounting proceeding and ask the court to reject the claim, or set aside a fund, as the case may be, and order distribution of the assets or the assets remaining after reservation of the fund, as the case may be. If the court does so, the claimant has no cause of action against the

8. See Matter of Burridge, 146 Misc. 527, 262 N.Y.S. 378 (New York County 1933), where the decedent had agreed to pay his ex-wife $50 per month, and the court ordered the executor to set aside a fund to make the monthly payment, refusing to allow the ex-wife a lump sum based on her estimated life span.

9. Matter of Runals, 68 Misc.2d 967, 328 N.Y.S.2d 966 (Cattaraugus 1972).

10. In Matter of Runals, 68 Misc.2d 967, 328 N.Y.S.2d 966 (Cattaraugus 1972), the decedent gave the executor this authorization and the executor tried to shift to the trustee of the trust created for the second wife the obligation to make annual payments to the decedent's first wife. The court forbade it, and ordered him to set aside a fund under McKinney's SCPA 1804.

11. McKinney's SCPA 1804(2); 1803, discussed this chapter supra at 146–47.

12. McKinney's SCPA 1804(2).

13. McKinney's SCPA 1804(3).

14. McKinney's SCPA 1804(3).

15. See discussion of state and federal estate taxes in chapter on "Estate Taxes," infra at 556 et seq.

16. See Matter of Rappaport, N.Y.L.J., May 20, 1985, at 19, col. 1. There the court then ordered payment of the money out of the reserve fund to beneficiaries who agreed to pay the taxes, and ordered the beneficiaries receiving the funds to file refunding bonds, in case the estate was later found to be liable for those taxes. The court later limited its order to allow payment out of the reserve fund of only the reimbursement of taxes actually paid by the beneficiaries. Matter of Rappaport, N.Y.L.J., July 10, 1985, at 13, col. 2 (Nassau).

fiduciary, and the court's rejection of his claim would be res judicata in another action on the same claim against the beneficiaries.

An executor administering a reserve fund has the same powers, duties and liabilities [17] he had while administering the estate.[18]

The Surrogates sometimes refuse to order a reserve fund where the claim is based on a negligence suit against the decedent.[19] The reasons are legion. Such claims are not "contingent" within the statute's contemplation. The statute should cover claims where the liability is clear but the amount of damages is either contingent or subject to a condition precedent (such as default by the person primarily responsible for the claim). The plaintiff in the negligence suit has no status as a creditor. In negligence cases often the demand is exaggerated, the judgment is covered by insurance, and the action is protracted by delays. The claimant does not present a formal claim [20] to the fiduciary. As a practical matter, therefore, the courts have sometimes determined not to allow such lawsuits to delay the finalization of an estate. If the liability and amount are later established and insurance does not cover the full indebtedness, the claimant has to pursue his claim against the beneficiaries.[21]

In the proper case, however, the court will order reservation of a fund in a negligence action. The elements of the "proper case" may be some or all of the following: [22]

1. the commencement of the accounting proceeding reasonably soon after the decedent's death;

2. the insurance carrier's offer to pay the full amount of its policy;

3. a seemingly meritorious claim in excess of the insurance;

4. the absence of dependent spouse or minor children;

17. A fiduciary has the powers granted by McKinney's EPTL 11–1.1, discussed in chapter on "Fiduciaries," infra at 402–05, as modified by the testator in the will. Fiduciaries' duties and liabilities are discussed in chapter on "Fiduciaries," infra at 405 et seq.

18. Matter of Runals, 68 Misc.2d 967, 328 N.Y.S.2d 966 (Cattaraugus 1972).

19. See Matter of Rosenfeld, 42 Misc.2d 117, 247 N.Y.S.2d 639 (New York County 1963); Matter of Zutell, 213 N.Y.S.2d 290 (Queens 1961); Matter of Schwartz, 19 Misc.2d 203, 191 N.Y.S.2d 810 (Kings 1959). See also Matter of Baldwin, 157 Misc. 538, 284 N.Y.S. 761 (Westchester 1935) (similar refusal to set aside a reserve fund in proceedings against decedent as corporate director).

20. The formal claim is required by McKinney's SCPA 1803, discussed this chapter supra at 146–47.

21. Arguably in these cases fiduciaries may lose their McKinney's SCPA 1802 "seven month" protection because they know of the claim when they distribute the estate assets to beneficiaries. See McKinney's SCPA 1804, Prac.Comm. at 32 (Supp. 1986). Only an accounting decree (or court approval in another proceeding) would fully protect the fiduciary.

22. See Matter of Biel, 103 A.D.2d 287, 479 N.Y.S.2d 740 (2d Dep't 1984), on remand N.Y.L.J., April 3, 1985, at 15, col. 4 (Suffolk) (entire estate held in reserve for payment of negligence claim); Matter of Berg, N.Y.L.J., March 8, 1985, at 16, col. 2 (Nassau); Matter of Vasquez, 122 Misc.2d 479, 471 N.Y.S.2d 780 (Bronx 1984); Matter of Keisler, 41 Misc.2d 991, 246 N.Y.S.2d 870 (Bronx 1964).

5. the unlikelihood that plaintiff will be able to recover on the judgment from beneficiaries (because, for example, they are non-New Yorkers) if no fund is reserved;

6. the plaintiff's diligent prosecution of his claim.

7. the relatively small percentage of the estate assets the plaintiff seeks to reserve.

The court will also weigh those factors in deciding how long the funds should be reserved.[23]

SECTION F. FIDUCIARIES' CLAIMS

If the decedent owed the fiduciary money, the fiduciary cannot ordinarily reimburse himself from the estate assets until he proves the claim and the court allows it in the final accounting proceeding.[1] The fiduciary has the burden of proving the debt by clear and convincing proof.[2] If someone controverts the claim, it will be treated like any other contested claim on the accounting.

Despite this general rule, the fiduciary may present an ex parte application to the court for advance payment of the claim,[3] and if the estate is solvent, he should do so promptly or risk being surcharged for any loss to the estate, such as the interest that accrues on the debt after letters are issued,[4] or increased commissions if the amount of the unpaid claim would push the estate into a multiple-commissions bracket.[5] The application should establish the claim and the interest rate clearly and should be supported by affidavits if necessary. The fiduciary should attach promissory notes or any other relevant documentary evidence to the petition and affidavits, or the court will deny the application. If questions of fact arise, the court may order a hearing at which those interested in the estate have an opportunity to be heard, even though the application was originally ex parte.[6] With or without a hearing, the fiduciary should prove his claim to the court's full satisfaction.[7] After the hearing, the court can allow the fiduciary to

23. See Matter of Biel, 103 A.D.2d 287, 479 N.Y.S.2d 740 (2d Dep't 1984).

Sec. F

1. McKinney's SCPA 1805(1).

2. Matter of Zalaznick, 90 Misc.2d 113, 394 N.Y.S.2d 347 (Bronx 1977); Matter of Effros, 43 A.D.2d 539, 349 N.Y.S.2d 688 (1st Dep't 1973).

3. McKinney's SCPA 1805.

4. Matter of Ludlam, 32 A.D.2d 948, 304 N.Y.S.2d 73 (2d Dep't 1969); Matter of Bender, 56 Misc.2d 585, 289 N.Y.S.2d 822 (Nassau 1968). See also Matter of Rubin, 7 A.D.2d 624, 179 N.Y.S.2d 465 (1st Dep't 1958), affirmed 5 N.Y.2d 1022, 185 N.Y.S.2d 548, 158 N.E.2d 249 (1959); McKinney's SCPA 1805, Prof. Powers, Practice Commentary at 35–36 (Supp.1986).

5. An estate of under $100,000 permits the payment of one full statutory commission, while an estate of $100,000 or more permits multiple commissions. See McKinney's SCPA 2307 and chapter on "Commissions," infra at 426–29. If an estate is $103,000 and one of the fiduciaries has a claim for $4,000, he should apply for advance payment to get the estate below the multiple commissions level. Matter of Robord, 69 Misc.2d 1026, 332 N.Y.S.2d 698 (1972).

6. McKinney's SCPA 1805(2).

7. Matter of Zalaznick, 90 Misc.2d 113, 394 N.Y.S.2d 347 (Bronx 1977).

pay his own claim and may require him to post a bond or to give notice to interested parties before making the payment.

In practice most applications are granted without notice so that the interest on the claim will stop accumulating and so that the claim can be used as an estate tax deduction.[8] If the fiduciary is a corporate trustee, the court does not require a bond, but if the fiduciary is an individual, the court often does require a bond. The order usually states that the allowance of the claims is subject to objections in the first accounting proceeding. If the objectants prevail, the fiduciary will have to refund the assets.

The fiduciary can also pay himself a claim due from the estate if all the beneficiaries are adults and consent to the payment.[9] Even in that case, however, the court must not allow the payment during the seven-month "creditor-protection" period unless the fiduciary files a refunding bond.[10]

If the fiduciary pays himself estate funds in satisfaction of a claim without court order or without the consent of the interested parties, he will be surcharged at the accounting for the amount he paid himself.[11]

The same rule applies to attorney-fiduciaries: if they pay their claims from the estate in advance without consent of all interested parties or without court approval, they will be subject to surcharge.[12] If an attorney is rendering legal services and is also a fiduciary, he can apply for advance payment of his legal fee,[13] and the court will usually grant his application. Additionally, an attorney-fiduciary may pay himself without a court order if there is a co-fiduciary not rendering legal services who consents to the payment.[14] There is no corresponding provision permitting a fiduciary with a claim other than legal services to satisfy his claim if he gets the consent of a co-fiduciary.[15] He must either obtain the consent of all parties or obtain a court order for the advanced payment. If the fiduciary obtains consents from some of those interested in the estate, but not others, and the court at the accounting denies his claim, only those who did not consent will share, pro rata, in the surcharge.[16]

8. See I.R.C. § 2053.

9. Ledyard v. Bull, 119 N.Y. 62, 23 N.E. 444 (1890); Matter of Bloom, N.Y.L.J., April 24, 1985, at 16, col. 2 (Nassau); Matter of Shapiro, 110 N.Y.S.2d 213 (Kings 1952). The consent cannot be implied when the executor includes it in his accounting, however, and no one objects. It should be in writing. Matter of Smith, 169 Misc. 615, 8 N.Y.S.2d 383 (Kings 1938).

10. E.g., Matter of Bloom, N.Y.L.J., April 24, 1985, at 16, col. 2 (Nassau).

11. See Matter of Bender, 56 Misc.2d 585, 289 N.Y.S.2d 822 (Nassau 1968).

12. Matter of Obst, 115 N.Y.S.2d 739 (Kings 1952).

13. McKinney's SCPA 2111(1). Advance payment of attorneys' fees is discussed in chapter on "Attorneys' Fees," infra at 379–81.

14. McKinney's SCPA 2111(2).

15. See McKinney's SCPA 1805.

16. Matter of Shapiro, 110 N.Y.S.2d 213 (Kings 1952); Matter of Zalaznick, 90 Misc. 2d 113, 394 N.Y.S.2d 347 (Bronx 1977). Errors or malfeasance by the fiduciary are not always treated so; sometimes a fiduciary is surcharged for the entire amount even though only some, or even none, of the beneficiaries object. These surcharges and their apportionment are discussed in chapter on "Accounting," infra at 213.

If a fiduciary advances money to pay administration expenses other than his own legal expenses, it would appear that he can reimburse himself without court approval or consent of the beneficiaries; these are seemingly not personal claims requiring a court order for payment.[17] A fiduciary may not, however, take advance payment of commissions without court approval unless all beneficiaries are adult and competent and they consent.[18]

If an estate is insolvent or may be, the fiduciary should not seek advance payment of his claim, and every application should include enough information to allow the court to determine whether the estate is solvent.

Because of the general rule prohibiting a fiduciary from satisfying his own claim against an estate, the statute of limitations is suspended on that claim from the death of the decedent until the fiduciary first obtains a judicial settlement of his account.[19] If the fiduciary with the claim took over the job from a previously appointed fiduciary, the statute of limitations is suspended only when his letters are issued, and resumes running at the time of his first accounting.

SECTION G. CLAIMANT'S REMEDIES TO ENFORCE CLAIMS

In the ideal case, the claimant presents his claim and the fiduciary pays it. To cover the less than ideal case, Article 18 has several rules to prod the fiduciary and the claimant if they do not act promptly to clarify their positions and to resolve the claims.

After a claimant has filed a written claim with the fiduciary, the fiduciary has to give prompt written notice to the claimant stating whether he allows or rejects the claim in whole or in part.[1] If the fiduciary fails within ninety days from receipt of the claim to tell the claimant whether he is allowing the claim, the claimant may force the fiduciary's hand by serving him with a demand to act on the claim and give the claimant notice of his position on it. If the fiduciary then fails to give notice of allowance or rejection within thirty days, the claim will be considered rejected on the expiration of the thirty days.[2] This gives the claimant some finality so that he may take steps to compel an

17. See McKinney's EPTL 11-1.1(b)(22).

18. McKinney's SCPA 2310, 2311. Advance payment of commissions is discussed in chapter on "Commissions," infra at 447-49.

19. McKinney's SCPA 1805(3).

Sec. G

1. McKinney's SCPA 1806(1). There is, however, no penalty for violation of this promptness rule. McKinney's SCPA 1806(4), which allows the fiduciary to reject a claim any time before the accounting. It was because this "promptness" requirement had no teeth that the legislature amended the statute to add paragraph (3), discussed in the text accompanying this footnote, giving the claimant a way to force a rejection from the fiduciary so he can then pursue his claim either in the Surrogate's Court (under McKinney's SCPA 1808) or in another civil court (under McKinney's SCPA 1810). L.1970, c. 396, § 6.

2. McKinney's SCPA 1806(3).

accounting [3] in the Surrogate's court or start a proceeding in another court of competent jurisdiction,[4] steps we discuss shortly. If a fiduciary allows a claim but delays in making payment, the claimant's remedy is to commence a proceeding to compel payment [5] or to petition for a compulsory accounting.[6]

If the claimant does not demand action by the fiduciary, the fiduciary can give notice of allowance or rejection any time until the eve of the accounting,[7] despite the promptness rule just discussed. If the fiduciary files his account without having rejected or allowed the claim, the claim is deemed allowed.[8] The allowance establishes the validity of the claim.[9] This is, however, only a prima facie establishment of validity, attackable in the accounting proceeding by other interested parties.[10] If the claim is for a debt owed by the decedent, the objectants bear the burden of proving that the claim is invalid,[11] and if it is for administration expenses, the fiduciary bears the burden of sustaining their validity.[12] If the adversely affected party does not object at the accounting, he cannot do so on appeal.[13] If a claim is allowed on an intermediate accounting and the parties do not object, they cannot later object at the final accounting.

If the fiduciary rejects the claim, the court often determines its validity at the accounting proceeding. The fiduciary must give notice of rejection of the claim,[14] because while an unpaid creditor is entitled to process,[15] he usually does not receive a copy of the accounting, and the citation does not always specify that the claim has been rejected; the prayer for relief is simply to settle the account as filed. Thus, except for this requirement that the fiduciary give notice of rejection to the claimant, the claimant may not in fact know it. To be safe, many of the Surrogates direct that the citation served on a rejected claimant in the accounting proceeding order him to show cause why his claim should not be rejected.

3. McKinney's SCPA 2205. Compulsory accountings are discussed in chapter on "Accountings," infra at 183–86.

4. McKinney's SCPA 1810, discussed in this chapter infra at 162.

5. McKinney's SCPA 2102(4), discussed in chapter on "Miscellaneous Proceedings," infra at 332–33.

6. McKinney's SCPA 2205, discussed in chapter on "Accounting, infra at 183–86.

7. McKinney's SCPA 1808(3) requires that notice of rejection be completed before the accounting that lists the rejected claim.

8. McKinney's SCPA 1806(4).

9. McKinney's SCPA 1807.

10. Matter of Deitch, 92 Misc.2d 942, 401 N.Y.S.2d 732 (Nassau 1978), affirmed 67 A.D.2d 839, 412 N.Y.S.2d 532 (2d Dep't 1979).

11. Matter of Smith, 84 A.D.2d 664, 444 N.Y.S.2d 325 (3d Dep't 1981) (objectants to attorneys' fees for services rendered to decedent before his death failed to sustain burden of proof).

12. Matter of Zalaznick, 90 Misc.2d 113, 394 N.Y.S.2d 347 (Bronx 1977) (objectants to surcharge for administration expenses failed to sustain burden of proof).

13. Matter of Gil, 67 A.D.2d 779, 412 N.Y.S.2d 682 (3d Dep't 1979) (appellate court unable to pass on issue not raised at accounting).

14. McKinney's SCPA 1808(3). Notice of rejection of the claim is required by McKinney's SCPA 1806.

15. McKinney's SCPA 2210(1), discussed in chapter on "Accounting," infra at 189–92.

The fiduciary must then, after service of process and delivery of the notice of rejection, list in the accounting itself all rejected claims and the reasons for rejection.[16] A rejected claimant has eight days from the return date of process to object to the account.[17] If he does object, he must serve objections on the fiduciary and file them with the court, along with a copy of the claim and any supporting documents he initially filed with the fiduciary. If the fiduciary has any affirmative defenses not set forth in the account, he can raise them in a reply filed in court and served on the claimant within five days after service of the objections on him. Parties adversely affected by the claimant's objections can also, within eight days of the service of claimant's objections, file and serve a reply containing any additional defense.[18]

If anyone objects to the accounting, every party who has appeared is entitled to service of the objections. If a fiduciary has paid a claim, he does not serve the claimant in the accounting proceeding, but he must serve the claimant with a copy of any objections to the claim, either in person or by mail, whether the claimant has appeared or not.[19] When the objectant serves the non-appearing claimant with a copy of objections, the claimant does not become a party to the proceeding and is in no danger of defaulting. The notice simply allows the claimant to come forward and help the fiduciary prove that the claim was valid. The court can decide the contested claims at a trial during the accounting proceeding.[20]

If the court sustains objections to a claim that was allowed but not yet paid, it will dismiss the claim.[21] If the fiduciary paid the claim, the court will surcharge him for damage to the estate caused by his fraud, negligence, mistake or collusion in paying it.[22] The objecting party may also petition to have the claimant refund any excess over the amount that was due to him.[23]

Similarly, if a claimant obtained a judgment in another court of competent jurisdiction by fraud, negligence, mistake or collusion, an adversely affected party can object and the Surrogate can surcharge the fiduciary for the damages to the estate.[24] This is the objectant's only recourse in the Surrogate's Court, which does not have jurisdiction to set aside the judgment of another court. For that relief, the objecting party would have to make the appropriate motion in the court that rendered the judgment.

16. McKinney's SCPA 1808(2).

17. McKinney's SCPA 1808(4).

18. McKinney's SCPA 1808(4).

19. McKinney's SCPA 1807(1).

20. McKinney's SCPA 1808(1). See Maki v. Ziehm, 55 A.D.2d 454, 391 N.Y.S.2d 705 (3d Dep't 1977), where the court recognized its broad jurisdiction in trying contested claims and allowed a stockholders' derivative action.

21. McKinney's SCPA 1807(1).

22. For the opinion that the scope of inquiry and breadth of litigation is broader for the claim improperly allowed but not yet paid than for the claim negligently or fraudulently paid, see McKinney's SCPA 1807, Prac.Comm. at 126–27 (1967).

23. McKinney's SCPA 2215(3), discussed in chapter on "Accounting," infra at 216.

24. McKinney's SCPA 1807(2).

In either case, the burden of proving the fiduciary's wrong-doing is on the person objecting to payment of the claim.[25]

If a surcharge against the fiduciary results from the objections, it will normally be limited to the damages incurred by the objecting party because of the wrongful allowance of the claim.[26]

If no accounting proceeding is pending, a rejected claimant can petition the court to compel the fiduciary to account.[27] If the contested claim is the only real issue and the estate is solvent,[28] the fiduciary may want to avoid a complete accounting and may ask the court in his answer to determine the claim as a preliminary step to an accounting proceeding.[29] To do so, he must say why he rejected the claim. The court has the option to entertain the application or not, and if it does it will first determine whether the estate is solvent and then allow or reject the claim, taking into account the priority of other creditors, and decide related issues.

The claimant has the burden of proving the claim by clear and convincing evidence.[30] If, however, the estate concedes that the decedent was liable for a claim, but contends that the claim was paid, the executor has the burden of proving that payment.[31] If the claimant was also a beneficiary, whether the legacy is in satisfaction of the debt is a question of fact. The testator's intent controls, and it is not dispositive that the legacy and the claim are in different amounts.[32]

This preliminary hearing is usually inappropriate in an insolvent estate, unless all creditors are made parties to the proceeding. In most insolvent estates a formal accounting is required.[33]

25. Matter of Smith, 84 A.D.2d 664, 444 N.Y.S.2d 325 (3d Dep't 1981) (burden of proving attorney's fees excessive is on objecting party). This is not clear from the face of the statute but is a sound decision and SCPA's predecessor, SCA 210, which McKinney's SCPA 1807 was not meant to change substantively, was clear that the objectant had to show that the fiduciary paid the claim negligently or fraudulently. See McKinney's SCPA 1807, Prac.Comm. at 127 (1967).

26. Matter of Zalaznick, 90 Misc.2d 113, 394 N.Y.S.2d 347 (Bronx 1977) (on the theory that "beneficiaries who sit on the sidelines should not share in the fruits of victory earned by the touchdowns scored by the labors, burdens and expenses incurred by objectants").

27. McKinney's SCPA 1808(5). Compulsory accountings are governed by McKinney's SCPA 2205 and discussed in chapter on "Accounting," infra at 183–86.

28. Accountings are almost always required in insolvent estates, so this simplified procedure is not used. The predecessor to McKinney's SCPA 1808(5), SCA 211–a, permitted its use only in solvent estates, and the omission in McKinney's SCPA 1808(5) has little practical effect. See McKinney's SCPA 1808, Prac.Comm. at 140–41 (1967).

29. McKinney's SCPA 1808(5).

30. Matter of Gorden, 8 N.Y.2d 71, 202 N.Y.S.2d 1, 168 N.E.2d 239 (1960); Matter of Adamoski, 7 A.D.2d 864, 182 N.Y.S.2d 221 (2d Dep't 1959) (dissenting opinion), modified on basis of dissent 6 N.Y.2d 927, 190 N.Y.S.2d 999, 161 N.E.2d 213 (1959); Matter of McCormack, 43 A.D.2d 794, 350 N.Y.S.2d 247 (4th Dep't 1973), affirmed 35 N.Y.2d 888, 364 N.Y.S.2d 890, 324 N.E.2d 359 (1974); Matter of Modell, N.Y.L.J., May 6, 1982, at 12, col. 1; Matter of Phillips, 12 Misc.2d 402, 176 N.Y.S.2d 918 (New York County 1958), and cases cited therein.

31. Matter of Lurje, 64 Misc.2d 569, 315 N.Y.S.2d 476 (New York County 1970).

32. Matter of Revson, 86 A.D.2d 872, 447 N.Y.S.2d 297 (1982).

33. Matter of Perry, 123 Misc.2d 273, 473 N.Y.S.2d 335 (Nassau 1984).

SECTION H. CLAIMANT'S RIGHT TO ACTION IN ANOTHER COURT

A claimant against an estate does not have to bring his action in the Surrogate's Court; he may bring it in the Supreme Court or any other civil court with subject matter jurisdiction.[1] If the claimant wishes to proceed in another court, he must bring the action in the other forum within sixty days of the fiduciary's rejection, or the Surrogate's Court will be the only court with jurisdiction to decide the claim.[2] The sixty days starts to run after the claimant has presented the claim and received notice of rejection from the fiduciary. It runs whether the rejection is by a "permanent" fiduciary or by a preliminary executor[3] or temporary administrator.[4]

Significantly, the filing of a claim against the decedent's estate and subsequent rejection by the fiduciary do not constitute the commencement of an action for any purpose other than the statute of limitations.[5] For limitations purposes, the filing of the claim puts the parties in the same position as if an action had been commenced and issue joined.[6] The claimant, if he acts within sixty days of the rejection, can institute an action in a proper civil court.

The short statute of limitations does not apply to tax claims by the United States against the estate.[7]

If a claimant wishes he may sue the estate in another forum without presenting his claim to the fiduciary. This will, of course, turn out to be uneconomical and unwise if the fiduciary is going to allow the claim.

Sec. H

1. Matter of Nutter, 280 App.Div. 1035, 117 N.Y.S.2d 207 (4th Dep't 1953).

2. McKinney's SCPA 1810.

3. Matter of Cooper, 55 Misc.2d 159, 284 N.Y.S.2d 464 (Kings 1967), affirmed 30 A.D.2d 642, 292 N.Y.S.2d 820 (2d Dep't 1968).

4. McKinney's SCPA 905(2) provides that a temporary administrator can be sued without court permission. L.1975, c. 280. See McKinney's SCPA 1810, Prac. Comm. at 47–48 (1986).

5. E.g., Matter of Feinberg, 18 N.Y.2d 499, 277 N.Y.S.2d 249, 223 N.E.2d 780 (1966) (federal government's filing notice of claim for taxes within six year statute of limitations tolled the statute).

6. See Matter of Schorer, 272 N.Y. 247, 5 N.E.2d 806 (1936), where a physician presented a claim for medical services and the executor refrained from paying it, telling the doctor that if they could not ultimately decide the issue, they would litigate it. When the doctor finally petitioned for an accounting, the executor asserted the statute of limitations as a defense. The court rejected the executor's argument on the ground that the doctor's filing of the claim had tolled the statute of limitations.

7. Matter of Feinberg, 18 N.Y.2d 499, 277 N.Y.S.2d 249, 223 N.E.2d 780 (1966). See also Matter of Smathers, 249 App.Div. 523, 293 N.Y.S. 314 (2d Dep't 1937) (United States cannot be brought into Surrogate's Court by supplemental citation on tax matter); Matter of Sabha, 65 A.D.2d 917, 410 N.Y.S.2d 463 (4th Dep't 1978) (if United States does not start an action in federal court, the Surrogate should resolve the issue on the accounting and the United States will be bound by it. This holding should be limited to cases where the United States appears in the Surrogate's Court proceeding).

SECTION I. FIDUCIARY'S REMEDIES TO DETERMINE THE ENFORCEABILITY OF CLAIMS

Occasionally the fiduciary knows of the existence of a possible claim against the estate which the claimant has not formally submitted. Sometimes a claimant gives notice of a claim, the fiduciary has reason to question its validity, and the claimant does not institute a proceeding to enforce it. For instance, the claimant may allege a contract with the decedent which the fiduciary believes does not satisfy the statute of frauds.[1] The fiduciary can settle the matter by petitioning the court to order the claimant to show cause why the claim should not be disallowed.[2] A rejected claimant has sixty days after rejection to commence an action in a civil court,[3] and presumably the fiduciary cannot petition the Surrogate to resolve the claim until the sixty days have passed.[4]

Only the fiduciary may start this proceeding, and even he has no automatic right to do so.[5] The court can entertain the proceeding or decline to do so, and if it does, it will issue process for service on the claimant.[6] In most cases, only the fiduciary and the claimant are parties,[7] but if the claim is large, that is, more than the lesser of $10,000 or twenty-five percent of the estimated gross probate estate, the court must also order service on all adversely affected parties.[8] Normally this includes other claimants and residuary beneficiaries, since in a solvent estate, they would be adversely affected by the allowance of the claim. The pre-residuary beneficiaries need not be served, since their interests are not affected, unless the estate is insolvent and their interests are therefore subject to abatement if the claim is paid.

Sec. I

1. E.g., Matter of Schaeffner, 96 Misc. 2d 846, 410 N.Y.S.2d 44 (Nassau 1978) (oral agreement for sale of newsstand subsequently confirmed in suicide note).

2. McKinney's SCPA 1809(1).

3. McKinney's SCPA 1810.

4. Matter of Unseld, 43 Misc.2d 106, 250 N.Y.S.2d 353 (Nassau 1964). The reason is, of course, to avoid multiplicity of proceedings.

5. See discussion of entertainment of proceedings in chapter on "Miscellaneous Proceedings," infra at 327–28.

6. Matter of Denberg, 66 Misc.2d 508, 321 N.Y.S.2d 763 (New York County 1971).

7. Matter of Gregory, 102 Misc.2d 735, 424 N.Y.S.2d 641 (1980) (Attorney General not allowed to intervene in 1809 proceeding between creditor and estate, despite fact that his interests coincided with administrator's); Matter of Denberg, 66 Misc. 2d 508, 321 N.Y.S.2d 763 (1971).

8. McKinney's SCPA 1809(2), added L.1981, c. 135. The late Professor Paul J. Powers criticized this amendment in his Practice Commentary to McKinney's SCPA 1809 at 46 (1986) on the ground that it was likely to add unnecessary expense and that the court's liberal allowance of intervention in proceedings would usually obviate the need for it. The amendment was involved in Matter of Perry, 123 Misc.2d 273, 473 N.Y.S.2d 335 (Nassau 1984), where the court, fearful that the estate might be rendered insolvent by payment of the claim, converted a proceeding under McKinney's SCPA 1808, which allows an ex parte proceeding to determine a claim's validity, into one under McKinney's SCPA 1809(2) requiring notice to other creditors.

Virtual representation can also limit the number of those entitled to process.[9]

Within eight days of the return date, those cited may file an answer.[10] If the claimant answers, he must include a copy of the notice of claim he presented, and any supporting materials he filed with the fiduciary. The court will then, at a hearing, determine the validity of the claim. If the claimant does not answer, he defaults. Within five days of service of an answer, the fiduciary is permitted to serve and file a reply containing facts and evidence of the claim's invalidity.[11]

If a fiduciary intends to close the estate by a formal accounting,[12] he will often choose not to commence this proceeding but to wait for the accounting proceeding to determine the validity of the claim.[13] Some fiduciaries may use this procedure in addition to (and prior to) formal accounting despite the expense if they have declared a claim as a deduction on the federal estate tax return,[14] and the government will not issue a closing letter until the claim is finally resolved. This expedited proceeding is more often useful, however, for a fiduciary who intends to close out the estate informally and not to have a judicial settlement of his account.[15] Though the statute is phrased in terms of a decision preliminary to the accounting,[16] in fact this proceeding is often in lieu of a formal judicial accounting. Resolution of the single issue in this proceeding often avoids the unnecessary expense of a full accounting. Hence, if a claimant petitions for a compulsory accounting, the court can, if the estate is solvent and the claim is the only issue to be resolved, convert it into an SCPA 1809 proceeding instead.[17]

SECTION J. PRIORITY OF CLAIMS

In an estate large enough to pay all outstanding debts and claims, no statement of priorities among claimants is necessary. In insolvent estates, however, a fiduciary needs to know which claims to pay first.

Article 18 sets up the order of priority,[1] and that order will be discussed presently, but on the top of the priority list, before any of the claimants, is the recipient of "exempt" or "set-off" property, namely the

9. McKinney's SCPA 315, discussed in chapter on "Procedure," supra at 60–70.

10. McKinney's SCPA 1809(2).

11. McKinney's SCPA 1809(2).

12. See chapter on "Accounting," infra at 182 et seq.

13. For example, if an estate is insolvent, an accounting usually occurs and McKinney's SCPA 1809 can rarely be used; the contested matters would be decided on the accounting.

14. See I.R.C. § 2053.

15. See chapter on "Accounting," infra at 180–82.

16. McKinney's SCPA 1809(3).

17. The court has the power to do so under McKinney's SCPA 202, discussed in chapter on "Jurisdiction," supra at 23–24. See, by analogy, Matter of Perry, 123 Misc. 2d 273, 473 N.Y.S.2d 335 (Nassau 1984), discussed in note 8 supra.

Sec. J

1. McKinney's SCPA 1811.

decedent's surviving spouse or minor children.[2] Next follows the Article 18 hierarchy.

Administration and funeral expenses have priority over all other claims[3] and must be paid by the fiduciary out of the first funds received before the fiduciary makes any distribution or gives a preference to any other claimant.[4] In fact, courts have not construed this "first money received" provision literally, and have allowed a fiduciary to invest estate funds before paying administration and funeral expenses.[5]

1. ADMINISTRATION EXPENSES

Administration expenses are the reasonable costs of marshaling the estate assets, paying the creditors, distributing the property and accounting. Typical examples of administration expenses are premiums on the fiduciary's bond, commissions, attorney's fees and disbursements,[6] and costs of audit of, or litigation over, estate tax returns.

The courts recognize and allow various other administration expenses. For example, the fiduciary's travelling expenses are permitted when they are necessary for the proper administration of the estate. Costs of maintaining property so it can be sold are allowed, and that can include salaries of persons hired to maintain it.[7] Brokers' commissions on the sale of property are also permissible.[8]

Some expenses are not for the estate's benefit, however, and are not permitted to be paid from the estate funds. For example, in cases where real property is not sold, but passes to the distributees or devisees, expenses of maintaining it,[9] or demolishing it,[10] are theirs.

2. McKinney's EPTL 5–3.1; Matter of Sanchez, 58 N.Y.S.2d 230 (Westchester 1945). Exempt property is discussed in chapter on "Miscellaneous Proceedings," infra at 329–31. The reason for this de facto priority over all claims is that the exempt property is not even a part of the estate; it is exempt from creditors. It is not preferred, however, over a lien perfected prior to decedent's death. Matter of Rosenfield, 36 Misc.2d 284, 232 N.Y.S.2d 610 (Westchester 1962) (federal lien for income taxes prior to decedent's death has priority over widow's right to set-off property). In addition, the $1,000 cash component of the exempt property is available for the payment of funeral expenses if the estate has insufficient assets to pay them. McKinney's EPTL 5–3.1(a)(5).

3. McKinney's SCPA 1811(1) states that funeral expenses, "subject to the payment of expenses of administration," have top priority. This appears to put administration expenses first, followed by funeral expenses. Matter of Mowbray, 4 Misc.2d 844, 159 N.Y.S.2d 123 (Westchester 1956); Matter of Amelio, 153 Misc. 52, 274 N.Y.S. 484 (Kings 1934). But see Matter of Reilly, 165 Misc. 214, 300 N.Y.S. 1285 (Kings 1937). As a practical matter, a fiduciary or family member usually pays for the funeral with no objections and no court order.

4. Matter of Scheuer, 94 Misc.2d 538, 405 N.Y.S.2d 189 (New York County 1978).

5. Matter of Scheuer, 94 Misc.2d 538, 405 N.Y.S.2d 189 (New York County 1978).

6. See Matter of Dinger, 118 Misc.2d 781, 461 N.Y.S.2d 713 (Richmond 1983), where the attorney's fee was given preference over unpaid real estate taxes.

7. Matter of Watson, 86 Misc. 588, 148 N.Y.S. 902 (New York County 1914) (four months salary permitted).

8. Matter of Larson, 87 Misc.2d 397, 385 N.Y.S.2d 720 (Chattaugua 1976).

9. Matter of Kaufman, N.Y.L.J., Jan. 21, 1966, at 16, col. 4 (temporary administrator living in decedent's house retained servants for fourteen months. The court stated that employees of decedent had to be terminated promptly, and ordered the

The cost of upkeep and storage of the decedent's automobile, which passed to his widow as exempt property,[11] is not a proper charge against the estate.[12] Similarly, legal and accounting fees incurred in seeking to have the decedent's widow released from liens filed by the Internal Revenue Service against both spouses prior to the decedent's death benefited only the widow, not the estate.[13]

The courts have been reluctant to award fees to accountants when the attorney could have done the work. Accounting fees are generally part of the attorney's fees unless the estate has special problems (that is, more than merely the completion of tax returns) requiring an accountant or tax accountant.[14] Services that are merely clerical or that are clearly part of the fiduciary's duties are likewise not separately compensable.[15]

Persons in the business of locating heirs for estates have met with mixed fates in the category of allowable administration expenses. In a case where the heir-finder located two heirs and an asset of the estate that otherwise would have gone undiscovered, the court permitted him a quantum meruit recovery from the estate, but not the percentage of the found asset he had requested.[16] In another case the detective, who was simply trying to prevent the estate from escheating to the state, located no heirs, and the court refused to allow a fee. The court theorized that his only function would have been to diminish the size of the estate by his fee.[17] This may be a harsh result because it is incumbent on the fiduciary to make some effort to locate heirs, and ascertaining their non-existence is just as important as ascertaining their existence.

The allowance of administration expenses under state law is important not only because it determines the estate's liability, but also because it is a factor in whether the claim will be deductable from the federal and state estate tax returns. Because the federal law permits the deduction of administration expenses allowable under state law,[18] usually the Internal Revenue Service and the federal courts adopt the state's determination of what is allowable.[19]

temporary administrator to pay $2,000 per month toward rent and expenses).

10. Matter of Offermann, 90 Misc.2d 346, 394 N.Y.S.2d 119 (Erie 1977) (no claim against estate for cost of demolishing buildings, since that obligation passed directly to distributees).

11. McKinney's EPTL 5–3.1, discussed in chapter on "Miscellaneous Proceedings," supra at 329–31.

12. Matter of Purcell, 39 Misc.2d 852, 241 N.Y.S.2d 998 (Kings 1963) (wife responsible for storage costs of exempt property).

13. Matter of Watson, 88 Misc.2d 1051, 390 N.Y.S.2d 355 (Erie 1976).

14. Matter of Kramer, 78 Misc.2d 662, 356 N.Y.S.2d 984 (New York County 1974); Matter of Rich, 27 Misc.2d 364, 211 N.Y.S.2d 68 (New York County 1960). See chapter on "Attorneys' Fees," infra at 369.

15. Matter of Tuttle, 4 N.Y.2d 159, 173 N.Y.S.2d 279, 149 N.E.2d 715 (1958).

16. Matter of Greenberg, N.Y.L.J., April 20, 1978, at 11, col. 6.

17. Matter of Pedersen, N.Y.L.J., April 12, 1978, at 16, col. 3 (Bronx).

18. I.R.C. § 2053(a).

19. But see Tr.Reg. 20.2053–3(d)(2), which requires that an expense be necessary in addition to allowable under state law. Compare Smith v. Commissioner, 57 T.C. 650 (1972), affirmed 510 F.2d 479 (2d Cir.1975), certiorari denied 423 U.S. 827, 96

Under this rule giving first preference to administration expenses, New York fiduciary income taxes validly incurred during administration of an estate have priority over taxes incurred by the decedent during his lifetime, although those taxes were federal.[20] It has also been held that the expenses of running a business properly continued by the estate [21] are administration expenses entitled to preference over general creditors,[22] and the expenses of running a business improperly continued by the estate are not.[23]

2. FUNERAL EXPENSES

Funeral expenses must be reasonable,[24] and a funeral director seeking payment must bear the burden of proving that the expenses are reasonable.[25]

The fiduciary has to pay the funeral expenses either directly to the funeral director or to the person who paid for the funeral. The estate has primary liability to pay for the funeral expenses.[26] The decedent's surviving spouse has an obligation to arrange for the burial, but can get reimbursement from the estate.[27] A spouse can waive the right to

S.Ct. 44, 46 L.Ed.2d 44 (1975), and Vatter v. Commissioner, 65 T.C. 633 (1975), affirmed per curiam 556 F.2d 563 (2d Cir.1976), with Estate of Park v. Commissioner, 475 F.2d 673 (6th Cir.1973). See Flynn, "Interplay of Federal and State Law in Determining Deductible Administration Expenses," St. John's L.Rev. 357 (1975); Note, "Estate of Smith—Deductibility of Administration Expenses under the Internal Revenue Code and under the Treasury Regulations: Resolving the Conflict," 17 William and Mary L.Rev. 363 (1975).

20. Matter of Stone, 108 Misc.2d 235, 437 N.Y.S.2d 249 (New York County 1981).

21. For an executor's power to continue a business, see chapter on "Miscellaneous Proceedings," infra at 354–56.

22. Matter of Henke, 39 Misc.2d 705, 241 N.Y.S.2d 788 (Nassau 1963).

23. They are, rather, personal debts of the executor. Matter of Begent, 37 A.D.2d 310, 325 N.Y.S.2d 317 (3d Dep't 1971). The court found, however, that federal withholding taxes incurred in running that business were administration expenses entitled to a preference over pre-death debts.

24. McKinney's SCPA 1811(1); see Weil v. Schneider, 154 Misc. 797, 278 N.Y.S. 593 (App.Term 1st Dep't 1935); Matter of Kircher, 123 Misc.2d 397, 473 N.Y.S.2d 679 (Kings 1984).

25. Coleman and Daniels Funeral Home v. Estate of Guiles, 53 Misc.2d 449, 278 N.Y.S.2d 665 (Tioga 1967); Matter of Siciliano, 32 Misc.2d 789, 223 N.Y.S.2d 824 (Westchester 1961) (burden of proving reasonableness of funeral expenses is on funeral director). Reasonable funeral expenses cover the customary ceremonies and can also include the cost of a meal following the funeral. Matter of Kircher, 123 Misc.2d 397, 473 N.Y.S.2d 679 (Kings 1984) (husband entitled to reimbursement for his undisputed payment of his wife's funeral expenses and a luncheon immediately following the burial); Matter of DiNezzo, 49 Misc.2d 237, 267 N.Y.S.2d 67 (Erie 1966). The following have been denied as funeral expenses: a trip to Israel to visit the decedent's grave, Matter of Lurje, 64 Misc.2d 569, 315 N.Y.S.2d 476 (New York County 1970), masses for the repose of the decedent's soul, Matter of Gerringer, 58 Misc.2d 867, 296 N.Y.S.2d 448 (Erie 1969) (though mass as part of funeral service would be allowable), and a bill of $372 for guards to protect the decedent's home during the funeral (deemed excessive and reduced to $72), Matter of Hart, 32 A.D.2d 961, 303 N.Y.S.2d 82 (2d Dep't 1969), affirmed 27 N.Y.2d 560, 313 N.Y.S.2d 128, 261 N.E.2d 268 (1969).

26. E.g., Riverside Memorial Chapel v. Albert, 76 Misc.2d 1070, 352 N.Y.S.2d 581 (Civ.Ct.New York County 1974); Jaudon v. White, 60 Misc.2d 86, 302 N.Y.S.2d 281 (Civ.Ct.N.Y.1969).

27. Patterson v. Patterson, 59 N.Y. 574 (1875); Matter of Grasso, 20 Misc.2d 202, 189 N.Y.S.2d 281 (Kings 1959). See Coleman and Daniels Funeral Home v. Estate of Guiles, 53 Misc.2d 449, 278 N.Y.S.2d 665

reimbursement, but it must be by a positive act indicating a gift to the estate.[28]

The Social Security Administration pays $255 in a lump sum to the surviving spouse of a decedent, and it has been held that that sum should not be deducted from the reimbursement for funeral expenses.[29]

Where an estate is insolvent or very small, the court will strictly enforce the reasonableness requirement. If the decedent's will specifies the maximum amount to be spent for the funeral, the court will enforce that amount unless it is clearly insufficient.

3. PRIORITY OF CLAIMS AFTER ADMINISTRATION AND FUNERAL EXPENSES

After payment of these administration and funeral expenses, the order of priority is as follows:

1. Debts entitled to preference under federal and New York laws.[30] This section automatically gives preference to federal claims, because federal law provides that debts of the United States have priority over all other debts.[31] The priority arises at the moment of the decedent's death.[32]

If the fiduciary distributes estate assets without paying federal claims and the Surrogate finds him personally liable, the Surrogate can also order a refund by the person to whom the distribution was made.[33]

After federal claims, state claims have next priority. The statutory wording is "debts entitled to a preference under New York law,"[34] and although it gives a preference to New York State claims, it operates differently from the federal preference. First, there is no New York state statute giving automatic preference to claims by New York State. Because there is not, New York State is entitled to a preference only when New York law grants it, either by common law or by statute. Under the common law, the state succeeds to the Crown's prerogative

(Tioga 1967), where a husband and wife died simultaneously, the husband's liabilities exceeding his assets, and the court held that the priority for funeral expenses extended only to the cost of his funeral, not hers.

28. Matter of Stadtmuller, 110 App.Div. 76, 96 N.Y.S. 1101 (2d Dep't 1905) (where no gift given, there is no legal impediment to prevent reimbursement); Matter of Kircher, 123 Misc.2d 397, 473 N.Y.S.2d 679 (Kings 1984).

29. Stein v. Flemming, 187 F.Supp. 1 (E.D.Mo.1959); Matter of Kircher, 123 Misc.2d 397, 473 N.Y.S.2d 679 (Kings 1984).

30. McKinney's SCPA 1811(2)(a).

31. 31 U.S.C.A. § 191. For a discussion of a fiduciary's liability for federal estate taxes, see Ferguson, The Fiduciary's Personal Liability for Federal Taxes of the Decedent and His Estate: The Problems of Distribution and Partial Distribution, 25 N.Y.U.Inst. on Fed.Tax. 1185 (1967).

32. Matter of Gruner, 295 N.Y. 510, 68 N.E.2d 514 (1946). Hence it does not prevail over liens that existed before the decedent's death. Brent v. Bank of Washington, 35 U.S. (10 Pet.) 596, 9 L.Ed. 547 (1836).

33. Matter of Berg, 91 Misc.2d 939, 398 N.Y.S.2d 948 (New York County 1977).

34. McKinney's SCPA 1811.

right of priority.[35] It operates whenever the state acting in its sovereign capacity renders services to the decedent.[36] That common law preference can be abrogated, but only by specific mention in a statute.[37] Secondly, unlike the preference accorded to federal debts, which arises at the date of death, the priority of state debts arises only when the state seeks to enforce its right and may be lost if the state fails to take action before another creditor becomes secured.[38]

The fact that state estate taxes are due before federal estate taxes (the state taxes six months after death and the federal nine months) does not create a preference for the state taxes. In an insolvent estate, the federal taxes would be payable in full before the state taxes.[39]

If the state has two claims against an insolvent estate, each entitled to priority, they will abate ratably.[40]

Courts have held that state claims have preference over city claims [41] and county claims [42] on the common law prerogative theory. For example, where both the state and the city have claims against the estate for income taxes, it is probable (but not settled) that the state's claim should prevail over the city's.[43]

2. Taxes assessed against the property of the decedent prior to death.[44] If the taxes are on property that passes to a beneficiary, the beneficiary must reimburse the estate for the taxes unless

35. See Marshall v. New York, 254 U.S. 380, 41 S.Ct. 143, 65 L.Ed. 315 (1920); Matter of Warren, 53 N.Y.2d 118, 440 N.Y.S.2d 609, 423 N.E.2d 32 (1981); Matter of Carnegie Trust Co., 206 N.Y. 390, 99 N.E. 1096 (1912). That right is guaranteed by N.Y. Const. art I, section 14.

36. Matter of Bloomfield, 53 N.Y.2d 118, 440 N.Y.S.2d 609, 423 N.E.2d 32 (1981); Matter of Gallucci, 87 A.D.2d 818, 448 N.Y.S.2d 767 (2d Dep't 1982); Matter of Melvin, 126 Misc.2d 900, 483 N.Y.S.2d 941 (Onondaga 1984). Though the debtor in Bloomfield was an incompetent and in Gallucci a conservatee, the same rule applies to decedents, since McKinney's SCPA 1811 does no more than codify the state's common law preference.

37. McKinney's Cons. Laws of New York, Book I, Statutes, section 115, states that "a statute does not apply to the State, where its sovereign rights, prerogatives, or interests are involved, unless it is specifically mentioned therein or included by necessary implication." See Matter of Bloomfield, 53 N.Y.2d 118, 440 N.Y.S.2d 609, 423 N.E.2d 32 (1981), where neither the amendment to N.Y.Soc.Serv. Law 104 giving New York City a preference over general creditors, nor the amendment to the Mental Hygiene Law omitting reference to the State's preferred creditor status, L.1972, c. 251, was sufficient to abrogate the State's preference. Matter of Kielbeiwicz, 88 Misc.2d 476, 389 N.Y.S.2d 82 (Erie 1976), which holds to the contrary, is effectively overruled by Matter of Bloomfield, 53 N.Y.2d 118, 440 N.Y.S.2d 609, 423 N.E.2d 32 (1981).

38. Matter of Gruner, 295 N.Y. 510, 68 N.E.2d 514 (1946).

39. See Matter of Froelich, 98 Misc.2d 1, 416 N.Y.S.2d 744 (Nassau 1979).

40. Matter of Rubin, 74 Misc.2d 503, 344 N.Y.S.2d 153 (Erie 1973).

41. Matter of Bloomfield, 53 N.Y.2d 123, 440 N.Y.S.2d 609, 423 N.E.2d 32 (1981) (state claim for services under Mental Hygiene Law had a common law preference over city claim for services under Social Services Law section 104 despite repeal of statute giving state preference); Matter of Colwin, 98 Misc.2d 676, 414 N.Y.S.2d 469 (New York County 1979); Matter of Solomon, 18 Misc.2d 984, 187 N.Y.S.2d 573 (Westchester 1959).

42. Matter of Melvin, 126 Misc.2d 900, 483 N.Y.S.2d 941 (Onondaga 1984).

43. See Matter of Colwin, 98 Misc.2d 676, 414 N.Y.S.2d 469 (New York County 1979). See also McKinney's SCPA 1811, Prac.Comm. at 51–52 (1986).

44. McKinney's SCPA 1811(2)(b).

the will directs otherwise.[45] Similarly, if the property was jointly owned, the taxes are not a proper expense of the estate, but of the other joint owner, who receives the property by operation of law and subject to any outstanding indebtedness on it.[46] This provision operates differently from the provision that a beneficiary takes a decedent's property subject to an outstanding mortgage or lien.[47] In the mortgage or lien case, the estate does not have liability for the debt; the beneficiary takes the property and must satisfy the lien or pay the mortgage and his liability is limited to the value of the property. In the real estate taxes case, the estate is liable for the taxes [48] and can seek reimbursement from the beneficiary. The beneficiary is liable for all the real estate taxes, even if they exceed the value of the property, unless he refuses the devise.

3. Judgments docketed and decrees entered against the decedent during his lifetime, the priority depending on the timing of the docketing or entering.[49] If, however, a creditor who had obtained a judgment later than another creditor executed on the debtor's property first, he would have a priority over the earlier judgment creditor, provided he obtained the execution during the decedent's lifetime.

4. All other claims, including recognizances, bonds, sealed instruments, notes, bills and unliquidated demands and accounts.[50] This category includes all other obligations of the decedent. Unsecured obligations and secured obligations are lumped together here, although the secured creditors have a right to the security; the excess of the debt over the security is treated along with the unsecured creditors.

Except for judgments and decrees obtained during the decedent's lifetime, whose priority depends on the time of the judgment or decree, all claims of the same class are treated equally and abate pro rata if the assets are insufficient to cover them all.[51] For example, wages due to a claimant do not have priority over general claims against a decedent.[52]

45. McKinney's SCPA 1811(2)(b).

46. Matter of Hoover, 71 Misc.2d 438, 336 N.Y.S.2d 110 (Erie 1972).

47. McKinney's EPTL 3–3.6(a).

48. McKinney's EPTL 3–3.6(a) contains an express exception for McKinney's SCPA 1811.

49. McKinney's SCPA 1811(2)(c). See Matter of Cornez, 27 Misc.2d 671, 207 N.Y.S.2d 343 (Kings 1960), where a hospital had obtained a lien against wrongful death proceeds and the court held that claims should be paid in the following order:

1. widow's exemption
2. administration expenses
3. funeral bills
4. hospital bill
5. other claims, including that of the Department of Welfare.

See also Matter of Homer, 122 Misc.2d 908, 472 N.Y.S.2d 275 (Onondaga 1984), where a hospital obtained a judgment before decedent's death and before Department of Social Services filed its claims. The court held the hospital's judgment was entitled to priority over claim of Department of Social Services.

50. McKinney's SCPA 1811(2)(d).

51. McKinney's SCPA 1811(3).

52. Matter of Livingston, 14 A.D.2d 264, 220 N.Y.S.2d 434 (1st Dep't 1961).

A debt already due is not preferred over a debt not yet due.[53] If the fiduciary pays debts not yet due he can deduct the amount of interest for the unexpired term.[54]

If someone has a claim for rents due from the decedent on leases during his lifetime, the court can give it priority over other claims if this treatment would be beneficial to the overall administration of the estate.[55]

Even if a claimant starts a lawsuit for recovery of a claim after the decedent's death, his claim will not acquire a preference over all other claims of the same class, nor will an after-death judgment have priority over other claims, for judgments have priority only when they were obtained against the decedent prior to death.[56]

A fiduciary's claim naturally does not have priority over others of the same class.[57]

4. SECURED OBLIGATIONS

Priority is granted to claims secured by deeds,[58] liens, mortgages,[59] promissory notes or other forms of collateral to the extent of the collateral. If the decedent owed a debt secured by property which was sold before his death to satisfy the debt, any deficiency judgment because of the insufficiency of the collateral is a claim of the obligee against the decedent's estate.[60]

A fiduciary whose claim is secured by collateral may apply to the court to surrender the collateral to the estate and pay himself on the claim.[61] A non-fiduciary who has collateral may request the fiduciary to exchange the collateral for its value, but the fiduciary can refuse and demand that the issue await an accounting.

In insolvent estates, if a secured creditor is holding property that earns dividends, the dividends payable to the secured creditor are computed only on the difference between the face amount of the claim without security and the value of the security itself, unless the creditor surrenders the security to the fiduciary, in which case the dividend is computed on the full face amount.[62] This is in effect an apportionment of the income from the security between the creditor and the estate. For example, if the claimant is holding income-earning property as

53. McKinney's SCPA 1811(3).

54. McKinney's SCPA 1811(3).

55. McKinney's SCPA 1811(3).

56. McKinney's SCPA 1811(3). See Matter of Klupt, 65 Misc.2d 822, 319 N.Y.S.2d 79 (Nassau 1971) (judgment against an estate obtained after decedent's lifetime has no greater preference than a valid claim against an estate).

57. McKinney's SCPA 1811(3).

58. Wicks v. Carmichael, 172 Misc. 924, 16 N.Y.S.2d 395 (Broome 1939) (debt arising from assumption by a deed of mortgage indebtedness).

59. Emigrant Industrial Savings Bank v. New Rochelle Trust Co., 297 N.Y. 996, 80 N.E.2d 455 (1938).

60. Jemzura v. Jemzura, 36 N.Y.2d 496, 369 N.Y.S.2d 400, 330 N.E.2d 414 (1975) (if mortgage is foreclosed and sale does not yield enough to satisfy mortgage, the estate is liable for difference).

61. McKinney's SCPA 1811(3).

62. McKinney's SCPA 1811(4).

collateral, the value of the collateral must be deducted from the face value of the indebtedness to determine the proportionate dividends due to the creditor. The court will fix the date on which the creditor's rights begin.

SECTION K. VALIDITY OF CLAIMS

Naturally, a fiduciary can pay only valid claims. If he wrongfully pays an invalid claim, he will have to repay the amount to the estate in the form of a surcharge when he accounts.[1]

A claimant must prove the validity of his claim by clear and convincing proof.[2]

The costs of hospital, medical service, drugs and food provided to the decedent in his last illness are valid claims for which the estate is liable. Fees the decedent owed to his attorney,[3] promissory notes,[4] deficiency judgments on mortgage foreclosures,[5] and alimony arrears[6] are examples of valid claims, if proved by clear and convincing evidence. If the decedent was survived by a spouse with responsibility for the decedent's medical bills, the court can permit the estate to pay the bills and then seek reimbursement from the spouse.[7]

On occasion, courts have allowed claims against the estate by persons the decedent was supporting even without an obligation to support. In one case, for example, the decedent had been supporting his incompetent former spouse even after the annulment of their marriage, and the court ruled that the estate was liable for her continued care.[8] In another the court found that an estate may be liable for continuation of court-ordered support payments for an illegitimate child.[9]

Sec. K

1. See chapter on "Fiduciaries," infra at 412–13.

2. Matter of McCormack, 43 A.D.2d 794, 350 N.Y.S.2d 247 (4th Dep't 1973), affirmed 35 N.Y.2d 888, 364 N.Y.S.2d 890, 324 N.E.2d 359 (1974); Matter of Modell, N.Y.L.J., May 6, 1982, at 12, col. 1, and cases cited in footnote 30, Sec. G supra.

3. Matter of Anninger, 35 Misc.2d 493, 230 N.Y.S.2d 910 (New York County 1962) (estate obligated to pay for legal services rendered to decedent at his request to secure payment for shares of stock of a corporation confiscated by Yugoslav government).

4. Matter of Morrell, 38 Misc.2d 518, 237 N.Y.S.2d 14 (New York County 1962).

5. Emigrant Industrial Savings Bank v. New Rochelle Trust Co., 297 N.Y. 996, 80 N.E.2d 455 (1948) (trustee-legatee liable for amount of deficiency judgment to extent of assets paid to it).

6. Matter of Fox, 109 Misc.2d 634, 440 N.Y.S.2d 811 (New York County 1981), reversed on another ground 94 A.D.2d 662, 462 N.Y.S.2d 464 (1st Dep't 1983) (separation agreement provided that decedent's former wife had the right to proceed against security upon written notice); Matter of Torr, 29 Misc.2d 772, 218 N.Y.S.2d 318 (New York County 1961) (arrears of alimony due and unpaid at time of husband's death determined to be obligation of his estate).

7. Matter of Rubin, 30 Misc.2d 790, 217 N.Y.S.2d 447 (New York County 1961) (when credit was extended to the wife and not the husband, the creditor may recover from the wife's estate).

8. Matter of Lichtenstein, N.Y.L.J., Dec. 14, 1964, at 17, col. 7 (New York County).

9. See Matter of Blumberg, 83 Misc.2d 523, 372 N.Y.S.2d 93 (New York County 1975) (court set case on calendar for hear-

An estate may be liable to fulfill a charitable pledge made by the decedent when the pledge is properly documented and the intent of the decedent was clearly to fulfill it. In one case the decedent died after paying $3.5 million of a $5 million pledge to a museum, and the court allowed the museum's claim for the rest, despite the fact that the museum presented only the written gift advices accompanying the previous payments and received a substantial bequest under the decedent's will. The court warned charities and estate planners to be more careful about adhering to the Statute of Frauds.[10]

Alleged claims between husbands and wives are most carefully scrutinized because of their potential to defraud creditors. If, for example, a husband gives his wife promissory notes for loans in order to put her in a position of priority over the many other creditors, the court will refuse to grant the priority.[11]

An estate may be held liable to pay a debt previously discharged in bankruptcy if the decedent writes a letter to the creditor reviving the debt.[12]

Claims for compensation for the physical care of the decedent raise many problems. If a person claims that the decedent agreed to bequeath him a sum of money in return for the services, he must produce a written contract or it will not be enforceable.[13] If no written contract exists, the claimant can recover the reasonable value of his services.[14] The court implies a promise by the recipient of the services to pay for their value,[15] unless it can find an inference that the care-giver rendered the services gratuitously.[16] This inference arises if the care-giver was the decedent's relative [17] or close friend,[18] because the court as-

ing on issue of whether child support payments would continue).

10. Matter of Payson, N.Y.L.J., July 26, 1978, at 14, col. 3 (Nassau).

11. Matter of Plotkin, N.Y.L.J., June 12, 1968, at 15, col. 4 (New York County).

12. Matter of Maher, N.Y.L.J., Nov. 17, 1970, at 21, col. 6 (Queens).

13. McKinney's EPTL 13–2.1; Dombrowski v. Somers, 51 A.D.2d 636, 378 N.Y.S.2d 825 (3d Dep't 1976), reversed 41 N.Y.2d 358, 393 N.Y.S.2d 706, 362 N.E.2d 257 (1977) (payment for housekeeping chores).

14. E.g., Peters v. Morse, 96 A.D.2d 662, 466 N.Y.S.2d 504 (3d Dep't 1983), appeal after remand 112 A.D.2d 559, 491 N.Y.S.2d 495 (1985) (nursing, medical and household duties); Silberberg v. Haber, 42 A.D.2d 552, 345 N.Y.S.2d 558 (1st Dep't 1973) (quantum meruit for services).

15. Matter of McArdle, N.Y.L.J., March 29, 1985, at 14, col 5 (Kings).

16. E.g., Robinson v. Munn, 238 N.Y. 40, 143 N.E. 784 (1924) (action against executor to recover on an implied contract for services rendered as a nurse).

17. Collyer v. Collyer, 113 N.Y. 442, 21 N.E. 114 (1889) (where person lived with relative and it was clear neither party had expectations board would be paid, law will not imply a promise to pay board); Matter of Schultz, 18 Misc.2d 1012, 188 N.Y.S.2d 144 (New York County 1959) (decedent's sister presumed to have cared for decedent out of love and affection); Matter of Harvey, 15 A.D.2d 834, 224 N.Y.S.2d 767 (3d Dep't 1962) (claimant rendered services to her husband's uncle, and the court awarded her reasonable compensation); Matter of Lutz, 55 Misc.2d 226, 284 N.Y.S.2d 945 (Oneida 1965) (claim of decedent's stepdaughter denied; services not rendered with expectation of payment).

18. Matter of Cooke, 45 Misc.2d 365, 256 N.Y.S.2d 819 (Onondaga 1965) (banker with close personal relationship to decedent not entitled to payment for portfolio management); Matter of McArdle, N.Y. L.J., March 29, 1985, at 14, col. 5 (Kings).

sumes that friendship or duty prompted the care, and disallows the claim. The inference can be overcome by a showing that the parties mutually expected that the decedent would compensate the care-giver for the services.[19] In one case, a registered nurse who claimed she had rendered care to the decedent but never billed him for it presented a claim to the estate. The court would not allow it because her claim was too vague and the evidence presented to support it too fragmentary.[20]

Oral agreements often fail because they are subject to the Dead Man's Statute[21] and the claimant cannot testify as to the oral contract.[22]

It is not always impossible, however, for a relative to prove an enforceable contract to render services to the decedent. When a stepdaughter, for example, presented a claim for seven years services caring for decedent, she produced evidence to show that she had performed substantial services and her claim was allowed.[23] A daughter of another decedent produced a letter written by the decedent which implied a contract to pay for care provided to her mother, including room, board and personal care. She produced evidence of what this care would have cost in a nursing home and the court awarded her over $39,000. The respondents' failure to object to the daughter's testimony had waived the Dead Man's Statute.[24]

The value of the services is based on the wages received by persons supplying similar services in the community at the same time.[25] If no such comparable wage can be determined, courts sometimes compute the services by using the minimum wage.[26]

The court usually demands some showing of the decedent's consent to the care provided, except perhaps if the decedent was incompetent and therefore unable to consent.[27]

In considering claims presented to the fiduciary, the court considers prior actions of the decedent as an indication of his agreement to be subject to a claim. For example, in one case a physician had authorized his bank to grant an automatic overdraft on his checking account which would be recouped from his next deposit. When the physician

19. See Matter of Phelps, 58 A.D.2d 988, 397 N.Y.S.2d 485 (4th Dep't 1977) (letter signed by decedent indicated intention to pay son for services); Matter of McArdle, N.Y.L.J., March 29, 1985, at 14, col. 5. (Kings).

20. Matter of Heigman, 25 Misc.2d 238, 201 N.Y.S.2d 281 (New York County 1960) (objectant resided in same apartment and cared for decedent).

21. McKinney's CPLR 4519 (1963).

22. See Matter of McArdle, N.Y.L.J., March 29, 1985, at 14, col. 5 (Kings), where the care-giver could not testify but disinterested witnesses' testimony proved her claim.

23. Matter of Aronsohn, N.J.L.J., Nov. 16, 1978, at 12, col. 4 (New York County).

24. Hamar v. Isachsen, 58 A.D.2d 988, 397 N.Y.S.2d 485 (4th Dep't 1977).

25. Morone v. Morone, 50 N.Y.2d 481, 429 N.Y.S.2d 592, 413 N.E.2d 1154 (1980); Matter of McArdle, N.Y.L.J., March 29, 1985, at 14, col. 5 (Kings).

26. Matter of McArdle, N.Y.L.J., March 29, 1985, at 14, col. 7 (Kings); Matter of Augustyn, N.Y.L.J., Nov. 1, 1983, at 12, col. 4 (Kings).

27. See Matter of Cytryn, N.Y.L.J., Mar. 24, 1976, at 12, col. 2 (Queens).

died, the bank was in fact carrying such an overdraft on its books and the court ruled it a debt of the estate.[28]

The court does not customarily grant summary judgment on the issue of a claim's validity, but occasionally it does so.[29]

SECTION L. EXECUTION AGAINST DECEDENT'S REAL PROPERTY

If a creditor has obtained a judgment against the decedent, he may not execute against the decedent's real property unless he petitions the Surrogate's Court, setting forth the relevant facts and the names of those adversely affected.[1] This is true whether the creditor has obtained an "in rem" judgment (foreclosure) or a money judgment.[2] The purpose of this rule is to insure that other claimants are not adversely affected, and that those who have rights prior or equal to the judgment-creditor will not lose their preferred status.[3] The court will use its discretion to direct the issuance of process and the manner of service of process. Ordinarily, the court directs personal service.

SECTION M. COMPROMISE OF CLAIMS

Fiduciaries have the power to compromise claims by or against the estate,[1] whether or not any interested persons (or all the interested persons) object to it.[2] In the absence of bad faith or fraud, settlement of disputed claims in private proceedings, even out of court, has been given vigorous support by the courts,[3] so long as it does not interfere with the priorities among creditors.[4]

28. Matter of Marine Midland Bank, 67 A.D.2d 1081, 415 N.Y.S.2d 130 (4th Dep't 1979).

29. See Matter of Bellantoni, N.Y.L.J., June 12, 1985, at 17, col. 1 (Westchester), where the court granted summary judgment to the claimant who produced documentary proof of the claim, and the petitioner offered no evidence of any kind.

Sec. L

1. McKinney's SCPA 1812. McKinney's CPLR 5208 parallels McKinney's SCPA 1812 and requires permission of the Surrogate before a creditor can execute on a money judgment. In Matter of Scott, 125 Misc.2d 1024, 480 N.Y.S.2d 1018 (Monroe 1984), the court held that the city needed court permission to enforce an in rem judgment against a decedent's real property and that any excess over what was needed to satisfy the debt should be paid to the estate.

2. See McKinney's EPTL 11–4.6.

3. Priorities are governed by McKinney's SCPA 1811 and discussed this chapter supra at 164–72.

Sec. M

1. McKinney's EPTL 11–1.1(b)(13). This is a codification of the power to compromise which the fiduciary had at common law. E.g., Matter of Leopold, 259 N.Y. 274, 181 N.E. 570 (1932) (negotiation to compromise suit pending against decedent); Scully v. McGrath, 201 N.Y. 61, 94 N.E. 195 (1911) (settlement by fiduciary can be set aside only on showing of bad faith).

2. Matter of Leopold, 259 N.Y. 274, 181 N.E. 570 (1932); Transit Casualty Co. v. Estate of Rappaport, 102 Misc.2d 910, 424 N.Y.S.2d 675 (Nassau 1980).

3. Matter of Shubert, 110 Misc.2d 635, 442 N.Y.S.2d 703 (New York County 1981).

4. Priorities are governed by McKinney's SCPA 1811 and discussed this chapter supra at 164–72.

If the compromise is wrongful, objectants at the fiduciary's accounting can obtain a surcharge against him. To avoid the possibility of objections and surcharge, if a fiduciary has negotiated a settlement with a creditor or debtor of the estate, he may petition the court to approve the compromise. The compromise can relate to a debt, claim or demand, whether due or not. The proceeding is available if the estate cannot be settled without such action,[5] but that requirement is not difficult to meet, since claims eventually must be settled before the estate can be closed. The court may authorize the compromise ex parte, but it usually directs notice to parties adversely affected by the compromise, who are the same parties entitled to notice in an accounting proceeding.[6]

If the fiduciary gets court approval, no one can charge him with negligence or imprudence; he will escape liability unless he acted fraudulently.

The court may also direct that any uncollectible, stale or doubtful debt or claim belonging to the estate be auctioned, on notice tailored by the court to be most effective,[7] usually by publication or by mail to professional buyers and interested parties. Any party not given notice under this section may file objections in the accounting proceedings.

Because the fiduciary has the power to compromise,[8] the Surrogate's role is merely to approve the compromise or disapprove it; he cannot substitute his own discretion for the fiduciary's.[9] The Surrogate has the power to disapprove the settlement even if all the parties to the lawsuit consent to it,[10] and to approve the settlement even if all the parties oppose it.[11]

The Surrogate can also approve the settlement of an infant's claim or cause of action pending in the Supreme Court if a Supreme Court Justice would have been authorized to do so, when there is no resident Justice of the Supreme Court qualified to act and when there is no term of the Supreme Court then in session.[12] This subparagraph is useful in rural areas; in metropolitan areas it is rarely used because there is usually a resident Supreme Court Justice seated in a court in session.

5. McKinney's SCPA 1813(1).

6. See chapter on "Accounting," infra at 189–92.

7. McKinney's SCPA 1813(1).

8. McKinney's EPTL 11–1.1(b)(1).

9. Matter of Leopold, 259 N.Y. 274, 181 N.E. 570 (1932); Levine v. Mellin, 79 A.D.2d 584, 434 N.Y.S.2d 355 (1st Dep't 1980), modified 81 A.D.2d 523, 440 N.Y.S.2d 538 (1st Dep't 1981).

10. Matter of Muccini, 118 Misc.2d 38, 460 N.Y.S.2d 680 (Queens 1983) (compromise of wrongful death action).

11. Transit Casualty Co. v. Estate of Rappaport, 102 Misc.2d 910, 424 N.Y.S.2d 675 (Nassau 1980).

12. McKinney's SCPA 1813(2). This is another exercise of the legislature's right under the New York State Constitution to assign additional duties to a Surrogate. See discussion in chapter on "Jurisdiction," supra at 2.

SECTION N. APPLICATION OF ARTICLE 18

Article 18 does not apply to trusts and their administration.[1] It governs claims against an estate and the payment of administration expenses of an estate. The legislature felt it necessary to add this provision when it conferred on the Surrogates jurisdiction over inter vivos trusts by statute.

Arguably, though, the Surrogate has jurisdiction under Article 2, notwithstanding the limitation in Article 18, over claims against trusts if the trustee, for example, initiates a proceeding to obtain judicial approval of his actions, and the claimant and the fiduciary in that case would not be bound to follow the procedural and timing requirements of Article 18.[2]

SECTION O. CREDITORS' RIGHTS AGAINST NON-PROBATE ASSETS

Many decedents hold their property in ways that cause it to pass outside the will or the laws of intestacy, such as Totten Trusts (bank accounts in the decedent's name "in trust for" a named beneficiary), jointly owned property with right of survivorship, inter vivos trusts, and insurance policies. The question arises whether these assets are available to pay administration expenses, funeral expenses and debts when the testamentary assets are insufficient to pay those obligations.

As a general rule, a decedent's creditors must look to his testamentary assets for satisfaction of claims. There are a few significant exceptions.

The first exception is that property the decedent transferred with the intent to defraud creditors is available for payment of claims,[1] if other assets are insufficient. It is treated as though the transfer had not been made.

The second exception is the Totten Trust. Money in a Totten Trust account is available for the payment of debts and expenses. The

Sec. N

1. McKinney's SCPA 1814.

2. See McKinney's SCPA 1814, Prac. Comm. at 61 (Supp.1986).

Sec. O

1. See, e.g., McKinney's EPTL 13–3.6 and McKinney's Real Property L. § 268, permitting a creditor the right to void such transfers. See also Granwell v. Granwell, 20 N.Y.2d 91, 281 N.Y.S.2d 783, 228 N.E.2d 779 (1967) (illusory trust over which grantor retained right to revoke and change beneficiaries); Boshart v. Kirley, 34 Misc. 241, 69 N.Y.S. 623 (Sup.Ct. Lewis County 1901), affirmed 67 App.Div. 624, 74 N.Y.S. 1121 (4th Dep't 1901) (chattel mortgage given in fraud of creditors); Matter of Chaikowsky, 94 Misc.2d 70, 404 N.Y.S.2d 510 (1978) (Totten Trusts created when creator was insolvent); Matter of Jacob, 92 Misc.2d 1027, 401 N.Y.S.2d 986 (1978) (accord with Chaikowsky); Matter of Plotkin, 57 Misc.2d 754, 290 N.Y.S.2d 46 (1968); Matter of Sanchez, 58 N.Y.S.2d 230 (1945) (transfer of corporate stock leaving transferor unable to meet obligations under separation agreement).

beneficiary is entitled only to the residue of the fund after payment of the obligations.[2]

A third exception is, under some circumstances, property owned jointly by the decedent and someone else. If a decedent created a bank account and named another person as joint owner solely as a matter of convenience (so the person could make withdrawals for the creator), the account belongs to the decedent and is subject to his creditor's claims. The same is true if the decedent was insolvent when he created it, or intended to defraud creditors.[3] In other cases, however, the decedent created a "true" joint account and made a bona fide gift at the time of creation of one-half the value of the property on deposit to the noncontributing joint tenant. If the donor predeceases the other joint tenant and dies insolvent, it would appear that one-half of the jointly-held property would be subject to creditors' claims.[4]

A fourth exception is, under certain circumstances, insurance and annuity benefits. Although they are usually exempt from creditors' claims,[5] if an assignment, change of beneficiary or other transfer was made with the actual intent to hinder, delay or defraud creditors, the proceeds and interest will be available to creditors' claims.

Gifts causa mortis are also subject to creditors' claims.[6]

A fiduciary has to try to recover fraudulent transfers in his process of marshalling assets of an estate.[7]

2. Matter of Halbauer, 34 Misc.2d 458, 228 N.Y.S.2d 786 (Suffolk 1962), affirmed 18 A.D.2d 966, 238 N.Y.S.2d 511 (2d Dep't 1963).

3. McKinney's Debtor and Creditor L. § 273; McKinney's EPTL 7-3.1.

4. Matter of Granwell, 20 N.Y.2d 91, 281 N.Y.S.2d 783, 228 N.E.2d 779 (1967). Accord, Anderson v. Massachusetts Mutual Life Insurance Co., 77 A.D.2d 248, 432 N.Y.S.2d 959 (4th Dep't 1980). Granwell has reconciled the prior conflict. Compare Matter of Dunleavy, 41 Misc.2d 28, 244 N.Y.S.2d 730 (1963) (when an estate is insolvent, all jointly-owned property is subject to creditors' claims), with Matter of Ruben, N.Y.L.J., Nov. 30, 1965 (Nassau), and Matter of Mayer, N.Y.L.J., Nov. 30, 1965 (Nassau) (jointly held property was not subject to creditors' claims).

5. McKinney's Ins. Law § 166.

6. Wetmore v. Brooks, 18 N.Y.S. 852 (1891).

7. Matter of Mellan, 106 Misc.2d 113, 431 N.Y.S.2d 269 (1980); Matter of Turner, 179 Misc. 217, 38 N.Y.S.2d 769 (1942).

Chapter Six

ACCOUNTING

SECTION A. INTRODUCTION

An accounting is the procedure that enables a fiduciary to make disclosure of what he has done, to show what assets he has received and what he has paid out, and to absolve himself from further liability. An executor usually accounts when the estate has been completely administered and the final assets are ready to be paid out to beneficiaries. A trustee accounts at the termination of the trust (final accounting), and at various intervals throughout the duration of the trust (often about ten-year intervals) and at other times when an accounting is appropriate, such as at the resignation or death of a trustee or beneficiary (intermediate accountings). Guardians account every year unless the appointing instrument exempts them,[1] and finally account at the end of the guardianship. Interested parties who fear wrongdoing can ask the court to compel an accounting from a fiduciary.[2]

This chapter discusses the possible methods of accounting (informal accounting on receipts and releases, decree on receipts and releases, voluntary judicial accounting, compulsory judicial accounting), the accounting proceeding (petition, service of process, necessary parties, right to object), various accountings in special circumstances such as death or resignation of a fiduciary or death of a beneficiary, and the form of the accounting itself (schedules of the account, computations).

Usually the accounting fiduciary, his attorney or his accountant prepares the account, obtaining the necessary information from bank statements, the fiduciary's ledger book, the checking account statements, the estate tax return (form 706) (in an estate accounting), and similar sources.

A final preliminary comment is that although this chapter covers the accounting aspects of the accounting proceeding, in fact the accounting proceeding is an appropriate time to bring up other unresolved issues, such as the propriety of appointing the preliminary executor, the validity of the surviving spouse's right of election, the construction of the will, the fiduciary's entitlement to commissions and

Sec. A

1. See chapter on "Guardianships," infra at 269–71. As we discuss there, a guardian need not account annually if he holds the ward's property jointly with the court or a bank appointed by the court.

2. Compulsory accountings are discussed this chapter infra at 183–86.

the reasonableness of the attorneys' fees, to name a few. We discuss these proceedings in their own respective chapters, and the attorney should be aware that if the issues are ripe, they can also be litigated in the course of an accounting proceeding.

SECTION B. WAYS TO SETTLE AN ACCOUNT

A fiduciary can settle his account in any of three ways: by an informal accounting on receipts and releases, by obtaining a decree on the receipts and releases, or by a formal judicial accounting.

1. INFORMAL ACCOUNTING ON RECEIPTS AND RELEASES

A fiduciary can prepare an account, give copies of it to interested persons, including legatees, devisees, distributees, beneficiaries, and creditors, and obtain from the interested persons instruments known as receipts and releases, which absolve the fiduciary from liability on the matters contained in the accounting. These instruments release the fiduciary partially (on an intermediate account or partial distribution) or completely (on a final account).

The accounting fiduciary can use a simple procedure under SCPA 2202 to file and record the receipts and releases in court and settle an account informally.[1] He can do so both in intermediate and in final accountings, and both when the interested parties are competent adults and when they are under a legal disability. The guardian, conservator or committee of a person under disability can execute the receipt and release so long as the disabled person has received his share. In practice when there are persons under disability, the fiduciary uses this simplified procedure mostly when the person under disability has received a specific or general legacy of a stated amount, not when he shares in the residuary. In that case the fiduciary usually seeks a formal judicial accounting.[2]

The fiduciary may file the instruments or record them.[3] He does not have to do either, and many practitioners opt instead to retain the receipts and releases in their own file. There is no fee for filing the receipts and releases without the accounting, and the fee for recording them is three dollars per page. If they are recorded, they must be acknowledged before a notary public. Some practitioners do not want the responsibility of storing the documents so they use the court as the depository, and in that case it is better to record then to file, because the record of the instrument (or a certified copy) creates a presumption of its due execution and the accuracy of its contents. Filing does not create that presumption. Neither the filing nor the recording procures

Sec. B

1. McKinney's SCPA 2202.

2. See McKinney's SCPA 2202, Practice Commentary at 29 (1967); McKinney's SCPA 2203, Practice Commentary at 4 (Supp.1986).

3. McKinney's SCPA 2202.

any judicial approval of the account; for that, the petitioner must seek a formal judicial accounting, discussed later in this chapter.

If an interested person claims that the fiduciary induced him to sign the receipt and release by fraud, the fiduciary has the burden of proving that he dealt with the beneficiary fairly.[4] Fraud or failure to make full disclosure renders the receipt and release ineffective.[5] The fiduciary should therefore always attach the account to the receipts and releases when he sends them to the beneficiaries for signature.

If the receipts and releases and the accounting are filed or recorded, the filing fee is based on the amount of the estate or trust being accounted for, a sliding scale of $20 (for an estate or trust of less than $10,000) to $600 (for an estate or trust of more than $500,000).[6]

2. DECREE ON FILING RECEIPTS AND RELEASES

On a middle ground between informal accounting and a formal judicial settlement of account,[7] a fiduciary can use the procedure set forth in SCPA 2203 to obtain judicial approval of his account based on the receipt and releases executed by the interested parties. This procedure is available only for final accountings. The fiduciary must submit a petition to the court, showing the names and addresses of all persons interested in the estate, indicating that any taxes imposed have been paid, stating that the petitioner has given full disclosure in writing and a full accounting of his administration of the estate to all interested persons on whom service of process would have been required if there had been a judicial accounting proceeding,[8] and praying for a decree releasing and discharging him.

In the petition, any fiduciary other than a trustee or guardian must state that his letters have not been revoked and that he has not been removed from office, that the time for creditors to present their claims has expired, and that all administration expenses and known debts of the decedent have been paid.[9] A trustee must indicate whether or not the trust has been fully executed,[10] and a guardian must indicate whether the ward has reached majority or died.[11]

The fiduciary must file, and should record,[12] with the petition acknowledged receipts and releases from all those persons who would have been cited in a formal judicial accounting proceeding, which may include sureties on the bond, co-fiduciaries, successor fiduciaries, the

4. Matter of Amuso, 13 Misc.2d 686, 176 N.Y.S.2d 175 (Nassau 1958).

5. Matter of Gee, 46 N.Y.S.2d 662 (Queens 1943).

6. See McKinney's SCPA 2402(5), (8).

7. Formal accountings are discussed this chapter infra at 183–88.

8. See McKinney's SCPA 2210 and discussion of service of process this chapter infra at 189–92.

9. McKinney's SCPA 2203(2)(a).

10. McKinney's SCPA 2203(2)(b).

11. McKinney's SCPA 2203(2)(c).

12. The suggestion is made to record these instruments because, under McKinney's SCPA 2202, only recorded instruments enjoy the presumption that the contents are true and that the instrument was duly executed.

attorney general, distributees, devisees, trustees, unpaid legatees (or their legal representatives), guardians and their infant wards, and trust beneficiaries.[13] A fiduciary for a person under disability who has been paid can execute the receipt and release, but usually does so only when the ward's share was a specific legacy or a general legacy of a stated amount.[14] If the ward's share is a portion of the residuary estate or a distributive share, the court will usually in its discretion order a full judicial accounting rather than issue a decree on receipt and releases. After examining the petition and the receipts and releases, the court may make a decree releasing and discharging the fiduciary (and his surety on the bond) from further liability.[15]

The filing fee in a proceeding for a decree on receipts and releases depends on the amount of the fund being accounted for; it starts at $20 (for an estate or trust of less than $10,000) and goes up to $600 (for an estate or trust of more than $500,000).[16]

As a practical matter, this proceeding is used infrequently. Most attorneys either account informally on receipts and releases or obtain a formal judicial settlement.

3. JUDICIAL SETTLEMENT OF ACCOUNT

In addition to the informal accounting permitted on receipts and releases and the "middle ground" judicial decree on receipts and releases, a fiduciary can account formally and get a judicial settlement of the account. As a matter of fact, most estates are settled on an informal basis on receipt and releases. Only a relatively small number of estates, approximately one out of ten, is judicially settled. A formal judicial accounting may be necessary because the parties refuse to agree to an informal settlement, or an issue requires court participation [17] or the necessary parties are legally disabled or very numerous or scattered widely about.

A judicial settlement of account can come about in three ways: first, when the court decides to compel an accounting on its own motion, secondly, when an interested person petitions the court to compel an accounting; [18] and thirdly, when the fiduciary wants the protection and finality of a decree and voluntarily petitions the court to approve his account.[19]

13. This class of persons entitled to service under McKinney's SCPA 2210 is discussed in greater detail this chapter infra at 189–92.

14. See McKinney's SCPA 2202, Practice Commentary at 29 (1967); McKinney's SCPA 2203, Practice Commentary at 4 (Supp.1986).

15. McKinney's SCPA 2203(4).

16. McKinney's SCPA 2402(6), (8).

17. See Matter of Jones, 38 N.Y.2d 189, 379 N.Y.S.2d 55, 341 N.E.2d 565 (1975); Matter of McCarthy, 49 A.D.2d 204, 374 N.Y.S.2d 203 (4th Dep't 1975).

18. Compulsory accountings are discussed infra at 183–86.

19. Voluntary accountings are discussed infra at 187–88.

a. Accounting on the Court's Motion

The court has broad discretion to require a judicial settlement of a fiduciary's account on its own motion if to do so would serve the best interests of the estate.[20] On the other hand, its power to refuse to approve an accounting in a case where all the interested parties are competent adults and have waived process and consented to the relief sought is limited.[21]

b. Compulsory Accounting

As a preliminary word, an interested person should, before petitioning the court for a compulsory accounting, simply ask the fiduciary to account voluntarily, because most fiduciaries will do so. This request is, however, not a statutory prerequisite to a petition to compel an accounting; the petitioner may request an intermediate or final accounting without asking the fiduciary first, and the courts are fairly liberal in granting compulsory accountings. Another alternative is to commence discovery proceedings [22] to obtain information from the fiduciary concerning the assets and administration of the estate.

If, after all, a compulsory accounting is necessary, interested persons can petition for an order compelling the fiduciary to account.[23] It is because a party always has a right to petition for a compulsory accounting that the statute does not mandate periodic judicial settlement of accounts. The class of persons with an interest sufficient to give them standing to petition for a compulsory accounting is broad: [24] it includes creditors whose claims are not time-barred,[25] persons monetarily interested,[26] the public administrator or county treasurer,[27] any person on behalf of an infant or after-born child interested in the estate, the fiduciary of a deceased person with an interest in the estate,[28] a surety on the bond of the fiduciary, a successor fiduciary, a

20. McKinney's SCPA 2205. See, e.g., Matter of Natham, N.Y.L.J. Nov. 29, 1979, at 11, col. 6 (Bronx).

21. See Matter of DeVany, 205 N.Y. 591, 98 N.E. 1101 (1912); Matter of Veccio, 49 A.D.2d 380, 375 N.Y.S.2d 637 (3d Dep't 1975) (where commissions were paid out of specific legacies instead of residuary estate, and all beneficiaries consented, the Surrogate erred in refusing to approve the account).

22. These discovery proceedings are authorized by McKinney's SCPA 2101 and 2102 and discussed in chapter on "Miscellaneous Proceedings," infra at 326–36.

23. McKinney's SCPA 2205.

24. McKinney's SCPA 2205.

25. See Matter of Thom, 76 Misc.2d 132, 350 N.Y.S.2d 568 (Monroe 1973) (creditor whose claim was barred by statute of limitations not proper petitioner under McKinney's SCPA 2205).

26. Under McKinney's SCPA 103(39), this includes "[a]ny person entitled either absolutely or contingently to share as beneficiary in the estate or the trustee in bankruptcy or receiver of such person." This includes a decedent's out-of-wedlock child in cases where an order of filiation had established paternity, Matter of McLeod, 105 Misc.2d 1012, 430 N.Y.S.2d 782 (Westchester 1980), or where other proofs sufficient to allow the child to inherit had been made. See McKinney's EPTL 4–1.2, discussed in chapter on "Administration," supra at 130–32.

27. Participation of the public administrator or county treasurer is rare; it may occur when a public administrator working on one estate has a claim against another estate.

28. An interesting quandary arises when the fiduciary of a post-deceased beneficiary is a beneficiary of the same estate, for example, when two brothers are sole

co-fiduciary who has already accounted, or the attorney general as representative of a charitable beneficiary or in a case where any of the estate may escheat.[29]

The statute permits the court to order the filing of the account,[30] and in practice the courts also require that the petitioner also move for a judicial settlement of the account.

When a party files a petition to compel an accounting (or when the court directs a compulsory accounting on its own), the fiduciary is entitled to process.[31] The petitioner submits the citation to the court, the court issues it, and the petitioner arranges for its service on the fiduciary. On the return date the fiduciary may appear and do a variety of things: file his account, petition for the determination of the validity of a claim as a preliminary matter to accounting,[32] petition for a voluntary accounting,[33] or show good cause why he cannot file an accounting, because, for example, some matter is still outstanding, such as an estate tax proceeding, sale of property or a lawsuit. In some cases where it appears that an immediate accounting is necessary, the court will order it notwithstanding the unsettled matters.[34] In others the court finds that the fiduciary has not been dilatory and refuses to order an accounting because too many matters still require administration.[35]

If, as usually happens, a fiduciary against whom a party has sought a compulsory accounting petitions for a voluntary accounting by the return date, the court will consolidate the two proceedings and the fiduciary will not have to serve further process on the person who petitioned for the compulsory accounting. In practice the courts give the fiduciary the opportunity to account voluntarily rather than compel him to account,[36] prescribing a time, usually sixty days, within which

distributees of their parent's estate, one then dies after the parent and the other is the administrator of the deceased brother. In that case the beneficiaries of the deceased brother's estate should receive process, because the surviving brother has an irreconcilable conflict and cannot be trusted to object to overpayment of his own share. This situation arose in Matter of White, 125 Misc.2d 436, 479 N.Y.S.2d 702 (Nassau 1984), and the court ordered service on the guardian of the deceased brother's minor daughter.

29. See McKinney's SCPA 2222–2225, discussed this chapter infra at 224–30.

30. McKinney's SCPA 2205.

31. McKinney's SCPA 2206.

32. McKinney's SCPA 1809, discussed in chapter on "Claims," supra at 163–64. See Matter of Thom, 76 Misc.2d 132, 350 N.Y.S.2d 568 (Monroe 1973).

33. McKinney's SCPA 2208, discussed this chapter infra at 187–88.

34. Matter of Richardson, N.Y.L.J., April 25, 1985, at 13, col. 3 (Bronx) (court ordered fiduciary to account despite her request to await resolution of a real property proceeding. The court noted that the petitioner sought an accounting of property other than the realty); Matter of Donnelly, N.Y.L.J., March 29, 1985, at 5, col. 5 (Nassau) (court ordered fiduciary to account despite pendency of estate tax proceeding because no distributions had been made and bonds had been sold below market value).

35. Matter of Greenstein, N.Y.L.J., Feb. 21, 1985, at 12, col. 6 (Westchester).

36. If the fiduciary's voluntary accounting is satisfactory, the court will entertain it. If not, it will usually order the fiduciary to file an acceptable account within a specified period or be compelled by the court to file one. See Matter of Usdan, 125 Misc.2d 494, 480 N.Y.S.2d 81 (Nassau 1984), where the decedent's grandson petitioned to compel an accounting covering

the fiduciary must serve process on those who would be necessary parties to a voluntary accounting proceeding [37] and to move for judicial settlement of the account, or if he does not, the court will compel him to account, usually within ten days, and the court has discretion to extend that time.[38] In practice the petitioner for the compulsory accounting can submit the proposed order with the petition and serve it on the fiduciary when the judge signs it. If the fiduciary fails to account within sixty days, he is under a compulsory order to account within ten days thereafter, and if he does not, he will be subject to contempt proceedings.[39]

The court, after hearing the proof of all the parties, can make such order as justice requires, even if the fiduciary has failed or refused to file an account or to procure its settlement.

The court may hold the fiduciary in civil contempt if it finds that the fiduciary's failure to account has prejudiced (or was calculated to prejudice) the rights of the person seeking the accounting,[40] and may impose a fine of the greater of $250 or the actual loss caused.[41] The court may hold the fiduciary in criminal contempt if it finds the disobedience was willful,[42] and in that case can impose a fine of $250.[43] The court can hold the fiduciary in both civil and criminal contempt,[44] and can dispense with personal service of the order to show cause why the fiduciary should not be punished for contempt, ordering service by an alternative manner instead.[45]

The accounting fiduciary must attach to the account an affidavit [46] swearing that the statement in the account of receipts and disbursements is true to the best of the petitioner's knowledge, that the account

the entire (eighteen-year) period of administration, and the executors proposed a voluntary account that would show satisfaction of the grandson's $25,000 legacy plus interest. The court refused to entertain the voluntary accounting on the theory that the executors, who were also primary beneficiaries of the estate, (properly) continued the decedent's business and may therefore have been liable to the decedent's grandson for profits generated by his $25,000.

37. See McKinney's SCPA 2210, discussed this chapter infra at 189–92.

38. See Matter of Seymour, N.Y.L.J., May 24, 1985, at 17, col. 1 (Nassau) (Surrogate ordered fiduciary to obtain new counsel when fiduciary requested three month extension because of his attorney's hospitalization).

39. See, e.g., Matter of Stanton, N.Y. L.J., March 29, 1985, at 15, col. 4 (Nassau) (court allowed executrix to purge herself of contempt by filing an accounting by stated date two weeks after order); Matter of Cinqueman, N.Y.L.J., Oct. 2, 1978, at 13, col. 4 (Bronx) (court held in contempt fiduciaries who, in response to order, filed an account covering a period that ended three years before they filed it).

40. Powell, v. Clauss, 93 A.D.2d 883, 461 N.Y.S.2d 413 (2d Dep't 1983).

41. McKinney's Jud.Law §§ 753 (1975) 773 (Supp.1986); New York v. Unique Ideas, 44 N.Y.2d 345, 405 N.Y.S.2d 656, 376 N.E.2d 1301 (1978).

42. Powell v. Clauss, 93 A.D.2d 883, 461 N.Y.S.2d 413 (2d Dep't 1983).

43. McKinney's Jud.Law 750, 751 (1975).

44. McCormick v. Axelrod, 59 N.Y.2d 574, 466 N.Y.S.2d 279, 453 N.E.2d 508 (1983).

45. McKinney's SCPA 607(2); Matter of Drimmer, 97 A.D.2d 792, 468 N.Y.S.2d 533 (2d Dep't 1983) (service by mail on fiduciary's attorney).

46. This affidavit is set forth in McKinney's SCPA Official Forms 12, 13 and 14.

covers all money and other estate assets that he has received or any other person has received for his use, and that he does not know of any error or omission in the account that prejudices any creditor or other person interested in the estate.[47]

It is worthwhile to recall a general point of procedure here. Under SCPA 509, allegations in a petition or account are deemed accepted unless denied in an answer or objections. On the other hand, allegations in an answer or objections are automatically deemed denied because no pleadings responsive to them are required.[48] This rule may create a trap for the unwary in a compulsory accounting proceeding. In a voluntary accounting proceeding,[49] the accounting fiduciary submits a petition and the accounting as affirmative pleadings, and their allegations are deemed accepted unless refuted. Where the account is compulsory, the accounting fiduciary is the respondent and his accounting is a responsive pleading. Accordingly, in the context of a compulsory accounting, the interested parties should always file any objections to the account by the return date, or under a strict reading of SCPA 509, the materials contained in the account may be deemed to be accepted.

Sometimes a fiduciary wants to assert the statute of limitations or the doctrine of laches as a defense to a compulsory accounting proceeding. Since the SCPA is silent, the CPLR's six-year statute of limitations [50] applies, and it begins to run when the fiduciary clearly and unequivocally repudiates his duties as fiduciary of the estate and the beneficiary knows it.[51] Mere passage of time without an act of repudiation is not sufficient to start the running of the statute.[52] The fiduciary has the burden of proof that the statute of limitations has run.[53] Even if the statute of limitations has not run, the fiduciary can plead the defense of laches, but to do so he must prove delay as well as resultant injuries or change of position.[54]

47. McKinney's SCPA 2209. Compare the less detailed affidavit attached to a guardian's annual account under McKinney's SCPA 1719.

48. See McKinney's SCPA 509, Prac. Comm. at 465 (1967).

49. Voluntary accountings are discussed infra at 187–88.

50. McKinney's CPLR 213(1).

51. Matter of Barabash, 31 N.Y.2d 76, 334 N.Y.S.2d 890, 286 N.E.2d 268 (1972), reargument denied 31 N.Y.2d 963, 341 N.Y.S.2d 1029, 293 N.E.2d 258 (1972) (no repudiation by trustee who, after receiving letter threatening compulsory accounting if informal accounting was not forthcoming within two weeks, hinted in correspondence that he would offer a settlement); Matter of Menahan, 224 App.Div. 139, 229 N.Y.S. 706 (2d Dep't 1928); Matter of Jackson, N.Y.L.J., Dec. 14, 1984, at 14, col. 2 (Bronx).

52. Matter of Ashheim, 111 A.D. 176, 97 N.Y.S. 607 (1st Dep't 1906), affirmed 185 N.Y. 609, 78 N.E. 1099 (1906).

53. Matter of Lewin, 41 Misc.2d 72, 245 N.Y.S.2d 254 (Suffolk 1963); Matter of Sakow, N.Y.L.J., May 10, 1985, at 15, col. 2 (Bronx).

54. Weiss v. Mayflower Doughnut Corp., 1 N.Y.2d 310, 152 N.Y.S.2d 471, 135 N.E.2d 208 (1956); Matter of Sakow, N.Y. L.J., May 10, 1985, at 15, col. 2 (Bronx).

c. *Voluntary Accountings*

A fiduciary winding up an estate or trust may want to obtain a judicial settlement of his account. If it is a final account, he has a right to a judicial settlement.[55] If he wants an intermediate account, he must meet the following time requirements, and in addition the court has discretion whether to entertain it.

(1) Fiduciaries Other Than Guardians or Trustees

Reference to executors and administrators in this section includes administrators c.t.a., administrators d.b.n., preliminary executors and temporary administrators.

When seven months have elapsed from the appointment of the first fiduciary, the executor or administrator can petition to account.[56] This seven-month period is the same period during which the fiduciary is personally liable to creditors if he pays out estate assets without first satisfying the claim.[57] If instead of waiting the seven months, he publishes notice to creditors, he can petition for the accounting when the publication period ends (fourteen weeks in a large city, three months elsewhere).[58] Because fiduciaries usually do not publish notice,[59] in most cases the seven-month period has elapsed before the fiduciary moves for a voluntary settlement of his final account.

The executor or administrator can also petition if his letters have been revoked.[60] The court can revoke a fiduciary's letters for various wrong-doing, such as wasting assets and refusing to obey court orders,[61] and can also revoke letters because the fiduciary's serving was, under the terms of the appointing instrument, to cease on the occurrence of a contingency which has in fact occurred.

An executor or administrator can also account where it appears that real property has to be sold to pay expenses, taxes or debts of the estate[62] and the court entertains the fiduciary's petition to account within six months of issuance of original letters.[63] Real estate proceedings are rare and thus accountings commenced solely for the purpose of selling real property are also rare.

In other cases, the executor or administrator does not have a right to an accounting; he must ask the court to entertain the accounting

55. McKinney's SCPA 2208.

56. McKinney's SCPA 2208(1)(a).

57. McKinney's SCPA 1802, discussed in chapter on "Claims," supra at 148–50.

58. McKinney's SCPA 1801, discussed in chapter on "Claims," supra at 150–51.

59. The reason is that only four months can be saved by this publication of notice and most fiduciaries are not ready to wind up the estate for at least seven months anyway.

60. McKinney's SCPA 2208(1)(b).

61. See McKinney's SCPA 711 and 719 and chapter on "Fiduciaries," infra at 393–400.

62. Such sale would be required under SCPA 1902, discussed in chapter on "Real Estate Transactions," infra at 470 et seq.

63. McKinney's SCPA 2208(1)(c). The six month period was more useful historically, when a fiduciary could not account for one year from the issuance of letters, than it is currently, when a fiduciary can account seven months after letters.

proceeding, and the court can do so if the fiduciary's account has not been judicially settled within one year.[64]

(2) Guardians

A guardian may, like any fiduciary, voluntarily account where an interested party has petitioned for his compulsory accounting[65] or he has spent all of the infant's property in his possession and the court believes it appropriate to discharge him.[66] In practice, this final judicial accounting occurs when the ward reaches majority. In the intervening years the guardian submits an annual account or, in the alternative, holds the ward's property jointly with a bank or the court clerk.[67] If the guardian does annual accounts, they are reviewed by the court but they are not judicially approved. When the ward reaches majority, the fiduciary submits a final accounting and the ward signs a waiver based on the annual accounts and the last accounting, and the court then judicially settles the account.

(3) Trustees

A trustee can voluntarily account whenever a trust under his supervision (whether created by will or inter-vivos instrument) is ready to be terminated.[68] The court can also entertain the application for an intermediate accounting at an earlier time if there has been no judicial settlement of account within one year.[69]

SECTION C. PROCEDURE

We couch this discussion of the procedure in an accounting proceeding in terms of a voluntary account. Appropriate changes would have to be made for a compulsory accounting on the court's motion.

The voluntary accounting proceeding resembles the typical proceeding in the Surrogate's Court. The fiduciary petitions the court for a judicial settlement of account and submits an affidavit that the account is accurate.[1] He pays a fee set by the SCPA if it is an estate or testamentary trust accounting,[2] and by the CPLR if it is an inter vivos trust accounting.[3] He obtains waivers of citation from all parties amenable to settlement of the account, and he submits to the court citations for all other necessary parties. The judge or the clerk issues the citations, and the fiduciary arranges to serve them personally or by

64. McKinney's SCPA 2208(1)(d).

65. McKinney's SCPA 2208(2)(a).

66. McKinney's SCPA 2208(2)(b).

67. McKinney's SCPA 1709. These alternatives are discussed in the chapter on "Guardianships," infra at 269–71.

68. McKinney's SCPA 2208(3)(a).

69. McKinney's SCPA 2208(3)(b).

Sec. C

1. See discussion of the affidavit in section on "Compulsory Accountings," this chapter supra at 183–86.

2. McKinney's SCPA 2402(1).

3. McKinney's SCPA 2402(4), incorporating McKinney's CPLR 8018.

an alternative means with a court order.[4] If the fiduciary wants any additional relief in the course of an accounting proceeding, such as construction of the will or determination of the validity of the surviving spouse's right of election, the citation should so state. On the return date, objectants have a chance to be heard, and the court issues a decree settling the account.

1. NECESSARY PARTIES

In a solvent estate, before a fiduciary accounts he should try to reduce the number of persons cited by paying valid claims against the estate, paying general and specific dispositions and obtaining receipts and releases where possible from residuary legatees.

The persons entitled to process are listed in SCPA 2210:

(i) unpaid creditors or persons claiming to be creditors of the decedent.[5] This should include plaintiffs in personal injury actions against the decedent. The petitioner should specifically ask the court in the petition to approve the rejection of the creditor's claim.

(ii) the fiduciary's surety, if any.[6]

(iii) all co-fiduciaries who have not joined in the account.[7]

(iv) the decedent's intestate distributees where the decedent died intestate as to any property, except those who have been paid and have submitted releases; [8]

(v) all devisees, trustees of any trust created under a will or inter vivos trust, and all legatees who have not been paid and who have not waived (themselves or through their fiduciaries).[9] If a legatee is under disability, he will not be entitled to process if his share was paid on his behalf to a parent or other adult for an infant,[10] or to a custodian under the Uniform Gifts to Minors Act,[11] and the person who received the payment on his behalf executed a waiver of citation.

(vi) any appointed successor fiduciaries where the petitioner's letters have been revoked or he has been removed, and if no successor has been appointed, all persons interested who would otherwise have been entitled to process under SCPA 2210.[12] The clear implication here is that if the court has appointed a successor fiduciary, the "persons interested" are not entitled to service, on

4. Waivers and service of process are discussed in chapter on "Procedure," supra at 37–49.

5. McKinney's SCPA 2210(1).

6. McKinney's SCPA 2210(2).

7. McKinney's SCPA 2210(3).

8. McKinney's SCPA 2210(6).

9. McKinney's SCPA 2210(7). If a beneficiary-necessary party signed a power of attorney delegating power over estate matters, the attorney-in-fact can assert objections for him. Matter of DelVecchio, N.Y. L.J., June 23, 1978, at 15, col. 6 (Suffolk).

10. Under McKinney's SCPA 2220 and McKinney's EPTL 11–1.1(b)(19), a parent or adult with custody of a child can receive $5,000 on the child's behalf.

11. McKinney's EPTL 7–4.8.

12. McKinney's SCPA 2210(4).

the theory that the fiduciary will represent their interests. The phrase "persons interested," however, includes beneficiaries (the distributees, devisees and legatees referred to in (iv) and (v) above), but not creditors, sureties, and other persons listed in SCPA 2210,[13] so this latter group must be cited even if the court has appointed a successor.[14]

(vii) the attorney general where he is required to be given notice of an accounting proceeding in the context of a charitable trust; [15]

(viii) the attorney general where the decedent, infant or beneficiary died intestate leaving unknown distributees or distributees whose whereabouts are unknown; [16]

(ix) the infant in guardianship proceedings.[17]

(x) in trustee's accounting proceedings, all those entitled to share absolutely or contingently by the terms of the will or inter vivos trust, or by operation of law. Thus even contingent income beneficiaries or remaindermen are necessary parties. SCPA 315's virtual representation provisions apply here,[18] reducing the number of necessary parties and guardians ad litem.

If the accounting fiduciary is accounting to himself in a separate capacity (fiduciary of a deceased beneficiary, trustee, guardian of an infant beneficiary, committee of an incompetent beneficiary, or conservator of a beneficiary-conservatee), it is not sufficient to serve himself with process or obtain an appearance from himself in the separate capacity. He also has to serve all persons interested in the trust or in the estate of the deceased beneficiary, the infant, the incompetent, or the conservatee, unless there is a co-fiduciary (or more than one) serving with him in his non-accounting capacity and not serving with him in his accounting capacity.[19] For example, if a fiduciary is submitting his final accounting as executor, and has to account to himself as trustee of a testamentary trust, he will have to cite the trust beneficiaries. If, however, there is an independent co-trustee serving with him, he can cite the other trustee alone, just as he could if he were not trustee.[20] If a conflict of interests appears to exist, such as in the case

13. McKinney's SCPA 103(39) defines "persons interested" as "[a]ny person entitled either absolutely or contingently to share as beneficiary in the estate or the trustee in bankruptcy or receiver of such person. A creditor shall not be deemed a person interested."

14. See Matter of May, 111 Misc.2d 51, 443 N.Y.S.2d 359 (Nassau 1981).

15. McKinney's EPTL 8–1.4(e)(1)(D); McKinney's SCPA 2210(5).

16. McKinney's SCPA 2210(5). See discussion of estates where there are no beneficiaries or they are unknown in section on "Escheat," this chapter infra at 224 et seq.

17. McKinney's SCPA 2210(8).

18. Virtual representation is discussed in chapter on "Procedure," supra at 60–70.

19. McKinney's SCPA 2210(10).

20. However, if the executor's accounting seeks incidental relief that would discharge the "independent" co-trustee as well, the court will require all the beneficiaries to be cited. See Matter of Seidman, 124 Misc.2d 1053, 478 N.Y.S.2d 798 (Nassau 1984) (co-executors sought in final estate accounting to serve only the independent co-trustee of residuary trust rather than all beneficiaries, but court refused to allow it because the estate accounting also

where the co-fiduciary is also the accounting party's attorney, the court will order the beneficiaries to be cited.[21] Absent such a conflict, however, the independent co-trustee is likely to protect the interests of the beneficiaries, and the adequacy of that representation is reviewable when the co-trustee later accounts on his own behalf. SCPA 315's virtual representation provisions apply even in this case.[22]

To avoid application of this rule and to keep expenses to a minimum, it may be advisable to designate only one person as executor and that person and another as trustees rather than designating both to serve in both capacities.[23]

If a person entitled to process dies, process goes to his fiduciary, or if there is none, to his distributees, and if he has a will filed in the court, to his nominated fiduciaries and named legatees and devisees.[24]

The court may dispense with the service of process on any person whose interest does not exceed $500 if good cause is shown,[25] and the expense of service can be sufficient good cause. The court may dispense with service even if the party's name and address are known, but it ordinarily requires service by registered mail [26] to any beneficiary whose whereabouts are known, to avoid constitutional challenges.[27] When the court dispenses with process, the decree settling the account is not conclusive against the party not served unless he has waived process or appeared in the proceeding before the entry of the decree. Because it is the responsibility of the fiduciary to cite all proper parties, and because he will be liable to those not cited, it may be wise to serve those whose names or whereabouts are unknown by publication rather than to dispense with service under this subparagraph, in order to put the matter finally to rest.

sought approval of trust principal invasions made by all three trustees).

21. See Matter of Hammond, 94 Misc. 2d 760, 405 N.Y.S.2d 594 (Dutchess 1978).

22. The 1967 enactment of McKinney's SCPA 2210(13), L.1967, c. 739, § 5, specifying that McKinney's SCPA 315's virtual representation provisions apply to McKinney's SCPA 2210, eliminated the ambiguity surrounding that issue. The question was whether vested remaindermen could virtually represent contingent remaindermen in view of McKinney's SCPA 2210's requirement that all trust beneficiaries be served if the executor was accounting to himself as trustee. See, for example, Matter of Snyder, 54 Misc.2d 695, 283 N.Y.S.2d 326 (Erie 1967), where the court ruled that if McKinney's SCPA 315 was applicable, the representation of contingent remaindermen by vested remaindermen was possibly inadequate, but that in any event it believed that 2210 did not permit virtual representation.

23. See McKinney's SCPA 2210, Practice Commentary at 16 (Supp.1986). Despite the existence of the rule dispensing with service on the trust beneficiaries if a fiduciary is accounting to a co-fiduciary, some courts find the rule discretionary and order service on the beneficiaries on the theory that the trustees serve as a single entity or person. See Matter of United States Trust Co. of New York, 71 Misc.2d 996, 337 N.Y.S.2d 534 (New York County 1972). This should be seen as an aberration rather than as the rule, a throw-back to the view of trustees as a single entity, see, e.g., Matter of Miles, 31 Misc.2d 464, 221 N.Y.S.2d 43 (Nassau 1961), which McKinney's SCPA 2210 was specifically enacted to overcome.

24. McKinney's SCPA 2210(11).

25. McKinney's SCPA 2210(12).

26. See McKinney's SCPA 2210, Practice Commentary at 16 (Supp.1986).

27. See Matter of Galvin, 153 Misc. 11, 274 N.Y.S. 846 (Monroe 1934).

When the accounting party is the public administrator or county treasurer and there are no known beneficiaries, and it appears that the value of the interests of all beneficiaries is less than $2,500, the court may dispense with the service of process on the beneficiaries.[28] No publication need be made and no guardian ad litem appointed. In such a case the attorney general receives process and may make any objections to the account that the beneficiary could have made. Usually after the accounting, the estate funds are paid to the state as custodian for the unknown beneficiaries.[29] The decree is binding on any person ultimately determined to be entitled to share in the estate. This section can probably also be used in cases where a beneficiary's whereabouts are unknown, although the statute does not specifically say that it is.[30]

When an accounting proceeding is pending, a supplemental account may be filed without serving a further citation,[31] unless the supplemental account reports substantial transactions, in which case the court must issue a supplemental citation.

The virtual representation rules of SCPA 315 [32] apply in accounting proceedings. The general rule is that the court will dispense with process and appointment of a guardian ad litem only when the presence of the cited parties will necessarily protect the persons under disability, unborns and unknowns. Thus, if a person is a remainderman of a testamentary trust, he could normally represent the contingent remaindermen even if he was also a permissible income beneficiary, because their mutual interest at the accounting proceeding would be to have the trust funded to the maximum degree. However, if that remainderman actually received income during estate administration, he cannot represent the contingent remainderman because his interest in justifying the income payments would conflict with theirs in maximizing principal.[33]

2. EXAMINATIONS AND OBJECTIONS

On the return of process the court must take the account, hear the relevant testimony of the parties, and make whatever order or decree justice requires.[34] Any party may examine the fiduciary under oath on all estate matters, either before or after the filing of objections,[35] and a guardian ad litem may also do so before filing his report.[36] The party naturally does not waive that right by inspecting, or having his attor-

28. McKinney's SCPA 2210(13).

29. See McKinney's SCPA 2223 and 2224, discussed infra at 224 et seq.

30. McKinney's SCPA 2210, Prac. Comm. at 17 (Supp.1986).

31. Matter of Hickey, 73 N.Y.S.2d 508 (Rensselaer 1939).

32. McKinney's SCPA 315 is discussed in chapter on "Procedure," supra at 60–70.

33. See Matter of Sage, 54 Misc.2d 779, 283 N.Y.S.2d 442 (New York County 1967).

34. McKinney's SCPA 2211(1).

35. McKinney's SCPA 2211(2). See, e.g., Matter of Golding, N.Y.L.J. Dec. 13, 1979, at 11, col. 5 (New York County), where the court ordered an examination of the attorney, who was serving as the fiduciary of the deceased trustees, on his proposed payment of legal fees.

36. Matter of Alpert, N.Y.L.J. July 30, 1985, at 6, col. 4 (New York County).

ney or accountant inspect, the pertinent books and records kept by the fiduciary.[37] If there is a question whether a piece of property is part of the estate or trust, the court can decide that issue as a preliminary matter before the accounting or as part of the objections to the account.

On the return date the respondent's attorney may request an opportunity to examine the fiduciary. The court usually assigns a date for that examination and directs the time for filing objections (often ten days after the court reporter files the transcript of the examination). This examination must be held at the courthouse before the official court reporter,[38] because it is a quasi-hearing. In the larger counties, the court (often through a member of the law department in his capacity as referee), supervises the disclosure and makes rulings as the examination progresses. The scope of this examination is broad; the court will permit questions on all issues that could be the subject of a CPLR Article 31 examination.[39] However, once a fiduciary is examined under 2211, the court usually does not allow a second examination under Article 31.[40] If other parties are examined in an accounting proceeding, it is CPLR Article 31 and not the SCPA that permits it.[41]

Any person entitled to process in the accounting proceeding has standing to object to the accounting. The objections must be specific enough to give notice of the issues. If the objectant fails to give notice of an issue, the court cannot try that issue.[42] Objections must be verified, since they are pleadings.[43]

In most cases the respondents interpose no objections and the matter goes to decree, or goes to decree subject to the report of a guardian ad litem. The petitioner drafts and submits the proposed decree granting the relief he sought (approving the account, allowing the commissions and attorneys' fees, ordering distributions). In rare cases the petitioner or the objectant moves for summary judgment.[44] The Surrogates of some counties do an audit of the accounting before the matter proceeds to decree even if no one objects to the account.

Even in counties where the Surrogate does not do a thorough audit of the uncontested account, the judge at least checks commissions, computations and the special prayer for relief to ascertain the overall accuracy of the account. The fiduciary should be prepared to produce

37. Matter of Sheirr, N.Y.L.J. Jan. 24, 1979, at 11, col. 3 (New York County).

38. See Uniform Rules of the Surrogate's Court 207.28.

39. For a discussion of the Article 31 examination, see D. Siegel, New York Practice at 228 et seq.

40. Matter of Coyle, 61 Misc.2d 720, 306 N.Y.S.2d 161 (Albany 1969).

41. The CPLR governs Surrogate's practice where the SCPA is silent. McKinney's SCPA 102. See Matter of Laflin, 105 A.D.2d 747, 481 N.Y.S.2d 179 (2d Dep't 1984) (proper to direct non-party witness to appear for examination on objectant's counsel's showing that he needed that witness's deposition to prepare for trial).

42. Matter of Gil, 67 A.D.2d 779, 412 N.Y.S.2d 682 (3d Dep't 1979).

43. McKinney's SCPA 303.

44. McKinney's CPLR 3213. See, e.g., Matter of Schmitz, N.Y.L.J. April 16, 1985, at 13, col. 2 (Westchester).

cancelled checks, releases, income tax returns, securities transactions data, and any other papers supportive of the figures in the accounting.

After the examination of the fiduciary, if a party interposes objections, a pretrial conference will be scheduled to narrow the issues for trial or settlement.[45] The petitioner can also move to dismiss the objections.[46] If the matter is not settled, the court will set a hearing date to hear evidence on the outstanding objections; the Surrogate usually presides, though in some cases the hearing is before a "law assistant to hear and report." [47] There is ordinarily no right to a jury trial.[48]

If the accounting is unacceptable, the court can remedy the situation in several ways. It can deny the fiduciary commissions or surcharge him to make the estate whole,[49] or it can remove him from his office.[50]

The court can exercise all of its constitutional and statutory jurisdiction in an accounting proceeding,[51] and the fiduciary therefore often uses the accounting proceeding to wind up all outstanding issues, such as questions of construction, right of election, tax computation, commissions, propriety of the sale of assets, amount of distributions, validity of claims, abandonment of assets, stockholders' agreements, and payment of administration expenses. After a hearing the court will determine the issues and, where necessary, surcharge the fiduciary for losses caused by improper acts or omissions.[52]

SECTION D. THE ACCOUNT

The account is a listing of all the money and property under the fiduciary's control. It is divided into schedules that show what was in the fund when the fiduciary took over, the increases or decreases to the value of that property, and the expenditures the fiduciary made. The purpose of the account is to balance the charges to the fiduciary, namely the property received, the realized increases in its value, and the income received, with the credits to the fiduciary, namely expenses and claims paid, distributions, realized decreases in value of property, and the value of the property still in the fiduciary's hands. These schedules show what the fiduciary did and how prudently (or imprudently) he acted. In addition, the account contains informational schedules that are neither charged against nor credited to the fiduciary: computation of commissions (usually not paid until after the account-

45. Uniform Rules of the Surrogate's Court Sec. 207.29.

46. McKinney's CPLR 3211.

47. See discussion of the "law assistant to hear and report" in chapter on "Trials," infra at 504–06.

48. See chapter on "Trials," infra at 497–499.

49. See chapter on "Commissions," infra at 436–41.

50. McKinney's SCPA 711, discussed in chapter on "Fiduciaries," infra at 393–400.

51. McKinney's SCPA 202.

52. For a discussion of surcharges, see chapters on "Commissions," infra at 436–41, and "Fiduciaries," infra at 412–13.

ing),[1] listing of interested persons, allocation of estate taxes, other pertinent facts and cash reconciliation.

In an estate accounting, the fiduciary is chargeable with all the property that would pass under a will (probate assets) such as cash, securities, bank accounts, personal property, partnership interests, as well as property payable to the estate, such as life insurance proceeds and death and retirement benefits if the decedent named the estate as beneficiary.

The fiduciary does not have to account for non-probate assets: property that passes outside the will, such as life insurance payable to someone other than the estate, jointly owned property, Totten Trusts, other transfers in trust, or death or retirement benefits payable to a designated beneficiary. He is not accountable for real property that is not sold, although he must include it in one of the informational schedules.[2] Out-of-state real property should also be listed for informational purposes.

The SCPA contains official forms for an estate accounting when the will did not create a trust,[3] for an estate accounting when the will created a testamentary trust,[4] for a trustee's accounting,[5] and for the annual accounting of a guardian.[6] Most Surrogate's Courts supply their own accounting forms to attorneys who request them.

This discussion of the following accounting schedules will assume that the fiduciary is an executor accounting for an estate in which the will did not create a testamentary trust. Following the estate accounting schedules are samples of schedules used in trust accountings or estate accountings where the will created a testamentary trust.

1. SCHEDULE A: PRINCIPAL RECEIVED

The fiduciary must list the date of death value of all principal received, and the date of receipt. In many contexts it is easy to identify principal: the property owned by the decedent, including any accrued income through the date of death, which came under the fiduciary's control. Sometimes the question of what is principal (as distinguished from income) is a little harder to answer, and EPTL 11–2.1 details the types of property that are income and the types that are principal.[7]

The value of the principal received is the date of death value, even if the fiduciary opted for alternate valuation for tax purposes;[8] he

Sec. D

1. See chapter on "Commissions," infra at 425 et seq.

2. Schedule J, discussed infra at 207.

3. McKinney's SCPA Official Form 12.

4. McKinney's SCPA Official Form 14.

5. McKinney's SCPA Official Form 13.

6. McKinney's SCPA Official Form 10.

7. The details of McKinney's EPTL 11–1.2 on principal and income are discussed in chapter on "Fiduciaries," infra at 413–424.

8. Matter of Hoff, 186 Misc. 684, 65 N.Y.S.2d 234 (New York County 1945), affirmed 270 A.D. 891, 62 N.Y.S.2d 577 (1st Dep't 1946), affirmed 296 N.Y. 650, 69 N.E.2d 814 (1946); Matter of Baker, 92 Misc.2d 934, 399 N.Y.S.2d 871 (1977).

must report and account for actual increases and decreases in value from the date of death through the cut-off date of his account.

Real property has to be listed as principal received only if it was sold, and if it was, the amount chargeable against the executor is only the net value (corroborated by the closing statement, which should be attached to the account). If the fiduciary did not sell it, the realty passes by operation of law to the beneficiary or beneficiaries entitled to it under the will or the laws of intestacy; the fiduciary never takes control of it and is not accountable for it. He must, however, list it in schedule J ("Other Pertinent Facts"), and list the amount of mortgages or liens on it at the decedent's death.

All principal received by the executor is listed on this schedule, even if discovered after the decedent's death. The fiduciary should cross-check this schedule against the federal and state estate tax returns, if any, to ensure consistency and accuracy. He should also explain any delay in collecting estate assets, such as debts.[9]

The following is a sample of schedule A:

SCHEDULE A

STATEMENT OF PRINCIPAL RECEIVED

9–12–84	Empire Federal Savings and Loan Ass'n Greenville, New York Savings Account # 3–23–22	$100,000.00
9–26–84	Valley View Trust Company Walestown, New York Checking Account # 33782	787.23
9–28–84	Internal Revenue Service Refund of Income Tax Overpayment	113.00
9–28–84	30 shares ABM Corp. stock	32,194.62
9–28–84	6 shares ATC Corp. stock	636.00
9–28–84	Cash	392.00
10–20–84	Cash	9.60
11–12–84	Travellers Insurance Policy # 45893902	731.99
12–9–84	Prudential Insurance Policy # 37237237	728.04
1–4–85	Blue Cross/Blue Shield Claim Payment	80.00
3–12–85	New York Telephone Company Credit balance	15.06
4–27–85	Internal Revenue Service Refund of Income Tax Overpayment	275.00

9. In the chapter on estate taxes, we discuss briefly the "Q–Tip" marital deduction trust, whose beneficiaries are liable for ratable shares of the estate taxes imposed on the estate of a surviving spouse at her death. I.R.C. § 2207A. The fiduciary should indicate on Schedule A that he received these amounts.

4–27–85	Proceeds of sale of real property located at 222 Main St., Walestown, New York	71,581.86
	Total of Principal Received:	$207,544.40

2. SCHEDULE A–1: INCREASES ON SALES, LIQUIDATION OR DISTRIBUTION

In Schedule A–1, the fiduciary charges himself with any realized increases on the sale or distribution of an asset. For instance, if an asset is worth $10,000 at decedent's death, and seven months later when its value has appreciated to $12,000, the executor distributes it to a beneficiary in satisfaction of a legacy in the will, he must include the $2,000 increase in value in schedule A–1. The market value at the date of distribution is given ($12,000) and its inventory value in the estate is subtracted ($10,000), resulting in the increase realized.

If the executor incurred a brokerage fee on the sale, that fee is subtracted from the increase in value, and only the net increase is included in Schedule A–1.

The schedule should explain any failure of the fiduciary to realize reasonable profits because of untimely or imprudent sales.

A sample of Schedule A–1 follows:

SCHEDULE A–1

STATEMENT OF INCREASES ON SALES, LIQUIDATION OR DISTRIBUTION

	Proceeds	Inventory Value	Increase
30 shares ABM Corp. stock— sold 7–6–85	34,397.62	32,194.63	2,203.00
Total increase:			2,203.00

3. SCHEDULE A–2: INCOME COLLECTED

All income must be listed on this schedule. It may either be listed chronologically or, preferably, broken down by the asset from which the income was produced. Any income accrued before decedent's death is principal [10] and is listed on schedule A. A full year's income may be listed for each asset.

In a trust, a sharp division between income and principal is crucial because the two are separate interests belonging, in many cases, to different persons (income beneficiaries or remaindermen). The distinction is less important in an estate accounting, because with a few exceptions discussed in the next paragraph, all the property, income and principal, is distributable to the beneficiaries under the terms of the will or the laws of intestacy. Consequently, for some purposes, such as Schedule F (Personal Property Remaining on Hand), income and principal are lumped together in an estate accounting. Nevertheless,

10. McKinney's EPTL 11–2.1(b)(2).

principal and income received by the executor are listed separately in schedules A and A–2, respectively, because different classes of beneficiaries under the will are entitled to income under the following rules:

The beneficiary of a specific disposition is entitled to income earned by the property from the date of death.[11] For example, the rental income from specifically devised real property goes to the specific devisee.

An income beneficiary of a trust has the right to the income from the date the property becomes subject to the trust (unless the trust provides otherwise). In a testamentary trust, property becomes subject to the trust on the date of death.[12]

A beneficiary of a general bequest of money is entitled to no interest for the first seven months after the issuance of letters; this is tied to the seven month period creditors have to present their claims.[13] After the seven month period, the beneficiary (if he petitions to compel payment of his disposition) is entitled to six percent interest for a period during which distribution would be reasonable, then the legal rate.[14] The executor has the option instead to segregate the beneficiary's bequest and allow the beneficiary to take the accrued interest at the time of distribution.

All other beneficiaries share whatever interest the estate earns during administration in proportion to their interests in the undistributed assets, computed at the time of distribution.[15] If the estate contains real property not specifically devised, its income is payable to the residuary beneficiaries in proportion to their interests under the will.[16]

To illustrate these rules, assume a will leaves Blackacre to X, a general bequest of 1,000 shares of XYZ Corp. to Y, $100,000 to Z and the residue one-half to A, one-quarter to B and one quarter in trust, income to C, remainder to D. Assume further that during estate administration the rental income from Blackacre is $100x, dividends from the 1000 shares of XYZ Corp. stock are 200x, and that the other assets of the estate are Whiteacre, whose rental income was $300x, and $500,000 cash, which earned $400x interest, and another 1000 shares of XYZ Corp., which earned $200x.

X would be entitled to the $100x income from Blackacre. C would be entitled to the income from the date of death of one-quarter of the residue. Z would be entitled to six percent annual interest on $100,000 starting seven months after the appointment of a fiduciary if he petitioned for payment. The income from Whiteacre would be divided

11. McKinney's EPTL 11–2.1(d)(2)(A).

12. McKinney's EPTL 11–2.1(c)(1).

13. McKinney's SCPA 1802, discussed in chapter on "Claims," supra at 148–50.

14. McKinney's EPTL 11–1.5(d), amended L.1985, c. 634, to provide for interest of six percent instead of three percent, and to start it running from seven months after preliminary letters or temporary letters are granted, instead of letters testamentary or letters of administration.

15. McKinney's EPTL 11–2.1(d)(2)(B).

16. McKinney's EPTL 11–2.1(d)(3)(A).

among the residuary beneficiaries pro rata (one-half to A, one-quarter to B and one-quarter to the trust for C) unless the fiduciary, under his power to distribute property in kind,[17] allocates Whiteacre to the trust for C; in that case the income from Whiteacre from the date of death goes to the trustee. The remaining income (that is, the dividends from the XYZ stock and the interest on the cash not paid to Z under the six percent rule discussed above), is payable to the beneficiaries pro rata.

In a trust accounting, the fiduciary must treat the income beneficiaries and the remaindermen fairly and this schedule should reflect that. It should also show whether any allocation is made to income because of underproductive property.[18]

A sample of Schedule A–2 follows:

SCHEDULE A–2

STATEMENT OF ALL INCOME COLLECTED

10–20–84	Interest on Savings Account (Empire Federal Savings Bank, Account # 2001) 9–12–84 to 9–30–84	547.03
1–4–84	Interest on Savings Account 10–1–84 to 12–31–84	2,509.78
4–27–85	Interest on Savings Account 1–1–85 to 4–1–85	1,792.10
9–30–84	Interest on Checking Account (Empire Federal Savings Bank Account # 057482977)	36.07
12–31–84	Interest on Checking Account	205.03
3–31–84	Interest on Checking Account	194.92
	Total of Income Collected	$5,284.93

4. SCHEDULE B: DECREASES

Schedule B lists decreases realized on distribution or sale of assets, so that if a piece of property worth $10,000 at death had depreciated in value to $8,000 when sold or distributed to a legatee, Schedule B is the place to credit the fiduciary with the $2,000 realized loss.

Schedule B has an additional task. Assets whose values have not changed between the date of death and the date of distribution are listed in Schedule B (with zero listed as the amount of decrease), and worthless assets which the executor intends to abandon are also listed there. These assets are also listed in Schedule A, at their date of death value (which may be zero). The fiduciary should indicate whatever facts are necessary in Schedule B to prove his prudence.

17. McKinney's EPTL 11–1.1(c)(20).

18. McKinney's EPTL 11–2.1(k), discussed in chapter on "Fiduciaries," infra at 421–22.

A sample of Schedule B follows:

SCHEDULE B

DECREASES ON SALE OR DISTRIBUTION

	Inventory Value	Proceeds	Decrease
6 shares ATC Corp. stock— sold 4–8–85	$631.00	$600.00	$31.00
Total Decrease:			$31.00

5. SCHEDULE C: ADMINISTRATION AND FUNERAL EXPENSES CHARGEABLE TO PRINCIPAL

Some administration and funeral expenses are chargeable to income and others to principal.[19] An accounting contains two schedules to cover these expenses. The expenses chargeable to principal [20] are generally the "expenses incurred in connection with the settlement of a decedent's estate," and they include debts, funeral expenses, estate taxes (and interest and penalties on taxes), attorneys' fees, fiduciaries' commissions (except for commissions on estate income),[21] and court fees.

If any commissions have been paid on account to an executor by court order,[22] they are listed in schedule C. The computation of total commissions is included for information purposes in schedule H, and unpaid commissions are listed as unpaid administration expenses in schedule C–1.

The court will allow reasonable expenses only, so this schedule should reflect that. The fiduciary also should not pay expenses that should be paid by a beneficiary.

The testator can by will direct a different allocation of administration and funeral expenses.

If the will directs the payment of estate taxes out of the residuary estate as an administration expense, the tax payment should be listed on Schedule C. If the will contains no such directive, the taxes are apportioned against the beneficiaries pro rata,[23] and they will not be shown as a credit in schedule C, but rather will appear as an informational item in schedule H (Allocation of Estate Taxes) to be deducted from the beneficiaries' shares when distributions are made. If partial distributions have been made, they will appear on schedule E (Distribution of Principal) with an indication of the amount of estate taxes charged against each beneficiary's share.

19. McKinney's EPTL 11–2.1.

20. McKinney's EPTL 11–2.1(d)(1).

21. See chapter on "Commissions," infra at 425 et seq.

22. Payment of commissions on account is allowed with court permission. McKinney's SCPA 2310, 2311.

23. See McKinney's EPTL 2–1.8 and discussion of allocation of estate taxes in chapter on "Estate Taxes," infra at 602–06.

A sample of Schedule C follows:

SCHEDULE C

ADMINISTRATION AND FUNERAL EXPENSES

9–12–84	Salton Funeral Home	$2,918.08
9–21–84	United Lighting Company	240.40
9–21–84	New York Telephone Company	105.51
9–21–84	Valley View Water Company	30.00
9–25–84	Prudential (for Homeowners Insurance)	242.00
9–30–84	Kenneth Lombardi (Guardian ad litem in probate proceeding)	400.00
10–12–84	J.B. Service Company (for oil delivery)	334.92
10–24–84	Onondaga Tax Collector	413.39
10–24–84	Town Tax Collector	1,008.48
11–5–84	Lowe Jewelers (appraisal)	37.89
12–9–84	New York State Tax Commission (estate taxes)	4,667.20
12–9–84	Mullally Realtors (appraisal)	150.00
12–15–84	New York Telephone Company	32.14
1–3–85	J.B. Service Company	582.80
1–3–85	United Lighting Company	187.84
1–14–85	New York State Tax Commission (interest)	70.61
1–23–85	Town Tax Commissioner	830.39
3–16–85	Peter Levine, C.P.A. (preparation of decedent's final income tax return and estate fiduciary income tax return)	120.00
4–12–85	Internal Revenue Service (fiduciary income taxes)	851.95
4–12–85	New York State Tax Commission (fiduciary income taxes)	204.00
4–27–85	American Title Company (transfer tax, release of lien)	304.00
4–29–85	Star Publications (advertisements for sale of house and contents)	37.00
5–21–85	Frances Long (advance of attorney's fee and disbursements)	4,423.00
Total funeral and administration expenses:		$18,191.61

6. SCHEDULE C–1: UNPAID ADMINISTRATION EXPENSES

Schedule C–1 is an information section, representing neither a charge against nor a credit to the fiduciary. Items such as unpaid attorneys' fees, costs in connection with the accounting, and unpaid commissions are listed in this schedule. As with Schedule C, the court will read this schedule with an eye to reasonableness and the executor's liability as opposed to a beneficiary's liability for the expense.

The following is a sample of schedule C–1:

SCHEDULE C–1

STATEMENT OF UNPAID ADMINISTRATION EXPENSES

Frances Long—Attorney's fees	$3,250.00
Preparation of fiduciary income tax returns	60.00
State and federal fiduciary income taxes	1,100.00
Total unpaid administration expenses:	$4,410.00

7. SCHEDULE D: CREDITORS' CLAIMS

Schedule D gives the fiduciary an opportunity to list and allow or reject creditors' claims. The failure to list a claim in the accounting causes it to be deemed allowed.[24]

Claims are divided into five groups in Schedule D: claims allowed and paid, claims allowed and not yet paid, claims rejected, including the date and reason for rejection, claims that are contingent or unliquidated, and claims by the fiduciary, which automatically require court approval. To the extent that the claims listed in schedule D have been paid, they are a credit to the fiduciary and will appear in the summary statement.[25]

The fiduciary should give information that would show whether the statute of limitations has run.

If the estate is not sufficient to pay all debts, this schedule will list the order of priority of claims, if any. If a fund has to be reserved for a contingent claim, this schedule should give information to allow the court to decide whether to order a reservation and in what amount.[26]

A sample of schedule D follows:

SCHEDULE D–1

STATEMENT OF ALL CREDITORS' CLAIMS

9–21–84	Dr. Kern (services to decedent in hospital) Paid on 9/21/84	75.00
9–21–84	County Neurological (services to decedent in hospital) Paid on 9/21/84	125.00

SCHEDULE D–2—NONE
SCHEDULE D–3—NONE
SCHEDULE D–4—NONE
SCHEDULE D–5—NONE

24. See chapter on "Claims," supra at 146 et seq.

25. A sample summary statement appears in McKinney's SCPA Official Forms Numbers 12, 13, 14.

26. Priority of claims and reservation of funds are discussed in chapter on "Claims," supra at 164–172.

8. SCHEDULE E: DISTRIBUTION OF PRINCIPAL

Any distributions made to beneficiaries are listed in schedule E at their date of distribution value. This schedule is a credit; the charges against the fiduciary are in Schedules A, A–1 and A–2, and in the summary statement the charges of those schedules will offset the credits of Schedules D, E, and F.

This schedule should state when the distributions were made and whether they were made in cash or in kind.

If the will does not contain a clause exempting the will beneficiaries from sharing in the estate tax burden, they have to share the taxes pro rata.[27] If they do, Schedule E will reflect the apportionment of estate taxes charged against the distributions.

A sample of schedule E follows:

SCHEDULE E

DISTRIBUTIONS OF PRINCIPAL

Date	Distributee	Amount
12–15–84	Hazel Barren	$8,750.00
	Fran Lawrence	7,000.00
	Ralph Barren	8,750.00
	Teresa Torrent	1,750.00
	Gary Lambert	1,750.00
	Edwina Hildock	1,750.00
	Ralph Barren, Jr.	875.00
	Carl Barren	875.00
	Kristen Barren	875.00
	Frances Horne	875.00
	Grant Horne	875.00
3–26–85	Hazel Barren	$8,750.00
	Fran Lawrence	7,000.00
	Ralph Barren	8,750.00
	Teresa Torrent	1,750.00
	Gary Lambert	1,750.00
	Edwina Hildock	1,750.00
	Ralph Barren, Jr.	875.00
	Carl Barren	875.00
	Kristen Barren	875.00
	Frances Horne	875.00
	Grant Horne	875.00
	Total Distributions Made:	$59,500.00

27. See McKinney's EPTL 2–1.8 and discussion in chapter on "Estate Taxes," infra at 602–06.

9. SCHEDULE F: PERSONAL PROPERTY REMAINING ON HAND

The property set forth in this schedule, when added to the credits listed in schedule B (realized decreases in value of principal), schedule C (expenses), schedule D (paid claims), and schedule E (distributions), should equal the charges listed in schedule A (principal received), schedule A–1 (realized increases in value of principal) and schedule A–2 (income). Schedule F should also list uncollected property rights and receivables.

If the fiduciary acquired any of the property listed in schedule F by purchase, transfer or exchange, he must state the date and cost of the purchase.

The following is a sample of schedule F:

SCHEDULE F
STATEMENT OF ALL PERSONAL PROPERTY
REMAINING ON HAND

Empire Federal Savings Account # 23–2	$134,596.31
Empire Federal Checking Account # 874	2,544.41
Total Personal Property Remaining on hand	$137,140.72

10. SCHEDULE G: INTERESTED PARTIES

The official directions require a fiduciary to identify all persons as legatee, devisee, trustee, surviving spouse, distributee or other person entitled to share in the estate, and the latter phrase "or otherwise" should include all those entitled to process under SCPA 2210.[28] The fiduciary must also give each party's address, relationship to the decedent, and interest in the estate.

The fiduciary must state that he has searched the records of the court for any transactions by the persons listed in Schedule G that affect their interests in the estate: assignments, powers of attorney, or encumbrances. If he has found any, he must give details about the transactions, including pertinent names, addresses and dates. If he has any knowledge of a non-recorded power of attorney, encumbrance or assignment, he must also reveal it on schedule G.

A sample of schedule G follows:

SCHEDULE G: INTERESTED PARTIES

Name and Relationship	Nature of Interest	Address
Jean Fredericks, as executrix for Hazel Barren Niece Died March 13, 1985	25% of residue	40 Main St. Valley View New York 10000

28. See discussion of McKinney's SCPA 2210 this chapter supra at 189–92.

Fran Lawrence Grand-niece	20% of residue	29 Elm Ave. Valley View, New York 10000
Ralph Barren Grand-nephew	25% of residue	549 Hill Blvd. Valley View, New York 10000
Teresa Torrent	5% of residue	2231 8th Ave. Longview, New York 10000
Gary Lambert Brother	5% of residue	45 Nancy Dr. River Run, New York 10000
Lance Maher, as executor for Hazel Barren Smith Died Jan. 3, 1985	Burial plot	50 Main St. Valley View, New York 10000
Ralph Barren, Jr.	2½% of residue	549 Hill Blvd. Valley View, New York 10000
Carl Barren Great-grand-nephew	2½%	549 Hill Blvd. Valley View, New York 10000
Frances Horne Great-grand-niece	2½% of residue	29 Elm Ave. Valley View, New York 10000
Grant Horne Great-grand-nephew	2½% of residue	29 Elm Ave. Valley View, New York 10000
Edwina Hildock Friend	5% of residue	978 Grand Ave. Big Gorge, New York 10000
Gerald Horne Great-grand-nephew	2½% of residue	549 Hill Ave. Valley View, New York 10000
Kristen Barren Great-grand-niece	2½% of residue	29 Elm Ave. Valley View, New York 10000.

11. SCHEDULE H: ESTATE TAXES PAID AND THEIR ALLOCATION

If the estate incurred a federal or state estate tax, the fiduciary must show those taxes on Schedule H and attach the final receipt for New York estate taxes, if any were paid. If none were paid, he must append an order of exemption from tax.[29]

29. See chapter on "Estate Taxes," infra at 556 et seq.

If the taxes were apportioned ratably against the beneficiaries[30] (because the will did not direct otherwise), the fiduciary has to set forth the computation used in apportioning the taxes and the amount to be charged against each beneficiary, as well as the amounts due to the estate from each beneficiary on whose behalf a tax payment was made.

A sample of schedule H follows:

SCHEDULE H:

STATEMENT OF ESTATE TAXES PAID AND ALLOCATION THEREOF

New York Estate Taxes Paid	$4,737.81
Total	$4,737.81

The taxes were paid out of the residuary estate as directed by the will.[31]

12. SCHEDULE I: COMMISSIONS

The fiduciary must include in Schedule I the computation of his commissions. The fiduciary's commissions are based on a percentage of property he received (receiving commissions) and a percentage of property he paid out (paying commissions).[32]

The base for computing receiving commissions is arrived at by first deleting specific legacies from Schedule A (principal received), and then adding the result to Schedules A–1 (realized increases) and A–2 (income). The statutory percentages are then applied to that sum. For paying commissions, the fiduciary should add Schedules C (expenses paid), D (debts paid), E (not including specific dispositions), and F (not including specific dispositions).

SCHEDULE I

STATEMENT OF COMPUTATION OF COMMISSIONS

Commissions for Receiving Property	
Total property received:	$215,032.33
(all subject to commissions, since real property was sold on April 27, 1985)	
2½% on first $100,000.00	2,500.00
2% on next $115,032.33	2,300.65
Total receiving commissions	4,800.65
Commissions for Paying Out Property	
2½% on first $100,000.00	2,500.00
2% on next $115,032.33	2,300.65
Total paying commissions	4,800.65
Total Commissions	9,601.30

30. McKinney's EPTL 2–1.8. Tax apportionment is discussed in chapter on "Estate Taxes," infra at 602–06.

31. See discussion of estate tax apportionment and sample of the computation in chapter on "Estate Taxes," infra at 602–06.

32. See McKinney's SCPA 2307–09 in chapter on "Commissions," infra at 426–36.

13. SCHEDULE J: OTHER PERTINENT FACTS AND CASH RECONCILIATION

The fiduciary must give in Schedule J any other facts that affect estate administration or the rights of the parties. He must list unsold real property in this schedule for informational purposes, though he is not accountable for it, and must state whether the realty was encumbered by mortgages or liens when the decedent died. Another pertinent fact might be the existence of jointly owned property or other non-probate property which, although the fiduciary is not accountable for it, may affect tax apportionment.[33] Similarly, if the surviving spouse has asserted a right of election, the fiduciary should list testamentary substitutes such as Totten Trusts, joint property, gifts causa mortis and revocable transfers,[34] despite his lack of fiduciary responsibility for them.

A cash reconciliation should appear here in which the sum of Schedules A, A–1, and A–2 should equal the sums of Schedules B, C, D, E and F.

A sample Schedule J follows:

SCHEDULE J

OTHER PERTINENT FACTS AND CASH RECONCILIATION

Carl Barren is a minor. His share of the estate is less than $5,000 and is being paid to his father, Ralph Barren, 549 Hill Blvd., Valley View, New York 10000 under the authority of the Surrogate's Court Procedure Act, section 2220.

The real estate listed in Schedule A was sold in order to pay administration expenses and claims.

CASH RECONCILIATION

Schedule A		$207,544.40
Schedule A–1		2,203.00
Schedule A–2		5,284.93
Schedule B	31.00	
Schedule C	$18,160.61	
Schedule D	200.00	
Schedule E	59,500.00	
Schedule F	137,140.72	
Total:	215,032.33	215,032.33

33. Tax apportionment is discussed in chapter on "Estate Taxes," infra at 602–06.

34. Testamentary substitutes are discussed in chapter on "Surviving Spouse's Right of Election," infra at 307–11.

14. SOME ADDITIONAL SCHEDULES RELATING TO TRUSTS

a. Schedule F: New Investments and Stock Distributions

Schedule F is an informational schedule used in accountings where trusts are involved. Its purpose is to enable the court to evaluate the prudence of the fiduciary's investment decisions. All investments and reinvestments will appear on this schedule. The charges resulting from these investments will appear on schedule A–2 (increases in value of principal) or schedule A–1 (income received).

The fiduciary should cross-check this schedule with the estate income tax returns to see if the gains and losses are consistent and accurate.

Schedule F also lists all stock distributions and stock dividends. To determine whether to include the new stock in principal (Schedule A) or income (Schedule A–2), the executor must ascertain whether the stock distribution or dividend is at a rate of more than six percent or less than six percent of the shares of the company on which the distribution is made. If less, it is all income. If more, it is all principal.[35]

This schedule should reflect whether the fiduciary left cash uninvested for a long period.[36] The court will review the investments to see whether "churning" (investing, reselling and reinvesting and delaying the termination of the estate or trust to get increased commissions) occurred and whether the investments were prudent.

b. Schedule C–2: Administration and Funeral Expenses Chargeable to Income

This section must appear in a trust accounting. The fiduciary has to list ordinary expenses of trust administration in Schedule C–2, including regularly recurring taxes assessed against trust property, water costs, insurance premiums, interest paid by the trustee, ordinary repairs and income taxes.[37]

SECTION E. ACCOUNTING IN NEGLIGENCE ACTIONS

If the decedent had a cause of action for personal injuries, the personal representative has the authority to continue that action or to commence it if the decedent had not, provided it is not barred by the statute of limitations. If the decedent died because of another's negligence the personal representative has a right to commence a wrongful death action on behalf of the distributees.[1] The substantive aspects of

35. McKinney's EPTL 11–2.1(e)(2).

36. See Cooper v. Jones, 78 A.D.2d 423, 435 N.Y.S.2d 830 (4th Dep't 1981).

37. McKinney's EPTL 11–2.1(*l*)(1), (2), (3), (5).

Sec. E

1. See chapter on "Wrongful Death," infra at 527 et seq.

the wrongful death actions in the Surrogate's Court are covered by EPTL Article 5, Part 4, and SCPA 2204 provides for judicial settlement of the fiduciary's account after he obtains a recovery in a negligence or wrongful death action.[2] The EPTL provides for a hearing to determine who is entitled to share in the proceeds of the action.[3] SCPA 2204 works together with the EPTL, permitting a judicial settlement of the fiduciary's account.

We discuss wrongful death and negligence actions in another chapter,[4] and a brief synopsis will suffice here to give the context for the accounting proceeding in such actions. In a wrongful death action the recovery is payable to the distributees in the proportion the decedent's death caused them pecuniary loss. The decedent's executor or administrator commences the action. Frequently, in intestate estates, an administrator's letters are limited:[5] he can negotiate but cannot enter into a settlement until the court gives an order approving it. Because of the fiduciary's limited powers and the uncertainty of the amount of recovery, the fiduciary does not have to obtain a bond.[6] When he has negotiated a settlement with the defendants, he then petitions for an accounting and seeks a court order approving the compromise and settling his account. If the court approves, it either orders distribution directly to the beneficiaries and dispenses with a bond, or lifts the restrictions of the limited letters, permits the fiduciary to collect and administer the assets, and orders him to file a bond.

If there is an executor in place with unlimited letters, he has the authority to compromise the action without a court order and can receive the proceeds without filing a bond. He can then seek an accounting to determine how to distribute the proceeds.

In a survival action (for the decedent's personal injuries, medical expenses, pain and suffering), the proceeds of the action are payable to the estate and are distributed to the will beneficiaries or the intestate distributees like other estate assets. A fiduciary with limited letters must get a court order approving the compromise. If the estate is not ready for distribution, the fiduciary has to post a bond; otherwise the court order can direct distribution to will beneficiaries or distributees and dispense with a bond. An executor with full letters can receive the proceeds without filing a bond and administer them as part of the estate.

Thus, the fiduciary has to account for the proceeds, whether he has limited or full letters, and whether the action was for wrongful death or personal injuries or both. In practice he usually combines everything in one petition: the compromise of the action, the accounting, an award

2. See discussion of McKinney's EPTL 5–4.4 and McKinney's SCPA 2204 in chapter on "Wrongful Death," infra at 554–55.

3. McKinney's EPTL 5–4.4.

4. See chapter on "Wrongful Death," infra at 527 et seq.

5. McKinney's SCPA 702.

6. If there are other assets in the estate and the fiduciary has the power to collect them, he may have to file a bond as to those assets.

of attorneys' fees and disbursements, apportionment of the proceeds between the wrongful death and personal injury elements of the action, apportionment of the proceeds among the beneficiaries entitled to share, and discharge of the fiduciary (and the defendants) from liability upon his complying with the court's decree for payment.

The fiduciary must cite all the necessary parties or can obtain waivers of process from those who are competent adults.[7] If a judgment directs payment of a lump sum to the estate and does not specify the division between the wrongful death and conscious pain and suffering causes of action, the court must decide that matter before settling the account, and the parties who could be adversely affected by that determination, including the State Tax Commission, are necessary parties.[8] The State Tax Commission is a necessary party because the wrongful death proceeds are not part of the taxable estate, while the conscious pain and suffering (or other survival causes of action) is included in the taxable estate.[9]

On the return date of process, the court can settle the account and direct payment of the recovery proceeds. After the fiduciary files receipts for payment from all the interested parties, the court can discharge the fiduciary and the defendants from all future liability.

The fiduciary receives full statutory commissions on the personal injury recovery but is limited to commissions on the net recovery (that is, the full amount recovered less disbursements, attorneys fees, and funeral and medical expenses) in wrongful death actions.[10]

SECTION F. ACCOUNTING BY FIDUCIARY OF DECEASED FIDUCIARY

If a person serving as fiduciary dies, three problems arise: first, someone must step in to preserve the property that was under his control. Second, there must be an accounting for the actions of the deceased fiduciary, and third, the court must decide whether it needs to appoint a successor fiduciary to serve or whether the fiduciary of the deceased fiduciary can wind up the estate. SCPA 2207 governs these issues.[1] The terminology in this chapter refers to the "estate" under the fiduciary's control, and it refers to all fiduciaries, including conservators and committees.[2]

It is the obligation of a fiduciary of a deceased fiduciary to preserve the assets that were under the control of the deceased fiduciary at death.[3] He does not, however, take on the duties of the deceased

7. McKinney's SCPA 2204. Necessary parties are listed in McKinney's SCPA 2210 and discussed supra at 189–92.

8. See Matter of Franco, 108 Misc.2d 1084, 439 N.Y.S.2d 278 (Bronx 1981).

9. Matter of Connecticut Bank and Trust Co., 465 F.2d 760 (2d Cir.1972).

10. McKinney's EPTL 5–4.4(b).

Sec. F

1. McKinney's SCPA 2207.

2. McKinney's SCPA 2207(8).

3. Matter of Hogeboom, 219 App.Div. 131, 219 N.Y.S. 436 (3d Dep't 1927).

fiduciary unless the court orders him to do so. In fact, the law severely restricts the powers of the deceased fiduciary's fiduciary, prohibiting him from commencing or maintaining actions relating to the estate and from taking charge or control of such actions.[4]

It is also the responsibility of the deceased fiduciary's fiduciary to account for the deceased fiduciary's actions. The ways of accounting for the deceased fiduciary's actions parallel those for a living fiduciary: the representative can voluntarily account for the deceased fiduciary's actions,[5] or an interested party can compel the representative to account for the deceased fiduciary.[6] If the fiduciary of a deceased fiduciary voluntarily petitions to account for the fiduciary, he must cite all the persons the deceased fiduciary would have had to cite, as well as the successor fiduciary, if one has been appointed.[7] A petition for a compulsory accounting can be brought by an interested party (that is, one entitled to process in a voluntary accounting proceeding)[8] to compel the fiduciary of a deceased fiduciary to account in the same manner that the fiduciary himself could have been compelled to account.[9]

In either a voluntary or compulsory accounting proceeding, the deceased fiduciary's fiduciary accounts for the assets the deceased fiduciary collected and also for those assets that have come into his possession as the result of his status as fiduciary of a deceased fiduciary. However, his accountability is limited to the extent that the assets of the deceased fiduciary have come into his possession.[10] If estate assets are in the hands of others it is up to the new fiduciary to collect them unless the court grants powers to the fiduciary of a deceased fiduciary to do so. The representative accounting for the deceased fiduciary should use the standard accounting forms.[11]

If the fiduciary died while a voluntary or compulsory accounting proceeding was pending, the court may continue the proceeding if the deceased fiduciary's fiduciary or a successor fiduciary appointed to complete the administration of the estate has voluntarily made himself a party or has been made a party by supplemental process. The court can proceed to determine all questions and grant all appropriate relief as though the fiduciary had not died.[12]

The court may allow reasonable compensation to the fiduciary of a deceased fiduciary, but that compensation, when added to any commissions retained by the deceased fiduciary or payable to his estate, may

4. McKinney's EPTL 13–3.4.

5. See McKinney's SCPA 2208 and discussion of voluntary accountings this chapter supra at 187–88.

6. See SCPA McKinney's 2205 and 2206 and discussion of compulsory accountings this chapter supra at 183–86.

7. McKinney's SCPA 2207(4).

8. McKinney's SCPA 2210.

9. McKinney's SCPA 2207(1).

10. McKinney's SCPA 2207(2).

11. See the discussion of the form of account and the sample schedules, supra at 194–208.

12. McKinney's SCPA 2207(3).

not exceed one full fiduciary's commission.[13] The court in the exercise of its discretion can award nominal (or no) commissions for dilatory or inadequate work.[14]

The court does not always appoint a successor fiduciary; if distribution can be made without much ado, the court may empower the fiduciary of a deceased fiduciary to do it, and decide what security, if any, is required.[15] It can grant to a fiduciary of a deceased fiduciary all the rights and powers of the deceased fiduciary and permit him to wind up the estate. If the testator named a successor in the will, and the court determines it is necessary to have a full fiduciary at the helm of the estate because the decedent desired it and the estate still needs additional administration, the court will name the successor.[16] Without a court order, the fiduciary of a deceased fiduciary does not have a right to assume the duties of the deceased fiduciary. The court typically deputizes the deceased fiduciary's fiduciary to act when there is very little left to do to complete the estate administration. If a substantial amount remains to be done, the court ordinarily requires the appointment of a successor fiduciary.[17] The matter is completely within the Surrogate's discretion.[18]

SECTION G. ACCOUNTING FOR PROFIT AND LOSS

A fiduciary may not profit from increases in the portfolio during his management of the estate, nor is he liable for any losses that result without his fault. He is charged with the increases and credited with the decreases on the settlement of his account.[1] The standard of care is the "Prudent Man Rule," which means that the fiduciary must have acted with such diligence and circumspection as prudent men of discretion and intelligence employ in their own affairs.[2] The rule has been

13. Commissions are allowable under SCPA 2307, 2308, and 2309 and are discussed in chapter on "Commissions," infra at 426–36. See Matter of Sawyer, 46 A.D.2d 48, 361 N.Y.S.2d 51 (3d Dep't 1974), where the court awarded the full commission to the successor executor because he did virtually all the work in marshaling, administering and distributing the estate. See also Matter of Jadwin, 58 Misc.2d 809, 296 N.Y.S.2d 901 (Suffolk 1969) (full commissions awarded to successor executor who took over immediately at primary executor's death despite the fact that he made distributions before letters were issued to him).

14. See Matter of Simpson, 61 Misc.2d 307, 305 N.Y.S.2d 339 (New York County 1969) (fiduciary appointed in 1957 did not file accounts until 1968 and 1969; court awarded no commissions).

15. McKinney's SCPA 2207(5).

16. See Matter of Zalaznick, 76 Misc.2d 43, 349 N.Y.S.2d 879 (Bronx 1973).

17. See, e.g., Matter of Mraz, 111 Misc. 2d 804, 445 N.Y.S.2d 405 (Nassau 1981).

18. Matter of Mann, 86 Misc.2d 1028, 382 N.Y.S.2d 906 (Westchester 1976).

Sec. G

1. See discussion of Schedules A–1 and B, and sample schedules this chapter supra at 197, 199–200.

2. Matter of Clark, 257 N.Y. 132, 177 N.E. 397 (1931); Matter of Delamater, 266 App.Div. 200, 41 N.Y.S.2d 715 (1st Dep't 1943), affirmed 292 N.Y. 518, 54 N.E.2d 205 (1944).

codified.[3] If a fiduciary deviated from this standard, he may be subject to loss of commissions, removal or a surcharge.[4]

Ordinarily a surcharge is imposed pro tanto and those who consent to an accounting, either by signing a waiver and consent or by failing to object or join in objections, will not share in the reduction of credits; that is, the amount of the surcharge is limited to the damages sustained by the objecting party or parties.[5] For example, if only three out of eight interested parties establish grounds for a $24,000 surcharge against the fiduciary, then the surcharge will be reduced to $9,000 and will benefit the three objectants equally.[6] However, this pro tanto rule will not be applied if it results in unjust enrichment of the fiduciary. For example, it does apply when the court disallows credits claimed by the fiduciary (such as excessive funeral expenses paid in good faith) but it does not if the fiduciary failed to charge himself with assets in the first instance (such as failure to account for an automobile or bank account). He must fully account to all interested parties for those assets, not just to those who objected.[7]

Analogously, a court may direct an attorney to refund the entire excess above a reasonable fee for the services rendered even if only some of the interested parties object.[8] This is not true, however, if the non-objecting parties have specifically consented to the fee.[9]

If the objectants are unsuccessful, occasionally a court has ordered them to pay the fiduciary's cost of defending himself against the objections, so that those costs will not be charged against the estate assets generally.[10] The theory is that those who have not interposed objections should not have to share in the costs of settling them.

3. McKinney's EPTL 11–2.2(a)(1) states: "A fiduciary holding funds for investment may invest the same in such securities as would be acquired by prudent men of discretion and intelligence in such matters who are seeking a reasonable income and preservation of their capital * * *"

4. Loss of commissions and surcharges are discussed in chapter on "Commissions," infra at 436–41. Removal is discussed in chapter on "Fiduciaries," infra at 393–400.

5. Matter of Fuller, 10 A.D.2d 938, 201 N.Y.S.2d 116 (1st Dep't 1960), affirmed without opinion 9 N.Y.2d 943, 217 N.Y.S.2d 101, 176 N.E.2d 107 (1961). The theory is that the non-objecting by-standers should not profit from the labors of the objectants. Matter of Rosenbaum, 76 N.Y.S.2d 715 (New York County 1947), modified 277 App.Div. 199, 97 N.Y.S.2d 871 (1st Dep't 1950), modified 303 N.Y. 715, 103 N.E.2d 338 (1951).

6. Matter of Zalaznick, 90 Misc.2d 113, 394 N.Y.S.2d 347 (Bronx 1977).

7. Matter of Goodliffe, 29 Misc.2d 1067, 195 N.Y.S.2d 461 (Westchester 1959).

8. Matter of Mette, 273 App.Div. 740, 80 N.Y.S.2d 221 (2d Dep't 1948), affirmed 298 N.Y. 789, 83 N.E.2d 475 (1948).

9. Matter of La Grove, 31 A.D.2d 928, 299 N.Y.S.2d 80 (2d Dep't 1969), affirmed 30 N.Y.2d 624, 331 N.Y.S.2d 439, 282 N.E.2d 329 (1972).

10. See Matter of Penney, 60 Misc.2d 334, 302 N.Y.S.2d 886 (Erie 1969) (because two of the three remaindermen of the trust consented to accounting, legal fees incurred in litigating unsuccessful objections were charged to the objectant). But see Matter of Povlsen, 62 Misc.2d 239, 308 N.Y.S.2d 168 (Kings 1970) (contra).

SECTION H. ACCOUNTING FOR FUNERAL EXPENSE CLAIM

Under the priority rules applicable to claims, a fiduciary must first pay administration expenses, and then funeral expenses if there are assets still available.[1] If he could have paid the funeral expenses but did not, the court cannot discharge him on the accounting.[2]

A funeral director may petition the court to require the fiduciary to pay reasonable funeral expenses if funds remain after payment of administration expenses,[3] and the court may fix the amount either in the special proceeding brought by the funeral director or in the accounting proceeding.[4] Except for administration expenses, no other debts or claims against the decedent may be credited to the fiduciary until the funeral bill has been paid.

SECTION I. DIRECTION TO TURN OVER ASSETS

The court can always compel a fiduciary or his successor or the fiduciary of a deceased fiduciary to turn over estate property in his possession or control.[1] In addition, if a fiduciary has died, absconded with estate property, or become incompetent, or if his letters have been revoked, the court can direct either the fiduciary or anyone else holding estate property to deliver it to the court or to a successor fiduciary appointed by the court. The court may direct the turn-over even if it has an accounting proceeding before it.[2] The statute merely confirms the Surrogate's jurisdiction over the fiduciary to monitor the possession and control of assets.

SECTION J. DECREE FOR PAYMENT AND DISTRIBUTION

Where an account is judicially settled under Article 22, the court issues a decree directing distribution of any remaining assets of the estate to those entitled to them (legatees, distributees, claimants, assignees).[1] It is the court's decree, and not the fiduciary's accounting, which authorizes the distribution.[2] The SCPA creates a time limita-

Sec. H

1. McKinney's SCPA 1811(1) states, "The reasonable funeral expenses of the decedent *subject to the payment of expenses of administration* shall be preferred to all debts and claims against his estate and shall be paid out of the first moneys received by his fiduciary" (emphasis added).

2. McKinney's SCPA 2213(1).

3. McKinney's SCPA 2102(3), discussed in chapter on "Miscellaneous Proceedings," infra at 331–32.

4. McKinney's SCPA 2213(2).

Sec. I

1. McKinney's SCPA 2214.

2. See McKinney's SCPA 2214, Prac. Comm. at 229 (1967).

Sec. J

1. McKinney's SCPA 2215(1).

2. Matter of Knapp, 141 Misc. 540, 253 N.Y.S. 409 (Wayne 1931).

tion, however, in cases where real property had to be sold under Article 19 (for payment of estate expenses or debts); in those cases if the accounting proceeding was commenced within six months of letters, the court cannot decree distribution until the time for presentation of claims by creditors has expired (seven months from letters, or the last day of publication for creditors).[3] If all creditors were served with process when the accounting petition was filed, the court may issue the decree and direct the distribution. If some creditors were not cited, the court will issue a supplemental citation and issue its decree subsequently.

The accounting proceeding is the appropriate vehicle for resolving many issues before the estate is finally settled, even those that could have been resolved earlier in another proceeding, such as construction of a will, propriety of attorneys' fees, allowance of fiduciary's commissions, status as a surviving spouse, status as distributee.[4] For example, SCPA 2215(2) specifically authorizes the court to award to a surviving spouse or child "set-off" or "exempt" property, though SCPA 2102 is another vehicle for that relief. When a person dies leaving a surviving spouse or minor children, the spouse or children are allowed to take certain items of property considered so personal or so vital for the period immediately following the decedent's death that the family should not be without them.[5] They are therefore "set off" for the family and exempt from claims.[6] They include up to $5,000 worth of housekeeping utensils, musical instruments, furniture and appliances, fuel, provisions and decedent's clothing, up to $150 worth of books and photographs, including the family bible, up to $10,000 worth of domestic animals, food for them, farm machinery and a tractor, and a car worth up to $10,000.[7] If the decedent did not own such items, no cash allowance or other property is substituted.[8] The spouse or minor children are also entitled to up to $1,000 in cash or other personal property (invadable by the fiduciary if the rest of the estate is insufficient to pay funeral expenses).[9] The accounting is an appropriate time to settle the issue of the survivors' entitlement to this property.

The court cannot order a distribution other than the one prescribed by a probated will or the laws of intestacy, despite an agreement among all interested parties to a different distribution.[10] If a deceased beneficiary is entitled to a share of the estate, that share must be paid to the

3. See discussion of the timing requirements for presenting claims to a fiduciary in chapter on "Claims," supra at 148–51.

4. See McKinney's SCPA 202 and chapter on "Jurisdiction," supra at 23–24.

5. McKinney's EPTL 5–3.1.

6. This is so even if the surviving spouse is incompetent. See Matter of Schoenfelder, 161 Misc. 654, 292 N.Y.S. 647 (Kings 1937).

7. McKinney's EPTL 5–3.1(b).

8. McKinney's EPTL 5–3.1(c).

9. McKinney's EPTL 5–3.1(a)(5).

10. See Matter of Monsen, 204 Misc. 245, 123 N.Y.S.2d 358 (New York County 1953); Matter of Horst, 148 Misc. 160, 266 N.Y.S. 507 (Queens 1933), affirmed 240 App.Div. 982, 268 N.Y.S. 865 (2d Dep't 1933), reversed on other grounds 264 N.Y. 236, 190 N.E. 475 (1934).

deceased beneficiary's fiduciary, and if none is serving, one will have to be appointed.[11]

If the accounting party has paid any creditor or other person interested in the estate an amount in excess of what is due, the accounting decree can direct repayment of the excess.[12] The accounting party need not start a separate proceeding but may join the overpaid party to the accounting proceeding. If an overpayment was made to a creditor, the other creditors should be cited in the proceeding so that the statutory preferences are preserved.[13] For example, in one case the fiduciary paid taxes to the state and the federal government attempted to recover from the state in the accounting proceeding. The court denied the relief unless all general creditors were joined.[14] The government can make its demand for a refund from other creditors for satisfaction of taxes after the audit and issuance of the final tax assessment. Even though much time has passed since the decedent's death, the government will not be barred by laches if it acts reasonably soon after the final assessment.[15]

If the fiduciary made an overpayment of property and that property earned any interest or dividends after it was paid, it is within the Surrogate's discretion to order repayment of the interest or dividend as well as the property itself.[16]

An overpaid beneficiary must reimburse the estate,[17] or the fiduciary can be held personally responsible for the overpayment and be surcharged.[18]

Even if the fiduciary is aware at the time of the final accounting that a judgment is outstanding against a distributee, he has no responsibility to provide for direct payment to the judgment creditor. He can, and usually does, pay the estate property directly to the distributee.[19]

SECTION K. DISTRIBUTION IN KIND

Except for specific legacies, fiduciaries frequently pay dispositions in cash, but they can make distributions in kind (that is, in property),[1]

11. See Matter of Merrill, 188 Misc. 441, 64 N.Y.S.2d 241 (Westchester 1946); Matter of Lane, 20 N.Y.S. 78 (1892).

12. McKinney's SCPA 2215(3).

13. See discussion of order of priority among claims in chapter on "Claims," supra at 164–72.

14. Matter of Schmuckler, 58 Misc.2d 418, 296 N.Y.S.2d 202 (1968).

15. Matter of Fisch, 58 Misc.2d 193, 294 N.Y.S.2d 397 (1968).

16. Matter of Dewar, 62 A.D.2d 352, 404 N.Y.S.2d 750 (3d Dep't 1978). But see Matter of Fisch, 58 Misc.2d 193, 294 N.Y.S.2d 397 (New York County 1968) (creditors refunding payments to satisfy United States' claim for taxes did not have to pay interest).

17. Matter of Peters, 189 Misc. 222, 72 N.Y.S.2d 583 (New York County 1947).

18. Matter of Berg, 91 Misc.2d 939, 398 N.Y.S.2d 948 (New York County 1977).

19. Matter of McClure, N.Y.L.J. April 1, 1969, at 20, col. 5 (Nassau). The judgment creditor can, however, obtain a garnishee order to secure payment.

Sec. K

1. McKinney's EPTL 11–1.1(b)(20) states that a fiduciary may "distribute in kind any property at its fair market value at the date of distribution."

and they often do so when they do not need to reduce all assets to cash to pay debts and expenses or to provide for distribution. They do not have to get court permission to distribute in kind. SCPA 2216 governs the procedural aspects of such distributions. Its function is to allow the court to direct the distribution in kind despite a beneficiary's objections. For example, a surviving spouse exercising a right of election may object to receiving stock in a close corporation in satisfaction of the elective share because it will result in a minority (and therefore subordinate) position to that of the other shareholders, but the court has discretion to order such distribution anyway.[2]

The statute permits the court during any phase of estate administration to direct payment of estate property in kind, including unsold realty or chattels, uncollected demands or other personal property to persons entitled to payment or distribution, in place of the money value of the property at the date of distribution. The court will order such distribution when a sale of the property is impracticable or unprofitable. If the property is securities, the same valuation method (opening price, closing price, mean price for the day) should be used for all the stock distributed.[3]

When a decedent died survived by a surviving spouse and gave money to his spouse in the will, either in a dollar amount or in an amount determined by a formula, the fiduciary may distribute property in kind to satisfy the pecuniary dispositions. However, if the bequests to the spouse are eligible for the marital deduction,[4] the fiduciary must give the spouse property valued at the date of distribution or, if the will directs valuation at a different date, the fiduciary must choose for distribution to the spouse assets which are at least the amount stated in the will and to the extent possible, no more than that.[5] To illustrate, if the decedent left $500,000 to his spouse, and some stock valued at $500,000 at decedent's death had diminished in value to $400,000 by the time the fiduciary was ready to distribute it, it would satisfy only $400,000 of the bequest. Even if the decedent directed valuation of property at the date of death, the fiduciary would have to give the spouse cash or other property to boost the spouse's legacy to at least (and if possible, not more than) $500,000. The reason for this rule is to preserve the marital deduction;[6] if the executor had discretion to distribute assets that had depreciated since the date of death to a surviving spouse, it would make that bequest to the surviving spouse a terminable interest ineligible for the marital deduction.

2. Matter of Hoffman, 98 Misc.2d 732, 414 N.Y.S.2d 863 (Albany 1979).

3. See Matter of Baker, 92 Misc.2d 934, 399 N.Y.S.2d 871 (Nassau 1977).

4. See discussion of marital deduction in chapter on "Estate Taxes," infra at 592–96.

5. McKinney's EPTL 2–1.9.

6. McKinney's EPTL 2–1.9 was enacted to meet the requirements of Rev.Rul. 64–19, which describes the powers of a fiduciary that can make property passing to a surviving spouse a non-deductible terminable interest and gives alternatives restricting the fiduciary's powers, one of which was incorporated into McKinney's EPTL 2–1.9, which preserves the marital deduction.

SECTION L. DEPOSIT IN COURT FOR THE BENEFIT OF A LEGATEE, DISTRIBUTEE OR BENEFICIARY

Occasionally a New York decedent leaves money to a person living in a country hostile to the United States. If the United States has issued an executive order or regulation saying that no money can be sent to that country,[1] the Surrogate can direct payment of the property into court for the benefit of the alien beneficiary or his successors in interest.[2] Once the funds are paid into court, they can be paid out only on a court order. If the alien attempts to assign his interest to another, the assignee has no greater right than the alien had.

In SCPA 2218's second paragraph, the court also has discretion to withhold money from a beneficiary if it appears that he will not benefit from the use of it.[3] The beneficiary has the burden of proving that he will get the use of the money or property.[4]

The purpose of this provision is to prevent the transmittal of funds to a beneficiary in a country where they are likely to be confiscated.[5] This provision got a fair amount of use during the "cold war" to avoid delivering assets to a resident of an Iron Curtain country. Because of treaties and policy decisions by the Department of State, fiduciaries now use this provision less frequently. The United States has closer relations now with Iron Curtain countries; a general policy of free trade prevails, and in some instances treaties direct the distribution of estate assets to nationals residing in these countries.

In some cases, the will gives directions on what standard the fiduciary should use in determining whether the legatee will have the use of property, and courts tend to honor these directives, though they still try to determine whether the beneficiary will actually have the use of the property.[6] The courts may accept such evidence as memoranda

Sec. L

1. The government issues such regulations or orders when the United States is at war with another country.

2. McKinney's SCPA 2218(1).

3. McKinney's SCPA 2218(2). Compare, e.g., Matter of Padwordski, 53 Misc. 2d 1043, 281 N.Y.S.2d 276 (Dutchess 1967) (money distributed to decedent's widow and children in Russia), and Matter of Henseling, 70 Misc.2d 610, 334 N.Y.S.2d 553 (Erie 1972) (money distributed to beneficiaries in East Germany), with Matter of Harmoza, 57 Misc.2d 40, 292 N.Y.S.2d 488 (Nassau 1968) (uncertainty in issue of beneficiary's ability to use the property resolved in favor of withholding the funds).

4. McKinney's SCPA 2218, Prac.Comm. at 254 (1967). See Matter of Kolodij, 85 Misc.2d 946, 380 N.Y.S.2d 610 (Monroe 1976); Matter of Krasowski, 28 A.D.2d 180, 283 N.Y.S.2d 960 (3d Dep't 1967), appeal denied 22 N.Y.2d 827, 292 N.Y.S.2d 919, 239 N.E.2d 658 (1968).

5. Matter of Leikind, 22 N.Y.2d 346, 292 N.Y.S.2d 681, 239 N.E.2d 550 (1968), appeal dismissed 397 U.S. 148, 90 S.Ct. 990, 25 L.Ed.2d 182 (1970) (will provided that executor's good faith determination that beneficiary would not have control of assets would be binding. Surrogate found that the executor's determination was in good faith, and the Court of Appeals affirmed).

6. See Matter of Danilchencko, 37 A.D.2d 587, 323 N.Y.S.2d 150 (2d Dep't 1971), affirmed 30 N.Y.2d 504, 329 N.Y.S.2d 820, 280 N.E.2d 650 (1972).

of law from attorneys specializing in the interest of heirs from the country in question, letters from the state department and regulations of that country's trade organizations.[7] It is ultimately a question of fact, however, and the court has discretion to order payment to the county comptroller or fiscal officer pending resolution of that factual issue.[8]

Doubts about the constitutionality of this provision have been laid to rest by case law. The United States Supreme Court, in Zschernig v. Miller,[9] invalidated a similar statute in Oregon because the state was attempting to legislate in an area in the exclusive domain of Congress and the President. In a companion case it withheld its decision on the constitutionality of the New York statute [10] remanding the case for further consideration.[11] Subsequently, a federal district court ruled that the withholding of funds from an alien without a hearing violated the alien's procedural due process rights [12] and ordered a three-judge court convened to decide the statute's constitutionality. Before that court had convened, the New York County Surrogate ruled that the alien had the burden of proof, and hence the right to a hearing, in all cases where his property might be paid into court rather than sent to him in his country, even under the statute's discretionary second paragraph.[13] The three-judge federal court [14] ruled that the statute could be construed to require a hearing if the beneficiary applied for withdrawal of the funds, and hence the beneficiary's due process rights were protected.

In addition, the New York Court of Appeals reviewed the statute in light of Zschernig v. Miller, and upheld the constitutionality of the statute,[15] finding that the Supreme Court had not invalidated the Oregon statute on its face, but had found that, as the Oregon courts applied it, the statute unduly interfered with foreign affairs, a peculiarly federal domain. Needless to say the Surrogates may not interfere with foreign policy or the relationship between the United States and another country, which are solely within the federal government's domain.

It is conceivable that, under the discretionary second paragraph, the court could withhold funds even from one other than an alien of a

7. See Matter of Ficek, N.Y.L.J. Mar. 1, 1985, at 15, col. 4 (Queens).

8. See Matter of Ficek, N.Y.L.J. Mar. 1, 1985, at 15, col. 2 (Queens).

9. 389 U.S. 429, 88 S.Ct. 664, 19 L.Ed.2d 683 (1968), rehearing denied 390 U.S. 974, 88 S.Ct. 1018, 19 L.Ed.2d 1196 (1968).

10. That is, McKinney's SCPA 2218's predecessor, S.C.A. 269–a.

11. Goldstein v. Cox, 389 U.S. 581, 88 S.Ct. 694, 19 L.Ed.2d 781 (1968), on remand 299 F.Supp. 1389 (D.N.Y.1968).

12. Bjarsch v. DiFalco, 300 F.Supp. 960 (E.D.N.Y.1969).

13. That is, in cases under paragraph (1) where it is apparently mandatory that the court must withhold assets because of an executive order or regulation by the United States, and in cases under paragraph (2) where such withholding is discretionary.

14. Bjarsch v. DiFalco, 314 F.Supp. 127 (S.D.N.Y.1970).

15. Matter of Leikind, 22 N.Y.2d 346, 292 N.Y.S.2d 681, 239 N.E.2d 550 (1968), appeal dismissed 397 U.S. 148, 90 S.Ct. 990, 25 L.Ed.2d 182 (1970).

country with which the United States does not have a favorable relationship (such as a person detained in a friendly country), but in fact it is very rarely used that way.

Even if the inheritance laws of the other jurisdiction make the government a substitute heir for the beneficiary, that government may not claim the property for itself under any theory.[16] The net effect of this 1977 amendment [17] is that if an escheat eventually occurs, New York, and not the foreign jurisdiction, benefits.[18]

SECTION M. COURT ORDER TO RETAIN PROPERTY

Sometimes a fiduciary is ready to account but there is an outstanding debt he cannot pay before the accounting. It may be, for example, that he disputes the legitimacy of a claim not yet due but ascertainable in amount, or that a debt admittedly owed by the estate and ascertainable in amount is not yet due. In those cases, a fiduciary can account and the court has discretion to order the fiduciary to retain a sum sufficient to satisfy the claim, the probable interest and any probable costs, for example, the cost of resolving the disputed claim.[1]

This section of Article 22 does not cover claims for unascertainable amounts. Under a different (but similar) section in SCPA Article 18,[2] the court can order the retention of assets for the payment of contingent and unliquidated claims (including estate taxes).

Specifically, Article 22 allows the court to order the retention of money in the following circumstances:

(i) when a fiduciary admits owing a debt that is not yet due and the creditor refuses (usually for income tax purposes) to accept payment early with an appropriate rebate of interest. For example, a decedent may have made a purchase on the installment basis and the creditors do not want to accelerate capital gains taxes by accepting early payment.[3]

(ii) when a fiduciary disputes or rejects the validity of a debt not yet due whose amount is ascertainable.

(iii) when an action is pending between a person claiming to be a creditor and the estate.[4]

(iv) in a trustee's accounting, when a controversy exists on a party's right to share in the property.[5]

16. McKinney's SCPA 2218(4).

17. L.1977 c. 496.

18. See discussion of when property escheats, this chapter infra at 224 et seq.

Sec. M

1. McKinney's SCPA 2217.

2. McKinney's SCPA 1804, discussed in chapter on "Claims," supra at 153–56.

3. See McKinney's SCPA 2217, Prac. Comm. at 250 (McKinney 1967).

4. Matter of Biel, 103 A.D.2d 287, 479 N.Y.S.2d 740 (2d Dep't 1984).

5. McKinney's SCPA 2217(1)(a), (b), (c), (d).

The court chooses an appropriate arrangement for safekeeping the property. It can direct the fiduciary to hold on to the assets, or deposit them in a bank, or pay them into the court. When the unresolved matter has been resolved, the fiduciary can, with another court order, use the funds to pay the debt or claim or to satisfy any judgment recovered, and distribute the balance to those entitled to share in the estate.[6]

Any party may petition for distribution of the retained assets to those entitled to them.[7]

SECTION N. ADJUSTMENT OF ADVANCEMENTS

Sometimes a testator advances funds to a beneficiary or donee in partial payment of what the beneficiary would otherwise have received under the will or the laws of intestacy. The substantive law of advancements is governed by the EPTL, which defines an advancement as an irrevocable gift which the donor intends as an anticipatory distribution in complete or partial satisfaction of the donee's interest in the donor's estate, either as a distributee in intestacy or as a beneficiary under the donor's will.[1] When the testator makes the gift, if either he or the donee signs a writing that acknowledges the gift as an advancement, that amount will be subtracted from the donee's share of the estate. If neither the testator nor the donee signs a writing at the time of the gift, it is not an advancement but simply an additional gift, and the donee will also take the full amount given under the will, or his full intestate share. If the gift was an advancement (that is, there is a contemporaneous signed writing) and it exceeds what the donee was supposed to get under the will, he can keep the advancement and does not have to repay the excess. In that case the other beneficiaries' interests in the estate abate pro rata. For example, if a person with five children for reasons of his own gives child A $200,000 during his lifetime, without a contemporaneous writing, and later dies without a will and with an estate of $300,000, child A, like each of the other four, is entitled to $60,000 of the estate. If the decedent or child A had acknowledged the gift in writing, child A keeps the $200,000 and gets nothing more in intestacy, and the other four take $75,000 each (that is, their shares of $100,000, or one-fifth of the total pre-advancement wealth of $500,000, reduced ratably to $75,000 each). If the advancement to child A had been $499,990, the other four would get $2.50 each. If the property left after the $200,000 advancement was $1,200,000, child A would keep the $200,000 advancement and take an additional $80,000, and the other four would take $280,000 each (that is, one-fifth of the pre-advancement estate of $1,400,000).

6. McKinney's SCPA 2217(1).

7. McKinney's SCPA 2217(1).

Sec. N

1. McKinney's EPTL 2–1.5.

The procedural law on advancements is covered by the SCPA,[2] which provides that if the decedent made an advancement in the form of personal property and the estate contains personal property waiting to be distributed, the court must in its decree make appropriate adjustments for the advancement. Similarly, if the decedent gave to a beneficiary an advancement of real property that exceeds his benefits under the will, and as a result legacies of personal property have to be reduced pro rata, the court must make that adjustment. If another court (for example, the Supreme Court in case of an inter vivos trust) has already adjusted the advancements, the Surrogate will not do so.

If a person affected by this decree was not made a party to the proceeding, the court must order supplemental process to be served on him.

SECTION O. PAYMENT OF SHARE OF PERSON UNDER LEGAL DISABILITY

When an infant, incompetent or other person under disability has a financial interest in an estate, wrongful death or personal injuries recovery, or settlement of any cause of action, the court must, with the exceptions discussed presently, direct the fiduciary to pay the money to the disabled person's guardian, committee, or conservator, who either has to post a bond sufficient to cover the assets or has to hold and administer the property jointly with the court or a bank appointed by the court.[1]

The statute makes an exception for small amounts. The court can order amounts of $5,000 or under to be paid to the disabled person's father or mother, or to a competent adult person living with the disabled person who has some interest in his welfare. The recipient does not have to file a bond. In either case the court orders the person receiving the funds to hold them for the disabled person's use and benefit.

This section states the court's power to order such payment of $5,000 or less, but does not imply that such an order is necessary. In fact a fiduciary is allowed to pay amounts under $5,000 on behalf of the disabled person under the EPTL without a court order.[2] If the fiduciary decides to get a court order, this section is the way to proceed.

If the person under disability has no guardian, committee or conservator, the court will direct that the fiduciary pay the money into court, deposit it in specified banks, or invest it in certificate accounts in insured savings and loan associations subject to the court's further order. Neither the interest nor the principal can be withdrawn without a court order.[3]

2. McKinney's SCPA 2219.

Sec. O

1. See chapter on "Guardianships," infra at 257 et seq.

2. McKinney's EPTL 11–1.1(b)(19).

3. Levin v. United Air Lines, Inc., 279 F.Supp. 860 (S.D.N.Y.1967).

When an infant reaches eighteen years, the fiduciary can turn over assets to him without a court order, unless the court's initial order directing the deposit provides otherwise. In Surrogate's practice, it usually does, so the bank cannot pay the eighteen-year old until it receives a further court order. Under most other civil practice, this further court order is unnecessary. The Surrogates limit the banks this way to assure that an accounting will take place and to preserve the rights of the fiduciary to commissions on the minor's property.

Rather than ordering the money paid into court, under certain circumstances the court may instead appoint a conservator to receive the money. Three criteria must be met:

(i) the disabled person must live in the county where the accounting proceeding is pending;

(ii) the disabled person must be a person for whom a conservator would be appropriate, and

(iii) the disabled person must not already have a conservator, committee or guardian. The fiduciary does not have to start a proceeding in the Supreme Court for appointment of a conservator. The Surrogate can appoint a conservator [4] who can then receive payment of assets for a person under disability, exercise the right of election for him if authorized by the appointing court, and disclaim property for tax purposes. The procedure is also useful when a mentally retarded minor reaches majority and the guardianship ends. If for some reason the court does not appoint a guardian for a mentally retarded person,[5] it can appoint a conservator to continue to represent the incompetent major.

If the sum exceeds $5,000, the court either has to appoint a fiduciary or order the money deposited into court. Ordering the money to be paid into court is very rare; the court may do so if an infant is just a few weeks away from majority, but ordinarily it requires appointment of a fiduciary.

The Mental Hygiene Law [6] authorizes the director of an institution in the State Department of Mental Hygiene to receive funds (currently $5,000) on behalf of a patient. The Surrogate's order or decree may authorize the director to receive a sum of money on behalf of the ward up to the amount authorized by the statute.

If the infant or person under disability lives in another jurisdiction and the court has reason to question whether the funds, if transmitted, would actually be used for the child's benefit, it can hold a hearing to consider such matters as whether the child has a fiduciary, and if so,

4. McKinney's SCPA 2220(4); McKinney's Mental Hygiene L. 77.01 (Supp.1984–85).

5. See chapter on "Guardianships," infra at 285–88.

6. McKinney's Mental Hygiene L. 29.23.

what the fiduciary's powers are, what the investment plan is, and whether the payment is proper.[7]

SECTION P. PAYMENT TO FOREIGN FIDUCIARIES

When a beneficiary of an estate is a nondomiciliary infant, incompetent, conservatee or decedent, the court may order payment to the fiduciary, committee, conservator or person with a comparable title and comparable duties in the beneficiary's domicile. The court must satisfy itself that the foreign fiduciary is entitled to receive the assets under the EPTL,[1] which prohibits the New York fiduciary from paying money to a foreign fiduciary if the beneficiary will not get the benefit of those assets, or if the beneficiary has a fiduciary (principal or ancillary) here, or if the beneficiary has creditors in this state. The foreign fiduciary must also have filed security in his domicile sufficient to cover the amount to be received if the domicile requires such security.[2]

The EPTL allows the fiduciary to make this payment without a court order,[3] but if the fiduciary does seek a court order to relieve himself of liability, then SCPA 2221 is the procedure to use.

The directive to pay the funds to the foreign fiduciary may come in one of two forms: by a decree in a judicial settlement of the fiduciary's account, or by an order when the fiduciary applies to the court for permission to deliver assets to a foreign fiduciary.

SECTION Q. ESCHEAT

If no one is in existence entitled to succeed to a decedent's property, that property will escheat to the state.[1] If property from an estate is payable to persons whose existence or whereabouts are unknown, SCPA 2222, 2223, 2224 and 2225 create various safeguards to protect those unknowns, to avoid escheat and to give some finality to estate proceedings that might otherwise go on indefinitely.

SCPA 2222 covers unknown beneficiaries; SCPA 2223 covers beneficiaries whose whereabouts are unknown; SCPA 2224 permits an expedited procedure in cases where the beneficiary's whereabouts are unknown; and SCPA 2225 permits a judicial declaration of the death of

7. See McKinney's SCPA 2221; Matter of Faki, 73 A.D.2d 689, 423 N.Y.S.2d 235 (2d Dept. 1979).

Sec. P

1. McKinney's EPTL 13–3.4.

2. McKinney's EPTL 13–3.4 disallows transfer of assets to any person under disability when there are known creditors in New York, and SCPA 2221 reiterates the rule for cases where the beneficiary is deceased.

3. McKinney's EPTL 13–3.4.

Sec. Q

1. McKinney's Const. Art. 1, section 10; McKinney's Abandoned Property Law 200 (1944); Johnston v. Spicer, 107 N.Y. 185, 13 N.E. 753 (1887); Matter of Hammond, 2 A.D.2d 160, 154 N.Y.S.2d 820 (2d Dep't 1956), affirmed 3 N.Y.2d 567, 170 N.Y.S.2d 505, 147 N.E.2d 777 (1958) (veteran's funds paid to state should be turned over to federal government).

a long-missing beneficiary. These statutes are the subject of our next few sections.

1. UNKNOWN PERSONS

If a beneficiary of an estate is unknown, under SCPA 2222 the accounting decree must direct the fiduciary to pay that unknown beneficiary's share to the comptroller of the State of New York as custodian for the beneficiary should he later appear. This covers cases where the fiduciary does not know whether the beneficiary is alive or dead and cases where the beneficiary is dead but the fiduciary does not know whether he left issue entitled to his share.[2] It also applies when a person claiming to be a distributee has come forth but has not proven his relationship to the decedent.[3] If a person comes forward and proves that he is a distributee, but cannot prove that all other distributees with the same relationship with the decedent predeceased, the court will require a hearing on that issue and will not make distribution of the entire estate to the distributee who appears until it determines who the other distributees are.[4] If the others do not show up for three years and cannot be found after a diligent search, the court can declare them dead under SCPA 2225, discussed presently. If the fiduciary believes that the beneficiary is alive, he will look to SCPA 2223 and 2224, also discussed presently, rather than this section.

When he makes the payment to the comptroller, the fiduciary must file a certified copy of the decree, deducting the fee for that certified copy from the beneficiary's share before payment to the comptroller. The comptroller deposits the property in the state's abandoned property fund. This is not escheat, but merely a custodial arrangement.[5]

If the beneficiary returns, or if someone learning of the deposit claims to have an interest in it (such as issue of a predeceased beneficiary), that person may petition the Surrogate's Court or the Supreme Court for the withdrawal of the funds.[6] There is no statutory time limit to commence such a withdrawal. The petitioner must give fourteen days' notice and serve a copy of the petition on the attorney general (as counsel for the state comptroller),[7] the state comptroller, and the public administrator.[8] The court will either direct a referee's hearing [9] or a trial to ascertain the rights of the beneficiary or other

2. See McKinney's SCPA 2222, Prac. Comm. at 39 (Supp.1986).

3. See McKinney's SCPA 2222, Prac. Comm. at 282 (1967); Matter of Sloat, 141 Misc. 710, 253 N.Y.S. 215 (Kings 1931).

4. See Matter of Rollock, N.Y.L.J. Feb. 2, 1985, at 12, col. 6 (Kings), where the court appointed the one distributee, a cousin of decedent's, administrator and ordered her to obtain proof of death of all other maternal and paternal aunts, uncles and cousins before it would distribute the estate to her.

5. Matter of Braslowsky, N.Y.L.J. Oct. 29, 1976, at 13, col. 3 (Kings).

6. McKinney's SCPA 2222(2).

7. McKinney's SCPA 2222(2).

8. In counties with no public administrator, the fiduciary must give notice to the county treasurer.

9. The referee's hearing is discussed in chapter on "Trials," infra at 504–06.

claimant. The court in its discretion can direct a trial by jury but usually does not. If the result of the hearing or trial is that the beneficiary is entitled to the funds, the court orders the comptroller to release the funds, without interest, to the beneficiary after deducting all expenses incurred by the state.

When the comptroller receives a certified copy of the order, he draws a warrant from the abandoned property fund payable to the person entitled to the funds.

The court may direct that notice of the claim and a copy of the petition be given to any persons it believes should be made aware of the claim. While SCPA 2222 funds are treated as abandoned property [10] and may become part of the general treasury of the state, they are still subject to the rights of those who later appear and are entitled to them. Passage of time with no claims presented for their recovery makes such a temporary custodial arrangement permanent which, for practical purposes, amounts to an escheat.[11]

Unpaid creditors may petition for the funds held by the comptroller, and their claims, if proved, will be paid after deduction of any costs incurred by the state.[12]

If a distributee eventually turns up, but dies before the state comptroller has paid the funds, his administrator or executor is entitled to the funds after deduction of all costs incurred by the state.[13]

When a decedent dies in a Veterans' Administration Hospital and is not survived by intestate distributees, under federal law [14] his personal property escheats to the federal government, not to the State of New York. Similarly, if the fiduciary has funds of the decedent which he received through Veterans' Administration benefits, they also escheat to the federal government if he dies without heirs (regardless of where he dies),[15] but the state estate taxes are deducted first, since the federal statute provides that the federal government gets whatever would otherwise have escheated to the state.[16] Property passing to a designated beneficiary under a Veterans' Administration insurance policy does not escheat, but goes to the named beneficiary.[17] Federal law does not cover real property in New York, which would escheat to the state, not to the federal government.

10. McKinney's Abandoned Prop.L. 600(1)(b) (Supp.1984–85).

11. Matter of Menschefrend, 283 App. Div. 463, 128 N.Y.S.2d 738 (1st Dep't 1954), affirmed 8 N.Y.2d 1093, 208 N.Y.S.2d 453, 170 N.E.2d 902 (1960).

12. See Matter of Fredericks, 17 Misc. 2d 145, 169 N.Y.S.2d 853 (Westchester 1957).

13. Matter of Elliott, 51 Misc.2d 1056, 1057, 275 N.Y.S.2d 40 (Nassau 1966).

14. 38 U.S.C.A. 5220(a).

15. Matter of O'Brine, 37 N.Y.2d 81, 371 N.Y.S.2d 453, 332 N.E.2d 326 (1975); Matter of Hammond, 2 A.D.2d 160, 154 N.Y.S.2d 820 (2d Dep't 1956), affirmed 3 N.Y.2d 567, 170 N.Y.S.2d 505, 147 N.E.2d 777 (1958).

16. 38 U.S.C.A. § 5220(a) ("personal property").

17. Matter of Strahler, 79 Misc.2d 134, 359 N.Y.S.2d 481, affirmed 51 A.D.2d 746, 379 N.Y.S.2d 475 (1976).

If the decedent is a domiciliary of another jurisdiction and dies without known heirs, leaving New York property, the property will be paid to the state comptroller unless the law of the decedent's domicile also claims it by escheat, in which case the decedent's domicile should prevail over New York.[18]

There are persons whose occupation is to search for heirs; they try to locate beneficiaries with an interest in property that will escheat unless heirs appear and petition for withdrawal. When an heir-searcher petitions the court for payment of his fee out of the estate, he must prove that he had a private contract with a beneficiary to obtain a recovery. An heir-hunter who proves that there are no known distributees thereby justifying the escheat of the assets to the State, is not entitled to compensation from the estate for his services without a contract.[19] In short, whether or not the heir-searcher finds an heir, he will not be paid unless he had a contract.

A person claiming to be an heir must prove it, and if he relies on records or documents from other jurisdictions, they must be properly attested and certified,[20] and if he relies on a kinship hearing, the transcript or report of that hearing must be offered as proof.[21]

2. KNOWN PERSONS WHOSE WHEREABOUTS ARE UNKNOWN

Unlike the case of unknown beneficiaries whose funds are paid to the state comptroller,[22] if the fiduciary informs the court at or before the accounting that a beneficiary (or creditor or deceased beneficiary's successor in interest) is known but his whereabouts are not, under SCPA 2223(1) the decree must direct that the fiduciary pay the assets into court if he does not locate the beneficiary and pay him within a certain time (maximum six months).

It is always advisable for the fiduciary to ascertain early whether any beneficiaries are unavailable, so he can proceed under 2223(1), which provides the quickest relief and allows the earliest release from

18. See Matter of Utassi, 15 N.Y.2d 436, 261 N.Y.S.2d 4, 209 N.E.2d 65 (1965) (Swiss domiciliary, who was legatee of New York resident, died in Switzerland leaving no heirs, and Swiss law directed payment of securities located in New York to the city in which decedent died. New York court held that Swiss law should prevail and ordered securities delivered to the Swiss city). But see Matter of Menschefrend, 283 App.Div. 463, 128 N.Y.S.2d 738 (1st Dep't 1954), affirmed 8 N.Y.2d 1093, 208 N.Y.S.2d 453, 170 N.E.2d 902 (1960), remittitur amended 8 N.Y.2d 1156, 209 N.Y.S.2d 836, 171 N.E.2d 909 (1960), certiorari denied 365 U.S. 842, 81 S.Ct. 801, 5 L.Ed.2d 808 (1961) where the decedent was a California domiciliary with no distributees, and the Appellate Division ruled that the decedent's New York assets should escheat to New York, not to California, after determining that the New York assets were not needed to pay the California administration and funeral expenses.

19. See Matter of Maxson, 66 A.D.2d 635, 413 N.Y.S.2d 676 (1st Dep't 1979), affirmed 52 N.Y.2d 725, 436 N.Y.S.2d 274, 417 N.E.2d 568 (1980).

20. McKinney's CPLR 4542; see Matter of Lorre, 39 A.D.2d 731, 332 N.Y.S.2d 115 (2d Dep't 1972).

21. Matter of Lorre, 39 A.D.2d 731, 332 N.Y.S.2d 115 (2d Dep't 1972).

22. See discussion of McKinney's SCPA 2222 in preceding section.

liability for the fiduciary. If the fiduciary has not told the court about the unlocated beneficiary, then he must, under SCPA 2223(2), wait six months after the court issues the accounting decree and advise the court that he cannot make the payments to the beneficiary, either because he cannot locate the beneficiary or for another reason.[23] The court then orders the fiduciary to pay the funds into court.[24] If the fiduciary does not, the state comptroller may petition the Surrogate to compel the fiduciary to deposit the money into court.[25]

Once paid into court, the funds cannot be paid out without a further order of the court or another court of competent jurisdiction,[26] except that in counties outside of New York City, if the payment does not exceed $50, the county treasurer may pay it without a court order to a person entitled to it.[27]

When the fiduciary pays the money into court, the court delivers it to the county treasurer and ultimately, (usually after six months or, if the court directs, a shorter period),[28] if no one entitled to it appears, the treasurer pays it over to the comptroller of the State of New York subject to a claim by those interested.[29]

When the fiduciary pays more than $250 into court, and the money eventually goes to the state comptroller as abandoned property,[30] the court can subsequently order the payment of such funds out of the abandoned property fund only upon notice to the state comptroller and all other persons claiming an interest in the funds.[31]

3. OTHER GROUNDS FOR PAYMENT INTO COURT

If the fiduciary did not advise the court before the accounting decree as permitted by subparagraph (1) that he could not locate the beneficiary, but the amount in question is small and he prefers not to wait the six months required by subparagraph (2), because the wait will pile up expenses such as a bond and legal fees, he has the alternative of commencing a proceeding under SCPA 2224.

Under Section 2224, when the name or the whereabouts of a person interested in the estate as a beneficiary or an assignee [32] are unknown, despite the fiduciary's diligent search, and that person's interest does

23. See, e.g., Matter of Ridings, 91 Misc. 2d 946, 398 N.Y.S.2d 973 (Schenectady 1977), where the beneficiary refused to accept the payment.

24. McKinney's SCPA 2223(2).

25. McKinney's SCPA 2223(5).

26. McKinney's SCPA 2223(3).

27. McKinney's SCPA 2223(4).

28. McKinney's SCPA 2223(5).

29. See discussion of McKinney's SCPA 2222 supra at 224 et seq.

30. McKinney's Abandoned Property Law 600(1)(a) (Supp.1986). When assets are paid into court, they are deposited with the county treasurer or the commissioner of finance of the City of New York, and if the assets and their increments remain unclaimed for five years, they are considered abandoned.

31. McKinney's SCPA 2223(6).

32. Although McKinney's SCPA 2224 refers to "beneficiary or assignee," and 2223 refers to "legatee, distributees, creditors or other persons," no substantive difference was intended.

not exceed $1,000, the court on its own or on the fiduciary's petition may order the fiduciary to pay the funds into court and then discharge him from all further liability. The court has discretion whether to order notice of the application to interested persons or to dispense with it.[33]

Once paid into court, the funds cannot be paid out without a further order of the court or another court of competent jurisdiction,[34] except that in counties outside of New York City, if the payment does not exceed $50, the county treasurer may pay it without a court order to a person entitled to it.[35]

SECTION R. DETERMINATION OF DISTRIBUTEES AND DISTRIBUTIVE SHARES

When a decedent dies intestate, his property passes to his intestate distributees.[1] If any issue arises as to the identity of the distributees, the Surrogate naturally has jurisdiction to determine that issue. It may arise in the administration proceeding, or in a probate proceeding (because distributees are entitled to process) or in an accounting proceeding.

A serious problem could arise if one of the decedent's distributees has not been seen or heard from for a long time. Conceivably an estate could be held up indefinitely because of questions as to whether or not the decedent was survived by distributees. The property would go to the county treasurer or the state comptroller and those with a beneficial interest could not receive their distributions because of a cloud caused by unknown or unlocatable distributees. SCPA 2225 offers a solution to this problem: it permits distribution of the estate after three years both when there are distributees whose whereabouts are unknown (paragraph a) and when there is a question about the existence of any other distributees (paragraph b). Because of these sections, enacted on September 1, 1975,[2] the fiduciary can now after three years have the court determine finally who the distributees are and direct distribution.

SCPA 2225 provides that whenever the court in any proceeding has to establish who the decedent's intestate distributees are, the petitioner may also request the court as incidental relief to adjudge that a person who might otherwise be a distributee is dead and that he predeceased the decedent without issue or that no distributees other than those stated in the record exist.[3] The person named and any unknown distributees of the decedent are entitled to service of process, which will

33. McKinney's SCPA 2224(3).

34. McKinney's SCPA 2224(4).

35. McKinney's SCPA 2224(5).

Sec. R

1. McKinney's EPTL 4–1.1 discussed in chapter on "Administration," supra at 125.

2. L.1975, c. 156, section 3, amended L.1985, c. 106 to reduce the previous five-year requirement to three years.

3. McKinney's SCPA 2225.

have to be made by publication.[4] Without this service of process, the court does not have jurisdiction over necessary parties and cannot exercise its powers under SCPA 2225.

If the court is satisfied that despite a diligent search to discover whether the missing distributee is still living, the distributee has not been heard of for at least three years after the decedent's death, it may make a determination that such a person be presumed dead and that he predeceased the decedent without issue.[5]

Similarly, if no one is certain whether there were distributees other than those who have appeared, and the court is satisfied that no distributees have been found despite diligent and exhaustive efforts, after three years have elapsed since the decedent's death the court may make a determination that no distributees exist except those whose status the court has already accepted.

Upon making either of the findings just discussed, that there are no other distributees than those stated or that all others are presumed to be deceased without issue, the court may direct distribution of the assets to the proven distributees. If there are none, the property will escheat to the state.

When a fiduciary accounts and pays the money into court but fails to ask the court for the finding that the missing distributees predeceased the decedent without issue, he cannot come back after three years and seek a determination to that effect at that point, because the initial citation did not seek that relief. He must start a new proceeding and serve process on those interested, in particular on the distributees who it is contended are dead or those whose whereabouts are unknown.[6]

This section does not deal with absentees, whose fate is determined by SCPA Article 9. It also deals only with distributees and not with legatees. The legislature should consider amendments to the statute in the future to cover legatees.

SECTION S. RIGHTS OF ALLEGED DECEDENT UPON RETURN

When a person has mysteriously disappeared and his family has diligently but fruitlessly searched for him, and there is no feasible

4. Matter of Prunder, 95 Misc.2d 370, 407 N.Y.S.2d 810 (New York County 1978).

5. McKinney's SCPA 2225, amended by L.1985, c. 106, section 1 to reduce the time period from five years to three. See, e.g., Matter of Solomon, N.Y.L.J., Aug. 8, 1985, at 6, col. 6 (New York County) (distributee not heard from for three years, not located after diligent search, who would have been 100 years old, considered to have died without issue); Matter of Venecia, N.Y.L.J., May 17, 1985, at 13, col. 1 (New York County) (diligent search for distributee missing for twenty-three years fruitless; court declared distributee dead and ordered distribution to decedent's other distributees); Matter of O'Brien, N.Y.L.J., Feb. 21, 1980, at 11, col. 5 (Bronx) (distributee missing more than five years); Matter of Dehn, N.Y.L.J., April 6, 1978, at 17, col. 1 (Westchester) (distributee missing for sixty years had last been seen in Russia during the revolution; court declared him dead and distributed funds on deposit to surviving distributee).

6. Matter of Dashew, 105 Misc.2d 391, 432 N.Y.S.2d 325 (1980).

explanation for his absence other than his death, after five years the court can decree him dead, probate his will, appoint an executor or administrator, and order distribution of his estate. This process is governed substantively by EPTL 2–1.7 and procedurally by SCPA 2226. If that person later returns, he may get back his property then in the fiduciary's hands, after deduction of any unpaid administration expenses. Beyond that he has only the rights to compel the fiduciary to account, to enforce decrees made on the accounting, and to recover from any persons who received distribution of his assets from the fiduciary either the property or its value. The fiduciary is not liable for what he spent or distributed in good faith. The returning person cannot review anything in the account of the fiduciary which has been finally settled by decree entered before the time the fiduciary became aware that the missing person was not dead.

This differs conceptually from the administration of the estate of an absentee, a person whose disappearance does not lead inexorably to a conclusion of death. After ten years absence, the court can probate a will and permit distribution of the assets under the will or the laws of intestacy, just as in the estate of an alleged decedent, but there is no finding, or even presumption, of death, and if the absentee returns he cannot get his property back.

SECTION T. SUMMARY STATEMENT OF ACCOUNT

Each decree judicially settling an account must contain a summary statement of the account.[1] Those who received process and had an opportunity to be heard are bound by the accounting decree, but the settlement of an account is binding only to the extent of matters contained in the account.[2] When the court issues the decree, the fiduciary is discharged based on it, but his letters are not revoked. He must collect any new assets that come to his attention under the authority of his original letters, and he must account for the new assets.

If no objections are filed to an account and no parties are under disability, the court may not inquire into the validity of the account,[3] but where infants are parties, the court may.[4]

Sec. T

1. McKinney's SCPA Official Form # 12, 13, 14.

2. Krimsky v. Lombardi, 78 Misc.2d 685, 357 N.Y.S.2d 671 (Supreme Court Albany County 1974), affirmed 51 A.D.2d 600, 377 N.Y.S.2d 785 (3d Dep't 1976).

3. Matter of Veccio, 49 A.D.2d 380, 375 N.Y.S.2d 637 (3d Dep't 1975).

4. Matter of DeVany, 147 A.D. 494, 132 N.Y.S. 582 (3d Dep't 1911), modified on other grounds 148 App.Div. 932, 132 N.Y.S. 1126 (1912).

Chapter Seven

APPEARANCES

SECTION A. INTRODUCTION

Once the court has acquired personal jurisdiction over a party through the service of process on him, the party has the option to default (acquiescing in the relief requested) or to appear. This chapter discusses appearances; SCPA Article 4 governs them.

SECTION B. HOW APPEARANCES ARE MADE

1. ADULT, COMPETENT NATURAL PERSONS

For adult, competent natural persons, appearances may take one of several forms: [1]

a. Appearance by Waiver of Process

A petitioner's attorney, when commencing a proceeding, should send a waiver of process to each interested person who the attorney believes will have no objection to the petition.[2] In it the signing party waives service of process and consents to the relief requested. The waiver, when filed with the clerk, constitutes an appearance [3] and, like all appearances, it completes the court's jurisdiction over that person.[4]

A party signing the waiver is presumed to understand it and can withdraw the waiver only on a showing of fraud, misrepresentation or coercion.[5] However, to avoid subsequent attacks on its validity, the attorney requesting the waiver should explain its nature and its binding effect on the party signing it.[6]

In probate proceedings the waiver must state the date of the will being offered for probate or its filing will not effect an appearance.[7] The attorney should also check court rules to see whether the waiver must contain any other information.[8]

Sec. B

1. See Matter of Maroney, 20 A.D.2d 678, 246 N.Y.S.2d 280 (4th Dep't 1964).

2. Some attorneys representing executors in large estates do not use waivers, but instead serve all necessary parties with process as an extra precaution in assuring the finality of a decree.

3. McKinney's SCPA 401(4).

4. Matter of Frutiger, 29 N.Y.2d 143, 324 N.Y.S.2d 36, 272 N.E.2d 543 (1971).

5. Matter of Celantano, 31 Misc.2d 727, 221 N.Y.S.2d 47 (Nassau 1961).

6. See Matter of Sturges, 24 Misc.2d 14, 202 N.Y.S.2d 737 (Nassau 1960).

7. McKinney's SCPA 401(4).

8. In Queens County, for example, the court requires waivers in a probate pro-

b. Appearance by Pleading

A party submitting a pleading (petition, answer or objections) makes an appearance and completes the court's jurisdiction over him.[9] A limited exception exists for "special appearances" in which the appearing party does no more than contest the court's jurisdiction.[10]

c. Appearance in Person or by Attorney

An adult competent party may appear in person or by an attorney.[11] An appearance made in person must be noted on the record in open court. More frequently, an attorney makes the appearance by filing a notice of appearance with the clerk and serving it on the petitioner's attorney. Although the statute requires that the notice of appearance be filed with the clerk,[12] sometimes substantial compliance has been found to be sufficient. For example, in one case an attorney submitted to the court an affidavit that the party had retained him, and he advised the petitioner's attorney of the retainer. The court considered these acts equivalent to the filing of a notice of appearance.[13]

Some courts will provide the attorney with a form for the notice of appearance. The attorney appearing for the party must sign it, and as a matter of good practice, it should be acknowledged, though the statute does not require acknowledgment. The attorney must be admitted to practice in New York State,[14] and must maintain an office in this state.[15] If he is not admitted or does not maintain an office in New York, he must apply to the court to appear pro hac vice.

In certain cases the attorney cannot file a notice of appearance without written authorization from his client. If the appearing party is not a New York domiciliary or was not served personally within the state, the court may (and customarily does) require an acknowledged authorization by the party [16] to resolve any questions about the appearance and to ensure personal jurisdiction. That authorization must include a statement of whether the party had ever previously executed a power of attorney relating to the estate, or assigned his interest in the

ceeding to state that the signing party received a certified copy of the will. It is likely that this will eventually become a statutory requirement.

9. McKinney's SCPA 401(2).

10. This exception is discussed this chapter infra at 237.

11. McKinney's SCPA 401(1).

12. McKinney's SCPA 401(2).

13. See Matter of Hamilton, 81 Misc.2d 40, 364 N.Y.S.2d 950 (Cattaraugus 1974).

14. Matter of Smith, 3 Misc.2d 642, 149 N.Y.S.2d 124 (Kings 1956).

15. McKinney's Judiciary Law 470 (1983); Matter of Fordan, 5 Misc.2d 372, 158 N.Y.S.2d 228 (New York County 1956).

16. McKinney's SCPA 401(3). See, e.g., Matter of Mackey, 91 Misc.2d 736, 398 N.Y.S.2d 605 (Dutchess 1977) (necessary party refused service of process and an attorney later filed a notice of appearance on his behalf; court required acknowledged authorization by party to attorney); Matter of Agioritis, 80 Misc.2d 108, 362 N.Y.S.2d 338 (New York County 1974). This authorization was, under the old Surrogate's Court Act section 41, mandatory, both for the protection of the client against actions by an unauthorized attorney, and for the protection of the attorney against repudiation of his retainer. L.1922, c. 653; Matter of Lehmeyer, 112 Misc. 670, 204 N.Y.S. 767 (New York County 1924).

estate. The authorization may be implied. For example, if a respondent has submitted a verified answer to the petition and has named his attorney in that answer, the court may accept that pleading as an authorization for the attorney to act.[17] The court can require the authorization in other cases, in its discretion. For example, even if the respondent is a New Yorker served within the state, if something sparks the judge's suspicion about the attorney's appearance, such as the respondent's refusal to accept service, the court can require an authorization.

The filing of the notice of appearance confers personal jurisdiction even if the appearing party has not previously been served with process,[18] and has not in fact authorized his attorney to appear.[19] His remedy for the unauthorized appearance is against the attorney. However, the practice in the Surrogate's Court is to require an authorized notice of appearance whenever a party has not been served.

An attorney-in-fact may also appear for a competent adult.[20]

2. PARTIES OTHER THAN ADULT, COMPETENT, NATURAL PERSONS

a. Infants, Incompetents, Conservatives and Incapacitated Persons.

Infants, incompetents and conservatees cannot appear in person.[21] Appearances for them, and for incapacitated persons,[22] are governed by the interworkings of SCPA 401 and 402 and can be made in three ways: (i) in person by the guardian of the property for an infant, the conservator for a conservatee, or the committee of the property for an incompetent; (ii) by the attorney for the guardian, conservator or committee; or (iii) by a guardian ad litem for an infant, incompetent, conservatee, or incapacitated person.

Parents are natural guardians, not general guardians, and hence unless they are judicially appointed as guardians,[23] they cannot appear in the Surrogate's Court on behalf of their infant children, although that practice is sometimes permitted in other civil practice.[24] They (and some other adults) are authorized to receive process for the

17. See Matter of Martin, 29 Misc.2d 274, 216 N.Y.S.2d 883 (Kings 1961).

18. See, e.g., Matter of Fobac, 266 App. Div. 80, 41 N.Y.S.2d 780 (4th Dep't 1943), appeal dismissed 291 N.Y. 671, 51 N.E.2d 940 (1943).

19. Petker v. Rudolph, 168 Misc. 909, 6 N.Y.S.2d 296 (Bronx 1938), affirmed 258 App.Div. 1040, 17 N.Y.S.2d 1020 (1st Dep't 1940); Matter of Hamilton, 81 Misc.2d 40, 364 N.Y.S.2d 950 (Cattaraugus 1974).

20. See Uniform Rules of the Surrogate's Courts 207.48; Matter of Schaich, 55 A.D.2d 914, 391 N.Y.S.2d 135 (2d Dep't 1977), appeal denied 42 N.Y.2d 802, 397 N.Y.S.2d 1026, 366 N.E.2d 293 (1977).

21. McKinney's SCPA 401(1).

22. Incapacitated persons are discussed just below.

23. Appointment of a guardian is governed by SCPA Article 17 and discussed in Chapter on "Guardianships," infra at 257 et seq.

24. See, e.g., McKinney's CPLR 1202.

child,[25] but not to appear for him. Only his court-appointed guardian or a guardian ad litem can do that.[26]

If a disabled person is appearing by a representative, the representative may sign the notice of appearance in court. If that representative appears by attorney, the attorney signs the notice. If the representative received process out-of-state or is a non-New Yorker, he will sign on behalf of his ward an authorization for the attorney to act, if the court asks for one.[27]

An appointed guardian, conservator or committee is not required to appear as representative for the ward.[28] If he does not, however, the court will appoint a guardian ad litem, who must appear.[29] Moreover, the court can direct a guardian ad litem to appear even when the disabled person has a guardian, conservator or committee appearing, if the court finds a potential conflict of interest or other reason.[30] Even if a guardian ad litem is appointed, the guardian, conservator or committee can also appear. If he wants to avoid the appointment of a guardian ad litem, he and his attorney should each file by the return date an affidavit showing (i) that he is qualified to protect the rights of his ward, (ii) whether he has connections with any party to (or attorney in) the proceeding, (iii) whether he is entitled to share in the estate in which his ward has an interest, (iv) whether he has a conflict of interest with his ward, and (v) any additional facts the court requires.[31] If a guardian ad litem appears for the disabled person and later a conservator or committee is appointed, the conservator or committee can then appear for the ward.[32]

While SCPA 401(1) appears to authorize an incapacitated person to appear in person, the court is nonetheless required to appoint a guardian ad litem to represent his interests under SCPA 402(2).[33] Sections 402(2) and 403(2) provide for the appointment of guardians ad litem for all persons under disability, a class which, in addition to infants,

25. McKinney's SCPA 307, discussed in chapter on "Procedure," supra at 45.

26. McKinney's SCPA 402.

27. See discussions of notice of appearance and authorization to appear in the section entitled "Adults Competent Natural Persons" just preceding this section.

28. Prior to 1971, appearances by those representatives were mandatory. L.1966, c. 953. While 402(1) reads "An infant may appear by the guardian of his property * * *," its predecessor stated, "An infant must appear * * *."

29. McKinney's SCPA 402(2). The failure to have a guardian ad litem appear for a disabled person with no other representative is a jurisdictional defect. The infant, conservatee or incompetent can void the decree when the disability is removed. See Matter of Adoption of X, 84 Misc.2d 770, 376 N.Y.S.2d 825 (Cattaraugus 1975).

30. See Matter of Holquin, 101 Misc.2d 174, 420 N.Y.S.2d 670 (Queens 1979), where the court appointed a guardian ad litem for an infant in a wrongful death action because it suspected that the surviving spouse's interests might be adverse to the infant's. See also Matter of Berger, 61 Misc.2d 81, 304 N.Y.S.2d 911 (1969), where the infant-contingent-remainderman's guardian ad litem had to object to the exercise of the spouse's right of election when the child's parents, who were primary remaindermen, consented to it.

31. McKinney's SCPA 402(1).

32. McKinney's SCPA 402(1); Matter of Winston, 92 Misc.2d 208, 399 N.Y.S.2d 999 (New York County 1977).

33. See, e.g., Stane v. Dery, 86 Misc.2d 416, 382 N.Y.S.2d 607 (Supreme Court New York County 1976).

incompetents and conservatees, includes incapacitated persons (persons who "for any cause [are] incapable adequately to protect [their] rights * * * "[34]), unknowns, and persons confined to prison.[35] As we discussed above, infants, incompetents and conservatees may appear either by their representatives or by guardians ad litem. Incapacitated persons, unknowns and prisoners do not have appointed representatives and thus must appear by guardians ad litem.[36]

To justify the appointment of a guardian ad litem, the party's incapacity should be mental, not purely physical.[37] Where one party disputes another's capacity, the courts tend to appoint a guardian ad litem to assure the protection of the party whose capacity is questioned, even if that party objects to the appointment.[38] Its decree will then be binding even if the person is determined to be incapacitated.

The courts will ordinarily appoint a guardian ad litem only when the ward is not otherwise properly represented. Often the court designates an attorney to receive process for the disabled person [39] and on the return date appoints that attorney as guardian ad litem. Because of this early involvement, the guardian ad litem can start his work without delay, from the time he is designated to receive process, and he can often submit his report on the return date when he is formally appointed guardian ad litem or shortly after the return date.

When an infant reaches eighteen, the guardian ad litem's representation ceases and the infant must receive notice of the termination so that he can retain independent counsel.[40] The guardian ad litem should advise the court that the child has reached majority to ensure that the former ward receives the statutory notice. The normal procedure would be to continue the action or proceeding in the name of the infant-turned-adult. If the infant makes no move to substitute himself as the appearing party, the judgment rendered should still be valid.[41]

34. McKinney's SCPA 103(25).

35. McKinney's SCPA 103(40). See Matter of Schaich, 55 A.D.2d 914, 391 N.Y.S.2d 135 (2d Dep't 1977), appeal denied 42 N.Y.2d 802, 397 N.Y.S.2d 1026, 366 N.E.2d 293 (1977), where the court decided not to appoint a guardian ad litem for a prisoner because there was no evidence that the prisoner would have appeared in person at the hearing had he not been in prison at the time.

36. See Matter of Shifrel, 57 Misc.2d 860, 293 N.Y.S.2d 818 (Nassau 1968), where a guardian ad litem was appointed for the decedent's widow because she was in prison pending trial for her husband's homicide.

37. Southern Industries, Inc. v. Esskay Fabrics, Inc., 81 A.D.2d 647, 438 N.Y.S.2d 341 (2d Dep't 1981).

38. See Matter of Winston, 92 Misc.2d 208, 399 N.Y.S.2d 999 (New York County 1977), where the petitioners questioned the respondent's capacity and she appeared by attorneys who opposed the appointment of a guardian ad litem. The court appointed the guardian ad litem. Accord, Matter of Kaufmann, N.Y.L.J., March 11, 1980, at 11, col. 1 (guardian ad litem appointed over ward's objections).

39. McKinney's SCPA 311, discussed in chapter on "Procedure," supra at 46.

40. McKinney's CPLR 321(c); Matter of Fassig, 58 Misc.2d 252, 295 N.Y.S.2d 146 (Nassau 1968). See also McKinney's SCPA 1707, which provides that the appointment of a general guardian terminates at the infant's majority.

41. See McCarthy v. Anable, 169 Misc. 595, 7 N.Y.S.2d 887 (Supreme Court Greene County 1938).

Though they arise less frequently, cases where disabilities other than infancy disappear should be similarly treated.

It seems clear that, for purposes of determining who is an infant, New York's age of majority (eighteen) would apply to cases in the Surrogate's Courts, even if the party, at nineteen or twenty, is still an infant in his domicile.[42]

b. Corporations or Voluntary Associations

A corporation or voluntary association must appear by an attorney.[43]

c. Aliens

A consular official may appear on behalf of a non-domiciliary alien.[44] The consul usually acts as attorney-in-fact for the national, but his appearance ends if an attorney, or an attorney-in-fact under a power of attorney recorded in the Surrogate's Court, later appears for the alien.

If the alien is an infant and a consular official is appearing for him, the Surrogate will nonetheless appoint a guardian ad litem unless the public administrator is already a party to the proceedings and the Surrogate believes the public administrator can properly represent the infant alien.[45]

SECTION C. GENERAL VERSUS SPECIAL APPEARANCES

A person can make a special appearance solely to contest the court's personal or subject matter jurisdiction without submitting himself to the court's jurisdiction.[1] For example, a person moving under CPLR 3211 to dismiss for lack of personal or in rem jurisdiction or absence of an indispensible party does not submit to the Surrogate's jurisdiction. If the person swerves from the mere jurisdictional objection and begins to attack or defend the merits of the case, the appearance becomes general and completes the court's jurisdiction over the person making it.[2]

42. See Matter of Agioritis, 80 Misc.2d 108, 362 N.Y.S.2d 338 (New York County 1974), where two Greek citizens, who were minors under Greek law but adults in New York (21 and 18), were, permitted to appear as adults by attorney under SCPA 401 in a proceeding to which they were necessary parties.

43. McKinney's SCPA 401(1).

44. McKinney's SCPA 1120.

45. McKinney's SCPA 403(3)(c). Cases have split on who, as between the consular official and the guardian ad litem, should represent the infant. Compare Matter of Ostrowski, 160 Misc. 482, 290 N.Y.S. 174 (Kings 1936), with Matter of Gruner, 149 Misc. 341, 267 N.Y.S. 388 (Bronx 1933).

Sec. C

1. See, e.g., Matter of Esser, 38 Misc.2d 963, 239 N.Y.S.2d 585 (Ontario 1963).

2. See Matter of Katz, 81 A.D.2d 145, 439 N.Y.S.2d 941 (2d Dep't 1981), order affirmed 55 N.Y.2d 904, 449 N.Y.S.2d 29, 433 N.E.2d 1277 (1982) (California resident wrote letter to Surrogate's court unequivocally stating that he did not intend to come to New York to litigate the matter and that his letter did not constitute an appear-

SECTION D. GUARDIANS AD LITEM

1. APPOINTMENT

Whenever a person under disability is a necessary party to a proceeding and does not appear by guardian, committee or conservator, the court appoints a guardian ad litem [1] (formerly referred to as a "special guardian"). A guardian ad litem may be appointed in two ways, by nomination (for infants) or by the court on its own initiative.[2] An infant over the age of fourteen years or his parent or guardian may petition the court before the return date of process for the appointment of a named attorney as guardian ad litem.[3] If the nomination is not submitted before the return date, the court will appoint a guardian ad litem of its own choosing. The nominated attorney must submit an affidavit indicating that he is qualified to protect the rights of, and has no conflict of interests with, the infant, and explaining the circumstances leading to his nomination.

Only an infant or his parent or guardian can nominate a guardian ad litem, though it would be logical to permit a conservatee, a prisoner, or a non-infant who suffers a disability to nominate a guardian ad litem as well.

An appropriate adult, namely the parent with whom the infant resides, or the person with legal custody, or the adult with whom the infant resides, has to consent to the nomination. The adult must also submit an affidavit stating either that he has no interest adverse to the infant's or, if he does, that he has not influenced the infant in the nomination.

If the adult does have a potentially adverse interest, the court does not automatically disqualify the nominated guardian ad litem, but it certainly scrutinizes the nomination carefully.[4] The court ordinarily will appoint the nominated attorney unless it is satisfied that adversity or conflict of interest would leave the ward unprotected. In that case it appoints an independent guardian ad litem.

ance; the court did not acquire jurisdiction over him though he then went into a discussion of the merits); Matter of Orkin, 16 Misc.2d 454, 182 N.Y.S.2d 966 (New York County 1958), affirmed 8 A.D.2d 720, 187 N.Y.S.2d 324 (1st Dep't 1959).

Sec. D

1. McKinney's SCPA 402(2), discussed in preceding section. When the disabled persons are trust beneficiaries, the court may appoint one guardian ad litem to represent the disabled persons with an income interest, and another to represent those with an interest in principal.

2. McKinney's SCPA 403. McKinney's CPLR 1202(a)(2), which permits a relative or friend to apply for the appointment of a guardian ad litem, does not apply, because the SCPA has a contrary provision. SCPA 403.

3. Matter of Polinsky, 11 A.D.2d 738, 204 N.Y.S.2d 951 (2d Dep't 1960), rehearing denied 11 A.D.2d 941, 206 N.Y.S.2d 540 (1960).

4. See Matter of Reifler, 22 Misc.2d 242, 200 N.Y.S.2d 182 (Dutchess 1960) (court refused to appoint brother of person with adverse interest as guardian ad litem); Matter of Friedman, N.Y.L.J., Nov. 29, 1978, at 13, col. 1 (Bronx) (court refused to appoint former member of proponent's law firm as guardian ad litem).

If an infant was made a party to a proceeding and later it is claimed that another party can virtually represent the infant under SCPA 315,[5] the court should continue the representation by the guardian ad litem, whether the infant is a necessary party or a proper party.[6]

2. PROCEEDINGS WHERE GUARDIANS AD LITEM ARE NOT NEEDED

In some proceedings the Surrogate does not appoint a guardian ad litem to represent the disabled person because his interests in the estate do not warrant it. They are as follows:

(1) In an uncontested probate proceeding where the ward will receive a greater share under the will than he would have received had the decedent died intestate, no guardian ad litem is needed.[7] Since the statute states that the interest must be the same as what the party would have received under the laws of intestacy, by necessary implication the share must be outright, not in trust. However, if the donee of a power during the child's minority receives the property, the appointment of a guardian ad litem would appear to be unnecessary, since the infant's interest is vested.[8]

(2) In the rare proceedings where the public administrator receives process or notice on behalf of the person under disability, no guardian ad litem is needed.[9] This would occur when the public administrator is already in the proceeding and in addition the court directs him to represent the person under disability.

(3) In an accounting proceeding when the accounting party can prove that the ward has received his specific bequest or devise or his general legacy in full or will receive it under the court's decree.[10] If, in an accounting proceeding, however, the ward is expected to receive less than his due because the estate is partially insolvent, he must be cited and a guardian ad litem appointed. Additionally, a guardian ad litem would always be necessary in an accounting proceeding when the ward receives the residuary estate or a share of it and is not otherwise represented.

If no guardian ad litem is necessary, the disabled person is bound by the court's decree to the same extent as he would have been bound had he not been under disability.[11]

5. McKinney's SCPA 315 is discussed in chapter on "Procedure," supra at 60–70.

6. See Matter of O'Connor, 72 Misc.2d 490, 339 N.Y.S.2d 726 (New York County 1973).

7. McKinney's SCPA 403(3)(a).

8. See Matter of Cosgrain, N.Y.L.J., June 25, 1976, at 11 (Suffolk); Matter of Paris, N.Y.L.J., Nov. 29, 1973, at 20, col. 4; Matter of Lippner, N.Y.L.J., Jan. 17, 1979, at 17, col. 2 (Bronx); Matter of Famera, N.Y.L.J., April 13, 1981, at 17 (Suffolk); Matter of Desdon, 68 Misc.2d 1012, 328 N.Y.S.2d 927. Donees of a power during a child's minority are governed by SCPA 1714 and discussed in chapter on "Guardianship," infra at 282.

9. McKinney's SCPA 403(3)(b).

10. McKinney's SCPA 403(3)(c).

11. McKinney's SCPA 406.

The protection of persons under disability is of vital concern under New York law,[12] and hence we have special rules in Article 3 for serving them with process and in Article 4 for appointing representatives to appear on their behalf. Both phases are crucial; if a disabled person has not been properly cited, the court does not have personal jurisdiction over him and cannot appoint a guardian ad litem.[13]

3. APPOINTMENT OF GUARDIANS AD LITEM IN PROCEEDINGS FOR TERMINATION OF PARENTAL RIGHTS

Under the Social Services Law,[14] abandonment and permanent neglect proceedings can be commenced in the Surrogate's Court or the Family Court to terminate parental rights and free a child for adoption if that is found to be in the child's best interests. The court in these cases must appoint as guardian ad litem for the infant an attorney admitted in New York. SCPA 403(1)(a) provides for the appointment at no cost to the infant.

The legislature authorizes the courts to create a pool of guardians ad litem for these termination proceedings. This pool can be created in several different ways. The Court can, for example, appoint an attorney under County Law "18–b" list and the county then pays the attorney a rate prescribed under that section. The Office of Court Administration can contract to have legal aid attorneys act as guardians ad litem for infants and for parents in termination proceedings. The appellate division can create a panel of qualified guardians ad litem, or can invite the local bar association to make recommendations for the position. To date these procedures have not been followed, and the guardians appointed in the termination cases are the qualified attorneys the Surrogate uses for other cases, and either the petitioner pays the guardian ad litem's fee or the guardian ad litem serves in a pro bono capacity.

4. QUALIFICATIONS OF GUARDIANS AD LITEM

The guardian ad litem must be an attorney admitted to practice in New York, and he must file with the court a consent to act and a statement that he has no conflicts of interest with the person he represents.[15] The court provides the form for this consent and statement.

5. DUTIES OF GUARDIANS AD LITEM

a. *In General*

The guardian ad litem's duties are to file an appearance on behalf of his ward, investigate the facts of the proceeding, review all papers

12. See Matter of Arneson, 84 Misc.2d 128, 374 N.Y.S.2d 973 (Westchester 1975).

13. See Matter of Beckley, 92 Misc.2d 965, 402 N.Y.S.2d 295 (Cattaraugas 1978), modified 63 A.D.2d 855, 405 N.Y.S.2d 861 (4th Dep't 1978).

14. McKinney's Soc.Serv.L. § 384–b (1983).

15. McKinney's SCPA 404(1), (2).

filed with the court, do any necessary legal research in order to ascertain his ward's interest and to enable him to take all necessary steps to protect the ward's interests, and file a report of his activities and his recommendations with the court.[16] The guardian ad litem must confirm that the court has subject matter jurisdiction and personal jurisdiction over all necessary parties, review the file thoroughly, including the relief sought, determine whether the court has all the information it needs to grant such relief, and make his own recommendations as to whether the relief should be granted.

The guardian ad litem's primary duty is to protect the best interests of his ward. He must take steps to protect the ward whether those steps coincide with the wishes of the ward or not.[17] In this light, while it is true the ward may be represented both by a guardian ad litem and also by an attorney, their roles are somewhat different. Ordinarily the attorney should follow his client's subjective wishes, if proper, whether or not they are in the client's best interests.[18]

The rules of the Surrogate's Courts direct that the report be filed within five days of the guardian's appointment, unless the court directs otherwise.[19] When a ward receives property under a decree, the guardian ad litem has to supplement his report within sixty days after the settlement of the decree to show whether his ward has actually received the property.[20]

In some cases the court works closely with the guardian ad litem in deciding what services are appropriate.[21] After reviewing the file, if the guardian ad litem is uncertain, he should discuss the case with the Surrogate's law department to delimit his duties and learn whether or not he will need court approval to hire experts, such as accountants, appraisers, investigators or actuaries.

If the guardian ad litem obtains material information in the course of his investigation, the court may require him to disclose it to the other parties to avoid surprise.[22] The reason is that the guardian ad litem makes a full written report to the court, which is a non-privileged matter of public record.

When the guardian ad litem is appointed, he must complete a form, supplied by the court, giving information about himself and his appointment.[23] Then when the court issues decree, the guardian ad litem has to file a statement, also supplied by the court, about his compensation.

16. McKinney's SCPA 404(3).

17. See Matter of Aho, 39 N.Y.2d 241, 383 N.Y.S.2d 285, 347 N.E.2d 647 (1976).

18. Matter of Aho, 39 N.Y.2d 241, 383 N.Y.S.2d 285, 347 N.E.2d 647 (1976).

19. Uniform Rules of the Surrogate's Court 207.13.

20. See Uniform Rules of the Surrogate's Court 207.13(b).

21. See, e.g., Matter of Rappaport, N.Y. L.J., March 4, 1975, at 15, col. 1 (New York County); Tate v. McQuade, 83 Misc.2d 951, 373 N.Y.S.2d 263 (Westchester 1975); Matter of Layh, 55 Misc.2d 92, 284 N.Y.S.2d 511 (Nassau 1967).

22. Matter of Roe, 65 Misc.2d 143, 316 N.Y.S.2d 785 (Suffolk 1970).

23. McKinney's Jud.L. § 37a (1983).

b. Duties in Specific Proceedings

In probate proceedings, the guardian ad litem should review the will and speak to the attesting witnesses and the attorney-drafter to satisfy himself that the will was properly executed and witnessed,[24] and that the decedent had testamentary capacity and was free of restraint. If his review raises serious questions, he should request an examination of the attesting witnesses.[25] After the examination, he can decide whether to file formal objections.[26]

If the guardian ad litem represents a disabled surviving spouse who may have a right to elect against the will or to take an elective share, he must inform the spouse, and any person interested in the spouse's welfare, of this possible right, although the guardian ad litem cannot file a right of election for his ward.[27]

If the ward is an after-born child, the guardian ad litem should determine whether or not the child is entitled to a portion of the estate.[28]

If the sale of real property is in issue, the guardian ad litem should ascertain that an independent appraisal has been made, that the offer for the property and the terms of sale are favorable, and that the sale is in the best interests of the ward.

In an accounting proceeding, the guardian ad litem should fully review the accounts, cross-check them with bank statements, bank books, brokerage statements, securities, income tax returns and insurance applications to determine whether all assets are accounted for. If questions are raised, the guardian ad litem should examine the fiduciary and demand proof of claims and expenditures,[29] and if he is still not satisfied, he should file objections.

In an adoption proceeding where the natural mother is an infant, the guardian ad litem must investigate all the circumstances of the adoption and determine whether the natural mother's interests have been protected throughout the proceeding.[30]

A guardian ad litem has no duty to protect his ward's interests in matters outside the scope of the proceeding for which he was appointed.[31]

24. See generally McKinney's SCPA 404, Practice Commentary at 401–02 (1967).

25. McKinney's SCPA 1404, discussed in chapter on "Probate," supra at 90–93.

26. McKinney's SCPA 1411, discussed in chapter on "Probate," supra at 101–09.

27. See chapter on "Surviving Spouse's Right of Election," infra at 302 et seq.

28. The rights of after-born children are set forth in EPTL 5–3.2.

29. This examination is authorized by McKinney's SCPA 2211, discussed in chapter on "Accounting," supra at 192–94.

30. See Matter of Adoption of X, 84 Misc.2d 770, 376 N.Y.S.2d 825 (Cattaraugas 1975).

31. See Tate v. McQuade, 83 Misc.2d 951, 373 N.Y.S.2d 263 (Westchester 1975) (no duty to contest excess charitable gift in a probate proceeding).

6. COMPENSATION OF GUARDIANS AD LITEM

The general rule, subject to an exception we discuss presently, is that the guardian ad litem is entitled to a reasonable fee set by the court.[32] In practice, the guardian ad litem proposes a fee and often after consultation with the attorneys for the petitioners (who submit their views to the court by letter or affidavit) the court either approves it or reduces it. The reasonableness of the fee is judged by the same criteria used to determine the fairness of legal fees generally:[33] the time spent, the complexity of the issues, the stature and experience of the lawyer, the nature and extent of the services, and the results achieved.[34] In small estates, the court may award fees lower than what the legal services are actually worth.[35]

The guardian ad litem should keep detailed time records and prepare a statement for the court justifying the time spent and describing the results. Although it may not always be required, it is good practice for the guardian ad litem to submit an affidavit setting forth the nature and extent of his services.[36]

A guardian ad litem's fee comes from the estate or from the ward's interest, or partially from both, as the court directs. In practice, the Surrogates usually charge this expense against the estate rather than against the ward, although some cases state that the charge will be made against the estate only when the guardian ad litem's services benefit the other estate beneficiaries as well as the ward.[37]

While the Surrogate has discretion to apportion the guardian ad litem's fee against the estate or the ward, it cannot charge that fee against another party to the proceeding, no matter how fair it would seem to do so.[38]

If the person under disability appears by his guardian, committee or conservator, the court may also allow that representor a reasonable

32. McKinney's SCPA 405.

33. See Matter of Potts, 213 App.Div. 59, 209 N.Y.S. 655 (4th Dep't 1925), affirmed without opinion 241 N.Y. 593, 150 N.E. 568 (1925), discussed in chapter on "Attorneys' Fees," infra at 366–69.

34. Matter of Burk, 6 A.D.2d 429, 179 N.Y.S.2d 25 (1st Dep't 1958); Matter of Meade, N.Y.L.J., Dec. 5, 1978, at 13, col. 2 (Bronx).

35. See Matter of Kaufmann, 51 Misc. 2d 560, 273 N.Y.S.2d 533 (New York County 1966), affirmed 26 A.D.2d 818, 273 N.Y.S.2d 902 (1st Dep't 1966), affirmed 23 N.Y.2d 700, 296 N.Y.S.2d 146, 243 N.E.2d 751 (1968); Matter of Cook, 102 Misc.2d 691, 424 N.Y.S.2d 330 (Nassau 1980).

36. Matter of Burk, 6 A.D.2d 429, 179 N.Y.S.2d 25 (1st Dep't 1958).

37. See, e.g., Matter of Burk, 6 A.D.2d 429, 179 N.Y.S.2d 25 (1st Dep't 1958); Matter of Thaw, 182 A.D. 368, 169 N.Y.S. 430 (1st Dep't 1918).

38. See Matter of Niedelman, 6 A.D.2d 291, 175 N.Y.S.2d 694 (1st Dep't 1958), where the court refused to reduce the widow's elective share by the amount of the fees of the guardian ad litem representing the children in a proceeding to elect against the will. See also Guardianship of Mark V., 80 Misc.2d 986, 365 N.Y.S.2d 463 (Nassau 1975). The child had been supported by the Department of Social Services and the court could not find the authority in McKinney's SCPA 405(1) to charge the guardian ad litem's fee against the city. It urged the legislature to amend SCPA 405 to permit the court to assess costs (including the guardian ad litem's fee) against any party. McKinney's SCPA 405's counterpart in the CPLR, section 1204, allows it.

sum for his counsel fee and for expenses incurred in protection of the ward's interest.[39] The exception to the general rule of fees in the court's discretion is the case of a guardian ad litem appointed to represent an infant in a proceeding that could result in a termination of parental rights. Those fees are governed exclusively by SCPA 403(1)(a), which permits the use of legal aid attorneys or "18–b" attorneys paid by the government, not the infant. As we mentioned, under SCPA 403(1)(a), in practice the guardian ad litem often serves pro bono or the petitioner pays his fee.

7. BINDING EFFECT OF PROCEEDINGS

When a guardian ad litem appears for a person under disability or where a guardian, committee or conservator appears for an infant, incompetent or conservatee, the proceedings bind the disabled parties as if they were under no disability. Therefore, absent fraud, misrepresentation or other misconduct by the guardian ad litem, the decree is final and safe from subsequent direct or collateral attack.[40] The disabled person is also bound where appointment of a guardian ad litem or legal representative is not required or the SCPA dispenses with it.

SECTION E. ASSIGNMENT OF COUNSEL FOR INDIGENT PERSONS

Certain categories of parties have a right to be represented by an attorney and to have court-appointed counsel if they cannot afford to retain an attorney.[1] These parties are (i) parents in proceedings which may lead to termination of parental rights,[2] (ii) natural parents in surrender proceedings,[3] and (iii) natural parents opposing adoption in an adoption proceeding. The right to counsel also extends to an appeal of these proceedings. The court advises these parties of their right to counsel when they first appear, and if appropriate, grants a period of adjournment to give them time to consult with counsel. When the party is indigent and the court appoints a lawyer, it does so in the same manner as it appoints guardians ad litem; that is, it chooses from a list of qualified attorneys. Their fees, however, are payable under 18b of the County Law.

1. REMOVAL OF A GUARDIAN AD LITEM

Although the SCPA does not specifically permit a court to remove a guardian ad litem once appointed, the power to remove is undoubtedly inherent in the power to appoint.[4] A party seeking removal of a guardian ad litem should make a motion on notice to all parties,

39. McKinney's SCPA 405(3).

40. See, e.g., Matter of Silver, 72 Misc. 2d 963, 340 N.Y.S.2d 335 (Kings 1975).

Sec. E

1. McKinney's SCPA 407.

2. McKinney's Soc.Serv.L. 384–b (1983).

3. McKinney's Soc.Serv.L. 384–b (1983).

4. Ford v. Moore, 79 A.D.2d 403, 436 N.Y.S.2d 882 (1st Dep't 1981).

including the guardian ad litem. The motion should set a return date, at which time the court hears evidence and the guardian ad litem has the opportunity to respond to the motion. The court should not remove the original guardian ad litem if these procedural requirements are not met. In practice, if the court finds the representation is inadequate, it will rescind the order of appointment and substitute a new attorney to represent the best interests of the ward.

Chapter Eight

ADMINISTRATION OF SMALL ESTATES

SECTION A. INTRODUCTION

Some estates consist solely of assets that do not require any formal (that is, court-supervised) administration. For example, if a decedent died owning a car, a house in joint name with his spouse, and a small amount of cash in a joint bank account with the spouse, it will be unnecessary for anyone to obtain letters. The Motor Vehicles Department does not require letters for transfer of title of the car; the surviving joint tenant can obtain a release of the state's tax lien, if any, on the house without obtaining letters; and the bank is authorized to pay out bank accounts under $30,000 (or an unlimited amount to a surviving spouse) to the joint owner without requiring a tax waiver or a fiduciary's letters.[1] If the amount in the joint account is larger and the joint owner is not the decedent's surviving spouse, the bank can pay it out to the surviving joint tenant on receipt of a tax waiver, and that too can be procured without letters.

Other estates, though small, may contain an asset that cannot be transferred without the authority of a fiduciary. Because a formal proceeding for appointment of an executor or administrator would, in these small, relatively simple estates, waste time and money, the legislature enacted the predecessor of Article 13 of the Surrogate's Court Procedure Act to expedite the administration of small estates.[2]

The threshold amount for an Article 13 small estate proceeding, or "voluntary administration," is $10,000 of personal property,[3] not includ-

Sec. A

1. See discussion of state estate tax proceedings in chapter on "Estate Taxes," infra at 563–75.

2. L.1963, c. 495, section 1, enacted Article 8B of the Surrogate's Court Act entitled "Settlement of Small Estates Without Administration." Because Article 13 works properly, there are not many reported cases under it. An example of its application can be found in Matter of Gary, 79 Misc.2d 419, 358 N.Y.S.2d 488 (1974) (decedent's only asset was a portion of a wrongful death lawsuit payable because of the death of decedent's son, and it was administered under Article 13).

3. McKinney's SCPA 1301(1). In 1981 the threshold amount was raised from $5,000 to $10,000. L.1981, c. 221, section 1, subdivision 1. Before that it had been raised to $5,000 from $3,000 in 1975. L.1975, c. 276, section 1.

Before the 1981 increase to $10,000, the threshold amount in voluntary administration proceedings was always equal to the "off-the-top" amount the surviving spouse got in intestacy under McKinney's EPTL 4–1.1 (currently $4,000) plus the $1,000

ing the exempt property set off for the decedent's spouse or minor children under EPTL 5–3.1.[4] That $10,000 figure may be deceptive for two reasons. A decedent may actually have a large estate consisting of real property and non-testamentary assets, such as property held jointly with another person, and his family (or survivors) can still use the simplified Article 13 procedure if his individually owned personal property was worth less than $10,000. The attorney should not misunderstand: only the sub-$10,000 personal property can be administered under the simplified Article 13 procedures; the point is that the real property above the threshold amount does not knock the estate out of voluntary administration for the personal property.[5]

In addition, the set-off property of EPTL 5–3.1, which does not have to be counted for purposes of voluntary administration, can be quite substantial. Specifically, it may include $5,000 worth of housekeeping utensils, musical instruments, sewing machine, household furniture, appliances, fuel, provisions and clothing; $150 worth of books and family pictures, $10,000 worth of domestic animals with food for sixty days, farm machinery, and one tractor; a motor vehicle worth up to $10,000; and $1,000 in money or other personal property.[6] Thus, an estate valued at $36,150 (the $26,150 of EPTL 5–3.1 and the $10,000 of SCPA 1301) can fall conceivably within the voluntary administration limit.

If the decedent's property is above the threshold amount, the estate must be administered either under Article 14 (probate)[7] or Article 10

cash and personal property under McKinney's EPTL 5–3.1. See Matter of Kolasinski, 59 Misc.2d 533, 299 N.Y.S.2d 905 (Erie 1969). The intestacy amount was not changed when the small estate threshold was increased in 1981, so the two figures are now out of kilter.

4. The amendment excluding exempt property from the threshold amount was added in 1973, L.1973, c. 285, section 1, because frequently the decedent's furniture and car would boost his estate above the (then) $3,000 limit even though his disposable assets were well below the threshold. See Surrogate's Association Note appended to L.1973, c. 285. It was amended in 1985 to correct a technical error under which not all paragraphs of EPTL 5–3.1 were listed in McKinney's SCPA 1301(1). L.1985, c. 9.

5. McKinney's SCPA 1302. If an intestate decedent owned real property in his sole name, it passes automatically to the decedent's distributees under McKinney's EPTL 4–1.1. No formal proceedings are necessary unless the property is sold and the title company insists on some form of letters. In most cases the title company will accept a death certificate and affidavits of heirship proving the identity of distributees. Formal proceedings may also be necessary to prove kinship where it is uncertain. See McKinney's SCPA 2113 and discussion of probate of heirship in chapter on "Miscellaneous Proceedings," infra at 357–58. If the decedent died testate the will must be probated to effectuate the devise of real property. If the decedent owned real property in joint name, a release of lien should be obtained unless the surviving joint tenant is the surviving spouse. Releases of lien are discussed in chapter on "Estate Taxes," infra at 571–75. If the joint owner does not intend to sell it, he does not theoretically need a release of tax lien, but if he is not the decedent's surviving spouse, it is advisable to obtain it anyway because on his death, releases will be required both for his estate and the estate of the former joint owner, which may be difficult to obtain after a passage of time.

6. See chapter on "Miscellaneous Proceedings," infra at 329–31, for a discussion of exempt property.

7. See chapter on "Probate," supra at 71 et seq.

(administration).[8] If the voluntary administrator discovers after appointment that the estate is larger than $10,000, he should tell the court and commence proceedings for appointment of an administrator or executor.[9] Another person interested in the estate can also seek removal of the voluntary administrator if the estate is larger than the Article 13 threshold amount.[10]

Voluntary administration is available whether the decedent was a domiciliary or a non-domiciliary of New York,[11] and whether he died testate or intestate.[12] A voluntary administrator derives his status, powers and duties solely from Article 13.[13] In fact Article 13 grants some of the powers and imposes some of the liabilities of a full fiduciary, and we discuss those powers and liabilities shortly.

SECTION B. PERSONS WHO MAY SERVE AS VOLUNTARY ADMINISTRATOR

The class of persons who may serve as voluntary administrator used to be severely limited, but has been expanded a bit under SCPA 1303.

The applicable classes of those eligible to serve depend on whether the decedent died testate or intestate. If he died intestate, the voluntary administrator must be a distributee (as listed below)[1] and a New York domiciliary,[2] and the order of priority is as follows:[3]

(i) the decedent's surviving spouse;

(ii) the decedent's competent adult children;

(iii) the decedent's competent adult grandchildren;

(iv) the decedent's parent;

(v) the decedent's brother or sister;

(vi) the decedent's niece or nephew.[4]

If a person from a prior class is legally disabled, and there are no competent members of his class who can serve, his guardian, conserva-

8. See chapter on "Administration," supra at 125 et seq.

9. McKinney's SCPA 1307, Practice Commentary at 35 (Supp.1986).

10. See Matter of Terrano, N.Y.L.J., July 12, 1985, at 15, col. 3 (Westchester) (court removed decedent's son as voluntary administrator and granted letters testamentary to decedent's surviving spouse on uncontroverted evidence that the probate estate was $130,000, not $3,000 as the son had stated).

11. This was not always so, but the statute was amended to include non-domiciliaries in L.1971, c. 312, section 2.

12. Voluntary administration used to apply only to intestate estates. This was changed by L.1970, c. 998, sections 1 and 2.

13. This is because the voluntary administrator is not included among the fiduciaries entitled to exercise the powers in McKinney's EPTL 11-1.1.

Sec. B

1. McKinney's SCPA 1303(a).

2. McKinney's SCPA 1303(c).

3. McKinney's SCPA 1303(a).

4. The class of niece or nephew was added by L.1984, c. 224, section 1, effective June 19, 1984.

tor or committee may serve and has a prior right to serve over an adult competent member of a subsequent class.[5]

Unlike a distributee in an administration proceeding,[6] a distributee in an Article 13 voluntary administration proceeding cannot designate a non-distributee to serve as voluntary administrator. If no distributee (or representative of a legally disabled distributee) qualifies, the public administrator can serve as voluntary administrator.[7]

If the decedent died testate, the executor (or alternate executor) named in the will has the first right to act as voluntary administrator after filing the will with the Surrogate's Court,[8] but only if he is a New York domiciliary.[9] The will of course need not be probated; Article 13 is a device to avoid probate. If the named fiduciary renounces or does not qualify within thirty days after filing the will,[10] then any adult person who would be entitled to petition for letters of administration with the will annexed under SCPA 1418, namely any person interested in the probate proceeding, may file the required affidavit and serve as voluntary administrator.[11]

Although the statute says that only those mentioned can serve,[12] in the proper case the court can use its discretion. In one case, for example, where a decedent wrote a will of one sentence, leaving her entire estate to a sole beneficiary, the court construed that as an implied appointment of the beneficiary as executor and allowed the sole beneficiary to serve as voluntary administrator.[13]

SECTION C. PROCEDURE FOR VOLUNTARY ADMINISTRATION

The procedure to start a voluntary administration proceeding is for the decedent's spouse or other eligible person to file with the court clerk an affidavit, described presently, a certified copy of the death certificate [1] and a one-dollar filing fee.[2] The affidavit can be filed immediately after the decedent's death [3] in the county of the decedent's domicile, or if the decedent was not a New York domiciliary, in the

5. See Matter of Armstrong, 95 Misc.2d 406, 407 N.Y.S.2d 434 (Nassau 1978) (guardian of decedent's minor child had prior right to serve over decedent's mother).

6. McKinney's SCPA 1001(5), (6), discussed in chapter on "Administration of Intestate Estates," supra at 136.

7. McKinney's SCPA 1303.

8. McKinney's SCPA 1303(b).

9. McKinney's SCPA 1303(c).

10. He would qualify by filing the affidavit discussed in the next section of this chapter.

11. Those persons include any party interested in the probate proceeding and are discussed in chapter on "Probate," supra at 115–18. Before their addition as persons eligible to serve as voluntary administrators in 1976, L.1976, c. 263, it was uncertain who could serve if the named executor did not. See McKinney's SCPA 1303, Practice Commentary at 30–31 (Supp.1986).

12. McKinney's SCPA 1303(c).

13. Matter of McElroy, 110 Misc.2d 792, 443 N.Y.S.2d 46 (Nassau 1981).

Sec. C

1. McKinney's SCPA 1304(3).

2. McKinney's SCPA 1304(4).

3. McKinney's SCPA 1304(1).

county where his personal property is located.[4] Official Form Number 5 to the SCPA sets forth the requirements of the affidavit for settlement of a small estate, and a form of the affidavit is also available from the court clerk. The affidavit requires the name and address of the affiant and his relationship to the decedent, the name, domicile and date of death of the decedent, the fact that he died testate or intestate, a list of the decedent's personal property and a statement that it was worth less than $10,000, the names and addresses of his distributees or will beneficiaries, and a statement that the affiant will honestly discharge his duties as voluntary administrator. The affidavit must be notarized.

The clerk files the affidavit, assigns a number to it, and enters it into an index book entitled "Small Estates Settled without Administration." [5] The clerk issues to the voluntary administrator a certified copy of the affidavit (usually a certification of a carbon copy of the affidavit); its purpose will be discussed presently. The clerk mails to each distributee and beneficiary mentioned in the affidavit a post-card notice of the proceedings. The notice is informational, not jurisdictional,[6] so failure to mail it does not affect the voluntary administrator's authority to act. The clerk also gives the voluntary administrator copies of a certificate, issued by the court, which gives him authority to act.[7] The voluntary administrator does not have to file a bond.[8]

SECTION D. THE VOLUNTARY ADMINISTRATOR'S DUTIES

The voluntary administrator is charged with collecting the decedent's property from debtors, transfer agents or banks, and to do so he delivers the short form certificate and a receipt for the property to that person or entity. The person gives the money or property to the voluntary administrator, and endorses on the back of the voluntary administrator's certified copy of the affidavit a list of the property delivered.[1] The person is then discharged from liability for the payment, just as he would have been had he delivered the property to a true fiduciary. He does not have to worry about how the assets are applied.[2]

The procedure is the same if the voluntary administrator wants to gather the contents of a safe deposit box.[3] A representative of the State Tax Commission has to be present, and once that official has released the contents of the box, the safe deposit company endorses on

4. McKinney's SCPA 1304(3).

5. McKinney's SCPA 1304(4).

6. McKinney's SCPA 1304(4).

7. The voluntary administrator has to pay twenty-five cents per certificate. McKinney's SCPA 1304(5).

8. McKinney's SCPA 1304(2).

Sec. D

1. McKinney's SCPA 1305(2).

2. McKinney's SCPA 1305(1); McKinney's SCPA 1309(3).

3. See discussion of the opening of a safe deposit box under McKinney's SCPA 2003 in chapter on "Probate," supra at 74.

the back of the certified copy of the affidavit a release of the contents of the box. Itemization is not required. When the voluntary administrator takes the contents of the box, the bank is completely discharged from further liability.[4]

If the voluntary administrator collects any of the decedent's money, he must open an estate account in a New York bank[5] and deposit all the money into it. He must sign checks in his own name, as voluntary administrator of the estate. He has to pay all necessary administration expenses, the reasonable funeral bill of the decedent, and the decedent's debts.[6] If the estate is insufficient to pay all debts, he must pay them in the proper (Article 18) order of priority.[7] He then has to distribute the balance of the estate to the decedent's beneficiaries:[8] that is, to the intestate distributees if the decedent died intestate[9] or to the persons named in the will if a will is filed and is valid on its face. "Valid on its face" presumably means signed and attested by two witnesses.[10] Any person affected by the distribution has the right to contest the will at any time.[11] The voluntary administrator is not paid for his services.[12]

When he completes the administration of the small estate, the voluntary administrator must account by filing with the clerk of the court the certified copy of the affidavit with the endorsements on the back, along with a statement of all assets collected and all payments and disbursements made, supported by receipts and cancelled checks. Official Form Number 6 gives the format of this "Report and Account." There is no court fee for filing the accounting.[13]

SECTION E. THE VOLUNTARY ADMINISTRATOR'S POWERS

The voluntary administrator is like a true fiduciary in some ways, except that the assets he is administering are of a very limited amount and the voluntary administrator is subject to a couple of specific restrictions.

Since one of the duties of the voluntary administrator is to marshal assets, he can bring an action or proceeding against a person who has the decedent's personal property if that person refuses to deliver it. The action or proceeding may be to compel the delivery of the property or to enforce a contractual or quasi-contractual claim the decedent had, so long as the underlying assets do not exceed the $10,000 threshold of

4. McKinney's SCPA 1305(3).

5. He must, under McKinney's SCPA 1307(1), open an estate account in a "bank, trust company, savings bank, savings and loan association or federal savings and loan association in this state."

6. McKinney's SCPA 1307.

7. See McKinney's SCPA 1811 and discussion of priority of claims in chapter on "Claims," supra at 164–72.

8. McKinney's SCPA 1307(1).

9. See McKinney's EPTL 4–1.1.

10. See McKinney's SCPA 1307, Practice Commentary at 35 (Supp.1986).

11. McKinney's SCPA 1307(1).

12. McKinney's SCPA 1307(1).

13. McKinney's SCPA 1307(2).

Article 13.[1] In such action or proceeding a certified copy of the affidavit will be prima facie proof of the facts stated in it.[2]

The voluntary administrator may sell the decedent's personal property for its reasonable value [3] as long as it is not specifically bequeathed by will.[4]

The voluntary administrator is the fiduciary of the decedent's estate and he has all the rights, powers and duties of an administrator with respect to the decedent's personal property.[5] He cannot, however, bring an action for wrongful death or personal injuries to the decedent.[6] An administrator must be appointed to do that. The rationale is twofold: the recovery is likely to be above $10,000, and the administrator represents the distributees suffering a pecuniary loss,[7] a function the voluntary administrator cannot perform. One court has held that he can settle a cause of action against the decedent's estate by a person injured because of the decedent's negligence.[8] The voluntary administrator's power to compromise should be, however, limited to the voluntary administration threshold amount ($10,000).[9]

SECTION F. THE VOLUNTARY ADMINISTRATOR'S LIABILITY

The voluntary administrator is like a true fiduciary in terms of his liability: he is responsible and accountable to all persons aggrieved by his actions, including creditors, distributees if the decedent died intestate, beneficiaries named in the decedent's will, and a fiduciary appointed after him.[1]

If a person makes a false affidavit to obtain personal property of the decedent under Article 13, he is subject to a perjury conviction.[2]

Sec. E

1. McKinney's SCPA 1306(1).

2. McKinney's SCPA 1306(1).

3. McKinney's SCPA 1306(2).

4. McKinney's EPTL 11–1.1(b)(5).

5. McKinney's SCPA 1306(3).

6. McKinney's SCPA 1306(3).

7. McKinney's EPTL 5–4.4.

8. Matter of Essenberg, 120 Misc.2d 993, 467 N.Y.S.2d 127 (Suffolk 1983).

9. Matter of Essenberg, discussed in the preceding footnote, held to the contrary. In Essenberg the court permitted a voluntary administrator to settle a claim against an estate for $10,000 at a time when the Article 13 threshold was $5,000. The Surrogate's reasoning was that McKinney's SCPA 1306 prohibited only three things: the commencement of a wrongful death action, the commencement of a negligence suit, and the commencement of a lawsuit to recover more than the Article 13 threshold amount of personal property. McKinney's SCPA 1306 was silent on the voluntary administrator's power to compromise actions against the estate. Hence, the court looked to McKinney's EPTL 11–1.1(b)(13) which permitted fiduciaries to compromise claims against the estate.

The case was wrongly decided. The voluntary administrator's very function is to manage funds of less than $10,000, and McKinney's SCPA 1307 should not be read to confer authority to settle claims for more than that amount.

Sec. F

1. McKinney's SCPA 1308(1).

2. McKinney's SCPA 1308(2).

SECTION G. GENERAL PROVISIONS OF SMALL ADMINISTRATION

Small administration is permissible, not mandatory,[1] so the court can require letters testamentary or letters of administration even though the estate could have qualified for small administration under Article 13.[2]

To expedite the administration of small estates, the statute permits New York debtors, transfer agents, safe deposit box companies and trust companies or other persons holding a non-domiciliary's personal property to honor the equivalent of an Article 13 affidavit from another state. The rule is that New York will honor affidavits from states which honor New York affidavits, and not those from states which do not.[3] A person turning over property to a foreign voluntary administrator is discharged as he would have been had the voluntary administrator been a New Yorker acting under Article 13.[4] If a bank has the property, the bank's counsel checks whether the voluntary administrator is from a state with reciprocity. The bank or a private debtor who pays over the property to a person whose state does not have reciprocity is liable for the wrongful payment.

SECTION H. PAYMENT OF DEBTS WITHOUT COURT INTERVENTION

The reverse side of voluntary administration is the case where a debtor wants to pay a debt but no fiduciary has been appointed. SCPA 1310 allows the debtor to do so.

Section 1310 permits certain kinds of debtors to discharge up to $10,000 of their obligations to a deceased creditor by paying it to the decedent's spouse or other family members without the formality of administration proceedings. For example, a hospital could use this section to pay the decedent's spouse money belonging to the decedent left in its custody after the decedent's death.

The debtors who are apt to use SCPA 1310 are banks, insurance companies, corporations, employers of the decedent, governments and

Sec. G

1. McKinney's SCPA 1309(1).

2. See, e.g., Matter of Mundinger, 103 Misc.2d 243, 425 N.Y.S.2d 520 (Bronx 1980), where almost fifty years had passed since the decedent's death and the estate was valued very close to the threshold amount for voluntary administration ($4,724 when the threshold was $5,000). The court required administration under Article 10.

3. The reciprocity can be a matter of statute or merely a matter of practice, since McKinney's SCPA 1309(2) allows New Yorkers to pay out property to a non-New Yorker with a foreign affidavit so long as "debtors, transfer agents, safe deposit companies, banks, trust companies or persons in such other state holding personal property of a domiciliary decedent shall, *whether pursuant to statute or otherwise,* recognize and pay or transfer his personal property pursuant to a short certificate of the court made under this article" (emphasis added).

4. McKinney's SCPA 1309(3).

governmental agencies. Thus, bank accounts, insurance proceeds, employee death benefits, unpaid wages and retirement obligations are usually the subject matter of this section, if the decedent designated a beneficiary from among the family members listed in SCPA 1310. The rationale for this simplified procedure is that there is no reason for these banks and corporations to act fraudulently, and that they usually keep accurate records of payments.

The section covers debts less than $10,000 and the first $10,000 of larger debts. It gives the debtor the right to make the payment, up to $10,000, to the decedent's surviving spouse or his adult children, his father or mother, his brother or sister, or his niece or nephew.[1] The debtor has a right to pay the debt to any of the persons listed, and must give priority to them in the order listed only if more than one makes a request for payment.[2]

In the alternative, if one of the decedent's relatives listed in this section requests it, the debtor can pay the money to a creditor of the decedent's, including the person who paid for the funeral expenses.[3]

The debtor who makes the payment to a relative or creditor must get an affidavit from the relative who received the payment or authorized payment to another.[4] The affidavit states the date of decedent's death, the relationship of the party signing it to the decedent, the fact that no fiduciary is serving, the names and addresses of the persons to whom the money will ultimately be paid, and the fact that the payments being tendered under this section (including those paid by other debtors) are within the $10,000 threshold.[5]

The debtor offering payment should be aware of SCPA 1310's timing provisions. If the debtor is paying the debt to the surviving spouse, he can make the payment immediately on the decedent's death.[6] If he is paying the debt to the decedent's children, parents, siblings or nieces and nephews, or to a creditor on a relative's authorization, he must wait for thirty days after the death of the decedent.[7]

If the decedent was not survived by a spouse or minor children,[8] and the debtor has not paid the debt to any of the decedent's relatives

Sec. H

1. Nieces and nephews were added to this class in 984. L.1984, ch. 224, section 2. This roughly follows the intestate distribution scheme of McKinney's EPTL 4–1.1, except that in McKinney's SCPA 1310 the decedent's issue other than children are left out, as are his minor children. The reason for this is simply a legislative judgment call. This is a simplified procedure to facilitate the payment of debts, and the appointment of guardians or production of proof of one's relationship with the decedent would complicate it.

2. McKinney's SCPA 1310(3)(a)–(e).

3. McKinney's SCPA 1310(3)(f).

4. McKinney's SCPA 1310(3).

5. McKinney's SCPA 1310(3).

6. McKinney's SCPA 1310(2). The rationale is that the legislature wanted to expedite the procedure for a surviving spouse.

7. McKinney's SCPA 1310(3).

8. The presence of minor children here is due to the exempt property provision, McKinney's EPTL 5–3.1, which keeps certain property set aside for a surviving spouse or minor children, insulated from creditors and other beneficiaries. See discussion of exempt property in chapter on

as just discussed, he can pay other distributees (that is, grandchildren, grandparents, aunts, uncles and first cousins), but under even more restrictive conditions. First, he may pay no more than $1,500, and second, he may pay it only after six months from decedent's death.[9] Subject to the six month and $1,500 restrictions, the voluntary administrator can also pay the debt (or the first $1,500 of it) to a creditor of the decedent's, so long as the claim is not exempt from creditors.[10] As in the preceding subsection, the debtor must obtain an affidavit from the person he pays, in this case giving the decedent's date of death and stating that no fiduciary is serving, that no spouse or minor child survived the fiduciary, that the person signing the affidavit is entitled to the payment, and that the debts payable under this section (including those of other debtors) do not exceed $1,500.[11]

A payment made in good faith discharges the debtor, even if the affidavit is false, but the debtor must strictly comply with the time requirements and be sure that the payee has the relationship to the decedent required by the statute (or alternatively, that the payee is indeed a creditor).[12]

This section is meant only to protect the debtor. Thus, once a debtor makes the payments, the personal representative can always go against the person receiving the fund if the estate rightfully deserves the money.[13] The spouse, of course, is always entitled to her $1,000 of exempt property and need not account to the fiduciary for it.[14]

The person to whom the offer of payment is made should contact the attorney for the debtor to find out the requirements of the debtor's company or organization.[15] It may have certain forms it wants completed or require documents, such as the death certificate or loan agreement.

SECTION I. ADMINISTRATION OF FUNDS PAID UNDER SOCIAL SECURITY AND UNEMPLOYMENT INSURANCE

The public administrator of every county can receive up to five hundred dollars in social security, unemployment insurance, or workmen's compensation payments.[1] If the public administrator collects these funds, he must use them to pay the expenses of administration and funeral expenses not otherwise paid, and if there is any excess, he

"Miscellaneous Proceedings," infra at 329–31.

9. McKinney's SCPA 1310(4), increased from $500 to $1500 by L.1986, ch. 81, sec. 1.

10. A claim would be exempt from creditors' claims if a spouse or minor child survived and the property was exempt under McKinney's EPTL 5–3.1.

11. McKinney's SCPA 1310(4)(a)–(e).

12. McKinney's SCPA 1310(5).

13. McKinney's SCPA 1310(6).

14. McKinney's SCPA 1310(6).

15. McKinney's SCPA 1310, Prac. Comm. at 38 (Supp.1986).

Sec. I

1. McKinney's SCPA 1311(1). If there is no public administrator, the county treasurer can collect these funds.

distributes it to the beneficiaries entitled to it.[2] He need not account.[3]

If an infant's or incompetent's share is $1,000 or less, it may be paid for his use or benefit to a parent or some competent person living with him or interested in his welfare.[4]

If the sum payable to a patient in a state institution is within the amount the director of the institution is authorized to receive under the Mental Hygiene Law,[5] it may be paid to the director for use as provided in that section.[6]

SECTION J. LIBERAL CONSTRUCTION

Because its purpose is to facilitate the administration of small estates, Article 13 is liberally construed.[1]

2. McKinney's SCPA 1311(2).
3. McKinney's SCPA 1311(2).
4. McKinney's SCPA 1311(3).
5. McKinney's Ment.Hyg.L. 29.23.
6. McKinney's SCPA 1311(4).

Sec. J

1. See Matter of Cohen, 68 Misc.2d 445, 326 N.Y.S.2d 595 (Nassau 1971), where a person filed for voluntary administration for a testate decedent a week before the enactment of an amendment to the statute extending it to estates of testate decedents. The court permitted the use of Article 13 administration on the liberal construction theory.

Chapter Nine

GUARDIANSHIPS

SECTION A. INTRODUCTION

A child starts out with two natural guardians, a mother and a father. The natural guardians make decisions about the child's personal welfare and also manage his property, except that if he inherits a large asset or gets such an asset through a lawsuit or by operation of a statute, the natural guardians do not have the right to manage it.[1] When one natural guardian dies, the other remains the guardian.[2]

When a child finds himself without a natural guardian, when his natural guardian is not adequately safeguarding his best interests, or when he receives assets requiring the appointment of a guardian, the court must appoint some person or persons to take care of the child or his property or both. The person who takes care of the child is the guardian of the person, and the one who manages the property is the guardian of the property.[3] The same person usually serves in both capacities, but not necessarily; fiduciaries can serve respectively as guardian of the child's person and property.

In practice, guardianships are most often used when both parents die, when they are absent, when they become unable to care for the child because of mental or physical problems, or when the child becomes entitled to more than $5,000 by gift or inheritance or as a recovery from a lawsuit.[4] Guardians are also frequently appointed for mentally retarded persons either before or after they reach eighteen. Without appointment of a guardian, no one would be authorized to sign for medical treatment for the retarded person because the natural guardianship of the parents ends when the child reaches majority.

Sec. A

1. Decker v. Pouvailsmith Corp., 225 App.Div. 489, 233 N.Y.S. 407 (3d Dep't 1929), reversed on other grounds 252 N.Y. 1, 168 N.E. 442 (1929) (natural guardian is guardian of person of child, not guardian of property suddenly acquired). A child's parent can receive on his behalf a sum of $5000 or less without being appointed guardian of the child's property. McKinney's SCPA 2220; McKinney's EPTL 11–1.1(b)(19).

2. McKinney's Domestic Relations Law section 81 (1977).

3. Besides a natural person, a trust company may serve as guardian of an infant's property. McKinney's Banking Law section 100–a(2)(a) (1971).

4. A child's parent is allowed to receive $5000 on his behalf without being appointed guardian. McKinney's SCPA 2220.

The kind of guardian contemplated by Article 17 (and discussed in this chapter) is what used to be called a "general" guardian,[5] and now includes a court-appointed guardian of the person and guardian of the property. It is the person entrusted by the court to take care of the child and to manage his property. It does not include the guardian ad litem, a "special" guardian appointed to protect a child's interest in an action or proceeding.[6] In this chapter we discuss the guardianship proceeding and the powers, duties and liabilities of the guardian.

SECTION B. THE COURT'S POWER TO APPOINT A GUARDIAN

The Surrogate's Court can appoint a guardian of the person and property, or both, of an infant,[1] even if the child's parents are alive.[2] The power given to the Surrogate is discretionary, and the court will exercise it only for legitimate purposes. For example, frequently parents will have a friend or relative petition for guardianship of the person of their child because they hope to have the child enrolled in a school district other than the one in which they live. The courts are reluctant to grant such applications unless the school district is given an opportunity to be heard on the issue [3] and to object on the ground that the child's residence in the school district is not bona fide and hence the guardianship is invalid.[4]

Guardianship proceedings, unlike adoption proceedings, are "ambulatory," so the court can always undo the appointment of a guardian.[5] The court therefore has somewhat less concern in guardianship proceedings than in adoption proceedings about subject matter jurisdiction and personal jurisdiction over the parties.

SECTION C. THE COURT'S JURISDICTION IN GUARDIANSHIP PROCEEDINGS

The New York Constitution gives the Surrogate's Court jurisdiction over the guardianship only of the property of infants,[1] but the legisla-

5. The definition of guardian in McKinney's SCPA 103(23) is "any person to whom letters of guardianship, whether of the person, property or both, of an infant have been issued by a court of this state."

6. Guardians ad litem are discussed in chapter on "Appearances" supra at 238–44.

Sec. B

1. McKinney's SCPA 1701.

2. See Matter of Caseres, 67 A.D.2d 630, 412 N.Y.S.2d 599 (1st Dep't 1979).

3. See Matter of Sussman, N.Y.L.J., May 29, 1985, at 15, col. 4 (Nassau) (application granted); Matter of Moncrieffe, 121 Misc.2d 395, 467 N.Y.S.2d 812 (Nassau 1983) (application granted); Matter of Proios, 111 Misc.2d 252, 443 N.Y.S.2d 828 (Nassau 1981) (application denied).

4. See Drayton v. Baron, 52 Misc.2d 778, 276 N.Y.S.2d 924 (Nassau 1967). See also Plyler v. Doe, 457 U.S. 202, 102 S.Ct. 2382, 72 L.Ed.2d 786 (1982), rehearing denied 458 U.S. 1131, 103 S.Ct. 14, 73 L.Ed.2d 1401 (1982) (persons entitled to establish residence wherever they wish notwithstanding that choice might establish right to attend certain school).

5. See Matter of Jacqueline, 94 Misc.2d 96, 404 N.Y.S.2d 790 (Bronx 1978).

Sec. C

1. McKinney's Const. Art. 6, section 12.

ture is authorized to broaden the jurisdiction of the Surrogate's Court,[2] and has done so by giving the Surrogate's Court jurisdiction to appoint a guardian of the person as well.[3] The Surrogate's jurisdiction is broad in guardianship matters.[4]

The court's jurisdiction to appoint a guardian of the person or of the property is based on the child's domicile; the Surrogate can appoint a guardian if the infant is domiciled in the county or had sojourned there just before the application.[5] In practice, the proceeding is almost always brought in the county of domicile, not where the child has sojourned. Once a proceeding is commenced in one county, that court should retain jurisdiction to decide all guardianship issues.[6] The court has the power to change the venue of the proceeding or transfer it to another court if that would serve the interests of justice.[7] It can also revoke letters of guardianship to promote the best interests of the child.[8]

An infant is presumed to be domiciled in the same place as his parents, or as the parent who has custody.[9] The court has taken jurisdiction when the parent with custody resided in New York even though the child did not.[10] If the child's parents are living, his domicile is rebuttably presumed to be with them even if he resides with his grandparent in another county.[11] If he has no parents, his domicile is normally with the person who has custody of him.[12]

If the child is not a domiciliary of New York, the Surrogate nevertheless has jurisdiction over a guardianship proceeding if the child has property in that county.[13] In that case, the court will usually exercise its jurisdiction only over the guardianship of the property

2. McKinney's Const. Art. 6, section 30.

3. McKinney's SCPA 1701. The Surrogate's jurisdiction is concurrent with that of the Family Court and the Supreme Court, and this is discussed infra at 271–72.

4. The only reported case restricting the Surrogate's powers in guardianship proceedings is Matter of D.D., 64 A.D.2d 898, 408 N.Y.S.2d 104 (2d Dep't 1978), appeal dismissed 49 N.Y.2d 879, 427 N.Y.S.2d 990, 405 N.E.2d 233 (1980), where the appellate division held that the Surrogate did not have jurisdiction to order the surgical sterilization of a mentally retarded girl.

5. McKinney's SCPA 1702. The former one-year sojourn requirement was changed by L.1973, c. 286.

6. See Matter of Lavender, N.Y.L.J., June 12, 1985, at 14, col. 4 (Bronx) (court revoked guardianship letters on finding that a guardianship proceeding had previously been commenced in Westchester).

7. McKinney's CPLR 510; CPLR 327; Matter of V.S., 90 Misc.2d 139, 394 N.Y.S.2d 128 (New York County 1977); Matter of Michael, N.Y.L.J., May 8, 1985, at 16, col. 4 (Nassau).

8. McKinney's SCPA 711(9). See Matter of Jacqueline F., 94 Misc.2d 96, 404 N.Y.S.2d 790 (Bronx 1978).

9. See Backstatter v. Backstatter, 66 Misc.2d 331, 320 N.Y.S.2d 613 (Nassau 1971). This presumption is rebuttable, but the burden is on the person claiming that the child's domicile is other than the parent's.

10. Louise G. v. Peter C., 97 Misc.2d 338, 411 N.Y.S.2d 101 (Fam.Ct.Kings 1978).

11. See Matter of Delaney, 282 App. Div. 280, 123 N.Y.S.2d 255 (3d Dep't 1953).

12. See First Trust Co. v. Goodrich, 3 N.Y.2d 410, 165 N.Y.S.2d 510, 144 N.E.2d 396 (1957) (grandmother who, in good faith, had changed the domicile of her orphaned grandchildren to her own could petition for letters of guardianship in her own county); Matter of Stange, 38 Misc.2d 170, 236 N.Y.S.2d 718 (Kings 1962) (accord).

13. McKinney's SCPA 1702(2).

located there, and not over the person of the child. The court's jurisdiction would be concurrent with that of the Surrogate in the county where the child had sojourned, if he had, and the first court to entertain a proceeding then becomes the proper court for all matters relating to the guardianship.

If the child is domiciled in one county and has property in another, the court of the county of the child's domicile has jurisdiction.

A guardian appointed in another state cannot exercise guardianship authority in New York.[14] If a local guardian is needed, New York court must appoint an ancillary guardian.[15]

Both the Family Court and the Supreme Court have concurrent jurisdiction with the Surrogate over guardianships, but while all three courts can appoint a guardian, the supervision of the guardian and all proceedings commenced after the appointment of the guardian are under the jurisdiction of the Surrogate's Court.[16] If, however, a matrimonial proceeding is pending in the Supreme Court, the Surrogate will not entertain a petition to appoint a guardian until the Supreme Court determines the custody issue, unless a special reason exists to warrant the Surrogate's intervention.[17]

The Commissioner of Social Services has jurisdiction over abandoned children.[18] While that jurisdiction does not oust the Surrogate if someone petitions for the child's guardianship,[19] if the Family Court is supervising the child's placement and progress in foster care, the Surrogate may defer exercise of its jurisdiction.[20]

There are alternatives to appointment of a guardian to hold and administer the child's property. The Supreme Court or another civil court in which a child recovers money in a negligence action, for example, can order the money deposited into court and withdrawn only on a further court order.[21]

SECTION D. THE PETITION

Any person may petition on the infant's behalf for the appointment of a guardian of the person or property, or both, of the infant.[1] The infant may petition if he is fourteen years old or older, and apparently

14. Wuesthoff v. Germania Life Insurance Co., 107 N.Y. 580, 14 N.E. 811 (1888); Matter of Farrell, 97 Misc.2d 18, 410 N.Y.S.2d 775 (Bronx 1978).

15. Ancillary guardianships are discussed in this chapter infra at 283–85.

16. McKinney's SCPA 1709, discussed in section on "Appointment of Guardian by Supreme Court or Another Court," this chapter infra at 271–72.

17. See Matter of Sussman, N.Y.L.J., May 29, 1985, at 15, col. 4 (Nassau), where the court appointed a temporary guardian to permit the child to enroll in school and then stated that future adjudications should be made by the Supreme Court which had jurisdiction of the divorce and custody issues.

18. McKinney's Soc.Serv.L. §§ 371(2), 398 (1983).

19. Matter of Caseres, 67 A.D.2d 630, 412 N.Y.S.2d 599 (1st Dep't 1979).

20. See Matter of Thomas, N.Y.L.J., July 3, 1985, at 13, col. 6 (Bronx).

21. See McKinney's CPLR 1211.

Sec. D

1. McKinney's SCPA 1703.

an infant under fourteen can also petition, since the statute says that "any person" may do so.[2]

Every petition in the Surrogate's Court must set forth the facts that give the court jurisdiction and must also contain all the information required under Article 3,[3] and in addition a guardianship petition must set forth the names of the surviving father and mother and their domiciles,[4] the names and addresses of the persons living with the infant and of the nearest adult domiciliary distributees, if both parents are dead. The petition must indicate whether a guardian was ever acting for the child.[5] It must set forth the estimated value of the child's real and personal property and any income from that property to which the infant is entitled.

If the child is a non-domiciliary and is married, the petition must give the name and domicile of the spouse, and if the petition relates only to personal property, it must state whether the property is subject to the spouse's control under the laws of the marital domicile.

The petition must say why the person nominated is a good choice for guardian, and why the parent, if living, is not.

If the infant is not the petitioner, his consent should be attached to the petition if he is fourteen or older, and it is good practice to get the consent of the child if possible even if he is under fourteen, if he is relatively mature. The petitioner should also mention the religious faith of the child, the proposed guardians and the parents, since it is the public policy of the state to appoint guardians of the same religion as the child when possible.[6] The SCPA contains official forms for the guardianship proceeding,[7] and forms are available at the Surrogate's Court. As a matter of practice the attorney should use these forms

2. See Matter of Ingersoll, 192 Misc. 158, 78 N.Y.S.2d 513 (1948).

3. McKinney's SCPA 304, discussed in chapter on "Procedure," supra at 54–55.

4. McKinney's SCPA 1704.

5. Specifically, McKinney's SCPA 1704 requires that the petition state "[w]hether the infant has had at any time a guardian appointed by will or deed or an acting guardian in socage or a guardian of the person appointed pursuant to section 384 or 384–b of the social services law." A guardian in socage was, at common law, a guardian with custody of lands coming to the child by descent and the guardian of the person of the infant until he reached fourteen. See McKinney's Dom.Rel.L. 80 (1977).

6. McKinney's Const. Article 6, section 32 states that when a court places a child in the custody of another person, the child shall be placed, when practicable, in the custody of a person of the same religion as the child. Social Services Law section 373 provides that a court appointing a guardian must where practicable appoint a person of the same religious faith as the child; see Matter of Starr, 29 A.D.2d 662, 286 N.Y.S.2d 313 (2d Dep't 1968), order affirmed 24 N.Y.2d 1011, 302 N.Y.S.2d 835, 250 N.E.2d 240 (1969); and see Matter of Crickard, 52 Misc. 63, 102 N.Y.S. 440 (Monroe 1906), where the child's aunt, though the same religion as the child, was married to a man of a different faith. An additional factor was that she was, in the court's language, "narrow-minded, quick-tempered and obstinate." The court granted letters of guardianship to the child's grandparents, both of whom were of the same faith as the child.

7. Official Forms Number 8 (petition), Number 9 (renunciation, waiver of process and consent), Number 10 (annual account) and Number 11 (petition to close guardianship account.

provided by the court, one for children under fourteen and one for children fourteen and older.

SECTION E. NECESSARY PARTIES

In a guardianship proceeding, as in any Surrogate's Court proceeding, the petitioner should always attempt to get waivers of citation from necessary parties.[1] If he cannot, the court will issue process and he must arrange to serve it on the infant's parents and, if there is one, the spouse, if they are in New York and their addresses are known. If there is no parent or spouse, service must be made on the grandparents if they are within the county in which the proceeding is brought. In addition, the persons with custody of the infant or with whom the infant resides are entitled to service. This will include, where appropriate, the Commissioner of Social Services or an authorized agency to whom the child's custody has been committed.[2] If the infant is fourteen or over (and is not the petitioner), he too is a necessary party and must be served.[3]

There are exceptions. If a parent has abandoned the child, has been deprived of his civil rights, or has been divorced from the other parent (who was given legal custody of the child), he is not a necessary party and need not be cited. Service is also unnecessary on an incompetent or a person otherwise judicially deprived of the infant's custody. Similarly, if the infant is married, the spouse need not be served if he has abandoned the infant, has been deprived of civil rights, has been divorced from the infant, or is incompetent.[4]

If the child resides with relatives, the court must ascertain (to the extent practicable) which relatives are domiciled within the county and which without, and may issue process to any relative or class of relatives to show cause why the petition should not be granted.[5]

When the infant's nearest relative is the petitioner, the court will usually not require that notice be given to other relatives in the county, but when the petitioner is not the nearest relative, or there are some others of equal degree, the court will usually direct that they be given notice of the application even if they reside outside the county.[6]

Sec. E

1. See discussion of waivers of process in chapter on "Procedure," supra at 37.

2. See Matter of Thomas, N.Y.L.J., July 3, 1985, at 13, col. 6 (Kings), where the court vacated letters of guardianship issued to children's grandmother because she failed to list the Commissioner of Social Services, who had custody, as a necessary party.

3. McKinney's SCPA 1705(1).

4. McKinney's SCPA 1705(2).

5. McKinney's SCPA 1705(3). The attorney may note that these process requirements are not especially onerous and that they give the court some flexibility. The reason is that the legislature intended guardianship proceedings to be expeditious, so that someone could be put in place to take care of the child. Since a guardianship is always revocable, this flexibility is well warranted.

6. Matter of Crickard, 52 Misc. 63, 102 N.Y.S. 440 (Monroe 1906).

To illustrate, if a minor child receives an inheritance larger than $5,000, his parents can apply for letters of guardianship and no other parties will have to be cited. If only one parent petitions for guardianship, he can obtain a waiver of citation from the other, or if he cannot, he will have to cite the other parent. If the parents die and an aunt petitions for guardianship, she will have to cite the grandparents if they are in the county, and, if the court directs, any close relatives residing in the county.

Significantly, even a person without any rights to notice of a guardianship proceeding has a right to petition to revoke the letters of guardianship, since the SCPA allows any person acting on an infant's behalf to do so.[7]

An unwed father is a necessary party to guardianship proceedings.[8]

Failure to cite a necessary party is a jurisdictional defect, and the defect is not cured by the necessary party's constructive or even actual knowledge of the proceeding,[9] but only by service of process on him. However, as we have stated, guardianship proceedings are easily revocable, so jurisdictional defects are not so grave as in adoption proceedings, which are permanent.

SECTION F. THE GUARDIANSHIP HEARING

A hearing is not required in every guardianship case. If no persons have had to be cited, or if, on the return date of process, no one contests the petition, the court will ordinarily not require a hearing.[1] If there is a contest, the court must conduct a hearing to determine whether or not a guardian is needed and, if so, who ought to be appointed.[2]

Whether or not there is a contest, the court must satisfy itself that a guardian is needed and must review the qualifications of the applicant, set forth in the petition and the other data submitted. The court must determine the age of the infant, the amount of his personal property and, if applicable, rents due to the infant from real estate, and the sufficiency of the security offered by the proposed guardian.[3]

7. McKinney's SCPA 711(9). See Matter of Goulden, 41 A.D.2d 684, 342 N.Y.S.2d 737 (4th Dep't 1973), where the child's father-in-law, not a necessary party to the guardianship proceeding, nevertheless had standing to petition for removal of the infant's father as guardian because of unfitness.

8. Raysor v. Gabbey, 57 A.D.2d 437, 395 N.Y.S.2d 290 (4th Dep't 1977) (proof of paternity must be by clear and convincing evidence); Matter of Morgan, 70 Misc.2d 1063, 335 N.Y.S.2d 226 (Erie 1972).

9. Raysor v. Gabbey, 57 A.D.2d 437, 395 N.Y.S.2d 290 (4th Dep't 1977); Matter of Lord, 52 Misc.2d 904, 276 N.Y.S.2d 1021 (Onondaga 1967).

Sec. F

1. McKinney's SCPA 1706.

2. Matter of Snure, N.Y.L.J., October 23, 1967, at 23, col. 1 (Kings County).

3. Most often security is not an issue, since the court has joint control and no bond need be filed. See section on joint control, this chapter infra at 268–69.

If the child is fourteen or over, the court must ascertain his preference for a guardian.[4] In practice, the infant usually expresses his preference by joining in the petition and does not have to appear at a hearing.

The child, when interviewed by the court, need not be represented by counsel.[5]

SECTION G. WHO SHOULD BE APPOINTED GUARDIAN

The choice of guardian is within the court's discretion.[1] Ordinarily the court appoints a parent guardian, if a parent wants to be appointed.[2] Both parents are joint natural guardians of their child [3] and they have equal powers, rights and duties. Unless they have been deprived of their rights to participate in the guardianship proceeding,[4] they must be cited in the proceeding and they have priority over others in being appointed as guardian, so long as such appointment is in the child's best interests.

An attempt by one parent to have someone other than the other parent appointed guardian by will is void unless the surviving parent is statutorily disqualified.[5] Such a designation in the will is not useless, though, because if the will provides for a gift to the child to be held by the guardian, then the ineffective nomination of a guardian in the will is effective to appoint the named guardian as donee of the power during minority and will permit him to take possession during minority of assets that the infant takes under the will.[6] The donee has the power to invest and distribute the funds to the infant or on his behalf until he reaches majority.

When a parent is not petitioner, the court usually appoints the person nominated in the petition when there is no contest, unless that appointment seems clearly not to be in the child's best interests.[7] Though the court rarely does so, it also has the power to appoint a person other than the parent or the person nominated in the petition.

4. See Matter of Carbonaro, N.Y.L.J., June 21, 1985, at 15, col. 1 (Suffolk) (court appointed fifteen year old child's preferred choice of guardian).

5. See Matter of Lincoln, 24 N.Y.2d 270, 299 N.Y.S.2d 842, 247 N.E.2d 659 (1979).

Sec. G

1. Matter of Stuart, 280 N.Y. 245, 20 N.E.2d 741 (1939).

2. Eden M. v. Ines R., 97 Misc.2d 256, 410 N.Y.S.2d 997 (Kings 1978) (Family Court exercised jurisdiction over the custody of a child when the Surrogate had already appointed the grandmother as guardian without notice to the natural mother); Matter of Morgan, 70 Misc.2d 1063, 335 N.Y.S.2d 226 (Erie 1972).

3. McKinney's Dom.Rel.L. 81 (1977).

4. McKinney's SCPA 1705(2).

5. McKinney's SCPA 1705(2).

6. McKinney's SCPA 1714, discussed infra at 282.

7. See Matter of Best, N.Y.L.J., Aug. 8, 1985, at 11, col. 5 (Bronx), where the court refused to appoint the child's godmother, a welfare recipient with inadequate housing who was unsuccessful in motivating the child to attend school, although the Social Services Department stated that it had no alternative.

The test is always the best interests of the child.[8] A guardianship proceeding is not like an adoption proceeding, where the court must consider the rights of the natural parents before the best interests of the child.[9] For example, in one case where the natural father had been divorced by the mother on grounds of adultery and had been in arrears on support payments, had been married and divorced again and had fathered an illegitimate child,[10] after the mother's death the court appointed the grandparents as guardians in the child's best interests. Similarly, a court denied an application for guardianship of the teenage sister of a single woman with two out-of-wedlock children of different fathers and with no apparent source of support.[11] When both parents are deceased, the court will consider grandparents, who are then the natural guardians of the infants.[12] Since the best interests of the child are paramount, however, the court may appoint someone other than the grandparents of the orphaned grandchild if it finds that it would be in the infant's best interests to do so.[13]

In order to determine the best interests of the child when two relatives (or any two persons) vie for guardianship, the court must look thoroughly into the qualifications and motivation of each potential guardian.[14] It should order psychological examinations and should unearth all possible relevant information before deciding which choice would be in the best interests of the child.[15] The court, having chosen

8. Matter of Gustow, 220 N.Y. 373, 115 N.E. 995 (1917).

9. McKinney's Dom.Rel.Law section 111.

10. See Matter of LaFountain, 33 A.D.2d 586, 304 N.Y.S.2d 421 (3d Dep't 1969).

11. Matter of Maria Q., N.Y.L.J., March 21, 1985, at 11, col. 2 (Bronx). See also Matter of Morgan, N.Y.L.J., Jan. 10, 1979, at 12, col. 1 (Kings) (mother was unstable, unemployed for eight years, and living with a man who had struck the children); Matter of Maribel, N.Y.L.J., May 5, 1978, at 12, col. 2 (Bronx) (mother wanted guardianship of the child only because of the public assistance payments she would then receive).

12. First Trust and Deposit Co. v. Goodrich, 3 N.Y.2d 410, 165 N.Y.S.2d 510, 144 N.E.2d 396 (1957); Matter of Erhardt, 27 A.D.2d 836, 227 N.Y.S.2d 734 (2d Dep't 1967); see McKinney's Dom.Rel.L. section 80 (1977) (nearest and eldest relative of age of majority).

13. Matter of Ingersoll, 192 Misc. 158, 78 N.Y.S.2d 513 (Broome 1948).

14. See Matter of Marrero, N.Y.L.J., July 8, 1985, at 12, col. 4 (Bronx), where the court refused to appoint a guardian for a drug-abusing teenager without an investigation into the petitioner's qualifications on notice to the Department of Social Services and the drug center which had custody of the child.

15. See Bennett v. Jeffreys, 40 N.Y.2d 543, 551, 387 N.Y.S.2d 821, 356 N.E.2d 277 (1976), appeal after remand 59 A.D.2d 492, 399 N.Y.S.2d 697 (1977), where the court said, "[N]o psychological or other background examination of the mother had ever been obtained. There was, therefore, no consideration of whether the mother is an adequate parent, in capacity, motivation, and efficacious planning * * *. Thus a new hearing is required because the Family Court did not examine enough into the qualifications and background of the long-time custodian, and the Appellate Division did not require further examination into the qualifications and background of the mother." See also Matter of Unold, 86 A.D.2d 612, 446 N.Y.S.2d 99 (2d Dep't 1982), where the court reversed the Surrogate's decision to grant letters of guardianship to the grandfather, transferred the case to the Supreme Court, and mandated an examination into the respective merits of the uncle and the grandfather.

one to serve as guardian, retains jurisdiction and can entertain a petition to change the guardian in the child's best interests.[16]

Where relatives of equal rank, such as paternal and maternal grandparents, would both, in the court's opinion, be suitable guardians, the court can appoint them co-guardians.[17]

When an infant is fourteen or over, the court will consider his opinion in determining who should be guardian, even to the exclusion of a parent.[18] The court also gives some weight to the wishes of a minor under fourteen, although that preference is not considered paramount.[19] The CPLR requires the Supreme Court to examine an infant over fourteen years on the suitability of the nominated guardian.[20] Although the SCPA does not require such examination by the Surrogate,[21] it does require the Surrogate to determine the child's preference, which may be by affidavit or by the child's joining in the petition. Often the court does examine the child who is fourteen or over,[22] and should do so when anyone files objections to the proposed guardian.[23] In practice, however, even if the infant prefers a person other than his parent as guardian, the court exercises great restraint in overruling parental rights.[24] If a parent is incapable of caring for the child and later regains that capacity, the court will reconsider his application for guardianship.[25]

A court appointing a guardian other than a parent examines the past living habits of the child, the environment in which he lives, his schooling needs, the attempt to continue family relationships, his financial needs and his religious requirements.[26] If all other things are equal, the court will try to appoint a relative rather than a stranger as guardian, especially as guardian of the person. The court will also try to keep siblings together.

The court can also, in an appropriate case, appoint an attorney or the Public Administrator as the guardian of the infant's property, for example if no family member or friend is willing to serve and a trust company will not serve because the assets are limited.[27]

16. Matter of Sapanara, 89 Misc.2d 956, 392 N.Y.S.2d 825 (Queens 1977).

17. See Matter of Krayem, 177 Misc. 842, 32 N.Y.S.2d 70 (Ulster 1942).

18. Matter of Stuart, 280 N.Y. 245, 20 N.E. 741 (1939); Matter of Gustow, 220 N.Y. 373, 115 N.E. 995 (1917).

19. Metz v. Morley, 20 A.D.2d 462, 289 N.Y.S.2d 364 (4th Dep't, 1968).

20. McKinney's CPLR 1210(b).

21. See McKinney's SCPA 1706.

22. See Lipman, McKinney's SCPA 1706, Practice Commentary at 17 (1967) (court should examine the child).

23. Matter of Thoemmes, 238 App.Div. 541, 264 N.Y.S. 829 (4th Dep't 1933).

24. See Matter of Bock, 280 N.Y. 349, 21 N.E. 186 (1934); Matter of LaFountain, 33 A.D.2d 586, 304 N.Y.S.2d 421 (3d Dep't 1969) (court required compelling and substantial proof of natural parent's unfitness).

25. Matter of Cuddihy, 8 Misc.2d 450, 167 N.Y.S.2d 741 (Suffolk 1957) (mother received psychotherapy and recovered from alcoholism).

26. Matter of Bock, 280 N.Y. 349, 21 N.E.2d 186 (1939).

27. Matter of McCoyd, 112 Misc.2d 491, 447 N.Y.S.2d 230 (Nassau 1982).

SECTION H. THE DECREE APPOINTING GUARDIAN

After the court reviews the petition and accompanying documents, and completes the hearing if one is necessary, and if it believes that the child's best interests require appointment of the guardian, it will appoint one.[1] Often the decree appoints the same person as guardian of the child's person and guardian of his property, but if the court believes that someone who would be a good guardian of the child's person lacks the expertise to manage the child's large assets, it can appoint someone who has such expertise, including a corporate fiduciary, as the guardian of the child's property.

The court can set conditions on the appointment, such as instructions on religious training, education or visitation rights. This may be necessary, for example, because grandparents have a right to apply for visitation rights,[2] even if their child has died and the grandchildren have been adopted by the widow or widower's second spouse.[3]

SECTION I. TERM OF GUARDIAN'S OFFICE

Usually a guardianship ends when the infant reaches the age of majority (eighteen),[1] but there are two exceptions. Guardianship of a child's person ends when the child marries, even before reaching the age of majority, and the court can for good cause terminate a guardianship of the person or of the property before the child reaches majority.[2] For example, the court might set a shorter period if a parent is temporarily unable to care for a child because of illness or incarceration, or if the parent has to move and wants the child to finish out the school year. Similarly, if a child is under mental disability the court can direct that the guardianship will terminate at the appointment of a conservator for the child, ensuring that the ward will have a fiduciary beyond the age of majority if a guardian is not appointed under SCPA Article 17A (guardianships of mentally retarded persons), which we discuss later in this chapter. In these cases, the court provides in the decree that the guardianship will last for a fixed period, or until the end of the school year or the appointment of a conservator or some other contingency, and then automatically terminate without further court decree. In the alternative, the court may find that temporary guardianship is in the child's best interests and may grant open-ended temporary letters until some further proceeding is commenced.[3]

Sec. H

1. McKinney's SCPA 1707.

2. McKinney's Dom.Rel.L. § 72 (1977).

3. Scranton v. Hutter, 40 A.D.2d 296, 339 N.Y.S.2d 708 (4th Dep't 1973) (adoption by stepmother does not preclude grandparents from applying for visitation rights).

Sec. I

1. McKinney's SCPA 1707(2).

2. McKinney's SCPA 1707(2).

3. See Matter of Sussman, N.Y.L.J., May 29, 1985, at 15, col. 4 (Nassau), where the child (fifteen years old), the product of a bitter divorce between his physician-parents, petitioned for appointment of his for-

SECTION J. REMOVAL OF A GUARDIAN

After the court has appointed a guardian, any person, regardless of his relationship with the child, can petition the court for revocation of the guardian's letters.[1] The petitioner must show either that the guardian is about to remove the child's property from the state (or has removed it) or that appointment of a different guardian would serve the child's best interests. His petition for this relief must contain specific factual allegations, not just opinions and conclusory statements.[2]

SECTION K. JOINT CONTROL OF GUARDIANSHIP ASSETS

Like other fiduciaries, a guardian must post a bond before the court will issue letters of guardianship unless he falls within one of the exceptions that make a bond unnecessary. The bond must be at least the value of all the infant's personal property the guardian will receive, three years estimated rents from realty, and three years estimated income from property not in the hands of the guardian.[1]

There are three instances in which the guardian need not obtain a bond. If a parent nominates a guardian for his children in a will, he can exempt the guardian from a bond. The court can also dispense with the bond if it issues letters of guardianship restricting the guardian's powers.[2] Most frequently, the court dispenses with the bond for guardians on another ground: the guardian holds the infant's property jointly with a person or bank designated by the court.[3]

The court orders the guardian to deposit the money and property in a bank[4] in the name of the guardian. After depositing the property the guardian can make withdrawals only with a court order. When the infant reaches majority, he can withdraw the funds without court order, unless the court has directed otherwise. Most Surrogate's Courts do direct otherwise; they order the depository not to pay over the funds at the infant's eighteenth birthday unless the (former) infant obtains a court order. They do this to ensure that guardianship accounts cannot

mer nanny and her husband as guardians. The school district refused to allow him admittance until letters of guardianship were issued, and the child's parents consented, at least as a temporary arrangement. The court granted temporary letters of guardianship with no specific expiration date.

Sec. J

1. McKinney's SCPA 711(9).

2. Matter of Goulden, 41 A.D.2d 684, 342 N.Y.S.2d 737 (4th Dep't 1973).

Sec. K

1. McKinney's SCPA 801(1)(b).

2. McKinney's SCPA 801.

3. McKinney's SCPA 1708.

4. Under McKinney's SCPA 1708(1), the depository can be a bank, savings bank, trust company, industrial bank or safe deposit company, or a savings and loan association. The court can also order that the money be invested in the shares or savings account of a savings and loan association. No deposit of the child's funds in any single institution may exceed the maximum amount insurable by the Federal Deposit Insurance Corporation. The guardianship letters must contain the substance of the court's order.

be closed out without the Surrogate's knowledge and to protect creditors and fiduciaries with valid claims for debts and commissions.

A similar rule applies to life insurance proceeds; if they are payable to an infant as beneficiary, the court may dispense with a bond and direct the insurance carrier to issue joint checks to the guardian and a person designated by the court to receive them,[5] often a bank official or the guardianship clerk of the Surrogate's Court or, in the smaller counties where there is no guardianship clerk, the clerk of the court. The attorney must check with the local Surrogate's Court guardianship department to find out which procedure the court uses.

If a bank or insurance company violates the court's order and pays the guardian alone, it is liable for any loss to the infant.[6] The court should make the bank aware of its order appointing the bank as depository to hold the property jointly with the guardian, however, because the New York Court of Appeals has recently held that a bank which negotiates a check payable to the fiduciary without first establishing his authority to do so will not, without more, be liable for the fiduciary's negotiating the check and thus exceeding his powers.[7]

SECTION L. ACCOUNTING FOR GUARDIANSHIP PROPERTY

When a guardian has joint control of assets [1] either with the clerk or with a bank, he does not have to file an annual accounting unless the court directs one.[2] The reason is that the clerk or the bank has in its file the same information normally required by a guardian's accounting,[3] namely, an accurate record of deposits and withdrawals of principal or income in the infant's account. In addition, the court order always directs the bank to submit an annual report to the court when it has joint control. Thus, the only thing that the guardian has to supply on an annual basis is a request for a maintenance order if the child is not being supported by his parents. In fact, this contains an "accounting" of a sort, because it predicts future expenses for the upcoming year in affidavit form.

When the guardian does not hold the assets jointly, he must account annually.[4] In Nassau, Orange, Suffolk and Westchester counties, and in New York City's five boroughs, the account must be made within thirty days after the anniversary of the guardian's appointment. In all other counties, it must be made in January.[5]

5. McKinney's SCPA 1708(3).

6. See Matter of Cadena, N.Y.L.J., March 22, 1982 (Nassau); Duncan v. Mutual Life Insurance Co., 99 Misc. 280, 164 N.Y.S. 97 (App. Term 2d Dep't 1917).

7. Matter of Knox, 64 N.Y.2d 434, 488 N.Y.S.2d 146, 477 N.E.2d 448 (1985).

Sec. L

1. McKinney's SCPA 1708.

2. McKinney's SCPA 1719(5).

3. McKinney's SCPA 1719.

4. McKinney's SCPA 1719(5).

5. McKinney's SCPA 1719 (first paragraph).

The account must describe each item of personal property received by the guardian since appointment and since the filing of the prior annual account, state the value of the items remaining in his hands and the way he has disposed of any item not remaining in his hands, and describe each investment he has made.[6]

The guardian must list receipts and disbursements during the preceding year, charge himself with any balance remaining in his hands since the last accounting, and state the balance remaining at the end of the year.[7] He must name the sureties on his bond and if the surety is a natural person, state whether he is still living. He must state whether the security of the bond has become impaired.[8] The court may require him to produce all securities or evidences of deposit or investments.[9] If the guardian did not change investments during the year, a simple affidavit will suffice.

The annual account, though subject to SCPA Article 22 like all accountings,[10] is not a judicial settlement. Interested parties have access to the annual accounts and in theory can object to them, though such objections are rare in practice. At the end of the guardianship, the guardian must finally account, and at that time interested persons have another opportunity to review the annual accounts and make objections.[11]

The guardian must attach an affidavit, which only he can execute,[12] to the annual account, stating that to his knowledge the account is true.[13] In this respect, guardianship accountings do not differ from any other kind.

SECTION M. ANNUAL EXAMINATION OF THE GUARDIAN'S ACCOUNT

In February each year (and until completed), or at another time in the court's discretion, the court must examine the guardianship annual accounts filed for the preceding year.[1] Usually the guardianship clerk or the clerk of the court does the examinations, but the court has discretion to appoint a special examiner who, when appointed, must sign an oath that he will faithfully execute his duties and make a true report to the court.

6. McKinney's SCPA 1719(1).

7. McKinney's SCPA 1719(2).

8. McKinney's SCPA 1719(3).

9. McKinney's SCPA 1719(4).

10. See chapter on "Accounting," supra at 179 et seq.

11. See McKinney's SCPA 1719, Prac. Comm. at 68 (1967).

12. McKinney's SCPA 1720.

13. Under prior law, an attorney or an agent could execute it for the guardian on a showing of good cause if the guardian knew the facts. McKinney's SCA 191, L.1914, c. 443.

Sec. M

1. SCPA 1721.

1. DEFECTIVE ACCOUNTS

If the court discovers that a guardian of an infant's property has failed to file an annual account or the accompanying affidavit, or if the court feels that the account is inadequate or that the guardian should be removed, it may appoint a guardian ad litem or a special examiner as guardian ad litem to file a petition for the filing of an amended account or the removal of the guardian.[2] If the court appoints a special examiner, it can charge his fee against the guardian personally, against the funds in the guardian's hands, or against the county.[3]

SECTION N. APPOINTMENT OF GUARDIAN BY SUPREME COURT OR ANOTHER COURT

The Surrogate's Court has a position of supremacy in the area of guardianships.[1] Even if the appointment of the guardian was made in another court, it is the Surrogate who issues the letters of guardianship. When the Supreme Court or the Family Court[2] appoints a guardian of an infant's person or property, that court must file a certified copy of its order, and of the bond, with the Surrogate's Court of the county where the infant is domiciled, or if he is not a New York domiciliary, the county where the infant has property. The appointed guardian must qualify in the Surrogate's Court by signing an oath that he will faithfully discharge his duties and a designation of the court clerk to receive process on his behalf.[3] The Surrogate's Court supervises the guardians and reviews the annual accounts and all guardians are subject to the duties and liabilities of Article 17 of the SCPA.[4]

Thus the Surrogate's Court effectively acquires jurisdiction of all guardians, whether appointed in the Surrogate's Court or another court, and the appointing court surrenders its jurisdiction to the Surrogate's Court. The purpose of this transfer of jurisdiction is to centralize guardianships in the court with the most expertise in guardianships.[5]

2. McKinney's SCPA 1722. See, e.g., Matter of Polur, N.Y.L.J., April 23, 1980, at 11, col. 6 (Bronx) (court appointed guardian ad litem because guardian had collected rents from guardianship property without accounting for them). If the child is very close to eighteen, the court may refrain from appointing a guardian ad litem and may instead prohibit the guardian from making any further withdrawals. See Matter of Brown, N.Y.L.J., July 13, 1979, at 6, col. 5 (Bronx).

3. When the court assesses the fee against the county, the court certifies the items to the proper officers of the county (which is rare) and they are paid as other county or city charges. In the City of New York, the court certifies it to the proper officers. In other counties, it is certified to the treasurer of the county or the chief fiscal officer.

Sec. N

1. McKinney's SCPA 1709.

2. The statute says "any other court," but it is rare that a court other than the Supreme Court, the Family Court or the Surrogate's Court will ever appoint a guardian.

3. McKinney's SCPA 1709(3). A fiduciary qualifies by following the provisions of McKinney's SCPA 708, discussed in chapter on "Fiduciaries," infra at 391–92.

4. McKinney's SCPA 1709(3).

5. On the other hand, while the Surrogate has jurisdiction to appoint a guardian, it can defer to the Supreme Court when that court has exercised jurisdiction of the issue of the child's custody in a divorce action. See Matter of Sussman, N.Y.L.J., May 29, 1985, at 15, col. 4 (Nassau), where

In this interplay between the courts, a few statutory inconsistencies exist. The CPLR [6] and the Family Court Act [7] provide that the certified order of appointment from the Supreme Court and the Family Court, respectively, must be filed with the Surrogate of the county where the order was made. The SCPA,[8] as we have mentioned, states that the order of appointment must be filed in the Surrogate's Court of the child's domicile. If a proceeding on behalf of a child starts in the Supreme Court or Family Court of the child's domicile, as it often does, no inconsistency arises; the Supreme or Family Court appoints the guardian, and the Surrogate's Court of that county issues the letters. However, if the guardianship proceeding was begun in a county other than the child's domicile, the SCPA provision conflicts with the other two. Similarly, if the infant is not a domiciliary but has property in a New York county, and the guardian was appointed in a county other than the one where the child has property, the SCPA's requirement (that the certified copy be filed with the Surrogate's Court of the county where the property is) conflicts with the CPLR and Family Court Act provisions (that the copy be filed in the Surrogate's Court of the county where the guardianship proceeding was commenced).

The legislature is aware of this inconsistency, and is considering remedial legislation. A good way to harmonize the statutes would be to follow the SCPA and require filing with the Surrogate's Court of the child's domicile or of the county where the child's property is located, which would be consistent with the other statutory provisions relating to the Surrogate's jurisdiction.[9]

SECTION O. APPOINTMENT OF GUARDIAN BY WILL OR INTER VIVOS INSTRUMENT

Under the Domestic Relations Law,[1] both parents are natural guardians of their children. On the death of one of them, the other automatically becomes the sole natural guardian. A parent has a right to appoint a guardian for a child by will, subject to the surviving spouse's right to serve,[2] and, in most cases the courts honor the parent's wishes, provided that is in the child's best interests.[3] A parent's

the Surrogate appointed a temporary guardian to permit the child's immediate enrollment in school and then deferred to the Supreme Court for the future.

6. McKinney's CPLR 1210(e).

7. McKinney's Fam. Ct. Act § 663 (1983).

8. McKinney's SCPA 1709.

9. See McKinney's SCPA 205, 206 and 207, discussed in chapter on "Jurisdiction," supra at 1–9.

Sec. O

1. McKinney's Dom.Rel.L. 81 (1977).

2. This right is guaranteed by McKinney's Dom.Rel.L. 81 (McKinney 1977), and did not exist at common law. Matter of Sapanara, 89 Misc.2d 956, 392 N.Y.S.2d 825 (Queens 1977).

3. See Matter of Sapanara, 89 Misc.2d 956, 392 N.Y.S.2d 825 (Queens 1977). For a case in which the court found it not to be in the child's best interests to appoint a guardian approved by the mother, see Matter of Marrero, N.Y.L.J., July 8, 1985, at 12, col. 4 (Bronx), where the mother had in effect abandoned her drug-abusing daughter and consented to the appointment of a stranger as guardian.

attempt to appoint someone other than the surviving spouse as testamentary guardian will usually be void.[4] Similarly, any attempt by a person other than a parent to name a testamentary guardian is ineffective.[5] The ineffective designation of the guardian in the will, however, is not completely wasted; it is effective to designate that person as donee of a power to manage the property of the infant, formerly called the donee of a "power in trust."[6]

Although it is rare, a parent can nominate a guardian to serve immediately during the parent's lifetime by inter vivos instrument. As in the nomination by will, the other parent has priority over others.

Parents may, with mutual consent, execute wills during their lifetimes naming a third party to serve as guardian along with the surviving parent, so long as their mutual consent is motivated by the best interests of the child.[7] If the parents die simultaneously, naming different guardians, the court chooses the guardian whose appointment best serves the child's interests.

Nomination under a will does not automatically make the nominated person a guardian. The proper Surrogate's Court must admit the will to probate,[8] and the nominated guardian must petition and give facts showing why he should serve, must file his oath and designation, post a bond if one is required and receive letters of guardianship before he can serve as guardian.[9] Similarly, an inter vivos instrument naming a guardian must be acknowledged and recorded to be effective.[10] The proper place to record it is in the recording office of the county of the parent's domicile. A testamentary or inter vivos guardian may serve without a bond if the instrument so provides, but any property passing to him as guardian outside the instrument, such as insurance proceeds, pension payments, Totten Trusts and jointly owned property, must be secured.[11]

The guardian named in a will or deed is subject to the provisions of Article 17. There is no distinction between a testamentary guardian and the "general guardian" discussed elsewhere throughout this chap-

4. See Matter of Thorne, 212 App.Div. 654, 209 N.Y.S.2d 280 (2d Dep't 1925); Matter of Dedon, 68 Misc.2d 1012, 328 N.Y.S.2d 927 (New York County 1972).

5. Matter of Silvera, 27 Misc.2d 361, 211 N.Y.S.2d 378 (New York County 1960).

6. See "Donee of Power to Manage During Minority," this chapter infra at 282. The donee has the rights and duties of a general guardian with regard to the property the child takes under that instrument. Matter of Roy, 9 Misc.2d 991, 174 N.Y.S.2d 119 (Nassau 1957).

7. McKinney's Dom.Rel.L. 81 (McKinney 1977).

8. McKinney's SCPA 1710.

9. McKinney's SCPA 1710.

10. McKinney's SCPA 1710. The statute says that the deed must have "been recorded in the office for recording deeds in the county of domicile of the person making the appointment at the time of execution thereof." The phrase "at the time of execution thereof" apparently refers to "domicile," not "recorded." The deed will be effective if recorded within 3 months of the grantor's death at the domiciliary county. See McKinney's SCPA 1711; McKinney's SCPA 1710, Practice Commentary at 35–36 (1967).

11. The property may be secured either by a bond or by its deposit in joint custody of the guardian and another designated by the court. Each of these is discussed this chapter supra at 268–69.

ter.[12] The same parties have to be cited,[13] the same standard (best interests of the child) governs, and the same rules on the necessity of a hearing apply. The term of office of each ends when the child reaches majority. It is unclear in the statute and case law whether a testator can successfully appoint a guardian of the child or a donee of a power during minority whose term lasts longer than the child's minority,[14] although it appears acceptable to extend the period of "minority" to twenty-one years in New York, and this is routinely done.

If a guardian is nominated by will, he must qualify by filing his oath, designation and bond [15] within three months of probate unless the will provides otherwise.[16] If he does not, he is presumed to have renounced. Before or after the expiration of the three-month statutory period, the court can extend the time to qualify for good cause.[17] The nominated guardian can get this extension by filing an ex parte petition or affidavit. A nominated guardian who does not wish to serve can renounce by filing an acknowledged instrument in the court of original probate.

Similarly, if a guardian nominated in an inter vivos instrument does not record it within three months of the grantor's death, the law presumes that the person nominated has renounced his appointment, and that presumption is conclusive if the court appoints another guardian after the three-month period. In the case of a "presumed renunciation," process should be served on the guardian.

1. APPOINTMENT OF A SUCCESSOR

If a guardian appointed by will or inter vivos instrument resigns, dies, becomes incompetent or ceases to serve for another reason before the child's majority, the court can appoint a successor unless the instrument says otherwise.[18] The successor receives the infant's property and should request a settlement of the predecessor's account, either from the predecessor or his representative, as soon as possible.[19] The application for appointment of a successor should be made to the

12. Matter of Taylor, 252 N.Y. 218, 169 N.E. 282 (1929).

13. See Matter of Sapanara, 89 Misc.2d 956, 392 N.Y.S.2d 825 (Queens 1977), where a parent had nominated a guardian in his will. Prior to appointment of a guardian, the child's grandparents petitioned in another court for letters of guardianship. The proceeding was removed to the Surrogate's Court where the parent's will had been offered for probate, and the Surrogate found that the grandparents were not necessary parties to the guardianship proceeding because the child's parent had nominated someone else by will.

14. This issue is being reviewed by the legislature.

15. McKinney's SCPA 708, discussed in chapter on "Fiduciaries," infra at 391–92.

16. McKinney's SCPA 1711.

17. McKinney's SCPA 1711(4); Matter of Sapanara, 89 Misc.2d 956, 392 N.Y.S.2d 825 (Queens 1977) (court reminded nominated guardian to apply for extension).

18. McKinney's SCPA 1712.

19. See Matter of Russell, 43 N.Y.S.2d 839 (Madison 1943); McKinney's SCPA 1712, Practice Commentary at 41 (1967).

Surrogate's Court that either appointed the original guardian or issued the letters if another court appointed the guardian.[20]

SECTION P. USE OF THE INFANT'S PROPERTY

In New York, parents have to support with their own funds their unemancipated children under the age of twenty-one,[1] regardless of the existence of guardianship assets. Therefore, the child's funds can be used only when those primarily responsible for his education and support cannot provide them.[2] Each parent shares the obligation of support.[3] The cases split on whether the obligation of support extends to providing a private high school education when free public education is available, or providing a college education.[4]

Subject to that rule, the court can direct that the child's property, both income and principal, be used to support and educate the child.[5] "Support" is a flexible term; it has been held to include basic necessities such as food, clothing and shelter and medical care,[6] as well as proper recreation, vacation and traveling expenses,[7] the cost of summer camp,[8] wedding expenses for a minor bride,[9] moving expenses to move

20. Matter of Stein, 98 Misc. 493, 164 N.Y.S. 930 (Bronx 1915).

Sec. P

1. McKinney's Fam.Ct. Act 413 (1983).

2. Laumeier v. Laumeier, 237 N.Y. 357, 143 N.E. 219 (1924); Matter of Darlene C., 96 Misc.2d 952, 410 N.Y.S.2d 51 (Bronx 1978). See Matter of Keeting, N.Y.L.J., July 12, 1965, at 12, col. 3 (Westchester) (guardian's application to mortgage property to finance college education denied); Gaffney v. Constantine, 87 N.Y.S.2d 131 (Queens 1949) ("infant has a right to expect to receive the money awarded to him for his injury with interest and not a bundle of court orders showing his funds were spent for necessities of life which others were obligated by law to furnish to him"). See McKinney's SCPA 1713.

Grandparents are not legally responsible for support of their grandchildren, McKinney's Dom.Rel.L. 32 (McKinney 1977), enacted L.1965, c. 647, so guardianship funds can be used regardless of the grandparents' resources.

Even if the child's parent receives a very limited income, the guardianship property should not be used to support the parent. See Matter of Cooke, N.Y.L.J., April 10, 1985, at 12, col. 1 (Bronx).

3. Matter of Garcy, 19 A.D.2d 811, 243 N.Y.S.2d 464 (1st Dep't 1963) (mother as well as father has obligation to support). Cases such as Matter of Polinsky, 33 Misc.2d 1002, 225 N.Y.S.2d 855 (Kings 1962), which held that the mother need not present as strong a case for invasion of guardianship funds as the father, have now become obsolete.

4. Compare Wagner v. Wagner, 51 Misc.2d 574, 273 N.Y.S.2d 572 (N.Y. County 1966), affirmed without opinion 28 A.D.2d 828, 282 N.Y.S.2d 639 (1st Dep't 1967), motion dismissed 20 N.Y.2d 803, 284 N.Y.S.2d 460, 231 N.E.2d 135 (1967) (no obligation), with Kotkin v. Kerner, 29 A.D.2d 367, 288 N.Y.S.2d 244 (1st Dep't 1968) (3–2 decision finding obligation to provide private school education); Kern v. Kern, 65 Misc.2d 765, 319 N.Y.S.2d 178 (Fam.Ct. New York County 1970).

5. McKinney's SCPA 1713. See, e.g., Matter of Quintero, N.Y.L.J., April 3, 1984, at 13, col. 1 (Bronx), where the court authorized payment of parochial school tuition and uniform expenses.

6. See, e.g., Matter of Henry, N.Y.L.J., April 1, 1980, at 6, col. 6 (New York County) (court allowed withdrawal of $600 monthly for infant's support).

7. Matter of Vanderbilt, 129 Misc. 605, 223 N.Y.S. 314 (New York County 1927), affirmed 220 A.D. 830, 222 N.Y.S. 916 (1st Dep't 1927).

8. See Matter of Panciarello, N.Y.L.J., May 8, 1985, at 16, col. 4 (Nassau), where

9. See note 9 on page 276.

the child out of a bad neighborhood,[10] expenses of posting bail [11] and retaining an attorney [12] when the infant commits a crime, and expenses of buying life insurance on the guardian's life.[13] The court weighs all factors, including the ability of the parent to provide the money out of his own funds and the proportion of the child's property the expenditure represents.[14]

The guardian can also pay the funeral expenses of his ward's parent or of any other person who named the child beneficiary under an insurance policy or donee of any other property and whose other assets are insufficient to pay for the funeral.[15] Formerly, the guardian could use only insurance proceeds for burial purposes,[16] but the statute now provides that any assets the decedent left to the child can be used. This includes pension funds, profit-sharing funds, Totten trusts and jointly held property as well as probate assets. If the decedent's estate is enough to pay the funeral expenses, the court will not allow the guardian to spend the child's money.[17]

If the child is receiving Social Security payments, the guardian does not need a court order to use them for the child's support.[18]

The child's funds are ordinarily not available for family needs.[19] For example, the guardian cannot use the infant's funds to repay the

the guardian (the child's parent) requested withdrawal of $1,000 of the guardianship account of $6,000 to pay for summer camp. The court noted the parent's primary responsibility to pay that expense and his inability to pay the whole amount and the beneficial effect summer camp would have on the child, and allowed $600 to be withdrawn, which was approximately the interest earned on the account. The parent was responsible for the remaining $400.

9. Matter of Anonymous, 44 Misc.2d 38, 252 N.Y.S.2d 946 (Kings 1964).

10. Matter of Reid, N.Y.L.J., April 21, 1980, at 14, col. 6 (Bronx) (court allowed withdrawal of funds to cover broker's fee, security deposit and moving expenses to move child into a neighborhood likely to cause fewer developmental problems).

11. Matter of Rodriguez, 109 Misc.2d 1047, 441 N.Y.S.2d 327 (New York County 1981). But see Peterson v. New York, 107 Misc.2d 1055, 436 N.Y.S.2d 577 (Queens 1981), where the court denied the application to use guardianship funds to post bail.

12. Matter of Heyliger, 125 Misc.2d 915, 480 N.Y.S.2d 869 (New York County 1984) (court allowed payment of $15,000 legal fee from guardianship funds when infant was indicted for felony murder and other felonies).

13. Matter of Darlene C., 96 Misc.2d 952, 410 N.Y.S.2d 51 (Bronx 1978).

14. Matter of Monica L.R., N.Y.L.J., March 15, 1979, at 10, col. 2 (Bronx) (court allowed use of 50% of child's fund for private school); Matter of Anthony, N.Y.L.J., Dec. 28, 1978, at 12, col. 2 (Bronx) (court disallowed use of eighteen percent of child's account to pay for one year of kindergarten); Matter of Evans, N.Y.L.J., April 14, 1978, at 13, col. 1 (Bronx) (court disallowed withdrawal of $5,000 from child's estate of $13,600, to pay for child's secondary education). But see Matter of Sean Michael W., N.Y.L.J., Nov. 21, 1979, at 12 col. 2 (Bronx), where the court allowed withdrawal of seventy percent of child's estate for private school because the child flatly refused to go to public school.

15. McKinney's SCPA 1713. See, e.g. Matter of Davis, N.Y.L.J., May 22, 1985, at 12, col. 5 (Bronx) (court allowed payment of $2,221 for father's funeral out of child's estate which was received because of father's wrongful death); Matter of Blake, N.Y.L.J., June 19, 1978, at 20, col. 1 (Westchester) (accord).

16. L.1966, c. 953.

17. McKinney's SCPA 1713(2).

18. McKinney's SCPA 1713(3).

19. See Matter of Polinsky, 33 Misc.2d 1002, 225 N.Y.S.2d 855 (Kings 1962): Leon v. Walker, 1 Misc.2d 219, 147 N.Y.S.2d 331 (New York County 1955).

debts of the father.[20] Often after the payment of damages for personal injuries to a child, the guardian, usually a parent, wants to use some of the funds for a new house or other asset to be used by the whole family, but he cannot do so without a court order,[21] and the court will allow it only in extraordinary circumstances.[22] In practice if the only way to raise the child's substandard manner of living or the only way to avoid a foreclosure that would leave the child without a place to live is to permit use of guardianship funds, the court will allow it though that expenditure helps the other family members as well.[23] If the guardian applies for the use of the child's money as a down payment, the court closely scrutinizes the parent's subsequent ability to keep up the payments and maintenance.[24] When a family dwelling is not so structured to accommodate a child who has developed a physical handicap, and the parents' funds are limited, a court may allow guardianship funds to be used to make changes or buy a new home for the infant,[25] and in practice the court orders the guardian to take title in the infant's name or in the name of the guardian as fiduciary for the infant.

Occasionally a guardian reimburses a person who, without any obligation to do so, supported the child before the guardian was appointed, and the court has discretion to ratify such reimbursement.[26]

The guardian should obtain a court order whether he wants to use income or principal of the guardianship assets, although there is some authority that he can use income without a court order.[27] This is, in most cases, an academic question, since assets are held jointly and a court order is therefore necessary.[28]

The court can award an attorney legal fees out of the guardianship property, but they must be reasonable.[29]

The guardian who wants to use the property should petition in the Surrogate's Court, stating the amount of money he needs for the child

20. Matter of Richards, 44 Misc.2d 620, 254 N.Y.S.2d 490 (Westchester 1964).

21. See Arnstein v. Price, 285 App.Div. 557, 139 N.Y.S.2d 471 (2d Dep't 1955), affirmed 309 N.Y. 694, 128 N.E.2d 411 (1955).

22. Matter of DeLind, N.Y.L.J., March 11, 1977, at 12 (Bronx).

23. Matter of Mattei, N.Y.L.J., June 6, 1979, at 10, col. 3 (Bronx) (court allowed investment in real estate to alleviate crowded conditions); Matter of Allen, N.Y. L.J., March 15, 1978, at 12, col. 2 (Bronx) (court allowed withdrawal to prevent eviction and forestall foreclosure).

24. See Matter of Greer, N.Y.L.J., June 21, 1985, at 14, col. 5 (Suffolk) (guardian's own income precluded maintaining of mortgage payments); Matter of White, N.Y.L.J., Sept. 11, 1978, at 14, col. 2 (Westchester) (court disallowed withdrawal because subsequent monthly payments would consume seventy percent of parent's total income).

25. See Matter of Moroney, N.Y.L.J., June 10, 1985, at 15, col. 3 (Nassau) (court, which previously allowed purchase of home, permitted physical improvements to meet mentally retarded person's needs).

26. Matter of Russell, 43 N.Y.S.2d 839 (Madison 1943).

27. Matter of Jarvis, 259 App.Div. 843, 19 N.Y.S.2d 183 (Franklin 1940).

28. See "Joint Control of Assets," this chapter supra at 268–69.

29. See Matter of Quintero, N.Y.L.J., April 3, 1985 at 13, col. 1 (Bronx), where the court reduced the requested $2,000 attorney's fee to $900. See chapter on "Attorney's Fees," infra at 366–69.

and the reason he needs it, the total amount of money he holds for the ward, where it is invested and how much income it earns, and the child's parents' (if any) ability to support the child. If a court has ever issued a maintenance order, the guardian must advise the Surrogate of it and describe the disbursements under it.[30]

If a child whose property was being held by a guardian dies, the court may order payment of guardianship funds for his burial if the parents cannot afford to pay the entire funeral expenses.[31]

SECTION Q. PROTECTION OF GUARDIANSHIP FUNDS

Any person, including the child if he is fourteen or over, can petition to have the court appoint a guardian ad litem to commence a proceeding for protection of the child's interests, whether financial or personal.[1] The court has discretion to entertain the proceeding or not, and it usually does so, authorizing the guardian ad litem to take whatever action the court considers necessary. The court can also appoint a guardian ad litem on its own if it finds that the interests of the guardian are adverse to those of the infant or if there is another valid reason to examine the administration of the child's assets,[2] such as inaction on the guardian's part in collecting assets.[3] The need for this proceeding would arise because the natural guardian has an interest adverse to the child's in an estate.

A natural guardian cannot appear in a proceeding for an infant unless the court has appointed him guardian and issued letters of guardianship.[4] As a rule the court will not officially appoint a guardian ad litem until the return date, because a guardian of the property

30. See McKinney's SCPA 1713, McKinney's CPLR 1211, and Uniform Rules of the Surrogate's Court 207.14.

31. Matter of Yonnone, 72 Misc.2d 579, 339 N.Y.S.2d 212 (Orange 1972).

Sec. Q

1. McKinney's SCPA 1713(4).

2. See, e.g., Matter of Kaplan, N.Y.L.J., May 15, 1985, at 13, col. 6 (Nassau), where the court appointed a guardian ad litem to protect the child's interest after the guardian acquiesced in the decision of the trustee of a trust to halt discretionary income payments to the ward. Similarly, in Matter of Blattman, N.Y.L.J., Feb. 27, 1985, at 17, col. 4 (Westchester), the court appointed a guardian ad litem on a guardian's accounting when the guardian had, without a court order, withdrawn money from the guardianship account to repair damages to guardianship property caused by guardian's wrongdoing; and in Matter of Jenkins, N.Y.L.J., June 11, 1985, at 11, col. 1 (Bronx), the court appointed a guardian ad litem because the guardian was not adequately accounting for the ward's funds when the court inquired. See also, by analogy, Sutherland v. New York, 107 A.D.2d 568, 483 N.Y.S.2d 307 (1st Dep't 1985), where the appellate division refused to appoint a guardian ad litem in place of the child's mother to represent her interests in the settlement of a medical malpractice action when the only issue was the payment of the settlement in a lump sum or over a term.

3. Matter of Kiniel, N.Y.L.J., June 12, 1985, at 14, col. 5 (Bronx) (court on its own motion appointed guardian ad litem because guardian had not deposited insurance proceeds in designated bank or responded to the court's inquiry on that matter).

4. See chapter on "Appearances," supra at 232 et seq.

may be appointed before then, obviating the need for the guardian ad litem. However, the court will, when it anticipates a conflict of interest, request an attorney to act as guardian ad litem, or even appoint the attorney as designee to receive service for the minor,[5] and postpone formal appointment as guardian ad litem until the return date. If in fact the guardian and the child have conflicting interests, the court by this preliminary appointment of a designee to receive process has reduced delay, because the attorney can make a preliminary investigation before the return date and submit the report shortly after his appointment as guardian ad litem on the return date.[6]

SECTION R. POWERS OF GUARDIANS

1. GENERAL POWERS AND DUTIES OF A GUARDIAN OF THE PROPERTY

SCPA Article 17 [1] is the source of the guardian's powers, since the EPTL fiduciaries' powers provisions do not include guardians.[2] The guardian of an infant's property has the duty to protect, preserve and manage the infant's property.[3] If someone takes the property from the minor by duress or fraud, the guardian should take appropriate steps to get it back. He can invest the property, sell it and reinvest the proceeds, and dispose of investments, unless the court order or the appointing will says otherwise. A guardian can also, without court order, reimburse someone who has supplied necessaries to the ward unless assets are held jointly; in that case an order is necessary.[4]

In practice the guardian's powers are not very broad. Although theoretically the guardian may sell assets without court order, the guardian usually holds the assets jointly with the court clerk or a bank,[5] and a court order is necessary to dispose of them.[6] Except for the limited powers listed in the statute, the guardian has no power to act on the child's behalf without a court order.[7]

5. McKinney's SCPA 311.

6. Cf. Byrn v. New York City Health and Hospital Corp., 38 A.D.2d 316, 329 N.Y.S.2d 722 (2d Dep't 1972), affirmed 31 N.Y.2d 194, 335 N.Y.S.2d 390, 286 N.E.2d 887 (1972), appeal denied 411 U.S. 940, 93 S.Ct. 1889, 36 L.Ed.2d 404 (1973) (court may appoint guardian ad litem before natural guardians appear to protect infant's interests).

Sec. R

1. McKinney's SCPA 1723.

2. McKinney's EPTL 11–1.1.

3. McKinney's SCPA 1723. See Delafield v. Barret, 270 N.Y. 43, 200 N.E. 67 (1936).

4. See Matter of Ackerman, 116 N.Y. 654, 22 N.E. 552 (1889).

5. See "Joint Control of Assets," supra at 268–69.

6. McKinney's SCPA 1723's authorization to sell the child's property was added to the statute by L.1967, c. 685, to make it clear that guardians have that power. Guardians could not dispose of the infant's property under McKinney's EPTL 11–1.1, which excludes guardians, but case law permitted the guardian to do so. Clare v. Mutual Life Ins. Co., 201 N.Y. 492, 94 N.E. 1075 (1911).

7. For example, he cannot remove the guardianship assets from the state without a court order. Matter of Rodriguez, N.Y. L.J., Nov. 1, 1979, at 10, col. 5 (Bronx).

Under Domestic Relations Law 83, a guardian must preserve and maintain the infant's property, pay necessary taxes, keep the property in repair, and, when the child reaches majority, deliver it to the child in at least as good condition as it was when the guardian received it, except for reasonable wear and tear, along with any profits from it.[8] Again, since most guardians have joint rather than sole control, in practice the guardian has to get a court order to spend funds for repair of guardianship property.[9] The guardian must manage the child's property himself; delegating duties will not relieve him from liability for loss.[10]

A guardian must use the "prudent man" standard in managing the child's property.[11] In practice when the court receives a request to allow a specific investment, it will consider all the facts, including the liquidity of the proposed investment in case the infant should need the money during his minority.[12] When the guardian holds the funds jointly, the court usually specifies (by order) the banks where the funds should be invested and the types of account that are permissible. If a guardian places the funds in a bank other than the one directed by the court, the court can surcharge or remove him, but if the alternate investment does not cause a loss and the guardian acted in good faith, the court also has the power to ratify, retroactively, the guardian's investments if the guardian files a bond sufficient to cover the funds not held in the court-designated bank.[13]

A guardian who does not deliver the property to the child at majority arguably thereafter, holds the property in constructive trust for the child, and no statute of limitations should begin to run against the guardian unless he notifies the former ward that he is not holding the property for the ward's benefit.[14] The guardian should remain liable both to give the property back and to continue to manage it prudently.

8. See Feuring v. Siewers, 120 Misc. 720, 200 N.Y.S. 440 (Kings 1923) (unless rents and profits are available for such purposes, a guardian must get a court order to bind the corpus of an infant's estate for the expenses of repairs to real estate).

9. See Matter of Blattman, N.Y.L.J., Feb. 27, 1985, at 17, col. 4 (Westchester), where a young and inexperienced guardian withdrew from the guardianship account without a court order funds to repair damage to guardianship property, and on his accounting asked the court to approve it. The court noted his good faith and approved the expenditure, but denied him any commissions because his expenditure wasted estate assets.

10. Matter of Pinchefski, 179 A.D. 578, 166 N.Y.S. 204 (3d Dep't 1917).

11. The prudent man rule is discussed in chapter on "Fiduciaries," infra at 407–12.

12. See Matter of Ueda, N.Y.L.J., March 12, 1985, at 12, col. 2 (Bronx), where the court refused to allow a guardian to invest in an annuity under a plan that would impose substantial penalties for withdrawals during the child's minority; Matter of Blissitt, N.Y.L.J., March 20, 1985, at 13, col. 3 (Bronx), where the court did not interfere with the guardian's decision to invest the infant's money in zero coupon bonds (Certificates of Accrual on Treasury Securities), which would limit the guardian's access to the funds during the child's infancy, because it found that the mother's ability to support the child made resort to the guardianship funds unlikely.

13. See Matter of Morgan, N.Y.L.J., June 19, 1985, at 12, col. 1 (Suffolk).

14. See Matter of Wall, 179 Misc. 924, 38 N.Y.S.2d 879 (Nassau 1942).

A guardian has a fiduciary responsibility; he must adhere to the strictest standard and cannot use the property of his ward for his own purposes,[15] even with the ward's consent.[16]

2. POWER TO SELL, LEASE, EXCHANGE OR MORTGAGE GUARDIANSHIP PROPERTY

The court can authorize the guardian to sell, lease, exchange or mortgage a child's interest in real property.[17] The guardian can do so by filing a petition in which the child, if fourteen or over, can join. The petition must describe the realty, the interests of the child both in the realty and in other assets, and the financial needs of the child. The petition must also state why the sale, lease, exchange or mortgage is in the child's best interests. The court has discretion to entertain the proceeding; if it does, it issues process to the child (if not a petitioner), to the parents,[18] if there are no parents to the adult residing with the child, and if the child is married, to his spouse. If the guardian cannot serve the necessary parties, he must tell the court, in the petition or in an affidavit, that he does not know of their existence or whereabouts, or that he tried diligently to serve them but could not do so. The court can dispense with service of process and give whatever directions are necessary to protect the child's interests.

On the return date, the court hears proof and issues an order directing the executor to sell or take whatever other steps are required by justice and the child's best interests. Any instrument the guardian executes relating to the real property has the same effect as if the infant were of full age and executed it himself. The court can also ratify any leases made by the guardian on the infant's behalf, thus retroactively approving them.

Of course a guardian cannot commence this proceeding if it violates the terms of the will or deed creating the child's interest.[19]

Real Property Actions and Proceedings Law contains, in Article 17, rules on the disposition of realty of an infant or incompetent. Technically, a proceeding to obtain authorization to sell, lease, etc., can be brought in the Supreme Court under that statute. However, if a guardian has already been appointed, the Surrogate's Court controls that guardian wherever appointed,[20] and the guardian must bring the proceeding in the Surrogate's Court and get approval under SCPA

15. See Matter of Walker, 17 N.Y.S.2d 918 (Chinango 1940), affirmed 260 App.Div. 835, 22 N.Y.S.2d 420 (3d Dep't 1940); Rooney v. Wiener, 147 Misc. 48, 263 N.Y.S. 222 (Kings 1933).

16. A will or trust beneficiary of full age can consent to a breach of fiduciary duty, except that McKinney's EPTL 11–1.7 provides that a fiduciary cannot be exonerated from gross negligence.

17. McKinney's SCPA 1715.

18. Note that the exceptions of McKinney's SCPA 1705 for parents who have abandoned the child, etc., do not appear in this section.

19. McKinney's SCPA 1715.

20. See "Appointment of Guardian by Supreme Court or Another Court," supra at 271–72.

Article 17 rather than RPAPL Article 17. The latter is useful when a guardian has not been appointed for a child.

SCPA Article 19 also contains rules on the sale of real property to meet an estate's cash needs. It is expressly inapplicable to guardians.[21] Thus SCPA Article 17 is left to do the job.

SECTION S. POWER TO MANAGE PROPERTY VESTED IN AN INFANT

Often a will provides that an infant's interest in an estate should vest immediately on the decedent's death, but that the child should not actually get the property until the age of majority. Instead, the property is held until the child reaches majority by the person named in the will, usually the executor or the child's parent, guardian, or Uniform Gift to Minors Act custodian. This is called the granting of a power to manage funds during minority, formerly known as a power in trust, and the fiduciary is called the donee of the power to manage funds during minority. His powers are those the testator gave him by the will. Typically the powers are to apply income and principal in his discretion for the child's support and education until the child reaches twenty-one and then to pay the principal outright to the child.[1]

The power to manage funds during minority also springs into being when the testator ineffectually nominates someone as guardian, such as the case where a parent designates someone other than his spouse as guardian. The court will not grant the nominee letters of guardianship over the child, but it will grant letters as donee of a power to manage the child's property during minority.[2] His powers are not the (typically) broad powers of the fiduciary described in the last paragraph whom the testator deliberately appointed by will.[3] Rather he has the powers of a guardian of property with respect to the assets that pass to the child in the will; he must file annual accounts,[4] unless the will directs otherwise, and he is entitled to commissions allowed a guardian.[5] If the decedent improperly nominated someone other than the spouse as guardian, and the spouse consents to that appointment and waives process, the nominated guardian will serve as actual guardian of the child's property, not just as donee of the power to manage the child's property, but in practice their functions are the same.

21. McKinney's SCPA 1901. See chapter on "Disposition of Real Property," infra at 470 et seq.

Sec. S

1. See, e.g., Matter of Toerge, 102 Misc. 2d 592, 424 N.Y.S.2d 95 (Nassau 1980).

2. See McKinney's EPTL 10–3.1. As a guardian of the property, the donee of a power in trust must petition for letters appointing him donee of the power to manage funds during minority. See McKinney's SCPA 1714 (such guardian is subject to the provisions of Article 17); Matter of Biederman, 186 Misc. 625, 57 N.Y.S.2d 560 (N.Y. County 1945).

3. See Matter of Fuchs, 10 Misc.2d 997, 170 N.Y.S.2d 480 (New York County 1957).

4. See discussion of when annual accounts are required this chapter supra at 269–71.

5. See chapter on "Commissions," infra at 428–29.

SECTION T. GUARDIAN'S COMMISSIONS

A guardian is a fiduciary entitled to commissions for his services. The guardian's commissions are governed by SCPA 2307, the details of which we discuss in another chapter.[1] If the decree makes an allowance of more than $200 for the guardian, the guardian must file a form with the Office of Court Administration. The form (available from the court) is the same as that used by guardians ad litem.

SECTION U. FOREIGN GUARDIAN'S AUTHORITY TO ACT IN NEW YORK

Sometimes a child from another state[1] has a right to property in New York or a right to bring a lawsuit in New York. If the child has a guardian appointed in another state, that out-of-state guardian cannot exercise guardianship powers in New York unless he petitions for letters of ancillary guardianship.[2] That is true even if the child is a New York domiciliary whose guardian was appointed while the child temporarily resided in another state; that appointment is not binding in New York.[3] It does not, however, prevent an out-of-state guardian from receiving money located outside New York on the ward's behalf.[4]

1. THE PROCEEDING

The court can issue ancillary letters of guardianship, which give the ancillary guardian the authority to transact business on the child's behalf, if the petitioner demonstrates the need for the appointment. To be appointed, the foreign guardian must submit a petition showing that a court of competent jurisdiction in his own state has granted him letters of guardianship, and he must have given security in his home state at least equal to the value of the child's personal property and the rents and profits from real property. He must describe the initial appointment and list the child's assets and any debts to New York domiciliaries. The security posted in the other jurisdiction must be sufficient to cover the out-of-state property as well as the property the guardian hopes to obtain in this state.[5]

The petitioner must also submit authenticated copies of the papers properly sealed by the court proving due appointment and proof[6] of

Sec. T

1. See chapter on "Commissions," infra at 425 et seq.

Sec. U

1. McKinney's SCPA 1716 refers to an infant domiciled in a state of the United States, the District of Columbia, the Commonwealth of Puerto Rico or a territory or possession of the United States.

2. See Wuesthoff v. Germania Life Insurance Co., 107 N.Y. 580, 14 N.E. 811 (1888); Matter of Farrell, 97 Misc.2d 18, 410 N.Y.S.2d 775 (Bronx 1978).

3. Sengstack v. Sengstack, 4 N.Y.2d 502, 176 N.Y.S.2d 337, 151 N.E.2d 887 (1958).

4. McKinney's SCPA 1716(4). See Matter of Feltrinelli, 159 N.Y.S.2d 563 (N.Y. County 1956) (New York guardian accountable only for New York property).

5. McKinney's SCPA 1716(1).

6. McKinney's SCPA 1716(4).

adequate security in the other jurisdiction.[7] If he does, the petition and attached proofs will be conclusive evidence of the facts stated in them.

The court can even issue ancillary letters to a non-New York bank that would otherwise not be entitled to receive them [8] by ordering the bank to file a bond to secure the assets.[9]

A comparable set of rules exists for a child who resides in a foreign country with a right to New York property or a right to maintain a New York lawsuit. A foreign guardian may petition for, and receive, letter of ancillary guardianship even if he is a non-domiciliary alien, which he could not do for any other type of fiduciary letters.[10] The foreign guardian may petition for ancillary letters in the county where the property is located or where the action or proceeding would be brought. The petition requires the same facts regarding the appointment, debts and securities as those required of an applicant from another state. The petitioner must submit copies of the records of appointment, authenticated by the court or officer who made the appointment, and the signature of the judge or officer must be further authenticated by a sealed certificate under the principal seal of the Department of Foreign Affairs or the Department of Justice of the foreign country and attested by the signature or seal of the United States consul. If the appointment was by statute and not by a court, the petitioner must submit proof of the foreign law. Compliance with these rules will cause the petition and attached papers to be conclusive evidence of the facts they contain.[11]

If the court is satisfied that appointment of an ancillary guardian would be in the child's best interests, it may issue a decree appointing one.[12] The decree may be made without process, or the court may direct process to be served on parties it considers proper. Before granting ancillary letters, the court may direct that any debts owing from the child to a New York domiciliary be paid, or that security be given to cover the debt. The ancillary guardian must qualify by filing an oath and designation.[13] If adequate security was posted at the domicile, the court can issue ancillary letters without additional security.[14]

7. McKinney's SCPA 1716(4).

8. That is, under McKinney's Banking L. § 131 (1971).

9. McKinney's SCPA 1716(3).

10. McKinney's SCPA 707, governing fiduciaries, states:

> Letters may issue to a natural person or to a person authorized by law to be a fiduciary except as follows:
>
> (1) * * *
>
> (c) a non-domiciliary alien except in the case of a foreign guardian as prescribed in 1716(4).

11. McKinney's SCPA 1716(4).

12. McKinney's SCPA 1717.

13. McKinney's SCPA 708, discussed in chapter on "Fiduciaries," infra at 391–92.

14. McKinney's SCPA 1718.

2. THE ANCILLARY GUARDIAN'S POWERS

The ancillary guardian can collect personal property, the rents and profits of real property and the proceeds of sale, mortgage or lease of the infant's real property.[15] The letters also authorize the guardian to dispose of the infant's assets as a domestic guardian could, to remove them from the state, and to maintain any action or special proceeding in New York on the child's behalf. They do not, however, authorize an ancillary guardian to receive the child's money or other property from a New York guardian unless the domiciliary guardian's letters have been revoked or the court orders the delivery for good cause.[16]

SECTION V. SURROGATE'S JURISDICTION OVER CUSTODIANS

Under EPTL Article 7, New York's version of the Uniform Gifts to Minors Act,[1] a person may make a gift to a minor by transferring property to a custodian. The Surrogate's Court has jurisdiction of both the infants and the custodians.[2]

SECTION W. GUARDIANS OF MENTALLY RETARDED PERSONS

1. INTRODUCTION

A mentally retarded person's inability to make personal and financial decisions may, unlike a child's, very well continue past the age of majority. A special proceeding was added in Article 17A of the SCPA in 1969 to ensure that a guardian can serve for the entire lifetime of a mentally retarded person.[1] Under former practice, the guardianship lasted only until the age of majority of the mentally retarded person, and then a conservator or committee had to be appointed.

Occasionally even under the current law a court (frequently a court other than the Surrogate's Court) opts to appoint a conservator to manage a large personal injury recovery because it is clear that the mentally retarded child will not be able to manage his affairs upon reaching majority.[2] The appointment of a conservator is an alternative to an Article 17–A appointment, and both alternatives are proper.

While the Supreme Court and the Family Court have concurrent jurisdiction with the Surrogate to appoint guardians for minors, the 17–A guardian is appointed only by the Surrogate. The normal rules governing guardianships for children, contained in SCPA Article 17 and discussed in this chapter, also govern guardianships of mentally retard-

15. McKinney's SCPA 1718(2).

16. McKinney's SCPA 1718(3).

Sec. V

1. McKinney's EPTL 7–4.1 to 7–4.9.

2. McKinney's SCPA 1724.

Sec. W

1. L.1969, c. 1143.

2. See, e.g., Matter of Ramos, 111 Misc. 2d 1078, 445 N.Y.S.2d 891 (Bronx 1981).

ed persons unless Article 17A provides otherwise.[3] Article 17A provides for different levels of guardianship, depending on the extent of the mental retardation and the ability of the retarded person to manage his own affairs and gain employment. In most cases, either or both parents are named guardian of the mentally retarded person, but usually the court also names a "stand-by" guardian to take over on the death of the survivor of the parents. This stand-by guardian can qualify before the death of the parents and assume the duties of guardianship immediately on the death of the parent.

The guardian of a mentally retarded person is then authorized to make decisions in place of the mentally retarded person.

2. THE PROCEEDING

Proceedings for appointment of a guardian can be commenced at any time, regardless of the age of the mentally retarded person. A mentally retarded person is defined as one incapable of managing his affairs because of mental retardation,[4] and the court cannot appoint a guardian unless it is satisfied that the person is in fact mentally retarded.[5] Two licensed physicians, or one physician and one psychologist having qualifications to make such certification, must certify that the person is retarded, and that the condition is permanent.[6] The court may then appoint a guardian of the person or the property, or both.

The court may make the appointment without a hearing on the application of both parents or the surviving parent, or one parent with the consent of the other.[7] In addition, an interested person can apply, with the consent of each parent.[8]

If one parent petitions and the other has not consented, the court must hold a hearing, and the non-consenting parent must be cited. The court can also appoint a guardian on the petition of any interested person without the consent of the parents, so long as the parents have been cited and the court has held a hearing.[9]

If a parent has abandoned the mentally retarded person, the court can dispense with his consent and even the service of process and a hearing.[10] The abandonment may have been determined by another competent court, such as the Family Court, and even if proceedings were held elsewhere, the court can order a hearing on the issue of abandonment if it feels that is appropriate.

3. McKinney's SCPA 1755.

4. McKinney's SCPA 1750.

5. Because of this requirement, the court also observes the demeanor of the mentally retarded person and weighs that into the decision whether to appoint a guardian. See Matter of Krakoff, N.Y.L.J., Feb. 27, 1985, at 13, col. 4 (Bronx).

6. McKinney's SCPA 1750.

7. McKinney's SCPA 1750(1)(a), (b).

8. McKinney's SCPA 1750(1)(c).

9. McKinney's SCPA 1750(2).

10. McKinney's SCPA 1750(2).

In practice when the parents are the petitioners, the court usually does not require a hearing unless there is a contest, and when someone other than a close relative applies, the court does require a hearing.[11]

3. LIMITED GUARDIANSHIP

If a mentally retarded person is an adult who, though able to work, needs some protection, the court can issue limited letters of guardianship.[12] Under this arrangement the mentally retarded person can receive, spend and manage his wages, and the "limited guardian" will manage the funds that come from other sources. The mentally retarded person in that case can also bind himself by contract for a sum of money not exceeding one month's wages or $300, whichever is greater.[13]

4. DURATION OF GUARDIANSHIP

The guardianship of the property of a mentally retarded person continues for life unless the court terminates it. The guardianship of the person terminates on the ward's marriage.[14] If a "17–A" guardian was appointed during the mentally retarded person's minority, when he reaches eighteen he may petition the court, or someone else may petition on his behalf, for an order discharging the guardian and appointing a successor, or changing the status of the guardian to a limited guardian. Proper venue for this proceeding is in the Surrogate's Court that appointed the guardian or the Surrogate's Court in the county where the ward resides. The court will conduct a hearing, and the mentally retarded person is entitled to be present and to have the matter tried by a jury. The same is true if a proceeding is commenced for appointment of a guardian for a mentally retarded person over the age of eighteen. If he (or the person who commenced the proceeding) does not demand a jury trial, he waives it. If the certifying professionals state in their report that the ward is incapable of understanding the proceedings, the court may dispense with the ward's appearance.[15]

5. STAND–BY GUARDIANSHIP

The court can appoint a standby guardian of the mentally retarded person's property and person on the application of both parents, the survivor of them, or if they are both deceased, the guardian of the child.[16] The court can also name an alternate standby guardian whose duty will be to act if the standby guardian dies or becomes incapacitated or renounces. Under the statute, curiously, only the parent, and not a guardian, can petition for the appointment of an alternate standby. There is no logical reason for this distinction and the statute should be changed. The standby or the alternate standby usually qualifies (files

11. McKinney's SCPA 1750, Prac. Comm. at 21 (Supp.1986), for a discussion of the procedure if neither parent is living.

12. McKinney's SCPA 1751.

13. McKinney's SCPA 1751.

14. McKinney's SCPA 1752.

15. McKinney's SCPA 1752.

16. McKinney's SCPA 1753(1).

an oath and designation [17]) when the petition is filed, and if he has, on the death or resignation of his predecessor guardian, he can assume the guardianship duties immediately, and the court must then confirm his appointment within sixty days.

The court can appoint and issue letters to several alternate standby guardians at once, to take over successively as their predecessors resign.[18] If the mentally retarded person is over eighteen, the court will not confirm the standby guardian's appointment without a hearing at which the mentally retarded person appears and has a right to a jury trial. The court can dispense with his appearance if it is convinced that the mentally retarded person could not understand the proceeding.

The court retains jurisdiction over the mentally retarded person after the appointment of a standby, and can, on its own motion or on the petition of others, take steps to ensure that the retarded person's best interests are served.[19]

6. CORPORATE GUARDIANSHIP

Although no corporation can be appointed guardian of the person of a mentally retarded person, an exception is made for non-profit corporations whose charters include the power to act as guardian of mentally retarded persons.[20] In such cases, the corporation will serve as guardian only of the person, and not of the property, of the ward. Often organizations such as the Association for the Help of Retarded Children will have such corporate powers, and parents will designate those institutions as standby or alternate standby guardians in case close relatives cannot assume guardianship of the person of the mentally retarded person.

17. To qualify, the guardian must sign an oath that he will faithfully discharge his duties, designate the court clerk to receive process, and file a bond if necessary (usually unnecessary because assets are held jointly with bank or clerk of the court). See SCPA 708 and chapter on "Fiduciaries," infra at 391–92.

18. See Matter of Caldicott, N.Y.L.J., April 29, 1985, at 16, col. 3 (Suffolk) (letters issued to two guardians, a first alternate stand-by and a second alternate stand-by).

19. McKinney's SCPA 1753(2).

20. McKinney's SCPA 1754.

Chapter Ten

TEMPORARY ADMINISTRATION

SECTION A. INTRODUCTION

In an ideal world, a fiduciary would be appointed soon after a decedent's death. The named executor in the will would offer it for probate and would receive letters testamentary, or at least preliminary letters.[1] If the decedent had no will, an appropriate relative would petition for letters of administration.[2] The executor or administrator would then be able to collect the assets and take the steps necessary to preserve them: sell depreciating securities, exercise options or meet any deadlines relating to estate property.

It is not an ideal world, though, and sometimes the fiduciary's appointment is delayed. SCPA Article 9 creates a remedy for this delay: temporary administration. A temporary administrator can collect and conserve the assets of the estate which might otherwise be subject to waste.[3]

Article 9 allows temporary letters to be issued in four situations. The first two,[4] temporary administration of the estates of actual or alleged decedents, differ a great deal from the second two,[5] temporary administration of the estates of absentees or internees. The former two categories envision an administrator who is truly temporary, appointed to take care of an emergency (or something close to an emergency) when someone is dead, something needs to be done, and a "permanent" administrator is not yet in place. The second two categories envision (or at least allow for) a fiduciary relationship of longer duration, where a temporary administrator is appointed to administer the property of a person who cannot do it for himself, because he is either missing or imprisoned in an enemy country.

Like most proceedings in the Surrogate's Court, the proceeding for appointment of a temporary administrator is commenced by a petition, after which the court issues process, usually in the form of a citation (and rarely in the form of an order to show cause), for service on parties

Sec. A

1. Preliminary letters are discussed in chapter on "Probate," supra at 118–24.

2. See chapter on "Administration," supra at 125 et seq.

3. See Matter of Ort, 217 A.D. 422, 217 N.Y.S. 46 (3d Dep't 1926); Matter of Young, 133 N.Y.S.2d 387 (Suffolk 1954).

4. McKinney's SCPA 901(1).

5. McKinney's SCPA 901(2), (3).

whose interests would be affected by the appointment.[6] The procedure for obtaining temporary letters can vary a great deal, however, depending on whether they are for the estate of a true decedent, an alleged decedent, or an absentee or internee. Those procedures are the subject of this chapter.

SECTION B. TEMPORARY ADMINISTRATION—DECEDENTS

The Surrogate can grant temporary letters in a decedent's estate when a delay occurs in commencing a proceeding to obtain letters testamentary or letters of administration.[1]

Temporary administration occurs far more often in estates of intestate decedents than decedents who died with a will. The reason is that if the decedent had a will, the court usually appoints the named executor as preliminary executor if a delay occurs,[2] obviating the need for a temporary administrator. This helps to promote confidence on the part of the living that their estates will be administered, even temporarily, according to their wishes.[3] Statistically, most estates are administered by executors rather than administrators,[4] so when there is a delay, a preliminary executor is appointed more often than a temporary administrator. Occasionally, however, the court will for good cause refuse to grant the named executor preliminary letters,[5] and will appoint a temporary administrator.

6. For a discussion of the petition and process generally, see chapter on "Procedure," supra at 39–55.

Sec. B

1. McKinney's SCPA 901(1). In an interesting and correct interpretation of McKinney's SCPA 901, the appellate division ruled that the Surrogate could not grant letters of temporary administration to the public administrator after previously issuing preliminary letters testamentary to the executor named in the will, against whom a charge of undue influence had been leveled after his appointment as preliminary executor. Matter of Vermilye, 101 A.D.2d 865, 475 N.Y.S.2d 888 (2d Dep't 1984). The court reasoned that the situation was not one in which delays had occurred in probate, as required by McKinney's SCPA 901. The allegations of undue influence were "bald," and the Surrogate therefore should not have effectively revoked the preliminary letters.

The state Supreme Court has concurrent jurisdiction with the Surrogate to issue letters of temporary administration. See Faulk v. Aware, 35 Misc.2d 302, 315, 231 N.Y.S.2d 270 (New York County 1962), reversed on other grounds, 19 A.D.2d 464, 244 N.Y.S.2d 259 (1st Dep't 1963), affirmed 14 N.Y.2d 899, 252 N.Y.S.2d 95, 200 N.E.2d 778 (1964), remittitur amended 14 N.Y. 954, 253 N.Y.S.2d 990, 202 N.E.2d 372 (1964), certiorari denied 380 U.S. 916, 85 S.Ct. 900, 13 L.Ed.2d 801 (1965), rehearing denied 380 U.S. 989, 85 S.Ct. 1328, 14 L.Ed. 2d 282 (1965) where the Supreme Court in a defamation action properly appointed a temporary administrator after the death of a defendant. See also Matter of Malloy, 278 N.Y. 429, 17 N.E.2d 108 (1938).

2. McKinney's SCPA 1412, discussed in chapter on "Probate," supra at 118–24.

3. This has long been the policy in New York. Even prior to the enactment of McKinney's SCPA 1412, the courts tended to appoint the nominated executor, rather than an outsider, as temporary administrator. See Matter of Erlanger, 136 Misc. 793, 242 N.Y.S. 249 (New York County 1930), affirmed 229 App.Div. 778, 242 N.Y.S. 910 (1st Dep't 1930).

4. For instance, in Nassau County less than a quarter of the estates are administered by administrators and the balance are administered by executors nominated in wills of decedents.

5. E.g., Matter of Mastro, N.Y.L.J., May 4, 1979, at 15, col. 4 (Suffolk) (named exec-

The court will appoint a temporary administrator if something has come up that requires action, such as the need to exercise a conversion option on convertible debentures subject to strict time limits,[6] to pay rents and preserve real property,[7] or to protect the decedent's contractual rights under an agreement to sell his business.[8]

SECTION C. TEMPORARY ADMINISTRATION—ALLEGED DECEDENTS

If a person is missing continuously for five years, and his family has searched diligently for him, and there is no reasonable explanation of his absence, he can be "declared dead" by the court.[1] His official date of death is five years after the disappearance, or an earlier date if he was exposed to a specific peril[2] such as a shipwreck, boating accident,[3] or plane crash.[4] The petitioner bears the burden of proving all the elements,[5] and typically presents detailed evidence of the search and of the alleged decedent's positive state of mind, and testimony by the last persons to have seen the missing person. If the petitioner meets the burden, at the end of five years, or earlier in cases where he was exposed to a danger, the court can declare the missing person dead, probate his will, appoint an executor or administrator, order distribution of his estate and approve an accounting, not because of his absence, but because of his death. If he later returns, he can recover his

utor not appointed because she had induced decedent to sell major asset at low price and upset testamentary scheme); Matter of Mann, N.Y.L.J., Apr. 10, 1978, at 12, col. 1 (each nominated fiduciary charged the other with partiality). But see Matter of Iffland, N.Y.L.J., Jan. 20, 1979, at 14, col. 2 (allegation of fraud by named executor not ground for refusing to grant preliminary letters); Matter of Ellenberg, N.Y.L.J., June 12, 1978, at 13, col. 6 (named executor appointed despite claims against the estate).

6. See Timpone v. Concord Enterprises, 93 Misc.2d 691, 403 N.Y.S.2d 457 (Richmond 1978).

7. See Matter of Howard, 93 Misc.2d 620, 403 N.Y.S.2d 455 (Nassau 1978).

8. Matter of Gray, N.Y.L.J., Feb. 28, 1985, at 15, col. 5 (Nassau).

Sec. C

1. McKinney's EPTL 2–1.7; Butler v. Mutual Life Insurance Co., 225 N.Y. 197, 121 N.E. 758 (1919); Kutner v. New England Mutual Life Insurance Co., 57 A.D.2d 697, 395 N.Y.S.2d 540 (4th Dep't 1977).

2. McKinney's EPTL 2–1.7(a)(1).

3. See Matter of Vigilant, N.Y.L.J., June 24, 1985, at 27, col. 1 (Suffolk), where a man was declared dead on the date his ship was apparently destroyed in a storm; Matter of Rice, N.Y.L.J., June 19, 1985, at 12, col. 5 (Suffolk), where a man was declared dead on the date the boat on which he was riding overturned; Matter of Conrad, 109 Misc.2d 756, 440 N.Y.S.2d 991 (Westchester 1981) (accord).

4. See Matter of Votino, N.Y.L.J., June 21, 1985, at 14, col. 3 (Suffolk), where a man was declared dead on the date an airplane on which he was a passenger was apparently destroyed in a crash.

5. See Matter of Layh, 55 Misc.2d 92, 284 N.Y.S.2d 511 (Nassau 1967); Matter of Katz, 135 Misc. 861, 239 N.Y.S. 722 (Kings 1930); Matter of Krugman, N.Y.L.J., June 6, 1985, at 14, col. 5 (Nassau) (alleged decedent mixed up with criminals who committed the Lufthansa heist at Kennedy Airport, nine of whom had been murdered or had disappeared). If the petitioner believes that the insurance company which insured the missing person's life has information relevant to his fate, the petitioner should examine the insurance company, ascertain the nature of the documents and ask the Surrogate to order their production, which the Surrogate will do if they are not exempt as material prepared for litigation or attorney's work product.

property.[6] As in the case of a proven decedent, if a delay occurs in the granting of letters of administration or letters testamentary, the court can appoint a temporary administrator to handle an emergency situation that needs immediate attention.[7]

In addition, in the five-year period between the disappearance and the declaration of death, there will very likely be a need to make decisions and take actions in connection with the missing person's property. The alleged decedent can be treated as an absentee as soon as he disappears so that the court can appoint a temporary administrator to administer his affairs in his absence. We discuss absentees presently.

In practice, often a petitioner seeking to have a missing person declared dead petitions for a declaration of death and, in case the evidence of death is insufficient, alternatively seeks temporary letters in the estate of an absentee.

SECTION D. TEMPORARY ADMINISTRATION—ABSENTEES

If a person has disappeared but the disappearance does not point inexorably to his death, the court cannot declare him dead and issue letters testamentary or letters of administration in his estate.[1] In that case the remedy is to seek appointment of an administrator for an absentee. Whether or not a missing person is believed to be dead, a temporary administrator may be appointed to administer his property. The absence need not be mysterious; the absentee may in fact have hinted that his departure was related to dissatisfaction with his life style or other reasons. The absentee is simply a person who is missing without explanation and who has not been found despite a diligent search.[2] No one has to claim or believe that he is dead; upon his disappearance, the court can appoint a temporary administrator to handle his affairs [3] and if he fails to return within ten years, the court can distribute his estate as though he were dead.[4] The temporary administrator's role is not so much to deal with an emergency as to preserve the estate, which otherwise may be subject to waste. The petitioner seeks only appointment of a temporary administrator, not letters testamentary or letters of administration as he would for a person allegedly deceased.

After the petitioner has filed the petition, the court issues process for service on the absentee and his distributees (more precisely, those

6. McKinney's SCPA 2226.

7. McKinney's SCPA 901(1).

Sec. D

1. See, e.g., Matter of Gregory, N.Y.L.J., May 20, 1985, at 19, col. 1 (Nassau), where a man had not been seen by his wife or son for twenty years, but the court could not declare him dead because the petitioner (the missing man's wife) could not meet her burden of proof that there was no explanation for his absence other than death.

2. McKinney's SCPA 901(2).

3. McKinney's SCPA 902(6).

4. McKinney's SCPA 911(3).

who would have been his distributees if he had died the day the petition was filed).[5] On the return date the court holds a hearing at which it determines when the absentee was last heard from and sets that date as the date of the absentee's disappearance.[6] Ten years from that date, the court can start in motion a process in which the absentee loses all interest in his property: the court requires an accounting by the temporary administrator, requires (by publication) the absentee to show cause why his assets should not be distributed, and decrees that the estate be paid to persons who would have received it if the absentee had died at the end of the ten-year period.[7] If the absentee ever returns, he has no right to get his property back.[8]

The temporary administrator must be in office for at least one year before the court can make this decree. Thus, if no proceedings were commenced until nine or more years after the disappearance, the court would have to order at least one year of temporary administration.[9]

The court can order the temporary administrator to use the absentee's funds to support his dependents or to search for him.[10]

If the absentee (or his fiduciary) comes back before the final decree, he can get back whatever is left of his property.[11]

SECTION E. TEMPORARY ADMINISTRATION—INTERNEES

Like the absentee, an internee is a person who because of his absence cannot look after his own property. An internee is "one who has been made a prisoner of war or has been detained or interned by an enemy country or in an enemy-occupied country or by any force in a foreign country, whether legal or illegal * * *." [1] The country need not be officially at war with the United States.

A temporary administrator for an internee functions much like a guardian for a child. The temporary administrator must account annually for the internee's property, or in the alternative must keep it deposited jointly with a bank designated by the court.[2] The court can authorize the temporary administrator to use the internee's funds to support his dependents or to search for him.[3] Whenever the internee returns, even more than ten years after his internment, he can get his property back.[4]

5. McKinney's SCPA 902(3).

6. McKinney's SCPA 902(3).

7. McKinney's SCPA 911(3). See Matter of Battha, 97 Misc.2d 405, 411 N.Y.S.2d 531 (Erie 1978).

8. McKinney's SCPA 911(3).

9. McKinney's SCPA 911(3).

10. McKinney's SCPA 907.

11. McKinney's SCPA 911(2).

Sec. E

1. McKinney's SCPA 901(3).

2. McKinney's SCPA 910(1), (2); McKinney's SCPA 909. If he fails to account, interested parties can bring a proceeding against him as prescribed in McKinney's SCPA 1722, discussed in chapter on "Guardianships," supra at 271. McKinney's SCPA 910(3).

3. McKinney's SCPA 907(2).

4. McKinney's SCPA 910(4).

SECTION F. PROCEDURES FOR APPOINTMENT OF A TEMPORARY ADMINISTRATOR

1. WHO CAN PETITION

As a preliminary note, the Surrogate will not appoint a temporary administrator unless the petitioner can show real need for it.[1] If the court does find it necessary, it can appoint (i) any person interested as an absolute or contingent beneficiary of the decedent's estate or anyone who would be a beneficiary if the alleged decedent, absentee or internee were dead, (ii) a creditor,[2] (iii) a beneficiary named in a will of the decedent or alleged decedent on file in the court [3] (iv) a party to a lawsuit to which the decedent or absentee, alleged decedent or internee would have been a party, or (v) the public administrator and county treasurer.[4]

The statute does not create any priorities; the court has discretion as to the person to be appointed.[5] The court can also impose reasonable conditions on the appointment. If the parties all agree, the court's decision is easy. If a person objects to the appointment of the petitioner, he should make those objections known to the court or if the court has already appointed the petitioner, the objectant should appeal or move to vacate the order.[6] If objections are made, the court must determine whether the temporary administrator it is considering or has appointed will serve the best interests of the estate.[7] One of the factors the courts will consider are the expenses. Since the ultimate administrator or executor who also serves on an intermediate basis as temporary administrator will receive only one full commission,[8] the courts tend

Sec. F

1. See Matter of Curtis, 194 A.D. 334, 185 N.Y.S. 507 (1st Dep't 1920), affirmed 231 N.Y. 632, 132 N.E. 917 (1921); Matter of Larsen, 137 Misc. 271, 242 N.Y.S. 486 (Kings 1930).

2. McKinney's SCPA 902(7). See Matter of Gaul, 6 A.D.2d 949, 176 N.Y.S.2d 190 (1958), where the court ruled that the named corporate executor in the will, a creditor of the decedent, should be appointed temporary administrator, unless the contestants could prove that the trust company was not disinterested. The statute clearly states that a creditor can petition for appointment.

3. Under McKinney's SCPA 2508, the Surrogate will accept wills for safekeeping, either from the testator during his lifetime or from interested parties after his death.

4. McKinney's SCPA 902(7).

5. See Matter of Pearson, 228 A.D. 418, 239 N.Y.S. 653 (3d Dep't 1930) Matter of Watson, 123 Misc. 323, 205 N.Y.S. 380 (Westchester 1924), affirmed 209 A.D. 876, 205 N.Y.S. 382 (2d Dep't 1924); Matter of Gray, N.Y.L.J., Feb. 28, 1985, at 15, col. 5 (Nassau); Matter of McGuire, 47 Misc.2d 158, 261 N.Y.S.2d 974 (Nassau 1965).

6. See Matter of Briger, 95 A.D.2d 887, 464 N.Y.S.2d 31 (3d Dep't 1983) (widow's failure to appeal or move to vacate resulted in affirmance of Surrogate's order appointing named executor as temporary administrator).

7. See Matter of Craig, 8 Misc.2d 231, 166 N.Y.S.2d 101 (Nassau 1957), where the court appointed a business associate of the decedent's, over the contestant's objections, because it felt that his knowledge of the decedent's affairs would facilitate administration of the estate.

8. McKinney's SCPA 2307(5).

to appoint as temporary administrator the one most likely to be the eventual permanent fiduciary of the estate.[9]

If strong hostility exists among the parties, the court will appoint an "outsider" (such as a bank) as temporary administrator.[10] Similarly, if the contestants allege that someone forged the will or that the testator wrote it under duress or undue influence, the court will appoint a disinterested, neutral temporary administrator rather than the executor named in the will.[11]

2. VENUE

If the decedent, alleged decedent, absentee or internee was a New York domiciliary, the petitioner for temporary administration files in the court of the county of the decedent's (or alleged decedent's, absentee's or internee's) domicile.[12] If that person was not a New York domiciliary, the petitioner files in the county where the property is.[13] If the decedent, alleged decedent, absentee or internee left property in more than one county, the first county to entertain a proceeding becomes the proper venue for the proceeding.[14]

3. PERSONS ENTITLED TO PROCESS

After the petitioner files, the type of proceeding and the circumstances determine whether service of process is necessary; if it is, the court issues process, usually a citation or, less often, an order to show cause, which the petitioner then serves.

When the petitioner seeks temporary administration in probate or administration proceedings, the court decides who should get process and how it should be served,[15] and can dispense with process entirely if that serves the estate's best interests,[16] for example, if a fiduciary must

9. See Matter of Hillman, 280 App.Div. 310, 113 N.Y.S.2d 409 (1st Dep't 1952), affirmed 305 N.Y. 577, 111 N.E.2d 446 (1953), reargument denied 305 N.Y. 797, 113 N.E.2d 305 (1953); Matter of Erlanger, 136 Misc. 793, 242 N.Y.S. 249 (New York County 1930), affirmed 229 App.Div. 778, 242 N.Y.S. 910 (1st Dep't 1930).

10. See Matter of McGuire, 47 Misc.2d 158, 261 N.Y.S.2d 974 (Nassau 1965).

11. Matter of Mottek, 6 Misc.2d 934, 162 N.Y.S.2d 310 (Nassau 1957); Matter of Burnham, 114 Misc. 455, 186 N.Y.S. 520 (Westchester 1921). See also Matter of Weisberg, 286 App.Div. 850, 141 N.Y.S.2d 386 (2d Dep't 1955), where two of the three named executors were accused of fraud and undue influence, and the court appointed the third, who received nothing under the will and was a reputable attorney, as temporary administrator.

12. All Surrogates in New York have subject matter jurisdiction, but the only proper venue is the county of domicile. SCPA 205. See discussion of subject matter jurisdiction and venue in chapter on "Jurisdiction," supra at 2–8.

13. McKinney's SCPA 206(1).

14. McKinney's SCPA 206(2).

15. McKinney's SCPA 902(1).

16. McKinney's SCPA 902(5). See Matter of Bayley, 72 Misc.2d 312, 339 N.Y.S.2d 129 (Suffolk 1972), affirmed 40 A.D.2d 843, 337 N.Y.S.2d 500 (2d Dep't 1972), appeal dismissed 31 N.Y.2d 1025, 341 N.Y.S.2d 898, 294 N.E.2d 658 (1973). The named executor in a will, who failed to offer the will for probate, moved to vacate the decree appointing a temporary administrator on the ground that the application for temporary letters falsely represented that the executor had declined to file or probate the will. The court dismissed his motion to vacate the appointment, noting that even if the will had been offered for probate, the Surrogate had discretion to dispense with service on the executor, and it could dis-

be appointed to commence an action on behalf of the estate on which the statute of limitations is about to run.[17]

If no proceeding is pending and the petitioner seeks temporary letters in the estate of an intestate decedent or alleged decedent, the court issues process to the persons who would be entitled to receive process in an administration proceeding,[18] but the court can dispense with service on those persons in its discretion.[19]

If no probate proceeding is pending, and the petitioner seeks temporary letters in the estate of a decedent or alleged decedent with a will, the court issues process to the executor named in the last will on file in the Surrogate's Court and to the beneficiaries named in that instrument, and to such other persons it considers necessary. The court can in its discretion dispense with service on any of these persons.[20]

If the petitioner seeks temporary letters in the estate of an internee, the court issues process to the persons who would be his distributees if he had died on the date of the filing of the petition.[21] The court can in its discretion dispense with service on these parties.[22]

In all cases except the estate of an absentee, the court can appoint a temporary administrator without service of process or any notice to the parties. The reason is that the court must be able to put someone at the helm immediately if it finds that giving notice to all interested parties would cause a delay adverse to the best interests of the estate.

The court has no such discretion in the case of an absentee. There it must order process served on the absentee and the persons who would be his distributees if he had died on the date the petition was filed.[23] It must also appoint a guardian ad litem to receive process for the absentee and to represent his interests. If the circumstances warrant it, the court can, while the proceeding for appointment of a temporary administrator is pending, issue an injunction against the transfer of any of the absentee's property.[24]

While the court cannot dispense with process in the estate of an absentee, it may appoint a temporary administrator immediately after

pense with service under the facts at bar because the dispensation was in the best interests of the estate.

17. See, e.g., Matter of Bordeman, N.Y. L.J., Sept. 12, 1985, at 15, col. 2 (Nassau) (court appointed as temporary administrator the nominated successor executor to commence an action against the nominated executor who, it was alleged, had wrongfully transferred the decedent's property to himself).

18. SCPA 902(2)(a). Persons entitled to process in administration proceedings are set forth in SCPA 1003, and discussed in chapter on "Administration," supra at 139–41.

19. McKinney's SCPA 902(5).

20. McKinney's SCPA 902(2)(b).

21. McKinney's SCPA 902(4).

22. McKinney's SCPA 902(5).

23. McKinney's SCPA 902(3). No exception is made in McKinney's SCPA 902(5).

24. See, e.g., Matter of Baydal, N.Y.L.J., Aug. 6, 1985, at 12, col. 1 (Richmond), where the court enjoined banks and other agents from paying any property to the absentee's spouse, who was joint owner of some of the property, pending resolution of an indictment charging him with her murder.

process issues if it believes that the best interests of the absentee's estate require immediate action by a fiduciary.[25] That temporary administrator can serve for a maximum of six months from the date the citation issues, and the court has the power to revoke the temporary letters during the six months.

This six-month period is a sort of "temporary temporary administration" whose purpose is to deal with emergencies during the period after the absentee (and his distributees) have received notice but before the court has held the hearing which officially sets the date of his disappearance and "permanently" appoints the temporary administrator.

SECTION G. COMMISSIONS

The "temporary temporary administrator" is not entitled to commissions, but the court can award reasonable compensation, and in fact often the "temporary temporary administrator" is ultimately appointed as fiduciary and then gets one full commission for his administration of the estate.[1]

Other temporary administrators are entitled to statutory commissions.[2] The court sometimes sets a condition, however, either that a temporary administrator waive commissions or, if he is not ultimately appointed as executor or administrator, that the court be permitted to fix the reasonable compensation for services actually performed in lieu of statutory commissions. The court can also limit the assets that the temporary administrator can receive,[3] thus reducing his commissions.

SECTION H. POWERS OF THE TEMPORARY ADMINISTRATOR

1. GENERALLY

The powers of the temporary administrator, who was originally merely a "collector of estate assets," [1] remain restricted. He can take possession of assets to secure and preserve them,[2] or start a lawsuit for this purpose,[3] pay all taxes due, and accelerate the period of time the creditors have to present their claims by publishing a notice to them.[4] All other acts of the temporary administrator must be authorized by

25. McKinney's SCPA 902(6).

Sec. G

1. See chapter on "Commissions," infra at 425 et seq.

2. McKinney's SCPA 2307, discussed in chapter on "Commissions," infra at 426–29.

3. McKinney's SCPA 702(2).

Sec. H

1. See McKinney's SCPA 905, Prac. Comm. at 163 (Supp.1986).

2. McKinney's SCPA 903.

3. McKinney's SCPA 905.

4. McKinney's SCPA 903(2)(a), (b), 905(1). See McKinney's SCPA 1801, discussed in chapter on "Claims," supra at 150–51.

the court, including the payment of debts, funeral and administration expenses, and the care, custody and disposition or sale of property.[5]

The temporary administrator has full power to marshal the assets, conserve them, make sure they are properly invested and pay taxes, but he cannot make distribution to legatees or distributees or creditors (other than the taxing authorities) without court order.[6] By statute, he cannot make any payments, except for taxes, unless specifically directed by the court. Usually the temporary administrator does not make distributions until after the accounting. The court can order payment of a part of the estate to a beneficiary if circumstances warrant it, but the share would be limited to the smaller of the beneficiary's share under the will or under the laws of intestacy.[7] The court can also authorize the temporary administrator to pay the decedent's spouse or issue property exempt under EPTL 5–3.1.[8] The temporary administrator cannot hire experts without court permission, but if he does so, and if the fees are reasonable, a court has discretion subsequently to permit either their payment out of the estate, or if the temporary administrator has paid them, reimbursement to him.[9]

In cases of absentees and internees, one directive that the court frequently gives to temporary administrators is to use assets not needed for the payment of claims to provide for the health, maintenance, clothing or education of the internee or the spouse, child, or a dependent presumptive distributee of an absentee or internee.[10] Logic dictates that the court should be able to order this allowance can also be made in the case of a person believed to be dead, since that person is, at least initially, treated as an absentee.[11] In the case of an actual decedent, one case has held that a court cannot order such payments for the use of the dependents,[12] because the statute specifically authorized such payments only in cases of absentees and internees. The better view is to permit the court discretion to order support payments where they are needed during a delay in probate or administration of an estate. In practice, the provisions for exempt property, which allow

5. McKinney's SCPA 903(2)(c).

6. McKinney's SCPA 903; McKinney's SCPA 906. The temporary administrator's conservative role is illustrated by the holding of Bradley v. Roe, 282 N.Y. 525, 27 N.E.2d 35 (1940), where the court held that the temporary administrator properly held onto property claimed by another until the Surrogate could determine after a hearing who owned it. The claimant sued the temporary administrator for conversion, and the court dismissed the lawsuit.

7. Matter of Morland, 184 Misc. 435, 55 N.Y.S.2d 910 (New York County 1944).

8. See Matter of Levine, 157 Misc. 454, 284 N.Y.S. 255 (Kings 1935). Exempt property is discussed in chapter on "Miscellaneous Proceedings," infra at 329–31.

9. See Matter of Sheinman, 52 Misc.2d 220, 275 N.Y.S.2d 197 (New York County 1966).

10. McKinney's SCPA 907 authorizes this practice.

11. See Matter of Magre, 189 Misc. 246, 73 N.Y.S.2d 467 (New York County 1947), where the court directed that the temporary administrator pay for the living expenses of the sole distributee of a woman who had been arrested and sent to Auschwitz and who it was believed had been executed there.

12. Matter of Carll, 104 N.Y.S.2d 611 (Suffolk 1951).

payment of $1,000 and other necessaries to the spouse or minor children, usually take care of this problem.[13]

The court may also permit the temporary administrator to use estate assets in his attempt to find out the whereabouts or condition of an absentee or internee, and to treat such expenditures as administration expenses.

Since the temporary administrator is often bonded, the modern tendency of the Surrogates is to grant the temporary administrator powers similar to those of a preliminary executor.[14] The temporary administrator also has all the duties and liabilities of an administrator with respect to the property he administers.[15]

2. POWER AS TO REAL PROPERTY

The court can give a temporary administrator the power to take possession of real property in any county in the state and to receive the rents and profits from it, and to do anything else necessary for its preservation. The temporary administrator may also maintain or defend any action or special proceeding in furtherance of such order.[16] For example, a temporary administrator could bring an action to eject a person claiming adverse possession.[17] The court may grant him authority to lease the real property for a term of up to one year, and can grant him authority to mortgage or sell the real property if necessary to pay administration and funeral expenses, debts, judgments and mortgages, taxes, and distributive shares of the property itself.[18]

If an absentee or internee has an interest in real property as a tenant in common, joint tenant or tenant by the entirety, the temporary administrator can join with the other tenants in a sale, mortgage or lease of the property under terms and conditions set by the court, which also apportions the proceeds according to the interest of each of the parties.[19]

The statute says that the temporary administrator's acts bind the internee and the absentee if he is living, or his distributees or devisees if he is dead, in the same manner as the acts of a fiduciary bind his successor.[20] When a successor fiduciary takes over after his predecessor has resigned or died or been removed, he can require an accounting for the predecessor's actions, but if he does not, or if he does not make

13. McKinney's EPTL 5–3.1, discussed in chapter on "Miscellaneous Proceedings," infra at 329–31.

14. See McKinney's SCPA 903, Practice Commentary at 162 (Supp.1986). The powers of a preliminary executor are discussed in chapter on "Probate," supra at 122–23.

15. McKinney's SCPA 903(1). See chapter on "Fiduciaries," infra at 384 et seq., for a discussion of a fiduciary's duties and liabilities.

16. McKinney's SCPA 904.

17. See Matter of Ort, 217 App.Div. 422, 217 N.Y.S. 46 (3d Dep't 1926).

18. McKinney's SCPA Article 19 covers these real property proceedings, discussed in chapter on "Disposition of Real Property," infra at 470 et seq.

19. McKinney's SCPA 904(2).

20. McKinney's SCPA 904(3).

objections to the accounting, he is bound by the predecessor's actions.[21] Translated to the case of a temporary administrator, this means the absentee or internee can require an accounting and can obtain a surcharge or denial of commissions if the temporary administrator engaged in wrongful conduct, but if the absentee or internee does not, he is bound by his actions. (We repeat here that an absentee cannot get his property back if he returns more than ten years after his "disappearance date" has been set by the court if the temporary administrator has distributed it.[22])

3. ACTIONS OR PROCEEDINGS BY OR AGAINST A TEMPORARY ADMINISTRATOR

A temporary administrator may start a lawsuit relating to the property of a decedent, absentee or internee.[23] In addition, a temporary administrator can be sued for a debt of the decedent, absentee or internee, or for any cause of action to which the decedent, absentee or internee would have been a party.[24] It is unnecessary to get court approval before starting an action against a temporary administrator.[25] The practical effect of this is that as soon as the temporary administrator is appointed, the seven-month period to present claims against an estate begins to run.[26] Also, the sixty-day period under SCPA 1810 during which a claimant can start an action in the Supreme Court or another forum after rejection of his claim by the fiduciary begins to run at the time the temporary administrator rejects the claim.[27]

The temporary administrator can bring a wrongful death action,[28] though the court must approve any settlement before the temporary administrator can accept it.[29]

4. POWER TO PAY CLAIMS

A temporary administrator cannot pay claims without a court order. The usual procedure for getting the court order is that after the court has issued letters to a temporary administrator, a claimant for payment of a debt, funeral or administration expense petitions the court to issue process requiring the temporary administrator to show cause why he should not pay the claim.[30] The court reviews the proof and may dismiss the petition or may direct payment of the claim after

21. See chapter on "Fiduciaries," infra at 384 et seq.

22. McKinney's SCPA 911(3).

23. McKinney's SCPA 905(1).

24. McKinney's SCPA 905(2).

25. L.1975, c. 280, section 1, deleting from McKinney's SCPA 905(2) the requirement for court approval.

26. McKinney's SCPA 1802, discussed in chapter on "Claims," supra at 148–50.

27. McKinney's SCPA 1810. This amendment overrules case law. See Matter of DeRidder, 183 App.Div. 657, 170 N.Y.S. 765 (1st Dep't 1918); Brown v. Ingersoll, 226 N.Y.S.2d 479 (Monroe County 1962).

28. SCPA 905(1); see Merrick v. Murphy, 83 Misc.2d 39, 371 N.Y.S.2d 97 (Delaware County 1975); Matter of Hogan, 13 Misc.2d 270, 177 N.Y.S.2d 757 (Fulton 1958).

29. See chapter on "Wrongful Death Proceedings," infra at 527 et seq.

30. McKinney's SCPA 906.

determining that the assets of the estate exceed the debts, and may require the claimant to file a refunding bond.[31] The court's directive is not a ruling on the validity of the claim, which, if challenged, is an issue to be resolved in an accounting proceeding or in a preliminary "1809" proceeding to determine the validity of a claim against the estate.[32]

If a temporary administrator pays claims without court authorization and the estate in fact did not owe them, the court will surcharge the temporary administrator for them.[33]

SECTION I. ACCOUNTING OF A TEMPORARY ADMINISTRATOR

A temporary administrator's accounting is substantially like that of any other fiduciary.[1] If a temporary administrator is appointed permanent administrator or executor, he need not account at the time his roles switch; his eventual accounting will cover both his period of temporary administration and his period of "permanent administration." The final accounting can be either informal,[2] if all interested parties sign receipts and releases, or formal.[3]

If the temporary administrator is supplanted by someone else appointed as permanent fiduciary, he has to account at that time. He can do so either formally or informally.

If the "decedent" who was declared dead reappears, the absentee returns within ten years, or the internee is released, the temporary administrator must account, and can do so either formally or informally.

31. McKinney's SCPA 906; Matter of Reardon, 230 N.Y.S.2d 458 (Nassau 1962).

32. See Matter of Dix, 34 Misc.2d 421, 226 N.Y.S.2d 111 (Rensselaer 1962). McKinney's SCPA 1809 is discussed in chapter on "Claims," supra at 163–64.

33. Matter of Newin, 33 Misc.2d 72, 224 N.Y.S.2d 888 (Suffolk 1962). See also Matter of Johnson, 147 N.Y.S.2d 405 (New York County 1955), where the temporary administrator, without court permission, paid an attorney $20,000 out of his own funds for services rendered to the estate. The court awarded him reimbursement because the services were necessary and reasonable.

Sec. I

1. We discuss these procedures in chapter on "Accounting," supra at 179 et seq.

2. McKinney's SCPA 2202, 2203, discussed in chapter on "Accounting," supra at 180–82.

3. McKinney's SCPA 2205, 2206, discussed in chapter on "Accounting," supra at 183–88.

Chapter Eleven

SURVIVING SPOUSE'S RIGHT OF ELECTION

SECTION A. INTRODUCTION

Married persons cannot disinherit each other in New York, unless they waive their right to inherit, fail to assert it, or lose it because of some disqualifying conduct. Their right to inherit from their spouses is in the form of a right of election against a will attempting disinheritance.

This chapter discusses a surviving spouse's right of election, both its substantive and procedural aspects. It covers the law in effect before September 1, 1966, the changes in the law effective September 1, 1966 and the application of both pre-1966 and post-1966 law to current decedents. It omits discussion of the dower rights belonging to the surviving spouse of a person whose will was executed before September 1, 1930 because of their near-obsolescence.

SECTION B. WHEN A SURVIVING SPOUSE CAN EXERCISE THE RIGHT OF ELECTION

The EPTL contains the substantive law governing a surviving spouse's right of election.[1] It applies to the surviving spouses of decedents who were New York domiciliaries and of domiciliaries of other jurisdictions who opt in their will for application of New York law.[2] If a decedent survived by issue failed to give to the surviving spouse at least one-third of the net estate (either outright or in trust, as we discuss shortly), the surviving spouse can elect against the will.[3] This, anomalously, is true whether the decedent provides for the issue or disinherits them. If a decedent was not survived by issue, that

Sec. B

1. McKinney's EPTL 5–1.1.

2. McKinney's EPTL 5–1.1(d)(7). The legislature is currently reviewing certain parts of McKinney's EPTL 5–1.1, including the appropriateness of the general rule that a non-domiciliary's spouse has no right of election against New York real property.

We discuss whether a decedent can *limit* his spouse to the New York right of election when the domiciliary state's is more favorable in chapter on "Jurisdiction," supra at 32–34.

3. McKinney's EPTL 5–1.1(a)(1)(A) (pre-September 1, 1966 wills); McKinney's EPTL 5–1.1(c)(1)(B) (post-August 31, 1966 wills).

threshold figure is one-half of the net estate.[4] Adopted children are issue.[5] Children born out of wedlock are issue of their mother and are issue of their father if paternity was proved or notoriously acknowledged in a manner sufficient to permit them to inherit from their father under the law of intestacy.[6] The issue must be the decedent's; it does not matter if they are not the surviving spouse's.

If the decedent leaves the spouse less than that threshold amount of one-third or one-half in the will, she can elect against the will, and in some cases against non-testamentary assets and certain of the decedent's lifetime transfers.[7] The fund against which the surviving spouse can exercise the right of election is the net estate plus illusory transfers (for pre-1966 situations) or testamentary substitutes (for post-1966 situations). Illusory transfers and testamentary substitutes are described in detail shortly. The "base figure" is the decedent's net estate, that is, all the probate property less debts, administration expenses and reasonable funeral expenses. In the usual case the elective share is not reduced by estate taxes, because the surviving spouse's share is eligible for the marital deduction and hence does not bear any of the tax burden. If for some reason, however, the surviving spouse is responsible for a portion of the estate taxes under the "tax apportionment" statute,[8] because, for example, her share of the estate was left in trust in a way that does not qualify for the marital deduction,[9] and the will does not direct otherwise, the elective share will be reduced by the taxes apportioned against it. In other words, the elective share may be eligible for the marital deduction, but to the extent estate taxes are apportioned against it, the marital deduction is unavailable and the surviving spouse's share is reduced.

SECTION C. ELECTIVE SHARE IN TRUST

The decedent can satisfy the one-third or one-half share by leaving that amount in trust with the income payable to the surviving spouse for life.[1] The provisions of the statute on trusts apply equally to legal life estates, annuities for the surviving spouse's life, annuity trusts,

4. McKinney's EPTL 5–1.1(a)(1)(A) (pre-September 1, 1966 wills); McKinney's EPTL 5–1.1(c)(1)(B) (post-August 31, 1966 wills).

5. McKinney's EPTL 1–2.10(a)(2).

6. See McKinney's EPTL 4–1.2 and chapter on "Administration," supra at 130–32. An out-of-wedlock child can inherit from his father if a court has issued an order of filiation, if the father has signed an acknowledgment of paternity, or if the father notoriously acknowledged paternity and in addition there is clear and convincing proof of paternity.

7. See sections on testamentary substitutes and illusory transfers, this chapter infra at 307–12.

8. McKinney's EPTL 2–1.8(e), discussed in chapter on "Estate Taxes," infra at 602–06.

9. This could happen, for example, if the decedent set up a trust with income payable to the surviving spouse, remainder to the children, and the executor did not opt to treat the property as Qualified Terminable Interest Property under Internal Revenue Code 2056. See chapter on "Estate Taxes," infra at 595.

Sec. C

1. McKinney's EPTL 5–1.1(a)(1)(B); McKinney's EPTL 5–1.1(c)(1)(D).

unitrusts and all other testamentary provisions under which the surviving spouse receives income for life.[2] If the decedent opts to leave the property to the spouse in this form of trust, the surviving spouse has no right to elect against the will, but she does have a right, (the "limited right of election" [3]) to take some money or property outright. If the will was executed after August 31, 1966, that outright share is $10,000, whether through the will, or through the limited right of election, or a combination of the two, provided her elective share amounts to $10,000 or more. If her elective share is less than $10,000 she can withdraw only the amount of her elective share.

For example, if the will was executed after August 31, 1966 and the net estate is $100,000, and

(a) the decedent without issue left $50,000 in trust, income to surviving spouse, she can take $10,000 outright and the remaining $40,000 will remain in the trust for her benefit.

(b) the decedent without issue left $30,000 in trust, income to surviving spouse for life, she can take $20,000 outright, and $30,000 will remain in the trust for her benefit.

(c) the decedent without issue left $45,000 in a trust, income to surviving spouse for life, she can take $10,000 outright and $40,000 will remain in the trust for her benefit.

(d) the decedent left one child surviving and left $18,000 in trust, income to surviving spouse for life, she can take $15,333 outright and $18,000 will remain in the trust for her benefit.[4]

If the will was executed before September 1, 1966, the spouse has a limited right to take $2,500 outright. The examples in the preceding paragraph would be adjusted for a pre-September 1, 1966 trust as follows:

(a) surviving spouse can take $2,500 outright and the remaining $47,500 will remain in the trust for her benefit.

(b) no adjustment

(c) surviving spouse can take $5,000 outright and $45,000 will remain in trust for her benefit.

(d) no adjustment.

It is not surprising that many surviving spouses do not want to receive the elective share in the form of a trust, and consequently much litigation has arisen on whether the trust satisfies the criteria of the statute. For example, if the income will cease on the occurrence of a contingency, such as remarriage, the trust does not satisfy the statute and the surviving spouse is entitled to the share outright.[5] One

2. McKinney's EPTL 5–1.1(c)(1)(I).

3. McKinney's EPTL 5–1.1(a)(1)(B)–(F); McKinney's EPTL 5–1.1(c)(1)(D)–(G).

4. See, e.g., Matter of Handler, 82 Misc. 2d 482, 371 N.Y.S.2d 297 (Kings 1975).

5. Matter of Byrnes, 260 N.Y. 465, 184 N.E. 56 (1933).

enterprising testator left nothing to his surviving spouse, but provided that if she were able to establish her right of election, a trust would be created to satisfy her elective share. The court allowed the surviving spouse to take her share outright because the testator had left her nothing.[6] Another wiser (or luckier) testator left the spouse's share in trust, conditioned, however, on her having a right to share in the estate, and his widow's attempt to elect against that trust and take her whole share outright was unsuccessful (though she was permitted to take $10,000 outright under the limited right of election).[7] A bequest of a minimum amount to the spouse provided she has a right to share in the estate does not require her to elect against the will to take her bequest,[8] but she does have to prove her status as surviving spouse if it is challenged.[9]

Occasionally a testator conditions his surviving spouse's right to property on the spouse's surviving him for six months. He does so to minimize administrative inconvenience and expense without jeopardizing the federal or state marital deduction.[10] If a testator creates such a trust sufficient to satisfy his spouse's elective share but provides that the income of the trust is payable to the spouse immediately, the spouse will not be able to break that trust and take the elective share outright.[11]

A trust over which a trustee has a discretionary power to sprinkle income among the surviving spouse and children does not satisfy the spouse's elective share.[12] However, the trustee can be given fairly broad powers over the trust without conferring a right of election against the trust upon the surviving spouse. In a pre-September 1, 1966 trust, the trustee's permissible powers are specifically listed; he can serve without bond, sell assets, invest in other than legal investments, distribute property in kind, and allocate assets to the elective share.[13] The surviving spouse cannot elect against the trust simply because the trustee has those powers. The permissible powers of the trustee of a post-August 31, 1966 trust are not specifically listed, but certain powers given to a fiduciary are so forbidden that the trust will be considered a nullity and the spouse will be able to take the elective share from the capital value of the trust. These are [14] the power to invade principal for anyone other than the surviving spouse, to pay less

6. Matter of Filor, 267 App.Div. 269, 45 N.Y.S.2d 376 (2d Dep't 1943), affirmed 293 N.Y. 699, 56 N.E.2d 585 (1944).

7. Matter of Arlin, 120 Misc.2d 96, 465 N.Y.S.2d 491 (Nassau 1983), affirmed 100 A.D.2d 878, 473 N.Y.S.2d 1022 (2d Dep't 1984), appeal denied 62 N.Y.2d 605, 479 N.Y.S.2d 1025, 468 N.E.2d 57 (1984); Matter of Benin, 31 A.D.2d 747, 297 N.Y.S.2d 347 (2d Dep't 1969), appeal denied 24 N.Y.2d 738, 300 N.Y.S.2d 1026, 248 N.E.2d 453 (1969).

8. Matter of Collins, 13 N.Y.2d 194, 245 N.Y.S.2d 384, 195 N.E.2d 53 (1963).

9. See Matter of Cristiano, N.Y.L.J., Jan. 17, 1975 (Nassau).

10. Internal Revenue Code § 2056(b)(3)(a).

11. Matter of Berger, 61 Misc.2d 81, 304 N.Y.S.2d 911 (Kings 1969); contra, Matter of Fishman, N.Y.L.J., Oct. 1, 1963, at 15, col. 3 (New York County).

12. See Matter of Friedman, 67 Misc.2d 304, 323 N.Y.S.2d 499 (Westchester 1971).

13. McKinney's EPTL 5-1.1(a)(1)(H).

14. McKinney's EPTL 5-1.1(c)(1)(J).

than substantially all the income to the surviving spouse,[15] and to terminate the trust before the surviving spouse's death. If the trustee has any of these powers, the surviving spouse can break the trust and take the elective share outright. Any other powers that threaten the surviving spouse's security are subject to scrutiny by the Surrogate, who can approve the powers or make discretionary orders to protect the surviving spouse, including (but not limited to) orders to distribute the elective share outright to the spouse and orders not to exercise certain fiduciary powers.[16] If a trustee has no offensive power other than the right to allocate trust property between principal and income, the court can order the proper allocation to ensure that the spouse will get substantially all the income; she cannot automatically elect against such a will. However, if a testator directs that stock dividends for a corporation be principal, the spouse can elect against the will because stock dividends are sometimes income [17] and she is not assured of getting substantially all the income.[18] If a trustee can terminate the trust by invading principal for the surviving spouse, the surviving spouse has no right to elect against the will.[19] If, however, the trustee can invade in favor of the surviving spouse "and/or" another person, the spouse has a right of election.[20]

The testator cannot provide that unproductive property be used to fund the surviving spouse's trust,[21] but if the estate consists largely of unproductive property, a trust funded with that property has been held to satisfy the elective share.[22] In such a case a spouse may seek a court order causing the fiduciary to sell the property and invest it in income producing property that will benefit both the income beneficiary and

15. See Matter of Baileson, 16 N.Y.2d 757, 262 N.Y.S.2d 487, 209 N.E.2d 810 (1965) (decedent stipulated that income earned by widow's trust, but not yet payable to trustee, should not be paid to her. The court ruled that this did not deprive widow of substantially all the income so as automatically to give her a right of election).

16. See Matter of Nelson, 95 Misc.2d 215, 407 N.Y.S.2d 773 (Westchester 1977), where the court ruled that a trustee's power to administer three trusts (one of which was the trust satisfying the elective share) "in solido" as one trust would not permit the surviving spouse to take her share outright. See also Matter of Best, 62 Misc.2d 535, 308 N.Y.S.2d 930 (Erie 1970) (court directed trustees to pay all income to widow; testator's directive to use their discretion to meet her support needs not sufficient grounds for allowing right of election); Matter of Jacobsen, 61 Misc.2d 317, 306 N.Y.S.2d 290 (New York County 1969), affirmed 33 A.D.2d 760, 306 N.Y.S.2d 297 (1st Dep't 1969) (trustees' discretion to amortize bond premiums); Matter of Kirsch, N.Y.L.J., Oct. 14, 1960, at 17 (Westchester) (fiduciary's powers to set up a reserve fund for depreciation and apportion assets between income and principal).

17. See McKinney's EPTL 11–2.1(b)(2)(D), discussed in chapter on "Fiduciaries," infra at 416, 420.

18. Matter of Kunc, 43 Misc.2d 387, 251 N.Y.S.2d 112 (Westchester 1964), affirmed 22 A.D.2d 852, 255 N.Y.S.2d 467 (2d Dep't 1964). See generally Amend, The Surviving Spouse and the EPTL, 33 Brooklyn L.Rev. 530 (1967).

19. Matter of Niedelman, 6 A.D.2d 291, 175 N.Y.S.2d 694 (1st Dep't 1958), affirmed 5 N.Y.2d 1043, 185 N.Y.S.2d 802, 158 N.E.2d 498 (1959).

20. Matter of Aaronson, 20 A.D.2d 133, 246 N.Y.S.2d 61 (2d Dep't 1963).

21. Matter of Clark, 1 A.D.2d 567, 151 N.Y.S.2d 911 (4th Dep't 1956).

22. Matter of Shupack, 1 N.Y.2d 482, 154 N.Y.S.2d 441, 136 N.E.2d 513 (1956) (stock in closely held corporation); Matter of Anderson, 29 A.D.2d 621, 285 N.Y.S.2d 454 (1967).

the remainderman.[23] A gift of a life estate may satisfy the right of election statute but the will provisions may not deprive the surviving spouse of any income earned on the underlying property.[24]

Occasionally a testator attempts to give his spouse an annuity from the residuary estate, such as $500 per month for life. Because it is the size of trust corpus and not the capitalized value of income that determines the adequacy of the share left to the surviving spouse, some courts have allowed the spouse to exercise a right of election against such a will,[25] while others have construed the will to mean that all income should be paid to the widow, and have denied the right of election.[26]

If the combined bequests to the surviving spouse are enough to satisfy the elective share, the fact that estate taxes are apportioned against those bequests and that the decedent failed to take advantage of the full marital deduction are irrelevant. However, as a result of the new federal and New York estate tax laws dealing with both the qualitative and quantitative value of marital bequests, most such bequests can escape estate tax.[27]

A charitable remainder unitrust and a charitable remainder annuity trust whose corpus is at least the elective share, paying at least five percent of the fair market value of the trust annually to the surviving spouse for life, both satisfy the surviving spouse's elective share.[28]

SECTION D. PROPERTY AGAINST WHICH THE SURVIVING SPOUSE CAN ELECT

The right of election attaches to the decedent's probate estate. Thus, if the decedent made complete and absolute gifts of all his property during his lifetime, his surviving spouse has no recourse, even if he did it expressly to disinherit her.[1] In addition to the probate assets, the right of election attaches to "illusory transfers" if the pre-

23. See McKinney's EPTL 11–2.1(a)(1), McKinney's EPTL 5–1.1(c)(1)(J).

24. Matter of Brettschneider, 30 A.D.2d 59, 289 N.Y.S.2d 661 (1st Dep't 1968); Matter of Fike, 59 Misc.2d 1047, 301 N.Y.S.2d 394 (Erie 1969).

25. See In re Withall, 274 A.D. 846, 80 N.Y.S.2d 769 (4th Dep't 1948); Matter of Haubenstock, 28 Misc.2d 714, 212 N.Y.S.2d 312 (Kings 1961); Matter of Leekoff, N.Y. L.J., July 17, 1962, at 8, col. 1 (Kings). See Matter of Rosenzweig, 19 N.Y.2d 92, 278 N.Y.S.2d 192, 224 N.E.2d 705 (1966), reargument denied 19 N.Y.2d 862, 280 N.Y.S.2d 1025, 227 N.E.2d 408 (1967); Conway, Surviving Spouse's Right of Election in New York Where Trust Income May Be Diverted: The Need for a Further Change, 34 Fordham L.Rev. 593, 598 (1966); Amend, Surviving Spouse and the EPTL, 33 Brooklyn L.Rev. 530, 544 (1967).

26. Matter of Fisher, N.Y.L.J., April 29, 1971, at 19, col. 4 (New York County).

27. Internal Revenue Code § 2056; McKinney's Tax L. 249–s(2) (1966), discussed in chapter on "Estate Taxes," infra at 593–96.

28. McKinney's EPTL 5–1.1(c)(1)(K).

Sec. D

1. If a surviving spouse can prove that a lifetime gift was ineffective, because of, for example, lack of delivery, that incomplete gift will constitute part of the net estate for purposes of computing the right of election.

September 1, 1966 law applies, and to "testamentary substitutes" if the post August 31, 1966 law applies.

1. POST–AUGUST 31, 1966: TESTAMENTARY SUBSTITUTES

If the decedent's will was executed after August 31, 1966, or if a will is executed before September 1, 1966, and a codicil is executed after,[2] the surviving spouse can elect against any transfers made after the marriage and after August 31, 1966 that are "testamentary substitutes."[3] They are as follows:

(i) gifts causa mortis;

(ii) Totten Trusts created after August 31, 1966 and still on deposit at decedent's death;

(iii) money in joint bank accounts deposited after August 31, 1966 and still on deposit at decedent's death;

(iv) jointly owned property created after August 31, 1966 to the extent the decedent contributed the consideration for it;

(v) property transferred after August 31, 1966 if the decedent retained the right to revoke the transfer or invade its principal.[4]

All three criteria must be met, namely, the will and the transfer must be after August 31, 1966 and the transfer must be after the marriage, or the governing law will be the pre-September 1, 1966 law, which we discuss shortly.

Courts do not like to keep property exempt from the surviving spouse's right of election and they decide the cases accordingly when possible. For example, if a Totten Trust was created before September 1, 1966, but was transferred (lock, stock and barrel) to a different bank after, it is "created" after August 31, 1966 and is therefore a testamentary substitute.[5] Similarly, a "first-in, first-out" method is used to determine the date of creation. If the decedent created a Totten Trust of $10,000 in 1965, and over the next ten years deposited and withdrew $20,000, and at his death in 1976 $10,000 remained, the court assumes the remaining $10,000 was the last $10,000 deposited, not the original $10,000 in the account.[6] However, if the transfer was pre-September 1,

2. Matter of Berger, 61 Misc.2d 81, 304 N.Y.S.2d 911 (Kings 1969). The will is considered to be republished on the date of the codicil and therefore the post-August 31, 1966 law applies. See also Irving Trust Co. v. Day, 314 U.S. 556, 62 S.Ct. 398, 86 L.Ed. 452 (1942) (codicil to will allowed widow to take advantage of new state law).

3. McKinney's EPTL 5–1.1(b)(1)(A–E).

4. Matter of Twersky, N.Y.L.J., Sept. 16, 1982, at 10, col. 6 (New York County) (inter vivos irrevocable charitable annuity trust not a testamentary substitute because testator did not retain power to invade).

5. Matter of Agioritis, 40 N.Y.2d 646, 389 N.Y.S.2d 323, 357 N.E.2d 979 (1976).

6. Matter of Agioritis, 40 N.Y.2d 646, 389 N.Y.S.2d 323, 357 N.E.2d 979 (1976). But see Matter of Fox, 67 Misc.2d 470, 324 N.Y.S.2d 434 (Erie 1971), where a pre-September 1, 1966 transfer into tenancy by the entirety retained its exempt status despite the deposit of the proceeds of sale from the property into a joint bank account in 1969. The New York Supreme Court ordered the sale after the wife was judicially adjudged incompetent, and when the husband died, the wife's committee wanted to include the bank account in the elective "pot." The court refused, holding

1966, the transfer itself and the interest earned on it are exempt from the spouse's right of election, though the interest was earned after September 1, 1966.[7]

The surviving spouse has the burden of proving the decedent's contribution to a testamentary substitute, and the Dead Man's Statute [8] does not prevent her from making that proof.[9]

Moreover, while testamentary substitutes payable to the spouse must usually be set off against her elective share, to the extent the surviving spouse also contributed to the joint property and can prove it, she will not have to reduce her elective share. For example, if a decedent died with a net testamentary estate of $200,000 and also a home worth $100,000, paid for by him and held in joint name with his wife, her elective share of the estate if he has no issue is $150,000 (half of $300,000). The full value of the house is credited to her, because it passes to her as joint owner and she did not contribute toward its purchase, so she has a right to an additional $50,000 from the estate. If she could prove that she paid one-half the consideration for the house, one half of its value is excluded from the elective "pot," which is therefore $250,000. The surviving spouse's elective share is $125,000 (one-half of the "pot") and only $50,000 of the value of the house will be credited to her. She will take $75,000 from the testamentary estate.

The testamentary substitutes are invalidated only to the extent necessary to satisfy the elective share.[10] Thus, if a decedent placed his entire estate in a Totten Trust for his friend, the surviving spouse could exercise the right of election and take her share, and the friend would get the rest.

The surviving spouse is not entitled to interest on the testamentary substitutes during the period of administration,[11] but she is entitled to a share of the estate income proportionate to her fractional share of the probate assets.[12]

As we have stated, the burden of proving that the testamentary substitutes came from the decedent's funds is on the surviving spouse, and if the surviving spouse is the beneficiary of the testamentary substitutes, the burden is on her as well to prove her own contribution.[13]

that because of the forced sale, the property should retain its character as a pre-September 1, 1966 transfer.

7. See Matter of Kleinerman, 66 Misc. 2d 563, 319 N.Y.S.2d 898 (Kings 1971). Though Kleinerman was decided before the Court of Appeals decided Matter of Agioritis, discussed in the preceding footnote, the interest should in fact be exempt.

8. McKinney's CPLR 4519.

9. McKinney's EPTL 5–1.1(b)(3).

10. McKinney's EPTL 5–1.1(d)(1). See discussion of this point as it relates to illusory transfers, infra at 311–12.

11. See Matter of Spinelli, 86 Misc.2d 1039, 384 N.Y.S.2d 665 (Kings 1976).

12. McKinney's EPTL 11–2.1(d)(2)(B), discussed in chapter on "Accounting" supra at 197–99.

13. McKinney's EPTL 5–1.1(b)(3). The Surrogate can hear proof on this issue without the constraints of the Dead Man's Statute. Id.

The bank (or corporation or other person) with possession of the testamentary substitutes is permitted to pay them out unless it receives a court order enjoining it from doing so.[14] The surviving spouse, when filing her notice of election, should seek the injunction as well.

a. Excluded Property

The statute specifically excludes three kinds of property from the net estate; these assets are not subject to a surviving spouse's right of election. First, insurance policies are not part of the "elective pot." [15] If the decedent had life insurance payable to a third party, the surviving spouse has no rights in that insurance. If the decedent placed the insurance policy in a trust and retained powers over the trust sufficient to qualify the trust as a testamentary substitute, the insurance is nevertheless excluded from the net estate for elective purposes.[16]

The second exemption is for pension and retirement plans,[17] even if the decedent retained such powers as the right to change beneficiaries.

The third exception is for United States savings bonds.[18] The reason savings bonds are exempted is that payment of these bonds to the person named as beneficiary is mandated by federal law, and a state law to the contrary would cause a constitutional preemption problem. A testator could thus place his entire estate in bonds and defeat the surviving spouse's right of election.

In addition, completed gifts and irrevocable trusts are not testamentary substitutes,[19] nor is out-of-state real property part of the elective "pot"; it is subject to surviving spouse's rights, if any, in the state in which it is located.[20] Property transferred to minors under the Uniform Gifts to Minors Act [21] is an outright gift, not a testamentary substitute.[22]

14. McKinney's EPTL 5–1.1(b)(4).

15. McKinney's EPTL 5–1.1(b)(2).

16. See Matter of Brociner, N.Y.L.J., May 22, 1985, at 14, col. 1 (Nassau), citing the Third Report of Commission on Estates, Legis.Doc. No. 19, at 138–39, where the Bennett Commission decided to exempt all life insurance after having admitted, id. at 128, that the retention of rights to revoke and change beneficiaries could present a way of evading the statute.

17. McKinney's EPTL 5–1.1(b)(2)(A).

18. McKinney's EPTL 5–1.1(b)(2)(c).

19. Matter of Riefberg, 58 N.Y.2d 134, 459 N.Y.S.2d 739, 446 N.E.2d 424 (1983).

20. McKinney's EPTL 5–1.1(d)(8); McKinney's EPTL 3–5.1(b)(1). Thus, a surviving spouse of a New Yorker may wind up with no elective rights at all against out-of-state real property if the other state does not allow her to elect against it. For example, New Jersey's right of election for spouses of non-domiciliary decedents is governed by the law of the decedent's domicile. New York's right of election does not apply to non-New York realty. Hence a surviving spouse would have no right to include that New Jersey realty in her elective "pot." See Matter of Economides, 126 Misc.2d 879, 483 N.Y.S.2d 886 (New York County 1984). This feature of New York law, which excludes foreign realty from the elective pot even when the foreign jurisdiction is willing to allow application of domiciliary (New York) law, should be reconsidered by the legislature.

21. McKinney's EPTL Article 7, Part 4.

22. See Matter of Zeigher, 95 Misc.2d 230, 406 N.Y.S.2d 977 (Nassau 1978).

b. "Judicial" Testamentary Substitutes

Until the New York Court of Appeals decided Matter of Riefberg in 1983,[23] the testamentary substitutes enumerated in EPTL 5–1.1(b) were thought to be exclusive.[24] The court in Reifberg expanded the list of testamentary substitutes to include a corporate buy-sell agreement where a decedent retained a power similar to those retained by the grantor of a revocable trust. The decedent owned corporate stock, and signed an agreement under which on his death the corporation would buy the decedent's shares from the estate, paying the proceeds to the executor. On the day before decedent's death, he amended the agreement to provide for payment of proceeds of the sale to some named persons. The court found that this transaction was akin to the creation of a testamentary substitute, and allowed the surviving spouse to elect against it.

Although the Reifberg conclusion is not irresistible under the statute, it is equitable; a contrary decision would have left a loophole for diminishing the share of the surviving spouse. If the decedent had wanted the asset to be free of an elective right, he should not have retained any control. Had the agreement been truly irrevocable, the right of election probably would not have applied against the sale proceeds.

2. PRE–SEPTEMBER 1, 1966: ILLUSORY TRANSFERS

The concept of testamentary substitutes was a creature of EPTL 5–1.1, effective September 1, 1966, and was applicable prospectively only. Thus, if the decedent's will or the transfer was before September 1, 1966, or if the transfer was before the marriage, or if the intestate decedent died before September 1, 1966, the surviving spouse cannot elect against the testamentary substitutes, but can elect against all "illusory transfers," which was the pre-September 1, 1966 law.[25]

The "illusory transfer" doctrine was spawned in the notorious case of Newman v. Dore,[26] where an eighty-year old testator and his thirty-year old bride had a difference of opinion leading him to create a trust, shortly before his death, from which he was to receive all the income and over which he retained all control, including the power to revoke. Although in his will he gave his wife the minimum amount necessary to satisfy the elective share, he had transferred everything to the trust so there was no probate property against which she could elect. The court found that, in light of the powers and interests he had retained, he had not in good faith divested himself of ownership of the property.[27]

23. 58 N.Y.2d 134, 459 N.Y.S.2d 739, 446 N.E.2d 424 (1983).

24. Matter of Zeigher, 95 Misc.2d 230, 406 N.Y.S.2d 977 (Nassau 1978).

25. On the other side of the coin, illusory gifts which are not enumerated testamentary substitutes will not constitute elective property for estates of decedents that come under the criteria of McKinney's EPTL 5-1.1(c). Matter of Brociner, N.Y. L.J., March 2, 1984, at 16, col. 3 (Nassau).

26. 275 N.Y. 371, 9 N.E.2d 966 (1937).

27. For a good discussion of Newman v. Dore and its progeny, see Gillette v. Madden, 280 App.Div. 161, 112 N.Y.S.2d 543 (3d Dep't 1952).

True divestiture thus was the test, and still is, for transfers that fail to meet all the post-August 31, 1966 timing requirements discussed above. Motive of the transferor was (and is) immaterial; a decedent has the prerogative to disinherit his spouse, so long as he does it by truly divesting himself of the property. The "good faith" standard refers to the divestiture, not to his frame of mind.[28] The surviving spouse has the burden of proving that the transfer is illusory.[29]

The reason the legislature changed the law in 1966 was because the "illusory transfer" test was a fairly muddy one, but the amendments were prospective only and not all the questions raised have been clearly answered.[30] Money transferred into a joint bank account is not an illusory transfer unless it was merely for the decedent's convenience,[31] and Totten Trusts have been held not to be illusory,[32] although under the post-August 31, 1966 law, both are testamentary substitutes. The finding of an illusory transfer has been held to invalidate the entire transfer, not just the portion of it necessary to satisfy the elective share,[33] a curious notion overruled for post-August 31, 1966 cases by EPTL 5–1.1(d)(1), which states that the will or trust is effective except the extent needed to satisfy the right of election.

SECTION E. EFFECT OF ELECTION ON THE WILL

Sometimes the question arises what happens to the rest of the will once a surviving spouse elects against it. The rule is that the will remains effective after satisfaction of the elective share. Thus, if a testator executed a will leaving nothing to the spouse and his entire estate in equal parts to his three children, the spouse's elective share is paid first and whatever is left goes to the three children in equal shares. Any legacy to the spouse in the will remains effective, with one exception discussed presently, and is set off against the elective share. For example, if the widow's elective share is $25,000, and under the will she gets only one bequest, a ring worth $5000, and the residue goes to the decedent's three children in equal shares, she takes the ring and $20,000 from the estate, and the three children share what is left equally.

The exception is the case where the decedent attempted to satisfy the spouse's elective share by creating a trust, but did not succeed and

28. See generally Matter of Center, 61 Misc.2d 193, 304 N.Y.S.2d 944 (Kings 1969).

29. Matter of Chandler, 175 Misc. 1029, 26 N.Y.S.2d 280 (Kings 1941).

30. See Powers, Illusory Transfers and Section 18, 32 St. John's L.Rev. 193 (1957).

31. Inda v. Inda, 288 N.Y. 315, 43 N.E.2d 59 (1942).

32. Matter of Halpern, 303 N.Y. 33, 100 N.E.2d 120 (1951), distinguishing Kraus v. Kraus, 285 N.Y. 27, 32 N.E.2d 779 (1941) (where Totten Trust were found to be illusory) on the dubious ground that the beneficiary in Kraus was living in a foreign country.

33. Matter of Halpern, 303 N.Y. 33, 100 N.E.2d 120 (1951).

the spouse elects against the will.[1] For example, if a testator gave a spouse income from a trust until her death or remarriage, she would lose that interest by electing against the will, and would have the right to take her elective share outright. Similarly, a spouse who elects against the will forfeits a power of appointment[2] but not the right to serve as executor.[3]

The surviving spouse takes from the estate her elective share reduced by any amounts she otherwise receives from the estate (under the will, in testamentary substitute or in intestacy).[4] For example, if a decedent made a will in 1968, leaving his estate to his wife, and later deposited $40,000 in a joint account with a friend and $60,000 in a Totten Trust in his cousin's favor, and bought a $100,000 house in his name and his daughter's as joint owners with right of survivorship, the widow's elective share when he later dies with a testamentary estate of $10,000 is $60,000. The net estate of $210,000 includes the $10,000 cash and all the transfers made, since they were all after August 31, 1966, all after the marriage and all from the decedent's own funds. The $10,000 she receives under the will is credited to her, so she is entitled to an additional $60,000.

A surviving spouse gets the elective share pro rata from the beneficiaries under the will and the beneficiaries of the testamentary substitutes.[5] In the example just discussed, the friend got $40,000, the cousin $60,000 and the daughter $100,000 in testamentary substitutes. Because there are no will beneficiaries other than the wife, the beneficiaries of the testamentary substitutes bear the entire burden of satisfying the elective share. Their ratio to each other is 40:60:100, or 20%, 30% and 50% respectively. Thus the widow would receive twenty percent of her $60,000 from the decedent's friend ($12,000), thirty percent from the cousin ($18,000), and fifty percent from the daughter ($30,000). Had there been will beneficiaries, they also would have shared ratably in making up the elective share.

If any of the testamentary substitutes are in the surviving spouse's favor, they are added to the net estate to compute the elective share, and then deducted from the surviving spouse's share, just as a will bequest or intestate share would be. For example, if the net testamentary estate of a decedent without issue, consisting of testamentary assets and post-August 31, 1966 Totten Trusts to others, is $200,000,

Sec. E

1. Matter of Rosenzweig, 23 A.D.2d 427, 261 N.Y.S.2d 125 (1st Dep't 1965), reversed on other grounds, 19 N.Y.2d 92, 278 N.Y.S.2d 192, 224 N.E.2d 705 (1966), reargument denied 19 N.Y.2d 862, 280 N.Y.S. 2d 1025, 227 N.E.2d 408 (1967). See also Matter of Handler, N.Y.L.J., July 8, 1975, at 16, col. 4 (Kings) (where elective share was less than $10,000, the right to take elective share outright is in lieu of any trust bequest).

2. Matter of Friedman, N.Y.L.J., July 23, 1971, at 11, col. 7 (Westchester).

3. Matter of Rosenfield, 76 N.Y.S.2d 177 (New York County 1944).

4. McKinney's EPTL 5–1.1(d)(3)(A), (B). See Matter of Gerard, 84 Misc.2d 213, 377 N.Y.S.2d 394 (New York County 1975).

5. McKinney's EPTL 5–1.1(d)(3)(A), (B).

and in 1980 the decedent deposited $50,000 into a Totten Trust in his wife's favor, her elective share is $125,000 and she will receive $75,000 of it ratably from the will- and Totten Trust-beneficiaries.

Because the surviving spouse's claim "cuts across" the whole estate [6] including testamentary substitutes or illusory transfers as appropriate, the spouse cannot file a lis pendens against a piece of realty that is part of the estate.[7] The notion is that a lis pendens is inappropriate unless the proceeding "would affect the title to, or the possession, use or enjoyment of, real property," [8] and the right of election entitles the wife not to the real property itself, but to a portion of the entire estate, including one-third or one-half of the sales proceeds from the real property. Since the right of election is essentially a claim for money, there is no right to use a lis pendens.[9] In fact, lis pendens are quite rare in estate proceedings.[10]

SECTION F. RIGHT OF ELECTION IN AN INTESTATE ESTATE

A surviving spouse of a decedent who died partially or wholly intestate may also be entitled to a right of election.[1] Because a surviving spouse's share of an estate is larger in intestacy than under a right of election [2] she will exercise the right of election in an intestate estate only when the decedent transferred property in the form of a testamentary substitute.[3] The surviving spouse's share is then payable pro rata out of the shares of the beneficiaries of the testamentary substitutes.[4]

For example, if the decedent died intestate in 1985, survived by a widow and two children, leaving net estate property of $100,000, Totten Trusts opened after his marriage in 1970 of $400,000 in favor of a friend, and a joint account with his wife of $130,000 opened with his own funds in 1975, the widow's right of election is $210,000 (one-third of $630,000). She is credited with $130,000 in the joint account and her intestate share of $36,000 ($4,000 plus one-third of $96,000 [5]). The additional $44,000 to which she is entitled is payable completely from

6. Matter of Taliento, 9 Misc.2d 167, 168 N.Y.S.2d 13 (Kings 1957).

7. Cassia v. Cassia, 125 Misc.2d 606, 480 N.Y.S.2d 84 (Westchester 1984).

8. McKinney's CPLR 6501.

9. See Long Island City Savings and Loan Ass'n v. Gottlieb, 90 A.D.2d 766, 455 N.Y.S.2d 300 (2d Dep't 1982), modified 58 N.Y.2d 931, 460 N.Y.S.2d 513, 447 N.E.2d 61 (1983).

10. Matter of Sabatino, 90 Misc.2d 56, 393 N.Y.S.2d 671 (Albany 1977).

Sec. F

1. McKinney's EPTL 5–1.1(c)(2).

2. Compare McKinney's EPTL 4–1.1 (surviving spouse gets $4,000 plus one-half remaining estate if there are no children or one child or his issue, $4,000 plus one-third if there are two or more children or their issue), with McKinney's EPTL 5–1.1 (surviving spouse gets one-third if there are any children or their issue, one-half if there are none).

3. See, e.g., Matter of Spinelli, 86 Misc. 2d 1039, 384 N.Y.S.2d 665 (Kings 1976) (no testamentary assets; all property in Totten Trusts).

4. McKinney's EPTL 5–1.1(d)(3)(A), (B).

5. See McKinney's EPTL 4–1.1.

the friend's Totten Trust, not from the shares of the other two intestate distributees.

If the decedent died partially intestate, the same rules apply, except that any amounts the surviving spouse receives under a will are off-set against her elective share, and the elective share is apportioned ratably against the testamentary trust beneficiaries and the will beneficiaries.

SECTION G. CONFLICTS BETWEEN RIGHT OF ELECTION AND CONTRACTUAL INTERESTS IN DECEDENT'S ESTATE

There is a curious interplay between the surviving spouse's right of election and conflicting contractual rights possessed by others. For example, if the decedent had a joint will with his first spouse incorporating a contract not to revoke the joint will, and the first spouse dies, at the decedent's death the second spouse's right of election against the decedent's will is ineffective.[1] On the other hand, if the decedent contracted in a separation agreement with his first wife to make a bequest to her or another person, and at his death the estate assets are insufficient to cover both the contractual obligation and the second spouse's elective share, the second spouse will prevail.[2] This is a good argument against both joint wills and promised bequests in separation agreements.[3]

SECTION H. SURVIVING SPOUSE'S STATUS OR DISQUALIFICATION

The surviving spouse need not have been married to the decedent when the will was executed as long as they were married when the decedent died.[1] A common law marriage valid in the state where the couple entered into it can be a basis for asserting the right of election,[2]

Sec. G

1. Rubenstein v. Mueller, 19 N.Y.2d 228, 278 N.Y.S.2d 845, 225 N.E.2d 845 (1967); Wagner v. Wagner, 58 A.D.2d 7, 395 N.Y.S.2d 641 (1st Dep't 1977), affirmed 44 N.Y.2d 780, 406 N.Y.S.2d 38, 377 N.E.2d 482 (1978).

2. Matter of Dunham, 63 Misc.2d 1029, 314 N.Y.S.2d 29 (Greene 1970), affirmed 36 A.D.2d 467, 320 N.Y.S.2d 951 (1st Dep't 1971), appeal denied 29 N.Y.2d 485, 325 N.Y.S.2d 1025, 274 N.E.2d 753 (1971).

3. See Turano, Love and Death: Marital Problems, Wills and the Right of Election, 49 Brooklyn L.Rev. 405 (1983).

Sec. H

1. Matter of Grossman, 71 Misc.2d 1050, 337 N.Y.S.2d 712 (New York County 1972).

2. Mott v. Duncan Petroleum, 51 N.Y.2d 289, 434 N.Y.S.2d 155, 414 N.E.2d 657 (1980) (Georgia common-law marriage); Matter of Pecorino, 64 A.D.2d 711, 407 N.Y.S.2d 550 (2d Dep't 1978), appeal denied 46 N.Y.2d 708, 414 N.Y.S.2d 1025, 386 N.E.2d 1337 (1979) (Pennsylvania common-law marriage). See also Matter of Smith, N.Y.L.J., July 30, 1985, at 11, col. 4 (Kings), where the court refused to recognize the petitioner's assertion that he was married to decedent on his proof that they had slept together on weekend trips to Pennsylvania, a state that recognizes common law marriages, because, among other

and the surviving spouse seeking to rely on the common-law marriage has the burden of proving it.[3]

The court has the power to determine who is the surviving spouse. A second marriage is presumed valid, and the second spouse has a right of election unless the first spouse can produce enough evidence to rebut the presumption.[4] While the parties litigate the issue of the surviving spouse's status, the court can order temporary payments to the surviving spouse.[5]

A spouse who has been divorced from the decedent under a decree recognized in New York is no longer a surviving spouse and cannot exercise a right of election.[6] The same is true if the marriage was bigamous or incestuous or if it was a prohibited remarriage.[7] If the surviving spouse obtained a divorce not recognized in New York, that spouse is precluded from exercising the right of election.[8] That is not so, however, if it was the decedent who obtained the invalid divorce, unless the "innocent" spouse then remarries, in which case there is no right of election on the theory that the surviving spouse by remarrying is estopped from relying on the continued existence of the first marriage.[9] A surviving spouse who abandoned the decedent or failed to support him when there was a duty to do so [10] is disqualified unless the abandonment or failure to support ended before the decedent's death.[11] Abandonment has been defined as departure without consent, without

things, the decedent's income tax returns listed her as "unmarried head of household."

3. Matter of Benjamin, 34 N.Y.2d 27, 355 N.Y.S.2d 356, 311 N.E.2d 495 (1974), reargument denied 34 N.Y.2d 916, 359 N.Y.S.2d 1028, 316 N.E.2d 723 (1974).

4. Matter of Dugro, 261 App.Div. 236, 25 N.Y.S.2d 88 (1st Dep't 1941), affirmed 287 N.Y. 595, 38 N.E.2d 706 (1941); Matter of Bihanskyj, 55 A.D.2d 836, 390 N.Y.S.2d 322 (4th Dep't 1976); Matter of Kolodij, 85 Misc.2d 946, 380 N.Y.S.2d 610 (Monroe 1976). See also Matter of Brown, 49 A.D.2d 648, 370 N.Y.S.2d 262 (3d Dep't 1975), affirmed 40 N.Y.2d 938, 390 N.Y.S.2d 59, 358 N.E.2d 883 (1976), where the first spouse obtained a statement from the officer with custody of divorce records in the jurisdiction where the divorce was supposed to have taken place, that no divorce had occurred, and the court found that the presumption of validity of the second marriage was overcome; Matter of Hadley, 57 Misc.2d 652, 293 N.Y.S.2d 224 (Dutchess 1968), judgment affirmed 32 A.D. 2d 1078, 303 N.Y.S.2d 1012 (1969), where the presumption of the validity of the second marriage was overcome by the decedent's return to the first wife and continued cohabitation with her until his death.

5. Matter of Milbank, 83 Misc.2d 716, 373 N.Y.S.2d 440 (New York County 1975), modified on other grounds 49 A.D.2d 848, 374 N.Y.S.2d 105 (1st Dep't 1975).

6. McKinney's EPTL 5–1.2(a)(1), (2).

7. The prohibited remarriage no longer exists in New York, and hence this language of McKinney's EPTL 5–1.2(a) is quite musty.

8. McKinney's EPTL 5–1.2(a)(3). See Matter of Loeb, 77 Misc.2d 814, 354 N.Y.S.2d 864 (New York County 1974) (husband got ex parte Mexican divorce and therefore had no standing to file objections to probate).

9. Matter of Bingham, 178 Misc. 801, 36 N.Y.S.2d 584 (Kings 1942), affirmed 265 App.Div. 463, 39 N.Y.S.2d 756 (2d Dep't 1943), appeal denied 266 App.Div. 669, 41 N.Y.S.2d 180 (1943); accord, Matter of Goethie, 9 Misc.2d 906, 161 N.Y.S.2d 785 (Westchester 1957).

10. Under McKinney's Dom.Rel.L. § 32 (Supp.1983–84), spouses each have an obligation to support the other.

11. McKinney's EPTL 5–1.2(a)(5), (6). Cf. Matter of Reifberg, 58 N.Y.2d 134, 459 N.Y.S.2d 739, 446 N.E.2d 424 (1983); Cassia v. Cassia, 125 Misc.2d 606, 480 N.Y.S.2d 84 (Westchester 1984).

justification, and without intention to return,[12] and a spouse who goes through a marriage ceremony with another at a time when the first marriage is still valid has abandoned the first spouse.[13] The proponent of the will objecting to the surviving spouse's election has the burden of proving the surviving spouse's abandonment, non-support, divorce or other disqualification,[14] and has available the equitable defenses of laches and estoppel.[15] A surviving spouse against whom the decedent obtained a decree or judgment of separation recognized in New York is also disqualified.[16] If the surviving spouse obtained the decree of separation against the decedent, she can exercise a right of election unless the decree specifically states that it is waived.[17]

A surviving spouse living apart from the decedent under a separation agreement is not disqualified, unless the separation agreement incorporates a waiver of the right of election,[18] nor is a spouse who was "merely" unfaithful to the decedent.[19]

SECTION I. PERSONAL RIGHT

A right of election belongs to the surviving spouse of a New York domiciliary, whether or not the surviving spouse is domiciled in New York.[1] A New York domiciliary may not, by opting for application of the law of another jurisdiction to his will, eliminate his surviving spouse's right of election,[2] but arguably a non-New Yorker can place his assets in New York, provide a "right of election" trust for his spouse, opt for application of New York law, and avoid the more substantial right of election permitted by his own state.[3]

12. Matter of Prince, 36 A.D.2d 946, 321 N.Y.S.2d 798 (1st Dep't 1971), affirmed 30 N.Y.2d 512, 330 N.Y.S.2d 61, 280 N.E.2d 888 (1972).

13. See Matter of Oswald, 43 Misc.2d 774, 252 N.Y.S.2d 203 (Nassau 1964), affirmed 24 A.D.2d 465, 260 N.Y.S.2d 615 (2d Dep't 1965), affirmed 17 N.Y.2d 447, 266 N.Y.S.2d 807, 213 N.E.2d 888 (1965); Matter of Goethie, 9 Misc.2d 906, 161 N.Y.S.2d 785 (Westchester 1957).

14. Matter of Ruff, 91 A.D.2d 814, 458 N.Y.S.2d 38 (3d Dep't 1982); Matter of Fuller, 9 A.D.2d 565, 189 N.Y.S.2d 287 (3d Dep't 1959), reargument denied 9 A.D.2d 854, 194 N.Y.S.2d 454 (1959).

15. See Matter of Guido, 81 A.D.2d 614, 438 N.Y.S.2d 9 (2d Dep't 1981), where the first spouse waited twenty-one years (until decedent's death) before challenging decedent's foreign divorce and remarriage. She also acknowledged on various estate forms and returns the second wife and her own status as former wife. See also Matter of Bock, 70 Misc.2d 470, 333 N.Y.S.2d 801 (Erie 1972) (since wife did not contest the validity of the divorce decree for ten years, she was barred by laches and estoppel).

16. McKinney's EPTL 5–1.2(a)(4).

17. Matter of Gerke, 70 Misc.2d 280, 332 N.Y.S.2d 493 (Wayne 1972).

18. Matter of Martin, 45 Misc.2d 852, 257 N.Y.S.2d 668 (Westchester 1965); Matter of Archibald, 19 Misc.2d 705, 191 N.Y.S.2d 1021 (New York County 1959), appeal dismissed 10 A.D.2d 576, 200 N.Y.S. 2d 317 (1st Dep't 1959) (court dismissed proceeding without prejudice to renew on proper papers).

19. Matter of Holman, 46 Misc.2d 809, 260 N.Y.S.2d 885 (Erie 1965).

Sec. I

1. McKinney's EPTL 5–1.1(d)(7).

2. See Matter of Crichton, 20 N.Y.2d 124, 281 N.Y.S.2d 811, 228 N.E.2d 799 (1967).

3. See Matter of Renard, 108 Misc.2d 31, 437 N.Y.S.2d 860 (New York County 1981), affirmed 85 A.D.2d 501, (1st Dep't 1981), affirmed 56 N.Y.2d 973, 453 N.Y.S.2d 625, 439 N.E.2d 346 (1982), and

The right of election is a personal right to the decedent's spouse. If the surviving spouse dies without serving the notice of election, her administrator or executor cannot exercise the right of election.[4] This is true even if the surviving spouse had signed the notice of election before death but had not yet served it on the decedent's executor.[5] If she served it and later died before her share was paid, the right is preserved and the money is payable to her estate. The surviving spouse's creditors cannot force her to exercise her right of election.[6]

There is an important exception to this "exercise by spouse only" rule. If the surviving spouse is a minor, conservatee or incompetent, her representative (guardian, conservator or committee) can exercise the right of election for her during her lifetime with permission of the appointing court.[7] A will cannot prevent these representatives from exercising the right. If the incompetent or conservatee surviving spouse attempts to exercise the right of election herself, the exercise is invalid, but the court will then allow the committee or conservator to do it.[8] The committee or conservator cannot file the notice of election without court approval, but in one case where the incompetent died after the committee's unauthorized filing of the notice, the court granted retroactive leave to file.[9] In another, where the person who had petitioned to become the surviving spouse's conservator had, with court permission, filed the notice of election, the court allowed the exercise of the right despite the fact that the conservator was never appointed because the surviving spouse died during the conservatorship proceeding.[10] If no committee or conservator has been appointed for an incompetent or disabled spouse, the New York Supreme Court may appoint one, and the Surrogate has jurisdiction to appoint conservators under certain circumstances, including this one.[11] The Surrogate's Court has the authority to permit the committee of an incompetent spouse to file the notice of election any time before the first accounting.[12] A guardian ad litem is not authorized to exercise the right of election for the incompetent spouse,[13] but the guardian ad litem should

Matter of Clark, 21 N.Y.2d 478, 288 N.Y.S. 2d 993, 236 N.E.2d 152 (1968) (contra, but arguably overruled by *Renard*) and discussion in chapter on "Jurisdiction," supra at 32.

4. McKinney's EPTL 5–1.1(d)(4); Matter of Cohen, 12 Misc.2d 784, 177 N.Y.S.2d 245 (New York County 1958), affirmed 6 A.D.2d 1033, 178 N.Y.S.2d 1017 (1st Dep't 1958); Matter of Reich, 94 Misc.2d 319, 404 N.Y.S.2d 781 (New York County 1978).

5. Matter of Thornstrom, 95 N.Y.S.2d 42 (Queens 1950); Matter of Ward, 73 N.Y.S.2d 456 (Queens 1947).

6. Matter of Charkowsky, 89 Misc.2d 623, 392 N.Y.S.2d 368 (New York County 1977).

7. McKinney's EPTL 5–1.1(d)(4)(a), (b), (c).

8. See Matter of Hansen, 117 N.Y.S.2d 619 (Suffolk 1952).

9. Matter of Harris, 35 Misc.2d 443, 229 N.Y.S.2d 997 (Fulton County 1962).

10. Matter of Fabell, 121 Misc.2d 176, 467 N.Y.S.2d 792 (Bronx 1983).

11. McKinney's Mental Hygiene Law § 77.01(3) (Supp.1984–85).

12. McKinney's EPTL 5–1.1(e)(3).

13. Matter of Gilchrist, 93 Misc.2d 475, 403 N.Y.S.2d 175 (Rensselaer 1978); Matter of Fuller, 33 A.D.2d 1095, 308 N.Y.S.2d 193 (4th Dep't 1970).

note the possible existence of a right of election in his report [14] and notify the family, or if there is none, the Department of Social Services if no one has commenced a proceeding to appoint a conservator or committee.

A consul can exercise the right of election for a non-domiciliary alien if a treaty between the United States and the country of the surviving spouse's citizenship allows it.[15]

SECTION J. WAIVER OF RIGHT OF ELECTION

Spouses can waive their right of election in the other's estate before or after the marriage.[1] The waiver must be in writing and signed, and it should be acknowledged.[2] If it is not acknowledged, the statute also permits "[proof] in the manner required by the laws of this state for the recording of a conveyance of real property." [3] In the very rare case where the surviving spouse's waiver is in her will (an unacknowledged instrument), the subscribing witness can give this proof by acknowledging the will after the decedent's death.[4] One or both of the spouses may waive the right, and the waiver need not be supported by consideration.[5] If the waiver is part of a separation agreement and the couple later reconciles, unless they show a contrary intent the separation agreement is void and the waiver ineffective, and the surviving spouse can elect against the decedent's will.[6] Courts interpret these waivers much like any other contract,[7] and enforce them if they were made fairly, without fraud, and if their terms are not unconscionable.[8] A surviving spouse can attack the validity of a waiver on the grounds of fraud or lack of understanding,[9] and the courts will consider the intelligence and business experience of the contesting

14. The guardian ad litem's report is required by McKinney's SCPA 404 and is discussed in chapter on "Appearances," supra at 240–42.

15. Matter of Zalewski, 292 N.Y. 332, 55 N.E.2d 184 (1944).

Sec. J

1. McKinney's EPTL 5–1.1(f)(3)(A); see Matter of Falanga, 29 A.D.2d 169, 286 N.Y.S.2d 961 (1st Dep't 1968), affirmed 23 N.Y.2d 860, 298 N.Y.S.2d 69, 245 N.E.2d 802 (1969).

2. McKinney's EPTL 5–1.1(f)(2). See Matter of Warren, 16 A.D.2d 505, 229 N.Y.S.2d 1004 (2d Dep't 1962), affirmed 12 N.Y.2d 854, 236 N.Y.S.2d 628, 187 N.E.2d 478 (1962) (wife signed separation agreement waiving right of election, but did not acknowledge it; waiver ineffective); accord, Matter of Held, 24 A.D.2d 506, 261 N.Y.S.2d 674 (2d Dep't 1965).

3. McKinney's EPTL 5–1.1(f)(2).

4. Matter of Maul, 262 App.Div. 941, 29 N.Y.S.2d 429 (4th Dep't 1941), affirmed 287 N.Y. 694, 39 N.E.2d 301 (1942); Matter of Stegman, 42 Misc.2d 273, 247 N.Y.S.2d 727 (Bronx 1964).

5. McKinney's EPTL 5–1.1(f)(3)(C), (D).

6. Matter of Wilson, 50 N.Y.2d 59, 427 N.Y.S.2d 977, 405 N.E.2d 220 (1980). But see Matter of Granchelli, 90 Misc.2d 103, 393 N.Y.S.2d 894 (Monroe 1977) (reconciliation after separation decree, followed by a second split, did not restore right of election to surviving spouse).

7. Matter of Lemle, 30 A.D.2d 785, 291 N.Y.S.2d 443 (1st Dep't 1968).

8. Christian v. Christian, 42 N.Y.2d 63, 396 N.Y.S.2d 817, 365 N.E.2d 849 (1977); Matter of Davis, 20 N.Y.2d 70, 281 N.Y.S.2d 767, 228 N.E.2d 768 (1967).

9. Matter of Phillips, 293 N.Y. 483, 58 N.E.2d 504 (1944), motion denied 294 N.Y. 662, 60 N.E.2d 389 (1945).

spouse.[10] The very substantial burden of proof is on the party attacking the waiver, and it is especially difficult to meet that burden if each of the parties was represented by separate counsel.[11] The doctrine of equitable estoppel is applicable both to uphold the waiver,[12] and to defeat it.[13]

Because a waiver is a contract, it is subject to a six-year statute of limitations.[14] If the cause of action is based on fraud, the six years begins to run when the fraud is discovered.[15] The agreement does not remain executory until one of the parties dies.[16] A spouse can execute a waiver of her elective rights against any will, present or future, of the decedent,[17] or only against a particular will specified in the waiver.[18] If the waiver is ambiguous, it will be interpreted in favor of the surviving spouse,[19] and in that case the burden of proof is on the party asserting that the surviving spouse has waived.[20] A waiver of the right of election does not waive dispositions under the will. This means that if a couple enters into a separation agreement in which the spouses waive the right of election in each other's estate but do not specifically waive bequests under each other's wills, and then one spouse dies before the divorce and without changing will provisions in the other's favor, those

10. Hoffman v. Hoffman, 100 A.D.2d 704, 474 N.Y.S.2d 621 (3d Dep't 1984); Matter of Sunshine, 51 A.D.2d 326, 381 N.Y.S.2d 260 (1st Dep't 1976), affirmed 40 N.Y.2d 875, 389 N.Y.S.2d 344, 357 N.E.2d 999 (1976).

11. Matter of Sunshine, 51 A.D.2d 326, 381 N.Y.S.2d 260 (1st Dep't 1976), affirmed 40 N.Y.2d 875, 389 N.Y.S.2d 344, 357 N.E.2d 999 (1976).

12. Matter of Lemle, 30 A.D.2d 785, 291 N.Y.S.2d 443 (1st Dep't 1968); Matter of Hart, 53 Misc.2d 555, 279 N.Y.S.2d 119 (Suffolk 1967), affirmed 30 A.D.2d 781, 292 N.Y.S.2d 1017 (2d Dep't 1968), appeal dismissed 24 N.Y.2d 158, 299 N.Y.S.2d 182, 247 N.E.2d 148 (1969); Matter of Yaeger, N.Y.L.J., July 8, 1985, at 7, col. 1 (New York County) (surviving spouse tried to set aside the ante-nuptial agreement in which she waived her right of election on the ground, among others, that her husband had orally promised the agreement would be effective for only two years, and the court used her own attempts to change the agreement as an estoppel against her argument).

13. See Nassau Trust Co. v. Montrose Concrete Products Corp., 75 A.D.2d 866, 428 N.Y.S.2d 40 (2d Dep't 1980), reversed 56 N.Y.2d 175, 451 N.Y.S.2d 663, 436 N.E.2d 1265 (1982), reargument denied 57 N.Y.2d 674, 454 N.Y.S.2d 1032, 439 N.E.2d 1247 (1982); Rose v. SPA Realty Ass'n, 42 N.Y.2d 338, 397 N.Y.S.2d 922, 366 N.E.2d 1279 (1977).

14. McKinney's CPLR 213(2); Matter of Lemle, 30 A.D.2d 785, 291 N.Y.S.2d 443 (1st Dep't 1968).

15. McKinney's CPLR 213(8); see Sielcken-Schwarz v. American Factors Ltd., 265 N.Y. 239, 192 N.E. 307 (1934).

16. Pacchiana v. Pacchiana, 94 A.D.2d 721, 462 N.Y.S.2d 256 (2d Dep't 1983), appeal dismissed 60 N.Y.2d 586 (1983).

17. Matter of Marley, 3 A.D.2d 53, 158 N.Y.S.2d 566 (3d Dep't 1956); Matter of Peltz, 14 Misc.2d 18, 178 N.Y.S.2d 920 (Sullivan 1957).

18. Matter of Deffner, 202 Misc. 1, 114 N.Y.S.2d 600 (Monroe 1952), reversed 281 App.Div. 798, 119 N.Y.S.2d 443 (4th Dep't 1953), affirmed 305 N.Y. 783, 113 N.E.2d 300 (1953).

19. See Matter of LeRoy, 118 Misc.2d 382, 461 N.Y.S.2d 161 (Onondaga 1983), citing by analogy Matter of Maruccia, 54 N.Y.2d 196, 445 N.Y.S.2d 73, 429 N.E.2d 751 (1981) (spouse held not to have waived will bequests in separation agreement when waiver referred to all rights in spouse's estate, enumerating right of election and other statutory rights, but did not specifically refer to will bequests).

20. Matter of Colaci, 288 N.Y. 158, 42 N.E.2d 466 (1942).

will provisions are valid.[21] A divorce automatically revokes will provisions in favor of the divorced spouse.[22]

Sometimes an issue arises whether a surviving spouse who intends to assert, or has asserted, her right of election can accept any property from the estate before her right to elect has been established. In one case, for example, the decedent gave the surviving spouse the minimum amount necessary to satisfy the elective share in lieu of exempt property under EPTL 5–3.1. The spouse took possession of the exempt property, and the court held that she had not waived the right of election by accepting the exempt property, since that passes to the spouse by operation of law regardless of the terms of the will.[23] In another case, the court held that a spouse does not waive the right of election by accepting specific dispositions under the will.[24] If a spouse signed a waiver of the right of election but seeks to set it aside, her acceptance of some of the property the decedent gave her under the agreement should not affect her rights, if any, to set the agreement aside.[25]

It is possible for a surviving spouse to make a partial waiver of her right of election.[26]

Presumably, a surviving spouse who validly waived her right of election still has standing to object to probate of the will, since she is an intestate distributee and has a financial stake in seeing the will denied probate.[27]

SECTION K. PROCEDURE FOR ELECTING AGAINST WILL

The surviving spouse makes the election by serving a copy of the written notice on the administrator or executor (by mail without court order [1]) and by filing the original in the Surrogate's Court with an affidavit of service. While the statute does not specify the form of the written notice of election, and while it has been held that the notice need not be signed by the surviving spouse in her own handwriting [2] or acknowledged,[3] it is certainly advisable to do both to avoid litigation.

21. Matter of Maruccia, 54 N.Y.2d 196, 445 N.Y.S.2d 73, 429 N.E.2d 751 (1981).

22. McKinney's EPTL 5–1.4.

23. Matter of Tisnower, 16 N.Y.2d 906, 264 N.Y.S.2d 697, 212 N.E.2d 151 (1965), reversing 23 A.D.2d 535, 255 N.Y.S.2d 457 (1965), affirming 40 Misc.2d 778, 244 N.Y.S.2d 169 (1963).

24. Matter of Burr, 168 Misc. 240, 4 N.Y.S.2d 832 (Genesee 1938), affirmed 254 App.Div. 825, 6 N.Y.S.2d 152 (1938); Matter of Tannenbaum, 25 Misc.2d 287, 205 N.Y.S.2d 390 (Kings 1960).

25. Matter of Yaeger, N.Y.L.J., July 8, 1985, at 7, col. 1 (New York County).

26. See Matter of Grosser, N.Y.L.J., Nov. 9, 1979 (New York County) (widow waived her right of election against certain Totten Trusts, and her share was apportioned ratably among all).

27. See Matter of Schwartz, 94 Misc.2d 1024, 405 N.Y.S.2d 920 (1978); Matter of Levow, N.Y.L.J., March 23, 1962, at 17.

Sec. K

1. McKinney's EPTL 5–1.1(e)(1).

2. Matter of Charkowsky, 89 Misc.2d 623, 392 N.Y.S.2d 368 (New York County 1977).

3. Matter of Finn, 85 Misc.2d 274, 381 N.Y.S.2d 380 (Schenectady 1976).

If a will of the decedent is on file in the Surrogate's Court but has not been probated, the surviving spouse can, if she chooses, serve the notice on the executor named in that will.[4] A spouse in delicate health is likely to do so.

The spouse (or her representative) must make the election within six months from the issuance of letters testamentary or letters of administration.[5] Appointment of a successor fiduciary does not give the surviving spouse additional time.[6] On the other hand, the appointment of a preliminary executor or temporary administrator does not commence the six-month period.[7]

The surviving spouse will not be bound by the six-month period where an administrator has been appointed and a will is subsequently found,[8] or when a will is probated but the decree is later vacated.[9] Thus, although the surviving spouse can, if she chooses, serve notice on the executor named in a non-probated will on file in the Surrogate's Court, she has no obligation to do so because the six-month period does not start to run until the letters-in-chief are issued.

If the surviving spouse applies for an extension during the six-month period, the court can extend the time for another six months. If she does not apply during the six-month period, she has defaulted.[10] She, or her committee, conservator, guardian, or a guardian ad litem on her behalf,[11] can file a petition seeking relief from default. The court can order an extension of time for filing for reasonable cause, such as the surviving spouse's limited knowledge of English,[12] ignorance of inter vivos transfers made by decedent just before his death,[13] and complete ignorance of the value of the estate.[14] Ignorance of the law has been held not to constitute reasonable cause,[15] but if the failure to file was induced by fraud, the surviving spouse arguably should be relieved from default.[16] If the surviving spouse has not procured an extension within the six months or opened her default after the six months, she is absolutely foreclosed after twelve months,[17] except that if the surviving spouse was an infant or an incompetent or conservatee and the fiducia-

4. McKinney's EPTL 5–1.1(e)(1).

5. McKinney's EPTL 5–1.1(e)(1).

6. Matter of O'Shea, 45 Misc.2d 84, 255 N.Y.S.2d 729 (Suffolk 1965), affirmed 24 A.D.2d 845, 263 N.Y.S.2d 554 (2d Dep't 1965).

7. McKinney's EPTL 5–1.1(a)(1) starts the six months running from the issuance of "letters testamentary or letters of administration."

8. McKinney's SCPA 705, 1413.

9. Matter of Latowitzky, 56 Misc.2d 916, 290 N.Y.S.2d 667 (Kings 1968).

10. McKinney's EPTL 5–1.1(e)(2).

11. Matter of Fuller, 33 A.D.2d 1095, 308 N.Y.S.2d 193 (4th Dep't 1970).

12. E.g., Matter of Lamash, 8 Misc.2d 544, 49 N.Y.S.2d 434 (Queens 1941).

13. Matter of Koleda, N.Y.L.J., Feb. 6, 1978, at 12, col. 5 (New York County).

14. Matter of Crary, 283 App.Div. 760, 128 N.Y.S.2d 173 (3d Dep't 1954).

15. Matter of Zweig, 145 Misc. 839, 261 N.Y.S. 400 (Kings 1932).

16. See Matter of Schnabel, 77 N.Y.S.2d 593 (Queens 1947); Matter of Vogel, N.Y. L.J., Dec. 23, 1977, at 6, col. 2 (dictum). But see Matter of Goldstein, 176 Misc. 366, 27 N.Y.S.2d 288 (New York County 1941); Matter of Stultz, 4 Misc.2d 847, 159 N.Y.S. 2d 516 (New York County 1956).

17. McKinney's EPTL 5–1.1(e)(2).

ry has not accounted, the court can allow an extension at any time [18] until the executor or administrator has obtained a decree settling his account.[19] Though the statute calls for strict application of these time limits,[20] rare exceptions are allowed. For example, in one case the widow's failure to exercise her right of election was due to ongoing negotiations for a settlement, and she applied for relief from default one day before the expiration of a year from issuance of letters. In view of this, the court permitted her to file the notice after the expiration of the year.[21] If the court does extend the time to file, the order is then recorded like a notice of pendency of an action in every county where the decedent owned real property.[22]

Far more often the statutory requirements are strictly construed, and failure to comply results in the loss of the right of election.[23]

The court can also permit the surviving spouse to revoke the notice of election if the surviving spouse's creditors (or other persons) are not prejudiced.[24] In that case the Surrogate directs the manner of service and the persons to be served.

SECTION L. RIGHT OF ELECTION PROCEEDING

When court intervention is required, the EPTL [1] and the SCPA [2] operate together to govern the procedural aspects of the surviving spouse's right of election. A fiduciary has the right to pay a surviving spouse her elective share without court approval, but the fiduciary's action is subject to review in the accounting proceeding. He may be surcharged if the surviving spouse's right turns out to invalid, or if the fiduciary distributed the wrong assets in satisfying it.[3] Therefore, when there is a serious question about the validity of the right of election, the fiduciary should seek court approval under SCPA 1421, which allows the court to determine whether the surviving spouse has a valid right of election and if so, how the exercise of that right affects the other beneficiaries of the decedent's property. Sometimes the SCPA 1421 procedure is brought in the course of an accounting, and even when it is commenced as an independent proceeding the court usually does not direct payment of the elective share until the fiducia-

18. McKinney's EPTL 5–1.1(e)(3).

19. McKinney's EPTL 5–1.1(e)(2).

20. McKinney's EPTL 5–1.1(e)(3).

21. Matter of Silverman, 74 Misc.2d 399, 344 N.Y.S.2d 36 (Erie 1973).

22. McKinney's EPTL 5–1.1(e)(2).

23. See, e.g., Matter of Brookes, 9 A.D.2d 927, 195 N.Y.S.2d 389 (2d Dep't 1959) affirmed N.Y.2d 840, 216 N.Y.S.2d 88, 175 N.E.2d 457 (1961) (statute requires surviving spouse both to file and to serve notice of election and failure to do both within twelve months is a default of which the court has no power to relieve the surviving spouse); Matter of Allan, 5 N.Y.2d 333, 184 N.Y.S.2d 613, 157 N.E.2d 607 (1959).

24. McKinney's EPTL 5–1.1(d)(6).

Sec. L

1. McKinney's EPTL 5–1.1(e).

2. McKinney' SCPA 1421.

3. See chapters on "Accounting," supra at 212–13 and "Commissions," infra at 436–41.

ry's accounting, except in cases where the spouse's right of election attaches only to testamentary substitutes, when the court is likely to order payment sooner to protect the spouse's interest in property that is not in the hands of the fiduciary.

1. WHO MAY PETITION

When a spouse elects to take a share of the decedent's estate, any "person interested" may petition the Surrogate[4] to determine the validity of that election.[5]

Usually the interested person is the surviving spouse who hopes to receive the elective share, or the fiduciary who wants to avoid the possibility of surcharge if the payment was wrongful. However, other parties may also be interested, such as legatees under the will,[6] another person claiming to be the decedent's surviving spouse,[7] or the beneficiary of an inter vivos transfer by the decedent which the surviving spouse claims is a testamentary substitute.

This proceeding is useful when the fiduciary does not have custody of property that is part of the net estate for right of election purposes (that is, testamentary substitutes given to others during the decedent's life[8]). The court can fix the liability of the persons who have that property,[9] thus apportioning the property among the surviving spouse and the decedent's beneficiaries.

The person interested can ask for this determination in the course of an accounting proceeding,[10] or can, by filing a petition, start a separate proceeding expressly to contest the right of election.[11] Like many miscellaneous proceedings, the court has discretion whether to entertain the application; the petitioner does not have an automatic right to be heard. If the court entertains the proceeding, the petition must show the petitioner's interest, the names and post office addresses of other persons interested, all the other information required in petitions generally by the SCPA,[12] and the specific issues submitted for adjudication.[13]

2. PROCESS

The petitioner submits a citation along with the petition, and the court issues it and gives it back to the petitioner, who arranges for its

4. The Surrogate's Court with jurisdiction is the one in the county where the will was probated or letters of administration issued. SCPA 1421(1).

5. SCPA 1421(1).

6. See Matter of Lukas, 38 A.D.2d 784, 328 N.Y.S.2d 118 (4th Dep't 1972), where the decedent's niece, the primary legatee under the will, was permitted to object to the surviving spouse's filing of his notice of election on the ground that he was incompetent (though not judicially declared so) at the time of the filing.

7. See discussions of status and disqualification of surviving spouses, this chapter supra at 315–17.

8. See discussion of testamentary substitutes this chapter supra at 307–11.

9. SCPA 1421(5).

10. SCPA 1421(3).

11. SCPA 1421(1).

12. SCPA 304, discussed in chapter on "Procedure," supra at 54–55.

13. McKinney's SCPA 1421(1).

service.[14] All persons interested must receive process, except that the beneficiaries of an inter vivos trust claimed to be a testamentary substitute need not be cited; the trustee of such a trust must receive process and will protect the interests of the beneficiaries.[15]

On the return of process the court may take proof and make such decree as justice requires. The parties do not have a right to a jury trial in a right of election proceeding.[16] The rights of the surviving spouse are liberally construed to give the surviving spouse the broadest possible protection.[17] When the court determines that a surviving spouse is entitled to a right of election, the court can direct that the fiduciary use assets in his possession and subject to a right of election to satisfy the right of election. If he has no such assets, or insufficient assets, the court fixes the liability of the appropriate persons with an interest in estate property and directs that they make their contributions toward the surviving spouse's right of election.[18] The will beneficiaries and beneficiaries of testamentary substitutes, and not the intestate distributees, are responsible pro rata for making up the elective share.[19]

SECTION M. DISCOVERY OF ASSETS

If a surviving spouse is unsure whether she is entitled to elect under EPTL 5–1.1 because the extent of the assets of an estate is not known, she can examine the fiduciary under SCPA 2102 and any other party under CPLR Article 31 to determine whether or not she has a valid right of election.

14. Service of process is discussed in chapter on "Procedure," supra at 39–49.

15. McKinney's SCPA 1421(4).

16. See Matter of Santillo, 103 Misc.2d 937, 426 N.Y.S.2d 441 (Erie 1980).

17. Matter of Bartley, 83 Misc.2d 672, 370 N.Y.S.2d 990 (Cattaraugus 1975); Matter of Mescall, 54 Misc.2d 165, 281 N.Y.S.2d 394 (Erie 1967).

18. McKinney's SCPA 1421(5).

19. See section on "Right of Election in an Intestate Estate," this chapter supra at 314.

Chapter Twelve

MISCELLANEOUS PROCEEDINGS

SECTION A. INTRODUCTION

Frequently in estates practice someone needs a kind of relief not specifically provided for in the standard probate, administration or accounting proceeding. For example, a fiduciary may want to question persons who have estate assets or information about them. A creditor or beneficiary may want to question a fiduciary about his actions or nudge a dilatory fiduciary. A fiduciary may want the court's advice and direction on the best way to proceed in a doubtful situation or the court's approval to continue operating the decedent's business. Parties may want to settle a claim or a lawsuit. SCPA Article 21 provides for these (and other) miscellaneous proceedings.

While Article 21 lists specific miscellaneous proceedings, it is not exclusive; many miscellaneous proceedings are set forth in other articles.[1] In addition, the court has the (New York) constitutional jurisdiction to entertain any proceeding relating to the administration of an estate or the affairs of a decedent.[2] If the proceeding relates to a matter within the court's jurisdiction, but the SCPA does not specifically provide for such a proceeding, it can be brought under SCPA 202. For example, a fiduciary uncertain whether to sell estate property can,

Sec. A

1. For example, McKinney's SCPA 902 permits a proceeding for appointment of a successor temporary administrator when the office becomes vacant, McKinney's SCPA 1116 and 1210 permit a public administrator to apply for letters of administration or probate, McKinney's SCPA 1121 allows a distributee of a decedent to petition for letters superseding those granted to a public administrator, McKinney's SCPA 1304 allows a summary proceeding for the administration of small estates, McKinney's SCPA 1401 allows a proceeding to compel production of a will, McKinney's SCPA 1412 allows a proceeding for preliminary letters testamentary, McKinney's SCPA 1415 allows a proceeding for the issuance of supplementary letters testamentary, McKinney's SCPA 1420 allows a proceeding for construction of a will, McKinney's SCPA 1421 allows the exercise of a right of election by a surviving spouse, McKinney's SCPA 1507 allows a trustee to petition for authorization to release a claim, McKinney's SCPA 1602 allows a proceeding for ancillary probate, McKinney's SCPA 1703 and 1750 allow a proceeding for appointment of a guardian, McKinney's SCPA 1809 allows a fiduciary to petition to determine the validity of a claim, McKinney's SCPA 1904 allows a proceeding for the disposition of real property, McKinney's SCPA 2003 allows a proceeding for the opening of a safe deposit box, and McKinney's SCPA 2310 and 2311 allow a proceeding for payment on account of commissions.

2. See McKinney's Const. Art. 6, section 12, McKinney's SCPA 202, and chapter on "Jurisdiction," supra at 23–24.

under SCPA 2107, ask the court for advice and direction.[3] The fiduciary does not have the right under SCPA 2107 to seek advice and direction when other tough or questionable situations arise, but because of the jurisdiction given to the Surrogate by the New York Constitution and SCPA 202, he can seek advice and direction from the Surrogate anyway.[4]

SCPA 2101 sets forth the general provisions relating to all the miscellaneous proceedings. Unless a specific section of Article 21 sets forth different rules or procedures, SCPA 2101 controls. As a matter of good practice, parties should follow the procedural rules set forth in SCPA 2101 (regarding form of petition, process and parties) in all miscellaneous proceedings, even those brought under SCPA 202.

A fiduciary, creditor or any person interested[5] in an estate may commence an Article 21 proceeding.[6] However, these persons do not have an absolute right to start the proceeding; the court can refuse to entertain it.[7] The court usually entertains the matter if it raises an issue needing immediate resolution. The court has the options of entertaining the proceeding, refusing to entertain it, or electing not to entertain it but to decide it later in an accounting or other proceeding if the issue is one that is typically decided at the final accounting and not before.[8] The court will decline to entertain a proceeding if it feels it does not have jurisdiction,[9] or if the issue has already been determined in another court or another proceeding in the Surrogate's Court, or if the petitioner lacks standing, or if the proceeding would serve no useful purpose in the administration of an estate. Once the court entertains the proceeding, its jurisdiction over the proceeding continues until a decree or order is signed.[10]

The legislature gave the Surrogate the power to entertain or decline jurisdiction because most miscellaneous proceedings are equitable and the court ought to have the power to weigh the equities before

3. Advice and direction proceedings are discussed this chapter infra at 350–53.

4. See, e.g., Matter of Tapow, N.Y.L.J., April 3, 1985, at 13, col. 3 (Bronx); Matter of Colp, N.Y.L.J., Jan. 20, 1976, at 8, col. 2 (New York County); Matter of Raible, N.Y. L.J., May 10, 1977, at 14, col. 1 (Nassau). See also Matter of Rappaport, 121 Misc.2d 447, 467 N.Y.S.2d 814 (Nassau 1983), and Matter of Fales, 106 Misc.2d 419, 422, 431 N.Y.S.2d 763, 764 (New York County 1980), where the court gave fiduciaries guidelines on exercising their discretion in tax issues.

5. Person interested includes "[a]ny person entitled either absolutely or contingently to share as beneficiary in the estate or trustee in bankruptcy or receiver of such person." McKinney's SCPA 103(39).

6. McKinney's SCPA 2101(1)(a).

7. McKinney's SCPA 2101(1)(b).

8. Matter of Brodin, 32 Misc.2d 651, 224 N.Y.S.2d 748 (Nassau 1962).

9. See Matter of Mester, 69 Misc.2d 570, 330 N.Y.S.2d 737 (Nassau 1972), where the court lacked jurisdiction to entertain the petition to order the trustees of the estate to pay directly to the infant's mother money due the infant's father from a trust, because the interests of other parties not before the court would be directly affected; Matter of Wright, 58 Misc.2d 783, 296 N.Y.S.2d 489 (Westchester 1968), where the court lacked jurisdiction to approve a compromise of an infant's cause of action and could not grant authorization for the removal of money from the guardianship account for the payment of medical expenses.

10. McKinney's SCPA 2101(2).

agreeing to hear the case. Those equities include the convenience, urgency or practicality of proceeding immediately, and the expense and possible duplication of an independent proceeding compared with an inevitable later proceeding, when the issues and the facts are likely to be better developed.[11]

The Surrogate's decision not to entertain a proceeding is reviewable by the appellate division, which can reverse and require the Surrogate to entertain the proceeding if the refusal was an abuse of discretion.[12]

Like all proceedings in the Surrogate's Court, the Article 21 proceedings are commenced by a petition which must set forth the jurisdictional facts and the facts relevant to the relief sought.[13]

When the petitioner files the petition, the clerk usually stamps it with an "entertainment order" and submits it to the Surrogate, who either signs it or refuses jurisdiction. As a practical matter, if there is a serious question as to whether the Surrogate should entertain the proceeding or not, the matter will be submitted for a formal decision on the issue of entertainment. Otherwise, the Surrogate merely approves the petition by signing the entertainment request or by issuing a short decision or order entertaining the proceeding.

If the court entertains the petition, all persons interested in the proceeding are entitled to process and the court can direct service on any others as well. The exception is that in proceedings under SCPA 2102 for relief against the fiduciary, it is sufficient to serve the fiduciary unless the court directs otherwise, on the theory that the fiduciary is the only person interested.[14] After all parties have had an opportunity to appear, the court has broad discretion to grant in the form of a decree or order whatever relief justice requires. If someone receives money or property under the order, the court can order the filing of a refunding bond as a pre-condition.[15]

SECTION B. PROCEEDINGS FOR RELIEF AGAINST A FIDUCIARY

In SCPA 2102 are six proceedings commenceable against a fiduciary. Any person interested, creditor or fiduciary (such as a co-executor, guardian or trustee) can start these proceedings.

11. See McKinney's SCPA 2101, Practice Commentary at 334–35 (1967).

12. See Matter of Smith, 84 A.D.2d 664, 444 N.Y.S.2d 325 (3d Dep't 1981), where an attorney claimed a fee for legal services and the Surrogate refused to entertain it. The appellate division found the petition reasonable and the Surrogate's refusal to entertain it abusive of his discretion.

13. See McKinney's SCPA 304 and discussion of the contents and form of the petition in the Surrogate's Court in chapter on "Procedure," supra at 54–55.

14. McKinney's SCPA 2101(3), as enacted in L.1970, c. 396.

15. McKinney's SCPA 2101(4).

1. EXAMINATION OF THE FIDUCIARY

If a person with an interest in an estate has written to the fiduciary asking about his interest and has received no response from the fiduciary, he can petition for the information under SCPA 2102(1). The petitioner often needs the information to decide whether to file a right of election, contest a will, commence a construction or other miscellaneous proceeding, or make tax planning decisions.[1]

This provision changes prior practice, under which the fiduciary had to submit an inventory of estate assets before the accounting, and under which the court could direct an appraisal of the assets.[2] The earlier practice was uneconomical because in many cases none of the persons interested in the estate sought or needed this information. Now the fiduciary must supply it only when someone wants it.

The petitioner should submit, along with the petition, evidence that he asked for the information in writing but did not receive it, and a proposed order to the fiduciary to show cause why the examination should not take place. If the court entertains the proceeding and signs the order to show cause, the petitioner must then arrange to serve it.[3] On the return date, the court usually orders the examination. It is a quasi-hearing, held at the courthouse before the official court reporter.[4]

2. PROCEEDING TO SET ASIDE EXEMPT PROPERTY

A spouse or minor children of a decedent may be entitled to certain assets as exempt property under EPTL 5–3.1, including utensils, musical instruments, clothing, fuel, books, domestic animals, farm machinery and vehicles of specified values, and one thousand dollars in cash or personal property.[5] If the executor does not set apart the exempt property and turn it over to the spouse or children, they can start a proceeding to compel the turnover under SCPA 2101(2). Before doing so, they should make a demand for the exempt property in writing, although the statute does not mandate this step. If the fiduciary does not then deliver the property, the spouse or children (or their representative) may petition for a court order directing the fiduciary to turn the property over, or to pay its value if he has lost, damaged or disposed of it. The court ordinarily does not make the spouse or child wait until the accounting proceeding, because this set-off property is not subject to creditors' claims even if the estate is insolvent.

Sec. B

1. See Matter of Passannante, N.Y.L.J., March 29, 1979, at 12, col. 2 (New York County) (one co-fiduciary, claiming that a co-fiduciary, now deceased, had commingled the decedent's assets with the co-fiduciary's own, sought order requiring executor of other co-fiduciary to disclose all decedent's assets at the time of death).

2. L.1966, c. 953, amended L.1967, c. 685, section 119.

3. Service of process is discussed in chapter on "Procedure," supra at 39–49.

4. Uniform Rules for the Surrogate's Courts section 207.28.

5. Exempt property is discussed in chapter on "Miscellaneous Proceedings," infra at 329–31.

The court can order a hearing if necessary, for example, if the fiduciary challenges the status of the spouse or child to share in exempt property.[6] The parties are not entitled to a jury trial.[7] The burden of proving that assets are exempt property is on the petitioner [8] but if the fiduciary claims that the spouse is disqualified, he has the burden of proof.[9]

If the assets of the estate are insufficient to cover the funeral expenses, the thousand dollars in cash or personal property that would otherwise be set off under EPTL 5–3.1 and exempt from creditors' claims will be available for payment of the funeral costs.[10] While administration expenses may have statutory priority over funeral expenses,[11] in the context of set-off property, funeral expenses have priority. The reason is of course a practical one: something must be done with the decedent's body. The Surrogate thus has to determine before granting relief to the spouse or children in this proceeding that the funeral expenses have been (or will be) paid.

One point that may be litigated is the existence of exempt property at the time of death.[12] Under the statute, no substitute can be made if specific items of exempt property do not exist at the time of decedent's death.[13] Exempt property is treated differently from specific bequests and devises; if such property is destroyed before the decedent's death and insurance proceeds are paid after, the executor must pay the insurance money to the specific beneficiary.[14] The exempt property

6. See Matter of Chandler, 175 Misc. 1029, 26 N.Y.S.2d 280 (Kings 1941) (hearing held to determine whether the husband's departure with the wife's permission was abandonment).

7. Matter of Adler, 3 Misc.2d 631, 155 N.Y.S.2d 823 (Bronx1956).

8. See, e.g., Matter of Marri, 57 Misc.2d 793, 293 N.Y.S.2d 670 (Nassau 1968), where the decedent died of a heart attack during an accident in which his car, which would otherwise have been exempt property, was demolished. It was impossible to determine whether his death or the collision occurred first. The widow argued that the proceeds of the insurance settlement should have been paid to her as exempt property. McKinney's EPTL 5–3.1 says that no substitute can be made if specific items of exempt property do not exist as the time of death, but in this case that fact was unknown. The court tried to draw an analogy to McKinney's EPTL 3–4.5 which permits insurance proceeds on lost or destroyed specific legacies to be paid to a specific legatee, but since the court could not determine when the decedent's death occurred, it could not extend the analogy to the facts at bar.

9. Matter of Feinstein, 95 N.Y.S.2d 631 (1950); Matter of Chandler, 175 Misc. 1029, 26 N.Y.S.2d 280 (Kings 1941) (fiduciary failed to meet burden of proving abandonment because husband had left with wife's permission); Matter of Vogel, 251 App.Div. 741, 295 N.Y.S. 913 (2d Dep't 1937) (the fiduciary was aided in meeting his burden that the husband had not abandoned the decedent by the res judicata effect of dismissal of an action for divorce on the ground of abandonment brought by the wife).

10. Matter of Garrett, 5 Misc.2d 165 N.Y.S.2d 194 (New York County 1956) (widow's portion is available for payment of funeral expenses, but not for administration expenses).

11. SCPA 1811 and chapter on "Claims," supra at 164–72.

12. See Matter of Winkler, 112 Misc.2d 932, 447 N.Y.S.2d 642 (Westchester 1982), where the court, to avoid injustice to the surviving spouse, disregarded the subchapter S corporate entity, which it considered a fiction, and declared the corporate-owned car to be exempt property.

13. McKinney's EPTL 5–3.1.

14. McKinney's EPTL 3–4.5.

statute does not make such an exception; in fact it states that cash cannot be substituted for exempt property not in existence. Judges very seldom make exceptions.[15]

This proceeding can be brought against a temporary administrator,[16] and a fortiori, against a preliminary executor.[17]

3. PROCEEDING FOR PAYMENT OF FUNERAL EXPENSES

If the fiduciary has not paid the funeral expenses, the funeral director (or the person who paid for the funeral) may petition for payment under SCPA 2102(3). The petitioner has other options: he can present a claim for funeral expenses to the fiduciary,[18] or wait for an accounting, or compel an accounting.[19] Each of these options requires patience. If the funeral director presents the claim, the fiduciary has the right to delay payment for seven months from the decedent's death, which is the time creditors have to present their claims.[20] Waiting for an accounting is usually worse, since the accounting occurs when the estate administration is complete. Compelling an accounting also takes time.[21] Section 2102 creates a proceeding that allows the funeral director to accelerate payment. Although the statute does not require it, the funeral director should first demand payment from the fiduciary in writing, or the Surrogate is likely not to entertain the petition. He can file his petition any time, but as a matter of practice the court does consider the proceeding's timing and may decide not to entertain the proceeding (or not to grant the relief) if the estate administration has begun too recently.[22]

The petitioner must satisfy several requirements in order to succeed. First, he must show that the funeral expenses are reasonable.[23]

15. See Matter of Marri, 57 Misc.2d 793, 293 N.Y.S.2d 670 (Nassau 1968), discussed in note 8 supra.

16. Matter of Levine, 157 Misc. 454, 284 N.Y.S. 255 (Kings 1935) (the proceeding directing payment to the widow can be brought against a temporary administrator). See chapter on "Temporary Administration," supra at 289 et seq.

17. See discussion of preliminary letters in chapter on "Probate," supra at 118–24.

18. McKinney's SCPA 1803, discussed in chapter on "Claims," supra at 146–47. Because McKinney's SCPA 1811 directs the fiduciary to pay the funeral expenses out of the first monies received, the proceeding described in the text is not overused.

19. See McKinney's SCPA 2205 and discussion of compulsory accountings in chapter on "Accounting," supra at 183–86.

20. McKinney's SCPA 1802, discussed in chapter on "Claims," supra at 148–50.

21. Compulsory accountings are governed by McKinney's SCPA 2205 and discussed in chapter on "Accounting," supra at 183–86.

22. The predecessor to McKinney's SCPA 2102(3) required a person petitioning for payment of funeral expenses to wait sixty days after the issuance of letters to do so, and forbade a petitioner to reapply for payment within three months of his previous petition. L. 1938, c. 145. Those restrictions have been removed and the court now has discretion whether to entertain the petition or not, and will take the timing into account.

23. Matter of Cammarinese, 199 Misc. 831, 104 N.Y.S.2d 7 (Kings 1951) (objectant had paid for the funeral and the fiduciary (the public administrator) refused to reimburse him fully because the objectant failed to prove that decedent had directed a funeral more elaborate than the public administrator authorized); Matter of Siciliano, 32 Misc.2d 789, 223 N.Y.S.2d 824 (Westchester 1961).

If that point is disputed, the court can either direct a hearing or reserve judgment until the accounting proceeding. The reasonableness of funeral expenses depends on the size of the estate, the decedent's station in life, the solvency of the estate and the wishes of the testator, the effect of the expenditures on creditors and beneficiaries,[24] and to some extent, the request of the survivors.[25] The parties do not have a right to a jury trial on the reasonableness issue.[26]

Second, because administration expenses have priority over funeral expenses,[27] the petitioner has to show that the estate is sufficient to pay administration expenses and also that enough money is available at the time of the proceeding to make the payment for funeral expenses. However, as a practical matter, the executor, who is in a much better position to know this, has the burden of going forward to disprove it.

The court may grant the petitioner full payment or part payment, with interest from the date of the funeral,[28] or may reject the petition.

A spouse, child or another relative or friend may undertake the responsibility for the decedent's funeral expenses. However, the estate is primarily liable. If someone other than the fiduciary has paid the funeral expenses, he can commence these proceedings and get reimbursement from the estate.[29] If the estate does not have assets to pay the funeral expenses, the one who assumed the obligation remains liable for them.[30] In certain instances an infant's funds may be used to pay funeral expenses.[31]

4. PROCEEDING FOR ORDER REQUIRING FIDUCIARY TO PAY A CLAIM

Ordinarily, in solvent estates the fiduciary pays creditors when he learns of the claims.[32] If a fiduciary rejects a claim, the creditor may wait for an accounting to litigate the claim or, if he acts quickly, may proceed against the estate in a court of civil jurisdiction other than the Surrogate's Court.[33] When the fiduciary has allowed the claim or the claimant has a judgment establishing it, the claimant may expedite

24. Matter of Siciliano, 32 Misc.2d 789, 223 N.Y.S.2d 824 (Westchester 1961).

25. McCullough v. McCready, 52 Misc. 542, 102 N.Y.S. 633 (Appellate Term 1907), affirmed 122 App.Div. 888, 106 N.Y.S. 1135 (1st Dep't 1907).

26. Matter of Popek, 157 Misc. 421, 283 N.Y.S. 758 (Bronx 1935).

27. McKinney's SCPA 2102(3); McKinney's SCPA 1811; McKinney's SCPA 2213.

28. Matter of Lewis, 261 App.Div. 905, 25 N.Y.S.2d 155 (2d Dep't 1941); see Matter of Kulyk, 150 Misc. 307, 269 N.Y.S. 70 (Bronx 1934), reversed 243 App.Div. 443, 277 N.Y.S. 807 (1st Dep't 1935) (no interest allowed when claim was made seventeen years after decedent's death).

29. Matter of Stadtmuller, 110 App.Div. 76, 96 N.Y.S. 1101 (2d Dep't 1905) (husband entitled to recover funeral expenses from wife's estate).

30. See Ruggiero v. Tufani, 54 Misc. 497, 104 N.Y.S. 691 (Sup.Ct.App.Term 1907) (father who expressly contracted to pay for son's funeral is not discharged simply because estate paid part of funeral bill).

31. McKinney's SCPA 1713 and chapter on "Guardianships," supra at 276.

32. For a general discussion of claims, see McKinney's SCPA Article 18 and chapter on "Claims," supra at 146 et seq.

33. McKinney's SCPA 1810.

collection by commencing a proceeding under SCPA 2102(4). In his petition he must describe the claim and show that the fiduciary allowed it. The fiduciary may answer that the estate is insolvent, deny that he allowed it, challenge the claim's validity or assert that the underlying judgment was defective. If necessary the court will hold a hearing to determine whether the claim is valid and whether the estate has sufficient assets to pay it without prejudicing the rights of other creditors. The court can defer payment, grant partial or full payment, or refuse payment. If the court suspects that the rights of other creditors may be prejudiced, it will wait until the accounting, when all creditors have an opportunity to be heard.[34]

5. PROCEEDING FOR ORDER REQUIRING FIDUCIARY TO PAY ADMINISTRATION EXPENSES OR MAKE DISTRIBUTIONS TO BENEFICIARIES

A fiduciary has a perfect right to pay administration expenses and beneficiaries' distributions seven months after the court has issued letters, because at that point his personal liability to creditors who have not presented their claims ceases if he has no knowledge of their claims; if he is acting in good faith he may pay out the estate assets and the dilatory creditor has no recourse against him in his personal capacity.[35] In solvent estates the fiduciary usually does pay the creditors who are still unpaid and make the distributions to beneficiaries at that time. If the seven months have passed and still he does not pay administration expenses or make distributions to beneficiaries, the aggrieved creditor or beneficiary can petition under SCPA 2102(4) and EPTL 11–1.5 for payment.

This proceeding is available to beneficiaries (legatees, devisees, distributees or trust beneficiaries) and to claimants for administration expenses (such as attorneys, accountants, brokers and appraisers), and those who have advanced funds for the payment of administration expenses. Since administration expenses have priority over all other claims,[36] the petitioner seeking payment of administration expenses (or reimbursement for such payment) has a better chance for relief than the creditor seeking payment of other debts. The proceeding can be brought against an executor, administrator, trustee or any other fiduciary.

The petition should say why the petitioner has a right to the property. If the petitioner is a beneficiary, he should attach the trust agreement or will and prove that he has complied with any necessary conditions (such as survivorship or attainment of a certain age). If he is an intestate distributee, he should prove his right to inherit. If the

34. See Matter of Brodin, 32 Misc.2d 651, 224 N.Y.S.2d 748 (Nassau 1962) (court would not make a determination which could affect other creditors).

35. See McKinney's SCPA 1802 and discussion of the seven-month statute of limitations in chapter on "Claims," supra at 148–50.

36. See McKinney's SCPA 1811(1) and discussion of priorities in chapter on "Claims," supra at 164–72.

court orders the fiduciary to deliver the property, it may also require the recipient to post a refunding bond.[37] If a trustee cannot deliver the personal property, he must give the beneficiary its value.[38]

This section can sometimes be used even when a will contest delays probate. For example, if all parties agree that a specific bequest is valid and should be honored, the court may grant partial probate and direct the fiduciary to make the payment immediately.[39] If the fiduciary wishes to challenge the petition, his answer usually is that the estate is insolvent, that the beneficiary is not entitled to the property or has already received, assigned or released it, that a condition precedent has failed, that a construction is needed, or perhaps that the fiduciary has a right of set-off against the amount owed to the beneficiary.[40]

The court should not entertain a proceeding for payment of distributions under this section if another state or country has jurisdiction of the estate and the distribution sought would violate the law of that state or country.[41]

6. PROCEEDING FOR ORDER REQUIRING FIDUCIARY TO MAKE EARLY PAYMENT OF DISTRIBUTIONS

A fiduciary usually waits seven months from his appointment to distribute estate assets to beneficiaries, because in a solvent estate he has personal liability for failure to pay creditors' claims submitted during that time.[42] A fiduciary can transfer assets to beneficiaries sooner under EPTL 11–1.5(a). The EPTL language is merely an authorization; the fiduciary does not have to make the distributions early unless the will directs it or the court orders it. A beneficiary hopeful of getting the court to order it should do so under SCPA 2102(5).

If the fiduciary chooses not to make early distribution (that is, within seven months of letters), the beneficiary's job under SCPA 2102(5) is not easy. First, he must show that he needs the money or property for his own support or education or his family's. To do so he should list all his assets and sources of revenue and his expenses. Second, he must show that the estate is large enough so that his

37. Matter of Milbank, 49 A.D.2d 848, 374 N.Y.S.2d 105 (1st Dep't 1975) (as a condition precedent to receiving weekly partial payments while the issue of abandonment was being determined, decedent's widow was required to post a refunding bond).

38. This should be true of other fiduciaries as well, as failure to deliver the property would be a breach of fiduciary responsibility.

39. Matter of Atlas, 101 Misc.2d 677, 421 N.Y.S.2d 815 (Nassau 1979) (since only the residuary clause was being contested, the court granted partial probate to fund a trust for decedent's mother who was of advanced age.) The court would order the fiduciary to make the payment under McKinney's SCPA 2102(4) if the fiduciary refused.

40. McKinney's SCPA 2102, Practice Commentary at 342 (1967).

41. See Matter of Gyfteas, 36 A.D.2d 380, 320 N.Y.S.2d 540 (1st Dep't 1971), where the distribution to New York legatees under will of Greek domiciliary would have left the estate insufficient to pay Greek death taxes and contravened Greek law.

42. See McKinney's SCPA 1802 and discussion of the seven-month statute of limitations in chapter on "Claims," supra at 148–50.

disposition would almost assuredly be paid eventually, so that other interested parties are not put at risk. Specifically, he must prove that the property available for the payment of debts, legacies and expenses exceeds by at least one-third the amount of all known claims, and all legacies with priority over or equality to the petitioner's. This priority or equality refers to the order of abatement of dispositions; if the estate is not large enough to cover all expenses, debts and dispositions, specific dispositions abate last and thus have priority over general and residuary dispositions and shares in intestacy.[43] General dispositions are the next best protected in priority;[44] residuary dispositions are next[45] and distributions in intestacy have the lowest priority and abate first.[46] Demonstrative dispositions enjoy the highest priority and are treated like specific dispositions if the fund from which they were payable is still available, but their priority drops to that of a general disposition if that fund is gone.[47] Thus, if a beneficiary of a general bequest wants to apply for early distribution, he has to show that the estate assets are at least one third more than needed to pay the claims, general dispositions and demonstrative dispositions and specific dispositions, and in addition that he or his family needs the money for support or education. The court may direct that a refunding bond be filed as a precondition for granting the application.[48]

Even a beneficiary whose status is challenged can apply for advance payment under this provision if he can prove his need and the adequacy of estate assets. The court has the discretion to grant the relief, but in almost all cases will require a refunding bond.[49]

7. DISAGREEMENT AMONG FIDUCIARIES

When more than two fiduciaries serve together, in matters requiring the exercise of discretion, a majority of the fiduciaries must agree, and if only two are serving, both must agree.[50] If both must agree and they cannot do so, or if they need not agree but the fiduciary who has

43. A specific disposition is "a disposition of a specified or identified item of the testator's property," McKinney's EPTL 1–2.16, for example, "my 120 shares of ABC stock" (if that is what the decedent owned), "my green Volvo," "my house on Main St."

44. A general disposition is "a testamentary disposition of property not amounting to a demonstrative, residuary or specific disposition," McKinney's EPTL 1–2.8, for example, "100,000 in cash."

45. A residuary disposition is a disposition of the remainder of a testator's estate after all other dispositions have been made, for example, "the rest, residue and remainder of my estate."

46. McKinney's EPTL 12–1.2.

47. A demonstrative disposition is "a testamentary disposition of property to be taken out of specified or identified property," for example, "$10,000 to be paid out of my Merrill Lynch Money Market Fund," or "200 shares of ABC stock from my E.F. Hutton brokerage account."

48. Matter of Milbank, 49 A.D.2d 848, 374 N.Y.S.2d 105 (1st Dep't 1975).

49. See Matter of Milbank, 49 A.D.2d 848, 374 N.Y.S.2d 105 (1st Dep't 1975) (as a condition precedent to receiving weekly partial payments while issue of abandonment was being decided, decedent's widow was required to post a refunding bond).

50. McKinney's EPTL 10–10.7, 11–1.1(b)(13), 11–1.4; Fritz v. City Trust Co., 72 A.D. 532, 76 N.Y.S. 625 (2d Dep't 1902), affirmed 173 N.Y. 622, 66 N.E. 1109 (1903), motion for reargument denied 174 N.Y. 524, 67 N.E. 1082 (1903); Guthy v. Brandine, N.Y.L.J., May 17, 1985, at 16, col. 2 (Nassau).

decided to do something is insecure about it, or outsiders (such as banks or purchasers) are reluctant to deal with one co-fiduciary, the deadlock may prevent them from moving forward with the estate administration. If they cannot agree on the issue of custody of estate property, such as what to marshal, where to store assets, or how to invest or preserve assets, anyone interested in the estate may petition the court under SCPA 2102(6) to direct the fiduciaries to act.[51] If the fiduciaries disagree about an issue other than the custody of estate property, they cannot use this section, but they can resolve the issue by seeking advice and direction from the court where appropriate[52] or by waiting until the accounting.

Most well-drafted wills give specific directions to fiduciaries, and most relationships among fiduciaries are harmonious, so resort to SCPA 2102(6) is infrequent. It is useful if one fiduciary refuses to divulge information or show books and records to the others. There, the court can fashion appropriate relief such as directing the fiduciary to give the books and records to the clerk of the court so that all fiduciaries will have access to them.[53] This section may not be used to substitute the court's judgment for the fiduciaries' on investment of estate funds,[54] timing of payment of a claim,[55] or any other matter of business judgment,[56] but the court may direct that no matter how the funds are invested, the fiduciaries control them jointly.[57]

51. See Matter of Jacobs, N.Y.L.J., April 11, 1985, at 11, col. 4 (New York County), where trustees disagreed on how to dispose of the remainder of a testamentary charitable trust. The court found that, although it could not rule how the trustees should exercise their discretion, in view of the deadlock between them it could give advice. If the trustees chose to disregard the advice, the court said that it would appoint another trustee to break the tie, citing Stuart v. Continental Illinois National Bank and Trust Co., 68 Ill.2d 502, 12 Ill.Dec. 248, 369 N.E.2d 1262 (1977). See also. Matter of Leopold, 259 N.Y. 274, 181 N.E. 570 (1932) (Surrogate may approve the settlement despite dissent of one of the administrators); Barry v. Lambert, 98 N.Y. 300 (1885) (co-executor borrowed money from third party to combine with estate funds and purchase a mortgage. The dissenting executor could not deny the third party the right to the property).

52. Advice and direction is discussed this chapter infra at 350–53.

53. Matter of Stubing, 47 Misc.2d 174, 261 N.Y.S.2d 914 (Kings 1965) (all co-executors are entitled to inspect the books to enable them to render account).

54. Matter of Edelstein, 60 N.Y.S.2d 373 (Queens 1946) (court denied executor's petition for advice and instruction on sale of testator's interest in real property).

55. Matter of Bulova, 60 Misc.2d 151, 301 N.Y.S.2d 1008 (New York County 1969) (one co-executor sought to compel her co-executor to pay a claim she contended was an obligation of the estate, and the court declined to interfere).

56. Matter of Leopold, 259 N.Y. 274, 181 N.E. 570 (1932) (Surrogate refused to order co-fiduciary to join in compromise agreement).

57. Matter of Stukalo, 7 Misc.2d 1042, 166 N.Y.S.2d 478 (Kings 1957) (two of three executors deposited estate assets in an estate account in a Pennsylvania bank subject to their joint withdrawal. The court required them to place the estate account on deposit within this jurisdiction subject to the control of all three executors).

SECTION C. DISCOVERY PROCEEDINGS

One of the fiduciary's responsibilities is to gather the assets of an estate.[1] If a fiduciary suspects that someone is withholding estate assets or has information about them, he may start a proceeding to discover that property or information, and force the person who has it to deliver it (or impart it) to him.

This section refers to decedents, their estates and their fiduciaries, but applies equally to inter vivos trusts and trustees. In 1980 the legislature expanded the jurisdiction of the Surrogate's Court to include inter vivos trusts,[2] a jurisdiction the Surrogates had in fact exercised increasingly without legislative authority.[3] That extension of jurisdiction to inter vivos trusts was made expressly applicable to discovery proceedings, which before 1980 could be used only in decedent's estates.[4]

1. THE SURROGATE'S JURISDICTION IN DISCOVERY PROCEEDINGS

Before discussing the way to commence and proceed in discovery proceedings, we must comment on the court's jurisdiction over them.

Although SCPA 2103 on its face limits discovery proceedings to the discovery of money or other personal property, there has been a dramatic expansion of the scope of these proceedings. The discovery proceeding in SCPA 2103's predecessors envisioned a replevy action of money or personal property, and that property had to be a definite fund, not just an amount owing to the decedent.[5] The courts would not allow discovery of such assets as real property, insurance, contract actions, bank accounts or rents.[6] After the passage of the SCPA, the courts began to exercise the jurisdiction the state constitution granted to them (that is, jurisdiction over matters relating to the affairs of decedents and the administration of estates).[7] For example, in 1967, the court permitted discovery of rents and real property.[8] In 1970 the

Sec. C

1. See Estate of Kaufman, 83 Misc.2d 846, 848, 374 N.Y.S.2d 244 (New York County 1973) (dictum).

2. McKinney's SCPA 209, L.1980, c. 503, § 4.

3. See cases discussed in chapter on "Jurisdiction," supra at 12–13.

4. L.1980, c. 503, § 27.

5. McKinney's SCPA 2103, Practice Commentary at 365 (1967); Matter of Kadar, 3 Misc.2d 479, 154 N.Y.S.2d 280 (New York County 1956), affirmed 3 A.D.2d 654, 159 N.Y.S.2d 677 (1st Dep't 1957); Matter of Theirich, 11 Misc.2d 39, 165 N.Y.S.2d 642 (Nassau 1957); Matter of Sheridan, 39 Misc.2d 343, 240 N.Y.S.2d 481 (Seneca 1963) (discovery proceeding cannot be used to collect a debt owed to the decedent).

6. See, e.g., Matter of Sachs, 15 Misc.2d 537, 182 N.Y.S.2d 527 (New York County 1958) (contract rights in partnership context); Matter of Balthazar, 4 Misc.2d 800, 156 N.Y.S.2d 64 (New York County 1956) (contract rights in insurance context); Matter of Trevor, 309 N.Y. 398, 131 N.E.2d 561 (1955) (bank accounts).

7. McKinney's Const., Art. 6, section 12.

8. Matter of Hall, 54 Misc.2d 923, 283 N.Y.S.2d 540 (New York County 1967); accord, Matter of Rungo, 74 Misc.2d 239, 342 N.Y.S.2d 929 (Nassau 1973). See also Mat-

court allowed discovery of information under a stock agreement,[9] in 1972 insurance proceeds [10] and rescission of a contract agreement,[11] in 1975, royalties under a publishing agreement,[12] in 1977 the ownership of a title insurance policy.[13] The courts' theory was that while Article 21 did not specifically allow for discovery of all these kinds of property, SCPA 202's general grant of jurisdiction over all matters relating to a decedent's affairs would permit it. Since the Court of Appeals' decision in Matter of Piccione confirms the Surrogate's broad jurisdiction,[14] SCPA 2103 should be read as extending to any assets a fiduciary administers. It does not extend, however, to controversies between living parties.[15]

The Surrogate's Court has jurisdiction to order discovery if it has personal jurisdiction over the respondent (because he is in New York, is a New York domiciliary or has committed an act or omission in New York [16]) whether or not the assets are in New York. That is true even when the out-of-state assets are real property; [17] though the court does not have jurisdiction over the realty itself, it has jurisdiction over the respondent and can order him to do something that relates to that real property. The New York Constitution gives the Surrogate jurisdiction over the affairs of a decedent, and discovering assets that supposedly belonged to the decedent clearly meets this standard.

Under prior practice it was often expensive and burdensome to obtain personal jurisdiction over a respondent outside New York; the fiduciary had to arrange for service of an order to appear for examination and pay witness and mileage fees. Current practice differs, because the petitioner has the option to skip the inquisitorial stage of a discovery proceeding and to go right into the hearing stage, stages we discuss shortly. If he does, he can serve the respondent by citation, if necessary by mail (with a court order) on an out-of-state respondent.

ter of Poggemeyer, 87 A.D.2d 822, 449 N.Y.S.2d 12 (2d Dep't 1982).

9. Matter of Ryan, 63 Misc.2d 415, 311 N.Y.S.2d 719 (Erie 1970).

10. Matter of Robles, 72 Misc.2d 554, 339 N.Y.S.2d 171 (Orange 1972) (decedent was killed by her husband who was named as beneficiary of her life insurance policy. The administratrix claimed the proceeds. Surrogate can determine after a hearing who is entitled to the insurance proceeds).

11. Matter of Rothko, 69 Misc.2d 752, 330 N.Y.S.2d 915 (New York County 1972).

12. Matter of Young, 80 Misc.2d 937, 365 N.Y.S.2d 695 (New York County 1975).

13. Matter of London, N.Y.L.J., May 17, 1977, at 15, col. 3 (Nassau).

14. 57 N.Y.2d 278, 456 N.Y.S.2d 669, 442 N.E.2d 1180 (1982). Matter of Piccione is discussed in Chapter on "Jurisdiction," supra at 12–18.

15. Matter of Piccione, 57 N.Y.2d 278, 456 N.Y.S.2d 669, 442 N.E.2d 1180 (1983) (malicious prosecution action by tenant against executor individually). See also Matter of Pokrass, 105 A.D.2d 659, 481 N.Y.S.2d 861 (1st Dep't 1984), where the court would not allow discovery of claims between executor individually and corporation.

16. See discussion of personal jurisdiction in chapter on "Jurisdiction," supra at 25–28.

17. Matter of Carr, 113 Misc.2d 818, 450 N.Y.S.2d 141 (New York County 1982) (Surrogate refused to dismiss claims by petitioner seeking discovery of realty in Pennsylvania and California transferred to respondents because of their undue influence on decedent).

The petitioner must show that the court has a basis for personal jurisdiction, but he can easily do so if the respondent committed an act or omission in New York. In one case the court held that a respondent's control over securities in a New York bank was an act sufficient to subject him to the jurisdiction of the Surrogate's Court even though the fiduciary was a non-domiciliary not present in New York.[18] If the petitioner does allege this long-arm basis for jurisdiction, he must substantiate it, for example by the testimony of a party with knowledge of the jurisdictional facts.[19]

The discovery proceedings of SCPA 2103 should not be used to discover evidence for use in some other action unrelated to the administration of an estate.[20]

Several courts have pondered the question whether one fiduciary can discover against another fiduciary. Some have answered no on the theory that any controversy between them should be resolved in accounting proceedings.[21] Others have authorized one fiduciary to discover against another.[22] A fiduciary may commence a discovery proceeding against anyone he believes has property or information, including the fiduciary of another estate,[23] an attorney,[24] an attorney-in-fact,[25] a bank[26] or a bailee.[27]

2. THE DISCOVERY PROCEEDING

A fiduciary may, under SCPA 2103, file a petition stating that he knows or believes that the respondent has money or other personal property, or information, and is withholding it from the fiduciary. It does not matter whether the respondent obtained possession before or after the decedent's death, or before or after the creation of the inter vivos trust.[28] The courts tend to entertain this proceeding liberally because its purpose is to facilitate the fiduciary's job; the courts generally allow him to proceed if he reasonably believes that the respondent has property or information. Only a fiduciary may com-

18. Matter of Cooke, 112 Misc.2d 167, 446 N.Y.S.2d 189 (Nassau 1982).

19. See Matter of Katz, 81 A.D.2d 145, 439 N.Y.S.2d 941 (1981) affirmed 55 N.Y.2d 904, 449 N.Y.S.2d 29, 433 N.E.2d 1277 (1982); Matter of O'Brien, 54 A.D.2d 880, 389 N.Y.S.2d 2 (1st Dep't 1976).

20. Matter of Lifschutz, 54 Misc.2d 289, 282 N.Y.S.2d 328 (Kings 1967); Matter of Stiassni, 195 Misc. 668, 90 N.Y.S.2d 434 (New York County 1949), reversed on other grounds 277 App.Div. 848, 97 N.Y.S.2d 795 (1st Dep't 1950); Matter of Lowe, 148 Misc. 107, 265 N.Y.S. 420 (Westchester 1933).

21. E.g., Matter of Matheron, 207 Misc. 1061, 141 N.Y.S.2d 199 (Nassau 1955).

22. E.g., Matter of Freitag, N.Y.L.J., March 19, 1984, at 17, col. 6 (Nassau).

23. Matter of Goldfarb, 17 Misc.2d 976, 185 N.Y.S.2d 1014 (New York County 1959).

24. Matter of Present, 15 Misc.2d 759, 184 N.Y.S.2d 134 (Kings 1956).

25. Lalor v. Duff, 28 A.D.2d 66, 281 N.Y.S.2d 614 (3d Dep't 1967).

26. See Matter of Bock, N.Y.L.J. May 18, 1970, at 22, col. 2, where the bank demanded an indemnity bond before turning over proceeds of bank accounts, and the court ordered the bank to pay over the assets without a bond when no adverse claims had been made. The McKinney's Banking Law, § 238(3), permits such payment with a court order.

27. Matter of Guttman, N.Y.L.J. Dec. 11, 1972, at 17 (New York County).

28. McKinney's SCPA 2103(1)(a).

mence this proceeding, not the deceased's spouse or a beneficiary.[29] A preliminary executor can commence this proceeding,[30] as may any other fiduciary,[31] unless the court restricts the fiduciary's powers.[32]

The statute provides that the petitioner may include an affidavit or other written evidence to support the relief sought. In practice the petitioner must include that information if it is available.

Discovery proceedings potentially have two stages: one is the inquisitorial stage and the second is the hearing stage. The former is used if the fiduciary does not know whether or not the respondent has estate assets; he may ask the court to order the respondent to submit to an examination, and the court will order it if the petition convinces the court that the petitioner has reasonable grounds to examine the respondent.[33] Usually the court does so by an order to appear and be examined. The petitioner arranges personal service of a certified copy of the order on the respondent, and tenders a subpoena fee in the amount set forth under CPLR 8001, which is usually an administration expense payable out of the estate. Failure to serve the order or tender the witness fee is a jurisdictional defect.[34] The court may issue a supplemental citation on any person who appears to have an interest in the property.[35]

On the return date, whether or not the respondent answers, the petitioner may question him on the allegations in the petition. That "inquisition" is held at the courthouse before the official court reporter.[36] The scope of the examination is very broad.[37] During the examination, if an issue of title to any money or other property is raised, the court will direct the respondent to serve and file a verified answer [38] if he has not already done so, and the court can also direct that the examination continue.[39] For instance, a fiduciary may believe that a

29. Matter of Litman, 13 Misc.2d 108, 176 N.Y.S.2d 477 (Nassau 1958); Matter of Korowitz, 120 N.Y.S.2d 498 (Kings 1953); Wierdsma v. Markwood Corp., 53 A.D.2d 581, 384 N.Y.S.2d 836 (1st Dep't 1976).

30. Matter of Turner, 86 Misc.2d 132, 382 N.Y.S.2d 235 (Albany 1976).

31. McKinney's SCPA 2101(a); see McKinney's SCPA 103(21).

32. See chapter on "Fiduciaries," infra at 402–05.

33. McKinney's SCPA 2103(3).

34. Matter of Benowitz, N.Y.L.J., March 9, 1977, at 12, col. 2 (New York County).

35. McKinney's SCPA 2103(4).

36. Uniform Rules 207.28.

37. See Matter of Kevill, 166 Misc. 230, 2 N.Y.S.2d 191 (Kings 1938).

38. See Matter of Coon, 87 A.D.2d 966, 451 N.Y.S.2d 202 (3d Dep't 1982) (when respondent claimed ownership of property subject to discovery proceeding, petitioner sought order requiring respondent to file answer, and Surrogate denied motion. Appellate Division reversed). All pleadings in the Surrogate's Court must be verified, McKinney's SCPA 303, and McKinney's SCPA 2104(2) reiterates that requirement for answers in discovery proceedings.

39. McKinney's SCPA 2104(1); Matter of Jacobs, 263 A.D. 829, 31 N.Y.S.2d 536 (2d Dep't 1941); Matter of Pender, 197 Misc. 344, 94 N.Y.S.2d 447 (Kings 1949). Under prior practice, L.1920, c. 928, § 205, at that point the respondent would file his answer and the examination would end. If the fiduciary wanted to examine the respondent further, he would have had to use the predecessor of McKinney's CPLR Article 31. Under present practice, however, the court can direct that the examination continue.

respondent has information about the decedent's missing ring, so he obtains an order of discovery and examines the respondent. If the respondent does not file an answer and during the examination he states that the decedent gave him the ring, the court will direct the respondent to file an answer. After the examination, the proceeding enters the hearing stage and the question of title is tried as a litigated issue. All testimony that was part of the inquisitorial stage should be produced again at the hearing stage. This can be done by actual testimony or by introducing the earlier testimony into evidence at the trial stage.[40]

In the inquiry stages of the proceeding, a respondent can answer questions about communications with the decedent without waiving his right to invoke the Dead Man's Statute at the later hearing.[41] If the proceeding develops into a trial, however, the Dead Man's Statute is in full effect.[42] In practice this could occur when a respondent files an answer claiming title to the decedent's property.[43] If the respondent fails to appear, the court can hold him in contempt, and if he appears but refuses to answer after being directed to do so, the court may leave the burden on the fiduciary to prove his right of possession, or may order the respondent to show cause why the property should not be turned over, and so order if the respondent defaults.[44]

If the petitioner does not need to examine the respondent, because he is sure that the respondent has the property, the court can issue a citation ordering the respondent to show cause why he should not deliver that property, its proceeds or the information to the petitioner.[45] On the return date the court can hold a hearing to determine whether the respondent has the property and whether the fiduciary should get it. Any party may present proof concerning possession of property. If during the proceedings property is discovered and the respondent admits possession and does not claim title to the property by a verified answer, the court may make an interim decree directing its delivery to the fiduciary and continue the proceedings for a determination of any other litigated issue.[46] The fiduciary has the burden of establishing his claim, and if the respondent admits possession, the fiduciary makes a prima facie case by establishing that title was in the decedent.[47]

40. Matter of Detweiler, 121 Misc.2d 453, 467 N.Y.S.2d 766 (Cattaraugus 1983).

41. McKinney's SCPA 2104(6).

42. Lalor v. Duff, 28 A.D.2d 66, 281 N.Y.S.2d 614 (3d Dep't 1967).

43. See Matter of Detweiler, 121 Misc. 2d 453, 467 N.Y.S.2d 766 (Cattaraugus 1983).

44. See Matter of Anderson, N.Y.L.J., Feb. 27, 1985, at 13, col. 5 (Bronx), where the court refused to hold respondent in contempt because he had served a notice of motion for summary judgment and that motion stayed his own examination; Matter of Wilson, N.Y.L.J., Nov. 25, 1985, at 11, col. 4 (Bronx) (burden remained on fiduciary); SCPA 2104(3) (court may direct turn-over).

45. McKinney's SCPA 2103(3). See Matter of O'Brien, N.Y.L.J., Jan. 16, 1976, at 8, col. 1. (New York County).

46. McKinney's SCPA 2104(1).

47. Cf. Matter of Kircher, 123 Misc.2d 397, 473 N.Y.S.2d 679 (Kings 1984) (fiduciary met his burden by establishing that property was in decedent's possession at

Bills of particulars, inspection of documents and other CPLR-authorized disclosure devices are available to the parties in a discovery proceeding. They are inappropriate in the inquisitorial stage, however, and should be used in the hearing stage,[48] since Article 31 does not come into play until issue is joined.

If during the examination or after a hearing the court determines that the petitioner is entitled to possession of property, because the respondent admits possession but cannot persuade the court of his entitlement (for example, the respondent admits possession merely for safekeeping), it issues a decree directing delivery of the property to the fiduciary. If the property is gone, the court can make any determination which the Supreme Court might decree in a trust proceeding.[49] It may, for example, direct the payment of the proceeds or the value of the property to the fiduciary, or may impress a constructive trust on the proceeds, or issue an injunction.[50]

If at some point in the proceeding it becomes clear that the estate does not own the property and a person other than the respondent claims to own it, the Surrogate has jurisdiction to decide which claimant is the owner.[51] This power to decide the rights of living persons does not spring from the state constitutional grant of jurisdiction;[52] rather, the legislature, using its constitutional power to confer additional jurisdiction on the Surrogate's Court, gave the Surrogate this power in discovery proceedings. It did so because the issue of ownership arises in these cases only after the parties have adduced at least enough evidence to show that the estate does not own the property, and at that point the Surrogate should be in a position, without much ado, to determine who does have an ownership interest.

death, and decedent's husband claimed, but did not persuade the court, that it was later stolen from the apartment where he and the decedent had lived).

48. Matter of Lukas, 79 Misc.2d 24, 360 N.Y.S.2d 549 (Westchester 1974); Matter of Kuster, 12 Misc.2d 239, 152 N.Y.S.2d 742 (Nassau 1956); Matter of Kevill, 166 Misc. 230, 2 N.Y.S.2d 191 (Kings 1938).

49. McKinney's SCPA 2104(4).

50. See Matter of Chess, N.Y.L.J., Sept. 16, 1965, at 17 (dictum).

51. McKinney's SCPA 2103(4). This power to determine rights between third parties includes the power to determine the right of subrogation between them. Matter of Block, N.Y.L.J., April 2, 1975, at 18, col. 3 (New York County).

52. See, e.g., Matter of Piccione, 57 N.Y.2d 278, 456 N.Y.S.2d 669, 442 N.E.2d 1180 (1982) (no jurisdiction to decide malicious prosecution action between two living parties); Matter of Lainez, 79 A.D.2d 78, 435 N.Y.S.2d 798 (2d Dep't 1981), affirmed 55 N.Y.2d 657, 446 N.Y.S.2d 942, 431 N.E.2d 303 (1981) (no jurisdiction over claim by Department of Social Services against sole distributee of estate); Matter of Goelet, 28 A.D.2d 149, 283 N.Y.S.2d 545 (1st Dep't 1967) (no jurisdiction to compel enforcement of separation agreement between fiduciary of spendthrift trust and beneficiary's former wife). Contra, Matter of Zalaznick, 84 Misc.2d 715, 375 N.Y.S.2d 522 (Bronx 1975) (to prevent fragmentation and repetition of testimony, the Surrogate's Court should exercise its constitutional jurisdiction to the fullest extent).

3. BURDENS OF PROOF

The petitioner has the initial burden of proving that the property is part of the estate.[53] He is not entitled to recover merely because the respondent fails to answer. He must continue the inquiry and establish facts sufficient to justify a decree directing the respondent to turn over the property.[54] However, a respondent alleging a gift or pledge has the burden of proving it,[55] and the proof must be clear and convincing,[56] often an insurmountable burden because of the Dead Man's Statute.[57] The respondent must present independent proof of each element of a gift: donative intent, delivery and acceptance. Often such independent proof is unavailable because the decedent gave the property to the respondent privately.[58] If the fund is a joint bank account, the creation of the account is prima facie proof of the survivor's right to it,[59] rebuttable by proof that the account was created solely for the decedent's convenience.[60] If the respondent was in a confidential relationship with the decedent, the burden shifts to him to go forward with an explanation of the circumstances.[61]

If the respondent denies possession, the petitioner is entitled to a trial on that issue.[62]

Any party may demand a jury trial if the court determines a trial is necessary to determine title.[63] However, demand for the jury trial

53. Matter of Santalucia, 10 A.D.2d 715, 199 N.Y.S.2d 285 (2d Dep't 1960).

54. But see text at note 44, supra at 341, discussing the court's-power to order defaulting respondent to turn over property.

If the petitioner is alleging that the respondent exercised undue influence over the decedent, evidence of judgments against the respondent for exercising undue influence against other decedents is admissible to show a common scheme or plan. Matter of Brandon, 79 A.D.2d 246, 436 N.Y.S.2d 329 (2d Dep't 1981), affirmed 55 N.Y.2d 206, 448 N.Y.S.2d 436, 433 N.E. 2d 501 (1981).

55. Matter of Booth, 224 App.Div. 363, 231 N.Y.S. 218 (1st Dep't 1928); Matter of Rabinowitz, 5 Misc.2d 803, 159 N.Y.S.2d 492 (Nassau 1957); Matter of Hossan, 162 Misc. 333, 294 N.Y.S. 516 (Kings 1937).

56. Roberts v. Jossen, 99 A.D.2d 1002, 473 N.Y.S.2d 469 (Dep't 1984); Matter of Saltzman, 21 A.D.2d 892, 251 N.Y.S.2d 872 (2d Dep't 1964) (checks endorsed in blank insufficient to prove gift to brother). See Citibank v. Piccirillo, 99 A.D.2d 390, 473 N.Y.S.2d 179 (Dep't 1984) (borrower failed to prove that decedent had converted loan to gift before death). Compare Matter of Stuts, 20 A.D.2d 728, 248 N.Y.S.2d 92 (2d Dep't 1964), appeal denied 14 N.Y.2d 485, 251 N.Y.S.2d 1026, 200 N.E.2d 220 (1964) (checks endorsed by deceased payee were not assets of payee's estate where payee received, endorsed and delivered checks to the endorsee).

57. McKinney's CPLR 4519.

58. E.g., the Dead Man's Statute applied in Matter of Fishman, 32 A.D.2d 1063, 303 N.Y.S.2d 905 (2d Dep't 1969), affirmed 27 N.Y.2d 809, 315 N.Y.S.2d 866, 264 N.E.2d 356 (1969). There the decedent's widow had possession of bearer bonds. She could not testify because of the Dead Man's Statute. The decedent's attorney could not testify that the decedent had said that he had bought the bonds with his own money because of the hearsay rule of evidence and the attorney-client privilege.

59. McKinney's Banking Law § 675; Matter of Fenelon, 262 N.Y. 308, 186 N.E. 794 (1933).

60. See Matter of Camarda, 63 A.D.2d 837, 406 N.Y.S.2d 193 (1978); Matter of Coddington, 56 A.D.2d 697, 391 N.Y.S.2d 760 (3d Dep't 1977).

61. See Matter of McMurdo, 56 A.D.2d 602, 391 N.Y.S.2d 468 (2d Dep't 1977).

62. Matter of Akin, 248 N.Y. 202, 161 N.E. 471 (1928); Matter of Rosen, 173 Misc. 433, 17 N.Y.S.2d 794 (Kings 1940).

63. Matter of Sachs, 256 App.Div. 364, 10 N.Y.S.2d 78 (1st Dep't 1939). Matter of Goldfarb, 18 Misc.2d 773, 188 N.Y.S.2d 55

must be timely, that is, filed with the answer of objections if the respondent is demanding, and filed within six days of the service of the answer or objections if the petitioner is demanding.[64]

SECTION D. DISCOVERING TESTAMENTARY SUBSTITUTES

In a proceeding by a surviving spouse to elect against the will, the issue of entitlement to testamentary substitutes may arise. If it does, the party having control over those assets should be made a party to the proceedings.[1]

SECTION E. REVERSE DISCOVERY PROCEEDINGS

A person claiming property that the fiduciary is holding may commence a "reverse discovery" proceeding under SCPA 2105 to recover it. Although the statute specifies that the claim must be for money or personal property,[1] the courts have liberally construed it and read it in conjunction with SCPA 202 to allow not only the replevy type of proceeding originally contemplated but also recovery of rents, contract actions, royalties and similar assets.[2]

The aggrieved party commences the proceeding in the Surrogate's court with jurisdiction over the estate[3] by filing a petition and a citation and then arranging for service on the fiduciary when the court has signed the citation.[4] A reverse discovery proceeding can be brought only against a fiduciary. The petitioner does not have to cite other parties interested in the estate, unless the court orders such additional service. The petition must state how and why the fiduciary got the property (for example, the petitioner received property from the decedent as a gift and the executor fraudulently induced the petitioner to pay the executor money for it).[5]

Unlike the fiduciary's discovery proceeding, the reverse discovery proceeding does not have a built-in inquisitorial stage, but the parties can conduct examinations before trial and use all the other disclosure

(New York County 1959); Matter of Britton, 187 Misc. 70, 60 N.Y.S.2d 466 (Monroe 1946).

64. SCPA 502(2)(a), discussed in chapter on "Trials," infra at 499–500.

Sec. D

1. Matter of Riefberg, N.Y.L.J., Oct. 11, 1984, at 13, col. 1 (Nassau). See chapter on "Surviving Spouses," supra at 302 et seq.

Sec. E

1. McKinney's SCPA 2105(1).

2. See discussion of the expanded jurisdiction of the Surrogate in discovery proceedings, this chapter supra at 337–39, and of the Surrogate's Court's jurisdiction generally in chapter on "Jurisdiction," supra at 12–18.

3. McKinney's SCPA 2105(1). He could also commence the proceeding in another court of competent jurisdiction, such as the Supreme Court.

4. McKinney's SCPA 2105(2).

5. Matter of McNulty, N.Y.L.J. June 3, 1964, at 16, col. 3 (New York County).

devices afforded by Article 31 of the CPLR.[6] After the parties have completed discovery, the court will hold a hearing to determine whether the petitioner has a right to the assets or not. If the court finds that someone other than the fiduciary has the property, and if it can obtain personal jurisdiction over that person, it can make him a party to the proceeding by issuing a citation and can direct him to turn over the property to the petitioner.[7] As in the "straight" discovery proceeding, this power to litigate an issue between living persons was given to the Surrogate by the legislature exercising its constitutional right to expand the jurisdiction of the Surrogate's Court whether or not the issue relates to an estate. It did so on the theory that after the court has gone so far in determining title, it would be wasteful not to permit the court finally to determine that issue.

Naturally, if a dispute arises between a person claiming to own property and the fiduciary arguing that the property was the decedent's, the person claiming it cannot testify about transactions with the decedent because of the Dead Man's Statute.[8]

If the fiduciary's withholding of the property was wrongful, the court can order him to turn it over to the petitioner, and can then remove him from office.[9]

The parties are entitled to a jury trial on the issue of ownership if they demand it timely.[10] Despite older cases to the contrary,[11] the modern approach is to allow jury trials to all parties.

SECTION F. COMPROMISE PROCEEDINGS

The vast majority of proceedings in the Surrogate's Court are uncontested and many of the contested ones are settled; the parties reach a compromise and agree not to proceed with the litigation. The controversies can include the validity of a claim, the validity of the exercise of a spouse's right of election, construction proceedings, probate contests, accounting proceedings, appointment of the administrator in administration proceedings, tax apportionment, and myriad other issues.[1]

6. The CPLR applies where the SCPA is silent. McKinney's SCPA 102.

7. McKinney's SCPA 2105(3).

8. Matter of Marri, 57 Misc.2d 793, 293 N.Y.S.2d 670 (Nassau 1968) (widow claimed money in joint safe deposit box was hers, not decedent's, but could not prove it because she would have had to testify about amounts she and the decedent both deposited and withdrew).

9. Matter of Irwin, 60 A.D.2d 885, 401 N.Y.S.2d 289 (2d Dep't 1978) (affirmed decree removing the person serving as executor and trustee who wrongfully held the property of the petitioner).

10. Matter of Schneier, 74 A.D.2d 22, 426 N.Y.S.2d 624 (4th Dep't 1980). See McKinney's SCPA 502(2) and discussion in chapter on "Trials," infra at 499–500.

11. Matter of Leary, 175 Misc. 254, 23 N.Y.S.2d 13 (New York County 1940), affirmed 260 App.Div. 1000, 24 N.Y.S.2d 1000 (1st Dep't 1940), affirmed 285 N.Y. 693, 34 N.E.2d 383 (1941).

Sec. F

1. See Matter of Merrill, 50 A.D.2d 605, 375 N.Y.S.2d 388 (2d Dep't 1975), where a husband and wife, each with children by former marriages, agreed that the estate of the first to die would be placed in trust,

A couple of preliminary comments:

The Supreme Court has concurrent jurisdiction with the Surrogate to compromise claims relating to estate property, and if it entertains such a proceeding (which is rare), it is subject to the SCPA 2106 rules discussed presently.

SCPA 2106 does not cover the compromise of a creditor's claim against the estate or the estate's claim against a debtor. The EPTL gives the fiduciary the power to compromise claims without court order,[2] and SCPA 1813 permits the fiduciary to obtain court approval of such a compromise.[3] What is therefore left for SCPA 2106 is the compromise that shifts the interests among beneficiaries of the estate. The court cannot grant relief in a SCPA 2106 proceeding unless the controversy is real. If no real controversy exists, the court will not permit the parties to use this vehicle to shift interests in the decedent's property when his testamentary intent was clear.[4] If the parties do so without court approval, they are making gifts.

SCPA 2106 governs compromises in proceedings in which one or more of the parties is under legal disability. The court has the authority to approve compromises where all the parties are competent adults; that authority is found in SCPA 202, the general grant of jurisdiction over matters relating to a decedent's estate.

Compromise proceedings take two forms: those that occur during probate proceedings and those that arise in other contexts and relate to a claim to the same property by two or more parties. They are essentially similar but have an important difference or two.

1. COMPROMISE IN PROBATE PROCEEDINGS

Traditionally in the probate proceeding, the court had to authorize the compromise even if all signatories to it were adult, competent parties. The reason was that the very validity of the will was at stake; the testator had a plan, and parties could not get together and agree to change that plan. The court had to review it and give effect to the testator's intentions if it found the will valid. Courts are somewhat

income to the surviving spouse, remainder to the decedent's children. Since the husband's will had given the wife a general power of appointment over the remainder of a trust of which she was receiving income for life, the wife executed a codicil to her will renouncing her power of appointment and thus allowing it to pass by default to her husband's children. Although it was clear that the parties' intentions was to pay the estate taxes attributable to the husband's trust out of the trust, her attorney had neglected to put that provision in the codicil, and the will directed that her estate taxes be paid out of the residuary estate. The court allowed the compromise on the ground that it clearly reflected both testators' intentions. See also Matter of Shubert, 110 Misc.2d 635, 442 N.Y.S.2d 703 (1981).

2. McKinney's EPTL 11–1.1(b)(13)

3. McKinney's SCPA 1813 is discussed in chapter on "Claims," supra at 175–76.

4. See Matter of Sidman, 154 Misc. 675, 278 N.Y.S. 43 (Kings 1935), where the court noted that if parties could reach compromises in the absence of a controversy, the testator's intention would have no effect.

more liberal today in allowing pre-probate compromises if all parties are competent adults acting in good faith.[5]

When a proposed compromise arises in a probate proceeding, if the validity of the will is very questionable and the beneficiaries named in it agree with the intestate distributees on a disposition of estate assets, the court must evaluate that disposition and decide whether the expense of litigation and the likelihood of success justify the compromise. If the surviving spouse is compromising a claim to elect against the will, the court has to evaluate his chance of success, and the same is true of a person claiming the decedent's property under an agreement with the decedent.

The procedure for obtaining court authorization of a compromise during a probate proceeding is for the proponent of the will, or one of the parties to the compromise, to file a supplemental petition with the court,[6] in some cases submitting affidavits supporting the matters in the petition.[7] Within the probate proceeding, the way the parties arrive at a compromise can vary. The parties with a stake in the controversy, which means the will beneficiaries on one side, and the distributees, surviving spouse or person claiming property under an agreement with the decedent on the other,[8] may reach the compromise while the court "presides," or may arrive at it in private negotiations outside the court. If the court supervised the compromise, its terms usually will be placed on the record and the court will approve the compromise in open court on the record or will direct that a full compromise proceeding be commenced and approve the compromise in a later decree. If the matter was settled without court supervision, the petitioner must submit the agreement with the petition and serve process on all parties with an interest in the proceeding, not including nominated executors under the propounded will who have not received letters[9] or persons unaffected by the proposed compromise, or attorneys rendering services to the estate.[10] For example, if a person will receive

5. See Matter of Siegel, N.Y.L.J., March 6, 1985, at 13, col. 2 (Nassau).

6. McKinney's SCPA 2106(5).

7. See Matter of Hoffman, 66 Misc.2d 736, 323 N.Y.S.2d 12 (Nassau 1971) (because the rights of persons under disability may have been affected by the settlement of a probate contest, the parties had to submit a petition and affidavits pursuant to McKinney's SCPA 2106).

8. The nominated executor is not a necessary party. See McKinney's SCPA 2106(1)(b); Matter of Smith, 44 A.D.2d 851, 355 N.Y.S.2d 994 (2d Dep't 1974), appeal denied 35 N.Y.2d 644, 362 N.Y.S.2d 1026, 321 N.E.2d 555 (1974); McKinney's SCPA 2106, Revisers' Notes.

9. McKinney's SCPA 2106(1)(b). For a case where the Surrogate, as a precaution, permitted a nominated executor to object to probate on condition that he agree that he would not be a necessary party to any compromise proceeding under McKinney's SCPA 2106, see Matter of Molnar, 76 Misc. 2d 126, 350 N.Y.S.2d 855 (New York County 1973). The Surrogate acknowledged that this precaution was probably not necessary but decided to impose the condition to give effect to the legislative intent behind the 1971 amendment to McKinney's SCPA 1410 limiting the rights of nominated executors to object to probate because of the concern that the disappointed fiduciary might, if he were necessary party, try to thwart the compromise reached by the parties with a true economic interest in the estate.

10. Matter of Smith, 44 A.D.2d 851, 355 N.Y.S.2d 994 (2d Dep't 1974), appeal denied 35 N.Y.2d 644, 362 N.Y.S.2d 1026, 321 N.E.2d 555 (1974) (attorneys' interests in

the same under the will and under the compromise agreement, he is not a necessary party to the compromise agreement.

A guardian, guardian ad litem, committee or conservator should not execute a compromise agreement until the court authorizes him to do so on behalf of his ward.[11] Usually he will submit a report to the court indicating whether he approves or not. The court then reviews the compromise and, if it is acceptable, directs the ward's fiduciary or the guardian ad litem to sign it on the ward's behalf.

If the parties settle a probate contest and the settlement does not radically change the will provisions, the Surrogate may grant probate to the original will, subject to the conditions of the compromise agreement. The decree will refer to the settlement agreement and make the will provisions subject to it. In some instances the court may want the will redrafted to comport with the agreement. While most courts ordinarily do not fashion a new will incorporating the terms of the agreement and then admit that "will" to probate,[12] the court may have the compromised will provisions specifically set forth in the decree as a substitute for those set forth in the propounded instrument.

2. COMPROMISE OUTSIDE OF PROBATE PROCEEDINGS

If the compromise arises in a context other than a probate proceeding, court approval is not always necessary. If all the parties to the compromise agreement are competent adults and the compromise affects only their interests in the estate, they are free to agree as they wish, in effect to carve up the estate as they like. However, if their compromise affects the interests of persons under legal disability [13] or unborn persons, they cannot reach a settlement without court approval, and they can obtain court approval by using the procedure allowed by SCPA 2106. The fiduciary starts this proceeding, and he cannot obtain approval unless all the parties in being with an interest in the estate have agreed to the compromise in person or by their legal representatives (guardians, conservators or committees).

The mechanics of SCPA 2106 vary depending on whether the compromise among the interested persons arises in the course of a proceeding or in private negotiations. As we discussed in the preceding section on compromises within a probate proceeding, if the parties reach a settlement during a proceeding and the court has supervised it, a formal agreement is not necessary. Instead, the terms and conditions of the compromise are spread on the record before the court and the court either grants its approval on the record in open court or it

legal fees is not the type of interest that would permit them to prevent a compromise among the parties beneficially interested).

11. See Matter of Handsman, N.Y.L.J., April 11, 1985, at 16, col. 2 (Nassau).

12. See Matter of Calascione, 35 A.D.2d 568, 313 N.Y.S.2d 574 (2d Dep't 1970).

13. McKinney's SCPA 103(40) defines person under disability as "(a) an infant, (b) an incompetent, (c) an incapacitated person, (d) unknown or whose whereabouts are unknown or (e) confined as a prisoner who fails to appear under circumstances which the court finds are due to confinement in a penal institution."

submits the matter for decision and later authorizes or rejects the compromise in a decree or order. In some limited cases the court may direct that a full SCPA 2106 proceeding be commenced. On the other hand, if the parties reach the compromise independently (either out of court or in the course of a proceeding but without court supervision), the fiduciary will have to submit a formal petition along with the proposed agreement and serve all interested parties who have not waived citation or appeared.[14]

The courts vigorously support settlements of disputed claims if all parties are acting in good faith. The court has the power to approve a compromise that eliminates the rights of persons under legal disability and unborn contingent remaindermen if all the parties are acting in good faith.[15] However, any interested person under legal disability is a necessary party and if a guardian, conservator or committee does not appear for him, the court will appoint a guardian ad litem to appear;[16] virtual representation does not apply in compromise proceedings.[17] Similarly, the court will appoint a guardian ad litem to appear for an unborn person with a contingent future interest. The guardian ad litem or legal representative can then execute any necessary documents and bind the wards to the compromise. They cannot compromise the matter without court approval.[18] If the court approves the compromise, it binds the parties to the agreement and the persons under disability and unborns who are represented by a guardian ad litem.[19] Even if the disabled person (through his legal representative or guardian ad litem) renounces rights to property from an estate other than the one for which the proceeding is pending, the decree binds him unless he can, upon removal of the legal disability, show fraud or bad faith in the compromise.[20]

If a person has a child out of wedlock and places the child for adoption, that child loses the right to inherit under the intestacy law

14. See chapters on "Procedure," supra at 35 et seq., and "Appearances," supra at 232 et seq., for discussions of waivers and appearances.

15. See Fisher v. Fisher, 253 N.Y. 260, 170 N.E. 912 (1930) (no grandchildren alive at death of testator and so the compromise was permitted though it could affect the contingent rights of any future grandchildren); Matter of Shubert, 110 Misc.2d 635, 442 N.Y.S.2d 703 (New York County 1981) (compromise agreement valid though it extinguished rights of infants to property and future interests).

16. McKinney's SCPA 2106(2). See Matter of Shubert, 110 Misc.2d 635, 442 N.Y.S.2d 703 (New York County 1981) (guardian ad litem for minor children accepted cash settlement from estate of father and waived rights in large estate of grandfather in return for a declaration of legitimacy, a valuable consideration at the time it was bargained for (1963). Without the declaration of legitimacy, moreover, the children would have had no rights in the grandfather's estate anyway).

17. McKinney's SCPA 2106(2); SCPA 2106, Prac.Comm. at 104 (Supp.1986); see Matter of Wegner, N.Y.L.J., Aug. 14, 1985, at 14, col. 2 (Nassau) (guardian ad litem appointed for infant in contested probate proceeding). See discussion of virtual representation in chapter on "Procedure," supra at 60–70.

18. See Honadle v. Stafford, 265 N.Y. 354, 193 N.E. 172 (1934) (guardian ad litem).

19. McKinney's SCPA 2106(4).

20. The persons under disability will be bound only if properly represented in the proceeding. See McKinney's SCPA 2106(4) and see discussion of guardians ad litem and McKinney's SCPA Article 4 in chapter on "Appearances," supra at 238–44.

from the natural family,[21] and therefore is not a necessary party to the compromise proceedings. The same is true if a member of the child's biological family makes a provision in his will leaving property to the "issue" of the child's natural mother; that term has been interpreted to exclude non-marital children adopted into another family, unless the will expressly shows a contrary intent.[22] Thus a natural child adopted out of a family is not a necessary party to the compromise proceeding if the will leaves a disposition to the class of "issue" that includes him. A non-marital child not adopted out of a family does have a right to inherit under that language,[23] and hence is a necessary party to a compromise proceeding affecting his bequest or devise.

If under the compromise, money or property is payable for the benefit of an unborn or a person under disability, the court may direct that it be deposited in court subject to the further order of the court,[24] or a guardian or conservator may be appointed for a person under disability and payments can be made to that representative.[25]

The compromise proceeding is, naturally, started by a petition. If a proceeding is pending, such as probate, the petitioner files a verified supplemental petition,[26] thus avoiding the expense of serving citations and paying an additional filing fee.[27] If no proceeding is pending, the petitioner starts one by filing a verified petition, which must set forth (i) the provisions of any instruments under which someone claims the property in controversy, (ii) the identity and claims of the parties to the controversy, (iii) the possible contingent interests of persons not in being, and (iv) the reason court approval is needed.[28]

Sometimes the court entertains the application before the parties have executed the proposed agreement. It obtains jurisdiction over all necessary parties and then permits them to execute the agreement.[29]

After the petitioner commences the proceeding and the court obtains jurisdiction over the necessary parties, the court will hold a hearing if necessary, and after a full review of all the facts, it will approve or reject the compromise.

SECTION G. ADVICE AND DIRECTION

A preliminary word: This section deals primarily with the "formal" advice and direction proceedings allowed by SCPA 2107, which allows a fiduciary contemplating sale of estate property to seek the court's advice. The practitioner should keep in mind, however, that a

21. McKinney's EPTL 4–1.1(f); McKinney's Dom.Rel.L. 117.

22. Matter of Best, 64 N.Y.2d 605, 486 N.Y.S.2d 1025, 476 N.E.2d 340 (1985).

23. Matter of Hoffman, 53 A.D.2d 55, 385 N.Y.S.2d 49 (1st Dep't 1976).

24. McKinney's SCPA 2106(3).

25. See chapter on "Guardianship," supra at 257 et seq.

26. McKinney's SCPA 2106(5).

27. L.1979, c. 388 effected this change.

28. McKinney's SCPA 2106(5). In addition, all petitions must have certain basic information set forth in McKinney's SCPA 304 and discussed in chapter on "Procedure," supra at 54–55.

29. McKinney's SCPA 2106(6).

perplexed fiduciary can seek advice and direction from the court on other matters as well under the court's general jurisdiction over matters related to the affairs of a decedent.[1] Although the court refrains from substituting its own judgment or discretion for that of the fiduciary, it will often at least give the fiduciary some guidelines. Adherence to those guidelines will be viewed as prudent if anyone later objects to the fiduciary's actions.

A fiduciary has under EPTL 11–1.1 broad powers to administer an estate and broad discretion to sell estate assets. Because the decedent chose the fiduciary to exercise prudent judgment, the fiduciary cannot delegate his responsibility or the exercise of his discretion.[2] However, on occasion the fiduciary may have an asset of uncertain value; he may want to sell it, but may be nervous about a surcharge if a party questions his judgment on the accounting. SCPA 2107 allows a fiduciary to apply to the court for advice and direction on the propriety of selling the property, the appropriate price, and the time and manner of the sale.[3] If a fiduciary gets advice and direction from the court and substantially complies with it, he is relieved of any liability for loss on the sale.

Because the fiduciary has such broad powers under EPTL 11–1.1, SCPA 2107 is not overworked. In fact, the courts often refuse to entertain the proceeding on the ground that the fiduciary has the

Sec. G

1. See, e.g., Matter of Tapow, N.Y.L.J., April 3, 1985, at 13, col. 3 (Bronx), where the court entertained a petition seeking advice and direction on the identity of the charitable beneficiary and the application of the cy pres doctrine; Matter of Colp, N.Y.L.J., Jan. 20, 1976, at 8, col. 2 (New York County), where the court entertained a proceeding by a fiduciary seeking advice and direction on which date to choose for estate tax valuation, the date of death or the alternate valuation date six months later. 26 U.S.C.A. § 2032. The interests of the decedent's beneficiaries depended on the choice of valuation date, as did income tax considerations. Neither McKinney's SCPA 2102 nor McKinney's SCPA 2107 specifically allowed such advice and direction, but the court entertained it under McKinney's SCPA 202. It did not make the decision for the executor, for it did not have the power to interfere with the executor's discretion, but it did set forth guidelines for the executor's exercise of discretion. See also Matter of Raible, N.Y.L.J., May 10, 1977, at 14, col. 1 (Nassau), where the court similarly gave some guidelines to the executor on the selection of the estate tax valuation date. As in Colp, it refrained from giving advice and direction because it could not interfere with the executor's discretion. But see Matter of Fales, 106 Misc.2d 419, 422, 431 N.Y.S.2d 763, 764 (New York County 1980), where the same court that decided Colp retreated a bit from its position there and held that it should provide direction to fiduciaries presented with Colp-type tax elections; and Matter of Rappaport, 121 Misc.2d 447, 467 N.Y.S.2d 814 (Nassau 1983), where the court directed the fiduciaries to deduct all administration expenses on the estate tax return rather than on the fiduciary return. The Surrogate held that the court's broad jurisdiction permitted such direction.

2. Gates v. Dudgeon, 173 N.Y. 426, 66 N.E. 116 (1903); Roe v. Smith, 42 Misc. 89, 85 N.Y.S. 527 (Sup.Ct. Orange 1903), affirmed 97 App.Div. 633, 89 N.Y.S. 1115 (2d Dep't 1904). See also Matter of Badenhausen, 38 Misc.2d 698, 237 N.Y.S.2d 928 (Richmond 1963) (reasserting general rule and noting exception that executor can hire agents to perform special functions, such as evaluating stock of closely held corporation).

3. McKinney's SCPA 2107. See footnote 4, supra at 327, for cases allowing a fiduciary to ask for advice and direction on issues other than sale under the court's general jurisdiction over affairs of a decedent and administration of an estate.

power to sell and should be held to the prudent man standard in exercising it.[4]

Fiduciaries often petition the court for advice and direction where they have serious doubts about selling property, even though they suspect that the court will refuse to entertain the matter. Their very attempt to seek the protection of SCPA 2107 bolsters their good faith and reduces the possibility of a surcharge.

Fiduciaries also resort to SCPA 2107 when the only offers to buy a piece of property are below the appraised value or the estate tax value. Some fiduciaries purposely condition the sales contract on obtaining court approval. This does not, of course, confer subject matter jurisdiction on the court, which the parties cannot do, but the court already has subject matter jurisdiction under SCPA 202 because the matter relates directly to the affairs of a decedent.[5] When the contract calls for court approval, the court will usually entertain a SCPA 2107 proceeding but then dismiss the petition if everyone is competent and there is no special reason for the court to approve or disapprove.[6] Fiduciaries often use SCPA 2107 when they have received offers of varying quality, such as a lower all-cash offer versus a higher financed offer, or a broker-free transaction versus one requiring a broker's fee. These are usually issues of ordinary business judgment, and the courts often refuse to make the decision whether to go ahead or not, but instead give guidelines that aid the fiduciary in making the judgment. Courts have given advice and direction when the fiduciary has entered into more than one contract to sell the property,[7] and when beneficiaries constantly question his administration.

The Surrogate's advice on questionable valuation is an issue of fact and the Appellate Division can overturn it only if the Surrogate's finding was against the weight of the credible evidence.[8]

If the court entertains the petition, all interested persons (and the court is the judge of that) should receive citations.[9] On the return date the court looks at the facts and circumstances and hears evidence of value and the best arrangements for disposition. It may appoint appraisers or accountants to help determine the value of property.

4. Matter of Osterndorf, 75 Misc.2d 730, 349 N.Y.S.2d 275 (Nassau 1973). See discussion of the prudent man rule in chapter on "Fiduciaries," infra at 407–12.

5. See, e.g., Matter of Peck, 79 Misc.2d 1053, 362 N.Y.S.2d 120 (Monroe 1974).

6. Matter of Friedman, N.Y.L.J., March 19, 1985, at 14, col. 5 (Nassau) (though fiduciary proposed self-dealing, all parties consented and therefore there was no need for court approval).

7. Matter of Peck, 79 Misc.2d 1053, 362 N.Y.S.2d 120 (Monroe 1974) (court was even more confident of its jurisdiction because both contract vendees had agreed in the contracts that the sale was conditioned on the Surrogate's approval).

8. See Matter of Kane, 98 A.D.2d 851, 470 N.Y.S.2d 823 (3d Dep't 1983), appeal denied 61 N.Y.2d 607, 475 N.Y.S.2d 1025, 463 N.E.2d 1235 (1984).

9. See, e.g., Matter of Tapow, N.Y.L.J., Apr. 3, 1985, at 13, col. 3 (Bronx), where the court ordered service on decedent's distributees in a proceeding to determine whether to apply the cy pres doctrine to a charitable bequest in decedent's will.

After the hearing, the court gives whatever advice and direction it considers to be in the best interests of all parties.

The EPTL does not give the fiduciary the power to abandon, alter or demolish real property, even if such actions are necessary to effectuate a sale. In such cases, if the will does not confer the extraordinary power, the fiduciary may seek the court's advice and direction. Ordinarily the court will not entertain a petition to abandon property, which is usually reserved for the accounting proceeding, but in rare instances it will grant this extraordinary relief. For example, if the real property has many liens and judgments against it, and taxes and maintenance are high, the court could allow the fiduciary to abandon the property rather than to continue spending estate assets on it and incur a loss.

SCPA 2108, which we discuss shortly, permits a fiduciary to obtain court approval to continue the decedent's business. Before SCPA 2108 was enacted, fiduciaries used SCPA 2107 when they wanted to continue the decedent's incorporated business [10] because they wanted to sell the business as a "going concern." [11] If a fiduciary merely wants approval to continue the business, he should use SCPA 2108 but he can combine SCPA 2107 and 2108 proceedings if he needs both advice concerning a sale and court approval to continue a business.

The fiduciary can also use SCPA 2107 when he wants to purchase estate property himself. That purchase, of course, is disfavored because of its potential for grave conflict of interest, and hence the court's approval of the sale is necessary.[12] Similarly, when the will directs the retention of property but the fiduciary believes that circumstances have changed so much it should be sold, he can seek the court's advice and direction regarding a sale.[13]

A fiduciary can bring an independent proceeding for advice and direction, or he can incorporate it in another proceeding, such as an accounting or construction proceeding. Conversely, if the fiduciary does bring an independent proceeding under SCPA 2107, the court may also decide other matters within its jurisdiction, using SCPA 202's grant of authority to exercise its jurisdiction in any proceeding.

Like most of the miscellaneous proceedings, advice and direction proceedings vary greatly according to the circumstances presented; the petition, citations and orders or decrees are tailor-made, unlike standard proceedings like probate where the court provides standardized forms.

10. McKinney's SCPA 2108, discussed just below, covers the fiduciary's power to continue the decedent's unincorporated business.

11. See Matter of Graves, 197 Misc. 555, 95 N.Y.S.2d 809 (Erie 1950).

12. See Matter of Kramer, 101 Misc.2d 782, 421 N.Y.S.2d 975 (Bronx 1979), where the court says in dicta, "under appropriate circumstances a court will * * * give a fiduciary advice and direction with regard to a self-dealing transaction * * *."

13. Matter of Pulitzer, 140 Misc. 575, 251 N.Y.S. 549 (New York County 1931), affirmed 237 App.Div. 808, 251 N.Y.S. 954 (1st Dep't 1932).

SECTION H. CONTINUATION OF A BUSINESS

Sometimes a testator authorizes a fiduciary in the will to continue a business, and in such case the fiduciary can do so on his own, without any court order. It is good practice for a testator to confer this power by will, clearly defining the fiduciary's authority to continue the business and the general estate assets that can be used to do so.[1] If he does not, and the fiduciary believes it to be in the estate's best interest to continue the decedent's business, SCPA 2108 permits him to get court approval of this plan.[2] Without this provision, the fiduciary would have to proceed at his personal risk and most would be reluctant to do so.

The chapter refers to continuing the business of a decedent, but the whole discussion applies equally to continuing the business of an absentee.[3] The absentee's estate, like the decedent's, requires administration. The court accordingly may order the fiduciary to continue the business of either.

This section applies to businesses of which the decedent was sole owner. It does not apply to partnerships,[4] or to professions.[5]

The courts tend to entertain this proceeding and grant the relief when a fiduciary can show that continuation is a prudent decision, because, for example, no ready buyer is available, the market conditions are not favorable for a sale, liquidation is not economically advisable, or the decedent's beneficiaries depend on the business for their livelihood.

The fiduciary starts the proceeding by filing a petition, and if the court entertains the proceeding, it may initially make an intermediate order, without notice to anyone, authorizing the fiduciary to continue

Sec. H

1. The fiduciary is liable for improvidence or negligence in continuing the business even if the will authorizes continuation. See Matter of Etoll, 101 A.D.2d 935, 475 N.Y.S.2d 654 (3d Dep't 1984) (executor improperly continued decedent's business for several years, using estate funds to do so, and court said it would have surcharged him even if the will had authorized the continuation).

2. Before the enactment of the provision allowing the court to authorize the continuation of a business, L.1920, c. 938, a fiduciary had to liquidate the business if the testator did not authorize him in the will to continue it. Even if the will gave the fiduciary authority to continue, his personal liability was uncertain. McKinney's SCPA 2108, Prac.Comm. at 479 (1967).

Some businesses cannot be continued without the Surrogate's authorization. See McKinney's Real Prop.Law § 441–a(8) providing that a real estate broker's personal representative can continue his business on a limited basis if the Surrogate authorizes it. See Matter of Nelson, 122 Misc.2d 889, 472 N.Y.S.2d 73 (Nassau 1984) (court allowed continuation of business under that section even though the equitable and legal interests in the estate had merged in the executrix); Matter of Halperin, 76 Misc.2d 1012, 352 N.Y.S.2d 579 (Nassau 1974) (Surrogate authorized continuation of real estate brokerage business for one hundred twenty days after decedent's death).

3. See discussion of absentees in chapter on "Temporary Administration," supra at 292–93.

4. Matter of Saffioti, 77 Misc.2d 1052, 355 N.Y.S.2d 709 (Orange 1974).

5. McKinney's SCPA 2108.

the business during the period before the return of process and a final decree.[6] This, of course, is to avoid losses that could occur if the executor were hamstrung during that period. The fiduciary then serves all necessary parties (and any other persons specified by the court) with the citation the court has issued. Very often no one objects. In that case, the court can make its decree based on the petition and supporting affidavits. If, on the other hand, a controversy arises, any respondent may file an answer within eight days after the return date, or at another time if the court directs. The court may then look at the facts and hold a hearing. If the court is satisfied that the best interests of the estate require the business to continue, it may decree accordingly.[7]

If the court grants the petition, the decree will include any restrictions, conditions or requirements the court believes necessary, as well as any incidental relief, such as an order to incorporate the business.[8]

If the court authorizes that the business continue but not incorporate, it must in its decree specify the time period for such continuation [9] and direct the extent to which the other estate assets will be available for liabilities incurred in continuing the business. It must also direct the fiduciary to file with the County Clerk a certificate of doing business under an assumed name pursuant to General Business Law section 130. The certificate must describe the capacity in which the fiduciary is conducting the business and the extent to which liabilities incurred in the business are chargeable to the estate. If the fiduciary complies and acts within the authority granted by the court, he is relieved of personal liability; he is liable only in his fiduciary capacity unless he acts wrongfully or negligently.[10] Moreover, any person dealing with the business is on notice of the extent of the estate's liability and a person with a claim arising out of the continuation of the business is limited to the assets specified in the court's decree.

Whether the fiduciary continues the business because the will permits it or the court authorizes it, he must keep all business funds separate from the general estate assets.[11] He may not use estate assets for the business [12] unless the will allows it in "direct, explicit and unequivocal language * * *" [13] or the court authorizes such use to preserve the assets of an estate.[14] The court often severely restricts such use; it may set a limit on estate assets to be used, or it may direct

6. McKinney's SCPA 2108(1).

7. McKinney's SCPA 2108(2).

8. McKinney's SCPA 2108(3). See, e.g., Matter of Saionz, N.Y.L.J., March 25, 1983, at 12, col. 2 (Bronx Court directed continuation of decedent's studio-franchising business only to extent of granting the franchises already in process at decedent's death).

9. McKinney's SCPA 2108(4).

10. McKinney's SCPA 2108(5).

11. McKinney's SCPA 2108(6).

12. Matter of Muller, 24 N.Y.2d 336, 300 N.Y.S.2d 341, 248 N.E.2d 164 (1969).

13. Matter of Whalen, 146 Misc. 176, 261 N.Y.S. 761 (New York County 1932), affirmed 242 App.Div. 763, 275 N.Y.S. 341 (1st Dep't 1934), affirmed 267 N.Y. 537, 196 N.E. 567 (1935).

14. McKinney's SCPA 2108, Practice Commentary at 112 (Supp.1986).

that only those assets already part of the business be used. Under SCPA 2108, the court's authority does not permit the use of estate assets for an already incorporated business,[15] since it is a separate entity in which other stockholders may have an interest and the estate may be insulated from corporate creditors and liabilities. However, that does not preclude the fiduciary from obtaining such authorization through SCPA 2107 (the proceeding to obtain advice and direction). Although SCPA 2107 permits the fiduciary to ask for advice and direction on a sale, it should also be available when the court's approval is needed to preserve the value of the corporation before its sale.[16] Any creditor or person interested in the estate may petition at any time for an order requiring the fiduciary to wind up the business, and the court has broad discretion to do so or to give the fiduciary other directions.

A fiduciary may find himself asking the court for guidance when he is also a director or officer of the corporation of which the estate is majority shareholder. This is not an SCPA 2108 proceeding, but rather it is a request for advice and direction from the court on a matter related to a decedent's affairs. A corporate officer may, for example, be serving as the sole trustee of a testamentary trust funded by corporate stock, and the income beneficiary of that trust may petition for an order directing the corporate officer to distribute dividends. In one such case the corporate officer withheld the dividends because in a law suit he had commenced, the defendant had asserted a counterclaim against the corporation. Under the law governing corporations,[17] he could not declare dividends at a time when liabilities exceeded assets. On the other hand, under the law governing fiduciaries, he had to serve the best interests of the estate, and the Surrogate can intervene if the trustee clearly breaches his duty to the estate or trust.[18] This conflict situation is an appropriate one for seeking the court's guidance. The Surrogate's Court will not, however, substitute its own business judgment for that of the fiduciary.[19]

SECTION I. MONIES PAID INTO COURT

On the occasions when Surrogate orders that assets be paid into court, the CPLR rules governing such deposits govern in the Surrogate's Court as well.[1] Ordinarily, the funds are paid to the County Treasurer, in the City of New York to the City Treasurer, unless the court directs otherwise; it may, for example, direct delivery of property

15. McKinney's SCPA 2108, Practice Commentary at 112 (Supp.1986).

16. McKinney's SCPA 2108, Prac. Comm. at 112 (Supp.1986).

17. McKinney's Bus.Corp.Law § 719(a)(3).

18. See, e.g., Schwartz v. Marien, 37 N.Y.2d 487, 373 N.Y.S.2d 122, 335 N.E.2d 334 (1975); Matter of Muller, 24 N.Y.2d 336, 300 N.Y.S.2d 341, 248 N.E.2d 164 (1979); Matter of Hubbell, 302 N.Y. 246, 97 N.E.2d 888 (1951); Matter of Durston, 297 N.Y. 64, 74 N.E.2d 310 (1947); Matter of Cohen, 88 A.D.2d 290, 453 N.Y.S.2d 10 (1982).

19. Matter of Grove, N.Y.L.J., Feb. 22, 1985, at 12, col. 1 (New York County).

Sec. I

1. McKinney's SCPA 2109; McKinney's CPLR 2601–08.

to a warehouse or safe deposit box in a trust company. A party making the payment of funds or the delivery of property into court is ordinarily discharged from liability to the extent of the payment or property.[2]

The court's order or decree can direct the time of withdrawal of funds, but usually it does not, and a person claiming the right to withdraw needs a further court order. That application is usually made by a petition; all persons with an interest in the funds and the County Treasurer are necessary parties.

Either the party making the payment or the clerk (if the delivery is made directly to the court) delivers the property to the County Treasurer. Title vests in the County Treasurer for the benefit of interested parties and any securities that he may purchase as investments are in the County Treasurer's name.[3]

If something other than money or securities is to be paid into court, the court usually directs their storage in a warehouse or safe deposit box and the court can charge the cost of storage to the one making the deposit or the one who sought the deposit. In addition, the court can require a bond to guarantee the storage costs.[4] In Surrogate's practice the expense is usually treated as an administration expense.

Sometimes a party is entitled to income from property paid into court, such as income from a trust, but his whereabouts are unknown or he is under a disability and has no guardian, committee or conservator. That person is responsible for the cost of administering the property and for receiving and paying over the income.[5]

The application for payment out of court may be made in the form of motion or special proceeding but the person with custody of the property can pay amounts not exceeding fifty dollars without court order.[6] If he does so in good faith, he will have no liability for the payment. He is also relieved of liability if he pays greater amounts under the terms of the court order.

SECTION J. PROBATE OF HEIRSHIP

When a decedent fails to devise his real property, any New York real property passes automatically to his distributees. The distributees can sell the real property; they merely enter into a contract of sale with a vendee. The title company is often satisfied with a death certificate and an affidavit indicating who the decedent's distributees are. The distributees execute a deed and the property is conveyed. However, if a question arises concerning whether the decedent died testate or intestate, or what interest he had in the real property, or who his distributees are, SCPA 2113 permits a proceeding to clear up title and to determine who is entitled to the real property. The distributees

2. McKinney's CPLR 2601(a).

3. McKinney's CPLR 2601(b).

4. McKinney's CPLR 2602.

5. McKinney's CPLR 2603.

6. See McKinney's SCPA 2109, Prac. Comm. at 482 (1967).

may present either to the court with jurisdiction of the estate or to the court of the county where the real property is located a petition for a decree establishing the right of inheritance by the distributees. The petition has to describe the property and show the interest of the petitioner and the decedent's other distributees in the property. The petitioner also serves citations issued by the court to all the distributees to show cause why the petition should not be granted.[1] If the petitioner is also seeking letters of administration, he must petition for them either under SCPA Article 10 (for a domiciliary) or Article 16 (for ancillary letters).[2]

Usually when a Surrogate has exercised jurisdiction over an estate, that Surrogate retains jurisdiction over all estate matters and Surrogates of other counties refrain from exercising jurisdiction. SCPA 2113 specifically confers jurisdiction on both the county "with jurisdiction of the estate" and the county where the real property is located, and the latter county can exercise jurisdiction even if letters were granted in another county.[3]

The distributee bears the burden of proving that he is a distributee entitled to share in the real property.[4] While it has been held that a party is entitled to a jury trial,[5] jury trials are in fact rare. More often the Surrogate or a law assistant-referee conducts a hearing.

Sec. J

1. McKinney's SCPA 2113.

2. Article 10 is discussed in chapter on "Administration," supra at 125 et seq., and Article 16 is discussed in chapter on "Ancillary Administration," infra at 509 et seq.

3. Matter of Stevenson, 76 Misc.2d 313, 351 N.Y.S.2d 262 (Orange 1973) (Orange County Surrogate properly exercised jurisdiction because property was there, although Bronx Surrogate had issued letters).

4. Matter of Leslie, 175 App.Div. 108, 161 N.Y.S. 790 (1st Dep't 1916); Matter of Kennedy, 82 Misc. 214, 143 N.Y.S. 404 (New York County 1913).

5. Matter of Bringgold, 204 App.Div. 101, 198 N.Y.S. 282 (3d Dep't 1923).

Chapter Thirteen

ATTORNEYS' FEES

SECTION A. INTRODUCTION

Frequently, when a person named in a decedent's will as fiduciary or beneficiary retains an attorney, the attorney and the client agree on a fee for the legal services and the timing of payments. The fiduciary (provided he is not representing himself and is not a member of the firm representing him) can pay those fees, like any other administration expense, without a court order, and usually pays them periodically through the estate administration or after the accounting is done. Sometimes, however, the parties cannot agree and court has to fix the attorney's fees. The vehicle for fixing fees is SCPA 2110, and it is used, for example, if the parties dispute the amount of the fee, or if the attorney is also serving as fiduciary, or if the fiduciary fires the attorney, or if the attorney withdraws and refuses to deliver to the new attorney papers or funds belonging to the estate.[1]

SCPA 2110 is not the Surrogate's only authorization to review attorneys' fees. Even if no one starts a 2110 proceeding, the court can always review the reasonableness of an attorney's fee on an accounting (final or intermediate) if anyone objects to the fee. The court's authority to do so is found circuitously in Article 23, governing fiduciaries' commissions.[2] The court must allow the fiduciary to pay reasonable administration expenses, of which the attorneys' fees are one; implicit in this is of course the court's finding of reasonableness. In practice, if the fee is unconscionably high, even if no one objects to it the court will convene the parties to see whether they had actual knowledge of the fee. If infants or other persons under disability are parties, the court can review the reasonableness of the fee even if no objections are raised.

Section 2110, and the materials in this chapter, apply equally to attorneys' fees for estate matters and for other matters within the Surrogate's jurisdiction, such as trusts, guardianships and adoptions. For verbal economy, the discussion is in terms of estate proceedings.

Sec. A

1. McKinney's SCPA 2110(1). The retiring attorney may have a retaining lien on the estate papers, and a charging lien on estate assets, discussed this chapter infra at 376–77.

2. McKinney's SCPA 2307(1), 2308(1), 2309(1). These sections also give the court the authority to review the attorneys' fees of an attorney who is also serving as fiduciary, whether or not objections are raised. See chapter on "Commissions," infra at 425 et seq.

There are two situations outside the scope of SCPA 2110. First, although the statute applies to legal fees incurred in administering the estate, it does not apply to money the decedent owed the attorney for pre-death legal services.[3] In that case the attorney would have an Article 18 claim against the estate,[4] and would be in a much better position than the SCPA 2110 petitioner, since arguably he merely has to present the claim and the objectants have the burden of proving its invalidity.[5] Under SCPA 2110 the attorney has the burden of proving reasonableness of the fee.[6]

Secondly, this section does not apply when there are no estate assets or when the fiduciary does not have in hand funds of a legatee or distributee; the court cannot order payment out of any other fund,[7] unless the legal fees relate to a tax apportionment issue, in which case the court can apportion the legal fee between testamentary and non-testamentary assets.[8] An attorney can seek legal fees directly from his client and, if necessary, litigate the issue in another forum.

It is of course irrelevant that the attorney performed the services in a court other than the Surrogate's Court; the Surrogate can set the attorney's fees anyway,[9] as long as the services related to the estate. The Supreme Court has concurrent jurisdiction with the Surrogate [10] but exercises it quite sparingly,[11] usually only in cases where the legal services were rendered to an estate and to another entity as well, the other entity being within the Supreme Court's jurisdiction and the services for each being inseparable.

3. Matter of Luckenbach, 46 Misc.2d 864, 261 N.Y.S.2d 106 (Nassau 1965), affirmed 25 A.D.2d 852, 269 N.Y.S.2d 469 (2d Dep't 1966). See chapter on "Claims," supra at 146 et seq.

4. See chapter on "Claims," supra at 146 et seq.

5. See Matter of Smith, 84 A.D.2d 664, 444 N.Y.S.2d 325 (3d Dep't 1981) (burden of proving value of legal services rendered to decedent before his death is on objectant to claim). But see Matter of Taylor, 251 N.Y. 257, 167 N.E. 434 (1929) (executor may not, simply by allowing a claim, shift the burden of proof to the objectants).

6. See Matter of Spatt, 32 N.Y.2d 778, 344 N.Y.S.2d 959, 298 N.E.2d 121 (1973); Matter of Wilkinson, 41 A.D.2d 1024, 343 N.Y.S.2d 959 (4th Dep't 1973), on remand 75 Misc.2d 831, 348 N.Y.S.2d 734 (1973).

7. Matter of Adler, 285 App.Div. 889, 137 N.Y.S.2d 599 (2d Dep't 1955) (court could not fix attorney's compensation because executor had been discharged after complying with accounting decree and had no estate assets).

8. McKinney's EPTL 2–1.8. The apportionment of attorneys' fees in these proceedings are discussed in this chapter, infra at 375, and the proceedings themselves are discussed in chapter on "Estate Taxes," infra at 602–06.

9. Matter of Proffen, 175 Misc. 447, 24 N.Y.S.2d 889 (New York County 1940). But see Matter of Post, 155 Misc. 389, 279 N.Y.S. 408 (Kings 1935) (award of fee for services rendered in another court to recover note owing to decedent was not within Surrogate's jurisdiction).

10. Matter of Haas, 33 A.D.2d 1, 304 N.Y.S.2d 930 (4th Dep't 1969), appeal dismissed 26 N.Y.2d 646, 307 N.Y.S.2d 671, 255 N.E.2d 782 (1970); Matter of Matheson, 265 N.Y. 81, 191 N.E. 842 (1934).

11. Matter of Haas, 33 A.D.2d 1, 307 N.Y.S.2d 930 (4th Dep't 1969), appeal dismissed 26 N.Y.2d 646, 307 N.Y.S.2d 671, 255 N.E.2d 782 (1970); Crempa v. Oakley, 9 Misc.2d 583, 170 N.Y.S.2d 669 (Sup.Ct. New York County 1958). See also Matter of Moody, 6 A.D.2d 861, 176 N.Y.S.2d 1 (1st Dep't 1958), where the court found that the legal services provided to the estate and wholly-owned corporation were "so coincidental as to render it difficult to ascertain any clear distinction," and found sufficient specific circumstances to permit the Surrogate's Court to exercise jurisdiction.

SECTION B. THE PROCEEDING

1. THE PETITIONER

An attorney, a fiduciary or a person interested in the estate can commence an SCPA 2110 proceeding [1] by filing a petition. The petitioner can start the proceeding at any time during the administration of an estate, whether in the context of a pending proceeding or as an independent proceeding.[2] Fiduciaries sometimes use this proceeding to get court approval of the attorney's fee and avoid the possibility of surcharge at the final accounting.[3] The SCPA 2110 proceeding cannot be started by the attorney for a creditor seeking payment of the creditor's claim, because a creditor is not a person interested.[4] Nor can certified public accountants or other accountants use SCPA 2110 for the fixation of their fees [5] except in the rare case where they are attorneys and actually performed legal services,[6] or their services were part of the attorney's disbursements.

Generally, a non-resident attorney not admitted to the bar in New York may not receive a fee for services performed in New York.[7] Neither may a member of the New York bar with no office in New York.[8] Even if the fee is for an isolated service, the court will not grant the fee to the non-resident attorney for services rendered in New York.[9]

Sec. B

1. McKinney's SCPA 2110(2).

2. McKinney's SCPA 2110(1).

3. See Matter of Rosenberg, 263 N.Y. 357, 189 N.E. 452 (1934) (issue of attorneys' fees paid without court order had to be litigated).

4. McKinney's SCPA 103(39); Matter of Kreider, N.Y.L.J., Jan. 31, 1964, at 17, col. 1 (Kings) (attorney rendered services to people to whom the estate owed rent. They were creditors and hence not interested parties).

5. Matter of Kottle, 13 Misc.2d 970, 179 N.Y.S.2d 196 (Nassau 1958) (no statutory authority for proceeding to fix certified public accountant's fees. Executors should have paid it or allowed it or waited until accounting). See Blumenberg v. Neubecker, 15 A.D.2d 952, 226 N.Y.S.2d 452 (2d Dep't 1962), reversed 12 N.Y.2d 456, 240 N.Y.S.2d 730, 191 N.E.2d 269 (1963) (accountant and lawyer can both be paid for their services in prosecuting a matter in the Tax Court, but the lawyer may recover only for legal services and the accountant only for accounting services); Matter of Balsam, N.Y.L.J., August 21, 1969 (Nassau) (accord).

6. Matter of Stern, N.Y.L.J., April 28, 1970, at 17, col. 4 (New York County) (accountant who was admitted to practice before the Tax court rendered legal services in a Tax Court proceeding, and the court entertained proceeding to set accountant's fees).

7. Matter of Nunno, 161 Misc. 707, 293 N.Y.S. 827 (Richmond 1937) (McKinney's SCPA 2110's predecessor, SCA 231–a, did not afford relief to an attorney not admitted in New York for services performed in New York).

8. Matter of Fordan, 5 Misc.2d 372, 158 N.Y.S.2d 228 (New York County 1956); McKinney's Jud.Law § 470 (1983).

9. Spivak v. Sachs, 16 N.Y.2d 163, 263 N.Y.S.2d 953, 211 N.E.2d 329 (1965) (attorney had advised client that he would not appear for her and that his services would be limited; court refused to assist attorney in collecting fee because the services were performed illegally by a person not admitted to practice in New York). For a case discussing the rights of non-New York attorneys in federal actions, see Spanos v. Skouras, 364 F.2d 161 (2d Cir.1966 en banc), reversing 235 F.Supp. 1 (D.N.Y.1964), certiorari denied 385 U.S. 987, 87 S.Ct. 597, 17 L.Ed.2d 448 (1966). See generally "Geography and the Law," N.Y.L.J., June 7, 1966, at 1, col. 1.

If a non-New York-attorney renders services in a state where he is admitted, the New York court can compensate him from the estate,[10] so long as it is the same estate to which the services were rendered.[11]

2. THE PETITION

In practice, the proceeding should be brought either when the attorney's job is done or when he is discharged.[12] A court cannot set a fee for services the attorney expects to perform in the future.[13] The petition asks the court to fix the fees of the fiduciary's attorney or of a beneficiary's attorney,[14] and it asks the court to direct the source of the payment (from the general estate funds or from a beneficiary's share).[15] It must contain all the information required for petitions in the Surrogate's Court generally,[16] and in addition must conform to the rules governing all miscellaneous proceedings; that is, it must state the jurisdictional facts and the "facts applicable to the particular relief sought." [17] Those would include at a minimum the identity of the parties, the size and nature (that is, testamentary or non-testamentary nature) of the estate, the services and their value.

The petitioner ordinarily submits a detailed affidavit of services with the petition, since the burden is on the attorney to prove the value

10. Matter of Matheson, 265 N.Y. 81, 191 N.E. 842 (1934) (Surrogate, even without personal jurisdiction of parties, had subject matter jurisdiction to set attorney's fees of non-resident attorney who performed services in his own jurisdiction); see also Matter of Stern, 62 Misc.2d 730, 309 N.Y.S.2d 764 (New York County 1970), where the court allowed a fee to an accountant admitted to practice before the Internal Revenue Service. See Matter of Shea, 191 N.Y.S.2d 1014 (Westchester 1959).

For the reciprocal problem, see Matter of Grosner, 30 A.D.2d 652, 290 N.Y.S.2d 1010 (1st Dep't 1968), modified 24 N.Y.2d 789, 300 N.Y.S.2d 576, 248 N.E.2d 435 (1969), where the court received a request to set the fees of a person who rendered services in a trust litigation taking place in Washington, D.C., and directed the attorney to apply there for fixation of his fees.

See also Note, Retaining Out-of-State Counsel: The Evolution of a Federal Right, 67 Col.L.Rev. 731 (April 1967); Note, Unauthorized Practice of Law, 50 Cornell L.Rev. 360 (Winter 1965); Case Note, Legal Services, Admission Pro Hac Vice, 33 Fordham L.Rev. 483 (March 1965).

11. See Matter of Brannan, 66 Misc.2d 283, 321 N.Y.S.2d 49 (1971). There the Florida attorneys asked the court to order payment of their fees out of the estate of X, in whose favor Z had exercised a power of appointment. After checking, the court discovered that the work done by the attorney in Florida had been for Z's estate, not X's, and refused to allow payment out of X's estate.

12. Matter of Cook, 41 A.D.2d 907, 343 N.Y.S.2d 189 (1st Dep't 1973), affirmed 33 N.Y.2d 919, 352 N.Y.S.2d 935, 308 N.E.2d 451 (1973); Matter of Luckenbach, 46 Misc. 2d 864, 261 N.Y.S.2d 106 (Nassau 1965), affirmed 25 A.D.2d 852, 269 N.Y.S.2d 469 (2d Dep't 1966) (dicta); Matter of Rosenblum, 137 N.Y.S.2d 481 (Kings 1955).

13. Matter of Starbucks, 225 App.Div. 689, 231 N.Y.S. 378 (2d Dep't 1928); Matter of Cook, 41 A.D.2d 907, 343 N.Y.S.2d 189 (1st Dep't 1973); but see Matter of Secor, 39 A.D.2d 575, 331 N.Y.S.2d 754 (2d Dep't 1972), where the amount of legal work completed was significant and the amount not yet completed was minor, and the court awarded the attorney his fees for all services.

14. McKinney's SCPA 2110(2). The court will not dismiss the motion merely because the executor does not have assets belonging to the legatee against whom the fee is chargeable. Matter of McKay, 10 A.D.2d 887, 201 N.Y.S.2d 311 (2d Dep't 1960).

15. The source of the payments is discussed presently.

16. McKinney's SCPA 304, discussed in chapter on "Procedure," supra at 54–55.

17. McKinney's SCPA 2101(3).

of the legal services.[18] Moreover, although a beneficiary paying an attorney from his own share is free to agree to any fee, if the attorney is paid from the estate assets, the fee must be reasonable.[19]

The affidavit should cover the five criteria used to determine the reasonableness of attorneys' fees (discussed shortly) and should stress the unusual or difficult aspects of the case, if any. It should list legal services only. If the attorney is also a fiduciary, he should not list his executorial services (that is, the services any layman could perform).[20] Thus, if an attorney marshalled assets, prepared checks, paid creditors, made funeral arrangements or performed similar services, he cannot expect compensation from the estate for those services.[21] The fiduciary may be personally liable to the attorney for the value of those services, and may be required to pay for them out of his commissions.[22]

If the court must fix the fee, the attorney cannot charge items of overhead, such as lunches, traveling expenses (unless the attorney must travel great distances to aid in the estate administration), telephone calls, messenger service, postage, taxi fare and secretarial services, as disbursements.[23] Naturally, he cannot get compensation under SCPA 2110 for services for which he has already been paid.[24]

In practice, as a starting point, some courts arbitrarily divide the sum to be allowed for the attorney's fee into sixths and allocate one-sixth to probate, three sixths to tax proceedings, marshaling assets and generally administering the estate, and two-sixths to accounting.

18. See Matter of Spatt, 32 N.Y.2d 778, 344 N.Y.S.2d 959, 298 N.E.2d 121 (1973) (record must contain enough evidence on the value of fees to allow court to set them); Matter of Wilkinson, 41 A.D.2d 1024, 343 N.Y.S.2d 959 (4th Dep't 1973), on remand 75 Misc.2d 831, 348 N.Y.S.2d 734 (1973) (accord). The court can order the attorney to submit this affidavit in any proceeding (such as a proceeding to fix New York estate taxes) in which the attorneys' fees become an issue. See Matter of Maras, N.Y.L.J., July 8, 1985, at 14, col. 7 (Queens).

19. Reasonableness of attorneys' fees is discussed in this chapter infra at 366–69. See Matter of Woolfson, 158 Misc. 928, 287 N.Y.S. 12 (Kings 1936) (unless unreasonable on its face, contract between attorney and client enjoys presumption of reasonableness).

20. Matter of Hallock, 214 App.Div. 323, 212 N.Y.S. 82 (3d Dep't 1925) (claim reduced because much of attorney's work was executorial); Matter of Arguto, N.Y. L.J., April 19, 1985, at 7, col. 1 (Westchester).

21. Matter of Saperstone, 258 App.Div. 776, 14 N.Y.S.2d 816 (4th Dep't 1939); Matter of Owen, 144 Misc. 688, 259 N.Y.S. 892 (Richmond 1932). The fees of attorney-fiduciaries are discussed again in section on "Advance Payment of Attorney's Fees to Attorney-Fiduciaries," this chapter infra at 379–81.

22. Matter of Grace, 62 Misc.2d 51, 308 N.Y.S.2d 33 (Nassau 1970) (corporate executor which performed executorial duties was entitled to be paid by fiduciary, not by estate).

23. Matter of Lieberman, 151 N.Y.S.2d 166 (Westchester 1966). Paralegal services are also considered items of overhead. Matter of Laing, N.Y.L.J., December 6, 1979, at 13, col. 5 (Queens).

24. See Matter of Martin, 35 A.D.2d 513, 312 N.Y.S.2d 51 (1st Dep't 1970), affirmed 29 N.Y.2d 806, 327 N.Y.S.2d 366, 277 N.E.2d 413 (1941) (no duplication of fees).

3. NECESSARY PARTIES

The court can entertain the proceeding, refuse to entertain it, or defer its decision until the final accounting.[25] If the court decides to entertain the proceeding, it issues process (citation or order to show cause [26]) for service on all interested persons and whomever else it believes should be cited.[27] The court determines which parties are necessary by looking at the nature of the services for which the fee is claimed and the source of payment. If the petitioner expects the fee to be paid from the general assets of the estate, then all those adversely affected (and the fiduciary) must be served. If the petitioner seeks compensation out of the share of one beneficiary who retained him, he need serve only that beneficiary.

4. OBJECTIONS AND HEARING

Usually anyone opposing the attorney's fee submits answering affidavits. The court can order a hearing in a contested proceeding, and has the discretion to order a jury trial.[28] Usually the parties waive a hearing and the court can fix the fee after reviewing affidavits of service, replies to the affidavits, and memoranda submitted by the petitioners' and objectants' attorneys. If anyone insists on a hearing the court will hold one. In addition, if the affidavits raise serious questions of fact, the court must hold a hearing.[29]

If an objecting party does not submit verified objections, technically the court does not have to accept them and can view the attorneys' fee as uncontested.[30] However, in practice the Surrogates do take heed of such objections, even when they are oral or in the form of a letter from a layman upset by the size of the proposed fee. The safe rule seems to be that when any objections are made, the Surrogate will look carefully at all the proofs submitted before fixing a fee.[31] Moreover, even in some uncontested proceedings, the court can review the fee.[32] If there is a trial, in most cases all parties stipulate that if the attorney were to take the stand, his testimony would be the same as his affidavit of services, and the affidavit is then made an exhibit in evidence. The

25. McKinney's SCPA 2101(1)(b).

26. Matter of Fagan, 8 Misc.2d 1029, 167 N.Y.S.2d 272 (Nassau 1957) (notice of motion insufficient; citation and petition required).

27. McKinney's SCPA 2101(3).

28. Matter of Richards, 5 A.D.2d 124, 169 N.Y.S.2d 503 (4th Dep't 1958) (ordering jury trial was not abuse of discretion; jury verdict advisory only).

29. Matter of Gurland, 22 A.D.2d 696, 253 N.Y.S.2d 798 (2d Dep't 1964) (issues of fact when raised can be decided only by a hearing).

30. Matter of Gross, 79 Misc.2d 204, 359 N.Y.S.2d 484 (Queens 1974) (court considered McKinney's SCPA 2110 application unopposed because parties opposed to it failed to file a verified pleading).

31. Matter of Kittelberger, 4 A.D.2d 218, 163 N.Y.S.2d 856 (4th Dep't 1957), affirmed 4 N.Y.2d 740, 171 N.Y.S.2d 861, 148 N.E.2d 910 (1958) (court required proof by affidavits or testimony because objections were raised).

32. Matter of Bernheimer, 61 A.D.2d 761, 402 N.Y.S.2d 10 (1st Dep't 1978), appeal denied 45 N.Y.2d 710, 409 N.Y.S.2d 1028, 381 N.E.2d 616 (1978) (attorney-fiduciary). See discussion this chapter supra at 359.

court usually gives the attorney permission to add anything he thinks is necessary to what he stated in the affidavit, and then allows the objectant to cross-examine the attorney. Often the attorney is the only witness unless the objectant offers testimony by someone who can refute whether the services were performed or who performed them. Even expert witnesses on the value of legal services are rare, because the court can determine that issue itself.[33]

If a party objects to excessive attorney's fees, the parties who specifically consented to the fees cannot share in the surcharge.[34] However, the court can order the attorney to refund the whole fee, even if only one party objects [35] and even if some do not object but do not specifically consent to the fee either. The refunded money is then an estate asset and is paid ratably among all estate beneficiaries except those who consented to the legal fee.

5. THE COURT ORDER

The court's final determination of the attorney's fees is in the form of a decree or order, and it may condition its award on the petitioner's filing a refunding bond.[36] The decision is entirely within the Surrogate's discretion,[37] and will be overturned by the Appellate Division only on a finding that the Surrogate abused his discretion and acted arbitrarily.[38]

If the attorney has already received more than the amount fixed by the court, the court may direct a refund,[39] and the court's direction is

33. See McAvoy v. Harron, 26 A.D.2d 452, 275 N.Y.S.2d 348 (4th Dep't 1966), affirmed 21 N.Y.2d 821, 288 N.Y.S.2d 906, 235 N.E.2d 910 (1968) (expert testimony admissible but not conclusive).

34. Matter of La Grove, 31 A.D.2d 928, 299 N.Y.S.2d 80 (2d Dep't 1969), affirmed 30 N.Y.2d 624, 331 N.Y.S.2d 439, 282 N.E.2d 329 (1972) (only the party objecting to the attorney's fee entitled to refund of his pro rata (one-eighth) share).

35. Matter of Mette, 273 App.Div. 740, 80 N.Y.S.2d 221 (2d Dep't 1948), affirmed 298 N.Y. 789, 83 N.E.2d 475 (1948) (court directed refund of entire excess of attorney's fee to estate and surcharged executor).

36. McKinney's SCPA 2101(4); Matter of Aaron, 30 N.Y.2d 718, 332 N.Y.S.2d 891, 283 N.E.2d 764 (1972).

37. See Matter of Brehm, 37 A.D.2d 95, 322 N.Y.S.2d 287 (4th Dep't 1971).

38. Matter of Freeman, 40 A.D.2d 397, 341b N.Y.S.2d 511 (4th Dep't 1973), affirmed 34 N.Y.2d 1, 355 N.Y.S.2d 336, 311 N.E.2d 480 (1974); Matter of Greatsinger, 107 A.D.2d 873, 484 N.Y.S.2d 311 (3d Dep't 1985) (though Surrogate did not state his theory for the award, he had affidavit of services before him and his award was not abusive of his discretion); Matter of Brehm, 37 A.D.2d 95, 322 N.Y.S.2d 287 (4th Dep't 1971) (Surrogate arbitrarily reduced attorneys' fees despite lack of objections and submission of affidavits of services). The Court of Appeals does not review the reasonableness of attorneys' fees, which is a question of fact. See Matter of Aaron, 30 N.Y.2d 718, 332 N.Y.S.2d 891, 283 N.E.2d 764 (1972). See also Matter of Snell, 17 A.D.2d 490, 235 N.Y.S.2d 855 (3d Dep't 1962), where the Appellate Division reversed the Surrogate's reduction of a $150,000 legal fee in a $7,000,000 estate and reinstated the $150,000 fee. It did not mention an abuse of discretion by the Surrogate, but it did state that in view of the lack of objections to the fee, the Surrogate should have entered a pro forma order on the fee.

39. McKinney's SCPA 2110(3). See Matter of Sharkey, 64 A.D.2d 636, 406 N.Y.S.2d 1006 (2d Dep't 1978) (affirmed order fixing fee and requiring refund); Matter of Freeman, 40 A.D.2d 397, 341 N.Y.S.2d 511 (4th Dep't 1972), affirmed 34 N.Y.2d 1, 355 N.Y.S.2d 336, 311 N.E.2d 480

controlling so long as it is not arbitrary or unreasonable.[40] Similarly, the court can, during an SCPA 2110 proceeding, find an attorney liable for damages to the estate.[41]

The Surrogate has discretion to award interest on the attorney's fee and it can compute such interest from the date the petition is filed or another date in its discretion.[42]

SECTION C. REASONABLENESS OF ATTORNEYS' FEES

Matter of Potts [1] and Matter of Freeman [2] are the leading cases setting forth the criteria for fixing attorneys' fees: [3]

> (i) The size of the estate. The size of an estate [4] limits the legal fees. Thus if an estate is small, the attorney may earn less than the value of his services.[5] On the other hand, a large estate does not automatically justify a large fee; [6] there the attorney will earn the reasonable value of his services.[7] The attorney can consider both testamentary and non-testamentary assets when set-

(1974); Matter of Giddings, 96 Misc.2d 824, 410 N.Y.S.2d 16 (Onondaga 1978); Matter of Storm, 40 Misc.2d 390, 243 N.Y.S.2d 53 (New York County 1963) (court on summary motion of substitute trustee directed attorney of removed trustee to repay fees not allowed by court).

40. Matter of Freeman, 40 A.D.2d 397, 341 N.Y.S.2d 511 (4th Dep't 1972), affirmed 34 N.Y.2d 1, 355 N.Y.S.2d 336, 311 N.E.2d 480 (1974) (Surrogate must act reasonably, not arbitrarily); Matter of Bernheimer, 61 A.D.2d 761, 402 N.Y.S.2d 10 (1st Dep't 1978), appeal denied 45 N.Y.2d 710, 409 N.Y.S.2d 1028, 381 N.E.2d 616 (1978) (accord).

41. See Matter of Remsen, 99 Misc.2d 92, 415 N.Y.S.2d 370 (Nassau 1979), where the attorney filed the estate taxes late, incurring a penalty, and held estate assets in non-interest-bearing accounts. The court held him liable for both.

42. Matter of Aaron, 30 N.Y.2d 718, 332 N.Y.S.2d 891, 283 N.E.2d 764 (1972), remitting to appellate division which, in 39 A.D.2d 963, 333 N.Y.S.2d 767 (2d Dep't 1972), allowed interest in part; Matter of Mandel, 20 A.D.2d 719, 247 N.Y.S.2d 556 (2d Dep't 1964) (allowing interest from date of demand); Matter of Noble, 1 A.D.2d 900, 149 N.Y.S.2d 610 (2d Dep't 1956) (allowing interest from date of demand).

Sec. C

1. 213 A.D. 59, 209 N.Y.S. 655 (4th Dep't 1925) affirmed 241 N.Y. 593, 150 N.E. 568 (1925).

2. 40 A.D.2d 397, 341 N.Y.S.2d 511 (4th Dep't 1973), affirmed 34 N.Y.2d 1, 355 N.Y.S.2d 336, 311 N.E.2d 480 (1974).

3. Though this chapter discusses only attorneys' fees, the Potts and Freeman criteria are used to gauge the reasonableness of the fees of attorneys-in-fact, Matter of Reeve, N.Y.L.J., June 19, 1985, at 12, col. 3 (Suffolk), and guardians ad litem, Matter of Jackson, N.Y.L.J., May 14, 1985, at 13, col. 1 (Suffolk), as well.

4. The "size of the estate" in this discussion means gross taxable estate. Matter of Shalman, 68 A.D.2d 940, 414 N.Y.S.2d 70 (3d Dep't 1979) (Surrogate approved a lawyer's fee of four percent of gross taxable estate).

5. Matter of Kaufmann, 26 A.D.2d 818, 273 N.Y.S.2d 902 (1st Dep't 1966), affirmed 23 N.Y.2d 700, 296 N.Y.S.2d 146, 243 N.E.2d 751 (1978) (court stated that the size of the estate operates as limitation on full value of services rendered).

6. Matter of Young, 52 Misc.2d 398, 275 N.Y.S.2d 879 (Suffolk 1966) (value of services, not size of estate, determines fee; fee fixed at $26,000 in $800,000 estate).

7. Matter of Martin, 21 A.D.2d 646, 249 N.Y.S.2d 179 (1st Dep't 1964), affirmed 16 N.Y.2d 594, 261 N.Y.S.2d 54, 209 N.E.2d 102 (1965) (size of estate cannot increase value of services beyond reasonable compensation). See also Gelfand, Estate Attorneys' Fees, N.Y.L.J., June 17, 1974 at 23, col. 4.

ting a fee, but non-testamentary assets are usually weighed less heavily than testamentary assets.[8] The courts often approve attorney's fees ranging up to five percent of the estate for the first $50,000 or so and smaller percentages on higher amounts.[9] However, percentages or hourly rates are not conclusive, but are merely a guide to determine if the amount sought is reasonable. Local bar associations no longer suggest scales for attorneys' fees in estates, since the United States Supreme Court ruled such rate scales violative of anti-trust laws.[10]

(ii) The professional standing of the attorney. The court will consider the attorney's reputation and experience when it sets the attorney's fee.[11] If the attorney requests payment based on what he claims is his usual hourly rate, he must substantiate that rate.[12]

(iii) The complexity of the issues and the necessity for litigation. For example, if an estate is "bitterly, doggedly and uncompromisingly battled from the very first day of the proceedings," [13] and the attorney labors for years to resolve intricate questions of law that arise, the court will allow compensation for that labor. The same is true if an attorney had to research and brief issues in a construction proceeding, and negotiate with the Internal Revenue Service about reducing taxes.[14] On the other hand, if the litigation is not complex but routine, the court will reduce an excessive fee.[15]

(iv) The results achieved. For example, success in litigation and negotiation is a factor in the setting of attorneys' fees.[16]

8. See Matter of Bradley, N.Y.L.J., May 31, 1985, at 19, col. 6 (Nassau) (fee in estate of $144,000, most of it in non-testamentary assets, reduced from $3,500 to $750); Matter of Crotty, N.Y.L.J., Nov. 30, 1972 at 16, col. 3 (New York County) (Surrogate would not approve five percent fee on non-testamentary assets).

9. See Matter of Getsinger, 246 App. Div. 868, 284 N.Y.S. 881 (3d Dep't 1936) (approximately four percent); Matter of Ketcham, 199 App.Div. 244, 191 N.Y.S. 396 (2d Dep't 1921) (approximately five percent); Matter of Felton, 199 Misc. 507, 99 N.Y.S.2d 351 (Schenectady 1950) (five percent on first $50,000 and three percent on excess over $50,000).

10. Goldfarb v. Virginia State Bar, 421 U.S. 773, 95 S.Ct. 2004, 44 L.Ed.2d 572 (1975), rehearing denied 423 U.S. 886, 96 S.Ct. 162, 46 L.Ed.2d 118 (1975).

11. Matter of Potts, 213 A.D. 59, 209 N.Y.S. 655 (4th Dep't), affirmed 241 N.Y. 593, 150 N.E. 568 (1925); Matter of Brehm, 37 A.D.2d 95, 322 N.Y.S.2d 287 (4th Dep't 1971) (attorneys' substantial experience enabled them to complete the work in shorter time than other attorneys with less experience).

12. See Matter of Terry, N.Y.L.J., March 12, 1985, at 12, col. 1 (Bronx), where the attorney requested a fee based on a $100 hourly rate, but was unable to convince the court in his testimony that he customarily received that amount.

13. Matter of Sabatino, 66 A.D.2d 937, 411 N.Y.S.2d 439 (3d Dep't 1978).

14. Matter of Lieberman, 151 N.Y.S.2d 166 (Westchester 1956).

15. Matter of Giddings, 96 Misc.2d 824, 410 N.Y.S.2d 16 (Onondaga 1978).

16. Matter of Shalman, 68 A.D.2d 940, 414 N.Y.S.2d 70 (3d Dep't 1979) (dicta); Matter of Sabatino, 66 A.D.2d 937, 411 N.Y.S.2d 439 (3d Dep't 1978) (estate attorney prevailed in litigation); Matter of Rosenbaum, N.Y.L.J., November 23, 1979, at 13, col. 1 (New York County) (success in repatriating estate).

(v) The time spent. The time spent is an important factor [17] and is indeed a starting point for computation of the fee,[18] but it is not the only important factor, and the courts are critical of an approach that over-emphasizes it.[19] The attorney relying on time spent should document the claim amply with time records and diary entries.[20] The Surrogates tend to frown on the submission of a short (one or two page) affidavit accompanied by diary entries that are difficult to evaluate (such as "conference held-five hours").[21] The court will not accept an attorney's statement of the hours spent unsupported by time records clearly indicating what the time was devoted to and what result the work achieved.[22] The court can take judicial notice of the attorney's appearances in court.[23] The importance of the time spent diminishes if the estate is small.[24] Promptness and efficiency in performing the services are also a factor.[25]

The attorney's services must also be necessary.[26] If no court-supervised administration is necessary, or if the estate could be admin-

17. Matter of Lipsit, 21 A.D.2d 509, 251 N.Y.S.2d 979 (2d Dep't 1964), affirmed 15 N.Y.2d 588, 255 N.Y.S.2d 257, 203 N.E.2d 646 (1964) (court allocated fee between two attorneys, using time spent as the criterion).

18. Matter of Potts, 213 App.Div. 59, 209 N.Y.S. 655 (4th Dep't 1925), affirmed 241 N.Y. 593, 150 N.E. 568 (1925).

19. Matter of Brehm, 37 A.D.2d 95, 322 N.Y.S.2d 287 (4th Dep't 1971) (attorneys were so experienced in estates practice they accomplished the services in less time than less experienced attorneys); Matter of Snell, 17 A.D.2d 490, 235 N.Y.S.2d 855 (3d Dep't 1962) (time clock approach should not be used exclusively); Matter of Shalman, 68 A.D.2d 940, 414 N.Y.S.2d 70 (3d Dep't 1979) (though fees were less than customary in the county, the Surrogate did not abuse his discretion in reducing fees based too heavily on time spent).

20. Matter of Schaich, 55 A.D.2d 914, 391 N.Y.S.2d 135 (2d Dep't 1977), appeal denied 42 N.Y.2d 802, 397 N.Y.S.2d 1026, 366 N.E.2d 293 (1977) (Surrogate refused to accept attorney's assertion that he had spent one thousand hours especially when it was unaccompanied by time records); Matter of Giddings, 96 Misc.2d 824, 410 N.Y.S.2d 16 (Onondaga 1978) (court disregarded attorney's assertions of time spent after he first claimed that fire destroyed the file, and then produced time records).

21. Matter of Strupp, N.Y.L.J., Jan. 12, 1968, at 18, col. 1 (New York County) (two-page affidavit and 110 pages of diary entries).

22. Matter of Schaich, 55 A.D.2d 914, 391 N.Y.S.2d 135 (2d Dep't 1977); Matter of Geiger, 25 Misc.2d 397, 207 N.Y.S.2d 144 (Nassau 1960) (attorney who rendered services died, and his associates inspected files and estimated attorney had spent six hundred hours on estate; court discounts their estimate and reduced requested $12,000 fee to $2,000).

23. Matter of Mann, 41 A.D.2d 861, 342 N.Y.S.2d 617 (3d Dep't 1973), appeal denied 33 N.Y.2d 517, 348 N.Y.S.2d 1028, 303 N.E.2d 709 (1973).

24. Matter of Martin, 21 A.D.2d 646, 249 N.Y.S.2d 179 (1st Dep't 1964), affirmed 16 N.Y.2d 594, 261 N.Y.S.2d 54, 209 N.E.2d 102 (1965).

25. See Matter of Arguto, N.Y.L.J., April 9, 1985, at 7, col. 1 (Westchester).

26. E.g., Matter of Kaufman, 18 A.D.2d 977, 238 N.Y.S.2d 440 (1st Dep't 1963) (services related to an issue that should not have been submitted to the referee because it was a matter of business judgment; services were not necessary and no fee was allowed); Matter of Giddings, 96 Misc.2d 824, 410 N.Y.S.2d 16 (Onondaga 1978) (court conceded that there was much paper work done but found much of it unnecessary). See Matter of Sanford, N.Y.L.J., Feb. 27, 1985, at 15, col. 4 (Nassau), where the attorney for a conservatee represented her in criminal matter. The court had told her guardian ad litem that she needed an attorney, and she was ineligible for Legal Aid, so the court considered the representation necessary and allowed the attorney's fee.

istered under the facilitated Article 13 procedures for small estates,[27] an attorney will not be entitled to a fee for a full, formal administration.[28] The attorney will not be paid for performing services the fiduciary should have done, unless they require legal expertise,[29] though he can sue the fiduciary for payment of such services.[30]

If an attorney is also serving as fiduciary, he is allowed to represent himself and in addition to his fiduciary's commissions, he will be paid a legal fee for those services that are legal in nature. He can also hire counsel to perform the legal services, since he is not expected to perform legal services gratis.[31] If he hires an accountant the court usually includes the accountant's services in setting the attorney's fees (that is, the attorney is expected to pay the accountant out of his own fee), so there is no duplication of fees.[32]

Many Surrogates and their staffs keep diaries on how long a trial, pre-trial procedure or conference took. If the attorney's time records are inconsistent with the court's, it may arouse a suspicion that the attorneys' records are inaccurate.

The courts usually weigh all five factors in setting the attorney's fee in determining the reasonableness of the fee requested.[33]

Although contingency fees are not prohibited in the Surrogate's Court, they are usually used only in representation of contestants and objectants. The fee arrangements vary, but are usually at lower rates than those used in negligence cases.

SECTION D. RETAINER AGREEMENTS

It is sound practice for the attorney and the client to enter into a very specific retainer agreement,[1] but if a problem arises and someone

27. See chapter on "Small Estates," supra at 246 et seq.

28. Matter of Bradley, N.Y.L.J., May 31, 1985, at 19, col. 6 (Nassau) (fee in simple estate reduced from $8,500 to $750).

29. Matter of March, N.Y.L.J., November 2, 1978, at 13, col. 4 (Suffolk) (construction of family tree required attorney's services). See also Matter of Wiltshire, 4 A.D.2d 981, 167 N.Y.S.2d 852 (3d Dep't 1957), appeal denied 5 A.D.2d 797, 170 N.Y.S.2d 318 (1958), where the court said, "To the extent that an executorial duty requires legal evaluation, compensation for same is allowable."

30. Matter of Rosenberg, 147 Misc. 517, 266 N.Y.S. 99 (Richmond 1933), affirmed 241 App.Div. 601, 268 N.Y.S. 733 (2d Dep't 1934), affirmed 265 N.Y. 521, 193 N.E. 302 (1934).

31. Matter of Hallock, 214 A.D. 323, 212 N.Y.S. 82 (3d Dep't 1925).

32. Matter of Deitch, N.Y.L.J., March 8, 1985, at 16, col. 2.

33. See, e.g., Matter of Mann, 41 A.D.2d 861, 342 N.Y.S.2d 617 (3d Dep't 1973), appeal denied 33 N.Y.2d 517, 348 N.Y.S.2d 1028, 303 N.E.2d 709 (1973) (court considered time spent, litigation required, results obtained, amount of estate, and time period covered). See also Code of Professional Responsibility, E.C. 2–18; Canons of Professional Ethics, Canon 2.

Sec. D

1. Professional Code of Responsibility, Ethical Consideration 2–19; De Graff v. McKesson and Robbins, Inc., 31 N.Y.2d 862, 340 N.Y.S.2d 171, 292 N.E.2d 310 (1972) (formula for fixing fee on contingency basis should be clearly stated at time of retainer). See also Matter of Thaw, 60 Misc.2d 184, 302 N.Y.S.2d 661 (New York County 1969), where the decedent entered into an agreement with an attorney setting a fee, conditioned on the attorney's surviv-

invokes SCPA 2110, the court is not bound by the retainer terms and can set the fee in a different amount based on quantum meruit.[2] No retainer agreement can bind the estate to more than a reasonable fee,[3] and the attorney has the burden of proving reasonableness of the amount.[4] If the client agreed to pay the retainer out of his own share of the estate, it is arguable that unless there was mistake, fraud or overreaching, he is bound by it.[5] Other parties to the proceeding, who did not consent or did not have the capacity to consent, are not bound.[6] Even if the retainer amount was unreasonable and the court reduces the fee, the attorney may possibly recover the amount disapproved by the court from the fiduciary individually on an agency theory if the court's determination was without prejudice to pursue that amount.

On the other hand, if the retainer is low, an attorney may be bound by that on more than one theory: because it is in the nature of an admission,[7] or because the court does not have the power to pay an attorney a higher fee than he agreed to[8] unless the attorney was discharged by the fiduciary before completing his services, or other circumstances show that the services were worth more.[9] If the attorney was fired, he is no longer bound by the retainer agreement and can recover on a quantum meruit basis.[10] We discuss discharged attorneys and their remedies later in this chapter.

ing the decedent. The attorney predeceased the decedent, and the retainer agreement was held not to bind the deceased attorney's partners.

2. Matter of Schanzer, 11 Misc.2d 893, 177 N.Y.S.2d 124 (New York County 1958), reversed 7 A.D.2d 275, 185 N.Y.S.2d 475 (1st Dep't 1959), affirmed 8 N.Y.2d 972, 204 N.Y.S.2d 349, 169 N.E.2d 11 (1960) (court rejected retainer agreement of fifteen percent of the gross estate); Matter of Gasco, 27 A.D.2d 557, 275 N.Y.S.2d 871 (2d Dep't 1966) (court rejected a one-third retainer agreement).

3. Matter of Reisfeld, 227 N.Y. 137, 124 N.E. 725 (1919); Matter of Cook, 41 A.D.2d 907, 343 N.Y.S.2d 189 (1st Dep't 1973), affirmed 33 N.Y.2d 919, 352 N.Y.S.2d 935, 308 N.E.2d 451 (1973); Matter of Deitch, N.Y.L.J., March 8, 1985, at 16, col. 3 (Sup. Ct.Nassau).

4. Cohen v. Ryan, 34 A.D.2d 789, 311 N.Y.S.2d 644 (2d Dep't 1970); Matter of Schanzer, 7 A.D.2d 275, 182 N.Y.S.2d 475 (1st Dep't 1959), affirmed 8 N.Y.2d 972, 204 N.Y.S.2d 349, 169 N.E.2d 11 (1960); Matter of Wittenberg, N.Y.L.J., Feb. 26, 1979, at 26, col. 3 (Bronx).

5. Matter of Reisfeld, 227 N.Y. 137, 124 N.E. 725 (1919), dealt with a wrongful death action in which the decedent's father, who was administrator, retained an attorney and agreed to pay him fifty percent of the recovery. He personally was bound by it because he could not show fraud or mistake.

6. In Matter of Reisfeld, discussed in the preceding note, the decedent's mother was not bound by the retainer agreement signed by her husband; the court held that she was bound only by the administrator's reasonable contracts. Accord, Matter of DeLorenzo, N.Y.L.J., Jan. 13, 1978, at 12, col. 6 (Queens) (husband bound by retainer agreement of one-third but court allowed only one-quarter of infant daughter's share to be paid to attorney).

7. Prager v. New Jersey Fidelity and Plate Glass Insurance Co., 245 N.Y. 1, 156 N.E. 76 (1927).

8. See Matter of Kane, 2 A.D.2d 982, 157 N.Y.S.2d 805 (2d Dep't 1956) (court conceded that the quantum meruit value of attorney's services was $1,000 but awarded him the $500 he had contracted for).

9. Matter of Montgomery, 272 N.Y. 323, 6 N.E.2d 40 (1936).

10. Matter of Montgomery, 272 N.Y. 323, 6 N.E.2d 40 (1936). See Matter of Krooks, 257 N.Y. 329, 178 N.E. 548 (1931); Kronish, Lieb, Shainswit, Weiner and Hellman v. Howard Stores Corp., 44 A.D.2d 813, 355 N.Y.S.2d 426 (1st Dep't 1974); Matter of Balsam, N.Y.L.J., Aug. 21, 1969 (Nassau).

It is a fiduciary's prerogative to choose an attorney. This prerogative rises to the level of a public policy in New York, and the court will ignore the testator's wishes on the choice of attorney and monetary limitations on the attorney's fee.[11] However, if the testator designates an executor or trustee or attorney on condition that he waives commissions or accepts limited fees, and appoints alternative fiduciaries and attorneys if the originally nominated attorney does not accept the condition, the court will honor such limitations.[12]

SECTION E. SOURCE OF THE PAYMENT

1. GENERALLY

In the SCPA 2110 proceeding, the court may direct the source of the payment either out of the general assets of the estate or from the funds of a legatee, devisee, or distributee or person interested (such as the assignee of a beneficiary).[1] An attorney who is not representing the fiduciary in the fidiciary capacity may not be paid out of the general estate; he can look only to his own client for compensation.[2] For example, an attorney's services to the fiduciary in his other capacity as beneficiary are payable by the fiduciary personally.[3]

The exception to this rule is the case where the attorney can show that, though his services were for a beneficiary, they benefited the estate generally.[4] Some courts have held that the test of a benefit to the estate means an actual addition to the estate as opposed to mere

11. Matter of Olney, 255 App.Div. 195, 7 N.Y.S.2d 89 (4th Dep't 1938), appeal dismissed 281 N.Y. 98, 22 N.E.2d 252 (1939); See also Matter of Wallach, 164 App.Div. 600, 150 N.Y.S. 302 (1st Dep't 1914), affirmed 215 N.Y. 622, 109 N.E. 1094 (1915), remittitur amended 215 N.Y.S. 687, 109 N.E. 1094 (1915).

12. Matter of Roth, 291 N.Y. 1, 50 N.E.2d 281 (1943).

Sec. E

1. McKinney's SCPA 2110(2).

2. Matter of Della Chiesa, 23 A.D.2d 562, 256 N.Y.S.2d 519 (2d Dep't 1965) (attorney representing executors in their capacity as debtors of the estate); Matter of Loomis, 273 N.Y. 76, 6 N.E.2d 103 (1937) (attorney whose retainer specified fifty percent of recovery entitled only to fifty percent of recovery by his client, not fifty percent of entire recovery); Matter of Bacharach, 12 A.D.2d 938, 211 N.Y.S.2d 230 (2d Dep't 1961); Matter of Geiger, 25 Misc. 2d 397, 207 N.Y.S.2d 144 (Nassau 1960); Matter of Utter, 17 A.D.2d 868, 233 N.Y.S.2d 369 (3d Dep't 1962), affirmed 13 N.Y.2d 836, 242 N.Y.S.2d 356, 192 N.E.2d 230 (1963).

3. Matter of Lewin, 34 Misc.2d 789, 229 N.Y.S.2d 1001 (Suffolk 1962), appeal dismissed 18 A.D.2d 1138, 239 N.Y.S.2d 655 (2d Dep't 1963) (attorney collected insurance for the fiduciary in his individual capacity as beneficiary); Matter of Kramer, 70 N.Y.S.2d 239 (Monroe 1947) (attorney defended administratrix against charges of misconduct); Matter of Rosenzweig, 237 N.Y.S.2d 438 (New York County 1963) (attorney pursued widow-executrix's right of election); Matter of Rosenberg, 165 Misc. 92, 2 N.Y.S.2d 300 (Richmond 1937) (fiduciaries had personal claim for partnership interest in decedent's business).

4. Matter of Del Monte, 37 A.D.2d 827, 325 N.Y.S.2d 345 (1st Dep't 1971) (attorney's services saved the estate the disallowed commissions); Matter of Elias, Schewel and Schwartz, 55 A.D.2d 448, 390 N.Y.S.2d 739 (4th Dep't 1977) (compensation paid from general estate assets); Matter of Rizzo, 36 Misc.2d 60, 231 N.Y.S.2d 115 (Kings 1962) (attorney for administrator could not render services because the administrator was testifying against the estate; attorney for beneficiaries performed the services and the court allowed compensation for them).

reduction of attorney's fees [5] or fiduciaries' commissions,[6] or the elimination of the widow's right to elect against the will.[7] Other courts see such reductions as real benefits resulting in increased distributions to all the estate beneficiaries, even those who did not join in the litigation.[8] That determination has to be made on a case by case basis.

When the equities demand it, the court can allow attorneys' fees to an attorney for a beneficiary even when the services do not benefit the estate, if the services were necessary and the fiduciary was not performing them.[9] For example, occasionally relatives of a decedent who believe themselves to be the intestate distributees retain an attorney to represent them at the kinship hearing, and the attorney spends time and effort to represent them. If in the course of the proceeding a closer relative is found who ousts the petitioners as intestate distributees, the court has to decide whether the attorney's services benefited the estate. Usually it finds that they did, and orders compensation of the attorney from the estate. The rationale is that the court could have appointed an administrator to search for relatives and charged those costs against the estate, so it can also compensate the attorney who bore those costs.[10]

If the attorney rendered services both to the estate and to the individual beneficiary, he can recover those fees payable by the estate under SCPA 2110 and can then try to recover the rest from the client individually either within the SCPA 2110 proceeding or on a contract theory in another court.[11]

2. SOURCE OF PAYMENT IN SPECIFIC PROCEEDINGS

a. *Construction Proceedings*

If an attorney assists the court in a construction proceeding by participating in a trial or hearing and submitting memoranda, he may

5. E.g., Matter of La Grove, 31 A.D.2d 928, 299 N.Y.S.2d 80 (2d Dep't 1969), affirmed 30 N.Y.2d 624, 331 N.Y.S.2d 439, 282 N.E.2d 329 (1972); Matter of Heilbronner, 39 Misc.2d 912, 242 N.Y.S.2d 118 (New York County 1963). See generally Matter of Irvin, 24 Misc.2d 799, 804, 198 N.Y.S.2d 904, 910 (New York County 1960) and cases cited therein.

6. Matter of Bourne, N.Y.L.J., Feb. 2, 1965, at 18, col. 2 (Suffolk)

7. Matter of Allan, 16 A.D.2d 609, 226 N.Y.S.2d 281 (1st Dep't 1962) (attorney failed to prove that she was responsible for widow's withdrawal of right of election or that estate benefited).

8. Matter of Del Monte, 37 A.D.2d 827, 325 N.Y.S.2d 345 (1st Dep't 1971) (attorney for objectant succeeded in reducing fiduciary's commissions and was awarded a fee for such services); Matter of Ryder, N.Y. L.J., Feb. 26, 1985 at 11, col. 3 (Bronx) (attorneys' services resulted in $25,000 surcharge against executor and court awarded him attorneys' fees out of estate).

9. Matter of Rizzo, 36 Misc.2d 60, 231 N.Y.S.2d 115 (Kings 1962) (attorneys of beneficiaries were awarded legal fees from estate assets because executor had testified against estate and the beneficiaries' attorneys performed services that benefited the estate).

10. See, e.g., Matter of Wiltshire, 4 A.D. 2d 981, 167 N.Y.S.2d 852 (3d Dep't 1957); Matter of Herlihy, N.Y.L.J., June 2, 1982, at 11, col. 7 (Bronx); Matter of Hunter, N.Y.L.J., Dec. 27, 1960, at 7, col. 2 (Kings).

11. Matter of Dickinson, 10 Misc.2d 280, 169 N.Y.S.2d 920 (New York County 1957) (court allocated fees within the SCPA 2110 proceeding so beneficiaries would not escape paying their shares, and instructed the attorney to look to their clients for the excess not awarded).

be paid out of the general assets of the estate.[12] In construction proceedings, the grant of attorney's fees is completely discretionary with the court,[13] and the appellate court will overturn it only if the Surrogate's decision was an abuse of discretion.[14] The court can allocate the fee among the interested parties.[15] It will award the fees only if the attorney helped the court to reach a determination, and will therefore probably not do so if it dismisses the construction proceeding for lack of status after a finding that the client had no interest in the proceeding and was not a necessary party to it.[16] The court will award a fee commensurate with the size of the interest "at risk" in the construction proceeding,[17] giving consideration to the importance of the question presented.[18] If the state attorney general appears for ultimate charitable beneficiaries in a construction proceeding, the court will not award attorneys' fees because the attorney general does not assist the court to construe the will, but advocates for a construction benefiting the charities.[19] The success of the construction proceeding alone is not dispositive, but it may help the court in its decision to award attorney's fees.[20] The court may allow part of the fee and the attorney may still have a claim against his client for additional fees to compensate him for the full value of his services not chargeable against the estate.[21] If the court enters the decree without an award of attorney's fees, it is not likely to reopen the decree to allow them.[22] In some cases, the court

12. Matter of O'Brien, 28 A.D.2d 1040, 283 N.Y.S.2d 926 (3d Dep't 1967); Matter of Chodikoff, 54 Misc.2d 785, 283 N.Y.S.2d 555 (Renssalaer 1967).

13. McKinney's SCPA 2301; 2302(6); Matter of O'Brien, 28 A.D.2d 1040, 283 N.Y.S.2d 926 (3d Dep't 1967).

14. Matter of Hoffman, 22 A.D.2d 735, 253 N.Y.S.2d 513 (3d Dep't 1964).

15. Matter of Upjohn, 304 N.Y. 366, 107 N.E.2d 492 (1952) (allocation among testamentary trusts); Matter of Gordon, 65 Misc.2d 50, 316 N.Y.S.2d 879 (Broome 1970) (all parties shared attorneys' fees pro rata because residuary estate was small); Matter of O'Neil, 70 Misc.2d 445, 334 N.Y.S.2d 455 (Broome 1972) (pro rata effect achieved by charging fee against unpaid accumulated income rather than corpus of testamentary trust).

16. Matter of Hayden, 200 Misc.2d 758, 107 N.Y.S.2d 648 (New York County 1951) (employees of decedent were not parties to construction proceeding and their attorney could not recover his fee from the estate).

17. Matter of Griffing, 31 Misc.2d 266, 219 N.Y.S.2d 86 (Suffolk 1971) (fee depends on the size of the interest affected).

18. See Matter of Rothchild, 85 N.Y.S.2d 881 (New York County 1948), where the court disregarded the size of the trust because the litigated question, whether the trust was designed to incite a divorce, was one of public policy.

19. Matter of Dow, 90 Misc.2d 950, 396 N.Y.S.2d 979 (Monroe 1977). The court also found that the attorney general was representing the general public, not the estate, and therefore the attorney general's fee should be the public's burden, not the estate beneficiaries'.

20. Matter of Clark, 54 Misc.2d 1024, 284 N.Y.S.2d 254 (Kings 1967) (award not dependent on vindication of party's interpretation); Matter of Kaufman, N.Y.L.J., Jan. 28, 1975, at 17, col. 1 (Kings) and cases cited therein.

21. Matter of Jacobsen, 70 Misc.2d 355, 333 N.Y.S.2d 511 (New York County 1972); Matter of Storm, 35 Misc.2d 275, 230 N.Y.S.2d 348 (New York County 1962); Matter of Thall, 41 Misc.2d 1086, 247 N.Y.S.2d 153 (Westchester 1964), modified on other grounds 24 A.D.2d 494, 261 N.Y.S.2d 490 (2d Dep't 1965), modified on other grounds 18 N.Y.2d 186, 273 N.Y.S.2d 33, 219 N.E.2d 397 (1966).

22. See Matter of Heller, 33 Misc.2d 798, 226 N.Y.S.2d 260 (New York County 1962) (court will reopen or vacate only on finding of fraud, newly discovered evidence or other sufficient cause, not an attorney's failure to seek compensation from estate assets).

directs that all parties' attorneys' fees be paid from the general estate,[23] but if a generalization can be made, it is that the courts are not inclined to award counsel fees to anyone except the fiduciary's attorneys in construction proceedings, or that at least they will limit the amount.[24]

b. Probate

A probate contest that results in denial of the will to probate benefits the estate, as does a good faith but unsuccessful attempt by a named executor to probate a will,[25] so the attorney's fees can be paid out of the estate generally. If someone makes unfounded charges against the fiduciary, who resists the unjustified attempt to remove him, he can pay his attorneys' fees and expenses from the estate. The charges against him must really be groundless, however; denial of the petition to remove him does not necessarily mean that the removal proceedings were unjustified.[26]

On the other hand, if a named executor in a will propounds the instrument knowing of its invalidity, the executor individually (not the estate) must pay the attorney.[27] If a beneficiary causes meritless litigation, the court can charge the legal fee against that beneficiary.[28] Similarly, an errant or wrongdoing fiduciary may be charged with

23. See Matter of Ablett, 2 A.D.2d 205, 153 N.Y.S.2d 816 (4th Dep't 1956), affirmed 3 N.Y.2d 61, 165 N.Y.S.2d 63, 144 N.E.2d 46 (1957) (because construction clarified will and benefited whole estate, counsel fees for winners and losers were payable out of general estate assets).

24. See Matter of Sinclair, 56 Misc.2d 554, 289 N.Y.S.2d 54 (New York County 1968), where the court said that "[i]n general, in a [will] construction proceeding * * * parties must expect to bear their own attorneys' fees where, as here, (a) each attorney represents only his own client who is not acting in a representative capacity and who is not a 'person under disability,' SCPA 103, subd. 37, (b) the dispute is as to the disposition of an immediately available fund, (c) success will enure to immediate benefit of the attorney's own client only, and (d) there is no question of future interests involved (i.e. it is not case of a successful client having to wait a generation or so and the happening of some contingency before he can really benefit)."

25. Matter of Andersen, N.Y.L.J., Feb. 1, 1980, at 14, col. 5 (Queens) (services in unsuccessful attempt to sustain will); Matter of Yates, 30 Misc.2d 475, 219 N.Y.S.2d 357 (Ulster 1961) (accord); Matter of Krasner, 12 Misc.2d 814, 170 N.Y.S.2d 365 (Westchester 1957) (attorney's services in successfully objecting to appointment of a trustee).

26. Matter of Estricher, 202 Misc. 431, 111 N.Y.S.2d 295 (New York County 1952), affirmed 281 App.Div. 828, 118 N.Y.S.2d 922 (1st Dep't 1953).

27. Matter of Kaufmann, 51 Misc. 560, 273 N.Y.S.2d 533 (New York County 1966), modified 26 A.D.2d 818, 273 N.Y.S.2d 902 (1st Dep't 1966) (executor had used undue influence in procuring a will under which he was primary beneficiary, and court refused to allow attorneys' fees for probate).

28. Matter of Bishop, 277 App.Div. 108, 98 N.Y.S.2d 69 (1st Dep't 1950) (legal fees for groundless lawsuit brought by income beneficiaries against trustees charged against the income beneficiaries, not against the charitable remaindermen); Matter of Rourke, 2 Misc.2d 471, 152 N.Y.S.2d 338 (Herkimer 1956) (beneficiary charged with legal fee in non-meritorious suit despite his incompetence); see Matter of Penney, 60 Misc.2d 334, 302 N.Y.S.2d 886 (Erie 1969) (fee for resisting surcharge charged against objecting party because objections would not have benefited others). Matter of Stanton, 41 Misc. 278, 84 N.Y.S. 46 (Rensselaer 1903) (legal fees charged to executor who simply refused to perform enforceable contract). But see Matter of Povlsen, 62 Misc.2d 239, 308 N.Y.S.2d 168 (Kings 1970) ("where there is no attorney-client relationship, attorneys' fees cannot be charged against an adverse or co-party in any proceeding").

attorneys' fees where someone objects to his actions and he has to defend them.[29]

The court can award attorneys' fees out of the estate when the public administrator or county treasurer brings a probate proceeding.[30]

c. *Appeals*

An appellate court may direct the Surrogate to order the payment of attorneys' fees incurred in taking an appeal.[31]

d. *Accounting Proceedings*

The court can award a fiduciary attorneys' fees of up to $100 per day in New York City and up to $50 per day elsewhere in accounting proceedings.[32]

e. *Estate Tax Proceedings*

Unless a will provides otherwise, all beneficiaries of a decedent's estate must bear a pro rata portion of the state and federal estate taxes. EPTL 2–1.8 sets forth that basic rule and also provides for a special proceeding to determine liability for estate taxes.[33]

In matters other than tax apportionment, attorneys' fees incurred in connection with non-testamentary assets are not chargeable to the estate, but against the beneficiaries who get those assets;[34] the notion is that the Surrogate's Court does not have jurisdiction of property passing outside the probate estate and thus it cannot authorize payment for an attorneys' services relating to that property.[35] EPTL 2–1.8 makes an exception for attorneys' fees incurred in fixing and apportioning estate taxes; in those cases the court can apportion not only the taxes but also expenses and fees, and that is true even if no special proceeding under EPTL 2–1.8 occurs.[36]

29. Matter of Rothko, 84 Misc.2d 830, 885, 379 N.Y.S.2d 923, 976 (New York County 1975), modified 56 A.D.2d 499, 392 N.Y.S.2d 840 (1st Dep't 1977), affirmed 43 N.Y.2d 305, 401 N.Y.S.2d 449, 372 N.E.2d 291 (1977), on remand 95 Misc.2d 492, 407 N.Y.S.2d 954 (New York County 1978) (self-dealing); Parker v. Rogerson, 76 Misc.2d 705, 350 N.Y.S.2d 950 (Erie 1973), affirmed 49 A.D.2d 690, 373 N.Y.S.2d 1022 (4th Dep't 1975) (illicit acquisition of company); Matter of Hildreth, 274 App.Div. 611, 85 N.Y.S.2d 829 (2d Dep't 1949), affirmed 301 N.Y. 705, 95 N.E.2d 54 (1950) (self-dealing); Matter of Mead, 90 Misc.2d 144, 394 N.Y.S.2d 123 (Westchester 1977) (wrongfully retained commissions).

30. McKinney's SCPA 2302(4).

31. McKinney's SCPA 2302(5).

32. McKinney's SCPA 2302(7).

33. Tax apportionment is discussed in chapter on "Estate Taxes," infra at 602–06.

34. Matter of Pack, N.Y.L.J. May 10, 1963, at 20, col. 7 (Westchester) (attorneys' fees for services relating to Louisiana real property not payable out of estate).

35. Matter of Walsh, 23 Misc.2d 873, 200 N.Y.S.2d 159 (Nassau 1960).

36. Matter of Keating, 84 Misc.2d 39, 374 N.Y.S.2d 909 (Orange 1975).

SECTION F. DISCHARGE OR SUBSTITUTION OF ATTORNEYS

Attorneys in the Surrogate's Courts have, like attorneys in other courts, various rights to secure payment of their legal fees. The attorney has a charging lien against estate assets,[1] if there is a fund of estate assets relating to his services,[2] and against assets belonging to a beneficiary if the attorney rendered services to that beneficiary.[3] Attorneys have a retaining lien on all estate papers that come into their possession.[4] Although a client has an absolute right to discharge the attorney and substitute another, the attorney has a right to be paid for the services properly rendered,[5] and when a new attorney is substituted for the old, the Surrogate can refuse to order the replaced attorney to turn over the papers to the new one unless the legal fee is paid.[6] If the attorney represented the fiduciary or a party who will receive estate assets, when he is dismissed the court may order him to turn all papers over to the new attorney subject to a lien in an amount fixed by the court then or at a later date, such as the final accounting proceeding, of which the removed attorney must be given notice. Because the resigning attorney has a lien against the estate assets, when his fee is fixed on the accounting, it becomes a prior charge on the estate assets.[7]

Sec. F

1. E.g., Matter of Martin, 36 Misc.2d 1020, 234 N.Y.S.2d 573 (Kings 1962) (court refused to direct discharged attorney to turn over papers to executrix in absence of proceeding to fix attorneys' fees).

2. See Matter of Beckett, 112 Misc. 45, 182 N.Y.S. 571 (New York County 1920), affirmed 194 App.Div. 901, 184 N.Y.S. 908 (1st Dep't 1920) (no charging lien in will contest because the client had not established right to decedent's estate); Matter of Dawson, 110 Misc. 472, 180 N.Y.S. 271 (New York County 1920) (no lien on papers held by the attorney because he was holding them merely as custodian, and they were not necessary for the services he rendered).

3. Matter of Fitzsimmons, 174 N.Y. 15, 66 N.E. 554 (1903) (attorney had lien against share he obtained for his client); Matter of Ludwig, 20 Misc.2d 54, 192 N.Y.S.2d 708 (1959) (attorney had lien against Totten Trust account that he recovered for the fiduciary); but see Matter of Craig, 171 A.D. 218, 157 N.Y.S. 310 (1st Dep't 1916), affirmed 220 N.Y. 576, 115 N.E. 1036 (1917) (if services to fiduciary were not part of the administration proceeding but were for the fiduciary in his individual capacity, no lien against that person's share of the estate).

4. Matter of Cooper, 291 N.Y. 255, 52 N.E.2d 421 (1943); Matter of Streger, 12 A.D.2d 494, 208 N.Y.S.2d 904 (2d Dep't 1960); Matter of Present, 15 Misc.2d 759, 184 N.Y.S.2d 134 (Kings 1956).

5. Schwartz v. Schwartz, 25 Misc.2d 225, 205 N.Y.S.2d 34 (Sup.Ct.Nassau 1960) (matrimonial action).

6. See Bernstein v. Bedrick, 262 N.Y. 472, 188 N.E. 25 (1933); Matter of Theirich, 13 Misc.2d 155, 178 N.Y.S.2d 232 (Nassau 1958). Contra, Shatzkin v. Shahmoon, 19 A.D.2d 658, 242 N.Y.S.2d 72 (2d Dep't 1963) (if the client seeks an order from the court substituting attorneys but does not seek an order to compel the attorney to hand over the papers, the court cannot fix the attorney's fee; the attorney must bring a separate action for fixation of his fees).

7. The following would be a typical decision along this line:

> This is a motion to substitute the movant's attorney as the attorney for Mary Allman, the executrix herein, in place of Clarence N. Johnson, and directing him to turn over all papers and records of his former client in his possession. The respondent attorney requested the fixation of his fee. The motion for substitution is granted. The former attorney, Clarence N. Johnson, shall immediately turn over

If the attorney has already been paid the amount agreed upon in the retainer agreement, but is seeking more on a quantum meruit theory because he has been discharged, the court may, in view of the amount he has already received, require him to turn over the estate papers without payment of an additional fee, which can ultimately be determined in a separate proceeding or at the accounting.[8]

If an attorney is disbarred or abandons a client, he has no right to any fee;[9] his lien is automatically forfeited.[10] Similarly, if the client fires him with cause, he has no right to a fee. Malpractice on the attorney's part, either in the course of estate planning[11] or estate administration,[12] can result in reduction of the legal fees, as can bizarre overzealousness.[13]

An attorney is permitted to end the attorney-client relationship if he can show good cause,[14] and if the attorney's withdrawal is justified, the court will award compensation.[15] If the attorney is discharged without cause the court may award him a fee in excess of retainer on a quantum meruit basis,[16] and a client's unjustified attacks on an attorney's integrity may constitute a discharge of the attorney.[17]

to Maxwell Ross, the new attorney for the executrix, all papers and records in his possession pertaining to this estate. The lien of said Clarence N. Johnson for the amount of his fee for services rendered is retained and when fixed shall become a prior charge on the assets of the estate. Such fee and the amount of the lien shall be determined on the accounting to be rendered herein, notice of which shall be given to the said outgoing attorney. This shall be without prejudice to a further application to be made for an immediate payment on account of such fee.

8. Matter of Romanoff, N.Y.L.J., June 17, 1975, at 19, col. 3 (Kings).

9. Holmes v. Evans, 129 N.Y. 140, 29 N.E. 233 (1891) (attorney who abandoned client cannot recover fee); Tiringer v. Grafenecker, N.Y.L.J. Feb. 7, 1962, at 16, col. 5 (District Court Nassau) (attorney not entitled to recover his fee on contingency or quantum meruit basis).

10. Matter of Murphy, N.Y.L.J. Sept. 22, 1970, at 19.

11. Matter of Cook, N.Y.L.J. Jan. 23, 1980, at 14, col. 3 (Nassau) (malpractice in drafting will provision).

12. Matter of Remsen, 99 Misc.2d 92, 415 N.Y.S.2d 370 (Nassau 1979) (attorney's procrastination led to tax penalties and interest).

13. See Matter of Sherbourne, N.Y.L.J., July 17, 1985, at 14, col. 4 (New York county), where an attorney, without his client's consent, appealed an order of the Surrogate and commenced an Article 78 proceeding in Supreme Court against the Surrogate, appealed the Supreme Court's judgment against him in the Article 78 proceeding and, after losing both appeals, commenced a federal action alleging that the Surrogate, Supreme Court judge and Appellate Division judges had engaged in a conspiracy to violate his constitutional right to win his case. When he lost in the federal district court, he appealed to the United States Court of Appeals. The attorney also called his clients at midnight and told them they would go to jail if they did not get another lawyer. They did (understandably) get another lawyer, and the Surrogate reduced the zealot's fee from the requested $81,000 to $1,000, the value of the legitimate services rendered.

14. Matter of Dunn, 205 N.Y. 398, 98 N.E. 914 (1912); Isser v. Berg, 38 Misc.2d 957, 239 N.Y.S.2d 370 (Sup.Ct.Nassau 1963).

15. Matter of Murphy, N.Y.L.J., Sept. 22, 1970, at 19, col. 6 (Bronx) (client unreasonably refused to advance money to attorney, and his withdrawal from the case was justified).

16. Matter of Goldin, 104 A.D.2d 890, 480 N.Y.S.2d 392 (2d Dep't 1984); Matter of Dutchen, N.Y.L.J., July 3, 1985, at 11, col. 4 (Bronx).

17. Matarrese v. Wilson, 202 Misc. 994, 118 N.Y.S.2d 5 (Bronx 1952).

Attorneys representing estates must scrupulously avoid conflicts of interest and self-dealing or the court will not permit them to represent the estate [18] or will disallow their compensation.[19] For example, an attorney may not take a case against a former client in matters that relate to his representation (or his former firm's representation) of that client.[20] The theory is that the appearance of impropriety is so strong that the attorney must be disqualified. Despite this rule, however, some courts have refused to disqualify the attorney if he in fact had no confidential knowledge relating to the issue before the court and if the disqualification would impose an unreasonable hardship on the other parties.[21] The burden of proving that the attorney should be disqualified is on the party moving to disqualify him, because of the strong public policy in favor of the right to choose one's own attorney.[22] The application should be addressed to the court in which the proceeding is pending.[23]

If a probate proceeding is contested and the will contest proceeds to trial, the attorney-draftsman and his partners and the attesting witnesses should not represent the proponent on the trial.[24]

The attorney has, by the notice of appearance, the presumed authority to act for his client and the client is bound by the attorney's actions unless he can show fraud.[25]

If the attorney for the estate retains another attorney in an "of counsel" capacity, that "of counsel" has no independent standing to claim fees unless he contracted for them directly with the estate.[26] His

18. See Matter of Cousin, N.Y.L.J., May 25, 1984, at 7, col. 3 (Bronx) (petitioner's attorney disqualified because he had formerly represented respondent).

19. Matter of Clarke, 12 N.Y.2d 183, 237 N.Y.S.2d 694, 188 N.E.2d 128 (1962) (attorney accepted part of real estate brokerage commission); Matter of La Grove, 31 A.D.2d 928, 299 N.Y.S.2d 80 (2d Dep't 1969), affirmed 30 N.Y.2d 624, 331 N.Y.S.2d 439, 282 N.E.2d 329 (1972) (attorneys for life tenant aligned themselves with trustee's attorney; the court severely criticized them and denied payment from the trust corpus).

20. Cardinale v. Golinello, 43 N.Y.2d 288, 401 N.Y.S.2d 191, 372 N.E.2d 26 (1977), adopting the "substantial relation" test enunciated by the federal district court in T.C. Theatre Corp. v. Warner Brothers Pictures, 113 F.Supp. 265 (S.D. N.Y.1953); Edelman v. Levy, 42 A.D.2d 758, 346 N.Y.S.2d 347 (2d Dep't 1973). Cf. People v. Shinkle, 51 N.Y.2d 417, 434 N.Y.S.2d 918, 415 N.E.2d 909 (1980). See generally Midonick, Attorney-Client Conflicts and Confidences in Trusts and Estates, Record of the Association of the Bar of the City of New York 215 (April 1980).

21. See Berkowitz v. Roubicek, 122 Misc.2d 322, 471 N.Y.S.2d 208 (Nassau 1983); Lopez v. Precision Papers, Inc., 99 A.D.2d 507, 470 N.Y.S.2d 678 (2d Dep't 1984).

22. Young v. Oak Crest Park Inc., 75 A.D.2d 956, 428 N.Y.S.2d 69 (3d Dep't 1980).

23. Matter of Erlanger, 20 N.Y.2d 778, 284 N.Y.S.2d 84, 230 N.E.2d 727 (1967); Matter of Amann, N.Y.L.J., June 19, 1984, at 13, col. 6 (Suffolk).

24. Code of Professional Responsibility DR 5-102; Matter of Burke, N.Y.L.J., Feb. 28, 1985, at 16, col. 2 (Westchester); Matter of Runes, N.Y.L.J., Aug. 2, 1984, at 5, col. 3 (New York County); Matter of Discala, N.Y.L.J., July 17, 1984, at 14, col. 2 (Westchester); Matter of Brodsky, N.Y. L.J., October 1, 1980, at 14, col. 2 (Nassau).

25. Matter of Locke, 21 A.D.2d 248, 250 N.Y.S.2d 181 (3d Dep't 1964).

26. Matter of Sakel, 21 A.D.2d 666, 250 N.Y.S.2d 168 (1st Dep't 1964) (payment to attorney of record discharged estate obligation to the other attorney, who gave the attorney of record an affidavit of services and had no contract with the estate); Mat-

recourse is against the attorney who retained him. If the court fixes the fee of the attorney of record based on the counsel's affidavit, payment to record attorney discharges the "of counsel's" claim.[27]

In many cases each executor selects his own attorney and in those cases the court will allow only one legal fee to be shared among the attorneys.[28]

In some cases the attorney for the estate or a beneficiary also serves as fiduciary. In that case the attorney-fiduciary owes a duty not only to his client (the co-fiduciary or the beneficiary) but also to the other beneficiaries of the estate.[29] The fiduciary obligation owed to the beneficiaries may clash with the fiduciary obligation owed to the client (if their interests are in conflict) and in such a case the attorney cannot serve in both capacities.[30] For example, the attorney obviously cannot represent the objecting party in an accounting proceeding in which the attorney is the accounting party.[31] This is because an attorney with a financial interest in a lawsuit akin to the interest of a defendant cannot represent the party whose interest in akin to the plaintiff's.[32]

If an attorney withdraws from a case because of conflicts in his roles as fiduciary and attorney, his law firm should also be disqualified, on the theory that the firm would then be representing interests adverse to those of their former clients, who should be free from the risks of opposition by attorneys who were once privy to the client's confidences.[33] The resigning attorney cannot separate himself from the other members of his firm.

SECTION G. ADVANCE PAYMENT OF ATTORNEYS' FEES TO ATTORNEY-FIDUCIARY

An attorney retained by a fiduciary [1] can arrange for payment of the legal fee at a certain time, such as at the final accounting, or for

ter of Russ, N.Y.L.J., June 16, 1978, at 14, col. 5 (Bronx).

27. Ripley v. International Railway Co., 16 A.D.2d 260, 227 N.Y.S.2d 64 (1st Dep't 1962), affirmed, 12 N.Y.2d 814, 236 N.Y.S.2d 64, 187 N.E.2d 131 (1962); Matter of Howard, N.Y.L.J., May 19, 1975, at 18, col. 7 (Bronx).

28. Matter of Arguto, N.Y.L.J., April 9, 1985, at 7, col. 1 (Westchester); Matter of Mattis, 55 Misc.2d 511, 285 N.Y.S.2d 551 (New York County 1967); Matter of Scher, 147 Misc. 791, 264 N.Y.S. 579 (Westchester 1933); Matter of Lieberman, 151 N.Y.S.2d 166 (Westchester 1956).

29. Ethics Opinion No. 511, 51 A.B.A. Journal 515.

30. Code of Professional Responsibility DR5–105[B].

31. Code of Professional Responsibility DR5–101[A].

32. Greene v. Greene, 47 N.Y.2d 447, 418 N.Y.S.2d 379, 391 N.E.2d 1355 (1979).

33. Matter of Howard, 80 Misc.2d 754, 363 N.Y.S.2d 711 (Bronx 1975); Ethics Opinion No. 511, 51 A.B.A. Journal 515.

Sec. G

1. Fiduciary is defined in McKinney's SCPA 103(21) as an "administrator, administrator c.t.a., administrator d.b.n., ancillary administrator, ancillary administrator c.t.a., ancillary executor, ancillary guardian, executor, guardian, preliminary executor, temporary administrator, testamentary trustee, to any of whom letters have been issued, and also the donee of a power during minority and a voluntary administrator and a public administrator acting as

periodic payments on account. If the attorney is also serving as fiduciary, however, he cannot pay himself periodically on account unless one of three tests is met: either the will authorizes such periodic payments, or the co-fiduciaries serving with the attorney agree to it (and at least one of them is not rendering legal services), or the court authorizes it.[2] If the will allows it, or the co-fiduciaries consent, the attorney-fiduciary can simply make the payments to himself. If not, he has to request the court to authorize the payments.

The attorney who tries to get court authorization usually does so either because he needs the funds, or because the payment would benefit him or the estate for tax purposes.

The SCPA 2111 proceeding is expeditious and inexpensive. It is valuable to attorney-fiduciaries who do not wish to commence a full proceeding under SCPA 2110 [3] or wait for an accounting proceeding or an informal accounting on receipts and releases before getting paid.

Usually the one to bring this proceeding is the attorney-fiduciary serving alone or the fiduciary who cannot obtain the consent of his co-fiduciary.

The procedure is for the attorney-fiduciary to petition to receive partial payment of his fee for legal services. He can do so at any time during the administration of an estate, even if no proceeding is pending. The attorney must file the petition in the court that granted letters, and no notice is required to any other party. The court must decide whether to entertain the proceeding, and if it does, it may award a sum on account of the legal fee or make such other order as it deems appropriate. The petitioner must personally bear the expense of bringing the proceeding,[4] but unlike in the case of ex parte payments of commissions under SCPA 2311,[5] he need not file a bond.

Whenever an attorney takes an advance payment of legal fees, he must disclose it in his account. As a matter of good practice, he should also set it forth in the citation in the accounting proceeding, along with the total attorney's fee claimed.[6] Any persons interested in the estate can then object to the fee. Unlike the court-approved fee fixed by SCPA 2110, the fee taken under SCPA 2111 remains subject to attack. If the attorney wants the court to set a fee that is binding, he has to use the SCPA 2110 proceeding or wait until the final accounting.

administrator or a public administrator or county treasurer to whom letters have been issued, and a lifetime trustee."

2. McKinney's SCPA 2111(2). This is so despite the contrary dicta in Matter of Luckenbach, 46 Misc.2d 864, 261 N.Y.S.2d 106 (Nassau 1965).

3. Before the enactment of this provision, L.1963, c. 288, the attorney would have to bring a proceeding under McKinney's SCPA 2110's predecessor, citing all the interested parties, causing expense to the estate and delays in obtaining the advance payment, which was frequently being sought for the purpose of getting an income tax advantage, making time of the essence. See McKinney's SCPA 2111, Prac.Comm. at 567 (1967).

4. McKinney's SCPA 2111(1).

5. McKinney's SCPA 2311 is discussed in chapter on "Commissions," infra at 448.

6. McKinney's SCPA 2111, Practice Commentary at 124–25 (Supp.1986).

If the attorney-fiduciary takes an advance fee without court approval, the court will surcharge him at least for the interest that payment would have earned for the estate.[7]

In practice, attorney-fiduciaries often seek both full commissions and fees, and the court carefully segregates the services performed and allows full commissions if the fiduciary performed the services and in addition, an attorney's fee based on the legal services rendered, with no reduction for the commissions. The theory is of course that the duties are separate and that each role requires different services entitled to compensation.[8]

This proceeding is not available to attorneys who are not serving in the dual capacity of fiduciary and attorney. It is a rare (and very protracted) case in which the court will allow a person serving only as attorney to obtain this relief.[9]

SECTION H. FEES OF ATTORNEYS–IN–FACT

EPTL 13–2.3 permits a person to act under a power of attorney on behalf of a person interested in an estate.[1] The instrument authorizing the attorney-in-fact to act must be written, properly acknowledged,[2] and recorded in the Surrogate's Court that granted letters, or if no letters have been granted, in the Surrogate's Court having jurisdiction to grant letters. If the instrument has not been recorded, no one has the power to act under it. When the instrument is recorded, the Surrogate obtains jurisdiction over the grantor of the power of attorney, the attorney-in-fact named in the instrument, and any other person acting under it, such as agents of the attorney-in-fact.[3] The recording is a notice requirement, and failure to record is not a jurisdictional defect; that is, the court can exercise jurisdiction over the attorney-in-fact and grantor of the power if they are present in the state, domiciled there, or if they commit an act or omission there, despite their failure to record the instrument.[4] Powers of attorney are most often used by a benefici-

7. Matter of Anninger, 35 Misc.2d 493, 230 N.Y.S.2d 910 (New York County 1962); Matter of Levine, 26 Misc.2d 307, 203 N.Y.S.2d 643 (New York County 1960); but see Matter of Seskis, 6 Misc.2d 762, 160 N.Y.S.2d 197 (New York County 1956) (though advance payment was improper, no surcharge of interest because no one objected).

8. Matter of Lieberman, 151 N.Y.S.2d 166 (Westchester 1956); Matter of Free, 4 Misc.2d 463, 148 N.Y.S.2d 884 (Westchester 1956); Matter of Cochrane, 169 Misc. 138, 7 N.Y.S.2d 133 (New York County 1938). Contra, Matter of Cueff, N.Y.L.J., Jan. 19, 1984, at 14, col. 5 (Suffolk) (Surrogate is "obligated" to take commissions into account when fixing legal fees).

9. See Matter of Harris, 277 App.Div. 1030, 100 N.Y.S.2d 784 (1st Dep't 1950).

Sec. H

1. An executor cannot have an attorney-in-fact because he has no power to delegate his fiduciary duties. See chapter on "Fiduciaries," infra at 405.

2. Proper acknowledgment means acknowledgment in the form required for the recording of real estate deeds. The Surrogate may prescribe the form, content and manner of execution and conditions attached to the recording of the instrument. McKinney's EPTL 13–2.3(b)(1).

3. McKinney's EPTL 13–2.3(a).

4. Matter of Robinson, 52 Misc.2d 163, 275 N.Y.S.2d 337 (Kings 1966), affirmed 30

ary or other interested person who is in a foreign country or otherwise unavailable to appear, but wants to participate in the proceedings.

The person acting under the power of attorney (the "attorney-in-fact") may agree with the fiduciary and the beneficiary on a fee for his services, and under SCPA 2112 the Surrogate can approve that fee or set a different fee based on quantum meruit,[5] or if the attorney-in-fact did not contract for a specific fee, the Surrogate can set the fee.[6] The parties must get court approval; they have no authority to come to a private agreement on the issue of the fee of the attorney-in-fact.[7] This effectuates the public policy of keeping control over attorneys-in-fact.

SCPA 2112 essentially gives the court the same power to approve, reduce or fix the fee of the attorney-in-fact as it has under SCPA 2110 to approve, reduce or fix the attorney's fee. The court looks at the services rendered and their reasonable value.[8] The court can act on its own initiative or on the application of the fiduciary or a person interested. It can do so at any time during the administration of an estate whether or not a proceeding is pending.[9] If the attorney-in-fact has received more than a reasonable amount for services, charges and expenses, the court may direct a refund of the excess.[10]

If the attorney-in-fact retained an attorney, the court can also fix that attorney's fees under this section, and, as in the SCPA 2110 proceeding relating to attorneys, the court is not bound by any retainer agreement between the attorney-in-fact and the attorney.[11]

If the attorney-in-fact is not an attorney of the State of New York, this section does not authorize him to practice law.[12] If he is an attorney from another jurisdiction, he must apply to the court to practice before the Surrogate by making a motion to appear pro hac vice, and if he is not an attorney, he cannot practice in any case.

The Surrogate may prescribe the form, content, manner of execution and conditions attached to the recording of every power of attorney relating to an estate.[13] The New York State Uniform Rules for the Surrogate's Court contain statewide rules on powers of attorney.[14] Those rules state that the instrument must be in a form satisfactory to the Surrogate, and in addition the attorney-in-fact must file an affidavit

A.D.2d 702, 291 N.Y.S.2d 919 (2d Dep't), appeal dismissed 22 N.Y.2d 938, 295 N.Y.S.2d 62, 242 N.E.2d 95 (1968).

5. Matter of Dietsch, N.Y.L.J. June 25, 1975, at 16, col. 1 (Queens) (court refused to honor contingency fee agreement because there was no risk, and set quantum meruit fee).

6. McKinney's EPTL 13–2.3(b)(3).

7. Matter of Pia, 21 Misc.2d 464, 189 N.Y.S.2d 508 (New York County 1959).

8. Matter of Garrity, 167 Misc. 947, 5 N.Y.S.2d 168 (New York County 1938), affirmed 255 App.Div. 772, 7 N.Y.S.2d 570 (1st Dep't 1938).

9. McKinney's SCPA 2112(1).

10. McKinney's SCPA 2112(2).

11. Matter of Bargel, 5 Misc.2d 657, 163 N.Y.S.2d 175 (Richmond), affirmed 7 A.D.2d 645, 181 N.Y.S.2d 185 (2d Dep't 1958).

12. McKinney's SCPA 2112(3); McKinney's EPTL 13–2.3(d).

13. McKinney's EPTL 13–2.3(b)(1).

14. Uniform Rules of the Surrogate's Court 207.48.

stating the way he obtained the power of attorney, the grantor's address, the relationship of the attorney-in-fact to the decedent, his interest in the decedent's estate, the agreed-upon compensation, the disbursements chargeable to the grantor, and the name of any attorney representing the attorney-in-fact. If the parties have entered into a written compensation agreement, that must be attached. If the parties do not follow these rules, the Surrogate will not accept the validity of the instrument.[15]

The Surrogate may determine the validity of a power of attorney, require proof of the amount of compensation or expenses charged, and exact a bond to assure the payment of funds to the principal.[16]

A power of attorney may not be irrevocable, and the attorney-in-fact's compensation agreement may not create a power coupled with an interest in the subject matter.[17]

15. See Matter of Giannopoulos, 89 Misc.2d 961, 392 N.Y.S.2d 828 (Queens 1977).

16. McKinney's EPTL 13–2.3(b)(4).

17. McKinney's EPTL 13–2.3(c).

Chapter Fourteen

FIDUCIARIES

SECTION A. INTRODUCTION

Estates have administrators or executors, children have guardians, trusts have trustees, incompetents have committees, and some disabled persons have conservators. There are ancillary fiduciaries to manage the estates or administer the property of non-New Yorkers, and there are successor fiduciaries to replace deceased or resigning fiduciaries. All fiduciaries (except trustees of inter vivos trusts) need court-issued letters authorizing them to perform their fiduciary duties. This chapter discusses the appointment of fiduciaries, the issuance of their letters, their powers and duties, and the standards that govern them.

SECTION B. ISSUANCE OF LETTERS

The proceeding for appointment of a fiduciary shares much in common with other Surrogate's Court proceedings. A person interested in the estate or trust or minor child files a petition with the court, along with a copy of process (usually a citation). The court stamps the citation with its seal and gives copies to the petitioner for service on all necessary parties.[1] If anyone objects, the court gives all parties an opportunity to be heard at a hearing or a trial. When the objections are resolved, the court grants letters if someone is entitled to receive them.

The issuance of letters is a significant event, because the letters are conclusive evidence of the fiduciary's authority to act until the court revokes them or an appellate court reverses the decree that granted them.[2] The purpose of this "conclusive evidence" rule is to protect people dealing with the fiduciary. If the fiduciary wants to transfer stock, withdraw money from an account, or do another act in his fiduciary capacity, he has to show the person with whom he wants to deal a dated certificate of letters issued by the court, and the person has the right to rely on those letters for six months after the date of the certificate.[3] The certificate is no longer conclusive evidence of the

Sec. B

1. The procedure in the Surrogate's Court generally is discussed in chapter on "Procedure," supra at 35 et seq., and the petitions and necessary parties in each proceeding are discussed in the respective chapters on these proceedings.

2. McKinney's SCPA 703(1).

3. McKinney's SCPA 703(2).

fiduciary's authority to act after six months, and the person dealing with the fiduciary should insist on a current certificate. The fiduciary can obtain a "fresh" certificate from the court.

The judicial settlement of a fiduciary's account discharges the fiduciary from liability for all prior acts included in the account, but the letters remain in effect and his authority continues [4] unless the court revokes the letters in the accounting decree, which it rarely does.

The court issues the letters to the fiduciary in the name of the People of the State of New York. The letters are attested in the judge's name, embossed with the court seal and signed by the judge or the chief clerk.[5] The Surrogate's Court issues almost all fiduciary letters although in rare instances the Supreme Court appoints a successor trustee of an inter vivos trust when the initial trustee ceases to serve. The Family Court and the Supreme Court have jurisdiction to appoint guardians, but the Surrogate issues the letters.[6] Accordingly, in practice, even when the Supreme Court or the Family Court makes appointments, the Surrogate's Court issues the letters after a petitioner files a certified copy of the Supreme Court or Family Court order.[7]

Sometimes more than one court will decide matters relating to the same estate or family. For example, after a Surrogate has appointed a guardian for a child, the Supreme Court may decide the custody issue as part of a divorce action. In that case, the Supreme Court's matrimonial decree usually instructs the parties to advise the Surrogate of the custody award so the Surrogate can modify the letters of guardianship.[8]

If after the Surrogate has issued guardianship letters, the parties move in the Family Court to have them revoked, their attempt will fail; only the Surrogate who issues letters can revoke them.[9] This is true of letters of administration, letters of trusteeship and letters testamentary as well; only the court issuing letters to a fiduciary can revoke them, provided it had jurisdiction over the matter in the first place.[10]

If more than one person obtains letters from different courts in the same estate or trust or guardianship, the first person to receive letters has the exclusive authority to act, provided, of course, that the court that issued the letters had the jurisdiction to do so.[11] That fiduciary

4. See Matter of Sylvestri, N.Y.L.J., Feb. 1, 1978, at 13, col. 3 (Westchester).

5. McKinney's SCPA 701(1). The chief clerk can also designate another officer to sign the letters.

6. This procedure is discussed in chapter on "Guardianship," supra at 271–72.

7. See McKinney's SCPA 1503, discussed in chapter on "Trusts and Trustees," infra at 463; McKinney's SCPA 1709, discussed in chapter on "Guardianships," supra at 271–72.

8. Matter of Abeles, 65 Misc.2d 282, 316 N.Y.S.2d 752 (Nassau 1970). There is no res judicata effect of the Surrogate's appointment of a guardian because guardianships are ambulatory, subject to changes in custody, and the Supreme Court has jurisdiction to award custody.

9. McKinney's SCPA 701(3); Eden M. v. Ines R., 97 Misc.2d 256, 410 N.Y.S.2d 997 (Kings 1978).

10. McKinney's SCPA 701(3). See Holden v. Alexander, 39 A.D.2d 476, 336 N.Y.S.2d 649 (2d Dep't 1976). The court's jurisdiction over matters is discussed in a general way in chapter on "Jurisdiction," supra at 1 et seq., and more specifically in the chapters on the respective proceedings.

11. McKinney's SCPA 704.

can (and should) collect all the property held by a subsequently appointed fiduciary. However, until the second fiduciary gets notice of the first letters, his acts are valid. If he commences a lawsuit, the earlier-appointed fiduciary can substitute himself as a party and continue it.

SECTION C. LIMITED (RESTRICTED) LETTERS

Sometimes it is not necessary to appoint a full-fledged fiduciary, at least not initially, and the court has the power to grant limited or restricted letters allowing a fiduciary to take care of a particular discrete matter.[1] For example, if the fiduciary's sole task is to commence or continue a personal injury or wrongful death action, the court can grant limited letters, permitting the fiduciary to commence the action and negotiate a settlement, but not to bind the estate to the settlement until the court approves.[2] Typically, once he has entered into a settlement or tried the case, the limited fiduciary petitions the court to remove the restrictions and permit him to receive the proceeds of the lawsuit. Similarly, the court may limit a fiduciary to collecting a stated sum, enough perhaps to pay debts or expenses, pending resolution of some issue,[3] or may restrict the letters until more specific directions are given in a further court order or until the fiduciary posts security in an amount set by the court.

The court can also grant limited letters that allow the fiduciary to settle a claim in his fiduciary capacity in favor of or against the decedent or the fiduciary,[4] to perform an act necessary to discharge the estate from liability (such as paying a judgment or signing releases),[5] to file an accounting for the decedent who died while serving as a fiduciary (for example, as a trustee),[6] to execute necessary instruments to complete a transfer left incomplete by the decedent's death,[7] and to appear in a lawsuit in which the decedent or the fiduciary was a necessary party.[8] In addition, the court has broad power to grant limited letters in any other case it believes appropriate,[9] such as letters that authorize a fiduciary to continue a business. The advantage of limited letters is that the court can reduce the amount of the bond necessary to secure the fiduciary's performance or eliminate the bond completely.

Sec. C

1. McKinney's SCPA 702. The attorney should recall that there are two other types of "less than full" letters, temporary letters and preliminary letters, for use in special circumstances. Preliminary letters are governed by McKinney's SCPA 1412 and discussed in chapter on "Probate," supra at 118–24. Temporary letters are governed by McKinney's SCPA Article 9 and discussed in chapter on "Temporary Administration," supra at 289 et seq.
2. McKinney's SCPA 702(1).
3. McKinney's SCPA 702(2).
4. McKinney's SCPA 702(3).
5. McKinney's SCPA 702(4).
6. McKinney's SCPA 702(5).
7. McKinney's SCPA 702(6).
8. McKinney's SCPA 702(7).
9. McKinney's SCPA 702(8).

If there is an administrator or executor serving but he fails to start a lawsuit on the estate's behalf, or cannot do so because he has a conflict, the court can appoint a special administrator [10] to start the lawsuit and try the case or negotiate a settlement, but the special administrator must come back to the Surrogate for approval of the final recovery. He has no authority to administer the estate other than the limited power in connection with the lawsuit given to him by the court.

SECTION D. SUCCESSIVE FIDUCIARIES: TIME REQUIREMENTS

Some proceedings are subject to time limitations which begin to run on the appointment of a fiduciary. For example, a claimant has to present his claim against an estate within seven months of the appointment of a fiduciary or his rights to recover the claim are altered,[1] and a surviving spouse must file the notice of election against the deceased spouse's will within six months of the fiduciary's appointment or risk losing the right of election.

More times than not, the executor, administrator, trustee or guardian is appointed and continues his administration until the estate closes, the trust terminates, or the child reaches majority. In those cases the time period for filing a claim or notice of election is easy to compute, starting at the appointment of that fiduciary. In other cases, however, a successor fiduciary takes over for the original fiduciary who has died or resigned or has been removed for wrongdoing. In such cases, the time begins to run when the first letters are granted.[2]

If the time period has already run before the original fiduciary's resignation or death, the claimant or spouse does not get another chance with the successor fiduciary.

The statute contemplates successive letters, and "permanent" letters are not considered successive to temporary or preliminary letters.[3] If the first letters were issued to a preliminary executor, a temporary administrator or an administrator, and a will is later admitted to probate, the probate decree revokes the former letters,[4] and the former letters do not count in computing any time periods.[5] In effect, tempora-

10. McKinney's EPTL 5–4.1, discussed in chapter on "Wrongful Death," infra at 529.

Sec. D

1. McKinney's SCPA 1802, discussed in chapter on "Claims," supra at 148–50.

2. McKinney's SCPA 705.

3. See McKinney's SCPA 705, Prac. Comm. at 513 (1967); Matter of Young, 133 N.Y.S.2d 387 (1954).

4. McKinney's SCPA 1413.

5. McKinney's SCPA 705. Some statutes governing specific proceedings reiterate this notion. See, e.g., McKinney's EPTL 5–1.1(e)(1), giving a surviving spouse six months to file a right of election against the decedent's estate, and starting the six months from the appointment of an administrator or executor. See Matter of O'Shea, 45 Misc.2d 84, 255 N.Y.S.2d 729 (Suffolk 1965), affirmed 24 A.D.2d 845, 263 N.Y.S.2d 554 (2d Dep't 1965). Failure to file the notice of election during the tenure of a preliminary executor or temporary administrator does not preclude the spouse from filing it after the appointment of a permanent fiduciary. See discussion of the right of election in chapter on "Surviving

ry and preliminary letters do not start time periods running unless a specific statute states otherwise, such as the claimant's time period mentioned earlier in this subsection, where the governing statute states that the seven months start to run from the appointment of a temporary administrator or preliminary executor.[6]

SECTION E. FILLING VACANCIES IN OFFICE OF FIDUCIARY

If one of multiple co-fiduciaries can no longer serve, the court may not appoint a successor fiduciary unless directed by the terms of the will or trust.[1] The remaining fiduciary should continue the administration, and may continue any pending action or proceeding, and should file an ex parte petition to delete the name of the departed fiduciary from the letters.

The rule is, of course, different when no fiduciaries remain; in that case the court appoints a successor to continue the administration,[2] unless the estate or trust is almost wound up and the fiduciary of the deceased fiduciary can make final distribution.[3] The successor can continue actions and proceedings to which his predecessor was a party and enforce judgments in favor of his predecessor.[4]

SECTION F. ELIGIBILITY TO SERVE AS FIDUCIARY

To serve as a fiduciary, a person must be eligible, and every person is eligible except those listed in SCPA 707.[1] The ineligible persons are:

(i) Infants.[2]

(ii) Incompetents.[3]

(iii) Non-domiciliary aliens[4] (except guardians).[5] Although a resident alien can qualify,[6] one on a temporary or diplomatic visa may not.[7]

Spouse's Right of Election," supra at 302 et seq.

6. McKinney's SCPA 1802.

Sec. E

1. McKinney's SCPA 706(1); Matter of Stavin, 56 A.D.2d 68, 391 N.Y.S.2d 412 (1st Dep't 1977), affirmed 43 N.Y.2d 669, 400 N.Y.S.2d 817, 371 N.E.2d 535 (the mandatory language of McKinney's SCPA 706, "a successor * * * shall not be appointed," is not a rule of construction but a legislative mandate and accordingly the court should not appoint a successor fiduciary unless it is an absolute necessity).

2. McKinney's SCPA 706(2).

3. McKinney's SCPA 2207(5).

4. McKinney's SCPA 706(2).

Sec. F

1. "Person" in this context includes natural persons as well as non-natural persons authorized by law to serve as a fiduciary.

2. McKinney's SCPA 707(1)(a).

3. McKinney's SCPA 707(1)(a).

4. McKinney's SCPA 707(1)(c).

5. McKinney's SCPA 1716(4).

6. Tunas v. Municipal Gas Co., 88 A.D. 251, 84 N.Y.S. 462 (3d Dep't 1903).

7. Matter of Paderewski, 193 Misc. 688, 84 N.Y.S.2d 322 (New York County 1948); Matter of Gaffney, 141 Misc. 453, 252 N.Y.S. 649 (New York County 1931).

(iv) Convicted felons.[8] The statute is clear that to make a person ineligible a conviction is required.[9] The felony must be a felony under New York law; if it is a federal felony but would have been a misdemeanor under New York law, it will not make the named fiduciary ineligible.[10] The federal conviction may, however, be the ground for ineligibility because of dishonesty.[11]

(v) Persons incapable of fulfilling their fiduciary obligations because of habitual drunkenness,[12] dishonesty in money matters,[13] improvidence sufficient to render the estate unsafe,[14] or want of understanding.[15]

(vi) Persons who cannot read or write English if the court in its discretion declares them ineligible.[16]

An ineligible person cannot designate an eligible person to act in his place.[17]

If the nominated fiduciary's shortcomings do not fall within the SCPA 707 ineligibility categories, he is eligible.[18] For example, a physical disability, without additional factors that point to improvidence or want of understanding, does not make a person ineligible.[19] The fact that the named fiduciary is indebted to the estate does not make him ineligible,[20] nor does the fact that he has no assets of his own,[21] or has a claim against the estate.[22] Even the fact that the

8. McKinney's SCPA 707(1)(d).

9. Matter of Johnson, 202 Misc. 751, 112 N.Y.S.2d 866 (Kings 1952); Matter of Manley, 12 Misc. 472, 34 N.Y.S. 258 (Cattaraugus 1895).

10. Matter of Caperonis, 95 Misc.2d 690, 408 N.Y.S.2d 231 (Saratoga 1978); Matter of Kaufman, 77 Misc.2d 424, 353 N.Y.S.2d 355 (New York County 1974).

11. McKinney's SCPA 707(1)(e). See 26 Syracuse L.Rev. 326.

12. That the drunkenness must be habitual is supported by Matter of Manley, 12 Misc. 472, 34 N.Y.S.2d 258 (Cattaraugus 1895).

13. That the dishonesty must be in money matters is supported by Matter of Cohen, 254 A.D. 571, 2 N.Y.S.2d 764 (2d Dep't 1938), affirmed 278 N.Y. 584, 16 N.E.2d 111 (1938). The objectant arguing dishonesty alone does not have a right to a jury trial. Matter of Krom, 86 A.D.2d 689, 446 N.Y.S.2d 522 (1982). The dishonesty should also be more than an isolated incident. Matter of Cohen, 164 Misc. 98, 298 N.Y.S. 368 (1937) affirmed 254 App.Div. 571, 2 N.Y.S.2d 764 (1938), affirmed 278 N.Y. 584, 16 N.E.2d 111 (1938); Matter of Baragiano, N.Y.L.J., Aug. 6, 1985, at 12, col. 2 (Richmond).

14. That the improvidence must be sufficient to render the estate unsafe or liable to be lost or diminished is supported by Matter of Ferguson, 41 Misc. 465, 84 N.Y.S. 1102 (Kings 1903).

15. McKinney's SCPA 707(1)(e). For an example of a want of understanding sufficient to render a fiduciary ineligible, see Matter of Leland, 219 N.Y. 387, 114 N.E. 854 (1916), where the nominated fiduciary, though not adjudicated incompetent, had an incurable disease which made him unable to safeguard the interests of the beneficiaries.

16. McKinney's SCPA 707(2).

17. Matter of Dankerl, 12 A.D.2d 678, 207 N.Y.S.2d 514 (3d Dep't 1960). Compare Matter of Taomina, 2 A.D.2d 711, 153 N.Y.S.2d 250 (2d Dep't 1956), affirmed 2 N.Y.2d 878, 161 N.Y.S.2d 135, 141 N.E.2d 622 (1957).

18. E.g., Matter of Flood, 236 N.Y. 408, 140 N.E. 936 (1923); Matter of Leland, 219 N.Y. 387, 114 N.E. 854 (1916); 2 Jessup-Redfield, Surrogate's Law and Practice section 1284 (1947).

19. Matter of Decker, N.Y.L.J., Sept. 28, 1979, at 16, col. 1 (Westchester).

20. Matter of Rosenfeld, 157 Misc. 686, 284 N.Y.S. 491 (New York County 1935).

21. Matter of Riede, 138 App.Div. 83, 122 N.Y.S. 600 (2d Dep't 1910), affirmed 201 N.Y. 596, 95 N.E. 1127 (1911).

22. Matter of Ratner, 213 N.Y.S.2d 497 (Westchester 1961).

nominated fiduciary alleges that the will is a forgery does not make him ineligible.[23] The nominated fiduciary can serve even if he has a conflict of interest with the estate,[24] unless the conflict virtually assures the nominated fiduciary's inability to administer the estate.[25] If a problem arises after the appointment of a person with a conflict, persons affected can take steps to remove him.[26]

However, if a person is clearly unsuitable because, if he were appointed, an objectant to his serving as fiduciary could successfully petition for his removal,[27] some courts have declined to appoint him in the first place.[28]

A person need not be named to be eligible, as long as his identity is clear from the nomination, such as a description of his title or office.[29] He must, however, be a natural person, or a corporate trustee authorized by law to serve.[30] An example of a non-natural person authorized by law to act as fiduciary is found in SCPA 1418(4), where a corporation who is a sole or residuary legatee can serve as administrator c.t.a.[31] even if its charter does not authorize it and even if no other law authorizes it. If the corporation has no authorization, either in its charter or in the law, to serve as fiduciary, it cannot do so.[32]

One need never reach the issue of ineligibility if the clause nominating the executor was inserted in the will after its execution; there

23. Matter of Fodera, 96 A.D.2d 559, 465 N.Y.S.2d 65 (2d Dep't 1983) (X offered will for probate and Y objected on the ground the will was forged. The Surrogate admitted the will to probate after a jury trial, and held that Y was ineligible to serve as fiduciary. The Appellate Division reversed).

24. Matter of Foss, 282 App.Div. 509, 125 N.Y.S.2d 105 (1st Dep't 1953).

25. See Matter of Wehrli, 36 A.D.2d 488, 321 N.Y.S.2d 438 (1st Dep't 1971), affirmed 30 N.Y.2d 510, 330 N.Y.S.2d 60, 280 N.E.2d 887 (1972); Matter of Juelich, 81 A.D.2d 919, 439 N.Y.S.2d 394 (2d Dep't 1981); Matter of Bernich, 98 Misc.2d 1036, 415 N.Y.S.2d 201 (Dutchess 1979).

26. See McKinney's SCPA 711 and 719, discussed this chapter infra at 393–400.

27. McKinney's SCPA 711.

28. See Matter of Wehrli, 36 A.D.2d 488, 321 N.Y.S.2d 438 (1st Dep't 1971), affirmed 30 N.Y.2d 510, 330 N.Y.S.2d 60, 280 N.E.2d 887 (1972); Matter of Younker, 111 Misc.2d 599, 444 N.Y.S.2d 807 (New York County 1981) (dicta).

29. See Matter of Palmquist, 44 A.D.2d 897, 355 N.Y.S.2d 866 (4th Dep't 1974), where the decedent named "the pastor of the Swedish Lutheran Church of Buffalo" as a co-executor, and that church had moved from Buffalo, changed its name and changed pastors eight times before the decedent's death. The court held that the then-current pastor could serve.

30. See Matter of Klein, 87 Misc.2d 530, 386 N.Y.S.2d 321 (Orange 1976), where the fiduciary was a partner in a law firm whose partnership agreement provided that all commissions the partners earned by serving as fiduciary would be payable to the partnership. The court refused to sign a decree authorizing payment to the firm because the firm, as a non-natural person, was ineligible to serve. Accord, Matter of Bartholomew, 45 Misc.2d 815, 257 N.Y.S.2d 625 (Suffolk 1965) (law firm designated as fiduciary ineligible to serve).

31. Administration c.t.a. is discussed in chapter on "Probate," supra at 115–18.

32. Matter of Nichols, 124 Misc.2d 204, 475 N.Y.S.2d 787 (Clinton 1984) (church's charter did not authorize the church to serve, nor was the church sole or residuary beneficiary).

the clause itself is completely invalid regardless of the eligibility of the named fiduciary.[33]

SECTION G. QUALIFICATION OF FIDUCIARIES

The court will not issue letters to a fiduciary until he qualifies, that is, files in the Surrogate's Court his oath and designation together with a bond for security when required.[1] A fiduciary should qualify promptly.[2]

The designation is an acknowledged instrument setting forth the fiduciary's domiciliary address and designating the clerk of the Surrogate's Court to receive on the fiduciary's behalf service of any process issuing from that Surrogate's Court. The fiduciary has to notify the court promptly of any change of address, and if he cannot be found and served within the state with due diligence, service of process on the clerk is effective personal service on the fiduciary. The server must serve either the chief clerk or the deputy chief clerk. The designation is irrevocable and is effective as long as the fiduciary remains in office, until he is finally discharged by a decree of the court.[3] The clerk of the Surrogate's Court cannot receive on the fiduciary's behalf process issued from another court.[4]

The fiduciary also must submit his official oath, notarized, swearing that he will honestly discharge his duties and account for all property that comes into his hands. In practice the oath, like the designation, is part of the form provided by the court for the respective proceedings. It must describe the fiduciary relationship and state that the fiduciary is eligible to receive letters.[5] Corporate trustees do not file an oath but an acknowledged consent to the appointment.[6]

If a bond is required, either by law or by the direction of the court, the fiduciary cannot qualify until he secures and files the bond and the Surrogate approves it.[7] An executor ordinarily does not have to file a bond [8] unless the will requires it. If he also administers assets as a testamentary trustee, he must file a bond unless the will exempts him.[9]

33. Matter of Brumer, 96 Misc.2d 1054, 410 N.Y.S.2d 221 (Richmond 1978), affirmed, 69 A.D.2d 438, 419 N.Y.S.2d 155 (2d Dep't 1979).

Sec. G

1. McKinney's SCPA 708.

2. See, e.g., McKinney's SCPA 1416(1) (fifteen days after probate for executor).

3. McKinney's SCPA 708(1). In fact the court usually does not remove the fiduciary from office in the accounting decree. The decree discharges the fiduciary from all liability, but if any new assets come in, the fiduciary can collect them (and then has to account for them).

4. See Doughney v. Fauset, 9 Misc.2d 759, 170 N.Y.S.2d 419 (Sup.Ct. New York County 1958); Central Greyhound Lines v. Faust, 196 Misc. 53, 91 N.Y.S.2d 609 (Oneida 1949), affirmed 278 App.Div. 1012, 105 N.Y.S.2d 1010 (4th Dep't 1951).

5. McKinney's SCPA 708(2).

6. McKinney's SCPA 708(4).

7. McKinney's SCPA 708(3).

8. McKinney's SCPA 710(1).

9. McKinney's SCPA 806.

Other fiduciaries, except corporate trustees, ordinarily must file bonds.[10]

If a non-New York trust has been created in favor of a New York charity, the foreign trustee must qualify in New York and post a bond.[11] If the foreign fiduciary is a national trust company, the court can dispense with a bond.[12]

SECTION H. OBJECTIONS TO THE GRANT OF LETTERS

As a part of every proceeding leading to the appointment of a fiduciary (such as probate, administration, or guardianship proceedings), the necessary parties have an opportunity on the return date to object to the appointment of the fiduciary. The SCPA gives any interested person the right to object.[1] If someone does object, the court has the option of granting the letters or waiting until resolution of the objections.[2]

"Persons interested" who have a right to object include the class of absolute and contingent beneficiaries.[3] The term has also been held to include a non-distributee legatee in a probate proceeding. Although that person is not a necessary party to the probate proceeding and cannot object to probate of the will, he can object to the issuance of letters to a particular fiduciary.[4] This makes sense. He has no standing to object to probate of a will under which he gets a bequest, because without the will he would get nothing. On the other hand, once the will is established, he is pecuniarily interested in how the estate property is administered, so he should be able to voice his objections to the fiduciary under consideration.

The other person technically not entitled to object to the issuance of letters is the creditor, because he is not a "person interested."[5] However, when letters have been issued, the creditor has standing to seek their revocation,[6] and accordingly in practice the courts sometimes consider objections interposed by a creditor.[7]

10. McKinney's SCPA 805(1).

11. Matter of Weber, 22 Misc.2d 290, 195 N.Y.S.2d 337 (New York County 1959). McKinney's Banking L. § 100–a(5)–(7) gives a foreign trustee reciprocal rights to qualify, but McKinney's Banking Law § 13(3) does not absolve the foreign fiduciary from filing a bond. For rules governing the qualification of foreign trustees, see SCPA 1503, and for a discussion of the jurisdiction of the Surrogate's Court over foreign trusts, see McKinney's SCPA 1501, both discussed in chapter on "Trusts and Trustees," infra at 455–60, 463.

12. 12 U.S.C.A. § 92–A.

Sec. H

1. McKinney's SCPA 709.

2. McKinney's SCPA 709.

3. McKinney's SCPA 103(39).

4. Matter of Brumer, 69 A.D.2d 438, 419 N.Y.S.2d 155 (2d Dep't 1979).

5. McKinney's SCPA 103(39).

6. McKinney's SCPA 711, discussed presently; McKinney's SCPA 719, discussed this chapter infra at 398–99.

7. E.g., Matter of Nelson, N.Y.L.J., Dec. 26, 1984, at 11, col. 4 (New York County). But see Matter of Malkon, N.Y.L.J., July 15, 1985, at 15, col. 4 (New York County), where the same court dismissed the objections to the fiduciary's eligibility by a person claiming to be a creditor, distinguishing Nelson and relegating the alleged

If the proceeding is for the appointment of a trustee of a lifetime trust, the interested parties have a right to object. As a practical matter inter vivos trustees do not obtain letters. The court usually does not become involved unless the instrument fails to appoint a trustee, or the named trustee ceases to serve, and the court must therefore appoint one.

If, in a case where the will exempts the fiduciary from a bond, an interested party objects to the issuance of letters to named executor, testamentary guardian or testamentary trustee on the ground that he is a non-domiciliary or that he does not have enough responsibility to serve as fiduciary, the nominated fiduciary can overcome those objections by filing a bond to cover the property he will administer.[8] If, for example, a fiduciary is insolvent or has filed for bankruptcy, the court may direct that he file a bond. If a fiduciary moves out-of-state during his service as fiduciary, interested parties may object and the court may require a bond.[9]

When the will exempts a person from filing a bond, the burden of proof is on the objectant to prove that a bond is necessary to protect a creditor or a person interested in the estate.[10]

SECTION I. CHANGE OF SITUS OF ASSETS

If the fiduciary wants to remove property from the state, he must petition the court to do so. The court may require him to file a bond,[1] and in practice usually does. This ensures the court's continuing jurisdiction over the assets.

SECTION J. SUSPENSION, MODIFICATION OR REVOCATION OF LETTERS

Once the court has issued letters to a fiduciary, it can revoke, suspend or modify those letters if something goes awry. There are two procedures for revocation or modification of letters. One, governed by SCPA 711 and discussed in this section, is a procedure on notice to the fiduciary and any other persons whose interests are sufficient in the court's opinion to make those persons necessary parties. The other, governed by SCPA 719 and discussed later in this chapter, is an ex parte procedure used in more extreme circumstances.

creditor to a McKinney's SCPA 711 proceeding for removal of the fiduciary at which his status as creditor could be established.

8. McKinney's SCPA 710(2).

9. McKinney's SCPA 710(3).

10. Matter of Buono, 15 Misc.2d 694, 183 N.Y.S.2d 135 (Nassau 1959).

Sec. I

1. McKinney's SCPA 710(4).

1. SUSPENSION, MODIFICATION OR REVOCATION ON NOTICE

Under SCPA 711, the class of persons who can petition for revocation of letters is much broader than the class that can object to letters in the first place.[1] It includes creditors, persons interested, anyone on an infant's behalf, or the surety on the fiduciary's bond.[2] Moreover, even though SCPA 711 sets forth the persons who have standing to petition for revocation, arguably any person in the world can do so, not under this section but under SCPA 719, which permits the court to revoke letters whenever any ground for revocation set forth in SCPA 711 comes to its attention.[3]

When it receives a petition, the court may entertain or decline to entertain the proceeding.[4] The fiduciary is, of course, a necessary party. The court issues process and the petitioner arranges for its service on the fiduciary. The court may also direct service on all other persons interested in the estate[5] and it usually does, to ensure due process to interested persons.[6] Once process has issued, the court can suspend the fiduciary from exercising his powers. If it does so, the petitioner must serve the court order along with the process, and it is then binding on the fiduciary and on all other persons.[7]

The petition must state the petitioner's standing (person interested, creditor, surety or person on behalf of infant), and must list one or more of the statutory grounds for removal or modification.

On the return of process, the court hears proof and inquires into the fiduciary's actions, and the court will remove him, modify the letters or dismiss the petition.[8] The parties are not entitled to a jury trial in this proceeding.[9]

Sec. J

1. The class which can object in the first place is governed by McKinney's SCPA 709 and discussed this chapter supra at 392–93.

2. It does not include non-creditors with no interest in decedent's estate. Matter of Wagner, 106 A.D.2d 646, 482 N.Y.S.2d 904 (2d Dep't 1984).

3. McKinney's SCPA 719(10). This curious anomaly is illustrated by Matter of Guadagno, N.Y.L.J., Aug. 21, 1985, at 12, col. 5 (Richmond); where the court preliminarily decided that the petitioner for revocation of the fiduciary's letters did not have standing under McKinney's SCPA 711 and dismissed the petition, and then proceeded to grant the relief on its own under McKinney's SCPA 719 because a 711 ground had been brought to its attention. Accord, Matter of Prassas, N.Y.L.J., July 23, 1985, at 14, col. 1 (Queens). See Matter of Beattie, N.Y.L.J., Feb. 27, 1985, at 13, col. 3 (Bronx) (decedent's daughter-in-law permitted to petition on behalf of decedent's distributees).

4. McKinney's SCPA 712. See discussion of court's power to entertain proceedings in chapter on "Miscellaneous Proceedings," supra at 327–28.

5. Those persons must be listed in the petition, McKinney's SCPA 304, divided into classes of legally disabled persons and persons of sound mind and full age.

6. McKinney's SCPA 712. Under prior law, all persons interested in the estate were necessary parties, L.1966, c. 953; Matter of Bellinger, 35 A.D.2d 1078, 317 N.Y.S.2d 126 (4th Dep't 1970), and the statute was amended to require only the fiduciary as a necessary party. L.1973, c. 731. See Matter of Semon, N.Y.L.J., October 3, 1982, at 14, col. 3.

7. McKinney's SCPA 712.

8. McKinney's SCPA 713.

9. Matter of Ruggiero, 82 Misc.2d 211, 368 N.Y.S.2d 722, (Westchester 1975), af-

Even if the petitioner establishes his allegations to the satisfaction of the court, the court still has broad discretion to determine the appropriate relief and can dismiss the petition in the best interest of the estate.[10] Similarly, the court may surcharge a fiduciary instead of revoking letters and then permit the fiduciary to continue to administer the estate.[11]

a. Grounds for Removal of Fiduciary

The removal of a fiduciary is quite a serious step. There are less drastic sanctions to take against an errant or negligent fiduciary, namely denial of commissions and surcharge, which we discuss elsewhere. The court can impose all three penalties or any one or two it believes to be in the best interests of the estate. In fact, the courts exercise their power to remove fiduciaries very sparingly, typically in cases of serious misconduct or in cases where the safety of the fund is endangered.[12] Someone's complaint that the fiduciary has a claim against the estate or a conflict of interest with the estate is not sufficient to justify removal.[13] Sometimes rather than removing the fiduciary, the court requires a bond to secure his performance.[14]

As a preliminary statement to a discussion of removing a fiduciary from office, there is a curious tension between SCPA 707 and 708, under which the court issues letters if the fiduciary is not ineligible and if he qualifies, and SCPA 711, which allows the court to revoke letters or modify them (for example, by requiring a bond) under somewhat more relaxed standards. The reason is that prima facie, the courts want to grant letters to the person nominated by the testator or entitled under the law to serve as administrator unless there are clear grounds (such as fraud or undue influence) not to appoint that person. A proceeding for removing a fiduciary under SCPA 711 contemplates a more adversarial proceeding. The court will not, however, allow the parties to relitigate issues already raised.[15]

The court can remove the fiduciary or modify his letters in the following cases:

firmed 51 A.D.2d 969, 380 N.Y.S.2d 319 (2d Dep't 1976).

10. Stolz v. New York Central Railroad Co., 7 N.Y.2d 269, 196 N.Y.S.2d 969, 164 N.E.2d 849 (1959).

11. Cooper v. Jones, 78 A.D.2d 423, 435 N.Y.S.2d 830 (4th Dep't 1981).

12. Matter of Braloff, 3 A.D.2d 912, 162 N.Y.S.2d 620 (2d Dep't 1957), affirmed 4 N.Y.2d 847, 173 N.Y.S.2d 817, 150 N.E.2d 243 (1958).

13. Matter of Woodworth, 165 Misc. 770, 1 N.Y.S.2d 455 (New York County 1937), affirmed 254 App.Div. 852, 6 N.Y.S.2d 360 (1st Dep't 1938) (claim against the estate); Matter of Weiss, 33 Misc.2d 773, 227 N.Y.S.2d 378 (New York County 1962) (conflict of interest); Matter of Kent, 22 Misc.2d 66, 194 N.Y.S.2d 944 (New York County 1959) (conflict of interest).

14. E.g., Matter of Israel, 64 Misc.2d 1035, 315 N.Y.S.2d 453 (Nassau 1970).

15. Matter of Heilbronner, 22 Misc.2d 424, 199 N.Y.S.2d 753 (New York County 1960), appeal dismissed 11 A.D.2d 1022, 24 N.Y.S.2d 679, 214 N.Y.S.2d 672 (1st Dep't 1960).

(1) If the fiduciary was or has become ineligible [16] or disqualified [17] and the petitioner did not object before letters were issued.[18]

(2) If the fiduciary has engaged in some wrongdoing, namely has wasted or imprudently invested estate property,[19] acted dishonestly, improvidently or drunkenly.[20]

(3) If the fiduciary has refused to obey a court order.[21]

(4) If the fiduciary has obtained his letters by a false statement of a material fact,[22] even if he did so honestly.

(5) If the fiduciary failed to notify the court of a change in address within thirty days of moving.[23]

(6) If the fiduciary removed property from the state without prior court approval.[24]

16. McKinney's SCPA 707, discussed this chapter supra at 388–91. See, e.g., Matter of Holder, N.Y.L.J., Feb. 26, 1985, at 14, col. 3 (Nassau) (court revoked letters of husband-fiduciary convicted after his appointment as her fiduciary of murdering his wife); accord, Matter of Astolfo, N.Y. L.J., June 12, 1985, at 14, col. 5 (Nassau). If a fiduciary becomes an alien and leaves New York, the court may, but does not have to, revoke his letters. Matter of Clark, 136 Misc. 459, 241 N.Y.S. 520 (Ostego 1930).

17. McKinney's SCPA 708, discussed this chapter infra at 391–92.

18. McKinney's SCPA 711(1).

19. McKinney's SCPA 711(2).

20. McKinney's SCPA 711(2). The burden of proving dishonesty is on the party alleging it. Matter of Krom, 86 A.D.2d 681, 446 N.Y.S.2d 522 (1982); Matter of Baragiano, N.Y.L.J., Aug. 6, 1985, at 12, col. 2 (Richmond). Hostility is not a ground for removal unless it jeopardizes the estate, Matter of Miller, N.Y.L.J., Aug. 7, 1985, at 14, col. 2 (Nassau), and one factor the court considers is whether the fiduciary is at fault in creating the hostility. See Matter of Edwards, 274 A.D. 844, 80 N.Y.S.2d 807 (4th Dep't 1948).

21. McKinney's SCPA 711(3). The failure to obey a court order must amount to "willful resistance" or "neglect without good cause," or it should not be a ground for removal. See Matter of Oberstein, 103 A.D.2d 831, 478 N.Y.S.2d 70 (2d Dep't 1984) (Appellate Division reinstated removed fiduciary who asserted that she did not know of the court order requiring her to account).

22. McKinney's SCPA 711(4); Matter of Barasch, 32 Misc.2d 548, 222 N.Y.S.2d 722 (Nassau 1962). The purpose of McKinney's SCPA 711(4) is not to punish the fiduciary for the misrepresentation, but to protect the estate. See Matter of D'Onofrio, N.Y. L.J., November 30, 1978, at 15, col. 4 (Bronx), where the administrator's misstatement that he was the decedent's husband resulted in his obtaining letters of administration. Those letters were attackable seventeen years later when petitioner discovered the falsehood). See also Matter of Beattie, N.Y.L.J., Feb. 27, 1985, at 13, col. 3 (Bronx), where the decedent's niece represented that she and another niece were the decedent's sole distributees and received letters because of that misrepresentation. The court revoked those letters when the decedent's grandchildren, her true distributees, appeared. Accord, Matter of Wayne, N.Y.L.J., Dec. 13, 1978, at 12, col. 5 (Bronx) (father obtained letters of guardianship by alleging that mother's whereabouts were unknown, and court revoked them). See Matter of Prassas, N.Y. L.J., July 23, 1985, at 14, col. 1 (Queens), where the court removed both fiduciaries on the application of one of them to remove the other because the probate petition submitted by both had materially underestimated the estate assets.

23. McKinney's SCPA 711(6). See, e.g., Matter of Drimmer, 97 A.D.2d 792, 468 N.Y.S.2d 533 (2d Dep't 1983).

24. McKinney's SCPA 711(7). See Matter of Rothko, 84 Misc.2d 830, 379 N.Y.S.2d 923 (New York County 1975), modified 56 A.D.2d 499, 392 N.Y.S.2d 870 (1st Dep't), modified 43 N.Y.2d 305, 401 N.Y.S.2d 196, 372 N.E.2d 31 (1977).

(7) If the fiduciary's term has ended naturally, because of the occurrence of a contingency.[25]

(8) If the fiduciary is unbonded and the court finds that he does not have sufficient responsibility to act as fiduciary.[26]

(9) In a guardianship case, if the guardian has moved outside New York (or is about to) or if the court believes that a different guardian would better serve the child's best interests.[27]

(10) If the fiduciary is a testamentary trustee and he has violated his trust or is insolvent or if the court believes he is unsuitable for the job.[28]

(11) If the fiduciary is a trustee of a lifetime trust and the Supreme Court would have had jurisdiction to remove him.[29] A Supreme Court judge can discharge a trustee on such terms as he deems proper, which appear to be those set forth under SCPA 711, 719 and 720.[30] Specifically, the EPTL authorizes suspension, modification or removal if the trust is violated or a trustee threatens to violate a trust, is insolvent (or is about to become insolvent) or if the court believes the trustee is unsuited to execute the trust.[31]

The following is a sampling of cases in which fiduciaries were removed from office for wrongdoing:

—An administratrix started a wrongful death action on behalf of the decedent's distributees and then refused to settle it or to appear as a witness at the trial to give crucial testimony.[32]

—An administrator failed to disclose that the decedent was survived by a spouse.[33]

—An attorney who was both administrator of a wife's estate and the husband's conservator attempted to exercise the husband's right of election. The court required him to choose between the two positions because of the obvious conflict.[34]

25. McKinney's SCPA 711(5).

26. McKinney's SCPA 711(8).

27. McKinney's SCPA 711(9). See chapter on "Guardianships," supra at 257 et seq.

28. McKinney's SCPA 711(10). Insolvency will be a ground for removal if it jeopardizes the assets of the estate, and the court can require the insolvent fiduciary to file a bond rather than remove him. See Matter of Miller, N.Y.L.J., Aug. 7, 1985, at 14, col. 2 (Nassau).

29. McKinney's SCPA 711(11).

30. McKinney's EPTL 7–2.6; McKinney's EPTL 7–2.6, Prac.Comm. at 123 (Supp.1986).

31. McKinney's EPTL 7–2.6(2). Conservators and committees can also be removed for wrongdoing. See, e.g., Umscheid v. Simnacher, 106 A.D.2d 380, 482 N.Y.S.2d 295 (2d Dep't 1984).

32. Matter of Bosco, 106 Misc.2d 454, 431 N.Y.S.2d 972 (Richmond 1980).

33. Matter of Bailey, N.Y.L.J., July 2, 1980, at 11, col. 4 (Bronx).

34. Matter of Silber, 104 Misc.2d 574, 428 N.Y.S.2d 614 (Sup.Ct. Queens 1980).

—A fiduciary failed to file a proper account.[35]

—A fiduciary unduly delayed administration.[36]

2. SUSPENSION, MODIFICATION OR REVOCATION WITHOUT PROCESS

In cases where the "ordinary" revocation procedure cannot be used because the fiduciary is not amenable to personal service of process [37] or because his wrongdoing was so egregious, a different ex parte procedure is available. The court may revoke or modify a fiduciary's letters [38] regardless of which court made the initial appointment, or remove a lifetime trustee, in the following situations:

(1) If the court orders the fiduciary to account and he fails to appear on the return date without a good excuse.[39]

(2) If the fiduciary has absconded or hidden and cannot be served personally with process.[40]

(3) If the court ordered the fiduciary to supply information about estate assets in a discovery proceeding [41] and he has failed or refused to do so.[42]

(4) If another court with jurisdiction over the will or trust (such as the Supreme Court or a foreign court) declares the instrument to be invalid.[43]

(5) If an administrator has failed to post a necessary bond.[44]

(6) If a fiduciary has been convicted of a felony or judicially declared incompetent.[45]

(7) If a fiduciary commingles estate funds with his own or deposits estate funds in a bank in a name other than the estate's (that is, other than in his name as fiduciary).[46]

(8) If the fiduciary is an ancillary fiduciary and the primary letters granted in his own jurisdiction have been revoked.[47]

35. Kelly v. Sassower, 52 A.D.2d 539, 382 N.Y.S.2d 88 (1st Dep't 1976), appeal dismissed 39 N.Y.2d 942, 386 N.Y.S.2d 1029, 352 N.E.2d 897 (1976).

36. Matter of Caporuscio, N.Y.L.J., Jan. 2, 1979, at 12, col. 5 (Bronx) (preliminary executor, two-year delay).

37. Recall that a fiduciary, because he files a designation of the court clerk to receive process on his behalf, McKinney's SCPA 708, is always subject to the court's personal jurisdiction. This section contemplates a fiduciary who is avoiding personal service. See McKinney's SCPA 719(2).

38. Under prior law, Surrogate's Court Act 104, the court could only revoke letters if the McKinney's SCPA 719 circumstances arose, but the current McKinney's SCPA 719 permits the court to modify or suspend letters as well.

39. McKinney's SCPA 719(1).

40. McKinney's SCPA 719(2).

41. McKinney's SCPA 2102(1), which allows interested persons to examine a fiduciary about property over which he has control, is discussed in chapter on "Miscellaneous Proceedings," supra at 328–36.

42. McKinney's SCPA 719(3).

43. McKinney's SCPA 719(4).

44. McKinney's SCPA 719(5).

45. McKinney's SCPA 719(6).

46. McKinney's SCPA 719(7).

47. McKinney's SCPA 719(8). Ancillary letters are discussed in chapter on "Ancillary Administration," infra at 509 et seq.

(9) If the fiduciary is a temporary administrator for an absentee[48] and the absentee returns.[49]

(10) If the court learns that a ground for removal under SCPA 711 exists.[50]

In all of the above situations, the fiduciary has done something totally inconsistent with his duties as a fiduciary or circumstances have arisen which make it impossible, improper or unnecessary for him to continue. Neither notice nor a hearing is required, but where possible, the Surrogate acts only after service on the fiduciary.[51]

One can thus see a logical progression in Article 7: Under SCPA 707 a fiduciary has a right to serve unless he fits within one of the narrow categories that make him ineligible. Once the fiduciary is in office, under SCPA 711 there are somewhat broader grounds for removal, though they are still cautiously applied. Finally, in SCPA 719, the court can remove a fiduciary in an expedited proceeding if his misconduct has been very serious.

3. EFFECT OF DECREE

As soon as the court enters the decree, the fiduciary is removed or suspended, or his powers are modified, as the case may be.[52] The decree may also require him to account and to pay all property to a successor fiduciary or some other person. The removal of an executor or an administrator does not automatically revoke his letters as a testamentary trustee.[53] SCPA Article 15 permits a proceeding for removal of the fiduciary in both capacities,[54] but otherwise the removal as executor or administrator does not affect the fiduciary in his capacity as testamentary trustee.

The fiduciary must be served with any order of suspension or modification; otherwise his letters remain valid.[55] Moreover, the court can permit the fiduciary to perform certain acts after he has received process and those acts will be valid if both the fiduciary and the party with whom he deals are acting in good faith.

Occasionally a person missing for a long time without explanation is declared dead by a court decree (a proceeding we discuss in another chapter).[56] The court appoints an executor or administrator for that missing person, just as it would for a "truly" dead person. On his return, he has some rights to recover his property from the fiduciary

48. See chapter on "Temporary Administration," supra at 292–93.

49. McKinney's SCPA 719(9).

50. McKinney's SCPA 719(10).

51. McKinney's SCPA 719, Practice Commentary at 598 (1967).

52. McKinney's SCPA 720.

53. McKinney's SCPA 720.

54. McKinney's SCPA 1505, discussed in chapter on "Trusts and Trustees," infra at 465.

55. McKinney's SCPA 720, Practice Commentary at 142 (1967).

56. The judicial declaration of death is governed by McKinney's EPTL 2–1.7 and discussed in chapter on "Temporary Administration," supra at 291–92.

and the persons to whom it was distributed.[57] That fiduciary is subject to removal proceedings like other fiduciaries. In addition, despite the fact that the fiduciary acted properly in distributing assets either before or after receiving process in the removal proceeding, if a person whom the court judicially declared dead returns and attempts to recover his property from the persons to whom the fiduciary gave it, albeit properly, he can do so. SCPA Article 7 does not compromise that person's rights.[58]

SECTION K. ORDERS OF OTHER COURTS

The Supreme Court has jurisdiction to appoint a testamentary trustee, and the Supreme Court and Family Court have jurisdiction to appoint a guardian for an infant. When they do so, the order or decree appointing the fiduciary is sent to the Surrogate's Court, which then issues letters of trusteeship or guardianship.[1] If the Supreme Court or the Family Court which made the appointment later revokes it, or accepts the resignation of the fiduciary it appointed, a certified copy of that order or decree must be filed in the Surrogate's Court.[2] The clerk of the Supreme Court or Family Court must give written notice of the filing to the clerk of the proper Surrogate's Court.[3] The Surrogate indexes it in a book kept for that purpose. While the Surrogate's Court can revoke the letters (but not rescind the appointment) issued not only by itself but also by the Supreme Court and Family Court, those courts cannot revoke letters that were issued by the Surrogate as to the Surrogate's appointees.

SECTION L. APPLICATION TO RESIGN

Once he is appointed, a fiduciary may not resign as of right. He may petition at any time for permission to resign and settle his account as fiduciary.[1] The court may entertain or decline to entertain the proceeding. The petition must set forth the facts to justify the resignation, and the court will direct what service has to be given and how.[2] After the return of process the court decides whether it would be in the

57. See discussion of these rights in chapter on "Temporary Administration," supra at 291–92.

58. McKinney's SCPA 721.

Sec. K

1. McKinney's SCPA 1503 (trustees); McKinney's SCPA 1709 (guardians). See discussion of this point in chapters on "Trusts and Trustees," infra at 463, and "Guardianships," supra at 271–72.

2. The proper Surrogate's Court is the one with jurisdiction over the estate or testamentary trust or the infant's person. See chapter on "Jurisdiction," supra at 1–12.

3. McKinney's SCPA 714.

Sec. L

1. McKinney's SCPA 715.

2. McKinney's SCPA 715. See, e.g., Matter of Wood, N.Y.L.J., June 21, 1985, at 14, col. 6 (Suffolk), where the court decided the threshold question of whether virtual representation was applicable before the issue of whether the trustee should be allowed to resign.

best interests of the estate to allow the resignation,[3] and the appellate courts will usually not interfere with that.[4] The court frequently allows resignation because of advanced age of the fiduciary.[5] The court will not permit a fiduciary to resign simply because he disagrees with his co-fiduciaries about investment policies.[6]

1. PROCEEDINGS TO RESIGN

If the court entertains the petition, it may make an intermediate order permitting the fiduciary to resign, or may revoke his letters and remove him, appoint a successor and direct that the resigning fiduciary turn over all assets to his successor, file his account, and petition for its judicial settlement unless he obtains waivers from all necessary parties on an informal accounting to them.[7] In the accounting proceeding the successor is a necessary party if one has been appointed.[8] Once the resigning fiduciary has fully accounted and paid over all estate assets to his successor, the court makes a decree discharging him. The court may order the resigning fiduciary to bear the costs of an accounting[9] unless there is reason for accounting other than his resignation, such as the death of an income beneficiary or the passage of a considerable period of time, typically ten years, during which trust has been under administration.

SECTION M. SAFEGUARDING SECURITIES

If the court determines that a removed fiduciary made an illegal investment while serving as fiduciary, the court may surcharge him for the loss. For example, a fiduciary may have collected joint assets which should have gone to the surviving joint tenant or taken other non-testamentary assets and invested them. A successor fiduciary does not receive these assets. To safeguard them, the court will order them paid into court[1] or to the proper parties.

3. Barch v. Avco Corp., 30 A.D.2d 241, 291 N.Y.S.2d 422 (4th Dep't 1968) (court held that resignation of New York fiduciary and appointment of New Jersey fiduciary, because it would allow the parties to wrongful death lawsuit access to the federal courts on a diversity theory, was in best interests of estate); Matter of Busto, 173 Misc. 25, 19 N.Y.S.2d 4 (Queens 1939), affirmed 258 App.Div. 980, 17 N.Y.S.2d 591 (2d Dep't 1940).

4. See Matter of Tuttle, 4 N.Y.2d 159, 173 N.Y.S.2d 279, 149 N.E.2d 715 (1958).

5. E.g., Matter of Malkan, N.Y.L.J., July 15, 1985, at 15, col. 3 (New York County); Matter of Gates, 143 Misc. 83, 254 N.Y.S. 614 (1931), affirmed 239 App. Div. 666, 268 N.Y.S. 868 (1934); Matter of Szegezdy, N.Y.L.J., August 6, 1985, at 6, col. 6 (New York County).

6. Matter of Wacht, 285 App.Div. 402, 137 N.Y.S.2d 876 (1955). But see Matter of Sand, N.Y.L.J., July 10, 1985, at 11, col. 2 (New York County) (Surrogate granted fiduciary's application to resign because of differences of opinion between the trustees and between the trustees and the beneficiaries. All interested parties agreed to the resignation and the court found it to be in the trust's best interests.)

7. Informal accountings on receipts and releases and formal judicial accountings are discussed in chapter on "Accounting," supra at 180–88.

8. McKinney's SCPA 716.

9. Matter of Lamb, 66 Hun 631, 21 N.Y.S. 343 (1892).

Sec. M

1. McKinney's SCPA 722.

SECTION N. FIDUCIARIES' POWERS

The law gives fiduciaries broad powers over trust and estate property under their control [1] to enable them to perform their fiduciary duties of collecting assets, paying legitimate claims, debts and expenses, and carrying out the instructions in the instrument appointing them.

The powers discussed in this section, unless we specify otherwise, are exercisable by administrators, executors, preliminary executors, administrators d.b.n., administrators c.t.a., administrators c.t.a.d.b.n., ancillary executors, ancillary administrators and ancillary administrators c.t.a., trustees and successor fiduciaries.[2] The governing statute, EPTL 11–1.1, does not cover guardians, conservators, committees, temporary administrators or voluntary administrators, whose powers are set forth in different sections of the law.[3]

The will or trust can restrict the fiduciary's powers or can confer on him additional powers, which we will discuss presently. In the absence of such provisions in the will or trust, fiduciaries have the following powers:

—to accept additions from another source,[4] such as a pour-over trust, and acquire the rest of property of which the decedent was part owner; [5]

—to invest and reinvest assets; [6]

—to keep estate property insured; [7]

—to gather property not specifically bequeathed or devised, collect the rents from it and manage it,[8] sell it,[9] lease it for up to three years (executor or administrator or other non-trustee fiduciary) or up to ten years (trustee),[10] or mortgage it.[11] Even if the will or trust denies the fiduciary this power, he can nevertheless exercise it if the Surrogate deems it necessary for an Article 19

Sec. N

1. McKinney's EPTL 11–1.1.

2. McKinney's EPTL 11–1.1(a)(3).

3. Temporary administrators are governed by McKinney's SCPA Article 9 and discussed in chapter on "Temporary Administration," supra at 289 et seq. Guardians are governed by McKinney's SCPA Article 17 and discussed in chapter on "Guardianship," supra at 257 et seq. Voluntary administrators are governed by McKinney's SCPA Article 13 and discussed in chapter on "Small Estates," supra at 246 et seq. Conservators and committees are governed by the Mental Hygiene Law.

4. McKinney's EPTL 11–1.1(b)(1).

5. McKinney's EPTL 11–1.1(b)(2).

6. McKinney's EPTL 11–1.1(b)(3). See discussion of the prudent man standard of investment, this chapter infra at 407–12.

7. McKinney's EPTL 11–1.1(b)(4). This should be viewed as a duty as well as a power, since to leave valuables uninsured would be imprudent.

8. McKinney's EPTL 11–1.1(b)(5)(A).

9. McKinney's EPTL 11–1.1(b)(5)(B). If a beneficiary wants realty in kind, the executor should attempt to accommodate his wishes, or otherwise he should be able to justify the sale. See McKinney's EPTL 13–1.3, Prac.Comm. at 383 (1967); Matter of Sherburne, 95 A.D.2d 859, 464 N.Y.S.2d 531 (2d Dep't 1983) (executor prohibited from selling decedent's home when the devisees elected to take it in kind).

10. McKinney's EPTL 11–1.1(b)(5)(C).

11. McKinney's EPTL 11–1.1(b)(5)(D).

ment of administration expenses, debts,[12] fu- dispositions and distributions.[13] The fiducia- powers even if the exercise adversely affects share or a surviving spouse's elective share.[14]

's to estate or trust property; [15]

ıs for sale of estate property valid up to six

eclose mortgages or continue mortgages after ıewal or extension; [17]

York bank as custodian, and pay the resultant e; [18]

—to hire a broker-dealer as custodian; [19]

—to authorize a bank to hold securities in the name of a nominee without disclosing the fiduciary relationship; [20]

—to continue administration after the death of other fiduciaries unless the will specifies that a successor is necessary,[21]

—to assume, as successor fiduciary, all the powers of the original fiduciary; [22]

—to contest claims and compromise claims; [23]

—to vote shares of stock; [24]

—to pay legally enforceable charges on account of securities (such as calls or assessments); [25]

12. These debts include judgments and liens but exclude mortgages. McKinney's SCPA 1902(3). See chapter on "Real Property Proceedings," infra at 471.

13. McKinney's EPTL 11–1.1(b)(5)(E); McKinney's SCPA 1902(1), (2), (4), (5), (6). See chapter on "Real Property Proceedings," infra at 470 et seq.

14. McKinney's EPTL 11–1.1(b)(5)(F). The after-born child or surviving spouse may, for example, have to take the property subject to a lease or may have to take the proceeds of property instead of the property in kind if the fiduciary sells it.

15. McKinney's EPTL 11–1.1(b)(6). This means ordinary repairs, not capital improvements.

16. McKinney's EPTL 11–1.1(b)(7).

17. McKinney's EPTL 11–1.1(b)(8).

18. McKinney's EPTL 11–1.1(b)(9). The bank is fairly restricted: it must either keep the securities in the estate's name, separate from all other assets, McKinney's EPTL 11–1.1(b)(9)(A), or hold the estate's securities in bulk with the same securities owned by others, and follow the appropriate state or federal regulations. McKinney's EPTL 11–1.1(b)(9)(B), 11–1.6, 11–1.8, 11–1.9.

19. McKinney's EPTL 11–1.10, added L.1984, c. 911. The broker-dealer is then subject to the same limitations imposed on a bank or corporate trustee acting as custodian, found in McKinney's EPTL 11–1.1(b)(9), 11–1.6, 11–1.8, 11–1.9.

20. McKinney's EPTL 11–1.1(b)(10).

21. McKinney's EPTL 11–1.1(b)(11).

22. McKinney's EPTL 11–1.1(b)(12).

23. McKinney's EPTL 11–1.1(b)(13). Many fiduciaries ask the court to approve a compromise under McKinney's SCPA 2106, discussed in chapter on "Miscellaneous Proceedings," supra at 245–50, or enter into a stipulation of compromise with all interested parties, as alternatives to simply exercising the power granted by McKinney's EPTL 11–1.1(b)(13).

24. McKinney's EPTL 11–1.1(b)(14).

25. McKinney's EPTL 11–1.1(b)(15).

—to sell stock, exercise conversion rights, and participate in reorganizations, mergers and liquidations; [26]

—to execute agreements and other instruments; [27]

—to administer assets of two or more trusts together; [28]

—to pay up to $5,000 to the parent or adult in charge of an infant, incompetent, conservatee or person under disability; [29]

—to distribute property in kind at its date of distribution value; [30]

—to file joint income tax returns with the decedent's surviving spouse, and to consent to split-gift treatment of gifts made by the decedent's spouse before the decedent's death; [31]

—to pay administration expenses.[32]

The court can also grant other powers to a fiduciary to enable him to administer the estate,[33] and the beneficiaries of the trust cannot, by consent, restrict the trustee's powers.[34]

Broad as these powers are, they do not allow a fiduciary carte blanche; the following powers were specifically not included in the statute: [35]

—to abandon or demolish real property;

—to borrow money [36] (but a fiduciary can mortgage estate property [37])

—to pay outlawed debts;

—to rely on information deemed reliable;

—to keep funds uninvested;

—to advance income to a beneficiary; [38]

—to create reserves for depreciation or wasting assets;

—to lend personal funds to the estate and take back a lien on estate property;

26. McKinney's EPTL 11–1.1(b)(16).

27. McKinney's EPTL 11–1.1(b)(17).

28. McKinney's EPTL 11–1.1(b)(18).

29. McKinney's EPTL 11–1.1(b)(19).

30. McKinney's EPTL 11–1.1(b)(20). See discussion of McKinney's EPTL 2–1.9 on distributions in kind in satisfaction of a surviving spouse's share in chapter on "Accounting," supra at 217.

31. McKinney's EPTL 11–1.1(b)(21). The split-gift election causes the gift to be treated for gift tax purposes as though it had been made one-half by each spouse, and enables the donor spouse to take advantage of both spouses' annual exclusions and unified credits. I.R.C. § 2513. See generally chapter on "Estate Taxes," infra at 556 et seq.

32. McKinney's EPTL 11–1.1(b)(22).

33. McKinney's EPTL 11–1.1(c).

34. Matter of Wagner, 106 A.D.2d 646, 482 N.Y.S.2d 904 (2d Dep't 1984).

35. McKinney's EPTL 11–1.1 Revisers' Notes, reported in McKinney's EPTL 11–1.1, Practice Commentary at 9 (Supp. 1986).

36. See Matter of Rappaport, N.Y.L.J., March 24, 1977, at 11, col. 6 (Nassau) (court refused to compel preliminary executor to borrow).

37. McKinney's EPTL 11–1.1(b)(5)(e).

38. This should be interpreted to mean both advancements of income before it is earned and advancements of income before the beneficiary has a right to it under the instrument or under the law.

—to enter into a voting trust;

—to employ agents;

—to continue a business without authorization from the will or from the court; [39]

—to engage in self-dealing;

—to delegate authority.

Thus, if a testator wanted a fiduciary to have any of these powers, or other powers not included in the statute, such as the power to grant options for longer than six months, or the power to pay fiduciaries' commissions early without court order, he must authorize the fiduciary to do so in the will.

SECTION O. DUTIES OF A FIDUCIARY—STANDARD OF UNDIVIDED LOYALTY

Judge Benjamin Cardozo gave the classic definition of the duty of a fiduciary in Meinhard v. Salmon: [1]

> A trustee is held to something stricter than the morals of the market-place. Not honesty alone, but the punctilio of an honor the most sensitive, is then the standard of behavior. As to this there has developed a tradition that is unbending and inveterate. Uncompromising rigidity has been the attitude of courts of equity when petitioned to undermine the rule of undivided loyalty by the "disintegrating erosion of particular exceptions."

Some fiduciaries engage in nefarious conduct that violates that standard egregiously, such as self-dealing for personal gain at a loss to the trust or estate,[2] or "accepting" a gift from a disabled elderly person by signing it over to oneself under the authority of a power of attorney from the elderly person, and then qualifying as his administrator.[3]

The court can remove the fiduciary who breaches his duty of undivided loyalty, can surcharge him for any damages to the trust or estate, or can deny him commissions.[4] Often it does all three.

39. McKinney's SCPA 2108 allows the court to authorize continuation of a decedent's business even if the will does not authorize it. This proceeding is discussed in chapter on "Miscellaneous Proceedings," supra at 354–56.

Sec. O

1. Meinhard v. Salmon, 249 N.Y. 458, 164 N.E. 545 (1928).

2. The classic example of self-dealing is Matter of Rothko, 43 N.Y.2d 305, 401 N.Y.S.2d 449, 372 N.E.2d 291 (1977), on remand 95 Misc.2d 492, 407 N.Y.S.2d 954 (1978), where one executor of an estate consisting largely of artwork was a director and officer of an art gallery to which the estate sold the artwork for inadequate value, and another executor was an unsuccessful artist trying to sell his own paintings to that gallery. The court assessed over nine million dollars in damages against the executors, and in addition removed them and denied them commissions.

3. Matter of DeBelardino, 77 Misc.2d 253, 352 N.Y.S.2d 858 (Monroe 1974).

4. Removal of fiduciaries is governed by McKinney's SCPA 711, discussed this chapter supra at 393–400. Surcharges are discussed this chapter infra at 412–13. Denial of commissions is discussed in chapter on "Commissions," infra at 436–41.

A testator or settlor of a trust can exempt the fiduciaries from the undivided loyalty standard. If he does, the governing standard is good faith.[5]

If a testator or settlor nominates a person with a conflict of interest (either a conflict at the time of nomination or one that subsequently develops), that person can serve but must then act with undivided loyalty.[6] If he does not, he subjects himself to removal, surcharge and loss of commissions.

A fiduciary cannot deal with himself. This strict rule does not depend on a finding of fraud or wrongdoing; it is in effect to avoid the possibility of fraud and self-interest.[7] So strictly is a fiduciary's duty construed that if he owes money to the estate, it is simply charged against him; he is presumed to have paid it.[8]

If a fiduciary deals with himself, the courts do not even inquire any further into whether the deal was fair or the price adequate or whether the fiduciary had any personal gain.[9] The fiduciary must disgorge all profits and gains he realized because of the self-dealing. The testator or settlor can authorize self-dealing,[10] but if he does not, a fiduciary who wants to buy an asset or borrow money from the estate or trust must get court authorization to do so,[11] or do so with the consent of all the beneficiaries, who must be adult and competent.

A fiduciary must hold estate or trust funds separately from his own.[12] He can deposit securities in a central depository,[13] but he cannot merge them with his own assets.[14]

Sometimes a fiduciary who does nothing wrong nevertheless breaches his fiduciary duty, if he lets co-fiduciaries breach their duty without taking any action.[15] He must file his dissent promptly in

5. In Matter of Heidenreich, 85 Misc.2d 135, 378 N.Y.S.2d 982 (Nassau 1976), the decedent specifically authorized the fiduciaries to retain any assets, however they had been acquired. The retention by the corporate fiduciary (a successor trustee) of its own stock, done in good faith, was therefore not a breach of the fiduciary's duty. Accord, O'Hayer v. De St. Aubin, 30 A.D.2d 419, 293 N.Y.S.2d 147 (2d Dep't 1968).

6. Matter of Foss, 29 Misc.2d 876, 217 N.Y.S.2d 463 (New York County 1961) (fiduciary was also officer in corporation in litigation with estate).

7. Matter of Ryan, 291 N.Y. 376, 52 N.E.2d 909 (1943); Matter of Brownell, 112 Misc.2d 719, 447 N.Y.S.2d 591 (Delaware 1981).

8. Baucus v. Stover, 89 N.Y. 1 (1882); Matter of Israel, 64 Misc.2d 1035, 315 N.Y.S.2d 453 (Nassau 1970).

9. Matter of Rothko, 43 N.Y.2d 305, 401 N.Y.S.2d 449, 372 N.E.2d 291 (1977), on remand 95 Misc.2d 492, 407 N.Y.S.2d 954 (1978) (court did not have to resort to "no further inquiry" rule because the fiduciaries clearly violated the fairness doctrine). See also Matter of Ryan, 291 N.Y. 376, 52 N.E.2d 909 (1943); Meinhard v. Salmon, 249 N.Y. 458, 164 N.E. 545 (1928).

10. O'Hayer v. De St. Aubin, 30 A.D.2d 419, 293 N.Y.S.2d 147 (2d Dep't 1968) (self-dealing fiduciary held to fairness standard).

11. He can do so under McKinney's SCPA 2107, discussed in chapter on "Miscellaneous Proceedings," supra at 350–53. See Matter of Scarborough Properties Corp., 25 N.Y.2d 553, 307 N.Y.S.2d 641, 255 N.E.2d 761 (1969).

12. McKinney's EPTL 11–1.6(a).

13. McKinney's EPTL 11–1.9.

14. Matter of Coe, 80 Misc.2d 374, 363 N.Y.S.2d 265 (Nassau 1975).

15. See Matter of Rothko, 43 N.Y.2d 305, 401 N.Y.S.2d 449, 372 N.E.2d 291

writing,[16] or commence an action seeking advice and direction on how to proceed.[17]

SECTION P. PRUDENT PERSON RULE OF INVESTMENT

Fiduciaries must invest the assets under their control prudently. Unless a will or trust instrument gives them broader powers, they may invest estate, trust or guardianship funds "in such securities as would be acquired by prudent men of discretion and intelligence in such matters who are seeking a reasonable income and preservation of their capital * * *."[1]

The rule is a test of the fiduciary's conduct, not his performance.[2] The fiduciary must be cautious and avoid excessive risks; he must investigate the soundness of the investment; and he must have at least a modicum of skill in investment matters.[3] The prudent man rule does not permit a fiduciary to speculate.[4] He must investigate the safety of each investment and the income he expects it will yield.[5]

(1977), on remand 95 Misc.2d 492, 407 N.Y.S.2d 954 (1978), where the two executors were actively engaged in self-dealing and the third did nothing. The third was surcharged over six million dollars, removed and denied commissions. The others were surcharged even more.

16. McKinney's EPTL 10–10.7.

17. See, e.g., Matter of Frieman, N.Y. L.J., June 7, 1976, at 12, col. 3 (Kings). See discussion of advice and direction proceedings in chapter on "Miscellaneous Proceedings," supra at 350–53.

Sec. P

1. McKinney's EPTL 11–2.2(a)(1), codifying the common law rule adopted in King v. Talbot, 40 N.Y. 76 (1869). Prior to the enactment of McKinney's EPTL 11–2.2 in its current form in 1970, much stricter investment standards existed. Fiduciaries could invest in items on a "legal list," which consisted of conservative non-risk securities. Occasionally a court will approve an investment that was illegal when made if the accounting occurs after 1970 (that is, under the prudent man rule) and if the investment was in fact prudent. E.g., Matter of McGinty, N.Y.L.J., March 26, 1979, at 40, col. 1 (Bronx) (investment in real estate, though illegal at the time, was in fact prudent under current standards, and in addition all beneficiaries consented).

2. See Matter of Bank of New York, 35 N.Y.2d 512, 364 N.Y.S.2d 164, 323 N.E.2d 700 (1974); Matter of Morgan Guaranty Trust Co., 89 Misc.2d 1088, 396 N.Y.S.2d 781 (New York County 1977).

3. Restatement of Trusts, Second, section 174, states that

> [t]he trustee is under a duty to the beneficiary in administering the trust to exercise such care and skill as a man of ordinary prudence would exercise in dealing with his own property * * *.

4. See Memorandum of State Department of Banking, 1970 McKinney's Sessions Laws 2904:

> The prudent man rule is not a license to speculate. Instead, it applies the ultimate test of prudence to each investment. * * * It is especially in New York, where financial information and advice and competent legal advice are readily available, that fiduciaries should be expected to know or to learn how to invest prudently.

The appellate division in Matter of Newhoff, 107 A.D.2d 417, 486 N.Y.S.2d 956 (2d Dep't 1985), for example, affirmed the Surrogate's holding that the fiduciary's decision to invest a major part of the trust in fairly new Real Estate Investment Trusts (REITS), which were risky, was imprudent, especially when the REITS had not been in existence long enough to allow the trustee to evaluate their performance.

5. Restatement of Trusts, Second, Section 227(a), Comment.

A testator cannot exonerate the fiduciary from the duty of care, diligence and prudence,[6] but he can permit the fiduciary to invest in property which does not meet the prudent man standard. The language, however, must be definite and unambiguous to allow the fiduciary to depart from the prudent man rule,[7] and such language is strictly construed.[8] If fiduciaries invest imprudently, they face one or more of three possible sanctions: removal as fiduciary,[9] surcharge for any losses [10] and denial of commissions.[11]

Whether an investment is prudent is a question of fact; [12] when someone challenges the prudence of a fiduciary's investment, that objectant has the burden of proving it,[13] and the court must consider all the relevant circumstances at the time the fiduciary made the investment,[14] including whether the security was a seasoned one with a history of a productive return over a long period.[15]

6. McKinney's EPTL 11–1.7(a)(1).

7. See Matter of Ridings, 297 N.Y. 417, 79 N.E.2d 735 (1948) (clearly authorized fiduciary to retain any investments). For example, the instrument could permit the fiduciary to invest in non-traditional assets, including "investments that would otherwise be forbidden by the prudent man rule," and then could list the conduct that is acceptable, such as failure to diversify, speculation, favoring some beneficiaries over others.

8. Matter of Ridings, 297 N.Y. 417, 79 N.E.2d 735 (1948). But see Matter of Stillman, 81 Misc.2d 747, 366 N.Y.S.2d 934 (New York County 1975), where the testator instructed the fiduciary to invest as he saw fit, or with the consent of the beneficiaries, and the court construed that to mean that the beneficiaries' consent was needed only if the fiduciary wanted to invest in something other than what was permitted by law (at that time the legal list).

9. Removal of the fiduciary is governed by McKinney's SCPA 711 and discussed this chapter supra at 393–400. See e.g., Matter of Davis, 54 Misc.2d 1065, 284 N.Y.S.2d 414 (New York County 1967), where the court refused to remove the fiduciary for delaying collection of bond interest and its payment to the beneficiary. Such negligence was simply not of the scope necessary for removal.

10. Surcharge is discussed in this chapter infra at 412–13.

11. Courts generally deny commissions in cases where the fiduciary has engaged in fraud or self-dealing or has commingled funds; his behavior must show some bad faith. See Matter of Hildreth, 274 App. Div. 611, 85 N.Y.S.2d 829 (2d Dep't 1949), affirmed 301 N.Y. 705, 95 N.E.2d 54 (1950) (bad faith not established, so court refused to deny commissions). Loss of commissions is discussed in chapter on "Commissions," infra at 436–41.

12. See, e.g., Matter of Fleschner, N.Y. L.J., April 26, 1985, at 13, col. 1 (New York County), where the Surrogate refused to grant summary judgment because of the contested facts.

13. Matter of Barnett, 84 N.Y.S.2d 105 (Kings 1948). See generally Matter of Kane, 98 A.D.2d 851, 470 N.Y.S.2d 823 (3d Dep't 1983), appeal denied 61 N.Y.2d 607, 475 N.Y.S.2d 1025, 463 N.E.2d 1235 (1984), where the fiduciary sold the decedent's real property to the first bidder, a friend of the estate attorney's, without advertising. The court dismissed the objection to that sale because there was no proof that the property had been sold under market value or that the fiduciary could have gotten a better price if he had advertised.

14. Matter of Bank of New York, 35 N.Y.2d 512, 364 N.Y.S.2d 164, 323 N.E.2d 700 (1974).

15. Matter of Hall, 164 N.Y. 196, 58 N.E. 11 (1900); Matter of Newhoff, 107 A.D.2d 417, 486 N.Y.S.2d 956 (2d Dep't 1985); Current Investment Questions and the Prudent Person Rule, 13 Real Prop., Prob., and Trust J. 650.

Historically, the prudent man standard was the same for corporate trustees and individual trustees,[16] but currently, if a fiduciary has special investment skills, he must exercise those skills.[17]

In a trust, the fiduciary's duty is the preservation of the fund and production of a reasonable income, rather than the enrichment of the beneficiary.[18] He must consider the income beneficiaries (that is, consider the amount of income and its character, including the proportion that is tax-exempt) and the remaindermen (that is, consider the amount of principal and its nature).[19] In a guardianship, on the other hand, the child's welfare is the priority, and consequently an investment where the income and principal may be tied up during the child's minority may be imprudent.[20] In an estate, the fiduciary's duties are to marshal assets, pay claims and distribute the estate expeditiously, and the focus of his investments should be to prevent waste. It may, therefore, be imprudent for an executor to invest in six-month or other long-term certificates of deposit unless the will authorizes it or unless he is also testamentary trustee and the invested funds are part of the trust.[21]

Within the framework of the prudent man investment standard, the fiduciary must balance the rights of income beneficiaries with those of the remaindermen. These competing interests will help the fiduciary to determine how and whether to apportion the investments between high-yield or high-growth securities. The fiduciary has to analyze the risks of the security, its marketability and its volatility, as well as the anticipated effects of inflation and taxes.[22] He must also consider whether the fund as a whole has sufficient liquidity to meet expenses,[23] such as taxes (income, estate and generation-skipping) and principal invasions if the trust instrument authorizes them.

16. See Matter of Pate, 84 N.Y.S.2d 853 (New York County 1948), affirmed 276 App.Div. 1008, 95 N.Y.S.2d 903 (1st Dep't 1950), appeal denied 277 A.D.2d 768, 97 N.Y.S.2d 542 (1950); Matter of Flint, 240 App.Div. 217, 269 N.Y.S. 470 (2d Dep't 1934), affirmed sub nom. Matter of Central Hanover Bank and Trust Co., 266 N.Y. 607, 195 N.E. 221 (1935); Laurino, "Investment Responsibility of Professional Trustees," 51 St. John's L.Rev. 717 (1977). But see Midonick, Coping with the Increased Risk of Trust Litigation, Trusts and Estates 10 (October 1980), where former Surrogate Midonick expresses the view that a corporate trustee in fact is subject to a higher standard of prudence because of its expertise.

17. McKinney's EPTL 11–2.2(a), effective Jan. 1, 1986. The Uniform Probate Code, section 7–302, also provides for a higher standard of care for corporate trustees, and the Restatement of Trusts, Second, section 174, states that "if the trustee has or procures his appointment by representing that he has greater skill than a man of ordinary prudence, he is under a duty to exercise such skill."

18. Matter of Young, 249 App.Div. 495, 293 N.Y.S. 97 (2d Dep't 1937), affirmed 274 N.Y. 543, 10 N.E.2d 541 (1937).

19. Matter of Stillman, 107 Misc.2d 102, 433 N.Y.S.2d 701 (New York County 1980).

20. Matter of Ueda, N.Y.L.J., March 12, 1985, at 12, col. 2 (court would not allow guardian to invest in insurance policy under which substantial penalties would result if the guardian withdrew funds in the early years of the contract).

21. See Radigan, Note for Estate Practitioners, N.Y.L.J., Apr. 21, 1980, at 2.

22. For a discussion of investment strategies within the prudent man rule, see Investment Planning during Administration, Estate Planning 227 (July 1985).

23. Matter of Scheuer, 94 Misc.2d 538, 405 N.Y.S.2d 189 (New York County 1978).

The court will consider whether the fiduciary invested an unusually large proportion of the fund in a single type of security,[24] although failure to diversify is not, in itself, an act of imprudence.[25] The courts tend to apply a different (more relaxed) standard when the fiduciary retains assets owned by the decedent, as distinct from those that he acquired,[26] particularly if the will or trust specifically permits retention.[27] Such retention is not exempt from the prudent man rule, however. Even if the will permits a fiduciary to retain assets, he must exercise prudence in doing so.[28] He must consider the marketability of such securities and the strength of the company in making his decision.

If a fiduciary gets the consent of the beneficiaries before making the investment or ratification from them afterwards, the court will not surcharge him,[29] provided the consent was valid.[30] Similarly, if the fiduciary obtained expert advice (from a stockbroker, for example), the court will consider that favorably in its decision on whether an investment was prudent.[31]

A fiduciary is not liable for investment losses simply because his judgment was wrong.[32] The fact that in retrospect the fiduciary's

24. See Matter of Newhoff, 107 A.D.2d 417, 486 N.Y.S.2d 956 (2d Dep't 1985); Durant v. Crowley, 197 App.Div. 540, 189 N.Y.S. 385 (1st Dep't 1921), affirmed 234 N.Y. 581, 138 N.E. 455 (1922); Matter of Silberman, N.Y.L.J., June 17, 1975, at 18, col. 3 (New York County); Restatement of Trusts, Second, section 228.

25. E.g., Matter of Mendleson, 46 Misc. 2d 960, 261 N.Y.S.2d 525 (Albany 1965); Matter of Montant, 72 N.Y.S.2d 318 (New York County 1947), affirmed 274 App.Div. 751, 80 N.Y.S.2d 357 (1st Dep't 1948); Matter of First National Bank, 25 N.Y.S.2d 221 (Sup.Ct. New York County 1941). Compare the Employee Retirement Income Security Act of 1974, Section 404(a)(1), 29 U.S.C.A. § 1104(a)(1)(c), which requires diversification unless that would be clearly imprudent; and New York State Banking Board Regulation 22.60, which requires for common trust funds that not more than ten percent of fund be invested in any one security, except for United States obligations or obligations fully guaranteed by the United States.

26. Matter of Clark, 257 N.Y. 132, 177 N.E. 397 (1931); Matter of Newhoff, 107 Misc.2d 589, 435 N.Y.S.2d 632 (Nassau 1980), affirmed 107 A.D.2d 417, 486 N.Y.S.2d 956 (2d Dep't 1985).

27. See Matter of Kettle, 73 A.D.2d 786, 423 N.Y.S.2d 701 (4th Dep't 1979), appeal after remand 79 A.D.2d 860, 434 N.Y.S.2d 833 (1980), where the testator directed the fiduciary to retain his stock unless a compelling reason arose for selling it. Though no such reason arose and though the stock was a good investment, the fiduciary sold it, citing a good faith business decision to diversify as his reason. The court required him to buy back the stock and to pay the expenses of sale and the legal fees and court costs incurred in the proceeding.

28. See Matter of Hahn, 62 N.Y.2d 821, 477 N.Y.S.2d 604, 466 N.E.2d 144 (1984); Matter of Westerfield, 303 N.Y. 916, 105 N.E.2d 497 (1952); Matter of Hubbell, 302 N.Y. 246, 97 N.E.2d 888 (1951).

29. Vohmann v. Michel, 185 N.Y. 420, 78 N.E. 156 (1906); Matter of Hall, 164 N.Y. 196, 58 N.E. 11 (1900).

30. See Matter of Ryan, 291 N.Y. 376, 52 N.E.2d 909 (1943); Cowee v. Cornell, 75 N.Y. 91 (1878). See also Matter of Newhoff, 107 Misc.2d 589, 435 N.Y.S.2d 632 (Nassau 1980), affirmed 107 A.D.2d 417, 486 N.Y.S.2d 956 (2d Dep't 1985), where the trustee obtained releases without giving the beneficiaries any meaningful information and the court refused to give effect to the releases; accord Matter of Amuso, 18 Misc.2d 936, 187 N.Y.S.2d 519 (Nassau 1959).

31. See Matter of Newhoff, 107 Misc.2d 589, 435 N.Y.S.2d 632 (Nassau 1980), affirmed 107 A.D.2d 417, 486 N.Y.S.2d 956 (2d Dep't 1985); Matter of Berg, N.Y.L.J., Aug. 31, 1976, at 8, col. 3 (New York County).

32. Matter of Bank of New York, 35 N.Y.2d 512, 364 N.Y.S.2d 164, 323 N.E.2d 700 (1974); Matter of Clark, 257 N.Y. 132,

decision caused losses does not, in itself, point to a finding of imprudence.

The usual measure of the loss incurred by the estate because of the fiduciary's wrongful retention of stock and imprudent failure to sell is the value of the stock when it should have been sold (that is, the decrease in its value) plus interest, less the amount actually realized.[33] The measure of damages for the purchase of an imprudent investment is usually what the value of a proper investment would have been, less the present value of the investment made.[34]

The New York Court of Appeals has ruled that when the fiduciary not only acted negligently, but also engaged in self-dealing, the court can surcharge him with appreciation damages, that is, the rise in value of the property from the date of sale to the date of the trial.[35] In addition, in the case of a corporate trustee which used trust funds to attract additional deposits, arguably the trust company should disgorge those profits in favor of the trust even if the trust had no resultant losses.[36]

If the Surrogate rules on the prudence of an investment or the adequacy of the sales price of an asset, the Appellate Division can overturn the Surrogate's ruling only if it was against the weight of the credible evidence.[37]

The fiduciary may be surcharged for the losses incurred because of a single bad investment, even though his investments caused an overall gain to the trust or estate.[38]

117 N.E. 397 (1931). See also Stark v. United States Trust Co., 445 F.Supp. 670 (S.D.N.Y.1978), where the federal court applying New York law refused to surcharge a fiduciary despite substantial losses because the decision to retain the stocks was the result of careful and informed deliberation.

33. Matter of Kellogg, 35 Misc.2d 541, 230 N.Y.S.2d 836 (Erie 1962).

34. Matter of Kellogg, 35 Misc.2d 541, 230 N.Y.S.2d 836 (Erie 1962) (dicta). See also Matter of Newhoff, 107 Misc.2d 589, 435 N.Y.S.2d 632 (Nassau 1980), affirmed 107 A.D.2d 417, 486 N.Y.S.2d 956 (2d Dep't 1985) (surcharge should be measured by the amount invested plus interest from date of investment, less amount received on account of investments); accord, Gould v. Gould, 126 Misc. 54, 213 N.Y.S. 286 (New York County 1925).

35. Matter of Rothko, 43 N.Y.2d 305, 401 N.Y.S.2d 449, 372 N.E.2d 291 (1977), on remand 95 Misc.2d 492, 407 N.Y.S.2d 954 (1978).

36. See Midonick, Coping with the Increased Risk of Trust Litigation, Trusts and Estates 10 (October 1980). But see Securities and Exchange Act of 1934, section 28(e)(1); 15 U.S.C.A. § 78bb (1975), which permits fiduciaries to pay somewhat inflated brokerage fees in return for research services benefiting the trust.

37. E.g., Matter of Kane, 98 A.D.2d 851, 470 N.Y.S.2d 823 (3d Dep't 1983), appeal denied 61 N.Y.2d 607, 475 N.Y.S.2d 1025, 463 N.E.2d 1235 (1984); see also Conti v. Henkel, 60 A.D.2d 678, 400 N.Y.S.2d 27 (3d Dep't 1977), motion for leave to appeal denied 44 N.Y.2d 641, 404 N.Y.S.2d 1025, 376 N.E.2d 205 (1978).

38. Matter of Bank of New York, 35 N.Y.2d 512, 364 N.Y.S.2d 164, 323 N.E.2d 700 (1974). But see Matter of Morgan Guaranty Trust Co., 89 Misc.2d 1088, 1091, 396 N.Y.S.2d 781 (New York County 1977), decided after Bank of New York, where the court held, in a case where the fund showed overall substantial gains but several individual investments showed losses, that "the test to be applied is one of conduct rather than performance as reflected more expressly in the legislative declaration of McKinney's EPTL 11–2.2 (subd. [a], par. [1]). The all-over performance of the common trust fund in this case is a factor

Such investments as artwork, metals, commodities, natural resources and limited partnerships may be permissible if the investment is, under the circumstances, prudent when made. The lack of income or the inferior position of the income beneficiaries will be a factor in any decision on prudence, and it may be an insuperable problem unless the instrument authorizes such investments. In most cases these kinds of investments are not prudent at least for executors and administrators.

Custodians of gifts to minors under the Uniform Gifts to Minors Act may retain any property given to the minor with no liability. Subject to that exception, they must invest within the prudent man guidelines.[39] Case law has interpreted this rule to subject a custodian to liability for losses when he acted in bad faith or with gross negligence.[40]

In practice corporate trustees have systems of approving securities or rating them for purposes of the prudent man rule, with ample documentation to attempt to justify their position. The court still has the power to evaluate the prudence of each investment. Individual trustees should similarly prove that they obtained guidance (from journals and periodicals or from brokers) to aid them in their investment decisions.

SECTION Q. FIDUCIARIES' NEGLIGENCE

In the chapter on fiduciaries' commissions directly following this chapter, we discuss in some detail the kinds of actions that are sufficient grounds for denying a fiduciary commissions.[1] As we mention there, the overlap between denial of commissions and surcharges is enormous, and frequently the court denies commissions and also surcharges the fiduciary, or surcharges him with instructions that he be paid commissions to the extent they exceed the surcharge. The following are some of the situations in which courts have surcharged an executor:

—The fiduciary kept funds uninvested.[2]

—The fiduciary filed tax returns late.[3]

—The fiduciary made a disadvantageous tax election.[4]

to be weighed along with others in reviewing the prudence of individual investments."

39. McKinney's EPTL 7–4.4(e).

40. Matter of Levy, 97 Misc.2d 582, 412 N.Y.S.2d 285 (Nassau 1978).

Sec. Q

1. See chapter on "Commissions," infra at 436–41.

2. E.g., Matter of Welling, 26 Misc.2d 182, 203 N.Y.S.2d 98 (New York County 1960).

3. E.g., Matter of Newhoff, 107 Misc.2d 589, 435 N.Y.S.2d 632 (Nassau 1980), affirmed 107 A.D.2d 589, 486 N.Y.S.2d 956 (2d Dep't 1985).

4. E.g., Matter of Fales, 106 Misc.2d 419, 431 N.Y.S.2d 763 (1980).

—The fiduciary improperly computed and overpaid commissions.[5]

—The fiduciary failed to collect estate or trust assets.[6]

SECTION R. COMMON TRUST FUNDS

The law allows fiduciaries to invest in common trust funds; the intent of this provision was to make available to smaller estates the services of expert corporate fiduciaries and the diversification otherwise available only to larger investors.[1]

Every six years the fiduciaries of the common trust fund must file an account in the Supreme Court or Surrogate's Court.[2] The beneficiaries receive notice by mail and by advertisement.[3] A guardian ad litem is appointed to represent those who have an interest in income.[4] The guardian ad litem's services are similar to those of a guardian ad litem appointed to represent a person under disability in a fiduciary's accounting proceeding. The guardian ad litem reviews the investments to see if they were prudent; he ascertains that administration expenses and attorneys' fees are proper; and he addresses any special relief that may be sought in the proceeding. When the account is judicially settled, that settlement is res judicata against any of the beneficiaries.[5]

In practice the guardian ad litem's task, the evaluation of a corporate trustee's performance in a large diversified fund over a six-year period, is most difficult.[6]

SECTION S. PRINCIPAL AND INCOME

1. GENERAL RULES

When a trustee receives money or other property, he must allocate it to the proper account, either income or principal, and he must also charge expenses against one account or the other. To know how to make these allocations, the fiduciary must know EPTL Article 11's hierarchy. First, the fiduciary must follow the instructions given in the trust instrument.[1] That instrument may set guidelines itself or it

5. E.g., Matter of Smith, 82 N.Y.S.2d 468 (1948).

6. E.g., Cooper v. Jones, 78 A.D.2d 423, 435 N.Y.S.2d 830 (1981); Matter of Kitznes, 109 N.Y.S.2d 673 (1951).

Sec. R

1. See Matter of Central Hanover Bank and Trust Co., 75 N.Y.S.2d 397 (1947), affirmed 274 App.Div. 772, 80 N.Y.S.2d 127 (1948).

2. McKinney's Banking Law § 100(c) (10). The period was four years until amended by L.1975, c. 195, sec. 2.

3. McKinney's Banking L. § 100(c)(12).

4. Under prior law, changed by L.1981, c. 115, § 9, two guardians ad litem were appointed, one to represent those interested in income and one to represent those interested in principal.

5. McKinney's Banking L. § 100(c)(14).

6. See Matter of Jennings, N.Y.L.J., Aug. 8, 1985, at 14, col. 3 (Queens), where Judge Laurino states that "a chore that at one time was awesome [that is, when two guardians ad litem had to review a four-year period] is now downright impossible."

Sec. S

1. McKinney's EPTL 11–2.1(a)(1). See Matter of Pross, 90 Misc.2d 895, 396 N.Y.S.

may give the trustee the discretion to determine where to allocate a receipt or an expense.[2]

Secondly, if the trust does not contain instructions on a particular point, EPTL 11–2.1 governs.[3] Hence a trustee has to follow the rules of the EPTL on principal and income only if the trust instrument does not set different rules, and conversely, if the trust instrument is silent, the trustee's conformity with Article 11's principal and income rules fulfills his obligation in this regard.

Finally, if the trust instrument does not give the trustee a standard to follow, and EPTL 11–2.1 is silent on the allocation of a certain item, the trustee must be guided by what is fair and by what a prudent person would do with the item.[4] Such a standard was applied in one case, for example, to the proceeds of liquidation of non-income producing closely-held businesses held in trust;[5] because they were not covered specifically by the statute, they fell into the "fairness and prudence" clause.

Underlying this set of alternative rules is the general principle that a trustee must administer a trust "with due regard to the respective interests of income beneficiaries and remaindermen."[6] That standard is satisfied if the trustee follows the directive in the trust instrument, and if the trust instrument gives him discretion to allocate a receipt to income or principal or to charge an expense against income or principal, he can exercise that discretion without reference to the EPTL at all. No inference of improper conduct arises simply because he exercises his discretion in a way that is contrary to EPTL 11–2.1.[7]

If the fiduciary violates the "due regard" rule, he may be surcharged.[8]

The rules governing principal and income are always relevant to trustees, and frequently also applicable to executors, who must allocate the income earned during estate administration among the appropriate beneficiaries,[9] and who must also make adjustments in the use of deductions for income tax purposes versus estate tax purposes.

2d 309 (Westchester 1977); Matter of Shoenhair, 34 Misc.2d 884, 229 N.Y.S.2d 517 (New York County 1972).

2. Matter of Grover, 24 Misc.2d 857, 205 N.Y.S.2d 537 (Onondaga 1960).

3. McKinney's EPTL 11–2.1(a)(1)(B).

4. McKinney's EPTL 11–2.1(a)(1)(C).

5. Matter of Grove, 86 A.D.2d 302, 449 N.Y.S.2d 721 (1st Dep't 1982).

6. McKinney's EPTL 11–2.1(a)(1).

7. McKinney's EPTL 11–2.1(a)(2).

8. See discussion of surcharge this chapter supra at 412–13 and in chapter on "Commissions," infra at 436–41.

9. Estate beneficiaries are sometimes entitled to income. McKinney's EPTL 11–2.1(d). A beneficiary of a specific disposition gets the income earned by it, and general beneficiaries of money get income at the rate of three percent beginning seven months after the issuance of letters to a fiduciary, and at the legal rate after the passage of a reasonable time for distribution. Other beneficiaries share in the income in proportion to their respective interests in the assets remaining in the estate at the time of distribution. The income from any real property not disposed of is payable to the residuary beneficiaries pro rata or, if the realty is allocated to a testamentary trust, the income is instead payable to the trustee. McKinney's EPTL 11–2.1(d).

2. INCOME

Income is "the return in money or property derived from the use of principal * * *." [10] It includes the standard types of income such as interest earned on bank accounts, dividends paid on stock, and interest earned on bonds. It also includes rents, amounts received for cancellation of a lease, and amounts received for renewal of a lease.[11] It includes interest on a loan owing to the trust and amounts received in exchange for the right to prepay the loan.[12] It also includes insurance proceeds in the rare instances where there was insurance on the separate interest of an income beneficiary.[13]

In one case a testator created a trust whose income was to be used as "scholarships" which were in effect interest-free loans to deserving students. The court held that when they were repaid, the receipts were income.[14] Had the loans been made from principal, their repayment would have been principal, and had they been interest-paying loans, the interest would be income regardless of the source of the loan.

Receipts from income-producing assets are income [15] even if they had accrued before the transfer of the property to the trust,[16] except that in wills and testamentary trusts, receipts due but not yet paid at the date of death are principal.[17] If the receipts are in the form of periodic payments such as rents, they are deemed to accrue day to day and the portion that accrued up to the date of death is principal,[18] except for corporate distributions and bank dividends. This is not to say, however, that an income beneficiary has a vested interest in the accumulated, unpaid earnings of a corporation.[19]

The estate of a deceased income beneficiary (or the income beneficiary if he survives the termination of the income interest) is entitled to undistributed income and accrued income unless the will or trust says otherwise.[20]

10. McKinney's EPTL 11–2.1(b)(1).

11. McKinney's EPTL 11–2.1(b)(1)(A).

12. McKinney's EPTL 11–2.1(b)(1)(B). Though bonds are analogous to loans by the estate or trust, they are governed not by this section but by McKinney's EPTL 11–2.1(f), discussed this chapter infra at 418.

13. McKinney's EPTL 11–2.1(b)(2)(c).

14. Matter of Vail, 91 Misc.2d 398, 398 N.Y.S.2d 82 (1977).

15. McKinney's EPTL 11–2.1(c)(3).

16. McKinney's EPTL 11–2.1(c)(3).

17. McKinney's EPTL 11–2.1(c)(2)(A). See Matter of Wacht, 32 N.Y.S.2d 871 (1942) for an example of this allocation of receipts.

18. McKinney's EPTL 11–2.1(c)(2)(B).

19. See Matter of Ward, 58 A.D.2d 606, 395 N.Y.S.2d 671 (2d Dep't 1977) (though a corporation is successful, its earnings may never reach the dividend stage or an earned surplus account).

20. McKinney's EPTL 11–2.1(c)(4); see Matter of Watson, 262 N.Y. 284, 186 N.E. 787 (1933) (when trust instrument directed trustee to pay, at life beneficiary's death, all principal and accumulated income to remainderman, and remaindermen were absent at life beneficiary's death, accrued income was payable to deceased income beneficiary's estate); Matter of Bernstein, 94 Misc.2d 898, 405 N.Y.S.2d 958 (New York County 1978) (when will said deceased income beneficiary's share of income was payable to surviving beneficiaries, the accrued income was payable to deceased beneficiary's estate).

a. Corporate Distributions

The general rule on distributions from corporations or associations is that all distributions from them are income, including cash dividends, preferred or guaranteed dividends, options, share distributions, distributions of stock from another corporation or association (or the proceeds of such a distribution), and distributions made from ordinary income of a regulated investment trust or real estate investment trust.[21] The will can of course alter this general rule.[22] The rule is also riddled with exceptions.

When a company makes distributions of cash dividends, that is income.[23] If a corporation declares a stock split or a stock dividend, that receipt of stock is not divided between income and principal, but will be all income or all principal, depending on whether the new stock issued amounted to more than six percent of the shares of the issuing company on which the distribution is made. If it is six percent or less, the whole amount is income. If it is more than six percent, it is all principal.[24] The will or trust instrument can provide for a different rule,[25] but a will which provides for a different rule for "stock dividends" or "stock splits" without specifying a percentage will be con-

21. McKinney's EPTL 11–2.1(e)(9).

22. Matter of Lloyd, 292 N.Y. 280, 54 N.E.2d 825 (1944) (will authorized trustee to treat as income all dividends and all rights to subscribe for additional stock); the will can also provide that "extraordinary" dividends be apportioned to income, and it will then be a question of interpretation whether the receipt is principal or income, depending on its source of payment. See Matter of Muller, 14 A.D.2d 439, 221 N.Y.S.2d 424 (1st Dep't 1961), affirmed 12 N.Y.2d 851, 236 N.Y.S.2d 627, 187 N.E.2d 477 (1962). Sometimes the language of the will is not entirely clear and the court then decides how to allocate the corporate receipt. See, e.g., Matter of Grace, 51 Misc.2d 531, 273 N.Y.S.2d 514 (Nassau 1966), where the will said that "insofar as is permitted by law * * * all unusual or extraordinary cash dividends shall also be considered to be principal." The court evaluated extra dividends which were made from annual earnings in fairly small amounts and determined that, since they were not extraordinary, they were properly credited to income. Similarly, in Matter of Davis, 54 Misc.2d 1065, 284 N.Y.S.2d 414 (New York County 1967), the testator gave his fiduciaries full power to allocate receipts and expenses to income or principal, and the court approved the trustee's deduction of depreciation from income in determining net income for dividend purposes. See also Matter of Fox, 50 Misc.2d 1070, 272 N.Y.S.2d 495 (New York County 1966) (creator of inter vivos trust directed that excess income and creator's reversion be treated the same and become part of creator's estate at the creator's death, and consequently when the excess income was paid over to the executor, he was justified in treating it as corpus).

23. Where the testator stated in his will that all cash dividends were income, but did not refer to distributions from the corporation which were partially return of capital, the fiduciary properly apportioned the distribution between principal and income. Matter of Hart, 32 A.D.2d 961, 303 N.Y.S.2d 82 (2d Dep't 1969), affirmed 27 N.Y.2d 560, 313 N.Y.S.2d 128, 261 N.E.2d 268 (1970).

24. McKinney's EPTL 11–2.1(e)(2). This changes the very unwieldy rule created in Matter of Osbourne, 209 N.Y. 450, 103 N.E. 723 (1913).

25. McKinney's EPTL 11–2.1(e)(3)(C); Matter of Lustig, 59 Misc.2d 901, 300 N.Y.S.2d 880 (Westchester 1969) (two and a half percent stock dividend treated as principal pursuant to instructions in will). See Matter of Smith, 87 Misc.2d 868, 386 N.Y.S.2d 755 (Schenectedy 1976), and Matter of Kelchner, 56 Misc.2d 315, 289 N.Y.S.2d 35 (Westchester 1968), and Matter of Lettis, 54 Misc.2d 681, 283 N.Y.S.2d 252 (Otsego 1967), for discussions of the prospective and retroactive application of this six percent rule.

strued to mean only distributions of six percent or less,[26] and a will which provides that all dividends be applied to income is arguably not broad enough to cover stock dividends.[27]

If the entity is a regulated investment company or real estate investment trust, its distributions from ordinary income are income.[28]

A trustee can rely on the company's statement of the source of the distributions in deciding whether to allocate the receipt to income or principal.[29] If the trustee is initially unsure of the proper allocation, he can in the meantime treat the property received as principal, and if it is later determined to be income, he can then allocate it (or its proceeds) to income.[30] This is to ensure that the trustee can invest the property and make it productive to avoid lost opportunities while he is making a decision on the proper allocation of the property.[31]

Although when a company is liquidated, the distributions to shareholders are usually principal, if the corporation states that part of the distribution is in satisfaction of preferred dividends, that part is income.[32] Similarly, if the liquidation is pursuant to court order and the company indicates that part of the distribution is in lieu of an ordinary cash dividend, that part is income.[33]

If a company gives an option to take a distribution in cash, or in stock, or in an option to buy new shares, whatever the shareholder chooses, it is income.[34] Contrast the corporation's issuance of a right to subscribe to shares in the issuing company or another company, which is principal.[35]

The dispositive date in determining whether something is income or principal is the "accrual" date, which is the date on which the company specifies that shareholders of record are entitled to the

26. McKinney's EPTL 11–2.1(e)(3)(A). Matter of Ward, 58 A.D.2d 606, 395 N.Y.S.2d 671 (2d Dep't 1977).

27. Matter of Kelchner, 56 Misc.2d 315, 289 N.Y.S.2d 35 (Westchester 1968).

28. McKinney's EPTL 11–2.1(e)(7).

29. McKinney's EPTL 11–2.1(e)(10). See, e.g., Matter of Chase Manhattan Bank Trust Investment Funds, N.Y.L.J., Jan. 16, 1980, at 10, col. 6 (New York County) (extraordinary dividends characterized as capital adjustment was allocated to principal).

30. McKinney's EPTL 11–2.1(e)(12).

31. See Matter of Stillman, 82 Misc.2d 736, 371 N.Y.S.2d 78 (New York County 1975), where objectants to the fiduciary's account contested his right to take income commissions on the property which, when received, was subject to a dispute as to whether it was income or principal. The court held that the income commissions should be computed notwithstanding that as of the date of receipt of the property by the trustees, it was allocated to principal pending resolution of where it properly belonged. Thus this temporary allocation does not ultimately affect the fiduciary's right to commissions.

32. McKinney's EPTL 11–2.1(e)(6).

33. Id.

34. McKinney's EPTL 11–2.1(e)(8); Matter of Hurd, 203 Misc. 966, 120 N.Y.S.2d 103 (Rensselaer 1953).

35. McKinney's EPTL 11–2.1(e)(4).

distribution.[36] If the company does not specify, the accrual date is the date of declaration of the distribution.[37]

If a dividend is declared, payable to shareholders of record before the termination of a trust, it is income even if it is not payable until a date after the termination.[38]

b. Bonds

When a bond is issued at a discount and does not pay interest but is payable at a future maturity date in an amount greater than its cost at the time it was issued, the increments in value are income. If it accrues on a regular schedule, the trustee can periodically transfer the accrued amount out of the principal account and pay it to the income account.[39]

All other bonds are simply principal.[40] No reserve need be made of some of the income to make up for the difference in the market value of the bond at the time of the funding of the trust and the lower par or redemption value.[41]

c. Income from Principal Used in Business

A trustee can, with the authorization of the will or trust instrument or with a court order, continue the business of the testator or creator of the trust.[42] If he continues the decedent's sole proprietorship or partnership, the net profits from that business operation are income. Net losses are charged to principal in the year incurred and, for income and principal purposes, cannot be carried over to offset income in any other year.[43]

d. Natural Resources

If a trust or estate owns mineral rights and receives payments when those minerals are removed from the land and sold, the allocation to income or principal depends on the arrangement under which the payments are made.[44] If the receipts are rents on a lease, they are income. If they are production payments, there are two components to the income: first, the receipts are income to the extent the governing instrument so provides, and second, the rest of the receipts are principal in the ratio that the unrecovered costs of the production payment

36. See Matter of Donahue, 78 Misc.2d 923, 357 N.Y.S.2d 777 (New York County 1974), affirmed 48 A.D.2d 815, 370 N.Y.S.2d 67 (1st Dep't 1975), where the decedent died Nov. 1 at 6:30 AM; a previously declared dividend was payable to shareholders of record at close of business on November 1. The dividend, paid on December 1, was part of principal, not income.

37. McKinney's EPTL 11–2.1(e)(11).

38. Matter of Lowry, 39 Misc.2d 591, 241 N.Y.S.2d 703 (Onondaga 1963).

39. McKinney's EPTL 11–2.1(f)(2).

40. McKinney's EPTL 11–2.1(f)(1).

41. McKinney's EPTL 11–2.1(f)(1).

42. See discussion of fiduciaries' powers, this chapter supra at 402–05, and see chapter on "Miscellaneous Proceedings," supra at 354–56.

43. McKinney's EPTL 11–2.1(g).

44. McKinney's EPTL 11–2.1(h)(1).

bears to the balance owed on the production payment, and the rest is income. If not otherwise provided for, receipts will be allocated between principal and income in the same manner as the Internal Revenue Service treats them at the time of receipt.[45]

e. Timber and Other Property Subject to Depletion

If a trust receives payments for the sale of timber, the amount allocable to income will be determined by what is fair to the income beneficiaries and the remaindermen, and the trustee must be governed by what a person of ordinary prudence would do if he were managing his own affairs.[46] Similarly, the trust may contain property subject to depletion, such as patents, copyrights, royalty rights, deferred compensation payments, and leaseholds. If it does, the trustee has to allocate the receipts from that property in a way that maintains a fair balance between income beneficiaries and remaindermen, guided by what a prudent person would do if he were managing his own affairs.[47] In practice this means following the common customs of the marketplace.

The trust instrument may specify the date at which an income beneficiary is entitled to start receiving income. If it does not, that right arises on the date the asset becomes subject to the trust, which, in the case of a testamentary trust, is on the date of the decedent's death.[48]

3. PRINCIPAL

Principal is the property in the trust that earns the income to be paid or accumulated under the terms of the trust instrument. It is the property that ultimately passes to the remaindermen.[49]

Principal includes property received in exchange for principal, the proceeds of sale of principal, the repayment of a loan, a tax refund if the tax was paid out of principal,[50] the refund of principal and the change in the form of principal,[51] the proceeds of condemned property,[52] insurance proceeds on principal,[53] and profits that result from the change in form of principal.[54] Under this definition, capital gains received by an estate are principal when distributed to a legatee.[55]

45. McKinney's EPTL 11–2.1(h)(1)(C); McKinney's EPTL 11–2.1, Practice Commentary at 40 (Supp.1986).

46. McKinney's EPTL 11–2.1(i), incorporating McKinney's EPTL 11–2.1(a)(1)(C).

47. McKinney's EPTL 11–2.1(j), incorporating EPTL 11–2.1(a)(1)(C).

48. McKinney's EPTL 11–2.1(c). See Matter of Osterlof, 74 Misc.2d 877, 343 N.Y.S.2d 896 (Nassau 1973), where the court refused to allow the fiduciaries to set an arbitrary date for the creation of the trust at the time of their first distribution, which would have altered the rights of a beneficiary whose rights were contingent on surviving the creation by five years. The court ruled that the trust was created on the date of decedent's death.

49. McKinney's EPTL 11–2.1(b)(2).

50. Matter of Mendleson, 46 Misc.2d 960, 261 N.Y.S.2d 525 (Albany 1965).

51. McKinney's EPTL 11–2.1(b)(2)(A).

52. McKinney's EPTL 11–2.1(b)(2)(B).

53. McKinney's EPTL 11–2.1(b)(2)(C).

54. McKinney's EPTL 11–2.1(b)(2)(H).

55. Bank of Richmondville v. Graves, 259 App.Div. 4, 18 N.Y.S.2d 133 (3d Dep't 1940), affirmed without opinion 284 N.Y. 671, 30 N.E.2d 720 (1940). See also Simon v. Hoey, 88 F.Supp. 754 (S.D.N.Y.1949), affirmed 180 F.2d 354 (2d Cir.1950), certiora-

Receipts from income-producing assets are income[56] even if they had accrued before the transfer of the property to the trust,[57] except that in wills and testamentary trusts, receipts due but not yet paid at the date of death are principal.[58] If the receipts are in the form of periodic payments such as rents, they are deemed to accrue day to day and the portion that accrued up to the date of death are principal,[59] except for corporate distributions and bank dividends.

a. *Corporate Distributions*

As we discussed earlier in the section on income, if a corporation declares a stock split or a stock dividend, that distribution will be all principal if it is at a rate of more than six percent of the shares of the corporation on which the distribution is made. If the distributed shares represent more than six percent, all the distributed stock is principal. If the distributed stock represents six percent or less, it is all income.[60] The governing instrument can provide for another allocation.[61]

Principal also includes the right to subscribe to shares of the company issuing the right or another corporation, the proceeds of sale of that right,[62] and the stock issued to replace shares after a call-in of stock, a merger, consolidation or reorganization.[63] In a liquidation, cash or other property paid to shareholders is principal unless the corporation allocates part of it to income.[64] Distributions made by a regulated investment company or a real estate investment trust out of any source other than ordinary income, including capital gains, depreciation or depletion, are principal, whether they are paid in cash or options.[65] Capital gains are principal.

We have already discussed the accrual date and the power of the trustee to invest and hold receipts as though they were principal until he ascertains their correct allocation.[66]

b. *Bonds*

As we discussed earlier in the section on income, the entire fair market value ("inventory" value) of bonds is principal,[67] except that the increments in value which occur in the case of discount bonds (issued

ri denied 339 U.S. 966, 70 S.Ct. 1001, 94 L.Ed. 1374 (1950), where the federal court interpreting New York law in the context of a tax question ruled it impermissible to distribute capital gains as income.

56. McKinney's EPTL 11–2.1(c)(3).

57. McKinney's EPTL 11–2.1(c)(3).

58. McKinney's EPTL 11–2.1(c)(2). See Matter of Wacht, 32 N.Y.S.2d 871 (New York County 1942) for an example of this allocation of receipts.

59. McKinney's EPTL 11–2.1(c)(2).

60. McKinney's EPTL 11–2.1(e)(2).

61. McKinney's EPTL 11–2.1(e)(1), (3)(C).

62. McKinney's EPTL 11–2.1(e)(4).

63. McKinney's EPTL 11–2.1(e)(5).

64. McKinney's EPTL 11–2.1(e)(6).

65. McKinney's EPTL 11–2.1(e)(7).

66. See McKinney's EPTL 11–2.1(e)(11), (12), discussed this chapter supra at 417.

67. McKinney's EPTL 11–2.1(f)(1).

below face value with no interest payments and a future maturity date) are allocated to the income account.[68]

c. Natural Resources

As we discussed in the section on income, when a trustee receives cash or other property because the trust owns mineral rights, if the receipts are production payments, the trustee must allocate to income any amount the agreement specifies, and of the balance, a fraction of the receipts is allocated to principal which the unrecovered cost of the production payment bears to the balance owed on the production payment.[69] The trustee must add to the principal any deduction allowed on the federal income tax return. The balance of the receipts are income.

d. Timber and Other Property Subject to Depletion

As we discussed in the section on income, the fiduciary receiving cash or other property from the sale of timber, copyrights, leaseholds, patents or other property subject to depletion must allocate the proceeds between income and principal under the fairness and prudence standards set forth in the statute generally.[70]

4. UNDERPRODUCTIVE PROPERTY

If a trust corpus includes property that does not produce at least an average net income of one percent per year, that property is considered underproductive and the law creates an artificial income component[71] to satisfy the general rule of administering the trust property in a way that maintains an equitable balance between income beneficiaries and remaindermen. The rule does not apply to securities listed on a national exchange or traded over the counter since those securities can easily be sold and the proceeds used to purchase normally productive property. Its usual application is to such assets as unproductive real estate, closely held corporations, certain partnership interests and oil wells.

The rule is that when underproductive property is sold, part of the proceeds will be considered delayed income.[72] That amount will be the difference between the net proceeds and the amount that would have been earned had those proceeds been invested at five percent per year for the period the property was in the trust.[73] The trustee has to subtract from that sum any income the property actually did earn, and add to it any charges against income while the property was under-

68. McKinney's EPTL 11–2.1(f)(2). See Matter of Coulter, 204 Misc. 473, 121 N.Y.S.2d 531 (New York County 1953), affirmed 283 App.Div. 691, 128 N.Y.S.2d 539 (1st Dep't 1954).

69. McKinney's EPTL 11–2.1(h)(1).

70. McKinney's EPTL 11–2.1(i), (j), direct the fiduciary back to McKinney's EPTL 11–2.1(a)(1)(C).

71. McKinney's EPTL 11–2.1(k)(1).

72. McKinney's EPTL 11–2.1(k)(1). See e.g., Matter of Axe, N.Y.L.J., Nov. 8, 1979, at 12, col. 5 (Westchester).

73. McKinney's EPTL 11–2.1(k)(2).

productive. If the income beneficiary had the use of the property, the value of that use will also be subtracted from the amount allocated to income. For example, if a piece of unproductive raw land were held for five years and then sold for $1000, $200 would be paid to the income beneficiary as delayed income. The computation would be as follows: the amount that would, if invested at five percent interest over five years, yield a total of $1000 (principal and interest) is $800, that is:

$1000 divided by [100% + (5% times five years)]

= 1000 divided by 125%

= 800.

If the proceeds of the sale of the underproductive property are realty or other difficult-to-apportion property, the income beneficiary is entitled to the net income from that newly acquired property while the property is held, and not to the "delayed income" portion of the proceeds of that property when it is sold.[74]

The delayed income is considered to have accrued from day to day.[75]

5. CHARGES AGAINST INCOME

Unlike in estates, where all administration costs are charged against principal, in trusts the income account bears the brunt of the day-to-day expenses.[76] Income pays the ordinary expenses incurred in the administration and management of the trust, including income taxes [77] (but not capital gains taxes [78]), other regularly recurring taxes such as school or municipal taxes, insurance premiums, bond premiums, ordinary repairs and interest.[79] Moreover, although principal usually bears the burden of court costs and attorneys' fees in proceed-

74. McKinney's EPTL 11–2.1(k)(4). Strict application of the statute could conceivably cause the following results: Assume two persons are income beneficiaries of underproductive property. In one case the property is sold and part of the proceeds are paid to the income beneficiary as delayed income. In the other the property is sold and the sellers take back a purchase money mortgage, with five annual payments, then a balloon payment in year six. Arguably, that second income beneficiary would get nothing more than the five annual payments.

75. McKinney's EPTL 11–2.1(k)(3).

76. McKinney's EPTL 11–2.1(*l*)(1). See e.g., Matter of Satterwhite, 262 N.Y. 339, 186 N.E. 857 (1933) (where testatrix directed that unproductive property be sold within three years of her death, during that period before the sale the charges and taxes are paid out of income, and from directed date of sale until actual conveyance the carrying charges are paid out of principal). See also Matter of Jackson, 258 N.Y. 281, 179 N.E. 496 (1932) (principal of a trust should not be impaired by carrying charges unless intent of creator is otherwise).

77. See Matter of Mendleson, 46 Misc. 2d 960, 261 N.Y.S.2d 525 (Albany 1965); Matter of Holloway, 68 Misc.2d 361, 327 N.Y.S.2d 865 (1972), where the court directed reimbursement from income into principal of income taxes paid by principal on the "equitable principle that the burden of income taxes should be charged to the account into which the taxes item goes."

78. McKinney's EPTL 11–2.1(*l*)(4)(C). But see Matter of Pross, 90 Misc.2d 895, 396 N.Y.S.2d 309 (Westchester 1977), where the gain to the trust was only a paper gain and the capital gains taxes were therefore apportioned against the persons who actually received the gain.

79. McKinney's EPTL 11–2.1(*l*)(1).

ings relating to the trust,[80] the court has discretion to assess the costs of a proceeding and the attorneys' fees against income if the proceeding relates substantially to income, such as a proceeding to determine the status of an income beneficiary.[81] The trustee can arrange to spread the payments out of the income account over a period of time if the charges are large.[82]

Ordinarily the costs of recurring investment advice is chargeable against income, unless it is advice relating to a specific purchase or sale, in which case principal should bear the cost.[83]

The testator can give the trustee discretion to allocate charges differently.[84]

6. CHARGES AGAINST PRINCIPAL

a. Estates

All expenses of administering an estate are charges against principal. These expenses include debts, attorneys' fees, funeral expenses, commissions (except for commissions on estate income [85]) taxes (and interest and penalties), filing fees, costs of litigation, family allowances under EPTL 5–3.1 and comparable expenditures. The court can deny the award of attorneys' fees out of trust principal if the attorneys' services were for the benefit of particular beneficiaries.[86] In that case the beneficiaries individually should bear them.

b. Trusts

The every-day expenses of running a trust are charged against income.[87] Charges against principal in a trust are those expenditures not chargeable out of income; [88] they relate specifically to principal, such as court costs and attorneys' fees (unless the Surrogate in his discretion charges them against income because the proceeding is peculiarly related to income), the cost of investing principal, and the repayments on the principal of a loan. A good example of the rationing of costs between income and principal is the case where the trust receives real property in unlivable condition. The costs of rehabilitating the property are charges against principal, and the costs of maintaining it afterward are charges against income.[89] The test of whether

80. McKinney's EPTL 11–2.1(*l*)(4).

81. McKinney's EPTL 11–2.1(*l*)(2).

82. McKinney's EPTL 11–2.1(*l*)(3).

83. Matter of Cohen, 67 Misc.2d 447, 323 N.Y.S.2d 721 (New York County 1971).

84. Matter of Lecompte, 52 Misc.2d 549, 276 N.Y.S.2d 208 (New York County 1966).

85. See discussion of commissions in chapter on "Commissions," infra at 425 et seq.

86. Matter of Ward, 58 A.D.2d 606, 395 N.Y.S.2d 671 (2d Dep't 1977) (fees for income beneficiaries' attorneys in final accounting not charged against principal account). See chapter on "Attorneys' Fees," supra at 371–76.

87. McKinney's EPTL 11–2.1(*l*)(1).

88. McKinney's EPTL 11–2.1(*l*)(4)(A).

89. Matter of West, 175 Misc. 1044, 26 N.Y.S.2d 622 (New York County 1941), affirmed 264 App.Div. 701, 34 N.Y.S.2d 405 (1st Dep't 1942), affirmed 264 App.Div. 701, 34 N.Y.S.2d 405 (1st Dep't 1942), affirmed 289 N.Y. 423, 46 N.E.2d 501 (1943), affirmed 321 U.S. 36, 64 S.Ct. 384, 88 L.Ed. 526 (1944). See also Matter of Trimbey, 138 Misc. 662, 247 N.Y.S. 845 (Oneida

the cost of a repair or improvement is chargeable to principal has been said to be whether it is likely to outlast the life estate.[90]

If the will directs that all of the income, including stock dividends, is to be payable to the income beneficiary, the courts can construe the will to mean that the testator wanted all expenses allocated to principal.[91]

1930), for a nice break-down of expenses between income and principal.

90. Matter of Trimbey, 138 Misc. 662, 247 N.Y.S. 845 (Oneida 1930).

91. See Matter of Simmons, 30 Misc.2d 1022, 220 N.Y.S.2d 515 (New York County 1961) (court approved trustee's allocation of capital gains to principal account).

Chapter Fifteen

COMMISSIONS

SECTION A. INTRODUCTION

A fiduciary's commissions are a creature of statute,[1] and they depend on the fiduciary's title; SCPA 2308 and 2309 cover trustees generally, SCPA 2312 covers corporate trustees, and SCPA 2307 covers all fiduciaries who are not trustees, including executors, guardians, administrators, temporary administrators, administrators c.t.a., administrators d.b.n., ancillary fiduciaries other than trustees, and persons with the power to manage an infant's property during minority.[2] Certain other non-trustee fiduciaries are not within SCPA 2307 because specific statutes so provide. For example, the compensation of public administrators is fixed by statute,[3] and voluntary administrators are not compensated.[4] Preliminary executors' commissions are governed by SCPA 2307 if the preliminary executor completes the administration as executor, and are within the court's discretion if he does not.[5] Though the definition does not include conservators, to whom the court can award compensation on a quantum meruit basis,[6] they are typically compensated under SCPA 2307.[7]

The purpose of the statutory commissions provided in Article 23 is to compensate the fiduciary for taking the property under his administration and assuming the risk of personal liability for it.[8] Unless the governing instrument provides otherwise, the fiduciary is entitled to the commissions allowable under the law as it exists when the commissions are awarded, not the commissions allowable when the governing instrument was written or when the fiduciary was appointed.[9]

Sec. A

1. Matter of Nelson, 105 Misc.2d 747, 433 N.Y.S.2d 314 (Westchester 1980) (no inherent common law right to compensation); Matter of Gildersleeve, 75 Misc.2d 207, 347 N.Y.S.2d 96 (Orange 1973) (accord).

2. McKinney's SCPA 103(21).

3. McKinney's SCPA 1105 and 1207.

4. McKinney's SCPA 1307(1), discussed in chapter on "Small Estates," supra at 251.

5. McKinney's SCPA 1412(7).

6. See McKinney's Mental Hygiene L. § 77.27 (1978).

7. Matter of Merrick, 119 Misc.2d 886, 464 N.Y.S.2d 683 (1983); Matter of Huffard, 85 Misc.2d 399.

8. Matter of LoBono, N.Y.L.J., March 21, 1985, at 15, col. 5 (Queens) (no commissions where fiduciary never administered the property nor did his duties in the estate administration); Matter of Tucker, 75 Misc.2d 318, 347 N.Y.S.2d 845 (New York County 1973).

9. Matter of Barker, 230 N.Y. 364, 130 N.E. 579 (1921); Matter of Cullen, 127

If interested parties enter into a contract to pay the fiduciary higher commissions than the statutory rates, they cannot bind the estate by the contract but they can bind themselves personally.[10]

SECTION B. FIDUCIARIES WHO ARE NOT TRUSTEES

1. COMMISSIONS ON PROPERTY RECEIVED AND PAID OUT

The general rule is that executors and administrators [1] are paid commissions for all sums of money and all property they receive and pay out, including the estate assets and income, and additional commissions if they manage and collect rents on real property.[2] The rates are as follows:

5% for receiving and paying out up to $100,000.

4% for receiving and paying out the next $200,000.

3% for receiving and paying out the next $700,000.

2½% for receiving and paying out the next $4,000,000.

2% for receiving and paying out sums above $5,000,000.[3]

One-half the statutory rate is applied to the assets received and the other half to the amounts paid out. If the fiduciary winds up the estate by a formal judicial accounting, he usually takes commissions then,[4] unless he has obtained court approval for advance payments.[5] If he opts to settle the estate informally by receipts and releases, the fiduciary takes his commissions at that time, unless he has requested and received advance payments.

For example, if the fiduciary has received assets valued at $1,175,000 (net) and has paid out assets valued at $1,180,000 (the extra $5,000 representing income or appreciation), the commissions would be computed as follows:

Misc.2d 105, 485 N.Y.S.2d 454 (Suffolk 1985). See Matter of Miller, 99 A.D.2d 780, 471 N.Y.S.2d 877 (2d Dep't 1984), where the court held that the language in the boilerplate provision of the will to the effect that "[a]ll laws referred to in this will shall, unless otherwise indicated, refer to said laws as they exist at the time of my death" included commission rates and allowed the trustees the lower commissions in effect at decedent's death. On remand, Matter of Miller, N.Y.L.J., July 10, 1985, at 13, col. 3 (Nassau), the Surrogate surcharged the fiduciaries the interest on the overpayment and reduced the commissions.

10. Matter of Baehm, 110 Misc.2d 499, 442 N.Y.S.2d 755 (Nassau 1981) (two co-fiduciaries and residuary beneficiary entered into a valid contract agreeing to compute commissions on all property included in the gross estate, and because residuary beneficiary was only party affected, the court enforced the contract.

Sec. B

1. For simplicity, the fiduciaries compensable at 2307 rates (listed in the text in the introductory paragraph to this chapter) will be simply called "executors," "administrators" or "fiduciaries" in this section.

2. McKinney's SCPA 2307(6) discussed shortly.

3. McKinney's SCPA 2307(1).

4. McKinney's SCPA 2307.

5. Advance payments of commissions are governed by McKinney's SCPA 2310 and discussed this chapter infra at 447–49.

For receiving:

2½% on the first $100,000	$ 2,500
2% on the next $200,000	$ 4,000
1½% on the next $700,000	$10,500
1¼% on the next $180,000	$ 2,250
Total receiving commissions:	$19,250

For paying:

2½% on the first $100,000	$ 2,500
2% on the next $200,000	$ 4,000
1½% on the next $700,000	$10,500
1¼% on the next $180,000	$ 2,250
Total paying commissions:	$19,250
Total Commissions:	$38,500

When an asset is commissionable, the commissions are calculated on the net or equity value of the property.[6] Thus, if real property is subject to a mortgage or securities are subject to a lien, the fiduciary will compute commissions only on the net value.

2. MULTIPLE FIDUCIARIES

If two or more fiduciaries are serving, they can each take a full commission, up to three full commissions if there are three or more fiduciaries, if the value of the estate is more than $300,000.[7] If the estate is between $100,000 and $299,999.99, two commissions are allowed, to be divided among the fiduciaries depending on the services they provided, or under an agreement among them, but in no case can a fiduciary take more than one full commission. In the estate of $1,180,000 discussed in the preceding paragraph, each of three fiduciaries could receive $38,500, or if more than three were serving, they could divide three $38,500 commissions ($115,500) among them, as long as no fiduciary received more than $38,500.

3. COMMISSIONS FOR MANAGING REAL PROPERTY

In addition to the receiving and paying commissions, fiduciaries who manage real property can get an additional commission of five percent of the gross rents collected.[8] This permits, to some degree, double commissions on the rents, since their net value is also subject to commissions as property received and paid out.[9] The executor or administrator can retain five percent of the rents collected without waiting for the settlement of the account. Contrary to the rule allowing multiple commissions on assets received and paid out, only one commission for management of real property is allowed even if more than one fiduciary is serving.[10]

6. Matter of Mattis, 55 Misc.2d 511, 285 N.Y.S.2d 551 (New York County 1967).

7. McKinney's SCPA 2307(4).

8. McKinney's SCPA 2307(6).

9. McKinney's SCPA 2307(1).

10. McKinney's SCPA 2307(6).

The fiduciary can also reimburse himself for "reasonable and necessary expenses actually paid," and if the fiduciary is a lawyer and has rendered legal services, reasonable legal fees are allowed in addition to commissions.[11] A fiduciary is expected to do the normal administrative tasks necessary to settle an estate or run a trust, and if he hires someone else to do these tasks he will not be reimbursed for the expense. Where the administration requires extraordinary services, however, the fiduciary may hire an expert to do it and may be reimbursed from the estate or trust.[12]

4. SPECIAL RULES FOR GUARDIANS

A guardian of an infant's property must file an annual accounting of the infant's assets, if he holds those assets alone in his capacity as guardian.[13] He need not file the annual account if he holds the assets jointly with the court clerk or a bank approved by the court,[14] which is the far more common arrangement. In either case, if the guardian received income from the child's property he can take annual commissions on the income received and paid out at the SCPA 2307 rates. At the final accounting the guardian receives the paying commissions on the income he accumulated. If the guardian holds the assets alone and fails to file the account, he does not automatically forfeit commissions; he may take commissions on the judicial accounting if sufficient income is still on hand for the year for which the commissions are claimed. To the extent the income on hand for that year is insufficient, the guardian has waived commissions.[15]

At the end of his guardianship the guardian must file a formal accounting [16] and at that time the guardian is entitled to commissions on the principal of the ward's property received and paid out.

The commissions just discussed are payable to the guardian of the infant's property. The court has the power to award additional compensation to the guardian of the person,[17] whether that is the same person or different. If the court makes such allowance, the guardian of the child's property pays it from the child's funds. The paucity of case law on this topic is probably because the guardian of the person is usually a close relative of the child who does not want compensation for

11. McKinney's SCPA 2307(1).

12. For instance, ordinarily an attorney or fiduciary should do the ordinary accounting work for an estate, but if the services are extraordinary, they may hire an accountant and have the estate pay his fee. Matter of Musil, 254 App.Div. 765, 4 N.Y.S.2d 577 (2d Dep't 1938). See also Matter of Tuttle, 4 N.Y.2d 159, 173 N.Y.S.2d 279, 149 N.E.2d 715 (1958).

13. McKinney's SCPA 1719, discussed in chapter on "Guardianships," supra at 269–71.

14. McKinney's SCPA 1719(5); 1708, discussed in chapter on "Guardianships," supra at 268–69.

15. McKinney's SCPA 2307(4). Receiving commissions are allowed on income received and accumulated. 5th Rep. Temp. Comm'n on Est., Leg. Doc. (1966), No. 19 App. K, p. 136 at 192–95.

16. See chapter on "Accounting," supra at 188.

17. McKinney's SCPA 2307(3).

his services, or is satisfied with the commissions he receives as guardian of the child's property.

5. CUSTODIANS' COMMISSIONS

Custodians of an infant's property under the Uniform Gift to Minors Act are entitled to commissions only if they are also guardians of the minor's property.[18] The rate of such a custodian's compensation depends on whether he was named custodian before or after August 31, 1978.[19] For custodianships created on or before that date, commissions for persons serving as both custodian and guardian of the minor's property are computed under SCPA 2307 as if the custodianship property were guardianship property (that is, annual commissions on income if an annual account is filed, and receiving and paying commissions on principal at the judicial settlement of the account).[20] In practice most custodians neither file annual accounts nor take commissions. For custodianships created on September 1, 1978 or later, the custodian-guardian's commissions are computed under SCPA 2309, discussed shortly, as though the custodianship property were part of a trust created after August 31, 1956 (that is, annual principal commissions and commissions for paying out principal).

SECTION C. TRUSTEES

The commissions allowed to trustees depend on whether the trust was created before or after September 1, 1956.[1]

1. POST-AUGUST 31, 1956 TRUSTS

Trustees of trusts created by will of persons dying after August 31, 1956, and of inter vivos trusts created after August 31, 1956, are entitled to commissions under SCPA 2309.

a. Private (Non-charitable) Trusts

The general rule is that trustees of Post-August 31, 1956 trusts get (i) "one-shot" commissions, generally at the time of accounting, for paying out principal, (that is, money and other property [2] (ii) annual commissions based on the amount of principal in the trust each year,[3] and (iii) additional commissions on gross rentals if they manage or collect the rents on real property.[4]

18. McKinney's EPTL 7-4.5(b).

19. See L.1978, c. 694, § 1.

20. McKinney's SCPA 2307(1); 2307(4); McKinney's EPTL 7-4.5(c).

Sec. C

1. L.1956, c. 931.

2. McKinney's SCPA 2309(1).

3. McKinney's SCPA 2309(2).

4. McKinney's SCPA 2309(1), (2), (7).

i. Commissions for Paying Out Principal

The trustee is allowed commissions at the rate of 1% on all principal paid out.[5] These commissions are usually taken at the accounting unless the fiduciary applies to the court for advance payment.[6]

Properly accumulated income (and the income it earns as well) is subject to commissions when the fiduciary distributes it, at the rate of 2% on the first $2,500 and 1% of all amounts above $2,500. The trustee can retain these commissions at the time he distributes the accumulated income.[7]

ii. Annual Principal Commissions

In addition, the trustee may, subject to conditions discussed below, retain annual principal commissions at the following rates:

$8.50 per $1,000 on the first $400,000;

$4.50 per $1,000 on the next $600,000;

$3.00 per $1,000 on all principal above $1,000,000.[8]

The annual commissions are computed on a twelve-month period that starts from the date of death or the date of the creation (that is, the funding) of an inter vivos trust. The commission rates apply to the value of the principal at the end of the twelve month period, unless the trustee opts for the beginning of the period, an option he must make during the first twelve month period or lose the right to make it.[9] For example, if a trust is created by the will of a decedent dying on January 16, the twelve-month commissions period will end on January 15, unless the trustee has opted for January 16.[10] If the trustee does opt for the beginning of the year valuation, that option sticks, and even successor trustees must use it.[11]

If the amount of principal changes during the year (for example, if principal is distributed or additional principal is received), or if the first or last commissions period is shorter then twelve months, the amount of annual commissions payable will go up or down proportionately.[12] For example, in a March 1 to February 28 commissions period, if the principal on hand on March 1 is $700,000 and the fiduciary properly

5. McKinney's SCPA 2309(1).

6. Advance payments of commissions are discussed this chapter infra at 447–49.

7. McKinney's SCPA 2309(8).

8. McKinney's SCPA 2309(2). Increments of $500 or more are counted as $1,000. Before August 6, 1984, the rates were

$7.00 per $1,000 on the first $300,000

$3.75 per $1,000 on the next $500,000

$2.50 per $1,000 on all principal above $800,000.

The commissions were increased by L.1984, c. 936.

9. McKinney's SCPA 2309(2).

10. The trustee might choose that option to maximize his commissions in a case where the assets' value changed between the two dates.

11. McKinney's SCPA 2309(2).

12. McKinney's SCPA 2309(2).

distributes $250,000 of principal on June 1, the annual principal commissions would be computed as follows:

.0085 × $400,000	$3,400.00
1/4 × (.0045 × 300,000)	$ 337.50
3/4 × (.0045 × 50,000)	$ 168.75
Total annual commissions	$4,006.25

If in the final year of the trust, the trustee distributes all the remaining principal ($450,000) on June 1, his annual commissions for the fiscal year will be computed as follows:

1/4 × (.0085 × 400,000)	$ 850.00
1/4 × (.0045 × 50,000)	$ 56.25
Total annual commissions	$ 916.25

In addition, as we discussed in the preceding section, the trustee would receive 1% of all the principal ($700,000) he paid out.[13]

In computing commissions, the trustee is permitted to use the "presumptive value" of principal assets, that is, their value when received by the trust. He may, in the alternative, use the actual value of the assets [14] at the beginning or end (depending on which option he has chosen) of the commissions period. Thus, if an asset has depreciated in value, the fiduciary can still compute commissions on the higher value unless someone objects. Regardless of which value is used, on the accounting any interested person may dispute the valuation and the commissions claimed or retained. The burden of proof on the issue of valuation is on the person (trustee or person interested) who claims that a value is different from the "presumptive value." [15]

The trustee need not wait until the accounting to take these annual commissions: he may retain them each year if he furnishes two annual statements. The first, called an annual rest, shows the principal assets on hand. The fiduciary must file it no earlier than thirty days before the end of the commissions period.[16] The second is a statement showing all receipts of income and principal during the period, the amount of commissions retained, and the basis for computing them. The fiduciary can file this more often than annually if he chooses. He must give the statements to all current income beneficiaries and to any other persons interested in income or principal who demand them. If a current income beneficiary waives the statements in writing, the trustee is excused from furnishing them unless the beneficiary requests them again.[17]

If the trustee fails to furnish the annual statements, he is not entitled to annual commissions unless the income beneficiary waives the annual statement in writing.

13. McKinney's SCPA 2309(1).

14. McKinney's SCPA 2309(2).

15. McKinney's SCPA 2309(2).

16. McKinney's SCPA 2309(4).

17. McKinney's SCPA 2309(4).

A fiduciary who fails to retain commissions at the time he earns them does not automatically waive them. The annual commissions are payable one-half from principal and one-half from income unless the will provides otherwise,[18] and the trustee who fails to take commissions waives the commissions payable from income if no income remains on hand for the relevant year. Thus, if a trustee neglected to take commissions in 1986, and all income earned by the trust in 1986 was distributed, he is entitled only to the one-half of the annual commissions payable from principal.

iii. Multiple Fiduciaries

If more than one trustee is serving, the same rule of multiple commissions applies as applied to executors and administrators.[19] If the trust corpus is less than $100,000, only one commission is allowed (that is, one annual commission each year and one paying commission) even if more than one trustee is serving.[20] Between $100,000 and $199,999.99, two commissions are allowed, if there are at least two trustees, to be divided among all the trustees according to the services they performed, or by their agreement, as long as no trustee receives more than one full commission.[21] If the trust is $200,000 or above, three commissions are allowed, if there are at least three trustees, to be divided among them.[22]

If the fiduciary distributes or receives money in the course of the year, it is possible that the amount of principal might shift from the one-commission level (under $100,000) to a two- or three-commission level (under $200,000 or $200,000 and over, respectively). If that happens, the two segments of the trust year are treated separately.[23] For example, if the principal of a trust administered by three trustees is $120,000 on March 1, the beginning of the commissions period, and a distribution of $30,000 principal is properly made on June 1, annual commissions on $120,000 for one quarter of the year would be computed ($255),[24] and two such commissions would be allowed, divided among the fiduciaries based on the services they performed or based on their written agreement, provided that no trustee can take more than $255. For the remaining three-quarters of the year, three-quarters of a single annual commission would be allowed ($765),[25] to be divided among the three trustees. The same procedure is used to determine commissions for the trust to which principal is added during the trust year, hurtling the principal value over the next level. For example, if a three-trustee

18. McKinney's SCPA 2309(3).

19. McKinney's SCPA 2309(6). See discussion of commissions payable to multiple executors and administrators, this chapter supra at 427.

20. McKinney's SCPA 2309(6)(a)(i), 2309(6)(b)(i).

21. McKinney's SCPA 2309(6)(a)(ii), 2309(6)(b)(ii).

22. McKinney's SCPA 2309(6)(a), 2309(6)(b).

23. McKinney's SCPA 2309(6)(b)(ii).

24. This figure is computed as follows: 25% × (.0085 × $120,000).

25. This figure is computed as follows: 75% × (.0085 × $120,000).

trust whose principal on March 1 was $150,000 receives a $70,000 addition to principal on June 1, annual commissions on $150,000 for one-quarter of the year would be computed ($318.75),[26] and two such commissions would be divided among the three fiduciaries. For the remaining three-quarters of the year, annual commissions on $220,000 would be computed ($1,320),[27] and three such commissions would be allowed.

iv. Commissions for Managing Real Property

In addition to commissions for paying principal and annual commissions, a trustee who is required to manage and collect rents from real property may retain five percent of gross rents as compensation for those services.[28] Only one such commission is allowed regardless of the number of fiduciaries serving.

b. Charitable Trusts

The statute does not permit either receiving or paying commissions nor annual principal commissions for trusts "created solely for public, religious, charitable, scientific, literary, educational or fraternal uses" [29] because such trusts are typically of long duration and principal invasion would deplete them. The trustee can, however, take annual commissions of six percent of the annual income.[30]

Different rules govern trusts that are partly charitable and partly private. If the trust provides for payment to a private beneficiary for life or a term of years, after which it is solely for charitable uses, the trustee, during the private beneficiary's lifetime (or term as beneficiary), is entitled to the commissions allowed by SCPA 2309 generally, payable out of income and principal, except that he gets no commissions for principal paid out to a charity.[31]

Annual commissions allowed under this section are payable one-half out of income and one-half out of principal, unless the trust is a charitable remainder annuity trust or unitrust,[32] in which case annual commissions are payable from the corpus after allowance for the annuity or unitrust amounts.[33]

If a trustee of a charitable trust is managing and collecting the rents on real property, he includes the net rentals in the income of the trust and receives six percent commissions on them,[34] and in addition, he receives six percent of gross rentals.[35] Only one commission on gross rentals is allowed no matter how many fiduciaries are serving.[36]

26. This figure is computed as follows: 25% × (.0085 × $150,000).

27. This figure is computed as follows: 75% × (.0085 × $220,000).

28. McKinney's SCPA 2309(7).

29. McKinney's SCPA 2309(5)(a).

30. McKinney's SCPA 2309(5)(a).

31. McKinney's SCPA 2309(5)(c).

32. U.S.C.A. § 664; I.R.C. § 664.

33. McKinney's SCPA 2309(3).

34. McKinney's SCPA 2309(5)(a).

35. McKinney's SCPA 2309(7).

36. McKinney's SCPA 2309(7).

2. PRE–SEPTEMBER 1, 1956 TRUSTS

Trustees of trusts created by wills of person dying before September 1, 1956 or of inter vivos trusts created before September 1, 1956, are entitled to commissions under SCPA 2308.

a. Private (Non-charitable) Trusts

The general rule is that trustees of trusts created before September 1, 1956 receive (i) "one-shot" commissions, generally at the time of accounting, for paying out principal, (that is, money and other property) [37] and (ii) annual commissions based on the amount of principal in the trust each year, and (iii) additional commissions on gross rentals if they manage or collect the rents on real property.[38]

i. Commissions for Receiving and Paying Out Principal

Unlike the trustee of the post-August 31, 1956 trusts who receives as commissions one percent of all principal paid out, the trustee of a pre-September 1, 1956 trust is allowed both receiving and paying commissions as follows:

For receiving principal:

3% of the first $2,000

1½% of the next $10,000

1¼% of all amounts above $12,000.[39]

For paying out principal:

1% on all amounts paid out.[40]

ii. Annual Principal Commissions

A trustee is also entitled, subject to conditions noted below, to take annual principal commissions at the following rates, which are the same as the rates for post-August 31, 1956 trustees:

$8.50 per $1,000 on the first $400,000

$4.50 per $1,000 on the next $600,000

$3.00 per $1,000 on all principal above $800,000.[41]

The rules governing pre-September 1, 1956 trusts parallel those governing post-August 31, 1956 trusts, just discussed, in several ways:

The commissions period is twelve months, and valuation of principal occurs at the end of the period, or if the trustee elects, at the beginning of the period.[42] When the size of the principal changes during the commissions period, or when the first or last commissions period is shorter than a year, the commissions are proportionately

37. McKinney's SCPA 2308(10).

38. McKinney's SCPA 2308(1), (7).

39. McKinney's SCPA 2308(1)(a).

40. McKinney's SCPA 2308(1)(b).

41. McKinney's SCPA 2308(2).

42. McKinney's SCPA 2308(2). Under McKinney's SCPA 2308(2), if a trustee was in office before June 1, 1965, the option to use the beginning of the trust period for principal valuation was permitted during the first period ending after June 1, 1965.

increased or reduced.[43] Either "presumptive" or actual values can be used, and interested persons can object to commissions on accounting.[44]

The trustee may retain his annual commissions each year if he files an annual statement,[45] and the commissions are payable one-half out of income and one-half out of principal, unless the will directs that they should be otherwise apportioned.[46]

iii. Multiple Fiduciaries

The rules permitting payment of multiple commissions also track those applicable to other fiduciaries: If the trust is less than $100,000, only one commission is allowed (that is, one annual commission each year, one receiving commission and one paying commission) even if more than one trustee is serving.[47] Between $100,000 and $199,999.99, two commissions are allowed, if there are at least two trustees, to be divided among all the trustees according to the services they performed, or by their agreement, with no trustee receiving more than one full commission.[48] If the trust is $200,000 or above, three commissions are allowed, if there are at least three trustees, to be divided among them.[49]

As in the post-August 31, 1956 trusts just discussed, if the amount of principal changes in the course of the year, the two segments of the commissions period are treated separately for purposes of ascertaining whether one, two, or three commissions are allowable to multiple trustees.[50]

iv. Commissions for Managing Real Property

In addition to commissions for receiving and paying principal and annual commissions, a trustee of a pre-September 1, 1956 trust who is required to manage and collect rents from real property may retain six percent of gross rents as compensation for those services.[51] Only one such commission is allowed regardless of the number of fiduciaries serving.

b. Charitable Trusts

The treatment of pre-September 1, 1956 charitable trusts parallels that of post-August 31, 1956 charitable trusts. The statute does not permit either receiving or paying commissions nor annual principal commissions for trusts created solely for charitable uses.[52] The trustee can, however, take annual commissions of six percent of the income collected each year.[53]

43. McKinney's SCPA 2308(2).

44. McKinney's SCPA 2308(2).

45. McKinney's SCPA 2308(4).

46. McKinney's SCPA 2308(3).

47. McKinney's SCPA 2308(6)(a)(i), 2308(6)(b)(i).

48. McKinney's SCPA 2308(6)(a)(ii), 2308(6)(b)(ii).

49. McKinney's SCPA 2308(6)(a), 2308(6)(b).

50. See discussion of this issue and illustrations, this chapter supra at 432.

51. McKinney's SCPA 2308(7).

52. McKinney's SCPA 2308(5)(b).

53. McKinney's SCPA 2308(5)(a). Before the amendment of this section in 1984, L.1984, c. 936, the rates were seven percent

Different rules are created for trusts that are partly charitable and partly private. If the trust provides for a payment to a private beneficiary for life or a term of years, after which it is solely for charitable uses, the trustee, during the private beneficiary's lifetime (or term as beneficiary) is entitled to the commissions permitted in SCPA 2308 generally, payable out of income and principal, except that he gets no commissions for paying out principal to a charity.[54] Thus, if a trust provides income to X (a non-charity) for life, remainder to St. John's University, during X's life the fiduciary is entitled to commissions for receiving principal and annual principal commissions, and after X's death to commissions of six percent of annual income.

If the trust provides for a charitable use for a term, followed by payment to a non-charitable remainderman, the fiduciary is entitled to six percent commissions during the charitable term and ordinary commissions, that is, principal receiving and paying commissions and annual principal commissions, after the termination of the charitable interest.[55]

If a trust has multiple trustees, a single commission is allowed if the income is less than $4,000, and a maximum of two commissions are allowed if the income is $4,000 or more.[56] The two commissions are divided between or among the beneficiaries in accordance with the services they rendered, or according to their own agreement, provided that no fiduciary may receive more than a full statutory commission. An exception is made for charitable trust created before April 1, 1948, in which case a maximum of three commissions are allowed for trusts whose annual income exceeds $4,000.[57]

If a trustee of a charitable trust is managing and collecting the rents on real property, he includes the net rentals in the income of the trust and receives commissions on them, and in addition, he receives six percent of gross rentals,[58] to be divided among the fiduciaries, no matter how many are serving.

3. INTER VIVOS TRUSTS

The fiduciary's compensation is usually fixed by the terms of the trust. If not, the statutory provisions for testamentary trustees apply.[59]

SECTION D. RIGHT TO RECEIVE COMMISSIONS

SCPA 2307(1), 2308(1) and 2309(1), state that the court must award the statutory commissions to the fiduciary on the settlement of his account. However, the courts have never hesitated to deny or reduce

of the first $2,000 of income and five percent of all income over $2,000.

54. McKinney's SCPA 2308(5)(c).

55. See 4B Warren's Heaton, 418A par. 4 at 75–77.

56. McKinney's SCPA 2308(6)(c).

57. McKinney's SCPA 2308(6)(c).

58. McKinney's SCPA 2308(7).

59. McKinney's CPLR 8005.

commissions for a job poorly done.[1] Often someone raises objections to the payment of commissions on an accounting, and the court evaluates the fiduciary's actions or omissions and their effect on the estate in deciding whether to grant or deny commissions. If the court finds wrongdoing, it has several options. It can remove the fiduciary from office, deny him commissions, or surcharge the fiduciary in order to make the estate whole; it can apply one or all of these sanctions, and several variations. For example, some Surrogates have imposed a surcharge on the fiduciary with a direction that it be satisfied out of the commissions if not satisfied otherwise.[2] Though we treat the issue of the fiduciary's surcharge and removal for wrongdoing in a separate chapter,[3] and the denial of commissions here, in fact the two issues are woven tightly together, and in many cases the court both surcharges the fiduciary and denies commissions.

The decision whether to disallow commissions is within the Surrogate's discretion, and the best that case law can do is to give some guidelines. The fiduciary in all of the following situations was denied commissions:

—The administrator failed to keep records of receipts and disbursements and allowed another person to manage the estate irresponsibly.[4]

—The executor retained property for an unreasonable length of time and sustained a loss on its eventual sale.[5]

—The executor ran up excessive and extravagant administration expenses, including two trips to France, totalling three hundred fifty-three lavish days, charging the estate for chocolates and perfume as well as more traditional administration expenses; and he delayed the administration of the estate, allowing penalties to accrue and losses to occur.[6]

Sec. D

1. See, e.g., Matter of Ganns, N.Y.L.J., Jan. 23, 1985, at 13, col. 4 (Bronx).

2. See text accompanying notes 26–31 infra. The court can also remove the fiduciary from office if he has engaged in any of the misconduct proscribed by McKinney's SCPA 711, discussed in chapter on "Fiduciaries," infra at 393–400. Briefly, they are ineligibility on the grounds listed in McKinney's SCPA 707 (infancy, incompetence, status as a felon or non-domiciliary alien, incompetence because of drunkenness, dishonesty, improvidence or want of understanding), wasting or improperly investing estate assets, refusal to obey a court order, obtaining letters by false suggestion of material fact, refusing to notify the court within thirty days of a change of address, removing assets from the state without court approval.

3. See chapter on "Fiduciaries," infra at 393–400.

4. Matter of Penzato, 200 Misc. 751, 106 N.Y.S.2d 74 (Ulster 1951).

5. Matter of McDonald, 201 Misc. 844, 106 N.Y.S.2d 171 (Bronx 1951) (realty); Matter of Clark, 259 App.Div. 821, 19 N.Y.S.2d 72 (2d Dep't 1940) (bonds); Matter of McIlwaine, 255 App.Div. 978, 8 N.Y.S.2d 1 (2d Dep't 1938), affirmed 280 N.Y. 775, 21 N.E.2d 615 (1939) (margin account); Matter of See, 38 N.Y.S.2d 47 (Westchester 1942) (corporate business).

6. Matter of Ducas, 109 N.Y.S.2d 17 (New York County 1950), affirmed 279 App.Div. 730, 108 N.Y.S.2d 1016 (1st Dep't 1950).

—The administrator paid excessive amounts in funeral bills and waited for three years to sell the decedent's automobile.[7]

—The executor kept no records, did not attempt to resolve disputed claims, made substantial payments to his sister, a beneficiary, without regard to the claims against the estate, failed to petition the court to fix the widow's elective share, and delayed payment even after the court directed him in the course of a compulsory accounting to pay the widow her share.[8]

—The corporate fiduciary retained shares of stock through a long period of depreciation.[9]

—The executor failed to use good faith and reasonable business judgment in obtaining the best price for an estate assets. This led to litigation, and the executor attempted to pay for the appeal out of estate assets.[10]

—The executor let his interest in the residuary estate dominate over his duty to the pre-residuary beneficiaries.[11]

—The executrix failed to keep account of what she had received and paid, promoted unnecessary litigation, pushed unreasonable claims and frequently and unnecessarily changed attorneys during the trial.[12]

—The executor misappropriated funds and failed to account for the profit realized from them.[13]

—The executor failed to deposit estate money in the estate account and to file a timely accounting.[14]

—The executrix knew that the will was fraudulent but offered it for probate.[15]

7. Matter of De Filippis, 113 N.Y.S.2d 724 (Warren 1952).

8. Matter of Welling, 26 Misc.2d 182, 203 N.Y.S.2d 98 (New York County 1960). The court found that the executor had a "cynical disregard for the rights of the beneficiaries," causing loss and expense to them. It allowed the widow six percent interest on her elective share from eighteen months after issuance of letters, which was not only a reasonable time for payment of distributions, but also the time at which the executor had made distributions to his sister, who was also a beneficiary. The interest was payable out of estate income, and, to the extent the income was insufficient, out of the executor's own funds.

9. Matter of Junkersfeld, 244 App.Div. 260, 279 N.Y.S. 481 (2d Dep't 1935). If an executor had held onto stock in the hope that it would appreciate, the court implied that it would not have intervened. In this case there was no such decision; the trust company simply took no action on the stock.

10. Matter of Stevens, 92 N.Y.S.2d 226 (Monroe 1949).

11. Matter of Frame, 245 A.D. 675, 284 N.Y.S. 153 (1935).

12. Stevens v. Melcher, 152 N.Y. 551, 46 N.E. 965 (1879).

13. Cook v. Lowry, 95 N.Y. 103 (1884).

14. Matter of O'Byrne, 65 N.Y.S.2d 417 (Ontario 1946).

15. Matter of Gould, 6 Misc.2d 26, 116 N.Y.S.2d 269 (New York County 1952). The executrix was, however, compensated for services rendered in selling the corporation of which decedent was shareholder. The court's rationale was that those services were unrelated to the fraud and would have been required in any event.

—The executrix placed her own convenience and interests above her duties to the estate beneficiaries, delayed sale of the estate assets, attempted to charge the estate with fines she incurred by violating real property laws, refused to follow the court's directions, delayed liquidating and distributing assets so she could get more income commissions, and refused to account until the court ordered her to do so, and then did so only reluctantly.[16]

—The executor procured execution of the will by fraud and undue influence and then fought it as far as the New York Court of Appeals.[17]

—The executor treated estate assets as his own although other persons were beneficially interested in the estate.[18]

—The attorney-executor paid his own fees from estate funds without getting approval from the court.[19]

—The executor failed to cite the widow of the decedent, though he could have located her by conducting a limited search, and he engaged in an extensive search to find more distant relations.[20]

Undue delay can be a reason for denying commissions even in a case where there is no detriment to the beneficiaries.[21]

A court will deny commissions both to the wrong-doing executors and also to the co-executors who passively sit back and fail to stop the others from wrong-doing.[22] Even an unsophisticated fiduciary is liable for negligence or wrong-doing if it occurs.[23]

Not every mistake or act of negligence by a fiduciary precludes commissions for the fiduciary. The general rule is summed up as follows: [24]

> An executor may be denied commissions for misconduct, breach of trust or mismanagement. * * * In the absence of bad faith, neglect of duty or wanton disregard of rights of persons interested, commissions should not be denied an executor. * * * An executor is not "expected to be infallible in his judgments or decisions. Like all mortals, he is liable to make mistakes." * * * Even if the fiduciary

16. Matter of Geffen, 129 N.Y.S.2d 311 (Kings 1954).

17. Matter of Limberg, 281 N.Y. 463, 24 N.E.2d 127 (1939).

18. Matter of Rees, 277 App.Div. 839, 97 N.Y.S.2d 606 (1st Dep't 1950), modified on other grounds, 302 N.Y. 647, 98 N.E.2d 114 (1951).

19. Matter of Maas, 38 N.Y.S.2d 261 (New York County 1942).

20. Matter of Roberts, 19 A.D.2d 391, 243 N.Y.S.2d 780 (4th Dep't 1963).

21. See, e.g., Matter of Simpson, 61 Misc.2d 307, 305 N.Y.S.2d 339 (New York County 1969).

22. Matter of Rothko, 43 N.Y.2d 305, 401 N.Y.S.2d 449, 372 N.E.2d 291 (1977), on remand 95 Misc.2d 492, 407 N.Y.S.2d 954 (1978).

23. Matter of Junkersfeld, 244 App.Div. 260, 279 N.Y.S. 481 (2d Dep't 1935) (elderly widow with no business experience surcharged and denied commissions). For a discussion of the prudent man rule which governs fiduciaries, see chapter on "Fiduciaries," supra at 407–12.

24. Matter of Kramer, 78 Misc.2d 662, 356 N.Y.S.2d 984 (New York County 1974) (citations omitted).

acted erroneously, if there is no evidence of bad faith, he should not be denied his commission. * * *

If the negligence causes a loss to the estate, the court may require the fiduciary to make the estate whole and to apply his commissions to the surcharge, but may permit the fiduciary to take any commissions left after the surcharge has been paid.[25] The Surrogates applied that solution in each of the following situations:

The executor failed to account for withdrawals from the decedent's bank account.[26]

The administrator had received but not accounted for $760 of the proceeds of sale of the decedent's interest in real property. The court, noting that the records available to the administrator were in very poor shape, allowed commissions in excess of the $760.[27]

The executor was negligent in accepting an inadequate bid for real property.[28]

The fiduciary, who knew of the existence of judgments against the estate, negligently paid out estate assets after the statutory period for filing claims.[29] Though she acted negligently, she believed she was acting properly, so the court allowed her to take the statutory commissions reduced by the surcharge.

The fiduciary paid his own commissions in advance without a court order.[30] When someone objects to the early payment, the courts allow the commissions but surcharge the fiduciary the amount of interest that estate lost because of that payment.[31] If no one objects, the court may waive such interest.

Thus, the rule seems to be that the court will examine the conduct of the fiduciary. If it is grossly negligent, or if the fiduciary acted in

25. If commissions are applied against a surcharge, the fiduciary cannot waive his commissions. Matter of Fewer, 177 Misc. 788, 31 N.Y.S.2d 810 (Kings 1941).

26. Matter of Muller, 183 Misc. 957, 49 N.Y.S.2d 767 (Westchester 1944).

27. Matter of Jackson, 127 N.Y.S.2d 469 (Westchester 1953).

28. Matter of Shurtleff, 206 Misc. 255, 134 N.Y.S.2d 668 (St. Lawrence 1954).

29. Matter of Lukin, 26 Misc.2d 176, 207 N.Y.S.2d 318 (Nassau 1960). Accord, Matter of Spade, 28 A.D.2d 552, 280 N.Y.S.2d 205 (2d Dep't 1967) (overpayment of federal and state income taxes); Matter of Berg, 91 Misc.2d 939, 398 N.Y.S.2d 948 (New York County 1977) (negligent prepayment of widow's share); Matter of Cohen, 98 N.Y.S.2d 883 (Rockland 1950) (mistaken application by widow for letters of administration when the decedent had in fact died testate). Occasionally a court finds a mistake understandable on the ground that the will was ambiguous, and allows commissions despite the mistake. See Matter of Kramer, 78 Misc.2d 662, 356 N.Y.S.2d 984 (New York County 1974), where a will construction was eventually required to resolve the issue of tax apportionment, and the court awarded the fiduciary commissions despite the mistake he had made in apportioning taxes.

30. Matter of Benneche, N.Y.L.J., April 19, 1985, at 17, col. 6 (Westchester).

31. See Matter of Sealy, N.Y.L.J., June 19, 1985, at 12, col. 2 (Suffolk); Matter of Mattes, 12 Misc.2d 502, 172 N.Y.S.2d 303 (1958). But see Matter of Schmitt, 69 Misc.2d 1021, 319 N.Y.S.2d 869 (Nassau 1971), where the court denied commissions but did not charge the executor interest, since the executor, an attorney, did not charge legal fees for probate. The court found this waiver to be a generous act. See also Matter of Crippen, 32 Misc.2d 1019, 224 N.Y.S.2d 116 (1962).

bad faith, the court will deny commissions even if the estate did not sustain a loss. If, however, the fiduciary made a simple mistake, the court will generally require that the fiduciary reimburse the estate for any loss but will usually allow commissions. If the amount of the surcharge exceeds the commissions, the fiduciary will not get commissions but if the surcharge is less than the statutory commissions, the fiduciary can take the difference.

SECTION E. PROPERTY INCLUDED IN THE COMMISSION BASE

Whether a fiduciary is an executor or a testamentary trustee, the general rule is that he is permitted commissions on property only if he actually receives the property and pays it out. Thus the real issue in a discussion of the kinds of property subject to commissions is whether the fiduciary actually "receives" the property. Under the case law, specific bequests and real property pass directly to the beneficiary; the fiduciary does not receive them. Nor does the fiduciary receive property that passes by operation of law, such as joint bank accounts, jointly owned property with right of survivorship, Totten Trusts, "exempt property" [1] insurance policies and pension plans not payable to the estate, and consequently those assets are outside the commission base.

This section will discuss these general rules and their exceptions.

1. RULES FOR REAL PROPERTY

Although the statutes expressly permit commissions on the value of any property received or distributed by the fiduciary [2] and the word "property" includes both real and personal property,[3] case law has generally held that the fiduciary does not receive real property and consequently it is not part of the base for computing commissions,[4] unless it is sold.[5] Fiduciaries always have the power to sell realty, unless the will prohibits it,[6] but that power does not confer the right to

Sec. E

1. Exempt property is governed by McKinney's EPTL 5-1.3 and discussed in chapter on "Miscellaneous Proceedings," supra at 329–31.

2. McKinney's SCPA 2307, 2308, 2309.

3. McKinney's SCPA 103(41).

4. An early New York Court of Appeals case held that McKinney's SCPA 2307's predecessor, in conjunction with 103(41)'s predecessor, authorized commissions on real property. Matter of Barker, 230 N.Y. 364, 130 N.E. 579 (1921). A later case, Matter of Salomon, 252 N.Y. 381, 383–84, 169 N.E. 616 (1930), held that the executors were not entitled to commissions "because they had not received, distributed or delivered the real property in question. Title to it vested in the [legatee] by operation of law without any act on the part of the executors." This was true even though the will said that for purposes of the payment of legacies, the realty should be considered personal property. Myriad other cases are in accord with Salomon. See, e.g., Matter of Phelps, 79 Misc.2d 99, 359 N.Y.S.2d 614 (Westchester 1974); Matter of Smith, 62 Misc.2d 537, 308 N.Y.S.2d 980 (Erie 1970); Matter of Harriott, 32 Misc.2d 437, 222 N.Y.S.2d 587 (Nassau 1961).

5. See, e.g., Matter of Hildreth, 274 App.Div. 611, 85 N.Y.S.2d 829 (2d Dep't 1949), affirmed 301 N.Y. 705, 95 N.E.2d 54 (1940); Matter of Schaich, 55 A.D.2d 914, 391 N.Y.S.2d 135 (2d Dep't 1977), appeal denied 42 N.Y.2d 802, 397 N.Y.S.2d 1026, 366 N.E.2d 293 (1977).

6. McKinney's EPTL 11-1.1(b)(5)(B).

take commissions; the rule is that the fiduciary must actually have sold the property.[7] The commissions are then on the proceeds of sale, which he does receive, and not on the real property. Thus, when the executor had to sell the realty to pay debts of the decedent, commissions are allowed.[8] Similarly, when real property is part of the residuary estate and the executor sells it to one of the estate beneficiaries, he is entitled to commissions on the sales price.[9]

In some cases, the "no sale, no commission" rule is strictly construed. For example, in one the executor tried to sell the real property, but was unsuccessful, and finally distributed it in kind to the beneficiary. The court denied commissions.[10] In another case [11] the executors had the right to sell the property and refrained from doing so at the request of the beneficiaries. Although the executors had performed many duties in connection with managing the property, and although they refrained from exercising their power of sale, commissions were denied, except for the five percent management commissions.[12] Similarly, in another case [13] the court had ordered distribution in kind pursuant to SCPA 2216, which permits the court to direct the conveyance of any unsold realty to a person entitled to payment or distribution in lieu of the money value of the property at the fair market value at the date of distribution. The court denied commissions on the real property because the fiduciary had not sold it, albeit he refrained from doing so because of the court order of distribution.[14]

In many other cases, however, Surrogates have relaxed the "no sale, no commission" rule, and awarded commissions to an executor

7. See Matter of Alcott, 36 Misc.2d 264, 232 N.Y.S.2d 371 (Ontario 1962); Matter of Woods, 251 App.Div. 141, 295 N.Y.S. 718 (4th Dep't 1937).

8. Matter of Ryan, 45 N.Y.S.2d 227 (Bronx 1943).

9. See Matter of Robord, 69 Misc.2d 1026, 332 N.Y.S.2d 698 (Broome 1972), where the will permitted the residuary legatees to purchase a cottage which was part of the residuary estate if either of them desired to live in it; the court found that this arrangement had more characteristics of a sale than of a specific devise, and allowed commissions; Matter of Condax, 11 Misc.2d 819, 173 N.Y.S.2d 108 (New York County 1958) ("sale" was the result of a settlement of a partition action).

10. Matter of Tenney, N.Y.L.J., June 20, 1973, at 20, col. 6 (Suffolk). See also Matter of Saphir, 73 Misc.2d 907, 343 N.Y.S.2d 20 (Kings 1973). There the testator had owned income-producing property of which he gave a life estate in one-third to the widow for life, the remainder to the son. The remaining two-thirds was put in trust for the sister's benefit, income payable to the sister, remainder to the son at age 35. The real property could not be sold according to the terms of the will. When the son turned 35, the Surrogate ordered distribution of the property to the son with a mortgage that would pay the mother's life estate. The executor wanted to receive commissions on the ground that the Surrogate had signed an order denying him the right to sell the property. The court denied commissions because the property was not sold.

11. Matter of Paddison, 53 Misc.2d 2, 277 N.Y.S.2d 599 (Nassau 1967).

12. The five percent commissions for managing real property are allowed by McKinney's SCPA 2307(6) and 2309(7) and discussed this chapter supra at 427, 433.

13. Matter of Schaich, 55 A.D.2d 914, 391 N.Y.S.2d 135 (2d Dep't 1977).

14. The legislature in 1914 suggested a provision that real property "distributed without sale, at the election of a devisee, legatee or distributee, or pursuant to a consent filed, shall be considered as money in making the computation of commissions." It was not, however, enacted.

who did not sell the real property if he performed certain executorial duties in connection with it. For example, when a decedent left all real and personal property to the beneficiaries in equal shares and they decided that one would take all the realty in satisfaction of his share, the court allowed the executor, who executed the instruments necessary to make this transfer, commissions for receiving and paying out the realty.[15] Sometimes the executorial duties are fairly minimal; in one case [16] the executor needed money to pay debts and expenses, and could have sold the real property to do so, which would have entitled him to commissions. Instead, he decided to use the income the real property earned to pay debts and expenses of the estate, and then distribute the real property. The court allowed commissions on the theory that he would have been entitled to them if he had sold the real property and the result should be the same though he had used a different procedure.

Similarly, in another case [17] the bulk of the gross estate was real property. The executors had the choice of selling the property or dividing it between two trusts, and they chose the latter option. To do so they had to take possession of the property, arrange for payment of taxes, pay the debts and expenses since there were not sufficient other assets to make the payments, and make provisions to satisfy obligations toward all beneficiaries. They also assumed personal liability for the property during the time they held it. The court permitted commissions on the real property.

In a case where the decedent had commenced a partition action before his death and the executors continued it, eventually reaching a settlement under which a share of the real property was allocated to the estate, the court allowed the executors commissions on its value, though the property had not been sold.[18] On the other hand, an agreement among the devisees of realty to partition it does not make it part of the commission base.[19]

If real property is damaged by fire after the decedent's death and the executor receives the insurance, repairs the property and then sells it, he is entitled to commissions only on the sale proceeds, not additionally on the insurance proceeds.[20]

15. Matter of Kennedy, 133 Misc. 904, 234 N.Y.S. 734 (Saratoga 1929) (beneficiaries entered into agreement to take their shares in kind; fiduciary executed contracts to effectuate the will and the agreement).

16. Matter of Robinson, N.Y.L.J., June 30, 1978, at 19, col. 3 (Westchester).

17. Matter of Tucker, 75 Misc.2d 318, 347 N.Y.S.2d 845 (New York County 1973). The court in Tucker said that the rules enacted in Article 23 represented an attempt on the part of the legislature properly to value the services rendered by the fiduciary and at the same time minimize the expense to the estate.

18. Matter of Condax, 11 Misc.2d 819, 173 N.Y.S.2d 108 (New York County 1958).

19. Matter of Ross, 33 Misc. 163, 68 N.Y.S. 373 (New York County 1900). The court held that the executors had not received the property and that the devisees could not by an agreement with the executors increase the commissions beyond what the law prescribed.

20. Matter of Del Sordo, N.Y.L.J., June 13, 1978, at 12, col. 6 (Queens).

If under the terms of a will, title to realty vests in the executor, he is entitled to commissions on distribution. For example, in one case the testator specifically instructed his executors to convey the stock of his corporation that owned real estate to his trustees. On the liquidation of the corporation, the executors were vested with title to the real property, and they conveyed it to the trustees. The court held that they were entitled to commissions.[21]

This does not mean, necessarily, that an executor has "received" real property simply because his testator leaves the property to his executor under the will. Rather, his executorial duties will determine whether commissions are permitted on the realty or not. That is, the court will not allow commissions unless the executor has to take charge of the property, pay taxes, care for it and arrange for its distribution.[22]

2. RULES FOR SPECIFIC BEQUESTS

The general rule is that a fiduciary is not entitled to commissions on property specifically bequeathed to a beneficiary.[23] For example, a bequest of "all my interest in an agency account" was held to be specific and no commissions were allowed.[24]

However, just as exceptions are made for commissions on real property where the executor had to perform some executorial duties relating to the property, courts have allowed commissions to executors who have any active duty to perform in the collection or distribution of specific bequests, even more liberally than they have in the case of unsold realty.

Such duties may include dividing up property among the beneficiaries,[25] selling mortgages on the specifically bequeathed property,[26]

21. Matter of Rosenblum, 10 Misc.2d 1014, 171 N.Y.S.2d 619 (Kings 1958).

22. Compare Matter of Rich, 27 Misc.2d 364, 211 N.Y.S.2d 68 (New York County 1960) (executor not entitled to commissions on unsold realty) with Matter of Tucker, 75 Misc.2d 318, 347 N.Y.S.2d 845 (New York County 1973) (executors entitled to statutory commissions on value of realty which at their discretion they conveyed to themselves as trustees).

23. McKinney's SCPA 2307(2). See, e.g., Schenck v. Dart, 22 N.Y. 420 (1860) (executor not entitled to commissions on stock specially bequeathed); Matter of Volckening, N.Y.L.J., August 13, 1973, at 11, col. 4 (Kings), where the decedent made a specific bequest of his family corporation to his family and no commissions were allowed.

24. Matter of Povlsen, 62 Misc.2d 239, 308 N.Y.S.2d 168 (Kings 1970). See also Matter of Volckening, N.Y.L.J., August 13, 1973, at 11, col. 4 (Kings) (testator made specific bequest of family corporation and no commissions were allowed).

25. See Matter of Lane, 55 Misc.2d 88, 284 N.Y.S.2d 371 (Broome 1967), where the executor had to divide bank accounts among beneficiaries; Matter of Kuker, 22 Misc.2d 63, 192 N.Y.S.2d 1014 (New York County 1959) (executor granted compensation when will imposed active duties on the executor regarding assets); Matter of Brooks, 119 Misc. 738, 197 N.Y.S. 637 (New York County 1922), affirmed 212 App.Div. 868, 208 N.Y.S. 837 (1st Dep't 1925), where a specific bequest of clothing and furs to be divided among three beneficiaries was held to be subject to commissions; Matter of Roth, 53 Misc.2d 1066, 281 N.Y.S.2d 225 (New York County 1967), modified 29 A.D.2d 941, 289 N.Y.S.2d 575 (1st Dep't 1968). Significantly, in Roth the will had specifically excluded commissions on specific legacies, but the court said the executor had received stock and divided it, and

26. See note 26 on page 445.

and paying taxes out of the specific bequests because the residuary estate is insufficient.[27]

Even if specific legacies abate because there are insufficient assets in the estate, it has been held that if executorial duties are performed, commissions are allowed to the extent the bequests abate.[28]

The line between specific and general legacies is not always clear, and their characterization will sometimes determine whether or not commissions are awarded on them.[29] For example, one testator had three bank accounts, one in trust for X. His will noted that X had died and bequeathed the account to Y, and provided that if the account contained less than $500, Y was to receive $500. The court found this to be a general bequest of $500, subject to commissions.[30]

The rule that no commissions are available on property specifically bequeathed does not apply to trustees because the gift is given to the trustee who must manage, administer, sell or distribute the property.[31]

3. COMMISSIONS ON PROCEEDS OF WRONGFUL DEATH ACTION

In wrongful death actions, the court fixes the commissions at the SCPA 2307 rates on the basis of the net recovery after payment of expenses.[32] Commissions on the recovery from a personal injury cause of action are also computed under SCPA 2307 but they are based on the full amount of the recovery since the recovery is part of the estate. The wrongful death recovery is not part of the estate; it is the property of the distributees, created by statute, and the legislature decided to allow commissions only on the net recovery.

4. COMMISSIONS ON PROPERTY ENCUMBERED BY DEBTS OR MORTGAGES

When computing commissions, the fiduciary uses the net value of the property received and paid out, deducting mortgages and liens.[33]

because that was a typical executorial duty, he was entitled to commissions on its value. See also Matter of Doehla, 104 Misc.2d 176, 427 N.Y.S.2d 718 (Nassau 1980) (executor entitled to commissions on stock when will imposed responsibility on executor to determine if stock should be sold or distributed in kind).

26. Matter of Cannavo, 59 Misc.2d 889, 300 N.Y.S.2d 731 (Westchester 1969).

27. Matter of Doehla, 104 Misc.2d 176, 427 N.Y.S.2d 718 (Nassau 1980) (executor entitled to commissions on stock when will imposes on executor responsibility to determine if stock should be sold or distributed in kind); Matter of Weil, N.Y.L.J., June 29, 1973, at 13, col. 2 (Kings).

28. See Matter of Lewis, 115 N.Y.S.2d 791 (Queens 1952).

29. As one Surrogate phrased it, "[S]ome specific legacies and devises are more specific than others." Matter of Lane, 55 Misc.2d 88, 284 N.Y.S.2d 371 (Broome 1967).

30. Matter of Lane, 55 Misc.2d 88, 284 N.Y.S.2d 371 (Broome 1967).

31. See Matter of Schwartz, 73 N.Y.S.2d 756 (New York County 1946); Matter of Walker, 53 N.Y.S.2d 102 (New York County 1944).

32. McKinney's EPTL 5–4.4(b). See chapter on "Wrongful Death," infra at 527 et seq.

33. Matter of Mercantile Trust Co., 210 N.Y. 83, 103 N.E. 884 (1913); Matter of Mann, 41 A.D.2d 861, 342 N.Y.S.2d 617 (3d Dep't 1973), appeal denied 33 N.Y.2d 517, 348 N.Y.S.2d 1028, 303 N.E.2d 709 (1973) (decedent pledged collateral from broker-

5. COMMISSIONS ON PROPERTY PASSING OUTSIDE THE WILL

If a decedent owned joint property, Totten Trusts, life insurance pensions or other non-probate property, the fiduciary normally does not take commissions on it, on the theory that those assets pass directly to the beneficiary and the fiduciary does not receive them.[34]

Withheld income taxes, though they pass outside the estate, are included in the base for commissions purposes.[35]

6. COMMISSIONS ON RECEIPTS FROM DECEDENT'S BUSINESS

A fiduciary may be authorized to continue a decedent's business either because the decedent authorized it in the will or because the court directed it in the best interest of the estate.[36] If the executor continues the business without authorization either by the terms of the will or by court order, no commissions are allowed.[37] If the fiduciary continues the decedent's business properly, he is entitled to commissions only on the net profits, not on all receipts and disbursements.[38] Thus, no commissions are allowed for a business operating at a loss.[39]

If the decedent entered into a buy-sell agreement with his partners, and the proceeds are payable to the estate, they are commissionable.[40]

SECTION F. TIME TO TAKE COMMISSIONS

1. GENERAL RULE

a. Trustees

The trustee of a testamentary trust may, and usually does, take his principal receiving and paying commissions at the settlement of the

age accounts to secure debts, and the pledged shares were not part of the commission base).

34. Matter of McEntee, 82 Misc.2d 580, 372 N.Y.S.2d 532 (Nassau 1975); Matter of Roese, 36 Misc.2d 643, 232 N.Y.S.2d 592 (Westchester 1962); Matter of Rosenblum, 10 Misc.2d 1014, 171 N.Y.S.2d 619 (Kings 1958). See Matter of Reich, 94 Misc.2d 319, 404 N.Y.S.2d 781 (Sup.Ct. New York County 1978) (no commissions were allowed to a conservator who took Totten Trust passbooks into his possession, for he did not have to invade the accounts for the conservatee's benefit).

35. McKinney's SCPA 2307(2).

36. Continuation of a business is discussed in chapter on "Miscellaneous Proceedings," supra at 354–56.

37. Matter of Ferrante, 190 Misc. 788, 74 N.Y.S.2d 778 (Bronx 1947).

38. Beard v. Beard, 140 N.Y. 260, 35 N.E. 488 (1893).

39. Matter of Bates, 167 Misc. 641, 4 N.Y.S.2d 444 (New York County 1938), reversed on other grounds 255 App.Div. 615, 8 N.Y.S.2d 548 (1st Dep't 1938).

40. See Matter of Langbein, N.Y.L.J., March 8, 1972, at 20, col. 4 (Kings), where a long litigation ensued because the guardian ad litem objected to the buy-sell agreement between the decedent and his partners. The case was settled. The settlement was paid to the executor who was the last surviving partner and commissions were allowed on the amount added to the estate.

account.[1] If he wants advance payment of these commissions, he must start a special proceeding, discussed presently, for that purpose.[2]

As we discussed earlier in this chapter, trustees of testamentary trusts can simply retain annual commissions if they furnish two annual statements to current income beneficiaries who have not waived the statements and to other persons interested in the trust who demand the statements.[3] If a trustee fails to take his annual commissions during a trust year, he may still take his annual commissions payable from income to the extent income from the year the trustee failed to take commissions remains in the trust.[4]

Unless the trust instrument provides otherwise, the law governing the commissions of inter vivos trustees is the same as that governing testamentary trustees.[5]

b. Guardians

A guardian who receives income and pays it out is entitled to retain annual commissions on that income if he files an annual account of receipts and disbursements or holds the guardianship assets jointly with the court or a court-approved depository.[6] If he fails to file the account in any year, he may still get income commissions for that year upon the final settlement of his account if sufficient incomc from that year remains on hand.

c. Executors and Other Fiduciaries

A fiduciary other than a trustee usually receives commissions at the settlement of his account.[7] If he wants advance payments of commissions, he may commence a special proceeding for that purpose.[8]

2. ADVANCE PAYMENT OF COMMISSIONS

Often the payment of commissions in a lump sum at the final accounting is disadvantageous for the estate and the fiduciary. Consequently, two statutes allow advance payment of commissions. SCPA 2310 permits advance payment on service of process to all persons whose interests would be affected by the payment. SCPA 2311 permits advance payments without notice. Since SCPA 2311 is the far more often employed of the two statutes, we discuss it first.

Sec. F

1. McKinney's SCPA 2308(1) (pre-September 1, 1956 decedent); McKinney's SCPA 2309(1) (post-August 31, 1956 decedent).

2. McKinney's SCPA 2310, 2311.

3. McKinney's SCPA 2308(4); McKinney's SCPA 2309(4), discussed in sections on "Post-August 31, 1956 Trusts," supra at 429–33, and "Pre-September 1, 1956 Trusts," supra at 434–36.

4. McKinney's SCPA 2308(4); McKinney's SCPA 2309(4).

5. McKinney's CPLR 8004.

6. McKinney's SCPA 2307(4), discussed in section on "Special Rules for Guardians," this chapter supra at 428–29.

7. McKinney's SCPA 2307(1).

8. McKinney's SCPA 2310; McKinney's SCPA 2311.

a. Ex Parte Application for Advance Payment of Commissions

If paying the commissions in a lump sum on final accounting would have bad income tax consequences either for the fiduciary or the estate,[9] or would cause hardship or inconvenience,[10] the fiduciary may periodically apply to the court for the commissions he has earned to the date of the application. The court can, without notice to the interested parties, use its discretion in awarding commissions but cannot award more than the receiving commissions unless all interested persons are competent adults who have consented.[11] Even without the adverse tax consequences, hardship or inconvenience, the fiduciary can make this application if all the parties are adult and competent and they consent.

If the court allows commissions, the interested parties can object to them on the accounting, and the fiduciary has to file a bond to secure their return if they are eventually disallowed, except in the following circumstances:

(i) if the fiduciary already filed a bond, or

(ii) if it is a corporate fiduciary, or

(iii) if all persons affected by the payments are competent adults and consent to the waiver of a bond, or

(iv) if the will dispenses with a bond.

The court uses its discretion in apportioning the expenses of filing this ex parte application between the fiduciary and the estate according to the benefits derived from the advance payment.[12]

b. Advance Payment of Commissions on Notice

A fiduciary has, under SCPA 2310, another vehicle to get advance payment of commissions. Fiduciaries can use the SCPA 2310 proceeding either when the ex parte application of SCPA 2311 is inappropriate or when the fiduciary wants a binding award of commissions not attackable on the final accounting. In fact they use this proceeding rarely because they must bear its full costs.

Under SCPA 2310, the fiduciary requests the commissions he has earned to the date of the application. The petition must show "the facts upon which the application is founded," that is, the reason for the advance payment.[13] The petitioner submits the citation, the court issues it, and the fiduciary arranges for its service on the persons affected by the proposed payment. The citation orders those persons to show cause why the commissions should not be paid.[14]

The court has discretion to grant any amount of commissions that does not exceed the receiving commissions owing to the fiduciary, or more if all persons affected by the payment are competent adults who

9. McKinney's SCPA 2311(1).

10. McKinney's SCPA 2311(1).

11. McKinney's SCPA 2311(2), (3).

12. McKinney's SCPA 2311(4).

13. McKinney's SCPA 2310(1).

14. McKinney's SCPA 2310(2).

consent.[15] The petitioning fiduciary must file a bond if advance commissions are paid, subject to the same exceptions that apply to the ex parte application for advance payment of commissions: no bond is necessary if the fiduciary has already filed a bond or is a corporate fiduciary, or if the will dispenses with a bond, or if all persons affected are competent adults who consent to the advance payments.[16]

The fiduciary receiving advance payment bears the costs of the proceeding, whether the court grants or denies the petition.[17]

A fiduciary who takes unauthorized advance commissions risks being charged with interest from the date of the taking.[18]

SECTION G. SUCCESSIVE FIDUCIARIES

Two situations can arise in which administration of an estate or a trust is split between two fiduciaries. The first occurs when the same person serves under two different types of letters. A person may initially be appointed temporary administrator and later become administrator or executor; he may be named preliminary executor and later be appointed executor, or he may become administrator and later, when a will is found, be appointed executor. Where successive letters are issued to the same person in the same estate, he gets the commissions due to a fiduciary who administers the estate fully in a single capacity.[1]

The second occurs when one fiduciary ceases to act and another takes over in the middle of administration. As a general rule, commissions are payable only to fiduciaries who have completed their duties. The SCPA has no formula for commissions for fiduciaries who, because of death, resignation, or removal, do not complete the administration of the trust or estate. Their compensation is in the discretion of the court, which theoretically awards compensation on a quantum meruit basis, but in practice usually relies on the statutory commission rates to determine the worth of the fiduciary's services.

1. PRELIMINARY EXECUTORS

The preliminary executor's commissions depend in part on whether he is finally appointed executor of the will or not. If he is, he is entitled to receive the full commissions allowable to an executor for completing the administration of the estate.[2] On the other hand, if the court denies the will probate or revokes the fiduciary's letters, he is not

15. McKinney's SCPA 2310(3).

16. McKinney's SCPA 2310(5).

17. McKinney's SCPA 2310(4).

18. See, e.g., Matter of Crippen, 32 Misc.2d 1019, 224 N.Y.S.2d 116 (New York County 1961) (fiduciary improperly took advanced payment and was surcharged interest on amount taken); but see Matter of Schmitt, 65 Misc.2d 1021, 319 N.Y.S.2d 869 (Nassau 1971) (court in its discretion did not charge interest because executor had rendered legal services to estate without charge).

Sec. G

1. McKinney's SCPA 2307(4).

2. McKinney's SCPA 2307(6); McKinney's SCPA 1412(7).

entitled to statutory commissions, but the court can grant reasonable compensation for his services not to exceed an executor's commission.[3]

While "reasonable compensation" is often computed by using the statutory rates,[4] in some cases the courts will take into account the length of time the preliminary executor served and the services performed.[5]

A preliminary executor can be awarded reasonable compensation for services even if he is not entitled, under the will, to commissions as executor.[6] The same is true of temporary administrators.[7]

2. TEMPORARY ADMINISTRATORS

If the temporary administrator is ultimately appointed administrator or executor for the estate, he is entitled to one full commission at SCPA 2307 rates for completely administering the estate.[8] Frequently the temporary administrator accounts for his actions at the time of his appointment as executor or administrator, and the court has considerable discretion on what proportion of the commissions to allow at that time.[9] The court may not, however, award the temporary administrator commissions for paying to himself (as executor or administrator) the estate assets; the statute allows paying commissions only for sums paid "for debts, expenses of administration or to beneficiaries." [10] The theory is that he will be compensated on those sums on the settlement of his account as "permanent" fiduciary, and that it should remain as an incentive to performing his fiduciary duties.[11]

A temporary administrator who is not finally named executor or administrator is entitled to commissions under SCPA 2307.[12] A tempo-

3. McKinney's SCPA 1412(7). The provision that a preliminary executor's commissions cannot exceed those of an executor is strictly construed. See Matter of Birch, 80 Misc.2d 230, 362 N.Y.S.2d 811 (Schenectady 1974) reversed 50 A.D.2d 951, 376 N.Y.S.2d 25 (3d Dep't 1975).

4. See McKinney's SCPA 1412, Practice Commentary at 351 (McKinney 1967): "As commissions often bear little relationship to the responsibility involved or to the services actually performed, there is no reason why this same standard should not be applied to a preliminary executor, provided that the court considers him entitled to compensation. Although SCPA and the Revisers' Notes are silent as to the method by which compensation is to be fixed, there appears to be some relationship between the compensation and commissions as the last sentence of subdivision 7 limits any compensation paid to no more than the amount of commissions that would have been involved."

5. In Matter of Bernstein, 97 Misc.2d 898, 405 N.Y.S.2d 958 (New York County 1978), the preliminary executrix died after serving thirteen days; she had worked for four and a half months prior to her appointment locating assets, taking inventory and preserving the estate. An executor would have been entitled to $39,600 receiving commissions. In view of her short tenure, the court awarded commissions of $10,000.

6. Matter of Lowenstein, 72 Misc.2d 193, 338 N.Y.S.2d 335 (Queens 1972).

7. Matter of Hillman, 280 App.Div. 310, 113 N.Y.S.2d 409 (1st Dep't 1952).

8. McKinney's SCPA 2307(5).

9. McKinney's SCPA 2307(5).

10. McKinney's SCPA 2307(5).

11. Matter of Wendel, 159 Misc. 900, 289 N.Y.S. 290 (New York County 1935), affirmed 248 App.Div. 713, 289 N.Y.S. 294 (1st Dep't 1936); Matter of McGuire, 51 Misc.2d 56, 272 N.Y.S.2d 637 (Nassau 1966).

12. McKinney's SCPA 2307 refers to "fiduciaries," defined in SCPA 103(21) to

rary administrator who is appointed for only six months to administer the estate of an absentee, and then not appointed as "permanent" temporary administrator to administer the absentee's estate until it is wound up,[13] is not entitled to statutory commissions,[14] but the court may award "just, reasonable and proper" compensation for his services, not to exceed a full statutory commission. As a matter of practice, his commissions are usually based on the full amount of the assets he received, and assets he paid out for debts, for administration expenses, and to beneficiaries, and assets he paid over to the ultimate fiduciary.[15]

Courts frequently allow a temporary administrator to be compensated on the full value of the estate even though he does not reduce it to possession. A temporary administrator can do very little without court order, and the notion is that he is being paid primarily to conserve the estate until it can be paid over to a fiduciary who will administer it. Courts have therefore awarded temporary administrators commissions on stocks,[16] bank accounts [17] and cash [18] never actually reduced to possession. Courts have also allowed commissions on specific legacies on the theory that the property was not the subject of a specific legacy until the will was admitted to probate.[19]

If a temporary administrator dies while serving, his compensation (payable to his estate) is likely to be computed on the amount he received and paid out during his life.[20]

To avoid double commissions, sometimes the court gets a waiver of commissions from the temporary administrator and an agreement to accept, in lieu of commissions, reasonable compensation for services if he is not ultimately named fiduciary of the estate.[21]

A temporary administrator can be awarded reasonable compensation for services even if the will denies him commissions as executor.[22]

include temporary administrators. See Matter of McGuire, 51 Misc.2d 56, 272 N.Y.S.2d 637 (Nassau 1966).

13. McKinney's SCPA 902(3), discussed in chapter on "Temporary Administration," supra at 296–97.

14. McKinney's SCPA 902(6).

15. Matter of King, 122 App.Div. 354, 106 N.Y.S. 1073 (3d Dep't 1907); Matter of McGuire, 51 Misc.2d 56, 272 N.Y.S.2d 637 (Nassau 1966).

16. Matter of King, 122 App.Div. 354, 106 N.Y.S. 1073 (3d Dep't 1907).

17. Matter of King, 122 App.Div. 354, 106 N.Y.S. 1073 (3d Dep't 1907).

18. Matter of Hurst, 111 App.Div. 460, 97 N.Y.S. 697 (2d Dep't 1906); Matter of Hanson, 142 N.Y.S.2d 385 (Suffolk 1955) (compensation of temporary administrator based on value of entire estate for which he has acted as temporary administrator, not on actual money received).

19. Matter of Newins, 33 Misc.2d 72, 224 N.Y.S.2d 888 (Suffolk 1962); Matter of Egan, 7 Misc. 262, 27 N.Y.S. 1009 (New York County 1894).

20. Matter of Wendel, 159 Misc. 900, 289 N.Y.S. 290 (New York County 1935), affirmed 248 App.Div. 713, 289 N.Y.S. 294 (1st Dep't 1936); Matter of Newins, 33 Misc.2d 72, 224 N.Y.S.2d 888 (Suffolk 1962).

21. See Matter of Melcher, N.Y.L.J., August 16, 1974, at 12, col. 1 (New York County).

22. Matter of Hillman, 280 App.Div. 310, 113 N.Y.S.2d 409 (1st Dep't 1952); Matter of McVoy, 203 Misc. 33, 114 N.Y.S.2d 230 (New York County 1952).

3. ADMINISTRATORS AND EXECUTORS WHOSE LETTERS ARE LATER REVOKED

If a person receives letters of administration and a will is later found appointing someone else as executor, or if a nominated executor offers the will for probate and obtains letters testamentary, and later the decree of probate is reversed on appeal or vacated, that deposed fiduciary may be entitled to compensation if he believed that he had a right to act and if he properly performed his fiduciary duties.[23] The compensation awarded is ordinarily based on the statutory receiving commissions for amounts actually reduced to the fiduciary's possession,[24] and statutory paying commissions for amounts paid to beneficiaries or for debts or administration expenses, but not for paying over to the successor fiduciary.

4. DECEASED EXECUTORS OR ADMINISTRATORS

When an executor or administrator dies before completion of his duties, he is not entitled to statutory commissions.[25] The court has discretion to award reasonable compensation measured by the value of the services rendered, and its award may not exceed statutory commissions. In practice the court often computes the commissions by applying the statutory rates to the property received by the deceased fiduciary. The court has discretion to allow the deceased fiduciary's fiduciary to wind up the estate, and if it does, the commissions awarded to the fiduciary's fiduciary are within the court's discretion.[26]

The court usually fixes the compensation by applying the statutory rates to amounts actually received and paid out by the deceased fiduciary. In any event the deceased fiduciary's commissions and the commissions the court awards to his fiduciary for winding up the estate cannot exceed one statutory commission permitted by SCPA 2307, 2308 and 2309.[27]

23. Matter of Hurst, 111 App.Div. 460, 97 N.Y.S. 697 (2d Dep't 1906) (administrator removed because will found and probated); Matter of Staiger, 249 N.Y. 229, 164 N.E. 33 (1928) (executor removed because probate decree vacated).

24. In Hurst, for example, the administrator was denied commissions on bank accounts he had never collected. He unsuccessfully argued that he was more like a temporary administrator than an administrator, and that therefore actual receipt of property should not be a factor in determining commissions.

25. See Matter of Barker, 230 N.Y. 364, 230 N.E. 579 (1921); Matter of McGrath, 74 Misc.2d 92, 344 N.Y.S.2d 688 (New York County 1973), and cases cited therein.

26. McKinney's SCPA 2207(6). See Matter of Sawyer, 46 A.D.2d 48, 361 N.Y.S.2d 51 (3d Dep't 1974); Matter of O'Neil, 68 Misc.2d 634, 327 N.Y.S.2d 725 (Broome 1972); Matter of Jadwin, 58 Misc. 2d 809, 296 N.Y.S.2d 901 (Suffolk 1969); Matter of Vigeant, 29 Misc.2d 569, 215 N.Y.S.2d 187 (Dutchess 1961).

27. McKinney's SCPA 2207(6). The courts can award a deceased fiduciary commissions on property paid out by his successor if the deceased fiduciary did the bulk of the work. Matter of Vigeant, 29 Misc.2d 569, 215 N.Y.S.2d 187 (Dutchess 1961).

The court will look to the services provided by the deceased fiduciary's fiduciary successor to arrive at a fair payment.[28] Where the executorial duties were split, the court usually bases compensation on the services each fiduciary actually performed. For example, the deceased fiduciary's estate might be awarded receiving commissions and his fiduciary paying commissions for distributing the property.[29]

If the court appoints a successor fiduciary to replace the deceased fiduciary, he is entitled to the full commissions allowed by SCPA 2307, 2308 or 2309, whichever applies, regardless of the compensation the court awarded to his predecessor.[30]

5. EXECUTORS PAYING OVER TO TRUSTEES

Frequently, a testator leaves property in trust and names the same person as executor and trustee. When the executor accounts, an issue arises whether he is entitled to paying commissions for turning the property over to himself as trustee.

A general rule has been stated on this question of double commissions:

> To be entitled to double commissions as to the fund included in the corpus of any trust, there must be a complete severance of duties of the executors and of the trustees as to such fund. The will must show an intention on the part of the testator to end the executors' duties at some point of time and require executors thereupon to constitute and set up a trust to be held and managed as such for the benefit of the beneficiaries.[31]

The testator must have envisioned a severance of trust funds from the general assets of the estate and an actual severance must have occurred; in short he must have intended a separation of the duties of executor and trustee.[32]

When a testator appoints property under a power of appointment, it will be part of the commission base for the executor only if the testator clearly left it to the executor to be administered as part of the estate. If a testator leaves appointive property to trustees to be held in

28. See Matter of O'Neil, 68 Misc.2d 634, 327 N.Y.S.2d 725 (Broome 1972).

29. See Matter of O'Neil, 68 Misc.2d 634, 327 N.Y.S.2d 725 (Broome 1972).

30. See Matter of Sawyer, 46 A.D.2d 48, 361 N.Y.S.2d 51 (3d Dep't 1974), where full statutory commissions were allowed to successor because he had marshaled the assets, paid the taxes and distributed the estate. The court noted that it was appropriate to award statutory commissions not only because he had completely administered the estate, but also because he had been named successor by the testatrix and was serving in that capacity. It was, hence, not appropriate to look to McKinney's SCPA 2207(6), which applied to fiduciaries of deceased fiduciaries, not to successor fiduciaries. Accord, Matter of McGrath, 74 Misc.2d 92, 344 N.Y.S.2d 688 (New York County 1973).

31. Matter of Knoop, 283 N.Y. 267, 28 N.E.2d 832 (1940).

32. Matter of Daniels, 32 A.D.2d 986, 302 N.Y.S.2d 30 (3d Dep't 1969).

further trust, even if the trustee is also the executor, no executor's commissions will be allowed.[33]

Unsold real property distributed by an executor to himself as trustee is not subject to commissions as a result of the distribution.[34]

6. TRUSTEE PAYING OVER TO EXECUTOR

Sometimes a testator creates an inter vivos trust and directs payment of estate taxes and administration expenses directly from the trust. If the decedent named the same person as trustee and executor, and the trustee does in fact pay administration expenses, it is highly unlikely that the testator would intend that person to take paying commissions as trustee and receiving commissions as executor.[35]

SECTION H. CORPORATE TRUSTEES

The legislature in 1984 made a significant amendment to the laws governing the commissions of corporate trustees.[1]

SCPA 2312 allows corporate trustees to get "reasonable" commissions on trusts of more than four hundred thousand dollars,[2] and the court has the power to review the reasonableness if anyone contests it. A direction in the will or trust instrument setting the rate of commissions would, of course, prevail over the statute;[3] parties are free to contract with each other for services whether the fee is reasonable or not. If the governing instrument is silent and the parties have no agreement, the reasonableness rule prevails. The case law evolving from this section will give us guidelines on the criteria the courts use in fixing reasonable commissions.

The statutory amount permitted for individual trustees is the minimum measure of the reasonableness of commissions on trusts of four hundred thousand dollars or less,[4] and the corporate trustee is also entitled to annual commissions on principal at a rate of no more than 1%.[5]

33. Matter of Del Monte, 66 Misc.2d 458, 321 N.Y.S.2d 167 (New York County 1971).

34. Matter of Phelps, 79 Misc.2d 99, 359 N.Y.S.2d 614 (Westchester 1974).

35. See Matter of Mead, 90 Misc.2d 144, 394 N.Y.S.2d 123 (Westchester 1977).

Sec. H

1. L.1984, c. 936, enacting McKinney's SCPA 2312, effective August 6, 1984.

2. McKinney's SCPA 2312(2).

3. McKinney's SCPA 2312(1).

4. McKinney's SCPA 2312(4)(a).

5. More accurately, ten dollars per thousand or major fraction thereof. McKinney's SCPA 2312(4)(6).

Chapter Sixteen

TRUSTS AND TRUSTEES

SECTION A. INTRODUCTION

The Surrogate's Court has jurisdiction over trusts, as well it must, for many trusts are created by wills and are thus squarely within the Surrogate's domain and area of expertise. Article 15 of the SCPA governs trustees, their appointment and qualification,[1] their power to renounce their appointment and retract the renunciation,[2] their status when serving in a dual role as executor and trustee,[3] their liability for acts of their predecessors,[4] and their powers.[5] We discuss those points here, and we also direct the reader's attention to our chapter on "Fiduciaries," which covers the appointment of trustees, the issuance of their letters and the standards that govern them.

The Surrogate's Court has jurisdiction of, and Article 15 expressly applies to, trustees of testamentary trusts and inter vivos (lifetime) trusts whether they relate to an estate or not. The statute was amended in 1980 to give the Surrogates jurisdiction over inter vivos trusts concurrent with the jurisdiction of the Supreme Court, which previously had exclusive jurisdiction.[6] The Surrogates had in fact been exercising jurisdiction increasingly over inter vivos trusts in the years preceding the statutory conferral of jurisdiction,[7] so that the amendment was a welcome codification of this jurisdiction.

SECTION B. TRUSTS GOVERNED BY ARTICLE 15

SCPA Article 15 applies to the following trusts:

1. a testamentary trust created by a New York domiciliary; [1]

Sec. A

1. McKinney's SCPA 1502, 1503, discussed this chapter infra at 460–63.

2. McKinney's SCPA 1504, discussed this chapter infra at 463–64.

3. McKinney's SCPA 1505, discussed this chapter infra at 465.

4. McKinney's SCPA 1506, discussed this chapter infra at 465–66.

5. McKinney's SCPA 1507, discussed this chapter infra at 467.

6. L.1980, c. 503.

7. See, e.g., Matter of Fornason, 88 Misc.2d 736, 389 N.Y.S.2d 1003 (Nassau 1976); Matter of Bleier, N.Y.L.J., Nov. 17, 1978, at 12, col. 2 (New York County). See Midonick, Do Surrogates Have Jurisdiction in Cases Involving Inter Vivos Trusts?, N.Y.L.J., June 16, 1975, at 19, col. 1. See generally chapter on "Jurisdiction," supra at 10–12.

Sec. B

1. McKinney's SCPA 1501(1)(a).

2. a lifetime trust, no matter when created, if the trust situs is in New York or real property held by the trust is in New York.[2] The trust situs is here if the property is in the state at the testator's death or at the creation of the lifetime trust, or if it is brought here for administration; [3]

3. a testamentary trust of a non-domiciliary if the will is probated in New York; [4]

4. a testamentary trust of a non-domiciliary if the will was admitted to probate or proved in another jurisdiction where it was executed or where the testator was domiciled at death, if the trust situs is in New York or real property held by the trust is in New York or is brought into New York after the testator's death; [5]

5. a lifetime trust of which the Supreme court would also have jurisdiction.[6] That includes a trust created by a New York domiciliary and a trust whose trustee is a New York resident or has its principal office here.

The trustee need not be a New York domiciliary for Article 15 to apply.[7]

SECTION C. THE SURROGATE'S JURISDICTION OVER NON-DOMICILIARY TESTAMENTARY TRUSTS

If a Surrogate in New York grants original probate [1] or ancillary probate [2] to a non-domiciliary's will, that court will have exclusive jurisdiction over a trust created by the will.[3] In other cases, including all lifetime trusts, jurisdiction will be in the Surrogate's Court of the county in which the real property subject to the trust is located, or if there is no real property, in the Surrogate's Court of the county in which any trustee has a residence or its principal place of business.[4] If more than one Surrogate's Court could entertain jurisdiction over the trust, the first Surrogate to entertain a proceeding relating to the trust gets exclusive jurisdiction.[5]

2. McKinney's SCPA 1501(1)(b).

3. McKinney's SCPA 1501(2).

4. McKinney's SCPA 1501(1)(b).

5. McKinney's SCPA 1501(1)(b). If the Surrogate has jurisdiction under the statute, the court's jurisdiction is exercised as though it were the will of a domiciliary. Matter of DeVoe, 118 N.Y.S.2d 432 (New York County 1952); Matter of Vanneck, 158 Misc. 704, 286 N.Y.S. 489 (New York County 1936).

6. McKinney's SCPA 1501(1)(c).

7. McKinney's SCPA 1501(1).

Sec. C

1. Original probate of a non-domiciliary's will is governed by McKinney's SCPA 1605 and discussed in chapter on "Ancillary Proceedings," supra at 522–24.

2. Ancillary probate of a non-domiciliary's will is governed by McKinney's SCPA Article 16 and discussed in chapter on "Ancillary Proceedings," supra at 513–19.

3. McKinney's SCPA 1501(3).

4. McKinney's SCPA 1501(3).

5. McKinney's SCPA 1501(3).

The jurisdiction conferred in SCPA 1501 should be viewed together with the jurisdiction conferred by SCPA 206 and 207.[6] SCPA 206 grants to any Surrogate in the state jurisdiction over the will of a non-domiciliary if the decedent left property in New York or a wrongful death lawsuit against a New Yorker. SCPA 206 makes no distinction between real and personal property. The proper venue in such a case is the county where the property is located or where the defendant is domiciled, or the first of the proper counties to entertain a proceeding.

If a court exercises its SCPA 206 jurisdiction by granting original or ancillary probate to the will, SCPA 1501(2) gives that court exclusive jurisdiction of the trust created by that will. This parallels the strictly-enforced venue rules under which the Surrogate of each county entertains proceedings relating to the wills of domiciliaries of that county, regardless of where the assets are located. Alternatively, if there has not been original or ancillary probate, SCPA 1501 gives the Surrogate in a county where real property is located prior jurisdiction over the Surrogate in a county where the personal property is. If there is realty in two counties, the first Surrogate to exercise jurisdiction obtains exclusive jurisdiction. If there is no realty, the Surrogate of a county where the trustee resides has jurisdiction. If a trustee does not reside within any county in New York, SCPA 1501 does not specify which court has jurisdiction, so SCPA 206's directive that the county where the domiciliary's property is located would permit the court of the county where personal property is located to exercise jurisdiction. If there is more than one such court, the first court to exercise jurisdiction would be the proper venue.

Similarly, with respect to inter vivos trusts, SCPA 1501(3) does not dovetail perfectly with SCPA 207, which confers jurisdiction on any Surrogate if the trust had assets in the state or if the grantor was domiciled in New York or if the trustee was residing in New York (or had its principal office here). The proper venue is the county where the assets are, the grantor is domiciled or the trustee resides, and if more than one Surrogate's Court is a proper forum, the first to exercise its jurisdiction has priority. Regarding non-domiciliary grantors, SCPA 1501(3) states that the county where real property is located has jurisdiction, not the county where personal property is located, and if there is no realty, the trustee's county. Presumably if a non-domiciliary's inter vivos trust consisted of personal property, the Surrogate of that county could exercise jurisdiction under SCPA 207, since SCPA 1501 is silent.

The conflict between Article 2 and SCPA 1501 has been brought to the attention of the legislature for clarification. It would appear that Article 2 should conform to SCPA 1501.

6. McKinney's SCPA 206 and 207 are discussed in chapter on "Jurisdiction," supra at 1–9.

To illustrate these rules, assume a Florida domiciliary creates a lifetime trust into which he places two pieces of New York real property, one located in Dutchess County, one in Suffolk County. Both Dutchess and Suffolk have jurisdiction, and if a proceeding is commenced in Suffolk and the Surrogate entertains it, jurisdiction over the trust vests there. If the Florida person had created the trust by will and that will had been admitted to probate in Suffolk County (because, say, Florida discriminated against New York fiduciaries)[7], the Suffolk Surrogate would have exclusive jurisdiction. If the Florida decedent's will created a trust containing the two pieces of realty and some personalty located in New York and the will had not been admitted to probate in New York, the counties where the realty was located could exercise jurisdiction. If the trust contained only the personalty, jurisdiction would be in the county of residence of the trustee (or its principal place of business). If the trustee does not reside (or have its principal place of business) in New York, presumably the court of any county where personal property was located could exercise jurisdiction.

The parties interested in the trust cannot by mutual consent change the situs of the trust to another jurisdiction if the creator's apparent intent was to have the trust administered in New York.[8] They must apply to the court to allow a change in the situs of trust assets[9] under the notion that the move would be consistent with the testator's intent and would facilitate trust administration.[10] For this reason, the practitioner is well advised to include an authorization to change the trust's situs in the governing instrument.

SECTION D. SURROGATE'S DISCRETION TO DECLINE JURISDICTION

A Surrogate may decline jurisdiction over the administration of a testamentary or lifetime trust of personal property created by a nondomiciliary.[1] As with many special proceedings in the Surrogate's

7. See McKinney's SCPA 1605.

8. See Matter of Turrentine, 83 Misc.2d 170, 371 N.Y.S.2d 615 (Schenectady 1975), where the decedent's widow, beneficiary of his testamentary trust, had moved to Texas and requested an order permitting a Texas bank to serve as trustee instead of the New York trustee nominated by the decedent. The court denied her application, noting the testator's intent to have the trust administered in New York.

9. The court has jurisdiction to order this transfer of trust situs under McKinney's SCPA 202 (the general jurisdiction-conferring section, discussed in chapter on "Jurisdiction," supra at 23–24). See also McKinney's SCPA 209(11).

10. Matter of Hudson, 23 N.Y.2d 834, 297 N.Y.S.2d 736, 245 N.E.2d 405 (1969) (court would not allow change of situs "in the absence of either an express provision for a change of situs or a necessary implication of an intent that the situs could be changed," unless the petitioner could show that it would facilitate trust administration). See also Matter of Weinberger, 21 A.D.2d 780, 250 N.Y.S.2d 887 (1st Dep't 1964) (trust created by will which neither sanctioned nor barred transfer moved to California because trustees lived there).

Sec. D

1. McKinney's SCPA 1501(4).

Court, the petitioner must ask the court to entertain it,[2] and his request must set forth whether anyone ever applied for such relief before in New York and whether the court granted it.[3] The petitioner must submit the petition, a copy of the will and foreign letters, if any were issued,[4] or a copy of the inter vivos trust. If the court entertains the application, it records the will or trust in its office.[5]

Once a court admits a will to probate, that Surrogate retains jurisdiction over all matters relating to the estate and the testamentary trust unless the court transfers the situs to another jurisdiction for the convenience of all the parties. For example, that Surrogate would be the one to entertain an application of a trustee to resign, a will construction, and an accounting.

New York has sole sovereignty over real property located in New York; a foreign court admitting a will to probate cannot vest a testamentary trustee with any rights over the New York realty. The foreign fiduciary must obtain letters to administer the real property[6] unless one merely wishes to establish title, in which case the Surrogate admits the will to probate but does not grant letters.[7]

A 1975 addition to the EPTL is relevant here. EPTL 10–6.9[8] provides that where a donee of a power of appointment exercises the power in favor of a trust created by a will other than the will granting him the power of appointment, the appointed property is paid over to and administered by the trustees of the trust in favor of which the power was exercised, and the court with jurisdiction over the "payee" trust thereafter has jurisdiction over that property. For example, assume that grandfather G creates Trust G, giving his son S income for life and a power of appointment over the remainder. Assume that S's wife W predeceased him, creating by will Trust W, income to S for life, then income to their children for life, then remainder to their surviving issue per stirpes. Assume further that S exercises his power of appointment under Trust G in favor of Trust W. It is not necessary for the trustees of Trust W to go to G's jurisdiction and obtain letters in order to accept the property. Once the funds are transferred, jurisdiction rests with the court with jurisdiction of the receiving trust.[9]

Applicability of Article 15 to a trust merely establishes the jurisdiction of the New York Surrogate over the trustee; it does not necessarily

2. See, e.g., the proceedings discussed in chapter on "Miscellaneous Proceedings," supra at 326 et seq.

3. McKinney's SCPA 1501(4).

4. The foreign letters must be authenticated by the appropriate officer in the other jurisdiction, McKinney's CPLR 4540(c), and must conform with the requirements of McKinney's SCPA 1614.

5. McKinney's SCPA 1501(4).

6. Matter of Sabin, 155 Misc. 507, 280 N.Y.S. 211 (Kings 1935). There the decedent was a New Jersey resident who owned realty in New York. His will was probated in New Jersey. The Surrogate issued letters of trusteeship to the trustees named in the will for administration of the New York real property.

7. See chapter on "Ancillary Administration," infra at 513.

8. Enacted in L.1975, c. 114.

9. See McKinney's SCPA 1501, 1975 Prac.Comm. at 143 (Supp.1986).

dictate the application of New York substantive law governing the trust and the trustee, except of course for issues relating to real property.[10] That determination is made by application of conflicts of law and choice of law principles beyond the scope of this work.[11]

SECTION E. APPOINTMENT OF TRUSTEES

Although a trust will fail if it has no beneficiaries [1] or if it has no purpose,[2] it will not fail merely because it has no trustee. The court may appoint a trustee whenever there is no trustee able to act, for example, if a will or trust instrument fails to name a trustee, or if the named trustee dies before qualifying. If a trustee, or all of them, are unable to act, the court can appoint a successor or co-trustee if necessary,[3] as long as the appointment does not contravene the express terms of the will or trust [4] and carries out the testator's general intent.[5] If the testator nominated only one trustee, the court can nevertheless appoint a co-trustee if the named trustee has a power to invade the trust for his own benefit. Under the EPTL,[6] a trustee's power to distribute principal to himself may not be exercised by him, but only by a co-trustee. The court may therefore appoint a co-trustee for that purpose.[7]

The court does not have unbridled discretion in making appointments of trustees. If the will or trust designates a person to act and

10. McKinney's EPTL 3–5.1(b)(1) provides that the law of the situs of real property governs its disposition.

11. See, e.g., Matter of Vanderbilt, 31 Misc.2d 1086, 221 N.Y.S.2d 93 (1961) (jurisdiction of New York Surrogate under SCPA 1501's predecessor, coupled with settlor's residence in New York settlor's direction for application of New York law governing fiduciary's investments, and presence of trust in New York mandated application of New York law to question of validity of power of appointment); Matter of DeVoe, 118 N.Y.S.2d 432 (1953) (New York contacts, including decedent's domicile, mandated application of New York law to trustee's conduct, although decedent had been Massachusetts domiciliary when he executed will). For a discussion of choice of law principles in the context of a surviving spouse's right of election, see chapter on "Jurisdiction," supra at 32–34.

Sec. E

1. E.g., Holland v. Alcock, 108 N.Y. 312, 16 N.E. 305 (1888).

2. E.g., Matter of Brockman, 236 N.Y.S.2d 923 (Kings 1963) (trust created for beneficiary's college education; beneficiary had left high school in ninth grade and said that he had no intention of going to college).

3. McKinney's SCPA 1502(1). This includes trustees and successor trustees. Both the Supreme Court and the Surrogate, whichever has jurisdiction over the trust, have this power to appoint trustees.

4. McKinney's SCPA 1502(2). See Matter of Belford, N.Y.L.J., June 21, 1985, at 15, col. 1 (Suffolk) (successor appointed because such appointment did not contravene the terms of the will); Matter of Keech, 187 Misc. 154, 61 N.Y.S.2d 435 (1946), where the testator had named two trustees and had provided for replacement by a trust company if one of the trustees resigned or declined to serve. The court refused to appoint the corporate trustee when one of the trustees died, on the ground that that was not one of the contingencies for which the trustee had provided.

5. See Matter of Wallace, N.Y.L.J., May 22, 1985, at 14, col. 4 (Westchester) (court appointed successor trustees in a manner and with age restrictions that comported with the testator's intent). Accord, Matter of Wertheim, N.Y.L.J., July 1, 1985, at 15, col. 2 (New York County).

6. McKinney's EPTL 10–10.1.

7. Matter of Seidman, 58 A.D.2d 72, 395 N.Y.S.2d 674 (2d Dep't 1977).

that person is not disqualified to act, the court may not appoint a trustee other than that person.[8] The court also cannot appoint a trustee if there are no trust functions left to be performed.[9] If two or more trustees are serving, and one ceases to serve, the court cannot replace the deceased or resigning co-trustee when another co-trustee remains in office, unless the will provides for (or by clear implication permits) the appointment of a successor.[10] The remaining trustees can continue to administer the trust.[11] If the remaining single trustee is also the sole beneficiary, however, the court will appoint another co-trustee to prevent destruction of the trust by application of the doctrine of merger, which turns it into a legal life estate.[12] If other circumstances (such as the advanced age of the remaining trustees) indicate appointment of an additional trustee, and a petition is filed requesting such appointment, the court can appoint a co-trustee even if the will specifies that the surviving trustees can act alone.[13]

Until the court appoints a successor or co-trustee, the trustees who are serving may continue to administer the trust.[14]

8. McKinney's SCPA 1502(2). But see Matter of Johnson, 59 N.Y.2d 461, 465 N.Y.S.2d 900, 452 N.E.2d 1228 (1983). There a testator had created a gender-discriminatory trust and named a school district as trustee. The school district did not want to serve because it feared it would lose state and federal funding. The court appointed a private trustee to administer the trust, holding that the trust's purpose (to give scholarships to young men) was not against public policy and that appointment of an independent trustee would allow implementation of the trust.

9. Matter of Astor, 2 Misc.2d 385, 152 N.Y.S.2d 102 (Columbia 1956).

10. McKinney's SCPA 706. See discussion of this section and relevant cases in chapter on "Fiduciaries," supra at 388. See Dexter v. McAllister, 64 N.Y.2d 1149, 490 N.Y.S.2d 729, 480 N.E.2d 343 (1985), where the trust instrument specified the way of filling vacancies.

11. See McKinney's SCPA 706; McKinney's EPTL 11-1.1(b)(11); McKinney's SCPA 1502(3).

12. Matter of Phipps, 2 N.Y.2d 105, 157 N.Y.S.2d 14, 138 N.E.2d 341 (1956) (doctrine of merger not applied with rigidity; the court will appoint another trustee to prevent its application where the testator intended trust to stay in effect); Reed v. Browne, 295 N.Y. 184, 66 N.E.2d 47 (1946). See Matter of Seidman, 88 Misc.2d 462, 389 N.Y.S.2d 729 (Kings 1976), affirmed 58 A.D.2d 72, 395 N.Y.S.2d 674 (2d Dep't 1977); Matter of Duskis, 76 Misc.2d 411, 351 N.Y.S.2d 97 (New York County 1973), where the wife left her estate in trust, income to her husband, who was also named trustee and had unlimited power to invade principal. The court held that it was unnecessary to appoint the husband as trustee, since as sole beneficiary and sole trustee he became the owner of a legal life estate; Matter of Bleakley, N.Y.L.J., March 8, 1985, at 17, col. 1 (Westchester) (court appointed trustee nominated by interested parties to prevent merger of interests). See also Matter of Schwartz, N.Y. L.J., Aug. 13, 1985, at 11, col. 6 (Bronx), where the settlor's son, the income beneficiary, had not been named as trustee but was appointed by the court to fill a vacancy, and the court held that there was no merger since the testator clearly wanted the trust to continue for the son's life. For a discussion of this merger doctrine, see McKinney's SCPA 1502, Prac.Comm. at 136–39 (Supp.1986).

13. See Matter of Jones, 91 Misc.2d 143, 397 N.Y.S.2d 558 (New York County 1977), where the decedent's will provided on the death of any trustee the remaining trustees should continue to act without appointment of a successor. To protect and preserve the trust, the court appointed a successor to the deceased trustee because the remaining two trustees were octogenarians and requested appointment of a successor third trustee.

14. McKinney's SCPA 1502(3).

The procedure is for a person interested in the trust to petition for the appointment of a trustee. The court will decide who has to get notice,[15] which is usually by citation or order to show cause.

If a trust terminates by its own terms (for example, the trust was to end on the death of the income beneficiary, and that person has died), and no trustee is serving, the court may appoint a successor trustee to complete the administration or distribution of the trust.[16] If the reason for the vacancy in office is the death of the trustee and very little remains to be done, the court may grant powers to the fiduciary of the deceased trustee to wind up the administration of the trust.[17]

A successor trustee is, of course, a true fiduciary, subject to the same duties to account and to administer the trust as all trustees.[18] He may spend reasonable sums necessary for the trust administration. The court decides his commissions, which may not exceed those allowed by statute.[19]

If the court decides to appoint a trustee, no person has priority over any other under article 15.[20] The matter is within the court's discretion.[21] Anyone who would be eligible under SCPA 707 [22] may receive letters although the court ordinarily will appoint a person with an interest in the trust, or a person suggested by someone with an interest.[23] If all logical choices have conflicts of interest, the court will consider appointing a corporate fiduciary.[24] If the fitness or qualification of a nominee is questioned, the court will hold a hearing on the issue.[25]

15. McKinney's SCPA 1502(4).

16. McKinney's SCPA 1502(5).

17. McKinney's SCPA 2207.

18. McKinney's SCPA 1502(6); McKinney's EPTL 11-2.1.

19. McKinney's SCPA 1502(6). See McKinney's SCPA 2308 and 2309, discussed in chapter on "Commissions," supra at 429-36.

20. Matter of Eggsware, 123 Misc. 548, 206 N.Y.S. 24 (Clinton 1924).

21. Matter of Andrews, 233 App.Div. 547, 253 N.Y.S. 590 (3d Dep't 1931); Matter of Hayden, 141 Misc. 644, 253 N.Y.S. 641 (Jefferson 1931).

22. McKinney's SCPA 707 provides that all persons are eligible except:

(a) an infant

(b) an incompetent

(c) a non-domiciliary alien except in the case of a foreign guardian

(d) a felon

(e) one who is incompetent to execute the duties of his office by reason of drunkenness, dishonesty, improvidence or want of understanding.

See chapter on "Fiduciaries," supra at 388-91.

23. Matter of Gunther, 197 App.Div. 28, 188 N.Y.S. 615 (1st Dep't 1921) (while the beneficiaries cannot by consent oust the court of its jurisdiction to choose a trustee, the court should exercise its discretion with due regard to the beneficiaries' reasonable wishes).

24. Matter of Hawke, 222 App.Div. 643, 228 N.Y.S. 165 (1st Dep't 1928) (court invited parties to agree on a disinterested person or corporate trustee).

25. Matter of Wiltse, 24 Misc.2d 398, 203 N.Y.S.2d 298 (Nassau 1960) (court will decide on fitness of trustee at hearing, regardless of parties' stated choice of trustee).

SECTION F. QUALIFICATION OF TRUSTEE APPOINTED BY ANOTHER COURT

The Supreme Court has jurisdiction to appoint testamentary trustees although it rarely does so.[1] Even if it does issue the order appointing a trustee, however, it is the Surrogate who issues the letters of trusteeship.[2] As with guardians, the Surrogate's Court is the central depository of information relating to testamentary trustees, even if their appointment was by the Supreme Court. The certified copy of the order and decree of appointment and the bond given by the trustee, if any, must be filed in the Surrogate's Court of the county with jurisdiction of the trust, and a record (minute) must be indexed in the Surrogate's Court's book containing orders and decrees appointing trustees. The trustee has to file in the Surrogate's Court his oath (individual trustee), consent to serve (corporate trustee) and designation,[3] and a bond if necessary. A bond is not always necessary. The court can appoint a trustee without requiring the filing of a bond if the will dispenses with it.[4] Conversely, the court can require a trustee to post a bond even if the will exonerates him from doing so, if he is a nondomiciliary or a person the court feels lacks financial responsibility.[5]

Once the fiduciary files the oath and designation, and a bond if required, the Surrogate will then issue letters to him and he will be subject to all the duties and liabilities of the testamentary trustee appointed by the Surrogate's Court.[6]

SECTION G. RENUNCIATION OF APPOINTMENT

A testamentary trustee is not obligated to accept his appointment and may renounce by an acknowledged instrument.[1] The nominated

Sec. F

1. See Matter of Grey, 14 Misc.2d 57, 177 N.Y.S.2d 111 (Sup.Ct. Westchester 1958), where the Supreme Court in dicta said that the Supreme Court ordinarily will not appoint a testamentary trustee when relief is easily available from the Surrogate's Court. The Supreme Court in Grey in fact retained jurisdiction because the question was not raised, and the Supreme Court had appointed the trustee and had exercised control over the trust for fifty years.

2. McKinney's SCPA 1503.

3. McKinney's SCPA 1503. These documents are discussed in chapter on "Fiduciaries," supra at 391–92.

4. See McKinney's SCPA 806; Matter of Solomon, 18 Misc.2d 1029, 189 N.Y.S.2d 831 (Kings 1959).

5. See McKinney's SCPA 708(3), 710(2), discussed in chapter on "Fiduciaries," supra at 391.

6. That is, a designation of the clerk of the court to accept process for the trustee if he cannot be located in New York. McKinney's SCPA 708(1). See chapter on "Procedure," supra at 391–92.

Sec. G

1. McKinney's SCPA 1504(1), (3). If the renunciation was based, however, on a mistaken conception of who would replace the renouncing trustee, the court may request that the renouncing party retract. See Matter of Turrentine, 83 Misc.2d 170, 371 N.Y.S.2d 615 (Schenectady 1975), where the court asked the nominated New York corporate fiduciary to retract its renunciation after the court refused to allow the other fiduciary to move the trust assets out

trustee does not have to give a reason for renouncing an appointment, and the court ordinarily permits renunciations on the papers presented.

If the testator or creator imposes obligations on a nominated trustee which the trustee does not want to accept, his remedy is to renounce his appointment. He cannot refuse to accept those obligations and expect to qualify as trustee.[2]

After renouncing, a nominated trustee may retract his renunciation by an acknowledged instrument filed in the court with jurisdiction of the trust at any time before letters have issued to another in his place [3] or, if letters have been issued, he may retract his renunciation when the other is no longer serving.[4] If the court issues letters to the person retracting, it may use its discretion in ordering notice on persons it considers interested.[5]

The trustee trying to retract his renunciation has to give a reason, since the court has discretion whether to allow the retraction or not. Therefore, along with the instrument retracting his renunciation, the trustee should submit an affidavit explaining his change of heart. The court has the power to refuse to accept the retraction.[6] The trustee should show persuasive reasons for allowing the retraction, and the appellate court will not overturn the Surrogate's decision unless the Surrogate abused his discretion.[7]

Once the court has issued letters to the trustee, he cannot resign without court permission.[8]

of New York and to appoint a Texas fiduciary.

2. Matter of Witz, 95 Misc.2d 36, 406 N.Y.S.2d 671 (Nassau 1978) (testator imposed obligations on trustee which trustee could not disclaim without renouncing his right to letters of trusteeship).

3. It is significant that he must retract before letters have been issued to another trustee in his place. Thus, if a nominated trustee renounced and later a vacancy occurred and he tried to retract the renunciation, he would have to show that the retiring trustee is the one who was appointed because of the renunciation. McKinney's SCPA 1504; Matter of Statler, 81 N.Y.S.2d 916 (Erie 1948), affirmed 276 App.Div. 818, 93 N.Y.S.2d 709 (4th Dep't 1949), affirmed 301 N.Y. 645, 93 N.E.2d 921 (1950) (it must be shown that the deceased trustee was appointed to fill the vacancy caused by the petitioner's renunciation).

4. That is, that person has had his letters revoked, has become unable to serve or has become disqualified. McKinney's SCPA 1504(2).

5. McKinney's SCPA 1504(2).

6. Matter of Statler, 81 N.Y.S.2d 916 (Erie 1948), affirmed 276 App.Div. 818, 93 N.Y.S.2d 709 (4th Dep't 1949), affirmed 301 N.Y. 645, 93 N.E.2d 921 (1950) (court has power to refuse to accept trustee's retraction of his renunciation); Matter of Wetzel, 125 N.Y.S.2d 808 (New York County 1953) (corporate trustee was permitted to retract its renunciation upon death of sole remaining trustee and upon request of all parties interested).

7. Matter of Statler, 81 N.Y.S.2d 916 (Erie 1948), affirmed 276 App.Div. 818, 93 N.Y.S.2d 709 (4th Dep't 1949), affirmed 301 N.Y. 645, 93 N.E.2d 921 (1950) (Surrogate's discretion, under McKinney's SCPA 1504's predecessor, would not be overruled unless abused); Matter of Parker, 27 Misc.2d 652, 209 N.Y.S.2d 254 (Nassau 1961) (dissatisfaction with the investment yield and the remainderman's reaching the age of majority were not sufficient reasons to permit widow's retraction of renunciation).

8. We discuss the fiduciary's application for permission to resign in chapter on "Fiduciaries," supra at 400–01.

SECTION H. EFFECT OF FIDUCIARY SERVING IN TWO CAPACITIES

Often a testator creates a will and nominates the same person as executor of the estate and trustee of the testamentary trust. That person has two separate jobs which for most purposes are kept separate. For example, a decree revoking letters as personal representative does not revoke letters of trusteeship; [1] commissions are payable separately for both services; [2] and proceedings taken by or against a person as trustee do not affect him in his role as executor or administrator,[3] with the following two exceptions:

First, a person nominated as executor and trustee seeking to renounce appointment can petition for renunciation of both in the same petition.[4] This avoids two separate proceedings. The court will issue process both to those interested in the estate and to those interested in the trust.[5]

Second, if someone seeks to remove the executor-trustee (or administrator-trustee), he may make both applications in the same petition.[6] The court will issue process for service on the persons interested in both entities, the estate and the trust.

The court can, however, in either of these consolidated proceedings, sever them if necessary, for example, if the fiduciary has some duties left to perform in one capacity or the other.[7]

SECTION I. NON-LIABILITY FOR ACTS OF PREDECESSOR EXECUTOR

If two persons are named respectively as executor and trustee of a testamentary trust, the trustee is not liable for the executor's wrongdoing in any of the following cases: [1]

(1) He received the assets of the trust pursuant to a final decree of the court. His freedom from liability in this case stems from his thorough review of the accounting on which the decree was based. If he failed to review the accounting and object to the executor's acts, he can no longer blame any losses on the executor's

Sec. H

1. McKinney's SCPA 720.

2. McKinney's SCPA 2307 and McKinney's SCPA 2308–09.

3. McKinney's SCPA 1505(1); See Matter of Massimino, 143 Misc. 119, 256 N.Y.S. 32 (Bronx 1932) (where executor and trustee are separate entities, receipt by trustee of property discharges the executor as to payment of trust legatees).

4. McKinney's SCPA 1505(1)(a).

5. McKinney's SCPA 1505, Prac.Comm. at 596 (1967).

6. McKinney's SCPA 1505(1)(b).

7. McKinney's SCPA 1505, Prac.Comm. at 596 (1967).

Sec. I

1. McKinney's SCPA 1506.

wrongdoing; it is nonfeasance on his own part, and he is not absolved.[2]

(2) He did not know of the executor's wrongdoing and did not improperly allow it to continue.

(3) He took proper steps to compel the executor to deliver trust property to him.

(4) He took proper steps to redress the executor's wrongdoing.

In other words, a trustee is liable for his own non-feasance or malfeasance, not that of his predecessor.[3]

The statute creating this limited rule of non-liability for a predecessor's acts is not overused, because in many instances the executor is the trustee or a co-trustee. Although the statute addresses only a trustee's liability for acts of an executor,[4] in practice the same rule applies when a successor trustee assumes office. In practice all that is said in this statute about the executor-trustee relationship also applies to the trustee-successor trustee relationship, and the rest of this discussion, phrased in terms of the former, will apply equally to the latter.

The wording of the statute makes it clear that the trustee has a responsibility to determine whether the executor's actions caused a loss or dissipation of trust property. The trustee has a duty to marshal the trust assets and reduce them to his possession. If he has difficulty doing so, he should compel the executor to account.[5] Similarly, if on receiving the assets he observes that the investments were imprudent, he should obtain an accounting.[6] His failure to do so is viewed as wrongdoing on his part.[7]

A fortiori, if the trustee knows of an actual breach of trust by the executor, he must take steps on behalf of the trust to recover the property, and if he does not, he will be personally liable for the loss.[8]

2. McKinney's SCPA 1506, Prac.Comm. at 599 (1967).

3. This reflects the view espoused in the Restatement of Trusts, section 223, relating to a successor trustee's liability for acts of his predecessor trustee.

4. McKinney's SCPA 1506. See Matter of Brunner, 49 Misc.2d 139, 267 N.Y.S.2d 332 (Kings 1966), affirmed 26 A.D.2d 838, 274 N.Y.S.2d 414 (2d Dep't 1966).

5. Matter of Chalmers, 163 Misc. 142, 297 N.Y.S. 176 (Albany 1937) (court directed executor to account and to turn over sufficient assets to fund the trust). See discussion of McKinney's SCPA 2205 (compulsory accountings) in chapter on "Accounting," supra at 183–86.

6. See discussion of the "prudent man" rule governing investments by fiduciaries in chapter on "Fiduciaries," supra at 407–12. See Villard v. Villard, 219 N.Y. 482, 114 N.E. 789 (1917), where the executor improperly invested estate property and eventually paid it to the trustee who simply held it. Its depreciation was a surcharge against the trustee, who had a duty to discover the executor's improper acts and to remedy them.

7. See Matter of Chalmers, 163 Misc. 142, 297 N.Y.S. 176 (Albany 1937).

8. Villard v. Villard, 219 N.Y. 482, 114 N.E. 789 (1917); Bank of New York v. New Jersey Title Guarantee and Trust Co., 256 App.Div. 609, 11 N.Y.S.2d 181 (1st Dep't 1939) (successor trustees could maintain an action for conversion against predecessor trustee for breach of the trust agreement).

SECTION J. AUTHORITY TO MORTGAGE, SELL, LEASE OR EXCHANGE

If a will or trust instrument contains a long "fiduciaries' powers" clause, and includes all the standard boiler-plate provisions, the trustee of an inter vivos or testamentary trust invariably has the power to sell, mortgage, lease or exchange real property. If it does not, the trustee must look to the provisions of EPTL 11–1.1 for permissible powers.[1]

Though the EPTL powers are broad,[2] they are not unlimited, and they place some restrictions on trustees dealing with real property. For instance, a trustee cannot exchange real property without a court order.[3] He can lease real property for no more than ten years.[4] If a will or trust is silent and the trustee wants to exchange real property or lease it for more than ten years, the trustee must petition for a court order authorizing it.[5]

A trustee will also want court authorization when the will or trust explicitly prohibits a particular act and he wishes to do it in the best interests of the trust.

When the fiduciary petitions the Surrogate's Court for the desired relief, the Surrogate decides whether to entertain the application. If it does so, it will issue process (citation or order to show cause) to all persons interested in the trust to show cause why the relief should not be granted,[6] and the petitioner will arrange for service of the process.[7] Virtual representation applies,[8] and when no party can virtually represent unborns or a persons under disability, the court appoints a guardian ad litem for them.[9]

After the return date and after a hearing if anyone objects, the court will decide what is in the best interests of the trust and, if appropriate, order the fiduciary to exchange or lease the property or to proceed with whatever it was he wanted to do. When the fiduciary follows the court order, his action is binding on all persons interested in the trust who received process or appeared or consented, including those with present interests in the trust, those with remainders and reversions, and those under legal disability or not in being who were represented either virtually or by a guardian ad litem.[10]

Sec. J

1. McKinney's EPTL 11–1.1 states that a fiduciary must first follow the directions in the will or trust, and if the power is not covered by that instrument, must then look to McKinney's EPTL 11–1.1. If that statute does not list the power, he must then look to McKinney's SCPA 1507 or 1508.

2. McKinney's EPTL 11–1.1 is discussed in chapter on "Fiduciaries," supra at 402–05.

3. McKinney's EPTL 11–1.1(b)(5)(E).

4. McKinney's EPTL 11–1.1(b)(5)(c).

5. McKinney's SCPA 1507(1).

6. McKinney's SCPA 1507(2).

7. See chapter on "Procedure," supra at 39–49.

8. See McKinney's SCPA 315 and discussion of virtual representation in chapter on "Procedure," supra at 60–70.

9. See discussion of guardians ad litem in chapter on "Appearances," supra at 238–44.

10. McKinney's SCPA 1507(3).

SECTION K. CONDEMNATION PROCEEDINGS

If the state condemns real property belonging to a trust, the trustee must compromise that condemnation proceeding and receive the proceeds on behalf of the trust. He usually has the power to do this on his own, either under the boiler-plate fiduciaries' powers language in the will or trust, granting either the right to compromise a condemnation proceeding or the general right to sell estate assets, or, if not pursuant to powers in the will or trust, then under the EPTL which gives fiduciaries the power to compromise any claim [1] and the power to sell trust property.[2] It is therefore very rare that the fiduciary must resort to SCPA 1508 to obtain court approval for the compromise of a condemnation proceeding. In fact, the only time the fiduciary should resort to SCPA 1508 is when the will expressly prohibits such settlement, either specifically or in a general prohibition against sale of property.

The fiduciary starts this proceeding by petition, and the court has discretion to require notice to interested persons.[3] The petitioner also submits, either in affidavits or by oral testimony of two disinterested witnesses, evidence of the value of the condemned property, the damages sustained by the trust because of the condemnation, and the positions of the interested parties. The court evaluates the settlement offer and if it is acceptable, it approves the settlement and directs the trustee to give to the state any documents necessary to release the state upon receipt by the trustee of the agreed-upon amount.

If the trustee follows the court order, and if all interested persons received process, appeared, consented or were represented, either virtually or by a guardian ad litem, the trustee is exonerated from liability for his actions.

SECTION L. LIFETIME TRUSTS

The Surrogate's Court with jurisdiction over a lifetime trust has the same powers over the trust and the trustee as a Supreme Court justice has.[1] In practice, although the SCPA applies to lifetime trusts, they are not administered with the same formality as testamentary trusts. Lifetime trusts come into being at the time of execution of the instrument; letters do not issue to the trustee. The Surrogate (or the

Sec. K

1. McKinney's EPTL 11–1.1(b)(13).

2. McKinney's EPTL 11–1.1(b)(5)(E). The omission from the SCPA of a predecessor statute, L.1944, c. 761, SCA 250–c, that specifically permitted fiduciaries to settle condemnation proceedings is mysterious but probably meaningless, since such a power seems clearly to be allowed under the "settlement" power, McKinney's EPTL 11–1.1(b)(13), or the "sale" power, McKinney's EPTL 11–1.1(b)(5)(E). See McKinney's SCPA 1508, Prac.Comm. at 607 (1967).

3. The court usually orders process (a citation or order to show cause) rather than mere notice. McKinney's SCPA 1508, Prac.Comm. at 608 (1967).

Sec. L

1. McKinney's SCPA 1509.

Supreme Court justice) issues orders or decrees relating to a lifetime trust only when something specific is needed, for instance when a successor trustee has to be appointed because the instrument does not provide for one, or a construction problem arises, or an accounting is needed, or some other miscellaneous proceeding has to be commenced.

Chapter Seventeen

DISPOSITION OF REAL PROPERTY

SECTION A. INTRODUCTION

Under traditional common law principles, on a decedent's death, real property passes immediately by operation of law to the person entitled to it,[1] whether the joint owners, the devisees under the will or the distributees in intestacy. A fiduciary appointed for the estate therefore does not take title to it.[2] In practice the fiduciary treats real property like any other estate property; he has the broad powers conferred by EPTL 11–1.1 when necessary to administer the real property, including the power to sell it.[3] The general rule is that the fiduciary may sell real property to pay administration expenses and taxes and to make distributions to beneficiaries whether or not the estate also contains personal property that could be sold for that purpose.[4] He must resort to personal property first, however, if the real property is specifically devised and the personal property is not.[5] In addition, if real or personal property is part of the residuary estate and the residuary beneficiaries unequivocally express a desire to take it in kind, the fiduciary loses his power to sell it if other assets suffice for payment of expenses.[6]

Sec. A

1. Matter of Cunniff, 272 N.Y. 89, 4 N.E.2d 946 (1936).

2. This is the reason the fiduciary is not entitled to commissions on real property except in circumstances where real administrative duties are required. See chapter on "Commissions," supra at 441–44.

3. McKinney's EPTL 11–1.1(b)(5).

4. McKinney's EPTL 13–1.3(a), (b). The attorney should beware here that, if more than one piece of real property is available for sale, a hierarchy exists among the types of real property: that passing under the laws of intestacy, that passing under the residuary clause, and that passing to a specific devisee. See discussion this chapter, infra at 482.

5. See McKinney's EPTL 13–1.3(c).

6. Trask v. Sturges, 170 N.Y. 482, 63 N.E. 534 (1902); Mellen v. Mellen, 139 N.Y. 210, 34 N.E. 925 (1893). See Matter of Fello, 88 A.D.2d 600, 449 N.Y.S.2d 770 (1982), affirmed 58 N.Y.2d 999, 461 N.Y.S.2d 1009, 448 N.E.2d 794 (1983) where one residuary beneficiary unequivocally expressed the desire to take the real property in kind but the other did not. There the court held that the fiduciary's power of sale was not nullified. The agreement must be unequivocal and unanimous. See also Matter of Southwick, N.Y.L.J., Aug. 14, 1985, at 15, col. 3 (Suffolk), where the court ordered a sale despite an "understanding" between the beneficiaries that one would take the property and pay the other one-half its value in cash. Because the beneficiary had not asserted her right under the agreement before the executor entered into a contract to sell to a third party, the court held that she did not extinguish the fiduciary's right to sell.

Article 19 sets forth the Surrogate's power to entertain a request by a fiduciary to sell real property if necessary to pay debts, taxes, administration expenses and similar expenses, to make distributions to beneficiaries, or to accomplish some other necessary goal. In fact fiduciaries almost never have to resort to Article 19, both because wills frequently give them the power to sell the real property, and because the EPTL's powers are usually sufficient.[7] This chapter discusses the workings of Article 19, the rare occasions on which it is necessary, and the other occasions fiduciaries use it despite the existence of other sources of power to dispose of real property.

SECTION B. FIDUCIARY'S INVOCATION OF ARTICLE 19 PROCEEDING

Under SCPA 1902 a fiduciary may dispose of real property if he needs cash to:

(1) Pay administration expenses.

(2) Pay funeral expenses.

(3) Pay the decedent's debts, judgments and liens, except mortgage liens on the real property. The rationale here is that the beneficiary takes the property subject to the mortgage.[1]

(4) Pay estate taxes.

(5) Pay any debt or legacy charged on the real property; for example, "I give to X $5000 payable out of the proceeds of the sale of Blackacre," and "I direct that my debt to Y be paid out of the proceeds of sale."

(6) Make a distribution to beneficiaries. Even when multiple beneficiaries are entitled to the real property, the court in its discretion can order it sold and distribute the proceeds among the beneficiaries to avoid a partition.[2]

(7) In addition, the fiduciary can invoke Article 19 for "any other purpose the court deems necessary," for example, to clear title when a beneficiary wants to sell real property and another beneficiary arguably has a life interest in the property under an ambiguous will clause.[3]

7. See Matter of Osterndorf, 75 Misc.2d 730, 349 N.Y.S.2d 275 (Nassau 1973).

Sec. B

1. McKinney's EPTL 3–3.6. The will can provide otherwise.

2. See Matter of Lynch, 80 A.D.2d 959, 437 N.Y.S.2d 789 (3d Dep't 1981), appeal denied 53 N.Y.2d 606, 440 N.Y.S.2d 1026, 422 N.E.2d 835 (1981), where the court ordered the sale of the property for distribution to the intestate distributee on the theory that avoidance of the expenses of partitioning the property was in the best interests of the estate, despite the fact that the partition would have been more beneficial to the issue of a deceased distributee.

3. See Matter of Perkins, 55 Misc.2d 834, 286 N.Y.S.2d 586 (Albany 1967); Matter of Bolton, 79 Misc.2d 895, 362 N.Y.S.2d 308 (Tompkins 1974).

Article 19 applies to all fiduciaries except trustees,[4] guardians,[5] donees of a power during minority [6] and voluntary administrators.[7] It therefore does apply to executors and administrators (including ancillary), preliminary executors and temporary administrators.[8] Executors and administrators, because of their broad powers, do not use Article 19 very often. It is more likely to be used by temporary administrators, preliminary executors, and administrators who are not bonded.[9] It is also used by committees and conservators.[10]

SECTION C. THE COURT'S POWERS

Article 19 gives the Surrogate the power to authorize the fiduciary to sell, mortgage, exchange or lease real property, to confirm a lease made without court approval, to release the government from further claims in a condemnation proceeding, to transfer the property to a beneficiary, and to take possession of real property, collect the rents and use them as the court directs, and if the estate is a co-owner of property, to bring a partition action or participate in one.[1] The Surrogate may entertain an application even if the proposed disposition is authorized by will or statute.[2]

Because Article 19 does not mention jurisdiction or venue, the provisions of Article 2 govern. If the decedent was a New York domiciliary, every Surrogate in the state has jurisdiction but the proper venue is the county of decedent's domicile.[3] If the decedent was not a New Yorker but left property in New York, all counties have jurisdiction and the proper venue is the first of those counties where he left property to exercise its jurisdiction by entertaining a proceeding.[4] As a practical matter, the Article 19 proceeding is not the first proceeding commenced, so the proper venue will be in that court which has already exercised jurisdiction (usually in a probate or administration proceeding).

The court has the power to order disposition even if persons who may eventually become entitled to a remainder interest or the proceeds of the sale of real property are not in being.[5] As we will discuss

4. A trustee can bring a similar proceeding under SCPA 1507.

5. A guardian can bring a similar proceeding under SCPA 1715.

6. A donee of a power during minority obtains whatever powers he has from the will nominating him.

7. McKinney's SCPA 1901(3). A voluntary administrator's powers are limited to those enumerated in McKinney's SCPA 1306, discussed in chapter on "Small Estates," supra at 251–52.

8. McKinney's SCPA 103(21).

9. No bond is required for formal administration of estates of $10,000 or less, nor for voluntary administrators. McKinney's SCPA 801, Practice Commentary at 610 (1967).

10. See, e.g., Matter of Dessert, N.Y. L.J., Aug. 1985, at 16, col. 2 (Nassau) (conservator).

Sec. C

1. McKinney's SCPA 1901(2)(a)–(i).

2. McKinney's SCPA 1901(1).

3. McKinney's SCPA 205.

4. McKinney's SCPA 206.

5. McKinney's SCPA 1904(6).

shortly, those unborns must be represented either by virtual representation [6] or by appointment of a guardian ad litem to receive service on their behalf and appear for them in the proceeding, or the order will not bind them. The court can also order disposition even if, at the time of the disposition, a life tenant or some other person has a reversion; [7] the reason is that article 19 is primarily for the protection of creditors.

As in other special proceedings, the Article 19 proceeding is commenced by a petition; the court issues process and the petitioner arranges to serve it; and on the return date the court hears objections and eventually issues an order granting or denying the relief.[8]

The fiduciary is usually the petitioner in the Article 19 proceeding, since he is the one with liability for real property wrongfully sold. The petition can also be filed by "persons interested" in the estate,[9] and they usually do so if the fiduciary fails to or if a partition action has begun and they want to try to stop it.[10] In the Article 19 context, the persons interested are the persons entitled to share in the estate under the will or in intestacy, and guardians (or other legal representatives) of persons entitled to share. The public administrator can petition for sale if no interested person is available.[11] Creditors are not interested persons. If they have not availed themselves of a remedy under Article 18,[12] they have to wait for an accounting proceeding (or compel one) [13] to obtain relief. Co-owners of the property are also not interested parties. Unless they also take through the estate, their remedy is to seek a partition of the property.[14]

The court can entertain or refuse to entertain the application, and if it does entertain the petition, it can, of course, deny the application.[15] Often the fiduciary already has the power under EPTL 11–1.1 to dispose of real property, but wants court approval.[16] The court will

6. McKinney's SCPA 315, discussed in chapter on "Procedure," supra at 60–70.

7. McKinney's SCPA 1904(6).

8. See chapter on "Procedure," supra at 35 et seq.

9. McKinney's SCPA 103(39). See Matter of Bolton, 79 Misc.2d 895, 362 N.Y.S.2d 308 (Tompkins 1974) (life tenant has right to petition). Obviously a distributee is a person interested. Matter of Van Etten, 105 A.D.2d 961, 482 N.Y.S.2d 100 (3d Dep't 1984).

10. Under a 1975 amendment, the Surrogate can authorize a fiduciary's commencement of, or participation in, a partition action, which typically takes place in the Supreme Court. SCPA 1901(2), amended by L.1975, ch. 283. The Surrogate need not dismiss a proceeding to sell even when a partition proceeding is pending in the Supreme Court. Matter of Wendland, 35 N.Y.S.2d 622 (Orange 1942). See also McKinney's R.P.A.P.L. § 901.

11. This is true even if the property will escheat to the state. Matter of Clark, 69 Misc.2d 498, 329 N.Y.S.2d 995 (Albany 1972). See McKinney's Public Lands Law § 33(4), requiring authorization and consents by certain state officials before realty which is part of an estate that escheats can be sold. See also McKinney's SCPA 1901, Prac.Comm. at 63 (Supp.1986), where Paul J. Powers suggested that the McKinney's Public Land Law 33(4) procedures were overly cumbersome and should perhaps be changed.

12. See chapter on "Claims," supra at 146 et seq.

13. See discussion of compulsory accountings in chapter on "Accounting," supra at 183–86.

14. Matter of Baur, 135 N.Y.S.2d 105 (1954).

15. McKinney's SCPA 1905(1).

16. Even if the court refuses to entertain the proceeding, the fiduciary's attempt

bestow its approval only in extraordinary circumstances, not wishing to substitute its own judgment for the fiduciary's. Except in unusual circumstances, the fiduciary should exercise his EPTL 11–1.1 powers, his business judgment, and the powers given to him under the will or trust without the court's intervention.[17]

The petitioner must give the names and domiciles of the decedent, the petitioner, all interested persons and creditors. If he is considering a contract or if he has signed a contract contingent on the court's approval, he should attach it to the petition, along with a copy of the will. If the will provides a power of sale, the petitioner should state why he seeks court authorization and why he cannot rely on the will clause and the powers clause of EPTL Article 11.

An Article 19 proceeding is not the only way for the fiduciary to obtain approval of his conduct. The court can also decide the issue during the judicial settlement of the fiduciary's account. A party to that proceeding (usually a creditor [18] because a creditor cannot bring an Article 19 proceeding and is not even a party to it unless the court directs the service of process) may show facts which make a disposition of the decedent's real property desirable and petition for that disposition.[19]

If the court entertains this petition in the course of an accounting, it will adjourn the accounting proceeding until the fiduciary sells the real property under the authority of the court order.[20] After the fiduciary sells the property, he has to file by the adjourned date a supplemental account of the proceeds received from, and the expenses incurred in, the sale.[21] When the court receives this supplemental account, it proceeds with the accounting proceeding and orders distribution of the decedent's property, including the proceeds of the real property sale.[22]

In practice, if the request for disposition of real property is made in an accounting proceeding, the citation issued in the accounting proceeding has to give notice of the request, or if the process was served before

to get court approval tends to illustrate his good faith if the action is later challenged at the accounting.

17. Matter of Osterndorf, 75 Misc.2d 730, 349 N.Y.S.2d 275 (Nassau 1973).

18. See Matter of Cuniffe, 272 N.Y. 89, 4 N.E.2d 946 (1936) (Surrogate may properly grant a creditor's application for an order directing a sale of real property to which the devisee still has title).

19. McKinney's SCPA 1904(3).

20. McKinney's SCPA 1914. But see Matter of Troll, N.Y.L.J., April 16, 1985, at 13, col. 2 (Westchester). There an accounting was pending and a party objected to the executrix's management of assets, alleging that the mismanagement had caused losses which in turn necessitated the sale of real property. The will had given the real property to the objectant with directions to pay one-half its value to the executrix (surviving spouse). The court refused to entertain the Article 19 application, directing the parties to wait until the issue had been resolved on the accounting.

21. The supplemental account should also outline the steps taken in the Article 19 proceeding. See McKinney's SCPA 1914, Prac.Comm. at 306 (1967).

22. McKinney's SCPA 1914(2).

the request for Article 19 approval was made, the court will have to issue a supplemental citation.

If the applicant wants to dispose of real property, but it is clear to the court that the disposition may become unnecessary within a reasonable time because the net income from the real property is sufficient to cover expenses, the court can adjourn the application periodically and authorize the fiduciary to take possession of the property, receive the rents and apply them appropriately.[23] This may occur if the real property hosts crops almost ready to be harvested, lumber almost ready to be cut, or minerals about to be mined, or if the market conditions are changing favorably, or in other similar situations likely to bring money into the estate to pay expenses. This situation can come up either because someone raises objections, or because the court makes such an order in the absence of objections. Courts are likely to choose this course when the real property is specifically devised,[24] but it is not so limited.[25] It may also do so in cases where the real property passes under the laws of intestate distribution and where it passes as part of the residuary estate under a will.

SECTION D. PROCESS

If the Surrogate entertains the petition, process will issue to all persons interested (persons entitled to share in the estate under the will or in intestacy, and guardians (or other legal representatives) of persons entitled to share). The court may also order the petitioner to serve creditors.[1] As a matter of practice the court always directs service on creditors. A person designated as an appointee of the real property under a power of appointment with no other interest in the estate is not a necessary party.[2]

If a person is a necessary party but is unknown, the court must appoint a guardian ad litem to protect his interests.[3]

The court can refuse to entertain the application in the interests of justice.[4] For example, if an interested person offers to file a bond to pay all the costs and expenses that the fiduciary claims are necessary,

23. McKinney's SCPA 1905(2).

24. The specifically devised real property abates (along with specifically bequeathed personal property) after all other dispositions have been exhausted, McKinney's EPTL 13–1.3, and even if all other funds have been exhausted, the court, because it wants to protect the testator's plan, will delay ordering disposition if it believes, as discussed in the text, that the income will cover expenses.

25. A 1968 amendment to McKinney's SCPA 1905 expressly eliminated language that made this section applicable only to specifically devised real property. L.1968, c. 280, section 2.

Sec. D

1. McKinney's SCPA 1904(2). If the creditors are not parties, they may complain later that the sale price was too low. Matter of Hartman, 125 Misc. 656, 211 N.Y.S. 700 (Albany 1925) (creditors entitled to notice of proceeding to sell realty).

2. McKinney's SCPA 1904(5).

3. McKinney's SCPA 1909(2).

4. McKinney's SCPA 1905.

the court may very well refuse the application to dispose of the real property to pay such expenses.[5]

A judgment creditor of the distributee or devisee entitled to the real property subject to sale is a necessary party,[6] but is not entitled to payment out of the proceeds. That is simply not the executor's responsibility.[7]

Article 19 contains its own miniature virtual representation provisions. If a class of persons is interested in the reversion or remainder on a limited basis, only those members of the class at the time of the application need be served with process.[8] For example, if contingencies will eventually determine who is entitled to the reversion or remainder interest, the only members of the class necessary to the proceeding are those who would have been entitled to the interest if the contingency had happened immediately before the application for sale of the real property was made. However, because the general virtual representation provisions of SCPA 315 [9] apply to these proceedings, the Article 19 provisions are of historical interest and somewhat superfluous.

If it appears that the property may have escheated to the state, or if the state has a lien on a beneficiary's interest, the state must receive process like any other interested person.[10] The petition must show the nature of the state's interest and the reason for making the state a party. Failure to comply can result in the dismissal of the proceeding as against the state. The net effect of this dismissal would be to preclude the Surrogate from ordering a disposition, but in practice the Surrogate will cure the defect by ordering the petitioner to serve process on the state.

SECTION E. THE ORDER

On the return date of process, interested parties can object to the proposed disposition of the real property, and persons whose interests would be affected by allowance of a claim can object to its allowance.[1] The court weighs the advisability of allowing it by inquiring into the

5. Matter of O'Donnell, 121 Misc. 496, 201 N.Y.S. 463 (Kings 1923), reversed 208 App.Div. 374, 203 N.Y.S. 882 (2d Dep't 1924), reversed on other grounds 240 N.Y. 99, 147 N.E. 541 (1925).

6. Matter of Townsend, 203 N.Y. 522, 96 N.E. 1105 (1911) (judgment creditor has a substantial interest to protect and therefore must be made a party).

7. Matter of McClure, 59 Misc.2d 111, 298 N.Y.S.2d 96 (Nassau 1969) (proposed decree settling administrator's account should not direct that a part of the distributee's share be paid to judgment creditor of distributee, but should provide for payment to the distributee directly).

8. McKinney's SCPA 1904(4).

9. McKinney's SCPA 315 is discussed in chapter on "Procedure," supra at 60–70.

10. For a discussion of the special requirements when it appears that the realty will escheat to the estate, see McKinney's Public Lands Law § 33(4) and McKinney's SCPA 1901, Prac.Comm. at 63 (Supp.1986). For the manner of serving process on the state by service on the State Attorney General, see chapter on "Procedure," supra at 47.

Sec. E

1. McKinney's SCPA 1906(1). Thus in a solvent estate one creditor cannot object to the allowance of another's claim because his interest is not adversely affected.

amount of claims, the funds available to pay them and the extent of the deficiency.[2] It evaluates the defenses, which usually relate to the necessity of liquidating the real property to pay claims or provide for distribution, and the objectant's claim that there are sufficient assets available without resort to the proceeds of sale. The court may require an appraisal of the value of the property, or in some instances, testimony on the value, the best manner of disposition and the optimum time for the sale. In practice the petitioner usually includes a contract with the petition, and in most cases, the contract of sale contains a clause making it contingent on the court's approval. The court must try to get the best price possible. Ideally it does so by keeping the vendee in and getting extra bidders. There are several ways of doing this. Very often the courts provide the fiduciary with a form of notice and order to conduct an auction sale, and the court conducts the auction at the courthouse. The court usually sets a minimum amount, for example, the price set by the contract that was initially submitted for approval (called the upset price), and directs the fiduciary to advertise in several local papers and to give notice by mail to brokers in the neighborhood of the parcel. The notice directs that all persons who want to bid must deposit a certain amount, usually ten percent of the upset price, with the clerk of the court on the auction date, or they will not be permitted to bid.[3] On the auction date the court will list those who have posted the down payment and will then open up the bidding at the upset price as a starting point and then proceed to conduct an auction by oral bids.

The court can also set the contract price (subject to verification by appraisals[4]) as the upset price and give the vendee (or other interested persons, such as family members) the option to meet the price at the close of auction within a short period of time (perhaps thirty minutes). However, since such a procedure may discourage bidding, the courts do not use it often.

The court may in its order determine the rights of the respective parties or may postpone the determination until the final estate accounting.[5]

The court can direct the disposition of all or part of the property and specify whether the sale should be public or private. It may fix the manner, the terms and conditions of the sale.[6] Sometimes the court

2. McKinney's SCPA 1907(1).

3. See, e.g., Guthy v. Brandine, N.Y. L.J., May 17, 1985, at 16, col. 2 (Supreme Ct. Nassau). See also Matter of Kinder, N.Y.L.J., Aug. 8, 1985, at 14, col. 5 (Queens), where Surrogate Laurino advocates sale at public auction by the public administrator where several parcels are sold at once rather than the "costly and arcane method of public sale on the courthouse steps * * *."

4. Needless to say, the appraisal should be made by a disinterested outsider, to avoid the problems that arose in Matter of Kane, 98 A.D.2d 851, 470 N.Y.S.2d 823 (1983), appeal denied 61 N.Y.2d 607, 475 N.Y.S.2d 1025, 463 N.E.2d 1235 (1984). In that case the appraiser, the fiduciaries, the buyer, the Surrogate and the estate attorney all knew each other. The appellate division held that the facts did not point to a genuine conflict of interests sufficient to invalidate the sale, but warned against such transactions.

5. McKinney's SCPA 1909(1).

6. McKinney's SCPA 1907(2)(3).

allows the fiduciary to decide the public or private nature of the sale and the credit terms, security, and time of sale. However, usually the fiduciary has negotiated a conditional contract and submits it with the petition for the court's approval, and the court can direct the sale under the contract terms or modify them. If the sale is private, it should always be made subject to the Surrogate's approval. The court's rejection of the sale is usually because of the inadequacy of the price obtained, some irregularities in the sale, or evidence of bad faith.

In practice, if after the court approves a contract, a title search reveals a cloud on title, the purchaser must seek relief from the court on notice to all interested parties.

The order approving a contract to sell real property may provide for a real estate broker's fee and a guardian ad litem's fee for any parties under disability.[7]

As an alternative to ordering the property sold, the court may direct the fiduciary to go in and take possession of the property and collect the rent so that he can pay the obligations of the estate and avoid the necessity of a sale.

The court's order is binding on all persons interested in the real property, whether their interest takes the form of a present interest, a remainder, a reversion, a future interest or a trust interest, and it is binding on all persons under disability, absentees, internees, and persons not in being who have consented or appeared, or have been served, or have been represented either by a guardian ad litem or by a virtual representative.[8]

SECTION F. CREDITORS' RIGHTS

A fiduciary cannot distribute the proceeds of the disposition until the statutory period of time for the presentations of claims has expired.[1] That time is seven months from the appointment of a fiduciary, or if the fiduciary published notice for creditors, three months.[2] In addition, the fiduciary cannot make distributions, even after the seven-

7. If the court authorizes the sale under McKinney's SCPA 1902, the selling expenses should be deductible from the estate tax return. Matter of Larson, 87 Misc.2d 397, 385 N.Y.S.2d 720 (Chautaugua 1976). As a matter of tax law, this question of which expenses are deductible is far from settled. Compare Smith v. Commissioner, 57 T.C. 650 (1972), affirmed 510 F.2d 479 (2d Cir.1975), certiorari denied 423 U.S. 827, 96 S.Ct. 44, 46 L.Ed.2d 44 (1975), Vatter v. Commissioner, 65 T.C. 633 (1975), affirmed per curiam 1977–1 U.S.T.C. par. 13,169 (2d Cir.1976), and Hibernia National Bank v. United States, 581 F.2d 741 (9th Cir. 1978), with Estate of Park v. Commissioner, 475 F.2d 673 (6th Cir.1973). See Flynn, Interplay of Federal and State Law in Determining Deductible Administration Expenses," 50 St. John's L.Rev. 357 (1975); Note, "Estate of Smith—Deductibility of Administration Expenses under the Internal Revenue Code and under the Treasury Regulations: Resolving the Conflict," 17 William and Mary L.Rev. 363 (1975).

8. McKinney's SCPA 1913.

Sec. F

1. See McKinney's SCPA 1802 and discussion of this limited statute of limitations in chapter on "Claims," supra at 148–50.

2. McKinney's SCPA 1911(4) was amended in 1983, L.1983, c. 457, section 1, to conform with SCPA 1801's three-month time period for publication to creditors.

or three-month period has passed, until all known creditors or persons interested have had an opportunity to be heard on the disposition of the proceeds.[3]

If an interested person challenges a claim, debt, demand, charge or expense, the court can determine the validity of the claim, whether the fiduciary admitted or rejected it.[4] In that case the claimant would be a necessary party.[5] Where a claim has been allowed or reduced to judgment, the objectant has the burden of disproving the claim or showing that it was obtained through fraud or collusion.[6] The court can also determine the priority of claims, thus obviating the necessity for a full accounting proceeding. If the relief is sought in an accounting proceeding, the court usually will adjourn the judicial settlement of the account until the proceedings are complete, which may obviate the need for continuing the accounting.

Where a party objects to the fiduciary's allowance of a claim on the ground that the statute of limitations has run, the claim is deemed to be rejected by the fiduciary at the time the objection is interposed.[7] The fiduciary cannot waive the defense of the statute of limitations.[8] However, the statute of limitations is tolled for the period between the presentation of the claim and the time of the objections. That time is deducted from the time the cause of action arose to determine whether the statute of limitations has expired.[9]

Even if the court rules against the sale, it may determine the rights of the parties before it and direct a conveyance to them in whole or in part.[10]

SECTION G. PROCEDURE AFTER THE COURT SIGNS THE ORDER

Once the court signs the order of disposition, the fiduciary must execute it. If the petitioner already had a contract and attached it to

3. Naturally, if a person interested has received process in the proceeding or has appeared, that suffices for that person's opportunity to be heard. See McKinney's SCPA 307, discussed in chapter on "Procedure, supra at 39–49, and McKinney's SCPA Article 4, discussed in chapter on "Appearances," supra at 232 et seq.

4. McKinney's SCPA 1906. For a discussion of allowance or rejection of claims, see chapter on "Claims," supra at 146 et seq.

5. McKinney's SCPA 1904, Prac.Comm. at 279 (1967). The statute does not require such service, which is nevertheless necessary under general principles of due process.

6. See Matter of Smith, 84 A.D.2d 664, 444 N.Y.S.2d 325 (3d Dep't 1981); McKinney's SCPA 1807, Prac.Comm. at 127 (1967); McKinney's SCPA 1906, Prac. Comm. at 289–90 (1967).

7. McKinney's SCPA 1906(2).

8. Matter of O'Rourke, 12 Misc. 248, 34 N.Y.S. 45 (Westch.1895) (executor or administrator has no power to waive legal defenses of statute of limitations or statute of frauds).

9. McKinney's SCPA 1906(2). Under McKinney's SCPA 1810 a creditor may commence an action in another court of competent jurisdiction, such as the Supreme Court, by acting within sixty days of the rejection. It is an interesting question whether the creditor could argue, under McKinney's SCPA 1906, that the sixty day statute of limitations should start to run from the time the objections are filed.

10. McKinney's SCPA 1907(5).

the petition, after the court signs the order he merely has to execute the deed.[1] If he did not attach a contract, the fiduciary must report the eventual disposition to the court.[2]

The court may direct the fiduciary to furnish a bond to insure that he will execute the order and account for the proceeds of the sale.[3] Ordinarily wills exempt an executor from filing a bond, but the court can direct him to file one anyway.[4]

Usually an administrator's letters do not restrict his power to sell real property, but even if they do, the restrictions will be lifted to permit the sale after the fiduciary files the court-ordered bond. The court can dispense with a bond but usually does not if the administrator is going to receive the proceeds in his fiduciary capacity. The court can also reduce the amount of the bond on condition that the administrator deposit the proceeds in a specific bank or trust company subject to the further order of the court.[5] As an alternative, the court sometimes directs the contract vendees to draw checks payable to named persons other than the administrator, such as creditors, devisees or distributees. In that case it can dispense with the bond or reduce the bond to the amount the fiduciary will receive in his fiduciary capacity.

After the fiduciary has reported back to the Surrogate, the court will confirm or reject the disposition. It will confirm if the fiduciary followed the terms of the order. If it became impossible for the fiduciary to comply with the initial order, the court can change the terms and conditions of the order.[6] The court can also extend the order to other parcels, if the sale of the first parcel turned out to be insufficient.[7]

The court can also relieve a purchaser from his obligation to buy the property and can compel specific performance by either a purchaser or the fiduciary, just as the Supreme Court could.[8]

SECTION H. OBLIGATIONS OF LIFE TENANTS

Unless the will provides otherwise, a right to occupy premises under the terms of a will requires the life tenant to pay the ordinary expenses of maintenance, taxes and insurance.[1]

Sec. G

1. McKinney's SCPA 1911(3).
2. McKinney's SCPA 1911(1).
3. McKinney's SCPA 1910(1).
4. McKinney's SCPA 1910(2).
5. McKinney's SCPA 1910(3).
6. McKinney's SCPA 1911(2).
7. McKinney's SCPA 1911(2).
8. McKinney's SCPA 1911(2).

Sec. H

1. Matter of Gaffers, 254 A.D. 448, 5 N.Y.S.2d 671 (3d Dep't 1938) (direction in will that life tenant pay these expenses does not make payment a condition failure of which will lead to divestiture, because these conditions are imposed by law on the life tenant unless the will directs otherwise).

SECTION I. PURCHASER'S LIABILITY FOR DECEDENT'S DEBTS OR ADMINISTRATION EXPENSES

A person buying real property from a distributee or devisee is faced with a potential danger: if that real property is needed to satisfy the decedent's debts or estate administration expenses, it could be the subject of an Article 19 proceeding. Someone could petition for the sale of property under Article 19 even though it had already been sold. SCPA 1903 creates time limitations that expose the purchaser to liability for those debts but limit the time of such exposure. The statute says that if someone purchases real property from a distributee or devisee before an Article 19 proceeding is commenced, his title cannot be affected by the proceeding unless it is commenced within eighteen months from the date letters were issued to the original fiduciary and unless such letters were granted within two years after the date of death of the decedent.[1] Thus, if a devisee or distributee sells real property more than eighteen months after letters have issued, no liens attach to the sale. Similarly, if no letters issue and more than two years have elapsed since the decedent's death, no lien attaches.

Conversely, the purchaser's title to real property bought before the expiration of these time periods is subject to liens for the decedent's debts and may be subject to divestment. A person can, of course, commence an Article 19 proceeding after that time,[2] but if the property has been transferred, it will not affect the transferee. While it will be too late to go against the transferee, the proceeds received by the transferor will be subject to claims and expenses.

A judgment creditor has an additional right, not under Article 19 but under Article 18: he can petition the Surrogate to issue an execution against real property the decedent owned.[3] The court issues process and directs service on the persons it considers necessary.

Article 19 proceedings may not be commenced to satisfy a debt when the real property is exempt by law from levy and sale because of an execution;[4] for example, a judgment may have been obtained

Sec. I

1. McKinney's SCPA 1903(1).

2. See Wagner v. Wagner, 25 A.D.2d 796, 269 N.Y.S.2d 177 (3d Dep't 1966) (proceeding to sell realty was timely despite passage or more than eighteen months from decedent's death).

3. McKinney's SCPA 1812, discussed in chapter on "Claims," supra at 175. This proceeding is authorized by McKinney's CPLR 5208, whose general rule states that no execution can be levied after the judgment debtor's death, except that the Surrogate can do so under the provisions of SCPA 1812. See Matter of Chester National Bank, 72 Misc.2d 310, 339 N.Y.S.2d 174 (Orange 1972) (court was authorized to issue the execution even though the judgment creditor had not first filed a claim because the claim was based on the judgment of a court of competent jurisdiction).

4. McKinney's SCPA 1903(2).

during the decedent's lifetime, or the property may have been exempt from levy because of a homestead exemption or burial plot exemption.[5]

The final paragraph of SCPA 1903 is an actual statute of limitations. A proceeding to satisfy a legacy expressly or impliedly charged to the real property must be commenced within ten years from the date of the decedent's death.[6] This will not affect a bona fide transferee; the legatee can pursue his legacy only out of the proceeds of sale.

SECTION J. ORDER IN WHICH THE PARCELS ARE TO BE SOLD

Article 19 proceedings are rare to begin with, and even rarer is the case where the decedent owned more than one parcel of real property whose proceeds are necessary for debts or expenses. If he did, SCPA 1908 determines the order of sale.[1] This order is mandatory:

1. real property passing under the laws of intestacy [2] not conveyed by the distributees.

2. real property passing under the laws of intestacy and conveyed by the distributees.

3. real property devised under the residuary clause. If one person received two parcels under the residuary clause and conveyed one, the other is sold first. If, however, two persons received a parcel each under the residuary clause and one conveyed his, they are equally subject to sale.

4. real property specifically devised.

SECTION K. EFFECT OF THE DEATH OF A FIDUCIARY

A vacancy in the office of fiduciary will not end the Article 19 proceeding. If a fiduciary ceases to serve (because of death, disqualification or removal from office [1] before the court has signed its order to dispose of real property, the court may order the successor fiduciary to be substituted, and the proceeding will continue by or against the successor.[2] The deceased fiduciary's fiduciary would submit a motion and a proposed order of substitution (usually substitution by him) for the Surrogate's signature with an affidavit describing the need for the

5. See Matter of Driscoll, 12 Misc.2d 427, 176 N.Y.S.2d 463 (1958); McKinney's CPLR 5206.

6. McKinney's SCPA 1903(3).

Sec. J

1. If more than one parcel is subject to the Article 19 proceeding, the petition should specify the order of sale under McKinney's SCPA 1908.

2. Real property passes under the intestate scheme if the testator did not have a will. It also passes in intestacy if he failed to dispose of property in the will (for example, the will did not have a residuary clause disposing of all property not otherwise disposed of). See McKinney's EPTL 4–1.1 and chapter on "Administration," supra at 125 et seq.

Sec. K

1. See chapter on "Fiduciaries," supra at 384 et seq.

2. McKinney's SCPA 1912(1).

substitution, and serve a notice of motion on parties to the original proceeding.

If the original fiduciary ceases to serve after the court has granted the order to dispose of real property but before the fiduciary has executed it, the successor may proceed without further order to complete the transaction.[3]

If no successor fiduciary is serving, the court can authorize the fiduciary of the deceased fiduciary to complete the transaction or continue the proceeding.[4] In any case, the successor or the fiduciary of the deceased fiduciary must give security for the performance of his duties if the court directs.

SECTION L. PROCEDURE WHEN AN INTERESTED PARTY PURCHASES THE PROPERTY

It is not uncommon for a family member or a beneficiary or creditor of the estate to want to buy the real property that is the subject of an Article 19 proceeding. The court can permit the spouse, beneficiary or creditor to buy it, and can offset the elective share, legacy, distributive share or claim against the purchase price.[1] Since in practice the exact amount due to the spouse, beneficiary or creditor is often not known until the final accounting, the fiduciary can, at the time of the sale, allow an estimated credit to the bidder.[2] If the proceeds of sale are insufficient to cover administration expenses, debts and funeral expenses, the beneficiary's share is reduced, since those costs have priority over his legacy or elective share.[3] In that case, the fiduciary on the accounting credits the beneficiary only with an amount that represents the true offset after the deficiency is considered. The beneficiary has to repay the difference between what was originally credited to him and the amount he is actually entitled to receive.[4]

Because of these uncertainties, if the fiduciary gives the purchaser an offset credit on his bid, the purchaser will not receive a deed until the judicial settlement of the fiduciary's account, when his entitlement

3. McKinney's SCPA 1912(2).

4. See McKinney's SCPA 2207 authorizing the fiduciary of a deceased fiduciary to wind up certain business of a fiduciary, discussed in chapter on "Accounting," supra at 210–12.

Sec. L

1. McKinney's SCPA 1915(1). Since it refers to the spouse, beneficiary or creditor as a purchaser, it contemplates a post-contract application for the court's approval.

2. McKinney's SCPA 1915(1). Even a preliminary executor can enter into such a contract. Matter of Glazer, 86 A.D.2d 982, 448 N.Y.S.2d 322 (4th Dep't 1982) (the Surrogate's order authorized the preliminary fiduciary to enter into an agreement with a beneficiary and granted the beneficiary immediate possession although the deed would not be delivered until the final accounting).

3. See discussion of abatement in chapter on "Claims," supra at 151–52.

4. McKinney's SCPA 1915(2).

and any deficiency are finally established and he has made up any deficiency.[5] The courts are, naturally, conservative about this credit.

SECTION M. PROVISIONS FOR PAYMENT OF UNDETERMINED CLAIMS AND DEBTS NOT YET DUE

Sometimes when a fiduciary petitions for the sale of real property, a claim is uncertain or a debt is not yet due and the creditor does not want accelerated payment. In that case the court in its decree will direct that the fiduciary retain sufficient funds to pay the claim when determined or the debt when due. The decree will also instruct the fiduciary how to distribute any amounts left over after payment of the claim or debt,[1] since the courts typically require the fiduciary to withhold a larger amount than it thinks is necessary to cover the claim or debt.

The retention of funds under SCPA 1916 is similar to SCPA 2217,[2] applicable whether or not real property has to be sold to pay the claim. It is also somewhat similar to SCPA 1804, applicable when assets have to be retained to cover a contingent or unliquidated claim.[3]

SECTION N. EFFECT OF A DECEDENT'S DEATH BEFORE CLOSING

If a decedent entered into a contract during his lifetime to buy or sell real property, and died before the closing, his rights and liabilities and those of the other party to the contract are governed by Article 19.[1]

5. McKinney's SCPA 1915(3). For an example of the workings of McKinney's SCPA 1915, see Matter of Glazer, 86 A.D.2d 982, 448 N.Y.S.2d 322 (4th Dep't 1982), where two wills had been offered for probate in a decedent's estate, and the court had appointed two preliminary executors to start administration during the will contest. The decedent's home was part of the estate and the preliminary executors wanted to dispose of it. In each will Jerome Glazer, who was an intestate distributee and one of the preliminary executors, had been given an option to buy the real property at the same price. He petitioned the court to approve his purchase of the real property at the option price and the objectant urged that the purchase price should be fair market value. The Surrogate ordered the preliminary executors to have the property appraised, and then to convey it to Jerome Glazer at the option price if either will was admitted to probate. In the first will the legacy completely offset the option price and in the other the legacy was less. The court ordered Jerome Glazer to pay the difference if the latter will was admitted to probate. It further ordered that if both wills were denied probate, Jerome Glazer should pay the appraisal price. Thus, under the Surrogate's order, the estate would be paid in any contingency. The court ordered immediate conveyance to Jerome Glazer, who was entitled to immediate possession, but the fiduciary could not transfer the deed to Jerome Glazer until the final accounting. See also McKinney's SCPA 1915, Prac.Comm. at 69–70 (Supp. 1986).

Sec. M

1. McKinney's SCPA 1916.

2. See chapter on "Accounting," supra at 220–21.

3. See chapter on "Claims," supra at 153–56.

Sec. N

1. McKinney's SCPA 1917 governs the case where the decedent was purchaser, and McKinney's SCPA 1921 where he was seller.

1. DECEDENT AS BUYER

If the decedent signed a contract to buy real property and died before the closing, the fiduciary has a right to enforce that contract.[2] In addition, he can assign the decedent's interest in the contract for appropriate consideration, and the assignee then has the same interest the decedent would have had if he had not died,[3] including the right to specific performance. Legal title at the death of the decedent under such circumstances is in the vendor. The decedent, as vendee, had equitable ownership and his rights are those that he bargained for under the executory contract, subject to the vendor's lien for the unpaid purchase price from the decedent. The fiduciary can assign less than the decedent's entire interest (such as a life estate or fractional share of the property)[4] and if so, he retains the portion that is not assigned for the benefit of those interested in the estate.[5] In that case both the assignee and the fiduciary have a right to specific performance.[6]

If the decedent specifically devised the contracted-for property under his will or if it passes by intestacy, the specific devisee or distributee must pay any balance due under the contract (unless the will provides otherwise) if he is to accept the devise.[7] If the real property was part of the residuary estate, the fiduciary is free to complete the purchase or assign the contract. If he completes the deal, title to the real property will be in the estate for the beneficiaries' benefit. If he assigns the contract, the consideration paid for the assignment will be an asset of the estate. The fiduciary holds the property for the beneficiaries (subject to the dower or curtesy interest of the spouse, in the rare cases where such interests still exist.[8] If a decedent rented an apartment which turned cooperative after his death, his estate does not have the right to purchase, since the decedent did not possess that right.[9] If he did have the right but had not exercised it, the estate can do so.[10]

2. DECEDENT AS SELLER

If a decedent dies after signing a contract to sell real property, his fiduciary has the power to convey the real property according to the contract terms without resort to an Article 19 proceeding.[11] The

2. Baker v. Struck, 130 Misc. 62, 223 N.Y.S. 613 (Monroe 1927) (executrix has capacity to sue for specific performance of contract by testator to buy real property).

3. McKinney's SCPA 1917(1).

4. McKinney's SCPA 1917(2).

5. McKinney's SCPA 1917(4).

6. McKinney's SCPA 1917(3). The persons interested and the fiduciary would have to act in concert to obtain specific performance. See McKinney's SCPA 1917, Prac.Comm. at 310 (1967).

7. McKinney's EPTL 3–4.3.

8. McKinney's SCPA 1917(4).

9. Lomnitz v. 61 E. 86 St. Equities Group, Aug. 21, 1985, at 6, col. 5 (Sup.Ct. New York County).

10. DeKovessey v. Coronet Properties Co., N.Y.L.J., July 23, 1985, at 11, col. 1 (Sup.Ct. New York County); Bunim v. 300 Central Park West Apartments Corp., N.Y. L.J., June 30, 1982, at 6, col. 3 (Sup.Ct. New York County).

11. McKinney's EPTL 11–1.1(b)(3); McKinney's SCPA 1921(2).

fiduciary simply has to convey a deed to the purchaser,[12] and the contract should be attached to the deed. His ratifying the contract is subject to review on the accounting proceeding, so occasionally the fiduciary prefers to get court approval by bringing an Article 19 proceeding.[13] He may do so after the sale by starting a separate proceeding,[14] or at the final accounting. He may also be able to avoid the contract if the decedent's capacity to contract is questionable.[15] If, however, the decedent had capacity and the other party negotiated in good faith, the estate is bound by the contract even if objectively the price is too low.

In addition, the purchaser also has a right to use Article 19 to compel specific performance of the contract.

The procedure is for the prospective purchaser [16] or the prospective seller [17] to file a petition seeking confirmation of the sale under the contract terms.[18] In the alternative, the decedent's fiduciary can seek the same relief in the proceeding for settlement of his account. The vendee could also assert such a cause of action in the accounting proceeding, although it is not stated in the statute. The petitioner submits a citation, which the court issues and orders served on interested parties, and a proposed order for the Surrogate's signature. On the return date the Surrogate hears any objections, evaluates the contract,[19] adjudicates the rights of the parties, determines how much is still payable under the contract,[20] and makes whatever decree or order justice requires.[21]

The vendee should argue that his rights vis a vis the fiduciary are the same as the rights he would have had if the decedent had not died.[22]

12. McKinney's SCPA 1921, Prac. Comm. at 318 (1967).

13. McKinney's SCPA 1921(2). The Surrogate's jurisdiction stems from the McKinney's Constitution, Article 6, section 12, which grants the Surrogate jurisdiction over all matters relating to the affairs of a decedent.

14. McKinney's SCPA 1921.

15. See Matter of Gebauer, 79 Misc.2d 715, 36 N.Y.S.2d 539 (Cattaraugus 1974), affirmed 51 A.D.2d 643, 378 N.Y.S.2d 653 (4th Dep't 1976), where the court faced with such a challenge found that the testator did have testamentary capacity. See West McKinney Forms, ESP section 12:232.

16. That is, the contract vendee, his fiduciary, distributees, devisees or assigns. McKinney's SCPA 1921.

17. That is, the decedent's fiduciary, distributees, devisees or assigns. McKinney's SCPA 1921.

18. The statute is actually somewhat less clear than the text states. It does not specifically give the vendee (or his fiduciary, distributees, devisees or assigns) the right to seek confirmation of the deal. Only the decedent's successors in interest have that. The statute gives the vendee only the right to petition for the conveyance of the real property. The statute probably allows the vendee to get the confirmation, however, because its predecessor, SCA 227, clearly did, and the Revisers Notes to SCPA 1921 state that "[n]o change in substance is intended." The attorney for a vendee who wants the court's confirmation to avoid title problems later should petition for it.

19. The court can review the competency of the decedent to enter into the contract. See Matter of Gebauer, 79 Misc.2d 715, 361 N.Y.S.2d 539 (Cattaraugus 1974), affirmed 51 A.D.2d 643, 378 N.Y.S.2d 653 (4th Dep't 1976).

20. McKinney's SCPA 1921(3).

21. McKinney's SCPA 1921(4).

22. See Matter of Finkle, 44 A.D.2d 731, 354 N.Y.S.2d 169 (3d Dep't 1974),

If the decedent had executed a will specifically devising real property to a beneficiary and then entered into a contract to sell it, the devisee inherits the real property subject to the contract. He has to convey the real property under the terms of the contract, and he is entitled to that part of the sale proceeds paid after the decedent's death.[23]

SECTION O. RIGHTS OF LIFE TENANT IN DISTRIBUTION OF ASSETS

A decedent may have had an interest in real property in which someone else also had an interest, either as a life tenant or a tenant for a term of years. The fiduciary may believe that the sale of that property is necessary to pay debts or administration expense, and it is within the court's Article 19 jurisdiction to order the sale.[1] The reality is that an attempt to sell the property encumbered by a life interest reduces both its desirability to potential buyers and its value. The court therefore has a choice; it can order the property sold subject to the life interest, or it can order the sale of the property as a whole and then compensate the life tenant for the loss of his life interest or interest for years.[2] It can do so only if it finds "that the interests of all the parties will be better protected or a more advantageous disposition can be made of the real property. * * * "[3]

Typically there are two circumstances that will satisfy those requirements: first, if the property is subject to foreclosure for failure to pay a mortgage, tax or other upkeep, and second, if the life tenant no longer wants or needs to live there, because he is moving elsewhere.[4]

Obviously, before the court can order destruction of a life tenant's interest in property, it must make that person a party to the proceeding and allow him to object to the sale of his interest.[5]

where the buyer had been in default during the decedent's lifetime in exercising an option, but the decedent had not terminated the contract. The buyer was held to have a right to enforce it after the decedent's death.

23. McKinney's EPTL 3-4.2.

Sec. O

1. McKinney's SCPA 1918.

2. McKinney's SCPA 1918(1). The court in its order should specify that the sale encompasses the property as a whole; the mere waiver of process and consent by the life tenant does not effect a conveyance of the life tenant's interest. Milligan v. Gabbet, 101 Misc. 253, 167 N.Y.S. 558 (Onondaga 1917) (purchaser at judicial sale who finds others in possession cannot assume that they are his tenants without further proof).

3. McKinney's SCPA 1918(1).

4. See Matter of Christie, N.Y.L.J., Dec. 4, 1979, at 11, col. 1, where the testator gave the beneficiary a life interest in property and the beneficiary decided she no longer wanted to live there. Though the petitioner was the trustee of the testamentary trust, and though McKinney's SCPA 1901 excludes trustees as persons entitled to use Article 19, the court entertained the proceeding, and ordered the property sold and the money invested for the life tenant's benefit. They viewed her as the effective petitioner because she had waived process and consented to the relief. See also Matter of Bolton, 79 Misc.2d 895, 362 N.Y.S.2d 308 (Tompkins 1974) (accord).

5. See Matter of Bolton, 79 Misc.2d 895, 362 N.Y.S.2d 308 (Tompkins 1974) (life tenant is an interested person and can be considered to have petitioned for the relief because she waived service of process and consented to the relief).

The compensation due a life tenant or a tenant for a term of years is determined as though the proceeding were one for partition.[6] The solution might be a lump-sum payment based on annuity principles.

If the court finds that inequity lurks in the lump sum payment, because for example such a payment effectively accelerates the remainder interest and cuts out contingent remaindermen, the court may instead direct investing the proceeds and paying the income to the life tenant.[7] The value is computed at the date of sale, not the date of death. That plan would protect the contingent remaindermen if the first-line remainderman predeceased the life tenant.[8] If no such inequity exists and all the parties agree either to a lump-sum payment or the investment of the proceeds, the court usually orders accordingly.[9]

This discussion of the person with a life interest or an interest for a term of years applies equally to a person with a dower or curtesy interest in the decedent's real property. It also applies to a person with a lease for a term.[10] Applications under this section are very rare indeed.

It bears noting here that if a decedent's estate included an interest in real property for a term of years (such as a lease), his fiduciary could sell it freely, and need not show any of the SCPA 1902 exigencies before such sale.

SECTION P. RESTITUTION TO THOSE ADVERSELY AFFECTED BY THE SALE

Occasionally a piece of real property is sold to satisfy administration and other expenses and later additional money or personal property belonging to the estate is unearthed. A person adversely affected by the sale may maintain a proceeding for reimbursement from those newly discovered assets.[1] For example, if the fiduciary sold (pursuant to the Surrogate's Article 19 order) specifically devised real property to pay claims because he thought there was no residuary estate, and

6. McKinney's SCPA 1918(2); see also McKinney's RPAPL § 967, which provides that a party with a future or inchoate interest in real property is entitled to have a proportion of the sales proceeds invested, secured or paid over in a way calculated to protect his interests.

7. Recall that the typical Article 19 proceeding is brought because the fiduciary needs cash to pay for administration expenses and debts. McKinney's SCPA 1902. In that case the proceeds would be needed to pay those expenses and would not be available for investment. The court would order investment when it is ordering the sale under McKinney's SCPA 1902(7), for "any other purpose the court deems necessary." That could be a case, for example, where the life tenant intends to move out and the property is depreciating in value. The investment solution would avoid further loss to the estate while still protecting the life tenant's interests.

8. Matter of Kearns, 139 Misc. 877, 249 N.Y.S. 340 (Bronx 1931).

9. See McKinney's SCPA 1918, Prac. Comm. at 313 (1967).

10. See Matter of Hyland, 20 N.Y.S.2d 567 (Yates 1940).

Sec. P

1. McKinney's SCPA 1919.

assets later come into the residuary estate, the specific devisee can seek reimbursement from the residuary estate,[2] since his specific devise abates only after the residuary estate has completely abated.[3]

The person seeking reimbursement petitions for it, and submits a citation for service on all parties interested in the new fund along with a proposed decree for the court's signature. If an accounting proceeding is pending, the person seeking reimbursement may request such relief in that proceeding.

SECTION Q. DISPOSITION OF SURPLUS IN AN ACTION TO ENFORCE A MORTGAGE OR OTHER LIEN

It is not a permissible Article 19 purpose to sell real property to satisfy the mortgage encumbrance on it.[1] However, sometimes another valid Article 19 need exists, such as a need to pay estate taxes, administration expenses or legacies, and to satisfy it the fiduciary chooses to sell real property encumbered by a mortgage. The fiduciary has the right to do so. However, the mortgagee has the first priority to the amount of the proceeds necessary to satisfy the mortgage. The excess can be used for Article 19 purposes; SCPA 1920 provides for the disposition of such excess.

In many cases, the fiduciary can pay the surplus directly to the creditors or beneficiaries, but in the following situations he cannot:

(1) If less than eighteen months have passed since the issuance of letters.

2) if another Article 19 proceeding or accounting proceeding is pending and it was started within eighteen months of the issuance of letters.

3) if no fiduciary has received letters and less than two years have passed since the decedent's death.[2]

In these cases the fiduciary has to pay the excess money directly to the Surrogate with jurisdiction of the estate.

As a practical matter, this section is used very rarely.

The reason for these time limitations is to protect creditors. After the fiduciary has paid the funds to the Surrogate, the Surrogate then may allow them to be paid out to creditors before the eighteen months if it is satisfied that all creditors are known.

2. Recall that no priority exists between real and personal property for payment of claims, so this proceeding would not be available simply because real property in the residuary estate was sold and later personal property came into the estate. McKinney's SCPA 1919.

3. See discussion of order of abatement in chapter on "Claims," supra at 151–52.

Sec. Q

1. McKinney's SCPA 1902(3).

2. The same time limitations appear in McKinney's SCPA 1903, governing the rights of a bona fide purchaser from a distributee or devisee. They are discussed in this chapter, supra at 481–82.

Sometimes another court will order excess money on the sale of realty to be paid to the Surrogate. For example, the mortgagee may have foreclosed the mortgage in a court with jurisdiction over such actions and the foreclosure sale may have yielded more than enough to satisfy the mortgage, or a piece of real property may have been sold to satisfy tax arrears and the proceeds were more than enough to satisfy the taxes. In that case the Surrogate may pay the money to the fiduciary and order him to account for it at the judicial settlement of his account or in a special proceeding brought just for the purpose of accounting for the money. The court may also order distribution to the creditors or beneficiaries if sufficient time has passed, namely, eighteen months since the issuance of original letters or two years since the decedent's death if no fiduciary has received letters.[3]

Judgment liens are subject to a ten-year statute of limitations,[4] and the time limitations of this section add nothing to that period.

If the property itself would not have been subject to an Article 19 proceeding, because, for example, it was specifically devised and there is intestate or residuary real property available for Article 19 purposes, the fiduciary does not pay the surplus into court but to the persons entitled to the property.

To illustrate the workings of this section:

(1) If mortgaged real property is sold before eighteen months from letters, the person interested can get the excess proceeds from the court only with the consent of all interested persons, including the fiduciary, and only if the court believes all prior liens and funeral expenses have been paid.

(2) If mortgaged property is sold more than eighteen months from letters, the excess proceeds can be distributed immediately to those entitled.

(3) When mortgaged property is sold before eighteen months and then the eighteen months expire, the person entitled can petition the court to distribute the entire proceeds.

(4) If the two year period has not expired and the purchaser pays the surplus into court and the two years then does expire before a fiduciary is appointed, the purchaser of the interest of a beneficiary receives the property free of all claims of creditors and beneficiaries.[5]

3. McKinney's SCPA 1920(2).

4. Douglass v. Chisholm, 142 Misc. 869, 255 N.Y.S. 15 (New York County 1931), affirmed 236 App.Div. 668, 257 N.Y.S. 1030 (1st Dep't 1932), affirmed 261 N.Y. 632, 185 N.E. 769 (1933) (judgment more than ten years old ceases to be lien on real property).

5. McKinney's SCPA 1903.

SECTION R. CONCLUSIVE PRESUMPTION OF JURISDICTION

If someone wants to attack an order to set aside a disposition of real property granted under Article 19 [1] on the ground that the court lacked personal jurisdiction over an interested person or on any other procedural ground, that person must commence the action or proceeding within ten years of the date of the order. The court's jurisdiction over all interested persons and the regularity of its order are conclusively established after that time.[2]

Sec. R

1. The statute, McKinney's SCPA 1922, refers to an Article 19 order or an order granted under the Surrogate's Court Act article 13, which has become obsolete.

2. McKinney's SCPA 1922.

Chapter Eighteen

TRIALS

SECTION A. INTRODUCTION

When a person has filed a petition in a proceeding in the Surrogate's court and served process on interested parties, those parties have the right to serve an answer or objections. If the contested issues cannot be resolved, the parties proceed to a trial or hearing. This chapter gives a brief outline of pre-trial procedures [1] and covers Article 5's rules on trials and hearings in the Surrogate's Court—when a proceeding can be transferred there by another court, when proceedings can be consolidated or severed, when a case will be heard by the court, when a party is entitled to a trial by jury, and when a case may be heard before a referee.

SECTION B. A SUMMARY OF PRE–TRIAL PROCEDURES

Except in the few sections when the SCPA states rules relating to discovery and trials, such as the procedure for examining attesting witnesses,[1] and Article 5 generally on trials, the CPLR governs discovery and trial practice.[2] In addition, the Uniform Rules for the Surrogate's Court have rules dealing with transfer of actions, examinations before trial, examinations of attesting witnesses, examinations of parties in accounting and miscellaneous proceedings, notes of issue, statements of readiness, jury trials, and orders framing issue.[3]

If the petitioner commences the proceeding and an interested party files an answer or objections, either party may serve the other with a demand for a bill of particulars on issues on which the other has the burden of proof.[4] For this discussion we assume that the proceeding is probate and the issues are fraud and undue influence, so the burden is

Sec. A

1. For an incomparable treatise covering trial practice generally, see D. Siegel, New York Practice (1978).

Sec. B

1. McKinney's SCPA 1404, discussed in chapter on "Probate," supra at 90–93.

2. McKinney's SCPA 102 states that the CPLR applies unless the SCPA provides otherwise.

3. Uniform Rules for the Surrogate's Courts, Sec. 207.26, 207.27, 207.38, 207.29, 207.30, 207.31.

4. It is at that point that issue is joined, and the demand for the bill of particulars may be made at any time after the joinder of issue. McKinney's CPLR 3041; Updike v. Mace, 156 A.D. 381, 141 N.Y.S. 587 (2d Dep't 1913); Gross v. Price, 208 Misc. 899, 148 N.Y.S.2d 375 (Nassau 1955).

on the contestant.[5] All that we say applies equally when the contestant serves the demand for a bill of particulars on the petitioner relating to issues on which the petitioner has the burden of proof.

The petitioner demands that the contestant furnish the particulars within a stated time (usually ten days) and serves the demand on the contestant's attorney. The contestant has ten days to move to vacate or modify the demand.[6]

If the contestant is late in serving the bill of particulars, the petitioner can move to preclude the contestant from testifying about any facts on which he failed to supply particulars.[7] Along with the motion, the petitioner submits an affidavit stating that he made a demand for, and that the contestant refused to give, a bill of particulars. He also submits a proposed order of preclusion for the court's signature. The contestant can then submit an affidavit in opposition, stating, perhaps, that he needs to conduct discovery before giving the bill of particulars, or that the facts are particularly within the petitioner's knowledge, not his. The court reviews the motion and affidavits and determines whether to issue an order of preclusion. The court, in an attempt to accommodate the good faith efforts of both parties, may issue a conditional order of preclusion. For example, the court may give the contestant a period, perhaps thirty days, to conduct discovery and furnish the bill of particulars demanded by the petitioner,[8] or the court may require an affidavit from the petitioner explaining the facts and imparting the knowledge which only he has. In most cases, even if the party was plainly delinquent in filing the bill, the order of preclusion is at a minimum conditioned on receipt of the bill of particulars, so that if the party files it within a stated time, the court vacates the preclusion order.

If the contestant furnishes an inadequate or incomplete bill of particulars, timely or otherwise, the same procedures would be followed: petitioner can make a motion to preclude and the contestant's attorney can submit his affirmation or his client's affidavit in opposition. If the court issues an order to preclude, it is usually conditioned on the party's submission of an amended bill of particulars. If the party does submit it, the court vacates its preclusion order.[9]

The petitioner must give notice to the contestant at each stage: notice of motion when he moves to preclude, notice of settlement when he submits the order for the judge's signature, and notice of entry when the judge signs it.[10]

5. E.g., Matter of Burke, 82 A.D.2d 260, 441 N.Y.S.2d 542 (2d Dep't 1981).

6. McKinney's CPLR 3402.

7. McKinney's CPLR 3402.

8. See Matter of Unger, N.Y.L.J., July 23, 1985, at 14, col. 5 (Westchester) (where court noted that the objectant in an accounting proceeding ordinarily furnishes the bill of particulars only after examining the executor, denied the executor's motion for preclusion, and ordered the objectant to file a bill of particulars within fifteen days after the examination of the executor.

9. McKinney's CPLR 3042.

10. See McKinney's CPLR 2103 (service); McKinney's CPLR 2214 (motions); McKinney's CPLR 2209 and 2220 (orders and decrees).

In addition to the bill of particulars, the parties may use all the discovery devices allowed in civil practice, including discovery and inspection [11] and examinations before trial.[12] Both sides may conduct examinations before trial on any relevant material, either before or after demanding a bill of particulars. Parties may examine non-parties only in circumstances that make it likely that the non-party's testimony will otherwise be lost, such as imminent departure or extreme illness, or in other "special circumstances," which the courts tend to construe liberally.[13]

The party seeking an examination before trial does so either by stipulating a date and place with the party to be examined, or by notice of deposition addressed to that party. The notice need not state the issues the party intends to cover in the examination, although most attorneys do give such notice as a matter of good practice.[14] The party seeking the deposition arranges to have a stenographer there.

The parties can move for a protective order if the examination is being used for harrassment.[15]

The deposition of a party can be used at trial as evidence,[16] and depositions can be used to impeach the credibility of a witness who contradicts his examination testimony at the trial. Under special circumstances, usually relating to the witness's unavailability, any person's deposition can be used at trial.[17]

When the parties have finished discovery, the petitioner files a note of issue, indicating his readiness for trial.[18] He may also submit a proposed order framing the issues, which we discuss shortly.

At any stage, the parties may reach a compromise and the executor can enter into an agreement incorporating the compromise or can commence a proceeding to obtain court approval of it.[19] If the parties do not settle, they proceed to trial. If they proceed to trial, the CPLR rules governing privileges, such as the physician-patient privilege [20] and the attorney-client privilege [21] govern, as do the rules of the Dead Man's Statute.[22]

11. McKinney's CPLR 3120.

12. McKinney's CPLR 3101.

13. McKinney's CPLR 3101; see Matter of Laflin, 105 A.D.2d 747, 481 N.Y.S.2d 179 (2d Dep't 1984) (showing by objectant's counsel that he needed witness's pretrial deposition to prepare fully for trial suffices as a "special circumstance" under McKinney's CPLR 3101(a)(4)); Downey v. Tunney, 80 Misc.2d 535, 365 N.Y.S.2d 355 (Nassau 1975); Kelly v. Shafiroff, 80 A.D.2d 601, 436 N.Y.S.2d 44 (2d Dep't 1981).

14. McKinney's CPLR 3102.

15. McKinney's CPLR 3103.

16. McKinney's CPLR 3117(a)(1)(2); Matter of Schaich, 55 A.D.2d 914, 391 N.Y.S.2d 135 (2d Dep't 1979), appeal denied 42 N.Y.2d 802, 397 N.Y.S.2d 1026, 366 N.E.2d 293 (1977); Wojtas v. Fifth Ave. Coach Corp., 23 A.D.2d 685, 257 N.Y.S.2d 404 (2d Dep't 1965).

17. McKinney's CPLR 3117(a)(3).

18. Uniform Rules for the Surrogate's Court 207.29.

19. Compromise proceedings are discussed in chapter on "Miscellaneous Proceedings," supra at 345–50.

20. McKinney's CPLR 4504.

21. McKinney's CPLR 4503.

22. McKinney's CPLR 4519.

SECTION C. TRANSFER, CONSOLIDATION AND SEVERANCE

1. TRANSFERS

If an action is pending in a court other than the Supreme Court, and it relates to the administration of an estate, any party can move to transfer it for trial to the Surrogate's Court with jurisdiction over the estate.[1]

The New York State Constitution does not confer this power to receive actions from other courts of limited jurisdiction. The constitution does, however, empower the legislature to give the Surrogate's Court powers not enumerated in the constitution, and this is an example of it.[2]

In addition, the Surrogate can consent to receive for trial any action pending in the Supreme Court if it relates to the administration of a decedent's estate.[3]

In fact, under the constitution the Supreme Court can transfer such actions to the Surrogate's Court whether the Surrogate consents or not.[4] This section does not attempt to thwart the constitution, but merely creates a procedure under which the Surrogate advises the Supreme Court whether or not the transfer would be beneficial to the estate.[5] The Supreme Court is free to transfer it in any case, so long as the matter relates to estate administration,[6] but will invariably defer to the Surrogate's opinion.

The typical situation where the Supreme Court transfers actions to the Surrogate's Court is when the matter is clearly within the Surrogate's special competence and the Supreme Court's retention is likely to delay the fiduciary's final accounting in the Surrogate's Court.[7]

Sec. C

1. McKinney's SCPA 501. See Matter of Kleefeld, N.Y.L.J., July 19, 1985, at 11, col. 5 (New York County) (court removed actions for attorneys' fees from New York City Civil Court to Surrogate's Court). The statute was amended by L.1980, c. 503, section 7, effective June 24, 1980, to replace the words "decedent's estate" with the word "estate," so trials relating to minors' incompetents' and conservatees' estates and inter vivos trusts are now within the scope of SCPA 501.

2. See Matter of Howard, 52 A.D.2d 536, 382 N.Y.S.2d 59 (1st Dep't 1956) (transfer of trial from New York City Civil Court to Bronx Surrogate's Court).

3. McKinney's SCPA 501(1)(b). Unlike in paragraph (a), no amendment was made in 501(1)(b) to permit transfer of matters relating to an estate other than a decedent's estate; consequently, under (b) it looks as if the matter must relate to a decedent's estate. However, the New York Constitution, Article 6, section 19, authorizes the Supreme Court to transfer to the Surrogate's Court any matter relating to an estate (guardianships, inter vivos trusts, etc.), not just to a decedent's estate.

4. McKinney's Const. Art. 6, section 19(a).

5. Matter of Dick, N.Y.L.J., July 2, 1985, at 11, col. 2 (New York County); Matter of Suchoff, 55 Misc.2d 284, 285 N.Y.S.2d 134 (Nassau 1967).

6. See McKinney's SCPA 501, Practice Commentary at 91 (Supp.1986); Matter of Cox, N.Y.L.J., March 22, 1979, at 10, col. 4 (New York County).

7. E.g., Rodman v. Krosner, N.Y.L.J., Aug. 14, 1985, at 14, col. 3 (Nassau) (Surrogate conceded that the transfer lay in the Supreme Court's discretion but urged the

The motion to transfer from Supreme Court to Surrogate's Court can be made by any party, and it is good practice to bring the motion on notice to other parties rather than ex parte. The party seeking transfer moves in the Surrogate's Court on notice to all interested parties, and if the Surrogate agrees, the party then moves in the Supreme Court on notice, and the Supreme Court decides whether to make the transfer or not. The Surrogate will refuse to entertain the motion by a person who was not a party to the Supreme Court action.[8]

2. CONSOLIDATION

Whenever two or more proceedings contain a common question of law or fact, the court can, on its own motion or on the motion of a party, order a joint trial "to avoid unnecessary cost or delay." [9]

The Surrogate can consolidate proceedings pending before him and he can also join matters from other counties relating to the same estate or matter.[10] Consolidation in the Surrogate's Court normally joins two proceedings relating to the same estate. Consolidation of proceedings in two separate estates is very rare.

When the court orders consolidation, it directs whether or not the caption should be single or double. Ordinarily, the proceedings are commenced independently and the petitioner or petitioners must pay the required filing fee for each proceeding before the court will order consolidation.

3. SEVERANCE AND SEPARATE TRIALS

The court may order issues severed and tried separately if in its discretion it believes that severance will avoid inconvenience or prejudice to a party.[11] The court may do so on its own or on the motion of a party. If the issues are common, however, the court would be abusing its discretion to sever them.[12]

A Surrogate may find it appropriate to sever issues when one is triable before a jury and one is not, although the court could, as an

Supreme Court to order the transfer because a protracted litigation in the Supreme Court would delay settlement of the estate); Matter of Quirk, N.Y.L.J., April 2, 1985, at 13, col. 5 (Nassau) (actions pending in Supreme Court on debts owed to and by the decedent transferred to Surrogate's Court so fiduciary's final accounting could proceed).

8. Matter of Israel, 88 Misc.2d 999, 390 N.Y.S.2d 577 (Bronx 1977).

9. McKinney's SCPA 501(2)(a).

10. Prior to the amendments to McKinney's SCPA 205–207, L.1984, c. 128, the Surrogate could not have done so because the court lacked subject matter jurisdiction over matters in another county. Now the Surrogate's subject matter jurisdiction is state-wide. See chapter on "Jurisdiction," supra at 1–9.

11. McKinney's SCPA 501(2)(b).

12. See, e.g., Matter of Kessler, 28 A.D.2d 962, 283 N.Y.S.2d 123 (1st Dep't 1967); Matter of Zalaznick, N.Y.L.J., Nov. 19, 1976, at 11, col. 1 (Bronx) (court denied severence of malpractice claim because it would result in unnecessary repetition of testimony). Since the New York Court of Appeals decision in Matter of Piccione, 57 N.Y.2d 278, 456 N.Y.S.2d 669, 442 N.E.2d 1180 (1982), reargument denied 58 N.Y.2d 824, 459 N.Y.S.2d 1030, 445 N.E.2d 657 (1983), the court would probably sever the malpractice claim because it does not have jurisdiction over actions between third parties.

alternative, use the jury merely as an advisory jury [13] on the non-jury issue.[14]

SECTION D. TRIAL BY JURY

1. RIGHT TO A JURY TRIAL

A party may have a right to a jury trial on a controverted issue of fact under two theories: first, because the statute grants it (as it does in contested probate proceedings [1]) or second, because he has a constitutional right to it.[2] It is therefore useful for the attorney to know when the constitutional right to a jury is available.

The New York State Constitution states that "[t]rial by jury in all cases in which it has heretofore been guaranteed by constitutional provision shall remain inviolate forever." [3] Those include (i) all cases where the right to a jury trial existed at common law before 1777, and (ii) all cases where the right to jury trial was granted by statute between 1777 and 1894.

Consequently, when no statute grants a jury trial but a party seeks one, the Surrogate's first inquiry is whether the issue is one which would have been entitled to a jury trial before 1777. That was determined by deciding whether it is an issue essentially equitable or legal in nature; equitable issues were not tried by a jury, while legal issues were.

The New York Court of Appeals has clarified this "equitable versus legal issue" standard in Matter of Garfield.[4] There, a law firm petitioned for a compulsory accounting after filing a claim for fees for legal services rendered to the decedent. The executrix demanded a jury trial and the law firm, conceding that the executrix would have been entitled to a jury trial in the Supreme Court because the action was for labor and services (that is, legal in nature), nevertheless opposed her demand on the theory that accounting proceedings are equitable. The court settled the issue by holding that a party who would have been entitled to a jury trial in the Supreme Court is entitled to one in the Surrogate's Court. The nature of the claim was legal, not equitable, and while it is true that the Surrogate's Court was originally a court of

13. Jury trials and advisory juries are discussed in the next section of this chapter.

14. McKinney's SCPA 501, Practice Commentary at 414 (1967).

Sec. D

1. McKinney's SCPA 502(1).

2. For example, the right to a jury trial in discovery proceedings (McKinney's SCPA 2103, 2104, 2105) is assured under the New York Constitution, discussed presently in text. See, e.g., Matter of Wilson, 252 N.Y. 155, 169 N.E. 122 (1929); Matter of Wisniewski, 88 Misc.2d 76, 387 N.Y.S.2d 603 (Erie 1976). In fact contested probate and discovery proceedings account for the vast majority of jury trials in the Surrogate's Court. This is so because many of the proceedings in the Surrogate's Court are special proceedings, in which the right to trial by jury is rare. See Matter of Santillo, 103 Misc.2d 937, 426 N.Y.S.2d 441 (Erie 1980).

3. McKinney's Const. Art. 1, section 2.

4. Matter of Garfield, 14 N.Y.2d 251, 251 N.Y.S.2d 7, 200 N.E.2d 196 (1964).

equity,[5] its jurisdiction had expanded both under the state constitution and under the statute.[6] The court recognized that the legislature, in giving an equity court jurisdiction over a matter essentially legal in nature, would not have intended to deprive a party of a right to jury if that party pursued his right in the Surrogate's Court. Therefore, it is not the court but the nature and substance of the case that determines the right to a jury.

The attorney should note, however, that in a proceeding on a claim against the estate, only the fiduciary is entitled to demand a jury trial in the Surrogate's Court; the claimant is not.[7] If the claimant wants a jury trial, he must, within sixty days of rejection of his claim, bring an action in the Supreme Court or some other forum.[8] By contrast, in a contested probate proceeding the contestant may demand a jury trial.[9]

Even with the guidance of Garfield, the question of entitlement to a jury trial is sometimes close, as cases following Garfield illustrate. In one, for example,[10] an attorney discharged by the executrix petitioned the court to set his fees for services rendered to the estate.[11] The court held that this payment, if allowed, would be an administration expense of the estate, not a claim for services rendered during the decedent's lifetime, and hence was an item of the fiduciary's accounting and equitable in nature. On that ground it distinguished Garfield and denied the executrix's demand for a jury trial.

Similarly, in another case,[12] the United States objected to the fiduciary's account on the ground that he had failed to pay payroll and unemployment taxes on the decedent's business. The fiduciary demanded a jury trial but the court denied it, because taxes are an administration expense and claims for administration expenses are equitable.

The courts have also denied a jury trial on the ground that the issue was fundamentally equitable in the following situations:

—The decedent agreed to buy securities and hold them until the seller reimbursed him. The seller's claim against the estate was, essentially, that the decedent was holding the securities in a constructive trust for the seller.[13]

—The decedent's widow claimed that securities held in the decedent's sole name should have been placed in joint name with

5. Matter of Walsh, 147 Misc. 103, 264 N.Y.S.2d 621 (Erie 1933).

6. See discussion of the court's expanded jurisdiction in chapter on "Jurisdiction," supra at 12–18.

7. See, e.g., Matter of Cohen, N.Y.L.J., Feb. 7, 1979, at 13, col. 4 (Kings).

8. McKinney's SCPA 1810, discussed in chapter on "Claims," supra at 162.

9. McKinney's SCPA 502(1).

10. Matter of Pepi, 47 Misc.2d 137, 261 N.Y.S.2d 803 (Nassau 1965).

11. The attorney petitioned under SCA 231–a, L.1923, c. 526, the predecessor to McKinney's SCPA 2110, discussed in chapter on "Attorneys' Fees," supra at 259–79.

12. Matter of Ford, 78 Misc.2d 213, 356 N.Y.S.2d 952 (Erie 1974).

13. Matter of Johnson, 46 Misc.2d 285, 258 N.Y.S.2d 892 (Westchester 1965).

her. Her claim was that the decedent was holding the securities in a constructive trust for her.[14]

—The decedent's supposed common law widow claimed his entire estate in intestacy. The issue of status as surviving spouse is equitable, not legal, in nature.[15]

—Although the statute grants a jury trial in contested probate cases,[16] the right extends only to the probate issues, not to status,[17] kinship, domicile, right of election, right to property,[18] issuance of letters to the named executor in the will,[19] the fiduciary's eligibility to serve,[20] or the fiduciary's mismanagement of the property.[21]

The courts have found the following to be essentially legal and have allowed jury trials:

—The fiduciary of the estate claimed to have received a gift from the decedent, and the petitioner questioned the validity of the gift.[22]

—A party commenced a "reverse discovery" proceeding (in which a party attempts to compel delivery of property by the executor [23]). Because the claim sounded in replevin, which is legal in nature, he could have obtained a jury trial in the Supreme Court, and consequently he was entitled to a jury trial in the Surrogate's Court.[24]

2. DEMAND FOR A JURY TRIAL

Even if a party has a right to a jury trial, he must make a timely demand for a jury or he impliedly waives his right to a jury trial. If a proceeding begins in the Surrogate's Court, the respondents must demand a trial by jury in their answers or objections.[25] Even if the respondents have demanded a jury trial, the petitioner must file his

14. Matter of Luria, 63 Misc.2d 675, 313 N.Y.S.2d 12 (Kings 1970). In Luria the alleged agreement was that any new securities bought with funds from the sale of jointly owned securities would be placed in their joint names. The widow claimed that jointly owned securities were sold to buy the stock in issue in the case.

15. Matter of Fay, 70 Misc.2d 51, 332 N.Y.S.2d 322 (New York County 1972), affirmed 41 A.D.2d 703, 340 N.Y.S.2d 861 (1st Dep't 1973). Accord, Matter of Ruggiero, 82 Misc.2d 211, 368 N.Y.S.2d 722 (Westchester 1975), affirmed 51 A.D.2d 969, 380 N.Y.S.2d 319 (2d Dep't 1976) (issue of status in proceeding to revoke letters).

16. McKinney's SCPA 502(1).

17. Matter of Luria, 63 Misc.2d 675, 313 N.Y.S.2d 12 (Kings 1970).

18. Matter of Lacon, 58 Misc.2d 869, 296 N.Y.S.2d 711 (Westchester 1968) (right to real property).

19. Matter of Krom, 86 A.D.2d 689, 446 N.Y.S.2d 522 (3d Dep't 1982), appeal dismissed 56 N.Y.2d 505, 451 N.Y.S.2d 1027, 436 N.E.2d 1346 (1982).

20. Matter of Mastro, 100 Misc.2d 866, 420 N.Y.S.2d 166 (Suffolk 1979).

21. Matter of Nelson, 105 Misc.2d 747, 433 N.Y.S.2d 314 (Westchester 1980).

22. Matter of Wisniewski, 88 Misc.2d 76, 387 N.Y.S.2d 603 (Erie 1976).

23. McKinney's SCPA 2105, discussed in chapter on "Miscellaneous Proceedings," supra at 344–45.

24. Matter of Schneier, 98 Misc.2d 183, 413 N.Y.S.2d 568 (1979), modified 74 A.D.2d 22, 426 N.Y.S.2d 624 (4th Dep't 1980).

25. McKinney's SCPA 502(2)(a).

own demand within six days after service of the answers or objections. If a respondent has not submitted objections or an answer and he wants a jury trial on the issues raised by another respondent who has filed an answer, the non-answering respondent must file a separate demand within six days after receiving a copy of the other respondent's answer or objection.[26]

If the proceeding was commenced in another court and a party demanded a jury trial there, his demand will carry over to the Surrogate's Court.[27] Similarly, if he has waived or let his time to demand expire, he cannot get a jury trial in the Surrogate's Court.[28] If the party moving for transfer has not demanded a jury trial and if he has not waived or let the time for demand expire, he must demand the jury trial in his moving papers.[29] If another party has not demanded a jury and has not waived or let the time expire, he must file his demand in the Surrogate's Court within ten days after service of the order of transfer and notice of entry.[30]

Each party seeking a jury trial must pay a seventy dollar jury fee.[31]

A jury determination in the Surrogate's Court is valid on a vote of five of the six jurors. Unless the court otherwise directs a party may request one or two alternate jurors.[32] In practice the court will determine whether to have one or two alternate jurors based on the complexity of the matter and length of time the trial is expected to take. The judge presides over the jury selection but usually does not question prospective jurors. The attorneys receive bare information, such as the name, age and employment of each jury panel member, and then question the panel members, the attorney with the burden of proof questioning first. Each party has three peremptory challenges, where a juror may be dismissed without cause, and unlimited challenges for cause. Each party also has one peremptory challenge against each alternate juror.[33] If more than one party opposes the petitioner (for example, if there are several contestants in a probate contest), the Surrogate in his discretion can permit the petitioner extra challenges.

3. WAIVER OR WITHDRAWAL OF DEMAND FOR JURY TRIAL

A party waives a right to a trial by jury by: 1) failing to make a timely demand, 2) failing to appear at the trial, 3) filing a waiver signed by him or his attorney with the clerk of the court, or 4) orally waiving a

26. McKinney's SCPA 502(2)(a).

27. McKinney's SCPA 502(2)(b).

28. Matter of Bellak, N.Y.L.J., Nov. 19, 1979, at 16, col. 5 (Queens).

29. McKinney's SCPA 502(2)(b).

30. McKinney's SCPA 502(2)(b).

31. McKinney's SCPA 2402(10); 502(3) The same is not true when multiple parties object to a proceeding. See Calabrese v. Tomlinson, 106 A.D.2d 843, 484 N.Y.S.2d 242 (3d Dep't 1984) (when seven persons object on the same grounds, only one filing fee required).

32. McKinney's CPLR 4106.

33. McKinney's CPLR 4109.

trial by jury in open court or at a pre-trial conference if the waiver is entered in the minutes taken at the time.[34]

A party may withdraw his demand for a jury trial without the consent of other parties and if only one party requests a jury trial and then withdraws the request, the withdrawal is binding on all other parties.[35] This is the reverse of practice in other civil courts, where the withdrawal of a jury demand is binding only if the other parties consent.[36] Therefore, in the Surrogate's Court a party cannot rely on the fact that another party has requested a jury trial; he must independently demand his own jury trial. If he fails to do that, and the other party's demand is withdrawn, he will not be entitled to a jury trial. This is true whether the proceeding was commenced in the Surrogate's Court or was transferred there after commencement.

If a party fails to demand a jury, the court in its discretion may relieve the party of the omission and permit him to file a demand for jury trial if there is no undue prejudice to other parties.[37] For example, if the delay is short and the omission inadvertent and no prejudice demonstrated against any party, the court will grant the application.[38] The court ordinarily will not grant such an application on the eve of a trial.

4. ADVISORY JURIES

The court can empanel an advisory jury and submit to it any issue of fact required to be decided by the court.[39] If the jury cannot agree after a reasonable time, the court dismisses them and orders a new trial.[40] The advisory jury's findings are not binding. On the motion of any party, made within fifteen days after the jury's verdict, or on the court's own motion, the court can confirm or reject in whole or in part the verdict of the advisory jury.[41] The court may make new findings with or without taking additional testimony, or may order a new trial. Where there are no other issues remaining, the court will then give a written decision.[42]

5. ORDER FRAMING ISSUES

The court will not set a trial date until it has signed an order framing issues.[43] After issue is joined and a party has demanded a jury trial, any party can submit a proposed order framing issues, and the

34. McKinney's SCPA 502(5)(a).

35. McKinney's SCPA 502(5)(b).

36. McKinney's CPLR 4102(c).

37. McKinney's CPLR 4102(e). See Matter of Flamm, N.Y.L.J., Jan. 30, 1978, at 12, col. 3 (Queens) (court refused to grant jury trial when prejudice was probable and party did not demand jury trial until after note of issue had been filed and after six month delay).

38. Matter of Mirsky, 81 Misc.2d 9, 365 N.Y.S.2d 122 (New York County 1975).

39. McKinney's SCPA 502(6); McKinney's CPLR 4212.

40. McKinney's CPLR 4113.

41. McKinney's CPLR 4405.

42. McKinney's SCPA 502(6).

43. Uniform Rules of the Surrogate's Court 207.31.

court can direct any party to submit such an order.[44] The party submitting it must give five days notice of settlement to the attorneys for the other parties who have not appeared. Frequently the petitioner submits the proposed order, but very often both the petitioner and the respondent submit orders framing issues and the court makes an appropriate choice between them. The order must state plainly and concisely the controverted questions of fact for the jury in a form that elicits a "yes" or "no" answer. The party whose order the Surrogate signs will usually be required to serve it on all parties who have appeared and pleaded. In the order, the court may fix a date for trial or may place the matter on the calendar for a pre-trial conference to fix a date for trial. At least fifteen days before the trial date or the date of the calendar call, the signed order must be served on all parties who have appeared and pleaded. Although the statute says that service of the proposed order framing issues need only be made on those who have appeared and pleaded,[45] nevertheless, it is best to serve it on all parties who have appeared, even those who have not pleaded, and the Uniform Rules for the Surrogate's Court so provide.[46] Proof of service must be filed at least ten days before the date of the trial or calendar call.

The Surrogate's Courts have forms for orders framing issues, so the attorney should consult with the clerk of the court before drafting the order.

The person with the burden of proof opens and closes the trial. In a contested probate proceeding, that would ordinarily be the proponent, unless the only issues are undue influence or fraud.[47]

6. TRANSFER OF TRIAL ALONE

Under a constitutionally questionable statute,[48] the Surrogate may direct that the jury trial take place in the trial term of the Supreme Court within the county, or in the County Court if there is one. Unless the Supreme Court or the County Court sets aside the verdict after the jury trial, the clerk of that court then certifies the verdict to the Surrogate's Court, and it is then conclusive except upon appeal.

It is very rare, especially in the greater metropolitan area, for a Surrogate to order a jury trial to be tried in another forum. This procedure dates back to a time when the Surrogate's Court did not have jurisdiction to conduct a jury trial.

When this procedure is used, its effect is to transfer only the trial to the transferee court, the Surrogate retaining the case for every other purpose, including entering the order or decree. The only order or

44. McKinney's SCPA 502(4).

45. McKinney's SCPA 502(4).

46. Uniform Rules of the Surrogate's Court 207.31(c).

47. See Matter of McNamara, N.Y.L.J., April 1, 1976 at 8, col. 1 (New York County).

48. See McKinney's SCPA 502, Practice Commentary at 423–24 (1967).

decree permitted by the Supreme Court or the County Court is one to set aside the verdict.[49]

7. PROCEEDINGS ON A JURY TRIAL

During the course of the trial, on a motion of any party or on its own initiative, the court may direct judgment on one or more issues, or on the whole case, if it determines as a matter of law that the evidence does not create an issue of fact for the jury. The court will then treat the issue as though it had been withdrawn from the jury, which may not render a verdict or make any findings concerning it.[50] The court can also do this on consent of all parties. The court's verdict, order and decision must be entered in the minutes of the court and if the trial was held outside the Surrogate's Court, the verdict, order and decision must be certified to the Surrogate's Court by the clerk of the outside court, and the Surrogate's Court will enter a final decree based on it.

As a practical matter, the court will usually wait at least until the party with the burden of proof completes the presentation of the case and at that time will entertain motions for directed verdicts. Very often the court reserves decision until the entire case is in, or until the jury makes its determination, after which it hears the motions for directed verdict.

If no motions are made at the trial or after the jury renders its verdict, post-trial motions must be made within fifteen days of the completion of the trial.[51]

8. SELECTION OF JURORS

Jurors are selected from a panel in attendance at any trial term of the Supreme Court or County Court of the county. Most counties have central jury parts and jurors are sent over to the Surrogate's Court upon request of the clerk when a jury trial is about to begin.

SECTION E. TRIAL BY THE COURT

The court can decide all issues not required to be tried by a jury.[1] Its decision usually sets forth the findings of facts and conclusions of law, and so the order or decree need not repeat them unless the court in its decision so directs.[2] The court's decision is normally written but

49. Matter of DeLano, 34 A.D.2d 1031, 311 N.Y.S.2d 134 (3d Dep't 1970), affirmed 28 N.Y.2d 587, 319 N.Y.S.2d 844, 268 N.E.2d 642 (1971). There a necessary party was absent from a proceeding in the Supreme Court, and the appearing parties who fully litigated moved unsuccessfully to have the Supreme Court set aside the verdict. The defect had existed before and after the transfer and had to be cured by the Surrogate. The missing party had to be given a chance to litigate but the Supreme Court verdict was valid as to those parties who appeared there.

50. McKinney's SCPA 503.

51. McKinney's CPLR 4405.

Sec. E

1. McKinney's SCPA 505.

2. This is opposite of McKinney's CPLR 4213(b) which requires a statement of the facts found.

it may be oral.[3] If it is oral, the court reporter enters it in the minutes and files it.

The court must render a decision within sixty days after final submission.[4] That period starts to run when the transcript of the hearing has been filed and the parties have submitted any memoranda and replies requested by the court.

SECTION F. REFERENCE TO HEAR AND REPORT

In civil practice outside the Surrogate's Court, parties may present their case to a referee appointed by the court and the referee can decide the case. This procedure is the "reference to determine."[1] Appeal from the referee's decision is through the appellate courts. In the Surrogate's Court, only a limited version is permitted, the "reference to report."[2] It is, in effect, an advisory report which the court is free to reject. In any non-jury case, except for a probate proceeding,[3] the court may appoint a referee to report to the court on the facts, or on the law and the facts. In practice, the report usually contains the facts found and the conclusions of law.

The referee may issue subpoenas, administer oaths, direct and supervise disclosure and conduct a hearing on an issue as the court would do in non-jury cases.[4]

The referee must file his report within thirty days after the matter has been submitted. The transcript of testimony and the exhibits (or copies of the exhibits) are filed with the report. Opponents need not file exceptions to the report.[5] The court may accept or reject the report of the referee in whole or in part, either sua sponte or on any party's motion. It can make new findings, can take additional testimony, and can even order a new reference.[6]

After the referee has filed his report, any party may serve notice of the filing, and it will be deemed confirmed unless a party moves in the Surrogate's Court to reject it within sixty days from the filing of the report. If the report is confirmed and no other issues remain, the court may file its decision in writing.

The court has the discretion to set an appropriate fee for the referee.[7] It will do so in its order appointing a referee, or the parties can stipulate the fee. If the court or the parties do not set the

3. McKinney's SCPA 505(2)(b).

4. McKinney's CPLR 4213(c).

Sec. F

1. McKinney's CPLR 4317.

2. McKinney's SCPA 506.

3. A referee cannot be appointed in a probate proceeding even if the parties have waived their right to a jury trial. In cases where a party has a constitutional right to a jury trial but does not demand one, the court can appoint a referee. McKinney's SCPA 506(1).

4. McKinney's CPLR 4201; McKinney's SCPA 506(3).

5. McKinney's SCPA 506(6).

6. McKinney's SCPA 506(4).

7. McKinney's CPLR 4321.

compensation, the referee is entitled to fifty dollars per day.[8] An exception is made for accounting proceedings where the amount in issue is de minimis (estates of less than $1,000 or aggregate amounts at issue less than $200).[9] No referee can be appointed in such a case unless he serves without compensation.

As a practical matter, it is very rare that the Surrogate will appoint as referee anyone other than an attorney on his staff. This is permitted in non-jury cases [10] so long as the attorneys for all parties who have appeared consent.[11] If they do, the court will appoint a member of the law department, the chief clerk or deputy chief clerk, or sometimes other attorneys employed by the court, to serve as referee.

The procedure does not differ drastically from the one used when an outside attorney is appointed, except that the parties have a shorter time to object to the report (ten days instead of sixty). The lawyer will report in writing to the court on the facts, or on the law and the facts, and will file the report. The report must state the essential facts but need not make findings of fact. Usually the report sets forth the facts and makes recommendations of findings of fact and conclusions of law. The opponents need not file exceptions to the report. The referee may issue subpoenas, administer oaths, direct disclosure and conduct the hearing in the way the court would try the matter without a jury.[12] A copy of the report is sent to each party's attorney who has appeared at the hearing with a notice that the report will automatically be considered confirmed unless a party moves to modify or overrule it within ten days. The ten-day period begins to run when the report is mailed, so the attorney should move quickly to make his objections to it. If he misses the ten-day limit, he can request an extension and the court can grant it.[13] On the motion of any party or on its own initiative, the court may confirm, modify or reject the report in whole or in part, make new findings, take additional testimony or order a new hearing. It is not necessary to file a transcript of the testimony with the report of the referee, but if a party moves to modify or overrule the report, that party may file a copy of the transcript.

A judicial employee does not receive a fee from an estate or from any party for acting as a referee, but his necessary expenses can be paid.[14]

Very often, the attorneys agree in a stipulation to have a member of the law department hear and report to the court. They waive the

8. McKinney's CPLR 8003.

9. McKinney's SCPA 506(2).

10. McKinney's SCPA 506(6).

11. This section was added at the recommendation of the Surrogate's Association of the State of New York to keep down the costs to estates. See note appended to L.1971, c. 361.

12. McKinney's SCPA 506(6); McKinney's CPLR 4201.

13. See McKinney's CPLR 2004; McKinney's SCPA 506, Practice Commentary at 99 (Supp.1986).

14. McKinney's SCPA 506(6)'s erroneous reference to McKinney's SCPA 2609(3)(2) was amended in 1985 to refer to 2609(3)(a). L.1985, c. 8, section 1.

filing of the report by the referee and ask the court to render its decision based on the transcript of the hearing.

Surrogates will appoint referees on consent only when the calendar is heavy and delay would jeopardize the court's policy to keep the calendar current.

Typical of cases where the court will appoint a referee are kinship hearings, Putnam hearings, claims, some contested adoptions and accountings, and status hearings.

SECTION G. TESTIMONY OUTSIDE THE COURTROOM

When a witness is called upon to testify at trial, ordinarily the testimony is taken at the courthouse, but sometimes because of the witness's infirmity or distance, the testimony can take place at a different location.[1] The party who wants the witness's testimony taken outside the courthouse must give whatever notice of the time and place of taking the examination the court prescribes and must pay the Surrogate his actual and necessary expenses of travelling and taking the testimony.[2]

As a practical matter, when testimony must be taken in another location, the court usually designates a commission; the court by order directs one of the attorneys on its staff to preside over the taking of the testimony out of court.[3] The court has the power to designate certain other officers and attorneys to take testimony,[4] but it rarely designates anyone other than a member of the staff. The member of the law department acts as a commissioner and the court can grant him the same powers as a referee.[5] The order may direct him to supervise disclosure and to take testimony and make rulings, subject to review by the court at the trial or before.

In any uncontested matter where a witness (usually an attesting witness) is in another county of the state and cannot conveniently come to the court, the court can by order direct the witness to be examined in the Surrogate's Court of another county and specify the nature and the manner of the examination.[6] A copy of the order is sent to the

Sec. G

1. McKinney's SCPA 507.

2. McKinney's SCPA 507(1).

3. This is authorized by McKinney's SCPA 508(1). It is very rare for the Surrogate to go to another county for this purpose.

4. McKinney's CPLR 3113(a) permits the following persons to take depositions:

1. in New York, a person authorized to administer oaths;

2. elsewhere in the United States or its territories, a person authorized to take acknowledgments of deed by the law of the place where the testimony will be taken;

3. in a foreign country, by a United States diplomat, or a person appointed by commission or letters rogatory, or an officer of the armed forces authorized to take the acknowledgment of deeds.

See McKinney's SCPA 508, Practice Commentary at 465 (1967).

5. See McKinney's SCPA 506(1).

6. McKinney's SCPA 507(2).

Surrogate, along with the original will or a court-certified reproduction of it, if the examination is of an attesting witness. The Surrogate or one of the clerks of the court can take the examination. Usually attesting witnesses' affidavits signed at the time of the will execution and affidavits signed at the time of probate are acceptable in lieu of the examination described in this paragraph, but if a party insists on a full deposition of a witness who is not available to testify locally, the court can order this alternative procedure.

The examination must be reduced to writing and subscribed by the witness, certified by the judge or clerk who took it and attested with a seal, and returned to the court that directed the examination, where it is filed.[7]

If a witness is uncooperative, the court can issue a commission and empower the commissioner to seek remedy in the local courts where the testimony is sought. New York has a provision for aiding other jurisdictions in obtaining testimony within New York,[8] and reciprocal provisions are found in many states and foreign jurisdictions.

If a court hopes to get testimony in a jurisdiction without such a provision, letters rogatory may have to be used.[9] It is, preferable, however, to obtain oral examinations under the supervision of court personnel.

SECTION H. EFFECT OF UNCONTROVERTED ALLEGATIONS OF FACT

The facts set forth in a petition and account are deemed to be true unless denied by an answer, objection or other proof.[1] Thus, although the parties cannot confer subject matter jurisdiction upon the court, if a jurisdictional fact is set forth in a petition or a pleading and is not denied, the court has a right to assume its truth and any party over whom the court has personal jurisdiction will be bound if he fails to refute that fact.[2]

SECTION I. APPEALS

Appeals in the Surrogate's Court are governed by SCPA Article 27, which essentially states that the CPLR rules governing appeals (CPLR Article 55) govern in the Surrogate's Court.[1] A party may appeal from

7. McKinney's SCPA 507(2).

8. McKinney's CPLR 3102(3).

9. McKinney's CPLR 3108.

Sec. H

1. McKinney's SCPA 509. See, e.g., Matter of Speno, N.Y.L.J., Aug. 8, 1985, at 15, col. 6 (Westchester).

2. See McKinney's SCPA 509 Prac. Comm. at 466 (1967).

Sec. I

1. McKinney's SCPA 2701. McKinney's SCPA 2701 gives the following necessary changes in terminology in applying McKinney's CPLR Article 55 to Surrogate's practice:

"Action" in the CPLR should be read "proceeding."

"Judgment" in the CPLR should be read "decree."

a verdict or from an order denying a motion for a direction of a judgment.

An appeal may be taken on an issue of law or an issue of fact, or a mixed issue of fact and law.[2]

The time limitation for an appeal is a maximum of thirty days after service of the copy of a decree or order with notice of entry.[3] The appellant may raise as an issue any intermediate orders leading to the decree provided he states them explicitly in the notice of appeal.[4] If the Surrogate directed a verdict, the Appellate Division can order a retrial of all the issues in its discretion.[5] If there was a jury trial, the appellate division can direct a retrial.[6] When the appellate division has decided the appeal, the Surrogate enters a judgment consistent with the appellate division's ruling.

"Plaintiff" in the CPLR should be read "petitioner" or "applicant."

"Defendant" in the CPLR should be read "respondent."

2. McKinney's CPLR 5501.

3. McKinney's CPLR 5513, 5515.

4. McKinney's CPLR 5501; Matter of Weston, 15 A.D.2d 410, 224 N.Y.S.2d 643 (1962).

5. McKinney's CPLR 5522.

6. Matter of Saterlee, 281 App.Div. 251, 119 N.Y.S.2d 309 (1953), appeal denied 1 A.D.2d 774, 149 N.Y.S.2d 215 (1956).

Chapter Nineteen

ANCILLARY PROCEEDINGS

SECTION A. INTRODUCTION

A will is usually probated in the jurisdiction where the decedent was a domiciliary.[1] If a decedent was domiciled in one jurisdiction and had assets in another, the fiduciary often has to start proceedings in both jurisdictions. Typically this means the principal administration (or original probate) occurs in the domicile and ancillary proceedings in the other jurisdiction.

This chapter discusses estates with multi-jurisdictional contacts, stressing the ancillary proceedings allowed in New York for the estates of non-New Yorkers.

Sec. A

1. See Restatement Second, Conflicts of Law (1971), section 314 and 315:

Section 314. Where Will May Be Probated and Representative Appointed

(a) where the decedent was domiciled at the time of his death; or

(b) where there are assets of the estate at the time of the decedent's death or at the time of the appointment of the executor or administrator; or

(c) where there is jurisdiction over the person or property of one who is alleged to have killed the decedent by his wrongful act, if the statute under which recovery is sought permits suit by an executor or administrator appointed in that state.

Section 315. Where Administrator May Be Appointed in Case of Intestacy

An administrator will customarily be appointed in the case of intestacy in any state in which a will would have been admitted to probate.

At times more than one state claims to be the decedent's domicile. See Matter of Dorrance, 309 Pa. 151, 163 A. 303 (1932), certiorari denied 287 U.S. 660, 53 S.Ct. 222, 77 L.Ed. 570 (1932); same case 172 A. 900 (1933), certiorari denied 288 U.S. 617, 53 S.Ct. 507, 77 L.Ed. 990 (1933) (Pennsylvania and New Jersey both found decedent to be domiciliary, and levied $14,000,000 and $12,000,000 state estate taxes respectively, a result upheld by the Supreme Court, which held that as long as the executor received a fair trial on the issue of domicile, the inconsistent results were constitutionally allowable); Texas v. Florida, 306 U.S. 398, 59 S.Ct. 563, 83 L.Ed. 817 (1939) (Supreme Court determined domicile because conflicting claims would have exhausted the entire estate).

The Uniform Probate Code 3–202 attempts to solve the problem of more than one state's asserting that it is the decedent's domicile by the following provisions:

> If conflicting claims as to the domicile of a decedent are made in a formal testacy or appointment proceeding commenced in this state, and in a testacy or appointment proceeding after notice pending at the same time in another state, the Court of this state must stay, dismiss or permit suitable amendment in, the proceeding here unless it is determined that the local proceeding was commenced before the proceeding elsewhere. The determination of domicile in the proceeding first commenced must be accepted as determinative in the proceeding in this state.

In practice, the two states claiming domicile are likely to compromise the claim. See McKinney's Tax L. § 249–o (1966), the uniform law governing such compromises.

As a preliminary matter, in practice ancillary proceedings are used almost exclusively for real property. They are available for personal property as well, but personal property is usually transferred to the domiciliary fiduciary without the need for appointment of an ancillary administrator.[2]

SECTION B. PURPOSE OF ANCILLARY PROCEEDINGS

When a non-domiciliary of New York dies with real or personal property in New York needing administration, some person interested in his estate has to bring a proceeding in New York. It is usually a proceeding for ancillary administration, but that depends on whether the decedent had a will or not and whether any estate proceedings have occurred in the domiciliary court, issues we discuss presently.

The New York court's subject matter jurisdiction in ancillary proceedings is based on the decedent's property located here.[1] Article 2 gives the court subject matter jurisdiction if the property was here at the decedent's death or was moved here after death, so long as the move was not for a fraudulent or collusive reason.[2] All the Surrogates in the state have subject matter jurisdiction; the proper venue is the court where the property is, or if the decedent's property is in more than one county, the first county where the Surrogate exercises jurisdiction.[3]

The purpose of the Article 16 ancillary administration is to gather the New York property, pay the state estate taxes and creditors' claims, and then deliver the property to the fiduciary in the decedent's domicile, or, more commonly, execute the necessary instruments for the transfer of real property.[4]

The goal underlying Article 16 is to centralize the estate administration; to do so the legislature has structured Article 16 in a way to insure that New York courts will have a "respect for domiciliary procedure and administrative acts."[5] Article 16 is, in effect, an at-

2. McKinney's EPTL 13-3.4.

Sec. B

1. McKinney's SCPA 206, discussed in chapter on "Jurisdiction," supra at 6-9.

2. See Matter of Guadagno, N.Y.L.J., Aug. 21, 1985, at 12, col. 5 (Richmond), where the court revoked ancillary letters of administration when it discovered that the decedent's husband had placed $30 in a Totten Trust in his own name in trust for his wife while she was comatose just before her death.

3. See Matter of Walsh, 128 Misc.2d 694, 491 N.Y.S.2d 84 (Bronx 1985) (where decedent left realty in Bronx and Westchester, Bronx Surrogate refused to entertain ancillary proceeding when proceeding had already been started in Westchester).

4. A fiduciary appointed in another state has authority limited to that state and not recognizable in New York. Steele v. Connecticut General Life Insurance Co., 31 App.Div. 389, 52 N.Y.S. 373 (4th Dep't 1898), affirmed 160 N.Y. 703, 57 N.E. 1125 (1899).

5. Uniform Probate Code, Art. IV, General Comment. The Supreme Court has held that each state has the right to administer the personal assets of a decedent within its borders and to satisfy debts due to its citizens. Baker v. Baker, Eccles and Co., 242 U.S. 394, 37 S.Ct. 152, 61 L.Ed. 386 (1917).

tempt to give practical application to the doctrine of comity.[6] Thus, while ancillary proceedings may be occurring in various locations where the decedent left property, the main administration will occur in the decedent's domicile.[7] The very word "ancillary" connotes a secondary administration, supplemental to the one at the domicile.

In the first section of Article 16, the legislature incorporated its intention to keep the administration centralized. That section says that the New York court cannot appoint an ancillary administrator unless actual administration is taking place in the decedent's domicile. If it is not, the New York court will refuse to grant ancillary administration or probate. This is so even if the decedent requested that primary administration take place somewhere other than in his domicile and proceedings are in fact pending in that other jurisdiction.

There are two major exceptions to this rule of centralization in the decedent's domicile. The first is when the decedent makes two separate wills disposing of separate property.[8] In that case each of two jurisdictions can grant original probate to one of the wills. The other is when the decedent places some (usually most) of his property in New York and directs in his will that the will be probated in New York and that New York law govern the disposition of his New York assets. The New York court has discretion to grant original probate to that will. We discuss both of these cases below in the section of this chapter entitled "Original Probate."

SECTION C. WHEN ANCILLARY PROCEEDINGS CAN BE COMMENCED IN NEW YORK

The first issue in deciding whether ancillary administration is appropriate is whether an actual administration is taking place in the domicile. This is not always simple to determine. If the decedent's domicile is a sister state or a foreign country that follows the Anglo-American system of probating the will and appointing a formal fiduciary, then of course actual administration is occurring if the domiciliary court has done so. However, not all jurisdictions have such formal administration proceedings, so SCPA 1601 permits ancillary proceed-

6. Matter of Manias, N.Y.L.J., July 23, 1985, at 14, col. 1 (Queens). There the petitioner for ancillary letters, a designee of the decedent's father, stipulated that the decedent's father was sole distributee. To prove that actual administration was going on in Greece, the decedent's domicile, the petitioner submitted a decision by the Greek court finding that the decedent's sisters and brothers were also distributees. The Surrogate refused to grant the ancillary letters on the ground that approving a stipulation contrary to the domiciliary court's holding without notice would not further comity.

7. See Matter of Turton, 8 N.Y.2d 311, 206 N.Y.S.2d 761, 170 N.E.2d 190 (1960), reargument denied 9 N.Y.2d 758, 214 N.Y.S.2d 1025, 174 N.E.2d 612 (1961) (though decedent's domicile, British Honduras, had right to probate will and administer estate, New York could administer, on an ancillary basis, property located in New York).

8. The decedent might do so because his domicile restricts the transfer of assets out of the jurisdiction or has a burdensome rule governing inheritance, or similar circumstances. These are discussed in section on original probate, infra at 522–24.

ings here if the domiciliary court has appointed the equivalent of our fiduciary, or if there is (even in the absence of any court proceeding) a person in whom estate property vests, subject to the obligation to pay the decedent's debts and expenses and to distribute his assets. That person may have a title, such as a "universal heir" or "universal legatee," or he may simply be a person (or group of persons) with title to property and the duty to marshal assets, pay debts and distribute the balance under the decedent's will or the intestacy laws of the domicile state.[1] If the New York court finds that some de facto fiduciary is acting, and that person can show either that he took the procedural steps necessary to obtain authority to act as a fiduciary, or if no formal steps were required, that he is actually administering the decedent's property at the domicile or anticipates that he will do so soon, it can give him ancillary letters to act here. In practice, the court will usually grant ancillary letters only where original proceedings, or their equivalent, are pending in the domicile state.

An example of this "de facto" type of administration appears in Matter of Theodoropoulos.[2] Greek law has no statutory proceedings for the appointment of an administrator or other fiduciary. The decedent's heirs petition for a certificate of heirship or inheritance, which identifies and certifies the decedent's distributees, and those certified heirs have full power to administer the property of a decedent, collect the assets, pay liabilities and provide for distribution. The New York court held that the role of the heirs in Greece made them the equivalent of administrators in New York and therefore granted ancillary letters to the designee of the Greek distributees.[3]

Similarly, in Matter of Hahnel,[4] the court found that the will had been "established" in Germany. The court held a hearing on German law and found that the German court had rendered final judicial decrees (not mere administrative certificates) for which a finding of German domicile was a prerequisite.[5]

If the decedent had a will, the nominated fiduciary or a person interested can seek ancillary probate of it. If the decedent died intestate, any distributee can petition for ancillary administration.

Sec. C

1. McKinney's SCPA 1601, Prac.Comm. at 611 (1967).

2. 93 Misc.2d 551, 402 N.Y.S.2d 927 (New York County 1978).

3. A person entitled to serve as fiduciary in the domicile can serve as ancillary fiduciary in New York or can designate someone to serve. McKinney's SCPA 1608.

4. 88 Misc.2d 524, 389 N.Y.S.2d 970 (New York County 1976), affirmed 58 A.D.2d 531, 395 N.Y.S.2d 395 (1st Dep't 1977), motion for leave to appeal denied 43 N.Y.2d 644, 402 N.Y.S.2d 1026, 373 N.E.2d 995 (1978).

5. See also Matter of Martinez, N.Y. L.J., May 1, 1985, at 11, col. 4 (Bronx), where the court granted ancillary letters to the designee of the decedent's surviving spouse because it found that, although Spain did not have formal administration proceedings, the surviving spouse had started a proceeding, obtained a decree declaring her interest in the estate, and assumed control of the assets. It was, in effect, an "actual administration" in Spain and the designee of that "actual administrator" was appointed in New York as ancillary administrator.

Differences exist between the two, and the following discusses the proceedings and their differences.

SECTION D. ANCILLARY PROBATE

1. GENERAL RULES

If the decedent had a written will,[1] the court can grant ancillary probate in New York if the will has been probated or "established" (an approximation of probate under the laws of the foreign jurisdiction [2]) in the decedent's domicile, and if it is not contested.[3] The proceeding is similar to all Surrogate's Court proceedings: it starts with the filing of a petition by a creditor, a person interested in the estate, a person entitled to serve as ancillary administrator, or the public administrator or county treasurer.[4] It must contain the information required for all petitions in the Surrogate's Court [5] and also a listing of all the decedent's property in the state, the amount of the bond the fiduciary gave when he was appointed in the decedent's domicile, and the names of all creditors who are New York domiciliaries and the amount of their claims.[6] The petitioner should state that the will was admitted to probate (or "established") in the decedent's domicile and that it is not being contested, and should attach an authenticated copy of letters as an exhibit to the petition.[7] If the court entertains the petition, it will issue process for service on necessary parties: the New York State Tax Commission,[8] all New York domiciliary creditors and any persons entitled to ancillary letters.[9] The court has discretion to issue additional process to creditors who are New York residents and to determine the manner of its service.[10]

If the petitioner is seeking probate only and not letters, the only necessary party is the state tax commissioner.[11]

Sec. D

1. Ancillary probate is not available for oral wills. McKinney's SCPA 1602(1), overruling Matter of Batsholts, 188 Misc. 867, 66 N.Y.S.2d 358 (New York County 1946), affirmed 271 A.D. 915, 67 N.Y.S.2d 687 (1st Dep't 1947).

2. The mere filing of the will in court of decedent's domicile, without proof or establishment, is an insufficient basis for ancillary probate. Matter of Connell, 221 N.Y. 190, 116 N.E. 986 (1917).

3. If the decedent's will has been admitted to probate in a jurisdiction other than his domicile, the New York court cannot grant ancillary probate. McKinney's SCPA 1602(1).

4. McKinney's SCPA 1609.

5. McKinney's SCPA 304, discussed in chapter on "Procedure," supra at 54–55.

6. McKinney's SCPA 1609(1). A reading of the statute may lead one to conclude that it is the creditors in the decedent's domicile who are entitled to process. That is not so; the "domicile" referred to in SCPA 1609 is New York. McKinney's SCPA 103(16).

7. See McKinney's CPLR 4540 et seq.

8. Tax Law 249–t(1). The tax commission is entitled to process because a New York estate tax is imposed on a non-domiciliary's real property and tangible personal property located in New York. See chapter on "Estate Taxes," infra at 556 et seq.

9. McKinney's SCPA 1609(2). Needless to say, any necessary party who waives service or appears need not be cited. See chapter on "Procedure," supra at 37–38.

10. McKinney's SCPA 1609(2).

11. McKinney's SCPA 1609(3).

On the return date of process, any party may object to ancillary probate, but only on three grounds:

(1) that the will was not probated or established in the decedent's domicile; or

(2) that the proponent has not proved that the will is not being contested at the decedent's domicile; or

(3) that the will has been denied probate in New York.[12]

The objectant cannot raise the issue of the testator's capacity, the will's due execution, the exertion of undue influence or the presence of fraud, on the theory that those issues were or should have been litigated in decedent's domicile. It is irrelevant whether the objectant was a party to the original probate. However, if the Surrogate is not satisfied with the manner in which the estate was handled at the domicile, because, for example, necessary parties failed to get notice, it can grant original probate, which we discuss shortly, and the objectant could raise the issues of undue influence and testamentary capacity at that proceeding.

After the court has heard and decided objections, it can issue a decree of ancillary probate and grant ancillary letters. The court can also estimate the state estate taxes it believes will be due and order their payment or require the fiduciary to file a bond to cover them.[13]

2. PERSONS ENTITLED TO SERVE AS ANCILLARY EXECUTOR

The following persons have the right, in the order listed, to serve as ancillary administrator: [14]

(1) The person the testator named to act as executor of the New York property (or his designee).

(2) The person appointed as fiduciary at the decedent's domicile or if no one has been appointed, the person the testator named as fiduciary (or the designee of that person).

(3) The person acting as executor in the decedent's domicile. This would be different from (2) if the nominated executor had died or had stopped serving as executor and a successor was appointed under local law.

(4) A person entitled to letters of administration c.t.a. under New York law [15] (or his designee).

The public administrator can also bring the proceeding when there are assets in New York and no one else petitions for ancillary letters.[16]

12. McKinney's SCPA 1602(2). See, e.g., Matter of Paterno, N.Y.L.J., May 15, 1978, at 18, col. 5 (Suffolk) (court could not deny probate unless will had previously been denied probate or unless SCPA 1602 was not complied with).

13. Tax Law 249–t(1).

14. McKinney's SCPA 1604.

15. The persons entitled to serve as administrator c.t.a. are discussed in chapter on "Probate," supra at 115–18.

16. McKinney's SCPA 1609.

The persons listed in this statute have a right to serve whether they file the petition or someone else does.[17] The person serving as executor or administrator or de facto fiduciary in the decedent's domicile has the authority to designate an eligible person in New York to act as ancillary fiduciary.[18] (This is an advantage that ancillary proceedings have over original in New York; in an original probate or administration proceeding, a non-resident alien cannot serve and cannot designate an eligible person to act.[19]) The designation must be done in an acknowledged writing and be filed in the Surrogate's Court before the designee can act.[20]

While the priority issue is governed by New York law, the New York court must look to the domiciliary law to determine whether the person who is proposing to serve is in fact the equivalent of an executor here.[21]

This high priority given to the person serving as executor in the decedent's domicile sometimes works an injustice in cases where the decedent's domicile discriminates against New York residents. Florida, for example, places serious restrictions on the class of out-of-state persons who can serve as fiduciaries of Floridians' estates. One solution to this problem is to permit original probate of such a will in New York, since such probate is allowed "where the laws of testator's domicile discriminate against domiciliaries of New York * * * as fiduciary" [22] Another alternative, if the only action one needs to take in New York is to clear title to real property, is for the nominated executor to petition for ancillary probate but not ask for the issuance of letters. Once the will is probated, it is proof of the devise for title purposes, and the property passes to the devisees. There is no need for a fiduciary, and the court need not issue letters unless the petitioner requests them.[23]

In practice, the proceeding is usually brought by the fiduciary from the decedent's domicile, who brings it in the county where the decedent's property is. If the decedent had property in more than one county, the first Surrogate to entertain the proceeding retains jurisdiction from that point.[24]

17. See Matter of Edwards, 87 Misc.2d 337, 385 N.Y.S.2d 253 (Nassau 1976).

18. McKinney's SCPA 1608.

19. McKinney's SCPA 1001(6); Matter of Paderewski, 193 Misc. 688, 84 N.Y.S.2d 322 (New York County 1948); Matter of Reit, 183 Misc. 261, 48 N.Y.S.2d 957 (New York County 1944).

20. McKinney's EPTL 13–2.3(a). See also McKinney's Real Prop.L. § 301–a (1968), which states that if the instrument was executed in a foreign country it must be accompanied by a certificate that it conforms with that country's laws.

21. See Matter of Gyfteas, 59 Misc.2d 977, 300 N.Y.S.2d 913 (New York County 1968), modified on other grounds 36 A.D.2d 380, 320 N.Y.S.2d 540 (1st Dep't 1971) (will did not name an executor and the New York court looked to Greek law to determine whether one person was effectively administering the decedent's estate).

22. McKinney's SCPA 1605(2)(c).

23. McKinney's SCPA 1604(1).

24. McKinney's SCPA 206 governs venue. Every Surrogate in New York has subject matter jurisdiction to entertain the proceeding if the decedent left property in

3. WILL NOT SUBJECT TO CONTEST IN DOMICILE

The proponent must also show that the will is either not subject to contest in the domicile or, if it is, that it is not currently being contested there. The reason for this requirement is that the New York court granting ancillary probate relies on the domiciliary court's finding that the will is valid and therefore wants to know that the period for contest is over.

It is not always possible to be sure there can never be a contest, and several provisions of the SCPA soften the impact of the no-contest rule. Without these provisions, it would often be difficult for a New York court to grant ancillary probate. The statute provides that if a contest is still possible,[25] the proponent must demonstrate that one is not in progress.[26] This was enacted to cover "probate in the common form," a form of probate allowed in some jurisdictions where the will is admitted to probate before interested persons have had an opportunity to be heard; they have a period of time after probate to contest the proceedings.

Moreover, if the petitioner for ancillary probate does not know how long the will remains subject to contest at the decedent's domicile, either because it was admitted to probate in common form or because the proponent cannot get an expert on the law of the decedent's domicile to state definitely that the time for contest has passed, he may proceed with the New York ancillary probate and invoke the protection of SCPA 1603's time limitations. To protect the ancillary executor hesitant to send assets to the domiciliary fiduciary for fear that he may be liable for them if a contest later arises, SCPA 1603 provides that the ancillary administrator can send property to the domiciliary fiduciary or distribute it to beneficiaries under the will if the ancillary (New York) court authorizes the distribution on proof that 1) seven months have passed since the New York court issued ancillary letters,[27] and 2) no will contest is pending at the testator's domicile, and 3) either the time provided in the domicile for contesting has expired, or one year has passed since the New York court admitted the will to ancillary probate.[28] All three conditions must be met.[29]

New York, and the proper venue is the county where the property is located or the first of such counties to exercise jurisdiction. See chapter on "Jurisdiction," supra at 6–9.

25. The ability to contest a decree or order on the ground of newly discovered evidence is not a deterrent to ancillary probate. Matter of Hahnel, 88 Misc.2d 524, 389 N.Y.S.2d 970 (New York County 1976), affirmed 58 A.D.2d 531, 385 N.Y.S.2d 395 (1st Dep't 1977).

26. McKinney's SCPA 1602.

27. This seven months comports with the period for presentation of claims by creditors. McKinney's SCPA 1802, discussed in chapter on "Claims," supra at 148–50.

28. The one-year limitation was added by L.1975, c. 194, sec. 1. The prior version of the statute required the expiration of the time for contest at the domicile, but that period was sometimes several years. This had the effect of leaving the ancillary proceedings in suspension. Hence, the amendment gave the one-year period as an alternative. See McKinney's SCPA 1603, 1973 Prac.Comm. at 155–56 (1986), where this amendment was recommended.

29. McKinney's SCPA 1603(1).

An ancillary fiduciary who in good faith gets court authorization to send or distribute assets is discharged from liability even if a will contest arises at the decedent's domicile and the will is set aside or revoked, no matter what the reason.[30]

4. EFFECT OF ANCILLARY PROBATE

If the New York court grants ancillary probate, the will is effective to dispose of all the property it attempts to dispose of, unless the laws of the testator's domicile would limit its effect because of the legal capacity of the testator.[31] For example, if the testator's domicile did not permit its citizens to execute a will before age twenty-one, New York will not give effect to the will of a nineteen-year old although under New York law such a testator could have executed a valid will.[32] The term "legal capacity" in theory of course also applies to mental disability, but since no jurisdiction grants probate to the will of a person without testamentary capacity, we have never needed that application of the statute.[33]

If the Surrogate grants ancillary probate to a will in New York, the rights granted in the decedent's domicile to persons to take against the will, such as a right to contest an excess gift to charity, rights of after-born children and a right to exempt property, "are not affected" by the ancillary probate.[34] What this means is uncertain on its face, and case law does not entirely resolve the issue,[35] at least in the area of a surviving spouse's right of election. New York law provides that a non-domiciliary's surviving spouse does not have a right of election against New York property unless the decedent opts for the application of New York law to the New York property under EPTL 3–5.1(h).[36] For example, if a non-New Yorker dies leaving property in New York and his will is offered for ancillary probate in New York, his surviving spouse is not entitled to exercise her right of election against the New York property unless the decedent stated in the will that New York law should apply to the administration of his estate.[37] If he did not provide for application of New York law (and a testator usually does not unless he intended to have original probate in New York), under the EPTL provision she does not have a right to elect against the New York

30. McKinney's SCPA 1603(2).

31. McKinney's SCPA 1602(1).

32. McKinney's EPTL 3–1.1. New York would not be so restricted if it granted original probate to such a will, McKinney's EPTL 3–5.1, an anomaly which led Prof. Powers to suggest in his Practice Commentary to McKinney's SCPA 1602 at 615 (1967) that the grounds for original probate be expanded to include cases where the decedent's domicile imposes limitations inconsistent with our own.

33. The late Prof. Paul Powers, in his Practice Commentary to McKinney's SCPA 1602, at 614 (1967), raises the possibility of another jurisdiction's denying a person legal capacity to make a will because of race, gender, religion or political affiliation. The statute would on its face require New York to deny probate to such a will, but obviously such interpretation of the statute would be against public policy.

34. McKinney's SCPA 1602(1).

35. See discussion of the "not affected" language in McKinney's SCPA 1602, Prac. Comm. at 616–17 (1967), and at 153–54 (Supp.1986).

36. McKinney's EPTL 5–1.1(d)(7).

37. McKinney's EPTL 3–5.1.

realty, leaving some doubt about the meaning of the SCPA language that the right of election granted by the decedent's domicile is "not affected" by the ancillary probate. The Court of Appeals has spoken peripherally [38] twice on this issue, once in Matter of Clark,[39] where it held that a decedent could not opt to have New York's less favorable right of election apply to the New York assets rather than his domicile's more favorable one, and then again in Matter of Renard,[40] where it held that a decedent could opt for New York law which does not allow a forced share for heirs rather than the domicile's law allowing a forced share.[41] We must await either legislation or further appellate review to clarify the matter. At the same time the legislature should consider coordinating the non-domiciliary's rights with the New York domiciliary's rights, which currently do not include the right to elect against out-of-state real property.

5. QUALIFICATION OF THE ANCILLARY EXECUTOR

The ancillary executor must be eligible,[42] and before receiving letters he must qualify [43] by filing a designation of the court clerk to receive process if he cannot be served, filing an oath that he will faithfully perform his duties, and obtaining a bond in an amount set by the court. The court can dispense with a bond if the will dispenses with it or if there are no New York creditors and no New York estate taxes due. When the court dispenses with a bond, it usually requires the ancillary executor to publish notice for creditors.

The court can and often does require the petitioner to serve notice on New York beneficiaries who have not received or waived process or appeared. This notice is like the notice of probate,[44] and failure to give the notice does not jeopardize the decree; its purpose is to give the beneficiaries an opportunity to protect their interests.

38. These cases were peripheral in that they dealt with original, not ancillary probate, and with personal, not real property. Moreover, Matter of Renard was not a right of election case, but one which dealt with a forced share for issue.

39. 21 N.Y.2d 478, 288 N.Y.S.2d 993, 236 N.E.2d 152 (1968).

40. Matter of Renard, 108 Misc.2d 31, 437 N.Y.S.2d 860 (New York County 1981), affirmed without opinion 85 A.D.2d 501, 447 N.Y.S.2d 573 (1st Dep't 1981), affirmed 56 N.Y.2d 973, 453 N.Y.S.2d 625, 439 N.E. 2d 341 (1982).

41. See discussion of these two cases in chapter on "Jurisdiction," supra at 32–34.

42. McKinney's SCPA 1608(4) states that all SCPA provisions on eligibility are applicable to ancillary fiduciaries. McKinney's SCPA 707, discussed supra at 388–91 governs eligibility. A non-resident alien is not eligible. Under McKinney's SCPA 1608(6), the court may appoint as ancillary executor or administrator even a bank not entitled under the Banking Law to serve as fiduciary. Under McKinney's Banking Law § 131(3), trust companies incorporated in other jurisdictions cannot serve in New York unless their state extends reciprocal powers to New York trust companies.

43. McKinney's SCPA 1608 requires an ancillary fiduciary to qualify just as a New York fiduciary must. McKinney's SCPA 708, discussed supra at 391–92 describes the steps of qualification.

44. McKinney's SCPA 1409, discussed in chapter on "Probate," supra at 82–84.

If a creditor or a person interested wants the ancillary executor removed, the court can revoke ancillary letters on the same grounds it could revoke original letters.[45]

SECTION E. ANCILLARY LETTERS OF ADMINISTRATION

The rules for non-domiciliary intestate decedents who left property in New York requiring administration parallel those for non-domiciliary decedents who had a will. If the decedent's domicile has granted letters of administration, the Surrogate in New York may grant ancillary letters of administration.[1] If the law of the domicile does not provide for letters of administration, but some person is in fact administering the decedent's estate in the domicile under the laws of the domicile (marshalling assets, paying debts, and performing other fiduciary functions), the Surrogate in New York may issue ancillary letters of administration.[2] Occasionally the court has already granted original probate to a non-New Yorker's will, or is entertaining a proceeding for original probate, when someone petitions for appointment of an ancillary administrator. In that case, the court can do whatever is necessary in the interests of justice. It may, for example, continue the letters, or restrict them, to ensure that the executor will administer the new assets.

The order of priority for ancillary letters of administration is as follows: First, the administrator in the domicile (or the equivalent under the domicile's law), or a person designated by the administrator; secondly, any person entitled to original letters of administration under New York law, or a person designated by him.[3]

The proceeding is like the proceeding for ancillary probate; it is commenced by a petition, the court issues process, and the petitioner serves it on necessary parties: the state tax commission, all domiciliary (New York) creditors or those claiming to be, and other persons entitled to letters or entitled to designate an administrator if the court directs service on them.[4] Those parties have an opportunity to object, and if they do the court will hold a hearing and make an appropriate ruling. The person who serves as ancillary administrator must be eligible,[5] and before receiving letters he must qualify by designating the court clerk

45. See McKinney's SCPA 711 and 719, discussed in chapter on "Fiduciaries," supra at 393–400. See also Matter of Haim, N.Y. L.J., Dept. 11, 1979, at 7, col. 1 (New York County), where the court refused to revoke ancillary letters both because the petitioner, who was neither a creditor or a person interested, lacked standing and because petitioner had not shown fraud or other exceptional circumstances for revocation.

Sec. E

1. McKinney's SCPA 1607(1).

2. McKinney's SCPA 1607(1). See Matter of Theodoropoulos, 93 Misc.2d 551, 402 N.Y.S.2d 927 (New York County 1978).

3. McKinney's SCPA 1607(2).

4. McKinney's SCPA 1609.

5. McKinney's SCPA 1608; McKinney's SCPA 707. See discussion in note 42 supra at 518.

to receive process if he cannot be served, filing an oath that he will faithfully perform his fiduciary duties, and filing a bond in an amount set by the court.[6] The court can dispense with a bond if the prospective fiduciary swears in an affidavit that there are no New York creditors and no New York estate tax due. The court can require the petitioner to publish notice to creditors and can dispense with a bond. In practice, if there is a doubt, the court requires a bond.

As in the ancillary probate proceeding, the court can (and usually does) require the petitioner to serve notice on New York beneficiaries who have not received process or waived it or appeared. Failure to give the notice is not a jurisdictional defect, since its purpose is merely to give the beneficiaries the opportunity to protect their rights. The form is the same as that required for notice in an administration proceeding.[7]

SECTION F. POWERS AND DUTIES OF ANCILLARY FIDUCIARIES

The ancillary fiduciary has all the rights, powers, duties and liabilities of a fiduciary.[1] It is the usual job of an ancillary administrator to marshal the assets, pay New York claims and deliver the estate assets to the domiciliary fiduciary.[2]

The Surrogate may direct an ancillary fiduciary to pay New York creditors from assets he receives in New York. When the debt exceeds the property the ancillary fiduciary holds, the court may allocate the property among the creditors [3] using the Article 18 rules governing the priority of claims.[4] The Surrogate also has the power to decide the claims of non-domiciliaries,[5] though out-of-state claimants do not usually come to an ancillary jurisdiction for such relief.

If any property is left after the payment of all claims, the court may direct the ancillary fiduciary to distribute those assets to the beneficiaries,[6] to forward them to the decedent's domicile for administration by the fiduciary there,[7] or otherwise dispose of them as justice requires.[8] The usual course is to direct payment to the fiduciary at the domicile except when most of the property and beneficiaries are in New

6. McKinney's SCPA 1608 requires an ancillary fiduciary to qualify just as a New York fiduciary must. McKinney's SCPA 708, discussed supra at 391–92, describes the steps of qualification.

7. McKinney's SCPA 1005, discussed in chapter on "Administration," supra at 142–43.

Sec. F

1. See chapter on "Fiduciaries," supra at 384 et seq.

2. McKinney's SCPA 1610(1).

3. McKinney's SCPA 1610(2).

4. McKinney's SCPA 1610(2); McKinney's SCPA 1811, discussed in chapter on "Claims," supra at 164–72.

5. Matter of Meyer, 244 N.Y. 598, 155 N.E. 913 (1927).

6. See Matter of Van Allen, N.Y.L.J., Feb. 10, 1977, at 11, col. 6 (New York County) (giving fund to domiciliary fiduciary would cause delay and financial restrictions on beneficiaries); Matter of Heller-Baghero, 26 N.Y.2d 337, 310 N.Y.S.2d 313, 258 N.E.2d 717 (1970) (accord).

7. McKinney's SCPA 1610(4).

8. McKinney's SCPA 1610(3).

York and the extra step would be inefficient and wasteful.[9] If both the domiciliary fiduciary and the beneficiary ask the ancillary fiduciary for the property, he may ask the court which course to follow.[10]

If the ancillary fiduciary collects substantial assets in New York and the domiciliary fiduciary needs them, and if seven months have not passed since the issuance of ancillary letters, the Surrogate can direct the ancillary fiduciary to pay New York taxes and New York creditors, to post a bond, and to transmit the funds to the domiciliary fiduciary.[11] If no claims arise, after the seven months the bond can be rescinded. The court can also require notice to the domiciliary court which can then revise the domiciliary fiduciary's bond, if necessary.

A person in possession of the decedent's property can deliver it to a foreign fiduciary unless he knows of the existence of either creditors or an ancillary fiduciary in New York.[12] If creditors are in fact in New York, they must find out whether the decedent had assets here and pursue the assets, because any person who in good faith (that is, without knowledge of creditors) pays the property over to a foreign fiduciary is discharged, unless he knew that the beneficiary would not have the use of the property.[13]

Frequently, someone has a cause of action against the estate because, for example, of the decedent's negligence. If the only "asset" in New York is the cause of action against a New Yorker, a fiduciary appointed in another state can commence that action or proceeding without first obtaining ancillary letters [14] but a fiduciary appointed in another country cannot.[15] The foreign fiduciary must file a copy of his letters or an affidavit explaining his authority to act on the decedent's behalf.[16] He must also submit an affidavit that the decedent did not owe money to New Yorkers.[17] If the decedent had New York creditors, the fiduciary must notify them of the lawsuit.[18] The fiduciary must also swear that at least six months have passed since the decedent's death and that no one has petitioned for ancillary letters.[19] If the domiciliary fiduciary starts the proceeding or action and an ancillary

9. See Matter of Horwich, 10 Misc.2d 79, 170 N.Y.S.2d 472 (New York County 1957) (court ordered distribution directly to beneficiaries because there were nineteen New York beneficiaries and two non-New Yorkers, and more than eighty-five percent of property was in New York); Matter of Menschefrend, 283 App.Div. 463, 128 N.Y.S.2d 738 (1st Dep't 1954), affirmed 8 N.Y.2d 1093, 208 N.Y.S.2d 453, 170 N.E.2d 9022 (1960), remittitur amended 8 N.Y.2d 1156, 209 N.Y.S.2d 836, 171 N.E.2d 909 (1960), certiorari denied 365 U.S. 842, 81 S.Ct. 801, 5 L.Ed.2d 808 (1961) (if there are no heirs, ancillary fiduciary should turn property over to state, not deliver it to domicile).

10. Matter of Bourne, 82 Misc.2d 824, 370 N.Y.S.2d 462 (New York County 1975).

11. Matter of Martin, N.Y.L.J., March 17, 1983, at 12, col. 2 (Bronx).

12. McKinney's EPTL 13–3.4.

13. McKinney's EPTL 13–3.4(b).

14. McKinney's EPTL 13–3.5.

15. McKinney's EPTL 13–3.5 is expressly limited to representatives who are "duly appointed or authorized by the law of any other state, territory or other jurisdiction of the United States * * *."

16. McKinney's EPTL 13–3.5(a)(1); see also McKinney's CPLR 4542.

17. McKinney's EPTL 13–3.5(a)(2)(A).

18. McKinney's EPTL 13–3.5(a)(2)(C).

19. McKinney's EPTL 13–3.5(a)(2)(B).

fiduciary is later appointed, the ancillary fiduciary has a right to be substituted for the original petitioner or plaintiff.[20]

If someone has a cause of action against a decedent from another jurisdiction and wants to sue the foreign representative, he can do so in New York only if there is a basis for personal jurisdiction either of the representative or the decedent.[21]

The ancillary administrator has to account for his actions, and he is subject to the same sanctions for wrongdoing or negligence as a domiciliary fiduciary: surcharge, denial of commissions, and removal.[22]

SECTION G. ORIGINAL PROBATE OF NON-DOMICILIARY'S WILL

In some cases, a Surrogate will grant original probate rather than ancillary probate to a non-domiciliary's will. If the Surrogate admits the will to probate, it operates on property located in New York and is treated as though it was executed in New York.[1] Admission of a foreign will to original probate in New York depends on whether it has been probated (or established) in the decedent's domicile. If it has, original probate in New York is not undertaken lightly: the proponent must show that one of the exceptions of SCPA 1605 (discussed presently) exists. If the will has not been probated in the decedent's domicile, the court has jurisdiction to grant it original probate. It is then a matter of the court's discretion whether the New York connections make it appropriate to probate the will here. Both of these alternatives are discussed in this section.

1. ORIGINAL PROBATE WHEN THE DOMICILIARY COURT HAS GRANTED PROBATE

If the will has been admitted to probate (or established) at the testator's domicile, the New York court may not admit it to original probate unless (1) ancillary probate would be impossible or unduly expensive or inconvenient;[2] or (2) the testator directed in his will that the will should be offered for probate in New York;[3] or (3) the laws of

20. McKinney's EPTL 13-3.5(a)(4).

21. See McKinney's SCPA 210 and chapter on "Jurisdiction," supra at 25-28.

22. See chapters on "Commissions," supra at 436-41, and "Fiduciaries," supra at 393-400, 412-13. See also Matter of Bourne, 82 Misc.2d 824, 370 N.Y.S.2d 462 (New York County 1975), where stock depreciated in value while the ancillary fiduciary was holding it. The court refused to surcharge the ancillary fiduciary who had received conflicting orders from the primary fiduciary and the charitable beneficiary on the proper distribution of the stock; and Matter of Guadagno, N.Y.L.J., Aug. 21, 1985, at 12, col. 5 (Richmond), where the court removed the ancillary administrator for misstating a material fact in his petition for letters.

Sec. G

1. McKinney's SCPA 1605(1).

2. The kind of situation contemplated is a state of war, the destruction of the records at the domicile, prosecution of minorities, or similar cases. See McKinney's SCPA 1605, Practice Comm. at 632 (McKinney 1967).

3. McKinney's SCPA 1605(2)(b). See Matter of Renard, 100 Misc.2d 347, 417 N.Y.S.2d 155 (New York County 1979).

the testator's domicile discriminate against domiciliaries of New York either as beneficiaries or as fiduciaries.[4]

Even if it has the power, the court can refuse to entertain the proceeding if it believes that to be in the best interests of the estate.[5] That usually depends on the significance of the New York contacts.

If the will was offered for probate (or its equivalent) at the testator's domicile and the court there denied the will probate, the New York court cannot admit it to probate if the reason for denying probate is also a ground for rejection of a New York testator's will.[6]

2. ORIGINAL PROBATE WHEN THE DOMICILIARY COURT HAS NOT GRANTED PROBATE

If the will has not been probated in the domicile, the New York courts have the power to probate it here[7] and whether they exercise their power is a matter of discretion depending on the New York contacts. The court considers such factors as the location of the assets (in practice the most important consideration), the residence of the nominated fiduciary and the beneficiaries, the expense of proving the will at the domicile, the testator's request, if any, for New York probate, and the good faith of the proponent (illustrating that there is no attempt to thwart the law of the domicile).[8]

A common scenario is that the testator writes two wills, a foreign will to dispose of the foreign property, and a New York will to dispose of the New York property.[9] The "New York will" is not probated in

4. McKinney's SCPA 1605(2). See, e.g., Matter of Siegel, 83 Misc.2d 1062, 373 N.Y.S.2d 812 (Erie 1975); Matter of Brown, 107 Misc.2d 970, 436 N.Y.S.2d 132 (New York County 1981) (Surrogate granted original probate to non-domiciliary's will because law of decedent's domicile discriminated against appointment of non-residents as fiduciaries). For a discussion of the constitutional dimensions of such discrimination, see Matter of Harrison, 81 Misc.2d 807, 366 N.Y.S.2d 755 (Bronx 1974).

5. Matter of Oakley, N.Y.L.J., March 29, 1978, at 17, col. 6 (Westchester) (although court had authority to assume jurisdiction over the estate despite the admission of the will to probate in another jurisdiction, full faith and credit dictated that consideration be given to the actions of the Pennsylvania court).

6. McKinney's SCPA 1605(3).

7. Their jurisdiction stems from McKinney's SCPA 207. McKinney's SCPA 1605 prohibits New York original probate only when the domicile has granted probate.

8. Matter of Heller-Baghero, 26 N.Y.2d 337, 310 N.Y.S.2d 313, 258 N.E.2d 717 (1970); Matter of Renard, 100 Misc.2d 347, 417 N.Y.S.2d 155 (New York County 1979). The court denied original probate in Matter of Brunner, 72 Misc.2d 826, 339 N.Y.S.2d 506 (New York County 1973), because most of the assets were outside New York and because litigation was pending outside New York. But see Matter of Grushovetz, 84 Misc.2d 356, 375 N.Y.S.2d 518 (Albany 1975), where the New York court in its discretion granted original probate although almost none of the assets were in New York. Special circumstances compelled the court to act: the decedent had been a long-time New York domiciliary until his niece moved him to Pennsylvania shortly after his wife's death and shortly before his own. She also moved all of his possessions and the only asset left in New York was the (now empty) marital abode. The decedent had named a New York executor who offered the will for probate in New York. The niece obtained letters of administration in Pennsylvania. Because of the recent severance of the New York connections and because no court had reviewed the will, the court granted it original probate in New York.

9. A frequent reason for this plan is the desire to avoid the application of the domi-

the domicile because it does not relate to property in the domicile. Thus the New York court has the power to grant original probate to it, and usually does so because all (or much) of the property is located in New York.[10]

The person seeking original probate does so by filing a petition and serving the court-issued process on all necessary parties. The contents of the petition and the necessary parties are the same as those discussed above in connection with the petition for ancillary probate. The person who wants to serve as fiduciary must be eligible and qualify, just as the ancillary executor did.

In a proceeding for original probate of a non-domiciliary's will, the petitioner does not have to produce the original will if it has been probated in the place where it was executed; in that case the proponent can offer an authenticated copy of the will and evidence of its probate. That will be sufficient to prove the contents and compliance with the laws at the place of execution unless someone objects, and then the proponent must prove the contents of the will and its legal sufficiency. In that case the court may also order the proponent to obtain the original will.[11]

SECTION H. ANCILLARY ADMINISTRATION OF THE ESTATE OF AN ABSENTEE

If a New Yorker has disappeared, persons interested in his property can take steps to obtain a judicial finding of his death and to probate his will or administer his estate under the laws of intestacy.[1] If such a person was not a New York domiciliary but had property in New York requiring administration, ancillary proceedings are available. Ancillary proceedings for probate or administration are started by a petition. Process then issues to the absent person (by publication), to the public administrator, or if there is none, to the county treasurer. The court appoints a guardian ad litem to protect the interests of the absentee.

cile's laws on forced heirship. Some testators want to avoid the domicile's law on the right of election as well. For a discussion of whether this can work or not, see Matter of Renard, 108 Misc.2d 31, 437 N.Y.S.2d 860 (New York County 1981), affirmed without opinion 85 A.D.2d 501, 447 N.Y.S.2d 573 (1st Dep't 1981), affirmed 56 N.Y.2d 973, 453 N.Y.S.2d 625, 439 N.E.2d 341 (1982); Matter of Clark, 21 N.Y.2d 478, 288 N.Y.S.2d 993, 236 N.E.2d 152 (1968), and discussion of the issue in chapter on "Jurisdiction," supra at 32–34.

10. See, e.g., Matter of Heller-Baghero, 26 N.Y.2d 337, 310 N.Y.S.2d 313, 258 N.E.2d 717 (1970); accord, Matter of Lipin, N.Y.L.J., July 1, 1981, at 12, col. 1, where the decedent had a New York will and a Swiss will, and the Swiss court had not probated the New York will, and consequently the New York Surrogate granted original probate to the New York will. Both cases relied on Matter of Gifford, 279 N.Y. 470, 18 N.E.2d 663 (1939), which holds that where there are separate wills disposing respectively of property in separate countries, "the courts in each country probate the will or wills referring to property there. Even the courts of the country where the testator was domiciled do not grant probate or issue letters testamentary on a will which refers only to personal property in another jurisdiction."

11. McKinney's SCPA 1606.

Sec. H

1. See chapter on "Temporary Administration," supra at 291–93.

On the return of process the court examines the facts, and if it is satisfied that the missing person is dead, it may make a decree determining that fact and grant ancillary letters of administration.[2] If a judicial determination of death has occurred at the domicile, the New York court may accept that determination.[3]

SECTION I. EFFECT OF ADJUDICATION FOR OR AGAINST A FIDUCIARY

To maintain some order, the statute creates a privity between the primary fiduciary and the ancillary fiduciary. Without that privity, decisions in proceedings against one would not be res judicata on the other.[1] If the domiciliary court adjudicates an issue, that decision is binding on the ancillary fiduciary in New York just as though he had been a party to that adjudication,[2] unless the adjudication was a result of the fiduciary's fraud or collusion and it prejudices the estate. The statutory provision does not apply to an adjudication in another jurisdiction admitting or refusing to admit a will to probate. That issue can be relitigated in New York.[3]

SECTION J. APPLICATION OF OTHER PROVISIONS OF LAW

All the substantive and procedural laws concerning wills, probate contests, and the administration of an estate apply to ancillary proceedings, unless specific sections of the statute provide otherwise.

SECTION K. ANCILLARY PROCEEDINGS IN ANOTHER JURISDICTION FOR THE ESTATE OF A NEW YORK DOMICILIARY

If a New Yorker left property in other jurisdictions that needs administration, the New York fiduciary usually has to commence ancillary proceedings in the other jurisdiction. The law of the other jurisdiction governs the type of proceeding required, the process or notice required to persons interested, the fees, and the eligibility of fiduciaries. In many cases the law of the other jurisdiction parallels Article 16; the New Yorker can be appointed ancillary administrator (though often the law of the other state requires appointment of a local resident) and his task is to marshal the property, notify creditors, and pay local death taxes. The court in the other jurisdiction will usually

2. McKinney's SCPA 1611.

3. McKinney's SCPA 1611.

Sec. I

1. Matter of Zietz, 85 N.Y.S.2d 668 (New York County 1948), affirmed 275 App.Div. 748, 88 N.Y.S.2d 494 (1st Dep't 1949).

2. See, e.g., Matter of Kellner, 108 Misc. 2d 667, 438 N.Y.S.2d 705 (Nassau 1981) (domiciliary court determined that legacy should be paid without interest, and ancillary fiduciary was bound by that determination).

3. McKinney's SCPA 1605(3).

take steps to protect the taxing authority and local creditors, and will then order the property to be sent to New York, sold, delivered to beneficiaries or whatever else the New York fiduciary has requested.[1]

Sec. K

1. See American College of Probate Counsel, Rights of Nonresident Individuals To Act As Fiduciaries in Various States (Schaefler, ed. 1982), for a listing of which states permit nonresidents to act as administrators, ancillary administrators, executors, ancillary executors, testamentary trustees, ancillary testamentary trustees, guardians of property of minors, ancillary guardians of property of minors, committee of incompetent, and ancillary committee of incompetent.

Chapter Twenty

WRONGFUL DEATH PROCEEDINGS

SECTION A. INTRODUCTION

Whenever the negligence, omission or other tortious action of one person causes the death of another, the decedent's representative can commence an action on behalf of the distributees [1] for compensation of the pecuniary loss caused by the decedent's death.[2] Wrongful death proceedings are a "child of statute," [3] not permitted under common law, and have been constitutionally guaranteed in New York since 1894.[4]

Most often the decedent's fiduciary commences a personal injury action simultaneously with the wrongful death action. Though both actions are tried (or settled) together, conceptually there are vast differences between the two causes of action. The personal injury action was in a theoretical sense the decedent's property; he sought (or his personal representative seeks for him) compensation for medical expenses, pain and suffering, loss of earnings and other damages resulting from his injuries. He gives the cause of action to his beneficiaries and it is an asset of his estate. If the estate succeeds in the personal injuries part of the lawsuit, that recovery passes under the terms of the decedent's will or under the laws of intestacy, like any other property he owned. (It is also part of his gross estate for tax purposes [5] and subject to his creditors' claims.[6]) By contrast, the decedent and his estate have no ownership interest in wrongful death proceeds; the wrongful death cause of action is not part of the estate; [7]

Sec. A

1. A decedent's distributees are those listed in EPTL 4–1.1, discussed in chapter on "Administration," supra at 125 et seq.

2. McKinney's EPTL 5–4.1.

3. George v. Mount Sinai Hospital, 47 N.Y.2d 170, 417 N.Y.S.2d 231, 390 N.E.2d 1156 (1979). The statute governing wrongful death proceedings is McKinney's EPTL, Article 5, Part 4.

4. Under McKinney's Const. Art. 1, section 16, the right to recover damages for wrongful death shall never be abrogated and the amount recoverable cannot be limited by statute.

5. Matter of Franco, 108 Misc.2d 1084, 439 N.Y.S.2d 278 (Bronx 1981) (tax commission must be given notice of allocation hearing).

6. Matter of Franco, 108 Misc.2d 1084, 439 N.Y.S.2d 278 (Bronx 1981) (pain and suffering portion of recovery available for creditors' claims, wrongful death portion not).

7. Central New York Coach Lines v. Syracuse Herald Co., 277 N.Y. 110, 13 N.E.2d 598 (1938) (wrongful death proceeds are for sole benefit of distributees, not part of estate).

it belongs to such of the decedent's distributees who suffer a pecuniary loss.[8] Thus, if the estate succeeds in the wrongful death part of the lawsuit, that recovery goes to the distributees who experience a loss, regardless of how the decedent disposed of his property by will. (The wrongful death recovery is also excluded from his gross estate for tax purposes [9] and insulated from the claims of the decedent's creditors. [10])

Typically the parties, through their attorneys, attempt to negotiate a settlement to avoid a trial. Though the action is virtually never commenced in the Surrogate's Court, but rather in the Supreme Court or another civil court, if the case is settled, the Surrogate [11] sometimes reviews the settlement. Moreover, appointment of a fiduciary is a prerequisite for starting the action, and that appointment must come from the Surrogate. Because the trial itself usually takes place in the Supreme Court or another court of civil jurisdiction,[12] that court has the authority to approve a settlement that occurs during the trial. Even if there is a trial in the Supreme Court, the Surrogate may continue to oversee certain parts of the proceedings, including the allocation of the assets to the proper distributees, the fixing of commissions, and the settling of the fiduciary's account.[13] In effect, if the case is tried, or even if an action is merely commenced, there may be a flip-flopping of jurisdiction between the trial court and the Surrogate's Court.

The wrongful death proceeding, whether tried or compromised, is bifurcated into a "damages" portion and an "allocation" portion. The two interrelate heavily because the amount of damages is based on the pecuniary losses of the decedent's surviving distributees, and so is the allocation of damages among them.

This chapter discusses the jurisdiction and the special role of the Surrogate in wrongful death proceedings and personal injury actions,

8. See Baer v. Broder, 86 A.D.2d 881, 447 N.Y.S.2d 538 (2d Dep't 1982). In fact the decedent could not waive or relinquish rights to it during his lifetime. Western Union Telephone Co. v. Cochran, 277 App. Div. 625, 102 N.Y.S.2d 65 (3d Dep't 1951), affirmed 302 N.Y. 545, 99 N.E.2d 882 (1951), reargument denied 303 N.Y. 665, 102 N.E.2d 586 (1951). But see Hodge v. Rutland R. R. Co., 112 App.Div. 142, 97 N.Y.S. 1107 (3d Dep't 1906), reversed on other grounds 115 App.Div. 881, 100 N.Y.S. 764 (3d Dep't 1906), affirmed 194 N.Y. 570, 88 N.E. 1121 (1909). The proportion of wrongful death proceeds payable to the respective distributees is discussed in this chapter infra at 545–48.

9. Connecticut Bank and Trust Co. v. United States, 465 F.2d 760 (2d Cir.1972) (wrongful death proceeds excludible even in those states where the wrongful death action is, unlike in New York, a survival action).

10. Schwabacker v. International Salt Co., 272 App.Div. 173, 70 N.Y.S.2d 370 (3d Dep't 1947), affirmed 298 N.Y. 726, 83 N.E.2d 140 (1948).

11. The Surrogate's Court which appointed the fiduciary is the court with jurisdiction over the compromise of the wrongful death proceeding. McKinney's EPTL 5–4.4(a)(1). Since the venue requirement is strictly construed, that Surrogate is the only one who would entertain jurisdiction.

12. Ordinary rules of civil practice on venue, pre-trial discovery, trial procedure, function of the judge and jury, and motion practice govern. See generally Carmody-Wait 2d, Chapter 130, Section 130:70–130:81.

13. The trial court has concurrent jurisdiction to approve the compromise and allocate the proceeds.

the procedure for compromising the action, the allocation and distribution of the proceeds, and the fiduciary's accounting for the proceeds.

SECTION B. THE FIDUCIARY'S ROLE

Only the personal representative of a decedent survived by distributees may commence a wrongful death action.[1] Hence, unless an executor or administrator is serving, the first step in a wrongful death action is a proceeding in the Surrogate's Court for appointment of a fiduciary. The fiduciary's role is to try or to settle the action, to determine who the injured parties are and the amount of their damages, to get approval from the Surrogate of his allocation and distribution, and then to account for the distribution of the proceeds.

The petitioner may seek "full" letters of administration [2] or "limited" letters for the sole purpose of prosecuting the wrongful death claim.[3] In either case, necessary parties to an administration proceeding have a right to object to the grant of letters.[4]

If the decedent was a New York domiciliary, all the Surrogates in the state have jurisdiction to appoint an administrator, but the proper venue is in the county of the decedent's domicile.[5] If the decedent was a non-domiciliary, the foreign representative can bring the personal injury [6] or wrongful death [7] lawsuit in New York without seeking any letters, ancillary or original. If, however, a person does seek letters in New York, he can do so in any county if the decedent left property in New York or a cause of action against a New York domiciliary, and as a practical matter, the Surrogate will grant the letters. The proper venue is the county where the decedent's property is or where the New York defendant lives.[8] The New York Surrogate will not grant letters if someone objects on the ground that no New York court of competent

Sec. B

1. See McKinney's EPTL 5–4.1(1); Chong v. New York City Transit Authority, 83 A.D.2d 546, 441 N.Y.S.2d 24 (2d Dep't 1981); Boffee v. Consolidated Tel. and Electrical Subway Co., 171 A.D. 392, 157 N.Y.S. 318 (1st Dep't 1916), affirmed 226 N.Y. 654, 123 N.E. 856 (1919) (motion to dismiss granted because action was brought by nominated executor not duly appointed); Brosnan v. Allied Chemical Corp., N.Y.L.J., Jan. 4, 1980, at 12, col. 5 (Queens) (accord).

2. See Article 10, discussed in chapter on "Administration," supra at 125 et seq.

3. McKinney's EPTL 5–4.1. See discussion of limited letters in chapter on "Fiduciaries," supra at 386.

4. The parties necessary to an administration proceeding are governed by Article 10 and discussed in chapter on "Administration," supra at 139–41. See Matter of Cesario, 103 Misc.2d 1, 425 N.Y.S.2d 238 (Bronx 1980), where persons claiming to be decedent's out-of-wedlock children were necessary parties to the proceeding for appointment of an administrator for the purpose of bringing a lawsuit.

5. McKinney's SCPA 205.

6. McKinney's EPTL 13–3.5. Windbourne v. Eastern Airlines, Inc., 479 F.Supp. 1130 (E.D.N.Y.1979), reversed on other grounds 632 F.2d 219 (2d Cir.1980), which holds that an ancillary administrator must be appointed, is wrongly decided.

7. McKinney's EPTL 5–4.1(1) states that "[t]he personal representative, duly appointed in this state or any other jurisdiction" may commence the wrongful death action. See Provost v. International Giant Safety Coaster Co., 152 App.Div. 83, 136 N.Y.S. 654 (1st Dep't 1912), affirmed 208 N.Y. 635, 102 N.E. 1112 (1913). See chapter on "Ancillary Proceedings," supra at 521–22.

8. McKinney's SCPA 206.

jurisdiction, such as the Supreme Court, has personal jurisdiction over the defendant.[9]

If a nominated but not yet appointed fiduciary tries to commence an action, the defendant can have it dismissed.[10] However, that fiduciary can get a six-month extension after the dismissal (even if that extension goes beyond the two-year statute of limitations) to begin the lawsuit again, since a plaintiff who started a timely lawsuit which was then dismissed for reasons other than voluntary discontinuance, failure to prosecute or final judgment on the merits can always commence it again within six months of the dismissal.[11]

If the nominated executor is appointed and fails to bring an action for wrongful death, the distributees can petition the Surrogate to appoint a special administrator (either local or foreign [12]) to prosecute the action on their behalf.[13] Thus, a decedent's spouse or children could petition, or if a decedent has no children, his spouse or parents, or if he has no spouse or parents, his brothers and sisters.[14] The persons entitled to serve, in the order of priority, are the spouse, the children, the grandchildren, the parents, the brothers and sisters.[15] If the distributees are minors, conservatees or incompetents, their guardians, conservators or committees can petition for appointment of a fiduciary.[16] Even a distributee who negligently caused the death of a decedent can petition for appointment of a fiduciary.[17]

If one of the distributees is a minor out-of-wedlock child, that child's guardian can petition for appointment of (and can serve as) an

9. Money-Line, Inc. v. Cunningham, 80 A.D.2d 60, 437 N.Y.S.2d 816 (4th Dep't 1981) (three-step formula for personal jurisdiction under the constitution). Personal jurisdiction is discussed in chapter on "Jurisdiction," supra at 25–28. See Porcello v. Brackett, 85 A.D.2d 917, 446 N.Y.S.2d 780 (4th Dep't 1981), affirmed 57 N.Y.2d 962, 457 N.Y.S.2d 243, 443 N.E.2d 491 (1982) (New York does not have personal jurisdiction over a Massachusetts domiciliary in the case of an Ohio accident in which a New Yorker was killed by a Massachusetts domiciliary attending school in New York).

10. See, however, Huertas v. State, 84 A.D.2d 650, 444 N.Y.S.2d 307 (3d Dep't 1981), where an administrator filed a verified claim three days before her appointment, and then filed it after her appointment, and the court refused to dismiss it for lack of proper verification. See also Snay v. Cohoes Memorial Hospital, 487 N.Y.S.2d 899 (3d Dep't 1985) (widow served summons before her appointment, but filed complaint after, and court directed defendant to accept it).

11. McKinney's CPLR 205(a); Carrick v. Central General Hospital, 51 N.Y.2d 242, 434 N.Y.S.2d 130, 414 N.E.2d 632 (1980); Bernardez v. New York, 100 A.D.2d 798, 474 N.Y.S.2d 728 (1st Dep't 1984); Mogavero v. Stony Creek Development Corp., 53 A.D.2d 1021, 385 N.Y.S.2d 899 (4th Dep't 1976).

12. An executor or administrator from another jurisdiction has authority to commence the proceeding. McKinney's EPTL 5–4.1(1); McKinney's EPTL 13–3.5.

13. McKinney's SCPA 702(8).

14. The class of distributees is governed by McKinney's EPTL 4–1.1 and discussed in chapter on "Administration," supra at 125.

15. See more detailed discussion of who may serve as administrator in chapter on "Administration," supra at 129–33.

16. McKinney's SCPA 1002.

17. Unlike the intentional wrongdoer who is not allowed to profit from his own wrong, Riggs v. Palmer, 115 N.Y. 506, 22 N.E. 188 (1889), the negligent distributee who caused decedent's death is not precluded from inheriting. Guilmette v. Ritayik, 39 A.D.2d 339, 334 N.Y.S.2d 223 (2d Dep't 1972); Matter of Minetti, 65 Misc.2d 1011, 319 N.Y.S.2d 56 (New York County 1971).

administrator,[18] because that child is a distributee for wrongful death purposes.[19] This raises a curious anomaly in the law relating to non-marital children which bears especially heavily on wrongful death cases. If the decedent is a woman, her out-of-wedlock child can share equally with his "legitimate" siblings in both the personal injury recovery and in the wrongful death recovery, but when the decedent is his father, different levels of proof are required for personal injury and for wrongful death. To share in the personal injury recovery, which is part of his father's intestate or probate estate, an out-of-wedlock child must prove his relationship to the decedent in one of the following ways:

(1) a paternity order; or

(2) an acknowledgment of paternity by the father, filed in the Putative Father's Registry; or

(3) both clear and convincing evidence of paternity and open and notorious acknowledgment of paternity.[20]

On the other hand, the proof that the out-of-wedlock child must produce in a wrongful death case is much less stringent. EPTL 5–4.5 simply says that an out-of-wedlock child is his father's distributee for purposes of wrongful death distributions (and the father is the child's distributee as well). What this does, in effect, is to allow an out-of-wedlock child to share in the proceeds if he can prove by clear and convincing evidence that the decedent is his father.[21]

The Surrogate usually gives the special administrator limited letters which allow him simply to prosecute the wrongful death and personal injury action; he cannot compromise the action without the court's permission,[22] unless he files a bond for the full amount of the recovery or settlement. The severe restrictions in the administrator's letters make a bond unnecessary.[23] This elimination of the need for a bond is the real usefulness of limited letters, because the court has absolutely no idea what the recovery will be, and hence what the bond should be.

When the administrator (whether with limited letters or full letters) has brought the matter to a close, either through a trial or by

18. Matter of Brown, 101 Misc.2d 805, 421 N.Y.S.2d 983 (Bronx 1979).

19. McKinney's EPTL 5–4.5.

20. McKinney's EPTL 4–1.2.

21. For the constitutional underpinnings of this dual standard, see Labine v. Vincent, 401 U.S. 532, 91 S.Ct. 1017, 28 L.Ed.2d 288 (1971), rehearing denied 402 U.S. 990, 91 S.Ct. 1672, 29 L.Ed.2d 156 (1971); Levy v. Louisiana, 391 U.S. 68, 88 S.Ct. 1509, 20 L.Ed. 436 (1968), rehearing denied 393 U.S. 898, 89 S.Ct. 65, 21 L.Ed.2d 185, on remand 253 La. 73, 216 So.2d 818 (1968); Matter of Lalli, 38 N.Y.2d 77, 378 N.Y.S.2d 351, 340 N.E.2d 721 (1975), judgment vacated 431 U.S. 911, 97 S.Ct. 2164, 53 L.Ed.2d 220 (1977), on remand 43 N.Y.2d 65, 400 N.Y.S.2d 761, 371 N.E.2d 481 (1977); Matter of Murray, 90 Misc.2d 852, 396 N.Y.S.2d 149 (Erie 1977) (decedent's non-marital son could share in wrongful death recovery but not in personal injury recovery.

22. McKinney's SCPA 702(1), discussed in chapter on "Fiduciaries", supra at 386–87.

23. McKinney's SCPA 801(1)(d).

settlement, he petitions the court to approve the amount and to issue an order directing him to receive the proceeds and pay it to the proper recipients and, in the case of limited letters, remove the restrictions from the limited letters.[24] If the court orders the money paid to distributees and creditors, it ordinarily does not require the administrator to post a bond.[25] It may require a bond, however, if it orders any of the proceeds to be paid to the administrator.

If the personal representative dies, the successor administrator or executor of the decedent's estate can continue the proceeding.[26]

Only the personal representative can extinguish the action,[27] with a court order if his letters are restricted. A person beneficially interested in the proceeds can relinquish or assign his interest, however,[28] and if the sole distributee releases his rights against the defendant, or all the distributees release theirs, the personal representative cannot commence (or continue) the wrongful death action,[29] except to recover his expenses of bringing the action.[30]

The plaintiff brings the lawsuit against the person who caused the injuries and death; he may name the same defendants the decedent could have named had he not died as a result of the wrongful conduct.[31] If the defendant dies, the plaintiff may substitute the defendant's personal representative in his place.[32]

SECTION C. THE COMPLAINT

The fiduciary must plead [1] and prove by a preponderance of the evidence [2] all the elements of a wrongful death action: the death of a

24. See, e.g., Matter of Pargament, N.Y. L.J., March 8, 1985, at 13, col. 5 (Bronx).

25. See, e.g., Matter of Aguirro, N.Y. L.J., April 11, 1985, at 16, col. 2 (Nassau).

26. Meekin v. Brooklyn Heights Railway Co., 164 N.Y. 145, 58 N.E. 50 (1900).

27. See Rice v. Postal Telegraph-Cable Co., 174 App.Div. 39, 160 N.Y.S. 172 (4th Dep't 1916), affirmed 219 N.Y. 629, 114 N.E. 1081 (1916).

28. Quin v. Moore, 15 N.Y. 432 (1857).

29. Edwards v. Sullivan, 200 Misc. 488, 102 N.Y.S.2d 951 (Erie 1949) (widow-sole distributee released her rights against defendant, and decedent's mother as personal representative was not permitted to bring a wrongful death lawsuit).

30. Davis v. New York Central & H. Railroad Co., 233 N.Y. 242, 135 N.E. 277 (1922).

31. The statute says "person," and "person" includes entity or municipality. See Priebe v. Canandaigua, 91 Misc.2d 1047, 399 N.Y.S.2d 179 (Ontario 1977).

32. McKinney's EPTL 11-3.2(a).

Sec. C

1. Chong v. New York City Transit Authority, 83 A.D.2d 546, 441 N.Y.S.2d 24 (2d Dep't 1981) (complaint dismissed for failure to plead survival by distributees who suffered pecuniary loss, and appointment of personal representative).

2. Williams v. New York, 81 A.D.2d 559, 438 N.Y.S.2d 333 (1st Dep't 1981). The plaintiff, however, is held to a somewhat lesser degree of proof than if the decedent had survived to describe the facts, Zellman v. Metropolitan Transportation Authority, 83 A.D.2d 144, 443 N.Y.S.2d 666 (2d Dep't 1981); Franco v. Zingarelli, 72 A.D.2d 211, 424 N.Y.S.2d 185 (1st Dep't 1980); Jamison v. Walker, 48 A.D.2d 320, 369 N.Y.S.2d 469 (2d Dep't 1975), and is entitled to the benefit of every favorable inference that can be drawn to make a prima facie case. Carpino v. Baker, 66 A.D.2d 201, 412 N.Y.S.2d 617 (1st Dep't 1979), appeal after remand 75 A.D.2d 540, 427 N.Y.S.2d 225 (1980). In addition, the circumstantial evidence may be weighed more heavily than usual. Noseworthy v. New York, 298 N.Y. 76, 80 N.E.2d 744

human being, the defendant's wrongful act that caused the decedent's death,[3] the survival of distributees [4] who have suffered a pecuniary loss because of the decedent's death,[5] and the appointment of a personal representative of the decedent's estate.[6] The complaint must also state why the New York statute (or the law of another jurisdiction) should apply, and if the defendant is a municipality that requires notice of claim, a statement that the notice has been given.

Two factors need not be included in the complaint, and we discuss each of them briefly now: the statute of limitations and the decedent's negligence.

First, although the wrongful death action must be commenced within two years of the decedent's death,[7] that is not an element of the cause of action and need not be pleaded. It is a limitation on the remedy and must be raised by the defendant.[8]

Despite the two year statute of limitations, if the defendant is also being criminally prosecuted for the death, the personal representative has at least a year from the termination of the criminal action [9] to begin the action, even if the statute of limitations has expired on the underlying substantive claim, or has less than a year to run.[10] If a ninety-day notice of claim is required (because the lawsuit is against a municipality [11]) in a wrongful death lawsuit the ninety days run from the personal representative's appointment,[12] while in the personal

(1948); Horne v. Metropolitan Transit Authority, 82 A.D.2d 909, 440 N.Y.S.2d 695 (2d Dep't 1981).

3. See Prosser, Torts [4th ed.] 41–42; Horne v. Metropolitan Transit Authority, 82 A.D.2d 909, 440 N.Y.S.2d 695 (2d Dep't 1981). See also LaMaine v. Grey, 35 A.D.2d 541, 313 N.Y.S.2d 180 (2d Dep't 1970) (dismissal of cause of action after plaintiff's case because no causal connection shown).

4. Powe v. Wise, 70 A.D.2d 654, 417 N.Y.S.2d 12 (2d Dep't 1979) (complaint dismissed for failure to state that the decedent was survived by distributees).

5. McKinney's EPTL 5–4.1; Chong v. New York City Transit Authority, 83 A.D.2d 546, 441 N.Y.S.2d 24 (2d Dep't 1981) (complaint dismissed for failure to plead survival by distributees who suffered pecuniary loss, and appointment of personal representative). In practice in some cases none of the distributees suffered a pecuniary loss, and there the court will divide the proceeds among them as though the proceeds were assets passing under the laws of intestacy.

6. Chong v. New York City Transit Authority, 83 A.D.2d 546, 441 N.Y.S.2d 24 (2d Dep't 1981).

7. McKinney's EPTL 5–4.1.

8. See Sharrow v. Inland Lines, Ltd., 214 N.Y. 101, 108 N.E. 217 (1915).

9. The termination of the criminal action is when a sentence is imposed (or other final disposition is reached) for the crime or crimes in the last accusatory instrument. McKinney's Crim.Proc.L. § 1.20.

10. McKinney's EPTL 5–4.1(2) (effective July 17, 1983).

11. The notice of claim requirements apply to wrongful death actions. Hawkins v. County of Oneida, 297 N.Y. 393, 79 N.E.2d 458 (1948) (failure to notify municipality of pending claim is fatal and mandates dismissal).

12. Erickson v. Town of Henderson, 30 A.D.2d 282, 291 N.Y.S.2d 403 (4th Dep't 1968); Joseph v. McVeigh, 285 App.Div. 386, 137 N.Y.S.2d 577 (1st Dep't 1955); Buduson v. Curtis, 285 App.Div. 517, 139 N.Y.S.2d 392 (1955), order affirmed 309 N.Y. 879, 131 N.E.2d 290 (1955). Some abbreviated statutes of limitations and notice of claims statutes apply to specific municipal entities. See, e.g., McKinney's Public Authorities Law § 1276 (1982) (thirty-day notice of claim and one year statute of limitations for suits against the Metropolitan Transportation Authority); Andersen v. Long Island Rail Road, 88 A.D.2d

injury action, it starts running from the date of the injury.[13] If an administrator files the notice of claim before his official appointment, he can amend it after the ninety days to reflect his appointment.[14] The fiduciary should beware: if he is suing in his individual capacity for injuries he sustained and also for the wrongful death of the decedent, in the lawsuit for his own injuries the ninety days starts to run at the date of injury, not the date of appointment as fiduciary.

The two-year wrongful death statute of limitations prevails over the one-year ninety day statute of limitations usually applicable to municipalities,[15] and over the one-year statute of limitations ordinarily applicable to lawsuits against a sheriff.[16]

Infancy of a distributee will not toll the statute of limitations,[17] because the cause of action belongs to the personal representative, not the distributees.

If the statute of limitations ran on a personal injury action before decedent's death, there can be no wrongful death action.[18] If it did not, his representative has at least one year from the decedent's death to commence the personal injury action.[19] If the defendant dies within two years of the decedent's death, the statute of limitations is tolled until the appointment of a personal representative for the defendant's estate, not to exceed eighteen months.[20] Of course, if more than two years had passed since the decedent's death, the defendant's estate is not entitled to an additional eighteen months.

328, 453 N.Y.S.2d 203 (2d 1982), order affirmed 59 N.Y.2d 657, 463 N.Y.S.2d 407, 450 N.E.2d 213 (1983), reargument denied 60 N.Y.2d 586, 467 N.Y.S.2d 1031, 454 N.E.2d 127 (1983).

13. See Antoine v. State, 103 Misc.2d 664, 426 N.Y.S.2d 917 (Ct.Claims New York 1980), where a mother as fiduciary of her infant's estate sued for wrongful death and the infant's personal injuries. The ninety days in the wrongful death action started to run from the date of the mother's appointment as fiduciary, McKinney's Court of Claims Act § 10(2), and in the personal injury action from the date of the child's injury. McKinney's Court of Claims Act § 10(3).

14. Bernardez v. New York, 100 A.D.2d 798, 474 N.Y.S.2d 728 (1st Dep't 1984).

15. McKinney's Gen.Mun.L. § 53–i, amended Sept. 1, 1981. See Puliafico v. New York, 87 A.D.2d 512, 447 N.Y.S.2d 731 (1st Dep't 1982). The law in effect prior to Sept. 1, 1981 covered personal injury and damages to property but not wrongful death, and the Court of Appeals held that the two-year statute of limitations for wrongful death prevailed over the abbreviated one-year ninety day period applicable to personal injuries and damages to property. Collins v. New York, 55 N.Y.2d 646, 446 N.Y.S.2d 258, 430 N.E.2d 1311 (1981), on remand 89 A.D.2d 992, 454 N.Y.S.2d 327 (1982).

16. The one-year statute of limitations is found in CPLR 215. The holding that it is preempted by the two-year wrongful death statute of limitations is supported by Dixon v. Seymour, 62 A.D.2d 444, 405 N.Y.S.2d 320 (3d Dep't 1978).

17. Ratka v. St. Francis Hospital, 44 N.Y.2d 604, 407 N.Y.S.2d 458, 378 N.E.2d 1027 (1978). This case expressly does not resolve the question whether the statute is tolled for the personal injuries action, which should, however, be treated the same as wrongful death action; that is, the statute of limitations should not be tolled.

18. Johnson v. Stromberg-Carlson Tel. Mfg. Co., 250 App.Div. 352, 297 N.Y.S. 173 (4th Dep't 1937), affirmed 276 N.Y. 621, 12 N.E.2d 607 (1938), certiorari denied 305 U.S. 645, 59 S.Ct. 150, 83 L.Ed. 416 (1938).

19. McKinney's CPLR 210.

20. McKinney's CPLR 210(b); see McDonough v. Cestare, 3 A.D.2d 201, 159 N.Y.S.2d 616 (2d Dep't 1957), appeal denied 3 A.D.2d 861, 163 N.Y.S.2d 376 (1957).

If the decedent timely commenced a personal injury action and his death intervened before its conclusion, the personal representative can amend the complaint to include the wrongful death cause of action on the decedent's death, even after the expiration of the two-year statute of limitations, so long as the original complaint gave the defendant notice of the events that caused the death,[21] and the medical testimony proves the causal connection between the injuries and the death.[22]

The defendant will not be permitted to amend his answer after the running of the statute of limitations if to do so would leave the plaintiff without a remedy.[23]

If the defendant committed tortious acts within the state but is continuously absent from the state for two years, the statute of limitations is not tolled because he is subject to the court's jurisdiction under the long-arm statute of CPLR 302.[24]

The second factor that does not have to be pleaded in the complaint is the decedent's freedom from contributory negligence. Since September 1, 1975, New York has had a rule of comparative negligence.[25] Under that rule, the decedent's contributory negligence will not bar recovery, but the recovery will be diminished in the proportion the decedent's culpable conduct contributed to the damages. Such conduct is an affirmative defense to be pleaded and proved by the defendant.[26] The decedent's contributory negligence is attributed to his personal representative in the lawsuit.[27]

If a lawsuit was started before September 1, 1975, the plaintiff's contributory negligence completely bars his recovery. In those cases,

21. See Caffaro v. Trayna, 35 N.Y.2d 245, 360 N.Y.S.2d 847, 319 N.E.2d 174 (1974), where the court held that the two-year statute of limitations on a wrongful death action was a procedural point, not an element of the cause of action, and permitted the plaintiff to amend the complaint, finding that the original complaint gave notice of the events leading to decedent's death as required by McKinney's CPLR 203(e). Under this theory the cause of action relates back to the time the original complaint was filed, which is conceptually interesting because the wrongful death cause of action did not exist on the date it relates back to. See McKinney's CPLR 203, McLoughlin, Practice Commentary at 69 (Supp. 1986).

22. Mahoney v. Sharma, 110 A.D.2d 627, 487 N.Y.S.2d 114 (2d Dep't 1985) (improvident abuse of discretion to allow amendment of pleading when no causal connection between injuries and death was shown); Fiorentino v. Cobble Hill Nursing Home, 475 N.Y.S.2d 148 (2d Dep't 1984) (accord); Wood v. Southside Hospital, 45 A.D.2d 1052, 358 N.Y.S.2d 170 (2d Dep't 1974) (accord).

23. See Souchu v. J.I. Hass Co., 81 A.D.2d 884, 439 N.Y.S.2d 56 (2d Dep't 1981), where the defendant moved to amend his answer to withdraw the admission that he had provided the defective item which caused decedent's death.

24. See Immediate v. St. John's Queens Hospital, 65 A.D.2d 783, 410 N.Y.S.2d 328 (2d Dep't 1978), affirmed 48 N.Y.2d 671, 421 N.Y.S.2d 875, 397 N.E.2d 385 (1979), reargument denied 48 N.Y.2d 975, 425 N.Y.S.2d 1029, 401 N.E.2d 433 (1979).

25. McKinney's CPLR 1411.

26. McKinney's CPLR 1412; Padula v. State, 48 N.Y.2d 366, 422 N.Y.S.2d 943, 398 N.E.2d 548 (1979); Northrop v. Smith, 37 A.D.2d 1014, 325 N.Y.S.2d 491 (3d Dep't 1971); Sawyer v. United States, 436 F.2d 640 (2d Cir.1971); Jamison v. Walker, 48 A.D.2d 320, 369 N.Y.S.2d 469 (2d Dep't 1975). Gilliam v. Lee, 32 A.D.2d 1058, 303 N.Y.S.2d 966 (2d Dep't 1969).

27. Maidman v. Stagg, 82 A.D.2d 299, 441 N.Y.S.2d 711 (2d Dep't 1981).

the decedent's contributory negligence is a defense to be pleaded and proved by the defendant.[28] In the negligence survival action, the burden of pleading and proving freedom from contributory negligence is on the estate unless the survival action is combined with the wrongful death action, where the rule is that the defendant has the burden for both causes of action.[29]

Having filed a complaint with all necessary information, the fiduciary will proceed with the trial either until the judge or jury decides on the amount of damages or until the defendant makes a settlement offer acceptable to the fiduciary. In either case the fiduciary has to get court approval and a court order directing the allocation of the proceeds between wrongful death and personal injury and among the beneficiaries.

For the fiduciary to have a wrongful death action, the decedent must have had a cause of action at the time of his death.[30] If the decedent pursued to final judgment a personal injury action in his lifetime, the judgment in that action, whether for or against the decedent, is res judicata and no wrongful death action will lie.[31]

SECTION D. DAMAGES

A discussion of damages in wrongful death personal injury lawsuits has three issues: first, what are the compensable damages; second, who should share in the recovery; and third, how should the damages be allocated between the wrongful death and personal injury causes of action.

The first and second issues are so interrelated they must be discussed together. The third issue, allocation between personal injury

28. McKinney's EPTL 5–4.2.

29. McKinney's EPTL 11–3.2(b).

30. Kelliher v. New York City and Harlem Railroad Co., 212 N.Y. 207, 105 N.E. 824 (1914); Zinman v. Newman, 51 N.Y.S.2d 132 (Bronx 1942), affirmed 265 App.Div. 998, 39 N.Y.S.2d 999 (1st Dep't 1943), leave to appeal denied 265 App.Div. 1052, 41 N.Y.S.2d 193 (1st Dep't 1943). Hence there can be no wrongful death action if the death resulted from suicide. Prink v. Rockefeller Center, Inc., 48 N.Y.2d 309, 422 N.Y.S.2d 911, 398 N.E.2d 517 (1979) (allowing decedent's psychiatrist's testimony on whether death was by suicide), unless the plaintiff can show a strong causal connection between the defendant's actions and the suicide. See Cauverien v. DeMetz, 20 Misc.2d 144, 188 N.Y.S.2d 627 (New York County 1959) (plaintiff argued that decedent's suicide was induced by irresistable impulse resulting from defendant's actions; court held it to be a sufficient allegation to state a case of proximate cause); Herold v. State, 15 A.D.2d 835, 224 N.Y.S.2d 369 (3d Dep't 1962) (patient moved from well-supervised ward to open ward, and state institution held liable for his suicide because it could not prove that he had lost his suicidal tendencies). See Hirsh v. State, 8 N.Y.2d 125, 202 N.Y.S.2d 296, 168 N.E.2d 372 (1960) (state mental hospital held not negligent when decedent committed suicide by taking a drug not prescribed in the hospital. Dissent said that because of the decedent's suicidal tendencies, the hospital staff should have been more careful and found the drugs). See also Cabezudo v. New York's Eldorado, Inc., 50 A.D.2d 794, 378 N.Y.S.2d 75 (1st Dep't 1975) (court describes the proper use of circumstantial evidence where the decedent's fall was believed to be a suicide).

31. See McGahey v. Nassau Electric R. Co., 51 App.Div. 281, 64 N.Y.S. 965 (2d Dep't 1900), affirmed 166 N.Y. 617, 59 N.E. 1126 (1901).

and wrongful death causes of action, is at least somewhat discrete, and we will dispose of it immediately.

1. ALLOCATION BETWEEN WRONGFUL DEATH AND PERSONAL INJURY CAUSES OF ACTION

In the personal injury action, the decedent had, and the estate inherits from him,[1] a right to recover medical expenses, loss of income, and damages for pain and suffering. If the decedent was unconscious at all times after the injury, the court will not allocate any damages to pain and suffering.[2] The damages awarded in the wrongful death action, on the other hand, are meant to compensate the decedent's distributees for their pecuniary losses resulting from the decedent's death.

In practice, when making the allocation between wrongful death and personal injury, the court considers the time decedent survived after the injuries, the severity of his pain and suffering, the pecuniary needs of his distributees, and the fair treatment of his creditors.[3]

The personal injury recovery is a part of the decedent's probate or intestate estate and his gross taxable estate. It is available to satisfy the decedent's debts,[4] claims against his estate, and administration expenses. Fiduciaries are entitled to full commissions on the recovery. The wrongful death recovery is not part of the estate for probate, intestacy or tax purposes. It is subject to the reasonable expenses of the litigation or settlement, including attorneys' fees (for the lawsuit and the accounting),[5] court costs and expert testimony,[6] but it is not available to creditors,[7] with two exceptions: Funeral expenses and medical expenses caused by the injury resulting in the decedent's death can be paid out of the wrongful death recovery if the judgment states that they are compensable damages, or if there was no personal injury

Sec. D

1. McKinney's EPTL 11–3.2 permits the survival action.

2. Huertas v. State, 84 A.D.2d 650, 444 N.Y.S.2d 307 (3d Dep't 1981); Guiltinan v. Columbia Presbyterian Medical Center, 97 Misc.2d 137, 410 N.Y.S.2d 946 (New York County 1978). See Matter of Halpern, N.Y.L.J., April 10, 1985, at 12, col. 2 (Bronx) (no allocation to personal injury action because decedent remained comatose for entire period between accident and his death).

3. Matter of Lu, N.Y.L.J., May 14, 1985, at 11, col. 4 (Bronx) (entire proceeds allocated to wrongful death; court noted that no one was prejudiced by the allocation).

4. See Matter of Franco, 108 Misc.2d 1084, 439 N.Y.S.2d 278 (Bronx 1981).

5. Attorneys' fees are fixed by the court and discussed in this chapter, infra at 553–54, and in chapter on "Attorneys' Fees," supra at 359 et seq.

6. EPTL 5–4.4(b).

7. E.g., Matter of Ward, 84 Misc.2d 196, 375 N.Y.S.2d 243 (Rockland 1975). There may be specific statutory exceptions. E.g., McKinney's Workmen's Compensation Law 29 (lien for workmen's compensation repaid to carrier from the respective shares of the distributees who receive it).

The Department of Social Services, although a preferred creditor, does not have a claim against the wrongful death recovery unless it seeks reimbursement for funeral expenses advanced to a distributee who paid for them or was liable to pay for them. They, as other creditors, will share in the recovery if none of the distributees suffered a pecuniary loss. Matter of Payne, 12 A.D.2d 940, 210 N.Y.S.2d 925 (2d Dep't 1961), appeal denied 13 A.D.2d 688, 215 N.Y.S.2d 714 (1961).

recovery. Moreover, even if the recovery does not specifically include funeral and medical expenses and a distributee is not seeking reimbursement, sometimes courts allow their payment from wrongful death proceeds if there are no other assets in the estate to pay them.[8] If a sum was received for personal injury, or if the estate has other assets, the fiduciary will pay the funeral and medical expenses from those assets first.[9] If the will directs the executor to pay funeral expenses, the court cannot order them paid out of the wrongful death proceeds.[10] Fiduciaries are entitled to commissions only on the net amount available for distribution to the distributees, that is, the total proceeds less attorneys' disbursements and fees, the guardian ad litem's fee, funeral expenses and medical expenses.[11]

The Surrogate's Court and the trial court have concurrent jurisdiction to make the allocation between wrongful death and personal injury.[12] The Surrogate [13] will make the allocation if the parties negotiated a settlement without ever going to trial. If the case has been tried or if the parties settled the case during the trial, the jury or the judge as trier of the facts can specify the proportions of the damages allocable to personal injuries and to wrongful death, and that proceeding must be on notice to all interested parties.[14] As a matter of practice, the trial courts, when they settle the causes of action, usually do not make an allocation but leave it to the Surrogate, or make an allocation subject to the Surrogate's review.

The Surrogate (or the Supreme Court judge) fixes the statutory commissions [15] either after a hearing for that purpose or at the final accounting, and orders them deducted from the recovery.

8. See, e.g., Matter of Riley, 45 Misc.2d 658, 257 N.Y.S.2d 775 (Broome 1965); Matter of Woods, 144 N.Y.S.2d 880 (Westchester 1955). If the funeral expenses are paid out of the personal injury action, they are subject to a three-year statute of limitations, whereas if they are paid out of the wrongful death proceeds, they are subject to the two-year statute of limitations.

9. Matter of Iglima, 13 Misc.2d 910, 178 N.Y.S.2d 473 (Kings 1958). But see Matter of Pargament, N.Y.L.J., March 8, 1985, at 13, col. 5 (Bronx), where the court ordered the funeral expenses to be paid out of the wrongful death proceeds rather than the $2,000 no-fault death benefit paid under McKinney's Ins. Law § 672(a)(d), which is an estate asset.

10. Matter of Goyette, 141 Misc. 80, 252 N.Y.S. 566 (Clinton 1931).

11. McKinney's EPTL 5–4.4(b).

12. McKinney's EPTL 5–4.4(a)(1).

13. The Surrogate who issued letters to the fiduciary is the one with jurisdiction. McKinney's EPTL 5–4.4(a)(1). See Riley v. Capital Airlines, Inc., 42 Misc.2d 194, 247 N.Y.S.2d 427 (Monroe 1963), affirmed 20 A.D.2d 682, 246 N.Y.S.2d 1021 (4th Dep't 1964).

14. McKinney's EPTL 5–4.4(a)(1). See Matter of Judkins, N.Y.L.J., May 30, 1985, at 7, col. 6 (Bronx), where the court found that the Supreme Court's allocation was invalid because all necessary parties had not been joined.

15. See McKinney's SCPA 2307, discussed in chapter on "Commissions," supra at 426–29.

2. MEASURE OF DAMAGES

Since the first wrongful death statute in New York,[16] damages have been measured by pecuniary losses of distributees [17] who had a reasonable expectation of receiving pecuniary benefits from the continued existence of the decedent. Thus the first requirement for damages is that there be a distributee who suffered a pecuniary loss.[18]

As a preliminary observation on the practical reality of wrongful death actions, defendants and their insurance companies often settle cases even though no distributees actually had a pecuniary loss.[19] The reason is probably that, although the decedent may have been, say, an unmarried person survived only by adult children, the defendant was negligent and his negligence caused the decedent's death, and a finding of pecuniary injury, though doubtful, is certainly possible. The defendant and his carrier realize that a settlement may avoid the possibility of higher damages at a trial. When this happens the court orders the proceeds to be distributed to the decedent's distributees under the laws governing intestacy.[20]

But now back to the black-letter law: A distributee who did not have a reasonable expectation of pecuniary loss cannot share in the recovery, nor can a person who was dependent on the decedent but is not his distributee.[21]

A jury or a judge acts as the trier of facts [22] and determines an amount that is "fair and just compensation for the pecuniary injuries resulting from the decedent's death to the persons for whose benefit the action was brought" (that is, the distributees).[23] In addition, if the distributees paid for (or are responsible for) medical and nursing care

16. L.1847, c. 450.

17. McKinney's EPTL 4–1.1, discussed in chapter on "Administration," supra at 125 et seq.

18. This rule, that if no distributees suffered pecuniary injury, the fiduciary will recover only nominal damages, is venerable, perhaps even hoary. Quin v. Moore, 15 N.Y. 432 (1857).

19. See, e.g., Matter of Chernega, 54 Misc.2d 137, 281 N.Y.S.2d 908 (Broome 1967), where a boy died and his parents, neither of whom suffered a pecuniary loss, shared the recovery equally.

Once the trial court approves the compromise, that approval is conclusive evidence of the adequacy of the amount in any later accounting in the Surrogate's Court. McKinney's EPTL 5–4.6(b).

20. Matter of Langer, 10 Misc.2d 47, 171 N.Y.S.2d 530 (Kings 1958).

21. McKinney's EPTL 5–4.3, 5–4.4; Petrone v. United States Trucking Corp., 236 App.Div. 531, 260 N.Y.S. 671 (3d Dep't 1932), affirmed without opinion 262 N.Y. 540, 188 N.E. 55 (1933) (decedent's siblings not entitled to share wrongful death proceeds); Powe v. Wise, 70 A.D.2d 654, 417 N.Y.S.2d 12 (2d Dep't 1979) (complaint dismissed for failure to state that the decedent was survived by distributees); Morico v. Green Bus Lines, Inc., 429 F.Supp. 23 (E.D.N.Y.1977) (decedent's siblings could not recover because not distributees).

22. See Liddie v. State, 190 Misc. 347, 75 N.Y.S.2d 182 (Ct.Claims 1947).

23. McKinney's EPTL 5–4.3. Note that this criterion (a distributee who suffers a pecuniary loss) is used at the allocation-and-distribution stage of the proceeding as well as at the damages stage. As we will discuss in the section of this chapter on allocation of damages among distributees, the findings at the damages stage need not bind the court at the later stage.

made necessary by the injury that caused death, or reasonable funeral expenses, those expenses will be part of wrongful death damages.[24]

Damages are measured by the loss to distributees who had a right to anticipate the receipt of pecuniary benefits from the decedent's continued existence.[25] The distributee may have reasonably anticipated obligatory support payments (a spouse or minor child), or voluntary support (or other) payments.[26]

Actual dependency of the distributee on the decedent is not a precondition for recovery,[27] nor must the decedent have had an obligation to support the distributee. If it is likely that, had the decedent continued living, the distributee would have benefited financially, that distributee can successfully claim that he has been damaged by the decedent's death.[28]

While actual dependency on the decedent is not necessary to recovery, it has a bearing on the extent of damages.[29] If the distributees include persons whom the decedent had a legal obligation to support, or persons whom he was likely to support voluntarily, the court must make an allocation that is fair to all parties.[30] Usually the distributees who share in the recovery are those who were financially dependent on the decedent when he died, but potential future dependency is also considered by the court. For instance, a decedent's father (a distributee) was allowed to recover even though the decedent had not contributed to the father's support where the fiduciary showed that the father was unemployed and sick and had a reasonable expectation of receiving financial help from the son.[31] Similarly, a son of a decedent who was in the physical custody of the other parent at the time of the decedent's death was nevertheless entitled to share in the wrongful

24. McKinney's EPTL 5–4.3(a); Matter of Ward, 84 Misc.2d 196, 375 N.Y.S.2d 243 (Rockland 1975). McKinney's EPTL 11–3.3(a); Guiltinan v. Columbia Presbyterian Medical Center, 97 Misc.2d 137, 410 N.Y.S.2d 946 (New York County 1978). See Matter of Jackson, 71 Misc.2d 133, 335 N.Y.S.2d 587 (Kings 1972), for a discussion of the legislative history of McKinney's EPTL 5–4.1 and McKinney's EPTL 11–3.3(a) which allow recovery of funeral expenses under two different theories and with two different statute of limitations.

25. McKinney's EPTL 5–4.4. The distributees are those entitled to share in the decedent's estate under McKinney's EPTL 4–1.1 as well as his out-of-wedlock children as prescribed by McKinney's EPTL 5–4.5. See Loetsch v. New York City Omnibus Corp., 291 N.Y. 308, 311, 52 N.E.2d 448, 449 (1943) (pecuniary injury defined as "reasonable expectancy of future assistance or support if life continues").

26. Parilis v. Feinstein, 49 N.Y.2d 984, 429 N.Y.S.2d 165, 406 N.E.2d 1059 (1980).

27. See Gross v. Abraham, 306 N.Y. 525, 119 N.E.2d 370 (1954); Matter of Avery, 111 Misc.2d 818, 445 N.Y.S.2d 672 (Wayne 1981) (child in custody of father and not dependent on deceased mother held entitled to share in wrongful death recovery); Matter of Silverstein, 48 Misc. 2d 1029, 266 N.Y.S.2d 553 (1966) (child by decedent's previous marriage adopted by ex-wife's new husband permitted to share in wrongful death damages).

28. Matter of Pridell, 206 Misc. 316, 133 N.Y.S.2d 203 (Jefferson 1954) (decedent's out-of-wedlock son entitled to share in wrongful death proceeds).

29. Gross v. Abraham, 306 N.Y. 525, 119 N.E.2d 370 (1954).

30. Matter of Mairowitz, 90 Misc.2d 854, 396 N.Y.S.2d 146 (Bronx 1977) (parents entitled to share because of close relationship and expectations of future support).

31. Kelley v. Cacace, 43 A.D.2d 573, 349 N.Y.S.2d 410 (2d Dep't 1973).

death proceeds because the custody issue was not finally settled and he had a reasonable expectation of receiving support from the decedent.[32] To determine pecuniary injuries, the court looks at the age of the decedent, sex, type of employment, amicability and relationship to those seeking recovery, earning capacity, pension benefits,[33] life expectancy, health, intelligence, and the number, age, sex and physical condition of his distributees.[34] For example, it is relevant that a husband and wife are very hostile to each other,[35] that a married [36] or emancipated [37] minor child may not have had a reasonable expectation of support by his parent, and that an adult disabled child may have,[38] unless he was supported by governmental assistance.[39]

When a woman running a home and raising children dies, the pecuniary loss is measured by the costs of the homemaking and child-care services she was providing.[40]

If the decedent has questionable ability to earn a livelihood, for example because he is a patient in a state mental hospital, the fiduciary must prove that the decedent had reasonable prospects of being released and becoming productive.[41] If the decedent has no ability to earn a living and no likelihood of recovering it, but had an independent source of income, such as a trust fund, which ended because of his death, the fiduciary should be able to recover. Even if the fiduciary fails to show pecuniary injury, he can still recover actual expenses resulting from the death, such as funeral expenses.[42]

32. See Matter of Avery, 111 Misc.2d 818, 445 N.Y.S.2d 672 (Wayne 1981) (son in mother's custody permitted to share in father's wrongful death proceeds).

33. See, e.g., Thoirs v. Pounsford, 210 Minn. 462, 299 N.W. 16 (1941); Kowtko v. Delaware and Harlem Railway Corp., 131 F.Supp. 95 (M.D.Pa.1955).

34. See Lyons v. DeVore, 48 A.D.2d 943, 368 N.Y.S.2d 887 (3d Dep't 1975), affirmed 39 N.Y.2d 971, 387 N.Y.S.2d 108, 354 N.E.2d 848 (1976), where the court considered, inter alia, the decedent's working habits, present position, potential for advancement, responsibility, life expectancy, and survivors' life expectancies.

35. See Loetsch v. New York City Omnibus Corp., 291 N.Y. 308, 52 N.E.2d 448 (1943) (wife had executed a will attempting to disinherit husband).

36. See Matter of Sintyago, 198 Misc. 776, 100 N.Y.S.2d 556 (Kings 1950).

37. See Matter of Lilien, 139 N.Y.S.2d 128 (Queens 1955).

38. Matter of Stanley, N.Y.L.J., June 1, 1985, at 12, col. 1 (Nassau); Matter of DeMartino, 142 Misc. 785, 255 N.Y.S. 650 (Kings 1932) (disabled adult children entitled to share in wrongful death proceeds).

39. See Matter of Gould, N.Y.L.J., Feb. 27, 1985, at 13, col. 4 (Bronx), discussed in note 95 infra, and Matter of Reynolds, 115 N.Y.S.2d 534 (Erie 1952), discussed in note 96 infra.

40. Griscti v. State, 35 A.D.2d 764, 314 N.Y.S.2d 932 (3d Dep't 1970), affirmed 30 N.Y.2d 782, 334 N.Y.S.2d 175, 285 N.E.2d 318 (1972).

41. Hassler v. State, 29 A.D.2d 1026, 289 N.Y.S.2d 483 (3d Dep't 1968); Didocha v. State, 54 A.D.2d 786, 387 N.Y.S.2d 752 (3d Dep't 1976); Grasso v. State, 264 App. Div. 745, 34 N.Y.S.2d 440 (3d Dep't 1942), affirmed 289 N.Y. 552, 43 N.E.2d 530 (1942). See Dimitroff v. State, 171 Misc. 635, 13 N.Y.S.2d 458 (Ct.Claims New York 1939).

42. E.g., Gaccione v. State, 173 Misc. 367, 18 N.Y.S.2d 161 (Ct.Claims 1940).

Decedent's consistent high performance on the job and the resulting annual profit-sharing bonuses can be considered in computing pecuniary loss to the decedent's distributees.[43]

The decedent's habits, positive or negative, if they affect the ability to earn a living, are relevant. The court can hear, for example, evidence on the decedent's drunkenness,[44] or on the high standard of nurture, instruction, and physical, moral and intellectual training the decedent gave to her children,[45] which is in effect given a pecuniary value.

Loss of consortium, defined as grief, loss of society, affection and conjugal fellowship, is not an element of the statutory wrongful death recovery,[46] but it is an element of personal injury and compensable from the date of the accident to the date of death.[47]

As a practical matter, in arriving at a figure to compensate for loss of decedent's life, the court will not permit the defendant to set aside the capitalized value in the form of an annuity sufficient to produce the income the decedent was earning at the time of death for the period of his life expectancy,[48] with anticipated increase in earnings,[49] since they are speculative.

Although injuries to an unborn child subsequently born alive are compensable under New York law,[50] parents (or other distributees) of a

43. Woodrung v. Board of Education, 79 A.D.2d 1022, 435 N.Y.S.2d 52 (2d Dep't 1981), appeal denied 53 N.Y.2d 603, 439 N.Y.S.2d 1027, 421 N.E.2d 854 (1981).

44. See, e.g., Fearon v. New York Life Insurance Co., 162 App.Div. 560, 147 N.Y.S. 644 (1st Dep't 1914); McIlwaine v. Metropolitan Street Railroad Co., 74 App. Div. 496, 77 N.Y.S. 426 (1st Dep't 1902).

45. Gross v. Abraham, 307 N.Y. 525, 119 N.E.2d 370 (1954); Matter of Mairowitz, 90 Misc.2d 854, 396 N.Y.S.2d 146 (1977); Matter of Svibruck, 3 Misc.2d 607, 153 N.Y.S.2d 662 (Westchester 1956). See Tilley v. Hudson River Railroad Co., 29 N.Y. 252 (1864); Sternfels v. Metropolitan Street Railroad Co., 73 App.Div. 494, 77 N.Y.S. 309 (1st Dep't 1902), affirmed 174 N.Y. 512, 66 N.E. 1117 (1903).

46. Liff v. Schildkrout, 49 N.Y.2d 622, 427 N.Y.S.2d 746, 404 N.E.2d 1288 (1980), reargument denied 49 N.Y.2d 1048, 429 N.Y.S.2d 1027, 407 N.E.2d 483 (1980), adopting the reasoning of Osborn v. Kelley, 61 A.D.2d 367, 402 N.Y.S.2d 463 (3d Dep't 1978), that "insofar as plaintiff is attempting to recover for loss of consortium for the period prior to decedent's death, a cause of action is stated." That action is derivative of the personal injuries action and is not an element of wrongful death. See also Loetsch v. New York City Omnibus Corp., 291 N.Y. 308, 52 N.E.2d 448 (1943); Tilley v. Hudson River Railroad Co., 24 N.Y. 471 (1862); Puliafico v. New York, 87 A.D.2d 512, 447 N.Y.S.2d 731 (1st Dep't 1982); Chang v. New York City Health and Hospitals Corp., 82 A.D.2d 764, 440 N.Y.S.2d 211 (1st Dep't 1981), appeal denied 55 N.Y.2d 603, 447 N.Y.S.2d 1026, 431 N.E.2d 977 (1981); Albarran v. New York, 80 A.D.2d 784, 437 N.Y.S.2d 4 (1st Dep't 1981); Long v. New York, 81 A.D.2d 880, 439 N.Y.S.2d 58 (2d Dep't 1981).

47. See Chang v. New York City Health and Hospitals Corp., 82 A.D.2d 764, 440 N.Y.S.2d 211 (1st Dep't 1981), appeal denied 55 N.Y.2d 603, 447 N.Y.S.2d 1026, 431 N.E.2d 977 (1981).

48. Cf. Hinsdale v. New York, N.H. & H. R.R., 81 App.Div. 617, 81 N.Y.S. 356 (1903).

49. Cf. Matter of Reynolds, 115 N.Y.S.2d 534 (1952); Mix v. Hamburg-American S.S. Co., 85 App.Div. 475, 83 N.Y.S. 322 (1903).

50. Woods v. Lancet, 303 N.Y. 349, 102 N.E.2d 691 (1951).

child born dead because of the injuries cannot bring an action for wrongful death.[51]

The death of a child too young to work may still represent a pecuniary injury to his parents.[52] His likelihood of ever supporting them (or otherwise helping them financially) is a question of fact. Although expert testimony is permitted on the potential earnings of a decedent, mere speculation by "experts" on the possible earnings of two children during the lifetime of their parents should not be admissible.[53] The courts have split on the issue of whether evidence of the juvenile delinquency of the minor can affect the amount of recovery.[54]

The wrongful death recovery is not reduced by the amount a distributee receives from the decedent's estate, by will or in intestacy; that amount is considered irrelevant.[55] The beneficiaries' receipt of insurance proceeds or social security benefits also should not reduce the wrongful death recovery.[56]

The trial judge can review a jury's verdict if it is inadequate or excessive, and the appellate division can similarly review the award of damages.[57] The appellate division can send the issue of damages back for a new trial,[58] or can offer the parties the alternatives of accepting a reduced or increased sum or having a new trial.[59] If there are no questions of fact (or almost no questions), the appellate division can simply reduce the damages itself.[60]

51. Endresz v. Friedberg, 24 N.Y.2d 478, 301 N.Y.S.2d 65, 248 N.E.2d 901 (1969) (action for funeral expenses for unborn infant were nevertheless allowed); Raymond v. Bartsch, 84 A.D.2d 60, 447 N.Y.S.2d 32 (3d Dep't 1981), appeal denied 56 N.Y.2d 508, 453 N.Y.S.2d 1027, 439 N.E.2d 401 (1982); Ryan v. Beth Israel Hospital, 96 Misc.2d 816, 409 N.Y.S.2d 681 (New York County 1978).

52. See Birkett v. Knickerbocker Ice Co., 110 N.Y. 504, 18 N.E. 108 (1888). See generally Murphy v. Erie R. Co., 202 N.Y. 242, 95 N.E. 699 (1911).

53. Franchell v. Sims, 73 A.D.2d 1, 424 N.Y.S.2d 959 (4th Dep't 1980).

54. Compare Hill v. Erie Railroad Co., 225 App.Div. 19, 232 N.Y.S. 66 (4th Dep't 1928) (court did not allow juvenile convictions of fifteen-year old to be admitted in wrongful death proceeding), with Russell v. Cirillo, 17 A.D.2d 1005, 234 N.Y.S.2d 67 (3d Dep't 1962) (court allowed evidence of juvenile delinquency of minor decedent).

55. See Terry v. Jewett, 78 N.Y. 338 (1879).

56. See, e.g., Lebel v. Swincicki, 354 Mich. 427, 93 N.W.2d 281 (1958).

57. See, e.g., Long v. New York, 81 A.D.2d 880, 439 N.Y.S.2d 58 (2d Dep't 1981); O'Brien v. Lehigh Valley R. Co., 177 Misc. 25, 30 N.Y.S.2d 287 (Monroe 1941), affirmed 264 App.Div. 831, 35 N.Y.S.2d 752 (4th Dep't 1942), affirmed 289 N.Y. 783, 46 N.E.2d 847 (1943); Kretschmar v. New York, 225 App.Div. 761, 232 N.Y.S. 387 (2d Dep't 1928).

58. See DeSantis v. New York, 268 App. Div. 874, 50 N.Y.S.2d 695 (2d Dep't 1944).

59. See Horne v. Metropolitan Transit Authority, 82 A.D.2d 909, 440 N.Y.S.2d 695 (2d Dep't 1981); Chang v. New York City Health and Hospital Corp., 82 A.D.2d 764, 440 N.Y.S.2d 211 (1st Dep't 1981), appeal denied 55 N.Y.2d 603, 447 N.Y.S.2d 1026, 431 N.E.2d 977 (1981) (award of $160,000 conditionally reduced to $110,000); Long v. New York, 81 A.D.2d 880, 439 N.Y.S.2d 58 (2d Dep't 1981); Saltzberg v. Kiamesha Concord, Inc., 24 A.D.2d 876, 264 N.Y.S.2d 428 (2d Dep't 1965), affirmed 17 N.Y.2d 847, 271 N.Y.S.2d 283, 218 N.E.2d 323 (1966).

60. See Tryon v. Willbank, 234 App. Div. 335, 255 N.Y.S. 27 (4th Dep't 1932).

The plaintiff is entitled to statutory interest from the date of decedent's death,[61] even if the ad damnum clause of the complaint or petition does not include it.[62] Interest on a personal injury judgment runs from the date of the judgment. The right to interest, however, is considered to be a substantive, not merely a procedural, matter, so if the law of another jurisdiction governs, its law on interest will also govern.[63]

While the New York courts have not decided the issue, a federal judge has allowed the defendants to present evidence of the effect of income taxes on the decedent's earnings.[64]

Punitive damages were not permitted in wrongful death proceedings until 1982,[65] when the legislature amended the law[66] to allow punitive damages in cases where the decedent dying after August 31, 1982 could have obtained them in his negligence action had he lived.[67] The legislature reasoned first that prohibiting the award of punitive damages in wrongful death actions anomalously imposed less liability on the defendant whose victim died than on one whose victim survived, and secondly, that punitive damages could well prevent "corporate recklessness."[68]

Many settlements in wrongful death and personal injury lawsuits are "structured" rather than lump-sum payments. Typically, these settlements provide for periodic payments of interest to the beneficiaries and lump sum "balloon" payments deferred until the future. The court has the authority to review and alter these settlements.[69] Structured settlements have income tax advantages and permit the payment of a lump sum at a time when the beneficiary will presumably

61. McKinney's EPTL 5–4.3; McKinney's CPLR 5002; Public Authorities L. § 1276(5). See Hegger v. Green, 91 F.R.D. 595 (S.D.N.Y.1981).

62. George v. Erie County, 66 Misc.2d 871, 322 N.Y.S.2d 278 (Erie 1971).

63. Davenport v. Webb, 11 N.Y.2d 392, 230 N.Y.S.2d 17, 183 N.E.2d 902 (1962).

64. Morgan Guaranty Trust Co. v. Texasgulf Aviation, 604 F.Supp. 699 (S.D.N.Y. 1985) There the court limited its holding to wrongful death actions, specifically excluding personal injury actions.

65. Hempel v. American Airlines, Inc., 102 Misc.2d 563, 423 N.Y.S.2d 778 (New York County 1979). But see Robert v. Ford Motor Co., 100 Misc.2d 646, 417 N.Y.S.2d 595 (Sup.Ct. St. Lawrence 1979) (allowing punitive damages under common law theory).

66. McKinney's EPTL 5–4.3, L.1982, c. 100, McKinney's EPTL 11–3.2. L.1982, c. 100.

67. L.1982, c. 100, legislatively overruling Antoine v. State, 103 Misc.2d 664, 426 N.Y.S.2d 917 (Ct.Claims 1980).

68. See Memorandum and Recommendation of the Law Revision Commission, Leg.Doc. (1982) (No. 65[G], 1982 Sess.L. at A198–A205).

69. A good example of the structured settlement is seen in Matter of Grimes, N.Y.L.J., May 7, 1985, at 13, col. 5 (Bronx), where the decedent left as sole distributee a seven-month old child. The present value of the wrongful death recovery was $280,000, and the proposed settlement was to pay income of $500 per month for the first year, increased by five percent annually until the child reached eighteen. Between the ages of eighteen and twenty-one, the beneficiary would receive $10,000 annually, at twenty-five, $25,000, and at thirty, $778,425. The court modified the payments to provide for much more during the formative years and a balloon payment of $210,175 at age thirty. See also Matter of Green, N.Y.L.J., March 29, 1985, at 15, col. 5.

be mature enough to use it well.[70] In deciding whether to approve them, the court considers their risks, their tax advantages, and the alternative uses of the money.[71]

3. ALLOCATION OF THE PROCEEDS AMONG BENEFICIARIES

Once the trier of the facts decides the amount of damages, those damages have to be allocated among the persons entitled to them. The whole net personal injury recovery is payable to the fiduciary for distribution as part of the estate. The wrongful death proceeds must be divided among the decedent's intestate distributees in the proportion that the decedent's death caused them pecuniary injury, so long as they are not disqualified because of some "wrongdoing" on their own part.[72] These proportions will be determined at a hearing, notice of which is given to all interested persons.[73]

Usually the persons suffering pecuniary losses are the surviving spouse and minor children. If those distributees do not survive the decedent, other distributees, such as adult children, parents, siblings or other relatives, must prove pecuniary injuries if they wish to share.[74]

The court has broad discretion in apportioning the wrongful death proceeds. If the decedent was survived by legal dependents (a spouse, minor children), and there are no special circumstances, the courts allocate the damages among them by using the "Kaiser" Rule,[75] which assigns each distributee a fraction. The denominator of the fraction is the aggregate number of years of anticipated pecuniary dependency of all distributees. Since a person is expected to support his children through age twenty-one and to support his spouse until the first of his death or hers, the denominator of the Kaiser fraction is the sum of the remaining years of the children's minority (for this purpose, age twenty-one [76] and the life expectancy of the decedent or the surviving spouse, whichever is shorter.[77] The numerator of the fraction is each distributee's anticipated years of dependency. The Kaiser case itself is a good example: a decedent aged forty-four was survived by a spouse aged

70. For a general discussion of structured settlements, see Kelner and Kelner, "Structured Settlements," N.Y.L.J., Nov. 14, 1984, at 1, col. 1; Krause, "The Benefits of Structured Settlements," N.Y. State Bar J., Jan. 1982, at 13.

71. Matter of Blanchet, N.Y.L.J., June 24, 1984, at 16, col. 6 (Suffolk).

72. See McKinney's EPTL 4–1.4 and 5–1.2 and discussion this section infra at 547–48.

73. McKinney's EPTL 5–4.4(a).

74. See Matter of Uravic, 142 Misc. 775, 255 N.Y.S. 638 (Kings 1932) (presumption that adult child is not entitled to share); Matter of Riley, 45 Misc.2d 658, 257 N.Y.S.2d 775 (Broome 1965) (decedent's sisters, brothers, nieces and nephews had to show pecuniary loss).

75. Matter of Kaiser, 198 Misc. 582, 100 N.Y.S.2d 218 (Kings 1950).

76. The reduction of the age of majority in New York to eighteen, L.1974, c. 262, section 2, McKinney's EPTL 2–1.10, had no effect on the age-21 rule used for wrongful death actions, because parents in New York are generally required to support their children through age 21, and support is, of course, one measure of damages in a wrongful death action.

77. Life expectancies are determined by the tables issued by the United States Dep't. of Health and Human Services (Office of Vital Statistics).

forty and a child aged one. The wife's period of expected dependency was 25.27 years (the life expectancy of a forty-four year old man), and the baby's was twenty years, so the denominator of the fraction was 45.27. The baby was entitled to 20/45.27 (.442) and the wife to 25.27/45.27 (.558) of the recovery.[78]

The court has discretion to veer from the Kaiser formula if special circumstances warrant it. In one case, for example, an adult child was permitted to share in the recovery because the decedent had lived in the child's house, paid for food and helped with household services.[79] In another, the widow's share was reduced because she was young and self-sufficient and had been married to the decedent for less than two years. The decedent's children's shares were increased beyond the Kaiser amount.[80]

Where the decedent's children are close to majority and their ages are close, the Kaiser formula would cause a disproportionate amount to go to one child over another. For example, if a husband and wife died leaving three children ages seventeen, eighteen and nineteen, application of the Kaiser formula would cause the seventeen-year old to receive almost twice as much as the nineteen year old. In such a case the court can substitute a more reasonable formula. It may, for example, set aside half of the recovery for all the children's support and divide the other half equally among them.[81]

Courts are sensibly flexible in other contexts as well. For example, in one case the petitioner (guardian of the property of decedent's minor children) sought to allocate the entire recovery to wrongful death, and the tax commission did not object.[82] Because of the application of the Kaiser formula, this allocation would have been more advantageous to the younger child than to the older ones. The court declined to appoint separate guardians ad litem for the children because the resultant fees would deplete the amount available for them.[83]

78. For other examples of the Kaiser allocation, see Matter of Avery, 111 Misc. 2d 818, 445 N.Y.S.2d 672 (Wayne 1981), where the husband's life expectancy was 34.8 years and two infant children's ages were 18 and 15 years respectively, giving them three and six years of dependency left. The husband's proportion was 51.33% and the children's were 26.55% and 22.12% respectively. In Matter of Powell, N.Y.L.J., March 27, 1985, at 13, col. 5 (Nassau), the widow was younger than the decedent, so his life expectancy was used. The decedent's life expectancy was 28 years, his daughter's 9.3 years, and his son's 16.4 years. Hence the widow was entitled to 60.6%, the daughter to 14.3% and the son to 25.1% .

79. Gross v. Abraham, 306 N.Y. 525, 119 N.E.2d 370 (1954).

80. Matter of Feldman, N.Y.L.J., May 13, 1985, at 16, col. 2 (Westchester) (Kaiser proportion of 71%, 12% and 17% to widow and children respectively changed to 56%, 19% and 25%). Accord, Matter of Stanley, N.Y.L.J., June 11, 1985, at 12, col. 1 (Nassau) (share of self-sufficient widow reduced, and disabled adult son's share increased).

81. Matter of Maerkle, 44 Misc.2d 617, 254 N.Y.S.2d 411 (Broome 1964).

82. The Tax Commission could have objected on the ground that the wrongful death recovery is excluded from the gross estate, while the personal injury recovery is included.

83. Matter of Green, 127 Misc.2d 266, 486 N.Y.S.2d 131 (1985).

In "professional" families or other appropriate cases, the court may extend the period of support past twenty-one on the assumption that the decedent would have provided the children with post-graduate education.[84]

The right to share in the recovery is a vested right at the decedent's death, so status as distributee is determined at the date of death, not at the date of the recovery.[85] The right to share is transferable during the beneficiary's life and descendible if the beneficiary dies before payment.[86]

If a distributee suffers a pecuniary injury, it is irrelevant that he also had other sources of income.[87]

A person disqualified under law from sharing in the estate of an intestate, because he divorced, abandoned or failed to support the decedent, is also disqualified from sharing in the wrongful death and personal injury recoveries.[88] Other behavior not specified in the statute as disqualifying a distributee, no matter how unbecoming, will not preclude that distributee from sharing in the recovery.[89]

The Surrogates have also precluded the following persons from sharing in the wrongful death recovery:

(1) a parent who fails to support a child.[90]

(2) A married infant not dependent on the decedent.[91]

(3) The estate of a wife who died immediately after her husband.[92]

84. See, e.g., Mahler v. American Airlines, 49 Misc.2d 693, 269 N.Y.S.2d 342 (Westchester 1966); Matter of Silverstein, 48 Misc.2d 1029, 266 N.Y.S.2d 553 (Nassau 1966).

85. Gore v. Northeast Airlines, Inc., 373 F.2d 717 (2d Cir.1967); Alberino v. Long Island Jewish-Hillside Medical Center, 87 A.D.2d 217, 450 N.Y.S.2d 857 (2d Dep't 1982) (child was entitled to share in the action for the wrongful death of his mother although he was adopted by a third party before the recovery. Domestic Relations Law 117 states that an adopted child is not a distributee of his natural parents, but of his adoptive parents).

86. See Baer v. Broder, 86 A.D.2d 881, 447 N.Y.S.2d 538 (2d Dep't 1982). Note, however, that a beneficiary's death pending recovery reduces his pecuniary loss and his proportion of the proceeds.

87. See Matter of Frank, 286 A.D. 986, 144 N.Y.S.2d 435 (4th Dep't 1955).

88. McKinney's EPTL 5–1.4 and McKinney's EPTL 4–1.2. See Matter of Avery, 111 Misc.2d 818, 445 N.Y.S.2d 672 (Wayne 1981), where the decedent's husband was not disqualified as distributee despite his marrying her before obtaining a divorce from his prior spouse and despite his conviction of a felony. He was, however, ineligible to serve as administrator because of the felony. SCPA 707. See Matter of Oswald, 43 Misc.2d 774, 252 N.Y.S.2d 203 (Nassau 1964), affirmed 24 A.D.2d 465, 260 N.Y.S.2d 615 (2d Dep't 1965), affirmed 17 N.Y.2d 447, 266 N.Y.S.2d 807, 213 N.E. 2d 888 (1965) (husband abandoned wife); Matter of Thompson, N.Y.L.J., June 21, 1985 at 74, col. 4 (Suffolk) (father abandoned son when son was seven).

89. See Matter of Erzinger, 183 Misc. 806, 51 N.Y.S.2d 551 (Kings 1944).

90. Matter of Frigenti, 6 Misc.2d 80, 162 N.Y.S.2d 659 (Kings 1957).

91. Matter of Sintyago, 198 Misc. 776, 100 N.Y.S.2d 556 (Kings 1950).

92. Matter of Ray, 208 Misc. 617, 143 N.Y.S.2d 447 (Queens 1955).

(4) A self-supporting adult.[93]

(5) A self-supporting minor who was not dependent on the decedent.[94]

(6) An incompetent child where a decedent had not contributed to the support of the ward and whose care was otherwise provided for,[95] and permanent wards of the state.[96]

(7) Siblings who are not dependent on the decedent.[97]

Death of a distributee before recovery reduces that distributee's damages to the actual pecuniary losses he experienced during the period between the decedent's death and his own,[98] but remarriage of a surviving spouse does not cause a reduction of the recovery.[99]

E. PROCEDURE FOR SETTLING LAWSUITS AND MAKING ALLOCATIONS AND DISTRIBUTIONS

1. PRELIMINARY WORD ON POWERS OF TRIAL COURT VERSUS SURROGATE'S COURT

The Supreme Court, where the lawsuit usually takes place, has concurrent jurisdiction with the Surrogate to approve the compromise, allocate the proceeds between the two lawsuits and among the distributees, and order distribution of the recovery, but it should, and most often does, defer to the Surrogate's Court that issued letters to decide the allocation and distribution of the proceeds after an accounting.[1] At

93. Matter of Uravic, 142 Misc. 775, 255 N.Y.S. 638 (Kings 1932).

94. Matter of Krakie, N.Y.L.J., August 2, 1966, at 10, col. 1.

95. See Matter of Gould, N.Y.L.J., Feb. 27, 1985, at 13, col. 4 (Bronx) where the court refused to allocate any part of wrongful death proceeds to institutionalized son where the share would have been immediately absorbed by the state to pay for care he had already received. The court noted that the son had, under those circumstances, no reasonable expectation that his father would support him. Accord, Matter of Stanley, N.Y.L.J., June 11, 1985, at 12, col. 1 (Nassau). See also Matter of Lilien, 139 N.Y.S.2d 128 (Queens 1955).

96. See Matter of Reynolds, 115 N.Y.S.2d 534 (Erie 1952). In this case an aged father had not been supporting his institutionalized child for years, and the entire recovery went to his spouse.

97. Matter of Bernardi, 119 Misc. 919, 102 N.Y.S.2d 851 (Kings 1951).

98. See, e.g., Sider v. General Electric Co., 238 N.Y. 64, 143 N.E. 792 (1924); Matter of Ray, 208 Misc. 617, 143 N.Y.S.2d 447 (Queens 1955).

99. Matter of Giambertone, 38 Misc.2d 784, 238 N.Y.S.2d 883 (Suffolk 1963). See also Rodak v. Fury, 31 A.D.2d 816, 298 N.Y.S.2d 50 (2d Dep't 1969).

Sec. E

1. See, e.g., Matter of Judkins, N.Y.L.J., May 30, 1985, at 7, col. 6 (Bronx), where the court held that the Supreme Court should exercise jurisdiction in the negligence action and defer to the Surrogate in the proceeding to allocate the proceeds; Fried v. Glueck, 16 Misc.2d 423, 181 N.Y.S. 2d 27 (Kings 1958), conceding that the allocation and distribution of wrongful death proceeds were not in the exclusive jurisdiction of the Surrogate's Court, but deferring to the Surrogate anyway because of that court's special expertise and competence in such matters.

the very least, it should require the fiduciary to file a bond before distributing the proceeds.[2]

Although once the Supreme Court settles a matter it is binding on the Surrogate's Court, very often the Supreme Court expressly makes the settlement subject to the Surrogate's approval, because the trial court has only the fiduciary and the defendants before it, not the distributees, creditors and others interested in the decedent's estate.[3] It is therefore unable to determine proper allocation between wrongful death and personal injuries and the overall distribution and apportionment of the wrongful death recovery.

In many counties the administrative judges in cooperation with the Board of Judges and the Surrogate have arranged to have many of the matters settled subject to the Surrogate's approval in order to protect the rights of all the parties interested in the recovery.[4]

2. THE COMPROMISE PROCEEDING

As a preliminary step, the court may have to determine a choice of law issue on the question of how to allocate the proceeds among the decedent's survivors. The New York rule is that the choice of law in torts is determined by the "grouping of contacts" test,[5] under which the court applies the law of the jurisdiction with the most compelling interest in the application of its law. An initial grouping of contacts analysis would be applied to the negligence action itself, and after a recovery has been obtained, the court may make a second analysis to determine how the proceeds will be distributed. The crucial contact there would be the domicile of the distributees. For instance, if a wrongful death recovery is obtained in New York and all of the distributees are domiciliaries of another state, the law of the domicile of the distributees suffering the pecuniary loss will determine the manner of distributing and apportioning the recovery. In one case, the decedent's widow and four infant children lived in Nevada, and two adult children lived in Connecticut, where the decedent died, and the court applied Nevada's law of distribution. "It seems logical in this instance to conclude that Nevada is the state most vitally concerned with the manner in which the widow and infant children of a Nevada decedent

2. Matter of Franco, 108 Misc.2d 1084, 439 N.Y.S.2d 278 (Bronx 1981).

3. The allocation would matter to these persons for various reasons. A legatee who is not a distributee, for example, would want more allocated to personal injury than to wrongful death, as would a creditor, because the personal injury recovery is part of the estate and subject to creditors' claims.

For a discussion of the respective roles of the Surrogate's Court and the Supreme Court in the post-compromise procedures, see Matter of Judkins, N.Y.L.J., May 31, 1985, at 14, col. 1 (Bronx).

4. McKinney's SCPA 2220(1). For a discussion of the roles of and the cooperation between the two courts, see Radigan, Settlement of Wrongful Death and Personal Injury Actions, The Jurist (Publication of the Association of Justices of the Supreme Court of the State of New York), Spring 1985 at 1.

5. Babcock v. Johnson, 12 N.Y.2d 473, 240 N.Y.S.2d 743, 191 N.E.2d 279 (1963), on remand 40 Misc.2d 757, 243 N.Y.S.2d 715 (1963).

will be compensated for their pecuniary loss." [6] In another case, the court refused to allow the decedent's mother (a non-distributee) to share in the proceeds despite her argument that under the law of her domicile (Greece) she would be entitled to share. The court considered the New York contacts and found that they outweighed her Greek connection.[7] New York will not be bound, however, by another state's limitations on the amount of recovery.[8] Those limitations are considered procedural or remedial provisions of a foreign state,[9] and because they are against New York policy, New York courts need not follow them.

The fiduciary obtains court approval of the settlement by commencing a compromise proceeding.[10] As a practical matter, this compromise proceeding is often part of an accounting proceeding, which we will discuss shortly. If he is a fiduciary without restrictions, he can settle the action himself, and does not need to get court approval via a compromise proceeding, but because of the risk of surcharge when he accounts for the proceeds, even an unrestricted fiduciary usually seeks court approval. If he had commenced a wrongful death action, he can begin the compromise proceeding either in the trial court or the Surrogate's Court. If he did not commence the lawsuit, he must petition in the Surrogate's Court. At this determination, whether it occurs in the Supreme Court or the Surrogate's Court,[11] all parties affected by the division among beneficiaries and the division between the two lawsuits, including distributees, the personal representatives of distributees who died after the decedent,[12] claimants,[13] beneficiaries under the will, assignees of beneficiaries, the plaintiff's attorneys,[14] and the State Tax Commissioner [15] have a right to be heard.

6. See Matter of Caccamo, 71 Misc.2d 391, 394, 336 N.Y.S.2d 77, 81 (Kings 1972). See also Matter of Layden, 92 Misc.2d 353, 400 N.Y.S.2d 282 (Queens 1977) (New York court applied Florida law on the distribution issue when decedent, who was killed in New York while living in New York, had purchased a home in Florida, moved his wife and seven children there, and was staying with his mother until his job transfer came through.

7. Matter of Hadzis, N.Y.L.J., April 1, 1985, at 16, col. 6 (Queens). See also Cousins v. Instrument Flyers, Inc., 44 N.Y.2d 698, 405 N.Y.S.2d 441, 376 N.E.2d 914 (1978) (applied New York law where New York resident rented airplane from New Jersey corporation and crashed in Pennsylvania).

8. Miller v. Miller, 28 A.D.2d 899, 282 N.Y.S.2d 35 (2d Dep't 1967), affirmed 22 N.Y.2d 12, 290 N.Y.S.2d 734, 237 N.E.2d 877 (1968).

9. Kilberg v. Northeast Airline, 9 N.Y.2d 34, 211 N.Y.S.2d 133, 172 N.E.2d 526 (1961); Holzsager v. Valley Hospital, 482 F.Supp. 629 (S.D.N.Y.1979).

10. McKinney's SCPA 2106, discussed in chapter on "Miscellaneous Proceedings," infra at 345–50.

11. See Matter of Judkins, N.Y.L.J., May 31, 1985, at 14, col. 1 (Bronx), where the court, conceding that the Supreme Court has jurisdiction to allocate wrongful death and personal injury recoveries among the beneficiaries, also noted that the Supreme Court must follow the EPTL 5–4.4(a) notice requirements.

12. Meekin v. Brooklyn Heights Railway Co., 164 N.Y. 145, 58 N.E. 50 (1900).

13. Creditors cannot share in wrongful death proceeds but can share in personal injuries proceeds—hence their interest in the allocation.

14. The attorneys hired to bring the wrongful death action are necessary par-

15. See note 15 on page 551.

If a person may be disqualified as a necessary party because of abandonment, failure to support, or other wrong-doing,[16] he has a right to be heard in this proceeding on that issue.[17] As in other proceedings, persons under legal disability appear through their personal representatives.[18] A distributee en ventre sa mere is a necessary party and the distribution will not occur until his birth.[19]

The petition and supporting affidavits in an application to compromise a wrongful death or personal injury claim must state the facts about the decedent's injuries, the age, date of birth, residence, occupation and earnings of the decedent at the time of his death, the names, addresses, ages and dates of birth of those distributees suffering a pecuniary loss, and a complete statement of the nature and extent of the disability other than infancy of any person. It must state the laws of the jurisdiction whose law controls if the injuries arose out of an action not covered by New York law, and must list the gross amount of the settlement, the attorneys' fees requested, the terms of any retainer agreement, the net amount to be received by the petitioner, the commissions, the funeral expenses, and the hospital, medical or nursing costs with the names of those who paid for them or the names of the creditors. It must state whether any balance remains to be paid on the claims and must list unpaid claims, including hospital liens and claims for undeserved public assistance, against the decedent or his estate.

The personal representative must give the court a tabulation showing the fraction or percentage proposed to be paid to each beneficiary, using the mortality tables published by the United States Department of Health and Human Services where any distributee expected support for his or the decedent's life.

Where the petition also seeks to compromise a personal injury claim, it should state the amount of recovery and the basis for the allocation to personal injury (as opposed to wrongful death).

The petitioner's attorney must submit a supporting affidavit indicating his connections, if any, with the defendant. He should state whether the administrator will pay his fee and whether any other person or corporation interested in the compromise has paid him anything or intends to, listing their names. The attorney must give a detailed description of his services, the amount owed him and the basis

ties because their fees are payable from the proceeds. McKinney's EPTL 5–4.4(b).

15. Matter of Franco, 108 Misc.2d 1084, 439 N.Y.S.2d 278 (Bronx 1981). The state tax commissioner has a right to appear because wrongful death proceeds are not part of the taxable estate, Connecticut Bank and Trust Co. v. United States, 465 F.2d 760 (2d Cir.1972), while proceeds of the personal injuries action are.

16. McKinney's EPTL 4–1.4 (disqualification of parent); McKinney's EPTL 5–1.2 (disqualification of spouse).

17. See Fraley v. Muller, 281 App.Div. 1016, 121 N.Y.S.2d 138 (1st Dep't 1953) (father had to be cited despite allegation of abandonment. Issue of abandonment would be decided at the proceeding).

18. See chapter on "Appearances," supra at 232 et seq.

19. See Matter of Rivera, 230 N.Y.S.2d 858 (Suffolk 1962).

of that amount (almost always a prior retainer agreement). If it is based on a retainer agreement, the attorney must list the persons with whom the agreement was made and its terms.

If the application is for the compromise of a personal injury action, the petition must contain all the information just discussed and must state when letters were issued and whether or not seven months have elapsed from that date. This information is theoretically not needed in a proceeding to compromise solely a wrongful death action because creditors are not entitled to the proceeds of a wrongful death action. In such an action, however, the decedent must have died instantaneously to eliminate the creditors' standing, because if he survived the accident, even for a short time, part of the proceeds of the recovery may be allocable to pain and suffering, which is available to creditors.

If the Surrogate has appointed an administrator and that administrator chooses the Surrogate's Court as the forum in which to seek approval, any proceeding in another court brought by a distributee is without legal effect.[20] Even if the fiduciary seeks approval of the settlement in the Supreme Court, after the Supreme Court approval, the Surrogate usually reviews the matter, oversees the distribution and supervises the accounting. If the fiduciary is acting under limited letters, the trial court should do no more than approve the settlement; it should not exercise its power to distribute the proceeds.[21]

Formal hearings in compromise proceedings are rare, either on the issue of compromise or allocation. In practice these matters are usually decided in a single proceeding, most often without a hearing. The court makes its determination on whether to allow the compromise and how to allocate and distribute the proceeds after reviewing the petition and other data submitted. If questions of fact arise, the court will order a hearing.[22]

If the matter goes to trial, and an award is made in the personal injury and wrongful death proceedings, that determination, subject to appeal or motions, is binding on the Surrogate.

If instead of referring the allocation to the Surrogate, the fiduciary applies for a compromise order in the court where the action for wrongful death is pending, that court, after inquiry into the merits in the amount of damages, may approve or disapprove the compromise. The written approval of the compromise is then conclusive evidence as to adequacy of the compromise in any proceeding in the Surrogate's Court for the final settlement of the account of an administrator or personal representative.[23] No party can then object to it nor can the Surrogate, sua sponte, alter it, or send it back to the Supreme Court.

20. Matter of Holquin, 101 Misc.2d 174, 420 N.Y.S.2d 670 (Queens 1979).

21. See Matter of Franco, 108 Misc.2d 1084, 439 N.Y.S.2d 278 (Bronx 1981).

22. See Matter of Pargament, N.Y.L.J., March 8, 1985, at 13, col. 5 (Bronx), where the attorneys for both parties waived the right to a hearing and the court acceded (seemingly reluctantly) to their request to decide the issues on the papers, because the amount of money was small.

23. McKinney's EPTL 5–4.6.

The court may consider disqualification of a distributee [24] or of a surviving spouse,[25] and if the settlement is not in the Surrogate's Court, those issues are usually transferred to the Surrogate for determination.

If the proceeds of the lawsuit are payable to an infant, conservatee or incompetent, the court will order payment to the guardian, conservator or committee,[26] unless the amount is less than $5,000, in which case the court can order it paid to the parent or adult person residing with the disabled person.[27]

The Surrogate's Court may decide an action for wrongful death based on a federal claim or may approve a compromise by the parties to that action. In that case it will apply the appropriate federal law.[28] State law will, however, determine commissions and attorneys' fees because the federal laws are silent on these issues.[29]

SECTION F. ATTORNEYS' FEES

The plaintiff's attorney is entitled to disbursements and a reasonable fee. Almost universally the arrangement between the attorney and the client is on a contingency basis [1] fixed by a retainer agreement, but the agreement is always subject to the reasonableness requirement and is not binding on the distributees other than the fiduciary in his individual capacity (as one of the distributees suffering a pecuniary loss) and adult competent parties who consent to a retainer.[2] The court often approves the retainer agreement as to those parties and reduces it as to legally disabled persons or non-consenting persons. The court may ask the attorney to agree to reduce the overall fee, even as it affects competent adults who have consented, but if the attorney refuses, the court often reduces the infant's share of the fee to a twenty-five percent rate,[3] particularly in cases that are settled rather than tried to judgment.

In fixing the attorney's fees the court deducts the attorney's rightful disbursements from the gross recovery, and then makes two allocations. It apportions the fee first between the personal injury and the

24. McKinney's EPTL 4–1.4(a), discussed supra at 547.

25. McKinney's EPTL 5–1.2, discussed supra at 547.

26. McKinney's SCPA 2220(1).

27. McKinney's SCPA 2220(1).

28. See Matter of Yocom, 193 Misc. 340, 80 N.Y.S.2d 853 (Westchester 1948).

29. Matter of Brewer, 150 Misc. 661, 270 N.Y.S. 50 (Orange 1934).

Sec. F

1. The retainer agreement is often the lesser of one-third or the following sliding scale: fifty percent of the first $1,000, forty percent of the next $2,000, thirty-five percent of the next $22,000, and twenty-five percent of any amounts above $25,000.

2. Roberts v. Moore, 74 Misc.2d 709, 346 N.Y.S.2d 75 (App. Term 1st Dep't 1973); Matter of Seabury, N.Y.L.J., March 20, 1985, at 13, col. 2 (Bronx) (attorney's fees agreed to by adult were approved, while fees attributable to children's shares were reduced to thirty-one percent); Matter of Dietsche, 29 Misc.2d 609, 216 N.Y.S.2d 731 (Nassau 1961).

3. See, e.g., Matter of Layden, 92 Misc. 2d 353, 400 N.Y.S.2d 282 (Queens 1977); Matter of Harrison, N.Y.L.J., April 11, 1985, at 13, col. 1 (Bronx).

wrongful death recoveries,[4] and then between or among the beneficiaries. It can either base its allocation among beneficiaries on the retainer agreement, if everyone is adult and competent and agrees to that, or can fix the percentage itself.

Even if the fiduciary loses the trial, the reasonable expenses of the litigation are chargeable to the decedent's estate. Naturally, if the attorneys' fee was on a contingency basis, none is payable if the attorney does not obtain a recovery.

SECTION G. THE FIDUCIARY'S ACCOUNTING

Recall that the Surrogate's Court was initially involved because only it could grant letters, which are a prerequisite to the lawsuit. At that point the trial court may have assumed jurisdiction of the case and even made an allocation of the proceeds.

The final step in the wrongful death proceeding is the accounting. Regardless of which court was the more active in exercising its jurisdiction, it is the Surrogate who must settle the fiduciary's account.

Essentially the accounting procedures for wrongful death and personal injury proceeds are like accountings in all other estate contexts; in fact, Article 22 specifically provides for an accounting for wrongful death proceeds.[1] This discussion will highlight the points peculiar to the wrongful death and personal injury recovery.

The fiduciary petitions for the accounting, and frequently [2] he also petitions to compromise the actions, allocate the proceeds between the two causes of action, apportion the recovery among the distributees suffering a pecuniary loss, direct the payment of all necessary medical expenses, commissions and funeral expenses, provide for distribution, determine whether any beneficiaries are disqualified, settle the account and discharge the fiduciary and the party paying the money from all further liability. If part of the recovery represents the proceeds of a personal injury action, the court will ordinarily not permit the distribution and accounting until at least seven months after it has issued letters to the fiduciary, so that all creditors have had the opportunity to present their claims.[3]

If a negligence recovery is payable not to the estate but to the decedent's legatees or distributees pursuant to statute,[4] the fiduciary may petition at any time to account for the proceeds. The same is true if the fiduciary is bonded and therefore has the power to receive the

4. Matter of Jackson, 71 Misc.2d 133, 335 N.Y.S.2d 587 (Kings 1972).

Sec. G

1. McKinney's SCPA 2204, discussed in chapter on accounting, supra at 208–10.

2. We say "frequently" because the trial court has concurrent jurisdiction with the Surrogate's Court and some of these issues may have been decided there.

3. The seven-month time period is governed by McKinney's SCPA 1802 and discussed in chapter on "Claims," supra at 148–50.

4. E.g., Federal Employers' Liability Act. See Matter of Dennison, 203 Misc. 1004, 124 N.Y.S.2d 668 (Onondoga 1953).

proceeds directly. In either case, after the fiduciary obtains waivers or serves process,[5] the court can settle the account and direct payment. After filing receipts from the parties who received the proceeds, the fiduciary is discharged from further liability for that cause of action.

In a wrongful death action, the fiduciary is usually serving with limited letters without a bond and must get a court order to settle the action and collect the recovery. The order directs payment of allowable expenses and distribution of set percentages to distributees suffering a pecuniary loss. If the fiduciary is seeking court approval of a partial settlement, the court can order a reserve to cover federal and state estate taxes, attorneys' fees and partial distributions to beneficiaries.[6] The court can order the defendant (or his insurance carrier) to pay the money directly to the creditors and distributees, or can order it to be paid to the administrator jointly with a bank, not to be released until the court's further order.[7] If the fiduciary is bonded, he can receive the proceeds directly and then petition to account.

If the fiduciary is combining a proceeding to account for all assets received during the administration of the estate and to compromise a claim for wrongful death and personal injuries, he should use the ordinary forms for the judicial settlement of accounts, but supplemented by the above additional information.

5. See chapter on "Procedure," supra at 37–49.

6. See Matter of Aguirre, N.Y.L.J., April 11, 1985, at 16, col. 2 (Nassau), where the judge approved a $1,150,000 settlement with some of the defendants, ordered a reserve of $150,000 for estate taxes, and permitted the payment of attorneys' fees and disbursements and interim distributions to the decedent's distributees.

7. Matter of Aguirre, N.Y.L.J., April 11, 1985, at 16, col. 2 (Nassau).

Chapter Twenty-One

OVERVIEW OF ESTATE TAXES—SUBSTANCE AND PROCEDURE

SECTION A. INTRODUCTION

When a person dies, the fiduciary administering the estate, or the person effectively "in charge," such as a surviving spouse, daughter or son, has to think about estate taxes in two contexts: first, whether any estate taxes, federal or state, are due, and second, even if no taxes are due, whether any estate property is held by an entity or person who cannot release it without authorization from the taxing authorities.

If the answer to both questions is "no," the fiduciary or person in charge need not do anything about estate taxes, except perhaps to file an informational federal estate tax return in certain circumstances.[1] If the answer to either question is "yes," the person in charge has to compute and pay the taxes, if any are due, and obtain authorization for the release of assets. This chapter discusses the computation of the state and federal estate taxes, the procedures for paying them, and the procedures for obtaining tax waivers and releases when necessary, whether or not taxes are due. It also discusses the apportionment of the tax burden among the appropriate beneficiaries.

With regard to the substantive tax law, it is beyond the scope of this book to discuss the innumerable ramifications, twists and turns of the estate tax provisions of the Internal Revenue Code. The discussion in this chapter is general; its purpose is to give the attorney in a New York estate a basic overview of estate taxation and the procedural rules necessary to conclude those aspects of estate administration that relate to, and are affected by, the estate taxes.[2]

Sec. A

1. For example, the executor of a married person who dies with an estate larger than the unified credit exemption equivalent (see Note 2 infra and accompanying text) and leaves his estate to his surviving spouse must file a return though the estate incurs no taxes.

2. An excellent treatise on federal estate taxes is Stevens, Maxfield and Lind, Federal Estate and Gift Taxation (5th ed. 1983).

SECTION B. GENERAL COMMENTS ABOUT THE FEDERAL AND STATE ESTATE TAXES

Recent changes in the federal estate tax law exempt many estates from federal taxation. Because of the "unified credit" available for every decedent's estate, a decedent dying in 1987 or after who did not make significant lifetime gifts may have a taxable estate of $600,000 without owing any federal estate taxes.[1] The tax-free federal estate threshold for the preceding years was as follows:

1986—$500,000;

1985—$400,000;

1984—$325,000;

1983—$275,000;

1982—$225,000;

1981—$175,625.[2]

In addition, if a decedent was married, any property he left to his spouse is completely exempt from federal estate taxes because of the unlimited marital deduction enacted in 1981.[3] Thus, if a person has $5,000,000 and leaves it to his spouse, his estate is completely free of taxation. If he leaves $600,000 to his children and $4,400,000 to his spouse and dies in 1987 or later, his estate is free from federal estate taxes because $4,400,000 is eligible for the marital deduction, and the tentative tax on $600,000 is $192,800, which is wiped out by the unified credit.

The tax rates are graduated, starting at thirty-four percent for estates of $400,000, to thirty-seven percent for estates of $600,000 and eventually going to fifty percent for estates over $5,000,000.[4]

Taxable lifetime gifts made after January 1, 1977 figure into the estate tax computation. They are added to the taxable estate, which is the gross estate minus deductions, and the tax is computed on the sum of the two. A tax credit is given for any gift taxes paid, so the real effect of this addition is to boost a decedent's estate into the highest possible tax bracket.

Sec. B

1. The reason is that every estate of a decedent dying in 1987 or after can take a credit (the unified credit) of $192,800, I.R.C. § 2010, which wipes out the taxes on a $600,000 estate.

2. That is, the credits for 1986–1981 respectively were, under I.R.C. § 2010(b), $155,800, $121,800, $96,300, $79,300, $62,800 and $47,000, which insulated from taxation estates of $500,000, $400,000, $325,000, $275,000, $225,000 and $175,625 respectively.

3. I.R.C. § 2056, P.L. 97–34, section 403(a)(1)(B). The marital deduction is discussed this chapter infra at 592–96.

4. I.R.C. § 2001. The actual tax rates start at 18%, but the effective rates start at 34% and by 1987 they will start at 37%. The top bracket will be 50% when it is fully phased in in 1988.

With a few vastly important differences such as rate of taxation and amount of credit against the taxes, the New York legislature has largely conformed its estate tax law with the federal. The law governing New York estate taxation is found in Article 26 of the Tax Law.[5] It has no provision which automatically incorporates changes made in the federal law; the New York legislature must act if it decides to incorporate a federal change into a New York law.[6]

While the federal estate taxes apply to estates in excess of $500,000 (1986) or $600,000 (1987 and after), the state estate taxes apply to estates over $108,000. The New York estate taxation rates[7] are graduated, starting at two percent of amounts under $50,000 and increasing to twenty-one percent of amounts over $10,100,000.[8]

If the estate is $108,000, it incurs a tentative tax of $2,750, which is wiped out by the general credit in that amount.[9] The state credit does not operate like the federal, however; it exempts estates of less than $108,000 from taxes, not the first $108,000 of larger estates. If the tentative tax is more than $2,750 and less than $5,000, the credit is the amount by which $5,500 exceeds the tax. If the tentative tax is $5,000 or more, the credit is $500. The effect of this is that for every dollar the tax increases, the credit decreases by one dollar.

To illustrate, if the taxable estate is $108,000, no tax is due. If the taxable estate is $150,000, the gross tax is $4,000, the credit is $1,500 ($5,500 minus $4,000), and the tax due is $2,500. If the taxable estate is $140,000, the gross tax is $3,700, the credit is $1,800 ($5,500 minus $3,700) and the tax is $1,900.

SECTION C. STEPPED–UP BASIS

If a person receives property from a decedent's estate and later sells that property, any gain on the sale will be income to him, taxable as a capital gain. He must therefore know the basis of the property in order to figure the gain.

Under IRC 1014, property passing to a beneficiary from a decedent's estate gets a basis stepped up to the date of death value (or

5. McKinney's Tax Law §§ 951–963 (Supp.1986).

6. The first section of the New York estate tax law, section 951, always states the date of the latest amendments to the federal law, and when other sections of the state law refer to the Internal Revenue Code, the reference includes amendments through the date mentioned in section 951.

7. McKinney's Tax Law § 952(a)(4).

8. Id. However, if the tax computed this way is less than the federal credit allowed for state death taxes under IRC 2011 the New York estate tax is increased to equal the federal credit allowed. The reason for this provision is that the federal credit for state death taxes reduces, dollar for dollar, the federal estate taxes an estate owes by the state estate taxes the estate pays (up to the I.R.C. § 2011 ceiling). This means that if the state imposes an estate tax lower than the federal credit, the estate has to pay the same amount of taxes, but part of it will go to the federal government rather than to the state. In effect, a state that imposes a tax less than the federal credit is funnelling part of the taxes its taxpayers pay out of the state coffers and into the federal. McKinney's Tax L. § 952(c).

9. McKinney's Tax L. § 952(b) (Supp. 1984–85).

alternate value [1] if that is used for estate tax purposes).[2] The beneficiary who receives the property takes as a basis the fair market value of the property on the date of death or alternate valuation date, and if he sells it then, he has no capital gains. Had the property been transferred as a gift during the decedent's lifetime, the donee would have taken the donor's basis (adjusted for any gift taxes paid), and if he had sold it then would have incurred a capital gains to the extent the selling price exceeded the basis.

All property included in the gross estate gets a stepped-up basis. Hence if property is included because the decedent transferred it within three years of death (such inclusions are very rare since 1981) [3] or transferred it with a "string" attached,[4] its basis will be stepped up because of its inclusion. Similarly, if property is included one-half in the decedent's estate because he owned it jointly with his spouse,[5] one-half gets a stepped-up basis.

The stepping-up of basis has led to a grisly estate planning device and some remedial legislation. The device was to transfer property to a dying person to get a stepped-up basis at his imminent death. The legislation provides that if someone transfers low-basis property to a decedent during his lifetime and on the decedent's death the property goes back to the donor under the decedent's will or otherwise, the basis will be stepped-up to the date of death value or alternate value only if the decedent survived for at least a year after the transfer.[6]

The New York law conforms with the federal on the stepped-up basis.

SECTION D. INTERACTION BETWEEN STATE PROPERTY LAW AND FEDERAL TAX LAW

Whether or not a decedent owned property is usually determined by state law. Whether that ownership (or lack of ownership) causes inclusion in (or exclusion from) the decedent's federal gross estate is a federal question. The federal court deciding a tax issue will not be bound by lower state court decisions on the ownership issue, although the federal court will give those decisions "proper regard." [1] If the

Sec. C

1. Alternate valuation is discussed this chapter infra at 561–62.

2. For a short period after Jan. 1, 1977, a carry-over basis was in effect, and for decedents dying between Jan. 1, 1977 and November 7, 1978, an option could be taken as to which basis to choose. P.L. 94–455, sec. 2005(a)(1), repealed by P.L. 96–223, sec. 401(a).

3. I.R.C. § 2035, discussed this chapter infra at 576–77.

4. I.R.C. §§ 2036, 2037, 2038 discussed this chapter infra at 584–88.

5. I.R.C. § 2040, discussed this chapter infra at 579–82.

6. I.R.C. § 1014(e).

Sec. D

1. Commissioner v. Estate of Bosch, 387 U.S. 456, 87 S.Ct. 1776, 18 L.Ed.2d 886 (1967), on remand 382 F.2d 295 (2d Cir. 1967) (where federal estate tax liability turns on character of property under state law, federal authorities are not bound by state court, except highest state court).

state's highest court has decided the issue, the federal court is bound by that decision.[2] If the state's highest court has not, the federal court must come to the conclusion that it thinks the highest state court would reach.

The reason for this is that the government was not a party to the action or proceeding in which the ownership of property was determined, and family members may be perfectly happy to forego ownership and refrain from objecting if that would result in the overall tax benefits to the family.

GROSS ESTATE

The federal gross estate includes the following elements:

(a) property in which the decedent had an interest; [3]

(b) in some cases, jointly owned property; [4]

(c) in some cases, annuities and pensions payable to the decedent's beneficiaries after his death; [5]

(d) in some cases, life insurance on the decedent's life; [6]

(e) in some cases, property transferred by the decedent with "strings attached"; [7]

(f) in some cases, property transferred by the decedent with "strings attached" if the decedent cut those strings within the last three years of his life; [8]

(g) property over which the decedent had a general power of appointment; [9]

(h) gifts taxes on any gratuitous transfers made after 1976 and within the last three years of the decedent's life.[10] The gratuitous transfers themselves are not part of the gross estate if the decedent died after December 31, 1981, but they may be part of the estate tax computation as we discuss shortly.[11]

The New York gross estate is the federal gross estate (even if the fiduciary did not have to file a federal estate tax return) [12] with the following modifications:

1. Real property outside New York is not included.[13]

2. Commissioner v. Estate of Bosch, 387 U.S. 456, 87 S.Ct. 1776, 18 L.Ed.2d 886 (1967), on remand 382 F.2d 295 (2d Cir. 1967).

3. I.R.C. § 2033, discussed this chapter infra at 575–76.

4. I.R.C. § 2040, discussed this chapter infra at 579–82.

5. I.R.C. § 2039, discussed this chapter infra at 582–83.

6. I.R.C. §§ 2042, 2035, discussed this chapter infra at 576–79.

7. I.R.C. §§ 2036, 2037, 2038, discussed this chapter infra at 584–88.

8. I.R.C. § 2035, discussed this chapter infra at 576–77.

9. I.R.C. § 2041, discussed this chapter infra at 588–92.

10. I.R.C. § 2035(c).

11. Infra at 576–77.

12. If the estate did not exceed the threshold amounts discussed above (that is, $600,000 for estates of decedents dying after 1986), no federal estate tax return need be filed. I.R.C. § 6018.

13. McKinney's Tax Law § 954(a)(1).

2. Tangible personal property outside New York is not included.[14] The intangible personal property of a New York domiciliary is included in the New York gross estate [15] even if the jurisdiction where it is located taxes it as well.[16] Since New York has no credit for foreign death taxes, double taxation can result. It does not often result, however, because many states refrain from taxing such property of non-domiciliaries.

A 1973 amendment to the New York Tax Law [17] gives an exemption for non-New Yorkers from taxation on intangible personal property located in New York if the state where the property is located grants New Yorkers the same exemption.[18] Thus, if a sister state refrains from taxing the intangible personal property of a New Yorker located within the sister state, then New York will likewise refrain from taxing the intangible personal property of the non-resident.[19] A majority of states have these reciprocity provisions.

The other differences between New York gross estate and federal gross estate relate to specific kinds of property included in the gross estate, discussed in some detail later in this chapter.

SECTION E. ALTERNATE VALUATION

1. FEDERAL

The fiduciary has the choice of valuing estate property at its fair market value on the date of death or on the date six months after death.[1] If the fiduciary chooses alternate valuation instead of the date

14. McKinney's Tax Law § 954(a)(1). New York could not, even if it wanted to, tax such property. Frick v. Pennsylvania, 268 U.S. 473, 45 S.Ct. 603, 69 L.Ed. 1058 (1925) (state's attempt to tax property over which it did not have jurisdiction violative of due process).

15. See Matter of McCarthy, 39 Misc.2d 915, 242 N.Y.S.2d 82 (New York County 1963) (non-domiciliary's intangibles in a custody and brokerage account in New York are not taxable under New York estate tax law). The issue of where a decedent is domiciled is a question of fact, discussed in chapter on "Jurisdiction," supra at 2–6.

16. Matter of Fuhrmann, 80 Misc.2d 751, 363 N.Y.S.2d 883 (Nassau 1975) (intangible personal property located in Canada and taxed by Canadian government includible in New York gross estate).

17. L.1973, c. 640, § 4; McKinney's Tax Law § 249–p–A.

18. New York could constitutionally tax such property. Utah v. Aldrich, 316 U.S. 174, 62 S.Ct. 1008, 86 L.Ed. 1358 (1942), on remand 102 Utah 233, 129 P.2d 887 (1942).

19. The New York State Constitution, article 16, section 3, provides for this exemption among states with reciprocal provisions. The legislature enacted N.Y. Tax Law 249–p–A in 1973 because some sister states were recognizing reciprocity only when it was statutory. The legislature believed that allowing the exemption by statute might eliminate some litigation on the existence of reciprocity in New York. In fact, the amendment did not change existing law. Matter of Barnett, 92 Misc. 2d 947, 401 N.Y.S.2d 969 (Bronx 1978).

Sec. E

1. I.R.C. § 2032. The alternate valuation date is the date of the month six months after death corresponding to the date of the month in which decedent died. Thus, if decedent died on Feb. 9, the alternate valuation date is Aug. 9. If there is no corresponding date, the alternate valuation date is the last day of the month six months after death. For example, if the decedent died on Aug. 31, the alternate

of death, any property distributed or sold within six months is valued at the date of distribution value.

The choice of valuation date is an all-or-nothing proposition: all assets must be valued as of the date of death or all as of the alternate valuation date, except those sold or transferred before the alternate valuation date.

Because all property owned by a decedent gets a stepped-up basis to the value used for estate tax purposes,[2] and because the threshold for estate taxability rose so drastically from 1976 to the present,[3] the legislature found it necessary to amend IRC 2032 for decedents dying after July 18, 1984. Alternate valuation can be used only if it results in a lower gross estate and reduces the taxes due.[4]

The alternate valuation provision contemplates reduction in the value of assets because of market conditions or the occurrence or non-occurrence of contingencies. The provision allowing alternate valuation was enacted after the stock market crash; its original purpose was to insure that estates which depreciated drastically shortly after death would be taxed on their realistic value. If an asset goes down in value merely because of the passage of time, such as a patent or an income interest for a person's life, then although alternate valuation can be chosen for all other assets in the estate, those naturally diminishing assets will be valued at the date of death value.[5]

2. NEW YORK

Even if a federal estate tax return was not filed, the person filing the state estate tax return can take advantage of the alternate valuation date (six months after death or the date of sale or distribution within six months of death).

SECTION F. PROCEDURE FOR FILING FEDERAL ESTATE TAX RETURN

The federal estate tax return is Form 706, and it is due nine months after the decedent's death.[1] Payment must be made when the

valuation date is Feb. 28. Rev.Rul. 74–260, CB 1974–1, 275.

2. Stepped-up basis is discussed this chapter supra at 558–59.

3. In 1976, an estate of more than $60,000 would have incurred a federal estate tax, while in 1987, estates under $600,000 will not incur federal estate taxes.

4. I.R.C. § 2032(c); P.L. 98–369, sec. 1023(a).

5. Treas.Reg. § 20.2032–1(f).

Sec. F

1. I.R.C. 6075. The nine-month date is the same date of the month nine months after decedent's death; for example, if the decedent died on Feb. 21, the due date for form 706 is Nov. 21. If there is no date of the month corresponding to the date of decedent's death, the due date is the last day of the month; for example, if the decedent died on Dec. 31, the due date is Sept. 30, and if he died on May 29, the due date is Feb. 28. If the due date is on a weekend or legal holiday, the return is due the next day that is not a weekend or holiday. Treas.Reg. § 20.6075–1.

return is filed.[2] A six-month extension of time to file can be granted for reasonable cause,[3] and the application for extension should be filed before the original due date. Regardless of the filing extension, the taxes are still due nine months after death.[4] The return should be filed at the Internal Revenue Service Center for the New York region.[5]

Unless the fiduciary can show that a return was filed late for reasonable cause, the penalty for late filing is five percent of the tax per month, up to twenty-five percent. If the tax is not paid when the return is filed, the penalty is one-half percent per month, up to twenty-five percent, but the one-half percent penalty for not paying will not be due in any month when the five percent penalty for not filing is due.[6]

Responsibility for filing is on the fiduciary, and if more than one fiduciary is serving, they should all sign the one return.[7] If no fiduciary has been appointed, the person who has the decedent's property has to file the return. The attorney should be careful to tell the fiduciary about the filing requirements; some courts have held that reliance on an attorney's advice does not relieve the fiduciary from the obligation of timely filing,[8] and presumably a fiduciary who incurs penalties to the estate could seek to recover those funds from the attorney under a malpractice theory.

Typically the return is audited and the estate representative and the Internal Revenue Service auditor often settle their differences by compromise. If after the audit the commission assesses a tax which the fiduciary claims is excessive, the fiduciary can bring an action in the Tax Court or Court of Claims before paying the taxes, or can pay the taxes and then sue in the federal district court for a refund. In the latter case he has a right to a jury trial.

SECTION G. NEW YORK ESTATE TAX PROCEEDINGS AND PROCEDURES

As a preliminary matter, the formal estate tax proceeding discussed in this section is not always necessary. In relatively small estates, the fiduciary or other interested person may be able to get

2. I.R.C. § 6151.

3. I.R.C. § 6081; Treas.Reg. § 20.6081–1(a).

4. Extensions of time to pay the tax can be obtained in certain estates with liquidity problems, see I.R.C. § 6161; I.R.C. § 6166, and in cases where reversionary interests or remainder interests are included in the gross estate under I.R.C. § 2033, but not payable until sometime in the future. I.R.C. § 6163.

5. New York City and Nassau, Suffolk, Westchester and Rockland Counties file in Holtsville, New York, and all other counties in Andover, Massachusetts.

6. I.R.C. § 6651(c)(1).

7. If they cannot do so, they must each file a return. Cs. I.R.C. § 6012(b)(5).

8. See, e.g., Matter of Boyle, ___ U.S. ___, 105 S.Ct. 687, 83 L.Ed.2d 622 (1985); Matter of Lillihei, 638 F.2d 65 (8th Cir. 1981); Matter of Fleming, 648 F.2d 1122 (7th Cir.1981). See also Matter of Rohrabaugh, 611 F.2d 211 (7th Cir.1979), where the fiduciary, once informed that the return was late, promptly filed, and the court refused to impose a penalty because of the fiduciary's good faith reliance on his attorney.

waivers and releases of lien (discussed shortly) without filing a formal petition. Moreover, even in estates where taxes are due, the fiduciary or person in charge can pay the taxes without a formal proceeding, and can obtain waivers or releases of lien to free the estate assets.[1]

If an estate tax proceeding is necessary, it does not always necessitate the appointment of a fiduciary; it can be brought by "any person in actual or constructive possession of any property required to be included in the gross estate or the New York gross estate * * *."[2]

As a final introductory word, SCPA 2002 confers on the Surrogate jurisdiction to hear issues relating to New York estate taxes,[3] and even without that authorization, the Surrogate would have such jurisdiction under SCPA 202.[4] Because of the state-wide subject matter jurisdiction conferred on Surrogates in 1984,[5] any Surrogate has the jurisdiction to hear estate tax matters, and the proper venue (which will be strictly enforced) is the county of decedent's domicile, or for a non-domiciliary, the county where his property is, or the first county where the decedent left property to exercise its jurisdiction by entertaining a petition. SCPA 2002 is a broad grant of authority;[6] under it the court can do whatever is necessary to determine the tax-related issues raised, even if it may not have had the right to decide those issues in another proceeding. For example, it can construe an unprobated will to determine whether a bequest to a spouse qualifies for the marital deduction,[7] or decide an issue of ownership of the remainder of an inter vivos trust arising between two living persons to determine whether that property passed from the decedent to his surviving spouse.[8]

1. PROCEEDING TO SET ESTATE TAX OR EXEMPT ESTATE FROM TAX

The attorney or fiduciary who finds it necessary to commence a proceeding does so in the form of a motion;[9] he files a petition[10] and notice of motion in the Surrogate's Court. The petition does not have to conform with the requirements of SCPA 304. The state tax commis-

Sec. G

1. Waivers and releases of lien are discussed this chapter infra at 570–75.

2. McKinney's SCPA 2001.

3. McKinney's SCPA 2002.

4. See McKinney's SCPA 202, discussed in chapter on "Jurisdiction," supra at 23–24.

5. See McKinney's SCPA 206, 207, L.1984, c. 128, section 2, and discussion in chapter on "Jurisdiction," supra at 1–9.

6. Matter of Ullman, 137 N.Y. 403, 33 N.E. 480 (1893) (speaking of McKinney's SCPA 2002's predecessor).

7. See Matter of Rothwachs, 57 Misc.2d 152, 290 N.Y.S.2d 781 (Kings 1968), where the court construed the decedent's will and determined that it was the joint will of the decedent and his wife containing an agreement not to revoke. Thus the wife was constrained on her death to leave what was left of the property to the named beneficiaries, and such a "terminable interest" did not qualify for the marital deduction.

8. See Matter of Conover, 46 Misc.2d 336, 259 N.Y.S.2d 618 (Westchester 1965).

9. McKinney's SCPA 2004.

10. The form for the estate tax proceeding is TT–86.5, for all decedents dying after July 1, 1978. Form TT–86, for pre-July 1, 1978 decedents whose estates required a federal estate tax return, and Form TT–87, for pre-July 1, 1978 decedents whose estates did not require a federal estate tax return, are thus superseded.

sion determines the requirements, and as a practical matter provides the forms to use as well. The petitioner also files a proposed order by which the Surrogate will either fix the tax or exempt the estate from tax "pro forma." [11] Copies of all three must be served on the state tax commission. Since in some counties the state tax commission has an office at the Surrogate's Court, the petitioner can make that service personally simply by filing the papers because the "department" of the Surrogate's Court with whom the papers are filed is in fact the state tax commission. In other counties, where the tax commission does not have an office at the court, the petitioner must file the original and a copy in the Surrogate's Court and send a copy by mail to the attorney for the state tax commission. It is a good idea to call the Surrogate's Court to find out the practice for the county.

The counties also require other documents, varying a bit from county to county, but usually including the death certificate, the federal estate tax return, if one was filed, copies of tax forms for insurance policies (Form 712), letters from employers about pensions, and similar documents. If the estate contains real property subject to a contract of sale, the petitioner has to submit the contract.

When served with the papers, the tax commission attorney can appear, consent or object.

This proceeding may be commenced shortly after death, but the usual practice, to avoid complications and problems, is to pay the New York taxes in full (estimated) within six months of the decedent's death to avoid interest,[12] and then start the tax proceeding after getting the federal closing letter. The legislature has not set a time limit for filing a state estate tax return, but the interest and penalties begin to run six months after death. In practice the fiduciary often pays the estimated taxes at that time, and then files the return after completion of the federal tax return (706).[13] No interest is charged if at least eighty percent of the tax finally determined is paid within six months and the balance is paid within nine months of death. If less than eighty percent is paid, the interest rate during the seventh month is one-half percent of unpaid tax, during the eighth month one percent, and during the ninth month one and one-half percent.[14] After nine months both interest and penalties are assessed. The interest rate changes each year on March 1 and may be adjusted on September 1. The rate of interest is equal to the yield for United States Treasury securities during the last quarter of the preceding year, but if the rate fluctuates more than two percent from the second quarter of the preceding year to the last quarter, the second quarter rate is used for the six months following September 1.[15] For example, if the interest rate for United

11. Form TP 394 (can be used for fixing or exempting from taxes); Form TP–394 (for fixing taxes); Form TP–149 (for exempting taxes).

12. McKinney's Tax L. § 249(i).

13. The federal estate tax return is due nine months after death. I.R.C. 6075, discussed supra at 562–63.

14. McKinney's Tax Law § 962.

15. McKinney's Tax L. § 262.

States Treasury securities in 1986 is eight percent during the second quarter and eleven percent during the last quarter, then from September 1986 through March 1987, the interest on unpaid taxes would be eight percent, and from March the interest would be eleven percent.

The penalty is one-half percent of the tax due for each month after nine months, but cannot exceed twenty-five percent of the tax due. The Surrogate can reduce or eliminate the penalty if he finds that the failure to pay was due to reasonable cause, or if payment was made during an extension period.

A fiduciary (or the person filing the motion) can get an extension to file the estate tax return or to pay the estate taxes. In practice no one applies solely for an extension of time to file; rather fiduciaries and attorneys seek an extension of time to pay. Obtaining the extension also forestalls the tax commissioner from appointing an appraiser if the fiduciary does not file a return within 15 months of the issuance of tax waivers. To get an extension of time to pay the taxes of up to four years from the date of death, the petitioner must show either that the total state estate taxes due exceed five percent of the net estate, or that payment within nine months of death would impose undue hardship on the estate.[16] If the extension is granted, the estate still pays the statutory interest, and the commissioner may require annual installment payments (of the taxes and interest), and it may also require a bond of up to twice the amount of unpaid taxes. The application for an extension is made to the central state tax commission office in Albany.[17]

The filing fee for an estate tax proceeding is a sliding scale starting at $20 on an estate of less than $10,000 and increasing to $600 for estates of $500,000 and over.[18]

Sometimes the federal taxes are not finally computed at the time of the state estate tax proceeding. This can happen because the federal estate tax return is due nine months after death while the state return is due six months after death (or more precisely, the interest starts to run on unpaid taxes at that point). In addition, finalization of a federal estate tax return might be delayed by the audit process, which can be protracted. When that happens, the prudent fiduciary pays the estimated state estate taxes and then waits for the conclusion of the federal proceeding. In the alternative, the Surrogate can fix the state estate taxes on the known facts, and if more state taxes become due or if the estate is entitled to a refund after completion of the federal return, the

16. McKinney's Tax L. § 249–2(6) (Supp. 1986).

17. The state has a publication entitled "Instructions for Completing Estate Tax Petition Form TT–86.5" that contains helpful information on penalties and interest payments and filing requirements. It is available from the Taxpayer Services Division in Albany. The state tax commission in Albany maintains an office for the computation of interest and penalties due on any given estate which will, upon request, compute the amount owed. Estate representatives can use this service when estimating the estate tax payments with or without interest and penalties.

18. McKinney's SCPA 2402(8).

Surrogate can under SCPA 2006 adjust the state taxes by issuing an order. Similarly, if new facts are unearthed,[19] the fiduciary (or the person in charge) or the state tax commission can apply for the supplemental determination [20] submitting a supplemental order fixing the tax for the Surrogate's signature.

The person making the motion can ask for remission of the penalty on the ground that, because of claims, litigation or other unavoidable cause of delay, the tax cannot be determined and paid.[21] The practice varies among the counties as to whether this can be part of the tax motion, or whether a separate petition must always be filed, whether a fee will be charged if the court has already entered the order fixing the taxes, and whether the taxes must be paid within a certain period to entitle the estate to a remission of penalty. If the request is not part of the original tax motion as some counties allow, the person seeking the remission of penalty files a petition for it and a proposed order. The tax commission can, of course, oppose the petition.

The applicant can seek an amended order by submitting a petition or affidavit and a proposed amended order. The petition must be submitted within two years of the original order, or within one year of the final determination of the federal taxes, if that is later.[22] The applicant will not succeed unless the tax commission consents.

2. DETERMINATION OF TAXES BY APPRAISAL

A second way of fixing the estate taxes, used quite rarely, is by appraisal. The court will order this procedure in two cases.[23] First, if a fiduciary or interested person has asked the court to fix the taxes by means of an SCPA 2004 motion, but the papers submitted in that motion do not give the court sufficient information to fix the taxes (for example, if the value of the assets is unclear or the commissioner challenges the value) and especially in estates for which a federal return was not required,[24] the court can appoint an appraiser. Secondly, if a fiduciary (or the person with possession of the decedent's property) does not commence a proceeding to fix estate taxes by eighteen months after death, and does not apply for an extension to pay estate taxes, the court can appoint an appraiser.

19. For example, the decedent may have been the beneficiary of the will of another person and final determination of that person's estate may have resulted in increased estate taxes and hence an additional credit in decedent's estate for tax on prior transfers. I.R.C. § 2013.

20. McKinney's SCPA 2006, Prac. Comm. at 330 (1967).

21. McKinney's Tax L. § 249–z(1)(f). We remind the attorney that in cases where appointment of a fiduciary is delayed, two procedures are available, one for appointment of a preliminary executor and one for appointment of a temporary administrator, and he should use those procedures to get a fiduciary in place to pay the taxes. See Matter of Jeromer, N.Y. L.J., June 12, 1985, at 13, col. 5, (New York County) (court refused to remit penalty and reminded attorneys of existence of preliminary letters).

22. McKinney's Tax Law § 962(b)(5).

23. McKinney's SCPA 2005.

24. McKinney's SCPA 2005, Prac. Comm. at 329 (1967).

The procedure is for the tax commission to file a petition seeking appointment of an appraiser, and to submit a proposed order appointing an appraiser for the Surrogate's signature. The court can direct notice to interested parties. The court directs the appraiser to fix the fair market value of the estate property and compute the taxes. The appraiser may go to the house, look at the jewelry and artwork, and evaluate the assets, or simply work from the papers the petitioner submitted to obtain waivers; it depends on the condition of the estate. After the appraiser gives his report to the court, the court issues an order fixing the tax or exempting the estate from tax. Frequently the appraiser's report fixing the tax does not consider deductions, and the taxpayer challenging this must move to vacate the order. As a matter of practice, the appraiser or the Surrogate usually consults with the estate representative before the court issues its order.

When the court fixes the tax, it must immediately give notice of it to the fiduciary (or person in charge of the estate) and to his attorney if the fiduciary has appeared by attorney.[25] No other notice is required.[26] The court must also send all orders fixing tax or exempting the estate from tax to the state tax commission.

The fiduciary or the state tax commission wishing to challenge the Surrogate's order fixing the tax or exempting the estate from tax may appeal within sixty days from entry of the order.[27] This is so whether the order was granted in an appraisal proceeding or a proceeding on a motion to fix or exempt from tax. Thus we have in New York the curious situation where the Surrogate sets the tax as a pro-forma assessing officer under SCPA 2004 and then can hear the appeal from his own order under SCPA 2008. For the procedure, the SCPA refers to section 249–x of the Tax Law, which prescribes that the fiduciary or state tax commission should file with the Surrogate a written notice of appeal stating the grounds for the appeal.[28] The Surrogate cannot hear or decide on the appeal any issues not raised in the notice of appeal.[29] The sixty day time limit does not apply if the return was fraudulent or did not include all the estate property.

The fiduciary is thus limited to the sixty-day period unless he is appealing on the ground of fraud for omitted property. He may, for example, want to collect a ratable part of the taxes from beneficiaries

25. McKinney's SCPA 2007, Practice Commentary at 75 (McKinney Supp.1986) advises fiduciaries to consult with their attorneys before paying the taxes so the attorney can ensure that the taxes are sent to the proper office with the proper interest added.

26. Prior to the enactment of McKinney's SCPA 2002, L.1966, c. 953, McKinney's Tax Law § 249–w required that interested persons also get notice. Persons interested in the McKinney's SCPA 103(39) sense have largely been eliminated as necessary parties in estate tax proceedings, since the fiduciary and the state tax commission are the only parties with a real interest.

27. McKinney's SCPA 2008.

28. McKinney's Tax Law § 249–x.

29. Matter of Rothwachs, 57 Misc.2d 152, 290 N.Y.S.2d 781 (Kings 1968) (issue of tax exemption for decedent's lineal descendants not raisable on appeal because it did not appear in the notice of appeal).

who have estate property,[30] and to avoid personal liability for missing assets.

Strict as the time limit may seem to be, the attorney may be able to avoid it by using a motion to vacate the order on the ground that it was erroneous, instead of filing an appeal. The reasoning is that the Surrogate's only jurisdiction to fix the estate tax is that prescribed by statute, and the statute does not confer jurisdiction to set the taxes erroneously. The order is, in a sense, void.[31] Although some courts have made a distinction between errors of law (where the remedy is appeal within sixty days)[32] and errors of fact (where the Surrogate can vacate his order beyond the sixty day limit),[33] it is arguable that "it is not necessary to appeal within the 60 day period where there is a mistake of law or fact and where motion has been made expeditiously upon the discovery of such error. In such a case, the Surrogate may vacate such an order and assess the proper corrected tax."[34] This rationale makes sense and is consistent with the court's general power to modify its decisions.[35]

The state tax commission has another alternative: within two years of entry of the order, he can, if he believes the order resulted from fraud, collusion or error, apply to a supreme court justice of the same county for reappraisal of the estate.[36] The appraiser reports to the Supreme Court justice who appointed him, and the justice can proceed as though it were a proceeding in the Surrogate's Court to fix taxes or exempt the estate from taxes.

A failure by the state tax commission to prosecute promptly will not necessarily result in a dismissal of the appeal if the original notice of appeal was filed timely,[37] and the state tax commission or the

30. McKinney's EPTL 2–1.8 requires that beneficiaries bear a ratable share of the estate taxes unless the will says otherwise. That section is discussed this chapter infra at 602–06.

31. Matter of Bradley, 84 Misc.2d 1007, 376 N.Y.S.2d 874 (Albany 1975); Matter of McNeil, 53 Misc.2d 677, 679, 279 N.Y.S.2d 650, 653 (Washington Co. 1967); Matter of Delafield, 109 Misc. 342, 179 N.Y.S. 762 (Bronx 1919). See also Matter of Morgan, 164 A.D. 854, 149 N.Y.S. 1022 (1st Dep't 1914), affirmed 215 N.Y. 703, 109 N.E. 1084 (1915), where the court held that the Surrogate was without jurisdiction to tax property that passed outside of decedent's estate by the terms of other instruments.

32. Matter of Palmer, 254 App.Div. 732, 6 N.Y.S.2d 139 (1st Dep't 1938).

33. Matter of Bradley, 84 Misc.2d 1007, 376 N.Y.S.2d 874 (Albany 1975).

34. Matter of Bradley, 84 Misc.2d 1007, 1011, 376 N.Y.S.2d 874, 878 (Albany 1975). But see Matter of Bunyan, 96 Misc.2d 227, 408 N.Y.S.2d 941 (Saratoga 1978) (erroneous dispensation with interest subject to appeal within sixty days).

35. McKinney's Tax Law § 249x (Supp. 1986); See H. Harris, New York Estate Practice ¶ 28:254 (4th Ed.).

36. An enterprising attorney argued in Matter of Bradley, 84 Misc.2d 1007, 376 N.Y.S.2d 874 (Albany 1975), that since McKinney's SCPA 209(9) gives the Surrogate in exercising his jurisdiction all the powers of a Supreme Court justice, he should have the power to hear the appeal up to two years after entry of the order, as a Supreme Court justice can. The court correctly ruled that he could not, because of the specificity of McKinney's Tax Law § 249–x's other language which states that the Surrogate can hear the appeal within sixty days, or without time limitations in specified exceptional circumstances.

37. Matter of Fuhrmann, 80 Misc.2d 751, 363 N.Y.S.2d 883 (Nassau 1975) (tax commission timely filed appeal but waited two and a half years until termination of federal audit before prosecuting it).

taxpayer can move for a supplemental determination of the taxes after the Internal Revenue Service audit has been finished and the final federal taxes determined.[38] If the taxpayer is entitled to a refund because of the supplemental determination, he has to apply for it within one year of the supplemental determination (or the appeal from it).[39] If the taxpayer files an amended federal return, he must within ninety days file an amended New York return, and when he gets a final determination of the federal taxes, he must report any changes within ninety days to the state tax commission.[40]

3. DISPUTE OVER THE DECEDENT'S DOMICILE

Seventeen states have enacted the Uniform Interstate Compromise of Death Taxes Act. In New York it is in Tax Law section 249–*o*. It provides that when two states claim that a decedent was domiciled there, the tax commission may enter into an agreement with the tax authorities of the other jurisdiction and with the fiduciary to pay a stated amount for state estate taxes to the two states. The tax commission or the fiduciary files the proposed agreement with the Surrogate.[41]

4. MARSHALLING ASSETS AND PAYING ESTATE TAXES WITHOUT FORMAL PROCEEDINGS

Sometimes a decedent's assets are held by an agent (such as an insurance company, corporation or bank) which is not authorized to pay the assets over without a state estate tax waiver. The law prohibits banks and other agents holding a decedent's property from delivering the property to the fiduciary or the surviving joint owner without ten days notice to the tax commission of the time and place of the intended delivery,[42] and the waiver is the statement of the tax commission waiving that ten-day notice and allowing the agent to deliver the property.

The requirement of waivers insures that the state tax authorities will be aware of the decedent's death and the extent of his property. The Department of Taxation and Finance issues these waivers, and it is entirely irrelevant whether any estate taxes are due or not. It issues waivers at the state tax commission's office at the Surrogate's Court or, in some counties, at other locations.

Waivers are not necessary when the surviving spouse receives the assets and they qualify for the marital deduction.

38. McKinney's Tax Law § 961, 962; Matter of Bomann, 66 Misc.2d 26, 319 N.Y.S.2d 757 (New York County 1971).

39. McKinney's Tax L. § 962.

40. McKinney's Tax Law § 962.

41. See H. Harris, New York Estates Practice ¶ 28:191 (4th Ed.).

42. McKinney's Tax Law § 249–cc. The bank or other agent who violates this law is responsible for the taxes, interest and penalties.

Waivers are necessary for (i) intangible assets exceeding $30,000 held by a bank or other agent,[43] (ii) life insurance exceeding $50,000 held by an insurance company payable to a beneficiary other than the surviving spouse, (iii) death benefits or pension proceeds under non-qualified plans exceeding $50,000 payable to a beneficiary other than the surviving spouse, and (iv) (currently) annuities or pension benefits under a qualified plan exceeding $100,000 payable to a beneficiary other than the decedent's estate or the surviving spouse.[44] Although waivers are not required for insurance of $50,000 or less or for annuities and pensions of $50,000 or less, whenever these assets exceed $30,000 the agent has to give notice to the state tax commission.

The waivers are needed whether the property was held by the decedent individually, in Totten Trusts ("decedent in trust for X"), or in joint name with a person other than the surviving spouse.[45] This is true even if the surviving joint owner created the account with his own funds, since the joint account is all included in the decedent's estate unless the survivor can prove his contribution.[46]

If a bank or other agent holds assets valued at $30,000 or less, it can release them without a waiver.

The reason waivers are not needed when the beneficiary is the decedent's surviving spouse is that effective October 1, 1983, the New York legislature enacted an unlimited marital deduction, so all the assets payable to the surviving spouse are free of estate taxation.[47] This exemption from waivers applies only if the surviving spouse was the only joint tenant with the decedent. If there were others, each party must prove his contribution in order to exclude the assets from gross estate.

a. Procedure for Obtaining Tax Waivers

There are two ways to get tax waivers: submitting form TT–30 or submitting form TT–102. Both can be used whether or not any taxes are due.

43. Waivers are not needed for tangible personal property held by a safe deposit company or bank because a state tax commission representative is present when the box is opened to inventory the contents. See discussion of the proceeding to open a safe deposit box in chapter on "Probate," supra at 74.

44. The $100,000 limitation is tied to the excludible amount for benefits receivable under qualified plans under McKinney's Tax Law § 954(a), (c). Since the federal law was amended on Jan. 1, 1985, P.L. 98–369 section 525(a) to eliminate this exempt amount, and consequently the federal gross estate includes all pension proceeds which fall within the I.R.C. § 2039 criteria, whether under qualified plans or not, we can expect that New York will amend its law in the near future to conform with the federal. Then the amount releasable by the employer or annuity company without waivers will undoubtedly be reduced to $50,000, with a requirement of notice to the tax commission if the amount is over $30,000. The exception when the spouse is beneficiary will stay in effect.

The same rule applies to Individual Retirement Accounts within the income tax limits.

45. See Dept. Taxation and Finance Pamphlet TT–861.

46. Jointly owned property is discussed this chapter infra at 579–82.

47. L.1982, c. 916, § 5, McKinney's Tax Law § 955.

i. TT–102

Form TT–102 is called the "Resident Affidavit." It is the only way to get waivers if no fiduciary is serving or if more than eighteen months have passed since the decedent's death. The TT–102 is used when the representative wants to obtain a release of lien on real property or tax waivers on other assets, wants to make an estimated tax payment to avoid interest and penalties, or wants to close out a relatively simple and small estate, where for example most of the assets are held jointly. It is useful in estates where the family does not intend to file for appointment of an executor or administrator because all the decedent's assets can be transferred without such appointment and the attorney's and filing fees for such appointment would be wasteful.

The TT–102 requires information about the decedent, his date of death, his domicile, and his assets. If a federal estate tax return was filed, it must be attached to the TT–102.[48] The TT–102 also includes a computation of the estate taxes. The TT–102 computation permits only four deductions: the funeral expenses, the marital deduction, the charitable deduction, and mortgages on real property. It does not allow deductions for administration expenses, losses during estate administration, or debts. This feature makes the TT–102 less attractive than the formal estate tax proceeding of SCPA 2004 in estates that have substantial deductions. The general credit of $2,750, which wipes out the tax on an estate of less than $108,000, is available on the TT–102.

Another disadvantage of the TT–102 procedure versus the formal SCPA 2004 proceeding in estates that are at or near the $108,000 threshold for state estate taxation is that although joint property can be excluded from the gross estate of a decedent when the surviving joint owner can prove a contribution, that proof is usually not allowed on a TT–102, and therefore the whole value of the joint property is considered to be part of the gross estate unless the joint owner was the decedent's surviving spouse.

The person submitting the TT–102 has to attach a death certificate and a copy of the will if there was one, and also must pay the taxes (plus interest and penalties)[49] if any are due.

The attorney may complete the affidavit for the client if he has obtained a power of attorney.[50]

If the decedent's will creates a trust, the applicant has to list the trust beneficiaries and their ages. The Tax Department will issue the waivers after it receives the form, the check, the death certificate and the will.

48. In that case the TT–102 need not be fully completed; the schedules listing assets (pages 2 and 3) may be omitted. If the taxpayer opts to complete only the first three pages of the federal estate tax return, however (permissible in estates less than $500,000), he must complete the entire TT–102.

49. Interest and penalties are discussed supra at 563.

50. A power of attorney specifically tailored for the TT–102 is available from the court.

The clerk in the tax office (which is in the Surrogate's Court in some counties, or otherwise at the regional office in Albany) can issue the waivers immediately to the applicant who brings in the form and the necessary documents if less than eighteen months have passed since the decedent's death and the decedent was a resident of the county where the application is made. If the gross estate is under $100,000, the clerk can issue waivers for all the assets. If the estate if over $100,000, the clerk will issue waivers on $50,000 worth of assets immediately if the applicant pays the taxes due, and the remaining waivers will be issued from the central office in Albany.

The applicant presents the waivers to the bank or other agent which is then authorized to release the assets.

When a decedent's real property is sold after his death, the title company will require a release of lien to show that all state estate taxes were paid. The fiduciary or person in charge can use the TT–102 to obtain a release of lien to authorize transfer of the property. The applicant has to check with the County Clerk's office in the county where the realty is located to find out what information is required for the recording of the release of lien. On the back of the TT–102, the applicant must list this information, which may include the address of the property, the section, lot and block number, the liber and page number, the tax map number (if available), or a description of the metes and bounds of the property. In practice the applicant can get this information from the deed. The applicant should submit an additional copy of the TT–102, a description of the property by metes and bounds on a separate sheet of letter-sized paper, and a check for $10.00 for the release of lien. If the decedent had real property in more than one New York county, the applicant can apply for releases for all the real property in the same form but must submit a $10 check for each county (even if more than one piece of real property is located in a county).

If the taxpayer applies for a release of lien and it is denied, the state estate tax lien on the property continues for six years from the denial.[51] If the taxpayer never applies for a release of lien, the lien on the realty continues for fifteen years from the date of death.[52]

If a decedent owned real property jointly with a survivor, most title companies accept the death certificate and do not require a release of lien to insure title. If the surviving joint owner is not the decedent's spouse, however, it is advisable to obtain the release of lien, because on the survivor's death, the persons entitled to the property have to get releases of lien on both estates, and information on the taxable assets of the first decedent may be difficult to obtain at the time of the later death. For joint owners married to each other dying after September 30, 1983, it is no longer necessary to obtain the release of lien when the surviving spouse succeeds to full ownership of the property, because the

51. McKinney's Tax Law § 249–11.

52. McKinney's Tax Law § 249–11.

unlimited marital deduction eliminates any estate taxes on that property in the first decedent's estate.[53]

If the fiduciary or other person submitting the TT–102 pays an amount for taxes which later turns out to be too much, he cannot get a refund without a formal tax motion under SCPA 2004 unless the error was made by the tax commission. He cannot get a remission of penalty or amend the TT–102 without starting formal tax motions for that relief. Nor are final receipts issued on a TT–102 as they are in a formal tax proceeding.[54]

The TT–102 is not a matter of public record. Unlike the formal tax motion, it is filed in the office of the state tax commission, not in the record room of the Surrogate's Court. Some practitioners prefer to make a motion to fix the tax because such a motion remains a matter of record and can assist in establishing the income tax basis of the property.

ii. TT–30

The other way of obtaining tax waivers is to use the TT–30, called the "Application for Waivers." It is a simpler form than the TT–102 and can be used only if an executor or administrator is serving and not more than eighteen months have passed since the decedent's death. It must be filed by the executor or administrator or an attorney-in-fact for the executor or administrator.

The application lists information about the decedent, including his domicile and marital status. It states whether a tax proceeding has been filed. It lists the value of the gross estate.

The fiduciary must attach to the TT–30 the death certificate and a copy of his letters testamentary or letters of administration. He need not compute the state estate taxes; if the estate is large enough that it is likely to incur a tax, the tax commission may withhold waivers on some of the property, although in practice it frequently issues waivers for all the assets as requested.

iii. Waivers for Non-domiciliaries

Naturally, New York banks and other agents cannot release assets belonging to non-domiciliary decedent's without waivers, and the application for waivers in those cases is the "Estate Tax Domicile Affidavit."[55] That form has to list specifically the real estate, bank accounts and other intangible assets located in New York, and the same rates of tax are applied to the New York situs property as for New York domiciliaries. The affidavit elicits information on the decedent's domicile: where he voted, whether he owned or rented his home, where his vehicles were registered, where his income taxes were filed, the nature

53. See discussion of the marital deduction this chapter supra at 592–96.

54. McKinney's Tax L. § 249z(b).

55. TT–141A.

of his business activities within and without the state, where the church and clubs of which he was a member were located. The applicant can also obtain a release of lien for New York real property by submitting this affidavit, and the information required with the TT–102, discussed above.

SECTION H. ELEMENTS OF THE GROSS ESTATE

The estate tax computation, both state and federal, starts with the gross estate. The next sections will discuss what assets are included in the gross estate.

1. PROPERTY OWNED

a. Federal

Under IRC 2033, the gross estate includes "property to the extent of the interest therein of the decedent at the time of his death." Thus, any property in the decedent's individual name, such as artwork, cash, furniture, stamp collections, bank accounts, including those in Totten Trust form ("decedent in trust for X"), insurance policies on lives of other people,[1] remainder interests in property,[2] automobiles, partnership interests, stocks and bonds,[3] and property owned by decedent as a tenant in common with others, are included in the gross estate.[4] If the decedent had no interest in the property at death, IRC 2033 will not include it in the gross estate. For example, if a decedent had nothing but a right to income for his life from a trust created by someone other than himself, at his death the property is not included in his estate;[5] the lump sum payment by Social Security to help defray funeral expenses is not included;[6] and the proceeds of a wrongful death cause of action are not included.[7]

Sec. H

1. Includibility of life insurance on decedent's own life is discussed this chapter infra at 577–79.

2. These interests are valued by use of the actuarial charts found in Treas.Reg. § 20.2031–1(10)(e).

3. Valuation of these assets is discussed in the Treasury Regulations to IRC 2031.

4. Includibility of property owned with others in joint ownership with right of survivorship is discussed this chapter, infra at 579–82.

5. Davis v. United States, 27 F.Supp. 698 (S.D.N.Y.1939).

6. Rev.Rul. 55–87, 1955–1 C.B. 112.

7. Matter of Connecticut Bank and Trust Co., 465 F.2d 760 (2d Cir.1972). Wrongful death proceeds are not included whether the state law governing wrongful death actions makes such causes of action a right of the distributees, as in New York, or whether they are an "asset" of the decedent's which passed from him to his distributees or beneficiaries. See Rev.Rule. 75–127, 1975–1 C.B. 297 (acquiescing in this point). The rationale for such largesse is that no one uses wrongful death as an estate planning technique. On the other hand, the decedent did have an interest in the personal injuries action, and that recovery is includible in his gross estate. See chapter on "Wrongful Death," supra at 527 et seq.

Interest on property accrued before the date of death is included, and dividends on stock declared to shareholders of record before the decedent's death are included.[8]

b. New York

New York law conforms with federal on the type of property included in gross estate. As we mentioned above, however, real property and tangible personal property located outside New York will not be included in the New York gross estate.

2. TRANSFERS WITHIN THREE YEARS OF DEATH

a. Federal

The current federal rule generally excludes gratuitous transfers of property within three years of death from the decedent's gross estate.[9] The exceptions can be grouped into two categories. First, if a decedent owned or had incidents of ownership in a life insurance policy, and within three years of death gave the policy away or gave up the incidents of ownership, the proceeds of the policy are included in his gross estate. Secondly, if a decedent had previously transferred property but retained an interest sufficient to cause inclusion in his gross estate under IRC 2036, 2037 or 2038,[10] such as an income interest, or a power to change a trust, or a 2037 reversionary interest, the release of that interest within three years of death will cause inclusion.[11]

Any gift taxes paid on any transfers within three years of death are included in the gross estate.[12] This was added to the law as of Jan. 1, 1977 because without this provision, a person could make a large taxable death-bed gift, and though the gift itself would figure into the estate tax computation (pre-1981 as part of the gross estate, or post-1980 as an adjusted taxable gift), the gift taxes would not, so the

8. Treas.Reg. § 20–2033–1(b).

9. I.R.C. § 2035(d). Before Jan. 1, 1977, the rule was that property transferred within three years of death was includible if transferred "in contemplation of death." This was a question of fact, and most taxpayers were astute enough to avail themselves of a jury trial (by paying the taxes and suing in the federal district court for a refund). When a jury was the trier of fact, the government had a rather low success rate. The taxpayers typically pointed to the decedent's vim and vigor (despite his advanced age), his zest, his income tax motives for the gifts; they would often prevail on a clergyman to testify about the decedent's love for life and upbeat attitude. See, e.g., Matter of Oliver Johnson, 10 T.C. 680 (1948) (decedent jumped up and clicked heels together, stood up without touching the arms of the chair, pitched horseshoes and made frequent ringers, sported a head of thick, iron-grey hair); Matter of Kniskern, 232 F.Supp. 7 (D.Fla.1964) (decedent emptied his own wastebasket, went for rides with his maid, showed home movies, worked with a sledgehammer).

From Jan. 1, 1977 through Dec. 31, 1980, all gratuitous transfers within three years of death were included in decedent's gross estate.

Since Jan. 1, 1981, no transfers except those mentioned in the text are included. I.R.C. § 2035.

10. Discussed this chapter infra at 584–88.

11. I.R.C. § 2035(d).

12. I.R.C. § 2035(c).

transferor would have successfully removed that sum as part of his taxable assets.[13]

Property included in the gross estate under IRC 2035 is included at its date of death value. Thus, if a decedent transferred shares of X Corporation valued at $5,000 to his son in 1983 and retained the right to the dividends, and in 1984 he relinquished that right, and he died in 1986 when the shares were worth $10,000, $10,000 would be included in his estate. If the son had sold the X stock and used the proceeds to buy Y stock, which at the decedent's death were worth $8,000, $10,000 would be included, since that was the date of death value of the actual property transferred.[14]

b. New York

The New York rule on transfers within three years of death is substantively the same as the federal, but the effective dates of the various changes are different. Gifts made through 1982 and within three years of decedent's death are included.[15]

3. LIFE INSURANCE

a. Federal

The federal gross estate includes proceeds of life insurance [16] on the decedent's life in four cases: first, if the proceeds are payable to the decedent's estate; [17] second, if the decedent owned the policy; [18] third, if the decedent had "incidents of ownership" in the policy; [19] and fourth, if he relinquished ownership or incidents of ownership within three years of his death.[20] Incidents of ownership are any economic controls over the policy, including the right to change beneficiaries, assign or surrender the policy, pledge the policy as collateral for a loan,[21] or change the time or manner of payment.[22] If the policy or the proceeds may revert to the decedent, that reversionary interest is considered an

13. This highlights an important difference between the gift tax and the estate tax. The estate tax is imposed on the whole estate available for transfer to the beneficiaries (including the estate tax), while the gift tax is imposed only on the property transferred, not including the gift tax.

14. See Rev.Rul. 72–282, 1972–1 C.B. 306.

15. McKinney's Tax Law § 954(a)(3) (Supp.1984–85).

16. Life insurance is an arrangement in which the risk of death is shifted away from the decedent and distributed among a class of people. Matter of Treganowan, 183 F.2d 288 (2d Cir.1950). See Rev.Rule 83–44, 1983–11 IRB 6 (death benefits under no-fault insurance policy included in the definition of life insurance for IRC 2042 purposes because risk was shifted and distributed). Life insurance includes accidental death insurance. Matter of Noel, 380 U.S. 678, 85 S.Ct. 1238, 14 L.Ed.2d 159 (1965).

17. I.R.C. § 2042(1). If the proceeds are payable to another party who, either voluntarily (perhaps a spouse) or under a discretionary power (such as a trustee) transfers part of the insurance proceeds to the estate to pay taxes and administration expenses or to alleviate liquidity problems, they will be included in gross estate to the extent they were paid to the estate. Treas. Reg. § 20.2042(1)(b)(1).

18. I.R.C. § 2042(2).

19. I.R.C. § 2042(2).

20. I.R.C. § 2035(d).

21. Treas.Reg. § 20.2042–1(c)(2).

22. Treas.Reg. § 20.2042–1(c)(4).

incident of ownership if it is actuarially worth more than five percent of the proceeds,[23] and the proceeds of that policy are includible in the gross estate. The reversion is considered to be worth less than five percent if someone other than the decedent had a right to cash the policy in just before the decedent's death.[24]

The contract of insurance (that is, the policy itself) determines whether the decedent had incidents of ownership. It is irrelevant that he never intended to exercise them,[25] or that it would have been physically impossible to exercise them.[26] It is therefore important to read the small print of the policy if the goal is to remove the insurance from the gross estate.

When a decedent has incidents of ownership only in his capacity as trustee of the trust that owns the policy, and when he cannot exercise them for his own benefit, the proceeds will not be included in his gross estate.[27]

If a decedent has a controlling interest in a corporation (more than fifty percent of the voting stock), the corporation's incidents of ownership are attributed to him if the proceeds are payable to a third party for a non-business reason, but they are not if the proceeds are payable to the corporation or to a third party for a business reason.[28] The rationale is that if the proceeds are payable to the corporation or to defray one of the corporation's obligations, their value will be reflected in the value of the corporation and hence the decedent's estate will include them in the value of the stock. If they are payable to third

23. I.R.C. § 2042(2).

24. Treas.Reg. § 20.2042–1(c)(3).

25. See Matter of Rhode Island Hospital Trust Co., 355 F.2d 7 (1st Cir.1966), where a father bought life insurance on his sons' lives to protect his wife if he predeceased her. It was everyone's intention that the father should retain and exercise all control over the policies, which he did, but the terms of the policies themselves gave incidents of ownership to the sons. When one of the sons died, the insurance was included in that son's estate.

26. See Matter of Noel, 380 U.S. 678, 85 S.Ct. 1238, 14 L.Ed.2d 159 (1965), where the husband bought life insurance to cover him on an airplane flight, and gave the policy to his wife. He did not have possession of the policies and therefore could not have changed the beneficiaries, but the proceeds were nevertheless included because he possessed the power.

If, however, under state law the decedent could not have exercised the powers, the proceeds may be excluded. See Matter of Morton, 457 F.2d 750 (4th Cir.1972) (decedent's irrevocable designation of beneficiary effectively made it impossible for him to exercise any of the incidents of ownership he technically had); Matter of Beauregard, 74 T.C. 603 (1980) (husband's separation agreement made his promise to keep insurance in effect for his children enforceable and he consequently could not exercise his power under the policy to change beneficiaries).

27. Rev.Rul. 84–179, 1984–53 I.R.B. 7. If the decedent bought the policy or participated in a pre-arranged plan under which the incidents of ownership were to devolve to him, Rev.Rul. 84–179 would include the proceeds. See Matter of Skifter, 468 F.2d 699 (2d Cir.1972), where the decedent's estate did not include insurance which decedent had transferred more than three years before his death to his wife, who subsequently died and left the policies to the trust of which decedent was trustee, and Matter of Hunter, 624 F.2d 833 (8th Cir.1980) (in accord with Skifter). Matter of Rose, 511 F.2d 259 (5th Cir.1975), where the court included the proceeds on facts similar to those in Skifter, and Matter of Terriberry, 517 F.2d 286 (5th Cir.1975), certiorari denied 424 U.S. 977, 96 S.Ct. 1484, 47 L.Ed.2d 748 (1976) (in accord with Rose), are no longer valid.

28. Treas.Reg. § 20.2042–1(c)(6).

parties for other reasons, however, the arrangement is peculiarly testamentary and the decedent's effective control of the corporation imputes to him whatever incidents of ownership the corporation had.

b. New York

New York law conforms with federal law on the includibility of life insurance. The inclusion of life insurance transferred by the decedent within three years of his death is consistent with federal law, though its effective date (Jan. 1, 1983) was later than that of the federal (Jan. 1, 1977).

4. JOINTLY OWNED PROPERTY

a. Federal

If a decedent had an interest in property as a tenant in common with other people, his share passes on his death to his will beneficiaries or intestate distributees and is included in his gross estate as property he owned under IRC 2033. If he owned the property with another with a right of survivorship, IRC 2040 governs.

The amount included under IRC 2040 depends on whether or not the joint owners were husband and wife. Married joint owners have the rule of one-half inclusion, and non-married joint owners have the rule of "consideration-tracing."

i. Married Joint Owners

If a husband and wife own property jointly with a right of survivorship or by the entirety, and if no one else has an interest in the property, when the first one dies, the estate includes one-half of all jointly owned property.[29] The one-half that is included in the decedent's gross estate is eligible for the marital deduction because it passes to the surviving spouse,[30] and only one-half of the property gets a stepped-up basis for income tax purposes.[31]

This rule of one-half inclusion has been effective since January 1, 1982. The law has changed fast and furiously in this area. For decedents dying before Jan. 1, 1977, the rule for all joint owners, regardless of their marital status, was that the survivor had to prove a contribution or the whole property would be included in the decedent's estate.[32] For decedents dying between Jan. 1, 1977 and Dec. 31, 1981, the married persons had an option. If they opted to do nothing when they first placed the property in joint names, at the death of the first spouse the survivor would have to prove a contribution to the property; or they could "qualify" the joint ownership, which meant treating it as

29. I.R.C. § 2040(b).

30. The marital deduction is discussed this chapter infra at 592–96.

31. I.R.C. § 1014, discussed this chapter infra at 558–59.

32. P.L. 94–455, sec. 2002(c)(1).

a gift when the joint ownership was created,[33] and then when the first spouse died one half would be included in the gross estate.

ii. Non-married Joint Owners

If the joint owners were not married to each other, or if there were joint owners in addition to a husband and wife, when the first joint owner dies, the property is included entirely in his estate unless the survivor can show that he contributed toward the property and that he did not receive the money or property he contributed from the decedent.[34] For example, if a mother makes yearly cash gifts to her daughter of $5,000, and after ten years they purchase a $100,000 house jointly with right of survivorship, the daughter paying the $50,000 she received from her mother, when the mother dies the whole value of the house will be included in her gross estate, since the daughter cannot prove any contribution that did not originate with the mother.

If the survivor can prove a contribution from his own funds, the amount excluded from the decedent's estate is that part of the date of death value of the property proportionate to the survivor's contribution.[35] For instance, if D and his friend F bought stock jointly, D contributing $5,000 and F contributing $10,000, and at D's death the stock had appreciated to $30,000, D's estate will include $10,000, as long as F can prove that he did not get any part of his contribution from D.

iii. Some Rules On Tracing The Consideration

A few rulings and cases address the issue of when money or property is considered to have come originally from the decedent and when it is not. If a person makes a gift of property outright to a donee, the property earns income, and the donee uses the income to purchase property jointly with the donor, the income is considered the donee's contribution.[36] Similarly, if after the gift to the donee the property appreciates in value and the donee sells it, the appreciation is considered to be the donee's contribution.[37] For example, if a decedent transfers X stock, valued at $10,000, to the donee, the donee later sells it at $30,000 and uses the $30,000 to buy property in joint name with the decedent, $20,000 of that $30,000 (two-thirds) is considered to be the donee's contribution. If when the decedent dies the property is worth

33. If a married person placed personal property in joint name with his spouse, he would have to file a gift tax return showing a gift of one-half of the property to the spouse. Creation of a joint tenancy in real property was not a gift from one spouse to another, but under I.R.C. § 2515 (repealed McKinney's P.L. 97–34, § 403), the donor spouse could opt to treat it as a gift and file a gift tax return. If the couple took the steps necessary to treat the joint tenancy as a gift when created, or after the enactment of 2515, on the death of the first it was included one-half in the gross estate with no requirement of tracing the consideration paid.

34. I.R.C. § 2040.

35. I.R.C. § 2040(a).

36. Matter of Goldsborough, 70 T.C. 1077 (1978).

37. Harvey v. United States, 185 F.2d 463 (7th Cir.1950); First National Bank v. United States, 223 F.Supp. 963 (W.D.Mo. 1963).

$60,000, only $20,000 will have to be included in the decedent's estate, because the other $40,000 is traceable to the donee's contribution.

On the other hand, if the donor does not transfer the property outright to the donee, but places in in joint name with the donee, income earned by the jointly owned property is attributed one-half to each, and appreciation is considered all the donor's.[38] For example, if the decedent placed stock valued at $10,000 in joint name with a friend, and the stock earned $2,000 in dividends and appreciated to $18,000, and the decedent sold it and used the $20,000 to purchase property in joint name with the friend, only one-twentieth would be traceable to the friend ($1,000 of the income and none of the appreciation).

If improvements are made to jointly owned property, their cost is attributed to the person who paid for them, as is the proportion of the appreciation attributable to the improvements. For example, if D placed a house valued at $60,000 in joint name with X, and when it had appreciated to $100,000, X added a wing at a cost of $60,000, and D later died when the house was worth $320,000, $200,000 would be included in D's gross estate (as long as X could prove that his contribution did not originally come from D). That figure represents D's original $100,000 contribution plus five-eighths of the $160,000 appreciation (that is, $100,000/$160,000, representing the proportion of his contribution to the total cost of the house).

If a mortgage remains on jointly owned property, and each of the joint owners has personal liability for it, the mortgage will be attributed proportionately to each joint owner for purposes of tracing consideration. For example, assume D and his friend bought a $100,000 house, paying $10,000 each as a down payment and obtaining a mortgage of $80,000. Assume further that D alone paid off $20,000 of the mortgage, and that at D's death the house was still worth $100,000. On these facts $60,000 would be included in D's estate:[39] his $30,000 actual dollar contribution plus one-half of the remaining mortgage. (That amount of the mortgage would also be deductible from the gross estate as a debt of the fiduciary, creating a "wash" situation.) If the house had appreciated to $180,000, D's estate would include $108,000: his actual dollar contribution ($30,000), plus one half of the remaining mortgage ($30,000) plus sixty percent of the appreciation ($48,000), because his contribution at the time of death was sixty percent of the total, and the friend's was forty percent (that is, the friend's $10,000 cash contribution plus $30,000 of the outstanding mortgage).

b. *New York*

As in the federal estate tax, property owned jointly by a husband and wife with right of survivorship and property they owned by the

38. Matter of Endicott, 305 F.Supp. 943 (N.D.N.Y.1969).

39. See Rev.Rul. 79–302, 1966–1 C.B. 221.

entirety is included one-half in the estate of the first of them to die.[40] This one-half inclusion is effective for decedents dying after September 30, 1983. New York law evolved like the federal, only later: For decedents dying through June 30, 1978, the consideration-tracing rule now applicable to non-married persons applied, so the survivor had to prove a contribution that did not come from the decedent,[41] and for decedents dying between July 1, 1978 and September 30, 1983, the married joint owners had the option to include one-half of the property if they "qualified" it by treating it as a gift at its creation, or to trace the consideration for jointly held interests that they did not qualify.[42] In other respects the New York law conforms with the federal.

5. ANNUITIES AND PENSION PLANS

a. *Federal*

Many decedents have retirement plans with their employers and some have commercial annuities. If post-death benefits are payable to a beneficiary, their value may be included in the decedent's gross estate under IRC 2039.

Pensions and annuities are includible if four elements are present. First, the decedent must have had a right to an annuity or other payment during his life. These payments need not be regular; they may be uneven in amount and sporadic.[43] The decedent's right to payments has been interpreted to mean the right to something other than salary, that is, the right to some post-employment benefits.[44] It is irrelevant that the decedent was not yet receiving them at his death, so long as he had a right to receive them later (for instance, at retirement).[45] The courts have split on includibility if the only payment to which the decedent had a right was a disability payment payable on the very remote possibility that the decedent became totally disabled before retirement.[46]

Second, the decedent's right to receive these payments must have been for life or for a period somehow measured by the time of his death.[47]

40. I.R.C. § 2040(b).

41. McKinney's Tax Law § 954(a), (d).

42. McKinney's Tax Law § 954(a), (d).

43. Treas.Reg. § 20.2039–1(b).

44. See Matter of Bahen, 305 F.2d 827 (U.S. Court of Claims 1962); Matter of Fusz, 46 T.C. 214 (1966), acq. 1967–2 C.B. 2.

45. Treas.Reg. § 20.2039–1(b)(1).

46. Compare Matter of Bahen, 305 F.2d 827 (U.S. Court of Claims 1962) (decedent's right to disability payments sufficient to cause inclusion of benefits received by beneficiary after decedent's death), and Matter of Schelberg, 612 F.2d 25 (2d Cir.1979) (decedent's remote possibility of receiving disability payments insufficient to meet the "right to payments" element of section 2039), with Matter of Looney, 569 F.Supp. 1569 (M.D.Ga.1983).

47. The statute prescribes three periods, "for life," (self-explanatory), "for a period not ascertainable without reference to his death" (for example, payments every quarter except the last quarter before his death, or payments for the rest of his life after A's death), or "for a period which does not in fact end before his death" (for example, payments for five years, and decedent dies in year 4). See Treas.Reg. § 20–2039–1(b)(1), incorporating § 20.2036–1(b)(1)(i), (ii).

Third, a beneficiary must, by surviving the decedent, succeed to a right to receive an annuity or other payment.

Fourth, the rights of the decedent and the beneficiary must stem from a contract or other arrangement, and in practice the courts will look to all the agreements the decedent had with his employer or the annuity company and read them together to see whether the elements necessary for inclusion are there.[48]

If a decedent's estate is caught under IRC 2039, the amount included is that part of the value of the payments receivable by the decedent's beneficiary that is proportionate to the decedent's contributions made by the decedent and his employer. Thus, if a decedent purchased an annuity for a lump sum, and the annuity company agreed to pay him $200 monthly for his life and his spouse $200 monthly for life after his death, the decedent's gross estate would include the present value, computed actuarially [49] of the right of a person the spouse's age to receive $200 monthly for life.

The rules just stated apply whether the plan is "qualified" for income tax purposes [50] or not, but that was not always the case. From Jan. 1, 1977 through Dec. 31, 1982, the proceeds of a qualified pension plan were excluded from the gross estate unless they were paid in a lump sum [51] or paid to the estate. From Jan. 1, 1983 to Dec. 31, 1984, only $100,000 from a qualified plan was excludible, and as of Jan. 1, 1985, the entire amount is includible. If the pension is payable to the surviving spouse, it is eligible for the marital deduction.

Individual Retirement Accounts are subject to the same rules as other annuities.[52] Their treatment has paralleled that of qualified plans; they were, until December 31, 1982, excluded from gross estate to the extent they qualified for income tax exclusion if they were payable over at least three years, and they were subject to the $100,000 exclusion from Jan. 1, 1983 through Dec. 31, 1984, and they are currently includible in the decedent's gross estate.

b. New York

New York law conforms with the federal law in the area of annuities.

48. See, e.g., Matter of Bahen, 305 F.2d 827 (U.S.Ct.Cl.1962) (court read together a "death benefit" plan which would not have caused inclusion and a "deferred compensation" plan to include the death benefits in decedent's gross estate); Matter of Montgomery, 458 F.2d 616 (5th Cir.1972), certiorari denied 409 U.S. 849, 93 S.Ct. 58, 34 L.Ed.2d 91 (1972) (court read together an annuity contract and a life insurance policy issued by the same company to satisfy all the elements of I.R.C. § 2039).

49. See Treas.Reg. § 20.2031-10(e). Actuarial computations as of November 30, 1983 are done on a unisex basis using a ten percent interest rate. Prior to that date they were computed along gender lines, and the interest rate was six percent.

50. I.R.C. § 401 et seq.

51. If they were paid in a lump sum, the beneficiary had a choice of foregoing a favorable income tax treatment (ten-year averaging) and if he did so, the pension proceeds could be excluded from the gross estate. If the beneficiary opted for ten year averaging, the value of the pension had to be included in the decedent's gross estate. I.R.C. § 2039(f).

52. I.R.C. § 2039.

6. TRANSFERS "WITH STRINGS ATTACHED"

Three sections of the Internal Revenue Code include in the gross estate property the decedent gratuitously transferred to others during his lifetime but over which he retained certain powers. The decedent's retained control makes the transfer look inherently testamentary and the theory is that it is therefore justifiable to tax it.

a. Transfers With Retained Powers—Federal

IRC 2036 and 2038 overlap a great deal and will therefore be treated first.

IRC 2036 includes in the gross estate property the decedent transferred for inadequate consideration if he retained the right to income, the right to determine who will get the income, the right to possession or enjoyment of the property, or the right to determine who will possess or enjoy the property. For example, if the decedent transferred his car to another but retained the right to use it whenever he wanted, or transferred stocks but retained the right to dividends, or, more frequently, transferred property to a trust and named himself income beneficiary, the car, stock and the entire trust corpus would be included in his gross estate. If a decedent directs that income be used to discharge his legal obligation, he has retained income to that extent. For example, if the decedent has a duty to support his son, and creates a trust directing the trustee to pay the income to support the son, if he dies while he still has the support obligation, the trust will be included in his estate.[53] Even an informal reservation of the right to enjoy the property will snag the decedent. If, for example, a decedent transferred his house to his daughter but they tacitly understood that he could stay in it, IRC 2036 would operate to include the house in the decedent's gross estate when he later died still living there.[54] An exception is made for spouses: the transfer of a house to a spouse with the informal understanding that the transferor will stay there is not considered a reserved interest because a person may have many non-tax reasons for living in the same house with his spouse.[55]

The decedent must have retained the power for his life or another period somehow measured in terms of his life.[56]

53. Treas.Reg. § 20–2036–1(b)(2).

54. See, e.g., Matter of McNichol, 265 F.2d 667 (3d Cir.1959), certiorari denied 361 U.S. 829, 80 S.Ct. 78, 4 L.Ed.2d 71 (1959); Matter of Honigman, 66 T.C. 1080, CCH Dec. 34,039 (1976). If the daughter also moved into the house and the decedent effectively retained an interest in only a part of the house, a good argument could be made that only a portion of the value of the house should be included.

55. See Matter of Gutchess, 46 T.C. 554, CCH Dec. 28,067 (1966).

56. The statute prescribes three periods, "for life" (self-explanatory), "for a period not ascertainable without reference to his death" (for example, payments every quarter except the last quarter before his death, or payments for the rest of his life after A's death), or "for a period which does not in fact end before his death" (for example, payments for five years, and decedent dies in year four). See Treas.Reg. § 20.2036–1(b)(1)(i), (ii).

If a decedent is snagged by section 2036, the property included is that proportion of the property over which he retained the power. For example, if the decedent retained the right to income from (or other IRC 2036 power over) one-half of the transferred property, then one-half of the entire property is included in his estate.

The decedent's estate must include such property even if the decedent needed the consent of another person to use or enjoy the property and even if that person had an interest in the property substantially adverse to the decedent's exercise of his retained power.[57]

A decedent is considered to have a 2036 "string" attached to the transferred property even if his right or power springs into being only upon the occurrence (or non-occurrence) of a contingency, and that contingency in fact had not yet occurred at his death.[58] For example, if the decedent created a lifetime trust, income to the spouse for life, then if spouse predeceased, income to decedent for life, remainder to their children, and the decedent predeceased his spouse, his estate will still be snagged by IRC 2036; it is irrelevant that the contingency (surviving the spouse) had not occurred. The estate would include the full corpus of the trust less the actuarial value of the spouse's intervening life income interest.

The general rule of IRC 2038 is that the decedent's gross estate includes property the decedent transferred for inadequate consideration if he retained a right to revoke, amend, alter or terminate the terms of the transfer, and if he possessed that power at the time of death.[59] or relinquished it within three years of death.

The focus in IRC 2038 is on the time of death rather than the "lifetime" periods of IRC 2036. Thus, if the decedent's power was contingent on an event which had not occurred at decedent's death, IRC 2038 does not snag the property.[60] For example, if the decedent created a trust and reserved the right to eliminate one of the remaindermen if that remainderman divorced his spouse, 2038 would not include the property if the remainderman had not divorced his spouse at the time of decedent's death.[61] If the decedent did possess a power to change or revoke the trust, however, his estate will have to include the trust even

57. Treas.Reg. § 20–2036–1(b)(3)(i). This rule is stricter than that applying to powers of appointment, which excludes property if the decedent could exercise his power only with the consent of a person with a substantial adverse interest. See discussion of powers of appointment this chapter infra at 588–92. The reason is that I.R.C. § 2036 property actually belonged to the decedent and the test should be stricter than for IRC 2041 property, which belonged to someone other than the decedent.

58. Treas.Reg. § 20.2036–1(b)(3)(iii).

59. If the decedent had the power but had to give notice to the trustee before exercising it, he is deemed to have had the power at death even though he had not given the notice. I.R.C. § 2038.

60. Treas.Reg. § 20.2038–1(b).

61. Arguably, neither would I.R.C. § 2036. Though the statute says that 2036 will include property over which the decedent retained the right to determine who will enjoy the property, the regulations, 20.2036–1(b)(3) state that 2036 will not include property unless the decedent had a right to affect the payment of the income during his lifetime.

though he could not possibly enjoy any economic benefits himself, and even if his only power was to alter the time or manner of the beneficiary's enjoyment or possession.[62] For example, if the decedent's only power was to accumulate the income of a trust and pay it to the income beneficiary later, the income component of the trust (the actuarial value of the income beneficiary's right to income) would be included in his gross estate at death.

It is irrelevant that the decedent could exercise his power only with the consent of another person, even if that person had a substantial adverse interest.[63] However, the retention by the creator of an inter vivos trust of a power to amend the trust with the consent of all the trust beneficiaries will not, by itself, cause 2038 inclusion of the trust in the decedent's gross estate.[64] The reason is that every New York creator of an inter vivos trust has that power under New York law,[65] and if such power were sufficient to trigger 2038, conceivably every inter vivos trust (except those that specifically denied the creator this power) would be includible under 2038.

Unlike 2036, which includes the entire underlying property when the decedent retained an income right, IRC 2038 snags only the part of the property (the value of the income, the value of the remainder) over which the decedent had a power. Thus if a decedent retained a right to sprinkle the income between A and B, but retained no right to alter the remainder interest, 2038 would include only the income interest, whereas 2036 would snag the entire property.

IRC 2036 and 2038 have several features in common. A decedent who creates a trust and names himself trustee is not trapped under either unless the trustee has under the instrument a power that amount to a 2036 or a 2038 power. Mere administrative or managerial powers will not cause inclusion.[66] If a decedent creates a trust and has the power to fill a vacancy if the trustee resigns, the trustee's 2036 and 2038 powers will be attributed to the decedent if he has the right, under the trust instrument or under state law, to name himself successor trustee.[67] That would not be so if the decedent could name only a corporate trustee or someone other than himself in case of vacancy.[68]

62. Treas.Reg. § 20.2038–1(a) (last three sentences).

63. Treas.Reg. § 20.2038–1(a).

64. Treas.Reg. § 20.2038–1(a)(2) states that property will not be included under I.R.C. § 2038 if the decedent's power could be exercised only with the consent of all the parties with a beneficial interest and if the power adds nothing to the rights of the parties under local law.

65. McKinney's EPTL 7–1.9.

66. See, e.g., Matter of Hager, 173 F.2d 613 (3d Cir.1949), where the court in dicta said that mere administrative powers will not cause inclusion, though the broader powers in Hager to accumulate income and add it to corpus, and to determine whether capital gains should be treated as income or principal, were not mere administrative powers and did trigger inclusion under I.R.C. § 2038.

67. Matter of Farrel, 553 F.2d 637 (Ct. Cl.1977) (2036); Matter of Mathey, 491 F.2d 481 (3d Cir.1974) (2038).

68. Rev.Rul. 77–182, 1977–1 CB 273 (settlor retained power to appoint successor corporate trustee only if trustee resigned or was removed; court held not a retained power).

If, however, the decedent could fire the trustee, the trustee's powers will be attributed to the decedent even if the decedent could appoint only another corporate trustee.[69]

Neither IRC 2036 nor 2038 will include a retained power that is limited by an ascertainable standard defined in terms of support, medical care or education.[70]

If each of two persons transfers the same amounts of property into a trust and gives the other the right to income, the courts are likely to unravel the interests and attribute a retained income right to the respective creators.[71]

i. Retention of Voting Rights

If a decedent transfers shares of stock but retains the right to vote those shares, his estate may be caught under 2036(b), which states that the "retention of the right to vote shares of stock in a controlled corporation shall be considered a retention of the enjoyment of transferred property." A controlled corporation is a "corporation of which the decedent owned or had a right to vote twenty percent of the voting stock after the transfer of the property or within three years of death." The purpose of this 1976 amendment to 2036 [72] was to close the loophole left by Matter of Byrum,[73] which found that retention of voting rights was not within the language of 2036.[74]

b. Transfers With Retained Powers—New York

New York law conforms with federal on the issue of property transferred with strings attached. A recent case raised an interesting question about the situs of property transferred outside of New York with strings attached. Assume D transfers jewelry to a New Jersey trustee but retains right to revoke the trust at any time. The jewelry is part of the trust corpus and remains in New Jersey. D does not revoke trust, and at his death the jewelry is included in the federal gross estate because of IRC 2038. It should not be included in the New York gross estate because it is tangible personal property located elsewhere. The

69. Rev.Rul. 79–353.

70. Matter of Jennings, 161 F.2d 74 (2d Cir.1947); Matter of Old Colony Trust Co., 423 F.2d 601 (1st Cir.1970).

71. Matter of Grace, 395 U.S. 316, 89 S.Ct. 1730, 23 L.Ed.2d 332 (1969), rehearing denied 396 U.S. 881, 90 S.Ct. 147, 24 L.Ed. 2d 141 (1969); Matter of Bischoff, 69 T.C. 32 (1977).

72. P.L. 95–600 sec. 702(i)(1), Nov. 6, 1978, effective for transfers made after June 22, 1976.

73. Matter of Byrum, 408 U.S. 125, 92 S.Ct. 2382, 33 L.Ed.2d 238 (1972).

74. Despite this amendment, it may still be easy to maintain control of a corporation without falling within 2036, simply by transferring non-voting stock and retaining the voting stock. See, e.g., Rev. Rul. 81–15, where the decedent transferred property to a corporation in return for shares of non-voting preferred stock and debentures, shares of voting stock and shares of non-voting common stock. The decedent retained the voting stock and transferred the non-voting stock to a trust for his children of which he was trustee. The transferred stock was not included in his gross estate because the voting rights he retained were not over the transferred stock.

analogous case [75] had slightly different facts: the decedent gave property away to a person out of state within three years of his death, at a time when such transfers caused inclusion in the gross estate. The court held the property to be part of the decedent's New York gross estate, a decision that appears to be erroneous.

c. *Retained Reversionary Interest—Federal*

IRC 2037 includes in the gross estate property the decedent transferred during his life for inadequate consideration in money or money's worth if two elements are present. First, some person has the right to get the property only if he survives the decedent, and second, the decedent had at the time of death a reversionary interest in the transferred property equal to more than five percent of the property.[76] For example, if the decedent created an irrevocable trust, income to A for life, remainder back to the decedent if living at A's death, or if not, remainder to B, IRC 2037 will include the value of the property less the actuarial value of A's income interest (as long as the decedent's chances of surviving A are worth more than five percent of the property, a valid assumption unless there is an extreme difference in the ages of decedent and B). Both 2037 elements are there: B has to survive the decedent in order to take his share, and D has a reversionary interest in the property.

The reversionary interest may be explicit in the trust instrument (income to A, reversion to decedent if he survives A, remainder to B if decedent fails to survive A), or it may arise from the operation of state law, for example because no ultimate remainderman is named.

The reason for including property transferred in a 2037 way is that it is so inherently testamentary in nature. The transferor relinquishes his reversion only at death, and the beneficiary's right to the property ripens only at the decedent's death.

The decedent's reversion will be considered less than five percent if some beneficiary had a general power of appointment over the property exercisable just before the decedent's death.[77]

d. *Retained Reversionary Interest—New York*

The New York law conforms with the federal law on 2037 transfers.

7. POWERS OF APPOINTMENT

a. *Federal*

Section 2041 of the Internal Revenue Code is unique in that it includes in the gross estate property the decedent never owned, but

75. Matter of Burden, 91 Misc.2d 368, 398 N.Y.S.2d 88 (New York County 1977).

76. A reversionary interest is the possibility that the property itself, or a right to dispose of the property, will revert to the decedent.

77. I.R.C. § 2037(b), Treas.Reg. § 20.2037–1(e), ex. 6.

over which he had a general power of appointment. A general power of appointment is one that is exercisable in favor of the holder of the power, or his estate, or his creditors, or the creditors of his estate.[78] The language is in the disjunctive; if a person can exercise the power in favor of any one of the four, it is a general power of appointment and the underlying property is included in the power-holder's estate when he dies. Thus if the decedent's father creates a trust, income to the decedent for life, remainder as the decedent appoints in his will, when the decedent dies the entire trust will be included in his gross estate, because he possessed a general power of appointment over the property when he died. A non-general (special) power, such as the power to exercise in favor of a class of persons like children or issue, will not cause inclusion.

A decedent's estate will include property over which he had a general power of appointment, even if it could be exercised only by his will (testamentary power of appointment) or only during his lifetime and not by will.[79]

Thus, if the decedent's father created a trust, income to the decedent for life and the decedent could also invade the principal to any extent he wanted during his lifetime, and at his death any property remaining in the trust would pass to X, at decedent's death the whole trust will be included in the decedent's estate.

It also appears to be irrelevant that the power-holder was, at all times, mentally incompetent to exercise the power.[80]

In four instances the decedent can possess a power of appointment that will not cause the property to be included in his gross estate.

First, if the exercise was limited by an ascertainable standard, defined in terms of support, maintenance, medical needs or education, it will not be considered a general power of appointment.[81] The

78. I.R.C. § 2041. The New York definition of a power of appointment appears in McKinney's EPTL 10–3.1:

> A power of appointment is an authority created or reserved by a person having property subject to his disposition, enabling the donee [the holder of the power] to designate, within such limits as may be prescribed by the donor [creator of the power], the appointees of the property or the shares or the manner in which such property shall be received.

The definition of a general power, McKinney's EPTL 10–3.2(b), traces the federal definition: A power of appointment is general to the extent that it is exercisable wholly in favcr of the donee, his estate, his creditors or the creditors of his estate.

79. See Rev.Rul. 69–342.

80. See Matter of Alperstein, 613 F.2d 1213 (4th Cir.1979). Contra, Matter of Finley, 404 F.Supp. 200 (S.D.Fla.1975), reversed on other grounds 612 F.2d 166 (5th Cir.1980).

81. I.R.C. § 2041(b)(1)(A); Treas.Reg. § 20.2041–1(c)(2). The ascertainable standard, to be successful in removing the property from gross estate under I.R.C. § 2041, should track the language of the regulations, namely, "support, maintenance or education." Otherwise, the government may take a hard-nosed position on the ascertainable standard issue. See Rev.Rul. 77–60, which found that the language "to continue" the power-holder's accustomed standard of living was not an ascertainable standard and included the underlying property in the power holder's gross estate, despite the language in the regulations that a power exercisable to support a person in his accustomed manner of living is an ascertainable standard. Apparently the missing concept of "sup-

rationale is that the ascertainable standard effectively removes the discretion necessary for the existence of the general power.

Second, if a decedent has a power of appointment exercisable only in conjunction with, or with the consent of, the creator of the power, the underlying property is not in his gross estate even if he dies with that power.[82] (It is, of course, included in the estate of the creator of the power, under IRC 2038,[83] because the creator has not relinquished control over the property.)

Third, the property is not included in the estate of the person with the power if he can exercise the power only with the consent of a person with a substantial adverse interest.[84] For example, if D has a power to invade the corpus of a trust with the consent of B, the remainderman, he does not have a general power of appointment; B is not likely to give his consent and diminish his own interest in the trust.[85] To have a substantial adverse interest, a person should have a beneficial interest, not just a legal interest as trustee of the trust that holds the property.[86]

Fourth, a hybrid rule of partial inclusion exists for a power exercisable only with the consent of a person who is a permissible appointee of the property.[87] In that case a fraction of the property is included. The numerator is one, and the denominator is the number of permissible appointees whose consent is needed (including the decedent). For example, if D has a power to appoint the remainder of a trust to anyone in the world with the consent of A, B and C, one-fourth of the property would be included in his estate. The rationale is that in real life each potential appointee would refuse to consent unless he received his proportionate interest, so to that extent he has a substantial adverse interest.

Although some cases hold that property payable after the decedent's death to the decedent's executor for distribution under the terms of the decedent's will is included in his estate because he had a power of

port" made the restriction insufficient. See, however, Matter of Sowell, where the power to invade in case of "emergency" was held to be an ascertainable standard.

82. I.R.C. § 2041(b)(1)(C)(i).

83. I.R.C. § 2038 is discussed this chapter supra at 584–88.

84. I.R.C. § 2041(b)(1)(C)(ii).

85. The statute specifies that a person who will get a general power of appointment after the power holder's death should be considered a person with a substantial adverse interest. Such a person does not have an interest but a power, and thus without the provision, he would not be considered to have a substantial adverse interest.

86. See Matter of Towle, 54 T.C. 368 (1970). Moreover, the substantial adverse interest should have been created simultaneously with the power, and not created by some arrangement by the power holder. See Matter of Witkowski, 451 F.2d 1249 (5th Cir.1971), certiorari denied 409 U.S. 891, 93 S.Ct. 115, 34 L.Ed.2d 148 (1972), where the holder of the power entered into agreements which she alleged prevented her from exercising her general power of appointment. The court found that those agreements were unenforceable, but said in dicta that whether they were or not, the power holder should not be able to create a substantial adverse interest which then eliminates the power.

87. I.R.C. § 2041(b)(1)(C)(iii).

appointment over it,[88] if such money represents the recovery in a wrongful death cause of action against the defendant who caused the decedent's death, it is not includible under a power of appointment (or any other) theory.[89]

If an independent trustee has the right, in his sole discretion, to invade corpus for a beneficiary, that power is not imputed to the beneficiary unless the beneficiary has the right to compel the trustee to exercise the power.[90]

In addition to property over which the decedent had a general power of appointment at his death, a decedent's estate also includes property over which the decedent at one time possessed a power of appointment if he exercised that power in such a way that, had it been his own property, it would have been included in his gross estate under IRC 2035, 2036, 2037 or 2038.[91]

To illustrate, if the decedent's father created a trust, giving to the decedent income for his life as well as the power to appoint the corpus of the trust during his lifetime or by will, and the decedent appointed the property to A during his lifetime but retained the right to the income for life, when D dies the entire trust is included in his estate. If he had transferred his own property that way, it would have been included in his gross estate under IRC 2036; therefore IRC 2041 will snag it.

The same rule is true for the release of a general power of appointment: if the decedent releases a power in a way that, had it been his own property, would have caused inclusion in his gross estate, IRC 2041 will include it.[92] Thus, if a decedent releases a power of appointment and retains a life estate, a right to income, a right to revoke, or a 2037 reversionary interest, the property will be included. Since the 1982 amendment to IRC 2035,[93] if a decedent releases a power of appointment and then dies within three years, the property will not be included. If he exercises a power in a 2036–, 2037–, or 2038–way, then releases the "string" (income right, right to revoke), and then dies within three years of releasing the string, the property will be included.[94]

Some powers of appointment are limited in duration. For example, a decedent may take a stated amount out of the corpus of a trust every year if he asks for it by December 31 or another date. If he does not, the power lapses; it is non-cumulative. Lapsed general powers of

88. Matter of Keeter, 461 F.2d 714 (5th Cir.1972); contra, Second National Bank v. Dallman, 209 F.2d 321 (7th Cir.1954).

89. Matter of Connecticut Bank and Trust Co., 465 F.2d 760 (2d Cir.1972). The recovery from the personal injuries action is included in the decedent's gross estate, however, as property in which the decedent had an interest under I.R.C. § 2033. See chapter on "Wrongful Death," supra at 527 et seq.

90. Rev.Rul. 76–368, 1977–1 CB 282.

91. I.R.C. § 2041(a)(1), (2). Each of these sections is discussed above in this chapter.

92. I.R.C. § 2041(a)(2).

93. I.R.C. § 2035(d) is discussed supra at 576–77.

94. Stevens, Maxfield and Lind, Federal Estate and Gift Taxation, 4–221 n. 91 (1983).

appointment are treated the same as exercised power and released powers; if a decedent allowed the power to lapse in a way that, had it been his own property, would have caused inclusion under IRC 2035, 2036, 2037, or 2038, then IRC 2041 will include it [95] subject to the "five or five" exception discussed presently.

An example of the treatment of lapsed powers (without, for the moment, considering the exception) is as follows: G creates a trust, income to D for life, and D has the non-cumulative right to take $30,000 out of the corpus each year. The other provisions are immaterial for the present discussion. If the corpus was valued at $300,000 at all times, and D never exercised his power, he has allowed a general power of appointment to lapse while retaining an income interest over the underlying property. If he had transferred his own property and retained such an interest, the property subject to the power would have been included under 2036. Hence it has to be included under 2041.

It is, however, subject to the "five or five" exception, which states that to the extent lapsed powers do not exceed the greater of $5,000 or five percent of the total property,[96] the underlying property is not included in the gross estate. In the above example of a right to invade a $300,000 trust to the extent of $30,000 each year, at his death his estate would have to include $15,000 for each year the power had lapsed before the year of death. It would also have to include the full $30,000 for the year of his death if the power had not yet lapsed that year, since that was a power he possessed at death, and the five or five exception applies only to lapsed powers. Regardless of how many years the power had lapsed, the maximum amount that can be included is the value of the trust corpus at the date of the decedent's death.

b. New York

New York law conforms with federal law on powers of appointment.

SECTION I. DEDUCTIONS

1. THE MARITAL DEDUCTION

A. Federal

Since Jan. 1, 1982, an estate is allowed an unlimited marital deduction for all property passing to the decedent's surviving spouse.[1]

95. I.R.C. § 2041(b)(2).

96. The five percent is applied to the property or that part of it over which the decedent had the power. For example, in the text the decedent had a right to invade the corpus of the trust to the extent of $30,000. If, instead, he had a right to invade the income of the trust to the extent of $30,000 each year, the five percent would be measured against the income earned, not the corpus. Matter of Fish, 432 F.2d 1278 (9th Cir.1970). In the textual hypothetical, then, only $5,000 per year would be excludible, since $30,000 far exceeds five percent of the income from a $300,000 trust corpus.

Sec. I

1. I.R.C. § 2056. P.L. 97–34 sec. 403(a)(1)(B).

To be eligible for the marital deduction, the property must be included in the decedent's gross estate.[2] It must pass from the decedent to the surviving spouse, and it is considered to pass from the decedent to the surviving spouse whether it goes under the decedent's will, under the laws of intestacy, or under the laws permitting a surviving spouse a right of election.[3] It also passes from the decedent to the surviving spouse in the following circumstances:

—decedent creates a lifetime trust, income to himself for life, remainder to surviving spouse; [4]

—decedent exercises a general power of appointment in favor of his spouse; [5]

—decedent fails to exercise a general power of appointment and the property goes to surviving spouse by default; [6]

—decedent and surviving spouse owned property jointly and on decedent's death it passed to surviving spouse (if the property is included in his gross estate); [7]

—decedent named spouse beneficiary of life insurance policy (if the insurance is included in his gross estate); [8]

—decedent gave property to someone other than surviving spouse, and the residue to surviving spouse, and the other person validly disclaimed the property so that it passes to the surviving spouse; [9]

—decedent names surviving spouse as beneficiary of pension plan (if the pension is included in the gross estate).[10]

Besides being included in the decedent's gross estate and passing to the surviving spouse, to qualify for the marital deduction property must pass unconditionally to the surviving spouse; if it passes in the form of a terminable interest, it may lose the deduction. To determine whether the marital deduction is available, one must ask three questions. First, is the interest passing to the spouse terminable? If so, is it a nondeductible terminable interest? If so, is there a statutory exception that allows the marital deduction anyway?

A terminable interest is one which ends on the occurrence or nonoccurrence of a contingency or the passage of time.[11] An example

2. I.R.C. § 2056(a).

3. I.R.C. § 2056(c). If the surviving spouse's right of election is challenged and the surviving spouse and the fiduciary settle the issue, the amount of settlement is eligible for the marital deduction. See Pastore v. United States, 386 F.Supp. 106 (E.D.N.Y.1974).

4. I.R.C. § 2056(c)(4); Treas.Reg. § 20–2056(e)–1(a)(5). At D's death spouse gets the property outright.

5. I.R.C. § 2056(c)(6); Treas.Reg. § 20.2056(e)(1)(a)(2).

6. I.R.C. § 2056(c)(6); Treas.Reg. § 20.2056(e)–1(a)(2).

7. I.R.C. § 2056(c)(5); Treas.Reg. § 20.2056(e)–1(a)(1).

8. I.R.C. § 2056(c)(7); Treas.Reg. § 20.2056(e)–1(a)(4).

9. Disclaimers are governed by IRC § 2518.

10. Treas.Reg. § 20.2056(e)–1(a)(6).

11. I.R.C. § 2056(b)(1).

would be a will provision: "I give my estate to my wife, but if she remarries, whatever she still has shall pass upon her remarriage to my daughter."

If the interest is terminable, the next question is whether it is the non-deductible type of terminable interest, which is defined as an interest in property in which the decedent also gave someone other than the surviving spouse an interest after the termination of the surviving spouse's interest.[12] Thus, although a patent is a terminable interest because it decreases and eventually loses its value because of the passage of time, it is not the non-deductible type because the decedent did not give anyone else an interest in it after the spouse's interest ends. The hypothetical from the preceding paragraph, where the decedent gave the spouse his estate unless she remarried, is a non-deductible terminable interest. Similarly, a bequest to decedent's spouse, "but my spouse must be alive at the time of distribution or the property will instead go to my son" is a non-deductible terminable interest.

The Internal Revenue Code makes five exceptions for interests that are eligible for the marital deduction despite their status as non-deductible terminable interests. The first is that a decedent can condition the spouse's bequest on the spouse's surviving him for a period up to six months.[13] A decedent would want to do this to avoid having the property pass through two estates if the spouses were to die in quick succession, with the attendant double administration costs and filing fees. If he did so and the spouse survived him by more than six months, the spouse would get the property and the decedent's estate would get the marital deduction. If the spouse died within six months of the decedent's death, the property would pass to the alternate beneficiary and the estate would not get the marital deduction.[14]

The second exception is that the decedent can condition the bequest on the spouse's not dying in the common disaster that killed the decedent.[15] The presence of that condition in the will does not make the bequest ineligible for the marital deduction. If the spouse died after the decedent from injuries incurred in the accident that killed the decedent, the alternate beneficiaries would get the property and the estate would not get the marital deduction.

The third exception is the classic "life estate—power of appointment trust," [16] which permits the decedent to create a trust, all the income to surviving spouse for life,[17] paid at least annually, and the spouse must have a power to appoint the remainder to herself or her

12. I.R.C. § 2056(b)(1)(A), (B).

13. I.R.C. § 2056(b)(3)(A).

14. I.R.C. § 2056(b)(3)(B).

15. I.R.C. § 2056(b)(3)(A).

16. I.R.C. § 2056(b)(5).

17. If the trust contains non-income producing property (such as vacant lots), the estate will to that extent be denied a marital deduction unless the surviving spouse has the right to demand that the trustee make the property productive or to pay the surviving spouse income from other assets. Treas.Reg. § 2.2056(b)–5(f)(4) and (5).

estate,[18] exercisable alone without restrictions, and no one else may have a power to appoint the property to anyone other than the surviving spouse.[19]

The fourth exception is a similar arrangement over life insurance proceeds.[20]

The fifth exception, enacted in 1981,[21] makes it possible for a decedent to leave property in a trust, income only to the spouse for life, remainder to other beneficiaries of the decedent's choice. The income must be payable at least annually. No one can have the power to appoint the property to anyone other than the surviving spouse during the surviving spouse's lifetime, and the decedent's executor has to elect on the estate tax return to treat the property as qualifying for the marital deduction.[22] (This is called "Qualifying Terminable Interest Property" or the "Q–TIP trust".) Because the property is subject to transfer taxes when the surviving spouse disposes of it or dies,[23] this enactment accomplishes the goal of causing property to be taxed once on the death of a married couple, but gives each spouse the opportunity to name other beneficiaries, such as the children from a prior marriage, as ultimate remaindermen of the trust.

As in other federal estate tax areas, the law governing the marital deduction has been changing quickly. For decedents dying between Jan. 1, 1976 and Jan. 1, 1982, the marital deduction was the greater of $250,000 and one-half the adjusted gross estate (the gross estate less administration and funeral expenses, debts, claims, mortgages and casualty losses).[24] For decedents dying before 1977, the marital deduction was one-half the adjusted gross estate. The following chart illustrates the three phases of the law. In each case the funeral and administration expenses, claims, debts, mortgages and losses were

18. I.R.C. § 2056(b)(5). Note that that is even narrower than a general power of appointment, where the property could have been payable to the creditors or the creditors of her estate.

19. I.R.C. § 2056(b)(5). If the surviving spouse has a right to a part of fraction of the income, and all the other requirements are met, that part or fraction of the corpus is eligible for the marital deduction. If the surviving spouse has a right to a dollar amount of income each year and all the other requirements are met, the amount of the corpus necessary to yield that amount of income is eligible for the marital deduction. Northeastern Pennsylvania National Bank and Trust Co. v. United States, 387 U.S. 213, 87 S.Ct. 1573, 18 L.Ed.2d 726 (1967) (invalidating Treas.Reg. § 20.2056(b)–5(c)).

20. I.R.C. § 2056(b)(6).

21. P.L. 97–34 sec. 403; I.R.C. § 2056(b)(7).

22. The executor can elect to treat all or part of the trust as Q–TIP property. Temp.Reg. § 22–2056–1.

23. If the property is qualified and its value is therefore deducted from the decedent's estate, it is included in the surviving spouse's gross estate under I.R.C. § 2044, enacted simultaneously with the Q–TIP provision, I.R.C. § 2056(b)(7). If the surviving spouse has a right to dispose of her income interest by gift during her lifetime, when she does so it is treated as a taxable gift under I.R.C. § 2519(b)(1). The surviving spouse or her estate, as the case may be, can recover from the property the amount of estate or gift taxes paid. I.R.C. § 2207A. Thus, the property is taxed as though the transfer was made by the surviving spouse (that is, at her bracket and using her unified credit), but the decedent's property bears the tax burden.

24. P.L. 94–455 sec. 2002. If the decedent made lifetime gifts of $200,000 or less, the estate tax marital deduction was reduced by the amount of the gift tax marital deduction that exceeded fifty percent of the gift.

$100,000. Column I is the gross estate; Column II is the amount the decedent left to the surviving spouse; Column III is the marital deduction in years before 1976; Column IV is the marital deduction in 1977–1981, and Column V is the marital deduction in years since 1982:

I	II	III	IV	V
$1,000,000	$500,000 outright	$450,000	$450,000	$500,000
$1,000,000	entire estate	$450,000	$450,000	$900,000
$ 400,000	entire estate	$150,000	$250,000	$300,000
$ 400,000	$200,000	$150,000	$200,000	$200,000
$ 650,000	one-half adjusted gross estate	$275,000	$275,000	$275,000
$1,200,000	one third gross estate in trust, income monthly to spouse for life, remainder to children	–0–	–0–	$400,000 (if executor elects to treat it as QTIP)

b. New York

The federal marital deduction is reduced by the amount of any real property or tangible personal property outside New York passing to the surviving spouse, that is, by any amounts eligible for the federal marital deduction not included in the New York gross estate.[25]

The marital deduction for estates of decedents dying before July 1, 1978 was one-half the adjusted gross estate, and the marital deduction for persons dying between July 1, 1978 and September 30, 1983 was the greater of $250,000 or one-half the adjusted gross estate.[26]

If the decedent's spouse left a Q–TIP trust, and the fiduciary of the spouse's estate elected to qualify it for the marital deduction on the spouse's federal estate tax return, for federal estate tax purposes the whole trust is included in the decedent's estate on the decedent's later death. For state estate tax purposes, only those assets includible in the New York gross estate (that is, all property in New York and intangible personal property, wherever located) are considered to have passed from the decedent.[27]

2. EXPENSES, CLAIMS, DEBTS AND LOSSES

a. Federal

i. Expenses, Claims and Debts

Unlike the marital deduction, which is the result of a legislative policy decision to tax property only once each generation, and the charitable deduction,[28] which is the result of a legislative policy decision to encourage philanthropy, the deductions allowed under IRC 2053 and 2054 for expenses, debts, claims and losses are for the purpose of

25. McKinney's Tax Law § 956(c).

26. If the decedent made lifetime gifts between July 1, 1978 and September 30, 1983 of $200,000 or less, the estate tax marital deduction was reduced by the amount of the gift tax marital deduction that exceeded fifty percent of the gift.

27. I.R.C. § 2044(b)(1)(A).

28. The charitable deduction is discussed infra at 598–99.

reducing the gross estate to a level that reflects the assets the decedent actually had: his net worth.

The general rule is that the gross estate will be reduced by funeral expenses actually paid (such as casket, flowers, limousine), administration expenses actually paid (such as attorneys' fees, fiduciaries' commissions, selling expenses), claims against the estate and decedent's debts, to the extent these expenses, claims and debts are allowable under state law.[29] Although the statute says that the expenses, claims and debts must merely be allowable under state law, the regulations add the requirement that they also be necessary for the administration of the estate, that is, necessary to collect assets, pay debts and distribute the property.[30] The cases have split on whether the regulation should prevail over the statute, that is, whether the expenses need only be allowable or whether they must also be necessary.[31]

If a decedent had non-probate property (property that does not pass under a will, such as insurance, pensions, revocable trusts, jointly owned property with right of survivorship), administration expenses are allowed if they are of a type that would be allowed for probate assets and if they are paid within three years after the estate tax return is filed.[32]

A few limitations exist to these general rules.

First, if an executor wants to take a deduction for a claim or debt, and that claim or debt is based on a promise or contract, it is not deductible unless the promise was supported by adequate consideration in money or money's worth.[33] For example, if a creditor has a claim against the decedent based on a contract under which the decedent agreed to pay for work done to the decedent's house, that claim, if valid, is deductible, but a claim based on a contract under which the decedent agreed to pay the claimant to stop smoking is not.[34]

Second, to the extent the expenses, claims and debts are larger than the probate assets and are paid out of non-probate assets, they are

29. For a discussion of what expenses are allowable under New York law, see generally chapters on "Accounting," supra at 179 et seq., "Claims," supra at 146 et seq., "Commissions," supra at 425 et seq., and "Attorneys' Fees," supra at 359 et seq.

30. Treas.Reg. § 20.2053–3(a), (d).

31. See Matter of Vatter, 556 F.2d 563 (2d Cir.1976); Matter of Smith, 510 F.2d 479 (2d Cir.1975), certiorari denied 423 U.S. 847, 96 S.Ct. 44, 46 L.Ed.2d 44 (1975); Matter of Marcus, 704 F.2d 1227 (11th Cir. 1983).

32. I.R.C. § 2053(b).

33. I.R.C. § 2053(c)(1)(A).

34. The relinquishment of rights in marital property and rights in a decedent's estate is not consideration in money or money's worth, I.R.C. § 2053(e), so if a decedent promised his surviving spouse a sum of money in exchange for such relinquishment, the executor cannot deduct the payment. An exception is made if the parties obtained a divorce within two years of the separation agreement or if the agreement is made within a year of the divorce, I.R.C. §§ 2053(b)(2), 2516, and another exception is made if the court that rendered the divorce decree had a right to change the terms of the agreement. In that case the surviving spouse's claim is founded on a court decree and not on a promise, and it is irrelevant that there was no consideration. See Matter of Gray, 541 F.2d 228 (9th Cir.1976), on remand 440 F.Supp. 684 (D.Cal.1977); Rev.Rul. 76–113. See also Natchez v. United States, 705 F.2d 671 (2d Cir. 1983) (unenforceable provision of separation agreement incorporated into divorce decree eliminated need to show consideration although court rendering decree had no power to alter terms of agreement).

deductible only if paid before the estate tax return is filed.[35] This exception applies to an insolvent estate that is, because of inclusion of non-testamentary assets in gross estate, subject to an estate tax. For example, if the decedent's estate consists mostly of life insurance and inter vivos trusts, and his debts and claims and the administration and funeral expenses exceed the amount of probate assets, the insurance beneficiaries or trust beneficiaries could pay the expenses, debts or claims and if they did so before the estate tax return was filed, the executor could deduct them. He could also deduct all expenses, debts and claims that do not exceed the probate assets, even if they are paid by the insurance beneficiaries and trust beneficiaries after the estate tax return was filed.[36]

ii. Casualty Losses

IRC 2054 permits a deduction for "losses incurred during the settlement of estates arising from fires, storms, shipwrecks, or other casualties, or from theft, where such losses are not compensated for by insurance or otherwise."

For example, if a decedent owned a house, and after his death the house is damaged by fire or electrical storm, the loss is deductible.

The regulations specify that if the property has already been distributed, no deduction is available, and that the executor and beneficiary must decide between them whether the loss will be claimed as an income tax deduction or an estate tax deduction, because it cannot be deducted on both.[37]

Needless to say, if the fiduciary opts for alternate valuation and includes the damaged property at its diminished value,[38] no casualty loss can be deducted.

b. New York

New York estate tax deductions are defined as the federal estate tax deductions except that expenses, claims, debts and mortgages relating to real or tangible personal property outside New York are not deductible from the New York gross estate.[39]

3. CHARITABLE DEDUCTION

a. Federal

The federal law allows an unlimited charitable deduction.[40] If a testator has created a trust under which the charity receives an income interest and the remainder is payable to someone other than a charity, or under which a non-charity receives the income and the charity receives the remainder, the trust must be fashioned as a unitrust,

35. I.R.C. § 2053(c)(2).

36. Treas.Reg. § 20.2053–1(c).

37. Treas.Reg. § 20.2054–1 states that "no deduction is allowed under this section if the estate has waived its right to take such a deduction pursuant to the provisions of section 642(g) in order to permit its allowance for income tax purposes.

38. I.R.C. § 2032.

39. McKinney's Tax Law § 956(b).

40. I.R.C. § 2055.

annuity trust or pooled income fund under the stringent requirements of IRC 2055.

b. New York

The New York charitable deduction is fashioned after the federal, except that the New York charitable deduction is reduced by the amount of any real property or tangible personal property outside New York passing to the charity, that is, by the amounts eligible for the federal charitable deduction not included in the New York gross estate.[41]

SECTION J. GENERATION–SKIPPING TRANSFERS TAX

In 1976 Congress enacted the generation-skipping transfer tax to close the loophole available to the very wealthy who previously could create a trust, income payable to their children for life, remainder payable to their grandchildren. At the death of the children, nothing would be included in the children's gross estates because the life interests would expire with the children. The device allowed those wealthy enough to sustain their children on the income from their property to skip a whole generation of estate taxes. The current law imposes a generation-skipping tax on the intermediate generation.[1] If the property passes because of the death of that intermediate generation, it is effectively taxed as though it were part of that decedent's gross estate. If it is given away by the intermediate generation, it is effectively taxed as a gift by that donor.

SECTION K. CREDITS

Every estate is entitled to subtract from the tentative tax ("gross estate tax") the unified credit against the federal estate taxes in the following amounts:

1987 and after	—$192,800
1986	—$155,000
1985	—$121,800
1984	—$ 96,300
1983	—$ 79,300
1982	—$ 62,800
1981	—$ 47,000 [1]

41. McKinney's Tax Law § 955(a). If property has to be included in the New York gross estate because of the existence of a limited power of appointment created before September 30, 1930, and it passes to a surviving spouse or charity, the marital deduction or charitable deduction is increased to that extent.

Sec. J

1. I.R.C. § 2601 et seq. For a thorough discussion of the generation-skipping transfer taxes, see Stephens, Maxfield & Lind. Federal Estate and Gift Taxation 12–1 through 14–13 (1983). For proposed amendments to the generation-skipping transfer taxes, see HR 3838.

Sec. K

1. I.R.C. § 2010. For persons who made lifetime gifts just before the effective date of the Tax Reform Act of 1976, specifically from Sept. 8, 1976 through December 31, 1976, a permanent reduction of the

The New York credit is $2,750, insulating an estate of $108,000 from state estate taxes.[2] Every estate which pays state estate taxes is entitled to a federal credit for state death taxes. The amount of the credit is the smaller of the amount set forth in IRC 2012 and the state estate taxes paid. For New York residents the amount of the federal credit is usually the 2012 amount, because the state estate taxes exceed the allowable credit under 2012.

If an estate contains property which previously incurred federal estate taxes because of its inclusion in another person's estate within the ten years preceding the current decedent's death, a credit is allowed for the tax on the prior transfer. Its amount is the full amount of taxes paid if the earlier death was within two years of the later one, eighty percent if within four years, sixty percent if within six years, forty percent if within eight years, and twenty percent if within ten years.[3]

New York has a similar credit for taxes on prior transfers.[4]

If a decedent owned property which incurred foreign estate taxes and which is also included in the decedent's gross estate for federal estate tax purposes, credit is available for the foreign death taxes payable.[5] No comparable New York credit exists.

SECTION L. COMPUTATION OF THE FEDERAL ESTATE TAX

The federal estate tax is computed by tallying the gross estate [1] and subtracting deductions [2] which results in the taxable estate, and then by adding "adjusted taxable gifts," which are the taxable portions of post-1976 gifts that are not included in the gross estate.[3]

unified credit occurs. The reduction is twenty percent of the amount of the gift, up to $6,000. The reason was that the 1976 Tax Reform Act, which was available for study in September 1976, eliminated the $30,000 lifetime exemption for gifts and instituted the unified credit of IRC 2010. Consequently, many people who had not made lifetime gifts used the opportunity to make gifts of up to $30,000 rather than to lose that exemption. The twenty percent reduction of the unified credit for such persons was an attempt to equalize those who did and those who did not make gifts.

2. McKinney's Tax Law § 952(b).

3. I.R.C. § 2013.

4. McKinney's Tax Law § 959 (Supp. 1986).

5. I.R.C. § 2014.

Sec. L

1. The components of the gross estate are discussed this chapter, supra at 575–92.

2. Deductions are discussed this chapter supra at 592–99.

3. Taxable gifts are gross gifts minus the marital and charitable deductions and the annual exclusion if the gift was of a present interest. The charitable deduction is unlimited. The marital deduction has been unlimited since October 1, 1983; before 1977 it was fifty percent of the gift, and from Jan. 1, 1977 through December 31, 1980 it was one-half the gift, except that the first $100,000 of post-1976 gifts were completely deductable under the marital deduction. The annual exclusion was $3,000 through December 31, 1981 and has been $10,000 since Jan. 1, 1982. Note, however, that if property is included on the gross estate line, it is not included on the adjusted taxable gift line. Thus, if property were transferred after 1976 and the donor retained a right to the income, although the value of the remainder interest was a gift, the property is included at its full value in the gross estate under I.R.C. § 2036, discussed supra at 584–88, and hence is not added as an adjusted taxable gift.

The adjusted taxable gifts are added back at their date of gift value; all appreci-

The sum of the taxable estate and the adjusted taxable gifts is the "unified tax base." IRC 2001 gives the rates of taxation which, when applied to the "unified tax base," results in a tentative tax. Then the unified credit [4] and other available credits [5] are subtracted for the tax payable.

Assume, for example, that a decedent made a gift of $15,000 cash to his son in 1978, a gift of $20,000 in stocks to his daughter in 1982, and a gift of $25,000 in bonds to his spouse in 1984, and then died in 1986 with a gross estate of $2,500,000 and with administration and funeral expenses, debts, mortgages and claims of $300,000. If in his will he gave $1,000,000 to his spouse, $100,000 to St. John's University School of Law, and the residue to his children in equal shares, the fiduciary would compute the federal estate taxes as follows:

	Gross estate:	$2,500,000
Less	2053 deductions:	(300,000)
Less	Marital deduction:	(1,000,000)
Less	Charitable deduction:	(100,000)
	Taxable estate:	1,100,000
Plus	Adjusted taxable gifts:	22,000 [6]
	Unified tax base:	1,132,000
	Tentative tax:	399,920 [7]
Less	Credit for gift taxes on adjusted taxable gifts:	(–0–) [8]
Less	Unified credit:	155,800 [9]
Less	State death tax credit:	38,800 [10]
	Tax due:	205,320

ation after the date of the gift escapes estate taxation. The estate tax saving resulting from this exclusion may be offset somewhat by the increased capital gains tax to the donee. If the decedent had owned the property until his death, its basis would have been stepped up to the date of death value, I.R.C. § 1014 and the beneficiary would have avoided capital gains taxes on appreciation.

4. I.R.C. § 2010, discussed this chapter supra at 599.

5. For example, credits are available for taxes on prior transfers, IRC 2013, state death taxes, IRC 2011, and foreign death taxes, IRC 2014.

6. That is, $12,000 of the $15,000 gift in 1978, since $3,000 is eligible for the annual exclusion, and $10,000 of the $20,000 gift in 1982, since $10,000 was eligible for the annual exclusion. None of the gift to the spouse is an adjusted taxable gift because the unlimited marital deduction rendered it all non-taxable.

On the gifts to the children, if the decedent had obtained the spouse's consent to treat the gifts as split gifts under I.R.C. § 2513, the adjusted taxable gifts would have included $9,000 of the 1978 gift and none of the 1982 gift, since the donor could have taken advantage of his spouse's annual exclusion as well as his own.

7. That is, $345,800 plus forty-one percent of $132,000. I.R.C. § 2001(c).

8. Because the credit in effect in 1978 wiped out the taxes on taxable gifts of $134,000, no taxes were due on the taxable gift to the son of $12,000. Similarly, the 1982 credit insulated from taxes cumulative gifts of $225,000, well above the total taxable gifts of $22,000 he had made to that date. Thus he paid no gift taxes. I.R.C. § 2505.

9. His partial use of the unified credit during his lifetime was effectively eliminated by addition of the adjusted taxable gifts to which the credit had applied, so allowing the estate the full unified credit at the decedent's death in 1986 does not permit him use of the credit twice.

10. That is computed by subtracting $60,000 from the federal taxable estate ($1,100,000) and applying the I.R.C. § 2011 rates to the result.

SECTION M. TAX APPORTIONMENT

A federal estate tax is imposed on all estates above a certain threshold, ($600,000 in 1987 and after),[1] and New York, like many states, also imposes estate taxes.[2] When estate or other death taxes are imposed on an estate, the executor must determine which estate beneficiaries should bear the burden of paying those taxes. The testator can in the will direct the payment of estate taxes from a certain source or sources, and if he does not, EPTL 2–1.8 governs.

1. THE WORKING OF EPTL 2–1.8 ABSENT A CONTRARY DIRECTIVE IN THE WILL

EPTL 2–1.8 provides that unless the will directs otherwise, the persons who receive benefits under the will must each bear a pro rata share of the estate and death taxes (including taxes imposed by the United States, New York, and other jurisdictions [3] to the extent their dispositions generated taxes. Thus, if a testator gave a diamond ring worth $100,000 to his sister, stock worth $200,000 to his brother, and the residuary estate ($700,000) to his niece, and if his total estate taxes, state and federal, amounted (for ease of arithmetic) to $150,000, EPTL 2–1.8 would apportion the estate taxes among the three beneficiaries in the proportion that their benefits bear to the aggregate benefits of all those whose dispositions generated taxes. Here, the sister would have to pay $15,000, the brother $30,000, and the niece $105,000. Since the sister's bequest is specific, she would either have to pay her share of the taxes from her own funds, or sell the ring to do so.

The statute goes on to say that if the testator made dispositions that are deductible from the decedent's gross estate because of the relationship between the decedent and the beneficiary, or because the beneficiary was a charity, those beneficiaries do not share in the tax burden.[4] That refers to the marital and charitable deductions. Thus, if in the preceding hypothetical the decedent also left a deductable bequest of $100,000 to a charity [5] then the sister would be responsible for one-ninth of the taxes, the brother for two-ninths, and the niece for two-thirds (six-ninths).[6]

On the other hand, if the estate is entitled to a credit unrelated to the relationship (marital) or status (charitable) of a beneficiary, such as a credit for gift taxes the decedent paid,[7] or a credit for property

Sec. M

1. I.R.C. 2010.

2. New York's estate tax is an excise tax on the transfer of property. Other states have inheritance taxes imposed on the receipt of property.

3. McKinney's EPTL 2–1.8(a).

4. McKinney's EPTL 2–1.8(c)(2).

5. The charitable deduction is covered by McKinney's EPTL 2055 and discussed this chapter supra at 598–99.

6. The will can provide that persons or charities who would otherwise be exempt must share pro rata in the tax burden and sometimes does so inadvertently. See Matter of Knox, N.Y.L.J., March 21, 1980, at 16, col. 3 (Suffolk).

7. I.R.C. § 2012.

previously taxed[8] the credit is subtracted from the taxes before the apportionment is made.[9]

Interest and penalties due on estate taxes paid late are apportioned just as the taxes are.[10] If a discount is allowed for prepayment of the tax, that is credited to the fund which made the prepayment, and if several beneficiaries share in that fund, it is apportioned among them pro rata.[11]

The value to be used for computing the proper tax apportionment is the value of the assets for estate tax purposes, usually the date of death value or the value six months after death.[12]

A creditor does not bear any portion of an estate's tax burden, so when a decedent leaves a bequest to his surviving spouse in satisfaction of a separation agreement, that bequest does not share in the tax burden.[13]

If the estate is insolvent, the taxes are apportioned ratably under the rules of EPTL 2–1.8, not under the ordinary abatement rules that require that the residuary dispositions abate first, the general dispositions next, followed by demonstrative and specific dispositions.[14]

2. DIRECTIVE IN THE WILL

The testator may eliminate the application of 2–1.8 by directing in his will that all the estate taxes be paid from a certain fund. In order to do so effectively, the testator's directive must be clear and unambiguous.[15] For example, if a testator directs that the residue should bear the entire estate tax burden, or that the taxes be paid from "the residue" or from the "general estate," he has clearly and unambiguously avoided tax apportionment to the pre-residual beneficiaries.[16] Similarly, if he directs that the taxes be paid as an administration expense, he has avoided tax apportionment because the taxes, like the administration expenses, will be paid out of the residuary estate.[17] On the other hand, if he generally directs the executor to pay all administration expenses, debts and taxes as soon as practicable, arguably he has not exonerated the beneficiaries from sharing the tax burden and the provisions of EPTL 2–1.8 will apply.[18]

8. I.R.C. § 2013.

9. McKinney's EPTL 2–1.8(c)(3).

10. McKinney's EPTL 2–1.8(c)(4).

11. McKinney's EPTL 2–1.8(c)(5).

12. McKinney's EPTL 2–1.8(c)(1).

13. See Matter of Darrow, 120 Misc.2d 924, 467 N.Y.S.2d 114 (New York County 1983); Matter of Vernon, 107 Misc.2d 1021, 437 N.Y.S.2d 562 (Suffolk 1981).

14. McKinney's EPTL 12–1.2(b).

15. E.g., Matter of Pepper, 307 N.Y. 242, 120 N.E.2d 807 (1954); Matter of McKinney, 101 A.D.2d 477, 477 N.Y.S.2d 367 (2d Dep't 1984), appeal denied 63 N.Y.2d 607, 482 N.Y.S.2d 1024, 472 N.E.2d 48 (1984); Matter of Dewar, 62 A.D.2d 352, 404 N.Y.S.2d 750 (3d Dep't 1978); Matter of Mescall, 54 Misc.2d 165, 281 N.Y.S.2d 394 (1967).

16. See, e.g., Matter of Schuchman, 51 Misc.2d 541, 273 N.Y.S.2d 548 (Nassau 1966); Matter of Becher, 204 Misc. 523, 123 N.Y.S.2d 589 (Kings 1953).

17. E.g., Matter of Hammer, 81 Misc.2d 25, 362 N.Y.S.2d 753 (Nassau 1974); Matter of Seeley, 50 N.Y.S.2d 548 (New York County 1943).

18. See, e.g., Matter of Robord, 69 Misc. 2d 1026, 332 N.Y.S.2d 698 (Broome 1972);

While the directive should be "clear and unambiguous," it can nevertheless be indirect.[19] For example, a bequest of the residuary estate after payment of all administration expenses and taxes has been found to exonerate the pre-residuary dispositions from sharing in the taxes,[20] as has a directive to pay the pre-residuary dispositions within a month (or other time period before taxes are due) after the testator's death.[21] It is of course vastly preferable to phrase a tax clause clearly and unambiguously than to leave it to a court's interpretation.

3. CODICILS

If a will contains a directive prohibiting apportionment against all testamentary dispositions, and a codicil contains additional dispositions but no further language on tax apportionment, the tax clause in the will governs the codicil as well, since a will and a codicil have to be construed together.[22] A codicil may also exonerate from sharing in tax apportionment gifts that were subject to taxes under the will.[23]

4. NON-TESTAMENTARY ASSETS

The gross taxable estate may, and often does, include assets other than those owned individually by the testator. Inter vivos trusts, life insurance policies, pensions annuities, jointly owned property and Totten Trusts, which may be part of the taxable estate but are unaffected by the will, are categorized as "non-testamentary" or "non-probate"

Matter of Bradley, 206 Misc. 383, 132 N.Y.S. 546 (New York County 1954). But see a contrary line of cases which hold that the testator's grouping together of taxes with debts and expenses is an indication that estate taxes should be considered administration expenses and hence considered a direction against apportionment both as to the residuary beneficiaries and within the residuary estate. Matter of Wheller, 25 Misc.2d 933, 203 N.Y.S.2d 787, affirmed 14 A.D.2d 549, 219 N.Y.S.2d 235 (2d Dep't 1961); Matter of Leonard, 9 A.D.2d 1, 189 N.Y.S.2d 422 (3d Dep't 1959); Matter of Morite, 48 Misc.2d 323, 264 N.Y.S.2d 734. See also Matter of James, 180 Misc. 441, 40 N.Y.S.2d 4 (New York County 1943), affirmed 267 App.Div. 761, 45 N.Y.S.2d 938 (1st Dep't 1943), appeal denied 267 App.Div. 820, 47 N.Y.S.2d 110 (1944) where the testator, in addition to including the "soon as practicable" language in the text, directed that the taxes be treated as an administration expense, and the court held that they should be paid out of the residue and not apportioned among the beneficiaries.

19. See Matter of Chodikoff, 50 Misc.2d 86, 270 N.Y.S.2d 175 (Renssalaer 1966) (context of will made clear that testator wanted his wife's share, both testamentary and non-testamentary, to pass to her without reduction for taxes). See cases holding to the contrary in note 18 supra.

20. Matter of Leonard, 9 A.D.2d 1, 189 N.Y.S.2d 422 (3d Dep't 1959).

21. For an example of a case where construction of the will was required, see Matter of Rappaport, N.Y.L.J., July 23, 1985, at 14, col. 5 (Westchester).

22. Matter of Nicholas, 33 N.Y.2d 174, 350 N.Y.S.2d 900, 305 N.E.2d 911 (1973); Matter of Duryea, 277 N.Y. 310, 14 N.E.2d 369 (1938). But see Matter of Williams, 2 Misc.2d 687, 150 N.Y.S.2d 238 (Kings 1956) (will provision prohibiting apportionment among "foregoing gifts" held not to apply to gift in later codicil); Matter of Wolf, N.J.L.J., Jan. 12, 1979, at 11, col. 4 (New York County) (directive to pay a beneficiary first does not exonerate him); Matter of Ballou, 206 Misc. 442, 132 N.Y.S.2d 797, (New York County 1954) affirmed 285 App. Div. 929, 139 N.Y.S.2d 883 (1st Dep't 1955) (will exonerated specific dispositions only; codicil contained both specific and other dispositions. Held not to exempt the non-specific dispositions in codicil).

23. Matter of Campe, 3 Misc.2d 34, 148 N.Y.S.2d 365 (New York County 1955).

assets. The beneficiaries of these assets must share ratably in the apportionment of taxes along with the will beneficiaries.[24] Thus, if a decedent's taxable probate estate is $900,000 and his taxable estate also includes life insurance proceeds of $100,000, the insurance beneficiary is responsible for one-tenth of the taxes. The will can exonerate the recipients of non-probate property from taxes, but it must specifically refer to them to do so.[25] This issue should not be left to a judge's discretion to decide: the language in the will should state precisely what assets are exonerated and what are not.

5. DIRECTIVES IN A NON-TESTAMENTARY INSTRUMENT

As we have just discussed, EPTL 2-1.8 applies unless a will provides otherwise. Its scheme can also be altered by an inter vivos trust; the statute applies unless a non-testamentary instrument directs a different tax apportionment within the fund created by the non-testamentary instrument.[26] The language of the statute was interpreted in Matter of Spencer,[27] where the decedent executed an inter vivos trust and a will simultaneously, directing payment of the residue under the will to the inter vivos trust. In the trust he directed that the residuary estate bear the whole tax burden, or if the residuary estate was insufficient to cover all the taxes, he directed apportionment among specific parts of the trust. The will contained no language at all regarding apportionment. When the testator died, it became apparent that the payment of taxes would completely wipe out the residue, and the court ruled that a non-testamentary instrument cannot shift the burden of the taxes it generates entirely onto another fund. The practical effect of this ruling may be that the non-testamentary instrument can do no more than apportion taxes among its own beneficiaries. Whether this will be upheld as more cases are decided remains to be seen.

6. CONFLICTING DIRECTIVES IN A WILL AND A NON-TESTAMENTARY INSTRUMENT

In Matter of Cord,[28] the decedent had executed an inter vivos trust many years before her death, apportioning to the inter vivos trust all death and estate taxes imposed because of its inclusion in the gross estate, which is in effect what would have occurred if EPTL 2-1.8 applied. Forty years later she executed a will, apportioning all taxes on probate and non-probate property to the residuary estate. The residuary beneficiaries wanted to apportion the taxes generated by the

24. McKinney's EPTC 2-1.8(c)(1); see, e.g., Matter of Smithers, 15 Misc.2d 701, 181 N.Y.S.2d 702 (Nassau 1959).

25. McKinney's 2-1.8(d); e.g., Matter of Pergament, 29 Misc.2d 334, 218 N.Y.S.2d 831 (New York County 1961), affirmed 19 A.D.2d 945, 245 N.Y.S.2d 312 (1st Dep't 1963); Matter of Ritzheimer, 25 Misc.2d 515, 204 N.Y.S.2d 301 (1960).

26. McKinney's 2-1.8(a).

27. 95 Misc.2d 512, 406 N.Y.S.2d 960 (Onondaga 1978).

28. 58 N.Y.2d 539, 462 N.Y.S.2d 622, 449 N.E.2d 402 (1983).

inter vivos trust to the trust, but the court held that the will provision superseded the contrary direction in the trust. It reasoned that the decedent must have known when she wrote the trust that she could change the tax burden by will, and did so.[29]

7. CONFLICTING DIRECTIVES IN A WILL AND CODICIL

A court trying to interpret a testator's directions on tax apportionment always looks to his intent, and this is true when a will and codicil contain different directions on tax apportionment, or when one is silent. If the will apportions all taxes to the residuary estate, and the codicil simply makes a change in the dispositions and ratifies the will in all other regards, the tax clause in the will exonerates the codicil beneficiaries as well.[30] If the will exonerates only specific bequests to named persons from sharing the taxes, and the codicil makes additional specific and general bequests, the beneficiaries in the codicil have to pay their pro rata share of the taxes, even a beneficiary whose will bequest was cancelled and another bequest made in the codicil.[31]

29. Accord, Matter of Collia, N.Y.L.J./ May 14, 1984, at 17, col. 1. See also Matter of Annesley, N.Y.L.J., Jan. 4, 1979, at 6, col. 2 (New York County).

30. See Matter of Nicholas, 33 N.Y.2d 174, 350 N.Y.S.2d 900, 305 N.E.2d 911 (1973) (codicil specifically incorporated will provision against apportionment).

31. Matter of Ballou, 206 Misc. 442, 132 N.Y.S.2d 797 (1954), affirmed 285 A.D. 929, 139 N.Y.S.2d 883 (1954).

Appendix

WESTLAW REFERENCES

Analysis

INTRODUCTION

This informational appendix is designed to aid the reader in the general use of the WESTLAW system and more specifically to demonstrate how WESTLAW can be used in conjunction with this text to help make research in the area of estate administration law swift and complete.

THE WESTLAW SYSTEM

WESTLAW is a computer-assisted legal research service of West Publishing Company. It is accessible through a number of different types of computer terminals. The materials available through WESTLAW are contained in databases stored at the central computer in St. Paul, Minnesota.

To use the WESTLAW service a "query" or search request, is typed into the terminal and sent to the central computer. There it is processed and all of the documents that satisfy the search request are identified. The text of each of these documents is then stored on disks and transmitted to the user via a telecommunication network. This data then appears on the user's terminal, where it may be reviewed and evaluated. The user must then decide if the displayed documents are pertinent or if further research is desired. If further research is necessary, the query may be recalled for editing, or an entirely new query may be sent. Documents displayed on the terminal may be printed or, on some terminals, the text may be stored on its own disks.

IMPROVING LEGAL RESEARCH WITH WESTLAW

The WESTLAW service is designed for use in conjunction with the more traditional tools of legal research. In principle, WESTLAW works as an index to primary and secondary legal materials. Yet it differs from traditional digests and indexes in that more terms can be researched, and more documents retrieved.

Through WESTLAW it is possible to index, or search for any significant term or combination of terms in an almost infinite variety of grammatical relationships by formulating a query composed of those terms. Unlike manual systems of secondary legal sources that reference only a few key terms in each document, WESTLAW is capable of indexing every key word. This enables documents to be located using terms not even listed in manual reference systems.

In addition to its expanded search term capabilities, WESTLAW, through its numerous databases, enables the user to research issues in any and every jurisdiction quickly and efficiently. Most of the queries that readers will formulate for issues discussed in this text will be designed to search WESTLAW's New York case law database. However, WESTLAW provides access to may other libraries as well. For example, WESTLAW contains comprehensive federal and state case law databases as well as seperate topical databases for areas of federal and state law such as tax, securities, energy, and government contracts.

WESTLAW also includes the text of the United States Code and the Code of Federal Regulations, the Federal Register, West's INSTA-CITE ™, Shepard's ® Citations, *Black's Law Dictionary* and many other legal sources. Furthermore, because new cases are continuously being added to the WESTLAW databases as they are decided by the courts, the documents retrieved will include the most current law available on any given issue.

In addition, WESTLAW queries augment the customary role of footnotes to the text by directing the user to a wider range of supporting authorities. Readers are encouraged to formulate their own queries in order to retrieve cases relevant to the points of law discussed throughout the text.

QUERY FORMULATION

a. General Principles

The art of query formulation is the heart of WESTLAW research. Although the researcher can gain technical skills by using the terminal, there is no strictly mechanical procedure for formulating queries. One must first comprehend the meaning of the legal issue to be researched before beginning a search on WESTLAW. Then the user will need to supply imagination, insight, and legal comprehension with knowledge of the capabilities of WESTLAW to formulate a useful query. Effective query formulation requires an alternative way of thinking about the legal research process.

Using WESTLAW is a constant balancing between generating too many documents and missing important documents. In general, it is better to look through a reasonable number of irrelevant documents than it is to be too restrictive and miss important material. The researcher should take into consideration at the initial query formulation stage what he or she will do if too many, or not enough documents are retrieved. Thought should be given as to how the query might be narrowed or the search broadened, and what can be done if the initial search retrieves zero documents.

Some issues by their very nature will require more lengthy queries than others; however, it is best to strive for efficiency in structuring the query. Look for unique search terms that will eliminate the need for a lengthy query. Keep in mind that WESTLAW is literal. Consider all possible alternative terms. Especially consider inherent limitations of the computer. It doesn't think, create, or make analogies. The researcher must do that for the computer. The computer is designed to look for the terms in the documents in relationships specified by the query. The researcher should know what he or she is looking for, at least to the extent of knowing how the terms are likely to show up in relevant documents. Always keep in mind the parameters of the system as to date and database content.

The WESTLAW Reference Manual should be consulted for more information on query formulation and WESTLAW commands. The Reference Manual is updated periodically to reflect new enhancements of WESTLAW. It provides detailed and comprehensive instructions on all aspects of the WESTLAW system and offers numerous illustrative examples on the proper format for various types of queries. Material contained in the Reference Manual enables the user to benefit from all of the system's capabilities in an effective and efficient manner.

b. The WESTLAW Query

The query is a message to WESTLAW. It instructs the computer to retrieve documents containing terms in the grammatical relationships specified by the query. The terms in a query are made up of words and/or numbers that pinpoint the legal issue to be researched.

An example of the kind of queries that readers may formulate to research the law of estate administration is reproduced below.

The query appearing below relates to legal issues discussed in Chapter 1 pertaining to The Surrogate Court's long-arm jurisdiction.

```
topic(106) & surrogate /p long-arm
```

This query instructs WESTLAW to retrieve documents containing the West Digest Topic 106 (Courts) and the term SURROGATE in the same paragraph as the term LONG-ARM.

This query illustrates what a standard request to WESTLAW looks like—words or numbers describing an issue, tied together by connectors. These connectors tell WESTLAW in what relationships the terms must appear. WESTLAW will retrieve all documents from the database that contain the terms appearing in those relationships.

The material that follows explains how users of New York Estate Administration can formulate WESTLAW queries to use in computerized research of the law of estate administration.

c. Selection of Terms

After determining the legal issue that is to be researched, the first step in query formulation is to select the key terms from the issue that will be used as search terms in the query. Words, numbers, and various other symbols may be used as search terms.

The goal in choosing search terms is to select the most unique terms for the issue. In selecting such terms it is frequently helpful to imagine how the terms might appear in the language of the documents that will be searched by the query. Moreover, it is necessary to consider the grammatical and editorial structure of the document. This involves a consideration of how the writer of the document (i.e., judge or headnote and synopsis writer) has worded both the factual and legal components of the issue involved in the case.

Although traditional book research generally starts with a consideration of the general legal concepts under which particular problems are subsumed, WESTLAW research starts with a consideration of specific terms that are likely to appear in documents that have addressed those problems. This is so because documents are retrieved from WESTLAW on the basis of the terms they contain. The more precise the terms, the more relevant the search results will be. For example, in researching the rule against perpetuities, inclusion of the unique term PERPETUITIES rather than the common term RULE, would retrieve more specific, and hopefully more pertinent documents.

Once the initial search terms have been selected for a query, it is important to consider synonyms, antonyms, and other alternatives for the search terms. A space left between each of these alternative terms will be read as an "or" in WESTLAW. (See section e: Query Formulation: Proximity Connectors.) The nature of the legal issue will determine which alternative terms are desirable.

d. The Format of Search Terms

Once the key search terms have been selected, it is necessary to consider the proper form in which the term should appear in the query. As WESTLAW is literal in its search for terms, and as a term may appear in a variety of ways, derivative forms of each search term must be considered. There are two devices available on WESTLAW for automatically generating alternative forms of search terms in a query. The first of these is the Unlimited Root Expander, the symbol (!). Placement of the ! symbol at the end of the root term generates other forms containing the same root. For example, adding the ! symbol to the root GUARDIAN in the following query:

```
guardian! /p infant minor child /p surrogate
```

instructs the computer to generate the words GUARDIAN, GUARDIANS, GUARDIANSHIP, and GUARDIANSHIPS as search terms for the query. Yet time and space are saved by not having to include each of these alternatives in the query.

The second device used to automatically generate alternative forms of search terms is the Universal Character, the symbol (*). This symbol permits the generation of all possible characters by placing one or more asterisks at the location in the term where the universal character is desired. For example, placing three asterisks on the root EXECUTOR* in the following query:

```
executor* /s will
```

instructs the computer to generate all forms of the root term with up to one additional character. Thus, the terms EXECUTORS and EXECUTORY would be generated by this query. The symbol * may also be embedded inside of a term as in the following query:

```
underst**d /s nature extent /s property
```

This will generate the alternative terms UNDERSTAND and UNDERSTOOD without the need to enter both terms. As WESTLAW automatically generates plural forms for search terms (e.g., the endings -s -es and -ies) it is generally unnecessary to use the root expansion devices to obtain plural forms of search terms.

e. Proximity Connectors

Once the search terms and alternate search terms have been selected the next consideration is how these terms may be ordered so as to retrieve the most relevant documents. The connectors and their meanings appear below.

1. *Space (or).* A space between search terms is read as an "or" by WESTLAW. For example, leaving a space between the query terms WILL and CODICIL:

will codicil

instructs the computer to retrieve documents that contain either the word WILL or the word CODICIL or both.

2. *& (ampersand).* The symbol & means "and." Placing it between two terms instructs the computer to retrieve documents that contain both of the terms without regard to word order. For example, inserting the & between the terms WILL and CODICIL:

will & codicil

commands the computer to retrieve documents that contain both the term WILL and the term CODICIL anywhere in the text. The ampersand may also be placed between groups of alternative terms. By placing an & between WILL or CODICIL and SIGN or EXECUTE:

will codicil & sign execute

documents containing the terms WILL and/or CODICIL and the terms SIGN and/or EXECUTE may be retrieved.

3. */p (same paragraph).* The /p symbol means "within the same paragraph." It requests that the terms to the left of the /p appear within the same paragraph as the terms to the right of the connector. For example, placing the /p between GIFT and SPOUSE:

gift /p spouse

instructs the computer to retrieve documents in which both the terms GIFT and SPOUSE appear in the same paragraph. The terms on each side of the /p connector may appear in the document in any order within the paragraph. As with the & connector the /p may be placed between groups of alternative terms. Thus, the query

gift bequest /p spouse

will succeed in retrieving all documents in which the terms GIFT and/or BEQUEST appear in the same paragraph as SPOUSE.

4. */s (same sentence).* The /s symbol requires that the search terms so connected occur within the same sentence. A /s placed between GIFT and SPOUSE

gift /s spouse

will retrieve documents that contain the words GIFT and SPOUSE in the same sentence, without regard to which of these terms occur first in the sentence. As with the previous connectors, the /s may be placed between groups of alternative terms. Inserting the /s between the terms GIFT or BEQUEST and SPOUSE

gift bequest /s spouse

instructs the computer to retrieve documents with the terms GIFT and/or BEQUEST and the term SPOUSE regardless of which terms appear first.

5. *+s (precedes within sentence).* The +s requires that the term to the left of the +s connector precede the terms to the right of the connector within the same sentence. The query

burden +s proof

instructs the computer to retrieve all documents in which the word BURDEN precedes the word PROOF where both words appear in the same sentence. This connector may also be used between groups of alternative terms. Thus, the query

burden weight +s proof persuasion

commands the computer to retrieve all documents in which the terms BURDEN and/or WEIGHT precede the terms PROOF and/or PERSUASION in the same sentence.

6. */n (numerical proximity—within n words).* The /n symbol means "within n words," where n represents any whole number between 1 and 255, inclusive. It requests that the term to the left of the /n appear within the designated number of words as terms to the right of the connector. For example, in the following query:

subscribing /3 witness

the computer is instructed to retrieve all documents in which the term SUBSCRIBING appears within 3 words of the term WITNESS, without regard to word order. In addition, the + symbol may be used to require that the terms to the left of the numerical proximity connector precede the terms to the right of the connector. Thus, the query above could be altered to require that SUBSCRIBING precede WITNESS by no more than 3 words by replacing the /3 connector with the +3 connector.

subscribing +3 witness

Both the /n and the +n connectors may also be used between groups of alternative search terms. For example:

subscribing attesting +3 witness

instructs the computer to retrieve all documents in which the words SUBSCRIBING or ATTESTING occur within the three words preceding the word WITNESS.

7. *" " (quotation marks).* The " " (quotation marks) symbol is the most restrictive grammatical connector. When used to enclose search terms it requires that the computer retrieve only those documents in which enclosed terms appear exactly as they do within the quotation marks. For example, placing the following words within quotation marks

"dead man's statute"

commands the computer to retrieve all documents in which the terms DEAD and MAN'S and STATUTE occur in precisely the same order as they do within the quotation marks.

The quotation marks symbol is especially effective when searching for legal terms of art, legal concepts, or legal entities that occur together as multiple terms. Some examples are:

"ex parte" "reasonable doubt" "voir dire"

8. *% (exclusion/but not).* The % symbol may be translated as "but not." It instructs the computer to exclude documents that contain terms appearing after the percentage symbol. For example, to retrieve documents containing the term BURDEN within the three words of PROOF but not the term CRIMINAL, the following query would be used:

burden /3 proof % criminal

Any document containing the word CRIMINAL would automatically be excluded in the document search.

The connectors described above may be used in a variety of combinations, enabling the user to fine-tune a query to meet his or her specific research needs.

ADVANCED SEARCH TECHNIQUES

a. The Field Search

Within any given database a more specialized search may be conducted. Rather than researching the entire text of a case for a designated query term, the search may be limited to specific portions of the case by conducting a "field search." A search may be restricted to a particular field (or portion) of a document by incorporating the field name into the query, followed by the field search terms enclosed in parentheses.

The fields available for WESTLAW case law databases are described below.

1. *Title Field:* The title field may be used to retrieve a particular case on WESTLAW. The ampersand, rather than the v. is used between the names of the parties. Thus, to retrieve the case entitled Lalor v. Duff the following query would be used:

title(lalor & duff)

2. *Citation Field:* The citation field may be used for any document for which a citation exists in the WESTLAW databases. The proper database must first be selected. A numerical proximity connector is then used instead of the publication name to separate volume and page number. For example, to retrieve the case appearing at 473 N.Y.S.2d 679, the New York cases database must be selected. The following query may then be used:

citation(473 +7 679)

3. *Court Field:* The court field permits searches for case law to be restricted to particular states, districts, or courts. The correct database in which to conduct the search must be chosen. For example, to restrict a search to cases appearing in the Atlantic Reporter from

Pennsylvania and New Jersey, the following query could be used in the "atl" database:

```
court(pa nj) & 409k801(5)
```

4. *Judge Field:* A search may be limited to the individual or majority opinion of a particular judge. To retrieve all cases in which Otto C. Jaeger has authored an opinion the following query would be used:

```
judge(jaeger)
```

5. *Synopsis Field:* The synopsis field consists of the editorially prepared summary of the case found immediately after the title. By reading the synopsis it may be determined if the decision generally encompasses the legal issue being researched without reading the entire decision.

The synopsis field search can be especially useful in focusing broad queries which might retrieve too many cases if the entire case was searched. For example, the following query would limit retrieval to cases in which an elective share was a key element:

```
synopsis(electi** /3 share)
```

6. *Topic Field:* The topic field contains the West topics and Key Numbers assigned to the headnotes in a case. A search in this field may be conducted by using either the West topic name or by using the West topic number designated for that topic. For example, the West digest topic of Wills has been given the number 409. Thus in order to retrieve cases on holographic wills either of these two queries could be used:

```
topic(wills) /p holograph**
```

or

```
topic(409) /p holograph**
```

7. *Digest Field:* The digest field contains digest paragraphs prepared by West editors. It includes headnotes, corresponding digest topics and Key Numbers, the title and citation of the case, courts, and year of decision. The digest field can be used to search for terms which are not among the West topic headings. For example, the following query may be used to research computation of elective shares.

```
digest(electi** /3 share /s comput!)
```

8. *Headnote Field:* A headnote search limits the search to the language of the headnote, exclusive of the digest topic and Key Number lines and case identification information. Thus, the headnote field is useful in conducting a search where exclusion of the topic name, the key number or the title of the case is necessary to retrieve only the most pertinent cases. For example, if the query includes statute or rule numbers the headnote field can be helpful to exclude unwanted citation and key numbers. The query found below is an illustration of this function. The search, run in the New York cases database, will

retrieve cases containing headnotes which discuss section 210(2)(a) of the Surrogate Court Probate Act.

```
headnote(210(2)(a) /s scpa)
```

9. *Opinion Field:* The opinion field contains the text of the case, court and docket numbers, and the names of the attorneys and judges participating. The opinion field search is useful in retrieving cases in which a particular attorney, judge or witness has been involved. The following format can be used to retrieve this information:

```
opinion(clarence +2 darrow)
```

NOTE: Terms may be searched for in clusters of fields by joining any number of field names by commas. This technique is illustrated below:

```
synopsis,digest("totten trust")
```

With this query, documents containing the terms TOTTEN TRUST in either the synopsis or digest portions of the case will be retrieved.

b. Field Browsing

The WESTLAW fields listed above may be used in yet another way. This second method, known as field browsing, may be used with any query. Once a search has been completed, the documents retrieved may be scanned by entering the "f" command. A list of fields available for browsing is then displayed. Once a field has been selected, WESTLAW will display only the specified field(s).

The WESTLAW Reference Manual should be consulted for further instruction on using WESTLAW fields for searching or browsing.

c. Date Restrictions

WESTLAW may be instructed to retrieve documents appearing before, after or on a specified date, as well as within a range of dates. To use the date restriction the term DATE, followed in parentheses by the words BEFORE and/or AFTER, or the abbreviations BEF and/or AFT, or the symbols < and > must be included in the query. Note that the month, day and year may be included to further restrict the search. Date restrictions should be connected to the query by an ampersand. The following are examples of how the date restriction may be used within a query:

```
date(after 1965) & nuncupat! /5 will
date(aft 1965) & nuncupat! /5 will
nuncupat! /5 will & date(bef 1975)
nuncupat! /5 will & date(aft may 10, 1965 and bef feb 28, 1981)
```

d. Key Number Searching

Searches may be performed using West Digest Topic and Key Numbers as search terms. When using this search technique, the query consists of the West Digest Topic Number followed by the letter k and then the Key Number classified as a subheading under the Digest

Topic and Key Number. For example, to retrieve cases under the Digest Topic classification of Wills (Digest Topic number 409), and under its subsection or Key Number for Intent to Revoke, (Key Number 170), the following query would be used.

```
409k170
```

A complete list of Digest Topics and their numerical equivalents appears in the WESTLAW Reference Manual and is also available on-line in the WESTLAW database directory.

e. The Find Command

The FIND command may be used at any point in a search to retrieve a particular case from WESTLAW. No matter what the database, a case may be displayed by typing FIND followed by the case citation. For example:

```
find 473 n.y.s.2d 679
```

will retrieve the case of *Lalor v. Duff* no matter what the database. To return to the original screen, the GOBACK command is then entered.

f. The Locate Command

The LOCATE command may be used when viewing documents retrieved by a search query, to identify documents within the search results which contain certain words. To locate a term, LOCATE or LOC is typed followed by the ENTER key. On the screen which follows the LOCATE terms are then typed. The terms may or may not be words contained in the query. WESTLAW will then search the documents retrieved by the query to find the LOCATE terms. For example, to search the documents retrieved by the query:

```
topic(409) /p "totten trust"
```

for those documents containing the term "bank" type LOCATE followed by the term BANK. Those documents containing the term BANK will then be displayed.

CITATION RESEARCH WITH WESTLAW

a. Shepard's® Citations on WESTLAW

From any point in WESTLAW, case citations may be entered to retrieve Shepard's listings for those citations. To enter a citation to be Shepardized, the following format is used:

```
sh 442 a2d 1327
```

or

```
sh 442 a.2d 1327
```

or

```
sh 442a2d1327
```

When the citation is entered, Shepard's listings for the citation will be displayed. To shepardize a citation it is not necessary to be in the same database as that of the citation. For example, a Supreme Court citation may be entered from the Pacific Reporter database.

b. WESTLAW as a Citator

It is possible to retrieve new cases citing previous decisions by using WESTLAW itself as a citator. Using WESTLAW as a citator complements Shepard's Citations by retrieving very recent decisions not yet included in Shepard's. Because citation styles are not always uniform, special care must be taken to identify variant forms of citations.

1. Retrieving Cases that Cite Other Court Decisions

WESTLAW can be used as a citator of other court decisions if the title of the decision, its citation, or both, are known. When only the title of case is known, use the following format:

This query instructs the computer to retrieve all documents citing the case of *Riggs v. Palmer.* The /5 numerical connector requires that the term RIGGS occur within five words of the term PALMER.

If the citation of the case is known, it may be added to the query to retrieve only those documents citing the correct case name and case citation. For example, to retrieve cases that have referred to the *Riggs* decision by its citation, 22 N.E. 188, the following format may be used:

If both the citation and the case title are known, one or both of the case name terms may be used to retrieve all documents citing this case. The queries below illustrate this format.

```
riggs /5 palmer /15 22 +7 188
```

or

```
riggs /15 22 +7 188
```

2. West's INSTA-CITE ™

INSTA-CITE, West Publishing Company's case history system, allows users to quickly verify the accuracy of case citations and the validity of decisions. It contains prior and subsequent case histories in sequential listings, parallel citations and precedential treatment.

Some examples of the kind of direct case history provided by INSTA-CITE are: "affirmed," "certiorari denied," "decision reversed and remanded," and "judgment vacated." A complete list of INSTA-CITE case history and precedential treatment notations appears in the WESTLAW Reference Manual.

The format for entering a case citation into INSTA–CITE consists of the letters IC followed by the citation, with or without spaces and periods:

```
ic 103 s.ct. 969
```

or

```
ic 103 sct 969
```

or

```
ic 103sct969
```

SPECIAL FEATURES

a. Black's Law Dictionary

WESTLAW contains an on-line version of Black's Law Dictionary. The dictionary incorporates definitions of terms and phrases of English and American law.

The dictionary may be accessed at any point while using WESTLAW by typing DI followed by the term to be defined:

```
di
```

To obtain definitions of a phrase, enter the command DI followed by the phrase without quotation marks:

```
di per stirpes
```

If the precise spelling of a term to be defined is not known, or a list of dictionary terms is desired, a truncated form of the words may be entered with the root expansion symbol (!) attached to it:

```
di testat!
```

This example will produce a list of dictionary terms beginning with the root TESTAT!. From the list of terms a number corresponding to the desired term can be entered to obtain the appropriate definition of TESTATRIX.

WESTLAW HORNBOOK QUERIES

a. Query Format

There is seldom only one "correct" way to formulate a query for a particular problem. There is a wide range of alternative ways that queries may be structured for effective research. Such variance in query style reflects the great flexibility that the WESTLAW system affords its users in formulating search strategies.

For some research problems, it may be necessary to make a series of refinements to a query, such as the addition of search terms or the substitution of different grammatical connectors, to adequately fit the particular needs of the individual researcher's problem. The responsibility remains with the researcher to "fine-tune" his or her queries in accordance with his or her own research requirements.

If a query does not retrieve any cases in a given database, it is because there are no documents in that database which satisfy the proximity requirements of the query. In this situation, to search another database with the same query, enter the letter S followed by the initials DB, followed by the new database identifier. Thus, if a query was initially addressed to the New York cases (ny–cs) database, but retrieved no documents, the user could then search the New Jersey cases database (nj–cs) with the same query by entering the following command:

s db nj–cs

The maximum number of cases retrieved by a query in any given database will vary, depending on a variety of factors, including the relative generality of the search terms and proximity connectors, the frequency of litigation or discussion of the issue in the courts and administrative bodies, and the number of documents comprising the database.

b. Textual Illustrations

Examples from the text of this edition have been selected to illustrate how readers may formulate WESTLAW queries to meet the specific needs of research in the area of estate administration. A portion of Chapter 12 section B.2. of this text appears below.

2. Proceeding To Set Aside Exempt Property

A spouse or minor children of a decedent may be entitled to certain assets as exempt property under EPTL 5–3.1, including utensils, musical instruments, clothing, fuel, books, domestic animals, farm machinery and vehicles of specified values, and one thousand dollars in cash or personal property.

This excerpt discusses family exemptions under EPTL 5–3.1. In order to retrieve documents which address this provision, a reader could formulate a WESTLAW query similar to the following:

exempt! /p 5–3.1

The paragraph below appears in the text of a case retrieved by this query in the New York cases database (NY–CS).

R 12 OF 21 P 2 OF 4 NY–CS T

352 N.Y.S.2d 136

162⚷180

EXECUTORS AND ADMINISTRATORS

⚷. Persons entitled.

N.Y.Sur.1974.

Only requirement for family **exemption** under statute is that there be a surviving spouse or minor child, so that where decedent was survived by his divorced wife, a daughter who had attained her majority, and a son who was still a minor, son was entitled to automobile as a family **exemption**, and automobile should not be included as part of estate which under terms of decedent's will was left to his two children. EPTL **5–3.1**.

In re Comparetto's Estate,

352 N.Y.S.2d 136, 76 Misc.2d 859

The query can be easily altered to retrieve cases involving the one-thousand dollar cash exemption specifically:

exempt! /p 5-3.1 /p one-thousand 1,000

By adding the alternative terms ONE-THOUSAND and 1,000, the query retrieves documents relating to the statutory cash exemption. An excerpt from one such document is shown below.

R 3 OF 3 P 2 OF 15 NY-CS T

287 N.Y.S.2d 907

162⚷182

EXECUTORS AND ADMINISTRATORS

⚷. Priority over other claims.

N.Y.Sur. 1968.

One thousand-dollar statutory **exemption** payable to decedent's husband was applied against his indebtedness on worthless claim to executor where husband did not object. EPTL 5-3.1(1) (4), 11-1.1(b) (21).

In re Connor's Estate,

287 N.Y.S.2d 907, 56 Misc.2d 10

RANKING DOCUMENTS RETRIEVED ON WESTLAW: AGE AND TERM OPTIONS

Documents retrieved by a query can be ordered in either of two ways. One way is to order documents by their dates, with the most recent documents displayed first. This is ranking by AGE. Using the AGE option is suggested when the user's highest priority is to retrieve the most recent decisions from a search.

Alternatively, documents can be ranked by the frequency of appearance of query terms. This is ranking by TERMS. When a search is performed with the TERMS option, the cases containing the greatest number of different search terms will be displayed first.

When a database is accessed by entering a database identifier, WESTLAW responds with a screen requesting that the query be entered. At this point the user may select which type of ranking, AGE or TERMS, is desired.

CONCLUSION

This appendix has demonstrated methods that can be used to obtain the most effective research results in the area of estate administration.

WESTLAW queries may be formulated as needed to meet the needs of researcher's specific problems. The power and flexibility of WESTLAW affords users of this publication a unique opportunity to greatly enhance their access to and understanding of the law of estate administration law.

*

Table of Cases

References are to Pages

Table of Statutes

McKINNEY'S NEW YORK CONSTITUTION

McKINNEY'S ABANDONED PROPERTY LAW

McKINNEY'S BANKING LAW

McKINNEY'S BANKING LAW

McKINNEY'S BUSINESS CORPORATION LAW

McKINNEY'S CIVIL PRACTICE ACT

McKINNEY'S CIVIL PRACTICE LAW AND RULES

McKINNEY'S CIVIL PRACTICE LAW AND RULES

McKINNEY'S COURT OF CLAIMS ACT

McKINNEY'S CRIMINAL PROCEDURE LAW

McKINNEY'S DOMESTIC RELATIONS LAW

McKINNEY'S ESTATES, POWERS AND TRUSTS LAW

McKINNEY'S ESTATES, POWERS AND TRUSTS LAW

McKINNEY'S ESTATES, POWERS AND TRUSTS LAW

McKINNEY'S ESTATES, POWERS AND TRUSTS LAW

McKINNEY'S ESTATES, POWERS AND TRUSTS LAW

McKINNEY'S ESTATES, POWERS AND TRUSTS LAW

McKINNEY'S ESTATES, POWERS AND TRUSTS LAW

McKINNEY'S ESTATES, POWERS AND TRUSTS LAW

McKINNEY'S SURROGATE'S COURT PROCEDURE ACT

McKINNEY'S SURROGATE'S COURT PROCEDURE ACT

McKINNEY'S SURROGATE'S COURT PROCEDURE ACT

McKINNEY'S SURROGATE'S COURT PROCEDURE ACT

McKINNEY'S SURROGATE'S COURT PROCEDURE ACT

McKINNEY'S SURROGATE'S COURT PROCEDURE ACT

McKINNEY'S SURROGATE'S COURT PROCEDURE ACT

McKINNEY'S SURROGATE'S COURT PROCEDURE ACT

McKINNEY'S SURROGATE'S COURT PROCEDURE ACT

McKINNEY'S SURROGATE'S COURT PROCEDURE ACT

McKINNEY'S SURROGATE'S COURT PROCEDURE ACT

McKINNEY'S SURROGATE'S COURT PROCEDURE ACT

Sec.	This Work Page
1502(1)	460
1502(2)	460
	461
1502(3)	461
	462
1502(4)	462
1502(5)	462
1502(6)	462
1503	385
	392
	400
	455
	463
1504	455
	464
1504(1)	463
1504(2)	464
1504(3)	463
1505	399
	455
	465
1505(1)	465
1505(1)(a)	465
1505(1)(b)	465
1506	455
	465
	466
1507	326
	455
	467
	472
1507(1)	467
1507(2)	467
1507(3)	467
1508	467
	468
1509	468
Art. 16	6
	29
	358
	456
1601	511
	512
1602	326
	514
	516
	517
1602(1)	513
	517
1602(2)	514
1603	516
1603(1)	516
1603(2)	517
1604	514
1604(1)	515
1605	29
	30
	456
	458
	522
	523
1605(1)	31
	522

McKINNEY'S SURROGATE'S COURT PROCEDURE ACT

Sec.	This Work Page
1605(2)	29
	31
	523
1605(2)(a)	29
1605(2)(b)	29
	522
1605(2)(c)	29
	515
1605(3)	523
	525
1606	524
1607(1)	519
1607(2)	519
1608	512
	515
	518
	519
	520
1608(4)	518
1608(6)	518
1609	513
	514
	519
1609(1)	513
1609(2)	513
1609(3)	513
1610(1)	520
1610(2)	520
1610(3)	520
1610(4)	520
1611	525
1614	459
Art. 17	234
	258
	271
	273
	279
	281
	282
	402
1701	2
	258
	259
1702	259
1702(2)	259
1703	260
	326
1704	261
1705	281
1705(1)	262
1705(2)	262
	264
1705(3)	262
1706	263
	265
1707	236
	267
1707(2)	267
1708	268
	428
1708(1)	268
1708(3)	269
1709	188

McKINNEY'S SURROGATE'S COURT PROCEDURE ACT

McKINNEY'S SURROGATE'S COURT PROCEDURE ACT

McKINNEY'S SURROGATE'S COURT PROCEDURE ACT

McKINNEY'S SURROGATE'S COURT PROCEDURE ACT

McKINNEY'S SURROGATE'S COURT PROCEDURE ACT

McKINNEY'S SURROGATE'S COURT PROCEDURE ACT

McKINNEY'S SURROGATE'S COURT PROCEDURE ACT

McKINNEY'S SURROGATE COURT PROCEDURE ACT OFFICIAL FORMS

LAWS

UNITED STATES

UNITED STATES CONSTITUTION

UNITED STATES CODE ANNOTATED

12 U.S.C.A.—Banks and Banking

15 U.S.C.A.—Commerce and Trade

26 U.S.C.A.—Internal Revenue Code

UNITED STATES CODE ANNOTATED

26 U.S.C.A.—Internal Revenue Code

UNIFORM PROBATE CODE

RULES

FEDERAL RULES OF EVIDENCE

UNIFORM RULES

REGULATIONS

REVENUE RULINGS

TREASURY REGULATIONS

*

Index

References are to Pages

References are to Pages

References are to Pages

References are to Pages

†